WORLDMARK ENCYCLOPEDIA *of* Religious Practices

Volume 3

COUNTRIES

M–Z

Thomas Riggs, Editor

Detroit • New York • San Francisco • San Diego • New Haven, Conn. • Waterville, Maine • London • Munich

Worldmark Encyclopedia of Religious Practices, Volume 3

Thomas Riggs

Product Managers
Carol DeKane Nagel, Bonnie Hawkwood

Project Editors
Michael L. LaBlanc, Thomas Carson, Jason M. Everett, Bernard Grunow

Editorial
Mary Rose Bonk, Andrew Clapps, Sara Constantakis, Angela Doolin, Anne Marie Hacht, Gillian Leonard, Stephanie Macomber, Ellen McGeagh, Ira Mark Milne, Rebecca Parks, Mark E. Rzeszutek, Jennifer York Stock.

Rights Acqusition and Management
Peg Ashlevitz, Jacqueline Key, Susan J. Rudolph

Manufacturing
Wendy Blurton

Imaging and Multimedia
Lezlie Light, Dan Newell, Christine O'Bryan

Product Design
Kate Scheible

For more information, contact
Thomson Gale
27500 Drake Rd.
Farmington, Hills, MI 48331-3535
Or you can visit our Internet site at
http://www.gale.com

LIBRARY OF CONGRESS CATALOGING-IN-PUBLICATION DATA

Worldmark encyclopedia of religious practices / Thomas Riggs, editor in chief.
p. cm.
Includes bibliographical refrences and index.
ISBN 0-7876-6611-4 (set hardcover : alk. paper)—
ISBN 0-7876-6612-2 (vol 1 : alk paper)—;
ISBN 0-7876-6613-0 (vol 2 : alk. paper)—;
ISBN 0-7876-6614-9 (vol 3 : alk. paper)
1. Religions. I. Riggs, Thomas, 1963-

BL80.3.W67 2006
200.9—dc22 2005027456

This title is also available as an e-book.
ISBN 0-7876-9390-1

Contact your Thomson Gale representative for ordering information.

Printed in the United States of America
10 9 8 7 6 5 4 3 2 1

Contents

VOLUME 3: COUNTRY ENTRIES M–Z

Editor's Preface

In 2001 Thomson Gale had a simple but ambitious goal: to produce an encyclopedia outlining the contemporary religious practices of every country in the world—from the very largest, such as China, India, Brazil, and Russia, to the smallest, such as Tuvalu, Andorra, and Antigua and Barbuda. Because this information has not been readily available in books or other sources in libraries, as well as on the Internet, the project required years of planning and hard work by a large group of people: our distinguished board of 10 advisers, the 245 scholars and other subject specialists commissioned to write essays or to review the text of their colleagues, and the editorial staff of Thomson Gale. The result was this publication, the *Worldmark Encyclopedia of Religious Practices.* It joins an already existing series of Worldmark encyclopedias, including the *Worldmark Encyclopedia of the Nations* and the *Worldmark Encyclopedia of Cultures and Daily Life.*

Organization

The *Worldmark Encyclopedia of Religious Practices* has three volumes. Volume 1 includes essays on the history, beliefs, and contemporary practices of 13 major faith groups—African Traditional Religions, Bahá'í, Buddhism, Christianity, Confucianism, Hinduism, Islam, Jainism, Judaism, Shinto, Sikhism, Taoism, and Zoroastrianism—and 28 of their subgroups, such as Anglicanism, Reform Judaism, Mahayana Buddhism, and Vaishnavism. These essay topics, selected by our advisory board, represent not only the world's largest religious groups but also smaller faiths that have had significant historical, cultural, or theological impact. Because of space limitations, we could not include essays on all groups worthy of discussion. Each essay in volume 1 is organized with the same subject headings—for example, "Moral Code of Conduct" and "Sacred Symbols"—allowing easy comparison of a topic from one religion or subgroup to another. Printed at the top of each essay in volume 1 is a population map displaying the group's distribution throughout the world.

By discussing broadly various religions and subgroups, volume 1 provides the background or context for more fully understanding the information in volumes 2 and 3. These subsequent volumes together contain 193 essays, each focusing on the contemporary religious practices of a particular country. Organizing the topic of religious practices by country assumes that geographical and, in particular, political boundaries—because in varying degrees they mark off areas of unique history, culture, and influence—encourage distinctive ways in which a religion is practiced, despite shared beliefs held by all members of a religion.

The essays in volumes 2 and 3 follow a standard format: statistical information, an overview of the country, one or more sections on major religions, a discussion of other religions, and a bibliography. The statistical information includes the country's total population and a breakdown by percentage of the major religious groups. The "Country Overview" section contains an "Introduction," providing a geographical or historical summary of the country needed to understand religious activities in the area, and a subsection on "Religious Tolerance," discussing such topics as freedom of worship, religious discrimination, ecumenical movements, and the relationship between church and state.

Every country essay then proceeds with a major religion section on each religion whose followers make up 25 percent or more of the country's population. In some countries just one religion, such as Christianity, Islam, or Buddhism, has at least this percentage of followers, but in other countries two or three religions each have more than 25 percent, thus resulting in the essay including two or three major religion sections. Exceptions to the rule were made for a small number of essays, most notably for China, where Buddhism, at 8 percent of the population, and Christianity, at 6.5 percent, were given their own sections. China's population, however, is immense, and Buddhism's 8 percent, for example, represents 103 million people, more than the entire population of most countries. In some essays the major religion section is on a religious subgroup; this occurs when a subgroup, such as Roman Catholicism, dominates the country or when the country, such as Sweden, has had a historically important state church.

Each major religion section is broken down into the following 18 subsections, which describe the religion's distinctive qualities in that country. "Date of origin," for example, refers to the year not when the religion was founded but when it was introduced into the country. "Major Theologians and Authors" discusses significant religious writers from the country. "Mode of Dress" details any clothing or styles distinctive to adherents in the country. Because each major religion section is divided into the same 18 subject headings, religions can be easily compared from one country to another.

1. Date of Origin
2. Number of Followers
3. History
4. Early and Modern Leaders
5. Major Theologians and Authors
6. Houses of Worship and Holy Places
7. What is Sacred?
8. Holidays and Festivals
9. Mode of Dress
10. Dietary Practices
11. Rituals (outlining such practices as worship services, prayer, and pilgrimages)
12. Rites of Passage
13. Membership (discussing ways of encouraging new members)
14. Social Justice (in relation to poverty, education, and human rights)
15. Social Aspects (focusing on marriage and family)
16. Political Impact
17. Controversial Issues
18. Cultural Impact (in the arts, such as literature, painting, music, dance, and architecture)

Each country essay ends with a summary of other religions—those that make up less than 25 percent of the population—and a bibliography, which recommends other books and articles for further reading.

Acknowledgments

I would like to express my appreciation to the encyclopedia's editorial staff. Among those in-house at Thomson Gale are Bonnie Whitaker, who helped identify the need for the book and develop its main outline; Bernard Grunow, who calmly guided the early in-house steps; Thomas Carson, whose wisdom and background in religious studies kept the encyclopedia on the right path; Rita Runchock, whose editorial judgment proved essential at various stages of the project; Carol Nagel, who in the final months provided editorial focus, in the process finding solutions to lingering problems; and Michael LaBlanc, whose good humor, common sense, and fine editorial skills helped bring the project to a needed and gentle ending.

I am also grateful to Stephen Meyer, the associate editor, who was involved from the very beginning of the project, helping develop the book's editorial plan, contacting scholars to write essays and working with them on their revisions, and involving himself in other tasks too numerous to list; Mariko Fujinaka, an assistant editor, whose day-to-day organizational skills made all our lives easier; Erin Brown, our other assistant editor, who was involved in photo selection, contacting and corresponding with peer reviewers, and many other areas; Joyce Meyer, who translated a number of essays from French into English; Robert Rauch, the senior line editor, who helped create the editing guidelines and oversee the other line editors; and the line editors themselves—Lee Esbenshade, Laura Gabler, Natalie Goldstein, Anne Healey, Elizabeth Henry, and Janet Moredock—who were asked to ensure that the text, even when containing challenging or esoteric information, be accessible to a wide range of readers.

Finally, I would like to thank the advisers and contributors. Much of the information in the essays cannot be readily found in any other source, and without the involvement of our advisers and contributors, this encyclopedia, of course, could not have been produced.

Thomas J. Riggs

Comments

Although great effort has gone into this work, we would appreciate any suggestions for future editions of the *Worldmark Encyclopedia of Religious Practices.* Please send comments to the following address:

Editor
Worldmark Encyclopedia of Religious Practices
Thomson Gale
27500 Drake Road
Farmington Hills, Michigan 48331

Introduction

While religion is universal throughout human culture, its variations are so extensive that authorities do not always agree on a definition. Scholars have identified more than 50 characteristics of religion, from belief in gods or God to sophisticated ideas about a philosophical worldview. Some authorities regard religion as a particular kind of human experience, as a special way of living together, or as offering answers to certain vexing questions, such as why there is something rather than nothing or whether there is a larger purpose for evil. Religion is sometimes held to be bound up with what a particular group chooses as sacred, whether that be an object (totem), a being (God), a text (scripture), or a fundamental law of nature. Some believers hold that religion is beyond comprehension by the human mind, with study of it reserved for specially gifted people, a view that makes religion an esoteric, or secret, activity. On the other hand, many languages have no specific word to identify the human sensibility we call "religion." In these cases, acts of piety are simply considered natural or ordinary, so that there is no need to identify a distinctive experience.

In addition, how are innovations in religion under the pressures of modern life to be understood? For example, is the cooking and eating of a wild boar by a contemporary urban Melanesian a religious rite, even if it is not accompanied by the ceremony and ideology that traditionally attended such an act? Is a pious attitude sufficient for the act to be called religious? Further, if ideas are modern, are they less religious than views established long ago? What, for example, is to be made of the belief held by some Muslims that the best community existed at the time of the Prophet Muhammad, that the Islamic community today is somehow "less Muslim" than it was then? Or how is one to understand ancient gods? Osiris, for example, was once widely worshipped in Egypt but has few, if any, followers today. Does this mean that the most powerful beings humans once identified with and worshipped can "die"? And is a rule dating from biblical times still applicable today, or can "timeless" revelations be modified in the light of new discoveries? Despite the fact that there seem to be thousands of new religions, is it possible to say that a new religion is "better" than an old one? These and other issues surrounding contemporary religion are staggering in their complexity.

In spite of the difficulties in defining religion, it is essential to understand the phenomenon, for it touches almost every facet of life, from themes in popular culture, to perceptions of well-being, to motivations for global terrorism. Even those who reject religion, who blame it for human problems, or who regard it as a relic of the past should understand contemporary religion. It is also important that people understand the history of religion, including its power and its spread. Consider Christianity, for example, which began as an obscure movement in a tiny place outside Jerusalem some 2,000 years ago but which spread to Byzantium and Rome, centers of the then-known world, where it was adopted as the state religion. It later spread throughout Europe and followed European movement into the New World, and it has since spread to virtually every part of the earth. In the late twentieth century, reform movements from countries outside its traditional home, as with the doctrines of the Korean evangelist Sun Myung Moon, began to return to the heartland of Christianity with a revitalized vision. Thus, there are Christians from the so-called Third World who are now challenging Western nations to become "religious" once again. Such dynamism cannot be ignored by those who wish to understand the forces that motivate societies today.

The *Worldmark Encyclopedia of Religious Practices* focuses on contemporary expressions of world religion. It accepts the fact that there are international communities of faith, along with numerous branches within them, and that these define the world of religion today.

Volume 1 contains articles on the following 13 major religious groups: African indigenous beliefs, the Bahá'í faith, Buddhism, Christianity, Confucianism, Hinduism, Islam, Jainism, Judaism, Shinto, Sikhism, Taoism, and Zoroastrianism. In addition, there are separate articles on a number of major branches within these groups—for example, in Buddhism, on the Mahayana, Theravada, and Tibetan traditions.

This organization may seem misleading, for it does not indicate that religious ideas interact with one another or that similar perceptions are found in several religions. In addition, there is far more variety within each of these religions and subgroups than this approach suggests. Such matters are dealt with in Volumes 2 and 3 of the encyclopedia, where the diversity of religious practices in the various countries of the world is discussed. Still, the organization of Volume 1 is useful in showing that the subject is not limitless. It is possible to sketch the main dimensions of religious practice according to the traditions with which believers identify, an approach that scholarship has come to accept.

Common Elements in Religious Practice

Given the religious diversity found throughout the world, how can one hope to gain adequate knowledge of the subject? Are there basic ways of approaching the study of religion? It is often said that religion insists on a certain kind of reality, something that is larger than the individual or the immediate community. Such a reality is usually defined as a force or person of greater "power," something beyond human creation. What results from human interaction with this power may be called "religious." It may not be possible to prove such a reality, or to "know" it, conclusively. Nonbelievers, for example, do not accept its existence or share in the relationship. What is possible, however, is to document how people act when they are acting religiously. Thus, what appears to be crucial in understanding religion is practice—that is, activity related to the experience of a greater power.

Consider prayer, for example. Although there are considerable variations in how people pray, normally it is possible to tell the difference between believers at prayer and believers acting in an "ordinary" way. In prayer there are certain ways of moving, stances adopted, demeanors assumed, and words uttered—all of which appear to indicate a direct relationship between the believer and the greater power. Prayer brings believers into communication with the transforming agent, or higher power, that is the basis of their religion and their world.

Every religion has a system that establishes how that religion is experienced (as, for example, in prayer), giving a structure to its activities and providing an intellectual basis for the believer's perception of reality. Students of religion have an number of terms for such systems, including "philosophy," "theology," "beliefs," "values," and "doctrines." In some religions these systems are spelled out in an elaborate manner, as, for example, in the doctrine of the Trinity (Father, Son, and Holy Spirit) in Christianity. They may be part of a larger system of teaching and learning, as with Dianetics in the Church of Scientology. In some religions, however, there is less emphasis on theory than on acts, with reference made to basic beliefs only when queries are raised or when disagreements arise. This can be seen, for example, among Japanese shamans who perform healing rituals but who seldom talk about the spirit world they are encountering.

It is important to note that many religious practices arose from ancient rituals related to major life passages—for example, rites for girls and boys when they reach puberty. Some practices, such as those surrounding birth, marriage, and death, are as old as humankind. For many believers there is something reassuring about religion's connection with the stages and cycles of life, and people may actively participate in such rites even when they are not sure about the meaning of what they are doing.

Although every religion has distinctive practices, several common features are discussed here.

RITUALS Throughout life, rituals are used to express meaning. There are formal words used when greeting someone of an official rank, for example; gifts for people on special occasions; and the shaking of a hand when it is offered. It is possible for a person to ignore these practices, but there may be repercussions in doing so. By providing a grounding for life, rituals, rites, and ceremonies take on critical importance.

One of the most important ways of expressing religious feeling is through rituals. Believers, for example, use rituals to interact with their conception of the source of life. The indigenous people of the Plains tradition in North America smoke a pipe as a means of sending their prayers to the Spirit World, and Tibetan Buddhists chant in meditation to encounter the

Thunderbolt reality that lies beyond ordinary perception. In conveying their concerns and feelings to their sacred entities, believers do not see themselves as "using" rituals to manipulate the situation. Rather, they believe that such acts are a way of communicating with the object of their religious sensibilities.

For those who hold that communication with the gods or God is the purpose of religion, worship is a basic ritual, and in most religions worship is demanded of the faithful. Even in Buddhism, where the basis of religion is not worship, loving adoration of the Buddha is ordinarily a crucial part of the believer's rituals. In addition, most religions have developed rites that chart the growth of a person from birth to death and beyond, thus providing activities called rites of passage. These rites move a person through various levels of privilege and responsibilities. In some religions the performance of rites and ceremonies is considered so critical that they can be carried out only by specially endowed people, usually called priests, who operate as mediators between divine power and the individual believer.

The practices and rituals of any religion are directly affected by its conception of the spiritual world, that is, by its system of beliefs. When theism (belief in God) is a central tenant, the resulting religious practices in one way or another invoke the deity in its rituals. Further, how people conceive of the gods or God directly shapes practices. Christians speak of God's love as revealed through Jesus Christ and hold that God offers spiritual fulfillment and personal redemption through the doctrines reflected in the Trinity. As a result, Christians have developed rituals that embrace this belief, such as the commemorations and celebrations of Easter or the rituals of baptism. Jews, on the other hand, stress the worship of "the God of our Fathers, the God of Abraham, Isaac and Jacob," emphasizing the importance of a spiritual lineage with God. For Jews this lineage is demonstrated through the reading of the laws of God as set forth in the Hebrew Scriptures. By contrast, Hinduism has embraced many names for the diversity of spiritual reality, and Hindus observe a great number of rituals to express this exuberance of deities. On the other hand, those religions that do not involve belief in gods, including those of certain indigenous peoples, have quite different rituals. For example, in the past, Inuit shamans and medicine people maintained a vigorous religious life that involved spirits of the "other" world. They performed ceremonies honoring and submitting to these spirits, although they did not "worship" them in the sense commonly understood in Western religious rituals.

CELEBRATIONS AND OBSERVANCES Festive occasions bring people together and foster a sense of belonging, reflecting the deep-seated need within humans to move beyond the everyday. People celebrate birthdays, couples toast each other on a wedding anniversary, and victories on battlefields give rise to ceremonies of remembrance and introspection. Likewise, religions pause throughout the year to celebrate those events that make them unique, the result being an array of religious holidays and festivities. From the wandering Hindu sannyasi (mendicant), whose presence is regarded as beneficial, to the reaction of an infant upon first seeing Santa Claus, celebrations bond people to their religious families.

Many religions also celebrate their founding. Such celebrations look to a defining time in the past and rejoice at its continuing influence. For believers such a celebration brings with it a sense of liberation and freedom. Sometimes such observances, along with their accompanying feasts and festivals, are criticized for the waywardness they encourage or for their expense on the public purse. Critics, for example, often single out Christmas decorations and gift giving as reflections of such extravagance. Despite this, they are treasured by people for the benefits they bestow.

SCRIPTURE Authoritative religious teachings are those sources of inspiration that embody a tradition's wisdom. They take on a hallowed character that puts them beyond normal human creativity. For believers such teachings are not exhausted through reading, for they can become the source of theology, meditation, or even healing, to say nothing of their use to provoke division and militancy. The teachings also reveal the standards by which the believer is to live. In most religions there is a written document, or scripture, that conveys this material. The oldest is thought to be the Rig Veda, which includes materials that may date from before the beginning of writing—that is, to around 4000 B.C.E. Scripture is sometimes held to be timeless, as, for example, with the Koran—thewords were delivered by the Prophet Muhammad but the message is believed to date to the very establishment of humans upon the earth.

Because writing is relatively recent in human history, religion has not always relied on a written text. Even some literate peoples have never assigned true authority to written forms, preferring instead the immediacy of the oral version. Devout Muslims, for example, pointing to the oral origins of the Koran, regard the oral version of "pure Arabic" as the only authoritative version. Others, like the Quakers, hoping to ward off dogma and worrying that a text might become frozen into literalism, have refused to accept anything but a flexible interpretation. Further, in certain religious contexts, such as ritual activity, there remains a preference for oral versions among some groups—for example, Buddhists—even though they have written texts. In place of a written canon some religions have sacred stories that are passed on orally from one authoritative speaker to another. The stories may take on the character of scripture, with people referring to them as the basis for their actions. In such traditions the authorities have the freedom of recasting the stories according to the audience and the spiritual need of the moment.

One of the most important uses of scripture is to provide the language of religious rites, with believers using its passages as a means of communicating with the living object of their faith. In this case the text becomes a vehicle of communication at another, perhaps deeper spiritual level than when it is simply used to affirm a specific doctrine. At this level scripture fosters a state of spiritual being and unites those focused upon it in ways that few other writings can. This is why it is difficult to disassociate scripture from the ritual life and personal piety of the group. The use of a scriptural text in scholarship outside the religious tradition is sometimes said to distort its original purpose, provoking criticism from believers that outsiders are trying to interpret what are essentially sacred sources.

Not all scriptures are conceived of as written by God. The Analects of Confucius, for example, are regarded as inspired writings that give details on a properly ordered life, but they are held up not as the word of God but rather as spiritually superior insights from a master. In addition, many practitioners of New Age beliefs argue that true religion is syncretic or eclectic, that people may pick and choose which scriptures or parts thereof are most meaningful and then make up their own authoritative text. Such individualism seems to violate the traditional sense of a sacred text as the focus of group loyalty. Thus, not only can scripture undergo transformation within the life of a tradition itself but its traditional meaning has been challenged in the contemporary world.

THEOLOGY In many religions it is particularly important to describe the intellectual basis of the faith. Throughout history great minds have wrestled with the problems of explaining the reality behind one or another religion, their efforts producing an interpretation of God and related terminology that is called "theology." As with activities like prayer or sacrifice, the theologies of the various religions show considerable diversity, and despite the attempt to use words and phrases that can be understood by ordinary people, the subject is sometimes difficult. Further, in some religions certain ideas are not discussed in a systematic way, even though they involve important doctrines of the tradition. Ideas surrounding death and life after death are examples.

Theology has been of particular importance in Western religions, especially in Christianity. In the Christian tradition theology is a highly organized profession, with the various churches exercising vigorous control over the ideas perpetrated in their names. At least in Western culture, theology has a long history separate from both philosophy and science, and it often involves intellectual activity at a sophisticated level. When theology addresses doctrine, it attempts to explain the principal ideas of a religion in a way that both adherents and interested observers can understand. It also develops ways of dealing with puzzles that are created by its own system of thought. For example, in Judaism, Christianity, and Islam, which as monotheistic religions embrace the doctrine of God as all-powerful and all-good, the existence of evil in the world is a problem. For the ordinary believer some of these complications may be beyond solution, and believers sometimes simply embrace such difficulties as part of the weakness of the human mind in trying to comprehend what is beyond the everyday.

ETHICS Every religion serves as the foundation for a system of ethics, or standards of moral behavior. For some religions adherence to such standards is regarded as the very basis of the believer's relationship with God, as, for example, with the Torah, or teachings, in Judaism. For others ethics promotes well-being and a healthy society. In the Confucian tradition, for example, devotees believe that the successful person is one who is neighborly and giving. In effect, that person's key moral goal in life is to express *ren* (or *jen*). Such a person is held to be dedicated to human relationships and consequently subjects all personal acts to the rule of moral conduct. Acting out that value in life is religion. Confucius thus summed up the standard for human relationships in the

Analects as "Never do to others what you would not like them to do to you," which is strikingly similar to the biblical adage "Do unto others as you would have others do into you" (Matt. 7:12). Islam also asserts that God has established the true way and that living according to the Shari'ah, or religious law, is the most basic responsibility of the Muslim.

Most religions share the concern that their moral values be expressed concretely in people's lives. There is, for example, an almost universal interest among religions in helping the poor and in providing education for children. Religion affirms that there are certain principles that should be enshrined in society, since the values they represent are the foundation of a beneficial community life. It is for this reason that religions advocate such qualities as honesty and truthfulness and oppose greed and materialism. Likewise, everywhere religion thrives there is concern for the uniqueness and sanctity of human life. Agreements on matters such as these suggest deeper patterns that transcend religious boundaries.

Ethical questions also arise in the relationship between religion and science. There was a time when science, seen as objective and free of "beliefs," was held to be a type of knowledge unfettered by religious convictions. Few people would agree with this view now, however, for modern science itself has come to be seen as the result of particular cultural assumptions. Science has developed in certain ways because of complex influences from the culture in which it has grown, with one of these influences being religion. The freedom to pursue research regardless of the consequences, for example, reflects an aggressive individualism that could not have developed without belief in the individual's responsibility for knowledge, a view derived from religion.

Scientists are themselves human, of course, and they respond to various religious sensibilities. Because science is a human activity, scientists are not "outside" culture or totally "objective," especially when they deal with human problems. Thus, science sometimes comes into conflict with a deeper sense of what is right. Issues like human cloning, for example, are debated by all people, and scientists must sometimes arbitrate between their religious feelings and values and what is scientifically possible. Further, questions have been raised about the legitimacy of any science that operates without social and cultural oversight—that is, outside a solidly- based ethics.

It has been argued that, since different religions promote different standards of moral behavior, ethics should not be grounded in religious belief. Further, some people have pointed to new problems, such as the international scourge of HIV/AIDS, faced by humans today as evidence that religion cannot handle modern ethical problems. Others have claimed that some of the problems of the modern world are legacies of religion itself.

Such critics usually advocate a system of secular ethics. Religious believers, however, argue that in a secular system people are not schooled in and do not internalize the age-old patterns that have undergirded human civilization. Believers maintain, for example, that secular ethics seems not to provide an educational grounding in matters of respect and dutifulness, which have traditionally been provided by religion as the foundation for relationships among people. Moreover, believers point out that charges of inadequacy against religious ethics are unfair, since the world is littered with failed attempts to shape a secular moral sensibility. The rise and fall of Marxism is a notable example. The history of such attempts gives little comfort to those making the secular argument, and the result has been a renewed attempt to reaffirm religious value as a foundation of modern life.

Thus, although the modern world poses many difficulties for believers in every culture, religious groups maintain that their perspective is essential for civilization. Most believers argue that religious tradition addresses issues in a more positive way than does any other approach. Using the tools of promotion and advertising, religions have entered into competition with other forces as they challenge individuals and societies to live according to a better plan. Seen from this perspective, religion has taken on a business hue, with the various traditions competing for followers in the marketplace of contemporary life.

OBSERVANCE AND EXPLANATION OF DEATH Most religions deal with death by providing rituals of condolence and assurances that life goes on, even if in a different way and on another level. Some religions claim to hold keys to eternal life as part of their mandate, while others claim to provide the means by which a person can face the next phase of life. Even those religions that do not maintain a belief in life after death provide means for a sense of closure and acceptance at the ending of life.

Most cultures accept the idea that death falls within the compass of religion. As in other matters, there is a wide variety of approaches. Indigenous peoples anticipate living on in an ancestral world, sometimes characterized by festivities that provide endless moments of delight before some part of a person once again takes on bodily form in this world. Hindus believe in a form of transmigration: with the death of the body in this world a movement into a transitory state from which a person, depending on his or her karma, ultimately exits in another form. Buddhists hope to achieve nirvana, a state that is not material. Western religions, on the other hand, are based on a strong sense of linear time, and although they hold that death is the end of earthly life, they believe that at least a spiritual element lives on. Such religions hold that following death there occur various events, including judgment, purification, and, ultimately for believers, a glorious life in a paradise, or heaven.

Geographic Variations in Religious Practice

In the contemporary world there is great diversity within religious groups, and religious practices often vary by country or region. Consider meditation, for example. As practiced across India in early Hinduism, meditation seems to have been associated with mendicants, those who left their families and homes, took vows, and became wandering holy men. When the practice was adopted by Buddhism, which spread from India to China, it seems initially to have been restricted to monks. In Zen Buddhism, which took root in Japan, meditation eventually took on much broader forms, for the possibility of instant awareness had the effect of weakening the commitment to a monastic life and made the benefits of meditation available to the lay population.

Volumes 2 and 3 of this encyclopedia, containing essays on the contemporary religious practices of individual countries, reveal that religions have frequently been influenced by and vary according to political and geographical boundaries. For example, people do not celebrate Christmas in the same way in Sweden, Uganda, and China. This "mixture" of forms is, however, a contentious issue, for postcolonial critics argue that contemporary political boundaries sometimes reflect the historical presence of imperialism, not the "natural" configuration of an ethnic or religious group. It is also true that religion seldom is restrained by national borders, as is seen by the spread of fundamentalism. Nonetheless, whatever its limitations, the view that political boundaries play a critical role in shaping religious life is commonly accepted, even as it makes analysis more difficult.

Trends in Contemporary Religion

One important trend in the contemporary world is the growth of local religious groups made up of small but highly engaged memberships. These groups, whose practices are especially diverse, claim to redefine traditional views, and they sometimes challenge tradition over the "proper" way to practice religion. The numbers of such groups are staggering, with perhaps thousands having sprung up throughout the world in the past quarter century alone.

Contemporary religion is also characterized by its close relation to politics. As religion has come to play an increasing role in political life, nearly every major government in the world now faces pressure from groups that form political movements clothed in religious mantles and that raise ethical questions over public policy. Further, the rise of radical religious groups like al-Qaeda or the Tamil Tigers of Sri Lanka has sometimes made religion a prime force in political events. All of this demonstrates that religion has not retreated, even in the face of the widespread embrace of secularism by governments. Even in countries that might be conceived as firmly advanced in secularism, such as France, the official banning of a religious symbol like the *hijab* can raise a storm of protest, signaling that religious sensitivities are far from quiescent. Indeed, many governments in Muslim countries have quietly abandoned their secular stance, with one eye toward the rising tide of religious revivalism.

Obviously not even Western democratic governments are free from religious influence. This is a striking change compared with, say, Europe during the sixteenth-century Protestant Reformation, when whole countries and peoples became Protestant or Roman Catholic at the conversion of a ruler and stroke of a pen. Today it tends to be the other way around, with the religious values of the people having a direct impact on the government. Religious issues, moreover, are receiving more and more attention in the media. Whereas newspapers, for example, once were restrained in their reporting of religious issues, such matters are now front-page news. At the same time powerful religious organizations like the Roman Catholic Church are no longer free from scrutiny by the public press.

Another feature of contemporary religion is the changing role of women. Holding everything from volunteer to executive positions, women are more important than ever before in religious organizations. While some organizations have been slow to revise their official policies on the role of women, women themselves often have developed their own ways of circumventing the system. Their influence in religion has also changed many people's views about the relationship between the sexes, despite the view of women in traditional theology.

Along with this challenge from women, religious groups have also faced greater demands from the laity. Many laypeople have come to insist that their understanding of tradition is just as valid as that of the professional religionist, something that has consequences for everything from ritual activity to doctrine and organization. Prominent in this movement is the use of the Internet and other modern technology to promote alternative religious views. Whereas a traditional religious organization tends to adopt this technology only to serve its existing structures and approaches, lay leaders often use it as a means for developing new ideas and ways of interacting, which further alienates them from the traditional centers of authority.

The practice of religion without the trappings of wealth and privilege, what is called "antiformalism," is another contemporary idea of global significance. Although it is difficult to see the outlines of the movement clearly, one noticeable feature is the rejection of elaborate settings for worship. In Christianity, for example, architecture has historically played a major role, with basilicas, monasteries, and other religious and educational edifices being central to the life of the Church. The trend in Christianity away from embodying tradition in ornate, expensive buildings may have important ramifications for all religions, as this movement can be seen as part of a broader challenge to established religious understanding and practice.

Hand in hand with these movements are those associated with fundamentalism. A complex phenomenon that arose in American Christianity in the early twentieth century, variations of this movement have spread to most major religions and countries around the world. Fundamentalism involves a militant return to first principles, even as its very existence requires the presence of modernity, with which it clashes. It is not a return to traditional views, for most fundamentalists see such views as hopelessly entwined with political and secular issues. Instead, for fundamentalists religion is primary. Resisting the concept of compromise, fundamentalism affirms a direct and literal interpretation of what is seen as essential in religion. While it is claimed that the roots of fundamentalism connect it to ancient religious founders, there is no mistaking the modern tone and strident individualism of the movement, regardless of the religion in which it occurs.

An Invitation to Explore

These, then, are some of the ways in which people have fashioned responses to their religious sensibilities. It is this material that is summarized, or, perhaps better, sketched in the *Worldmark Encyclopedia of Religious Practices.* The essays in the encyclopedia attempt to describe the rich detail of religious activity in an accessible way. Given the wealth to be found in contemporary religion, however, it is not possible in the essays to do more than provide a sampling, supplemented by suggestions for further reading in the bibliographies. In fact, given limitations of time and space and of human understanding, it is impossible ever to fully describe contemporary religious practices. While acknowledging these limitations, we invite you to engage in studying this cultural wealth with us.

Earle H. Waugh

Advisory Board

Notes on Contributors

ABELA, ANTHONY M. Contributor and peer reviewer. Associate professor of sociology and social policy, University of Malta; principal investigator, European Values Study, Malta; and member, European Values Steering Committee, Tilburg, The Netherlands. Author of *Transmitting Values in European Malta,* 1991, *Changing Youth Culture,* 1992, *Shifting Family Values,* 1994, *Secularized Sexuality: Youth Values in a City-Island,* 1998, *Women and Men in the Maltese Islands: A Comparative European Perspective,* 2000, *Youth Participation in Voluntary Organizations,* 2001, and *Women's Welfare in Society,* 2002. Essay: Malta.

AGUILAR, MARIO I. Contributor and peer reviewer. Dean, Faculty of Divinity, Saint Mary's College, University of Saint Andrews, Scotland. Author of *Being Oromo in Kenya,* 1998, *The Rwanda Genocide and the Call to Deepen Christianity in Africa,* 1998, and *Current Issues on Theology and Religion in Latin America and Africa,* 2002. Editor of *The Politics of Age and Gerontocracy in Africa: Ethnographies of the Past and Memories of the Present,* 1998. Essays: Rwanda, Uganda.

AKERS, DEBORAH S. Contributor. Assistant professor of anthropology, Miami University, Oxford, Ohio. Author, with Abubaker Bagader, of *They Die Strangers: Selected Works by Abdel-Wali,* 2001, *Whispers from the Heart: Short Stories from Saudi Arabia,* 2003, and *Oranges in the Sun: Short Stories from the Persian Gulf,* 2004. Essays: Qatar, Saudi Arabia.

AKINADE, AKINTUNDE E. Contributor. Associate professor of world religions, High Point University, North Carolina. Coeditor of *The Agitated Mind of God: The Theology of Kosuke Koyama,* 1996. Essay: Gambia.

AMAYA, BENJAMÍN. Contributor. Assistant professor of anthropology and sociology, University College of Cape Breton, Nova Scotia, Canada. Author of *Violencia y culturas juveniles en El Salvador,* 2002. Author of book reviews for the scholarly journals *Anthropologie et Société* and *Culture.* Essay: El Salvador.

ANDERSON, LEONA. Contributor and peer reviewer. Professor of religious studies, University of Regina, Saskatchewan, Canada. Author of *The Vasantotsava: The Spring Festivals of India: Texts and Contexts,* 1993. Producer of the video documentaries *The Kumbh Mela,* 1991, and *The Ganesh Festival: Ten Days in the Presence of God,* 1999. Essay: India.

ANDERSON, PAUL N. Contributor. Professor of biblical and Quaker studies and chair, Department of Religious Studies, George Fox University, Newberg, Oregon. Author of *The Christology of the Fourth Gospel: Its Unity and Disunity in the Light of John 6,* 1997, and *Navigating the Living Waters of the Gospel of John: On Wading with Children and Swimming with Elephants,* 2000. Editor of *Evangelical Friend,* 1990–94, and *Quaker Religious Thought,* since 2000. Contributor to such journals as *Semeia, Horizons in Biblical Theology, Review of Biblical Literature, Journal of Biblical Literature, Critical Review of Books in Religion, Princeton Seminary Bulletin,* and *Pastoral Theology,* as well as to various Friends journals and collections. Author of the *Meet the Friends* series, 2003. Essay: Religious Society of Friends (Quakers).

ANDREEVA, LARISSA A. Contributor. Senior research fellow, Department of Cultural Anthropology, Center for Civilizational and Regional Studies, Russian Academy of Sciences, Moscow. Author of the monographs, in Russian, *Religion and Power in Russia,* 2001, and *Vicarius Christi on the Royal Throne: The Christian Civilization Model of Power Sacralization,* 2002. Essays: Belarus, Russia.

APRAHAMIAN, SIMA. Contributor. Research associate and lecturer, Simone de Beauvoir Institute, Concordia University, Quebec, Canada. Author of articles on Armenia and Lebanon in numerous scholarly journals and edited volumes. Essay: Armenia.

ARENS, WILLIAM. Contributor and peer reviewer. Professor of anthropology and dean of International Academic Programs, State University of New York, Stony Brook. Author of *On the Frontier of Change,* 1979, *The Man-Eating Myth,* 1979, and *The Original Sin,* 1986. Editor of *A Century of Change in Eastern Africa,* 1976. Coeditor of *Creativity of Power,*

1989. Author of numerous articles and essays in scholarly journals and other publications. Essay: Tanzania.

ARMSTRONG, CHARLES. Peer reviewer. Associate professor of history, Columbia University, New York, New York. Author of *Korean Society: Civil Society, Democracy, and the State,* 2002, and *The North Korean Revolution, 1945–1950,* 2003. Contributor to journals, including *Journal of Asian Studies, Critical Asian Studies,* and *Acta Koreana.*

AZEVEDO, MARIO J. Contributor and peer reviewer. Chair and Frank Porter Graham Professor, Department of African-American and African Studies, University of North Carolina, Charlotte. Author of *The Returning Hunter,* 1978, *Roots of Violence: A History of War in Chad,* 1998, and *Tragedy and Triumph: Mozambique Refugees in Southern Africa,* 2002. Coauthor of *Chad: A Nation in Search of Its Future,* 1998, and *A Historical Dictionary of Mozambique,* 2003. Editor of *Cameroon and Chad in Historical and Contemporary Perspectives,* 1988, *Africana Studies: A Survey of Africa and the African Diaspora,* 1998, and *Kenya: The Land, the People, and the Nation,* 1993. Author of articles in numerous scholarly journals, including *African Studies Review, African Affairs, Current History, Journal of Negro History,* and *Science and Medicine.* Essays: Central African Republic, Chad, Kenya, Lesotho, Mozambique, Nigeria.

BAKER, DONALD L. Contributor and peer reviewer. Professor of Asian studies, as well as director, Centre for Korean Research, University of British Columbia, Vancouver, Canada. Coeditor of *Sourcebook of Korean Civilization,* 1996. Author of numerous journal articles and book chapters on the history of Korean religion and traditional science. Essay: North Korea.

BALISKY, E. PAUL. Contributor. Lecturer, Ethiopian Graduate School of Theology, Addis Ababa. Director, Serving in Mission (SIM) Ethiopia, 1999–2003. Author of articles for the 14th International Conference of Ethiopian Studies, 2000, and the online *Dictionary of African Christian Biography.* Essay: Ethiopia.

BARBOSA DA SILVA, ANTÓNIO. Peer reviewer. Professor of systematic theology, philosophy of religion, ethics, and health care ethics, Misjonshøgskolen, Stavanger, Norway. Author of *The Phenomenology of Religion as a Philosophical Problem with Particular Reference to Mircea Eliade's Phenomenological Approach,* 1982, and *Is There a New Imbalance in Jewish-Christian Relations?* Author, in Norwegian, of *Hva er religionsfenomenologi?* Author of numerous articles.

BARCLAY, HAROLD B. Contributor and peer reviewer. Professor emeritus of anthropology, University of Alberta, Edmonton, Canada. Author of *Buurri al Lamaab, a Suburban Village in the Sudan,* 1964, *The Role of the Horse in Man's Culture,* 1980, *Culture, the Human Way,* 1986, and *People without Government: An Anthropology of Anarchy,* 1990. Author of the chapters "Egypt: Struggling with Secularization" and "Sudan: On the Frontier of Islam" in *Religions and Societies, Asia and the Middle East,* edited by Carlo Caldarola, 1982. Essays: The Sudan, Tunisia.

BAREJA-STARZYNSKA, AGATA. Contributor. Assistant professor, Department of Inner Asia, Institute of Oriental Studies, University of Warsaw, Poland. Author of "The History of Ancient Tibet according to the 17th Century Mongolian Chronicle 'Erdeni-yin tobci' by Sagang Secen," in *Proceedings of the 5th International Seminar on Tibetan Studies in Narita, Japan, 1989,* edited by S. Ihara and Z. Yamaguchi, 1992, and "The Essentials of Buddhism in the 'Ciqula kereglegci,' the 16th Century Mongolian Buddhist Treatise," in *Proceedings of the International Seminar on Buddhism 'Aspects of Buddhism' in Liw, Poland, 1994,* edited by A. Bareja-Starzynska and M. Mejor, 1997. Essay: Mongolia.

BARLOW, PHILIP L. Peer reviewer. Professor of theological studies, Hanover College, Indiana. Author of *Mormons and the Bible: The Place of the Latter-Day Saints in American Religion,* 1991. Coauthor of *New Historical Atlas of Religion in America,* 2000. Editor of *A Thoughtful Faith: Essays on Belief by Mormon Scholars,* 1986, and *Religion and Public Life in the Midwest: Microcosm and Mosaic,* 2004.

BEBBINGTON, DAVID. Peer reviewer. Professor of history, University of Stirling, Scotland. Author of *Evangelicalism in Modern Britain: A History from the 1730s to the 1980s,* 1989, and *Holiness in Nineteenth-Century England,* 1998. Editor of *The Baptists in Scotland: A History,* 1988, and *The Gospel in the World: International Baptist Studies,* 2002. Coeditor of *Evangelicalism: Comparative Studies of Popular Protestantism in North America, the British Isles and Beyond, 1700–1990,* 1994, and *Modern Christianity and Cultural Aspirations,* 2003.

BERNAL, VICTORIA. Contributor. Associate professor of anthropology, University of California, Irvine. Author of *Cultivating Workers: Peasants and Capitalism in a Sudanese Village,* 1991. Author of articles in such scholarly journals as *American Ethnologist, American Anthropologist, Comparative Studies in Society and History, Cultural Anthropology, African Studies Review,* and *Political and Legal Anthropology Review.* Essay: Eritrea.

BERRY, MOULOUK. Contributor. Assistant professor of Arabic, as well as director of the Arab and Chaldean American Writers Series and the Quranic Forum, University of Michigan-Dearborn. Essay: Lebanon.

BESNIER, NIKO. Peer reviewer. Visiting professor, Department of Anthropology, University of California, Los Angeles. Author of *Literacy, Emotion, and Authority: Reading and*

Writing on a Polynesian Atoll, 1995, and *Tuvaluan: A Polynesian Language of the Central Pacific,* 2000. Contributor to numerous journals in anthropology and linguistics, including *American Ethnologist, American Anthropologist, Anthropological Quarterly, Ethnos, Social Anthropology, Journal of Anthropological Research, Annual Review of Anthropology, Language,* and *Language in Society,* as well as many edited volumes.

BLUMHOFER, EDITH. Contributor. Professor of history, as well as director, Institute for the Study of American Evangelicals, Wheaton College, Illinois. Author of *The Assemblies of God: A Chapter in the Story of American Pentecostalism,* 1989, *Aimee Semple McPherson: Everybody's Sister,* 1993, and *Restoring the Faith: The Assemblies of God, Pentecostalism, and American Culture,* 1993. Coeditor of *Modern Christian Revivals,* 1993, and *Pentecostal Currents in American Protestantism,* 1999. Essay: Pentecostalism.

BOELDERL, ARTUR R. Contributor. Assistant professor of philosophy, Private Catholic University of Linz, Austria. Author of *Alchimie, Postmoderne und der arme Hölderlin: Drei Studien zur Philosophischen Hermetik,* 1995, and *Literarische Hermetik: Die Ethik zwischen Hermeneutik, Psychoanalyse und Dekonstruktion,* 1997. Coeditor of several volumes, including *Rituale: Zugänge zu einem Phänomen,* 1999, and *Die Sprachen der Religion,* 2003. Essay: Austria.

BONK, JONATHAN J. Peer reviewer. Executive director, Overseas Ministries Study Center, New Haven, Connecticut, as well as editor, *International Bulletin of Missionary Research,* and project director, *Dictionary of African Christian Biography.* Author of *An Annotated and Classified Bibliography of English Literature Pertaining to the Ethiopian Orthodox Church,* 1984, *The World at War, the Church at Peace: A Biblical Perspective,* 1988, *The Theory and Practice of Missionary Identification, 1860–1920,* 1989, *Missions and Money: Affluence as a Western Missionary Problem,* 1991, and *Between Past and Future: Evangelical Mission Entering the Twenty-First Century,* 2003.

BOOLELL, SHAKUNTALA. Contributor. Senior lecturer in French, Department of Humanities and Social Sciences, University of Mauritius. Author of *La femme enveloppée et autres nouvelles de Maurice,* 1996, and *De l'ombre à la lumière: Sur les traces de l'Indo-Mauricienne,* 1998. Coauthor of *Fonction et représentation de la Mauricienne dans le discours littéraire,* 2000. Essay: Mauritius.

BOROWIK, IRENA. Peer reviewer. Professor of religion and post-Communist transformation, Institute of Religious Studies, Jagiellonian University, Kraków, Poland. Author, in Polish, of *Charyzma a codziennosc: Studium wplywu religii na zycie codzienne,* 1990, *Procesy instytucjonalizacji i prywatyzacji religii w powojennej Polsce,* 1997, and *Odbudowywanie pamieci: Przemiany religijne w Srodkowo-wschodniej Europie po upadku komun izm',* 2000. Coauthor, with Tadeusz Doktór, in Polish, of *Religijny i moralny pluralizm w Polsce,* 2001. Editor of *State Relations in Central and Eastern Europe after the Collapse of Communism,* 1999, and *Religions, Churches and the Scientific Studies of Religion: Poland and Ukraine,* 2003. Coeditor, with Miklos Tomka, of *Religion and Social Change in Post-Communist Europe,* 2001. Coeditor and contributor to *The Future of Religion,* 1995, and *New Religious Phenomena in Central and Eastern Europe,* 1997.

BOYARIN, DANIEL. Peer reviewer. Hermann P. and Sophia Taubman Professor of Talmudic Culture, Department of Near Eastern Studies and Rhetoric, University of California, Berkeley. Author of *Carnal Israel: Reading Sex in Talmudic Culture,* 1995, *A Radical Jew: Paul and the Politics of Identity,* 1997, *Unheroic Conduct: The Rise of Heterosexuality and the Invention of the Jewish Man,* 1997, *Dying for God: Martyrdom and the Making of Christianity and Judaism,* 1999, and *Border Lines: The Partition of Judaeo-Christianity,* 2004. Coauthor, with Jonathan Boyarin, of *Powers of Diaspora: Two Essays on the Relevance of Jewish Culture,* 2002. Coeditor, with Jonathan Boyarin, of *Jews and Other Differences: The New Jewish Cultural Studies,* 1997, and, with Daniel Itzkovitz and Ann Pellegrini, of *Queer Theory and the Jewish Question,* 2003.

BRATT, JAMES D. Peer reviewer. Professor of history, as well as director of the Calvin Center for Christian Scholarship, Calvin College, Grand Rapids, Michigan. Author of *Dutch Calvinism in Modern America: A History of a Conservative Subculture,* 1984. Coauthor of *Gathered at the River: Grand Rapids, Michigan, and Its People of Faith,* 1993. Editor of *Viewpoints: Exploring the Reformed Vision,* 1992, and *Abraham Kuyper: A Centennial Reader,* 1998.

BRINKMAN, INGE. Contributor. Research fellow, Ghent University, Belgium. Author of *Kikuyu Gender Norms and Narratives,* 1996, as well as various articles in such scholarly journals as *Journal of African History, Africa, Journal of South African Studies,* and *Historische Anthropoligie.* Editor of *Singing in the Bush: MPLA Songs during the War for Independence in South-East Angola (1966–1975),* 2001. Coeditor of *Grandmother's Footsteps: Oral Tradition and South-East Angolan Narratives on the Colonial Encounter,* 1999. Essay: Angola.

BROWERS, MICHAELLE. Contributor. Assistant professor of political science, Wake Forest University, Winston-Salem, North Carolina. Coeditor of *An Islamic Reformation?,* 2003. Essay: Syria.

BUCHENAU, KLAUS. Contributor. Research assistant, Eastern European Institute, Free University of Berlin. Author of two monographs, as well as various articles on religion in the former Yugoslavia. Essay: Bosnia and Herzegovina.

BUCKSER, ANDREW. Contributor. Associate professor of anthropology, Purdue University, Lafayette, Indiana. Author of *Communities of Faith: Sectarianism, Identity, and Social Change on a Danish Island,* 1996, and *After the Rescue: Jewish Identity and Community in Contemporary Denmark,* 2003. Coeditor of *The Anthropology of Religious Conversion,* 2003. Essay: Denmark.

CAHN, PETER S. Contributor. Assistant professor of anthropology, University of Oklahoma, Norman. Author of *All Religions Are Good in Tzintzuntzan: Evangelicals in Catholic Mexico,* 2003, and a chapter in *Chronicling Cultures: Long-Term Field Research in Anthropology,* 2002. Essay: Brazil.

CALKOWSKI, MARCIA. Contributor and peer reviewer. Associate professor and head, Department of Anthropology, University of Regina, Saskatchewan, Canada. Author of articles in edited volumes and journals, including *Canadian Review of Sociology and Anthropology, Anthropologica, American Ethnologist, Journal of Asian Studies, Tibetan Review,* and *Culture.* Essays: Myanmar, Thailand, Tibetan Buddhism.

CAMPBELL, SIRI. Contributor. Journalist. Author of *Inside Monaco,* 2000, and contributor to numerous television organizations and travel shows, including the Discovery Channel, BBC *Travel Show,* NBC *Today Show, CBS News,* and Denmark 2. Essay: Monaco.

CAMPO, JUAN E. Peer reviewer. Associate professor, Religious Studies Department, University of California, Santa Barbara. Author of *The Other Sides of Paradise: Explorations into the Religious Meanings of Domestic Space in Islam,* 1991. Contributor to *Merriam-Webster's Encyclopedia of World Religions,* 1999, and to journals, including *Traditional Dwellings and Settlements Review, Contention, Annals of the American Academy of Political and Social Science,* and *Muslim World.*

CAREY, PATRICK. Peer reviewer. Professor of theology, Marquette University, Milwaukee, Wisconsin. Author of *An Immigrant Bishop: John England's Adaptation of Irish Catholicism to American Republicanism,* 1982, *People, Priests and Prelates: Ecclesiastical Democracy and the Tensions of Trusteeism,* 1987, *The Roman Catholics,* 1993, and *The Roman Catholics in America,* 1996. Editor of *American Catholic Religious Thought,* 1987, and *The Early Works of Orestes A. Brownson,* 2000. Coeditor of *Theological Education in the Catholic Tradition: Contemporary Challenges,* 1997, and *Biographical Dictionary of Christian Theologians,* 2002.

CASEBOLT, JAMES. Contributor. Associate professor of psychology, Ohio University Eastern Campus, Saint Clairsville. Contributor to the edited volume *Measures of Religiosity,* 1999, and to various journals, including *AURCO Journal.* Essay: Unitarianism and Universalism.

CATE, SANDRA. Contributor. Lecturer, Department of Anthropology, San Jose State University, California. Author of *Making Merit, Making Art: A Thai Temple in Wimbledon,* 2003. Coeditor of *Converging Interests: Travelers, Traders, and Tourists in South East Asia,* 1999. Essay: Laos.

CAULKINS, D. DOUGLAS. Contributor. Earl D. Strong Professor of Social Studies, Department of Anthropology, Grinnell College, Iowa. Formerly a visiting researcher at the Institute for Social Research, Oslo, Norway, and at the universities of Trondheim, Norway; Bergen, Norway; Stirling, Scotland; and Durham, England. Author of numerous articles in journals, including *Cross-Cultural Research, Journal of Anthropological Research, Field Methods,* and *Practicing Anthropology.* Essay: Norway.

CHAKANZA, J.C. Contributor. Associate professor and head, Department of Theology and Religious Studies, Chancellor College, Zomba, Malawi. Author of *Voices of Preachers in Protest: The Ministry of Two Malawian Prophets: Elliot Kamwana and Wilfrid Gudu,* 1998, *Religion in Malawi: An Annotated Bibliography,* 1998, *Islam in Malawi Week,* 1999, and *Wisdom of the People: 2000 Chinyanja Proverbs,* 2001. Author of articles in various journals, including *Lamp.* Essay: Malawi.

CHEVANNES, BARRY. Contributor. Professor of social anthropology and dean of the Faculty of Social Sciences, University of the West Indies at Mona, Kingston, Jamaica. Author of *Rastafari: Roots and Ideology,* 1994, and *Learning to Be a Man: Culture, Socialisation and Gender in Five Caribbean Communities,* 2001. Editor of *Rastafari and Other African-Caribbean Worldviews,* 1995. Essay: Jamaica.

CHEYEKA, AUSTIN. Contributor. Lecturer in religious studies, University of Zambia, Lusaka. Author of articles in various scholarly journals, including *African Ecclesial Review (AFER)* and *African Christian Studies.* Essay: Zambia.

CHILTON, TUTII. Contributor. Assistant professor of social science, Palau Community College, Republic of Palau. Essay: Palau.

CHOKSY, JAMSHEED. Peer reviewer. Professor of central Eurasian studies, professor of history, and adjunct professor of religious studies, Indiana University, Bloomington. Author of *Purity and Pollution in Zoroastrianism: Triumph over Evil,* 1989, *Conflict and Cooperation: Zoroastrian Subalterns and Muslim Elites in Medieval Iranian Society,* 1997, and *Evil, Good, and Gender: Facets of the Feminine in Zoroastrian Religious History,* 2002. Contributor to *Women in Iran from the Rise of Islam to 1800,* edited by G. Nashat and L. Beck, 2003, *Jamshid Soroush Soroushian Memorial Volume,* edited by C. Cereti and F.J. Vajifdar, 2003, and the periodicals *Indo-Iranian Journal, Iranian Studies, Iranica Antiqua, Journal of the American Oriental Society, Journal of*

Ritual Studies, Journal of the Royal Asiatic Society of Great Britain and Ireland, and Studia Iranica, among others.

CINNAMON, JOHN. Contributor. Assistant professor of anthropology, Miami University, Hamilton, Ohio. Author of various articles on religion and political ecology in Gabon. Essays: Comoros, Equatorial Guinea, Gabon, São Tomé and Príncipe.

CLAYER, NATHALIE. Contributor and peer reviewer. Researcher, Centre Nationale de la Recherche Scientifique (CNRS), Paris. Author of *L'Albanie: Pays des derviches,* 1990, and *Mystiques, etat et société: Les halvetis dans l'aire balkanique de la fin du XVe siècle à nos jours,* 1994. Coeditor, *Le nouvel Islam balkanique: Les musulmans, acteurs du post-communisme,* 2001. Essay: Albania.

COLE, JUAN R. Peer reviewer. Professor of modern Middle East and South Asian history, Department of History, University of Michigan, Ann Arbor. Author of *Roots of North Indian Shi'ism in Iran and Iraq: Religion and State in Awadh, 1722–1859,* 1988, *Colonialism and Revolution in the Middle East: Social and Cultural Origins of Egypt's 'Urabi' Movement,* 1993, *Modernity and the Millennium: The Genesis of the Baha'i Faith in the Nineteenth-Century Middle East,* 1998, and *Sacred Space and Holy War: The Politics, Culture and History of Shi'ite Islam,* 2002. Translator of *Miracles and Metaphors,* by Mirza Abu'l-Fadl Gulpaygani, 1982, *Letters and Essays 1886–1913,* by Mirza Abu'l-Fadl Gulpaygani, 1985, *Spirit Brides,* by Kahlil Gibran, 1993, *The Vision,* by Kahlil Gibran, 1998, and *Broken Wings: A Novel,* by Kahlil Gibran, 1998. Contributor to and coeditor of *From Iran East and West: Studies in Babi and Baha'i History,* 1984. Coeditor of *Shi'ism and Social Protest,* 1986. Editor of *Comparing Muslim Societies,* 1992, and *Religion in Iran: From Zoroaster to Baha'u'llah,* by Alessandro Bausani, 2000. Author of articles in numerous journals and books.

COLEMAN, SIMON. Contributor. Reader in anthropology, University of Durham, England. Author of *The Globalisation of Charismatic Christianity: Spreading the Gospel of Prosperity,* 2000. Coauthor of *Pilgrimage: Past and Present in the World Religions,* 1995. Coeditor of *Tourism: Between Place and Performance,* 2002, *Religion, Identity, and Change: Perspectives on Global Transformations,* 2003, *Pilgrim Voices: Narrative and Authorship in Christian Pilgrimage,* 2003, *The Cultures of Creationism: Antievolution in English-Speaking Countries,* 2003, and *Reframing Pilgrimage: Cultures in Motion,* 2004. Essay: Sweden.

COLLINGE, WILLIAM J. Contributor. Knott Professor of Theology and professor of philosophy, Mount Saint Mary's College, Emmitsburg, Maryland. Author of *A Historical Dictionary of Catholicism,* 1997, and *The A to Z of Catholicism,* 2001, as well as articles in various journals, including *Horizons, Living Light, Faith and Philosophy,* and *Augustinian Studies.* Essay: Roman Catholicism.

COSENTINO, DONALD. Contributor and peer reviewer. Professor of world arts and cultures, University of California, Los Angeles, as well as editor of *African Arts,* since 1988. Author of *Defiant Maids and Stubborn Farmers: Tradition and Invention in Mende Story Performance,* 1982, and *Vodou Things: The Art of Pierrot Barra and Marie Cassaise,* 1998. Editor of *Sacred Arts of Haitian Vodou,* 1995. Author of articles in numerous journals, magazines, and catalogs, from *Aperture* to *Playboy.* Essay: Haiti.

COWE, S. PETER. Peer reviewer. Narekatsi Professor of Armenian Studies, University of California, Los Angeles. Author of *The Armenian Version of Daniel,* 1992, and *Catalogue of the Armenian Manuscripts in the Cambridge University Library,* 1994. Editor of *Mxit'ar Sasnec'i's Theological Discourses,* 1993, and *Ani: World Architectural Heritage of a Medieval Armenian Capital,* 2001. Coeditor of *Modern Armenian Drama: An Anthology,* 2001. Translator of *Commentary on the Divine Liturg,* by Xosrov Anjewac'I, 1991.

CROCCO, STEPHEN D. Adviser. James Lennox Librarian, Princeton Theological Seminary, Princeton, New Jersey. Editor, *The Essential Paul Ramsey: A Collection,* 1994.

DAIBER, KARL-FRITZ. Contributor. Professor emeritus, College of Protestant Theology, University of Marburg, Germany. Author of *Praktische Theologie als Handlungswissenschaft,* 1977, *Diakonie und Kirchliche Identitaet,* 1988, *Religion unter den Bedingungen der Moderne—Die Situation in der Bundesrepublik Deutschland,* 1995, and *Religion in Kirche und Gesellschaft: Theologische und Soziologische Studien zur Präsenz von Religion in der Gegenwärtigen Kultur,* 1997. Coeditor of *Religion in den Gegenwartsströmungen der Deutschen Soziologie,* 1983. Essay: Germany.

DAMATTA, ROBERTO. Peer reviewer. Professor emeritus, Department of Anthropology, University of Notre Dame, Indiana. Author of *Carnivals, Rogues and Heroes: An Interpretation of the Brazilian Dilemma* and *A Divided World: Apinayé Social Structure.* Contributor to *Revisão do paraíso: Os brasileiros e o estado em 500 anos de história,* edited by Mary Del Priori, 2000, and *Brazil 2001: A Revisionary History of Brazilian Literature and Culture,* 2001. Coauthor and coeditor of *The Brazilian Puzzle* and coauthor of *Aguias, burros e borboletas: Um estudo antropologico do jogo do bicho,* 1999.

DARROW, WILLIAM. Contributor. Jackson Professor of Religion, Williams College, Williamstown, Massachusetts. Author of articles in various edited volumes and journals, including *Journal of the American Academy of Religion, Harvard Theological Review,* and *History of Religions.* Essay: Zoroastrianism.

DAVIS, MARTHA ELLEN. Contributor. Affiliate associate professor of anthropology and music, University of Florida, Gainesville. Member, Dominican Academy of Sciences, and researcher, Museo del Hombre Dominicana, Santo Domingo, Dominican Republic. Author of *Afro-Dominican Religious Brotherhoods: Structure, Ritual, and Music,* 1976, *Cries from Purgatory: A Study of the Dominican "Salve,"* 1981, and *The Other Science: Dominican Vodú as Folk Religion and Medicine,* 1987. Essay: Dominican Republic.

DIAGNE, SOULEYMANE BACHIR. Contributor. Professor of philosophy, Northwestern University, Evanston, Illinois. Author of *Boole: 1815–1864: L'oiseau de nuit en plein jour,* 1989, *Reconstruire le sens: Textes et enjeux de prospectives africaines,* 2000, *Islam et société ouverte: La fidélité et le mouvement dans la philosophie de Muhammad Iqbal,* 2001, and *100 mots pour dire l'Islam,* 2002. Coauthor of *The Cultural Question in Africa,* 1996. Essay: Senegal.

DIALLO, GARBA. Contributor. Director of international programs, International People's College, Elsinore, Denmark. Author of *Mauritania, the Other Apartheid,* 1993, *Indigenous Learning Forms in West Africa: The Case of Mauritania,* 1994, *Entrance to Hell—The Concentration Camp (Goree) That Lasted for 400 Years,* 1996, and *Mauritania—Neither Arab nor African,* 2001, as well as articles in journals, including *Global Ecology* and *Kontakt.* Editor of *Educators' Contribution to the Peace Process in the Middle East,* 1998. Essay: Mauritania.

DOLAN, JAY. Adviser. Professor emeritus of history, University of Notre Dame, Indiana. Author of *The Immigrant Church: New York's Irish and German Catholics, 1815-1865,* 1975, *Catholic Revivalism: The American Experience, 1830-1900,* 1978, *The American Catholic Experience: A History from Colonial Time to the Present,* 1985, and *In Search of an American Catholicism: A History of Religion and Culture in Tension,* 2002. Coauthor of *The American Catholic Parish: A History from 1850 to the Present,* 1987, and *Transforming Parish Ministry: The Changing Roles of Catholic Clergy, Laity, and Women Religious in the United States, 1930-1980,* 1989.

DOUGLAS, IAN T. Contributor. Professor of mission and world Christianity, as well as director of Anglican, global, and ecumenical studies, Episcopal Divinity School, Cambridge, Massachusetts. Author of *Fling Out the Banner: The National Church Ideal and the Foreign Mission of the Episcopal Church,* 1993. Editor of *Waging Reconciliation: God's Mission in a Time of Globalization and Crisis,* 2002. Coeditor of *Beyond Colonial Anglicanism: The Anglican Communion in the Twenty-First Century,* 2001. Essay: Anglicanism.

EBERSOLE, GARY. Adviser, contributor, and peer reviewer. Professor of history and religious studies, as well as director of the Center for Religious Studies, University of Missouri-Kansas City. Author of *Ritual Poetry and the Politics of Death in Early Japan,* 1989, and *Captured by Texts: Puritan to Postmodern Images of Indian Captivity,* 1995. Author of articles in numerous journals, including *History of Religions, Religion, Journal of Religion, Journal of Japanese Studies,* and *Momumenta Nipponica.* Essays: Japan, Shinto.

EDGECOMBE-HOWELL, OLIVIA. Contributor. Head, University Centre, University of the West Indies, Basseterre, St. Kitts. Essay: Saint Kitts and Nevis.

EL-ASWAD, EL-SAYED. Contributor. Professor of anthropology and chair, Department of Sociology, Tanta University, Egypt, as well as adjunct professor, Wayne State University, Detroit, Michigan. Author of books in Arabic and English, including *Religion and Folk Cosmology: Scenarios of the Visible and Invisible in Rural Egypt,* 2002, and *Symbolic Anthropology,* 2002. Author of articles in journals, including *AAA Anthropology Newsletter* and *Anthropos.* Essay: United Arab Emirates.

EL-HASSAN, KHALID. Contributor. Research assistant professor and program coordinator, African Studies Resource Center, University of Kansas, Lawrence. Author of articles and book reviews in edited volumes and journals, including *Horizons, Journal of International Programs for the University of Kansas,* and *African Studies Quarterly.* Essay: Bahrain.

ELOLIA, SAMUEL K. Contributor. Associate professor of Christian doctrine and missiology, Emmanuel School of Religion, Johnson City, Tennessee. Author of articles in several edited volumes. Essays: Burundi, Djibouti.

ESPOSITO, JOHN L. Contributor. Professor, School of Foreign Service and Theology, Georgetown University, Washington, D.C. Author of *Islam and Politics,* 1998, and coauthor of *Islam and Democracy,* 1996. Editor of *Islam and Development: Religion and Sociopolitical Change,* 1980, *Voices of Resurgent Islam,* 1983, *Islam in Asia: Religion, Politics, and Society,* 1987, *The Iranian Revolution: Its Global Impact,* 1990, and *The Islamic World: Past and Present,* 2004. Coeditor of *Islam, Gender, and Social Change,* 1998, *Muslims on the Americanization Path?,* 2000, *Religion and Global Order,* 2000, *Islam and Secularism in the Middle East,* 2001, *Daughters of Abraham: Feminist Thought in Judaism, Christianity, and Islam,* 2001, *Iran at the Crossroads,* 2001, *Muslims and the West: Encounter and Dialogue,* 2001, *Religion and Immigration: Christian, Jewish, and Muslim Experiences in the United States,* 2003, and *Turkish Islam and the Secular State: The Gülen Movement,* 2003. Essay: Islam.

ESTGEN, ALOYSE. Contributor. Member, Centre Luxembourgeois de Documentation et d'êtudes MÇdiÇvales, and former instructor of medieval history.

Author of numerous articles, as well as coeditor of *Les Actes de Jean l'Aveugle,* 1997. Essay: Luxembourg.

ESTGEN, PAUL. Contributor. Sociologist, SESOPI-Centre Intercommunautaire, Luxembourg. Contributor to *Les valeurs au Luxembourg: Portrait d'une société au tournant du 3e millénaire,* 2002. Essay: Luxembourg.

FERNEA, ELIZABETH. Peer reviewer. Professor emeritus of English and Middle Eastern studies, University of Texas, Austin. Author of *Guests of the Sheik: An Ethnography of an Iraqi Village,* 1965, *A View of the Nile,* 1970, *A Street in Marrakech,* 1975, and *In Search of Islamic Feminism,* 1998. Coauthor, with Robert A. Fernea, of *The Arab World: Personal Encounters,* 1985, *Nubian Ethnographies,* 1991, and *The Arab World: Forty Years of Change,* 1997. Editor of *Women and the Family in the Middle East: New Voices of Change,*1985, *Children of the Muslim Middle East,* 1995, and *Remembering Childhood in the Middle East: Memoirs from a Century of Change,* 2001. Coeditor of *Middle Eastern Muslim Women Speak,* 1977, and *The Struggle for Peace: Israelis and Palestinians,* 1992. Ethnographer and consultant for the film *Some Women of Marrakech,* 1976. Producer of numerous documentaries, including *A Veiled Revolution, Women and Religion in Egypt,* 1982, *The Price of Change,* 1982, *Women under Siege,* 1982, *The Struggle for Peace: Israelis and Palestinians,* 1991, *The Road to Peace: Israelis and Palestinians,* 1995, and *Living with the Past: Historic Cairo,* 2001.

FINE-DARE, KATHLEEN. Peer reviewer. Professor of anthropology and women's studies, Fort Lewis College, Durango, Colorado. Author of *Cotocollao: Ideología, historia, y acción en un barrio de Quito,* 1991, and *Grave Injustice: The American Indian Repatriation Movement and NAGPRA,* 2002. Contributor to journals, including *Radical History Review* and *Anthropological Quarterly.*

FLAKE, KATHLEEN. Contributor. Assistant professor of American religious history, Graduate Department of Religion and Divinity School, Vanderbilt University, Nashville, Tennessee. Author of *The Politics of American Religious History: The Seating of Senator Reed Smoot, Mormon Apostle,* 2004. Essay: The Church of Jesus Christ of Latter-day Saints.

FOHR, SHERRY. Contributor. Assistant professor of world religions, Wofford College, Spartanburg, South Carolina, and board member, Southeastern Commission for the Study of Religions. Essay: Jainism.

GALINIER-PALLEROLA, JEAN-FRANÇOIS. Contributor. Member, Department of Theology, Institut Catholique de Toulouse, France. Author of *La religion populaire en Andorre,* 1990, and of articles in *Bulletin de Literature Ecclésiastique.* Essay: Andorra.

GATTAMORTA, LORENZA. Contributor. Research associate of the sociology of culture, University of Bologna, Forli, Italy. Author of *La memoria delle parole: Luzi tra Eliot e Dante,* 2002. Author of articles in numerous journals, including *Strumenti Critici, Lingua e Stile, Ideazione,* and *Sociologia e Politiche Sociali.* Essay: San Marino.

GAUSSET, QUENTIN. Contributor. Associate professor, University of Copenhagen, Denmark. Author of articles in numerous journals, including *Africa, Journal of the Royal Anthropological Institute, Cahiers d'Études Africaines, Social Sciences and Medicine,* and *Anthropos.* Essay: Cameroon.

GEFFEN, RELA MINTZ. Contributor. President, Baltimore Hebrew University, and editor of the journal *Contemporary Jewry.* Coauthor of *The Conservative Movement in Judaism: Dilemmas and Opportunities,* 2000. Editor of *Celebration and Renewal: Rites of Passage in Judaism,* 1993. Coeditor of *A Double Bond: The Constitutional Documents of American Jewry,* 1992, and *Freedom and Responsibility: Exploring the Challenges of Jewish Continuity,* 1998. Essay: Conservative Judaism.

GHANNAM, FARHA. Contributor. Visiting assistant professor of anthropology, Swarthmore College, Pennsylvania. Author of *Remaking the Modern: Space, Relocation, and the Politics of Identity in a Global Cairo,* 2002. Author of articles in various journals, including *Visual Anthropology, City and Society,* and *Middle East Report.* Essay: Egypt.

GIBBS, PHILIP. Contributor and peer reviewer. Faculty member, Melanesian Institute, Soroka, Papua New Guinea. Author of *The Word in the Third World,* 1996. Author of articles in journals, including *Point 24* and *Studia Missionalia.* Essay: Papua New Guinea.

GIBSON, KEAN. Contributor. Senior lecturer in linguistics, University of the West Indies, Cave Hill, Barbados. Author of *Comfa Religion and Creole Language in a Caribbean Community,* 2001, and *The Cycle of Racial Oppression in Guyana,* 2003. Author of articles in numerous journals, including *Lingua, American Speech, International Folklore Review, Mankind Quarterly, Lore and Language,* and *Journal of Caribbean Studies.* Essay: Guyana.

GILL, ANTHONY. Contributor. Associate professor of political science, University of Washington, Seattle. Author of *Rendering unto Caesar: The Catholic Church and State in Latin America,* 1998, and of articles in numerous journals, including *American Journal of Political Science, Rationality and Society, Politics and Society,* and *Journal of Church and State.* Essays: Argentina, Chile, Uruguay.

GIRARDOT, NORMAN. Adviser and peer reviewer. University Distinguished Professor, Department of Religious Studies,

Lehigh University, Bethlehem, Pennsylvania. Author of *Myth and Meaning in Early Taoism*, 1983, and *The Victorian Translation of China*, 2002. Editor of the section on China in the *HarperCollins Dictionary of Religion*, edited by Jonathan Z. Smith and William Scott Green, 1995. Coeditor of *Imagination and Meaning: The Scholarly and Literary Worlds of Mircea Eliade*, 1982, and *Daoism and Ecology*, 2001. Cotranslator of *Taoist Meditation*, 1993. Contributor to books, including *Self-Taught Artists of the 20th Century: An American Anthology*, edited by Elsa Longhauser, 1998, and *Changing Religious Worlds, the Meaning and End of Mircea Eliade*, edited by Bryan Rennie, 2001, and to journals such as the *Journal of the American Academy of Religion*.

GOLDSMITH, MICHAEL. Contributor and peer reviewer. Senior lecturer in anthropology, University of Waikato, Hamilton, New Zealand. Coauthor of *The Accidental Missionary: Tales of Elekana*, 2002. Coeditor of *Other Sites: Social Anthropology and the Politics of Interpretation*, 1992. Author of numerous book chapters and encyclopedia entries, as well as of articles in various journals, including *Journal of Pacific History*, *Journal of Pacific Studies*, and *Ethnologies Comparées*. Essay: Tuvalu.

GOOREN, HENRI. Contributor. Researcher, IIMO Utrecht University, The Netherlands. Coeditor of *Under Pressure: Essays on Development Research*, 1997. Author of chapters in books, as well as of articles in various journals, including *Journal for the Scientific Study of Religion* and *Dialogue*. Essay: Nicaragua.

GOOSEN, GIDEON. Contributor. Associate professor of theology, Australian Catholic University, Sydney. Author of *Religion in Australian Culture: An Anthropological View*, 1997, *Australian Theologies: Themes and Methodologies into the Third Millennium*, 2000, and *Bringing Churches Together: A Popular Introduction to Ecumenism*, 2001. Author of articles in numerous journals, including *Theological Studies*, *Compass*, *Australasian Catholic Record*, *Word in Life*, *St. Mark's Review*, and *Peace and Change*. Essay: Australia.

GOTHÓNI, RENÉ. Peer reviewer. Professor of comparative religion, University of Helsinki, Finland. Author of several books, including *Paradise within Reach: Monasticism and Pilgrimage on Mt. Athos*, 1993, and *Attitudes and Interpretations in Comparative Religion*, 2000.

GRANT, BRUCE. Peer reviewer. Associate professor of anthropology, Swarthmore College, Pennsylvania. Author of *In the Soviet House of Culture: A Century of Perestroikas*, 1995, and editor of and author of the foreword and afterword to *The Social Organization of the Gilyak*, by Lev Shternberg, 1999. Contributor to *Paranoia within Reason: A Casebook on Conspiracy as Explanation*, edited by George Marcus, 1999, and to journals, including *American Ethnologist*.

GREEN, KATHRYN L. Contributor. Independent scholar. Contributor to various publications on African and Middle Eastern history. Essay: Mali.

GROELSEMA, ROBERT. Contributor. Civil society analyst, U.S. Agency for International Development. Author of articles on African politics, culture, and current events for encyclopedias and other publications, as well as regular articles on Guinea and the Seychelles in *Africa Contemporary Record*. Essays: Republic of the Congo, Ghana, Guinea, Seychelles, Sierra Leone.

HAAR, GERRIE TER. Adviser. Professor of religion, human rights, and social change, Institute of Social Studies, The Hague, The Netherlands. General Editor, Religion in Contemporary Africa (series), as well as author of *Faith of Our Fathers: Studies on Religious Education in Sub-Saharan Africa*, 1990, *Spirit of Africa: The Healing Ministry of Archbishop Milingo of Zambia*, 1992, *African Traditional Religions in Religious Education*, 1992, *Halfway to Paradise: African Christians in Europe*, 1998, and *Worlds of Power: Religious Thought and Political Practice in Africa*, 2004.

HALE, JOE. Peer reviewer. General secretary, 1976–2001, then emeritus, World Methodist Council.

HAMM, THOMAS D. Peer reviewer. Professor of history and archivist and curator of the Friends Collection and College Archives, Earlham College, Richmond, Indiana. Author of *God's Government Begun: The Society for Universal Inquiry and Reform, 1842–1846*, 1995, *The Transformation of American Quakerism: Orthodox Friends, 1800–1907*, 1998, and *The Quakers in America*, 2003.

HEITZENRATER, RICHARD P. Contributor. William Kellon Quick Professor of Church History and Wesley Studies, Duke University, Durham, North Carolina. Author of *Mirror and Memory: Reflections on Early Methodism*, 1989, and of several books about John Wesley, including *John Wesley As Seen by Contemporaries and Biographers*, 1984, *Wesley and the People Called Methodists*, 1995, and *The Elusive Mr. Wesley*, 2003. Editor of *Diary of an Oxford Methodist, Benjamin Ingham, 1733–1734*, 1985, *The Poor and the People Called Methodists, 1729–1999*, 2002, and other volumes. Essay: Methodism.

HERMANSEN, MARCIA. Peer reviewer. Professor of theology, Loyola University Chicago, Illinois. Author of *The Conclusive Argument from God*, including a translation from the Arabic of *Hujjat Allah al-Baligha*, by Shah Wali Allah, 1996. Coeditor of *Encyclopedia of Islam and the Muslim World*, 2003. Contributor to books, including *Women and Revolution in Iran*, edited by G. Nashat, 1983, *God Experience or Origin*, 1985, *Muslims of America*, edited by Yvonne Haddad, 1991, *Muslim Communities in America*, edited by Yvonne Haddad, 1994, *New*

Trends and Developments in the World of Islam, edited by Peter Clarke, 1997, and *Teaching Islam,* edited by Brannon Wheeler, 2002. Contributor to numerous journals, including *Studies in Islam, Journal of Near Eastern Studies, Arabica, Islamic Quarterly, Studies in Religion,* and *Muslim Education Quarterly.*

HEZEL, FRANCIS. Peer reviewer. Director, Micronesian Seminar, Kolonia, Pohnpei, Federated States of Micronesia. Author of *The First Taint of Civilization: A History of the Caroline and Marshall Islands in Pre-Colonial Days, 1521–1885,* 1983, *From Conquest to Colonization: Spain in the Mariana Islands, 1690 to 1740,* 1989, *The Catholic Church in Micronesia,* 1991, *Strangers in Their Own Land,* 1995, and *The New Shape of Old Island Cultures: A Half Century of Social Change in Micronesia,* 2001.

HILL, JACK A. Contributor. Assistant professor of religion, Texas Christian University, Fort Worth. Author of *I-Sight: The World of Rastafari: An Interpretive Sociological Account of Rastafarian Ethics,* 1995, and *Seeds of Transformation: Discerning the Ethics of a New Generation,* 1998. Author of numerous articles in scholarly journals, including *Annual of the Society of Christian Ethics, Journal of Religious Thought, Journal of Beliefs and Values, Journal for the Study of Religion,* and *Pacific Journal of Theology and Missiology.* Essays: Fiji, Federated States of Micronesia.

HILLERBRAND, HANS. Peer reviewer. Professor of religion and history, Duke University, Durham, North Carolina. Author of numerous books, including *The Reformation: A Narrative History Related by Contemporary Observers and Participants,* 1964, *Christendom Divided: The Protestant Reformation,* 1971, *The World of the Reformation,* 1973, *Anabaptist Bibliography, 1520–1630,* 1991, and *Historical Dictionary of the Reformation and Counter-Reformation,* 1999. Editor of many books, including *Protestant Reformation,* 1968, *Oxford Encyclopedia of the Reformation,* 1996, and *Encyclopedia of Protestantism,* 2003. Contributor to numerous journals.

HJELM, TITUS. Contributor. Researcher, Department of Comparative Religion, University of Helsinki, Finland. Author of Finnish high school philosophy textbooks, as well as various articles on satanism and new religious movements in Finnish and English anthologies. Essay: Finland.

HOFFMAN, VALERIE. Adviser and contributor. Associate professor of religion, University of Illinois, Urbana-Champaign. Author of *Sufism, Mystics, and Saints in Modern Egypt,* 1995. Author of numerous articles in scholarly journals, including *International Journal of Middle East Studies, Journal of American Academy of Religion, Muslim World, Religion, Religion and the Arts,* and *Mystics Quarterly,* as well as for *Encyclopedia of Modern Islam, The Encyclopedia of the Qur'an, Holy People: An Encyclopedia, HarperCollins Dictionary of Religion,* and *The Dictionary of Feminist Theologies.* Essay: Oman.

HOLLAND, CLIFTON L. Contributor. Director of PROLADES (Latin American Socio-Religious Studies Program), San José, Costa Rica, and editor of *Mesoamerica,* a monthly news journal published by the Institute of Central American Studies (ICAS), San José. Author of *Religious Dimension in Hispanic Los Angeles: A Protestant Case Study,* 1974, as well as numerous published research reports, documents, and magazine articles. Editor of *World Christianity: Central American and the Caribbean,* 1981. Essays: Belize, Costa Rica, Mexico, Paraguay, Portugal, Spain, Suriname.

HOLMBERG, DAVID H. Contributor. Professor of anthropology and Asian studies, as well as chair of the Anthropology Department, Cornell University, Ithaca, New York. Author of *Order in Paradox: Myth, Ritual, and Exchange among Nepal's Tamang,* 1989, as well as articles in numerous journals, including *Journal of Asian Studies, Signs, American Ethnologist, Journal of Ritual Studies,* and *Himalayan Research Bulletin.* Essay: Nepal.

HOLT, JOHN C. Contributor and peer reviewer. William R. Kenan Professor of the Humanities and Religion, as well as chair of the Religion Department, Bowdoin College, Brunswick, Maine. Author of *Discipline: The Canonical Buddhism of the Vinayapitaka,* 1981, *Buddha in the Crown: Avalokitesvara in the Buddhist Traditions of Sri Lanka,* 1991, *The Religious World of Kirti Sri: Buddhism, Art, and Politics in Late Medieval Sri Lanka,* 1996, and *The Buddhist Visnu: Religious Assimilation, Politics, and Culture,* 2004. Essay: Sri Lanka.

HUDEPOHL, KATHRYN A. Contributor. Assistant professor of modern language and intercultural studies, Western Kentucky University, Bowling Green. Essay: Saint Lucia.

HURLEY, SCOTT. Contributor. Visiting assistant professor of religion, Department of Religion and Philosophy, Luther College, Decorah, Iowa. Coauthor of "Some Thoughts on the Theory of Religious Capital in a Global Era: The Tzu Chi Movement and the Praxis of Charity," in *The Annual Bulletin of the Japan Academy for Foreign Trade,* 2003, and "The Lotus of Capital: Tzu Chi Foundation and the Praxis of Charity," in *Kokushikan Journal of Asia,* 21, 2003. Essay: Taiwan.

HUSSAINMIYA, B.A. Contributor. Senior lecturer in history, University of Brunei Darussalam. Author of *Orang Rejimen: The Malays of the Ceylon Rifle Regiment,* 1990, and *Sultan Omar Ali Saifuddin and Britain: The Making of Brunei Darussalam,* 1995. Essay: Brunei.

ISAAK, PAUL JOHN. Contributor. Head, Department of Religion, University of Namibia, Windhoek. Author of *Religion and Society: A Namibian Perspective,* 1997. Editor of *The Evangelical Lutheran Church in the Republic of Namibia in the 21st Century,* 2000. Author of articles in numerous journals, including *Black Theology: An International Journal, African Theological Journal, African Bible Commentary, Journal of Religion and Theology in Namibia, Panorama, Journal of Constructive Theology, Southern Africa,* and *Ecumenical Review.* Essay: Namibia.

ISKENDEROVA, MAYA. Contributor. Doctoral candidate, Institute of History, Azerbaijan Academy of Sciences, Baku. Essay: Azerbaijan.

JACKSON, ROGER. Peer reviewer. Professor of religion and director of Asian studies, Carleton College, Northfield, Minnesota. Author of *Is Enlightenment Possible?,* 1993, and *Tantric Treasures,* 2004. Coauthor of *The Wheel of Time: Kalachakra in Context,* 1985. Coeditor of *Tibetan Literature: Studies in Genre,* 1996, and *Buddhist Theology,* 1999. Author of numerous articles and reviews.

JACOBS, CLAUDE. Contributor. Associate professor of behavioral science, University of Michigan-Dearborn. Coauthor of *The Spiritual Churches of New Orleans: Origins, Beliefs, and Rituals of an African-American Religion,* 1991. Author of articles in numerous journals. Essay: Panama.

JAFFEE, MARTIN. Peer reviewer. Professor, Henry M. Jackson School of International Studies, University of Washington, Seattle. Author of *Mishnah's Theology of Tithing: A Study of Tractate Maaserot,* 1981, *The Talmud of the Land of Israel: A Preliminary Translation and Explanation,* Vol. 7, 1987, *The Talmud of Babylonia: An American Translation,* 1987, *Early Judaism: Religious Worlds of the First Judaic Millennium,* 1997, and *Torah in the Mouth: Writing and Oral Tradition in Palestinian Judaism,* 2001. Coauthor of *Jews, Christians, Muslims: A Comparative Introduction to Monotheistic Religions,* 1998. Coeditor of *Innovation and Religious Traditions: Essays in the Interpretation of Religious Change,* 1992, and *Readings in Judaism, Christianity, and Islam,* 1998. Contributor to numerous books and journals.

JAHANBAKHSH, FOROUGH. Contributor. Assistant professor of religious studies, Queen's University, Kingston, Ontario, Canada. Author of *Islam, Democracy and Religious Modernism in Iran (1953–2000),* 2001. Author of articles in journals, including *Brown Journal of World Affairs, ISIM Newsletter,* and *Historical Reflection.* Essays: Iran, Shiism.

JAKSIC, IVAN. Peer reviewer. Professor of history, University of Notre Dame, Indiana. Author of *Academic Rebels in Chile: The Role of Philosophy in Higher Education and Politics,* 1989, and *Andres Bello: Scholarship and Nation Building in Nineteenth-Century Latin America,* 2001. Editor of *Selected Writings of Andres Bello,*1998, and *The Political Power of the Word: Press and Oratory in Nineteenth-Century Latin America,* 2002. Coeditor of *Filosofia e identidad cultural en America Latina,* 1988, *The Struggle for Democracy in Chile, 1982–1990,* 1991, and *Sarmiento: Author of a Nation,* 1994.

JOCHIM, CHRISTIAN. Contributor. Professor of comparative religious studies, as well as director, Center for Asian Studies, and chair of the Humanities Department, San Jose State University, California. Author of *Chinese Religions: A Cultural Perspective,* 1986. Author of articles in various journals, including *Journal of Chinese Religions, Modern China,* and *Philosophy East and West.* Essay: Confucianism.

JOHNSON, MICHELLE C. Contributor. Assistant professor of anthropology, Bucknell University, Lewisburg, Pennsylvania. Author of chapters in *Female Circumcision in Africa: Culture, Controversy, and Change,* 2000, and *A World of Babies: Imagined Child-Care Guides for Seven Societies,* 2000. Essay: Guinea-Bissau.

JOHNSON, RHONDA. Contributor. Assistant professor and head of access services, Hostos Community College Library, Bronx, New York. Researcher for *Encyclopedia of the United Nations and International Agreements,* by Edmund Jan Osmanczyk, 2003. Essay: Saint Kitts and Nevis.

JONES, STEVEN. Contributor. Associate director, Center on Religion and Democracy, as well as lecturer, Department of Sociology, University of Virginia, Charlottesville. Author of various articles on religion and democracy, including essays on Alexis de Tocqueville, the Nation of Islam, and the intersection of religion and globalization. Essays: Baptist Tradition, Honduras.

KAPLAN, DANA EVAN. Contributor. Visiting research fellow, University of Miami, Coral Gables, Florida. Author of *American Reform Judaism,* 2003, and coauthor of *Platforms and Prayer Books,* 2002. Editor of *Conflicting Visions: Contemporary Debates in American Reform Judaism,* 2001, and *Cambridge Companion to American Judaism,* 2004. Essay: Reform Judaism.

KAUFMAN, PETER IVER. Peer reviewer. Professor of religious studies, University of North Carolina, Chapel Hill. Author of several books, including *Augustinian Piety and Catholic Reform: Augustine, Colet, and Erasmus,* 1982, *The "Polytyque Churche": Religion and Early Tudor Political Culture, 1485–1516,* 1986, and *Prayer, Despair, and Drama: Elizabethan Introspection,* 1996.

KERKHOFS, JAN. Contributor and peer reviewer. Professor emeritus, Kotholieke Universiteit, Leuven, Belgium, and founder, European Values Study. Author of many books in Dutch, as well as *Europe without Priests,* 1995, and *A Horizon of Kindly Light,* 1999, both in English. Essay: Belgium.

KHAN, AISHA. Contributor. Associate professor, Department of Anthropology, New York University, New York. Author of articles and essays, including "Juthaa in Trinidad: Food, Pollution, and Hierarchy in a Caribbean

Diaspora Community," in *American Ethnologist,* 1994, "'Rurality' and 'Racial' Landscapes in Trinidad," in *Knowing Your Place: Rural Identity and Cultural Hierarchy,* edited by Barbara Ching and Gerald Creed, 1997, and "Journey to the Center of the Earth: The Caribbean as Master Symbol," in *Cultural Anthropology,* 2001. Essay: Trinidad and Tobago.

KHAZANOV, ANATOLY M. Contributor. Ernest Gellner Professor of Anthropology, University of Wisconsin, Madison. Author and editor of many books, including *Nomads and the Outside World,* 1984, *Soviet Nationality Policy during Perestroika,* 1991, and *After the USSR: Ethnicity, Nationalism and Politics in the Commonwealth of Independent States,* 1995. Essay: Kazakhstan.

KHODJIBAEV, KARIM. Contributor. Voice of America radio broadcaster. Author of *U.N. Special Report of Tajikistan,* 1994, as well as a series of radio features on American democracy, 1995, and articles in journals, including *Central Asia Monitor.* Essay: Tajikistan.

KIMMERLING, BARUCH. Contributor. George S. Wise Professor of Sociology, Hebrew University of Jerusalem, Israel. Author of numerous books and articles, including *Zionism and Territory,* 1983, *The Interrupted System: Israeli Civilians in War and Routines,* 1985, *The Invention and Decline of Israeliness: State, Society and the Military,* 2001, and *Immigrants, Settlers and Natives: Israel between Multiculturalism and Kulturkampf,* 2003. Coauthor of *The Palestinians: A History,* 2003. Essay: Israel.

KINNARD, JACOB. Contributor and peer reviewer. Assistant professor of religion, College of William and Mary, Williamsburg, Virginia. Author of *Imagining Wisdom: Seeing and Knowing in the Art of Indian Buddhism,* 1999. Coeditor of *Constituting Communities: Theravada Buddhism and the Religious Cultures in South and Southeast Asia,* 2003. Essay: Buddhism.

KIRKLAND, J. RUSSELL. Contributor. Associate professor of religion, University of Georgia, Athens. Author of *Taoism: An Enduring Tradition,* 2004, as well as articles in numerous journals, including *History of Religions* and *Journal of the American Academy of Religion.* Essay: Taoism.

KIVILU, SABAKINU. Contributor. Professor and president, Institut de Recherche et d'Études Historiques du Présent, University of Kinshasa, Democratic Republic of the Congo. Contributor to *Démocratie et paix en République Démocratique du Congo,* 2000, *Élites et démocratie en République Démocratique du Congo,* 2002, *Les consequences de la guerre de la République Démocratique du Congo en Afrique Centrale,* 2003, as well as to journals, including *Journal of African Studies,* 1999, and *Laurent Monnier,* 2000. Essay: Democratic Republic of the Congo.

KNOWLTON, DAVID. Contributor. Associate professor, Behavioral Science Department, Utah Valley State College, Orem, Utah. Essays: Bolivia, Colombia, Ecuador.

KNYSH, ALEXANDER. Peer reviewer. Professor of Islamic studies, as well as chairman, Department of Near Eastern Studies, University of Michigan, Ann Arbor. Author of *Ibn al-'Arabi in the Later Islamic Tradition: The Making of a Polemical Image in Medieval Islam,* 1998, and *Islamic Mysticism: A Short History,* 2000. Author, in Russian, of *Ibn al-'Arabi: The Meccan Revelations: Selected Translations of Ibn al-'Arabi's Early Works and a Chapter from al-Futuhat al-makkiya,* 1995. Contributor to books, including *History of Islamic Philosophy,* edited by S.H. Nasr and O. Leaman, 1996, *Hadhrami Traders, Scholars, and Statesman in the Indian Ocean, 1750s–1960s,* edited by U. Freitag and W. Clarence-Smith, 1997, *Companion to Arabic Literature,* 1998, and *Cambridge History of Arabic Literature: The Literature of al-Andalus,* edited by M.R. Menocal, R. Sheindlin, and M. Sells, 2000. Contributor to numerous journals.

KOLB, ROBERT. Contributor and peer reviewer. Missions Professor of Systematic Theology, Concordia Seminary, Saint Louis, Missouri. Author of *The Christian Faith: A Lutheran Exposition,* 1993, *Speaking the Gospel Today: A Theology for Evangelism,* 1995, *Luther's Heirs Define His Legacy: Studies on Lutheran Confessionalization,* 1996, and *Martin Luther as Prophet, Teacher, Hero: Images of the Reformer, 1520–1620,* 1999. Coeditor of *The Book of Concord: The Confessions of the Evangelical Lutheran Church,* 2000, and other books. Essay: Lutheranism.

KOLLAR, NATHAN R. Contributor. Professor of religious studies, Saint John Fisher College, Rochester, New York; senior lecturer, Department of Education and Human Development, University of Rochester, New York; and chair, Center for Interfaith Studies and Dialogue, Nazareth College, Rochester, New York. Author of *Death and Other Living Things,* 1973, and *Songs of Suffering,* 1982, as well as numerous articles in edited volumes and journals. Editor of *Options in Roman Catholicism: An Introduction,* 1983. Essay: Canada.

KRINDATCH, ALEXEI. Contributor. Research associate, Center for Geopolitical Studies, Institute of Geography, Russian Academy of Sciences, Moscow, and research associate, Institute for the Study of American Religion, University of California, Santa Barbara. Author of *Geography of Religions in Russia,* 1996, as well as articles in numerous journals, including *Osteuropa, Journal for the Scientific Study of Religion,* and *Religion, State, and Society.* Essays: Lithuania, Moldova.

KRÜGGELER, MICHAEL. Contributor. Project manager, Schweizerisches Pastoralsoziologisches Institut (SPI), Saint Gall, Switzerland. Author of *Individualisierung und Freiheit: Eine Praktisch-Theologische Studie zur Religion in der Schweiz,* 1999, and coauthor of *Solidarität und Religion: Was Bewegt Menschen in Solidaritätgruppen?*, 2002. Coeditor of *Religion und Moral: Entkoppelt oder Verknüpft?*, 2001. Essay: Liechtenstein.

KUBURIĆ, ZORICA. Contributor. Professor of the sociology of religion, Faculty of Philosophy, University of Novi Sad, Serbia and Montenegro, and president, Center for Empirical Researches of Religion, Novi Sad. Author of *Religion, Family, and Youth*, 1996, *Faith, Freedom, and Religious Institutions in Yugoslavia*, 2002, *Faith and Freedom: Religious Institutions in Yugoslavia*, 2002, and *Religion and Mental Health*, 2003. Editor of *Religion, Religious Education and Tolerance*, 2002. Essay: Serbia and Montenegro.

KVASNIĆKOVÁ, ADELA. Contributor. Lecturer in sociology, Comenius University, Bratislava, Slovakia. Author of an essay in the edited volume *Slovakia in the 90s*, 2003. Essay: Slovakia.

LAMB, CONNIE. Contributor. Middle East librarian, Brigham Young University, Provo, Utah. Coeditor of *Agricultural and Animal Sciences Journals and Serials: An Analytical Guide*, 1986, and *Jewish American Fiction Writers: An Annotated Bibliography*, 1991. Essay: Jordan.

LANG, KAREN C. Peer reviewer. Associate professor of religious studies, University of Virginia, Charlottesville. Author of *Four Illusions: Candrakirt's Advice to Travelers on the Bodhisattva Path*, 2002. Contributor to *Buddhist-Christian Studies*, 1982, *Feminist Studies in Religion*, 1986, and *Off with Her Head! The Denial of Women's Identity in Myth, Religion, and Culture*, edited by Howard Eilberg-Schwartz and Wendy Doniger, 1995.

LEFFERTS, LEEDOM. Contributor. Professor of anthropology, as well as director of the Asian Studies Department, Drew University, Madison, New Jersey. Cocurator of and coauthor of the catalog for *Textiles and the Tai Experience in Southeast Asia*, an exhibition at the Textile Museum, Washington, D.C., 1992. Author of numerous articles on textiles, social organization, and women's roles in Lao and Thai Theravada Buddhism and on Lao and Thai material culture. Essay: Laos.

LEGRAND, MICHEL. Contributor. Sociologist, SESOPI-Centre Intercommunautaire, Luxembourg. Editor of *Les valeurs au Luxembourg: Portrait d'une société au tournant du 3e millénaire*, 2002. Essay: Luxembourg.

LEHTSAAR, TÕNU. Contributor. Professor of practical theology, as well as vice rector for academic affairs, University of Tartu, Estonia. Author of *Religious Experiencing: A Psychological Study of Religious Experiences in the Lifelong Perspective*, 2000. Essay: Estonia.

LEUSTEAN, LUCIAN N. Contributor. Graduate research student, Interfaculty Institute of Central and Eastern Europe, University of Fribourg, Switzerland. Author of a book chapter, as well as articles in such journals as *Romania, Journal for the Study of Religions and Ideologies*, and *Romanian Military Thinking*. Essay: Romania.

LITTLEWOOD, ROLAND. Peer reviewer. Professor of psychiatry and anthropology, Department of Anthropology, University College, London. Author of *The Butterfly and the Serpent: Essays in Psychiatry, Race and Religion*, 1988, *Pathology and Identity: The Work of Mother Earth in Trinidad*, 1993, *Religion, Agency, Restitution: The Wilde Lectures in Natural Religion*, 1999, and *Pathologies of the West: An Anthropology of Mental Illness in Europe and America*, 2002. Coauthor, with Maurice Lipsedge, of *Aliens and Alienists: Ethnic Minorities and Psychiatry*, 1982, and, with Simon Dein, of *Cultural Psychiatry and Medical Anthropology*, 2000. Coeditor, with Jafar Kareem, of *Intercultural Therapy*, 1999. Contributor to numerous books and journals.

LOBBAN, JR., RICHARD. Contributor. Professor of anthropology and African studies, as well as director of the program in African and Afro-American studies, Rhode Island College, Providence, and vice president of the Rhode Island Black Heritage Society, Providence. Author of *Cape Verde: Crioulo Colony to Independent Nation*, 1995, *Cape Verde Islands*, 2001, and *Historical Dictionary of Ancient and Medieval Nubia*, 2004. Coauthor of *Cape Verdeans in Rhode Island*, 1990, and *Historical Dictionary of the Republic of Cape Verde*, 1995. Essay: Cape Verde.

LOVELL, NADIA. Contributor. Lecturer, University of Linkoping, Sweden. Author of *Locality and Belonging*, 1998, and *Cord of Blood: Possession and the Making of Voodoo*, 2002. Contributor to various journals, including *Ethnos*. Essay: Togo.

MAKRIDES, VASILIOS. Contributor and peer reviewer. Professor and chair of religious studies, Faculty of Philosophy, University of Erfurt, Germany. Author of *Die Religiöse Kritik am Kopernikanischen Weltbild in Griechenland zwischen 1794 und 1821: Aspekte Griechisch-Orthodoxer Apologetik Angesichts Naturwissenschaftlicher Fortschritte*, 1995, as well as numerous other books and articles in German, Greek, English, French, and Italian. Essays: Cyprus, Greece.

MALIK, SAADIA. Contributor. Independent researcher. Author of "Displacement as Discourse" in **Ìrìnkèrindò: A Journal of African Migration*. Essay: Bahrain.

MANN, GURINDER SINGH. Peer reviewer. Professor of Sikh and Punjab studies, University of California, Santa Barbara. Author of *The Goindval Pothis*, 1996, *The Making of Sikh Scripture*,

2001, *Sikhism,* 2004, and all Sikhism-related entries in *Merriam-Webster's Encyclopedia of World Religions,* 1999.

MANSURNOOR, IIK A. Contributor. Associate professor of history, University of Brunei Darussalam. Author of *Islam in an Indonesian World: Ulama of Madura,* 1990, as well as chapters in books and articles in numerous journals, including *Islamic Quarterly, Islamic Studies, Journal of Al-Islam, Oxford Journal of Islamic Studies, Prajna Vihara,* and *Islamic Culture.* Essay: Kuwait.

MARINOV, MARIO. Contributor. Assistant professor of sociology, South-West University "Neofit Rilski," Blagoevgrad, Bulgaria, and adjunct assistant professor, Sofia University "Saint Kliment Ohridski," Bulgaria. Author of articles in various publications, including the journal *Sociologicheski Problemi.* Essay: Bulgaria.

MARSTON, JOHN. Contributor. Professor and researcher, Centro de Estudios de Asia y África, El Colegio de México, Mexico City. Author of *Cambodia 1991–94: Hierarchy, Neutrality, and Etiquettes of Discourse,* 1997, as well as articles in numerous edited volumes and such journals as *Estudios de Asia y África, Southeast Asian Affairs,* and *Crossroads: An Interdisciplinary Journal of Southeast Asia.* Essay: Cambodia.

M'BAYO, TAMBA. Contributor. Ph.D. candidate, African history, Michigan State University, East Lansing. Author of articles and book reviews for journals, including *H-West-Africa* and *Historian.* Essays: Benin, Côte d'Ivoire.

MCCLYMOND, MICHAEL J. Contributor. Clarence Louis and Helen Irene Steber Professor of Theological Studies, Saint Louis University, Missouri. Author of *Encounters with God: An Approach to the Theology of Jonathan Edwards,* 1998, and *Familiar Stranger: An Introduction to Jesus of Nazareth,* 2004. Editor of *Embodying the Spirit: New Perspectives on North American Revivalism,* 2004. Coeditor of *The Rivers of Paradise: Moses, Buddha, Confucius, Jesus, and Muhammed as Religious Founders,* 2001, and *Dimensions of North American Revivalism,* 2002. Essay: Christianity.

MCKIM, DONALD K. Contributor. Academic and reference editor, Westminster John Knox Press, Louisville, Kentucky. Author of numerous books, including *What Christians Believe about the Bible,* 1985, *Ramism in William Perkins' Theology,* 1987, *Theological Turning Points,* 1988, *The Bible in Theology and Preaching,* 1994, *Westminster Dictionary of Theological Terms,* 1996, *Introducing the Reformed Faith,* 2001, *Presbyterian Beliefs: A Brief Introduction,* 2003, and *Presbyterian Questions, Presbyterian Answers: Exploring Christian Faith,* 2003. Editor of numerous books, including *The Authoritative Word: Essays on the Nature of Scripture,* 1983, *Readings in Calvin's Theology,* 1984, *How Karl Barth Changed My Mind,* 1986, *God Never Forgets: Faith, Hope, and Alzheimer's Disease,* 1997, *Historical Handbook of Major Biblical Interpreters,* 1998, and *The Cambridge Companion to Martin Luther,* 2003. Essays: Protestantism, Reformed Christianity.

MEADOW, MARY JO. Contributor. Professor emeritus, Minnesota State University, Mankato, and founder, Resources for Ecumenical Spirituality, Forest Lake, Minnesota. Author of *Other People,* 1984, *Gentling the Heart: Buddhist Loving-Kindness Practice for Christians,* 1994, and *Through a Glass Darkly: A Spiritual Psychology of Faith,* 1996. Coauthor of *Psychology of Religion: Religion in Individual Lives,* 1984, and *Purifying the Heart: Buddhist Insight Meditation for Christians,* 1994. Coeditor of *A Time to Weep, a Time to Sing: Faith Journeys of Women Scholars of Religion,* 1985. Essay: Theravada Buddhism.

MENDES-FLOHR, PAUL. Contributor. Professor of modern Jewish thought, Divinity School, University of Chicago, Illinois, and director, Franz Rosenzweig Research Center in German-Jewish Literature and Cultural History, Hebrew University of Jerusalem, Israel. Essay: Judaism.

MICALLEF, ROBERTA. Contributor. Assistant professor of language and literature, University of Utah, Salt Lake City. Coauthor of *Islam in Turkic Central Asia,* 1997, as well as articles in numerous edited volumes and journals. Essay: Uzbekistan.

MIŠOVIC, JÁN. Contributor. Researcher, Institute of Sociology of the Academy of Science of the Czech Republic, Prague. Author of articles in various edited volumes in Czech and English, including *New Religious Phenomena in Central and Eastern Europe,* 1997, and *Church-State Relations in Central and Eastern Europe,* 1999. Essay: Czech Republic.

MOFFIC, EVAN. Contributor. Rabbinic student, Jewish Institute of Religion, Hebrew Union College, Cincinnati, Ohio. Author of articles in *CCAR Journal.* Essay: Reform Judaism.

MOLNAR, ANDREA. Contributor. Associate professor of anthropology, Northern Illinois University, DeKalb. Author of *Grandchildren of the Ga'e Ancestors: Social Organization and Cosmology among the Hoga Sara of Flores,* 2000, as well as essays in various edited volumes and articles in journals, including *Anthropos* and *Antropologi Indonesia.* Essay: East Timor.

MOLNÁR, ATTILA KAROLY. Contributor. Assistant professor, Eötvös University and Pázmány Péter Catholic University, Budapest, Hungary. Author of the monographs *The "Protestant Ethic" in Hungary,* 1994, *Notes from the Chaotic Prison,* 1999, and *Edmund Burke,* 2000. Essay: Hungary.

MOSAAD, MOHAMED. Contributor. Anthropologist and director, Religion and Society Studies Center, Cairo, Egypt. Author of a biography of the Prophet Muhammad, 2000, and of *Islam and Postmodernity: The New Islamic Discourse in Egypt,* 2004. Author of articles in various publications, including the newspaper *Al Qahira* and the magazine *Ar-Risala* magazine. Essays: Algeria, Iraq.

MULLIN, ROBERT BRUCE. Peer reviewer. Subdean of academic affairs and the Society for the Promotion of Religion and Learning, professor of history and world mission, and professor of modern Anglican studies, General Theological Seminary of the Episcopal Church, New York, New York. Author of *Episcopal Vision/American Reality: High Church Theology and Social Thought in Evangelical America,* 1986, *Miracles and the Modern Religious Imagination,* 1996, and *The Puritan as Yankee: A Life of Horace Bushnell,* 2002. Coauthor of *The Scientific Theist: A Life of Francis Ellingwood Abbot,* 1987, and coeditor of *Reimagining Denominationalism: Interpretive Essays,* 1994.

MUZOREWA, GWINYAI H. Contributor. Professor and chair, Religion Department, Lincoln University, Pennsylvania. Author of *The Origin and Development of African Theology,* 1987, *An African Theology of Mission,* 1990, and *Mwari: The Great Being God: God Is God,* 2001. Essay: Zimbabwe.

NADEAU, KATHLEEN M. Contributor. Assistant professor of anthropology, California State University, San Bernardino. Author of articles in various journals, including *Philippine Quarterly of Culture and Society, East Asian Pastoral Review,* and *Journal for the Scientific Study of Religion.* Essay: Philippines.

NARAYANAN, VASUDHA. Adviser and contributor. Professor of religion, University of Florida, Gainesville, and former president, American Academy of Religion. Author of *The Way and the Goal: Expressions of Devotion in the Early Srivaisnava Tradition,* 1987, and *The Vernacular Veda: Revelation, Recitation, and Ritual,* 1994. Coauthor of *The Tamil Veda: Pillan's Interpretation of the Tiruvaymoli,* 1989. Coeditor of *Monastic Life in the Christian and Hindu Traditions: A Comparative Study,* 1990. Author of articles in various journals, including *Journal of the American Academy of Religion, Journal of Vaishnava Studies,* and *Daedalus: Journal of the American Academy of Arts and Sciences.* Essays: Hinduism, Vaishnavism.

NDLOVU, HEBRON. Contributor. Senior lecturer in theology and religious studies, as well as dean of the Faculty of Humanities, University of Swaziland, Kwaluseni. Author of *Phenomenology in Religion,* 1997, as well as articles in edited volumes and various journals, including *UNISWA Research Journal, Theologia Viatorum, ATISCA Bulletin,* and *Journal of Black Theology in South Africa.* Essay: Swaziland.

NELSON, JOHN K. Peer reviewer. Associate professor of theology and religious studies, University of San Francisco, California. Author of *A Year in the Life of a Shinto Shrine,* 1996, and *Enduring Identities: The Guise of Shinto in Contemporary Japan,* 2000.

NEUMAIER, EVA. Contributor. Professor emeritus, University of Alberta, Edmonton, Canada. Author of several volumes, some under the name Eva Dargyay, including *The Rise of Esoteric Buddhism in Tibet,* 1979, *Tibetan Village Communities: Structure and Change,* 1982, and *The Sovereign All-Creating Mind—the Motherly Buddha: A Translation of the Kun-byed rgyal po'i mdo,* 1992. Coauthor of *Ladakh: Innenansicht eines Landes,* 1980, and coeditor of *Gender, Genre, and Religion: Feminist Reflections,* 1995. Essay: Mahayana Buddhism.

NEUSNER, JACOB. Peer reviewer. Research professor of theology and senior fellow, Institute of Advanced Theology, Bard College, Annandale-on-Hudson, New York. Author of more than 900 books and articles. Editor of the *Encyclopedia of Judaism,* 1999, editorial board chairman of *Review of Rabbinic Judaism,* and editor in chief of the Brill Reference Library of Judaism.

NKOMAZANA, FIDELIS. Contributor. Senior lecturer and head, Department of Theology and Religious Studies, University of Botswana, Gaborone. Author of *A New Approach to Religious Education in Botswana,* 1999, as well as articles in various edited volumes and journals, including *PULA: Botswana Journal of African Studies, Scriptura, Journal of Religion and Theology in Namibia,* and *Religion and Theology.* Essay: Botswana.

NORDBECK, ELIZABETH C. Contributor. Moses Brown Professor of Ecclesiastical History, Andover Newton Theological School, Wolfeboro, New Hampshire. Author of *Thunder on the Right: Understanding Conservative Christianity,* 1990, and coeditor of *Living Theological Heritage of the United Church of Christ,* 1999. Essay: United Church of Christ.

NUMBERS, RONALD. Peer reviewer. Hilldale and William Coleman Professor of the History of Science and Medicine, University of Wisconsin, Madison. Author of numerous books, including *The Creationists,* 1992, and *Darwinism Comes to America,* 1998. Coeditor of *God and Nature: Historical Essays on the Encounter between Christianity and Science,* 1986, *Caring and Curing: Health and Medicine in the Western Religious Traditions,* 1986, *Disseminating Darwinism: The Role of Place, Race, Religion, and Gender,* 1999, and *When Science and Christianity Meet,* 2003. Contributor to numerous books and journals.

OLADIPO, CALEB. Contributor and peer reviewer. Assistant professor, Baylor University, Waco, Texas, and director of the Baylor in West Africa Program. Author of *Development of the Doctrine of the Holy Spirit in the Yoruba (African) Indigenous Christian Movement,* 1996, as well as articles in numerous edited volumes and journals, including *International Christian Digest,*

Chicago Studies, Interpretation: A Journal of Bible and Theology, and *Journal of Church-State Studies.* Essays: Somalia, South Africa.

OLDSTONE-MOORE, JENNIFER. Peer reviewer. Associate professor, Department of Religion, Wittenberg University, Springfield, Ohio. Author of *Confucianism: Origins, Beliefs, Practices, Holy Texts, Sacred Places,* 2002, and *Taoism: Origins, Beliefs, Practices, Holy Texts, Sacred Places,* 2003. Contributor to *World Religions: The Illustrated Guide,* edited by Michael Coogan, 1998, *China: Empire and Civilization,* edited by Edward Shaughnessy, 2000, and to journals and encyclopedias.

OLSON, ERNEST. Contributor. Associate professor of anthropology and religion, as well as chair of the sociology/anthropology major, Wells College, Aurora, New York. Author of articles in various journals, including *Journal of Ritual Studies.* Essay: Tonga.

OLUPONA, JACOB K. Contributor. Director, African and African-American Studies, University of California, Davis. Author of *Religion, Kingship and Rituals in a Nigerian Community,* 1991, editor of *African Traditional Religions in Contemporary Society,* 1991, and coeditor of *Religious Pluralism in Africa: Essays in Honor of John Mbiti,* 1993. Essay: African Traditional Religions.

OTTENHEIMER, MARTIN. Peer reviewer. Professor of anthropology, Kansas State University, Manhattan. Author of *Marriage in Domoni: Husbands and Wives in an Indian Ocean Community,* 1985, and *Forbidden Relatives,* 1996. Coauthor of *Historical Dictionary of the Comoro Islands,* 1994. Contributor to books, including *The Encyclopedia of Vernacular Architecture of the World,* 1997, and *The Encyclopedia of Sub-Saharan Africa,* 1997. Contributor to numerous journals, including *Journal of Cognition and Culture, Choice, Czech Sociological Review,* and *American Anthropologist.*

PAPONNET-CANTAT, CHRISTIANE. Contributor. Professor and chair, Department of Anthropology, University of New Brunswick, Fredericton, Canada. Author of articles in various French-, Spanish-, and English-language journals, including *Agalter, Anthropologica, Canadian Review of Sociology and Anthropology, Ciencias Agrarias, Culture, Egalité, Extension Rural,* and *Journal of Clinical Engineering.* Essay: France.

PATTERSON, MARY. Contributor. Senior lecturer in anthropology, University of Melbourne, Australia. Author of book chapters on the arts, sorcery, and witchcraft in Oceania, as well as articles in various scholarly journals, including *Anthropological Forum, Oceania,* and *Australian Journal of Anthropology.* Essay: Vanuatu.

PENTON, M. JAMES. Contributor. Professor emeritus, University of Lethbridge, Alberta, Canada. Author of *Jehovah's Witnesses in Canada: Champions of Freedom of Speech and Worship,* 1976, and *Apocalypse Delayed: The Story of Jehovah's Witnesses,* 1997, as well as articles in various edited volumes and journals, including *Journal of Church and State.* Essay: Jehovah's Witnesses.

PETERSON, WILLIAM. Contributor. Associate professor, California State University, San Bernardino. Author of *Theatre and the Politics of Culture in Contemporary Singapore,* 2001. Author of numerous articles on theater and politics in Singapore, Maori theater, Australian theater, Indonesian dance, and American performance art for journals, including *Contemporary Dramatists, Theatre Research International, Asian Theatre Journal, Australasian Drama Studies, Theatre Journal, Journal of Dramatic Theory and Criticism, High Performance,* and *Theatre Insight.* Essay: Singapore.

PÉTURSSON, PÉTUR. Contributor. Professor of theology, University of Iceland, Reykjavík. Author of numerous books and articles on modern Icelandic church history, new religious movements, and Christian themes in film, art, and literature. Essay: Iceland.

PHUNTSHO, KARMA. Contributor. Scholar of Buddhism and Bhutan studies, as well as a trained Tibetan Buddhist. Author of various articles on Buddhism, Bhutan, and Tibetan studies and of a book on Buddhist epistemology. Essay: Bhutan.

POLLAK-ELTZ, ANGELINA. Contributor. Professor, Universdad Católica A. Bello, Caracas, Venezuela. Author of numerous books, including *Umbanda en Venezuela,* 1989, *Los santos populares en Venezuela,* 1989, *La religiosidad popular en Venezuela,* 1993, *Religiones Afroamericanos,* 1994, *Trommel und Trance: Afroamerikanische Religionen,* 1995, *El pentecostalismo en Venezuela,* 2000, and *La medicina tradicional en Venezuela,* 2001. Essay: Venezuela.

POLLOCK, NANCY J. Contributor. Acting director of development studies, Victoria University, Wellington, New Zealand. Author of *These Roots Remain: Food Habits in Islands of the Central and Eastern Pacific since Western Contact,* 1992. Coeditor of *Social Aspects of Obesity,* 1995. Essays: Fiji, Marshall Islands, and Nauru.

POTOCNIK, VINKO. Contributor. Associate professor, Faculty of Theology, University of Ljubljana, Slovenia. Contributor to *Mate-Toth,* 2001, as well as to numerous journals. Essay: Slovenia.

PRANDI, CARLO. Contributor and peer reviewer. Professor of the sociology of religion, University of Parma, Italy. Author of *I dinamismi del sacro fra storia e sociologia,* 1990, *La* *tradizione religiosa,* 2000, and *La religione populare fra tradizione e modernita,* 2002. Essay: Italy.

RAUSCH, MARGARET JEAN. Contributor and peer reviewer. Assistant professor of religious studies, University of Kansas, Lawrence. Author of various scholarly articles on the social and spiritual role of women in Morocco. Coauthor of *Modern Literary Arabic,* 1981. Essay: Morocco.

REINSCHMIDT, MICHAEL C. Contributor. Lecturer, Department of Anthropology, California State University, Chico, and research associate, UCLA Fowler Museum of Cultural History, Los Angeles, California. Author of articles in various edited volumes and for conferences. Coeditor of *Strengthened Abilities: Assessing the Vision of Tosan Ahn Chang-Ho,* 1998. Essay: South Korea.

ROBBINS, JOEL. Peer reviewer. Associate professor, Department of Anthropology, University of California, San Diego. Coeditor of *Money and Modernity: State and Local Currencies in Contemporary Melanesia,* 1999. Coeditor of a special issue of the journal *Anthropology and Humanism,* 1997. Author of articles in journals, including *Ethnology, Social Analysis, Anthropological Quarterly,* and *Anthropology and Humanism.*

ROBERTS, ALLEN F. Peer reviewer. Director, James S. Coleman Center for African Studies, University of California, Los Angeles. Curator and contributor to exhibition catalogs, including *The Rising of a New Moon,* 1985, *Animals in African Art,* 1995, and, with Mary Nooter Roberts, *Memory: Luba Art and the Making of History,* 1996, and *A Sense of Wonder,* 1997.

ROEBER, A. GREGG. Contributor. Professor of early modern history and religious studies and head of the History Department, Penn State University, University Park, Pennsylvania, and member of the Orthodox Theological Society of America. Author of *Faithful Magistrates and Republican Lawyers: Creators of Virginia Legal Culture, 1680–1810,* 1981, and *Palatines, Liberty, and Property: German Lutherans and Colonial British North America,* 1993, as well as articles in edited volumes and in such journals as *Lutheran Forum* and *William and Mary Quarterly.* Essay: Eastern Orthodoxy.

SALAMONE, FRANK A. Contributor. Professor of sociology and anthropology, Iona College, New Rochelle, New York. Author of *Gods and Goods in Africa: Persistence and Change in Ethnic and Religious Identity in Yauri Emirate, North-Western State, Nigeria,* 1974, *The Hausa People, a Bibliography,* 1983, *Who Speaks for Yanomami?,* 1996, *The Yanomami and Their Interpreters: Fierce People or Fierce Interpreters?,* 1997, *Italians in Rochester, New York, 1900–1940,* 2000, and *Popular Culture in the Fifties,* 2001, as well as numerous articles for journals, including *American Anthropologist, African Studies Review, Popular Culture,* and *Eastern Anthropologist.* Essays: Liberia, Niger, Vatican City.

SAMSON, C. MATHEWS. Contributor. Visiting lecturer, Department of Anthropology, University of Oklahoma, Norman. Author of articles in various journals, including "Texts and Context: Social Context and the Content of Liturgical Texts in Nicaragua and El Salvador," in *Human Mosaic,* 1991, and "The Martyrdom of Manuel Saquic: Constructing Maya Protestantism in the Face of War in Contemporary Guatemala," in *La Fait Missionaire,* 2003. Essay: Guatemala.

SANDS, CANON KIRKLEY C. Contributor. Lecturer, School of Social Sciences, College of The Bahamas, Nassau, and associate priest, Holy Trinity Church, Nassau. Author of *The Christian Church and the Penal Code: A Christian Response to Crime in The Bahamas,* 1983, and contributor to *Bahamas: Independence and Beyond,* 2003, *Cultural Perspectives,* 2003, and *Junkanoo and Religion: Christianity and Cultural Identity in The Bahamas,* 2003. Essay: The Bahamas.

SARNA, JONATHAN. Peer reviewer. Joseph H. and Belle R. Braun Professor of American Jewish History, Department of Near Eastern and Judaic Studies, Brandeis University, Waltham, Massachusetts. Author of *Jacksonian Jew: The Two Worlds of Mordecai Noah,* 1981, *JPS: The Americanization of Jewish Culture,* 1989, and *American Judaism: A History,* 2004. Coauthor of *American Synagogue History: A Bibliography and State-of-the-Field Survey,* 1988, *The Jews of Cincinnati,* 1989, *Yahadut Amerika: American Jewry: An Annotated Bibliography of Publications in Hebrew,* 1991, *The Jews of Boston,* 1995, and *Religion and State in the American Jewish Experience,* 1997. Editor of *Jews in New Haven,* 1978, *People Walk on Their Heads: Moses Weinberger's Jews and Judaism in New York,* 1982, *Observing America's Jews,* by Marshall Sklare, 1993, *The American Jewish Experience: A Reader,* 2nd edition, 1997, and *Minority Faiths and the American Protestant Mainstream,* 1997. Coeditor of *Jews and the Founding of the Republic,* 1985, *Yehude Artsot Ha-Berit,* 1992, *Ethnic Diversity and Civic Identity: Patterns of Conflict and Cohesion in Cincinnati since 1820,* 1992, *A Double Bond: The Constitutional Documents of American Jewry,* 1992, *Abba Hillel Silver and American Zionism,* 1997, and *Woman and American Judaism: Historical Perspectives,* 2001. Contributor to numerous journals.

SAUL, MAHIR. Contributor. Associate professor of anthropology, University of Illinois, Urbana. Coauthor of *West African Challenge to Empire: Culture and History in the Volta-Bani Anticolonial War,* 2001. Author of articles in numerous journals, including *American Anthropologist, American Ethnologist, Journal of the Royal Anthropological Institute, Africa,* and *International Journal of African Historical Studies.* Essay: Burkina Faso.

SCHOEPFLIN, RENNIE. Peer reviewer. Professor of history, La Sierra University, Riverside, California. Author of *Christian Science on Trial: Religious Healing in America,* 2003.

SHANKLAND, DAVID. Contributor. Senior lecturer in social anthropology, University of Bristol, England. Author of *Islam and Society in Turkey,* 1999, and *The Alevis in Turkey: The Emergence of a Secular Islamic Tradition,* 2003. Editor of *The Turkish Republic at Seventy-Five Years: Progress, Development, Change,* 1999. Essay: Turkey.

SHIPPS, JAN. Peer reviewer. Professor emeritus of religious studies and history, Indiana University–Purdue University, Indianapolis. Author of *Mormonism: The Story of a New Religious Tradition,* 1985, and *Sojourner in the Promised Land: Forty Years among the Mormons,* 2000. Editor of *Religion and Public Life in the Mountain West: Sacred Landscapes in Tension,* 2004. Coeditor of *The Journals of William E. McLellin, 1831–1836,* 1994.

SIDKY, HOMAYUN. Contributor. Associate professor of anthropology, Miami University, Oxford, Ohio. Author of *Irrigation and State Formation in Hunza: The Anthropology of a Hydraulic Kingdom,* 1997, *Witchcraft, Lycanthropy, Drugs, and Disease: An Anthropological Study of the European Witch-Hunts,* 1997, *Bitan: Oracles and Healers in the Karakorams,* 2000, *The Greek Kingdom of Cactria: From Alexander to Eurcratides the Great,* 2000, *Halfway to the Mountain: The Jirels of Eastern Nepal,* 2000, *A Critique of Postmodern Anthropology—In Defense of Disciplinary Origins and Traditions,* 2003, and *Perspectives on Culture: A Critical Introduction to Theory in Cultural Anthropology, 2003.* Essays: Afghanistan, Pakistan, Turkmenistan.

SIMONTON, MICHAEL J. Contributor. Lecturer in anthropology, Northern Kentucky University, Highland Heights, and adjunct professor, Wilmington College of Ohio. Essays: Antigua and Barbuda, Ireland.

SINGH, PASHAURA. Contributor. Assistant professor of Sikh studies, University of Michigan, Ann Arbor. Author of *The Guru Granth Sahib: Canon, Meaning and Authority,* 2000, and *The Bhagats of the Guru Granth Sahib: Sikh Self-Definition and the Bhagat Bani,* 2003. Coeditor of *The Transmission of Sikh Heritage in the Diaspora,* 1996, and *Sikh Identity: Continuity and Change,* 1999. Author of articles in numerous journals, including *Journal of American Academy of Religion, Journal of American Oriental Society, Religious Studies Review,* and *Studies in Religion/Sciences Religieuses.* Essay: Sikhism.

SOTIRIU, ELENI. Contributor. Instructor in sociology and social anthropology, University of Erfurt, Germany. Author of various articles in Greek and English on women's issues and Orthodox Christianity. Essays: Cyprus, Greece.

SPINDLER, MARC. Contributor and peer reviewer. Professor emeritus of missiology and ecumenics, University of Leiden and University of Utrecht, The Netherlands, and research associate, Centre d'Étude d'Afrique Noire, Institut d'Études Politiques de Bordeaux, France. Author of *La mission, combat pour le salut du monde,* 1967, and *Pour une théologie de l'espace,* 1968. Coeditor of *Missiology: An Ecumenical Introduction: Texts and Contexts of Global Christianity,* 1995, *Cultures of Madagascar: Ebb and Flow of Influences,* 1995, *Chrétians d'outre-mer en Europe: Un autre visage de l'immigration,* 2000, *Dictionnaire oecuménique de missiologie,* 2001, and *Les relations églises-états; en situation post-coloniale,* 2003. Essay: Madagascar.

STENHOUSE, JOHN. Contributor. Lecturer in history, University of Otago, Dunedin, New Zealand. Coeditor of *Science and Theology: Questions at the Interface,* 1994, *God and Government: The New Zealand Experience,* 1999, and *Disseminating Darwinism: The Role of Place, Race, Religion, and Gender,* 1999. Contributor to journals, including *Journal of the History of Biology, Journal of Religious History, Journal of Law and Religion, New Zealand Journal of History,* and *British Journal for the History of Science.* Essay: New Zealand.

ST JOHN, RONALD BRUCE. Contributor and peer reviewer. Author and independent scholar. Author of numerous books, including *Qaddafi's World Design: Libyan Foreign Policy, 1969–1987,* 1987, *Boundaries, Trade, and Seaports: Power Politics in the Atacama Desert,* 1992, *The Foreign Policy of Peru,* 1992, *Historical Dictionary of Libya,* 1998, *The Land Boundaries of Indochina: Cambodia, Laos, and Vietnam,* 1998, and *Libya and the United States: Two Centuries of Strife,* 2002. Author of articles in numerous journals, including *Asian Affairs: An American Review, Asian Survey, Contemporary Southeast Asia,* and *Asian Affairs: Journal of the Royal Society for Asian Affairs.* Essays: Libya, Vietnam.

STILLMAN, NORMAN. Peer reviewer. Professor and Schusterman/Josey Chair in Judaic History, Department of History, University of Oklahoma, Norman. Author of *The Jews of Arab Lands,* 1979, *The Language and Culture of the Jews of Sefrou,* 1988, *The Jews of Arab Lands in Modern Times,* 1991, and *Sephardi Religious Responses to Modernity,* 1995. Coauthor, with Yedida K. Stillman, of *Samuel Romanell's Travail in an Arab Land,* 1989, and, with Yedida K. Stillman, of *From Iberia to Diaspora: Studies in Sephardic History and Culture,* 1998. Editor of *Arab Dress: A Short History,* by Yedida K. Stillman, 2000.

STOCKMAN, ROBERT. Contributor. Director, Institute for Bahá'í Studies, Wilmette, Illinois. Author of *The Bahá'í Faith in America,* Vol. 1, *Origins, 1892–1900,* 1985, *The Bahá'í Faith in America,* Vol. 2, *Early Expansion, 1900–1912,* 1995, and *Thornton Chase: First American Bahá'í,* 2002, as well as articles in various edited volumes and journals, including *World Order, Religion, The Bahá'í Studies Review, Iranian Studies, Bahá'í News,* and *Theosophical History.* Essay: Bahá'í Faith.

STOFFELS, HIJME C. Contributor. Professor of the sociology of religion, Faculty of Theology, Vrije Universiteit, Amsterdam, The Netherlands; member of the steering committee of the International Society for the Study of Reformed Communities and of the steering committee of the Hollenweger Center for the Study of Pentecostal and Charismatic Movements, Amsterdam. Author of *Walking in the Light: Values, Beliefs, and Social Positions of Dutch Evangelicals,* 1990. Coeditor of *Reformed Vitality: Continuity and Change in the Face of Modernity,* 1998, and *Reformed Encounters with Modernity: Perspectives from Three Continents,* 2001. Essay: The Netherlands.

STOLZ, JÖRG. Contributor and peer reviewer. Professor of the sociology of religion, University of Lausanne, Switzerland, and director of the Observatoire des Religions en Suisse (ORS). Author of *Soziologie der Fremdenfeindlichkeit: Theoretische und Empirische Analysen,* 2000, and of numerous articles on the sociology of religion and on migration. Essay: Switzerland.

STRAUGHN-WILLIAMS, MARITZA. Contributor. Assistant professor of anthropology and African-American studies, Colby College, Waterville, Maine. Essays: Barbados, Dominica.

SUÁREZ, MARGARITA. Contributor. Assistant professor, Department of Religion and Philosophy, Meredith College, Raleigh, North Carolina. Author of "Across the Kitchen Table: Cuban Women Pastors and Theology," in *Gender, Ethnicity and Religion: Views from the Other Side,* edited by Rosemary Radford Ruether, 2002, and "Cubana/os," in *Handbook on Latino/a Theologies,* edited by Edwin David Aponte and Miguel A. de la Torre, 2005. Essay: Cuba.

SUSANTO, BUDI. Contributor. Director, Realino Study Institute, Sanata Dharma University, Yogyakarta, Indonesia. Author of *People (Trick) Theater: Politics of the Past in Present Day Java,* 2000. Contributor to *Indonesian Heritage,* Vol. 9, *Religion and Ritual,* 1998. Essay: Indonesia.

SYNAN, VINSON. Peer reviewer. Professor and dean, Regent University Divinity School, Virginia Beach, Virginia. Author of *The Twentieth-Century Pentecostal Explosion: The Exciting Growth of Pentecostal Churches and Charismatic Renewal Movements,* 1987, *The Spirit Said "Grow,"* 1992, *The Holiness-Pentecostal Tradition: Charismatic Movements in the Twentieth Century,* 1997, *Oldtime Power: A Centennial History of the International Pentecostal Holiness Church,* 1998, *In the Latter Days: The Outpouring of the Holy Spirit in the Twentieth Century,* 2001, *Century of the Holy Spirit: 100 Years of Pentecostal and Charismatic Renewal,* 2001, and *Voices of Pentecost: Testimonies of Lives Touched by the Holy Spirit,* 2003.

TABYSHALIEVA, ANARA. Contributor. Chair, Institute for Regional Studies, Bethesda, Maryland. Author of articles on Kyrgyzstan and Central Asia in various edited volumes and journals, including *Anthropology and Archaeology of Eurasia, Nordic Newsletter of Asian Studies,* and *OSCE Yearbook.* Essay: Kyrgyzstan.

TAIVANS, LEONS. Contributor. Professor of religion, University of Latvia, Riga. Author, in Russian, of *Po Latgalyi,* 1988, and *Vostochnaya misteriya: Politiya v relifioznom soznanii indoneziycev,* 2001. Author, in Latvian, of *Teologijas vesture I. Primkristigo laikmets, AD 1–313,* 1995, as well as numerous articles in edited volumes and journals, including *Religion in Eastern Europe.* Essay: Latvia.

TAYLOR, CHRIS. Peer reviewer. Associate professor of anthropology, University of Alabama, Birmingham. Author of *Milk, Honey, and Money: Changing Concepts in Rwandan Healing,* 1992, and *Sacrifice as Terror: The Rwandan Genocide of 1994,* 1999. Contributor to *Culture and AIDS: The Human Factor,* edited by D. Feldman, 1990, *Anthropological Approaches to the Study of Ethnomedicine,* edited by M. Nichter, 1992, *Encyclopedia of Cultures and Daily Life,* 1997, *Annihilating Difference: The Anthropology of Genocide,* edited by Alex Hinton and Nancy Scheper-Hughes, 2002, and *Anthropology and Chaos Theory,* edited by Mark Mosko and Fred H. Damon, 2004. Contributor to numerous journals, including *Social Science and Medicine, Medical Anthropology, Political and Legal Anthropology Review,* and *Anthropos.*

TEAIWA, KATERINA. Contributor. Assistant professor, Center for Pacific Islands Studies, School of Hawaiian, Asian and Pacific Studies, University of Hawaii at Manoa, Honolulu. Member of the editorial board of *Contemporary Pacific: A Journal of Island Affairs.* Essay: Kiribati.

TITUS, NOEL. Contributor. Principal and professor of church history, Codrington College, St. John, Barbados. Author of *The Church and Slavery in the English-Speaking Caribbean,* 1983, *The Development of Methodism in Barbados, 1823–1883,* 1994, and *Conflicts and Contradictions,* 1998, as well as articles in various journals, including *Howard Journal of Religion, Journal of Negro History, Anglican and Episcopal History,* and *Mission Studies.* Essays: Grenada, Saint Vincent and the Grenadines.

TRANQUILLE, DANIELLE. Contributor. Lecturer, University of Mauritius, Reduit. Coauthor of *Anthologie de la littérature Mauricienne d'expression française,* 2000. Coeditor of *Rencontres: Translation Studies,* 2000. Essay: Mauritius.

TROMPF, GARRY W. Contributor. Professor of the history of ideas, University of Sydney, Australia. Author or coauthor of numerous books, including *Melanesian Religion,* 1991, *Payback: The Logic of Retribution in Melanesian Religions,* 1994, and *The Religions of Oceania,* 1995. Editor of various books, including *Cargo Cults and Millenarian Movements: Transoceanic*

Comparisons of New Religious Movements, 1990. Essay: Solomon Islands.

TUITE, KEVIN. Contributor. Professor of anthropology, Université de Montréal, Québec, Canada. Author of *Kartvelian Morphosyntax: Number Agreement and Morphosyntactic Orientation in the South Caucasian Languages,* 1988, as well as articles in various journals, including *Anthropos, Historiographia Linguistica, Lingua, Anthropological Linguistics, Journal of Indo-European Studies,* and *Cosmos.* Editor of *Anthology of Georgian Folk Poetry,* 1994. Essay: Georgia.

UDDIN, SUFIA MENDEZ. Contributor. Assistant professor of religion, University of Vermont, Burlington. Author of articles in various edited volumes and journals, including *Journal for Islamic Studies.* Essay: Bangladesh.

UHL, FLORIAN. Contributor. Professor of philosophy and head of the Philosophy Department, Private Catholic University of Linz, Austria, and president, Austrian Society for the Philosophy of Religion (ÖGRph), Linz. Editor of *Roger Bacon in der Diskussion,* 2001, and *Roger Bacon in der Diskussion II,* 2002. Coeditor of *Rituale: Zugänge zu einem Phänomen,* 1999, *Zwischen Verzückung und Verzweiflung: Dimenensionen religiöser Erfahrung,* 2001, and *Die Sprachen der Religion,* 2003. Author of articles in various edited volumes and journals. Essay: Austria.

UNDERBERG, NATALIE M. Contributor. Visiting assistant professor of folklore, University of Central Florida, Orlando. Author of articles in edited volumes and journals, including *Folklore Forum,* 1997. Essay: Peru.

URBAN, HUGH B. Contributor and peer reviewer. Associate professor, Department of Comparative Studies, Ohio State University, Columbus. Author of *The Economics of Ecstasy: Tantra, Secrecy and Power in Colonial Bengal,* 2001, and *Tantra: Sex, Secrecy, Politics and Power in the Study of Religion,* 2003. Essay: Saivism.

VA'A, UNASA L.F. Contributor. Senior lecturer in Samoan language and culture and anthropology, National University of Samoa, Apia. Author of *Saili Matagi: Samoan Migrants in Australia,* 2001, as well as articles in various edited volumes and journals. Essay: Samoa.

VALK, PILLE. Contributor. Docent of religious education, Faculty of Theology, Tartu University, Estonia. Author of *Uhest heledast laigust Eesti looli ajaloos 1918.1940,* 1997, and *Eesti kooli religiooniõpetuse kontseptsioon,* 2002. Author of articles in various journals, including *Panorama* and *International Journal of Practical Theology.* Essay: Estonia.

VAN BEMMELEN, PETER M. Contributor. Professor of theology, Andrews University, Berrien Springs, Michigan. Author of articles in various edited volumes, including *Adventist Missions Facing the 21st Century: A Reader,* 1990, *Women in Ministry: Biblical and Historical Perspectives,* 1998, and *Handbook of Seventh-day Adventist Theology,* 2000. Essay: Seventh-day Adventist Church.

VAN DOORN-HARDER, NELLY. Contributor and peer reviewer. Associate professor of world religions, Valparaiso University, Indiana. Author of *Contemporary Coptic Nuns,* 1995, and *Between Desert and City: The Coptic Orthodox Church Today,* 1997, as well as numerous articles about the Copts and Islam. Essay: Coptic Christianity.

VAN ROMPAY, LUCAS. Peer reviewer. Professor of Eastern Christianity, as well as director of the Center for Late Ancient Studies, Duke University, Durham, North Carolina. Coeditor of *After Chalcedon: Studies in Theology and Church History Offered to Professor Albert Van Roey for His Seventieth Birthday,* 1985, *Studies in Hebrew and Aramaic Syntax: Presented to Professor J. Hoftijzer on the Occasion of His Sixty-Fifth Birthday,* 1991, and *The Book of Genesis in Jewish and Oriental Christian Interpretation: A Collection of Essays,* 1997. Editor and translator of *Fragments syriaques du commentaire des psaumes,* by Théodore de Mopsueste, 1982, and *Le commentaire sur Genèse-Exode 9,32 du manuscript (olim) Diayrbakir 22,* 1986.

VICTOR, ISAAC HENRY. Contributor. Research fellow, Milan V. Dimic Institute for Comparative Literary and Cultural Studies, as well as visiting professor, University of Alberta, Edmonton, Canada. Author of articles in numerous journals, including *Sri Lanka Journal for South Asian Studies, Indian Church History Review,* and *Vidyajyoti.* Essay: Maldives.

VOAS, DAVID. Contributor. Simon Research Fellow, Centre for Census and Survey Research, University of Manchester, England, and lecturer in sociology, University of Sheffield, England. Author of *The Alternative Bible,* 1993, and *The Bad News Bible,* 1994, as well as articles in various journals, including *Transactions of the Institute of British Geographers, American Sociological Review,* and *British Journal of Sociology.* Essay: United Kingdom.

VOM BRUCK, GABRIELE. Contributor. Lecturer in the anthropology of the Middle East, University of Edinburgh, Scotland. Author of articles in various journals, including *Journal of Material Culture, Die Welt der Islams, History and Anthropology,* and *Annales, Histoire, Sciences Sociales.* Essay: Yemen.

WACKER, GRANT. Adviser. Professor of church history, The Divinity School, Duke University, Durham, North Carolina. Author of *Augustus H. Strong and the Dilemma of Historical Consciousness,* 1985, *Religion in Nineteenth Century America,* 2000 (expanded in *Religion in American life: A Short History,* 2003), and *Heaven Below: Early Pentecostals and American Culture,* 2001. Coeditor of *Pentecostal Currents in American Protestantism,* 1999, *Portraits of a Generation: Early Pentecostal Leaders,* 2002, and *The Foreign Missionary Enterprise at Home: Explorations in North American Cultural History,* 2003.

WALKER, RANDI. Peer reviewer. Associate professor of church history, Pacific School of Religion, Berkeley, California. Author of *Protestantism in the Sangre de Cristos 1850–1920,* 1991, and *Emma Newman: A Frontier Woman Minister,* 2000. Contributor to *Religion and Modern New Mexico,* edited by Ferenc M. Szasz and Richard W. Etulain, 1997, *Religion and American Culture,* 1998, and *The Evolution of a UCC Style: Essays on the History and Ecclesiology of the United Church of Christ,* 2004. Contributor to journals, including *Prism.*

WASSERSTEIN, BERNARD. Adviser. Harriet and Ulrich E. Meyer Professor of Modern European Jewish History, University of Chicago, Illinois. Author of *The British in Palestine: The Mandatory Government and the Arab-Jewish Conflict,* 1978, *Britain and the Jews of Europe, 1939-1945,* 1979, *The Secret Lives of Trebitsch Lincoln,* 1988, *Herbert Samuel: A Political Life,* 1992, *Vanishing Diaspora: The Jews in Europe since 1945,* 1996, *Secret War in Shanghai,* 1999, *Divided Jerusalem: The Struggle for the Holy City,* 2001, and *Israelis and Palestinians: Why Do They Fight? Can They Stop?,* 2003. Editor of two volumes of the letters of the Zionist leader Chaim Weizmann, as well as coeditor of *The Jews in Modern France,* 1985.

WAUGH, EARLE H. Chair of advisory board, contributor, and peer reviewer. Professor of religious studies, University of Alberta, Edmonton, Canada. Author of *Peace As Seen in the Qur'an,* 1986, and *The Munshidin of Egypt: Their World and Their Song,* 1989. Coeditor of *The Muslim Community in North America,* 1983, *Muslim Families in North America,* 1991, and *The Shaping of an American Islamic Discourse: A Memorial to Fazlur Rahman,* 1999. Essay: Sunnism.

WELLMAN, JAMES K., JR. Contributor. Assistant professor of Western Christianity and comparative religion, University of Washington, Seattle. Author of *The Gold Coast Church and the Ghetto: Christ and Culture in Mainline Protestantism,* 1999. Coeditor of *The Power of Religious Publics: Staking Claims in American Society,* 1999. Author of articles in various journals, including *Review of Religious Research* and *Journal of Presbyterian History.* Essay: World Evangelicalism.

WHITE, DAVID. Peer reviewer. Professor, Department of Religious Studies, University of California, Santa Barbara. Author of *Myths of the Dog-Man,* 1991, *The Alchemical Body: Siddha Traditions in Medieval India,* 1996, and *Kiss of the Yogini: "Tantric Sex" in Its South Asian Contexts,* 2003. Editor and author of the introductory essay, *Tantra in Practice,* 2000. Translator of *The Making of Terrorism,* by Michel Wieviorka, 1993, and cotranslator of *Ashes of Immortality: Widow-Burning in India,* by Catherine Weinberger-Thomas, 1999. Contributor to journals, including *Numen* and *History of Religions.*

WILLEMSEN, HEINZ. Contributor. Ph.D. candidate, Ruhr Universität, Bochum, Germany. Author of articles in various edited volumes and journals, including *Osteuropa, Südosteuropa,* and *Jahrbücher für Geschichte und Kultur Südosteruopas.* Essay: Macedonia.

WILLIAMS, PETER. Contributor and peer reviewer. Distinguished professor of comparative religion and American studies, Miami University, Oxford, Ohio. Author of *Houses of God: Region, Religion, and Architecture in the United States,* 1997, *America's Religions: Traditions and Cultures,* 1998, and *Popular Religion in America: Symbolic Change and the Modernization Process in Historical Perspective,* 2002. Essay: United States.

WOLDEMIKAEL, TEKLE. Contributor. Associate professor and chair, Department of Sociology and Anthropology, University of Redlands, California. Author of *Becoming Black American: Haitians and American Institutions in Evanston, Illinois,* 1989, as well as articles in various journals, including *African Studies Review.* Essay: Eritrea.

WU, SILAS. Contributor. Professor emeritus of Chinese and Japanese history, Boston College, Massachusetts, and associate, Fairbank Center for East Asian Research, Harvard University, Cambridge, Massachusetts. Author of *Communication and Imperial Control in China: Evolution of the Palace Memorial System, 1693–1735,* 1970, *Passage to Power: K'ang-hsi and His Heir Apparent, 1661–1722,* 1979, and *Dora Yu and Christian Revival in 20th Century China,* 2002, as well as articles in numerous journals, including *Harvard Journal of Asiatic Studies, American Historical Review, Tong Pao,* and *Academia Sinica.* Essay: China.

YOUSIF, AHMAD. Contributor. Associate professor, Institute of Islamic Studies, University of Brunei Darussalam. Author of *Muslims in Canada: A Question of Identity,* 1993, and *Religious Freedom, Minorities and Islam: An Inquiry into the Malaysian Experience,* 1998, as well as articles in various edited volumes and journals, including *Journal of Religious Studies and Theology, ISIM Newsletter,* and *Studies in Contemporary Islam.* Essay: Malaysia.

YURASH, ANDRIJ. Contributor. Assistant professor, Ivan Franko L'viv National University, Ukraine. Author, in Russian, of *Religious Organizations of Contemporary Ukraine,*1997, as well as articles in various edited volumes and journals in

Ukraine, Poland, Russia, Germany, The Netherlands, England, and the United States. Essays: Eastern Catholic Churches, Ukraine.

ZALECKI, PAWEL. Contributor. Assistant professor of sociology, Nicolaus Copernicus University, Toruń, Poland. Author, in Polish, of *Religious Community as a Primary Group,* 1997, and *Between Triumphs and the Feeling of Danger: The Roman Catholic Church in Contemporary Poland in the Eyes of Its Representatives,* 2001. Coeditor, in Polish, of *Cultural Tools of Rule,* 2002. Essay: Poland.

ZOHAR, ZION. Contributor. Associate director, Institute for Judaic and Near Eastern Studies, Florida International University, Miami. Author of *Song of My People: A High Holy Day Machzor,* 1995, as well as articles in various edited volumes and journals, including *Jewish Studies.* Essay: Orthodox Judaism.

ZRINŠČAK, SINIŠA. Contributor. Associate professor of comparative social policy, Department of Social Work, Faculty of Law, University of Zagreb, Croatia, and vice president, International Study of Religion in Central and Eastern Europe Association (ISORECEA). Author, in Croatian, of *Sociology of Religion: The Croatian Experience,* 1999, as well as numerous articles in edited volumes and journals. Essay: Croatia.

Chronology

C. 1800 B.C.E. Zarathustra, founder of Zoroastrianism, is born in Persia (modern-day Iran).

C. 1500 B.C.E. Vishnu, the supreme deity of Vaishnava Hinduism, appears in the Vedas, the earliest sacred compositions in India.

C. 587 B.C.E. Babylonian armies destroy the Temple in Jerusalem. The occupation of Palestine initiates the Jewish Diaspora.

C. 565 B.C.E. Siddhartha Gautama, founder of Buddhism, is born in a small village on the border of modern-day Nepal and India.

C. 551 B.C.E. Master Kong, or Confucius, is born in China.

C. 550 B.C.E. Lord Mahavira, an ascetic living in Bihar, India, first sets forth the doctrines and practices of Jainism.

C. 550 B.C.E. Rudra-Shiva is described as the lord and creator of the universe in the Upanishads, the final portion of the Hindu Vedas, laying the foundation of Shaivism.

C. 550 B.C.E. The Achaemenian dynasty, the first empire to adopt Zoroastrianism as a state religion, originates in Persia.

C. 525 B.C.E. In Varanasi, India, the Buddha introduces the Four Noble Truths to the public. These fundamental beliefs soon came to form the core of Theravada Buddhist teachings.

500 B.C.E. Vishnu is featured in two popular Indian epics, the *Mahabharata* and the *Ramayana.* By portraying Vishnu as the supreme being who alone can grant salvation, the epics help establish Vaishnavism as a distinct system of faith and practices within Hinduism.

C. 285 B.C.E. Scholars in China complete the *Tao-te Ching,* or *Lao-tzu,* a written record of the oral tradition of the southern land of Ch'u and the earliest foundation of Taoism.

C. 250 B.C.E. The emperor Ashoka, of the Mauryan dynasty, converts to Buddhism and soon begins propagating Buddhist precepts throughout India.

C. 247 B.C.E. Venerable Mahinda, son of the Indian emperor Ashoka, carries Theravada Buddhism to Sri Lanka.

C. 30 C.E. Roman authorities in Palestine execute Jesus of Nazareth.

C. 48 C.E. The evangelist Saint Mark introduces Christianity to Egypt, laying the foundation of the Coptic Orthodox Church.

95 C.E. A letter of Clement asserts the authority of the Christian church in Rome over the church in Corinth, laying the foundation of the Roman Catholic papacy.

C. 135 C.E. Simeon Bar Kokhba, the leader of a Jewish revolt against occupying Roman forces, is killed in battle. Jews are subsequently banished from Jerusalem, while the Land of Israel becomes a non-Jewish state.

175 C.E. The emperor Han Xiaoling orders that stelae inscribed with sacred texts of Confucianism be erected at the Chinese national university.

C. 200 C.E. The Indian monk Nagarjuna sets forth the fundamental precepts of Mahayana Buddhism.

c. 200 c.e. The Pashupata tradition, the earliest known Shaivite branch of Hinduism, originates in India.

c. 313 c.e. Emperor Constantine revokes the ban on Christianity in the Roman Empire.

325 c.e. Constantine calls the first ecumenical council of Christian bishops at Nicaea, leading to the formation of the Eastern Orthodox Church.

c. 400 c.e. The Shvetambara branch of Jainism establishes its principal doctrines at the Council of Valabhi, creating a permanent rift with the Digambara branch.

406 c.e. Lu Hsiu-ching, a scholar and sage who collected diverse Chinese scriptures and religious teachings to create a coherent Taoist tradition, is born.

431 c.e. The Council of Chalcedon accepts Pope Leo I's solution to the question of Jesus' divinity and humanity, solidifying the authority of the papacy over Christian churches.

c. 525 c.e. Bodhidharma, a disciple of Mahayana Buddhism, founds Ch'an, or Zen, Buddhism in China.

c. 610 c.e. On what is known in Muslim tradition as the Night of Power, Muhammad ibn Abdullah, a Meccan businessman and the founder of Islam, receives his first revelation from Allah.

617 c.e. King Songtsen Gampo, responsible for laying the foundation of Buddhism in Tibet, is born.

c. 622 c.e. Muhammad forms the first Muslim community in the northern Arabian city of Yathrib, later renamed Medinat al-Nabi (modern-day Medina), or "City of the Prophet."

632 c.e. Sunni Islam originates following the death of the Prophet Muhammad.

c. 650 c.e. Followers of Zoroastrianism flee Persia in the wake of the Muslim invasion, resettling in the Gujarat region of India.

c. 656 c.e. Ali, son-in-law of the Prophet Muhammad, becomes the fourth caliph of Islam. He is recognized as the first imam of Shiism.

680 c.e. Hussein, son of Ali and the third imam of Shiism, is martyred at the hands of the Umayyads in the Battle of Karbala.

c. 712 c.e. The *Kojiki* ("Record of Ancient Matters"), a narrative that contains the earliest known written record of Shinto mythology, practices, and beliefs, appears in Japan.

859 c.e. The Yoshida Shrine, one of the oldest and most revered holy structures in the Shinto tradition, is established in Kyoto, Japan.

1054 c.e. Cardinal Humbert of Rome excommunicates the patriarch of Constantinople, precipitating what is known as the Great Schism between Roman Catholicism and Eastern Orthodoxy.

1182 c.e. The Maronite Church declares unity with the Roman Catholic Church, establishing the Uniate, or Eastern Catholic, tradition.

c. 1200 c.e. Jagachandrasuri founds Tapa Gaccha (austere practices) branch of Jainism.

c. 1209 c.e. Saint Francis of Assisi forms the order of Franciscan friars, founded on principles of "holy poverty."

1435 c.e. Yoshida Kanetomo, a Japanese scholar and the founder of Yoshida Shinto, is born. His vigorous defense of purist principles helped define Shinto culture in Japan for centuries.

1463 c.e. Guru Nanak, the founder of Sikhism, is born to an upper-caste Hindu family in the village of Talwandi, India (modern-day Nankana Sahib, Pakistan).

1517 c.e. Martin Luther nails his "Ninety-five Theses," an attack on Roman Catholic practices, to a church door, thus planting the seeds of the Protestant Reformation.

1523 c.e. After public debate the canton of Zurich, Switzerland, moves to adopt the theological doctrines of Ulrich Zwingli, one of the founders of the Reformed movement in Christianity.

c. 1530 c.e. King Henry VIII of England severs ties with the Roman Catholic Church, laying the foundation for the creation of the national Church of England, or Anglican Church.

1536 C.E. John Calvin publishes *Institutes of the Christian Religion,* outlining the theology that would prove pivotal to the development of Reformed Christianity.

1565 C.E. The Minor Reformed Church, the first organized body founded on Unitarian theology, is established in Poland.

c. 1580 C.E. The Congregationalist Church, one of four groups making up the modern-day United Church of Christ, is formed in England in reaction to the liberal doctrines of the Anglican Church.

1596 C.E. The Brest Union Council leads to the formation of national Uniate churches in Ukraine and Belarus.

1606 C.E. Guru Arjan becomes the first Sikh martyr after his execution by the Mughal emperor Jahangir.

1609 C.E. John Smyth, a dissenting pastor and the founder of the Baptist tradition, rebaptizes himself in an act of protest against the Church of England.

1652 C.E. George Fox, an English preacher, founds the Religious Society of Friends (Quakers).

1656 C.E. "Dragon Gate" Taoism, widely regarded as the foundation of modern-day "Northern Taoism," is established at the White Cloud Abbey in Beijing by disciples of the Taoist sage Wu Shou-yang.

1666 C.E. Philipp Jakob Spener becomes the pastor of the Lutheran Church in Frankfurt. The founder of the movement known as Pietism, Spener preached a Christian faith based on the individual's personal devotion to Jesus Christ, a belief that lies at the core of modern-day evangelicalism.

1699 C.E. Guru Gobind Singh creates the Khalsa Panth, or "pure path," based on strict Sikh principles.

1729 C.E. John Wesley forms a religious society with fellow students in Lincoln College, Oxford, thus laying the foundation of the Methodist Church.

1741 C.E. George de Benneville, the founder of Universalism in England, emigrates to the United States, where he soon begins preaching Universalist theology.

1746 C.E. The American pastor Jonathan Edwards writes *A Treatise concerning Religious Affections,* which describes the principal characteristics of the evangelical experience.

1775 C.E. Anglicans in the United States break from the Church of England to form the Protestant Episcopal Church.

1776 C.E. At the Philadelphia Yearly Meeting members of the Religious Society of Friends move to prohibit American Quakers from owning slaves.

1795 C.E. The term "orthodox" is first used by Jewish reformers to disparage those who refuse to adapt their faith to modern society. Almost immediately the term comes to represent Jewish groups who adhere to traditional beliefs and practices.

1801 C.E. Israel Jacobson, a seminal figure in Reform Judaism, forms the first Reform prayer chapel in Westphalia, Germany.

1824 C.E. American Reform Judaism originates in Charleston, South Carolina.

1830 C.E. Joseph Smith founds the Church of Jesus Christ of Latter-day Saints, or Mormon Church.

1831 C.E. William Miller, a farmer in upstate New York, publishes the pamphlet *Evidences from Scripture and History of the Second Coming of Christ about the Year 1843, And of His Personal Reign of One Thousand Years.* Some of Miller's disciples would later found the Seventh-day Adventist movement.

1836 C.E. The rabbi Samson Raphael Hirsch publishes *Nineteen Letters,* in which he elucidates the central tenets of modern Orthodox, or Neo-Orthodox, Judaism.

1844 C.E. 'Alí-Muhammad of Shiraz, an Iranian merchant and the founder of the Bábiacute; movement, declares himself to be the "hidden Imam" of the Shiites, laying the foundation for the Bahá'í faith.

1845 C.E. American Baptists split into Northern and Southern conventions, with the Southern Baptist Convention eventually becoming the largest Protestant group in North America.

1850 C.E. Brigham Young becomes the governor of the Utah Territory, and the headquarters of the Church of Jesus Christ of Latter-day Saints is relocated in Salt Lake City.

1863 C.E. The Bábí leader Mírzá Husayn-'Alí of Núr, or Bahá'u'lláh, launches his public ministry, declaring himself the divine messenger of the Bahá'í faith.

1870 C.E. The doctrine of papal infallibility is established at the First Vatican Council.

1879 C.E. Charles Taze Russell, founder of the Bible Students (renamed Jehovah's Witnesses in 1931), establishes the journal *Zion's Watch Tower and Herald of Christ's Presence* in order to propagate his beliefs.

1881 C.E. The World Methodist Council is formed.

1886 C.E. With the establishment of the Jewish Theological Seminary in New York City, Conservative Judaism is founded in the United States.

1901 C.E. Charles Fox Parham, an evangelist living in eastern Kansas, preaches that speaking in tongues is evidence of baptism with the Holy Spirit, launching the Pentecostal revival in Christianity.

1913 C.E. Solomon Schechter founds the United Synagogue of America, a confederation of Conservative congregations in the United States and Canada.

1917 C.E. The Bolsheviks come to power in Russia, establishing a Communist government and pursuing a policy of forced atheism.

1918 C.E. The Sunday School Movement helps launch a major revival of Coptic Christianity in Egypt.

1921 C.E. The Chinese scholar Liang Shuming publishes *Eastern and Western Cultures and Their Philosophies,* a modern defense of traditional Confucian principles.

1928 C.E. Hasan al-Banna, an Egyptian schoolteacher, founds the Ikhwan al-Muslimin, or Muslim Brotherhood, in reaction to European colonial domination in the Middle East.

1947 C.E. British territory in the Indian subcontinent is partitioned along religious lines into two independent nations—India, with a majority of Hindus, and Pakistan, becoming the first modern state founded on Sunni Muslim principles.

1947 C.E. Shoghi Effendi authorizes representation of the Bahá'í′ faith, under the name Bahá'í International Community, at the United Nations.

1948 C.E. The modern Jewish state of Israel is founded.

1957 C.E. Four American groups—the Congregational Church, Christian Churches, German Reformed Church, and German Evangelical Church—join to form the United Church of Christ.

1959 C.E. In the wake of China's occupation of Tibet, the 14th Dalai Lama, Tibet's head of state and the spiritual leader of Tibetan Buddhism, is forced into exile.

1962 C.E. Pope John XXIII convenes the Second Vatican Council to reform and modernize the Roman Catholic Church.

1966 C.E. The Chinese Communist Party under Chairman Mao begins the Cultural Revolution, suppressing all religious activity in the world's most populous country and lasting until 1976.

1977 C.E. The Universal Church of the Kingdom of God is founded in Brazil, reflecting the growth of evangelical churches in Latin America.

1979 C.E. The Islamic Revolution, lead by Ayatollah Ruhollah Khomeini, overthrows the Shah of Iran and establishes an Islamic republic.

1991 C.E. The Union of Soviet Socialist Republics, composed of Russia and other Eastern European and Asian countries, dissolves, resulting in greater religious freedom in the area.

1994 C.E. In Memphis, Tennessee, white and black Pentecostal churches of the United States, long divided along racial lines, formally unify to create the Pentecostal/Charismatic Churches of North America.

2003 C.E. The Right Reverend V. Gene Robinson is consecrated in the United States as bishop of the Episcopal Diocese of New Hampshire, becoming the first openly gay, noncelibate bishop in the Anglican Communion.

List of Holy Days

2005

DECEMBER 2005

1 THURSDAY

New Moon

4 SUNDAY

Advent begins (Christian)

15 THURSDAY

Full Moon

21 WEDNESDAY

Winter Solstice

25 SUNDAY

Christmas (Christian)

26 MONDAY

Chanukah begins (Jewish)

31 SATURDAY

New Moon

Oharae, or Great Purification (Shinto)

Begin Maidhyaiya, mid-year/winter feast (Zoroastrian)

2006

JANUARY 2006

1 SUNDAY

Oshogatsu, or NewYear (Shinto)

2 MONDAY

Chanukah ends (Jewish)

4 WEDNESDAY

End Maidhyaiya, mid-year/winter feast (Zoroastrian)

5 THURSDAY

Parkash (Birthday) Guru Gobind Singh (Sikh)

6 FRIDAY

Epiphany (Christian)

10 TUESDAY

Id-al-Adha begins (Muslim)

12 THURSDAY

Id-al-Adha ends (Muslim)

14 SATURDAY

Full Moon

New Year (Mahayanan)

15 SUNDAY

Seijin no hi, or *Coming of Age Day* (Shinto)

20 FRIDAY

Id al-Ghadir (Shi'a)

27 FRIDAY

Tse Gutor (Tibetan Buddhist)

29 SUNDAY

New Moon

New Year (Tibetan Buddhist, Confucian)

31 TUESDAY

Muharram, New Year (Muslim)

FEBRUARY 2006

1 WEDNESDAY

Begin Mönlam Chenmo, the great prayer ceremony (Tibetan Buddhist)

2 THURSDAY

Setsubun no hi, Change of Seasons, (Shinto)

9 THURSDAY

Ashura (Shi'a Muslim)

13 MONDAY

Full Moon

Tu Bi-Shevat (Jewish)

20 MONDAY

End Mönlam Chenmo, the great prayer ceremony (Tibetan Buddhist)

26 SUNDAY

Maha Shivaratri (Saivism)

28 TUESDAY

New Moon

MARCH 2006

1 WEDNESDAY

Ash Wednesday, beginning of Lent (Christian)

2 THURSDAY

Annual Fast begins (Bahá'í)

3 FRIDAY

Hina matsuri Doll Festival, or Girls' Day (Shinto)

14 TUESDAY

Full Moon

Holi (Hindu, Vaishnava)

15 WEDNESDAY

Holi (Hindu, Vaishnava)

16 THURSDAY

Begin Hamaspathmaêdaya, feast of All Souls (Zoroastrian)

20 MONDAY

Annual Fast ends (Bahá'í)

End Hamaspathmaêdaya, feast of All Souls (Zoroastrian)

21 TUESDAY

Spring Equinox

Naw-Rúz, or New Year (Bahá'í, Zoroastrian)

29 WEDNESDAY

New Moon

APRIL 2006

5 WEDNESDAY

Qing Ming festival (Confucian)

6 THURSDAY

Ram Navami (Hindu, Vaishnava)

9 SUNDAY

Palm Sunday (Christianity)

11 TUESDAY

Mawlid-al-Nabi (Muslim)

13 THURSDAY

Full Moon

New Year (Theravadan)

Passover begins (Jewish)

14 FRIDAY

Good Friday (Christian)

Vaisakhi, Birth Anniversary of Khalsa, (Sikh)

16 SUNDAY

Easter (Christianity)

20 THURSDAY

Passover ends (Jewish)

21 FRIDAY

Ridván festival holy day (Bahá'í)

25 TUESDAY

Yom Hashoah, or Holocaust Memorial Day (Jewish)

27 THURSDAY

New Moon

29 SATURDAY

Ridván festival holy day (Bahá'í)

30 SUNDAY

Begin Maidhyõizarêmaya, mid-spring feast (Zoroastrian)

MAY 2006

2 TUESDAY

Ridván festival holy day (Bahá'í)

3 WEDNESDAY

Yom Ha'atzmaut, or Israel Independence Day: (Jewish)

4 THURSDAY

End Maidhyõizarêmaya, mid-spring feast (Zoroastrian)

5 FRIDAY

Tango no sekku, Boys' Day (Shinto)

13 SATURDAY

Full Moon

Vesak, Buddha's Birthday (Buddhist)

23 TUESDAY

Declaration of the Báb (Bahá'í)

27 SATURDAY

New Moon

29 MONDAY

Ascension of Bahá'u'lláh (Bahá'í)

JUNE 2006

2 FRIDAY

Shavuot (Jewish)

3 SATURDAY

Shavuot (Jewish)

4 SUNDAY

Pentecost, or Whitsunday (Christian)

11 SUNDAY

Full Moon

16 FRIDAY

Guru Arjan, martyrdom day (Sikh)

25 SUNDAY

New Moon

29 THURSDAY

Begin Maidhyõishêma, mid-summer feast (Zoroastrian)

30 FRIDAY

Oharae, or Great Purification (Shinto)

JULY 2006

3 MONDAY

End Maidhyõishêma, mid-summer feast (Zoroastrian)

9 SUNDAY

Martyrdom of the Báb (Bahá'í)

11 TUESDAY

Full Moon

Asalha Puja (Buddhist)

21 FRIDAY

Summer Solstice

25 TUESDAY

New Moon

AUGUST 2006

3 THURSDAY

Tishah be-Av (Jewish)

9 WEDNESDAY

Full Moon

13 SUNDAY

Obon, Festival of the Dead begins (Shinto)

16 WEDNESDAY

Obon, Festival of the Dead ends (Shinto)

Krishna Janmashthami (Hindu, Vaishnava)

23 WEDNESDAY

New Moon

27 SUNDAY

Ganesh Chaturthi (Hindu)

SEPTEMBER 2006

7 THURSDAY

Full Moon

12 TUESDAY

Begin Paitishaya, feast of bringing in the harvest (Zoroastrian)

16 SATURDAY

End Paitishaya, feast of bringing in the harvest (Zoroastrian)

21 THURSDAY

Autumn Equinox

22 FRIDAY

New Moon

Begin Ulambana, or Ancestor Day, (Mahayana)

23 SATURDAY

Rosh Hashana, New Year (Jewish)

Begin Navaratri (Hindu, Vaishnava)

24 SUNDAY

Rosh Hashana, New Year (Jewish)

Begin Ramadan (Muslim)

28 THURSDAY

Master Kong Birthday (Confucian)

OCTOBER 2006

1 SUNDAY

End Navaratri (Hindu, Vaishnava)

2 MONDAY

Yom Kippur (Jewish)

6 FRIDAY

End Ulambana, or Ancestor Day, (Mahayana)

7 SATURDAY

Full Moon

Begin Sukkot (Jewish)

12 THURSDAY

Begin Ayathrima, bringing home the herds (Zoroastrian)

13 FRIDAY

End Sukkot (Jewish)

14 SATURDAY

Shemini Atzeret (Jewish)

15 SUNDAY

Simchat Torah (Jewish)

16 MONDAY

End Ayathrima, bringing home the herds (Zoroastrian)

20 FRIDAY

Birth of the Báb (Bahá'í)

21 SATURDAY

Dipavali, Festival of Lights (Hindu, Vaishnava, Jain, Sikh)

22 SUNDAY

New Moon

24 TUESDAY

End Ramadan Id al-Fitr (Muslim)

NOVEMBER 2006

5 SUNDAY

Full Moon

Parkash (Birthday) of Guru Nanak (Sikh)

12 SUNDAY

Birth of Bahá'u'lláh (Bahá'í)

15 WEDNESDAY

Shichi-go-san, children's rite of passage, (Shinto)

20 MONDAY

New Moon

23 THURSDAY

Niiname-sai, harvest festival (Shinto)

24 FRIDAY

Niiname-sai, harvest festival (Shinto)

Guru Tegh Bahadur, martyrdom day (Sikh)

26 SUNDAY

'Abdu'l-Bahá, Day of the Covenant (Bahá'í)

28 TUESDAY

Ascension of 'Abdu'l-Bahá (Bahá'í)

DECEMBER 2006

3 SUNDAY

Advent begins (Christian)

5 TUESDAY

Full Moon

16 SATURDAY

Chanukah begins (Jewish)

20 WEDNESDAY

New Moon

21 THURSDAY

Winter Solstice

23 SATURDAY

Chanukah ends (Jewish)

25 MONDAY

Christmas (Christian)

31 SUNDAY

Id-al-Adha begins (Muslim)

Oharae, or Great Purification (Shinto)

Begin Maidhyaiya, mid-year/winter feast (Zoroastrian)

2007

JANUARY 2007

1 MONDAY

Oshogatsu, or NewYear (Shinto)

2 TUESDAY

Id-al-Adha ends (Muslim)

3 WEDNESDAY

Full Moon

New Year (Mahayanan)

4 THURSDAY

End Maidhyaiya, mid-year/winter feast (Zoroastrian)

5 FRIDAY

Parkash (Birthday) Guru Gobind Singh (Sikh)

6 SATURDAY

Epiphany (Christian)

10 WEDNESDAY

Id al-Ghadir (Shi'a)

15 MONDAY

Seijin no hi, or Coming of Age Day (Shinto)

19 FRIDAY

New Moon

20 SATURDAY

Muharram, New Year (Muslim)

29 MONDAY

Ashura (Shi'a Muslim)

FEBRUARY 2007

2 FRIDAY

Full Moon

Setsubun no hi, Change of Seasons, (Shinto)

3 SATURDAY

Tu Bi-Shevat (Jewish)

16 FRIDAY

Maha Shivaratri (Saivism)

Tse Gutor (Tibetan Buddhist)

17 SATURDAY

New Moon

18 SUNDAY

New Year (Tibetan Buddhist, Confucian)

21 WEDNESDAY

Ash Wednesday, beginning of Lent (Christian)

Begin Mönlam Chenmo, the great prayer ceremony (Tibetan Buddhist)

MARCH 2007

2 FRIDAY

Annual Fast begins (Bahá'í)

3 SATURDAY

Full Moon

Hina matsuri, Doll Festival, or Girls' Day (Shinto)

Holi (Hindu, Vaishnava)

4 SUNDAY

Holi (Hindu, Vaishnava)

12 MONDAY

End Mönlam Chenmo, the great prayer ceremony (Tibetan Buddhist)

16 FRIDAY

Begin Hamaspathmaêdaya, feast of All Souls (Zoroastrian)

19 MONDAY

New Moon

20 TUESDAY

Annual Fast ends (Bahá'í)

End Hamaspathmaêdaya, feast of All Souls (Zoroastrian)

21 WEDNESDAY

Spring Equinox

Naw-Rúz, or New Year (Bahá'í, Zoroastrian)

27 TUESDAY

Ram Navami (Hindu, Vaishnava)

31 SATURDAY

Mawlid-al-Nabi (Muslim)

APRIL 2007

1 SUNDAY

Palm Sunday (Christian)

2 MONDAY

Full Moon

3 TUESDAY

New Year (Theravadan)

Passover begins (Jewish)

5 THURSDAY

Qing Ming festival (Confucian)

6 FRIDAY

Good Friday (Christian)

8 SUNDAY

Easter (Christian)

10 TUESDAY

Passover ends (Jewish)

14 SATURDAY

Vaisakhi, Birth Anniversary of Khalsa, (Sikh)

15 SUNDAY

Yom Hashoah, or Holocaust Memorial Day (Jewish)

17 TUESDAY

New Moon

21 SATURDAY

Ridván festival holy day (Bahá'í)

23 MONDAY

Yom Ha'atzmaut, or Israel Independence Day: (Jewish)

29 SUNDAY

Ridván festival holy day (Bahá'í)

30 MONDAY

Begin Maidhyõizarêmaya, mid-spring feast (Zoroastrian)

MAY 2007

2 WEDNESDAY

Full Moon

Vesak, Buddha's Birthday (Buddhist)

Ridván festival holy day (Bahá'í)

4 FRIDAY

End Maidhyõizarêmaya, mid-spring feast (Zoroastrian)

5 SATURDAY

Tango no sekku, Boys' Day (Shinto)

16 WEDNESDAY

New Moon

23 WEDNESDAY

Declaration of the Báb (Bahá'í)

Shavuot (Jewish)

24 THURSDAY

Shavuot (Jewish)

27 SUNDAY

Pentecost, or Whitsunday (Christian)

29 TUESDAY

Ascension of Bahá'u'lláh (Bahá'í)

JUNE 2007

1 FRIDAY

Full Moon

15 FRIDAY

New Moon

16 SATURDAY

Guru Arjan, martyrdom day (Sikh)

29 FRIDAY

Begin Maidhyõishêma, mid-summer feast (Zoroastrian)

30 SATURDAY

Full Moon

Oharae, or Great Purification (Shinto)

JULY 2007

3 TUESDAY

End Maidhyõishêma, mid-summer feast (Zoroastrian)

9 MONDAY

Martyrdom of the Báb (Bahá'í)

14 SATURDAY

New Moon

21 SATURDAY

Summer Solstice

24 TUESDAY

Tishah be-Av (Jewish)

30 MONDAY

Full Moon

Asalha Puja (Buddhist)

AUGUST 2007

5 SUNDAY

Ganesh Chaturthi (Hindu)

12 SUNDAY

New Moon

13 MONDAY

Obon, Festival of the Dead begins (Shinto)

16 THURSDAY

Obon, Festival of the Dead ends (Shinto)

28 TUESDAY

Full Moon

SEPTEMBER 2007

4 TUESDAY

Krishna Janmashthami (Hindu, Vaishnava)

11 TUESDAY

New Moon

Begin Ulambana, or Ancestor Day, (Mahayana)

12 WEDNESDAY

Begin Paitishaya, feast of bringing in the harvest (Zoroastrian)

13 THURSDAY

Begin Ramadan (Muslim)

Rosh Hashana, New Year (Jewish)

14 FRIDAY

Rosh Hashana, New Year (Jewish)

16 SUNDAY

End Paitishaya, feast of bringing in the harvest (Zoroastrian)

21 FRIDAY

Autumn Equinox

22 SATURDAY

Yom Kippur (Jewish)

25 TUESDAY

End Ulambana, or Ancestor Day, (Mahayana)

26 WEDNESDAY

Full Moon

27 THURSDAY

Begin Sukkot (Jewish)

28 FRIDAY

Master Kong Birthday (Confucian)

OCTOBER 2007

3 WEDNESDAY

End Sukkot (Jewish)

4 THURSDAY

Shemini Atzeret (Jewish)

5 FRIDAY

Simchat Torah (Jewish)

11 THURSDAY

New Moon

12 FRIDAY

Begin Ayathrima, bringing home the herds (Zoroastrian)

Navaratri (Hindu, Vaishnava)

13 SATURDAY

End Ramadan, Id-al-Fitr (Muslim)

16 TUESDAY

End Ayathrima, bringing home the herds (Zoroastrian)

20 SATURDAY

Birth of the Báb (Bahá'í)

Navaratri (Hindu, Vaishnava)

26 FRIDAY

Full Moon

NOVEMBER 2007

9 FRIDAY

New Moon

Dipavali, Festival of Lights (Hindu, Vaishnava, Jain, Sikh)

12 MONDAY

Birth of Bahá'u'lláh (Bahá'í)

15 THURSDAY

Shichi-go-san, children's rite of passage, (Shinto)

23 FRIDAY

Niiname-sai, harvest festival (Shinto)

24 SATURDAY

Full Moon

Niiname-sai, harvest festival (Shinto)

Parkash (Birthday) of Guru Nanak (Sikh)

Guru Tegh Bahadur, martyrdom day (Sikh)

26 MONDAY

'Abdu'l-Bahá, Day of the Covenant (Bahá'í)

28 WEDNESDAY

Ascension of 'Abdu'l-Bahá (Bahá'í)

DECEMBER 2007

2 SUNDAY

Advent begins (Christian)

5 WEDNESDAY

Chanukah begins (Jewish)

9 SUNDAY

New Moon

12 WEDNESDAY

Chanukah ends (Jewish)

20 THURSDAY

Id-al-Adha begins (Muslim)

21 FRIDAY

Winter Solstice

22 SATURDAY

Id-al-Adha ends (Muslim)

24 MONDAY

Full Moon

25 TUESDAY

Christmas (Christian)

30 SUNDAY

Id al-Ghadir (Shi'a)

31 MONDAY

Oharae, or Great Purification (Shinto)

Begin Maidhyaiya, mid-year/winter feast (Zoroastrian)

2008

JANUARY 2008

1 TUESDAY

Oshogatsu, or NewYear (Shinto)

4 FRIDAY

End Maidhyaiya, mid-year/winter feast (Zoroastrian)

5 SATURDAY

Parkash (Birthday) Guru Gobind Singh (Sikh)

6 SUNDAY

Epiphany (Christian)

8 TUESDAY

New Moon

10 THURSDAY

Muharram, New Year (Muslim)

15 TUESDAY

Seijin no hi, or *Coming of Age Day (Shinto)*

19 SATURDAY

Ashura (Shi'a Muslim)

22 TUESDAY

Full Moon

New Year (Mahayanan)

Tu Bi-Shevat (Jewish)

FEBRUARY 2008

2 SATURDAY

Setsubun no hi, Change of Seasons, (Shinto)

5 TUESDAY

Tse Gutor (Tibetan Buddhist)

6 WEDNESDAY

Ash Wednesday, beginning of Lent (Christian)

7 THURSDAY

New Moon

New Year (Tibetan Buddhist, Confucian)

10 SUNDAY

Begin Mönlam Chenmo, the great prayer ceremony (Tibetan Buddhist)

21 THURSDAY

Full Moon

29 FRIDAY

End Mönlam Chenmo, the great prayer ceremony (Tibetan Buddhist)

MARCH 2008

2 SUNDAY

Annual Fast begins (Bahá'í)

3 MONDAY

Hina matsuri, Doll Festival, or Girls' Day (Shinto)

6 THURSDAY

Maha Shivaratri (Saivism)

7 FRIDAY

New Moon

16 SUNDAY

Palm Sunday (Christian)

Begin amaspathmaêdaya, feast of All Souls (Zoroastrian)

20 THURSDAY

Mawlid-al-Nabi (Muslim)

Annual Fast ends (Bahá'í)

End Hamaspathmaêdaya, feast of All Souls (Zoroastrian)

21 FRIDAY

Full Moon

Spring Equinox

Naw-Rúz, or New Year (Bahá'í, Zoroastrian)

Good Friday (Christian)

Holi (Hindu, Vaishnava)

22 SATURDAY

Holi (Hindu, Vaishnava)

23 SUNDAY

Easter (Christian)

APRIL 2008

5 SATURDAY

Qing Ming festival (Confucian)

6 SUNDAY

New Moon

14 MONDAY

Ram Navami (Hindu, Vaishnava)

Vaisakhi, Birth Anniversary of Khalsa, (Sikh)

20 SUNDAY

Full Moon

New Year (Theravadan)

Passover begins (Jewish)

21 MONDAY

Ridván festival holy day (Bahá'í)

27 SUNDAY

Passover ends (Jewish)

29 TUESDAY

Ridván festival holy day (Bahá'í)

30 WEDNESDAY

Begin Maidhyõizarêmaya, mid-spring feast (Zoroastrian)

MAY 2008

1 THURSDAY

Yom Hashoah, or Holocaust Memorial Day (Jewish)

2 FRIDAY

Ridván festival holy day (Bahá'í)

4 SUNDAY

End Maidhyõizarêmaya, mid-spring feast (Zoroastrian)

5 MONDAY

New Moon

Tango no sekku, Boys' Day (Shinto)

10 SATURDAY

Yom Ha'atzmaut, or Israel Independence Day: (Jewish)

11 SUNDAY

Pentecost, or Whitsunday (Christian)

20 TUESDAY

Full Moon

Vesak, Buddha's Birthday (Buddhist)

23 FRIDAY

Declaration of the Báb (Bahá'í)

29 THURSDAY

Ascension of Bahá'u'lláh (Bahá'í)

JUNE 2008

3 TUESDAY

New Moon

9 MONDAY

Shavuot (Jewish)

10 TUESDAY

Shavuot (Jewish)

16 MONDAY

Guru Arjan, martyrdom day (Sikh)

18 WEDNESDAY

Full Moon

29 SUNDAY

Begin Maidhyõishêma, mid-summer feast (Zoroastrian)

30 MONDAY

Oharae, or Great Purification (Shinto)

JULY 2008

3 THURSDAY

New Moon

End Maidhyõishêma, mid-summer feast (Zoroastrian)

9 WEDNESDAY

Martyrdom of the Báb (Bahá'í)

18 FRIDAY

Full Moon

Asalha Puja (Buddhist)

21 MONDAY

Summer Solstice

AUGUST 2008

1 FRIDAY

New Moon

10 SUNDAY

Tishah be-Av (Jewish)

13 WEDNESDAY

Obon, Festival of the Dead begins (Shinto)

16 SATURDAY

Full Moon

Obon, Festival of the Dead ends (Shinto)

24 SUNDAY

Krishna Janmashthami (Hindu, Vaishnava)

30 SATURDAY

New Moon

31 SUNDAY

Begin Ulambana, or Ancestor Day, (Mahayana)

SEPTEMBER 2008

2 TUESDAY

Begin Ramadan (Muslim)

3 WEDNESDAY

Ganesh Chaturthi (Hindu)

12 FRIDAY

Begin Paitishaya, feast of bringing in the harvest (Zoroastrian)

14 SUNDAY

End Ulambana, or Ancestor Day, (Mahayana)

15 MONDAY

Full Moon

16 TUESDAY

End Paitishaya, feast of bringing in the harvest (Zoroastrian)

21 SUNDAY

Autumn Equinox

28 SUNDAY

Master Kong Birthday (Confucian)

29 MONDAY

New Moon

30 TUESDAY

Rosh Hashana, New Year (Jewish)

Navaratri (Hindu, Vaishnava)

OCTOBER 2008

1 WEDNESDAY

Rosh Hashana, New Year (Jewish)

2 THURSDAY

End Ramadan, Id-al-Fitr (Muslim)

8 WEDNESDAY

Navaratri (Hindu, Vaishnava)

9 THURSDAY

Yom Kippur (Jewish)

12 SUNDAY

Begin Ayathrima, bringing home the herds (Zoroastrian)

14 TUESDAY

Full Moon

Begin Sukkot (Jewish)

16 THURSDAY

End Ayathrima, bringing home the herds (Zoroastrian)

20 MONDAY

Birth of the Báb (Bahá'í)

End Sukkot (Jewish)

21 TUESDAY

Shemini Atzeret (Jewish)

22 WEDNESDAY

Simchat Torah (Jewish)

28 TUESDAY

New Moon

Dipavali, Festival of Lights (Hindu, Vaishnava, Jain, Sikh)

NOVEMBER 2008

12 WEDNESDAY

Birth of Bahá'u'lláh (Bahá'í)

13 THURSDAY

Full Moon

Parkash (Birthday) of Guru Nanak (Sikh)

15 SATURDAY

Shichi-go-san, children's rite of passage, (Shinto)

23 SUNDAY

Niiname-sai, harvest festival (Shinto)

24 MONDAY

Niiname-sai, harvest festival (Shinto)

Guru Tegh Bahadur, martyrdom day (Sikh)

26 WEDNESDAY

'Abdu'l-Bahá, Day of the Covenant (Bahá'í)

27 THURSDAY

New Moon

28 FRIDAY

Ascension of 'Abdu'l-Bahá (Bahá'í)

30 SUNDAY

Advent begins (Christian)

DECEMBER 2008

9 TUESDAY

Id-al-Adha begins (Muslim)

11 THURSDAY

Id-al-Adha ends (Muslim)

12 FRIDAY

Full Moon

19 FRIDAY

Id al-Ghadir (Shi'a)

21 SUNDAY

Winter Solstice

22 MONDAY

Chanukah begins (Jewish)

25 THURSDAY

Christmas (Christian)

27 SATURDAY

New Moon

29 MONDAY

Muharram, New Year (Muslim)

Chanukah ends (Jewish)

31 WEDNESDAY

Oharae, or Great Purification (Shinto)

Begin Maidhyaiya, mid-year/winter feast (Zoroastrian)

2009

JANUARY 2009

1 THURSDAY

Oshogatsu, or NewYear (Shinto)

4 SUNDAY

End Maidhyaiya, mid-year/winter feast (Zoroastrian)

5 MONDAY

Parkash (Birthday) Guru Gobind Singh (Sikh)

6 TUESDAY

Epiphany (Christian)

7 WEDNESDAY

Ashura (Shi'a Muslim)

11 SUNDAY

Full Moon

New Year (Mahayanan)

15 THURSDAY

Seijin no hi, or *Coming of Age Day (Shinto)*

24 SATURDAY

Tse Gutor (Tibetan Buddhist)

26 MONDAY

New Moon

New Year (Tibetan Buddhist, Confucian)

29 THURSDAY

Begin Mönlam Chenmo, the great prayer ceremony (Tibetan Buddhist)

FEBRUARY 2009

2 MONDAY

Setsubun no hi, Change of Seasons, (Shinto)

9 MONDAY

Full Moon

Tu Bi-Shevat (Jewish)

17 TUESDAY

End Mönlam Chenmo, the great prayer ceremony (Tibetan Buddhist)

23 MONDAY

Maha Shivaratri (Saivism)

25 WEDNESDAY

New Moon

Ash Wednesday, beginning of Lent (Christian)

MARCH 2009

2 MONDAY

Annual Fast begins (Bahá'í)

3 TUESDAY

Hina matsuri Doll Festival, or Girls' Day (Shinto)

9 MONDAY

Mawlid-al-Nabi (Muslim)

11 WEDNESDAY

Full Moon

Holi (Hindu, Vaishnava)

16 MONDAY

Begin Hamaspathmaêdaya, feast of All Souls (Zoroastrian)

20 FRIDAY

Annual Fast ends (Bahá'í)

End Hamaspathmaêdaya, feast of All Souls (Zoroastrian)

21 SATURDAY

Spring Equinox

Naw-Rúz, or New Year (Bahá'í, Zoroastrian)

26 THURSDAY

New Moon

APRIL 2009

3 FRIDAY

Ram Navami (Hindu, Vaishnava)

5 SUNDAY

Palm Sunday (Christian)

Qing Ming festival (Confucian)

9 THURSDAY

Full Moon

New Year (Theravadan)

Passover begins (Jewish)

10 FRIDAY

Good Friday (Christian)

12 SUNDAY

Easter (Christian)

14 TUESDAY

Vaisakhi, Birth Anniversary of Khalsa, (Sikh)

16 THURSDAY

Passover ends (Jewish)

21 TUESDAY

Ridván festival holy day (Bahá'í)

Yom Hashoah, or Holocaust Memorial Day (Jewish)

25 SATURDAY

New Moon

29 WEDNESDAY

Ridván festival holy day (Bahá'í)

Yom Ha'atzmaut, or Israel Independence Day: (Jewish)

30 THURSDAY

Begin Maidhyõizarêmaya, mid-spring feast (Zoroastrian)

MAY 2009

2 SATURDAY

Ridván festival holy day (Bahá'í)

4 MONDAY

End Maidhyõizarêmaya, mid-spring feast (Zoroastrian)

5 TUESDAY

Tango no sekku, Boys' Day (Shinto)

9 SATURDAY

Full Moon

Vesak, Buddha's Birthday (Buddhist)

23 SATURDAY

Declaration of the Báb (Bahá'í)

24 SUNDAY

New Moon

29 FRIDAY

Ascension of Bahá'u'lláh (Bahá'í)

Shavuot (Jewish)

30 SATURDAY

Shavuot (Jewish)

31 SUNDAY

Pentecost, or Whitsunday (Christian)

JUNE 2009

7 SUNDAY

Full Moon

16 TUESDAY

Guru Arjan, martyrdom day (Sikh)

22 MONDAY

New Moon

29 MONDAY

Begin Maidhyõishêma, mid-summer' feast (Zoroastrian)

30 TUESDAY

Oharae, or Great Purification (Shinto)

JULY 2009

3 FRIDAY

End Maidhyõishêma, mid-summer feast (Zoroastrian)

7 TUESDAY

Full Moon

Asalha Puja (Buddhist)

9 THURSDAY

Martyrdom of the Báb (Bahá'í)

21 TUESDAY

Summer Solstice

22 WEDNESDAY

New Moon

30 THURSDAY

Tishah be-Av (Jewish)

AUGUST 2009

6 THURSDAY

Full Moon

13 THURSDAY

Obon, Festival of the Dead begins (Shinto)

14 FRIDAY

Krishna Janmashthami (Hindu, Vaishnava)

16 SUNDAY

Obon, Festival of the Dead begins (Shinto)

20 THURSDAY

New Moon

22 SATURDAY

Begin Ramadan (Muslim)

23 SUNDAY

Ganesh Chaturthi (Hindu)

SEPTEMBER 2009

4 FRIDAY

Full Moon

12 SATURDAY

Begin Paitishaya, feast of bringing in the harvest (Zoroastrian)

16 WEDNESDAY

End Paitishaya, feast of bringing in the harvest (Zoroastrian)

19 SATURDAY

New Moon

Rosh Hashana, New Year (Jewish)

Begin Ulambana, or Ancestor Day, (Mahayana)

Navaratri (Hindu, Vaishnava)

20 SUNDAY

Rosh Hashana, New Year (Jewish)

21 MONDAY

Autumn Equinox

End Ramadan, Id-al-Fitr (Muslim)

27 SUNDAY

Navaratri (Hindu, Vaishnava)

28 MONDAY

Master Kong Birthday (Confucian)

Yom Kippur (Jewish)

OCTOBER 2009

3 SATURDAY

Begin Sukkot (Jewish)

Ulambana, or Ancestor Day, (Mahayana)

4 SUNDAY

Full Moon

9 FRIDAY

End Sukkot (Jewish)

10 SATURDAY

Shemini Atzeret (Jewish)

11 SUNDAY

Simchat Torah (Jewish)

12 MONDAY

Begin Ayathrima, bringing home the herds (Zoroastrian)

16 FRIDAY

End Ayathrima, bringing home the herds (Zoroastrian)

17 SATURDAY

Dipavali, Festival of Lights (Hindu, Vaishnava, Jain, Sikh)

18 SUNDAY

New Moon

20 TUESDAY

Birth of the Báb (Bahá'í)

NOVEMBER 2009

2 MONDAY

Full Moon

Parkash (Birthday) of Guru Nanak (Sikh)

12 THURSDAY

Birth of Bahá'u'lláh (Bahá'í)

15 SUNDAY

Shichi-go-san, children's rite of passage, (Shinto)

16 MONDAY

New Moon

23 MONDAY

Niiname-sai, harvest festival (Shinto)

24 TUESDAY

Niiname-sai, harvest festival (Shinto)

Guru Tegh Bahadur, martyrdom day (Sikh)

26 THURSDAY

'Abdu'l-Bahá, Day of the Covenant (Bahá'í)

28 SATURDAY

Ascension of 'Abdu'l-Bahá (Bahá'í)

Id-al-Adha begins (Muslim)

30 MONDAY

Id-al-Adha ends (Muslim)

DECEMBER 2009

2 WEDNESDAY

Full Moon

8 TUESDAY

Id al-Ghadir (Shi'a)

12 SATURDAY

Chanukah begins (Jewish)

16 WEDNESDAY

New Moon

18 FRIDAY

Muharram, New Year (Muslim)

19 SATURDAY

Chanukah ends (Jewish)

21 MONDAY

Winter Solstice

25 FRIDAY

Christmas (Christian)

27 SUNDAY

Ashura (Shi'a Muslim)

31 THURSDAY

Full Moon

Oharae, or Great Purification (Shinto)

Begin Maidhyaiya, mid-year/winter feast (Zoroastrian)

Practices and Beliefs

Worldmark Encyclopedia of Religious Practices

Religion	Year founded	Prominent leaders	Place of origin	Primary texts	Number of followers
African Traditional Religions	200,000–100,000 B.C.E.	priests and priestesses, sacred kings and queens, prophets and prophetesses, and seers	Africa	• myths and oral narratives	84.5 million
Anglicanism	sixteenth century C.E.	King Henry VIII (1491–1547) Thomas Cranmer (1489–1556) William Tyndale (c. 1492–1536)	England	• Bible • Book of Common Prayer	84.5 million
Bahá'í Faith	1863 C.E.	'Alí-Muhammad, or the Báb (1819–50) Bahá'u'lláh (1817–92) 'Abdu'l-Bahá (1844–1921) Shoghi Effendi Rabbani (1897–1957)	Iran	• writings of Bahá'u'lláh, the Báb, and of 'Abdu'l-Bahá	6.5 million
Baptist Tradition	1690 C.E.	John Smyth (died in 1612) William Carey (1761–1834) Martin Luther King, Jr. (1929–68)	England	• Bible	117 million
Buddhism	fifth century B.C.E.	Siddhartha Gautama, or the Buddha (sixth century B.C.E.) Bodhidharma (sixth century C.E.) Padmasambhava (eighth century C.E.	northern India	• *Tipitaka* ("three baskets") • Additional books, such as the Lotus Sutra and the Prajnaparamita (Perfection of Wisdom) texts	390 million
Christianity	first century C.E.	Peter (died c. 64) Paul (died c. 64) Ignatius of Antioch (c. 35–c. 107) Constantine I (died 337) Saint Augustine (354–430) Saint Patrick (c. 390–c. 460) Pope Gregory I (reigned 590–604) Francis of Assisi (c. 1181–1226) Pope Innocent III (reigned 1198–1216) Martin Luther (1483–1546) Ulrich Zwingli (1484–1531) John Calvin (1509–64)	Palestine	• Bible	2.21 billion
Confucianism	c. 1050–256 B.C.E.	Confucius, or Master Kong (551–479 B.C.E.) Mencius, or Master Meng (c. 391–308 B.C.E.) Dong Zhongshu (c. 176–104 B.C.E.) Zhu Xi (1130–1200 C.E.) Wang Yangming (1472–1529 C.E.) Ngo Thi Nham (1746–1803 C.E.) Motoda Nagazane (1818–91 C.E.)	China	• *Yijing* (Book of Changes) • *Shujing* (Book of Documents) • *Shijing* (Book of Odes) • *Liji* (Book of Rites) • *Zhouli* (Rites of Zhou) • *Yili* (Book of Etiquette and Ritual) • *Lun yu* (Analects) • *Xiaojing* (Scripture of Filiality) • the Chinese dictionary *Erya* • *Mengzi* (Master Meng) • *Chunqiu* (Spring and Autumn Annals)	6.5 million
Conservative Judaism	1886 C.E.	Solomon Schechter (1847–1915) Cyrus Adler (1863–1940) Louis Ginzberg (1872–1953) Mordecai Kaplan (1881–1983)	United States	• Tanakh (Hebrew Bible) • Talmud (Oral Torah)	1.56 million

[continued]

Worldmark Encyclopedia of Religious Practices [CONTINUED]

Religion	Year founded	Prominent leaders	Place of origin	Primary texts	Number of followers
Coptic Christianity	48 C.E.	Saint Mark the Evangelist (first century) Athanasius (c. 293–373) Patriarch Cyril I (reigned 412–44)	Egypt	• Bible • Liturgy of Saint Basil, the Liturgy of Saint Gregory of Nazianzus, and the ancient liturgy of Saint Mark, also known as the Liturgy of Saint Cyril • *Katamaros,* a study of the stages of Christ's life • *Agbiya,* the book of the hours, contains the Psalms, prayers, and Gospels for the seven daily prayers • in addition, Copts use a psalmody, a book of doxologies (praise), and the *Synaxarium,* a book that commemorates Coptic saints	7.8 million
Eastern Catholic Churches	twelfth century C.E.	Patriarch Jeremias II al-Amshitti (early thirteenth century) Saint Josaphat Kuntsevych (died in 1623) Patriarch Abraham Pierre I (eighteenth century)	Lebanon and Armenia	• Bible • Euchologions, the Books of Needs, the Anthologions, the Festal Anthologies, the Floral and the Lenten Triodions, Oktoechos, Horologions, Typikons, Menologions, Menaions, the Books of Akathistos, and the Books of Commemoration	13 million
Eastern Orthodox Christianity	325 C.E.	Constantine I (died in 337) Saint Basil the Great (329–79) Saint John Chrysostom (347–407)	eastern half of the Roman Empire (now Turkey, Greece, Bulgaria, Romania, and Serbia)	• Septuagint Greek version of the Old Testament • Greek New Testament	227.5 million
Hinduism	before 3000 B.C.E.	Shankara (eighth century C.E.) Ramanuja (c. 1017–1137 C.E.) Madhva (c. 1199–1278 C.E.) Ram Mohan Roy (1772–1833 C.E.) Dayananda Sarasvati (1824–83 C.E.) Ramakrishna (1836–86 C.E.)	India	• Vedas • *Ramayana* ("Story of Rama") • *Mahabharata* ("Great Sons of Bharata") • *Purana*s ("Ancient Lore") • *Dharma Sastra*s	910 million
Islam	622 C.E.	Prophet Muhammad (570–632) **Four Rightly Guide Caliphs:** Abu Bakr (reigned 632–34) Umar (reigned 634–44) Uthman (reigned 644–56) Ali (reigned 656–61)	Mecca and Medina (now in Saudi Arabia)	• Koran	1.3 billion
Jainism	c. 550 B.C.E.	Lord Mahavira (sixth century B.C.E.)	India	• **Shvetambara tradition:** • 45 texts organized into five groups: • Angas ("Limbs") • Upanga ("Supplementary Limbs") • Chedasutras ("Delineating Scriptures") • Mulasutras ("Root Scriptures") • Prakirnaka ("Miscellaneous")	6.5 million

[continued]

Worldmark Encyclopedia of Religious Practices [CONTINUED]

Religion	Year founded	Prominent leaders	Place of origin	Primary texts	Number of followers
				• **Digambara tradition:** • it is believed that the original canon has been lost • Shatakanda Agama Kashayaprabhrita • others	
Jehovah's Witnesses	1879 C.E.	Charles Taze Russell (1852–1916) Joseph Franklin Rutherford (1869–1942)	United States	• Bible	15.6 million
Judaism	c. eighteenth century B.C.E.	Abraham (eighteenth century B.C.E.) Isaac Jacob Moses (fourteenth–thirteenth centuries B.C.E.) Joshua (twelfth century B.C.E.) Samuel (eleventh century B.C.E.) David (eleventh–tenth centuries B.C.E.) Solomon (tenth century B.C.E.) Elijah (ninth century B.C.E.) Isaiah (eighth century B.C.E.) Rabbi Johanan ben Zakkai (died c. 80 C.E.)	Mesopotamia	• Tanakh (Hebrew Bible), divided into three parts: the Torah (also called the Pentateuch), the Prophets (Nevi'im), and the Writings (Ketuvim or Hagiographa) • Talmud (Oral Torah)	16.25 million
Lutheranism	1517 C.E.	Martin Luther (1483–1546) Philipp Melanchthon (1497–1560) Johannes Bugenhagen (1485–1558)	Germany	• Bible	65 million
Mahayana Buddhism	c. 200 C.E.	Nagarjuna (born in 150) Tenzin Gyatso, the 14th Dalai Lama (born in 1935)	India	• Perfection of Wisdom Sutras	208 million
				• Bible	76 million
Methodism	1729 C.E.	John Wesley (1703–91)	England	• Bible	12.35 million
The Church of Jesus Christ of Latter-day Saints	1830 C.E.	Joseph Smith (1805–44) Brigham Young (1801–77)	Fayette, New York, U.S.A.	• Book of Mormon • Pearl of Great Price • Doctrine and Covenants	
Orthodox Judaism	nineteenth century C.E.	**Hasidic community:** Rabbi Israel ben Eliezer, also called the Baal Shem Tov (c. 1700–60), **non-Hasidic Haredi community:** Rabbi Elijah ben Shlomo Zalman, known as the Vilna Gaon (1720–97) **Modern Orthodox community:** Rabbi Samson Raphael Hirsch (1808–88)	Europe	• Tanakh (Hebrew Bible) • Talmud (Oral Torah)	2.6 million
Pentecostalism	1901 C.E.	Charles Fox Parham (1873–1929) William J. Seymour (1870–1922)	Kansas, U.S.A.	• Bible	552.5 million

[continued]

Worldmark Encyclopedia of Religious Practices [CONTINUED]

Religion	Year founded	Prominent leaders	Place of origin	Primary texts	Number of followers
Protestantism	1517 C.E.	Martin Luther (1483–1546) John Calvin (1509–64) Ulrich Zwingli (1484–1531) Menno Simons (1496–1561)	Germany	• Bible	377 million
Reformed Christianity	sixteenth century C.E.	John Calvin (1509–64) Ulrich Zwingli (1484–1531)	Switzerland	• Bible	77.35 million
Reform Judaism	early nineteenth century C.E.	Israel Jacobson (1768–1828) Rabbi Isaac Mayer Wise (1819–1900)	western and central Europe	• Tanakh (Hebrew Bible) • Talmud (Oral Torah)	3.9 million
Religious Society of Friends (Quakers)	1652 C.E.	George Fox (1624–91) William Penn (1644–1718)	England	• Bible	390,000
Roman Catholicism	first century C.E.	Peter (died c. 64) Saint Ignatius of Loyola (1491–1556) Pope Pius IX (reigned 1846–78) Pope John XXIII (reigned 1958–63) Pope John Paul II (reigned 1978–2005)	Rome	• Bible, with 46 books in the Old Testament—the 39 from the Hebrew canon as well as 7 deutercanonical books	1.105 billion
Seventh-day Adventist Church	1863 C.E.	Ellen Gould White (1827–1915) James Springer White (1821–81) Joseph Bates (1792–1872)	United States	• Bible	13 million
Shaivism	second century C.E.	Lakulisha (c. second century) Basava (died in 1167) Sathya Sai Baba (born in 1926)	South Asia	• Upanishads • Shaivite Puranas • individual Shaivite groups have various other texts	208 million
Shiism	632 C.E.	Prophet Muhammad (570–632) Ali (c. 600–661) Husayn (626–80) Ja'far al-Sadiq (702–65)	Medina (now in Saudi Arabia)	• Koran	143 million
Shinto	c. 500 C.E.	Yamazaki Ansai (1618–82) Keichū (1640–1701) Motoori Norinaga (1730–1801)	Japan	• none sacred to all Shinto worshippers	117 million
Sikhism	c. 1499 C.E.	Guru Nanak (1469–1539) Guru Gobind Singh (1666–1708)	the Punjab (now in India and Pakistan)	• Adi Granth (Original Book) • Dasam Granth (Book of the 10th Guru) • Works of Bhai Gurdas and Bhai Nand Lal Goya • *janam-sakhis* (birth narratives) • *rahit-namas* (manuals of code of conduct) • *gur-bilas* (pleasure of the Guru) literature	19.5 million
Sunnism	632 C.E.	Prophet Muhammad (570–632) **Four Rightly Guided Caliphs:** Abu Bakr (reigned 632–34) Umar (reigned 634–44) Uthman (reigned 644–56) Ali (reigned 656–61)	Medina (now in Saudi Arabia)	• Koran	975 million

[continued]

Worldmark Encyclopedia of Religious Practices [CONTINUED]

Religion	Year founded	Prominent leaders	Place of origin	Primary texts	Number of followers
Taoism	c. 450–500 C.E.	Lu Hsiu-ching (406–77) T'ao Hung-ching (456–536) Ssu-ma Ch'eng-chen (646–735)	China	• *Tao-tsang*	65 million
Theravada Buddhism	fifth century B.C.E.	Mahasi Sayadaw (1904–82 C.E.) Ajahn Chah (1918–92 C.E.)	India	• *Tipitika*	123.5 million
Tibetan Buddhism	seventh and eighth centuries C.E.	Santaraksita (eighth century) Padmasambhava (eighth century) Tenzin Gyatso, the 14th Dalai Lama (born in 1935)	Tibet	• *Kanjur* • *Tenjur*	195,000
Unitarianism and Universalism	1565 C.E. (Unitarianism) and 1723 C.E. (Universalism)	Ferenc Dávid (1510–79) Faustus Socinus (1539–1604)	Poland and Transylvania (now in Romania) (Unitarianism) England (Universalism)	• Bible • many congregations include the sacred writings of all religions in worship	325,000
United Church of Christ	1957 C.E.	**Congregational:** John Winthrop (1588–1649) Jonathan Edwards (1703–58) **Reformed:** John Williamson Nevin (1803–86) **German Evangelical:** Reinhold Niebuhr (1892–1971)	United States	• Bible	1.3 million
Vaishnavism	c. 500 B.C.E.	Ramanuja (c. 1017–1137 C.E.) Madhvacarya (1296–1386 C.E.) Chaitanya (1485–1533 C.E.) Ghanshyam, or Swaminarayan (born in 1781 C.E.)	India	• Vedas • *Ramayana* • *Mahabharata* • Vaishnava Puranas	617.5 million
World Evangelicalism	seventeenth century C.E.	Philipp Jakob Spener (1635–1705) Charles Grandison Finney (1792–1875) Aimee Semple McPherson (1890–1944) Billy Graham (born in 1918)	Germany	• Bible	780 million
Zoroastrianism	second millennium B.C.E.	Tansar, or Tosar (died in 240 C.E.) Kirdīr, or Kartir (third century C.E.) K.R. Cama (1831–1909 C.E.)	Central Asia or eastern Iran	• Avesta, containing the *Yasna, Yashts*, and *Vendidad*	149,500

Quotations on Beliefs

I. God or gods

"Acts of God are like riddles."

> ***African Traditional Religions***
> ***African proverb***

"To every discerning and illuminated heart it is evident that God, the unknowable Essence, the Divine Being, is immensely exalted beyond every human attribute, such as corporeal existence, ascent and descent, egress and regress. Far be it from His glory that human tongue should adequately recount His praise, or that human heart comprehend His fathomless mystery."

> ***Bahá'í Faith***
> ***Bahá'u'lláh***

"God then is infinite and incomprehensible and all that is comprehensible about Him is His infinity and incomprehensibility. . . . For when you speak of Him as good, and just, and wise, and so forth, you do not tell God's nature but only the qualities of His nature."

> ***Christianity***
> ***John of Damascus***

"Heaven/God [Tian] bestows one's inner nature; the Way [Tao] consists in following one's inner nature; the Teaching [Jiao] derives from cultivating the Way."

> ***Confucianism***
> ***Doctrine of the Mean 1***

"You are the supreme being, the supreme abode, the supreme purifier, the eternal one, the divine being. You are the Primordial deity without birth."

> ***Hinduism***
> ***Bhagavad Gita 10:22***

"Say: He is Allah, the One and Only; Allah, the Eternal, Absolute. He begetteth not, nor is He begotten; And there is none like unto Him."

> ***Islam***
> ***Koran 112***

"Hear, O Israel! The Lord our God, the Lord is one. You shall love the Lord your God with all your heart and with all your soul and with all your might."

Judaism
Deuteronomy 6:4-6

"Generally speaking, 'kami' denotes . . . all kinds of beings—including not only human beings but also such objects as birds, beasts, trees, grass, seas, mountains, and so forth—any being whatsoever which possesses some eminent quality out of the ordinary and awe-inspiring."

Shinto
Motoori Norinaga

"My Master is the One. He is the One, brother, and He alone exists."

Sikhism
Guru Nanak, Adi Granth, p. 150

"Then as holy I have recognized Thee, Ahura Mazda, when I saw Thee at first at the birth of life, when Thou didst appoint rewards for acts and words, bad for the bad, a good recompense for the good, by Thy innate virtue, at the final turning point of creation."

Zoroastrianism
Yasna 43:5

II. Prayer

"The prayer of the chicken hawk does not get him the chicken."

African Traditional Religions
Swahili proverb

"The state of prayer is the best of conditions, for man is then associating with God. Prayer verily bestoweth life, particularly when offered in private and at times, such as midnight, when freed from daily cares."

Bahá'í Faith
'Abdu'l-Bahá

"Sitting cross-legged,
They should wish that all beings
Have firm and strong roots of goodness
And attain the state of immovability.
Cultivating concentration,
They should wish that all beings
Conquer their minds by concentration
Ultimately, with no reminder.
When practicing contemplation,
They should wish that all beings
See truth as it is
And be forever free of oppression and contention."

Buddhism
Garland Sutra (Gandavyuha) 11

"When you are praying, do not use meaningless repetition, as the Gentiles do, for they suppose that they will be heard for their many words. Therefore do not be like them; for your Father knows what you need, before you ask Him."

Christianity
Matthew 6:7

"Knowing in what to abide, one can settle the mind; with settled mind, one can achieve quiet; in quietude, one can reach a state of calm; in calmness, one can contemplate; in contemplation, one can attain the goal."

Confucianism
Great Learning 1

"Lead me from unreality to reality; lead me from darkness to light; lead me from death to immortality. Om Peace, Peace, Peace."

Hinduism
Brihadaranyaka Upanishad 1:3:28

"Recite what is sent of the Book by inspiration to thee, and establish regular Prayer: for Prayer restrains from shameful and unjust deeds; and remembrance of Allah is the greatest [thing in life] without doubt. And Allah knows the [deeds] that ye do."

Islam
Koran 29:45

"Homage to the Jinas.
Homage to the perfected souls.
Homage to the renouncer-leaders.
Homage to the renouncer-teachers.
Homage to all renouncers."

Jainism
Namaskar Mantra

"What then is left for us to do except to pray for the ability to pray, to bewail our ignorance of living in His presence? And even if such prayer is tainted with vanity, His mercy accepts and redeems our feeble efforts. It is the continuity of trying to pray, the unspoken loyalty to our duty to pray, that lends strength to our fragile worship; and it is the holiness of the community that bestows meaning upon our individual acts of worship. These are three pillars on which our prayer rises to God: our own loyalty, the holiness of Israel, and the mercy of God."

Judaism
Abraham Joshu Heschel

"When [the Shinto priest] pronounces the ritual prayers,
the heavenly deities will push open the heavenly rock door,
and pushing with an awesome pushing,
through the myriad layers of heavenly clouds,
will hear and receive [these prayers]."

Shinto
From ninth-century norito (prayer)

"Nanak prays: the divine Name may be magnified;
May peace and prosperity come to one and all by your grace, O Lord!"

Sikhism
Ardas prayer

"Those Beings, male and female, whom Ahura Mazda knows the best for worship according to truth, we worship them all."

Zoroastrianism
Yenghe Hatam prayer

III. Duty toward other people

"A lone traveler is swept away by a stream."

African Traditional Religions
Tonga proverb

"Be generous in prosperity, and thankful in adversity. Be worthy of the trust of thy neighbor, and look upon him with a bright and friendly face. Be a treasure to the poor, an admonisher to the rich, an answerer of the cry of the needy. . . . Be unjust to no man, and show all meekness to all men. Be as a lamp unto them that walk in darkness, a joy to the sorrowful, a sea for the thirsty, a haven for the distressed, an upholder and defender of the victim of oppression. Let integrity and uprightness distinguish all thine acts. Be a home for the stranger, a balm to the suffering, a tower of strength for the fugitive. Be eyes to the blind, and a guiding light unto the feet of the erring. Be an ornament to the countenance of truth, a crown to the brow of fidelity, a pillar of the temple of righteousness, a breath of life to the body of mankind, an ensign of the hosts of justice, a luminary above the horizon of virtue, a dew to the soil of the human heart, an ark on the ocean of knowledge, a sun in the heaven of bounty, a gem on the diadem of wisdom, a shining light in the firmament of thy generation, a fruit upon the tree of humility."

Bah·á'í Faith
Bahá'u'lláh

"Hatred is never quelled by hatred in this world. It is quelled by love. This is an eternal truth."

Buddhism
Dhammapada 1:5

"You shall love your neighbor as yourself."

Christianity
Mark 12:31

"The duties of universal obligation are five . . . those between ruler and subject, father and child, husband and wife, older and younger siblings, and two friends."

Confucianism
Doctrine of the Mean 20

"Lack of enmity to all beings in thought, word, and deed; compassion and generous giving—these are the marks of the eternal faith; this is the eternal duty."

Hinduism
Mahabharata

"It is not righteousness that ye turn your faces towards east or west; but it is righteousness to believe in Allah and the Last Day, and the Angels, and the Book, and the Messengers; to spend of your substance, out of love for Him, for your kin, for orphans, for the needy, for the wayfarer, for those who ask, and for the ransom of slaves; to be steadfast in prayer, and practice regular charity; to fulfill the contracts which ye have made; and to be firm and patient, in pain (or suffering) and adversity, and throughout all periods of panic. Such are the people of truth, the Allah-fearing."

Islam
Koran 2:177

"The observer of vows should cultivate friendliness towards all living beings, delight in the distinction and honor of others, [show] compassion for miserable, lowly creatures and equanimity towards the vainglorious."

Jainism
Tattvartha Sutra

"Love your fellow as yourself: I am the Lord."

Judaism
Leviticus 19:18

"The hearts of all you encounter shall be as a mirror to you, reflecting the face you have presented to them."

Shinto
Kurozumi Munetada

"One should live on what one has earned through hard work and share with others the fruit of one's exertion." Guru Nanak

Sikhism
Adi Granth, p. 1,245

"The sage does not accumulate [for himself].
The more that he expends for others, the more does he possess of his own;
the more that he gives to others, the more does he have himself."

Taoism
Tao te ching 81

"I pledge myself to the well-thought thought, I pledge myself to the well-spoken word, I pledge myself to the well-acted act."

Zoroastrianism
Yasna 12:8

IV. Poverty and wealth

"The lack of money does not necessarily mean that one is poor."

African Traditional Religions
African proverb

"O CHILDREN OF DUST!
Tell the rich of the midnight sighing of the poor, lest heedlessness lead them into the path of destruction, and deprive them of the Tree of Wealth. To give and to be generous are attributes of Mine; well is it with him that adorneth himself with My virtues."

Bahá'í Faith
Bahá.'u.'lláh

"Goodwill, and wisdom, a mind trained by method
The highest conduct based on good morals
This makes humans pure, not rank or wealth."

Buddhism
Samyutta Nikaya

"For I was hungry, and you gave me something to eat; I was thirsty, and you gave me drink; I was a stranger, and you invited me in; naked, and you clothed me; I was sick, and you visited me; I was in prison, and you came to me."

Christianity
Matthew 25:35-36

"Facilitate their cultivation of fields, lighten their tax burden, and the common people can be made wealthy."

Confucianism
Master Meng [Mencius] VII:2:23

"This body—it is for the service of others."

Hinduism
Anonymous

"Alms are for the poor and the needy, and those employed to administer the [funds]; for those whose hearts have been [recently] reconciled [to Truth]; for those in bondage and in debt; in the cause of Allah and for the wayfarer: [thus is it] ordained by Allah, and Allah is full of knowledge and wisdom."

Islam
Koran 9:60

"Speak up for the dumb,
For the rights of all the unfortunate.
Speak up, judge righteously,
Champion the poor and the needy."

Judaism
Proverbs 31:8

"True service is the service of poor people; I am not inclined to serve others of higher social status; charity will bear fruit, in this and the next world if given to such worthy and poor people."

Sikhism
Guru Gobind Singh, Adi Granth, p. 1,223

"There is no guilt greater than to sanction ambition;
no calamity greater than to be discontented with one's lot;
no fault greater than the wish to be getting.
Therefore the sufficiency of contentment is an enduring and unchanging sufficiency."

Taoism
Tao te ching 46

"As the Master, so is the Judge to be chosen in accord with truth. Establish the power of acts arising from a life lived with good purpose, for Mazda and for the lord whom they made pastor for the poor."

Zoroastrianism
Ahuna Vairya prayer

V. Women

"And among the teachings of Bahá'u'lláh is the equality of women and men. The world of humanity has two wings—one is women and the other men. Not until both wings are equally developed can the bird fly."

Bahá'í Faith
'Abdu'l-Bahá

"Whoever has such a vehicle, whether it is a woman or a man, by means of that vehicle shall come to nirvana."

Buddhism
Samyutta Nikaya

"The knot of Eve's disobedience was loosed by the obedience of Mary. For what the virgin Eve had bound fast through unbelief, this did the virgin Mary set free through faith."

Christianity
Saint Irenaeus

"To be a woman, one must develop as a person; to do this, strive to establish one's purity and chastity. With purity, one remains undefiled; with chastity, one keeps one's virtue."

Confucianism
Analects for Women 2:1a

"If any do deeds of righteousness—be they male or female—and have faith, they will enter Heaven, and not the least injustice will be done to them."

Islam
Koran 4:124

"Jewish feminism focuses on three issues: attaining complete religious involvement for Jewish women; giving Jewish expression to women's experiences and self-understanding; and highlighting the imagery, language, rituals already present within the tradition that center around the feminine and the women. These efforts involve changing or eliminating aspects of Jewish law, customs, and teachings that prevent or discourage women from developing positions of equality to men within Judaism as well as bringing new interpretations to bear on the tradition."

Judaism
Susannah Heschel

"Woman is the foundation of the faith."

Shinto
Nakayama Miki

"Blessed are they, both men and women, who endlessly praise their Lord. Blessed are they in the True One's court; there shall their faces shine."

Sikhism
Guru Nanak, Adi Granth, p. 473

"The valley spirit dies not, aye the same;
The female mystery thus do we name.
Its gate, from which at first they issued forth,
Is called the root from which grew heaven and earth.
Long and unbroken does its power remain,
Used gently, and without the touch of pain."

Taoism
Tao te ching 6

"We call upon you the Waters, and you the milk cows, and you the mothers, giving milk, nourishing the poor, possessed of all kinds of sustenance; who are the best, the most beautiful. Down we call you, O good ones, to be grateful for and pleased by shares of the long-armed offering, you living mothers."

Zoroastrianism
Yasna 38:5

VI. Death

"The elephant has fallen."

African Traditional Religions
Yoruba metaphor for the death of an elderly person

"O SON OF THE SUPREME!
I have made death a messenger of joy to thee. Wherefore dost thou grieve?"

Bahá'í Faith
Bahá'u'lláh

"[D]eath, which we want nothing to do with, is unavoidable. This is why it is important that during our lifetime we become familiar with the idea of death, so that it will not be a real shock to us at the moment it comes. We do not meditate regularly on death in order to die more quickly; on the contrary, like everyone, we wish to live a long time. However, since death is inevitable, we believe that if we begin to prepare for it at an earlier point in time, on the day of our death it will be easier to accept it."

Buddhism
Dalai Lama

"Death has been swallowed up in victory. Where, O death, is your victory? Where, O death, is your sting? . . . Thanks be to God! He gives us the victory through our Lord Jesus Christ."

Christianity
1 Corinthians 15:54-55

"If one is not yet able to serve living persons, how can one serve spirits of the dead? If one does not yet understand life, how can one understand death?"

Confucianism
Analects of Confucius 11:12

"Just as one casts away old clothes and gets new ones, so too, after casting away worn-out bodies, the soul gets new ones."

Hinduism
Bhagavad Gita 2:22

"Every soul shall have a taste of death: And only on the Day of Judgment shall you be paid your full recompense. Only he who is saved far from the Fire and admitted to the Garden will have attained the object [of Life]: For the life of this world is but goods and chattels of deception."

Islam
Koran 3:185

"The physical body with all its sense organs, its health and youth, strength, radiance, good fortune and beauty—all resemble the rainbow which vanishes within seconds. They are impermanent."

Jainism
Acharya Kundakunda

"By the sweat of your brow
Shall you get bread to eat,
Until you return to the ground—
For from it you were taken.
For dust you are,
And to dust you shall return."

Judaism
Genesis 3:19

"Death proceeds from life, and life is the beginning of death. The [Ise] Shrine official informed me that this was handed down as the reason for the taboos surrounding both birth and death."

Shinto
Muju Ichien

"To whom should one complain, O Nanak, when death carries the mortal away without one's consent?"

Sikhism
Guru Nanak, Adi Granth, p. 1,412

"Death and life are not within our power, so we must be content with death. In this world we are like a foreign traveler and our body is just like a hired shell which we are in. From it man goes to his original abode. There should be no deep mourning for that. Everybody dies; others go before us, and we have to follow. Thus to be mournful is a sinful act."

Zoroastrianism
Dastur Erachji Sohrabji Meherjirana

Populations

Religion	Population
African Traditional Religions	79,913,910
Anglicanism	79,913,910
Baha'I	6,147,224
Baptist Tradition	110,650,029
Buddhism	368,833,430
Christianity	2,090,056,103
Church of Jesus Christ of Latter-day Saints	11,679,725
Confucianism	6,147,224
Conservative Judaism	1,475,334
Coptic Christianity	7,376,669
Eastern Catholicism	12,294,448
Eastern Orthodox Christianity	215,152,834
Evangelicalism	737,666,860
Hinduism	860,611,337
Islam	1,229,444,767
Jainism	6,147,224
Jehovah'S Witnesses	14,753,337
Judaism	15,368,060
Lutheranism	61,472,238
Mahayana Buddhism	196,711,163
Methodism	71,922,519
Orthodox Judaism	2,458,890
Pentecostalism	522,514,026
Protestantism	356,538,982
Reform Judaism	3,688,334
Reformed Christianity	73,151,964
Religious Society of Friends	368,833
Roman Catholicism	1,045,028,052
Seventh-day Adventist	12,294,448
Shaivism	196,711,163
Shiism	135,238,924
Shinto	110,650,029
Sikhism	18,441,671
Sunnism	922,083,575
Taoism	61,472,238
Theravada Buddhism	116,797,253
Tibetan Buddhism	184,417
Unitarianism	307,361
United Church of Christ	1,229,445
Vaishnavism	583,986,264
Zoroastrianism	141,386

Combined populations exceed total world population since some people qualify as members more than one religious group. A Buddhist, for example, may also practice Confucianism. Likewise, a Methodist might also be counted as a Christian, a Protestant, an Evangelical, and a Pentecostal, depending on their beliefs.

Glossary

10 paramitas (Buddhism) 10 perfections of the bodhisattva: (1) *dana* (generosity), (2) *sila* (morality), (3) *ksanti* (patience and forbearance), (4) *virya* (vigor, the endless and boundless energy that bodhisattvas employ when helping others), (5) *dhyana* (meditation), (6) *prajna* (wisdom), (7) *upaya* (skillful means), (8) conviction, (9) strength, and (10) knowledge

Abaluhya (African Traditional Religions) an ethnic group in Kenya

Achaemenian dynasty (Zoroastrianism) dynasty that ruled Iran from 550 to 330 B.C.E.

acharya (Hinduism) a formal head of a monastery, sect, or subcommunity

acharya (Jainism) head of a subsect or smaller group of renouncers

Adi Granth (Sikhism) Original Book; the primary Sikh scripture

Advent (Christianity) period of four weeks, beginning four Sundays before Christmas, sometimes observed with fasting and prayer

afrinagan (Zoroastrianism) Zoroastrian ceremony involving the distribution of blessings

Aggadah (Judaism) nonlegal, narrative portions of the Talmud and Mishna, which include history, folklore, and other subjects

ahimsa (Jainism) nonviolence

Ahura Mazda (Zoroastrianism) supreme deity of Zoroastrianism; likely an honorific title meaning "Wise Lord" rather than a proper name

Akal Purakh (Sikhism) Timeless One; God

al-hajj / al-hajji (Islam) pilgrim; prefix added to a name to indicate that the person has made the hajj

Allah (Islam) God

Amaterasu (Shinto) the sun goddess

Amesha Spentas (Zoroastrianism) the six entities that aid Ahura Mazda, sometimes with an additional figure, Spenta Mainyu, to compose the divine heptad (group of seven)

amrit (Sikhism) divine nectar; sweetened water used in the initiation ceremony of the Khalsa

anagarika (Buddhism) ascetic layperson

anekant (Jainism) doctrine of the multiplicity of truth

Anglicanism (Christianity) Church of England, which originated in King Henry VIII's break with Rome in 1534, and those churches that developed from it, including the Episcopal Church in the United States; with a wide spectrum of doctrines and practices, it is sometimes called Episcopalianism

Angra Mainyu (Zoroastrianism) primordial evil spirit, twin of Spenta Mainyu

Apocrypha (Christianity) books of the Old Testament included in the Septuagint (Greek translation used by early Christians) and Catholic (including the Latin Vulgate) versions of the Bible but not in Protestant or modern Jewish editions

arahitogami (Shinto) a *kami* in human form

arhat (Buddhism) worthy one

aryika (Jainism) a Digambara nun who wears white clothing

asha (Zoroastrianism) truth; righteousness

Ashkenazim (Judaism) Jews whose ancestors in the Middle Ages lived in Germany (Ashkenaz in Hebrew) and the surrounding countries

ashrama (Hinduism) one of the four stages of life

atashkadeh (Zoroastrianism) "place of fire"; fire temple; more narrowly, the enclosed chamber in a fire temple that contains a fire continuously fed by the priests

atman (Hinduism) the human soul

Atonement (Christianity) doctrine that the death of Jesus is the basis for human salvation

Avestan (Zoroastrianism) ancient East Iranian language

Ayurveda (Hinduism) "knowledge of a long life"; a Hindu healing system

Ba Kongo (African Traditional Religions) a group of Bantu-speaking peoples who largely reside in Congo (Brazzaville), Democratic Republic of the Congo (Kinshasa), and Angola

Ba Thonga (African Traditional Religions) a group of Bantu-speaking peoples who live in the southern African countries of Mozambique, Zimbabwe, Swaziland, and South Africa

babalawo (African Traditional Religions) a divination specialist in Yoruba culture

Babi (Bahá'í) a follower of Ali-Muhammad of Shiraz (1819–50), who took the title of the Bab (Arabic: "gate")

Baganda (African Traditional Religions) the largest ethnic group in Uganda

Baha (Bahá'í) glory, splendor, or light; the greatest name of God; the root word in Bahaullah, the title of the founder of the Bahá'í faith, and in Bahá'í

Bambara (African Traditional Religions) an ethnic group in Mali

Bantu (African Traditional Religions) a large group of languages spoken in central, eastern, and southern Africa

baptism (Christianity) sacrament practiced by Christians in which the sprinkling, pouring of, or immersion in water is a sign of admission into the faith community

bar mitzvah (son of commandment) (Judaism) initiation ceremony for boys at age 13, when they are held to be responsible for their actions and hence are obliged to observe all of the commandments of the Torah; bat mitzah, a similar ceremony for girls at age 12, is observed by some Jews

barashnum (Zoroastrianism) Zoroastrian purification ceremony used primarily by priests to prepare for their ordination

Bhagavad Gita (Hinduism) one of the most sacred texts of the Hindus; a book of 18 chapters from the epic the *Mahabharata*

bhakti (Hinduism) devotion; the practice of devotion to God

bhikkhu (Buddhism) monk

bhikkhuni (Buddhism) female monk

bodhi (Buddhism) enlightenment; awakening

bodhisattva (Buddhism) an enlightened being who works for the welfare of all those still caught in samsara

Brahma (Hinduism) a minor deity; the creator god

brahmacharya (Jainism) chastity in marriage or celibacy

Brahman (Hinduism) the upper, or priestly, caste

Brahman (Hinduism) the term used in the Upanishads to refer to the supreme being

Brit Milah (Judaism) circumcision of a male infant or adult convert as a sign of acceptance of the covenant

caliph (Islam) successor; deputy to the Prophet Muhammad

caste (Hinduism) a social group (frequently one that a person is born into) in Hindu society

casuistry (Christianity) type of moral reasoning based on the examination of specific cases

catechesis (Christianity) formal instruction in the faith

"Celestial Masters" tradition (T'ien-shih) (Taoism) Taoist tradition of late Han times, with which several later traditions, especially Cheng-i, claimed affiliation

Ch'an (Zen in Japan) (Buddhism) a school of Mahayana Buddhism

ch'i (Taoism) life-energy

ch'i-kung (qigong) (Taoism) the skill of attracting vital energy

Ch'ing dynasty (Taoism) dynasty that ruled China from 1644 to 1911; also called the Manchu dynasty

Ch'ing-wei (Taoism) "Clarified Tenuity"; a Taoism subtradition the emerged in the tenth century; it involves a system of therapeutic rituals

ch'uan-ch'i (Taoism) type of traditional Chinese literary tale

Ch'üan-chen (Taoism) "Integrating the Perfections"; practice that originated in the eleventh century and continued in modern "Dragon Gate" Taoism; sometimes called "Northern Taoism"

chai (Taoism) type of Taoist liturgy that originated in the Ling-pao tradition in the fifth century

charismatics (Christianity) major expression of Christianity that includes those who affirm the gifts of the Holy Spirit but who are not affiliated with Pentecostal denominations

chen (Taoism) perfection or realization; ultimate spiritual integration

Cheng-i (Taoism) "Orthodox Unity"; Taoist tradition that emerged during the conquest period (approximately the twelfth through fourteenth centuries) and became a part of "Southern Taoism"

chen-jen (Taoism) perfected ones; a term used both for angelic beings and for the human ideal of fully perfected or realized persons

chiao (Taoism) extended Taoist liturgy; a sequence of events over several days that renews the local community by reintegrating it with the heavenly order

Chin dynasty (Taoism) dynasty that ruled China from 266 to 420 C.E.

ching (Taoism) vital essence

Ching-ming (Taoism) "Pure Illumination"; a Taoism subtradition that emerged during the Ming dynasty; it was absorbed into the "Dragon Gate" tradition

chin-tan (Taoism) "Golden Elixir"; a set of ideas about spiritual refinement through meditation

chrismation (Christianity) anointing with oil

Chuang-tzu (Taoism) classical text compiled c. 430 to 130 B.C.E.

classical China (Taoism) the period before 221 B.C.E.

conciliar (Christianity) governance through councils of bishops

confirmation (Christianity) sacrament marking membership in a church

congregationalism (Christianity) self-governance by a local congregation

Conservative Judaism (Judaism) largest denomination of American Judaism, with affiliated congregations in South America and Israel; advocating moderate modifications of Halakhah, it occupies a middle ground between Reform and Orthodox Judaism

cosmogony (African Traditional Religions) a theory about the creation of the universe

cosmology (African Traditional Religions) an explanation of the nature of the universe

daeva (Zoroastrianism) demon

Dagara (African Traditional Religions) an ethnic group of the Niger region of western Africa

dakhma (Zoroastrianism) "tower of silence"; a tower in which a corpse is traditionally exposed

dan (Sikhism) charity; a person's relation with society

dana (Buddhism) proper giving; generosity

dar-i Mihr (Zoroastrianism) "the court of Mithra"; the room in a fire temple where the *yasna* is performed

Dashalakshanaparvan (Jainism) yearly Digambara festival during which the Tattvartha Sutra is read and that ends in atonement

dastur (Zoroastrianism) "master"; honorific title for a Zoroastrian priest

dawa (Islam) call to Islam; propagation of the faith

de (Confucianism) virtue; potential goodness conferred on a person by *Tian* (Heaven)

deva (Buddhism) deity; divine being; divine

deva (Hinduism) a divine being

Devi (Hinduism) in the Sanskrit literary tradition, the name for the Goddess

dharma (Hinduism) duty, or acting with a sense of what is righteous; sometimes used to mean "religion" and "ethics"

dharma (Pali, dhamma) (Buddhism) the teachings of the Buddha

Dharma Sastra (Hinduism) any of a set of treatises on the nature of righteousness, moral duty, and law

dhimmi (Islam) protected person, specifically a Jew or Christian

Diaspora (Judaism) communities of Jews dispersed outside the Land of Israel, traditionally referred to as the Exile

Digambara (Jainism) wearing the sky; sect of Jainism, largely based in southern India, in which full monks do not wear any clothing

diksha (Jainism) rite of initiation for a monk or a nun

divination (African Traditional Religions) any of various methods of accessing sacred knowledge of the deities; it often involves interpreting signs

"Dragon Gate" tradition (Lung-men) (Taoism) Taoist tradition that originated in the seventeenth century, incorporating Ch'üan-chen and Ching-ming; the dominant form of Taoism in mainland China today

dua (Islam) personal prayer

duhkha (Pali, dukkha) (Buddhism) suffering; unsatisfactoriness

Durga (Hinduism) a manifestation of the Goddess (represented as a warrior)

Edo (African Traditional Religions) an ethnic group of southern Nigeria

Eightfold Path (marga; Pali, magga) (Buddhism) a systematic and practical way to realize the truth and eliminate suffering, traditionally divided into three distinct phases that should be progressively mastered

Epiphany (Christianity) January 6, a celebration of the coming of the Magi and, in Orthodoxy, of the baptism of Jesus

eschatology (Christianity) doctrine concerning the end of the world, including the Second Coming of Christ, God's judgment, heaven, and hell

Eucharist (Communion; Lord's Supper) (Christianity) sacrament practiced by Christians in which bread and wine become (in Roman Catholicism and Orthodoxy) or stand for (in Protestantism) the body and blood of Christ

evangelicalism (Christianity) movement that emphasizes the authority of the Scriptures, salvation by faith, and individual experience over ritual

extreme unction (Christianity) sacrament; blessing of the sick

Fang (African Traditional Religions) an ethnic group of west-central Africa

fasli (Zoroastrianism) seasonal calendar that places New Year's Day in March; compare with *qadimi*

fast of Ramadan (Islam) fast during ninth month; fourth pillar

fatwa (Islam) legal opinion or judgment of a mufti, a specialist in Islamic law

Five Pillars of Islam (Islam) fundamental observances

Five Scriptures (Confucianism) *Wujing;* Confucianism's most sacred texts

Fon (African Traditional Religions) an ethnic group of Benin

Four Books (Confucianism) *Sishu;* central texts of Confucian philosophy and education

frashkard (Zoroastrianism) the renewal of the world at the end of history

Fukko Shintō (Shinto) the "pure Shinto" of the scholar Motoori Norinaga

Gāthā (Zoroastrianism) one of the 17 hymns traditionally ascribed to Zoroaster

gūji (Shinto) Shinto head priest

Gahambar (Zoroastrianism) one of six five-day Zoroastrian festivals

Ganesha (Hinduism) a popular Hindu god; a son of the goddess Parvati, he is depicted with an elephant head

Gathic (Zoroastrianism) older Avestan dialect

getig (Zoroastrianism) form; physical world

ghusl (Islam) ritual cleansing before worship

Goddess (Hinduism) a powerful, usually gracious, deity in female form sometimes seen as a manifestation of Parvati, the wife of Shiva; she is called any number of names, including Shakti, Durga, Kali, or Devi

gon-gūji (Shinto) Shinto assistant head priest

goryō (Shinto) haunting spirit of a wronged individual

gotra (Hinduism) a clan group

grace (Christianity) unmerited gift from God for human salvation

granthi (Sikhism) reader of scripture and leader of rituals in the *gurdwara*

gurdwara (Sikhism) door of the Guru; house of worship

Gurmukh (Sikhism) a person oriented toward the Guru

guru (Hinduism) a charismatic teacher

Guru (Sikhism) spiritual preceptor, either a person or the mystical "voice" of Akal Purakh

Guru Granth, or Guru Granth Sahib (Sikhism) the Adi Granth, or scripture, functioning as Guru

Guru Panth (Sikhism) the Sikh Panth, or community, functioning as Guru

Hachiman (Shinto) a Shinto-Buddhist deity popular with samurai

hadith (Islam) tradition; reports of Muhammad's sayings and deeds

Haggadah (Judaism) book used at the Passover seder, containing the liturgical recitation of the Passover story and instructions on conducting the ceremonial meal

hajj (Islam) pilgrimage to Mecca; fifth pillar

Halakhah (Judaism) legal portions of the Talmud as later elaborated in rabbinic literature; in an extended sense it denotes the ritual and legal prescriptions governing the traditional Jewish way of life

halal (Islam) meat slaughtered in a religious manner

Han dynasty (Taoism) dynasty that ruled China from 206 B.C.E. to 221 C.E.

Hand of the Cause of God (Bahá'í) one of 50 individuals appointed by Bahaullah, Abdul-Baha, or Shoghi Effendi whose duties included encouraging Bahá'ís and their institutions, advising them about the development of the Bahá'í community worldwide, and informing the head of the faith about conditions and developments in local Bahá'í communities

haoma (Zoroastrianism) sacred drink, now pressed from ephedra and pomegranate twigs

haoxue (Confucianism) love of (moral) learning

harae (Shinto) purification rites

Hasidism (Judaism) revivalist mystical movement that originated in Poland in the eighteenth century

hijab (Islam) Muslim dress for women, today often referring to a headscarf

hijra (hegira) (Islam) migration of early Muslims from Mecca to Medina

himorogi (Shinto) sacred space demarcated by a rope (*shimenawa*) or other marker

hitogami (Shinto) a living *kami* in human form

honji-suijaku (Shinto) Buddhist philosophy of the assimilation of Buddhas and *kami*

Hsiang-erh (Taoism) "Just Thinking"; text that is couched as a commentary on the *Lao-tzu*

hsin (Taoism) heart/mind

hsing (Taoism) inner nature; internal spiritual realities

hsiu chen (Taoism) cultivating reality; term by which Taoists frequently refer to religious practice

hsiu tao (Taoism) cultivating Tao; nearly synonymous with *hsiu chen*

hsiu-lien (Taoism) cultivation and refinement; an enduring Taoist term for self cultivation

hukam (Sikhism) divine order

huququllah (Bahá'í) "right of God"; a 19-percent tithe that Bahá'ís pay on their income after essential expenses

Ifa (African Traditional Religions) a form of divination that originated in West Africa

Igbo (African Traditional Religions) an ethnic group of Nigeria

imam (Islam) Shiite prayer leader; also used as the title for Muhammad's successors as leader of the Muslim community, consisting of male descendants through his cousin and son-in-law Ali

Inner Alchemy (Taoism) *nei-tan*; a generic term used for various related models of meditative self-cultivation

ishnan (Sikhism) purity

Islam (Islam) submission to the will of God; peace

iwasaka (Shinto) sacred stone circles

janam-sakhi (Sikhism) birth narrative; a hagiographical biography

jashan (Zoroastrianism) festival

jati (Hinduism) birth group

jihad (Islam) strive, struggle; a holy war

Jina (Jainism) victor or conqueror; periodic founder or reviver of the Jain religion; also called a Tirthankara (ford or bridge builder)

jingzuo (Confucianism) "quiet sitting"; meditation

jiva (Jainism) soul; every soul is endowed with perfect energy, perfect bliss, perfect perception, and perfect knowledge

jizya (Islam) poll, or head, tax paid by Jews and Christians

juma (Islam) Friday congregational prayer

Jurchen (Taoism) Manchurian tribe; founders of the Chin dynasty (1115–1234)

Kaaba (Islam) sacred structure in Mecca; according to tradition, built by Abraham and Ismail

Kabbalah (Judaism) mystical reading of the Scriptures that arose in France and Spain during the twelfth century, culminating with the composition in the late thirteenth century of the *Zohar* ("Book of Splendor"), which, especially as interpreted by Isaac Luria (1534–72), exercised a decisive influence on late medieval and early modern Jewish spiritual life

kagura (Shinto) Shinto ritual dances

Kaguru (African Traditional Religions) an ethnic group in Tanzania

kami (Shinto) Shinto deity or deities

kannushi (Shinto) lower-ranking Shinto priest

karah prashad (Sikhism) sanctified food, prepared in a large iron dish, or *karahi*

karma (Buddhism) law of cause and effect; act; deed

karma (Hinduism) literally "action"; the system of rewards and punishments attached to various actions

karma (Jainism) microscopic particles that float in the universe, stick to souls according the quality of their actions, and manifest a like result before becoming detached from them

karma (Sikhism) influence of a person's past actions on his future lives

kasruth (Judaism) rules and regulations for food and its preparation, often known by the Yiddish "kosher"

katha (Sikhism) a discourse on scripture in a *gurdwara;* homily

Kaur (Sikhism) female surname meaning Princess

kegare (Shinto) bodily or spiritual pollution

Khalsa (Sikhism) order of "pure" Sikhs, established by Guru Gobind Singh in 1699

ki (Shinto) vital spirit or energy

kirpan (Sikhism) sword

kirtan (Sikhism) devotional singing

Kojiki (Shinto) eighth-century Japanese mythological text

kokoro (Shinto) heart-mind

kokugaku (Shinto) Japanese nativist school of scholarship

Koran (Quran) (Islam) revelation; Muslim scripture

Krishna (Hinduism) a manifestation of the supreme being; one of the most popular Hindu deities, he is considered by many Hindus to be an incarnation of the god Vishnu

kuan (Taoism) Taoist abbeys or temples

kundalini (Hinduism) the power that is said to lie dormant at the base of a person's spine and that can be awakened in the search for enlightenment

kusti (Zoroastrianism) sacred cord worn around the torso by Zoroastrians and tied and untied during prayer

Lakshmi (Hinduism) a goddess; wife of the god Vishnu

langar (Sikhism) community dining

Lao-tzu (Taoism) the supposed author of the *Tao te ching*; also another name for the *Tao te ching*

Legalism (Taoism) Chinese school of philosophy that advocated a system of government based on a strict code of laws; prominent in the fifth through third centuries B.C.E.

Lent (Christianity) period of 40 days from Ash Wednesday to Easter, often marked by fasting and prayer

li (Confucianism) cosmic ordering principle

li (Confucianism) norms for the interaction of humans with each other and with higher forces (a different Chinese character from the other *li,* meaning "principle," above)

liangzhi (Confucianism) innate moral knowledge

libationers (Taoism) *chi-chiu*; men and women officiants in the early "Celestial Masters" organization

lien-shih (Taoism) refined master or mistress; an honorific term that was the highest Taoist title in T'ang times

Ling-pao (Taoism) "Numinous Treasure"; a set of Taoist revelations produced in the fourth century C.E.

Lixue (Confucianism) "study of principle"; Neo-Confucian philosophical movement

Lupupa (African Traditional Religions) a subgroup of the Basongye, an ethnic group of Democratic Republic of the Congo (Kinshasa)

madrasah (Islam) Islamic religious school

Magi (Zoroastrianism) priestly group that was initially active in western Iran under the Medes

Mahabharata (Hinduism) "Great Epic of India" or the "Great Sons of Bharata"; one of the two Hindu epics

Mahavira Jayanti (Jainism) celebration of the birth of Lord Mahavira, the 24th and last Jina of the current period, by Shvetambaras and Digambaras in March–April

Mahayana (sometimes called Northern Buddhism) (Buddhism) one of two major schools of Buddhism practiced mainly in China, Japan, Korea, and Tibet; evolved from the Mahasanghika (Great Assembly)

Man'yōshū (Shinto) eighth-century Japanese poetry anthology

mandala (Hinduism) a geometric design that represents sacredness, divine beings, or sacred knowledge or experience in an abstract form

manifestation of God (Bahá'í) an individual recognized in Bahá'í authoritative writings as a source of divine revelation and usually as the founder of a religion

mantra (Hinduism) a phrase or string of words, with or without meaning, recited repeatedly during meditation

Manyika (African Traditional Religions) an ethnic group of the southern African countries of Zimbabwe and Mozambique

marebito (Shinto) wandering spirits of the dead

Masai (African Traditional Religions) a nomadic people who inhabit Tanzania and Kenya

masjid (Islam) place for ritual prostration; mosque

matrimony (Christianity) sacrament; the joining of a man and woman in marriage

matsuri (Shinto) Shinto festivals

meng-wei (Taoism) covenant

Messiah (Christianity) the "anointed one," Jesus

Midrash (Judaism) commentary on the Scriptures, both Halakhic (legal) and Aggadic (narrative), originally in the form of sermons or lectures

mihrab (Islam) niche in mosque indicating the direction of Mecca

miko (Shinto) female medium or shaman

millet (Islam) protected religious community

minbar (Islam) raised platform in mosque; pulpit

ming (Taoism) destiny; the realities of a person's external life

Ming dynasty (Taoism) dynasty that ruled China from 1368 to 1644

Mishnah (Judaism) collection of the Oral Torah, or commentary on the Torah, first compiled in the second and third centuries C.E.

moksha (Hinduism) liberation from the cycle of birth and death

moksha (Jainism) nirvana; enlightenment achieved when practitioners purify themselves of all karma so that they will not be reborn

Mongols (Taoism) originally nomadic people who established the Yüan dynasty in China in the thirteenth century

muhapatti (Jainism) mouth guard worn by some renouncers to avoid harming insects and air beings

muni (Jainism) a Digambara monk who wears no clothing

Murtipujak (Jainism) a Shvetambara subsect that worships by means of images

Mwari (African Traditional Religions) a creator god worshiped in the southern African countries of Zimbabwe and Botswana

nam (Sikhism) the divine name

Namaskar Mantra (Jainism) the preeminent mantra that all Jains know and recite

negi (Shinto) senior Shinto priest

neisheng waiwang (Confucianism) "sage within and king without"; phrase used to describe one who is both a spiritual seeker and a social leader

nei-tan (Taoism) "Inner Alchemy"; the practice of spiritual refinement through meditation

Nei-yeh (Taoism) "Inner Cultivation"; an early Taoist text, likely a prototype for the well-known text *Tao te ching*

Neo-Confucianism (Taoism) Confucian teachings that were turned into a sociopolitical orthodoxy in China in the twelfth century

nigoda (Jainism) microscopic being

Nihon shoki (Shinto) eighth-century chronicle of Japanese history

Nineteen Day Feast (Bahá'í) a special meeting of the Bahá'í community held once every Bahá'í month, with devotional, business, and social portions

nirvana (Buddhism) the absolute elimination of karma; the absence of all states (the Sanskrit word literally means "to blow out, to extinguish")

norito (Shinto) Shinto liturgical prayers

Northern Sung dynasty (Taoism) dynasty that ruled China until 1126; part of the Sung dynasty

"Northern Taoism" (Taoism) modern term for Taoist traditions (Ch'üan-chen and Lung-men) that stress self-cultivation

odu (African Traditional Religions) poetic oral narratives memorized by *Ifa* diviners and recited during divination

Olódùmarè (African Traditional Religions) the Supreme Being in the religion of the Yoruba people

oni (Shinto) demon

opele (African Traditional Religions) a divining chain used in *Ifa* divination

ordination (Christianity) sacrament, in which a person is invested with religious authority or takes holy orders

orisa (African Traditional Religions) in the Yoruba religious tradition, the pantheon of deities

Orthodox Judaism (Judaism) traditional Judaism, characterized by strict observance of laws and rituals (the Halakhah)

Orthodoxy (Christianity) one of the main branches of Christianity, with a lineage that derives from the first-century apostolic churches; historically centered in Constantinople (Istanbul), it includes a number of autonomous national churches

Pahlavi (Zoroastrianism) middle Persian language of the Sasanian period; also the name of an Iranian dynasty (twentieth century)

pancha sila (Buddhism) five ethical precepts; the basic ethical guidelines for the layperson

panth (Sikhism) path

parahom (Zoroastrianism) sacred drink prepared during the *yasna*; a mixture of *haoma* and milk

Parsi (Zoroastrianism) member of a Zoroastrian group living mainly in western India and centered around Mumbai (Bombay)

Parvati (Hinduism) a goddess; the wife of the god Shiva

Paryushan (Jainism) yearly Shvetambara festival during which the Kalpa Sutra is read and that ends in atonement

Passover (Pesach) (Judaism) festival marking the deliverance of the Israelites from Egyptian bondage

pati (Sikhism) the core of a person, including self-respect

Pentecost (Christianity) seventh Sunday after Easter, commemorating the descent of the Holy Spirit on the apostles

Pentecostalism (Christianity) movement that emphasizes grace, expressive worship, evangelism, and spiritual gifts such as speaking in tongues and healing

People of the Book (Islam) Jews and Christians, who Muslims believe received divine revelations in the Torah and Gospels, respectively

Petrine primacy (Christianity) view that, as the successor to Peter, the bishop of Rome (pope) is supreme

prajna (Buddhism) wisdom

presbyterianism (Christianity) governance by a presbytery, an assembly of local clergy and lay representatives

Prophets (Nevi'im) (Judaism) second of the three parts of the Tanakh, made up of the books of 7 major and 12 minor prophets

Protestantism (Christianity) one of the main branches of Christianity, originating in the sixteenth-century

Reformation; rejecting the authority of the pope, it emphasized the role of grace and the authority of the Scriptures

puja (Jainism) rite of worship

puja (Buddhism) honor; worship

puja (Hinduism) religious rituals performed in the home

Purana (Hinduism) "Ancient Lore"; any of a set of sacred texts known as the old narratives

Purvas (Jainism) oldest scriptures of Jainism, now lost

qadimi (Zoroastrianism) "old" Zoroastrian calendar, which has New Year's Day in late July; compare with *fasli*

qi (Confucianism) matter-energy; life force pervading the cosmos

qiblih (Bahá'í) "point of adoration"; the location toward which Bahá'ís face when saying their obligatory prayer

rahit (Sikhism) code

Ramayana (Hinduism) "Story of Rama"; one of the two Hindu epics

raspi (Zoroastrianism) assistant priest, who feeds the fire during the *yasna*

reconciliation (Christianity) sacrament; the confession of and absolution from sin

Reconstructionist Judaism (Judaism) movement founded in the United States in the early twentieth century by Mordecai M. Kaplan (1881–1983) that holds Judaism to be not only a religion but also a dynamic "civilization" embracing art, music, literature, culture, and folkways

Reform Judaism (Judaism) movement originating in early nineteenth-century Germany that adapted the rituals and liturgy of Judaism to accommodate modern social, political, and cultural developments; sometimes called Liberal Judaism

ren (Confucianism) humaneness; benevolence

renyu (Confucianism) human desires

renzheng (Confucianism) humane government

riba (Islam) usury

Roman Catholicism (Christianity) one of the main branches of Christianity, tracing its origins to the apostle Peter; centered in Rome, it tends to be uniform in organization, doctrines, and rituals

Rosh Hashanah (Judaism) Jewish New Year; also known as the Day of Judgment, it is a time of penitence

sacrament (Christianity) any rite thought to have originated with or to have been sanctioned by Jesus as a sign of grace

sacramental (Christianity) devotional action or object

sadaqah (Islam) almsgiving for the poor, for thanksgiving, or to ward off danger

sadre (Zoroastrianism) sacred shirt; a thin, white, cotton garment worn that is worn under clothes and should never be removed

salat (Islam) prayer or worship; second pillar

sallekhana (Jainism) ritual fasting until death

salvation (Christianity) deliverance from sin and its consequences

samadhi (Hinduism) the final state of absorption into, and union with, the divine

samsara (Buddhism) the cyclical nature of the cosmos; rebirth

samsara (Hinduism) continuing rebirths; the cycle of life and death

samsara (Jainism) the cycle of reincarnation

samudaya (Buddhism) arising (of suffering); the second noble Truth

sanatana dharma (Hinduism) "eternal dharma"; in the *Dharma Sastras*, virtues common to all human beings; also, a word used to denote Hinduism in general after the nineteenth century

sangat (Sikhism) holy fellowship; a congregation

sangha (Buddhism) community of monks

Sanhedrin (Judaism) supreme religious body of ancient Judaism, disbanded by the Romans early in the fifth century C.E.

sansar (Sikhism) rebirth; transmigration

Sanskrit (Hinduism) a classical language and part of the Indo-European language family; the language of ancient India

Sasanian dynasty (Zoroastrianism) dynasty that ruled Iran from 224 to 651 C.E.

sati (Jainism) virtuous woman; a chaste wife or a nun

Sephardim (Judaism) Jews of Spain and Portugal and their descendants, most of whom, in the wake of expulsion in 1492, settled in the Ottoman Empire and in North Africa; in the early seventeenth century small groups of descendants of Jews who had remained on the Iberian Penin

shabad (Sikhism) the divine word

Shabuoth (Feast of Weeks) (Judaism) originally a harvest festival, now observed in commemoration of the giving of the Torah to the Israelites

shahadah (Islam) declaration of faith; first pillar

shakti (Hinduism) energy or power, frequently used for the power of the Goddess; also a name for a manifestation of the Goddess

shan (Taoism) goodness

Shang-ch'ing (Taoism) "Supreme Clarity"; a tradition involving visualization meditation

Shariah (Islam) Islamic law

shen (Taoism) spirit; spiritual consciousness

shen-hsien (Taoism) spiritual transcendence

Shiite (Islam) member of second-largest Muslim sect, believing in the hereditary succession of Ali, the cousin and son-in-law of Muhammad, to lead the community

shinjin goitsu (Shinto) the essential identity of *kami* and humans

shintai (Shinto) the "body" of a *kami,* the object into which it descends following a ritual summons

Shiva (Hinduism) "the auspicious one"; a term for the supreme being; one of the most important deities in the Hindu tradition

shramana (Buddhism) wanderer

Shvetambara (Jainism) wearing white; sect of Jainism, largely based in northwestern India, in which monks and nuns wear white clothing

sikh (Sikhism) learner

Sikh Panth (Sikhism) the Sikh community

Sikh Rahit Maryada (Sikhism) Sikh Code of Conduct

sila (Buddhism) ethics; morality

Singh (Sikhism) male surname meaning Lion

smriti (Hinduism) "remembered"; a set of sacred compositions that includes the two epics, the *Puranas*, and the *Dharma Sastras*

"Southern Taoism" (Taoism) modern term for the Chengi Taoist tradition that survives mainly in Taiwan and along China's southeast coast; it stresses public liturgies such as *chiao* rather than self-cultivation

Spenta Mainyu (Zoroastrianism) primordial good spirit, twin of Angra Mainyu

sruti (Hinduism) "that which is heard"; a set of sacred compositions more popularly known as the Vedas

Sthanakwasi (Jainism) Shvetambara aniconic subsect

Sufi (Islam) mystic

Sung dynasty (Taoism) dynasty that ruled China from 960 to 1279

sunnah (Islam) example of Muhammad

Sunni (Islam) member of largest Muslim sect, holding that the successor (caliph) to Muhammad as leader of the community should be elected

surah (Islam) chapter of the Koran

svastika (Jainism) well-being; symbol representing the four realms into which souls are reincarnated, the three jewels, the abode of enlightened beings, and the enlightened beings themselves

swami (Hinduism) "master"; a charismatic teacher

T'ai-ch'ing (Taoism) "Great Clarity"; a tradition involving ritual alchemy

t'ai-p'ing (Taoism) grand tranquillity; a classical Chinese term for peace and harmony throughout the world; the most common Taoist political ideal

T'ai-p'ing ching (Taoism) "Scripture of Grand Tranquillity," an important early Taoist text

T'ang dynasty (Taoism) dynasty that ruled China from 618 to 907 C.E.

t'ien-shih (Taoism) celestial master; historical title for certain eminent Taoists, especially figures related to Chang Tao-ling

Talmud (Judaism) also known as the Gemara, a running commentary on the Mishnah written by rabbis (called *amoraim,* or "explainers") from the third to the fifth centuries C.E. in Palestine and Babylonia; the

Tamil (Hinduism) a classical language of southern India that is still spoken

Tanakh (Judaism) anagram for Jewish Scriptures, comprising the Torah, Prophets, and Writings

Tantra (Hinduism) literally "loom" or "to stretch"; generic name given to varied philosophies and rituals that frequently involve mantras, meditation on mandalas, or forms of yoga, leading to a liberating knowledge and experience

Tao (Taoism) classical Chinese term for any school's ideals and practices; among Taoists a term generally used to suggest the highest dimensions of reality, which can be attained by practitioners of traditional spiritual practices

tao (also dao) (Confucianism) "the way"; the Confucian life path

Tao te ching (Taoism) classical Taoist text; also known as the *Lao-tzu*

Tao-chiao (Taoism) the teachings of the Tao; the Taoist's name for their religion

Taoism (Taoism) *Tao-chiao*; a Chinese religious tradition that emphasizes personal transformation and integration with the unseen forces of the universe

tao-shih (Taoism) Taoist priest or priestess; a person recognized by the Taoist community as having mastered a specific body of sacred knowledge and the proper skills and dedication necessary to put that knowledge into effect for the sake of the community

Tao-tsang (Taoism) today's library of Taoist literature

tap (tapas, tapasya) (Jainism) austerities performed to purify the soul of karma

tattva (Jainism) any of the nine realities that characterize the universe and that include souls (*jivas*), matter (*ajiva*), matter coming in contact with souls (*ashrava*), the binding of karma and the soul (*bandha*), beneficial karma (*punya*), harmful karma (*papa*), inhibiting the influx of karma (*samvara*), purifying the soul of karma (*nirjara*), and liberation (*moksha*, or *nirvana*)

Tattvartha Sutra (Jainism) the only Jain scripture shared by both Shvetambaras and Digambaras, composed by Umasvati in c. 300 C.E.

tawhid (Islam) oneness, or unity, of God; monotheism

Terapanthi (Jainism) Shvetambara aniconic subsect that has only one *acharya*

Theravada (sometimes called Southern Buddhism) (Buddhism) one of two major schools of Buddhism practiced mainly in Cambodia, Laos, Myanmar [Burma], Sri Lanka, and Thailand; evolved from the Sthavira (Elders)

Three Bonds (Confucianism) obedience of subject to ruler, child to parent, and wife to husband

three jewels (Jainism) right faith, right understanding, and right conduct

Three Refuges, or Triple Gem (Buddhism) the Buddha, the dharma, and the sangha; the taking of the Three Refuges is a basic rite of passage in Buddhism

Tian (Confucianism) "Heaven"; entity believed to represent cosmic and moral order

tianli (Confucianism) ultimate, Heaven-rooted cosmic ordering principle permeating all phenomena

tianming (Confucianism) Mandate of Heaven

Torah (Pentatuch or Law) (Judaism) first division of the Tanakh, constituting the five books of Moses

torii (Shinto) gate marking the entrance to the grounds of a Shinto shrine

Trinity (Christianity) God as consisting of three persons—the Father, Son, and Holy Spirit

tripitaka (Pali, tipitaka) (Buddhism) three baskets, or three sets; the Tripitaka (Pali, Tipitaka), a collection of the Buddha's teachings—the Vinaya (Discipline), the Dharma (Doctrine), and the Abhidharma (Pali, Abhidhamma; Advanced Doctrine—forms the basis of the Buddhist canon

ubasoku, or hijiri (Shinto) mountain ascetics and holy men

ulama (Islam) religious leader or scholar

ummah (Islam) the transnational community of followers of Islam

Uniate (Christianity) any group observing Eastern rites but recognizing the authority of the pope

Universal House of Justice (Bahá'í) the supreme governing body of the worldwide Bahá'í community

upadesa (Hinduism) the sacred teaching

Upanishad (Hinduism) any of the Hindu sacred texts composed in about the sixth century B.C.E.; generally considered to be the "last" and philosophically the most important part of the Vedas

upaya (Buddhism) the concept of skillful means

Vaishnava (Hinduism) a member of a group of people devoted to Vishnu; also used to describe an object or an institution devoted to Vishnu

Vajrayana, or Tantra (Buddhism) a school of Mahayana Buddhism

vak (Sikhism) divine command

varna (Hinduism) literally "color"; the social class into which a person is born

varna-ashrama dharma (Hinduism) the behavior recommended for each class and each stage of life

Veda (Hinduism) literally "knowledge"; any of a set of compositions dating from the second millennium B.C.E. that is the highest scriptural authority for many educated Hindus

Vedanta (Hinduism) a philosophical school within Hinduism

Vishnu (Hinduism) literally "all-pervasive"; a term for the supreme being; one of the most important deities in the Hindu tradition; his incarnations include Rama and Krishna

wai-tan (Taoism) alchemy; a process of self-perfection involving the preparation of spiritualized substances called *tan* (elixirs)

wali (Islam) friend of God; Sufi saint

Wheel of the Dharma (Buddhism) visual symbol representing the Buddha's preaching his first sermon and also, with its eight spokes, Buddhism's Eightfold Path Yogacara, or Consciousness-Only school of Buddhism

Writings (Ketuvim or Hagiographa) (Judaism) third division of the Tanakh, including the Psalms and other works said to have be written under holy guidance

wu-wei (Taoism) nonaction; in the *Tao te ching,* a behavioral ideal of trusting the world's natural processes instead of one's own activity

wudu (Islam) ablution before worship

xin (Confucianism) heart-mind; human organ of moral evaluation

xing (Confucianism) inner human nature

Xinxue (Confucianism) "study of mind"; Neo-Confucian philosophical movement

ya Baha ul-abha (Bahá'í) "O Glory of the Most Glorious"; a form of the greatest name of God

Yasht (Zoroastrianism) one of a group of hymns to Iranian deities

yasna (Zoroastrianism) main Zoroastrian ritual; also the name of the main liturgical text, which is recited during the ritual

yazata (Zoroastrianism) any of a number of Zoroastrian divinities, the two most important of which are Mithra and the river goddess Anahita

yi (Confucianism) rightness; to act justly

yoga (Hinduism) physical and mental discipline by which one "yokes" one's spirit to a god; more generally, any path that leads to final emancipation

Yom Kippur (Day of Atonement) (Judaism) end of 10 days of penitence that begin with Rosh Hashana; the most holy of Jewish days

Yoruba (African Traditional Religions) an ethnic group residing in Nigeria and parts of Benin and Togo

yuga (Hinduism) in Hindu cosmology, any of four ages into which each cycle of time is divided

yuitsu genpon sōgen shintō (Shinto) "unique original essence Shinto"

zakat (Islam) purification; tithe or almsgiving; third pillar

zaotar (Zoroastrianism) priest

Zardushti (Zoroastrianism) name for the Zoroastrian tradition in Iran

Zoroaster (Zoroastrianism) founder of the Zoroastrian tradition; his Iranian name is Zarathustra

Zoroastrianism (Zoroastrianism) religion of pre-Islamic Iran; now represented by two communities, Parsi (Indian) and Zardushti (Iranian)

zot (Zoroastrianism) chief priest who performs the *yasna*

Zulu (African Traditional Religions) a large ethnic group in South Africa

Macedonia

POPULATION 2,054,800

MACEDONIAN ORTHODOX 66.3 percent

MUSLIM 30 percent

SERBIAN ORTHODOX 1.9 percent

ROMAN CATHOLIC 0.5 percent

GREEK CATHOLIC 0.3 percent

PROTESTANT 0.3 percent

ATHEIST 0.3 percent

OTHER 0.4 percent

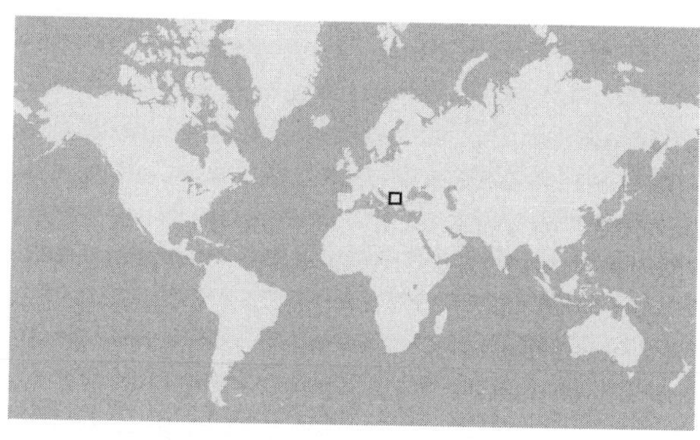

Country Overview

INTRODUCTION The Former Yugoslav Republic of Macedonia lies in the southern portion of Europe's Balkan Peninsula. A landlocked, mountainous country, Macedonia is bordered to the north by Serbia and Montenegro, to the east by Bulgaria, to the south by Greece, and to the west by Albania.

Christianity of the Byzantine rite prevailed in the region that includes modern Macedonia from the fourth century C.E. onward. Christian missions were successful among the Slavs who settled in the area in the sixth century. In the following centuries regional and imperial powers competed for control of Macedonia, which lay on the main route connecting Central Europe with the Aegean Sea. This contributed to the religious diversity of the region.

Besides the Orthodox Christians, a small, mainly Albanian, Roman Catholic minority has lived in Macedonia at least since the thirteenth century. When the Ottomans conquered Macedonia at the end of the fourteenth century, some Muslim colonists settled there. A significant number of Christians converted to Islam, and Islamic culture and customs permeated the whole society. Even so, the Christian majority continues to regard Islam as the religion of foreign rulers. With the penetration of European powers into the Ottoman Empire in the nineteenth century, Greek Catholic Unionism and Protestantism became established among Macedonia's Slavonic inhabitants. Most of Macedonia's several thousand Sephardic Jews were deported and murdered by the Germans during World War II.

Modernization during the period when Macedonia formed part of the Socialist Federal Republic of Yugoslavia (1946–91) led to a secularization of society. In keeping with its effort to develop Macedonia as a nation, however, the Yugoslav government supported an autocephalous (independent) Macedonian Orthodox Church. In 1992 the former Yugoslav republic became independent. More than two-thirds of the roughly 2 million inhabitants—mainly the Slavonic population,

A Macedonian Orthodox archbishop performs a holy service at St. Clement Cathedral in Skopje, Macedonia. AP/WIDE WORLD PHOTOS.

the Macedonians, and the small Serbian minority—are officially Orthodox Christians. About 616,000 Turks, Albanians, Roma, and Torbeši (Slavonic Muslims) together make up the country's Muslim population. A deep antagonism divides the Macedonian majority from the Albanian minority, and a military attack by Albanian rebels brought Macedonia to the brink of civil war in 2001. Although Macedonians are predominantly Orthodox Christian and the Albanians Muslim, this conflict is ethnic, not religious, in nature.

RELIGIOUS TOLERANCE Macedonia is a secular state with no official religion. The constitution guarantees freedom of worship, prohibits discrimination on the grounds of religious affiliation, and outlaws religious instruction in public schools. Despite these legal protections Macedonian nationalism has been significantly shaped by Christian elements. The Macedonian Orthodox Church seeks constitutional privilege in the country and has strongly opposed the expansion of Albanian minority rights since 2001. As a result, many Macedonian Muslims feel alienated from the state. In addition, a 1997 law requires that there be only one church organization for each confessional group. Although generally laxly enforced, this law is strictly enforced with regard to the Serbian Orthodox Church, the Macedonian Orthodox Church being considered the sole religious organization for all Orthodox in the country.

Major Religions

MACEDONIAN ORTHODOX CHURCH

ISLAM

MACEDONIAN ORTHODOX CHURCH

DATE OF ORIGIN 17–19 July 1967

NUMBER OF FOLLOWERS 1.4 million

HISTORY Christianity penetrated into Macedonia in the first century C.E., and the region became the center of missionary activity among the Slavonic population. To make this missionary activity easier, in the ninth century the scholars Cyril and Methodius, brothers from Thessalonica, Macedonia, introduced Old Church Slavonic as the liturgical language. With the Ottoman conquest at the end of the fourteenth century, distinct autonomous communities were established on the basis of religious affiliation. Under the new social system, the entirety of Orthodox Christianity was organized into one group. When the Ottoman's dissolved the archbishopric of Ohrid in 1767, the ecumenical patriarch of Constantinople became the head of all Orthodox Christians, and Greek was the liturgical language.

In 1870, under growing pressure from rival nationalist movements, the Ottomans were forced to recognize a separate Bulgarian Exarchate Church, the first ethnically based religious community in the empire. Thereafter, Ottoman Macedonia became a battleground where the Bulgarian Exarchate, the Orthodox Church of Greece, and the Ecumenical Patriarchate fought for the hearts of the Slavonic faithful. In the Balkan Wars of 1912–13, Macedonia came under Serbian rule, and the entire Orthodox Christian community in Macedonia was brought under the jurisdiction of Serbian Orthodoxy. While the authority of Serbian Orthodoxy in Macedonia was sanctioned by the Ecumenical Patriarchate in 1920, Serbia's ill treatment of the old exarchal priests and its assimilation policies did much to alienate the domestic Christian population from the Serbian church.

With the Bulgarian occupation of the greater part of Macedonia in 1941, Bulgarian Orthodoxy regained religious control of the country, and all clerics associated with Serbia were expelled. In 1943, in an effort to control all aspects of social life in the country, the Communist Partisan resistance, which fought against the Axis powers in World War II, installed a religious commission. After the war the Yugoslav Communists sought to rebuild the structure of the Orthodoxy as a common but federalist Yugoslav Orthodox Church, with the ecclesiastical organization of each Yugoslav republic as a federal subject of this common church. When this attempt failed, the atheist state promoted an independent Macedonian Orthodox Church. Beginning in 1958 Macedonia's efforts to assert its religious autonomy (treated as the revival of the archbishopric of Ohrid) were not resisted by the Serbian Church. In 1967 the Macedonian Orthodox Church declared its full independence, but, while the self-declared autocephaly of national churches has been customary since the nineteenth century, the Macedonian Church's independence has nonetheless gone unrecognized by other Orthodox churches. Unlike the Serbian Church, Macedonian Orthodoxy maintained close links with the socialist state. Also, unlike other Orthodox churches, Macedonian Orthodoxy has been greatly influenced by its lay members.

EARLY AND MODERN LEADERS In October 1943 the supreme command of the Partisan resistance appointed Veljo Mančevski, a priest and active Partisan, as the head of religious affairs. It was Dositej Stojković, however, who was elected head of the Macedonian Orthodox Church in 1958 and who led the church until his death in 1981. In 1951 Stojković had been appointed vicar-bishop of the Serbian patriarch to advocate for Serbian interests before the dissident clerics in Macedonia. It was planned that he should become the Serbian bishop of the Macedonian capital, Skopje, but resistance from the state and the Macedonian clerics prevented this. Seven years later he changed sides in the dispute. The current head of the Macedonian Orthodox Church, Archbishop Stefan (born Stojan Veljanovski in 1955), was elected in 1999. Stefan is closely affiliated with VMRO-DPMNE, the most important anti-Communist political party in the country.

MAJOR THEOLOGIANS AND AUTHORS Since the Macedonian Orthodox Church established its independence, the development of its religious life has been handicapped by the lack of educated clerics. While this state of affairs improved greatly with the establishment of the Macedonian Orthodox Seminary in 1967 and of the theological faculty at Saints Cyril and Methodius University in 1977, there have been no Macedonian theologians of international importance. The contemporary church has been mainly occupied with efforts to strengthen the national church tradition and the national awareness of Macedonian emigrants abroad. In 1980, for example, Boris Boškovski published *Verata na našite tatkovci* (The Belief of Our Fathers) to arouse popular religious and national feeling among the younger generations.

HOUSES OF WORSHIP AND HOLY PLACES The modern Cathedral of Saint Kliment of Ohrid in Skopje, built in the 1970s, is among the most notable Orthodox churches in Macedonia. Named after the medieval missionary who is considered the founding father of the church, the cathedral underscores the autocephaly of the Macedonian Church. The country is known for its many monasteries dating from the Middle Ages. Ohrid is famous for its 50 old churches, especially the dilapidated cathedral of Sveti Sofia.

WHAT IS SACRED? Macedonian Orthodox devotion centers around places—often monasteries—that are connected in popular belief with saints. Among these sacred sites are the tomb of Saint Naum in the monastery of Saint Naum at Lake Ohrid and the monastery of Sveti Bogorodica Uspenje (Sleeping God's Mother) in Berovo in eastern Macedonia.

HOLIDAYS AND FESTIVALS Besides the common Orthodox Christian holidays of Easter, Christmas, and Whitsunday, the highest Orthodox holidays in Macedonia are the commemoration days of the missionaries Saint Cyril (24 May) and Saint Methodius (24 May and 19 April) and their pupils Saint Kliment (9 August and 8 December) and Saint Naum (5 January and 3 July). Also, jubilee festivals are held on the anniversaries of important dates in the history of the national church.

Like other Orthodox churches, the Macedonian Orthodox Church celebrates certain secular national commemoration days as ecclesiastical ones. Significant among these are the birthdays of Goce Delčev (4 February) and Jane Sandanski (31 January), national revolutionaries of the Ottoman period. Ilinden (2 August), the religious holiday of Saint Elias, is likewise an important national holiday commemorating the anti-Ottoman Ilinden Uprising in 1903 and the founding of the Yugoslav People's Republic of Macedonia in 1944.

MODE OF DRESS Among the Macedonian Orthodox population, Western clothing styles are common. Traditional clothes are reserved for folkloric events and sometimes for rural marriages. Priests and bishops wear the common Orthodox black liturgical dress.

DIETARY PRACTICES Except for the period of fasting before Easter, which is observed casually by most people, there is no specific dietary practice among Macedonian Orthodox Christians.

RITUALS On *krsna slava,* the anniversary of the family saint characteristically celebrated in Serbian and Macedonian Orthodoxy, the distribution of *nafora* (blessed bread), the preparation of *žito* (wheatmeal cakes), and the lighting of candles are common rituals. Another ritual of Macedonian Orthodoxy is the traditional meal at the graves of loved ones on the anniversaries of their deaths. In rural areas with high rates of migration, however, the lack of people has often made observance of this ritual impossible. Since 1969 the head of the church has led a great delegation on an annual pilgrimage to the grave of Saint Kliment in Rome.

RITES OF PASSAGE There are no Orthodox rites of passage distinctive to Macedonia.

MEMBERSHIP The most recent figures for the membership of the Macedonian Orthodox Church are vague estimates from 1983. Many Macedonians are only Orthodox by social custom and not by religious belief. As a national church, Macedonian Orthodoxy does not actively missionize, except among Macedonian emigrants abroad, preferring instead to keep a closed society and to uphold a perceived responsibility to protect "our people" against a hostile world. Within Macedonia the church's methods of evangelization include Sunday schools, modern broadcast media, Orthodox Christian education, and an Internet site.

SOCIAL JUSTICE Macedonian Orthodoxy is a socially conservative force, not currently involved with any reform movement. First founded in Serbia in 1889, the renewal movement of the associations of Orthodox priests sought to strengthen the moral authority of the church by supporting social reforms within and without the church. These associations played an important role in the establishment of the church's independence and maintained close relations with the Communist state. Since the defeat of Communism, however, they have lost nearly all of their former importance.

SOCIAL ASPECTS Modernization has weakened the social influence of Orthodoxy. For example, rigid traditional rules regulating relations and contact between men and women have become a thing of the past. A majority of the Orthodox population shares the opinion that the Orthodox should not intermarry with members of other faiths. The two-child family is customary among the Orthodox and is regarded as a sign of modernity that distinguishes them from Muslim Albanians.

POLITICAL IMPACT Formed by post-Communist-era Social Democrats, who have led the country since its independence, and a party that emerged from among the Albanian rebels of 2001, the Macedonian government is secular. Nevertheless, since the end of Communism, the political leadership has made a point of demonstrating its Christian belief in public.

Religion is mainly regarded by politicians—and, to a certain extent, by ordinary members of the Macedonian Orthodox Church—as a way to strengthen national consciousness. But the strongest anticommunist party, VMRO-DPMNE, which ruled Macedonia from 1998 to 2002, has looked for a stronger Orthodox presence in the country's political and public life and has supported the church's ambition to be granted privileged status in the constitution.

CONTROVERSIAL ISSUES In 1992 the Serbian Orthodoxy declared its ecclesiastical jurisdiction over Macedonia and appointed an administrator for the country. Many Macedonians who have a reserved relationship with religion see this ecclesiastical dispute as an attempt to deny Macedonian nationhood. On the other hand, the Macedonian Orthodoxy declared itself responsible for the whole of Orthodoxy in Macedonia and, together with state authorities, prevented Serbian Orthodox clerics from serving the small Serbian minority, even while the Macedonian Church maintains its own right to serve Macedonians abroad. A new stage of the conflict erupted in 2002, when one of the eight Macedonian bishops, Jovan from Veles and Povardarje, declared his dioceses in liturgical and canonical union with the Serbian Orthodox Church. Jovan was impeached from office and heavily denounced in public, but this did not prevent three other bishops from voicing their own criticisms of the way the Macedonian autocephaly was gained in 1967. With regard to social issues that frequently arouse controversy in religious communities, the Macedonian Orthodox Church strongly rejects homosexuality.

CULTURAL IMPACT Macedonia is famous for the medieval icons in its churches and monasteries. To a limited extent, their influence is evident in the contemporary arts, a trend the nationalist members of the Macedonian Academy of Science and Arts avidly promote. In general, however, Macedonian arts and literature are most influenced by the modern secular West, though current literature and the humanities often reflect strong nationalist themes.

ISLAM

DATE OF ORIGIN Fourteenth century C.E.
NUMBER OF FOLLOWERS 616,000

HISTORY It has remained unclear whether the introduction of Islam in the Balkans was voluntary or compulsory, a sudden occurrence or a gradual process, and it has often been impossible to distinguish the Christians who converted from foreign colonists. Adherents of the Hanafi school of Sunni Islam predominated among Muslims in the region. Urbanization and the spread of Islam have been closely related since the turn of the sixteenth century. Many Macedonian towns, including Skopje, had a Muslim majority until the Balkan Wars of 1912–13. After 1912, when Muslims came under a Christian government, the internal structure of Sunni Islam in Macedonia was rebuilt after the model of the Christian churches.

The centralized structure of Islam in Macedonia corresponded with the Communist state's intention, after 1945, to strictly control the religious community. Outside of this community, Sufi orders like the Rifai, Halveti, Melami, and especially the heterodox Bektashi dervishes, who were strongly influenced by the Turkish Shiite sect of the Alevis, had to survive in a state of half-legality while many *tekkes* (monasteries) were closed. Although there was no official anti-Islamic law in Yugoslavia, the Shariah courts were abandoned in 1946, and public ceremonies like marriage became exclusive functions of the state. Furthermore, during heavy campaigns in the 1950s, Muslim women were urged to take down the traditional veil.

While the more urban Turks were the biggest Muslim minority in the period between the two world wars, they represent only 4 percent of the population of contemporary Macedonia, largely as the result of a 1950 state-sponsored exodus into Turkey of about 150,000 Muslims, who were mainly Turks but also Albanians and Torbeši. More than 22 percent of the population are Albanian Muslims. Most have remained in rural areas, unaffected by the modernizations of the socialist era because of their exclusion from economic and political power during the period. The Muslim population of Macedonia also includes more than 100,000 Albanians who have emigrated from Kosovo since 1980 and who lack Macedonian citizenship.

EARLY AND MODERN LEADERS In the period between the world wars Ferat Bej Draga led Cemiyet (Society for the Preservation of Muslim Rights), a Muslim confessional party active in Kosovo and Macedonia. Jakub Selimoski, who served as the first non-Bosnian head (Reis-ul-ulema) of the Yugoslav Islamic Community from 1990 to 1993, was the leader of the Islamic Religious Community of Macedonia for the country's Turkish, Slavonic, and Roma Muslims from 1993 until 2002. Sulejman Rexhepi led the Muslim Religious Community, whose members are Albanians, during the same period.

MAJOR THEOLOGIANS AND AUTHORS Because all Islamic trainee posts were closed after World War II and the first new *madrasah*, Isabeg-medresa in Skopje, was not opened until 1984, the level of Muslim theological culture in Macedonia is rather low. No theologians of broad significance exist, and few of the *hodžas* (spiritual teachers) and imams are able to read Arabic or Ottoman Turkish. Historically influential Muslim theologians in Macedonia were Mehmed Hayati (died in 1766), a sheikh of the Halveti order and founder of a suborder in Ohrid, and Muhammad Nur al-Arabi (1813–88), who spurred the diffusion of the Melami order in the Balkans.

HOUSES OF WORSHIP AND HOLY PLACES As elsewhere, the Muslim house of worship is the mosque. Many new ones have been built in Macedonia since the 1990s. The fifteenth-century mosque in Tetovo is considered one of the most beautiful painted mosques in the Balkans. The Bektashi's Arabati-Baba Dervish Tekke (monastery) is also located in Tetovo. Founded in the sixteenth century, this *tekke* has been converted to a commercial hotel, but dervishes have engaged in protests to restore it to its original religious function.

WHAT IS SACRED? Many popular observances of the dervish orders have survived from the pre-Christian era. These include sun and moon cults, the worship of rivers and streams, and the adoration of sacred trees in high places. Bektashi often identify the ninth-century Christian saint Elias with Ali, the Prophet Muhammad's cousin and son-in-law, who is called Abbas in the Balkans.

HOLIDAYS AND FESTIVALS An important Muslim holiday is the *bayram,* for the celebration of which many emigrant workers return to Macedonia. Many Muslim Roma celebrate Orthodox Christian religious festivals—such as Christmas, Saint George's Day, and Ilinden—partly to avoid offending the Christian majority but also because of the growing influence of the Bektashi and other Sufi orders (with their particular symbiotic tendencies regarding Christianity) among the Roma population. No Muslim holidays are observed by the state.

MODE OF DRESS While Muslim men and middle-class women in Macedonia wear Western clothing, women of the rural and lower urban classes often wear clothing regarded as more traditional. This includes a long gray coat and a headscarf. Veils, however, are not worn.

DIETARY PRACTICES In the public space the prohibition against drinking alcohol is widely respected. On the other hand, Muslims in the country do not generally observe the prohibition against eating pork.

RITUALS Most of the dervish rituals in Macedonia are now simplified, because nearly all of the new sheikhs are uneducated in religious affairs. Like Orthodox Christians, the Bektashi make pilgrimages to the Christian monastery of Saint Naum at Lake Ohrid.

RITES OF PASSAGE There are no Muslim rites of passage distinctive to Macedonia.

MEMBERSHIP Although Muslims do not seek a closed society, missioning in Macedonia is not the rule. Besides newspapers and radio and television programs, the Koranic schools are an important method of evangelization. Since the 1970s the growth of the dervish orders has rivaled that of official Islam, especially among the Roma population.

SOCIAL JUSTICE The Sufi orders—especially the Bektashi and Halveti—had a significant influence on the political and social renewal movement of the Young Ottomans or Young Turks at the end of the nineteenth century. Albanians were excluded from the power structure during the socialist era, and the Sufi orders served the needs of indigents among their Albanian adherents—by collecting donations, for example.

SOCIAL ASPECTS Less modernized than the Orthodox community in Macedonia, the Albanians tend to be more religious. The attitudes of urban middle-class Albanians toward family and marriage are similar to those of the Orthodox Christians. Among the rural majority of the Albanians, however, the traditional patriarchal family has survived with its strict hierarchy, including the subordinated role of women and rigid regulation of contacts between men and women. This hierarchy is often violated, though, because of the absence of young men, who play a decisive economic role and must often emigrate to find work. Macedonian Albanians have one of the highest birthrates in Europe. More than 70 percent of the Albanian population reject marriages between Christians and Muslims.

POLITICAL IMPACT The process of developing national consciousness was belated in Islamic society. In some rural areas the sense of religious communality among different Muslim ethnic groups has continued to predominate, with fluid boundaries between Albanian, Turkish, and Slavonic ethnicities. This has made the people in these areas a target for the pressure of Albanian, Macedonian, or Turkish nationalists. On the other hand, the Roma, many Slavonic Muslims, and especially the urban Turks are militantly anti-Albanian and side with the Macedonians in their ethnic conflict with the Albanians. While in Yugoslav times the entirety of Sunni Islam was united in one organization led by the Reis-ul-ulema in Sarajevo, since Macedonia's independence the Macedonian-Albanian conflict has become perceptible within the Islamic community. From 1995 until 2002 the community was split into two religious associations, one for the Albanians and one for the Turks, Roma, and Macedonian Muslims.

CONTROVERSIAL ISSUES Birth control for Albanians was vigorously propagated by the socialist state in the 1980s, along with administrative measures to enforce a two-child limit in families. Because of the resistance of the Muslim population, who regarded these measures as anti-Islamic, state intervention in family planning is prohibited by the constitution of independent Macedonia. Contraception is still not accepted in rural areas. Secular Albanian parties propagate the emancipation of women. Official Sunni Islam considers the admission of women to Bektashi religious meetings alongside men to be not in accordance with religious observance.

CULTURAL IMPACT Popular folk music in Macedonia was strongly influenced, at least in terms of melody, by the Ottomans. Since the 1960s "new composed music," a mixture of folk and light music, has become more popular than the traditional folk music. Nevertheless, Muslim influences are still apparent in the new composed music.

Other Religions

Catholicism of the Byzantine rite (Unionist) attracted a small but significant part of the Orthodox Slavonic population in the nineteenth century, though this development was not primarily influenced by religious motivations. Rather, French Catholic missionaries of the Order of Saint Lazarus exploited the dissatisfaction of the Slavonic faithful with the Ecumenical Patriarchate of Constantinople. The Slavonic population used the threat of conversion to exert pressure on the patriarchate to accede to their demand for Slavonic priests and bishops and the use of Old Church Slavonic—in place of Greek—as the liturgical language. With the founding of the Bulgarian Exarchate Orthodox Church in 1870, the number of Unionists drastically declined. Only about 5,000 Unionists remain in contemporary Macedonia.

American Protestant missionaries from the Methodist Episcopal Church and the Congregational Church were also active in nineteenth-century Macedonia. They established Episcopal stations and schools in many Macedonian towns, though they did not attract many adherents. The significance of their activity lies in the fact that they preached the gospel in the vernacular and translated the Bible into Bulgarian. This constituted an additional pressure on the Orthodox Church in Macedonia to instate Slavonic priests and to use Old Church Slavonic in its liturgy. The Orthodoxy and many ordinary members of the Macedonian Orthodox Church continue to regard the Protestant Christians as dangerous sectarians.

Among the overwhelmingly Muslim Albanians, there is a small minority of about 10,000 Roman Catholics. The most prominent has been Gonxhe Bojaxhiu (1910–97), known as Mother Theresa, who was born in Skopje. She became a nun in India in 1929 and began her lifelong ministry among the poor in Calcutta in the mid-1940s. In 2003 an agreement between Macedonia and Italy to build a memorial in Rome recognizing Mother Theresa (in Cyrillic) as a daughter of Macedonia drew many Albanian protests.

Heinz Willemsen

See Also Vol. I: *Christianity, Eastern Orthodoxy, Islam*

Bibliography

Alexander, Stella. *Church and State in Yugoslavia since 1945.* Cambridge: Cambridge University Press, 1979.

Clayer, Nathalie. "L'Islam, facteur des recompositions internes en Macédoine et au Kosovo." In *Le Nouvel islam balkanique: Les musulmans, acteurs du post-communisme, 1990–2000.* Edited by Xavier Bougarel and Nathalie Clayer, 177–240. Paris: Maisonneuve et Larose, 2001.

Clayer, Nathalie, and Alexandre Popovic. "Sur le traces des derviches de Macédoine yougoslave." *Anatolia Moderna 4: Derviches des Balkans, disparitions et renaissances* (1992): 13–63.

Dimevski, Slavko. *Istorija na Makedonskata Pravoslavna Crkva.* Skopje: Makedonska kn., 1989.

Ellis, Burcu Akan. *Shadow Genealogies: Memory and Identity among Urban Muslims in Macedonia.* Boulder, Colo.: East European Monographs, 2003.

Kraft, Ekkehard. "Die Religionsgemeinschaften in Makedonien." *Österreichische Osthefte* 40, no. 1–2 (1998): 339–76.

Pavlowitch, Stevan K. "The Macedonian Orthodox Church." In *Eastern Christianity and Politics in the Twentieth Century.* Edited by Pedro Ramet, 338–49. Durham, N.C., and London: Duke University Press, 1988.

Popovic, Alexandre. *L'Islam balkanique: Les musulmans du sud-est européen dans la période post-ottomane.* Berlin: Osteuropa-Institut an der Freien Universität Berlin; Wiesbaden: In Kommission bei O. Harrassowitz, 1986.

Thirkell, John. "Islamisation in Macedonia as a Social Process." In *Islam in the Balkans: Persian Art and Culture of the 18th and 19th Centuries.* Edited by Jennifer M. Scarce, 43–8. Edinburgh: Royal Scottish Museum, 1979.

Madagascar

POPULATION 16,473,477

CHRISTIAN 48 percent

TRADITIONAL RELIGION 46 percent

MUSLIM 5.4 percent

OTHER 0.6 percent

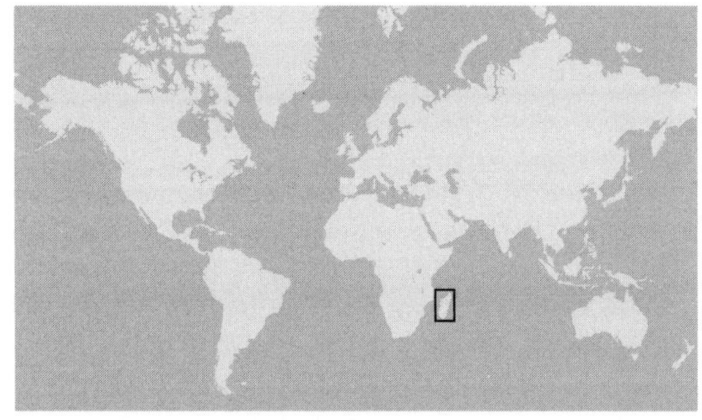

Country Overview

INTRODUCTION The island of Madagascar, which lies in the Indian Ocean off the southeastern coast of Africa, was uninhabited before the Common Era. Scholars generally agree that the island was first occupied by migrants from the Indonesian archipelago—hence the basically Austronesian character of Malagasy culture. Elements of Arabic culture were introduced among the island's coastal kingdoms between 1100 and 1400. The slave trade brought other influences, mainly from Africa. Conversely, many Malagasy were exported as slaves to every part of the world as a result of endless internecine wars between early Malagasy kingdoms.

The official prohibition of the slave trade by King Radama I in 1817, after a deal with the British, did not mean the end of the trade, but it did bring tremendous social changes. One of them was the effective adoption of Christianity in its Protestant (Congregationalist) form by the ruling elite of the central highlands. An original Malagasy culture was developed, with a comprehensive schooling network that included higher education (in the disciplines of law, economics, medicine, and theology) and a body of scientific literature in Malagasy. This culture prevailed until the French took possession of the island in 1895. The country became the Republic of Madagascar after it gained independence from France in 1960.

RELIGIOUS TOLERANCE Madagascar is a secular state without an official denominational affiliation, though its constitution does contain a reference to "God and the ancestors." In 1869 Queen Ranavalona II and her husband, Rainilaiarivony, the prime minister, were baptized, and the queen formally became the head of the Protestant Church in Madagascar. She decided to burn the royal idols but did not prohibit traditional rituals as practiced by families, villages, or federations of villages. This is the origin of the religious freedom that prevails in contemporary Madagascar.

Since the nineteenth century Christianity has been the most organized religion in Madagascar, whereas traditional ancestral rituals are commonly practiced either as genuine religious performances or as traditional folklore with little religious meaning. Islam is represented by a number of independent, genealogically linked groups. Statistics hardly begin to express the ambiguity and mobility of religious affiliations in Madagascar.

Major Religions

CHRISTIANITY

TRADITIONAL RELIGION

CHRISTIANITY

DATE OF ORIGIN 1613 C.E.

NUMBER OF FOLLOWERS 7.9 million

HISTORY In 1613 Luis Mariano, a Jesuit priest, arrived as the first Christian missionary in Madagascar. He stayed with a local king on the southeastern coast. Andria Ramaka, a son of the king, was sent to Goa, India, where he received clerical education but was not ordained. He eventually succeeded his father as king and welcomed other missionaries, including the Lazarist priests Charles Nacquart and Nicolas Gondrée, who arrived in 1648. Both Nacquart and Gondrée died soon after, and no church was planted, but a first catechism in Malagasy was composed. No new missionary project was entertained until the nineteenth century, when Welsh Protestant missionaries were sent by the London Missionary Society at the request of King Radama I, who reigned from 1810 to 1828. Protestants celebrate the year 1818 as the date of introduction of the gospel in Madagascar. The first Christian baptisms were held in 1831, and a Malagasy translation of the Bible was published in 1835.

These developments frightened Queen Ranavalona I, who, having succeeded Radama in 1828, decided to forbid the Christian religion and punish Malagasy Christians. The penalty was death, which is why the many victims of persecution during the period 1835–61 have been designated martyrs. From 1861 onward Christianity expanded quickly in various denominations as a result of spontaneous local movements. Protestantism was adopted by the monarchy and most of the nobility. Roman Catholicism won another part of the elite and became concentrated in the low-caste population.

In 1962, two years after Madagascar gained its independence from France, a state law on religion was promulgated. It enforced complete religious freedom for the churches. In 1968 three Protestant churches in the Reformed tradition merged to form the Church of Jesus Christ in Madagascar (FJKM). In 1980 the mainline denominations (Roman Catholic, Episcopal, United Reformed, and Lutheran) created the Council of Christian Churches in Madagascar (FFKM), which was instrumental in the political transition from the autocratic communist regime of Didier Ratsiraka toward democracy. Many Christian movements and denominations are active in Madagascar, including Pentecostal and Charismatic groups, the Baptist Church, the Orthodox Church, old popular revival movements, and a dozen independent churches. All churches and movements in Madagascar are self-governed. The country's Christian constituency is roughly half Roman Catholic and half Protestant.

People participate in the famidihana *ritual in Madagascar. During the ritual, the deceased are exhumed and wrapped in fresh shrouds.* © JOHN R. JONES; PAPILIO/CORBIS.

EARLY AND MODERN LEADERS Historical Christian figures in Madagascar include Rasalama (1798–1837), a high-caste woman who died as a martyr of the Christian faith, and Victoire Rasoamanarivo (1848–1894), who was beatified by the pope in 1989. Both exemplify the role of laywomen in Malagasy Christianity. Contemporary Christian leaders who have played a role in church and society, locally and globally, include the Reverend Richard Andriamanjato (born in 1930), a Reformed parish minister who is head of a political party, mayor of the capital, Antananarivo, and president of the National Assembly; Monsignor Jérôme Rakotomalala, who in 1969 became the first Malagasy cardinal; and Madeleine Ramaholimihaso, a businesswoman who heads a Roman Catholic think tank. Several Malagasy citizens have won leading positions in international religious organizations, including Peri Rasolondraibe, director of the Department for Mission and Development of the Lutheran World Federation in Geneva, Switzerland.

MAJOR THEOLOGIANS AND AUTHORS Local theologians as well as expatriate missionaries from many countries have contributed to the production of Malagasy theological and religious literature. Prolific authors among Protestants in the twentieth century have included Jean Williberton Rabemanahaka (born in 1921), Rakotonirainy Jonson (died in 1996), Joseph Ramambasoa, Paul Ramino, Michel Fety (1921–98), Daniel Ralibera (died in 2002), and Rakotobe-Andriamaro (born in 1912). Some younger theologians have achieved an international profile, such as Emmanuel Tehindrazanarivelo, the missiologist Laurent Ramambason, and the biblical scholar Rakotoharintsifa Andrianjatovo. Catholic authors have included the biblical scholar Léonard Ramaroson; the religious historian Pascal Lahady (died in 1995); the Benedictine monk Gilles Gaide, who was instrumental in a sweeping liturgical reform; Bruno Hübsch (1936–2003), the editor of an authoritative ecumenical history of Christianity in Madagascar, *Madagascar et le christianisme* (1993); and Adolphe Razafintsalama (1926–2001), a Jesuit anthropologist. The emerging generation of professional theologians includes Jean Germain Rajoelison, the editor of the theological quarterly *Aspects du christianisme à Madagascar* (Aspects of Christianity in Madagascar); the biblical scholar Hilaire Raharilalao; the anthropologist Robert Jaovelo; and the ecumenist Charles-Raymond Ratongavao. Unfortunately much theological literature in Madagascar has remained unpublished because of poor economic conditions there.

HOUSES OF WORSHIP AND HOLY PLACES Thousands of Christian churches in Madagascar catch the attention of the observer, their structures ranging from simple wooden sheds with thatched roofs to impressive cathedrals in hewed stone. The most famous are the Protestant memorial churches that were built in the 1860s on the four hills of the capital—Ambohipotsy, Ambatonakanga, Faravohitra, and Amboninampamarinana—where the Christian martyrs were killed.

The independent Protestant revival movements of the late nineteenth and twentieth centuries established holy villages or *toby* (camps) where pilgrims still come for spiritual exercises and healing sessions. Sick and disabled people reside almost permanently in these places. The most visited *toby* are Soatanana, which was established in 1894 by Rainisoalambo; Manolotrony, established in 1927 by Neny Ravelonjanahary; Ankaramalaza, established in 1941 by Germaine Volahavana (known as Nenilava, the Tall Mother); and Farihimena, established in 1946 by Daniel Rakotozandry. On special days (9 June and 10 August) crowds of disciples from all over the country gather at these places for worship, Bible study, healing, exorcism, and mutual encouragement. The Roman Catholic church has nothing comparable to the *toby* in Madagascar, though facsimiles of the Lourdes grotto have been built in the yards of many churches.

WHAT IS SACRED? In absolute terms there are no sacred animals, persons, or objects in Madagascar's Roman Catholic tradition except the elements of the Eucharist and, to a lesser degree, the relics of saints. In 2003 the Carmelite sisters organized a reverse pilgrimage in Madagascar for the relics of Saint Theresa of the Child Jesus, which are ordinarily kept in Lisieux, France, whereupon crowds of Malagasy Catholics had the opportunity to touch the sacred chest containing the saint's remains.

HOLIDAYS AND FESTIVALS Malagasy Christians have the same holidays as other Christians throughout the world, and their celebrations are not restricted by the state.

MODE OF DRESS There is no dress code for Christians in Madagascar. On Sundays dress is generally more elaborate than on weekdays. Women like to wear the traditional white silk *lamba* (scarf) on their shoulders over a Western-style blouse, dress, or suit. Trousers are not common attire for women. In the highlands men wear Western-style suits. On special occasions they may wear a colorful *lamba* on their shoulders. In villages and in the coastal provinces the tropical climate allows for lighter clothing. Men may wear a cotton robe called a *malabary,* which is actually a long white or colored shirt, with a long white cotton *lamba* on their shoulders. The *malabary* is worn over trousers.

Members of the revival movements in Madagascar follow a special dress code. Their clothing must be white, as a symbol of light, and their robes must be cut according to a particular pattern, with the seam through the chest, not along the loins.

DIETARY PRACTICES There are no special dietary practices among Malagasy Christians. The Roman

Catholic rule of fasting during Lent and on Fridays is largely followed by the faithful.

RITUALS There are no striking Christian rituals in Madagascar that accompany birth, marriage, or death. The dead are buried either in the family tomb or in communal graves or public cemeteries. Sometimes the deceased is buried in a provisional personal tomb until the next gathering of the extended family for second funerals. Cremation is not practiced.

RITES OF PASSAGE Malagasy Christians generally follow the traditional Christian rites of passage. They also practice male circumcision. Girls are not circumcised.

MEMBERSHIP Full church membership is granted, with access to Communion, after a teaching and testing period. Congregations are governed by the assembly of communicants (*mpandray ny Fanasan'ny Tompo*), but conversions of non-Christians are admitted and welcome. Evangelization campaigns aimed principally at nominal Christians are organized by many parishes and especially by revival movements.

SOCIAL JUSTICE Christians and non-Christians alike are keen on social justice in Madagascar, but the definition of injustice is disputed. According to indigenous tradition a person's social position is determined by his or her genealogy. Many can claim royal or noble ancestry, but still more people are said to be of slave (*andevo*) descent. The latter make up most of the low-caste population. The French colonial authorities abolished slavery in 1896, but the memory of slavery still lingers. In villages the descendants of slaves are not permitted to dwell near the homes of nobles. Low-caste people have generally accepted their condition and have not created social unrest. Modern social movements like nationalism and international socialism, however, have brought about a more militant attitude, which is now common in Christian milieus. The Catholic and Protestant churches have made numerous official statements on social justice in line with, respectively, the social teachings of the popes and the spirit of ecumenical bodies. At the grassroots level innumerable church-based nongovernmental organizations and other groups have helped the poor, including street children, and the disabled. New villages offering better housing and services have been created in order to break through the inherited social discrimination.

SOCIAL ASPECTS Marriages among Christians in Madagascar generally occur between people of the same social level who have compatible genealogies. But marriage outside the traditional custom is not prohibited. Interracial marriages may also occur. The penalty in these cases, however, is the exclusion of the foreign spouse from burial in the family tomb. New tombs can be built, however, and in public cemeteries members of nontraditional couples may be buried together; however, the number of public cemeteries is extremely limited. Some Christian communities have their own private burial grounds for members.

POLITICAL IMPACT Madagascar is a secular state, but it favors religious initiatives in the fields of rural development, general and professional education, social rehabilitation, medical services (including leprosy missions), journalism, and communications. There are no Christian political parties, but Christians take part in political life according to their own choice. Under the dictatorship of Didier Ratsiraka (1975–2001), the churches themselves became the only possible political voice of the people. In 1979 they joined the effort to push the resistance against Ratsiraka. A common political platform was set up, and a new constitution was drafted by a committee appointed by the Council of Christian Churches in Madagascar. The high point of the churche's political involvement came in October 1991, when church leaders stood as the brokers of democratization. Since then the political involvement of the church hierarchies has become less visible, but political statements are regularly issued by the Council of Christian Churches in Madagascar and by the bishops of the Roman Catholic Church.

CONTROVERSIAL ISSUES In the manner of other Austronesian cultures, Malagasy Christians belong to a culture of consensus and tend to avoid confrontation. Nevertheless, there have been heated discussions pertaining to the interpretation of social justice, the adaptation of a number of traditional practices by the Roman Catholic clergy, and the question whether ill-inspired political choices under the regime of Didier Ratsiraka should be punished or given a general pardon. Homosexuality has not been a topic of public debate in Madagascar.

CULTURAL IMPACT Malagasy people love singing. Christian worship and all kinds of formal and informal meetings offer countless opportunities for singers, musicians, composers, and choirs to perform. Musical styles range from slow, quasi-Gregorian liturgies to rapid, syncopated melodies and include adaptations of sentimental British tunes inspired by the nineteenth-century evangelists Dwight L. Moody and Ira D. Sankey. Electronic instruments have helped bring new forms of music into the churches and to so-called evangelical galas. While Protestants have generally adopted Westernized melodies in addition to cherished historical hymns, Catholics, in the name of inculturation, have retrieved old indigenous sounds and rhythms for use in their new hymns. The sounds of this music are rather rough and deep-seated in the chest. A mixture of indigenous and imported melodies is found in the so-called *zafindraony* (literally, "mixed") songs, which have been popular since the 1860s. They may be compared to musicals involving a leader and a choir.

A new kind of urban architecture was developed in the nineteenth century when British missionaries introduced the use of brick and stone for building houses. The missionary model of a two-story house with a veranda is still followed in contemporary Madagascar. Churches often bear the marks of the countries where missionaries came from or where Malagasy leaders have been educated: France, Italy, Norway, England, and Wales. Light, wooden buildings are typical in coastal regions. They are quickly destroyed by cyclones, which are very frequent in Madagascar, but they are equally quickly rebuilt.

Malagasy literature in written form has continued to draw heavily from the Bible. The original Malagasy version of the Bible, published in 1835, was the first literary monument of Madagascar and is considered a linguistic norm, though revised versions have been published in the meantime. The last version, an ecumenical translation, was launched in the beginning of 2003. Poems, plays, and novels inspired by biblical stories are countless and very popular. Even the political discourse in Madagascar is full of biblical references.

TRADITIONAL RELIGION

DATE OF ORIGIN Third or fourth century C.E.
NUMBER OF FOLLOWERS 7.6 million

HISTORY Traditional ancestral religion in Madagascar originated with the arrival of the first migrants from the Indonesian archipelago, probably in the third century C.E., though no written or material witness dates from that period. (The first reports on Malagasy pre-Christian and pre-Islamic religion were the work of European travelers and missionaries, who began to arrive in Madagascar in the sixteenth century.) On their way to the island, the Indonesian migrants, following the Indian Ocean rim, collected traditions, animals, and plants, and they probably also brought a number of men and women from various coastal territories along the way. This may explain why many Arab and Bantu and a few Chinese and Indian elements have been found in Madagascar since the Middle Ages. Islamic and Christian influences were adapted to the ancestral religion in their turn, and the process of adaptation continues today. Ancestral religion has its own dynamic history, and it is never static. Its focus is "God and the ancestors," which are globally identified with an unpredictable fate, or *vintana.*

EARLY AND MODERN LEADERS The origin of the tradition of the ancestors (*fomban-drazana*) is lost in the mist of prehistory. The beliefs are considered to be given by God and are not attributed to a single founder. The kings of the numerous former kingdoms of Madagascar, however, are celebrated as the key figures of the ancestral religion, and they are nearly worshiped, invoked by the faithful in endless litanies. In contemporary Madagascar there has been no living leader or official body (as in some African countries) representing ancestral religion as a whole.

MAJOR THEOLOGIANS AND AUTHORS Traditional religion in Madagascar does not rely upon written revelation but functions in the realm of oral culture under a shadow of secrecy. There are no theologians who speak authoritatively on its behalf. The exposition of ancestral religion is the work of outsiders. Pietro Lupo, a historian of religions at the University of Tulear, has shown the most genuine empathy with ancestral religion in Madagascar.

HOUSES OF WORSHIP AND HOLY PLACES Properly speaking, ancestral religion does not use houses of worship; instead it is focused on numerous meeting points, which may include isolated rocks in the mountains, where offerings are brought, animal sacrifices are performed, and prayers are said in the open air. A particular current within ancestral religion, the *tromba* (possession), is generally practiced indoors in private homes.

WHAT IS SACRED? Everything in nature has something sacred in it, according to ancestral religion. This is why every action that touches or changes nature requires permission from God and the ancestors before it can be undertaken. (If the permissibility of an action is in doubt, abstention is preferable.) By extension all of the Malagasy fatherland is said to be sacred (*masina ny tanindrazana*), meaning that no part of the territory should be sold to foreigners. There is no permanent clergy in Madagascar's traditional religion. Occasional officers are considered sacred at the time of the ceremony in which they are participating.

HOLIDAYS AND FESTIVALS There are no regular holidays in ancestral religion. The core of the religion lies in big festivals held at times that are decided upon by means of astrology. Intervals between celebrations of the same festival may last as long as several years. Festivals are never intended for the participation of the whole nation but are bound to particular ethnic groups, or to an extended family or a community of villages. Expatriate observers are generally welcome, but "foreigners," or people outside the relevant genealogies, are not.

On the northwestern coast, between the mouth of the river Betsiboka and the mouth of the river Onilahy (the traditional territory of the Sakalava, one of the 18 ethnic communities of Madagascar), the festival called Fitampoha is held every 7 or 10 years by the descendants of royal dynasties. Its main feature is the bathing of the relics (dry bones and paraphernalia) of old Sakalava kings.

Farther north on the coast the Antankarana, another Malagasy people, celebrate the Tsangantsaina, the mast-raising ceremony, every five or six years in their capital, Ambatoharanana. This festival dates from the eighteenth century. The 11-meter mast symbolizes the political and religious unity of the former kingdom.

On the east coast the Betsimisaraka, one of the major ethnic groups of Madagascar, celebrate their annual festival, Asarabe, at Foulpointe, a small port north of Toamasina (formerly Tamatave). The celebration lasts eight days following the new moon in September. It is conducted by a descendant of the former Betsimisaraka kings, under the auspices of the associations of *tangalamena* (clan chiefs).

Also on the east coast the Antambahoaka community celebrates the Sambatra, a huge collective ceremony accompanying the circumcision of all boys born during the seven years between festivals. The event, which lasts eight days, begins with the election of a boy as chief of the feast and the appointment of a man to hold a calabash containing a kind of alcohol needed for the mass operation. The traditional king of the tribe calls the royal ancestors to be present and bless the participants, who eat, drink, and dance day and night.

In the highlands the Merina royal lineages celebrate the Malagasy New Year with a festival called Alahamady. This includes a calling of the royal ancestors and the sacrifice of a specially prepared ox. The animal's blood is spread upon the participants, and the meat is shared among the families according to definite rules.

MODE OF DRESS Traditional religionists in Madagascar have no specific mode of dress. Rather, obvious differences in dress are related to the places where people live, whether in town or in the countryside, and to their social positions and professions. The use of masks, so common in African traditional religions, is unknown in Madagascar.

DIETARY PRACTICES Every family or clan has its own dietary practices, the staple food being rice or, in case of insufficient provisions of rice, cassava. Oxen meat is generally accepted when available, notably at festivals. Other kinds of meat—such as chicken, guinea fowl, some sorts of fish (specifically eels), and pork—may be forbidden among certain families or even for individuals who have received personal instruction from their parents or their traditional priest (*ombiasy*). Consumption of some vegetables—onion, for example—may be prohibited, too. There is no general dietary rule that applies to the whole of Madagascar.

RITUALS The most famous traditional ritual in Madagascar, which has been described in many books and reported in many films, is the *famadihana* (turning of the dead). The ritual consists of the solemn opening of the family tomb, the exhumation of the corpses, the cleaning of the bones, the wrapping of the dry bones in new, raw silk *lamba* (cloths) and mats, and the rearrangement of the dead in the tomb, which is finally closed again for several years. *Famadihana* takes place every five to ten years, depending on the wealth of the extended family and the inspiration received (in dreams) from the ancestors. The celebration is subject to change. Often Christian prayers are said and Christian songs are sung alongside traditional litanies. The Roman Catholic Church in Madagascar has produced a *famadihana* liturgy and organized special *famadihanas* for the gathering of the corpses of all the deceased bishops of Madagascar, including those of Europeans. It must be said, however, that this ritual is familiar to the Merina community only. Other groups have their own burial traditions, and people without family tombs in the Highlands, such as the descendants of slaves, are unable to make a *famadihana.*

RITES OF PASSAGE There are no special cycles of human life according to Malagasy traditional religion. The circumcision of boys is the main ritual occasion. It is the focus of big collective ceremonies among the Masikoro and Antambahoaka societies.

MEMBERSHIP Membership in Malagasy traditional religion is given at birth. The religion has no formal membership and no formal education or catechism for children and youth. The extended family and the clan provide an informal initiation into the customs. Transgression of ancestral rules, even by mistake, can lead to temporary or definitive exclusion and heavy penalties. Reintegration can be achieved by means of a confession of sins, a sacrifice and an offering to God and the ancestors, and the intercession of a traditional priest (*ombiasy*).

SOCIAL JUSTICE Malagasy traditional religion as such has made no contribution to social justice in the modern sense of the concept. However, ancestral wisdom, by means of proverbs and short stories, articulates a genuine concern for justice.

SOCIAL ASPECTS Women and men are almost equally active in the traditional religion of Madagascar. Possession periods happen more easily under the control of women than they do during regular royal festivals.

POLITICAL IMPACT Ancestral religion lost its political weight almost completely with the decline of the old ethnic kingdoms under the monarchy and, later, under the centralized colonial administration and the independent republican regime.

CONTROVERSIAL ISSUES At the local level controversies may arise among rival clans over the appointment of religious officers and the allocation of sacred land among the clans.

CULTURAL IMPACT Themes from ancestral religion are formally and informally present in Malagasy instrumental and vocal music and poetry. Modern Malagasy fiction written in French often mentions ancestral rituals.

Other Religions

Other religions in Madagascar include Islam, whose adherents number about 840,000, and Hinduism, with about 2,000 adherents. Hinduism has been present in Madagascar longer, as it was introduced at the beginning of human occupation. The small Hindu community in contemporary Madagascar is the result of a wave of Indian immigration in the nineteenth century. Hindus and other Indians in Madagascar are merchants, specialized artisans, and entrepreneurs. Hindu Indians are called Banìany. There are no Hindu holy places in Madagascar.

The most visible Hindu ritual in Madagascar is cremation. There is a special building on the outskirts of Antananarivo where a pyre can be installed. Membership in Hinduism is limited to the Hindu minority. Hindus do not proselytize. Marriage among Malagasy Hindus, as among practitioners of other religions in Madagascar, generally occurs within the limits of a person's authorized genealogy, though interreligious marriages may take place. Hinduism has no political impact in Madagascar.

Islam in Madagascar also has an old presence. Pre-Islamic Arab influences were evident in the use of geomancy and astrology, in the names of days (Alahady, Alatsinainy, Talata, Alarobia, Alakamisy, Zoma, Asabotsy), and in the technology of ancient navigation in the Indian Ocean. Another important legacy is the Arabic script, which was used at the courts of early kingdoms on the southeastern coast of Madagascar before the Malagasy language was rendered in Latin letters. No unified Islamic authority exists in Madagascar, but there is a loose national Muslim association, which held its first congress in Majunga in 1980.

Muslims on the island used to live in separate communities bound by genealogical links. Settlers from Comoros once formed the most populous and homogeneous Muslim community in Madagascar, which mainly occupied the northwestern region of Majunga and the capital, Antananarivo. Their form of Sunni Islam belongs to the Swahili culture of Eastern Africa. Xenophobic riots in 1976 in Majunga caused hundreds of casualties among Comorians, who subsequently fled the country in great numbers. Malagasy converts have joined the Sunni community and received formal religious education. Among these converts Hadjy Soulaiman Andriantomanga, who was educated in Egypt, is noted for his religious tracts, which were published in the 1960s.

Indians make up the other important Muslim community of foreign origin, but they have been largely integrated as Malagasy citizens. They are divided among four Islamic congregations, one representing the Sunni branch of Islam and three belonging to the Shiite tradition. Many Sunni Indians are artisans who interact easily with the rest of the Malagasy population. Many Shiites are more secluded and prosperous. Following three separate traditions, they are the Khodja, the most powerful group; adepts of the Aga Khan; and the Bohra. In 2003 the latter two groups were honored by visits from their respective spiritual leaders, Syedna Mohammed Bourhanuddin Saheb of the Bohra, who came from Bombay, and the Aga Khan IV (born in 1937), with the active cooperation of the Malagasy government, which is eager to promote foreign investment.

An interesting development has been the creation of Islamic missions at Morondava (in 1982) and Tulear (in 1985) and the ensuing gathering of indigenous Malagasy proselytes, who are recognizable by their dress, which consists of a long brown robe and a brown scarf on the head. They belong to the Khodja tradition, itself related to the Shiite martyr Husayn ibn 'Ali. The annual celebration of their religious festival, Ashura, is marked by a procession of flagellants in the streets. This form of militant Islam is a new but marginal phenomenon in Madagascar.

Indigenous forms of Islam are endemic on Madagascar's southeastern coast. The Antambahoaka and Antaimoro communities, for example, combine Islamic and Malagasy customs. The same can be said of the descendants of old Antalaotra clans in the Northwest. The Antankarana people in the North are a special case. The Antankarana became familiar with Islamic customs brought by Arab sailors and traders. But a turning point occurred in 1843, when their king, Tsimiaro, pressed by the army of Ranavalona I, made a vow to convert if he and his people could escape an attack. Officially, then, the Antankarana are Muslims, but they celebrate the traditional Tsangantsaina (mast-raising festival) nonetheless. Efforts have been made by Muslims from abroad to make the Antankarana better Muslims. For example, Ahmad al-Kabir, a Muslim missionary from the Comoros, worked among the Antankarana from 1896 to 1919.

Marc Spindler

See Also Vol. I: *African Indigenous Beliefs, Anglian/Episcopal, Christianity, Lutheran, Reformed Christianity, Roman Catholicism*

Bibliography

Estrade, Jean-Marie. *Un culte de possession à Madagascar: Le tromba.* Paris: Éditions Anthropos, 1977.

Evers, Sandra, and Marc Spindler. *Cultures of Madagascar: Ebb and Flow of Influences.* Leiden: International Institute for Asian Studies, 1995.

Gueunier, Noël Jacques. *Les chemins de l'islam à Madagascar.* Paris: Harmattan; Nanterre: Éditions Man Safara, 1994.

Hübsch, Bruno, ed. *Madagascar et le christianisme: Histoire oecuménique.* Paris: Karthala, 1993.

Lahady, Pascal. *Le culte betsimisaraka et son système symbolique.* Fianarantsoa, Madagascar: Ambozontany, 1979.

Lupo, Pietro. *Discours sur Dieu: Perceptions malgaches, africaines et chrétiennes.* Antananarivo, Madagascar: Ambozontany, forthcoming.

Middleton, Karen, ed. *Ancestors, Power and History in Madagascar.* Leiden: E.J. Brill, 1999.

Sauter, Jean. "Centres de guérison et leurs bergers dans les mouvements de réveil de Madagascar." In *L'espace missionnaire.* Edited by Gilles Routhier and Frédéric Laugrand, 213–27. Paris: Karthala, 2002.

Sharp, Lesley A. *The Possessed and the Dispossessed: Spirits, Identity, and Power in a Madagascar Migrant Town.* Berkeley and Los Angeles: University of California Press, 1993.

Spindler, Marc. "The Biblical Impact on Modern Malagasy Literature." *Exchange* 25, no. 2 (1996): 106–18.

———. "Theological Developments in Madagascar." *Exchange* 12, no. 35 (1983): 1–43.

Malawi

POPULATION 10,701,824

ROMAN CATHOLIC 29 percent

PRESBYTERIAN 25 percent

MUSLIM 13 percent

PENTECOSTAL/CHARISMATIC 8 percent

ANGLICAN 6 percent

AFRICAN INITIATED CHURCHES 5 percent

SEVENTH-DAY ADVENTIST 4 percent

BAPTIST 3 percent

OTHER (AFRICAN INDIGENOUS BELIEFS, JEHOVAH'S WITNESSES, BAHAI, RASTAFARIAN) 3 percent

NONRELIGIOUS 4 percent

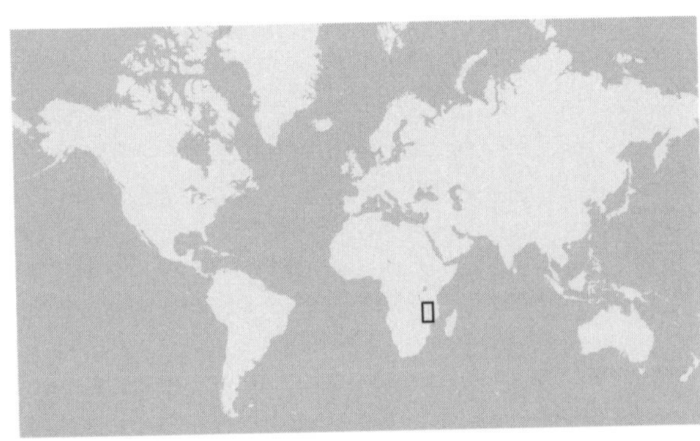

Country Overview

INTRODUCTION The Republic of Malawi, formerly known as Nyasaland (Land of the Lake), is a mountainous country in eastern Central Africa that includes Lake Malawi (Lake Nyassa). It shares borders with Zambia, Mozambique, and Tanzania. Agriculture is the backbone of Malawi's economy, with tobacco, tea, cotton, and sugarcane the main cash crops and maize, millet, cassava, and potatoes the main food crops. Malawi's varied ethnic groups include the Mang'anja (Nyanja), Yao, Sena, and Lomwe in the south; the Chewa and Ngoni in the central region; and the Ngoni, Tumbuka, Ngonde, Tonga, and Lambya in the north. The two official languages are Chinyanja (Chichewa) in southern and central Malawi and Chitumbuka in northern Malawi.

In 1859 David Livingstone, a Scottish missionary explorer, made Malawi known to Britain for evangelization. Protestant missionaries from Europe and South Africa began pouring into the country. Portuguese-sponsored Catholic missionaries arrived in 1889. To forestall a Portuguese attempt to annex Malawi to their possessions in Central and Southern Africa, Scottish missionaries prevailed on Britain to declare a protectorate over Malawi. The British established a colonial administration in Malawi in 1891.

In 1953 Malawi became part of the imposed Federation of Rhodesia and Nyasaland, which was so bitterly opposed by the Africans that it was terminated in 1958. This event gave impetus to a nationalist movement for self-rule. Britain granted Malawi independence in 1964. The Malawi Congress Party formed the first government under Dr. Hastings Kamuzu Banda, but it turned dictatorial and had a bad record of human rights abuses. The Catholic bishop's Lenten Pastoral Letter of 1992 exposed the regime's violations of human rights. A referendum held in 1993 showed that the majority of the people wanted a multiparty political government, which came into effect in 1994. In the 1994 and 1999 general elections, a Muslim presidential candidate, Dr. Bakili Muluzi of the United Democratic Front, won consecutively—a rare event in southern Africa.

Traditional African religions survive alongside Christianity, but few claim sole allegiance to them. Islam arrived in the 1840s and has a large following in Malawi. Bahai and Rastafarian groups are small.

RELIGIOUS TOLERANCE The 1964 constitution (revised in 1993) guarantees freedom of worship. Tensions between Christian churches and some traditional religionists, however, particularly over locally based traditional religious institutions such as possession cults, healing cults, and rites of transition, have sometimes led to confrontation. The Catholic Church and Protestant denominations (Anglicans and Presbyterians) have established ecumenical committees, such as the Christian Service Committee, the Christian Health Association, and the Public Affairs Committee for monitoring good governance (the latter includes Muslims), which foster unity of purpose. The election of a Muslim president in a Christian-dominated country is a significant mark of religious tolerance. Christian-Muslim relations have generally been good, though sporadic outbursts of violence occurred in 2000 (the burning of mosques by Christians in the north) and 2003 (the destruction of church property by Muslims).

Major Religion

CHRISTIANITY

DATE OF ORIGIN 1861 C.E.

NUMBER OF FOLLOWERS 8.6 million

HISTORY During his Zambezi Expedition (1858–64) the missionary explorer David Livingstone identified the Shire Highlands in Southern Malawi as an area suitable for European settlement, one he hoped might become the gateway to Africa for "Christianity and commerce." Inspired by this vision, Protestant missionaries

The cathedral of the Anglican Church in Malawi. Anglican missions established themselves in Malawi in 1861. © ANDREW BANNISTER; GALLO IMAGES/CORBIS.

from England, Scotland, France, the Netherlands, and South Africa began arriving in Malawi. Politically the missionaries carried out their work under the protection of the local chiefs. Between 1861 and 1901, 12 different Christian missions established themselves in various parts of Malawi: the Universities Mission to Central Africa (Anglican, 1861), the Livingstonia Mission of the Free Church of Scotland (1875), the Blantyre Mission of the Established Church of Scotland (1876), the Dutch Reformed Church (1889), the Seventh-day Baptist—Plainfield (1898), the Zambezi Industrial Mission (1892), the Nyasa Industrial Mission (1893), the Baptist Industrial Mission of Scotland (1895), the South African General Mission (1900), the Seventh-day Adventist Mission (1901), and the Roman Catholic Church (1901). In 1900 John Chilembwe, a Malawian, introduced the Providence Industrial Mission from the United States in his home area, Chiradzulu.

Catholicism arrived in Malawi in 1889. The Missionaries of Africa (the White Fathers), sponsored by the Portuguese, established the first Roman Catholic Mission at Mponda in Mangochi District. The Catholic mission was withdrawn in 1891, however, when Protestant missionaries (actively supported by Livingstone, who wanted the area reserved for Protestant work) pressured the British government to declare a protectorate over Malawi. In 1901 the Catholic Montfort Missionaries made a new beginning at Nzama in Ntcheu District.

The Catholic Church has overtaken the other denominations in numerical strength and infrastructure. The worldwide communion of the church has ensured a steady supply of highly organized missionary congregations and material resources for expansion. In the pioneering era (1861–1901), when different denominations laid claim to specific spheres of influence, the Catholics (as latecomers) were initially directed to take charge of the large influx of immigrant populations from Mozambique. Many, such as the Lomwe in the south, responded favorably because they needed patronage to integrate into their host country. Because Catholic conversions occurred mostly among the peasantry and neglected immigrants, Catholic Christians were slow to engage in the capitalist economy and become politically conscious. Catholicism's main attractions for Malawians have been the rituals associated with mystery; the moral teaching that does not forbid alcohol consumption; the absence of dietary regulations; and the authoritarian organization, which has some resemblances to traditional religions. Also, membership did not require literacy in the Bible but rather knowledge of doctrine.

Pentecostalism came to Malawi from South Africa in two waves. The first, in 1923, was a genuine indigenous religious movement called Zion. A decade later the Pentecostal churches arrived. Unlike the earlier churches these were introduced by returning Malawian labor migrants. During the 1920s Malawian-instituted churches began to emerge in some parts of the country.

EARLY AND MODERN LEADERS The achievement of Dr. David Livingstone, the great missionary explorer of south-central Africa, was honored in the creation of the Livingstonia Mission in northern Malawi by the Free Church of Scotland. Dr. Robert Laws, a minister and physician, was in charge of the Livingstonia Mission from 1878 until his retirement in 1927. Laws made the first coherent attempt to put Livingstone's enclave policy into action—to set up a nucleus for the introduction of legitimate commerce in opposition to the slave trade. He was convinced that the creation of a viable Christian community could be achieved only if higher training was offered. Under his inspiration the Overtoun Institution (named after Lord Overtoun, one of the Scottish businessmen who lent support to the mission) was founded at Khondowe in 1894, offering training in many skills and liberal arts to students both local and from neighboring countries. The Livingstonia Synod, which has founded Livingstonia University on the same premises, has carried Dr. Laws's vision further.

The Very Reverend Jonathan Sangaya, a village parish minister, became the first Malawian General Secretary for the Presbyterian Synod of Blantyre, serving from 1962 until his death in 1979. He was also elected Moderator of the General Synod of the Church of Central Africa Presbyterian. Through his leadership and initiative, important ecumenical service organs of the church (such as the Christian Service Committee, the joint Anglican-Presbyterian Chilema Lay Training Centre, the Private Hospital Association of Malawi, and the Theological Training by Extension in Malawi) came into being. He strengthened corporate work among Protestant Christians of various traditions through the Christian Council of Malawi. In the totalitarian regime of his day, he readily sacrificed his friendship and popularity with those in political power when the need to do so arose.

In the Catholic Church the devolution of authority into local hands allowed the Episcopal consecration in 1957 of Father Cornelius Chitsulo (died in 1984), who had become the first Malawian ordained priest in 1937. In 1959 Chitsulo became the Vicar Apostolic of Dedza, and when the national hierarchy was established, he was named the first indigenous bishop of Dedza. He helped establish a modern catechetical school and junior seminary and founded a women's religious congregation, the Presentation Sisters. He also presided over a process of liturgical renewal as mandated by the Second Vatican Council (1962–65).

MAJOR THEOLOGIANS AND AUTHORS Bishop Patrick Augustine Kalilombe, a member of the Society of the Missionaries of Africa, or White Fathers, and former bishop of Lilongwe Diocese (1972–76), has written extensively on basic Christian communities as a strategy for grassroots evangelization. Officials in Rome, suspicious of these communities and the liberation theology movement associated with them, accused Bishop Kalilombe of representing an anti-hierarchical, rebelliously popular, and near-Marxist ecclesiology. While in exile from 1976 to 1996, Bishop Kalilombe was elected vice president of the Ecumenical Association of Third World Theologians, a group charged with developing and practicing theologies appropriate for the needs of the Third World. The African Synod that met in Nairobi in 1995 unanimously adopted small Christian communities as a way of engaging the ordinary faithful in church life.

Dr. Isabel Apawo Phiri (born in 1957) has struggled on behalf of women for recognition of their personal relationship to God and for public manifestation of this in open ministry. General coordinator of the Continental Circle for Concerned African Women Theologians since 2002, Dr. Phiri also served as director of the Centre for Contextual Theology in Southern Africa from 1997 to 2001.

HOUSES OF WORSHIP AND HOLY PLACES Mjamba Park in Limbe, where Pope John Paul II first celebrated Mass during his pastoral visit in 1989, has now become a meeting place for ecumenical prayers, particularly during moments of political uncertainty. On Michiru Hill in Blantyre stands a huge cross solemnly erected by the Catholic archbishop of Blantyre. Pilgrims from all denominations and neighboring countries make stations of the Cross to the hilltop or simply go there to pray.

Malawian Presbyterians still maintain the more-than-century-old churches built by pioneer missionaries in Blantyre (Saint Michael and All Angels), Zomba, and Livingstonia. Anglicans go to Likoma Cathedral on Likoma Island. Catholics have prayer centers at Carmel in Kasungu and at the Poor Clare's Monastery in Lilongwe, which holds inculturated liturgical celebrations.

WHAT IS SACRED? Places of worship are regarded as sacred by all Christian denominations in Malawi. Malawian Christians also consider as sacred cemeteries; such consecrated persons as priests, ministers, pastors, and nuns; and objects reserved for worship. Any violation of the sacred is believed to provoke the wrath of God, as well as that of the spirits of the deceased, who may retaliate by inflicting misfortune.

HOLIDAYS AND FESTIVALS Malawian Christians celebrate the major holidays on the liturgical calendar, as well as some holidays unique to Malawi. National Day of Prayer (4 July) commemorates political independence from British rule and is celebrated with an interfaith worship service of thanksgiving. On a locally specified Sunday during the harvest (July or August), the faithful bring part of their produce for the year to church and join in thanksgiving prayers. Some of the food goes to the poor, while the remainder is left for the support of the church. All faith communities also celebrate John Chilembwe Day (15 January) and Martyr's Day (3 March) with prayer and laying of wreaths to commemorate nationalist heroes of all religious persuasions.

MODE OF DRESS Malawian Christian women generally cover their body from shoulder to knee in public. Most women wear a long dress or skirt and a blouse, with a large scarf wholly or partially covering their hair. Many women also wear a wrap called a *chitenje* below the shoulders. It has become fashionable for women to wear trousers, but Christians disapprove of tight trousers, and miniskirts are not allowed in public. Some local church communities have ruled that women may not wear trousers or shorts in church. Christian men wear trousers. People who belong to pious associations have their own uniforms, which they wear on special occasions.

DIETARY PRACTICES Apart from Seventh-day Adventists, Malawian Christians have no dietary regulations. In predominantly Muslim areas, Christians refrain from eating pork in order to maintain good neighborliness. Local custom remains strong in rural societies, where even among Christians certain plants or animals are considered totems, and to eat them would violates ancestral regulations.

RITUALS Malawian Christian worship services are held in the local language—Chichewa (Chinyanja) or Chitumbuka—and are led by ministers, priests, or church elders. The use of African music, drums, and rattles in Christian services is widespread. The Pentecostal and Anglo-Catholic traditions include dancing, hand clapping, and ululating (making loud, repetitive, high-pitched noises) in their services.

A customary engagement ceremony called a *chinkhoswe*, usually held in the bride's home, precedes a Christian church wedding. The highlight of the ceremony comes when the marriage representatives (*ankhoswe*) exchange a cock and a hen that symbolize the groom and the bride and share a roast chicken to emphasize the union of their respective extended families. Christian adults in good standing with the church may receive burial rites, preceded by an all-night vigil during which relatives and friends sing funeral hymns as a mark of respect. These traditional rituals have been incorporated into Christian practice.

RITES OF PASSAGE Many Malawian Christians celebrate birth, adulthood, marriage, and death by combining traditional African religious customs and Christian customs. Communities hold birth and puberty rites for both boys and girls. Newborn children are given a name and clan identity and are shown to the community. Certain denominations celebrate puberty rites in church to prevent their followers from reverting to the ancestral rites. A fair percentage of Christians prefer the ancestral practices, however, as they find the Christian version of the initiation not sufficiently detailed to address the crucial physical aspects of growing up in an African context.

Customary marriage—still recognized by the state—abounds in gift exchanges to emphasize new family ties and obligations. Burial rites are marked by the offering of food and drink to settle the spirit of the deceased. Not all Christian denominations have incorporated elements from the customary marriage and death rituals.

MEMBERSHIP Christian church membership is either real through baptism or assumed through association. With the rise of charismatic ministries, which are usually interdenominational, Christians from any denomination are free to have a supplementary membership to any group of their choice; the charismatic groups thrive on supplementary membership. Some, though, like the Living Waters, the Calvary Family, and the Charismatic Renewal Churches (founded respectively by Pastor Madalitso Mbewe, Pastor Stanley Ndovi, and Father Mark Kambalazaza), have become full-fledged churches and require their followers to become full members.

The Catholic Church has gained converts in many areas through its vast network of schools, hospitals, and other institutions that cater to people in need. Evangelization at grassroots level occurs through "inculturation of the Gospel" (expressing the Gospel through local culture), the key to church growth.

SOCIAL JUSTICE Malawian's awareness of social justice issues grew after a bitter experience with the oppressive Malawi Congress Party government (1964–1993). At the dawn of multiparty politics in 1994, a Catholic Commission for Justice and Peace was created to educate and sensitize Malawians to basic human rights and gender issues through Training for Transformation programs. The Presbyterian churches have a Church and Society program for civic education in their presbyteries. The Public Affairs Commission, created in 1992 and composed of Catholics, Presbyterians, and Muslims, monitors the consolidation of the democratic process and the governance of the country. Christian organizations, such as the Centre for Social Concern, the Centre for Youth and Children, and World Vision, work to alleviate poverty. Women within the churches run special committees on gender issues geared toward improving the lot of Malawian women in social, political, and economic life. A Violence against Women campaign is carried out in the streets of major towns and cities, where women carrying banners march in large numbers on certain occasions. The rights for the disabled are advanced by a special government ministry and the Malawi Council for the Handicapped.

SOCIAL ASPECTS Malawian customary law regards marriage as a union between two lineages and, therefore, ideally monogamous. Polygyny is accepted by local custom, however, for reasons of infertility, incompatibility, child care, and sometimes prestige. All mainstream Malawian Christian churches unequivocally condemn the practice. The churches require Christians to be married in church, over and above customary marriage; if they are not, church officials mete out sanctions. Customary law permits divorce and remarriage after all means for reconciliation have been exhausted. The Christian churches are divided on this issue.

POLITICAL IMPACT On various occasions Malawian churches have sent pastoral letters addressing the government on issues of national concern. Historically the state has listened to the voice of the churches, though sometimes reluctantly. The government has expressed its appreciation many times for the important role the churches are playing in the development of the country. The Anglican, Catholic, and Presbyterian Churches have sent official statements opposing and bitterly criticizing the 2002 constitutional amendment allowing an open or third term for the incumbent president.

CONTROVERSIAL ISSUES The national policy on population control supports all birth control methods, including birth control devices and voluntary abortion. The churches have condemned abortion and have advocated natural family planning methods in their health units. Government agencies also promote the use of condoms as a means of preventing the spread of HIV and AIDS, while the faith communities widely oppose the practice.

CULTURAL IMPACT By the early 1920s, the Bible and the cathechism had been translated into Malawi's vernacular languages, especially Chinyanja. Translated and nontranslated Euro-Christian hymns had also been introduced at religious gatherings and in all Malawian churches, to the extent that neighboring countries, including Portuguese-speaking Mozambique, adopted the hymns as well. The Malawi national anthem, which includes several references to God, was composed by a Catholic priest in the 1960s.

European-looking sacred buildings, such as the Catholic and Presbyterian Cathedrals in Blantyre and Lilongwe, are scattered throughout Malawi. Most of these relics of the Christian colonial past—some gothic, some more modern—are British in style, with yellowish or reddish brick (rarely painted), large entrances, and a bell tower.

In contrast to earlier intolerance, some Christian churches in Malawi have created museums of African art and history. Many churches have shown respect for traditional African artistic styles by training young Malawians as artists and preserving traditional masks, which early missionaries tried to eliminate.

Other Religions

Islam, the oldest nonindigenous religion, arrived in Malawi in the 1840s with the first Arabs from Zanzibar, who were traders in ivory and slaves. Malawi now has the largest number of Muslims of all the Central Africa nations. Until the mid-1970s the country was cut off from the Islamic world, with few connections to the wider *ummah* (Islamic community). Since then contact has been reestablished, occasioned by the Islamic revival in the Middle East, which insists on a return to Koranic orthodoxy. Some of the richer Muslim countries have given generous support to educational and mosque-building projects. All Malawian Muslims are Sunni and belong to the Shafiite school.

Most Malawian Christians have retained such traditional legacies as ancestor veneration, polygynous practices, and belief in sorcery and witchcraft as the explanation of disease, death, and calamity. Boy's and girl's puberty initiation rites (which largely do not involve circumcision and rarely clitoridectomy) are celebrated in all Malawian traditional societies. At the village level cults of possession or affliction (*vimbuza, malombo, nantongwe,* and *mabzyoka*), concerned with the exorcism or accommodation of ancestral spirits, perform dramatic séances. At puberty rites and the funerals of important people, masked dancers (*nyau*) represent ancestral spirits who have come back to the village to interact with the living. Christian missionaries abhorred and tried to eliminate *nyau,* because participants performed at night often covered only by banana leaves and instilled feared in the populace.

The Jehovah's Witnesses came to Malawi in 1908 through the preaching of a Malawian, Elliot Kenan Kamwana. Before the 1963 elections that led to independence and even later, the Malawi Congress Party regime persecuted the Jehovah's Witnesses for refusing, on religious grounds, to buy party membership cards, a nationwide symbol of political involvement. More than 10,000 fled to neighboring Mozambique and Zambia; many returned to Malawi after the regime fell in 1993.

The Bahai faith has established centers from which to proclaim its messages of peace. The Rastafari movement, originally from the West Indies, is popular among Malawian youth, but the ritual smoking of marijuana is frowned upon by Christians, Muslims, and other law-abiding citizens.

J.C. Chakanza

See Also Vol. 1: *Christianity, Islam, Roman Catholicism*

Bibliography

Breugel, J.W.M. van. *Chewa Traditional Religion.* Blantyre: Christian Literature Association in Malawi, 2001.

Chakanza, J.C., ed. *Islam Week in Malawi.* Blantyre: Christian Literature Association in Malawi, 1998.

Kalilombe, P.A. *Doing Theology at the Grassroots: Theological Essays from Malawi.* Gweru: Mambo Press, 1999.

Linden, I., and J. Linden. *Catholics, Peasants, and Chewa Resistance in Nyasaland.* Berkeley: University of California Press, 1974.

Livingstone, D., and C. Livingstone. *Narrative of an Expedition to the Zambezi and Its Tributaries, and of the Discovery of Lakes Shirwa and Nyassa, 1858–1864.* London: John Murray, 1865.

McCracken, J. *Politics and Christianity in Malawi 1875–1940: The Impact of the Livingstonia Mission on the Northern Province.* Cambridge: Cambridge University Press, 1977.

Phiri, Isabel A. *Women, Presbyterianism, and Patriarchy.* Blantyre: Christian Literature Association in Malawi, 1997.

Schoffeleers, J.M. *In Search of Truth and Justice: Confrontations between Church and State in Malawi, 1992–1994.* Blantyre: Christian Literature Association in Malawi, 1999.

Shepperson, G., and T. Price. *Independent African: John Chilembwe and the Origins, Setting, and Significance of the Nyasaland Native Rising of 1915.* Edinburgh: Edinburgh University Press, 1958.

Malaysia

POPULATION 23,274,690

MUSLIM 61 percent

BUDDHIST 19 percent

CHRISTIAN 9 percent

HINDU 6 percent

CHINESE RELIGIONS 3 percent

OTHER 2 percent

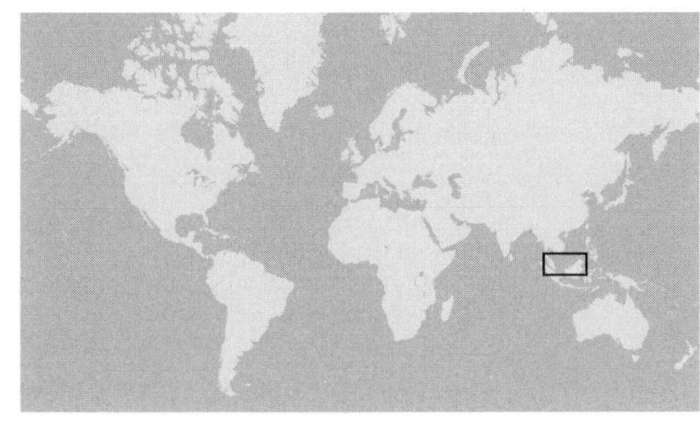

Country Overview

INTRODUCTION The Southeast Asian nation of Malaysia is home to an ethnically and religiously diverse population. Its complex ethnographic makeup can be attributed to its geographic situation and its long history as a maritime trading center. Malays, the overwhelming majority of whom are Muslim, make up about two thirds of the country's population. Ethnic Chinese form the largest minority population, and most of them are Buddhists or followers of traditional Chinese religions like Taoism and Confucianism. There are smaller groups of Indians, Pakistanis, Sri Lankans, and indigenous peoples. The Indians tend to be Hindu, and although its numbers are small, Christianity is the fastest growing religion in the country. The country is divided into two parts: Peninsular Malaysia (also known as West Malaysia or Malaya), on the Malay Peninsula, and East Malaysia, which occupies much of the northwestern coast of the island of Borneo. Peninsular Malaysia is bordered to the north by Thailand and is separated from the Republic of Singapore to the south by the Johor Strait. To the east of Peninsular Malaysia is the South China Sea; to the west are the Straits of Malacca and the Indonesian island of Sumatra. On Borneo East Malaysia shares land borders with Indonesia and the small sultanate of Brunei.

RELIGIOUS TOLERANCE Although Islam is the official religion of Malaysia, the Malaysian constitution guarantees all citizens the freedom to profess and practice their own faith, as well as the right to propagate their faith. Under a separate article, however, the constitution grants states—or, in Kuala Lumpur and Luaban, the federal government—the right to "control and restrict the propagation of any religious doctrine among persons professing the religion of Islam." The constitution also accords every religious group the right to establish and maintain institutions for the education of its children and to provide therein instruction in its religion. In addition federal law permits special grants of financial aid for the establishment and maintenance of Muslim institutions and for the instruction of Muslims in their professed faith. Nevertheless, the government is fairly intolerant of Muslims whom it perceives to be a threat to the country's security and unity and of non-Muslims

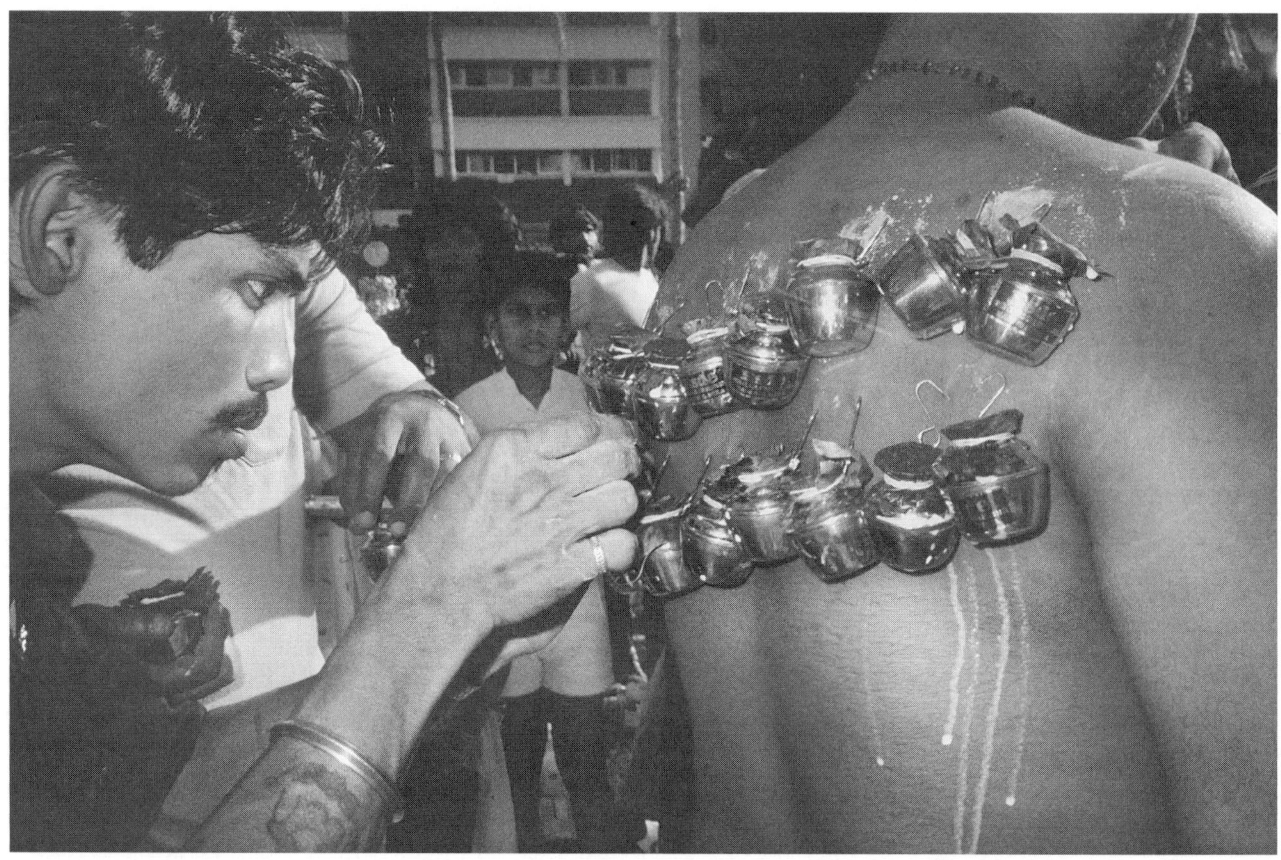

A Hindu man hooks jars of white liquid into the skin of another man's back during the Thaipusam festival. During the festival these celebrants do penance by piercing their cheeks and tongues with skewers and small spears and their bodies with hooks. © ROMAN SOUMAR/CORBIS.

who abuse their religious freedom or violate societal norms.

Major Religion

SUNNI ISLAM

DATE OF ORIGIN 1400 C.E.
NUMBER OF FOLLOWERS 14.2 million

HISTORY Before Islam spread to what is now Malaysia, the region's culture was largely influenced by Hindu-Buddhist traditions. According to some scholars Islam also entered Malaysia via India, while others argue it was introduced by traders who came by land from China. Whatever its source, by the beginning of the fourteenth century Islam had reached the Malay Peninsula and the neighboring Indonesian archipelago. The sultanate of Malacca, whose strategic port controlled shipping through the Strait of Malacca in the fifteenth century, was a key factor in the spread of Islam throughout Malaysia and beyond. Parameswara, who ruled Malacca from about 1400 until his death in 1424, converted to Islam upon his marriage to a Muslim princess and took the name Iskandar Shah. Other members of the Malay elite and merchant class followed his example, marrying Muslims exclusively, and the practice eventually spread among rural Malay farmers and traders who visited Malacca.

In 1511 the Malaccan sultanate fell to the Portuguese. In 1641 the Dutch took over Malacca, which they in turn conceded to the British in 1824. Thereafter—through treaties, relentless political pressure, and diplomacy—the British slowly extended their control over all the states of the Malay Peninsula. Islamic practices, including worship and the establishment of religious institutions, were not affected by the British colonial expansion.

During World War II the Japanese occupied the Malay Peninsula from 1941 to 1945. Soon after the war a number of Islamically-oriented Malay national movements and political parties were established in an effort to liberate the region from foreign control. The Federation of Malaya, which included all of the formerly British territories on the peninsula except Singapore, became independent in 1957. In 1963 the Bornean states of Sarawak and Sabah joined the Federation of Malaya to form Malaysia.

EARLY AND MODERN LEADERS A number of Muslims led Malaysia's struggle against British colonizers. In 1914 Hj Muhammad Hassan—also known by the nickname Tok Janggut—established an Islamic state within the northern peninsular state of Kelantan before being killed by British forces in 1915. In the neighboring state of Terengganu, Hj Abdul Rahman bin Abdul Hamid, a Muslim scholar and politician, revolted against the British Protective Agreement in 1928. Hj Ahmad Fuad bin Hassan became the first president and spiritual leader of the Parti Islam SeMalaysia (PAS), now a powerful Islamic political party, in 1951. Tuan Guru Dato Nik Abdul Aziz Nik Mat (born in 1932), the supreme advisor of PAS and chief minister of the state of Kelantan, and Dato Seri Tuan Guru Haji Abd Hadi Awang (born in 1946), president of PAS and chief minister of the state of Terengganu, are considered the most significant contemporary Islamic political figures in Malaysia.

MAJOR THEOLOGIANS AND AUTHORS Most of the contemporary literature on Islam in Malaysia has been written in Bahasa Melayu, the Malay language, by such Muslim authors as Sheikh Daud B. Abdullah B. Idris al-Fatani (eighteenth and nineteenth centuries), Seyd Alawi B. Tahir al-Haddad (1855–1907), and Mahayudin bin Hj Yahya (born in 1942). Notable writers in English include Muhammad Kamal Hassan (born in 1942), rector of the International Islamic University Malaysia since 1999 and an authority on Islam in Southeast Asia, and Syed Muhammad Naquib al-Attas (born in 1931), the founder of the International Institute of Islamic Thought and Civilization, who has written on Islamization theory, Islamic history and civilization, Sufism, and Islamic intellectual institutions in Malaysia.

HOUSES OF WORSHIP AND HOLY PLACES Islamic places of worship in Malaysia can be divided into two categories: large mosques like those found in Putra Jaya, Shah Alam, and Kuala Lumpur, and smaller prayer halls, or *suraus,* which are found throughout the country along highways and in such places as airports, hospitals, and government offices. All universities in Malaysia have their own mosques. In accordance with pre-Islamic customs of Hindu-Buddhist origin, some Muslims consider the tombs of certain saints holy.

WHAT IS SACRED? Like Muslims elsewhere Malaysian Muslims hold three places in the world sacred: Mecca and Medina in Saudi Arabia and Jerusalem. Each year, during the last month of the Islamic calendar, thousands of Malaysians perform their mandatory pilgrimage to Mecca, while many others pay optional visits (*umrah*) to the holy city at other times during the year.

Muslims in Malaysia observe certain taboos of Hindu-Buddhist, Islamic, and indigenous origin related to pregnancy and childbearing. Some Malay Muslims also believe that *bomohs,* or traditional healers, possess supernatural or magical powers and can cure their patients through the use of plant and animal parts.

HOLIDAYS AND FESTIVALS Muslims in Malaysia celebrate a number of religious holidays and festivals that take place according to the Islamic lunar calendar. The most significant are Hari Raya Aidilfitri, a festival that marks the end of the fasting month of Ramadan; Hari Raya Aidiladha, the festival of sacrifice; Awal Muharram, the Islamic new year; and Muhammad's birthday. The most popular Islamic holiday is Hari Raya Aidilfitri, which officially runs for two days but in fact is celebrated for almost a month. Houses are washed, new curtains are hung, and special foods are prepared—all for the monthlong open house, a time for visiting with friends and relatives. During the holiday all members of the household gather after the morning prayers and pay homage to the elders of the family. On Hari Raya Aidilfitri Muslims greet each other by saying "Selamat Hari Raya" ("Happy Hari Raya"), and children wear new clothes. At this time of year the public is allowed to visit the palaces of the Malay sultans, as well as the homes of government ministers and other officials who hold open houses. Other Muslim religious holidays—such as the first day of Ramadan, Nuzul al-Quran (Revelation of the Koran), and Israk Mikraj, which commemorates the ascension of Muhammad—are celebrated according to state laws.

MODE OF DRESS Muslim men in Malaysia often wear traditional Malay dress, particularly on ceremonial occasions. The outfit consists of two pieces, a *baju* (a loose shirt) and a pair of long pants. A colorful sarong (a long strip of cloth) is wrapped around the waist and draped over the pants. The accompanying head cover is a black *songkok* (a simple cap). During prayers men wear white caps.

Muslim women in Malaysia often wear the *baju kurung,* which consists of a loose blouse and a sarong, or the *baju kebaya,* which features a fitted blouse worn over a sarong. A headscarf is mandatory for Muslim women during prayers and other religious events. When performing prayers Muslim women wear a *telekong,* which consists of two pieces of white clothing that cover the entire body except for the face and hands.

Generally, Malays prefer shiny and colorful attire. Members of the royalty often wear gold, especially on official occasions. In urban areas many Muslim men and women wear Western clothing, though the number of women wearing the *tudung* (headscarf) has increased.

DIETARY PRACTICES Malaysian Muslims closely adhere to Islamic dietary restrictions. For the most part they do not drink alcohol or eat pork. They are also conscientious about ensuring that the slaughter of animals for food is carried out in accordance with Islamic law. The Malaysian government issues certificates to food outlets that sell *halal* (permissible) foods, and signs indicating the availability of *halal* foods are prominently displayed at the entrances of shops and restaurants, including stores operated by Western restaurant chains like McDonald's, KFC, and Pizza Hut.

RITUALS Muslim rituals related to worship services, prayer, pilgrimage, marriage, and burial in Malaysia are all conducted according to Islamic law and are performed in much the same way as they are in other Muslim communities. In addition Muslims in Malaysia practice *adat istiadat,* which are customs and traditions that pertain to such events as birth, marriage, and death. *Adat istiadat diraja* are the customs and traditions surrounding these events that are followed by the royal court.

Islamic rituals in Malaysia are performed according to the Shafiite school of law of the Sunni branch of Islam. As a rule most socio-religious events in the country, including official ceremonies, begin with a recitation of al-Fatiha, the opening chapter in the Koran, and end with a *doa,* or supplication, in Arabic. Malaysian Muslims also like to participate in the rituals of mystical orders called *tariqahs.* One such ritual is the *dhkir,* a special supplication that is made on certain occasions, including religious events, births, weddings, and deaths. *Dhkir* rituals usually last about one hour and usually are held in a local mosque or a house. Malay foods are served at the end of the session.

RITES OF PASSAGE There are no Muslim rites of passage that are distinctive to Malaysia.

MEMBERSHIP Most Muslims in Malaysia are members of the Sunni branch of Islam, though a small number of Shias are found there as well. There are also a number of Islamic deviationist groups called *ajaran sesat,* which are often found among mystic communities.

Dawah, or propagation, activities are undertaken by both the government and nongovernmental organizations (NGOs). Some NGOs in Malaysia that have been involved in Islamic propagation or working with new converts include Persatuan Darul Fitrah, Persatuan Al-Hunaffa, Angkatan Belia Islam Malaysia (ABIM), Jemaah Islam Malaysia (JIM), the Malaysian Chinese Muslim Association (MACMA), Belia Perkim, and Persatuan Ulama Malaysia (PUM). While religious propagation via modern media—including the Internet—in Malay, English, Tamil, Mandarin, and even Arabic has resulted in the growth of small ethnic Chinese and other ethnically-based Muslim communities, the majority of converts to Islam in Malaysia are the result of intermarriages among Muslim Malays and people of other faiths. In addition to Malay, Chinese, and indigenous Muslims, there are also a number of Muslims in Malaysia who trace their roots to India.

SOCIAL JUSTICE While economic power in Malaysia is in the hands of the ethnic Chinese community, the Malays control the country's political institutions and public sector. The Chinese tend to reside in towns and cities throughout the country, while the Muslim Malays predominate in the farming and coastal areas. Malays who live on the peninsula's east coast, the majority of whom work in low-paying farm or fishery jobs, generally have lower incomes than those on the west coast. Various quotas—including educational quotas—have been established to improve the economic status and social conditions of the *bumiputra,* or sons of the soil, as the Malays are known.

The legal system in Malaysia is based on British civil law, with a separate system of Shariah courts. Although the government has maintained a fair level of peace and stability in the country, its implementation of the Internal Security Act to quell tensions between religious groups has been of great concern to both Muslims and non-Muslims, especially because people can be detained without trial under the act and because the act is subject to abuse.

SOCIAL ASPECTS Marriage among Muslims in Malaysia is conducted according to Islamic law, which operates entirely within the state and addresses such other matters as divorce, dowers, maintenance, adoption, and legal guardianship. Generally, Malays prefer to have as many children as possible. A large percentage of Muslim women in Malaysia work in full-time jobs, in addition to maintaining their households.

POLITICAL IMPACT The first Muslim political party was established in Malaysia in 1948, as the country began to move toward independence, by Abu Bakar al-Bakir. Three years later the Parti Islam SeMalaysia (PAS; Islamic Party of Malaysia) was formed by Ahmad Fuad bin Hassan. Today PAS is the country's main opposition party.

As mentioned above, Malaysia is not an Islamic state, though Islam is the official religion of the nation. Nevertheless, many Muslims in the country believe that the freedom to practice their religion includes the freedom to set up Islamic legal and economic systems, as well as an Islamic state. Concerns that Malaysia might become an Islamic state grew in 1999, when PAS managed to form governments in the states of Kelantan and Terengganu on the northeast coast of Malaysia. The federal government has demonstrated its commitment to its own version of moderate Islam, as well as to the preservation of the current power structure, by dealing forcefully with alleged Islamic militants, in some cases detaining suspects without trial under the Internal Security Act.

CONTROVERSIAL ISSUES The question whether Malaysia may become an Islamic state is one of the most controversial issues in the country. Some scholars argue that because of the particularistic ethnic orientation of Islamic policies adopted by successive governments, it would be difficult for an Islamic social order to emerge. They contend that the government's preoccupation with protecting and preserving the interests of the Malays in multiracial Malaysia has shifted focus from the wider philosophical principles of Islam, such as its universality and its emphasis on equity and justice. Other political observers have noted the Malaysian government's long-held position that it is not feasible to implement Islamic legal and social principles in a multireligious and multicultural society like that of Malaysia, a position it has maintained since Tunku Abdul Rahman (1903–90) became the country's first prime minister in 1957.

CULTURAL IMPACT Islam's association with Malay traditional culture has influenced dress, marriage customs, architecture, music, and dance in Malaysia. Even the Malay martial art *silat* has some Islamic elements. Islamic literature, poetry, drama, and *nashyd* (song) groups like Raihan and Hijaz have flourished in recent years. Despite Malaysian's maintenance and promotion of their traditional Islamic cultural heritage, however, Western culture has grown to have a much greater influence on Malaysian youth.

Other Religions

Malaysia's other religious populations also tend to have strong ethnic associations. The majority of the ethnic Chinese population adheres to Buddhism and such traditional Chinese religions as Taoism and Confucianism. Indians in Malaysia are primarily Hindus, while some *orang asli* (native people) follow shamanist and other traditional belief systems.

Buddhists make up the second largest religious group in Malaysia. Although the majority of Chinese-educated Buddhists in Malaysia are Mahayana Buddhists, many do not distinguish between Buddhist and Chinese folk religious practices and tend to practice a mixture of the two. Consequently, a Malaysian Buddhist may follow the teachings of Confucius and Lao-tzu, participate in ancestor worship, burn papers, offer food and flowers to spirits, and light oil lamps—all of which have no connection with Buddhism in its original form.

There are more than 3,500 Buddhist temples and organizations in Malaysia. Buddhist temples are generally opened daily for devotees to pay homage to the image of Buddha. Attendance is especially high on such occasions as the new moon and full moon. Temples are also the primary venue for Wesak (the Buddha's birthday) and other Buddhist ceremonies, such as those marking the traditional Sinhalese New Year. Many temples hold weekly programs such as Dharma (good conduct or moral instruction) talks, meditation, language and public speaking classes, and religious seminars and talks. The main organization looking after the welfare of Chinese Buddhists in Malaysia is the Malaysia Buddhist Association.

The most important Buddhist festival is Wesak, which has been a public holiday in Malaysia since 1962. The festival's climax is Wesak Day itself, when gatherings are held at Buddhist temples throughout the country. Contributions are traditionally made at this time to schools, hospitals, and organizations for the blind and deaf. Another feature of Wesak is a six-mile candlelight procession around Kuala Lumpur. The procession is attended by a group of monks and nuns, and Buddhist organizations throughout the region contribute floats to the parade.

Many Chinese festivals tend to be localized and are often held in conjunction with the birthdays of different temple deities. Festivities often commence one to two weeks before the actual date of the god's anniversary and may feature processions, Chinese opera performances, the preparation of vegetarian foods, and entranced persons walking on burning coals.

In many Chinese Malaysian homes the family altar is the most important part of the house. These altars often contain a bronze urn for joss sticks, two tall candlesticks, and a small frame listing the date of death of each male ancestor. Family members come to the altar on festival and anniversary days to venerate deceased ancestors.

The Christian community is the fastest growing religious minority in Malaysia. In 1921 Christians made up only 1.7 percent of the country's population, but by 2000 they accounted for 9.1 percent. Although Christians still form a small minority of the population in most states, they make up 27 percent and 37 percent of the population in Sabah and Sarawak, respectively. Approximately 8 percent of the Chinese population of Malaysia is Christian, while a similar percentage of Indians in the country identify themselves as Christian. The primary religious organization representing the Christian community in Malaysia is the Council of Churches of Malaysia.

Domestic Christian rituals can be divided into the categories of individual prayer, family prayer, and house fellowship. In the former an individual may read the Bible alone and then close the session with a prayer. During family prayer, which is usually held in the mornings or in the evenings, one family member typically reads from the Bible, and this is followed by a few devotional songs and a prayer. Families may also open their homes for weekly worship. Malaysian Christians celebrate Christmas, New Year's Day, Good Friday, and Easter. Christmas is a national public holiday, and Good Friday is a public holiday in Sabah and Sarawak.

Hindus make up Malaysia's third largest religious community. Brahmanic Hinduism, which preceded Islam in Malaysia, was first spread among the region's elite and ruling classes. In contemporary Malaysia most Indians are descendants of contract laborers who immigrated during the nineteenth and twentieth centuries. They practice Tamil Nadu and Shaivite forms of Hinduism.

Malaysian Hindus celebrate three major festivals, Diwali, Thaipusam, and Thai Pongal. Diwali (Festival of Lights), which honors Laksmi, the goddess of wealth, is a national holiday and a day of new clothes, food, and fun for Malaysian Hindu children. Thaipusam, which originated in the southern Indian state of Tamil Nadu, is a public holiday in five states. The Thaipusam festival organized by the Maha Mariamman Temple in Kuala Lumpur has become a mammoth affair attended by hundreds of thousands of devotees and visitors, who gather to witness the procession of the great statue and chariot of Lord Murugan, the chief deity of the ancient Tamils, through the streets of the city to the Batu Caves eight miles away. On their shoulders some devotees carry *kavadis,* decorated frames hung with bells and baskets that contain offerings to the deity. Some *kavadi* bearers do penance during the festival by piercing their cheeks and tongues with skewers and small spears and their bodies with hooks. Other devotees bathe in a nearby stream or break coconuts to fulfill vows or to offer thanks to Lord Murugan. Upon reaching the Batu Caves the kavadi bearers complete their pilgrimage by climbing the 272 steps that lead to the temple there.

The Hindu community celebrates Thai Pongal, an annual harvest festival in honor of the sun god, for four days in mid-January. Hindu families reunite to share their joy and harvests with a *pongal,* a dish made with rice and milk. New clothes are prepared and homes are cleaned, painted, and decorated to welcome the festival. On the day of Pongal family members draw a decoration called a *kolam* on the floor with rice flour.

Ahmad Yousif

See Also Vol. I: *Buddhism, Islam, Mahayana Buddhism, Sunnism*

Bibliography

Ackerman, Susan E., and Raymond L.M. Lee. *Heaven in Transition: Non-Muslim Religious Innovation and Ethnic Identity in Malaysia.* Kuala Lumpur: Forum, 1990.

Alhabshi, Syed Othman, and Nik Mustapha Nik Hassan, eds. *Islam and Tolerance.* Kuala Lumpur: Institute of Islamic Understanding Malaysia (IKIM), 1994.

Endicott, Kirk Michael. *An Analysis of Malay Magic.* Oxford: Clarendon Press, 1970.

Hassan, M. Kamal. *Intellectual Discourse at the End of the 2nd Millennium: Concerns of a Muslim-Malay CEO.* Kuala Lumpur: International Islamic University Malaysia, 2001.

Laderman, Carol. *Taming the Wind of Desire: Psychology, Medicine, and Aesthetics in Malay Shamanistic Performance.* Berkeley and Los Angeles: University of California Press, 1991.

Lee, Raymond L.M., and Susan E. Ackerman. *Sacred Tensions: Modernity and Religious Transformation in Malaysia.* Columbia, S.C.: University of South Carolina Press, 1997.

Mutalib, Hussin. *Islam and Ethnicity in Malay Politics.* Singapore: Oxford University Press, 1990.

Muzaffar, Chandra. *Islamic Resurgence in Malaysia.* Petaling Jaya, Malaysia: Fajar Bakti, 1987.

Putra, Tunku Abdul Rahman, Tan Chee Khoon, Chandra Muzaffar, and Lim Kit Siang, eds. *Contemporary Issues on Malaysian Religions.* Petaling Jaya, Malaysia: Pelanduk Publications, 1984.

Yousif, Ahmad F. *Religious Freedom, Minorities and Islam: An Inquiry into the Malaysian Experience.* Kuala Lumpur: Thinker's Library, 1998.

Maldives

POPULATION 275,000

SUNNI ISLAM 100 percent

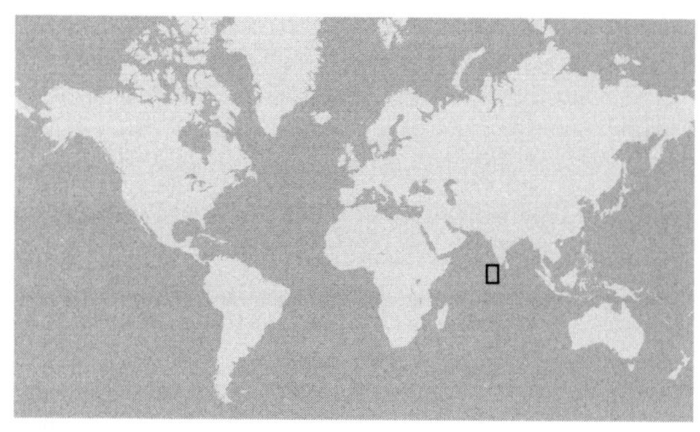

Country Overview

INTRODUCTION The Republic of Maldives, known officially as *Dhivehi Raajjeyge Jumhooriyyaa* and also called Maldive Islands until 1969, is a group of 19 coral atolls and about 1,200 islands in the Indian Ocean. It has a total land area of approximately 116 square miles (300 square kilometers). Only about 200 of the islands are inhabited. Maldives is about 420 miles (675 kilometers) southwest of Sri Lanka.

The Maldivian national language, Dhivehi, is related to Sinhalese, which is spoken in Sri Lanka, and includes words from Arabic and Indian languages. According to tradition, Sunni Islam has been the religion of the Maldivians since the twelfth century, when a visiting Islamic scholar converted King Sri Tribuvana Aditiya to Islam.

RELIGIOUS TOLERANCE Religious freedom is greatly restricted in Maldives, where the nation's constitution requires that the president and cabinet ministers be Sunni Muslims. Shariah (Islamic law) is observed and does not permit the public practicing or propagation of any other religious faith. Some reports indicated that two-dozen foreigners were expelled in 1998 on suspicion of spreading the Christian faith. Expatriate residents, however, are permitted to practice their religion in their private lives. Generally the government prohibits the importing of icons and religious statues, but it does not forbid the bringing in of religious books, such as Bibles, for personal use. In 1998, however, the government tried unsuccessfully to get the Seychelles to stop radio broadcasts of Christian programs in the Dhivehi language.

The government of Maldives does not permit the influence of Islamic fundamentalism, believing that standard Sunni Islam is one of the distinctive characteristics of the country, giving it religious harmony and a national identity. A Muslim converting to another faith is considered in violation of Islamic law, resulting in the loss of the rights to citizenship.

Major Religion

SUNNI ISLAM

DATE OF ORIGIN 1153 C.E.

NUMBER OF FOLLOWERS 275,000

HISTORY Islamization of Maldives was not accomplished without resistance. After his conversion in 1153

C.E., King Sri Tribuvana Aditiya became Sultan ibn Abdulla and constructed the first mosque in Maldives, leading to a rebellion of Buddhist monks, which was brutally suppressed. This was followed by the building of mosques at the sites of desecrated Buddhist monasteries and the forced conversion of many Buddhists to Islam.

A struggle ensued to keep the European powers and their religion—Christianity, both in its Roman Catholic and the varied Protestant forms—out of Maldives. *Tarikh,* an often-quoted chronicle in Arabic, describes some of the bloody battles fought in Maldives to keep the infidel Christians at bay.

Sunni Islam, along with its traditional institutions, was firmly established after the islands were placed under British protection in 1887. The entire present group of islands became the independent Republic of Maldives in 1965. Thereafter, the process of Islamization was very rapid, and the Maldivian government took full responsibility for this movement.

Maumoon Abdul Gayoom, elected in 1978, was president throughout the 1980s and '90s. Islamic fundamentalists who wanted to impose a stricter traditional way of life in the 1990s opposed Gayoom. Despite this opposition—and three coup attempts in 1980, 1983, and 1988—Gayoom continued to promote a more moderate form of Sunni Islam into the twenty-first century.

A Maldivian man removes his footwear before entering a mosque. Muslim rituals in Maldives are much like those in other Islamic nations. The ritual prayer, salat, *is conducted five times daily.* © ADAM WOOLFITT/CORBIS.

EARLY AND MODERN LEADERS Early Maldive history is obscure. A local Muslim leader, Muhammed Thakurufaan, helped free the islands from the Portuguese in the 1570s. In the latter part of the sixteenth century Sheikh Najeeb Habashee worked to strengthen Islam in the islands and contributed much to the religious and intellectual development of the Maldivian people.

MAJOR THEOLOGIANS AND AUTHORS President Maumoon Abdul Gayoom is a religious author whose works interpret the Koran and its message for the Maldivians. He is the editor of *Dheenuge Magu* (Path of Religion), published weekly in Dhivehi language. With a circulation of 7,500, this journal promotes an official Maldivian form of Sunni Islam.

Muhammad Luthfie, H.A. Maniku, A.S. Hassan, M.Waheed, and others are considered significant authors in Maldives. They write mainly in Dhivehi and work primarily on reconstructing the history of Maldives, weaving together the life and the religion of the islands.

HOUSES OF WORSHIP AND HOLY PLACES After King Sri Tribuvana Aditiya built the first mosque in the twelfth century, others followed quickly. As of 1991 there were 724 mosques for men and 266 mosques for women throughout the country. In Malé, the capital of Maldives, the Islamic Center and the Grand Friday Mosque were built in 1984, with major funding from outside Maldives. The gold-colored dome of this mosque is the first building sighted when approaching the capital.

WHAT IS SACRED? In Maldives sacredness is not limited to the mosque and the recitation of the Koran.

Fandita, a magico-religious system that coexists with Islam in the minds of ordinary people, provides an alternative way of dealing with their problems. This system, a mixture of folk medicine, charms, and black magic, as well as Koranic verses, gets its momentum from a widespread belief in *jinni,* or evil spirits. The Koran is seen as supporting this popular belief in *jinni.*

HOLIDAYS AND FESTIVALS Festivals in Maldives, though religious, also increase the sense of unity among Maldivians, as they involve communal worship, festivities, and entertainment. The two major Islamic festivals are the Bodu Eid (Id al-Adha), or the Feast of Sacrifice, and the Kuda Eid (Id al-Fitr), the feast celebrating the end of the Ramadan fast. Maldivians celebrate these festivals in the same way as Sunni Muslims elsewhere do, except on some Maldivian islands, where water is splashed on celebrants during Bodu Eid. Traditional music and traditional dances play a unique role in these holiday celebrations. The Prophet Mohammed's birthday is celebrated in Maldives, though without the same high spirit of festivity found during the Bodu Eid or Kuda Eid.

MODE OF DRESS Most poor men wear a shirt and the traditional sarong, an ankle-length cloth fastened around the waist. Many educated men now wear Western-style clothes. Men may choose to wear a head cloth, which also serves as covering during worship.

Styles for women include a long, shoulder-to-ankle dress or sometimes the *Salwar Khamiz,* similar to women's garb in India. Women may wear either a partial or a full veil. Schoolgirls may wear knee-length dresses without a veil.

DIETARY PRACTICES Eating habits have been greatly influenced by India, though this has more to do with availability than religion. Fish, rice, and coconuts are the staple foods. Reflecting Islamic dietary restrictions, alcoholic beverages, pork, and pork products are outlawed in Maldives (though alcohol is available in tourist areas).

RITUALS Muslim rituals in Maldives are much like those in other Islamic nations. The ritual prayer, *salat,* is conducted five times daily. Most shops and some offices in the islands close for about 10–15 minutes after the prayer call.

During the month of Ramadan, islanders fast during the daytime, and restaurants are closed. Working hours are also limited. Selling food during the daytime in the month of Ramadan is a punishable crime in Maldives. In addition to abstaining from food and drink, Maldivians also abstain from worldly pleasures such as listening to music or dancing. Yet at night and until dawn, the fast is broken, and the Koran and special prayers are recited.

Maldivian funerals are very simple ceremonies, with funeral prayers offered to the soul of the dead.

RITES OF PASSAGE A Maldivian baby is usually given an Arabic name on the seventh day after the birth. The naming ceremony is accompanied with ritual prayers followed by a celebration with close friends and relatives. Food is also frequently given to the poor. In some of the islands, it is also customary to shave a baby's hair on the day of naming.

Circumcision of boys between the ages of 7 to 10 is another rite of passage common in Maldives. The local doctor, known as the *hakeem,* performs this rite. In Malé this is normally done in a hospital. The circumcision ceremony takes place in the boy's home, which is decorated and visible to the community. The public is attracted to the celebrations by traditional drum music and dances; they are also treated to delicious food. This goes on while the boy lies in the middle of the room on a bed surrounded by relatives, who massage his feet and generally attempt to keep him comfortable. The boy also receives gifts. The festivities, typically a week, last until the boy is healed.

MEMBERSHIP The government does not aggressively propagate Islam among the expatriate non-Muslim workers in Maldives. The government does, however, expend a great deal of energy promoting the spirit and culture of Islam, largely to counteract certain Christian groups who try to proselytize among Maldivian Muslims.

SOCIAL JUSTICE The government's promotion of tourism, despite effects on the country's Islamic culture and the fisheries industry, has been much criticized. Critics, including Muslim leaders, have argued that tourism has led to a religious and cultural deterioration, as well as an increase in drug-related crimes, fights and murders among foreigners living in Maldives, child sexual abuse, pornography; and other social ills.

SOCIAL ASPECTS Despite the Islamic value on marriage and the family, there has been increasing rate of divorce, single-parent families, and cohabitation without marriage in Maldives, especially in Malé. Polygyny is allowed in Maldives, though only about 1 in 11 men have more than one wife.

POLITICAL IMPACT In Maldives Islam and politics are closely related. The nation's president must be a Sunni Muslim. Furthermore, the government considers the protection and promotion of Sunni Islam as one of its primary tasks; Islam, it believes, provides the glue that holds the islands together as one harmonious nation.

CONTROVERSIAL ISSUES The Maldivian courts apply a mixture of Shariah (Islamic law) and civil law. The government sanctions floggings and banishment to remote islands, which is very controversial, particularly for women, although it has been practiced in Maldives for centuries.

CULTURAL IMPACT Although Sunni Islam generally restricts arts such as music, traditional Maldivian music and dancing are permitted on the islands, particularly during festivals.

Other Religions

The only distinct religious minority, Shia Muslims, is found in Malé among the trading community of Indians, who settled there in the 1800s. There are no statistics regarding their numbers. A small number of Sri Lankans, with their Buddhist, Christian, and Hindu religions, have come to Maldives to work in the tourist resorts, because Maldivians, as devout Muslims, refuse to work in facilities serving alcoholic beverages.

Isaac Henry Victor

See Also Vol. 1: *Islam, Sunnism*

Bibliography

Heyerdall, Thor. *The Maldive Mystery: The Search for Ancient Civilizations in the Remote Islands of the Indian Ocean.* New York: Ballantine Books, 1986.

Maloney, Clarence. *People of the Maldive Islands.* Madras: Orient Longmans, 1980.

Phadnis, Urmila, and Ela Dutt Luithui. *Maldives: Winds of Change in an Atoll State.* New Delhi: South Asian Publishers, 1985.

Robinson, Francis, ed. *The Cambridge Encyclopedia of India, Pakistan, Bangladesh, Sri Lanka.* Cambridge: Cambridge University Press, 1989.

Wijesundera, G.D., J.B. Wijayawardhana, J.B. Disanayaka, Ahmed Hassan, and Mohamed Luthufee. *Historical and Linguistic Survey of Dhivehi: Final Report.* Colombo, Sri Lanka: University of Colombo, 1988.

Mali

POPULATION 11,340,480

MUSLIM 85 to 90 percent

AFRICAN INDIGENOUS BELIEFS 8 to 10 percent

CHRISTIAN 1 to 2 percent

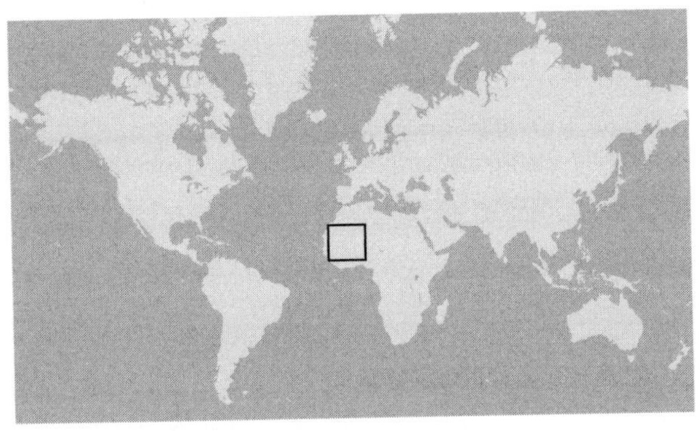

Country Overview

INTRODUCTION Located in West Africa, the Republic of Mali borders Algeria to the north, Mauritania and Senegal to the west, Guinea and Cote d'Ivoire to the south, and Burkina Faso and Niger to the east. Africa's second largest exporter of cotton, Mali depends on Niger River as a vital resource. Most inhabitants are farmers, stockherders, or fisherpeople. Mali is one of the poorest countries in the world; the United Nations estimates that 64 percent of the population lives in abject poverty.

Since early in the first millennium C.E. trade routes across the Sahara connected Mali with North Africa. Mali contains the centers of two great West African empires: the Mali (at its height in the thirteenth and fourteenth centuries) and the Songhai (Songhay; at its height in the fifteenth century). Influenced by Muslim traders and accompanying Islamic scholars, the leaders of both empires adapted early on the Islamic style of dress; some converted and even went on hajj (pilgrimage) to Mecca.

Morocco destroyed the Songhai power but could not exert control from across the Sahara. The eighteenth century saw the rise of the Bambara warrior states of Segu and Kaarta. The Bambara chiefs combined Islamic cultural traits—including the use of ulama (*karamotigiw*, or religious scholars) as mediators, geomancers (diviners), and advisers—with their traditional religious rituals and beliefs, which centered on controlling occult forces. In the nineteenth century a series of Islamic holy wars overthrew the Bambara states.

Western European imperial expansion reached Mali in the nineteenth century, and in 1904 it became the French Soudan. Mali achieved independence from France in 1960, with Bamako as its capital. Its first president, Modibo Keita, was overthrown in a 1968 military coup by Moussa Traoré, who ruled as a dictator until 1991. A coup led by Lieutenant Colonel Amadou Toumani Touré brought a democratic government to power, with a new constitution approved by referendum in 1992. The first president elected under the new constitution, Alpha Oumar Konaré, peacefully turned over power after two five-year terms to President Amadou Toumani Touré, elected with a turnout of less than 30 percent of the population in 2002.

Catholicism (which arrived in the late nineteenth century) and evangelical Protestant Christian groups (which arrived at various times during the twentieth

A man pushes a cart past the Jenné Mosque. The mosque is considered a masterpiece of the Sudanic style of mud architecture. © WOLFGANG KAEHLER/CORBIS.

century) are about evenly split in Mali, with most new Christian conversions occurring among western and southern populations that still practice traditional, usually locally specific African religions.

RELIGIOUS TOLERANCE Mali has a free press, with over 40 independent newspapers and 50 private (generally local) radio and television stations, as well as government-run print and broadcast media, allowing an open discussion of religion, freedom of worship, and noninterference by the state in religious affairs. All public associations, including religious organizations, must register with the government. The 1992 constitution defines the state as secular, prohibits discrimination based on religion, and mandates nonreligious public education. Since the 1950s intra-Islamic religious intolerance and even violence has pitted the overwhelming majority Sunni Muslims against the minority conservative, Wahhabi-influenced Muslims.

Major Religion

ISLAM

DATE OF ORIGIN Before 800 C.E.

NUMBER OF FOLLOWERS 9.6 to 10.2 million

HISTORY Soon after the birth of Islam in the seventh century C.E., Muslim traders began to cross the Sahara. Mali's ruling classes converted first but continued to perform traditional religious rituals. Indigenous religions generally included a belief in divine kingship that no ruler wanted to contest. Scholarly families did establish a tradition of Islamic study, and centers in Timbuktu (founded c. 1100) and Jenné (an ancient trading center; its learning center was founded soon after Timbuktu's) became renowned in the Islamic world for the quality of their scholarship and instruction. At the end of the sixteenth century, the Moroccan sultan invaded the Songhai empire, hoping to control West African gold. The conquest greatly damaged the two scholarly institutions, and many scholars were taken in chains across the Sahara to Morocco.

In the nineteenth century Islamic scholars and political leaders of the Fulbe/Tukolor ethnic group led two jihads (struggles, or holy wars) against the non-Muslim peoples of Mali and any Muslims the jihad leaders considered religiously lax or politically dangerous. The majority of non-Muslims converted to Islam at this time and maintained their acceptance of it even after the French defeated the descendants of the jihad leaders and established colonial control. Islamization actually increased during the colonial period, partially as a means of resisting the foreign occupiers.

Mali's Muslims continue to be well represented in the annual hajj and in North African and Arabian Peninsula Islamic learning centers. A Western-educated political elite, though professing to be Muslim, is oriented toward western Europe and North America. Other Muslims have begun to organize politically, establish a new media presence, and engage in public debate about Mali's stance on international issues related to Islam and Muslims peoples. They have criticized the government for the country's desperate economic state and demanded a reorientation of foreign policy, with closer ties to the Islamic world.

EARLY AND MODERN LEADERS Al-hajj Umar Tâl ibn Sadi al-Fûtî (c. 1794–1864), a nineteenth-century jihad leader, was the spiritual leader of the Tijaniyya Sufi brotherhood and a scholar in theology and Sufi thought. Many of his descendants continued in leadership roles. The Tâl family, who greatly extended the membership of the brotherhood, became known for their cooperation with the French colonizers. The Berber Kunta family of the Timbuktu area, northern Mali, Mauritania, and Niger has historically led the older Qadiriyya brotherhood.

Ahmad Hamadu llah b. Muhammad, a Sufi spiritual leader, developed a large following in Mali. His popularity and his unwillingness to participate in French gatherings made him a target of the French, and he died in exile in France in 1943.

Contemporary Muslim leadership is diffuse. Political activist and religious leader Imam Mahamoud Dicko, director of Bamako's Islamic Radio, uses the airwaves to critique the non-Islamic social mores of the political elite and their efforts to Westernize traditional Malian family structure. Sharif Haidara of the Ansar Dine movement and other charismatic popular leaders have attracted thousands of followers among poorer and frequently illiterate Malian Muslims, sometimes discomfiting more traditional Muslim leaders.

MAJOR THEOLOGIANS AND AUTHORS Ahmad Bâba, born into the Aquit family in Timbuktu in 1556, wrote over 50 works on Malikite law (one of four systems of interpreting Islamic law), grammar, and other Islamic sciences, as well as biographies of great West African Muslims. Taken in chains to Morocco in the late 1500s, Bâba was only allowed to return in 1607. He made the hajj and continued a productive scholarly and teaching career, leaving a large library at his death in 1627.

'Abd ar-rahman al'Sa'di, a seventeenth-century historian of Timbuktu, wrote a history of the city and of the Songhay empire, the *Ta'rîkh al-Sudân*; a late-nineteenth-century French translation brought it renown. Members of the scholarly Kati family, who settled in the Timbuktu area in the mid-fifteenth century, contributed to another historical work, the *Ta'rîkh al-Fattâsh,* completed around 1650. In September 2003 the new Mohamoud Kati library opened in Timbuktu.

The Kunta family produced many scholars, including Sidi al-Mukhtar (born Ahmad al-Kunti, he died in 1811); his son Sidi Muhammad (died in 1826), sometimes known as the "*shaykh* of peace" for his mediation activities in various conflicts; and his grandson Sidi Ahmad al-Bakka'i (died in 1865).

Cerno Bokhar Saalif Tâl was an influential early- to mid-twentieth-century Islamic leader and scholar famous for teaching Islamic studies to illiterate adult learners.

HOUSES OF WORSHIP AND HOLY PLACES The construction of the Djingareber mosque in Timbuktu is credited to Mana Mûsa, an emperor of Mali who made a much-touted and expensive hajj to Mecca in 1324. The Sankoré mosque, also in Timbuktu, was a center of university studies for the western Islamic world for hundreds of years. Both mosques are United Nations world heritage sites. The great mosques of Jenné and Mopti are masterpieces of the Sudanic style of mud architecture.

WHAT IS SACRED? Malian Muslims believe they receive *baraka* (blessings) by visiting the burial sites of important Muslims in history, including the grave of Shaehu Ahmadu in Hamdalayye. Timbuktu, known as the city of the 333 saints, has several hundred grave sites of sainted personages marked and mapped out for people to visit. Muslims may also receive *baraka* and even cures for physical ailments by drinking (or applying externally) the water used to clean Koranic writings from the wooden study boards of students. This water, called *nasi* among Mande speakers, is collected and placed in special bowls outside the entrances of Koranic schools for passersby to use as needed.

HOLIDAYS AND FESTIVALS Muslims in Mali celebrate the traditional Islamic festivals. At Id al-Fitr, the end of Ramadan, large communal prayers at mosques around the country are followed by great celebration and feasting. The girls and women dance; in some regions there are masking performances, which may include dance and song, celebratory holdovers from pre-Islamic times. Mali has declared Maouloud, the anniversary of the birthday of Muhammad, a civil holiday, and most Muslims return to their home villages to celebrate. On Tabaski (Id al-Adha, the feast of the sacrifice) Malian Muslims make efforts to see that no one goes hungry. Wealthier believers sacrifice many cows, sheep, and goats and distribute the meat to the less fortunate.

MODE OF DRESS Men wear long, voluminous robes, frequently with matching trousers underneath. Women wear similar robes with various headscarf coverings. Apart from desert dwellers (Tuaregs, among whom the men cover their faces as well, and Moors), Malian Muslim women have generally not worn a veil, except to prayer services and other specifically Islamic functions, but some conservative Muslim women have begun wearing full face veils as an outward sign of their Islamic observance.

DIETARY PRACTICES Muslims in Mali follow the traditional Islamic proscriptions against pork and alcohol and eat only halal meat (meat slaughtered according to Islamic law). Like other West African Muslims, Malian Muslims, both men and women, chew kola nuts. These small hard fruits of the kola tree contain high levels of caffeine and theobromine, a mild stimulant. Religiously "legal" stimulants, kola nuts are offered to visitors in Muslim homes and are a source of significant intra-African trade and connoisseurship.

RITUALS Muslims in Mali follow the same five daily prayers (with the prescribed ritual cleansing before the devotions), pilgrimage rituals, and funeral rites as are found throughout the Islamic world.

RITES OF PASSAGE Malian Muslims celebrate circumcision and naming ceremonies for both boys and girls. Some Malians see female genital circumcision as an Islamic rite, although it dates to pre-Islamic times; most Muslim scholars disagree. Children who complete their Koranic school education are given a celebration during which they recite portions of the Koran from memory.

Some Malian Muslims celebrate weddings with traditional African rituals, adding Islamic accoutrements. Among Islamic scholarly families of the Dyula/Bamana people, the men gradually untie large bunches of kola nuts, which are wrapped in banana leaves with long pieces of string. Each man makes a statement filled with Koranic prayers while untying and passing the nuts along, ensuring enough string remains for all male members of the two families to make their speeches.

Muslims follow the Islamic prescription of burial within a day or two of death, with no embalming or casket. The female members of the family wash the body and wrap it in a burial cloth; most older Muslims have a cloth picked out in readiness. Because of Mali's poor infrastructure, constraints on travel make it difficult for relatives to get to funerals, so families generally hold a prayer vigil and celebration of the life of the departed 40 days after the death.

MEMBERSHIP Because of Mali's high rate of illiteracy, Muslim leaders have made good use of nonprint media to attract followers and inspire adherents to commit more fully to a daily observance of Islam. The amount of time devoted to religious programming on radio and television has grown markedly. An increasing number of Muslims, both men and women, individually and in groups, listen to cassette tapes of sermons, discussions, and prayers.

SOCIAL JUSTICE Islamic education has been controversial in Mali since the French colonial period, when a small minority of the school-age population attended French-controlled public schools, a few attended mission schools, many did not attend school, and the vast majority attended parent-supported Koranic schools. Thousands of these schools still exist in Mali; an estimated 40 percent of all Malian boys and girls attend them, and most villages have one. The students spend hours each day begging in the streets or working in the fields of the schoolmaster, who justify this activity as teaching humility, modesty, and the importance of charity. After about six years those who are willing and financially able go on to the *madrasah* (*médersa*, Islamic religious school) to study advanced subjects in the Islamic sciences. The government provides little funding to these schools, which apply to Islamic states in the central Islamic lands for aid. The government has continued the colonial tradition supporting only secular state schools that instruct in French.

Islamic leaders have begun to address such issues as AIDS, which they formerly avoided. With the backing of international aid organizations, members of the Malian League of Imams and Islamic Scholars actively preach and educate about the disease and its control, as well as other public health, social, and political issues.

SOCIAL ASPECTS Malian family law is based on a mixture of local traditions and Islamic law and practice. Polygyny is legal and is one of the practices that differentiates Muslims and traditional African believers from Christians. Women participate in economic and political activity, but discrimination against them is institutionalized. A Malian woman cannot pass on her citizenship to her child; marital rape is not a crime; the minimum age for marriage is fifteen (and many village girls are married younger); and women have few rights in divorce and widowhood. The World Organization Against Torture issued a report in 2003 on violence against women in Mali and on existing Malian legislation that discriminates against women. The government subsequently attempted to introduce equal inheritance for men and women and equal status as leaders of the family, but the wrath of Muslims, both men and women, forced them to back down. The Islamic establishment sees the attempts to change family law as further evidence of the secular elite's desire to Westernize Malian culture.

POLITICAL IMPACT During the French colonial period and the first thirty years of independence, the government kept Muslim leadership at arm's distance. Beginning in 1974 the rise of OPEC allowed the oil-producing Islamic states to give significant aid to Mali's Muslims: Saudi Arabia funded the grand mosque in Bamako, and Libya helped build an Islamic Cultural Center; many Malians have been granted scholarships to study Arabic and Islamic theology in Cairo and other places, and *médersas* within Mali received funds to teach Arabic, among other subjects. The government, recognizing the possibilities of this Islamic generosity, created the Center for the Promotion of the Arabic Language within its Department of Primary Education in 1979. With one of the highest pupil-teacher ratios in the world (classes average 80 pupils per teacher), Mali's schools stand to benefit greatly from these changes. Conflicts over the teaching of religious subjects remain to be resolved.

In the early 1990s few Malian organizations proclaimed Islamic affiliation in their title. By 2003 more than 150 did, and Muslims were agitating against Mali's secular state. An umbrella group of 20 associations led by Imam Mamoud Dicko complained about the lack of Islamic input into state policies. After the terrorist attacks of 11 September 2001 and the onset of the United State's proclaimed "war on terror," an association of Islamic youth formed in support of Osama Bin Laden and al-Qaeda (accused of being responsible for the attacks), but older leaders who feared state violence against Islam pressured them to tone down their rhetoric.

Imams around the country have taken stances against government policies in their Friday sermons, entering into discussions they had carefully avoided before. The High Islamic Council, formed in Bamako in 2002, has vocalized discontent against the Malian elite and its alliances with the West, the United States in particular. In the 2002 elections Islamic leaders publicly ordered believers to vote for Ibrahim Boubacar Keita, who had agreed to a list of conservative demands they had presented to all the candidates. Though Keita was not successful, Malian Muslims are not likely to retreat from the political realm now that they have stepped into it.

CONTROVERSIAL ISSUES As elsewhere in the Islamic world, the issue of control over women galvanizes public opinion and pits western-oriented secularists against traditional Muslim believers. The government's attempt to change family law brought Muslims to the airwaves, meetings, and mosques to protest. The perceived dangers of state schools for Muslim girls cause many parents in Mali to place their daughters in Koranic schools and *médersas*.

CULTURAL IMPACT The Islamic mosque style that evolved in Mali and other savanna and desert areas of West Africa is frequently called "Sudanic." These mosques generally have two minarets made of solid mud (not used for the call to prayer since they have no interior), and their facades frequently suggest the ancestral earthen pillars found at traditional religion sanctuary sites. The walls have protruding wooden structural supports and pillared buttresses.

From the fifteenth century until the mid-nineteenth century, Timbuktu had a well-known book industry that produced beautifully bound volumes of Islamic scholarship, their prices rivaling the most luxurious products of the time. Malian family libraries and central local repositories have only just begun to garner the recognition and funding they need to maintain and preserve the books. Timbuktu has become a UNESCO world heritage site, both for its ancient mud architecture and for the thousands of Arabic-language manuscripts housed there, many uncatalogued and unknown to the outside world.

Other Religions

Long before the introduction of Islam, the people of Mali developed complex religious traditions. The various ethnic groups evolved similar belief systems, which generally propose a creator god removed from daily human existence. Lesser gods and spirits (frequently linked to natural forces and other living beings) and the souls of departed ancestors take an interest in, have a stake in, and exert influence over believer's daily lives. Geomancers and diviners, who are thought to be able to manipulate and appease these supernatural beings, have more or less power depending on their successes. Believers pay them to perform sacrifices, prayers, rituals, charms, and spells. The traditional art from Mali displayed in museums worldwide frequently serves a religious purpose and is not seen as art at all by practitioners.

In the late nineteenth century Catholicism was introduced in Mali by the White Fathers (The Order of Our Lady of Africa), a clerical order founded in Algeria in the nineteenth century. The anti-clerical French colonial governments discouraged and even undermined mission schools. The Catholic church in Mali has one archdiocese, Bamako, and five dioceses: Kayes, Mopti, San, Ségou, and Sikasso.

There were few Protestant Christians or missionaries in Mali until after the country gained its independence in 1960, though the Gospel Missionary Union dates its beginnings to 1918; the Christian Missionary Alliance to 1923; the Evangelical Baptist Union to 1949; and the United World Mission to 1952. Since 1961 the Association of Evangelical Churches of Africa and Madagascar has been the umbrella organization for most non-Catholic Christian churches in Mali. Christian groups have had difficulty converting long-standing Muslim populations; their greatest success has been in the newly Islamized south among the Bobo, Dogon, and Senufo and in the capital city of Bamako. The influence of foreign Christian mission groups, who proselytize while providing healthcare and literacy programs, causes concern in some Muslim circles.

Kathryn L. Green

See Also Vol. 1: *African Indigenous Beliefs, Islam*

Bibliography

Batran, A.A. "The Kunta, Sidî al-Mukhtar al-Kunti and the Office of Shaykh al-Tariq'al-Qadiriyya." In *Studies in West African Islamic History*. Vol. 1, *The Cultivators of Islam*. Edited by J.R. Willis. London: Frank Cass, 1979.

Baxter, Joan. "The Bin Laden Effect: Mali." *BBC Focus on Africa* 13, no. 1 (January–March 2002).

Brenner, Louis. *Controlling Knowledge: Religion, Power, and Schooling in a West African Muslim Society*. Bloomington: Indiana University Press, 2001.

———. *West African Sufi: The Religious Heritage and Spiritual Search of Cerno Bokar Saalif Taal*. Berkeley and Los Angeles: University of California Press, 1984.

Kaba, Lansiné. *The Wahhabiyaa: Islamic Reform and Politics in French West Africa*. Evanston, Ill.: Northwestern University Press, 1974.

Norris, H.T. *The Tuaregs: Their Islamic Legacy and Its Diffusion in the Sahel*. Wiltshire, England: Aris and Phillips, 1975.

Schulz, Dorothea E. "'Charisma and Brotherhood' Revisited: Mass-Mediated Forms of Spirituality in Urban Mali." *Journal of Religion in Africa* 33, no. 2 (2003): 146–71.

Zouber, Mahmoud Abdou. *Ahmad Bâba de Tombouctou (1556–1627): Sa vie et son oeuvre*. Paris: G.-P. Maisonneuve et Larose, 1977.

Malta

POPULATION 397,499

ROMAN CATHOLIC: 97.7 percent

PROTESTANT: 1.0 percent

OTHER: 1.3 percent

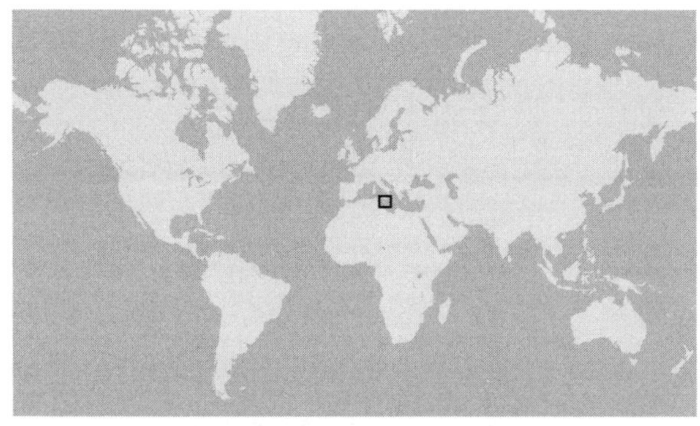

Country Overview

INTRODUCTION The Republic of Malta is an archipelago at the center of the Mediterranean, about 60 miles south of mainland Europe. It consists of three main islands that have a total area of 122 square miles. The islands have a series of low hills and terraced fields but no mountains or rivers. Malta's indented coastline provides numerous harbors, bays, and sandy and rocky beaches.

Archaeological remains indicate that in Malta there was a prehistoric temple civilization dating back to 5200 B.C.E. and then a Phoenician (c. 800 B.C.E.) and a Carthaginian presence (c. 480 B.C.E.). Later the islands were ruled by Roman, Arab, and Norman powers. The Order of Saint John of Jerusalem, also known as the Knights of Malta, left a rich cultural heritage (1530–1798). During successive foreign occupations that lasted until it achieved independence from British colonial rule in 1964, Malta developed a nationalism rooted in its language, cultural heritage, and religion. Malta was declared a republic in 1974. The vast majority of Maltese are Roman Catholic.

RELIGIOUS TOLERANCE The constitution of the Republic of Malta designates the Roman Catholic Apostolic Church as the official religion of the country. The constitution gives leaders of the Catholic Church the right to teach on morality, and religious education is provided in all schools. Members of minority religions also have freedom of worship. Compared to their European counterparts, however, most Maltese are less accepting of people belonging to different religions.

Major Religion

ROMAN CATHOLICISM

DATE OF ORIGIN 60 C.E.

NUMBER OF FOLLOWERS 388,400

HISTORY Although tradition traces the origin of Christianity in Malta to Saint Paul's shipwreck there in 60 C.E., there is no clear evidence of uninterrupted Christian practice on the islands. During the Muslim occupation (870–1048) in particular there seems to have been little Christian activity in Malta.

In the Great Siege of 1565 Malta was victorious over the Ottoman Empire. During World War II the islands survived severe bombardment and starvation. The Feast of Our Lady of Victories, celebrated every year on 8 September, marks both events. Since gaining independence Malta has been rapidly changing from a predominantly traditional fortress-island into an open, modern, service-oriented society. In 1990 Pope John Paul II was the first pope to visit the islands. In 2002 he beatified Gorg Preca (1880–1962), Sister M. Adeodata Pisani (1806–55), and Nazju Falzon (1813–65).

EARLY AND MODERN LEADERS Until 1828 the church in Malta was under the jurisdiction of the diocese of Palermo. There followed a succession of local bishops. Joseph Mercieca was appointed archbishop in 1976, and Annetto Depasquale became auxiliary bishop in 1998. Nikol G. Cauchi became bishop of the diocese of Gozo in 1972. Eight other Maltese bishops are in the service of the Holy See.

In the past priests in Malta often acted as political leaders. Gejtanu Mannarino led an unsuccessful rebellion against the grand master of the Order of Saint John in 1775, and in 1799 Mikiel Xerri was executed for leading an uprising against the French.

Although priests in Malta no longer run for office, they have remained socially active. In 1907 Gorg Preca opened a house for the teaching of catechism to youngsters by laymen; this later developed into a society for Christian doctrine, Magister Utinam Sequatur Evangelium Universus Mundus (MUSEUM; Master, Would That the Whole World Follow the Gospel). In 1954 Charles G. Vella set up the Cana Movement for family pastoral work, and in 1955 Fortunato P. Mizzi founded the Social Action Movement. Victor Grech founded the Caritas Drug Prevention and Rehabilitation Programme in 1984.

MAJOR THEOLOGIANS AND AUTHORS Pietru Pawl Saydon (1895–1971) stands out for translating the Bible from its original languages into Maltese. Maurice Eminyan is known for his articles in *The New Catholic Encyclopedia* (1967), and Edward G. Farrugia was the coauthor of *A Concise Dictionary of Theology* (1991). Benjamin Tonna has influenced local religious sociology, and Anthony M. Abela has contributed to comparative European Values Studies. George Grima was appointed dean of the Faculty of Theology in 1993.

HOUSES OF WORSHIP AND HOLY PLACES The Catholic Church in Malta has more than 360 churches.

Hooded men watch an Easter Week procession dedicated to Our Lady of Sorrows in the streets of Malta. During Easter time a few parishes hold Good Friday processions with statues representing Christ's passion and death. © BOB KRIST/CORBIS.

Major official services, including the inauguration of a new parliamentary legislature, are held at Saint John the Baptist Co-Cathedral in Valletta.

WHAT IS SACRED? Maltese Catholics give importance to the statues of patron saints and the shrines dedicated to the Madonna ta' Pinu (Our Lady of ta' Pinu) on the island of Gozo, the statue of the Redentur (Redeemer) in Senglea, the miraculous crucifix at Ta' Giesu Church in Valletta, and the crying effigy of the Madonna ta' l-Ghar (Our Lady of the Grotto) in Rabat. Priests in Malta bless homes, buildings, offices, machinery, animals, boats, cars, and other objects.

HOLIDAYS AND FESTIVALS Christmas, Easter, the Assumption of Our Lady (15 August), and the Feast of the Shipwreck of Saint Paul (10 February) are major holy days. During Easter time most Catholics attend Lenten sermons, and a few parishes hold Good Friday processions with statues representing Christ's passion and death. Most parishes also conduct processions for Corpus Christi, the Sacred Heart of Jesus, and Our Lady.

Every year parishioners have village feasts in honor of their town's patron saints. Priests and members of confraternities wear ornamental robes and walk in processions down decorated and illuminated streets. They bear a statue of their patron saint and are accompanied by band marches, tolling bells, and fireworks. To curb outbursts of rivalry between band clubs, church leaders regulate external festivities, emphasizing spirituality and solidarity.

MODE OF DRESS Most priests and religious men in Malta dress in dark grey clericals or a white shirt, dark trousers, and a small distinctive cross. Nuns wear traditional religious habits.

DIETARY PRACTICES There are no special dietary practices in Malta apart from those found in other Catholic countries.

RITUALS The majority of Maltese attend Catholic services at least once a week. A smaller number attend once a month or on special occasions such as Christmas and Easter. Prior to marriage Catholic couples exchange rings that have been blessed by a priest. They are required to attend marriage preparatory courses.

Catholic burial in Malta includes a funeral mass. The coffin is carried in a funeral cortege, blessed by a priest, and then buried. Tombs are adorned with flowers, candles, marble slabs, and statues representing Christian beliefs. People offer masses and prayers for the repose of the dead, and they visit graves in November and on anniversaries. The custom that requires close relatives to mourn the dead by wearing dark clothes and abstaining from public functions has become less popular.

RITES OF PASSAGE Almost all Maltese Catholics consider it important to hold religious services to commemorate births, marriages, and deaths. Families organize parties with gift giving to mark transitions in life; occasions include baptisms, first Communions, confirmations, engagements, and weddings. Church ministers anoint and give Communion to the sick in homes and hospitals.

MEMBERSHIP The church in Malta has retained its social relevance through its teachings and voluntary activities. People trust the church for its adequate response to spiritual needs and for its stances on family life and morality, but they rely on it less for its approach to social issues.

In 2003 a local synod displaced the traditional model of the church as "Mater et Magistra" (Mother and Teacher) with a more popular image of a sister, servant, and disciple of Christ. The new evangelization gives greater importance to the laity and to solidarity with the socially excluded. Pastoral activities attempt to reach families, youths, workers, immigrants, and refugees. The church's radio station is the third most popular in Malta, and weekly religious programs are broadcast on all local television stations.

SOCIAL JUSTICE The Catholic Church in Malta runs 55 charitable institutions, including homes for children, the elderly, battered women, persons in distress, the disabled, and refugees. In addition, more than 16,000 students (a third of the total student population) receive an education in one of the 82 church schools. Fundraising activities have broken new records every year. Church leaders have promoted social justice, the protection of the environment, national unity, and international solidarity.

SOCIAL ASPECTS The bishops of Malta defend the maintenance of traditional values. They resist consumerism and materialism, and they firmly oppose cohabitation, the legalization of divorce, same-sex marriages, and abortion. Church leaders constantly teach on the subject of family unity. Mothers of preschool children are encouraged to choose child rearing over a paid job.

POLITICAL IMPACT Until the second half of the twentieth century the Catholic Church influenced politics in Malta. In the 1960s the archbishop of Malta issued an interdict against the leaders and supporters of the Labour Party. This was followed by a series of church-state conflicts. After Vatican II the church contracted peace with the Labour Party and apologized for its past mistakes. It has since reached an agreement to transfer its immovable property to the state. It has also achieved state recognition of canonical marriage and a European Union protocol guaranteeing noninterference on matters of abortion in Malta.

The Maltese favor a relationship between religion and politics, insofar as the governmental decisions of religiously inspired politicians are not influenced by church leaders.

CONTROVERSIAL ISSUES The bishops oppose the Maltese Green Party's proposals for state recognition of cohabitation, same-sex relationships, illegitimate births, and divorce.

CULTURAL IMPACT Maltese baroque churches are adorned with paintings by renowned artists, including Michelangelo da Caravaggio, Mattia Preti, Giuseppe Calì, Emvin Cremona, and Willie Apap. Contemporary Maltese artists continue to draw their inspiration from Christian themes. Examples are the composer Charles Camilleri's *Missa Mundi* (1972; Mass on the World), Richard England's architecture, Antoine Camilleri's paintings and sculpture, Oliver Friggieri's literary works, David Azzopardi's folk guitar music, and popular dramas for radio and television.

Other Religions

Islam and Jehovah's Witnesses are the main minority religious movements represented in Malta. Greek Orthodox, Anglicans, and Church of Scotland members hold services in their churches in Valletta. The Muslim community worships in a newly constructed mosque in Paola. Baptists, Free Church members, and Bahai hold their services in their respective communities. Once a year representatives from all faiths participate in an ecumenical prayer service.

Anthony M. Abela

See Also Vol. 1: *Roman Catholicism*

Bibliography

Abela, Anthony M. *Transmitting Values in European Malta: A Study in the Contemporary Values of Modern Society.* Rome: Editrice Pontificia Università Gregoriana, 1991.

Archdiocese of Malta. 22 Dec. 2003. http://www.maltachurch.org.mt.

Bonnici, M.A. *History of the Church in Malta.* 2 vols. Valletta: Empire Press-Catholic Institute, 1967, 1968. Vol. 3. Zabbar: Veritas Press, 1975.

Clews, Stanley J.A., ed. *The Malta Year Book.* Sliema, Malta: De La Salle Brothers Publications, 2002.

Halman, Loek, comp. *The European Values Study: A Third Wave.* Tilburg, Netherlands: European Values Study, Work and Organization Research Centre, 2001.

Schiavone, Michael J., and Louis J. Scerri, eds. *Maltese Biographies of the Twentieth Century.* Pietà, Malta: Pubblikazzjonijiet Indipendenza, 1997.

Marshall Islands

POPULATION 73,630

CHRISTIAN 90 percent

OTHER 10 percent

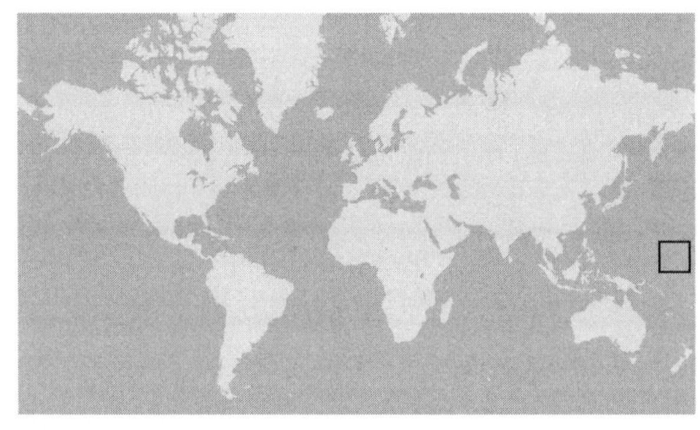

Country Overview

INTRODUCTION The Republic of the Marshall Islands consists of 29 low-lying coral atolls, along with other islands and islets, in the central Pacific Ocean. Two-thirds of the people live on two atolls: Majuro, the political center, and Kwajalein, a U.S. nuclear testing facility. The islands have been settled for approximately 2,000 years.

Beginning in the nineteenth century the islands came under European control, and Christianity was introduced. Some 80 percent of the population is Protestant, and 10 percent is Roman Catholic. There are smaller numbers of other faiths, including Bahais and members of the Church of Jesus Christ of Latter-day Saints.

RELIGIOUS TOLERANCE The constitution of the Marshall Islands expresses a strong adherence to Christian principles. There is tolerance, however, of non-Christian faiths.

Major Religion

CHRISTIANITY

DATE OF ORIGIN 1857 C.E.

NUMBER OF FOLLOWERS 66,000

HISTORY Indigenous beliefs that had persisted in the islands for some 2,000 years were disrupted by the arrival of new ideologies and political control in the nineteenth century. Following the island's contact with Spanish, German, British, and American traders, Germany established a protectorate in 1885, and the islands came under Japanese control after World War I. Following World War II the islands became part of the United Nations Trust Territory of the Pacific Islands, administered by the United States. They became independent in 1986 as the Republic of the Marshall Islands.

The Protestant Church was established on the islands in 1857 by Congregational missionaries sent from Boston, Massachusetts. They set up the first mission station on the southern atoll of Ebon. Other missionaries went to Jaluit, Majuro, Mili, and beyond, and by the 1880s missions were active on all of the major atolls.

In the 1890s German authorities sought the backing of the Vatican to establish German-speaking missionaries on the islands. The first Catholic missionaries opened a school on Jaluit, then the capital and administrative center of the archipelago, in 1899, and the first nuns arrived in 1902.

EARLY AND MODERN LEADERS George Pierson and Edward Doane established the Congregational mission on Ebon in 1857. Although the powerful chief Kaibuke initially opposed their work, he eventually became a member of the church. The Reverend Jude Samson, leader of the congregation at Uliga Protestant Church on Majuro, has been notable for maintaining the interest of young people and for keeping the outer-island churches in touch with the urban congregations through annual conferences.

Father August Erdland was one of the early German Catholic priests sent to the islands, where he worked alongside Father Friedrich Grundl. Erdland made a notable contribution to the Marshallese heritage by writing the first dictionary and grammar, and also by publishing detailed ethnographic accounts of the Marshallese ways of life.

Father Leonard Hacker is remembered for establishing a Catholic school on Majuro in 1954. Named Assumption School, it grew rapidly and attained a reputation for high academic standing as well as for its brass band, cooking classes, handicraft shop, and adult instruction, particularly for women. Hacker later built a school on Ebeye, where other outer-island migrants were congregating for job opportunities.

MAJOR THEOLOGIANS AND AUTHORS There are no especially prominent native-born theologians or authors of religious books. The American Board of Commissioners for Foreign Missions, the interdenominational organization based in Boston that first sent missionaries to the islands, developed its Pacific station in Hawaii in the 1820s. The reports of its missionaries, together with newsletters from Hawaii, provide a valuable archive for activities in the Marshall Islands. Catholic Church records are held on microfilm in several Pacific Island libraries. In *The First Taint of Civilization,* Father Francis X. Hezel has documented the origins of the Protestant Church in Micronesia.

HOUSES OF WORSHIP AND HOLY PLACES Early missionaries for the Congregational and, later, the Catholic Church established buildings on the main atolls. On Ebon, in 1857, George Pierson and Edward Doane built the first Congregational church of local materials, later replaced by a concrete structure. By the end of the twentieth century each major population settlement on an atoll had its own Protestant church, with two or three churches on a large atoll such as Jaluit and even more on Majuro. Uliga Protestant Church, in the commercial center of Majuro, is the most notable of these Protestant churches.

Like Protestant churches, Catholic churches are constructed of concrete and are painted white, although some colorful decoration may be added. Catholic churches are the center of a complex consisting of the pastor's rectory and a convent for nuns, along with a single elementary school and high school for students of both sexes.

Sacred sites from pre-Christian times persist in people's memories. These include rocks on the reef at Namu that represent the founding sisters of the Marshallese population. Each atoll has one or two such sites associated with its mythical past.

WHAT IS SACRED? There is no Marshallese word for the sacred, but the idea is conveyed by respect for the pastor as a representative of God (Anij) and of all associated with him. The nearest thing to a concept of the holy (*kojjarjar*) incorporates the notion of the church as a place to pray (*jar*). The concept of the taboo (*mo*) refers to general restrictions on relationships, places, and activities. For example, certain lands that must not be traversed because they belonged to a chief are designated as taboo, and the concept has been transferred to cemeteries, with the chief considered an earthly representative of God. Paramount chiefs are given a special place of honor in the front of the church. At the same time the world of the Marshallese is dominated by spirits (*jitob*), of which the new, Christian god, Anij, is supreme. Thus, former beliefs exist alongside those of Christianity.

HOLIDAYS AND FESTIVALS Christmas Day and Gospel Day are two major public holidays in the Marshall Islands. Gospel Day, the first Friday in December, commemorates the translation of the Gospels into Marshallese and is celebrated by Bible readings. Christmas is celebrated on the outer islands, particularly, by a singing competition between the two *jepta* (groupings), each made up of residents from one-half of the islet.

MODE OF DRESS People in the Marshall Islands wear their best clothes to church. A white dress and hat is the expected mode of dress for women, whereas men, particularly those who hold authority in the church, wear black suits. Children dress in white for special occasions, such as baptism and their first Communion. A deceased person is dressed in white for burial.

DIETARY PRACTICES No dietary restrictions are observed by Protestants or Catholics on the Marshall Islands. Seventh-day Adventists and Mormons, however, are strict in their rejection of stimulating drinks. In addition, Seventh-day Adventists, who follow old Jewish dietary restrictions, do not eat pork.

RITUALS The most important community ritual in the Marshall Islands is the funeral and burial of a deceased member. Very little ritual surrounds a birth, but when the baby reaches one year of age, the community celebrates with a special feast (*kemeem*), at which the local pastor blesses the child. Marriage is celebrated by some members of the community later in life, perhaps after they have had several children. Those who wish to be admitted to the church as full members, however, should be married in the church.

The Sabbath is a strictly enforced day of rest, for which food must be prepared the day before. Some families hold evening prayers on a regular basis, but this custom is diminishing. Meetings during the week are an important part of life for church members.

All community events begin and end with a prayer led by a senior member of a church, and all food at home and at a feast is blessed before it is eaten. Rituals celebrating the landing of a turtle or a very large fish are acknowledged by a senior person in the community, usually the chief.

RITES OF PASSAGE The two major rites of passage in the Marshall Islands are birth and death. A birth is celebrated after the first year of life. A funeral commemorates the passing of a community member, and the grave of the deceased is elaborately decorated immediately after burial and again a year later.

The first Communion is an important ritual for young Catholics. Acknowledgment of the successful completion of primary school has become an additional ceremony in some Congregational churches. The young people, dressed in white, are seated in front of the congregation, with special prayers offered for their success.

MEMBERSHIP Marshallese attend the church of their choice. Within the Protestant Church a distinction is drawn between *Eklesia,* who are full members, and *Rikabun,* literally "sinners," who, although they are not full members, may attend church. Only *Eklesia* can take Communion and be married in a church, however. Attendance at church to show active membership is more strongly enforced by some congregations than by others.

SOCIAL JUSTICE Pastors in the Marshall Islands work with the chiefs on the outer islands and with congregations in the urban centers to inform them on matters of social justice. Sermons preached at Sunday services usually address one or more social concerns, such as the plight of the needy or sick. The Reverend Jude Samson, for example, has spoken on the Christian community in a changing society, raising issues of globalization, capitalism, and individualism, as they affect the Marshallese people.

Both Protestant and Catholic Churches have opposed legislative proposals to legalize gambling in the Marshall Islands. They have cited both the financial and social damage suffered by islanders elsewhere when gambling has been legalized.

SOCIAL ASPECTS Church affairs dominate life in the Marshall Islands, particularly on the outer islands. Meetings for men and women, choirs, and youth groups draw members together several times a week. Ongoing fund-raising projects, whether for the maintenance of church facilities or other causes, are the duty of members, and the sums raised are acknowledged in weekly church news sheets.

The participation of young people in church activities is strongly encouraged through Sunday schools and attendance at Sunday services. They are taught to read the Bible and encouraged in proper, respectful behavior. Some young people find the services and activities of newer fundamentalist churches more lively, with singing to guitar accompaniment and a greater acknowledgment given to youth. This has led to some families being divided between two churches.

Both Protestant and Catholic missionaries were active in establishing formal education, and the church schools continued until they were taken over by the central government. Several schools, however, have retained their church affiliations. The Protestant school on Rongrong and the Catholic Assumption School on Majuro continue to be run as church schools. The Seventh-day Adventists and Mormons maintain primary schools alongside their churches.

POLITICAL IMPACT The chiefs of the islands initially resented the challenges to their authority by the missionaries and the new skills offered to their people, although they perceived the advantages in trade that the outsiders brought. The elevation of commoners to positions as deacons reinforced the chief's fears, and with education the teacher became a new mark of status in the community. Over time, however, these rivalries ameliorated as each sphere of leadership undertook its own pursuits. The churches, as the hub of social life in Marshallese communities, have come to be incorporated into the process of political consultation, and any political leader must have a strong church background to be successful.

CONTROVERSIAL ISSUES Minor rivalries between Protestants and Catholics have been overcome, but there is some resistance to the newer denominations that began arriving in the late twentieth century. Keeping the Sabbath has faced difficulties in urban centers, where tourism makes a vital economic contribution. Although government officials are not allowed to conduct business on the Sabbath, private businessmen are not so prohibited.

Control of reproduction has become a major issue facing members of the Catholic Church. The growth rate of the population of the Marshall Islands is believed to be too high for the limited resources available in such atoll communities. Family planning advice is offered, together with sex education in schools, but the Catholic Church takes its guidance from the Vatican on such issues.

CULTURAL IMPACT Church schools have supported the revival of traditional songs and dances as well as the production of artwork and music. The writing of songs, plays, and poems is encouraged. The brass band of Assumption School has become especially well known. Church events are featured in the exhibitions of the Alele Museum in Majuro.

Other Religions

Although Christianization began with the Congregational Church, by the end of the twentieth century there were some 20 Christian-based denominations on the Marshall Islands. Most of the newer churches are found only in the population centers of Majuro and Ebeye, where communities are large enough to support alternative teachings. Among them is the evangelistic Assemblies of God, with branches throughout Majuro, including the Rairok Living Water and Island Evangelism Outreach. This denomination offers an educational program using mainly volunteer teachers from overseas. The Salvation Army has a small, well-established following that offers the broad spectrum of social welfare programs for which it is known. The Church of Jesus Christ of Latter-day Saints has likewise established its church and mission structures on Majuro and Ebeye and on a couple of outer islands. With pastors drawn from the United States, it offers education and a broad-based program of social support. Seventh-day Adventists, Jehovah's Witnesses, and Bahais are active in the urban communities.

Nancy J. Pollock

See Also Vol. I: *Christianity, Reformed Christianity, Roman Catholicism*

Bibliography

Erdland, August. *Die Marshall Insulaner.* Münster, Germany: Anthropos Bibliotek, 1914.

Hezel, Francis X. *The First Taint of Civilization.* Pacific Islands Monograph Series, no. 1. Honolulu: University of Hawai'i Press, 1983.

Micronesian Seminar. *The Catholic Church in Micronesia.* Chicago: Loyola University Press, 1991.

Pollock, Nancy J. "The Origin of Clans on Namu, Marshall Islands." In *Directions in Pacific Traditional Literature.* Bernice P. Bishop Museum Special Publication, no. 62. Honolulu: Bishop Museum, 1975.

Sam, Harry. "A New Dawn: Christianity in the Marshall Islands." Pacific Theological College, Suva, Fiji, 1988. Mimeographed.

Mauritania

POPULATION 2,828,858

MUSLIM 100 percent

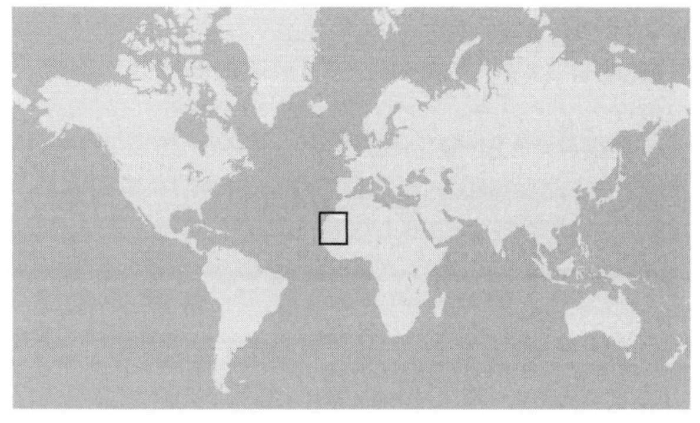

Country Overview

INTRODUCTION The Islamic Republic of Mauritania lies on the West African coast. Largely arid and flat, the country is bordered to the west by the Atlantic Ocean, to the northwest and north by the Moroccan-occupied territory of the Western Sahara, to the northeast by Algeria, to the east by Mali, and to the south by Mali and Senegal. Because of Mauritania's location at the ancient meeting point between Arab and Berber North African and black West African cultures, it was relatively easy for Islam to spread throughout the region with the advance of the Almoravids, the confederation of Berber tribes that built its empire in northwestern Africa and Muslim Spain in the eleventh and twelfth centuries. Like many North African countries, Mauritania continues to stand astride two worlds, Arab and African. The religions of its people cannot be fully separated from their historical and cultural contexts, and there is a dynamic cross-fertilization between Islam and the country's traditional African cultures.

RELIGIOUS TOLERANCE Because of the high degree of religious homogeneity, freedom of worship is not a major issue in Mauritania, which is surrounded by countries that are also overwhelmingly Muslim. The Mauritanian constitution states that "Islam shall be the religion of the people and of the State." Foreigners are allowed to practice their faiths freely.

Major Religion

ISLAM

DATE OF ORIGIN Eleventh century C.E.

NUMBER OF FOLLOWERS More than 2.8 million

HISTORY Since its introduction by the Almoravids in the eleventh century, Islam has been a unifying force and the base for political and social life in Mauritania. Islam provided the guiding principles for various political and anticolonial movements during the Charr Bubba wars (1644–74) against the Bani Hassan Arabs. It was also the ideological foundation for the Islamic state of Fouta-Toro in the eighteenth century and for the holy wars against French colonizers led by Al Hajji Oumar Tall (1794–1864) in the mid-nineteenth century. In addition Islam was used to support the later conflict between the French and Shaikh Hamullah, who refused to cooperate with the French and whom French authorities exiled several times between 1925 and 1941 on suspicion of fomenting anticolonial actions. Islam was also fundamental to the Al Falah educational movement initiated by Alhajji Mamoudou Ba (1908–78) of Diowol in the 1950s. Finally, the implementation of the Shariah (Islamic law) in 1980 served as the high-water mark of Islam's importance and influence in Mauritania.

EARLY AND MODERN LEADERS Mauritania has been home to many Islamic leaders and saints representing the different Sufi orders. As there is no clear separation between religion and politics or the state and the mosque, many of Mauritania's saints and scholars have also been political leaders. These have included Shaikh Nasir Al Din, who led the Charr Bubba wars; Suliman Ball, who founded the Fouta-Toro Almamate, which was governed by an imam (Muslim religious leader), in the 1770s; Abdoul Kader Kane, who mounted the fiercest resistance against the colonization of Fouta-Toro in the nineteenth century; and Abdoul Boukar Kane (1853–1891), who used Islam as an ideology to mobilize the people of Fouta-Toro against French colonial occupation. The scholar Shaikh Sidi Al Moukhtar (died in 1811) was well known for his criticism of military campaigns. Shaikh Saad Bou (died in 1917), the head of the Qadiriyya Sufi order in Trarza, was famous for issuing a fatwa in 1903 advocating submission to French colonial rule. In contrast, Saad Bou's brother Mal Ainin (died in 1910) took up arms against French rule in the Western Sahara. Cerno Amadou Mukhtar Sakho (1864–1934) was the best-known and longest-serving supreme judge (1905–1934) of Boghe in southern Mauritania.

The ranks of contemporary religious leaders in Mauritania are filled mainly by descendants of those named in the previous paragraph. They include the active ulamas Bouddah Ould Bousseïri (born in 1930), for decades the grand imam of Nouakchott; Mohamed Salem Ould Addoud; Bah Ould Abdallahi; Hamden Ould Tah (born in 1931); Amadou Nene; Amadou Boukar; Abdoulaye Dia; Tidiane Ly; and Shaikh Siddiya.

MAJOR THEOLOGIANS AND AUTHORS Mauritanian theologians and authors have included Sidiyya Baba (died in 1924) of the Trarza; Suliman Ball; Abdoul Boukar Kane; Amadou Boukar (1900–80); and Amadou Nene (born in 1914), who established religious schools in Ngijilon, Ganguel, Boki Diawe, Thilon, Boghe, Diatar, and Kaedi. The scholar and Islamic historian Shaikh Musa Kamara (1864–1945) is known for his ethnographic work *Zuhur al-Basatin, ou Histoire des noirs musulmans.* Other theologians have included Yaqouba Sylla (died in 1988), the head of the Hamalists (the followers of Shaikh Hamullah) in Kaedi; Alhajji Mamoudou Ba; Shaikh Saad Bou; Harun Ould Al Shaikh Sidiyya (1919–1977), who wrote an account of his family's history, *Kitab al-akhbar*; and Abdallah Ould Sidiyya, who founded the Islamic Institute at Boutilimit.

A Mauritanian man performs pre-prayer ablutions. Daily prayer and ablution are common Islamic rituals. © MARGARET COURTNEY-CLARKE/CORBIS.

HOUSES OF WORSHIP AND HOLY PLACES There are important mosques and religious centers throughout Mauritania. In the 1970s oil-rich Arab countries provided funds for the construction of huge mosques in the capital, Nouakchott. There are historical mosques in

Kaedi, Boghe, Chinguti, Boutilimit, Tijikhza, Walata, Tichit, and Mederdra. In addition to worshiping in mosques, Mauritanians also use public fields for communal prayers.

WHAT IS SACRED? The Koran and the hadith are among the religious sources considered sacred by Mauritanians. The saints of the various Sufi orders are revered as holy men because of their claim to be sharifs, or descendants of the Prophet Muhammad. Parents and older people are deferred to as sources of blessing and—potentially—serious curses. As a result of the thorough blending of Islam with local traditions, Mauritanian Muslims also believe in the power of ancestor spirits and consider certain locations, trees, and animals sacred.

HOLIDAYS AND FESTIVALS There are no Muslim holidays or festivals that are distinctive to Mauritania. But the use of music and dance during traditional Islamic feasts and the mingling of men and women are unique to African Islam.

MODE OF DRESS Mauritanian men and women dress modestly, as their religion requires. Both married black and Arab-Berber women cover their heads for religious reasons and to show respect for their in-laws. Men of all ethnic groups wear the West African boubou over pants, as well as a headdress, to protect them from the dry winds and recurrent sandstorms. During prayers and religious occasions, people wear their best clothes. Brides typically wear black. When people die, their bodies are washed and wrapped in white clothes before being placed directly in the grave.

DIETARY PRACTICES The Mauritanian diet consists of millet, sorghum, maize, milk products, rice, meat, fish, and fruits and vegetables. Meat comes primarily from such livestock as oxen, cows, goats, sheep, and camels and from gazelles and chickens and other birds. These must be slaughtered by an adult male in accordance with Islamic dietary principles. Meat from animals that have front teeth—such as pigs, horses, mules, donkeys, cats, and dogs—is prohibited. The consumption of alcohol or recreational drugs is also forbidden by Islamic law.

RITUALS Common Islamic rituals include the five daily prayers, ablution, and, for members of the Tijaniyya Sufi order, the recitation of a *wird* after prayers and especially on Friday evenings. Performed twice daily, *wirds* involve the repetition of specific sets of prayers and formulas. Other rituals include naming ceremonies for babies, which take place seven days after birth; the washing of hands before eating; bathing after sexual intercourse; fasting during the holy month of Ramadan; Friday prayers and the communal prayers that accompany such major annual festivals as the Id al-Fitr, which is celebrated at the end of Ramadan, the Id al-Adha, which takes place at the end of the pilgrimage to Mecca, and Mawlud, the birthday of the Prophet Muhammad; giving blessings during communal prayers; and burial ceremonies. Elaborate greetings containing religious elements—"peace be upon you" and "God be with you," for example—are common among Mauritanians.

RITES OF PASSAGE The first rite of passage is the naming ceremony for a newborn child. For boys the next turning point in life is marked by circumcision, which should take place before the age of 18. Men typically marry after their 18th birthday, but most young women marry at a much younger age. Other important rites of passage include initiation into the Tijaniyya Sufi order, during which the initiate receives the *wird,* and the obligatory pilgrimage to Mecca, after which a man is given the title hajji and a woman the title hajja.

MEMBERSHIP Like all Muslims, Mauritanians believe in the universal nature of Islam and actively try to spread their religion throughout the rest of Africa. The Almoravids in the eleventh century and the followers of Oumar Tall in the nineteenth century used force to convert people to Islam. Contemporary methods used to attract converts include trade; marriage to non-Muslim women, whose children will automatically become Muslims; mixing religion and magic in such practices as using verses copied from the Koran as amulets; and claiming to be a sharif. Mauritanian Sufis compete in the recruitment of members to the Qadiriyya and Tijaniyya orders.

SOCIAL JUSTICE Hospitality and generosity toward family members, neighbors, guests, fellow Muslims, and strangers are highly valued among all Mauritanian ethnic groups. Those who are better off are expected to be commensurately more generous to the poor and the less fortunate. As a result, individual destitution and isolation are uncommon in Mauritania, despite widespread material poverty.

SOCIAL ASPECTS In a society that has embraced Islam and blended it with indigenous West African and Berber traditions and beliefs, an adult life can not be complete without marriage. Even poor and disabled Mauritanians are expected to marry and have children. Unmarried women are often pressured to find a man with whom to pray—the expectation being that marriage will follow. When a person marries, people say he or she has joined the mosque, as though marriage were a precondition for being a good Muslim. Some Muslim social practices in Mauritania discriminate against women, especially those relating to polygamy, divorce, freedom of movement, child custody, inheritance, and witness testimony in a court of law.

POLITICAL IMPACT Although the constitution of Mauritania decrees that Islam shall be the religion of both the state and the citizens, the ruling elites have made it illegal to found political parties based in Islam. Islam is so pervasive, however, that politicians try to co-opt religious leaders for their political ends. The implementation of Islamic law in 1980 affected the political situation in Mauritania. Even though the formation of Islamic political parties is forbidden, the Mauritanian government itself has taken advantage of strict Islamic law to justify its actions. The controversial abolition of slavery in 1980, for example, was widely perceived to have been diluted by Islamic law, according to which the government found white Maur slave owners eligible for compensation for setting their black slaves free.

CONTROVERSIAL ISSUES The most vexing issues in Mauritanian society are collectively referred to locally as "la question nationale" ("the national question"), which primarily has to do with the continued coexistence of white and black Mauritanians. These issues focus on the sharing of political power, wealth, and employment and educational opportunities and the equal treatment of African languages and culture alongside those of the politically dominant Arab-Berber population. The military regime's imposition of strict Islamic law in 1980 was seen by the black community as another attempt by the Arab-Berbers to maintain their political monopoly by justifying human rights violations—including the compensation paid from public funds to former slave owners for freed slaves—through Islam. Islam has also been used to justify the imposition of Arabic as the country's sole official language, at the expense of the indigenous Pulaar, Soninke, Wolof, and Bambara languages.

CULTURAL IMPACT Whereas Mauritanian dance, music, and crafts are typically West African, the country's architecture, literature, and painting have been deeply influenced by Islam. In both the northern and southern regions of the country, people use African musical instruments to accompany songs the lyrics of which have Islamic and oriental characteristics. Mauritanian architecture—especially that of the mosques and some modern houses—and furniture design are closely derived from Islamic artistic traditions of the Middle East.

Other Religions

Officially there are no other religions in Mauritania besides Islam. Mauritanian Islam, however, represents a thorough blending of Islam with African and Berber spiritualism and traditional beliefs. The Christian community in Mauritania is extremely small and is made up entirely of European expatriates. There are a few Christian churches in Nouakchott, Rosso, Nouadhibou, Zouerat, and Atar. Christians may practice their faith freely as long as they keep a low profile, do not try to convert Muslims, and do not trade or consume alcohol in public.

Garba Diallo

See Also Vol. 1: *Islam*

Bibliography

Bâ, Amadou Hampaté. *Vie et enseignement de Tierno Bokar: le sage de Bandiagara.* Paris: Seuil, 1980.

Ba, Oumar. *Le Foûta Tôro au carrefour des cultures.* Paris: L'Harmattan, 1977.

Cotton, Samuel. *Silent Terror: A Journey into Contemporary African Slavery.* New York: Harlem Rivers Press, 1998.

Diallo, Garba. *Mauritania, the Other Apartheid?* Uppsala: Nordiska Afrikainstitutet, 1993.

Kane, Ousmane, and Jean-Louis Triaud. *Islam et islamismes au sud du Sahara.* Paris: Karthala, 1999.

Robinson, David. *Paths of Accommodation: Muslim Societies and French Colonial Authorities in Senegal and Mauritania, 1890–1920.* Athens, Ohio: Ohio University Press, 2000.

Robinson, David, and Jean-Louis Triaud, eds. *Le temps des marabouts: itineacute;raires et stratégies islamiques en Afrique occidentale française v. 1880–1960.* Paris: Karthala, 1997.

Sall, Ibrahima Abou. *Assassinat du Jaagorgal Abdul Bookar Kan.* Paris: n.p., n.d.

Mauritius

POPULATION 1,210,447

HINDU 52 percent

ROMAN CATHOLIC 26 percent

MUSLIM 16.6 percent

PROTESTANT 2.3 percent

OTHER 3.1 percent

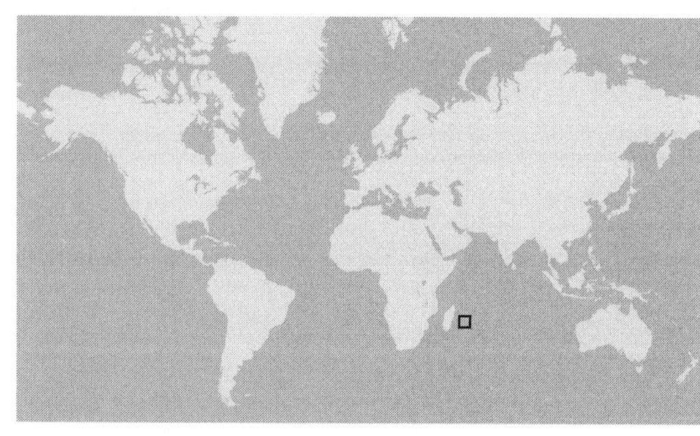

Country Overview

INTRODUCTION Mauritius is situated in the Indian Ocean and forms part of what is generally referred to as the Mascarene Islands (together with the islands of Rodrigues, Seychelles, and Réunion). Its history has been shaped over time by different colonial administrations. During the main part of the seventeenth century, the Dutch administered the island, from 1715 to 1810 it was a French colony, and from 1810 to 1968 it was under British administration. It became independent in 1968.

Because of the diversity of its culture and traditions, Mauritius is known as "the Rainbow Island." The first settlers came mainly from France during the period of French colonization, and they introduced slaves from Africa, Madagascar, and, to a lesser degree, India.

After slavery was abolished in 1835, there was an influx of Indian immigrants. The island also has a community of Chinese who arrived at different times during the colonial years.

The history of religion in the island was linked to that of political changes and colonial administration. During French colonial times, Catholicism was the state religion, and slaves were forced to give up their ancestral customs and traditions. In the nineteenth century the British administration encouraged the development of the Anglican Church but allowed the Catholic Church to continue with its mission. During the same period massive immigration from India changed the religious and cultural setting of the island thoroughly. These changes are visible today, with Hinduism being the main religion.

RELIGIOUS TOLERANCE In order to preserve the character of a multicultural country practicing different faiths and religious customs, Mauritius guarantees freedom of religious practice (according to section two of the constitution, which was ratified in 1968). Mauritians practice no fewer than five of the major world religions.

Major Religions

HINDUISM

ROMAN CATHOLICISM

HINDUISM

DATE OF ORIGIN 1640 C.E.
NUMBER OF FOLLOWERS 629,400

HISTORY Between 1728 and 1746 the French colonial government imported artisans, unskilled laborers, slaves, and sailors from South India. Many of them were Hindus who eventually remained in Isle de France (as Mauritius was then known). The first Hindu place of worship on the island was built in 1771 in Port Louis. In 1840 a Hindu temple was erected at Clemencia, and another, known as the Sinnatambou Temple, was later built at Terre Rouge.

Between the 1830s and the early 1930s, there was the mass importation of laborers from different regions of prepartitioned India. During this period Hindus in Mauritius suffered from prejudice and injustice. Few temples existed, and Indian culture was spread through teachings of the sacred books. Hindus struggled to maintain their values and cultural identities. Mauritius underwent a demographic revolution and saw the emergence of Hindu sacred places and other sites for social and cultural functions. Hinduism has become the most widely practiced religion in Mauritius.

EARLY AND MODERN LEADERS The island's first Hindu leader, Manilal Doctor, went to Mauritius to defend the rights of the indentured laborers. Between 1907 and 1911 he helped establish the Arya Samaj Movement in Mauritius. Chiranjiva Bhardwaj contributed to strengthening the local branch of Arya Samaj with the goals of preventing mass conversion of Hindus to Christianity or Islam, spreading the teachings of Swami Dayanand Saraswati, and promoting Indian culture. During the 1920s and 1930s, Pandit Cashinath Kistoe, Pandit Atmaram, R.K. Boodhun, and Dunputh Lallah combated illiteracy and social injustice in the Hindu communities of Mauritius.

Between 1939 and the 1950s, Basdeo Bissoondoyal brought about a Hindu cultural revival and protested British colonialism. From the 1950s until the early 1980s, the best-known Hindu political leader in Mauritius was Sir Seewoosagur Ramgoolam, head of the Labour Party and father of the nation. His successor, Sir Aneerood Jugnauth, formed the Mouvement Socialiste Mauricien (Mauritian socialist movement) in 1983. Outstanding spiritual leaders are Swami Ghanananda, who pioneered the Ramakrishna Mission in 1942, and Swami Krishnanand, who founded the Krishnanand Seva Ashram in Calebasses in 1980.

The most sacred place of worship for Hindus in Mauritius is the Ganga Talao (a lake that is also called Grand Bassin), to which more than 400,000 Hindus pilgrimage annually. © WOLFGANG KAEHLER/CORBIS.

MAJOR THEOLOGIANS AND AUTHORS Ramoo Sooriamoorthy (died in 1995) was a teacher and inspector of schools. His works include *Les Tamouls à l'Ile Maurice* (1977; "Tamils in Mauritius") and *Le but ultime* (1992; "The Ultimate Goal"). Pandit Atmaram Vishwanath (1884–1955) was an Indian journalist and writer who arrived in Mauritius in 1912 to work on Manilal Doctor's newspaper, the *Hindustani.* His books include a history of Mauritius (1923).

HOUSES OF WORSHIP AND HOLY PLACES Hindus in Mauritius worship in temples and at spiritual centers. The most popular Hindu temples are Shri Sockalingum Meenatchee Ammen in Port Louis, Siva Temple on the banks of the Ganga Talao (a lake that is also called Grand Bassin), and MamaToukay temple at Camp Diable. Centers that attract many devotees include Brahma Kumaris Raja Yoga Centre, the Sathya Sai Baba, and the Hare Rama Hare Krishna Centre. The most sacred place of worship for Hindus in Mauritius is the Ganga

Talao, to which more than 400,000 Hindus pilgrimage annually.

WHAT IS SACRED? Hindus in Mauritius follow the main rituals and customs as prescribed by Hinduism.

HOLIDAYS AND FESTIVALS The Maha Shivaratee Festival, in honor of the deity Shiva, is the most important Hindu festival in Mauritius. For this celebration devotees travel from all parts of the island to the sacred lake Ganga Talao in the south.

MODE OF DRESS There is no distinctive way of dressing for Hindus in Mauritius.

DIETARY PRACTICES The staple food of all Mauritian Hindus is rice. Hindus avoid eating beef and pork, and many are vegetarians.

RITUALS Mauritians of Hindu faith follow the rituals that are recommended by the sacred texts.

RITES OF PASSAGE Hinduism in Mauritius is based on what is set by the sacred texts, and there is no distinctive characteristic to be mentioned.

MEMBERSHIP Because of the multiracial, multilingual, and multicultural aspects of Mauritian society, Hindu membership is a complex issue. Different communities have set up their own doctrines, practices, and ways of life. Hindus are members of Sanatanist movements or of the Arya Samaj. Tamils belong to another society called Tamil Associations. Telugu, whose families came from the Indian state of Andhra Pradesh, have created their own organization, called Andhra Maha Sabha. The Marathis, whose ancestors were from the Maharashtra region in India, join the Marathi Mandali Federation.

SOCIAL JUSTICE Arya Samaj, the reformist wing of Hinduism, was introduced in Mauritius in 1903. Besides promoting and propagating the Vedic culture (based on the Vedas, the earliest Hindu scriptures), it did much to establish justice and human rights during the colonial period. In the 1930s and 1940s the Labour Party fought for the rights of Hindu workers. Furthermore, during the 1940s the Bissoondoyal brothers from India took the Jan Andolan (mass movement) to Mauritius to sensitize the Hindu community about their rights. The Voice of Hindu movement in the 1990s emerged for the same purpose.

SOCIAL ASPECTS Marriages are arranged within the caste system. Members of high castes continue to avoid marrying those of lower castes. Intercaste marriages have, however, become more common. Mixed marriages between Hindus and non-Hindus have also become common, although more traditional families tend to resist this trend.

POLITICAL IMPACT Early Hindus who were involved in Mauritius's political, social, and economic affairs paved the way for many more Indians to join politics and to be members of the assembly. In 1936 the Mauritius Labour Party played an important role in influencing Indo-Mauritian professionals and intellectuals. This influence increased in 1952 with the leadership of Sir Seewoosagur Ramgoolam. The Independent Forward Bloc, founded in 1958 and led by Sookdeo Bissoondoyal, also played a central role in molding a new generation of Hindu leaders. In the 1970s the MMM (Mouvement Militant Mauricien) offered young Hindu politicians an alternative to the Labour Party. During the 1980s and 1990s the Mouvement Socialiste Mauricien dominated Mauritian politics, and it was a mostly Hindu-controlled party.

CONTROVERSIAL ISSUES Since the 1950s and 1960s there has been a split in the Hindu groups in Mauritius. During this period the Tamils, Telegus, and Marathis began to feel that they had a different identity from that of the Hindi-speaking Hindus of Bihari origin. They celebrate their own religious festivals, and they have their own representatives in the parliament.

Before 1983 only Brahman priests were allowed to perform religious ceremonies, but now priests of other castes may also perform the rituals.

CULTURAL IMPACT Mauritian arts have been largely influenced by Hinduism. Hindu myths can be found in the novels and poems of Abhimanyu Unnuth, Robert Edward Hart, Malcolm de Chazal, and Marcel Cabon.

ROMAN CATHOLICISM

DATE OF ORIGIN 20 September 1715 C.E.

NUMBER OF FOLLOWERS 314,700

HISTORY During the French occupation of Mauritius (1715–1810), Catholicism was regarded as the state religion. All servile laborers imported from Africa, Madagascar, and India were converted by force to Catholicism.

When the British took over the administration of the island in 1810, they spared no effort for the promotion of the Anglican Church. They also, however, granted liberty of religious faith and practice to the inhabitants through Article VIII of the Capitulation Treaty.

The colonial office in London insisted that all ecclesiastical superiors in British colonies be of British origin. The Mauritian diocese was then separated from the Roman Curia, and a British vicar apostolic was nominated to look after religious matters in Mauritius, as well as in the lands of Saint Helena Island, the Cape of Good Hope, Madagascar, the Seychelles, Australia, Tasmania, and New Zealand. Priests serving in Mauritius either had to be British or to bear allegiance to the British flag. This situation caused tension between the church, the state, and the Franco-Mauritian community. Despite such difficulties, Catholicism continued to prosper, and it remains a stronghold of Christian faith in Mauritius.

EARLY AND MODERN LEADERS Allan Collier, bishop of Port Louis from 1841 to 1862, was the architect of the Catholic revival in Mauritius. He convinced the British administration to finance the building of new churches and schools. He brought congregations of nuns from France (Les Dames de Lorette) and founded the congregations Bon et Perpétuel Secours, La Confrérie du Rosaire, and Notre Dame des Victoires. He also started orphanages and special missions for the poor and the sick.

With James Leen and Daniel Liston at the head of the Mauritian Catholic Church (1926–49 and 1949–68, respectively), Catholicism thrived again. Both believed that the church had to meet the needs of a changing society. Liston pleaded for a new generation of Mauritian priests who would take up the challenge when independence was granted to Mauritius. Jean Margéot was the first Mauritian to be made head of the Catholic Church on the island. He became cardinal in 1988 and was succeeded as bishop by Maurice Piat.

Also important was the missionary work of Father Jacques Désiré Laval, known as the Apostle of Mauritius. He arrived in 1841, some seven years after the abolition of slavery, to take charge of the evangelization of the 80,000 blacks. Laval was beatified in 1979.

MAJOR THEOLOGIANS AND AUTHORS There have been no major Catholic theologians in Mauritius. However, the historical research conducted by Monsignor Amédée Nagapen is notable; his publications include a history of the Catholic Church in Mauritius.

HOUSES OF WORSHIP AND HOLY PLACES The main Catholic ceremonies in Mauritius are held in the Saint Louis Cathedral in Port Louis, which was inaugurated in 1782 after a long series of misfortunes that delayed its construction. It is dedicated to the patron saint of the town, Saint Louis.

The Marie Reine de La Paix (Mary, queen of peace) Square, inaugurated and dedicated to the Virgin Mary in 1940, is one of the main rallying places for ceremonies held in the open. Notable ceremonies there have included the beatification of Father Laval in 1979, the pastoral visit of Pope John Paul II in 1989, the ordination ceremonies of Mauritian priests, and the installation of both Cardinal Margéot and Monsignor Piat as bishops of Port Louis.

The burial place of Father Laval has become a place of devotion and pilgrimage for Mauritians of all faiths. On the eve of the anniversary of his death, thousands of pilgrims gather at his grave to pray.

WHAT IS SACRED? In terms of what is considered sacred, there is nothing distinctive about the way the Catholic faith is expressed in Mauritius.

HOLIDAYS AND FESTIVALS Apart from the usual Catholic holidays, Mauritians show much fervor and devotion on Assumption Day (15 August), held in celebration of the Virgin Mary. On Assumption Day, Mass is celebrated in all parishes. Families gather to mark the occasion and to share a meal after the traditional religious ceremony.

MODE OF DRESS Because the practice of Catholicism has been linked since colonial times to European culture, most Mauritian Catholics dress in European clothes. In the decades after independence, however, there has been a revival of traditional clothes among Indo-Mauritian Catholics who, for special Hindu celebrations such as the Divali (the festival of lights), dress in typical Indian clothes for a special Mass held on that occasion. The same is true for Chinese of Catholic faith, who, for special Chinese festivals, such as the Festival of the Moon, decorate their church in red and dress in typical Chinese costumes for religious celebrations.

DIETARY PRACTICES For the most part Mauritian Catholics follow Catholic traditions regarding dietary practices. Certain occasions are marked by special meals. On the Monday following Easter or on Christmas Day, Mauritians usually gather for a family lunch. Because Mauritian cuisine is multicultural, it is common to have as a main course *faratas* (Indian bread) and chicken curry. In villages the main dish could be a savory monkey curry.

On Assumption Day a special cake, *gâteau Marie* (Mary's cake), is baked and decorated in blue and white in honor of the Virgin Mary.

RITUALS Different ceremonies mark the lives of Mauritian Catholics, and there are traditions and customs linked to these occasions. At the birth of a child the family gathers for the christening, celebrating with a meal and festivities that can last a whole day.

When a family member dies, there is an elaborate system of customs. On the night of the death, family, friends, and neighbors gather at the home of the deceased for a vigil. Prayers are said, and for eight days family and friends pray together for the soul of the deceased. Masses are also said for the souls in purgatory and for deceased family members.

For the first Communion buns are baked and blessed. Families gather for a special lunch, and buns are distributed as the child receiving his or her first Communion is taken to visit neighbors, friends, and acquaintances.

RITES OF PASSAGE Mauritians of Catholic faith mark various life transitions by participating in the sacraments of the Catholic Church.

MEMBERSHIP The Catholic Church has done missionary work in the Indo-Mauritian and Chinese ethnic communities in Mauritius. Christians of Indian origin have been part of the Mauritian community since the initial colonization of the island. They were either slaves who had been baptized by force or free Indians from Pondichery who went to Mauritius as traders, masons, brick makers, workers, or *topaz* soldiers (born of a French father and an Indian mother).

The development of Catholicism within the Chinese community dates back to 1873, when Monsignor William Sacrisbrick evangelized to them. After World War II the Chinese Catholic Mission, which had been painstakingly developed over the years, counted some 2,700 members (25 percent of the Chinese population). It remains an active community in the Catholic Church of Mauritius.

SOCIAL JUSTICE In the 1950s Father Eugène Dethise launched the Ligue Ouvrière d'Action Catholique, which regrouped workers from the industrial sector. Affiliated with it are different associations, such as the Action Catholique des Enfants (for children's rights), La Ligue Ouvrière d'Action Catholique/Association Féminine Ouvrière (for women's rights), and La Commision Diocésaine du Monde Ouvrier (for the rights of industrial workers). Their main goal is to create an awareness among Catholics about their rights and duties as citizens of Mauritius.

With growing problems within Mauritian society, such as poverty, prostitution, drug addiction, and delinquency, the church encourages its members to join the different church movements to address such issues. The church actively participates in community life in trying to find solutions to these social ills.

SOCIAL ASPECTS Family life has remained quite traditional in Mauritius, with children leaving their parent's home only when they get married or when they go abroad to study. The conventional family setting is the nuclear family with an average of two children. Marriage being at the very heart of family life, it has both a religious and social function. The couple's entire family, neighbors, and friends are invited and actively take part in preparing the ceremony. Changes are slowly taking place, however. A small percentage of couples choose to live together without being married, and young professionals back from their studies tend to live on their own.

POLITICAL IMPACT Ethnicity has tended to play a key role in Mauritian politics, with citizens voting along ethnic lines and Hindus of Indian descent dominating the government. In 2003 Paul Bérenger, a Catholic of French descent, became the prime minister of Mauritius, the first non-Hindu to hold that position. He represented the Mouvement Militant Mauricien political party, which aims to transcend ethnic-based politics.

CONTROVERSIAL ISSUES Because of its educational policy, the Catholic Church in Mauritius has been engaged in a conflict with the state over the notion of "specificity" of Catholic education. The state maintains that all students, irrespective of their creed, should be given free access to schools as provided by the government grant system. The Catholics maintain, however, that 50 percent of their recruits should be Catholic in order to maintain the "specificity" of their educational program in the 11 secondary schools that they run. In December 2002 a complaint was lodged against the Catholic Church for discriminatory practices on religious grounds in the choice of their students.

Other Religions

The first Muslims in Mauritius were slaves from Senegal and Mozambique, but Islam was taken to Mauritius mainly by the Indian sailors and laborers who went to work on the island during the French occupation. With the mass arrival of traders from Gujarat, weavers from Bihar, and laborers from other parts of India, there was a steady increase in the Muslim community. The Muslim presence became permanent, and gradually there developed an awareness of the educational, cultural, and religious needs of the Muslim community. With the emergence of Muslim leaders such as G.M.D. Atchia, Hassen Sakir, and Sir Razack Mohamed, Muslims have become part of Mauritius's socioeconomic development and political progress.

The principal mosque in Mauritius is the Jummah mosque in Port Louis, erected in 1856. It is visited by thousands of Muslims for daily prayers, and most major religious festivals are celebrated there. The Al-Aqsa mosque in Plaine Verte, where the Muslim community is grouped, is also popular.

Noormamode Noorooya, editor of the newspaper *Islamisme,* had been in close contact with the Ahmadiyah movement (founded in Qadian, Punjab, India), and he initiated the Mauritian Ahmadiyah movement in 1913. The first missionary from India came 1915. After this, more Muslim families joined the movement and formed the Ahmadiyah Muslim Association of Mauritius. It is from Mauritius that Ahmadism has spread its influence on the other islands of the Indian Ocean.

The Anglican presence in Mauritius dates to the early months of the British occupation, when the soldiers and sailors attended religious services in the barracks on Sundays. Sir Robert Farquhar, having understood that the French plantocracy would not be easily converted to the Protestant faith, turned toward the slave population and the free "coloured" men. In 1814 he called upon Rev. Jean Lebrun to serve this community in particular. Lebrun developed a two-pronged approach, incorporating both education and conversion to Protestantism. With the support of the London Missionary Society and the Mico Society, a strategy for the rehabilitation of the slaves was undertaken. Lebrun succeeded in opening 28 schools. He was sent away in 1832 by the Franco-Mauritian antiabolitionists, who were close to the governor. His work was soon taken over by Jacques Désiré Laval, a Catholic priest. The mission of the Anglican Church then turned to the Indian immigrants. There has been a decline in the number of Mauritian Anglicans. In 1854 Mauritius became an Anglican diocese, and the bishop took the title of Bishop of Mauritius. Monsignor Ian Ernest was appointed bishop in 2001.

In Mauritius there has been a latent conflict between the Catholic Church and the Church of England concerning the status of both churches. Both the Catholic and Anglican churches, together with the Presbyterian Church, are actively engaged in ecumenism, hosting special ecumenical services in different churches each year during January.

The presence of the Presbyterian Church in Mauritius has been marked mostly by the work of Rev. Lebrun in the field of education. Another well-known Presbyterian minister was Rev. Patrick Beaton, who served from 1851 to 1857 and who wrote *Creoles and Coolies,* in which he depicted the living conditions of the latter. Despite a small congregation, the church remains active. Pastor Rodney Curpanen was appointed moderator of the church in 1999.

The Seventh-day Adventist Church also has a presence in Mauritius. Upon his arrival in Mauritius in 1914, French missionary Paul Badaut discovered frustration in the Catholic community, especially among the working class. Targeting this social group, he started his mission in different regions of the island. In 1949 the Adventist Church opened a secondary school in Phoenix. In 1982 Adventists opened a home for the elderly in Quatre-Bornes as well as a center for young people in Belle-Mare.

The Pentecostal Movement, especially the Assembly of God under the impulsion of Pastor Aimé Ciseron in 1967, has been actively involved in evangelization in Mauritius. Pentecostalists have places of worship in different regions of the island. The congregation seems to have been growing.

The Jehovah's Witnesses movement was launched in Mauritius in 1933 by an American, Robert Nisbet, and it gained momentum with the work started by the Canadian Ralph Bennett in 1953. The movement has become autonomous over the years, with elders being recruited from among the Mauritian community.

In 1953 an American woman, Ottilie Rherm, introduced the Bahai faith on the island. Since 1956 some 130 spiritual centers have been opened in the main towns and rural areas. In 1972 the Mauritian government acknowledged the Bahai faith, which is kept alive by more than 10,000 adepts.

Soon Fo Lim Fat sparked an interested in Buddhism among the Mauritian Chinese community. A small pagoda known as the Lim Fat was built in 1948 in Port Louis. With the growing number of followers, other pagodas were set up but have been influenced by popular cults of China. Mauritians have therefore blended Buddhism with Chinese rituals, and this new practice prevails among the Chinese community.

Shakuntala Boolell and Danielle Tranquille

See Also Vol. I: *Christianity, Hinduism, Islam, Roman Catholicism*

Bibliography

Beaton, Patrick. *Creoles and Coolies; Or, Five Years in Mauritius.* 1859. Reprint (2nd ed.), Port Washington, N.Y.: Kennikat Press, 1971.

Boodhoo, Sarita. *Kanya Dan: The Why's of Hindu Marriage Rituals.* Port Louis, Mauritius: Mauritius Bhojpuri Institute, 1993.

Burrun, Breejan. *Histoire des religions des îles Maurice et Rodrigues.* Vacoas, Mauritius: Editions le Printemps, 2002.

Catholic Church. *Le phénomène des sectes ou nouveaux mouvements religieux: Défi pastoral—Rapport intermédiaire basé sur les réponses (env 75) et la documentation au 30 octobre 1985 des conférences épiscopales régionales ou nationales.* Kinshasa: Editions Saint Paul Afrique, 1986.

Dukhira, Chit G. *History of Mauritius: Experiments in Democracy.* New Delhi: Brijbasi Art Press Ltd., 2002.

Emrith, Moomtaz. *History of the Muslims in Mauritius.* Vacoas, Mauritius: Editions le printemps, 1994.

Moutou, Benjamin. *Les chrétiens de l'île Maurice.* Port Louis, Mauritius: Best Graphics, Ltd., 1996.

Nagapen, Amédée. *Histoire de l'église, Isle de France—Ile Maurice, 1721–1968.* Port Louis, Mauritius: Diocese of Port Louis, 1996.

———. *Histoire de la colonie: Isle de France—Ile Maurice, 1721–1968.* Port Louis, Mauritius: Diocese of Port Louis, 1996.

———. *The Indian Christian Community in Mauritius.* Port Louis, Mauritius: Roman Catholic Diocese of Port Louis, 1984.

Mexico

POPULATION 103,400,165

ROMAN CATHOLIC 88.0 percent

PROTESTANT 5.8 percent

NONRELIGIOUS 4.3 percent

OTHER 1.9 percent

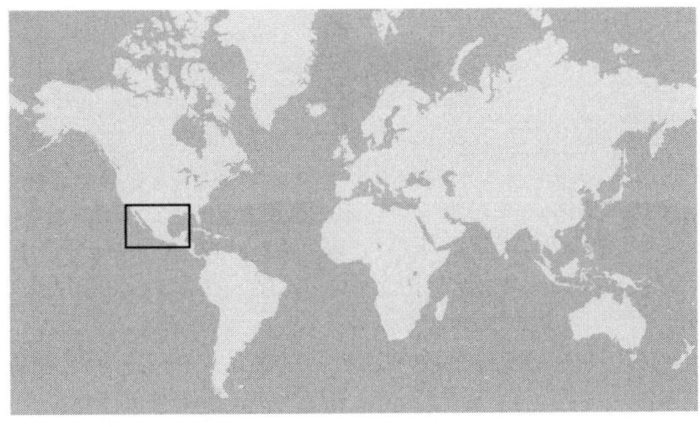

Country Overview

INTRODUCTION The United States of Mexico, located in North America, lies between the United States of America to the north and Guatemala and Belize to the southeast. Mexico is composed of a diversity of ethnic groups. The majority are mestizos (people of mixed Spanish-Indian blood), while the remainder include Amerindians (with 239 living languages), Caucasians, Afro-Americans, Middle Easterners, and Asians.

Spanish explorers arrived in Mesoamerica in the early sixteenth century C.E.. They discovered some of the greatest cultures in the history of the Americas, including the Olmec civilization, which began about 1200 B.C.E., and the Aztec empire, which dominated the central and southern regions of Mexico in the fifteenth and early sixteenth centuries.

Hernán Cortés (1485–1547) and his followers—Spaniards and a thousand allies from Tlaxcala (an Indian nation that had resisted Aztec rule)—conquered the Aztecs in 1519–21 and established Spanish rule in the region. During the colonial period the Roman Catholic Church dominated the religious life of the Viceroyalty of New Spain. A small number of Spanish Jews also arrived in the region during and after the Spanish conquest.

After Mexico achieved independence from Spain in 1821, the Catholic Church began to lose its privileged role in Mexican society, although it continued to monopolize the country's religious life. After the constitution of 1857 limited the power of the Catholic Church, Protestant denominations from the United States began establishing themselves in Mexico. The Mexican Revolution of 1910–17 brought a leftist government to power (the Institutional Revolutionary Party, known as PRI). This government established a separation between church and state.

Catholicism stands at the center of Mexican society and is the heart of its culture, which is highly syncretistic—a mixture of Roman Catholic beliefs and Native American animism. Other religious groups in Mexico include Protestant churches (whose adherents are known as Evangelicals in Mexico), other Christian groups such as Jehovah's Witnesses and Mormons, and non-Christian religions (including Native American religions, Judaism, Islam, Buddhism, Hinduism, Ancient Wisdom, and Psychic–Spiritualist–New Age groups).

Dancers perform outside of the Basilica of Our Lady of Guadalupe during the pilgrimage to the shrine of the Virgin of Guadalupe. The shrine is the most sacred relic in Mexico. © DANNY LEHMAN/CORBIS.

RELIGIOUS TOLERANCE The constitution provides for freedom of religion. Congress may not enact laws that establish or prohibit any religion. The constitution also provides for the separation of church and state. A provision was added to the constitution in 2001 that prohibited any form of discrimination, including discrimination against persons on the basis of religion.

Although the government generally respects this right, there are some restrictions at the local level. This is especially true within some of the Native American Indian communities in southern Mexico, where Evangelicals are occasionally persecuted by nominal Roman Catholics under the leadership of Mayan village elders, or *caciques.* Many of the most serious incidents have occurred in the state of Chiapas. The incidents of persecution, however, are not exclusively for religious reasons but rather are the result of a combination of political, cultural, and religious tensions, which limit the free practice of religion within some communities. Church leaders have been active in promoting interfaith understanding in the region.

Major Religion

ROMAN CATHOLICISM

DATE OF ORIGIN 1521 C.E.
NUMBER OF FOLLOWERS 91 million

HISTORY The evangelization of the Amerindian tribes of Mexico by Roman Catholic missionaries began with the arrival of the Franciscans (1524), Dominicans (1526), and Augustinians (1533). Between 1594 and 1722 the Jesuits worked among the Amerindians in northern Mexico, establishing mission centers there. During the seventeenth and eighteenth centuries the Franciscans organized a vast mission empire that included 11 districts, and the Dominicans established two important mission centers.

The first Catholic bishopric erected in Mexico was the See of Yucatán (c. 1518). In 1526 Pope Clement VII named Fray Julian de Garces the first bishop of New Spain. In 1545, at the solicitation of the Spanish king, Charles V, Pope Paul III separated the dioceses of New Spain from the Metropolitan See of Seville (in Spain) and established the Archdiocese of Mexico.

During the Spanish colonial period (1520–1821) there was a strict church-state relationship in Mexico. To facilitate conversion, Catholics frequently built churches on top of the ruins of ancient Indian worship centers. Catholic priests systematically established churches in nearly every village of Mexico prior to independence from Spain in 1821. The church accumulated extensive property in the growing cities and in the countryside.

In 1531 the Virgin of Guadalupe (the Virgin Mary) is said to have miraculously appeared to an Aztec Indian at Tepayac. The Catholic clergy attempted to bridge the gap between the Spanish and Indian cultures by establishing a chapel to Our Lady of Guadalupe at Tepeyac in 1555–56. This later became the most sacred site for Catholics in Mexico. Future generations of clerics embellished the legend of Our Lady of Guadalupe, so that by 1648 Mexican peasants considered the shrine to have supernatural significance and to be a sign that God had selected them as the new chosen people through the agency of the Virgin Mary. Today the Virgin of Guadalupe is a powerful symbol of Mexican national identity.

In 1571 Spanish authorities established the Office of the Holy Inquisition in New Spain for the purpose of defending the Catholic faith and rooting out any heresies that might exist within all levels of society. Any offenders could be detained, imprisoned, tortured, and killed by the inquisitors in their quest to maintain the purity of the faith and to protect its members from the influence of heretics (such as Jews, Muslims, and Protestants, the latter called "Lutherans"), blasphemers, bigamists, practitioners of witchcraft, and those committing acts against the Inquisition and other heretical activities. The tribunal of the Inquisition in Mexico was finally abolished in 1820.

After Mexico achieved independence from Spain in 1821, the power and influence of the Catholic Church began to decline because citizens no longer were obligated to pay tithes or to work for the church as peasants. Nevertheless, the Catholic Church maintained its monopoly on religion in Mexico, as seen in the constitution of 1824, which declared that the state religion "will perpetually be Catholic, Apostolic and Roman."

From independence (1821) to the Mexican Revolution (1910), the Catholic Church was aligned with conservative political parties, but certain church elements identified with the revolutionary struggle of peasants against the landed aristocracy. For instance, during the struggle for independence from Spain (1810–21), Father Miguel Hidalgo and other liberal-minded priests, such as Father José María Morelos, led uprisings against the Spanish colonial government. This period of Mexican history produced a division between the Catholic hierarchy and the "church of the people" that has continued up to the present.

During the nineteenth century the Catholic Church was heavily involved in politics on the side of the conservatives, who opposed the liberal movement and Freemasonry, which had gained popularity among the wealthy elite. The Catholic leadership strongly opposed the reform movement led by Benito Juárez and welcomed the French occupation of Mexico in 1862 under Maximilian of Hapsburg—which favored the Catholic Church. The French imperial venture was unable to survive the resistance of Mexican nationalistic forces and U.S. political pressures; in 1867, after capturing and executing Maximilian, Juárez returned to the presidency and enacted policies to limit the Catholic Church's power.

Church-state tensions eased considerably during the conservative administration of Porfirio Díaz (1876–1910), but they flared up again after the Revolution of 1910. The constitution of 1917 established a clear separation between church and state, guaranteed that public education would be secular and humanistic, and prohibited the clergy from participating in the nation's political life and from owning property.

The constitution of 1917 established certain antireligious laws that were opposed by the Catholic hierarchy. President Elías Calles, elected in 1924, strictly applied the constitution's anticlerical provisions (for example, deporting foreign clergy and closing Catholic schools). The church responded by suspending religious services, and in 1926 conservative Catholic forces in western states rebelled against Calles's government, a violent uprising known as the Cristero rebellion. The war ended in 1929 after the government promised to stop religious persecution.

Today Mexico has the second-largest Catholic population in the world after Brazil. Roman Catholicism in Mexico is extremely varied, ranging from traditional folk religious practices (especially in isolated rural communities, such as those in Chiapas) to the revolutionary ideas of liberation theology and from apolitical Catholic

Charismatic prayer groups to those who participate in the politicized Opus Dei movement. There are also various Catholic lay groups with different goals, purposes, and political orientations in modern Mexico, such as Mexican Catholic Action, the Knights of Columbus, and the Christian Family Movement, as well as a variety of organizations among university students and workers.

EARLY AND MODERN LEADERS Dominican friar Bartolomé de las Casas (died in 1566) defended the rights of the Indians in Chiapas during the 1500s. Dominican friar Pedro de la Peña (died in 1583) was the first professor of theology at the University of Mexico, founded in 1553; he later became the bishop of Quito, Ecuador.

The Spanish-born Franciscan priest Junípero Serra (1713–84) joined the missionary college of San Fernando, Mexico, in 1749. Between 1769 and 1782 he established and administered a chain of 21 missions in Alta California (present-day California).

Father Miguel Hidalgo y Costilla (1753–1811) revolted against Spain on 16 September 1810 (now celebrated as Mexican Independence Day). He marched against the capital with an ill-assorted, badly armed company of Indians. He was defeated, captured, and executed in 1811.

Father José María Morelos (1765–1815) led the liberation of much of southern Mexico from Spanish control and drafted a constitution calling for fair land distribution and racial equality. He was executed by Spanish forces in 1815. Bishop Samuel Ruíz García (born in 1924) worked for four decades to defend the human rights of the poor and the indigenous population in Chiapas. He played a fundamental role in peace negotiations between the Mexican government and the Zapatista National Liberation Army during the 1990s.

MAJOR THEOLOGIANS AND AUTHORS Monsignor Sergio Méndez Arceo (1907–92), bishop of Cuernavaca until 1982, was a progressive and, beginning in the 1960s, an early defender of liberation theology in Mexico; he was the only Catholic bishop to participate in the international conference Christians for Socialism in 1972. Enrique Dussel (born in 1934), a naturalized Mexican citizen from Argentina, is one of the leading Catholic philosophers and historians in the Americas. A defender of liberation theology, he wrote *A History of the Church in Latin America* (published in Spanish in 1972). Father Alfonso Navarro Castellanos (1935–2003) of the Congregation Missionaries of the Holy Spirit was a leader in the Catholic Charismatic movement in Mexico from the early 1970s. He had an international ministry as an author, speaker, philosopher, theologian, and evangelist. Roberto Blancarte (born in 1957) has written and edited many books and articles, including *History of the Catholic Church in Mexico* (1992).

HOUSES OF WORSHIP AND HOLY PLACES Throughout Mexico there are many Catholic shrines and sacred places, including caves, grottos, lakes, rivers, lagoons, crossroads, hills, and mountains. Many of these were sacred places for the Amerindians who inhabited the region prior to Spanish colonization, and they were clothed with Catholic symbols and renamed in honor of the Virgin Mary, Christ, or a Catholic saint. Some of the earliest Catholic churches were built on sites where the Amerindians worshiped their ancient gods and goddesses, such as the hill of Tepeyac on the shores of Lake Texcoco in Mexico City.

Many of the Catholic churches built in Mexico during the Spanish colonial period have survived and are revered by most Catholics. The shrine that is considered most holy is located at the hill of Tepeyac in Mexico City, where the Virgin Mary (in the form of Our Lady of Guadalupe) is alleged to have appeared to a poor Aztec, known today as Juan Diego, in 1531. The next two most important shrines are those dedicated to La Virgen de Juquila (the Virgin of Juquila) in Oaxaca and to Nuestro Señor Jesucristo y San Miguel de las Cuevas (Our Lord Jesus Christ and Saint Michael of the Caves) in Chalma in the state of México. Special celebrations are held annually in honor of the Virgin Mary, Christ, and Christian saints at other sites in Mexico.

WHAT IS SACRED? The concept of what is sacred among Roman Catholics in Mexico is in keeping with similar practices in other Catholic countries of the Americas and Europe, where there are numerous shrines and sacred places. These sanctuaries contain statues, paintings, and other symbols of the Virgin Mary, Christ, and the Catholic saints. Such shrines also include display cases of small metal representations of men, women and children; human arms, legs, eyes, and hearts; and animals, cars, boats, and other objects. People have left these behind as a testimony to their faith, either in thanksgiving or in supplication for divine intercession to cure a disease or to bring about some special favor. This is part of what is called "popular religiosity" among Roman Catholics in Mexico.

The most sacred relic in Mexico is the image of the Virgin of Guadalupe, which appears on a cloth that is alleged to be the actual cloak of Juan Diego, the sixteenth-century Aztec peasant who claimed to have witnessed an apparition of the Virgin Mary. This image is housed in the Basilica of Our Lady of Guadalupe, built at the foot of Tepeyac hill, which is now part of Mexico City. Juan Diego was canonized in 2002.

HOLIDAYS AND FESTIVALS Of nine public holidays, only two are associated with Christian religious events: Good Friday and Christmas Day. Most employers also grant holiday leave to their workers on Holy Thursday, All Soul's Day (31 October), Virgin of Guadalupe Day (2 August), and Christmas Eve. The most important Catholic holidays in Mexico are Easter Week and Virgin of Guadalupe Day, although every town and village also holds a festival on its patron saint's day.

MODE OF DRESS There is no special dress code for Roman Catholic parishioners in Mexico; however, the members of the various Catholic religious orders for men and women have their own traditional dress codes.

DIETARY PRACTICES There are no special dietary practices among Roman Catholics in Mexico; the variations in diet that exist are influenced by local customs and practices, mainly among the Amerindian communities.

RITUALS Traditional Roman Catholic rituals, imported from Europe during the Spanish conquest, are practiced by the majority of upper-class Catholics in Mexico today, but most middle and lower-class Catholics observe what is called "popular religiosity," a term used to describe the syncretistic belief system of Mexico's predominant Mestizo population of nominal Catholics. Also, the persistence of Indian cultures and belief systems is a vital force in Mexican society today, as seen in the prevalence of practices such as magic (*bujería*), herbal healing (*curanderismo*), and shamanism throughout Mexico, even in many non-Indian areas.

Mexican Catholics also hold a celebration in honor of the dead called Culto a los Muertos (21 October to 2 November). It is based on pre-Christian beliefs of the Amerindians and on Catholic beliefs from Spain. In villages, towns, and cities across the country, Mexicans take a variety of offerings (such as flowers, food, drink, and candles) to a family altar in their homes or to the graves of their dead relatives, and there is music, dancing, and fireworks in their honor.

RITES OF PASSAGE Although middle- and upper-class Catholics in Mexico observe the standard Roman Catholic rites of passage, such as baptism, first Communion, confirmation, marriage, and last rites, the marginalized people of Mexico often do not have the resources to pay for the cost of formal religious ceremonies in the Catholic Church.

MEMBERSHIP In Mexico there has been a steady decline in the size of the Catholic population (it dropped from 96 percent in 1970 to 88 percent in 2000). Despite the fact that the Catholic clergy have warned against the "invasion of the sects," many former Catholics have become members of other religious traditions or consider themselves nonreligious.

One of the challenges facing the Roman Catholic Church in Mexico today is how to combat the growth and influence of Protestant denominations, other Christian groups, and non-Christian religions that are eroding the cultural base of traditional Catholicism by creating a new climate of religious pluralism within modern Mexican society. Rather than confrontation, the moderate elements within the Catholic Church, inspired by the Second Vatican Council (1962–65), seek to "reevangelize those who are already baptized" in the Catholic faith and to improve pastoral care for Catholic parishioners who may be tempted to stray from the flock by the offer of new spiritual and religious alternatives.

SOCIAL JUSTICE In Mexico there are thousands of social service institutions sponsored by the Catholic Church or its various religious orders, including hospitals, clinics, literacy programs, orphanages, nursing homes, schools, women's ministries, migrant ministries, jail and prison ministries, and homeless shelters. One example is Casa Alianza, which works with homeless and at-risk children.

SOCIAL ASPECTS The Roman Catholic Church and popular Catholic religiosity dominated the political, social, and religious life of Mexico until the 1960s, when, as elsewhere, a large gap began to emerge between the moral and ethical teachings of the Catholic Church and the views of the Catholic population concerning marriage and family life. A growing number of Catholic couples are now opting for a civil rather than a religious ceremony. The Catholic population has also been experiencing a rising divorce rate and an increase of children born to single mothers, and millions of Catholic couples use unauthorized birth-control methods.

POLITICAL IMPACT The Mexican Episcopal Conference prohibits clergy members from joining political parties or becoming political leaders. The Catholic Church, however, also states that priests have a responsibility to denounce actions that violate Christian morality.

In 1992, under the administration of President Carlos Salinas (affiliated with the PRI), constitutional reforms were approved that officially recognized churches of all religious groups, restored land ownership rights to the Catholic Church, allowed for the wearing of Catholic vestments and robes in public, authorized the teaching of religion in private schools, and gradually restored diplomatic relations between the Vatican and the Mexican government. Nevertheless, tensions between the church and the state continued, particularly in southern Mexico. Local government and PRI officials and large landowners accused Catholic Bishop Samuel Ruíz of San Cristóbal de las Casas of having supported the Zapatista rebellion that began in Chiapas in 1994, a charge that the bishop strongly denied. In addition, the Vatican accused Ruíz of "theological and pastoral distortions" because of his support for an "Indian Theology," which is associated with the liberation theology. The Zapatista rebels insisted that Ruíz continue to serve as mediator in their negotiations with the federal government.

Strong Catholic support for the candidacy of right-wing businessman Vicente Fox in the 2000 presidential elections was essential in bringing the opposition National Action Party (PAN) to power in Mexico, overcoming the PRI's 70 years of dominance in the political arena. Under the presidency of Fox, who himself is a devout Roman Catholic, relations between the church and the state have thawed.

CONTROVERSIAL ISSUES A series of public opinion polls conducted in the 1990s revealed that many Mexican Catholics disagreed with the church's policies on certain issues, including birth control, divorce, remarriage, abortion, and the role of women in the church.

Although in Mexico, unlike in other Latin American countries, the Catholic Church is strong and largely self-sufficient, within the church there are many conflicting ideas about the church's nature and mission, creating debate and controversy among the hierarchy, the diocesan priests, the religious orders, and the laypeople. Especially controversial has been the tendency—supported by the Vatican's apostolic delegate to Mexico, Archbishop Jerónimo Prigione (served 1978–97)—to promote the appointment of moderate and conservative bishops while seeking to isolate the church's more progressive elements.

Great differences in approach exist among bishops in Mexico. Those based in the central states are distinguished by their concern for doctrinal and moral issues rather than for social causes. These bishops strongly support moralist and spiritualist initiatives by lay organizations. The bishops of the southern states of Oaxaca and Chiapas have been more concerned about the deteriorating socioeconomic conditions of the peasants and about government repression of the poor. They have supported the organization of progressive base communities (where progressive Catholics come together to pray, discuss social problems, and engage in other activities) and have sought to dismantle the paternalistic structures of the Catholic Church. They look to liberation theology for their inspiration.

Between the conservatives and progressive elements is a substantial group of moderates who identify with the principles of the Second Vatican Council. Associated with this group is the influential Catholic Charismatic movement, founded in the early 1970s, which is especially strong in Mexico City.

CULTURAL IMPACT Roman Catholicism has had a significant influence on all aspects of Mexican life, including music, the arts, and literature, despite the anticlerical attitude of the PRI, which ruled Mexico for most of the twentieth century. Catholic religious symbols are seen everywhere, but the most common ones are the cross and the image of Our Lady of Guadalupe. Spanish colonial architecture is in evidence throughout Mexico, especially in the form of the village church.

Other Religions

Other religious organizations and faiths in Mexico include the growing number of Protestant (Evangelical) churches, other Christian groups (such as Jehovah's Witnesses, Church of Jesus Christ of Latter-day Saints, and Light of the World Church), and non-Christian religions, including Native American religions, Judaism, Islam, Buddhism, Hinduism, Ancient Wisdom (for instance, Rosicrucians, Martinistas, and Gnostics), and Psychic–Spiritualist–New Age groups.

After the constitution of 1857 formalized liberal reforms, which limited the power of the Roman Catholic Church and broadened individual freedoms, the systematic penetration of Protestant groups began in Mexico. Various Protestant denominations from the United States were successful in establishing work in Mexico between 1850 and 1900, despite widespread opposition from the Mexican government and Roman Catholic authorities. The autonomous Mexican Church of Jesus was founded in 1850 by a dissident group of Catholic priests in Mexico City; in 1873 this church became affiliated with the Protestant Episcopal Church in the United States.

By 1900 about 20 Protestant denominations and mission agencies had been permanently established in Mexico. In 1910 there were about 24,000 baptized Protestants in Mexico, mainly Methodists, Presbyterians, Baptists, Congregationalists, Christian Churches (Disciples of Christ), and Quakers. By 1936, however, the total membership of these groups was only about 23,000, which reflects the difficulties encountered by these denominations during the Mexican Revolution and the Great Depression years. Between 1950 and 1985 at least 110 additional Protestant mission agencies arrived in Mexico, and scores of autonomous Mexican denominations also came into existence.

Since the 1960s the largest denominations have been Presbyterians, Methodists, Baptists, Christian Churches, Adventists, and Pentecostals (including various Apostolic Churches, Churches of God, Swedish Pentecostals, Assemblies of God, and MIEPI [Independent Evangelical Protestant Church Movement] groups). Most of the religious practices of these groups were similar to those observed by Protestants in other countries, especially in Latin America. There are numerous social-service ministries sponsored by Protestant denominations in Mexico. In 2000 Protestants formed an estimated 5.8 percent of the total Mexican population, compared to 1.8 percent in 1970.

Among the non-Protestant Christian groups is an indigenous religious tradition founded in Monterrey, Nuevo León, in 1926 by Eusebio Joaquín González (later known as the Apostle Aarón). He blended Mexican mysticism with Pentecostal fervor to create a unique religious movement that has spread throughout Mexico, to more than 20 countries in the Americas, and to Spain, Portugal, Italy, Germany, and Australia. The Light of the World Church, as the movement is known, grew from 80 members in 1929 to more than 4 million members in 22 countries in 1990, according to church sources. The official name of this organization is the Church of the Living God, Column and Pillar of Truth, Jesus the Light of the World, but its followers are popularly known in Mexico as "Aaronistas" (followers of Aarón).

Among the Psychic–Spiritualist–New Age groups is the Patriarch Elijah Mexican Church (Iglesia Mexicana Patriarca Elías), founded in 1869 by the psychic Roque Jacinto Rojas Esparza (1812–79). It is also known as the Spiritualist Trinitarian Marian Movement of the Prophet Elijah. Today this movement claims to have more than a million followers in Mexico.

Hundreds of Spanish Jews arrived in Mexico during and after the Spanish conquest, but the Jewish faith was not celebrated openly until after the 1850s. In 1990 the Jewish community in Mexico, one of the largest in Latin America, numbered about 64,500.

There is a small Muslim population in the city of Torreón, Coahuila, and a group of approximately 300 Muslims lives in the municipality of San Cristóbal de las Casas in Chiapas.

Clifton L. Holland

See Also Vol. I: *Roman Catholicism*

Bibliography

Blancarte, Roberto. *Historia de la Iglesia Católica en México.* Mexico City: Fondo de Cultura Económica, 1992.

Brading, D.A. *Mexican Phoenix: Our Lady of Guadalupe—Image and Tradition across Five Centuries.* New York: Cambridge University Press, 2001.

Dussel, Enrique D. *A History of the Church in Latin America: Colonialism to Liberation (1492–1979).* Grand Rapids, Mich.: Eerdmans, 1981.

Herring, Hubert. *A History of Latin America, from the Beginnings to the Present.* New York: Alfred A. Knopf, 1968.

McGavran, Donald. *Church Growth in Mexico.* Grand Rapids, Mich.: Eerdmans, 1963.

Poole, Stafford. *Our Lady of Guadalupe: The Origins and Sources of a Mexican National Symbol, 1531–1797.* Tucson: University of Arizona Press, 1995.

Scheffler, Lilian. *Magia y Brujería en México.* Mexico City: Panorama Editorial, 1994.

Micronesia

POPULATION 135,869

CHRISTIAN 98.5 percent

OTHER 1.5 percent

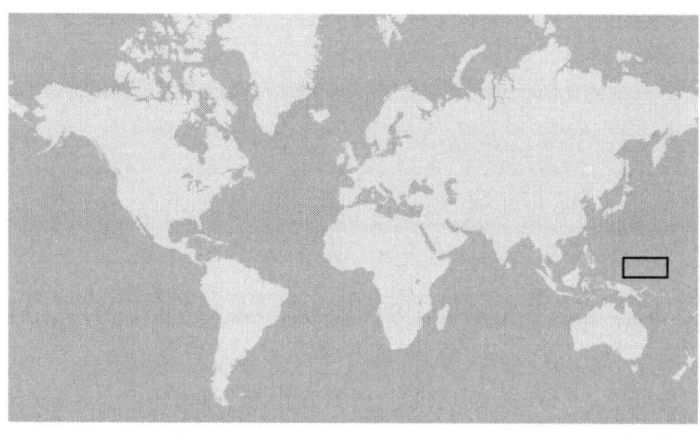

Country Overview

INTRODUCTION The Federated States of Micronesia (FSM), a sovereign, self-governing nation, consists of 607 islands in the central Pacific Ocean. Its four "states" are associated with four major island groups: Yap, Chuuk (called Truk until 1990), Pohnpei (called Ponape until 1984), and Kosrae (called Kusaie until the early 1980s). Once called the Carolines, the islands began to be known as part of the larger Micronesian chain of islands in the 1830s.

The population of more than 135,000, consisting of various Micronesian and Polynesian ethnolinguistic groups, is overwhelmingly Christian. Almost all Kosrae residents are United Church of Christ, and on Chuuk and Pohnpei about half are Protestant and half are Catholic. Historically there have been many more Catholics than Protestants on Yap, but the Protestant contingent is growing. Although English is the official and common language on the islands, church services are generally conducted in the local ethnic dialects.

Starting in the late 1800s the islands have been ruled by a succession of foreign powers—Spain, Germany, Japan, and the United States. Germany emphasized commerce, and a German evangelical church, the Liebenzell Mission, gained a small but significant foothold in Yap and Chuuk. Since the FSM and the United States formed the Compact of Free Association (which took effect in 1986), the islands have also proved to be fertile missionary soil for American evangelical Christian churches, including the United Church of Christ, the Assemblies of God, independent Baptists, and the United Pentecostal Church. The Nukuno Protestant Church in Chuuk is representative of a few emerging evangelical churches that have broken ties with historic mainline churches. Most immigrants are Filipino Catholics. The Iglesia Ni Christo churches are present on every FSM island having a sizable Filipino population.

A tiny remnant of Asian religious influences can be traced in part to the Japanese buildup of military bases in Chuuk, Yap, and Pohnpei leading up to World War II. Small groups of Jehovah's Witnesses, Mormons, and Seventh-day Adventists practice in the FSM, especially in Pohnpei and Chuuk. Also found in the FSM are followers of the Bahai faith, Buddhists, Shintoists, and Confucianists.

RELIGIOUS TOLERANCE The FSM constitution provides for freedom of religion, and the bill of rights forbids establishment of a state religion. The government generally promotes a climate of religious tolerance, and foreign missionaries operate without hindrance on all four islands. The essentially amicable relationship among religions in the FSM contributes to religious freedom.

Major Religion

CHRISTIANITY

DATE OF ORIGIN 1852 C.E.
NUMBER OF FOLLOWERS 133,800

HISTORY Some Micronesian islands were apparently sighted by European explorers in the 1500s, although the islands were peopled by immigrants from East Asia at least as early as 200 C.E. Medieval Pohnpei was ruled by the Saudeleurs (c. 1100–1600?), a tyrannical royal dynasty that reigned over Nan Madol, an elaborate city of stone fortresses. By 1400 Kosrae, the most stratified society in Micronesia, was unified under one *toskosra* (paramount chief).

No serious efforts were made to evangelize Micronesians until the nineteenth century, although Spanish Jesuits temporarily set up a colony in Yap in 1731. Benjamin Snow and Albert Sturges (Congregationalist missionaries from the American Board of Commissioners for Foreign Missions [ABCFM])—accompanied by Hawaiian "assistants"—established churches in Kosrae and Pohnpei in 1852. Beginning in the 1870s islander missionaries from Pohnpei working under the ABCFM built churches and schools in Chuuk. Capuchin missionaries, buttressed by Spanish military force, founded Catholic missions in Pohnpei and Yap in the 1880s. In Pohnpei they met resistance from the American missionaries and in collusion with the Spanish government ejected the latter, although local leaders kept the Protestant mission alive.

After Spain sold what would become known as the FSM to Germany in 1899, German Capuchins replaced their Spanish predecessors. In 1906 the German Protestant Liebenzell missionaries began work in Pohnpei and Chuuk. After taking control of the islands following World War I, Japan expelled all German missionaries (although the Liebenzellers later returned) but initially supported Congregational Christians from Japan and Jesuits and Mercedarian Sisters from Spain with government grants.

Micronesian villagers sit outside of a thatched church in the early 1980s. During the twentieth century islanders began substituting stone and concrete for thatch and matting. © JACK FIELDS/CORBIS.

After World War II the ABCFM came back with renewed commitment, the German mission became more American, and the Vatican transferred Spanish Jesuit responsibilities to the American Jesuits. Assisted by Maryknoll Sisters, Jesuits developed impressive programs in education, welfare, and social advocacy, opening the first four-year high school in Micronesia and establishing a research institute, the Micronesian Seminar, in Chuuk.

Most Protestant denominations, as well as Roman Catholic fellowships, are present on the four major islands. The historic mainline churches—those churches founded by the major missionary movements of the established denominations in Europe, Australia, New Zealand, and North America—represent the majority of Protestant adherents in the FSM. Most Kosrae residents are United Church of Christ, and on Chuuk and Pohnpei about half are Protestant and half are Catholic.

Historically there have been many more Catholics than Protestants on Yap, although the Protestant contingent is growing. Among Protestants in the FSM, the second largest group is the Assemblies of God. Most immigrants are Filipino Catholics, who join local Catholic churches. The Iglesia Ni Christo churches are present on every FSM island having a sizable Filipino population. Small groups of Jehovah's Witnesses, Mormons, and Seventh-day Adventists practice in the FSM, especially in Pohnpei and Chuuk.

EARLY AND MODERN LEADERS While Albert Sturges and Benjamin Snow were the early twin pillars of American Protestant work in Pohnpei and Kosrae, Elizabeth and Jane Baldwin—Presbyterians from the United States—were two of the most celebrated missionaries in the history of Christianity in Oceania. They were active during the late nineteenth century. For 40 years the multilingual Baldwin sisters lived simply, developed the training schools in Kosrae and Chuuk, and gently democratized Kosrae's hierarchical social system by stressing the priesthood of all believers. Elizabeth Baldwin was assisted in translating the entire Bible into Kosraean by an indigenous islander known by the name of Kefwas. Moses Teikoroi, a Sturges protégé, was a pioneer missionary in the Chuuk lagoon.

Henry Nanpei (1860–1928), a Pohnpeian, became Protestantism's leader during the rapid changes under the successive colonial regimes of Spain, Germany, and Japan. Although most Catholic priests have been expatriates, in 1940 Father Paulino Cantero from Pohnpei became the first indigenous Micronesian priest to be ordained.

MAJOR THEOLOGIANS AND AUTHORS Indigenous theologians and authors of religious practice have not yet emerged from the tiny, remote, and largely oral cultural contexts of the FSM. Following Vatican II the first meeting of the Vicariate Pastoral Planning Council in Micronesia (1971) focused on promoting the self-realization of islanders. Francis Hezel, Jesuit director of the Micronesian Seminar, has spearheaded liberating theological reflection on enculturation and indigenization in the region, including leadership training, financial responsibility, and the incorporation of cultural symbols in worship.

HOUSES OF WORSHIP AND HOLY PLACES FSM churches, the focus for kinship groups and social life, are invariably the largest buildings and are located near the center of each village or group of villages. Whereas in the nineteenth century churches had been constructed out of indigenous materials and according to indigenous styles, during the last century islanders substituted stone and concrete for thatch and matting. FSM islanders still retain architectural styles introduced by the early foreign missionaries, such as small windows and boxlike construction, even though such styles are ill suited for a tropical climate. Traditional ceremonial buildings, called *nahs* in Pohnpei and *pebai* in Yap, still function as community meetinghouses where transcendent power is evoked in prayers and oral traditions.

WHAT IS SACRED? The anthropologist William Lessa described Micronesian religion as "a mélange of many elements." Although basic aspects of missionary Christianity were accepted in the FSM, islander Christians still revere ancestors and the spirits of ancestors. In Chuuk, prior to the last half of the twentieth century, offerings to ancestor spirits were placed in model canoes suspended from the roof in men's houses. The spirits of certain animals—such as sharks, eels, and lizards—were sacred to the clan of which they were the totem. Heavenly spirits such as the Yapese Yalafath (a trickster god) and nature spirits associated with certain trees and plants were also sacred. *Tapuanu* masks were worn for ceremonial purposes. Only traces of these cultural forms remain.

Part of the Nan Madol ruins, Madol Powe, was an ancient religious center; many Pohnpeians believe it is still a *tabu* (forbidden) area. Today some Catholic liturgies include such traditional sacred symbols as the bestowal of the *mwaramwar* (head garland) at baptismal rites.

HOLIDAYS AND FESTIVALS Christians in Micronesia celebrate Good Friday, Easter, and Christmas in addition to Cultural Day, Constitution Day, United Nations Day, FSM Independence Day, and separate state holidays, such as Kosrae Liberation Day, commemorating the American defeat of the Japanese. These holidays feature singing, dancing, feasting, and sports competitions, such as canoe racing. Festivals are also held to raise money for churches. The completion of a major village project, such as a community house, is also a time for ritual festivity in Yap.

MODE OF DRESS While most Christians dress in Western clothes in Kosrae, many men and boys in the outer islands of Yap and Chuuk wear a brightly colored loincloth called a *thu*. Although the *thu* is not common in formal worship services, it is acceptable at informal religious gatherings. Similarly the traditional lavalava, or grass skirt, worn by Yapese women is not usually worn to Sunday services but will be featured at special religious occasions.

In Kosrae women wear white dresses and hats to worship. In Chuuk a few women can still be seen wearing a *nikautang* (a dress with puffed sleeves) to religious functions. Dancers at secular festivals will wear beaded necklaces and colorful ceremonial clothing that may evoke ancient religious meanings for participants.

DIETARY PRACTICES Local geography rather than distinct religious conventions dictates Micronesian Christian dietary practice, although feasting is an important part of any major religious celebration. At weddings and funerals relatives will contribute large amounts of local foodstuffs, especially rice and fish. Remnants of traditional agricultural festivals are still present in the offerings of first fruits in harvest worship services. Micronesian Christians are not vegetarians, but they are partial to breadfruit and yams. The Yapese eat taro for the most part.

RITUALS Before the missionaries arrived Micronesians performed a great variety of rituals, including breadfruit harvests in Chuuk, where trees were sanctified by herbs; rites of benediction in Yap, which preceded the felling of trees; and numerous *sakau* ceremonies prior to fishing journeys, warfare, or threats of typhoons. *Sakau* rituals were governed by strict rules, and the highest chief was served first. Women in Yap were secluded in huts during menstruation and childbirth. The Yapese *mitmit* was an all-out traditional feast accompanied by gift giving, singing, and dancing. One village would give a *mitmit* to another to reciprocate for one given to it in a previous year.

Church members arrive early for Sunday morning worship, and most of the day on Sunday is still devoted to services in Kosrae, Yap, and outer FSM islands. Men and women sit in different sections, and the choir is front and center. Occasionally island food and drink are substituted for the bread and wine in a Communion service. Nineteenth-century Western music (especially gospel hymns from America) makes up the bulk of congregational singing. Virtually all Protestant and Catholic pastors are local and preach in the indigenous language of their congregation. Typical services also include prayers, psalm readings, additional Scripture readings, announcements, and greetings to visitors. Weekday morning and evening prayers are still observed in many homes.

RITES OF PASSAGE Like Micronesians in general, islander Christians mark transitions between five stages in a person's life span: babyhood, childhood, young adulthood, middle age, and old age. Traditionally many taboos were associated with these and other rites of passage. For example, in the early 1900s, the family of a deceased person in Yap was separated from the community and prohibited from eating certain kinds of food. High priests in Pohnpei and Kosrae officiated at rites that entailed petitioning deceased family members for protection from spirits, especially during times of transition. Today in Yap, funeral services are still highly ritualized. When someone dies relatives and friends set up a formalized wail, singing songs of lamentation. The corpse is washed, decorated with flower garlands, and presented with gifts for the journey to Lang (the other world). Dirges are sung at the grave for three days, and on the fourth day a tomb is erected over the grave. Then the whole village observes a 10-day period of respect; those who washed the corpse observe a longer period. When close relatives have ended a five-month period of mourning, a rite called pay stone is held, in which those who assisted in the funeral are rewarded.

The practice of four-day funerals (as observed in certain parts of Micronesia, including Pohnpei) stems from the traditional belief that the soul of the dead did not depart the body for the heavens until the fourth day. Until that point it was necessary to appease the soul so it would not bring any misfortune to the family. Once the soul departed for the heavens, it served as the family's protector spirit.

MEMBERSHIP In Kosrae, until recently, to be a Kosraean was synonymous with being a Congregationalist. In the 1980s Jehovah's Witnesses, Mormons, and Seventh-day Adventists stepped up evangelization campaigns especially in Yap and Chuuk. Since each of the four state governments controls a radio station broadcasting primarily in the local language and only one religious group operates a private radio station, there is scant room for recruitment by radio. Television and the Internet also have not yet become a major factor in recruitment of church members. On Pohnpei clan divisions still affect religious conversion, with more Protestants living on the western side of the island, while more Catholics live on the eastern side.

SOCIAL JUSTICE Many Micronesians suspect that human rights language masks a neocolonial agenda. For example, although traditionally women were not the equals of men, they were protected, were honored, and exercised power over land selection. Christian missionaries, however, promoted gender equality in ways that may have contributed to the breakdown of the all-important extended family unit. For instance, by insisting that women receive equal pay for equal work and sanctioning women's work outside the home, Christian teaching undercut the authority of the lineage chief. The resulting increased parent-child tensions may well have contributed to child neglect, spousal abuse, and a high suicide rate, especially in Chuuk.

The church has also led the way in creating new opportunities for women. By attacking the traditional practice of confining women to separate menstrual houses, the church enabled women to join the rest of the community for prayers and other activities. Today the church advocates educating parents to affirm children, reduce sibling rivalry, and ameliorate domestic violence.

SOCIAL ASPECTS Traditionally social structures, such as the extended family unit, were viewed as divinely ordained. Missionary teachings, especially regarding the extended family in the Bible, were generally understood as reinforcing already existing family and kinship networks. The matrilineal system, however, had begun to break down prior to missionary contact, so that while Micronesian faith was challenged by the missionary ethic of individual rights, it already had a strong individualistic component while also paying due regard to the more traditional island emphasis on communal responsibility.

The churches recognize traditional arranged marriages, and old formalities usually supplement the church wedding. Some pastors and priests continue to honor the parent's wishes in regard to marriage and refuse to marry couples whose parents are opposed. Church leaders also recognize the social role of funerals as outlets for reinforcing the customary family circle meeting.

POLITICAL IMPACT The missionaries, in collusion with colonial civil authorities, often furthered cultural imperialism by censoring native dances and weakening chiefly prestige. But missionaries also eliminated certain objectionable practices, such as abortion, infanticide, and the *mispil,* where a woman captured from a neighboring village was used as a mistress for men's houses. Under missionary influence values associated with social status, transgression, and reconciliation were redefined in the life of the community, creating a homogeneous social order.

CONTROVERSIAL ISSUES Given a lack of economic development and an absence of an infrastructure to attract investment, Christians in Micronesia face a number of serious social issues, including food shortages, youth unemployment, black market alcohol, and pollution. In Chuuk sewage runs into the lagoon, and the streets are littered with trash. There, as well as in Kosrae and Pohnpei, the Congregational Christian Church has conducted workshops and extension education programs aimed at developing constructive responses to some of these issues, including an ecology campaign that entails picking up litter. Ongoing disputes concerning land ownership and land-use rights further complicate linguistic and ethnographic differences. As elsewhere in the region, Micronesia faces threats associated with sexual promiscuity, especially HIV and AIDS. The Catholic Church, through the Micronesian Seminar (originally in Chuuk but now in Pohnpei), has sponsored research on issues such as child abuse, economic injustice, and suicide. In general, however, Micronesia's Christian churches have been reluctant to address controversial issues.

CULTURAL IMPACT Christianity brought a number of foreign cultural influences to Micronesia, including the introduction of literacy in indigenous languages; Western hymns, clothing, and architectural styles; European conflicts between Catholics and Protestants; democratic approaches to problem solving; and abstention from work and trading on Sundays. FSM islanders are now reassessing some of their traditions in the light of their search for cultural identity. In particular, there has been renewed interest in incorporating traditional religious songs composed by Micronesians.

Other Religions

While Christianity (including new religious movements that are essentially Christian in origin) is the overwhelmingly predominant religion in the FSM, there are traces of other faith traditions. A few Buddhists and adherents of Chinese religious traditions (including Confucianism) are concentrated in Yap and Chuuk, with small groups in Kosrae. As a result of the Japanese occupation during World War II, there are a handful of believers in Shinto, an indigenous religious practice of Japanese origin once associated with emperor worship. The Japanese did not actively proselytize in Micronesia.

A few hundred Bahai adherents live in Chuuk and Pohnpei. During the 1997 International Women's Day Observance in Chuuk, Bahai believers drew more than 300 indigenous women from surrounding lagoons to workshops designed to promote the advancement of women. Like their Christian counterparts, Bahai adherents have had an impact on social justice in the FSM. For example, the Bahai faith credits one of their followers, a U.S. government official serving in the FSM, with pioneering legislation on domestic violence, hate crimes, rape, child care, and health research.

Jack A. Hill

See Also Vol. I: *Christianity, Reformed Christianity, Roman Catholicism*

Bibliography

Forman, Charles W. *The Island Churches of the South Pacific: Emergence in the Twentieth Century.* Maryknoll, N.Y.: Orbis, 1982.

Hanlon, David. *Remaking Micronesia.* Honolulu: University of Hawai'i Press, 1998.

———. *Upon a Stone Altar: A History of the Island of Pohnpei to 1890.* Honolulu: University of Hawai'i Press, 1988.

Haynes, Douglas, and William L. Wuerch. *Micronesian Religion and Lore: A Guide to the Sources, 1526–1990.* Westport, Conn.: Greenwood Press, 1995.

Hezel, Francis X. *The Catholic Church in Micronesia.* Chicago: Loyola University Press, 1991.

———. *The First Taint of Civilization.* Honolulu: University of Hawai'i Press, 1983.

Lessa, William A. *Ulithi: A Micronesian Design for Living.* New York: Holt, Rinehart and Winston, 1966.

Trumbull, Robert. *Paradise in Trust: A Report on Americans in Micronesia.* New York: William Sloane, 1959.

Wuerch, William L., and Dirk Anthony Ballendorf. *Historical Dictionary of Guam and Micronesia.* Metuchen, N.J.: Scarecrow Press, 1994.

Moldova

POPULATION 4,434,547

ORTHODOX CHRISTIAN 83.8 percent

OTHER CHRISTIAN 4.2 percent

JEWISH 0.8 percent

OTHER 1.0 percent

NONRELIGIOUS 10.2 percent

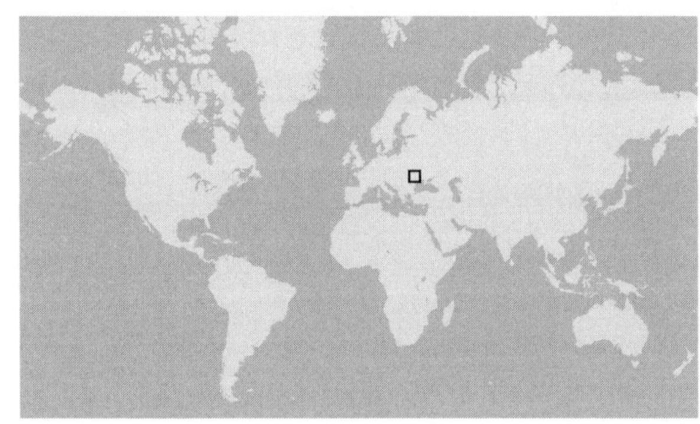

Country Overview

INTRODUCTION The Republic of Moldova, with an area of only a little over 13,000 square miles, lies between Ukraine and Romania in eastern Europe. The dominance of Orthodox Christianity in Moldova and in Romania is unique in that it exists within a Latin culture. Both Moldavians and Romanians are descended from the Vlachs, and the Moldavian and Romanian languages trace their origins to the Roman soldiers who occupied Dacia following Trajan's conquest in 106 C.E.

Christianity spread along the western shore of the Black Sea in the third century, but its history during the millennium following the withdrawal of the Roman administration in 271 is obscure. By the fourteenth century, however, Moldavian ethnic identity was identified with Orthodox Christianity and oriented toward Constantinople. The Orthodox Church in Moldova was originally influenced by the Romanian Orthodox Church, but in the nineteenth century it was incorporated into the Russian Orthodox Church. The question of the orientation of the church, whether toward Romania or Russia, surfaced again in the 1990s.

RELIGIOUS TOLERANCE Moldova is a secular state, and the constitution provides for freedom of religion. The Law on Religions of 1992, however, inhibits the activities of religious groups not registered with the state. Such groups cannot buy land, acquire construction permits for churches, or obtain space in public cemeteries.

Although there is no state religion, the Moldavian Orthodox Church, by far the largest religious organization in the country, receives special treatment. In the separatist region of Transdniester, local authorities endorse privileged relations with the Orthodox Church, while a number of minority religious groups, for example, Baptists, Jehovah's Witnesses, and Methodists, have been denied registration and even subjected to official harassment.

Major Religion

MOLDAVIAN ORTHODOX CHURCH

DATE OF ORIGIN Before 1350 C.E.
NUMBER OF FOLLOWERS 3.7 million

HISTORY By the mid-fourteenth century, at the time of the formation of the principality of Moldova between the Danube and Dniester rivers, Orthodox Christianity had become the dominant religion. Moldova experienced a short period of expansion and prosperity under the prince (*gospodar*) Stephen the Great (1435–1504). The best known of the country's rulers, Stephen was canonized by the Romanian Orthodox Church in 1992 and is recognized as the patron saint of Moldova. In the sixteenth century Moldova was overrun by the Ottoman Empire and turned into a vassal state. At the beginning of the nineteenth century the Russian Empire annexed Moldova from Turkey, and most of the Islamic Turkish residents were expelled.

After World War I, Moldova was contested between the Soviet Union and Romania. The land west of the Dniester, known as Bessarabia, became part of Romania, while that to the east of the Dniester, known as Transdniester, became part of the Soviet Union. In 1940 the Soviets annexed Bessarabia and in 1944 transformed the whole region into the Moldavian Soviet Socialist Republic, with the approximate borders of present-day Moldova. During the Soviet era, however, Moldova was less affected by the atheistic state policy than were the other republics, resulting in the preservation of its religious traditions.

After the breakup of the Soviet Union in 1991, Moldova became an independent state. The regions of Bessarabia and Transdniester had experienced different levels of Russification during the Soviet years, and these circumstances, combined with the pro-Romanian orientation of Moldova's first independent government, led to the secession of Transdniester. After bloody conflict in 1992, the Transdniestrian Moldavian Republic, with a territory of barely 1,600 square miles and a population of 750,000, became an unrecognized but a de facto independent state.

Also in 1992 a number of patriotically motivated priests broke away from the Moldavian Orthodox Church, which remained a part of the Russian Orthodox Church, and formed the Bessarabian Orthodox Church. This group regards itself as the successor to the pre-World War II Romanian Orthodox Church in Bessarabia and is subordinated to the Romanian church. The Bessarabian church is much smaller (fewer than 100 parishes) than the Moldavian church (more than 1,100 parishes), but its foundation has raised serious political and religious questions as to whether Orthodox Christianity in independent Moldova should be oriented toward Romania or Russia.

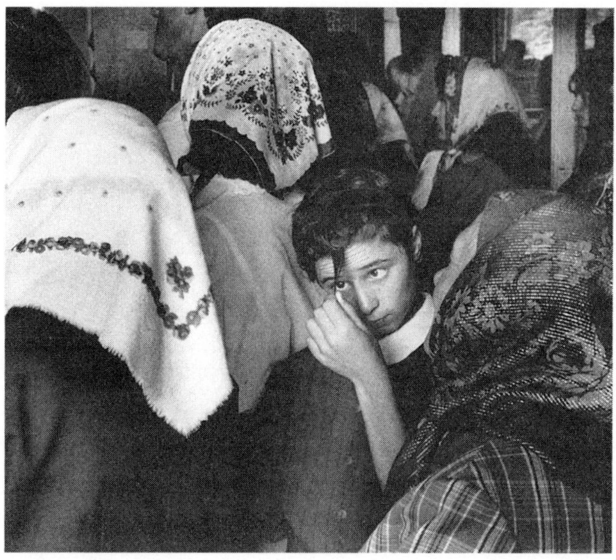

Older churchgoers at an Orthodox Christian mass surround a young girl. Moldovan women are required to cover their heads with kerchiefs and avoid wearing trousers when attending church services. © SHEPARD SHERBELL/ CORBIS SABA.

EARLY AND MODERN LEADERS The church in Moldova has generally not produced eminent historical leaders, but Orthodox self-consciousness and Moldavian national identity have been inseparably entwined for centuries. This link played an important role during the period of oppression under the Ottoman Empire, and it was the alliance between Orthodox bishops and noble landowners that served as the ideological and political base for the Moldavian resistance movement in the eighteenth century. One of most important figures from this period was Dmitry Kantemir (1673–1723), a ruler of Moldova (1710–11) who was also known as a prominent historian.

Metropolitan Vladimir (Kantarian) became the head of the Moldavian Orthodox Church in 1992. Under his leadership the church has obtained an autonomous status within the Russian Orthodox Church. His name has also become associated with the restitution of church property confiscated under the Soviet regime and with the reestablishment of hundreds of Orthodox parishes.

MAJOR THEOLOGIANS AND AUTHORS The Orthodox Church in Moldova has always been on the periphery of two influential national Orthodox churches, those of Russia and Romania. This situation and the rural character of Moldavian society—until the 1960s about 80 percent of Moldavians lived in the countryside—have resulted in a weak tradition of theological studies. Alexey Matievich, a Moldavian Orthodox priest from the beginning of the twentieth century, however, became well known for his literary works, specifically poetry. He is also the author of the national anthem.

HOUSES OF WORSHIP AND HOLY PLACES As in other Orthodox countries, the primary place of worship in Moldova is a local parish church that is generally dedicated to a particular saint or to a specific event from the life of Jesus or the Virgin Mary. There are some 1,400 churches in Moldova, half of which were built before the twentieth century. A group of approximately 20 wooden churches in northern Moldova is particularly distinct. These churches, which are built on headstones and have small windows, resemble rustic peasant houses.

Monasticism has always been a tradition of Orthodox Christianity in Moldova. Most monasteries are concentrated in the central part of Moldova, in the Codru forest zone. The monasteries of Varzaresti (1420), Rudi (1776), and Capriana (1429) are among the best known. There also are several ancient cave churches and monasteries dating to early Christian times. Three of these unique caves are situated on the right bank of the Dniester River near the villages of Jabca, Saharna, and Lalova.

WHAT IS SACRED? Reverence for icons and for the relics of saints, which are displayed in churches, is traditional in Orthodox Christian churches, and Moldova is no exception. The icon of the Herboveckaya Virgin Lady, in the Herbovecky monastery, is especially well known and is believed to possess healing power.

HOLIDAYS AND FESTIVALS Two national holidays in Moldova are religious by nature. Christmas is observed on January 7, according to the Julian church calendar, and Memorial Easter on the Monday after Easter.

In the former Soviet Union, Communist authorities encouraged the substitution of the secular holiday of New Year's Eve for the church event of Christmas. Nonetheless, many Christmas traditions, including the Christmas tree, Santa Claus, children walking from door to door to sing carols, and *plugushor* (a poetry reading describing all stages of agricultural work), survived in Moldova during the Soviet era.

Easter remains the most significant church event in Moldova. The Orthodox Church observes seven weeks of Lent before Easter, although only a small proportion of Moldavians adheres to this. For most people, celebrating Easter involves the preparation of traditional food (including painted eggs and special Easter cake), the bringing of the food to the church to be blessed by the priest, attendance on Saturday at a lengthy liturgy (the highlight of which is a procession with crosses and candles around the church, led by the clergy), and a great feast on Easter Sunday. On the following day, Memorial Easter, families take flowers to grave sites to remember those who have died.

MODE OF DRESS Both in cities and in villages, Moldavians wear Western-style clothing. The only requirements associated with attendance at church services are that women must cover their heads with kerchiefs and avoid wearing trousers, while men must enter the church without a hat.

DIETARY PRACTICES The diet of Moldavians is based on ethnic traditions, not religious prescription. There are no food or beverages forbidden by Orthodox teaching. The church calendar calls for fasting on Wednesdays and Fridays, and there also are longer periods of fasting. In modern Moldova, however, only a small number of the Orthodox follow these requirements.

RITUALS Besides the seven major sacraments (baptism, anointment with holy oil, penance, Eucharist, marriage, extreme unction, ordination to the priesthood), the principal regular ritual in any Orthodox church is the liturgy, celebrated by the clergy. The Eucharist is celebrated in a distinct way in Moldova. Before the ritual itself, the faithful touch the bowl containing the wine with their foreheads, as if making physical contact with the body of Christ.

In Moldova the Orthodox priest remains a socially important figure, present not only in the liturgy and at the sacraments but also, for example, invited to bless the construction of a well or a new home. In villages, however, official church rituals are mixed with many pre-Christian traditions. Most traditional folk celebrations, which often coincide with festival dates in the church calendar, are connected with cycles of agricultural production. These include *floriile* (a festival of vegetation), *dragajke* (of the harvest), and *barbe* (of the last sheaf).

Moldavian marriage rituals are particularly elaborate. The wedding itself is preceded by the folk traditions of *starostija* (matchmaking), *logodnja* (betrothal), and *respunsul* (the final agreement). During the wedding itself, which is performed by a priest, many special prayers are sung rather than recited. The official church ritual, however, is only a part of the numerous folk ceremonies that are celebrated over the course of several days.

RITES OF PASSAGE The baptism of newborn children in Moldova has continued to be a major rite of passage. In Moldova baptism is performed through immersion in holy water, although in some Orthodox regions this is being replaced with sprinkling.

MEMBERSHIP Most Moldavians have a clear religious identity, being Orthodox by birth and by social custom. The issue of formal membership in the Orthodox Church is controversial, however. According to surveys, more than 80 percent of Moldavians define themselves as Orthodox. At the same time fewer than 50 percent consider themselves religious, and only about 30 percent of believers attend services on a regular base. It has become common, therefore, to speak of "customary" Orthodoxy as opposed to active participation in the life of the church.

The Orthodox Church in Moldova gives major attention to catechization, that is, to teaching the basics of Orthodox Christian doctrine and involving people in day-to-day church life. The Orthodox Church is provided with regular weekly time on national radio and television, and there are mandatory or optional lessons on the Orthodox faith in a majority of the Moldavian state schools.

SOCIAL JUSTICE Human rights advocacy is not a part of the agenda of the Orthodox Church, which typically holds conservative attitudes toward social issues and emphasizes its loyalty to the state authorities. Orthodox doctrine has traditionally held a tolerant attitude toward the poor, and the entrances to churches during worship are often surrounded by beggars asking for alms.

In the past, during the period of the Russian Empire, elementary schools associated with Orthodox parishes were the only educational option for lower-class children in Moldavian villages. In the cities and towns many churches ran orphanages and hospitals for the poor. The Orthodox Church in Moldova is only beginning to recover from the Communist era, when it was required to refrain from social activities.

SOCIAL ASPECTS Orthodox morality remains conservative with regard to issues of family, marriage, and the social acceptance of sexual minorities. Present-day Moldavian society, however, is largely secular, and the social impact of conservatism within the Orthodox Church is limited.

POLITICAL IMPACT Despite the constitutional separation of church and state, the Orthodox Church has an essential impact on the internal politics in Moldova. At the time of armed conflict between Moldova and the self-proclaimed Transdniestrian republic in 1992, Orthodox priests were also divided by politics and encouraged soldiers on both sides. The tensions between the Moldavian Orthodox Church, subordinate to the patriarchate of Moscow, and the Bessarabian Orthodox Church, linked to the patriarchate of Bucharest, are hotly debated in Parliament, with right-wing nationalists supporting the Bessarabian church. The Orthodox Church officially requires its clergy to refrain from political activities, but during elections the priests in villages play an important role as people ask them for advice in voting.

CONTROVERSIAL ISSUES Most of the Orthodox faithful in Moldova belong to the Moldavian Orthodox Church. They are divided, however, along ethnic lines, with Moldavians making up 65 percent of the country's population, Ukrainians 14 percent, Russians 13 percent, Gagauzes (Christianized people of Turkish origin) 3 percent, and Bulgarians 2 percent. In independent Moldova, under conditions of growing nationalistic sentiments, the language of worship (Church Slavonic traditional for the Russian Orthodox Church as opposed to Romanian for ethnic Moldavians) and ethnic correlation between a priest and his flock have become problems.

CULTURAL IMPACT Orthodox Christian culture in Moldova manifests itself strongly in the painting of icons and frescoes, which provide rich decorations in churches. Domed village churches, decorated with wooden carvings, have shaped the Moldavian rural landscape for centuries. Church Slavonic, the old Slavic language that continues to be used in the Russian Orthodox Church, functioned as the literary language in Moldova until the sixteenth century. The oldest university-level school in Moldova was the Slavic-Greek-Latin Academy, established in the seventeenth century in Iasi, then the capital of the Moldavian principality, under the patronage of Petr Mohyla, the Orthodox metropolitan of Kiev.

Other Religions

The Orthodox Old Believers, an estimated 3 percent of the population, are a dissident branch of Russian Orthodox Christianity who did not accept various reforms introduced by Patriarch Nikon and ratified by councils in Moscow in the 1650s and 1660s. They have lived in Moldova since the early nineteenth century and traditionally have remained in isolated rural communities. The Roman Catholic Church was established in Moldova in 1993. Most Catholics, with estimates of adherents varying from 18,000 to 48,000, are of Polish, German, and Lithuanian descent and live in the cities of Kishinev and Beltsy. The Jewish community was heavily diminished during World War II by the Holocaust and in the 1970s and 1980s by emigration. At the beginning of the 21st century there were approximately 32,000 Jews remaining in Moldova, including 20,000 in the capital of Kishinev, and 8 synagogues, compared to 370 in 1940. Two public schools are open exclusively to Jewish students and receive the same funding as other state schools in addition to financial support from the community.

Of the various Protestant churches in Moldova, Baptists are the longest established and largest denomination. Baptist missionaries from Germany arrived in Moldova in 1876, and the first Russian congregation was formed in Kishinev in 1908. Baptists, who number about 20,000 members, are especially active in charitable activities. Jehovah's Witnesses, with some 15,000 members, is the group experiencing the most dynamic growth. Its aggressive door-to-door proselytizing has caused growing public resentment, however, and Jehovah's Witnesses typically experience difficulties in relations with state authorities, especially in separatist Transdniester.

Alexei Krindatch

See Also Vol. 1: *Christianity, Eastern Orthodoxy, Russian Orthodoxy*

Bibliography

Barrett, David. *The Encyclopedia of World Christianity.* 2nd ed. New York: Oxford University Press, 2001.

Bauman, Martin, and J. Gordon Melton, eds. *Religions of the World: A Comprehensive Encyclopedia of Beliefs and Practices.* Oxford: ABC-CLIO, 2002.

Bromlej, Jury, ed. *Strany i Narody: Sovetskij Sojuz—Respubliki Pribaltiki, Byelorussia, Ukraina, Moldavia.* Moscow: Mysl, 1984.

Dima, Nicholas. *From Moldava to Moldova: The Soviet-Romanian Territorial Dispute.* East European Monographs. New York: Columbia University Press, 1991.

Monaco

POPULATION 31,987

ROMAN CATHOLIC 90 percent

OTHER 10 percent

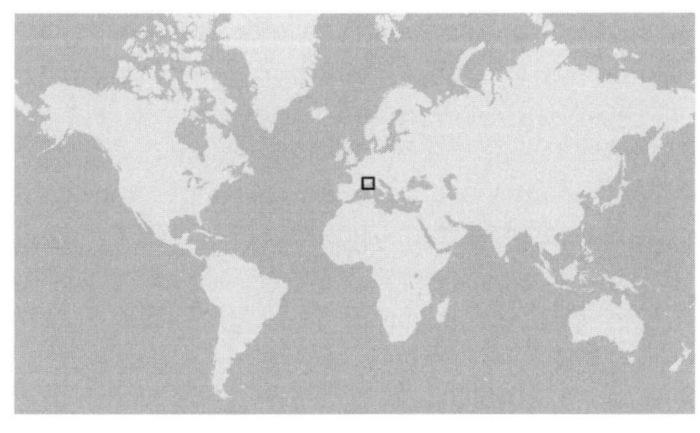

Country Overview

INTRODUCTION With an area of just 0.73 square miles, the Principality of Monaco is the second smallest independent state in the world, after Vatican City. It is located on the Mediterranean coast 11 miles east of Nice, France, and is surrounded on three sides by France. The Grimaldi family, which has ruled almost continuously since 1297, made Roman Catholicism the official state religion in 1848, and in 1911 religious freedom to all residents was made part of the constitution.

Only 19 percent of the population are citizens of Monaco. The majority are French, and Monaco maintains extensive economic and other ties to France.

RELIGIOUS TOLERANCE The constitution of Monaco provides for freedom of religion, and the government generally respects this right. In practice, however, there are some restrictions. No missionaries operate in Monaco, and proselytizing is discouraged, but religious organizations that are registered formally with the minister of state may recruit members. Organizations regarded as religious sects, however, are routinely denied registration. There are amicable relationships among the officially recognized religions in Monaco.

Major Religion

ROMAN CATHOLICISM

DATE OF ORIGIN 1061 C.E.

NUMBER OF FOLLOWERS 28,800

HISTORY From 58 to 51 B.C.E the region came under the influence of the Roman Empire and Julius Caesar. There is evidence of religious life from 1061, when Monaco came under the Catholic diocese of Nice. During the Middle Ages the Genoese, Monaco's nearest large neighbor, considered Monaco to be a part of their domain and obtained formal ownership from the German emperor Henry VI in 1191. The Genoese then built a fortress in Monaco to protect their interests. In 1247 Pope Innocent IV granted permission to the Republic of Genoa to build a chapel in Monaco. The Parish of Monaco was founded in 1252–53 and called Saint Nicolas.

The Grimaldis were one of the aristocratic families of Genoa and were considered the defenders of the pope's authority. They were forced out of Genoa by

On 26 and 27 January Monaco celebrates its patron saint with the Feast of Saint Dévote. A Te Deum is sung in the cathedral, followed by a procession through the streets of the Old Town. © SETBOUN/CORBIS.

supporters of the German emperor. On 8 January 1297 Francois Grimaldi disguised himself as a monk, and seeking shelter from the night with his band of men, he took control of the fortress. The Grimaldis have since ruled Monaco for more than 700 years (with a few hiatuses). Prince Honoré II, who ruled in the 1600s, was the first prior of the Brotherhood of the Black Penitents, and he founded the Misericorde Chapel (Chapel of Mercy). The diocese of Monaco was established in 1887.

While the minister of state must be a French citizen, the leader of the country is always a member of the Grimaldi family, which is devoutly Catholic.

EARLY AND MODERN LEADERS The first bishop of Monaco was Monsignor Bonaventure Theuret (appointed 1887), who had previously been the apostolic administrator. Since 1981 there have been three archbishops: Charles-Amarin Brand (served 1981–84), Joseph-Marie Sardou (served 1985–2000), and Monsignor Bernard Barsi (appointed 2000).

MAJOR THEOLOGIANS AND AUTHORS Monaco has not produced any notable Roman Catholic authors or theologians.

HOUSES OF WORSHIP AND HOLY PLACES The Church of Saint Dévote, the patron saint of Monaco, is the most important to the Monegasques (the 19 percent of the population who are citizens of Monaco). The Misericorde Chapel is the home of the White and Black Penitents. The Monaco Cathedral, built in 1875 in the Romanesque-Byzantine style, sits on the site of the former Saint Nicolas Church. The bell from the old church, dating from the 1200s, hangs on the outside of the northwestern nave. The cathedral contains the tombs of the royalty of Monaco. The royal family worships in the seventeenth-century Palatine Chapel, located in the palace.

WHAT IS SACRED? Anything to do with Saint Dévote is sacred. According to legend, in 304 C.E. the governor of Corsica, which was under Roman rule, tortured a young girl named Dévote. Christians put her in a small fishing boat and prayed that favorable winds would take her to safety. A storm came up, driving the boat to the shores of Monaco. As the boat landed, out of the mouth of Dévote came a dove. The inhabitants saw this as a miracle and erected a chapel in her honor.

HOLIDAYS AND FESTIVALS In addition to traditional Catholic holidays, Monaco has a number of local celebrations. On 26 and 27 January Monaco celebrates its patron saint with the Feast of Saint Dévote. To commemorate the legend, on the evening of 26 January a fishing boat is set ablaze by the reigning prince, and on 27 January a Te Deum is sung in the cathedral, followed by a procession through the streets of the Old Town.

In June is the Fête Dieu, which has been celebrated since 1260. The Corpus Christi procession goes through the streets of the Old Town and culminates at the palace, where the archbishop of Monaco gives his blessing.

Also in June Monaco celebrates Saint John's Feast. A salute to the Holy Sacrament is sung in the presence of the sovereign family and Monegasque authorities, followed by the lighting of a huge bonfire in the Palace Square. The Palladienne folk group dresses in native costumes to sing and dance to traditional songs.

The prince's saint day celebration takes place on 19 November. It is the saint day of the historical Saint Rainier d'Arezzo and also the country's national holiday (Principality National Day). It is celebrated the night before with fireworks and on the day itself with Mass in the cathedral for the prince's invited guests.

MODE OF DRESS Religion has little or no influence on everyday dress. Religious dress is casual, except for special holidays such as the prince's saint day celebration, when participants dress in their finest attire, with the women generally wearing hats and men in tuxedos, dark suits, or uniforms. This is an occasion when the Knights of Malta, distinguished ambassadors, consuls, and state officials wear their medal-laden uniforms.

DIETARY PRACTICES At Christmas a sweet bread, *pain de natale,* is made and blessed by the church. Sometimes it is prepared in the shape of a cross, and sometimes it is also made with walnuts. At Easter Catholics bake an unleavened bread with an egg in the center, which may never be cut with a knife and which must be broken by the head of the household.

RITUALS For the prince's saint day celebration, he chooses the music for the Mass. On 26 January every year, during the Feast of Saint Dévote, the prince sets a boat on fire.

RITES OF PASSAGE Religious weddings in Monaco are not legally binding. Only those people holding a resident's card may marry legally in Monaco, and the marriage ceremony must take place at the mayor's office.

MEMBERSHIP The catechism is an integral part of public school studies. The church also organizes activities, subsidized by the state, for young people in Monaco and in neighboring areas. These include leisure pursuits, cultural events, educational events, and moral guidance through the F.A.R. Association.

Since 1957 the Catholic Church has been involved in broadcasting *The Church Today* each Sunday on Radio Monte Carlo. Since 1958 the church has participated in presenting the UNDA (Association Catholique Internationale pour la Radio et la Télévision) Award at the International Television Festival of Monte Carlo. The criteria for the award are based on the human and cultural values of a film, not specifically on religion.

SOCIAL JUSTICE The Roman Catholic Church in Monaco espouses the principles outlined by Rome concerning education, human rights, poverty, and reproduction. The church, through voluntary associations, helps the handicapped and those in distress.

SOCIAL ASPECTS Marriage and family among Catholics in Monaco function as in the rest of Europe, especially France.

POLITICAL IMPACT Virtually all Monegasques are Catholic, and only Monegasques can be elected to the national assembly. Other government posts are also filled by Monegasques or by French citizens who are Catholic and appointed by the prince.

CONTROVERSIAL ISSUES The church in Monaco follows the teaching of the church in general and is strongly opposed to contraception and abortion. Most people in Monaco, however, practice contraception in opposition to church teachings.

CULTURAL IMPACT At the beginning of the seventeenth century, Prince Honoré II ordered a Spanish-style walnut altar decorated with gold leaf for Saint Nicolas Church. The altar is now located in the Blessed Sacrament Chapel in the cathedral. The chapel also owns an important collection of religious art, such as painted-wood Madonnas, damask chasubles, and gilded wood reliquaries. In the cathedral there are several reredoses of Saint Nicolas and Saint Dévote by the Nice painter Louis Brea dating to the 1500s. There are also two sixteenth-century paintings and a procession canopy bearing the coat of arms of Antoine I.

Under Antoine I (reigned 1701–31) the first vocal group with children's voices in Monaco was started and sang the liturgies at the Palatine Chapel. The Choir of Monaco (including children) became famous for its revival of early sacred musical works. In 1973 Prince Rainier III created the boy's choir Les Petits Chanteurs of Monaco (The Little Singers of Monaco), a part of the Monaco Cathedral Choir (which supplanted the Choir of Monaco). Because they travel around the world giving concerts, the prince refers to them as "his little singing ambassadors."

Other Religions

Other places of worship in Monaco include an Anglican church, an Orthodox synagogue, and a nondenominational Protestant church. There are several hundred practicing Episcopalians and other Protestants who have services in English, and several hundred practicing Orthodox or Conservative Jews have services in French.

Siri Campbell

See Also Vol. 1: *Christianity, Roman Catholicism*

Bibliography

Decaux, Alain. *Monaco and Its Princes: Seven Centuries of History.* Translated by Sylvia Carter and Anne Brav. Paris: Perrin, 1997.

Le Diocèse de Monaco, ses origines historiques. Monaco: Imprimerie Testa, 1987.

Duursma, J.C. *Fragmentation and the International Relations of Micro-States: Self-Determination and Statehood.* Cambridge: Cambridge University Press, 1996.

Edwards, Anne. *The Grimaldis of Monaco.* New York: Morrow, 1992.

"Monaco et la legende ou passion de Sainte Dévote." In *Contes, Legendes et Nouvelles d'Europe.* Strasbourg, France: Council for Cultural Cooperation, Council of Europe, 1998.

Mongolia

POPULATION 2,694,432

TIBETAN BUDDHIST 96 percent

OTHER (BAHAI, CHRISTIAN, JEHOVAH'S WITNESS, MUSLIM, SHAMANIST) 4 percent

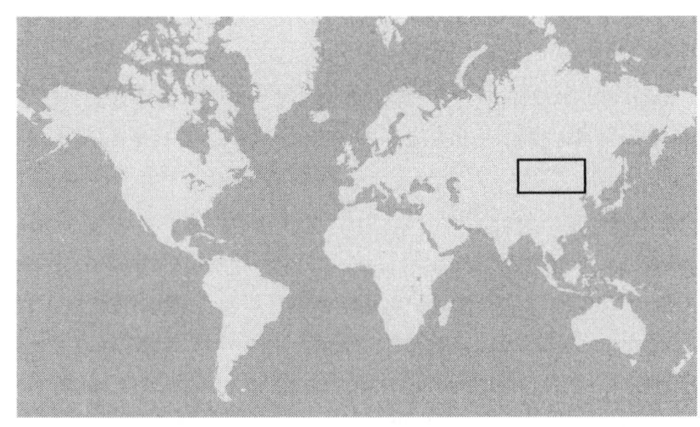

Country Overview

INTRODUCTION Mongolia is a landlocked country on the Mongolian Plateau in Inner Asia. It is sandwiched between Russia to the north and China to the south. The Gobi Desert covers much of southern Mongolia, and the Siberian taiga (coniferous forest) extends across the mountainous north. *Dzuds*, natural disasters caused by a lack of rain in summer or heavy snowfall in winter, are a constant threat to the livelihood of most Mongols, who are nomadic herders.

For centuries the Mongolian steppes were home to nomadic tribes that later migrated to the West: Scyts, Sarmats, Alans, Xiongnu, and Avars. Turkic tribes began building empires in Mongolia in the sixth century C.E. By the twelfth century both Turkic and Mongolian nomadic tribes inhabited the Mongolian Plateau. Thanks to the energetic efforts of the progenitors of Chinggis (Genghis) Khan and his own successful campaigns against neighboring tribes at the beginning of the thirteenth century, the Mongols united to become the leading group on the steppes. During the Mongolian Empire (1206–1370) the Mongols, who were mainly shamanists, became followers of Buddhism, Nestorianism, and Islam. Gradually Mongol minorities in different parts of the empire were assimilated into local cultures, and they began representing the interests of the local people, who tended to maintain their separate identities. On the Mongolian steppes the most important influence was that of conquered China, where Kubilai (Kublai) Khan (1215–94), a grandson of Chinggis Khan and the founder of the Yuan Dynasty (1271–1368), made Tibetan Buddhism a state-supported religion.

By the eighteenth century the Tibetan form of Buddhism had become the majority religion. Ties with Tibet were close, and the fourth incarnation of the Dalai Lama was recognized among Mongols in the grandson of Altan Khan. In 1635 part of Mongolia was directly incorporated into the growing Manchu Empire as Inner Mongolia. At the request of their Mongolian khans, lands farther north were added in 1691 as the autonomy of Outer Mongolia under the Manchu's Qing Dynasty. The Manchus favored the Tibetan Buddhist Gelukpa school in Mongolia.

In 1911 Mongolia gained independence from China, and the reincarnated lama Bogd Gegen became its ruler (Bogd Khan), following the Tibetan example

Lamas eat rice and drink tea before morning prayers at the Gandantegchenling monastery. © DEAN CONGER/CORBIS.

of theocracy, or hierocracy. The people's revolution of 1921 led to the establishment of the Communist Mongolian People's Republic in 1924. Since the fall of the Communist government in 1990, missionaries from different Christian groups, the Bahai faith, Ananda Marga, and the Jehovah's Witnesses have begun to proselytize in Mongolia. Reliable estimates of the current numbers of practitioners of different religions in Mongolia are unavailable, and the figures given above should be considered only rough estimates.

RELIGIOUS TOLERANCE Mongolia's 1992 constitution guarantees freedom of worship. Since the antireligious purges carried out by the Communist government in the 1930s, there have been no violent religious clashes.

Major Religion

TIBETAN BUDDHISM

DATE OF ORIGIN Thirteenth and fourteenth centuries C.E.
NUMBER OF FOLLOWERS 2.6 million

HISTORY Mongols came in contact with Tibetan Buddhism during their campaign against the Tangut people and Tibet in the thirteenth century. In the first dissemination of Buddhism among the Mongols, only khans (rulers) and aristocrats became followers, while the rest of society remained shamanists. Buddhist scriptures were translated into Mongolian, and the special priest-patron relationship was established, dividing power into religious and secular spheres represented by the hierarch of the Buddhist Sakyapa school and by Kubilai Khan, first emperor of the Yuan Dynasty. The "priest" secured religious services for the welfare of the ruler and the success of his war campaigns, and the ruler, as "patron," supported the activity of the Buddhist church, particularly the Sakyapa tradition.

After the fall of the Yuan Dynasty in 1368, Buddhism declined among Mongols, though it did not die out completely on the steppes. In the sixteenth century the second wave of Buddhist propagation began with contacts between individual khans and representatives of the different schools of Tibetan Buddhism. In 1587 a priest-patron relationship was established between the hierarch of the Gelukpa tradition, Sonam Gyatso (the future third Dalai Lama), and Altan Khan, from the Mongolian tribe of Tümed. It had a long-standing effect on religious and political relations between Mongolia and Tibet. The zealous campaign of Buddhist missionaries—combined with the khan's antishamanist edicts and, later, Manchu support—resulted in the almost complete conversion of the Mongols to Tibetan Buddhism by the eighteenth century. There were almost 800 Buddhist places of worship. The labor-intensive task of translating the Buddhist canon from Tibetan into Mongolian, which had begun in the thirteenth century, was completed, and the translated Word of Buddha (*Kanjur*) and its Commentary (*Tenjur*) were printed in Beijing. By this time, however, the Tibetan language had become the language of liturgy, and monks had become better educated in Tibetan. Many Mongolian reincarnated lamas appeared; some were native Tibetans who, once recognized as reincarnated lamas in Mongolia, had to remain there for the rest of their lives. Buddhism became the main factor in Mongolian's national and cultural identity and its monasteries the main source of Mongolian economic power. After the people's revolution of 1921, however, an antireligious Communist ideology was implemented in Mongolia. Persecutions of Buddhists culminated in the 1930s, when more than 20,000—and perhaps as many as 100,000—monks were killed, while others were imprisoned or secularized. Religious sites were also destroyed.

Democratic reforms in the late 1990s allowed for a Buddhist revival. By 2001 about 200 places of worship had been established, with almost 3,000 monks and dozens of nuns. The appearance of nunneries was a new phenomenon. Previously, a Manchu edict prohibited the establishment of nunneries in Mongolia. Today Buddhist activity is supported officially by the government, which recognizes Buddhism's importance as a national symbol. Old temples have been rebuilt and new ones founded. The most important historical sites receive state support. Old scriptures have been brought from hidden places back to the monasteries. Books have been published to educate people about Buddhism. The Gelukpa tradition is most widely represented, but there is one Sakyapa monastery and a few monasteries of the Nyingmapa tradition as well. The liturgy is conducted almost exclusively in the Tibetan language, with the exception of a few prayers recited in Mongolian. The exceptional Mongolian feature of Buddhism in the country is the widespread acceptance of marriage among the Gelukpa monks, who, according to the Tibetan standard, should live in celibacy. Lay management of some monasteries, the social involvement of several monasteries and nunneries, and a strong lay movement are some other peculiarities of revitalized Buddhism in Mongolia.

EARLY AND MODERN LEADERS Reincarnated lamas have played the most significant role as teachers and religious leaders in Mongolia. From the seventeenth century the main incarnation in Outer Mongolia was Jebtsundampa (in Tibetan, rJe-btsun-dam-pa, a title meaning "Reverend Holiness"). Most important for the development of Buddhism in Mongolia was the first Jebtsundampa, Zanabazar (also called Undur Öndör; 1635–1723). Zanabazar included several Mongolian elements in the Buddhist liturgy, designed the monk's robes, and was famous for casting beautiful bronze images. The eighth Jebtsundampa, Bogd Gegen (1870– 1924), became king of independent Mongolia in 1911. In Inner Mongolia the most important incarnation was Changkya Khutukhtu, who resided in Beijing. The second incarnation of Changkya Khutukhtu, Rolpe Dorje (1717–86), guided the Mongolian translation of Buddhist canonical writings.

Because the majority of reincarnated lamas and learned teachers of the twentieth century in Mongolia were executed by the Communists, key contemporary Buddhist leaders have since come from abroad. The ninth Jebtsundampa, who was born in 1925 in Tibet and now lives in India among exiled Tibetans, is treated by Mongols as the main religious figure. Ladakhi Kushok Bakula (1917–2003), India's ambassador to Mongolia from 1989 to 2000, actively supported the Buddhist revival. Gurudeva Rinpoche (Sogpo Lama; born in 1910) helped revive the monastery of Amarbayasgalant and is a contemporary Buddhist teacher. Born in Mongolia after the antireligious purges, Choijamts, the head lama of the Gandantegchenling monastery since 1993, has played a leading role among young Mongolian Buddhists.

MAJOR THEOLOGIANS AND AUTHORS The translation of the Buddhist scriptures and their interpretations and commentaries from the Tibetan language into Mongolian began in the thirteenth century and was completed by the eighteenth century. Later Mongolian Buddhist authors wrote mainly in the Tibetan language, which served as the lingua franca throughout Tibetan Buddhist civilization. There were, however, exceptions—Mongols still using the Mongolian language for composition in the eighteenth century. They included Mergen Diyanchi Lama, who made a translation and study of the Tibetan collection of aphorisms by Sakya Pandita, *Subhashitaratnanidhi.* Among the most eminent authors writing in Tibetan were the prolific Zaya Pandita Lobsang Prinlei (1642–1715) and Sumba Khamba Ishbaljir (also Sumpo Khanpo Yeshe Paljor; 1704–88), who wrote *Pagsam Jonzang* (The History of Buddhism in India, China, Tibet, and Mongolia), which is important for understanding Tibetan sectarian polemics.

HOUSES OF WORSHIP AND HOLY PLACES Quite often temples were housed in yurts (Mongolian tents). Such movable temples suited the monasteries of incarnations who moved according to the needs of herders and who benefited from their donations. Inside established monasteries, yurts served as monk's dwellings. In contemporary Mongolia many monasteries still begin their activity in a single yurt.

In the past the capital, Urga (now Ulaanbaatar), the headquarters of the Jebtsundampa incarnation, came to have the largest concentration of temples in Mongolia. The biggest was the Gandantegchenling monastery. It has again become the largest monastery, with approximately 400 monks. Founded in 1586, the oldest monastery is Erdeni dzuu in Kharkhorin. It served as an art museum during the Communist period. The huge, reactivated Amarbayasgalant monastery in the Selenge province was built in 1737 to house the relics of the first Jebtsundampa.

The most important holy places in Mongolia are sacred mountains like the Bogd-uul near Ulaanbaatar. Traditionally Mongols made pilgrimages to Tibet, a practice that is being revived in contemporary Mongolia.

WHAT IS SACRED? The majority of holy places are marked by an *obo,* a heap of stones and wood. Shamanist in origin, *obos* are worshiped by shamanists and Buddhists alike.

According to Buddhist principles the killing of any being is not welcome, but Mongols do slaughter domestic animals and hunt wild ones. Cattle marked by ribbons are offered to the gods, and they can not be killed or used by people in any way.

HOLIDAYS AND FESTIVALS The dates of Buddhist festivals in Mongolia are calculated according to the Tibetan lunar calendar. The main festival, which is also a state holiday, is Tsagaan Sar (White Month), the New Year. In a specifically Mongolian festival celebrated in May, Maitreya, the future Buddha, is invited to appear. In Tibet this formed part of the New Year celebrations.

MODE OF DRESS Monks wear either Tibetan-style robes with a maroon skirt, a sleeveless yellow shirt, and a long piece of maroon cloth that forms a shoulder covering, or they wear the Mongolian-style robe. The latter, which was designed by Zanabazar, consists of a maroon or yellow traditional Mongolian coat (*deel*), with no collar and with blue cuffs. Tibetan Buddhist orders are distinguished by the colors of the monk's hats: Most common are the high, upturned yellow hats of the Gelukpa, though hats with a Mongolian modification—yellow and maroon cups that cover the ears—are preferred in winter. Traditional boots with upturned toe caps—said to prevent injury to the earth but actually better for horse riding—are still worn by monks. Nuns wear Tibetan-style robes and shave their heads, while girls enrolled in nunnery schools wear maroon or yellow *deels* and keep their hair long.

DIETARY PRACTICES Buddhists traditionally avoid eating birds and fish because their eyes are believed to be similar to the Buddha's eyes. Due to their primary occupation as nomadic herders, Mongols eat mainly meat and milk products, though in cities they also eat bread, vegetables, and European foods. Meat is a staple food in monasteries as well. In summer the main food is *airag* (also known as *kumys*), a beverage made from fermented mare's milk that is also served in monasteries.

RITUALS Rituals are performed by monks on any important occasion, such as illness, birth, and especially death. In contemporary Mongolia astrologers (either monks or laypersons) who serve at monasteries decide which prayers and rites shall be performed for the laity. Monks used to take the body of the deceased to the cemetery or an isolated place, where it would be consumed by beasts. Nowadays astrologers and monks decide on the exact place of burial in a cemetery. *Chöd,* the practice of offering one's body as a temporary dwelling for beings lacking embodiment, which is seen as an act of compassion that may have future benefits, has been revitalized and has become extremely popular.

RITES OF PASSAGE In Mongolia the Indian model of fulfilling family duties and then turning to religious ones later in life can be traced. Old people, especially women, cut their hair and spend most of their time praying in monasteries. More important are the rites distinguishing monks from laypeople. Parents may decide to send a child to a monastery at age six or seven. Special rites, including hair cutting, are performed when the child enters the monastery. All novices and monks are obliged to observe monastic discipline, which consists of 250 rules that differ from those observed by laypeople.

MEMBERSHIP In contemporary Mongolia, after decades of Communism and forced atheism, people say that they are Buddhists because their ancestors were. Some do not know Buddhist precepts well or practice Buddhism, yet they still claim to be Buddhists. Buddhist associations publish books and newspapers and use radio and television to educate people about Buddhism and to counteract Christian proselytizing.

SOCIAL JUSTICE Traditionally Buddhists have not protested against poverty and misery. Instead they have practiced and prayed for better rebirths. Today, however, social involvement is evident in monasteries and nunneries that recruit orphans and street children. Some Buddhist teachers visit hospitals and prisons as well. Monasteries also serve as educational centers. In Ulaanbaatar the Buddhist medical college has been reestablished and operates a clinic.

SOCIAL ASPECTS The division between the lay community and Buddhist monks and nuns in Mongolia is becoming less important because of the shortage of dwelling places inside monastic compounds. Construction of new monasteries, and reconstruction of existing compounds, has been hampered by a lack of resources. As a result, many monks and some nuns have to stay with their families. The problem of married monks, a peculiar feature of Buddhism in Mongolia, is one of the most important social issues. Beginning in 1924 monks in Mongolia were allowed to marry. Although the principle was waived in 1994, the practice has continued to some extent and has met with criticism from the Tibetan Buddhist authorities.

Buddhist institutions do not concern themselves with marriage. As in other Tibetan Buddhist countries, monks may participate in prayers at a family's request.

POLITICAL IMPACT The government of Mongolia is secular. Nevertheless, the president and the prime minister take part in some important religious rites, like the Buddhist New Year celebration. As Mongols practice Tibetan Buddhism and most belong to the Gelukpa tradition, they view the Tibetan head of the Gelukpa order, the 14th Dalai Lama, as their leader. This poses a political problem with China, which views the Dalai Lama as one who "conducts separatist activity against China" and is thus wary of Mongolian's religious sentiment potentially evolving into political support for the Dalai Lama. Mongols would also like to invite the ninth Jebtsundampa to Mongolia, though some politicians fear that this could lead to an attempt to reinstate him as the ruler of Mongolia.

CONTROVERSIAL ISSUES Communist attempts to secularize Mongolian Buddhist monks included the 1924 law that enabled them to marry. The right to marry has been preserved, though it stands in opposition to the rule of celibacy in the Gelukpa tradition. Less controversial is the appearance of nunneries, which has been criticized nevertheless by many Mongols. Another dispute surrounds the question of the liturgical language: Some Mongols would prefer to have more prayers recited in Mongolian.

CULTURAL IMPACT Buddhism played a key role in Mongolia's cultural development from the sixteenth century until 1921. Monasteries served as educational and cultural centers where the visual arts also developed. Zanabazar, the first Jebtsundampa (1635–1723), cast masterpieces of Buddhist sculpture. Mongolian literature between the fourteenth and twentieth centuries was strongly influenced by Buddhism. The Buddhist revival in contemporary Mongolia has stimulated artistic development, partly by creating a great demand for Buddhist images. The construction of new monasteries and nunneries reflects different architectural trends. The Mongolian Institute of Buddhist Art teaches Buddhist iconography and Mongolian stylistic development. In contemporary literature and film production, historical themes with Buddhist elements are present. Mongolian pop music often mixes symbolic evocations of the life of Chinggis Khan—the sounds of horses, warriors, and battle, for example—with Buddhist ritual music.

Other Religions

Despite shamanism's long history in Mongolia, the number of contemporary shamanists is small. Under the Mongolian Empire shamanism remained the main religion. In the sixteenth century, however, Buddhist missionaries threatened the shamanist's domination. Shamans were persecuted and *ongons*, the shamanist images of house spirits, were destroyed. By the eighteenth century the shamanists were a banished religious minority that survived mainly in the northern region around Khubsugul Lake and among the Buriat people. During the antireligious campaigns led by Communists in the 1930s, shamanists and Buddhists were equally persecuted. In the 1990s shamanists revitalized their religion. Old shamans who had survived persecution by the Communists were called by local people to practice openly. At least two shamanist centers were established in Ulaanbaatar.

Islam is the religion of the Kazakh minority in Mongolia. This group was also persecuted by the communist government. With support from Muslim countries, in 1990 the Kazakh community established the Mongolian Muslim Association, which was renamed the Mongolian Islam Religious Center in 1992. The Kazakh Muslims live in the Bayan-Ölgiy district, where they opened a religious school (*medrese;* also *madrasah*) in 1993.

During the Mongolian Empire Nestorianism was the most popular Christian tradition among Mongols.

Limited mainly to the khan's family, however, it did not outlast the empire. In the 1990s foreign Christian missionaries began proselytizing in Mongolia. The Mongolian Bible Society was established in 1990. It has founded more than 50 centers and registered more than 4,500 believers. Other Christian groups active in Mongolia include Catholics, Russian Orthodox, Evangelicals, Baptists, Adventists, Mormons, and Nestorians.

Other religious groups represented in Mongolia since 1990 include the Jehovah's Witnesses and Christian Scientists. Ananda Marga, a yoga society founded in India in 1955, has attracted some practitioners. In 1992 the Mongolian Association of Ananda Marga and the Ananda Marga Union of Mongolian Students were established. The first congress of Mongolian Bahais was organized in 1993.

Agata Bareja-Starzynska

See Also Vol. I: *Buddhism, Tibetan Buddhism*

Bibliography

Barkmann, Udo B. "The Revival of Lamaism in Mongolia." *Central Asian Survey* 16 (1997).

"Buddhism in Mongolia." *Tibet Foundation Newsletter* 30–32 (2000–2001).

Heissig, Walther. "A Mongolian Source to the Lamaist Suppression of Shamanism in the Seventeenth Century." *Anthropos* 48 (1953): 1–29, 493–536.

———. "Odoogoor sergesen sum khiydiyn zhagsaalt." *Lavain egshig* 1996: 62–64.

Maiskii, Ivan M. *Mongoliya Nakanune Revolutsii.* Moscow: Akademiya Nauk SSSR, Institut Vostokovedeniya, 1959.

Moses, Larry William. *The Political Role of Mongol Buddhism.* Bloomington, Ind.: Asian Studies Research Institute, Indiana University, 1977.

Pozdneyev, Aleksei M. *Religion and Ritual in Society: Lamaist Buddhism in Late Nineteenth-Century Mongolia.* Edited by John R. Krueger and translated from the Russian by Alo Raun and Linda Raun. Bloomington, Ind.: The Mongolia Society, 1978.

Sagaster, Klaus. "Der Buddhismus bei den Mongolen." In *Die Mongolen.* Edited by Walther Heissig and Claudius C. Müller, 233–39. Innsbruck: Pinguin Verlag; Frankfurt am Main: Umschau-Verlag, 1989.

Morocco

POPULATION 31,167,783

MUSLIM 98.7 percent

CHRISTIAN 1.1 percent

JEWISH 0.2 percent

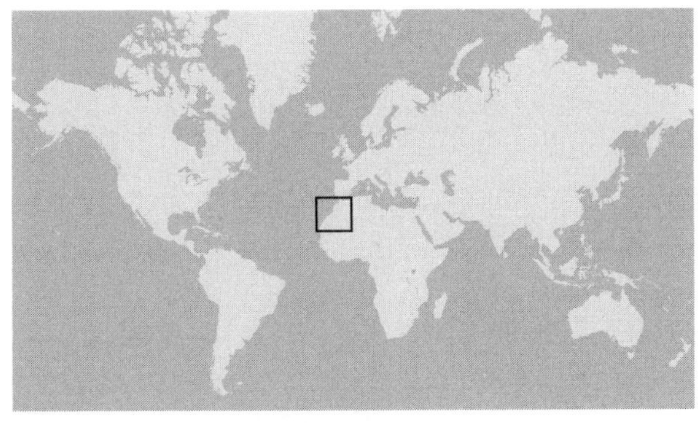

Country Overview

INTRODUCTION The Kingdom of Morocco is located in the northwestern corner of Africa, bounded on the north by the Mediterranean Sea and on the west by the Atlantic Ocean. Throughout history this location has made the region an attractive place for those seeking to settle or establish colonies. The earliest inhabitants of the area were Berbers, encompassing three separate groups distinguishable by their dialect, dress, and social customs. Tarifit Berbers inhabit northern, Tamazight western and central, and Tashilhit eastern and southern Morocco. The Berbers were originally polytheists, but when Jews and Christians migrated across North Africa, some Berbers converted to these religions. Phoenicians, Romans, Vandals, and Visigoths invaded the Atlantic and Mediterranean coastal regions successively between 1000 B.C.E. and 621 C.E.

Islam, particularly heretical Kharijism, was first introduced into the area by migrating Arab tribes beginning in the late seventh century C.E. From the founding of the Arab Shiite Idrisid dynasty in the late 780s onward, the history of the area was characterized by a long series of Arab and Berber dynasties, notably the Almoravids, Almohads, Marinids, Wattasids, Saadians, and Alawites. Often beginning as Islamic movements with varying doctrines, each succeeded in controlling larger or smaller portions of the territory within and outside the modern borders, including parts of Spain, Algeria, Tunisia, Libya, Mali, Spanish Sahara, and Mauritania. Islamic mystics, or Sufis, brought Sunnite Islam primarily to the rural population. Periodic attempts at colonization by Portugal, Spain, and France culminated in the French (and Spanish) Protectorate from 1912 to 1956.

RELIGIOUS TOLERANCE Conversion to Islam began in Morocco in the seventh century. Despite the protected status of Christians and Jews, Christianity disappeared completely within three centuries. Most Jews never converted, except nominally to avoid persecution. Some rulers treated Jews harshly, while others even employed them at their courts. Anti-Christian sentiment constituted the impetus for Moroccan deterrence of intermittent Spanish and Portuguese invasions and, together with salafism (Islamic puritanism), spurred the nationalist movement that ended the protectorate. The contemporary government controls Islamic revivalist activities while demonstrating tolerance toward other religions

Moroccan children are encouraged to attend Koran school before entering elementary school, and the public school curriculum includes lessons in religion. © CRAIG AURNESS/CORBIS.

and controversial Islamic practices like saint veneration. Nevertheless, most Jews migrated to Israel in the 1950s.

Major Religion

ISLAM

DATE OF ORIGIN Seventh century C.E.
NUMBER OF FOLLOWERS 30.8 million

HISTORY Founded in 789 C.E., the Idrisid dynasty claimed Prophetic lineage, introduced Shiite Islam, and established the city of Fez. In 828 its control weakened, and in 917 the Shiite Fatimids, ruling from Egypt, took the northeast. Inspired by Ibn Yasin, the Almoravid movement of the southern Sanhaja nomadic Berbers declared holy war. Aspiring to replace the paganism and heretical Islam of the Berber inhabitants with Sunnite Islam, the Almoravids conquered central Morocco (1053–69). By 1102 they controlled Algeria, Morocco, and Andalusia, but their power declined after 1142.

Between 1139 and 1146 the Almohad movement of the Masmuda Berbers, based on Ibn Tumart's doctrine of the absolute unity of Allah, conquered central Morocco and Andalusia, and by 1172 the empire stretched as far as Libya and Mauritania. The Almohads gradually lost all but Morocco to the Hafsids of Tunisia. Benefiting from this decline, the Banu Marin clan of the Zanata Berbers conquered Morocco between 1245 and 1269. Lacking special religious legitimacy, the Marinids institutionalized Islamic thought, which led to the creation of Sufi associations. Their extreme tolerance ushered in a golden age for Jews, and culture, trade, and architecture flourished. First serving as local rulers (1420–58), the Berber Wattasids ruled on their own from 1505 to 1550.

Prophetic lineage (sharifism) or saintly status became crucial for gaining popular support. Proclaiming sharifism and support from the Jazuliyya Sufi association, the Arab Saadians rose to power, capturing the south (1517–25), Agadir (1541), and Fez (1548). Upon the death of the sultan Ahmad al-Mansur in 1603, the dynasty declined. After conquering central Morocco (1659–69), Mulay al-Rashid established the Arab Alawite sharifian dynasty. King Mohamed VI's appointment in 2002 of Mohamed Taufiq, an Islamic scholar and a well-known Sufi, to head the Ministry of Islamic Affairs seemed to be an attempt to both mend broken bonds with Sufis and restrict the impact of Islamic revivalists.

EARLY AND MODERN LEADERS The powerful soothsayer Zaynab al-Nafzawiyya was the queen of Aghmat in southern Morocco when the Almoravids invaded in 1059 and killed her husband. She eventually married Yusuf ibn Tashafin, the Almoravid's second in command, and helped him become the first Berber conqueror of Morocco and Andalusia.

Sayyida al-Hurra governed the northern city of Tetouan from 1515 to 1542, launching raids on Spanish and Portuguese ships with the Ottoman pirate Barbarossa. The Sufi activist Aisha al-Idrisiyya (died in 1563) helped the Saadian take over Shafshawan in northern Morocco.

In 1923 the Berber religious judge Abdelkrim resisted the protectorate by establishing a modern Islamic state in northern Morocco. It was modeled on the Moroccan government but inspired by Middle Eastern reform movements. Outnumbered by the French, he surrendered on 27 May 1926.

Educated at al-Qarawiyin University in Fez, the legal scholar Mohamed Allal al-Fasi (1906–74) was the founder and greatest activist of both the nationalist movement against the French and of the independence party, which he headed from 1944 until his death. He also served as minister of Islamic affairs from 1962 to 1963.

The lawyer and political activist Mohamed Abderrahmane El Youssoufi (born in 1924) was active in the nationalist movement and cofounder in 1959 of the National (later Socialist) Union of Popular Forces. For his involvement in an antigovernment plot, he was forced to live in exile in France for 15 years (1965–80). From 1969 to 1990 he served as secretary general of the Arab Human Rights Organization. In protest against the manipulation of the 1993 elections, he resigned as head of the Socialist Union of Popular Forces and withdrew to France, but under pressure from friends he returned in 1995 to head a campaign for constitutional reform. He served as prime minister from 1998 to 2002.

MAJOR THEOLOGIANS AND AUTHORS Teaching the unquestionable authority of the imam (Allah's representative on earth), Ibn Tumart (died in 1130) drew on vast popular support to found the Almohad movement. A Spanish version of his Berber creed circulated in Spain until 1600. The Andalusian religious judge and physician Ibn Rushd (died in 1198) spent much of his time in Almohad Marrakech. He was known in Europe as Averroës, and his philosophy was taught in Paris. Born in Tunis, the scholar and court functionary Ibn Khaldun (died in 1406) was the most famous figure of Marinid Fez. He is widely known today for his theoretical explanation of the rise and fall of empires.

Al-Jazuli (died in 1465), Morocco's best-known mystic, revolutionized Sufi thought. His doctrine on sainthood and imitation of the Prophet Muhammad influenced almost every Moroccan Sufi tradition that followed and gave Moroccan sharifism its unique character.

Fatima Mernissi (born in 1940), a Moroccan sociologist and professor at Mohamed V University in Rabat, is known worldwide through her scholarship and public talks on the position of women in Islam. Some of her books have been translated into other languages.

Abdessalem Yassine (born in 1928), an Islamic revivalist scholar, preacher, political dissident, and author of numerous books and treatises, worked as a teacher, administrator, and school inspector for 30 years. Founder of the Justice and Spirituality Movement, which has criticized the Moroccan government for corruption, immorality, and human rights abuses, he was under house arrest without trial from December 1989 to May 2000. His daughter, Nadine Yassine, is a key figure in the national leadership of the organization.

HOUSES OF WORSHIP AND HOLY PLACES In Morocco, as elsewhere in the Muslim world, mosques constitute the primary place of worship. Moroccan mosques vary considerably in size, shape, and style of architecture. They are distinguishable by the minaret-a tall, narrow, square towerlike structure at one end-from which the call to prayer is transmitted. Mosques have a large carpeted prayer room that contains a *minbar,* or pulpit, from which the imam gives his Friday midday sermon, and a mihrab, or recess in one wall indicating the direction of Mecca, which is to be faced when praying.

A second place of worship is the *zawiya,* which varies in size and structure. It houses *dhikrs,* or remembrance ceremonies, and other activities of Sufi associations. Like certain caves, water sources, waterfalls, and trees, saint's tombs are also considered holy places.

WHAT IS SACRED? To Moroccans the *tasbih,* or prayer beads, and especially the Koran are considered sacred objects to be touched only when a person is in a state of ritual purity. This state is attained by two stages of ritual cleansing, *ghusl* and *wudu.* Ritual impurity results from the emission of bodily fluids. *Ghusl,* or bathing the entire body, is particularly necessary after menstruation, sexual intercourse, or childbirth. *Wudu* entails washing the hands, feet, and face and rinsing the body orifices of the nose, mouth, and ears. This state of ritual purity is also necessary for performing the five daily prayers and for entering a mosque or holy place.

HOLIDAYS AND FESTIVALS Like other Muslims, on the 10th of the month of the hajj, or pilgrimage to Mecca, Moroccans celebrate Id al-Adha to commemorate Abraham's sacrifice to Allah. They also celebrate Id al-Fitr at the end of the month of Ramadan. In both cases every family that can afford to do so slaughters a sheep and enjoys a meal together. Ramadan, the holy month of fasting, commemorates the revelation of the Koran to Muhammad. It entails purification of the mind by avoiding negative thoughts and of the body by refraining from eating, drinking, smoking, and engaging in sexual activities from sunrise until sunset. At sunset Moroccans break the fast with soup, dates, and other special dishes together with relatives, neighbors, or friends. Many Moroccans spend the entire night of the 27th, Laylat al-Qadr, or the night of destiny, in the mosque praying.

Additional holidays include New Year on the first and Ashura on the 10th of Muharram and the Prophet's birthday on the 12th of Rabi al-Awwal. Ashura is the annual occasion for collecting and distributing *zakat,* the obligatory 10 percent of one's income, to the needy. In the south it merged with an ancient Berber festival in which male youths masquerade as animals or women through the streets, eliciting laughter and money and temporarily reversing gender roles and power relations.

MODE OF DRESS There is no official dress code in Morocco, and styles vary from Western attire to modern and traditional indigenous clothing. Like other Muslims, most Moroccans believe that obligatory Islamic dress for the public sphere, especially for women, consists of loose clothing that covers the body entirely from the neck to the wrists and ankles. This code is always observed when praying and entering a mosque, even by those who do not feel obliged to do so at other times.

The two most common overgarments for women are the *jallaba* and the *lihaf.* The *jallaba* is a straight, loose ankle-length garment with a high neckline, long, full sleeves, and a hood. The hair is covered by a scarf. A small piece of cloth covering the face below the eyes may also be worn. The *lihaf,* a large piece of cloth about two yards by five yards, is wrapped around the waist and shoulders and then draped over the head and sometimes over the lower face.

Men are more likely to dress in European-style clothing. Some, however, especially older men, prefer to wear a loose ankle-length overgarment also known as the *jallaba.* Other men resort to traditional-style clothing only in cold weather, donning a loose ankle-length overgarment made of wool called the *salham.*

DIETARY PRACTICES Because Moroccans, like other Muslims, consider them to be gifts from Allah, food and drink are treated with respect and shared with others. There are two national dishes: couscous, a fine-grained hard wheat or barley pasta served with a vegetable and meat sauce, and *tajine,* a meat or fish and vegetable stew. In accordance with tradition, they are offered to anyone who is present, and both are eaten from a common platter. Moroccans follow the Muslim injunction not to consume pork or alcoholic beverages.

RITUALS Like most Muslims, Moroccans pray five times daily. A prayer rug is used at home or elsewhere, but any clean surface will do. Praying in mosques is optional except for the Friday midday prayer for men. Many Moroccan mosques have a separate room for women that is accessible exclusively through an outside door.

Besides the pilgrimage to Mecca, required once in the lifetime of every Muslim who is physically and financially able, Moroccans make pilgrimages to other holy places. These include saint's tombs, caves, water sources, waterfalls, and trees. While the saint's tombs honor humans, real or legendary, the other sites are dedicated to and inhabited by spirits. People visit such places regularly, occasionally, or only in times of need, as for problem solving, healing, or obtaining a *baraka,* or blessing. The recitation of special prayers is central to a visitation, and visitors sometimes make offerings of small personal items or sacrifice an animal to demonstrate their devotion.

Week-long pilgrimage festivals are held annually in honor of saints and some spirits. In addition to tomb visitations and prayer rituals, pilgrims shop and enjoy live entertainment provided by musical performers, storytellers, and acrobats.

Sufi ritual ceremonies take two forms in Morocco. The *dhikr* consists of eulogies chanted to Allah or Muhammad, sometimes to the accompaniment of drums and other instruments. The goal is to attain closeness to Allah. The second type of ceremony, the *hadra,* signifying presence, attempts to appease the spirits. Summoned by burning incense and by chanting to the accompaniment of drums and other instruments, the spirits take possession of the participants, causing them to sway to the beat faster and faster until they reach an ecstatic climax. Organized separately for women and men, both ceremonies are found throughout Morocco.

RITES OF PASSAGE On the seventh day after birth, a Moroccan child receives its name. This rite, *as-subu,* meaning "week," is celebrated by recitations from the Koran and by slaughtering an animal.

Male circumcision, which occurs between the ages of three and six, is undertaken as both a religious obligation and a hygienic measure, after which the boy is considered to be officially a Muslim. A local religious official performs the procedure privately or in groups and free of charge at pilgrimage festivals. Recitations from the Koran and a celebration follow.

Marriage is the most important rite of passage in Morocco. It involves decorating the bride's hands and feet with henna, a procession from the groom's to the bride's home, and a celebration.

At a funeral special prayers, unique to the occasion, are recited over the corpse in the mosque after it has been washed. The body is then placed in a coffin and transported in a procession to the cemetery. In the grave it is placed on its right side facing Mecca.

MEMBERSHIP With one exception, there are no recruitment strategies in Morocco. The Boudshishiyya, a branch of the Qadiriyya Sufi order established in the north in the early twentieth century, actively recruits members not only within Morocco but also in Europe, Asia, and the United States. The state, on the other hand, influences citizen's understanding of Islamic dogma and practice through both old and new measures, in part in an effort to limit participation in existing Islamist organizations and to ward off infiltration by new ones. Just before each of the five obligatory daily prayers, the call to prayer is chanted, often by microphone, from the minarets of mosques. In addition, national television broadcasts are interrupted with a version of the call to prayer. During Ramadan special entertainment programs are broadcast in the evenings, all restaurants and cafés are closed during daylight hours, and Moroccans can be fined for eating, drinking, or smoking in public. Children are encouraged to attend Koran school before entering elementary school, and the public school curriculum includes lessons in religion. National stations broadcast the king, dressed in traditional Muslim attire, praying with other officials in one of Morocco's large mosques and participating in other religious ceremonies. A new series discussing Islamic dogma and practice from a moderate point of view was aired in 2003.

SOCIAL JUSTICE Generosity is an important Islamic social value, and Moroccans are obligated to give to the needy whenever possible. In principle all human beings, regardless of their status, are to be treated with respect, as they are all Allah's creatures.

Education is generally considered a religious obligation, and by law Moroccan children are required to attend public school until the age of 12. Young girls, however, are often taken out of school early to help at home and to protect their honor. For at least a year before entering public school, most attend a Koran school to learn to recite, read, and write Koranic verses. Boarding facilities attached to some larger mosques prepare boys to become Koran teachers and low-level religious specialists through further training in Koranic recitation and interpretation and in Islamic law. Additional training in religious schools is required to become a religious instructor, an imam (mosque official), or an *adil* (religious registrar).

SOCIAL ASPECTS Marriage and procreation are considered to be religious obligations and are highly valued in Moroccan society. The same can be said of love and respect for elders, especially one's parents. Sexuality is considered to be a natural human need, but its expression is permissible only within the bonds of matrimony. Monogamy is preferable, but polygamy is acceptable when all wives can be treated equally.

POLITICAL IMPACT Politics and religion are closely linked in Morocco. Since the Idrisid dynasty Islam has been the sole source of legitimization for securing and wielding political authority. Throughout Moroccan history numerous groups have declared holy war on other groups or ruling dynasties.

Mohamed VI, who took the throne in 1999, is an Alawite. Ruling continuously since 1669, the Alawite dynasty traces its ancestry to the Prophet through his grandson al-Hasan, son of Ali and Muhammad's daughter Fatima. The king bears the title Amir al-Muminin, or Commander of the Believers. Muhammad and his first four successors, the so-called Rightly Guided Caliphs, as well as other early rulers of the Islamic empire, bore this title.

CONTROVERSIAL ISSUES Moroccan women are employed in a wide variety of positions in the public sphere. They may also hold official religious positions, for example, as a *qadi* (religious judge) or as an imam for an all-female congregation. This occurs infrequently, however.

Although marriage is considered to be a lifetime commitment, divorce is not uncommon in Morocco. Birth control and abortion are available with parental or spousal permission, but many Moroccans reject abortion as unacceptable in Islam.

CULTURAL IMPACT In keeping with the Islamic ban on the pictorial representation of humans and animals, Moroccan mosques, palaces, and other official buildings are decorated with floral and geometric designs and with Arabic calligraphy. Dating to pre-Islamic Arabia, the themes of unrequited love, nature, and beauty fill Arabic and Berber poetry and songs.

Other Religions

Christianity, brought to Morocco by tribes migrating from the east in the second or third century C.E., had completely disappeared by the eleventh century. The Portuguese, Spanish, and French living in coastal enclaves and throughout Morocco during the protectorate built churches. Some are still used by Christian foreigners living in larger cities.

Jewish tribes, arriving from the east in the first half of the second century B.C.E., lived segregated from Muslims in their own communities. Their intellectual exchange with Spanish Jewry was frequent, and their liturgical, educational, artistic, and musical traditions were highly developed. The Jewish practice of venerating saints paralleled that of Muslims. Most Jewish children attended Jewish schools, and while Hebrew was important as a liturgical language, Jews communicated in Berber and Moroccan Arabic. By 1960 the majority of Jews had left for Israel or elsewhere.

Margaret Jean Rausch

See Also Vol. I: *Islam, Shiism, Sunnism*

Bibliography

Baker, Alison. *Voices of Resistance: Oral Histories of Moroccan Women.* Albany: State University of New York Press, 1998.

Ben-Ami, Issachar. *Saint Veneration among Jews in Morocco.* Detroit: Wayne State University Press, 1998.

Brett, Michael, and Elizabeth Fentress. *The Berbers.* Cambridge, Mass.: Blackwell, 1996.

Cornell, Vincent J. *Realm of the Saint: Power and Authority in Moroccan Sufism.* Austin: University of Texas Press, 1998.

Ensel, Remco. *Saints and Servants in Southern Morocco.* Leiden: E.J. Brill, 1999.

Gerber, Jane S. *Jewish Society in Fez 1450–1700: Studies in Communal and Economic Life.* Leiden: E.J. Brill, 1980.

Kapchan, Deborah A. *Gender on the Market: Moroccan Women and the Revoicing of Tradition.* Philadelphia: University of Pennsylvania Press, 1996.

Mernissi, Fatima. *Beyond the Veil: Male-Female Dynamics in Modern Muslim Society.* Bloomington: Indiana University Press, 1987.

Park, Thomas K. *Historical Dictionary of Morocco.* Lanham, Md.: Scarecrow Press, 1996.

Shatzmiller, Maya. *The Berbers and the Islamic State: The Marinid Experience in Pre-Protectorate Morocco.* Princeton, N.J.: Markus Wiener, 2000.

Mozambique

POPULATION 19,607,519

AFRICAN INDIGENOUS BELIEFS 49.5 percent

CHRISTIAN 30 percent

MUSLIM 20 percent

HINDU 0.5 percent

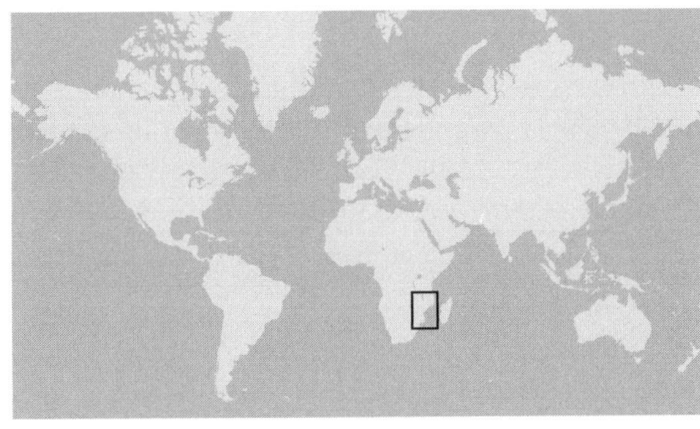

Country Overview

INTRODUCTION The Republic of Mozambique lies on the southeastern coast of Africa. It is bordered to the north by Tanzania; to the northwest by Lake Nyasa, Malawi, and Zambia; to the west by Zimbabwe; and to the southwest and south by South Africa and Swaziland. It is separated from the island of Madagascar to the east by the Mozambique Channel, an arm of the Indian Ocean.

For centuries before the arrival of Arab Muslim merchants in the 600s and European colonizers in the 1500s, virtually every Mozambican worshiped in ways prescribed by indigenous religious tradition, which consisted primarily of ancestor veneration and the belief in one, transcendental being (God) and in the existence of spirits. As Islam and Christianity have competed for the souls of the practitioners of traditional religion, many traditionalists have continued to practice their religion.

Islam was introduced in northern Mozambique via the Arabian Peninsula. Arab merchants, some of whom ventured into the interior, spread the new faith, sparing the Africans the full force of the jihad, or holy war. Muslim brotherhoods, such as the Qadiriyya and Tijaniyya, which were strong in West Africa, especially during the nineteenth century, were absent in Mozambique, however. The ethnic groups most receptive to Islam were the Macua and Makonde in the present-day provinces of Niassa and Cabo Delgado and in parts of Nampula, especially along the coast. As an indication of Islamic resistance to European colonialism, northern Mozambique surrendered to the Portuguese only during the 1920s.

Roman Catholicism was first introduced in Mozambique during the sixteenth century. In the 1930s a Catholic revival occurred in response to the accelerated activity of Protestant foreign missionaries, who had initiated their work in southern Mozambique as early as 1823, most notably through the Wesleyan mission in Lourenco Marques (now Maputo) and through Tsonga evangelists who came from the Transvaal region of South Africa in 1880. Christianity found its most fervent adherents on the southern coast of Mozambique, in Inhambane in particular, and along the Zambezi River, especially among the Anyungwe, Achuabo, and Asena peoples. It also made major inroads among the Ndao around what became Beira City (in Manica) and

Mozambique President Joaquim Chissano marries his bride in a Catholic ceremony in 2001. In Mozambique the Catholic Church is perceived by other churches as an institution that has always attempted to exert a religious hegemony over the rest of the country. © AFP/CORBIS.

Sofala. Except for a few pockets, however, the ethnic groups of the hinterland and the populations along the Manica Plateau (the Abarwe, the Karanga, and Atewe, for example) remained inaccessible to the early Catholic missionaries. When the Portuguese left Mozambique in 1975, there were some 4 million Christians in the country.

RELIGIOUS TOLERANCE Mozambique's 1995 constitution guarantees religious freedom and the separation of church and state. Historically, there was a fundamental difference in the state's behavior toward religion during the colonial period and during the period following the declaration of independence in 1975. Even though the churches, particularly the Catholic Church, and the state collaborated closely in the colonial period to preserve the status quo, religious persecution was rare. Following independence the Marxist-Leninist government attempted to simply eliminate religion as a superstition and an obstruction to the creation of a modern society. As a result, the Catholic Church was severely persecuted, its property confiscated, and vocal members of the clergy arrested and publicly humiliated. The late president Samora Machel once assembled in Maputo all religious leaders, including those of Islam, and publicly scorned the Catholic bishops, accusing them of having collaborated with the colonial oppressors and calling them "macacos" (monkeys). During the 1970s the persecution of Jehovah's Witnesses was vicious in Mozambique (and in most of southern Africa). Between 1975 and 1992 religious traditionalism also encountered a formidable opponent in the state, which used force to back up its antireligious campaign. Persons were not imprisoned on account of their traditionalist worship practices, but their lives were made difficult through ridicule, humiliation, and efforts to eliminate traditional power and respect for traditional values related to political and religious authority in the rural setting.

Although much touted, the ecumenical movement in Mozambique is virtually nonexistent. A semblance of ecumenism exists within the Protestant denominations; yet, apart from occasional meetings of the Conselho Cristão de Moçambique (CCM; Christian Council of Mozambique), established in 1948 mainly to counter Portuguese resentment of and discrimination against Protestant missions in the colony, interdenominational competition and jealousy is more evident than is harmony. True ecumenism entails efforts to reconcile doctrinal differences, concerted and meaningful liturgical integration, and coordination in the provision of social services. None of these is evident in interdenominational relations in Mozambique. Each church looks after its own interests, and the Catholic Church is perceived by all others as an institution that has always attempted to exert a religious hegemony over the rest of the country.

Major Religions

AFRICAN INDIGENOUS BELIEFS

CHRISTIANITY

AFRICAN INDIGENOUS BELIEFS

DATE OF ORIGIN 4000 B.C.E.

NUMBER OF FOLLOWERS 9.7 million

HISTORY Evidence suggests that Mozambique was one of the areas where religious practices and systems first emerged. At first, religious manifestations were simple, most likely taking the form of a polytheism (belief in the existence of many gods) associated with the forces of the universe and including the worship of hundreds of minor deities or spirits. As humans began to better understand and to take control of their environment, religious concepts became more complex, resulting in the worship of a transcendental or remote creator of the universe, who was believed to be caring, omnipresent, omniscient, and omnipotent. The creator was thought to be assisted by spirits and ancestors, who were sometimes called the living-dead and who also became the guardians of the traditional social order. These prevailing traditional beliefs were later infused with those of the Bantu-speakers, migrants from the area of Nigeria and Cameroon, who, through their superior weaponry and agricultural implements and knowledge, were able to overcome the first inhabitants of Mozambique as early, perhaps, as the first century C.E. Islam and Christianity have been unable to dislodge the grip of traditionalism on the population of Mozambique. The traditionalist's major religious and cosmological tenets have remained almost intact over the centuries and are associated with the powers of the medicine man, the witch, the sorcerer, the diviner, and the magician.

EARLY AND MODERN LEADERS Because of the absence of literate societies throughout much of Mozambique's history and the lack of organized proselytizing in the country, it is impossible to pinpoint the leaders of traditional religious movements. Political authorities and heads of families—who perform such rituals as pouring libations to the ancestors, offering sacrifices, and prayer—and some traditional healers and ancestors constitute, in a sense, the religious leadership. Because of the diversity of peoples in Mozambique, which harbors some 10 major ethnic groups, these religious authorities have no power beyond their village, clan, or ethnic group.

MAJOR THEOLOGIANS AND AUTHORS Given that traditional religion is not organized in the same discernible structure as Christianity, for example, and that traditional religious beliefs are only transmitted by word of mouth from one generation to another, no known theologians or authors have been nurtured or remembered as such in Mozambique's traditional religion.

HOUSES OF WORSHIP AND HOLY PLACES As is common in African traditional religions, places of worship in Mozambique usually include the back of the head of the family's house, where ancestral offerings are made; a special part of the forest that serves as a shrine; the cemetery or burial place; and a selected locality in the family compound or elsewhere, where the clan may have originated. In these places sacrifice, prayer, and thanksgiving ceremonies take place. In traditional Mozambique there is nothing comparable to Mecca or the Holy Land.

WHAT IS SACRED? Among Mozambican traditionalists, the dead, objects that are buried with the dead, the ancestors, the good spirits that mediate between God and man, and the animal that may be associated with the origins of the clan or the ethnic group are all considered sacred. Animals with clan associations may not be killed, eaten, or made to suffer.

HOLIDAYS AND FESTIVALS Each ethnic group has its own traditional holidays and festivals, even though, as a result of colonization, all groups observe Christian holidays. The birth of a child, harvest day, the day of a chief's enthronement, burial days (especially those of important persons in the village), and weddings are usually observed with religious rituals, rest from work, drumming, dancing, eating, and drinking. In these activities the religious and the secular interface.

MODE OF DRESS Traditionalism implicitly upholds decency in dress. Since religion permeates the daily life of a Mozambican, there is no need for special attire during worship. When someone is officiating during a religious ritual, however, he or she may be required to wear such items as beads, a cap, a cover made of animal skins, and amulets and to carry a symbolic stick.

DIETARY PRACTICES Religious traditions and secular cultural practices often overlap in Mozambique, and dietary practices offer an example of this. When a practitioner of traditional religion says, "I may not eat a crocodile," he is simply affirming an established tradition of his ethnic group, which may be based on ancestral practices. Because ancestors are linked to the supernatural and the divine and their moral sanction is part of the religious belief, the preceding statement is both a religious and a cultural affirmation.

RITUALS In Mozambique the nature and performance of traditional religious rituals varies depending upon the ethnic group and the clan, as well as the circumstances of the village or family on whose behalf the ritual is performed. Usually a ritual is considered religious in nature when the word for the divine is invoked—say, for example, Mulungu (God) among the Anyungwe of central Mozambique—or the spirits or the ancestors are summoned. Libations, prayers, hand washing (for purification), and partaking in a drink are religious acts. These activities are invariably officiated by a designated person, such as the head of the family or a "priest," who is thought to know and experience the divine world and to have a special relationship with the ancestors. Rituals may require large crowds, a small group, or just the individual presiding over the rite. They can have numerous purposes, such as placating the ancestors and spirits, atonement, giving thanks to the divine, calling the rain, stopping a calamity, finding a witch, or curing the sick. Spiritual possession occurs during some intense rituals and at dances. A possessed person may assume the nature of an animal or a spirit and behave accordingly.

RITES OF PASSAGE Even though it is almost impossible to separate traditional religion from other cultural practices in Mozambique, rites of passage from childhood to adulthood, and from the world of the living to the world of the ancestors, are social events rather than religious or spiritually required observances. Rites of passage are designed to teach youngsters to live according to the social and cultural norms that will ensure the survival of the family, the lineage, and the clan or to prepare the deceased to be properly received by the ancestors. In Mozambique adulthood rites, which are now fast disappearing, may last just a few days among some ethnic groups, while among others the initiation may take weeks. Most such rites of passage in Mozambique do not involve circumcision, which, among those ethnic groups that require it, takes place immediately after birth.

MEMBERSHIP There is no religious recruitment or proselytizing in Mozambique's traditional religion. Traditionalists do not use the radio or other sophisticated modes of communication to increase their religious membership. Children grow up in a religious atmosphere in which the divine, the spiritual, and the secular come to be known mainly through experience and participatory observation. Thus, the household guarantees membership in a traditional setting. Naturally tolerant, adherents of traditionalism in Mozambique rarely retaliate against those who decide to embrace Christianity or Islam.

SOCIAL JUSTICE The concepts of justice; responsibility for the care of the poor, the handicapped, and the elderly; and respect for the sanctity of human life are so intrinsically embedded in Mozambican traditions that a specific religious command or invocation is never needed. The community and the ancestors are responsible for upholding traditional religious concepts and precepts and applying them in daily activities.

SOCIAL ASPECTS Traditional religion in Mozambique upholds the sanctity of the (nuclear) family and (polygamous) marriage. Marriage and childbearing are obligations for those young men and women who have undergone the rites of passage, for they ensure the survival of the lineage and the clan. The sanctity of these cultural precepts is couched in myths and traditions related to the creation of man and woman and the origins of the clan.

POLITICAL IMPACT To the extent that the political authority of the king or chief is divine, religion plays a major role in the social order and ensures stability among Mozambican traditionalists. Traditionalists have never used their cohesion as a community, however, to oppose an enemy or to send adepts to vote for a specific political candidate. Thus, it is accurate to say that in village politics, where the government allows it, traditionalism has had an impact in several areas, but it has not had a direct impact on the conduct of modern politics in the country. Contemporary traditionalists are still scorned but are not persecuted by the government or by members of the other major faiths in Mozambique. Actions akin to religious cleansing, crusades, and jihads are totally alien to traditionalism in Mozambique. Thus, among traditionalists revolts against oppression and colonialism have been waged implicitly in the name of the dignity and the rights of human beings and only rarely in the name of religion.

CONTROVERSIAL ISSUES In traditionalism respect for the sanctity of human life undergirds traditional views of such practices as birth control, divorce, and abortion, as well as the traditional conception of the role of women. Anything that threatens the survival of the lineage or the clan must be avoided. The smaller the lineage is, the more strongly its members hold this belief. Birth control is seen as a Western conspiracy to ensure Western control based on demographic advantage, and divorce is made difficult by linking it to the return of the bridewealth and by requiring proof of adultery or infertility. The subordinate role of women is prescribed by tradition and preordained by God, the deities, or the ancestors and, therefore, cannot be altered easily.

Traditionalists do not oppose contraceptives or abortion because God forbids it. Rather, preordained order and "our tradition" will invariably be cited as the justification for such opposition in a religious traditionalist setting.

CULTURAL IMPACT In Mozambican traditionalism the secular and the divine are intrinsically intertwined and permeate all aspects of human life. The general absence of a literate tradition and the tendency not to question authority and the established order make it difficult to assess the historical impact of religion on cultural manifestations in traditional Mozambique. Certainly, however, traditional religion continues to influence wisdom literature through its proverbs, riddles, and stories, as well as music and art, especially with regard to themes and motifs in sculpture and painting.

CHRISTIANITY

DATE OF ORIGIN Sixteenth century C.E.
NUMBER OF FOLLOWERS 5.9 million

HISTORY Almost 50 years after Vasco da Gama disembarked there in 1498, the effort to Christianize Mozambique started in earnest, propelled by the work of Saint Francis Xavier in 1542 and the Jesuit priest Gonçalo da Silveira in 1560. Several religious orders—including the Jesuits, Capuchins, Augustinians, White Fathers, Burgos, Franciscans, and Cucujães—sent missionaries during the following centuries, even though the Catholic Church's effort was severely curtailed in the eighteenth and nineteenth centuries and between 1910 and 1926. The work of the Protestant churches began in the south during the 1820s.

By the 1940s Catholics and Protestants were fiercely competing for converts in Mozambique, even though Catholicism, as a de facto state religion, always had the upper hand. Elementary education, through which the Catholic Church exerted its greatest influence, was entrusted to the clergy, which received state subsidies. Thus, most Mozambican revolutionary leaders of the 1960s and '70s were educated in Catholic mission schools. They later renounced Catholicism in favor of atheistic socialism. Since the collapse of Communism and socialism during the 1990s, however, many of them have returned to the church.

In contrast to the Protestant churches, especially the Anglican Church, the Catholic Church had not seriously considered preparing an African clergy, a situation that created a severe shortage of local priests when most of the European missionaries were forced to return home after independence in 1975. Securing seminarians who will remain faithful to their vocation constitutes one of the greatest challenges facing churches in contemporary Mozambique, especially the Catholic Church, even though they are now "Africanized." The highest-ranking Catholic clergy in Mozambique include one retired cardinal, three archbishops, and nine bishops, who preside over 12 dioceses. The Anglican Church, the most influential of the Protestant churches, has two bishops, of whom one resides in Maputo and the other in Niassa.

EARLY AND MODERN LEADERS The Bishop's Conference of Mozambique includes the country's three Catholic archbishops—Francisco Chimoio of Maputo, Jaime Pedro Gonçalves of Beira, and Tomé Macueliha of Nampula—and nine bishops. The Anglican bishops, Dinis Salomão Singulane of Libombo (in Maputo) and Paulino Tomás Manhique of Niassa, receive their mandate directly from Cape Town, South Africa, and indirectly from the Anglican Church in England. Historical church leaders in Mozambique include Father Gonçalo da Silveira, one of the first Christian missionaries to the country, who was murdered there in 1561; the infamous Cardinal Clemente de Gouveia, who preached during the 1960s that the concept of independence for Mozambique was against the gospel; and the acclaimed Catholic bishop of Beira, Sebastião Soares de Resende, a critic of Portuguese colonial policies, who died in 1967.

MAJOR THEOLOGIANS AND AUTHORS Except for the bishops mentioned in EARLY AND MODERN LEADERS and some priests who have received further training in theology, philosophy, or canon law, no outstanding or renowned theologians have emerged in the country. Meager resources and facilities, lack of control of the media and publishing houses, and continued racism have prevented the Mozambican churches, Catholic and Protestant, from becoming major intellectual forces within the larger religious community.

HOUSES OF WORSHIP AND HOLY PLACES Except for the common churches, there are no outstanding Christian holy places in Mozambique. Catholic churches bear images of saints, and many have tinted windows and wooden pews. They sometimes provide areas where the faithful can light candles for a fee. As a result of the assault by the Frente de Libertação de Moçambique (FRELIMO; Mozambique Liberation Front) on religion during the 1970s and '80s and the precarious economic conditions in the country, few churches have been built in contemporary Mozambique, and most existing church buildings are decaying.

WHAT IS SACRED? In spite of Christianity's relatively long history in Mozambique, no local relics are venerated in the country, and no Mozambicans have ever been canonized or beatified.

HOLIDAYS AND FESTIVALS Christmas and Easter are the most important Christian holidays in Mozambique; they are also national holidays. Observance of major holidays includes church worship, a large meal, visits to family and friends, and perhaps a traditional or modern dance. Christmas is seen as a family festival, and wealthy families exchange small gifts on 25 December. Almsgiving at Christmas was common during the colonial period, and people were often seen extending their hands toward others while saying "bo festa" (a mispronunciation of the Portuguese "happy holiday" greeting). Holidays like Christmas and Easter are so associated with excessive eating and drinking that both Christians and traditionalists often say, "Comemos e bebemos Natal e Páscoa em casa" ("We ate and drank Christmas and Easter at home").

MODE OF DRESS No specific mode of dress is required of Christians in Mozambique, though decency is emphasized. Both the Catholic and Protestant clergy continue to wear the cassock or the white collar. Whereas Christians were expected to dress up on Sundays and holy days during the colonial period, nowadays poverty has forced the people to dress as poorly on Sunday as during the week.

DIETARY PRACTICES No specifically Christian dietary practices exist in Mozambique. Fasting and abstinence during Lent are poorly enforced and observed. There are certain meats that are usually avoided by religious traditionalists and Christians alike, such as lion, zebra, crocodile, monkey, leopard, hyena, snake, dog, donkey, and jackal. While some animals are not eaten because of their close association with humans, others are avoided because they consume human flesh.

RITUALS Like Christians throughout the world, Mozambique's Christians celebrate birth with baptism, the coming of age with the sacrament of confirmation, marriage with the rite of holy matrimony, and death with funeral ceremonies preceded by a mass or a special service. Because no officially acknowledged sacred shrine exists in the country, no local pilgrimages take place. A few wealthy Catholics might visit the Holy Land or Fátima in Portugal. Similarly, few Protestants or other Christians make pilgrimages to sites outside the country. Weddings, which take place in church, are followed by a major meal and a dance, or *baile,* and are therefore occasions for the rich to show off their opulence and power. Funerals are preceded by a church service and followed by a meal with invited guests. As during the colonial period, women tend to dress in black for funerals, and men wear a black band on the sleeves of their coats.

RITES OF PASSAGE Although several ethnic groups in Mozambique hold rites of passage for boys and girls, devout Christians do not. The closest rite vaguely resembling initiation is the instruction and preparation for First Communion and confirmation, or Chrisma, which is presided over by the bishop and begins when a youngster reaches the age of seven, considered to be the age at which children begin to think for themselves. Following the church ceremonies youngsters from wealthy families are received by relatives and guests, including the officiating priest or minister, in an elaborate festival of food, drinks, and gifts. There is singing, there may be dancing, and the parents and the godfathers usually make sentimental speeches in Portuguese.

MEMBERSHIP The Christian churches constantly send missionaries, preachers, priests, and catechists to convert Mozambican traditionalists and those belonging to other faiths, including Muslims. Conversion efforts are still largely made through word of mouth rather than through the modern media. Radio has become a tool for conversion but only in the hands of the more resourceful Catholic Church. No televangelists exist in Mozambique. Ideally and usually, religious instruction lasts three years and is conducted in groups led either by trained laymen or the clergy. Both Muslim and Christian groups have claimed tremendous success in converting potential adepts, even though in some areas very few Christians can be found.

SOCIAL JUSTICE Most of the Christian work in Mozambique has been related to restoring human dignity, preventing human rights abuses by the state, protecting religious freedom, speaking on behalf of the destitute, helping feed the hungry, and alleviating the misery of the masses. During the colonial period primary education and part of secondary education was largely entrusted to the Catholic Church. In 1996 the church opened its own private institution of higher learning, the Catholic University of Mozambique. Missions in colonial Mozambique were allowed to have their own hospitals and clinics, including leprosaria. The churches no longer operate hospitals in the country, but trained clerics, especially nuns, are found in most hospitals. The churches, especially the Catholic Church, have been highly outspoken in the country, as was the case during the civil war (1977–92), when religious leaders faulted both FRELIMO, the ruling party, and the rebel movement, RENAMO, for the war and human rights abuses. Such outspokenness has resulted in a permanent state of tension, and sometimes outright hostility, between church and state.

SOCIAL ASPECTS The churches in Mozambique have remained the strongest advocates of the nuclear, monogamous household, even though many men who were married in church have secret wives or clandestine concubines in the countryside. Extramarital and premarital sex are forbidden, even though more than 80 percent of those affected by these church directives have violated them. Church marriages are now acknowledged by the state, but a civil marriage can be contested by no one—not even the most remotely located Marxist administrator.

POLITICAL IMPACT By tradition members of the Catholic Church hierarchy, in contrast to the Protestant churches, are expected to stay out of politics and to let the faithful follow their own consciences. In practice and indirectly—and sometimes directly—through their pastoral letters and sermons, however, the Mozambican bishops have been politically active. During the civil war (1977–92) the Mozambican churches criticized both the government and the rebel movement and played an active role in the subsequent negotiations, in which Archbishop Jaime Gonçalves represented the Catholic Church and the Reverend Dinis Singulane the Anglican Church. It is accurate to say that the churches in contemporary Mozambique are deeply involved in politics as it relates to the issues of religious freedom, human rights, democracy, and corruption, and they inform the faithful which political candidates represent more closely the churche's respective positions. As a result, many bishops have met with government ire and, at times, incarceration, or they have been publicly denounced. Because the Protestant denominations have been less publicly vocal on political matters, none of their major leaders has ever been incarcerated by the government. Since 1995 the Christian Council of Mozambique has been helping to collect small firearms as part of the demobilization effort—referred to as "turning guns into plowshares"—that stemmed from the 1992 General Peace Accord.

CONTROVERSIAL ISSUES The Mozambican Catholic Church has followed the Vatican's teachings on the most important social issues, while the Protestant churches have emphasized individual consciousness and decision making. Catholics are forbidden to use condoms or other birth control, may not engage in abortion, and cannot divorce, lest they run the risk of excommunication. Lay Catholics, however, pay little attention to these teachings in the privacy of their homes and consciences. Family planning is allowed, but it must be practiced without artificial means. Women have only recently begun to play some role in church matters; yet they still may not be ordained as deacons or priests.

CULTURAL IMPACT Christianity has exerted considerable cultural influence in Mozambique. One of the churche's enduring legacies is found in the country's sacred music. During the colonial period Western sacred songs were introduced, and in the rural areas, especially in places where foreign missionaries evangelized, they were translated into the vernacular. Christians built hundreds of churches and chapels in the country, most of them Western in inspiration—with some Baroque and others Gothic in style. Christians translated the Bible into the vernacular, prepared the first dictionaries in African languages, and popularized an African alphabet.

Other Religions

Practitioners of Islam, which was introduced from the Arabian Peninsula during the seventh century, are said to account for 20 percent of the population, or about 3.9 million people. Most Muslims live in the north and in pockets of the north-central provinces—Niassa, Cabo Delgado, Nampula, and Quelimane. Islam appeals to Africans for several reasons. Islam teaches brotherhood and the equality of all mankind, regardless of race, and allows polygamy, permitting marriage to as many as four wives. Islam actively supports the concept of a large family and tolerates several African cultural practices that are not in line with Islamic tradition, such as those used in healing or in the veneration of ancestors. Equally important to the spread of Islam in Mozambique are the trappings of its rudimentary education, the lure of reciting the Koran in Arabic, and the religion's association with the cosmopolitan centers of the Middle East. Muslim influence in Mozambican politics and society has been growing. Muslims have their own political party, the Partido de Todos os Nativos Moçambicanos (PARTONAMO), whose leader is Mussaquy Abdul Ramane, and they have their own political representatives in the Assembleia da República (Assembly of the Republic). Politically prominent Muslims include Jose Ibraimo Abudo, the minister of justice, and Abdul Razak, the governor of Nampula. Muslims have also begun building their own institutions of higher learning in Mozambique.

Muslims have formed the Islamic Congress of Mozambique, which represents Sunni Muslims and is chaired by Hassane Makda, and the Islamic Council of Mozambique, which is led by Sheikh Abobakar Ismael Mangira. As in other parts of Africa, incidents of international terrorism have placed Mozambique's Muslim community on the defensive and slowed down even further the negligible ecumenical movement.

Muslims in Mozambique strive to observe the major external tenets of their religion, such as praying at the mosque on Fridays, fasting during Ramadan, wearing a cap and a white boubou, avoiding pork, and abstaining from alcohol and smoking, though this last teaching is often ignored. In an attempt to increase their numbers, Muslim communities encourage women to marry at an early age and bear as many children as they can. With this goal in mind Muslims in Mozambique are discouraged from using contraceptives, practicing abortion, and adopting family planning methods modeled on those of the West. Muslims have no elaborate rites of passage for boys or girls, and the circumcision of males is performed soon after birth.

Finally, even though worship associated with images is considered idolatrous in Islam, members of Muslim groups in Mozambique—such as the Yao, Macua, and Maconde—wear amulets, keep figurines believed to have spiritual powers, and often participate in traditional ritual practices, such as burial ceremonies, in the villages. Theoretically Islam shows great compassion for the poor and preaches equality and social justice. On Fridays Muslims pass out money among the poor, the sick, and beggars in the street. The irony is that most Muslims are as poor as the rest of the population, and almsgiving is like a drop of water amid an ocean of poverty and misery. Conversion to Islam has mainly become an urban phenomenon, attracting the poor, the unemployed, the underprivileged, the uneducated, former criminals (who converted in jail), and those who are disillusioned with the political and social order.

Hinduism is practiced by a few thousand Indians in Mozambique's major cities and towns. Hindus came to Mozambique from the Portuguese colonies of Goa, Damao, and Diu and from India. While many came as traders (Baneanes) and laborers, some were recruited as auxiliaries to the Portuguese colonial state and have been pejoratively called *monhes* (arrogant, clannish, or lacking in racial purity). Hindus have exercised a disproportionate influence on Mozambique's economy, especially the retail trade in such major cities as Maputo and Beira—to the point of eliciting resentment and scorn among the populace. They exercise overt political influence through financial means, including the banks they own in the country.

The numbers of Asian Buddhists and Shintoists in Mozambique are extremely small. They are found only in the major cities, where some work for international agencies while others live as traders and merchants.

Mario J. Azevedo

See Also Vol. I: *African Indigenous Beliefs, Christianity, Islam*

Bibliography

Africa South of the Sahara. 33rd ed. London: Europa Publishers, 2003.

Azevedo, Mario. *Historical Dictionary of Mozambique.* Metuchen, N.J.: Scarecrow Press, 1991.

———. "The Role of the Roman Catholic Church in the Politics of the Colonial and Post-Colonial State in Mozambique." In *Religion, State, and Society in Contemporary Africa: Nigeria, Sudan, South Africa, Zaire, and Mozambique.* Edited by Austin Metumara Ahanotou, 187–208. New York: P. Lang, 1992.

Butselaar, Jan van. *Africains, missionnaires, et colonialistes: Les Origines de l'Église presbytérienne du Mozambique (Mission suisse), 1880–1896.* Leiden: E.J. Brill, 1984.

Encyclopedia of Africa South of the Sahara. New York: C. Scribner's Sons, 1997.

Hanlon, Joseph. *Mozambique: The Revolution under Fire.* London: Zed Books, 1984.

Hastings, Adrian. "The Christian Churches and Liberation Movements in Southern Africa." *African Affairs* 80, no. 320 (1981): 348–59.

Isaacman, Allen, and Barbara Isaacman. *Mozambique: From Colonialism to Revolution, 1900–1982.* Boulder, Colo.: Westview Press, 1983.

Maquet, Jacques. *Africanity: The Cultural Unity of Black Africa.* Translated by Joan R. Rayfield. New York: Oxford University Press, 1972.

Mbiti, John S. *African Religions and Philosophy.* London: Heinemann, 1970.

———. *Introduction to African Religion.* London: Heinemann Educational, 1975.

Mondlane, Eduardo. *The Struggle for Mozambique.* Baltimore, Md.: Penguin Books, 1969.

Morier-Genoud, Eric. "Of God and Caesar: The Relation between Christian Churches and the State in Mozambique, 1974–1981." *Le Fait Missionnaire* (1996): 1–79.

The Oxford Encyclopedia of the Modern Islamic World. London: Oxford University Press, 1995.

Parrinder, Geoffrey. *Religion in Africa.* Baltimore, Md.: Penguin Books, 1969.

Ray, Benjamin C. *African Religions: Symbols, Ritual, and Community.* 2nd ed. Upper Saddle River, N.J.: Prentice Hall, 2000.

Rego, António da Silva. "Adaptação missionária e assimilação colonizadora no ultramar portugues." *Boletim geral do ultramar* 34, no. 402 (1958): 185–213.

Shorter, Aylward. *African Christian Theology: Adaptation or Incarnation?* Maryknoll, N.Y.: Orbis Books, 1977.

Suret-Canale, Jean. *Afrique noire: Géographie, civilisation, histoire.* Paris: Éditions Sociales, 1968.

Tempels, Placide. *Bantu Philosophy.* Paris: Présence africaine, 1959.

Voll, John Obert. *Islam: Continuity and Change in the Modern World.* Boulder, Colo.: Westview Press, 1982.

Myanmar

POPULATION 42,238,224

BUDDHIST 87.2 percent

CHRISTIAN 5.6 percent

MUSLIM 3.6 percent

HINDU 1.0 percent

OTHER 2.6 percent

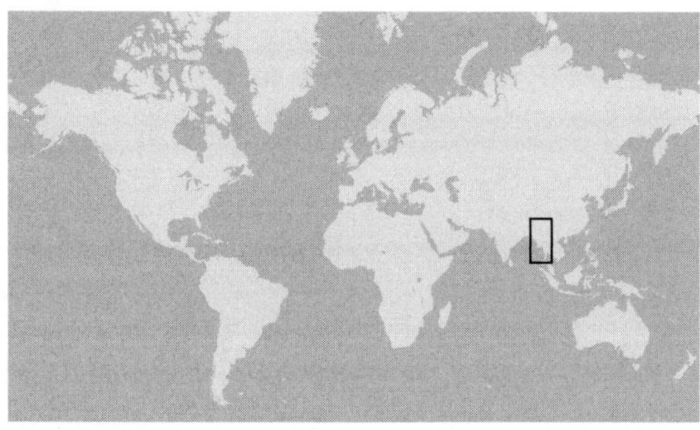

Country Overview

INTRODUCTION The Union of Myanmar, also called Burma, situated along the southeastern rim of continental Asia, is bordered by five countries: India and Bangladesh to the west, China to the north and east, and Laos and Thailand to the east. To the south of Myanmar and the west of peninsular Myanmar lies the Bay of Bengal. Myanmar is an economically undeveloped, semitropical, and mountainous country whose people have relied on rivers as the major travel routes. Buddhist monks accompanied Indian traders sailing to Myanmar's ports along the Bay of Bengal. Buddhist monks, however, also crossed mountains and used river routes to enter the country from the north.

Theravada Buddhism, the dominant religion in Myanmar, appeared about 2,000 years ago. Hinduism also dates back to this time. Christianity was encouraged during British colonial rule in the nineteenth century and has drawn the most converts from Myanmar's tribal animist populations. The ancestors of many of Myanmar's Muslims arrived during the British colonial period.

The impact of British colonial rule on the Buddhist sangha (community of monks) led monks to identify the precolonial past as a time when "pure" Buddhism flourished in Burma. The military coup in 1962 effectively sealed off the country from the rest of the world for about 20 years, which contributed to a perception of the purity of Burmese Buddhism. The current military regime, which chose the name Myanmar in 1989 to replace Burma as the official national designation, has identified its agenda as the fostering of Myanmar cultural heritage, which is effectively Buddhist culture. The government has invoked this agenda to rationalize its persecution of ethnic minorities.

As in other Southeast Asian countries, Buddhism has been used to legitimate historical and contemporary rulers. The current situation in Myanmar pits the ruling military regime, which has identified itself as a champion of Buddhism, against the 1991 Nobel Peace Prize laureate and leader of the political opposition, Aung San Suu Kyi, whom her followers view as a bodhisattva (future Buddha).

RELIGIOUS TOLERANCE Since the 1960s the military regime has been persecuting ethnic minority groups, which include the country's Muslim, Christian, and animist populations. The United Nations estimates that between 1 and 2 million displaced persons live in Myanmar, about 600,000 in camps and the rest in hiding. More than 600,000 refugees have fled Myanmar for Thailand, Laos, Bangladesh, and Malaysia since the late 1980s. Many have fled to escape conscription into forced labor projects, which the military regime defines as voluntary contributions to earn Buddhist merit. The military regime has recruited youths by portraying the army as defending pagodas and monasteries against attack by religious minorities.

Major Religion

THERAVADA BUDDHISM

DATE OF ORIGIN Second century C.E.
NUMBER OF FOLLOWERS 38.3 million

HISTORY Although Theravada Buddhism was introduced, along with Hinduism, to Burma by Indian traders who reached its shores during the first century C.E., Mahayana Buddhist missionaries from the Indian King Ashoka's court were the first Buddhist missionaries to influence mainland Southeast Asia. The first Buddhist kingdoms (100 B.C.E.–900 C.E.) established in Burma, however, were those of the Pyu, who had migrated from Tibet and incorporated Vajrayana, Mahayana, and Theravada Buddhism into their religious beliefs. The Mon, the Pyu's southern neighbors, who had migrated from the east, prospered from trade with Indian merchants, adopted Theravada Buddhism, and sent their own missionaries to propagate Buddhism throughout the region. By the ninth century the Pyu kingdoms were in decline, and a new wave of immigrants, the Burmans, settled in the north, establishing their own kingdom centered around the city of Pagan in 849.

By the eleventh century the Pagan kingdom succeeded in unifying Burma. The Pagan king Anawrahta defeated the Mon in 1057 and strove to legitimize his action by declaring himself to be a *dharmaraja,* a bodhisattva whose task as a monarch was to promote Buddhism. The Burmans, who learned the Pali language and Buddhist scriptures from Mon monks and Buddhist arts from Mon craftsmen, established Pagan as the new center of Theravada Buddhism.

Boys are initiated into monkhood at the Shwedagon Pagoda. The first monastic initiation occurs around the age of eight or nine, when a boy undergoes the shinbyu *ritual inducting him as a novice in the monastery.* © ALISON WRIGHT/CORBIS.

After the fall of the Pagan kingdom to the Mongols in 1287, no unified kingdom existed in northern Burma until the emergence of Ava in 1364. In the south the Mon forged another kingdom at Pegu (now Bago), which lasted until 1531 and became the chief center of Theravada Buddhism in Burma. Succeeding dynasties endeavored to unify Burma and wage war on the Ayutthaya kingdom of Thailand. The Ava kingdom was reestablished toward the end of the sixteenth century, and Ava kings attempted to re-create their state in the image of Pagan's former glory as a Buddhist kingdom. After Ava fell in 1752 the rulers of the succeeding Konbaung dynasty set themselves to conquering their neighbors. Their incursions into Assam resulted in the first of what would be three wars with the British in the nineteenth century, British colonization in 1885, and the transformation of Burma into a province of India until 1937.

The British rule in Burma severed the traditional relationship between the sangha and the state, revoking state patronage of the sangha and precipitating a series of rebellions led by Buddhist monks (1885–97, 1932–34). The sangha lost some of its traditional prestige, Christian missions were encouraged, and children were sent to secular schools, where their Christian teachers criticized Buddhism. The Young Monk's Association, which was effectively a political organization directed to national liberation, was founded in 1906. Burma became independent in 1948, and its first prime minister, U Nu, dedicated himself to strengthening Buddhism and ensured the passage of a constitutional amendment instituting Buddhism as the state religion. He convened the Sixth Buddhist Council in 1954.

In 1962 General Ne Win overthrew the government. Ne Win did not promote Buddhism and initially tried to transform Burma into an isolated, socialist state. The country's dismal economy, however, compelled him to put forward a new constitution, which would open the country to foreign aid. He resigned in 1988 after intensive protests (involving Buddhist monks) brought Burma close to revolution. The military took control, killed many demonstrators, and imposed martial law. The military regime promised a new constitution and called for elections in 1990. The overwhelming victor was Aung San Suu Kyi, daughter of General Aung San (1915–47), former hero of Burma's independence movement. She did not enjoy the fruits of her victory because she was placed under house arrest in 1989 and remained so until 1995. Nevertheless she was awarded the Nobel Peace Prize in 1991. Unlike the government of Ne Win, the current military regime publicly professes its support for Buddhism, as does Aung San Suu Kyi, who defines her political position in terms of the pursuit of Buddhist goals. She has argued that democracy and human rights are consistent with the Burmese Buddhist system and accused the military regime of violating the Buddhist precepts against lying and killing.

EARLY AND MODERN LEADERS Major historical leaders of Buddhism in Burma were often kings. Anawrahta (reigned 1044–77), who unified and expanded the Pagan empire, converted to Theravada Buddhism and maintained close relations with the Sri Lankan King Vijayabahu. Anawrahta sent monks to revive the sangha in Sri Lanka and, in return, obtained relics and a copy of the Pali canon, which he regarded as more correct than the copy he had obtained from his conquest of the Mon. Kyanzittha (reigned 1084–1113), Anawrahta's successor, built many of the most important Burmese temples. King Dhammazedi (reigned 1472–92) of the Pegu kingdom in Ava was a former monk who undertook a major reformation of the monastic order. In the first half of the seventeenth century, Manirathana Thera, a monk, translated numerous texts into the Myanmar language. These were subsequently introduced into school curriculums.

Most modern leaders of Buddhism in Myanmar have professed *vipassana* meditation (insight meditation). Sayagyi U Ba Khin (1899–1971), a layman, achieved such exceptional mastery of the techniques developed by Ledi Sayadaw that he was encouraged by a renowned Buddhist teacher, Webu Sayadaw, to offer instruction in this practice to laypeople. Among Sayagyi's students was Satya Narayan Goenka (born in 1924), whose Vipassana Research Institute was responsible for making the entire Pali canon available on the Internet and in various systems of writing.

MAJOR THEOLOGIANS AND AUTHORS Among the country's most influential theologians was Ledi Sayadaw (1846–1923), a prolific Buddhist scholar and influential teacher of meditation and scripture, who demonstrated particular ability in both the theory and practice of dharma (in the Pali language, *dhamma*). He departed from the scholarly traditions of his peers by writing many works in colloquial Burmese in order to make them accessible to laypeople. Another important theologian was Mahasi Sayadaw (1904–82), author of 67 Buddhist works and teacher of *satipathana vipassana* meditation (concentration meditation).

HOUSES OF WORSHIP AND HOLY PLACES Houses of worship are mainly temples and pagodas. Pagodas, which are relic chambers or stupas, are more plentiful in Myanmar than in other Buddhist countries. Particularly important pagodas include the Shwezigon Pagoda near Pagan, which houses a replica of the Buddha's tooth obtained by Anawrahta; Shwedagon Pagoda in Yangon (Rangoon), the largest gold-plated temple in the world, said to house eight hairs of the Buddha; Kuthodaw Pagoda in Mandalay, featuring the inscription of the Pali canon onto 729 white marble tablets; Mahazedi Pagoda in Bago (Pegu), enshrining a replica of the tooth relic and, purportedly, the Buddha's begging bowl; Arakan Pagoda in Mandalay, containing a sacred image of the Buddha; and Kyaiktiyo Pagoda in

Kyaiktiyo, perched atop a golden rock that is balanced on the edge of a cliff.

WHAT IS SACRED? Buddhist relics worshiped in Myanmar include eight hairs that, according to some legends, the Buddha purportedly gave to two Burmese merchants who had offered him refreshments; several replicas of the Buddha's tooth relic from Sri Lanka; and a replica of the tooth relic from the People's Republic of China. Consecrated images of the Buddha are objects of worship and may be attributed with special powers. For example, several images of a serpent-hooded Buddha are believed to protect victims of snake bites, and carved fish representing an incarnation of the Buddha are believed to have the power to bring rain. A symbol of the Buddha's renunciation of the world, the monk's yellow robe, is regarded as a sacred object with the power to protect the wearer from attacks by spirits or witches. The bo, or bodhi, tree (pipal tree) is particularly venerated and is ritually watered on the day commemorating the Buddha's enlightenment.

HOLIDAYS AND FESTIVALS The day of the Buddha's enlightenment is celebrated in Myanmar by such meritorious activities as catching fish in drying ponds in order to release them in fresh water. The onset of Buddhist Lent unites Myanmar villagers in collective efforts to honor monks about to enter retreat for three months. A lottery determines which layman shall have the privilege to present the collective offering to the monks in the communally owned gilded begging bowl. Another lottery decides how the collective offerings will be distributed among the monks. The First Festival of Lights, held at the end of Buddhist Lent, honors one's elder relatives with gifts of food or clothes. During the following month lay people accrue special merit by making collective public offerings of yellow robes to monks. This month also provides an occasion for the public offering of other items needed by monks. These items are conspicuously displayed with their donor's names on or under a wooden structure known as a wishing tree and taken in procession to the monastery. The Second Festival of Lights marks the end of the robe-offering season by commemorating the robe given to the Buddha by his mother. Villagers earn particular merit by collectively sewing a robe within one night to present to a monk or to cover a Buddha image.

MODE OF DRESS Six different types of robes are offered to monks or to the Buddha. The robe worn by a monk during his initiation, consisting of stitched-together patches of yellow cloth, is known as the great robe. Other robes include the two types that monks might receive during the Festivals of Lights, a robe adorned with a water-lily pattern that is offered to the Buddha, a "golden robe" made from white cloth covered by painted gilded flowers, and the "ownerless robe," which is left on the path frequented by a monk who vows not to accept a robe offering. Nuns wear pink robes, orange skirts, and brown stoles.

DIETARY PRACTICES Although Buddhism does not proscribe the eating of meat, some monks and renowned teachers in Myanmar have advocated vegetarianism.

RITUALS In Myanmar the daily practice of merit-making involves taking refuge in the Triple Gem (through which one relies on the Buddha, the dharma, and the sangha for help and guidance), reciting mantras, observing the *pancha sila* (Buddhist precepts), and offering cooked food to monks. Often it is not the monks themselves who beg from households but young novices who do so on their monastery's behalf. The food so collected is usually eaten by the novices and monastic visitors, not by the monks, who instead dine in the monasteries on ordered meals prepared by devout villagers. The daily food offering is an important expression of the relationship between the sangha and the laity. In village chapels, which are typically simple structures, laypeople may attend services led by a lay elder every evening.

Funerals offer the laity an opportunity to make merit and monks the opportunity to guide the soul to its future rebirth. In the event of an accidental death, the body is buried as quickly as possible and without ceremony, to discourage the dead person's ghost from returning to the former community of the deceased. When a nonaccidental death occurs in villages, people believe that the entire community is contaminated by the death and must work together to restore purity. Vigils following nonaccidental deaths provide community members with the opportunity to earn merit, because their presence reassures the departed spirit and drives off opportunistic ghosts. Just before the body is taken from a village house, laypeople place a mirror before its mouth to determine whether the soul has left the body, and they rock the body in a final obeisance to the Buddha. Relatives of the deceased usually do a meritorious act and then sponsor a ritual to transfer the merit to the deceased.

Although laypeople may be either buried or cremated, monastic funerals entail cremation and often separate final rites. During the latter, hired mourners weep and chant over the deceased monk's bones, which are laid in a kind of flower cradle. As the cradle is rocked, attending monks pray that the deceased will reach an auspicious destiny. The bones are then either interred or ground into a powder that is molded into a Buddha image to be placed in the monastery.

RITES OF PASSAGE Males who do not devote their lives to the sangha nonetheless typically participate in two monastic initiations. The first occurs around the age of eight or nine, when a boy undergoes the *shinbyu* ritual inducting him as a novice in the monastery. The initiate's parents might hire a band, offer guests a rich feast, and invoke the theme of Prince Siddhartha's departure from his secular, courtly life by dressing their son in the costume of a royal prince and building an imitation palace of cardboard and wood to house the festivities. Although a novice probably will not remain long in the monastery, his initiation is viewed as an essential basis for his ordination into monkhood when he is at least 20 years old. An ordination ceremony takes place in a temple chamber forbidden to laypersons. The candidate kneels before an assembly of at least four monks while one monk recites the ordination ritual. Following this recitation the presiding monk questions the candidate, the candidate formally requests admission to the sangha, and, barring objections from the assembly, the presiding monk then admits the candidate to the sangha, bestowing on him a new name.

MEMBERSHIP Burma began to attract Western converts to Theravada Buddhism around the beginning of the twentieth century. In 1908 Allan Bennet, the second Englishman to be ordained in Burma as a Theravada monk (Gordon Douglas was the first, in 1899), left Burma for England, where he founded a mission. Because members of the military government had been influenced by *vipassana* meditation, *vipassana* masters were permitted to leave Burma as missionaries from 1962 to 1988, when the country was closed (when foreigners were generally barred from entering the country and few citizens were permitted to leave). Since 1988 the Maha Bodhi meditation center and other traditions have attracted foreign disciples.

The Myanmar government has actively promoted missionary projects of its own. The most substantial of these is the International Theravada Buddhist Missionary University, which opened in 1998. Burmese monks living outside of the country convened in Malaysia in 1985 to establish the International Burmese Buddhist Sangha as a missionary organization. The Internet is an important tool for these various centers and organizations.

SOCIAL JUSTICE The country's military regime has generally tried to eliminate monks who might be active in the field of social justice. Under UNICEF auspices, however, monks and nuns have been training at Thailand's Sangha Metta Project (formed in 1998) to become educators in the prevention and social management of AIDS.

SOCIAL ASPECTS Myanmar Buddhists believe in a type of religious essence known as *pon*, which constitutes the power and glory of an individual and is mainly an attribute of men. Because men possess *pon* and women generally do not, women are expected to treat men with respect and defer to them in public. It is the wife's responsibility to guard and enhance her husband's *pon*. Although women enjoy parity with men in terms of inheritance rights, many choices of occupation, the ability to initiate divorce, and voicing their opinions, the view that *pon* is a male principle and associated with the capacity to attain *nibbana* (nirvana) influences relations between men and women.

POLITICAL IMPACT Buddhist monks periodically protested against British colonial rulers and the military regime that has controlled Myanmar since 1962. In 1990 monasteries organized an unprecedented boycott against the government. In response the government chose to avoid its earlier mistake of opposing Buddhism by declaring its program to support Buddhism by such actions as removing "vice" (meaning subversive monks) from the monasteries. Moreover, the government publicly associated the protests waged by monks in 1988 with the defilement of revered Buddhist shrines and argued that party politics should never be combined with religion.

Contemporary Myanmar politics reveals opposing interpretations of what constitutes meritorious activity. The military government, which has been censured internationally for its persecution of ethnic minorities and suppression of democracy, describes the forced labor it exacts from ethnic minorities to build temples and other state projects as voluntary labor given to gain Buddhist merit. The military government's chief opponent, Aung San Suu Kyi, has asserted that the struggle for democracy aids the Buddhist realm and, therefore, constitutes merit-making.

CONTROVERSIAL ISSUES Abortion, which is illegal in Myanmar, is considered to violate Buddhist ethics, but Buddhism does not oppose contraception. Buddhist nuns do not enjoy a high position in Myanmar society. They do not have the opportunity to pursue Buddhist studies, nor are they requested to perform religious functions.

CULTURAL IMPACT Buddhist literary genres in fifteenth-century Burma included verses based on stories of the Buddha's life but placed in a Burmese context, devotional poetry, and advisory epistles written by monks to kings. During the first millennium the Pyu devised a distinctive style of stupa known as a *cetiya,* which was continued in succeeding periods. In the eleventh century Buddhist architects began to build *cetiyas* with open bases and with domes that arose from the floor rather than the roof of these bases. This style transformed the base of the *cetiya* into a temple with internal halls that were decorated with Buddha images and paintings. These internal halls encompassed the lower part of the dome of the *cetiya,* which featured Buddha icons facing the four directions. The Ananda temple of Pagan is a noted example of this style. The Mandalay style of Buddha image depicts a standing Buddha with arms slightly spread at the base.

Other Religions

The propitiation of *nats* (designated as 37 anthropomorphic spirits associated with territories, villages, families, and activities) addresses worldly concerns, such as illness, bad luck, and prosperity. The Buddhist householder's worship of *nats* is oriented toward maximizing the potential of the present life, but maximizing the potential of one's present life ideally enables one to generate the merit that secures a better rebirth. Because the Buddhist householder in practice pursues the goal of a good rebirth rather than spiritual salvation, Buddhism and *nat* cults can be understood as reflecting complementary ethical notions and approaches to the supernatural. In Myanmar a *nat* shrine adorns each Buddhist village and many Christian villages. *Nat* cult leaders are mostly women, who serve as oracles, mediums, or diviners and consider themselves to be either married to or the lovers of *nats.* Several pagodas are dedicated exclusively to *nat* worship. Buddhists propitiate *nats* during the observance of rites of passage. The house *nat* must be honored when a child is born, and village *nats* receive offerings prior to a boy's initiation as a Buddhist novice, at weddings, and at funerals. *Nats* also receive offerings during the phases of the agricultural cycle and to prevent and cure illness. Significant parallels can be drawn between the hierarchy of *nats* and the political structure of historic Burmese kingdoms.

Hindu practitioners may participate in common Buddhist rituals in Myanmar. Brahman priests are occasionally hired to offer auspicious chants during *shinbyu* rituals, because the Buddhist sponsors believe that the Brahman priests are particularly adept at praising the ritual participants and guests and appeasing envious *nats.*

Because the ancestors of the majority of Myanmar's Muslim population arrived from India during the British rule, Myanmar Muslims cannot prove that their ancestors were residents of Burma before 1823 and thus meet the requirement for Myanmar citizenship and a national identity card. This, in turn, denies Muslims access to travel, education, and jobs. The construction of new mosques is prohibited, and, where anti-Muslim riots have occurred, Muslims are forbidden to assemble in groups of more than five. During 1991–92 about 250,000 Muslims fled to Bangladesh.

Like Muslims, Christians in Myanmar are prohibited from constructing or repairing churches; they are also prohibited from publishing or distributing religious literature. Bibles translated into local languages are forbidden. Many Christian churches have been closed or destroyed. Christian worship is only permitted in buildings more than 100 years old that display no external symbols of the cross. Christian ethnic minorities are being forced to convert to Buddhism. One group of Christian Karen tribal guerrilla fighters viewed the twin boys (born in 1988) leading them in their struggle (against the Myanmar army and the Myanmar regime's persecution of Christian tribal people) as messiahs.

Marcia Calkowski

See Also Vol. I: *Buddhism, Theravada Buddhism*

Bibliography

Houtman, Gustaaf. *Mental Culture in Burmese Crisis Politics: Aung San Suu Kyi and the National League for Democracy.* Study of Languages and Cultures of Asia and Africa Monograph Series, no. 33. Tokyo: Tokyo University of Foreign Studies, Institute of the Study of Languages and Cultures of Asia and Africa, 1999.

Nash, Manning. *The Golden Road to Modernity.* New York: John Wiley and Sons, 1965.

Sarkisyanz, E. *Buddhist Backgrounds of the Burmese Revolution.* The Hague: Martinus Nijhoff, 1965.

Smith, Donald Eugene. *Religion and Politics in Burma.* Princeton, N.J.: Princeton University Press, 1965.

Spiro, Melford E. *Buddhism and Society: A Great Tradition and Its Burmese Vicissitudes.* 2nd ed. Berkeley and Los Angeles: University of California Press, 1982.

———. *Burmese Supernaturalism.* Englewood Cliffs, N.J.: Prentice-Hall, 1967.

Namibia

POPULATION 1,820,916

LUTHERAN 44 percent

AFRICAN INDIGENOUS BELIEFS 20 percent

ROMAN CATHOLIC 18 percent

DUTCH REFORMED 4 percent

ANGLICAN 4 percent

MUSLIM 3 percent

OTHER (AFRICAN METHODIST EPISCOPAL, METHODIST, PRESBYTERIAN, BAPTIST, MORMON, JEWISH, HINDU, BAHAI) 7 percent

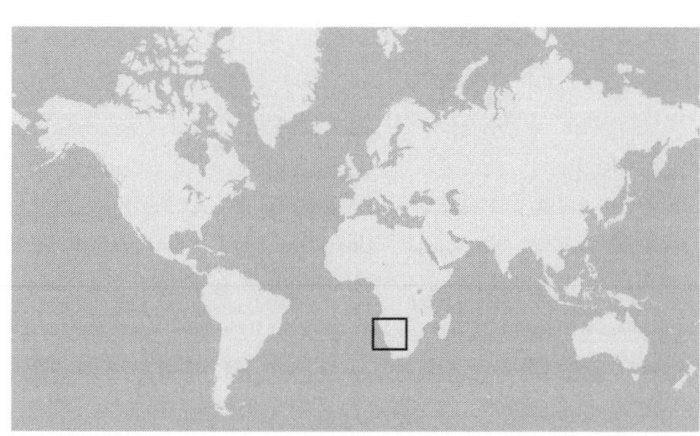

Country Overview

INTRODUCTION Namibia is a large, sparsely populated country on the Atlantic Ocean in southwestern Africa. It is surrounded by Angola, Botswana, and South Africa. The Damara-Nama word "Namib" (enclosure) describes the country's encompassment by deserts, the Namib in the west and the Kalahari in the east. Namibian ethnic groups include the Nama, Damara, Oshivambo, Kavango, Caprivian, Otjiherero, Tswana, San, Afrikaner, British, German, and Coloured (mixed-race).

With one of the world's biggest gemstone diamond deposits, large quantities of copper, zinc, uranium, and salt, vast tracts of land ideal for cattle farming, and fish-laden coastal waters, Namibia attracted European settlers from the 1840s onward. In 1884 the Germans made it a colony known as South West Africa and began a sustained drive to subdue the indigenous communities through "protection treaties." The settlers grew rich, but the indigenous people became impoverished. In 1920, after Germany's defeat in World War I, the country was given to the South African National Party to administer. When the minority white government's attempt to resettle black Namibians farther from white neighborhoods led to a massacre in Windhoek in 1959, Namibians formed the South West African Peoples Organization (SWAPO, a political party) and launched an armed struggle to force South Africa out of Namibia. In 1978 South Africa attacked a Namibian refugee camp in Angola, killing more than 1,000 people, mostly women and children. Namibia achieved independence in 1990, and a democratic government led by SWAPO began ruling Namibia. A white and emerging post-independence black elite lives mostly in urban areas and enjoys the income and amenities of a modern western European country. Namibia, however, has the most unequal distribution of wealth in the world, outdoing both Brazil and South Africa.

Students line up at a Lutheran mission school in Namibia. The adaptation of Christian rituals and icons to include indigenous music, songs, artwork, and forms of worship has particularly motivated Christian youth. © PETER JOHNSON/CORBIS.

Lutheran missionaries who arrived with the Germans made vigorous attempts on behalf of the colonial government to Christianize Namibia. Instead of rejecting Christianity on this basis, however, the Namibians Africanized Christianity. The process of indigenization was so successful that today Christianity is the dominant religion in Namibia. Most adherents of traditional African religion live in remote desert areas, though many indigenous Christians retain some traditional practices. Namibia has small communities of Muslims, Hindus, Jews, Mormons, and Bahais.

RELIGIOUS TOLERANCE The Namibian constitution of 1990 guarantees freedom of religious practice and expression. Any religion may conduct any type of religious activity, propagate its beliefs, gain converts, and express support for or criticism of the state. Christianity is the dominant religion, but Christians commonly have Muslims, Jews, Hindus, or adherents of traditional African religion as neighbors, friends, religious leaders, or healers. Religious communities seek interreligious dialogue, acknowledge differences, and abstain from passing judgment on people from other faith traditions. The Council of Churches in Namibia (CCN) was founded in 1978 by the Methodist, Anglican, Congregational, and Evangelical Lutheran Churches. The Roman Catholic Church joined the CCN in 1986, and the Dutch Reformed, Rhenish, and United Reformed Churches joined in 2000.

Major Religion

CHRISTIANITY

DATE OF ORIGIN After 1652 C.E.
NUMBER OF FOLLOWERS 1.4 million

HISTORY The Nama-speaking people from the Cape Area in present-day South Africa brought Christianity to Namibia, having learned it from the Dutch. They crossed the Orange River after 1652, settling in southern and central Namibia. The London Missionary Society (LMS) arrived in Namibia in 1812 and formed an interdenominational organization that included Anglicans, Methodists, Presbyterians, and Congregationalists. Their biggest achievement was the translation of the Bible into one of the Namibian languages, Khoekhoengowab (Damara-Nama). Lack of supplies and trouble with Namibians over grazing land led the LMS to request the Rhenish Mission (which consisted of various Lutheran and other Protestant churches in Germany) to take over their work in 1867. The Rhenish had arrived in 1842 with the first German colonists and were carrying out an aggressive campaign to convert Namibians, dismissing African religion and culture as inferior to Christianity and Western culture.

In the 1920s Namibian Christians began separating themselves from their German leaders, desiring to create a self-governing, self-supporting, and self-propagating body. In 1922 the first indigenous Lutheran pastors were ordained, and in 1954 the Lutheran Church was constituted as independent from the Rhenish Mission.

Anglican Church mission work in Namibia can be traced back to 1860, and the Roman Catholic Church arrived in 1882. Both these churches encountered many early difficulties, including German government prohibitions against working in the existing Lutheran mission fields. The first congregation of the Dutch Reformed Church was established in 1898 at Warmbad in southern Namibia.

In 1971, during the struggle for liberation from South African administration, the Lutheran Churches published their famous Open Letter. Addressed to the South African prime minister, John Vorster, the letter demanded that South Africa cooperate with the United Nations to make Namibia an independent state. The letter had strong support from several political parties (including SWAPO) and all other Christian denominations in Namibia except the Dutch Reformed and the German Evangelical Lutheran Churches, both with an exclusively white membership. The publication of the letter broke the silence of the church on social and political issues and sparked a wave of protests throughout the country (including strikes by workers in Walvis Bay, Windhoek, and Tsumeb), bringing Namibia international attention. Thereafter the churches provided institutionalized resistance to the South African regime: church buildings offered sanctuary, and pastors and laity formulated an ideology and action plan for liberation. Church newsletters spread the message to the country and beyond. Independence was achieved in 1990. The churches have continued to work openly for social and political change, taking stands against poverty and human rights abuses.

EARLY AND MODERN LEADERS Hendrik Witbooi (born in 1834 and killed by German troops in 1905), an elder and lay deacon in the Rhenish Mission Church, claimed that God appeared to him in a vision, exhorting him lead his people to power and glory. He believed in the Christian promise of salvation and liberation and saw Namibians as God's people to be led out of "Pharaoh's Egypt"—the German colonial government, against which he fought actively.

Contemporary Christian church leaders include Leonard Auala, ordained as the first indigenous Lutheran bishop in 1963, and Paulus Gowaseb, a Lutheran leader from 1967 to 1972. The two wrote the Open Letter of 1971 to the South African prime minister, demanding Namibian independence. Gerard Molelekwa became the first Namibian Roman Catholic priest in 1942, and Bonifatius Haushiku, the first Namibian bishop, was consecrated in 1979. The first leaders to challenge black oppression were the Anglican reverends Michael Scott and Theophilus Hamutumbangela, who lobbied at the United Nations for Namibian independence in the mid-1940s. The first indigenous Anglican bishop, James Kauluma, was consecrated in 1981.

MAJOR THEOLOGIANS AND AUTHORS Lukas de Vries (born in 1938), a Lutheran, wrote historical theology. He believed that Rhenish missionaries, loyal to the German administration and military, had spread colonialism rather than the liberating word of God and that the white German Lutheran Church of his time tacitly accepted South African apartheid policies.

The Lutheran Zephania Kameeta (born in 1945) was heavily involved in Namibia's liberation struggle. Through recreations of psalms and biblical texts, he called for direct engagement against the violations of human dignity in apartheid society.

Lutheran Paul John Isaak (born in 1947) has written on theoethics, stressing a humane God who sees sinners justified by faith. He has called on believers to alter their social relationships and become free men and women.

HOUSES OF WORSHIP AND HOLY PLACES Namibian Protestant churches, such as the African Methodist Episcopal, Dutch Reformed, and Lutheran Churches, keep decoration and trimmings to a minimum, believing that people come to church to hear the word of God. Roman Catholic and Anglican Churches in Namibia have stained-glass windows, statues, and candles to inspire worshipers in their liturgy, prayer, and meditation.

Namibian Christians regard cemeteries as holy places and often visit grave sites of family members. Many black Namibian Christians leave a bottle of water on the grave, believing the dead person is going on a long safari (trip). White Christians leave flowers, a European symbol of love.

WHAT IS SACRED? Namibian Christians regard the cross of Jesus Christ and the Bible as the most sacred symbols of their religion. Almost every Christian household has a sign of the cross, a Bible, and a hymnbook.

HOLIDAYS AND FESTIVALS All Christians in Namibia celebrate Good Friday, Easter, Ascension, and Christmas. Other national holidays that Christians celebrate include Independence Day (21 March); Cassinga Day, honoring the thousand-plus Namibians in refugee camps in Angola massacred by the South African army on 4 May 1978; Heroe's Day (26 August), honoring all Namibian heroes and heroines; and Human Rights Day, honoring the many Namibian Christians killed by the South African regime on 10 December 1959 because they refused to be resettled. These holidays provide occasions for family reunions; drama, music, and dance performances; the healing of strained relationships; and the transmission of knowledge.

MODE OF DRESS Christian men wear Western clothes. Christian women wear colorful dresses, the style based on the culture of their ethnic group. Otjiherero women in central and eastern Namibia wear Victorian-style dresses and head scarves shaped to resemble bull horns. Damara, Nama, and Coloured women in southern and western Namibia wear midlength dresses with matching head scarves or bonnets and aprons. Oshivambo women in northern Namibia wear voluminous dresses with or without sleeves. A range of colorful beads complement the dresses. Women wear Western-style dresses to work, and all Christians wear formal clothes to church services.

DIETARY PRACTICES The diet of most Namibian Christians is based on availability, not religious prescription.

RITUALS Namibian Christians consider baptism, confirmation, and marriage basic life requirements, and families gather to celebrate the associated rituals. Marriages are no longer arranged by parents or relatives; since Namibian independence people have tended to avoid traditional practices that might infringe on their freedom. After Christian funerals mourners are expected to return to the house of the deceased to wash their hands, symbolically washing off the death so it will not follow them to their own houses. The bereaved family then serves everyone food and drinks.

RITES OF PASSAGE The central Christian rites of passage in Namibia occur at birth, adulthood, marriage, and death. Celebrating these rites, however, involves social expectations (that everyone should be invited and provided with an abundance of food and drink) that cause financial burden to Christian families. Meeting the expectations is a question of honor, and families do everything possible, even taking out loans, to celebrate these occasions.

Most mainline churches practice infant baptism; Pentecostal and Charismatic churches only recognize adult baptism. Funerals are treated as major community events: everyone is expected to participate in the final ritual of the life of any other member of the community.

MEMBERSHIP Baptism is the means of attaining membership in a Christian church in Namibia. Church members are expected to lead a Christian life, observe church regulations and counsel others to do the same, make regular financial contributions and offerings, and propagate the teachings of the church in order to gain more members. Church membership has grown remarkably since independence as Namibian Christians take ownership of a religion received in difficult circumstances. The churches have challenged Namibian missionaries to carry Christianity from the African point of view into the world, particularly to Europe.

SOCIAL JUSTICE Denied formal education, health care, decent housing and jobs, pensions, social security, and social respect under colonialism and apartheid, indigenous Christians developed a strong resentment against oppression. Christian churches in Namibia, especially under the ecumenical leadership of the Council of Churches in Namibia (CCN), take stands on issues of land, the distribution of wealth, and the promotion and implementation of human rights. The CCN's goals are to foster the unity of the churches; to assist people in need; to coordinate the development of a culture of peace; and to promote self-help projects, the welfare of uprooted people in Namibia, and the role of women, children, and youth as full participants in church and society. Namibian churches have attempted to address the ever-growing gap between the whites and new elite (blacks in leadership positions in government and the private sector) and the majority of the black population, mostly rural, who live in abject poverty.

SOCIAL ASPECTS Namibian Christian churches have done little to address or challenge the growing financial costs of baptisms, marriages, and funerals. The majority of Namibian Christian couples (including those who still adhere to African traditional religion, with its emphasis on legitimacy and earning community approval) live together and have children without getting married. Weddings—those conducted according to traditional marriage customs as well as Christian church weddings—are expensive. The churches do not approve but have found no solutions.

POLITICAL IMPACT The political relationship between the Christian churches and the state in Namibia is one of institutional separation and functional interaction, a relationship that began with cooperation during the struggle for independence. Christian churches have had tremendous political impact by participating in nation building, promoting democratic principles and values, and speaking for the people. During apartheid the churches provided funds to Namibians who wanted to find better education abroad and to political prisoners who needed lawyers. The Lutheran Church newsletters *Immanuel* and *Omukewtu* and the Roman Catholic Church newsletters *Angelus* and *Omukuni* spread the message of liberation during the struggle for independence. In the contemporary period the churches have promoted programs dealing with HIV and AIDS, violence against women and children, democratic and human rights, and rights for disabled people.

CONTROVERSIAL ISSUES In the face of the AIDS epidemic in Namibia, many Christians want the church to recommend the use of condoms. Most churches, however, prefer to focus their campaign on abstinence and monogamy. Catholic Archbishop Bonafatius Haushiku changed the understanding of the pandemic among the religious communities by proclaiming AIDS a disease, not a sin.

Christian churches have also tried to have a voice in national reconciliation. Christians believe their churches have the credibility to negotiate with the government for them; they want churches to advocate for their rights to land, homes, and employment. The churches, while promoting these goals, have called upon all stakeholders to avoid violence and illegal land seizure and to have patience while the goals are pursued.

CULTURAL IMPACT Namibians have adapted Christian rituals and icons to include indigenous music, songs, artwork, and forms of worship. Drumming, singing, and dance have attracted people to Sunday services and church-sponsored youth gatherings. Such integration has particularly motivated Christian youth.

Other Religions

African traditional religion is given equal status in Namibia to other major religions, such as Christianity and Islam. The Himba (less than 1 percent of the population) in the desert northwest and the San (less than 3 percent of the population) near the Kalahari desert fully adhere to traditional beliefs. Indigenous religions are not based on doctrines but are a way of life, integrated into adherent's and the community's daily routines and made manifest in various rituals and rites of passage. Practitioners see the Supreme Being (known in various Namibian languages as Mukuru, Elob, and Kalunga) in all things and do not differentiate between sacred and secular.

Islam and Hinduism arrived after Namibian independence in 1990, and most followers are immigrants or descendants of immigrants, though some Hindus are Namibians who speak Indian languages. Some members of these communities are Namibians who have converted after recent proselytization. Judaism has existed in Namibia since the 1930s. Most Jews are Namibian or South African citizens. Members of all these groups live mainly in cities and towns.

Paul John Isaak

See Also Vol. 1: *African Indigenous Beliefs, Christianity, Lutheranism, Roman Catholicism*

Bibliography

Buys, G., and S. Nambala. *History of the Church in Namibia.* Windhoek: Gamsberg Macmillan, 2003.

De Vries, Lukas. *Mission and Colonialism in Namibia.* Johannesburg: Ravan Press, 1978.

Isaak, Paul John. *Religion and Society: A Namibian Perspective.* Windhoek: Out of Africa Publishers, 1997.

Kameeta, Z. *The Sun is Rising: Meditations and Prayers from Namibia.* Windhoek: Capital Press, 1993.

———. "Worshipping God as Africans." In *Worshipping God as Africans.* Edited by C. Lombard. Windhoek: University of Namibia, 1995.

Mbambo, S. "Religious Change in Namibia." In *Journal of Religion and Theology in Namibia.* Edited by J. Hunter. Windhoek: University of Namibia, 2000.

Nauru

POPULATION 12,329

CHRISTIAN 84 percent

BUDDHIST 15 percent

OTHER 1 percent

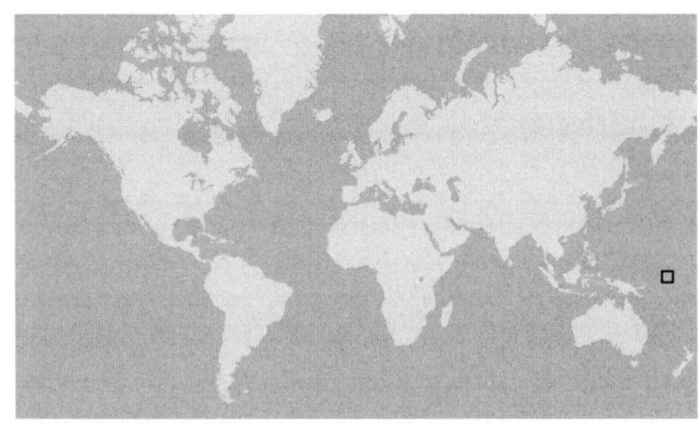

Country Overview

INTRODUCTION The Republic of Nauru, a single, raised coral island located in the Pacific Ocean, is 26 miles south of the equator and 165 miles east of its nearest neighbor, Ocean Island. With an area of just over 8 square miles, it is roughly circular and has a 22-mile-long coastline and narrow shore. Because of phosphate mining, which began in 1906, the interior four-fifths of the island now consists primarily of coral pinnacles and is unusable and cannot be traversed.

The people of Nauru are usually considered Micronesian, though their language differs markedly from all others in Oceania. The British explored the island in 1798, and it was annexed by Germany in 1888. At about the same time, Christian missionaries were sent to introduce Christianity. In 1906 phosphate mining commenced to supply the agricultural interests of Australia and New Zealand. The island was taken over by the British Phosphate Commissioners as a League of Nations Mandate in 1919, with administration in the hands of the Australians. Nauruans had no say in this political move for outsider's economic gains. Japan occupied the island during World War II, after which Nauru became a United Nations trust territory. It became independent in 1968. The phosphate was expected to run out in 1996, but a small amount is still being mined.

Although the island is predominantly Christian, there are small numbers of Buddhists and members of other faiths. Nauruans comprise two-thirds of the total population, with Chinese, Filipinos, Indians, Australians, and New Zealanders making up the rest.

RELIGIOUS TOLERANCE Although firmly Christian, Nauruans are tolerant of other religions, such as the Hindu practices of the small number of Indians working in government administrative positions. Nauruan government policy, however, has restricted access to most other religions, so the proliferation of non-conformist Christian churches, such as Seventh-day Adventists, which is found in many other Pacific Islands, has not happened on Nauru.

Major Religion

CHRISTIANITY

DATE OF ORIGIN 1887 A.D.

NUMBER OF FOLLOWERS 10,400

HISTORY Congregational Christianity was introduced to Nauru in the 1880s by missionaries from the American Board of Commissioners for Foreign Missions (ABCFM), based in Boston, and was readily received by the Nauruans. Three teachers from Kiribati (Gilber Islands) arrived on Nauru in 1887, and one of these pastors remained in charge of the mission until 1899. The mission schooner, the *Morning Star,* maintained contact with the Marshall Islands and Kosrae for supplies and spiritual support. It thus brought new missionaries from time to time, many of whom were from other islands in the Pacific. Christianity introduced the Nauruans to new ideologies and tenets, but they were adapted to include elements of traditional beliefs. These included cosmological beliefs in the original settlement of the island from the east and the existence of ancestral spirits in two rocks and caves, now removed by mining. The practice of capturing and nurturing frigate birds by specialist members of each clan as symbols of the beliefs and strength of that clan was the basis of a cult that continues to this day. The spiritual leadership of the chiefly class formed the basis of cooperation between the Nauruans and the missionaries. The Reverend Philip. Delaporte, sent to Nauru in 1899 by the ABCFM, gained the confidence of the Nauruans and successfully established a church and school.

The island's German administration favored the establishment of the Roman Catholic Church and sent Father Felix Grundl and Father P. Alois Kayser of the Order of the Sacred Heart to Nauru in 1903. Strong rivalry developed between the two religions, with each offering education and social services in addition to their pastorates. Father Kayser remained on Nauru, and he worked with other Catholic priests until he was deported by the Japanese in 1943.

The London Missionary Society (LMS) took over from the ABCFM in 1917 and continued to build the Congregational Church under a Nauruan pastor, Jacob Aroi, who was assisted by some of the local chiefs. Thus, the church became a Nauruan institution, even after an LMS pastor, Rev. Hannah, took over the mission. By 1925, of a total population of 1,239 Nauruans, 775 were Protestants, and 365 were Roman Catholics.

Throughout the twentieth century the phosphate mining industry was run on both Nauru and Ocean Island by the British phosphate commissioners (BPC). In 1970 Nauru sought control of the mine along with its political independence. Australia had been the administering nation on behalf of BPC but shared the profits from the sale of Nauruan phosphate with Britain and New Zealand as lesser partners in BPC. The mine attracted workers to Nauru from other Pacific nations, as well as from China, India, and the Philippines, thus bringing in diverse religious practices. People from both Kiribati and Tuvalu have their own Protestant churches, and those from Kiribati also have their own Catholic church.

EARLY AND MODERN LEADERS Nauru is notable among Pacific Island nations for having produced several strong, well-educated political leaders who were also firm upholders of Christian principles. In the 1920s Rev. Delaporte took Timothy Detudamo to Boston, where Detudamo learned valuable administrative skills. Detudamo was a young Nauruan (not a traditional leader) who had assisted Delaporte in his translations of the Bible into the Nauruan language. After four years in Boston, he returned home to establish a cooperative store in competition with the BPC store run by the Australians. He was jailed for this but gained recognition as a leader of the Nauruan people. As the Nauruan administrator, Detudamo effectively negotiated with the British phosphate commissioners to gain Nauruan rights. He was succeeded by Hammer DeRoburt, who later became the first president of Nauru and who was a strong upholder of the Protestant faith.

MAJOR THEOLOGIANS AND AUTHORS Father P. Alois Kayser is well remembered for the Catholic principles he promoted through Nauru's Sacred Heart Mission. He also wrote extensively on the language, traditions, and culture of the Nauruan people at the beginning of the twentieth century. The Reverend Philip Delaporte was another important figure, producing a short Nauru-German dictionary and translations of the New Testament, a Nauru hymn book, and a German hymn book.

Since the 1980s the Reverend James Angimea has been an outstanding leader of the Congregational Church on Nauru. He is pastor of the main church on the island and is recognized for his commitment to improving the social status of Nauruans.

HOUSES OF WORSHIP AND HOLY PLACES The main Protestant church is located in central Aiwo, the main district of Nauru where business activity and the port are situated. In contrast, the Catholic church complex has developed in the northwest corner of the island. All modern church structures are built of concrete, with cemeteries surrounding them.

WHAT IS SACRED? The foundation of the Protestant faith in Nauru, as elsewhere, is the sacredness of the Bible and its teachings, including the Godhead and all its spiritual aspects. Churches and cemeteries are places of reverence, with the latter being a matter of particular concern, as the small island is running out of space for them.

Christian beliefs dominate on Nauru, but even among Christians, many native beliefs also persist, particularly as spirits associated with the environment. The cultivation of Ibija fish (*Chanos chanos*) also follows ancient ritual and symbolic ideologies; these fish are served by the appropriate clan at festivities. Two sacred rocks, representing the founding ancestors of all Nauruans, were removed by mining, but their memory remains part of Nauruan cultural identity. The Nauruan culture maintains a close identification with birds as representatives of ancestral ties; the frigate bird is the national symbol and appears prominently on Air Nauru planes.

HOLIDAYS AND FESTIVALS As in most Christian cultures, Christmas and Easter are observed on Nauru as the major religious and public holidays. Both celebrations last several days and are marked by attendance at a series of church services, interspersed with much feasting and gift exchanges. Notable is the wearing of white by women and children, with hats specially purchased in Australia for the occasion. Weddings and funerals are islandwide festivals, with most of the population participating.

MODE OF DRESS Modern dress on Nauru is not directly influenced by religion. In the early days, however, missionaries forbade the wearing of the traditional *ridi,* a mat woven of pandanus leaves. They introduced long, white cotton dresses for women and suits for men.

Today women's Sunday attire for church is changing from traditional white dresses and hats to fashionable dresses from Australia. Men, especially church deacons, wear dark suits. Everyday clothing ranges from jeans and T-shirts to suits and fashionable office wear.

DIETARY PRACTICES Religion has little influence on the dietary practices of Christian Nauruans. There are no specific dietary practices observed on Nauru. Food is blessed before a meal, particularly at a civic event.

RITUALS Religious rituals on Nauru are syncretic, combining traditional ceremonies with Christian celebrations, as in weddings and funerals and first Communion for Catholics. Raising *Ibija* fish in the Buada lagoon and the capture and feeding of frigate birds on special platforms are cultural events that have been retained alongside Christianity.

RITES OF PASSAGE In earlier times the birth of a child was less celebrated than the onset of a girl's first menses, an event promising ongoing fertility for the Nauruan people. This occasion was commemorated with a feast. The birth of the 1,500th Nauruan in 1933 is still commemorated as a national holiday, with religious and civil ceremonies; it reminds the Nauruan people of the struggles they had in the past to build their population. Today births rather than first menses are celebrated with both civic and Christian events, including baptism. For Catholics first Communion is an important event for each family member.

The death of a community member is marked by a series of ceremonies conducted over a period of time. After the church service for the dead, several rituals are performed that combine Christian and traditional beliefs. Cemeteries are located near churches, as well as near the residences of the main clan families. The use of scarce land for cemeteries has been a matter of considerable debate involving the future development of the island's resources.

MEMBERSHIP Church membership is less universal than in the past, as today's young people question its value in their lives. Yet both Congregational and Catholic churches are full on Sundays, with members attending two or three other services during the week. In both churches the women's fellowship endeavors to reach young people and organizes social activities.

SOCIAL JUSTICE Each church serves as an advocate for its members. Concerns about land, payments from the Nauru Trust Fund, and the rights of immigrants working for the Nauru Phosphate Company are advocated largely through church supporters. Of the several trust funds established with royalties paid to Nauruan landowners for the phosphate extracted from their lands since the 1920s, the Nauru Trust Fund was expected to provide the families of these landowners with much needed cash. But the liquidity of the Nauru Trust Fund and the other funds is in serious doubt, owing to poor investment advice. The funds were established by the British Phosphate Commission, which set aside a small proportion of earnings from the sale of phosphate. One fund was used by the Australian administration to pay for administrative costs, another was set aside for rehabilitation of the mined areas, and yet another was designated as the Nauruan Community Long-term Investment Fund. The Nauruan government, in conjunction with the Nauru Phosphate Company, has taken control of these funds after independence.

SOCIAL ASPECTS The churches are an integral part of Nauruan community life, and their representatives are prominent at social events, where they offer the blessing for the day and, especially, for the food. Church representatives serve as a channel for developing leadership, as well as for expression of social concerns. The churches were the first to introduce formal Western-style education. For today's older family members church membership is still a central part of their lives. For many young people, however, religion is less important. The Sabbath is a day for relaxing, going to the one small beach, or having picnics in the center of the island; adults will attend church in the morning or evening, taking very young children. The women's groups of both the Protestant and Catholic churches try to encourage the young people to attend Sunday school.

POLITICAL IMPACT Christianity has been a significant influence on the modern state of Nauru. An early visitor in the 1860s referred to the island as the Garden of Eden for its lush vegetation and friendly population. In the 1990s a prominent Nauruan politician picked up this reference in describing how Nauru's environment should be restored after mining is completed on the island.

Strong leaders have been groomed by the church to follow Protestant principles. Each of Nauru's 12 districts has at least one church, though many Nauruans travel to the main Protestant church in Aiwo, where Rev. Aingamea presides. He carries on the tradition instituted by Timothy Detudamo in the 1920s of providing a moral platform for the people.

Many of the leaders of the 1950s and 1960s were educated at church schools in Australia and thus brought back to Nauru strong moral principles. The churches had direct political influence through their connection with the Nauru Local Government Council until that was disestablished in the mid-1990s. Religious ideology has thus been one of the attributes that a budding politician includes in his platform.

CONTROVERSIAL ISSUES Population growth was a major goal for Nauru during the early twentieth century. This policy has continued, despite attempts by outsiders, including missionaries, to reduce the birth rate on many other Pacific Islands. Unlike many Pacific Island nations, Nauru has a very small proportion of its population living overseas.

In contrast to the patriarchal base of Christianity, each child in Nauru becomes a member of its mother's lineage. Those children not born of a Nauruan mother have no direct rights either to land or to the trust funds, which is a matter of particular concern to men who have married non-Nauruan women. The persistence of phosphate mining is also a major and highly contentious issue among religious and political leaders as well as the Nauruan people, as the Nauruan economy is almost solely dependent on this nearly depleted resource.

CULTURAL IMPACT Protestant churches are a central feature in each of the 12 districts around the island. They offer a meeting place for both secular and religious events and are used for youth group activities, women's group meetings, and public discussions. Women's church committees have been active in hosting foreign visitors, in maintaining connections with churches in Australia (mainly in the Melbourne area), and in providing forums for political discussions. They are the pivotal group for organizing the annual meeting of all the Protestant churches on the island and for sending delegates to Kiribati and Fiji for meetings of the Council of Churches. Church music has been adopted from Australian sources, and the influence of Australia can also be seen in other aspects of Nauruan life, including church architecture.

Other Religions

Chinese brought in to work in the phosphate mines in 1906 still retain their Buddhist practices within the confines of their own community. Until the 1950s Chinese workers on Nauru were not allowed to bring their families to the island, as Nauruans did not want them to establish a permanent Chinese community. After a United Nations Trusteeship Council debate in 1947, Australia continued the policy of restricting the Chinese population; this policy was lifted only when Nauru won independence in 1968. Since 1970 the Chinese population on Nauru has increased.

There are a small number of Bahai on Nauru, as well as members of the Church of Jesus Christ of Latter-day Saints (Mormon). The latter has a smaller presence on Nauru than elsewhere in the Pacific. Indian and Southeast Asian workers observe their own religious (e.g., Hindu and Muslim) practices from their homes.

Nancy J. Pollock

See Also Vol. 1: *Buddhism, Christianity*

Bibliography

Kayser, Alois P. "Die Eingeborenen von Nauru (Sudsee)." *Anthropos* 12–13 (1917–18).

Kretzschmar, K.E. *Nauru.* Cyclostyled, 1913.

Viviani, Nancy. *Nauru, Phosphate and Political Progress.* Honolulu: University of Hawai'i Press, 1970.

Wedgwood, Camilla. "Report on Research Work in Nauru Island." Parts 1 and 2. *Oceania*6 (June 1936); 7 (September 1936).

Nepal

POPULATION 25,873,917

HINDU 81 percent

BUDDHIST 11 percent

OTHER (BAHÁ'Í, CHRISTIAN, MUSLIM, JAIN, SIKH) 8 percent

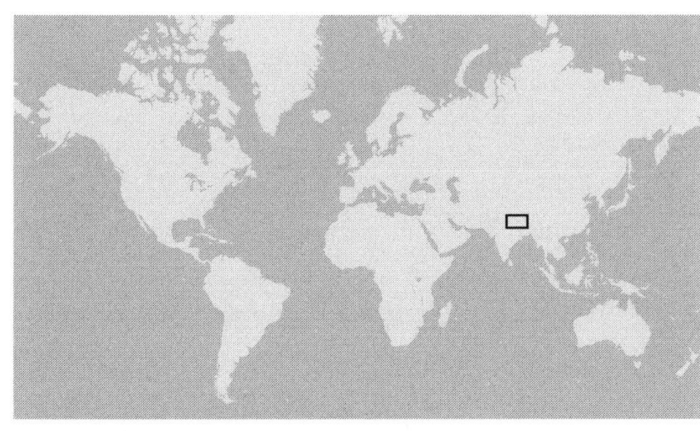

Country Overview

INTRODUCTION The Kingdom of Nepal lies on the southern slopes of the Himalayas in Asia. It is bordered by the Tibet Autonomous Region of China to the north and by India to the east, south, and west. Mountains cover about three-fourths of the country, and many of the world's highest peaks are found there.

Sixty-two ethnic groups are legally recognized in Nepal and are distinct from the country's dominant Hindu caste communities. These ethnic groups have their own religions, which synthesize practices of indigenous, Hindu, and Buddhist origin. The population remains largely rural, and most people do not identify their religious practices doctrinally. Figures from the 2001 census describing Nepal's religious groups are generally believed to be inaccurate. Other estimates indicate that as many as 20 to 25 percent of the people practice Buddhism in some form. Generally, most of the population is divided into three groupings: Indo-Nepali (Parbatiya), whose cultural and historical affinities are with greater Hindu South Asia; peoples living along the border with Tibet, whose cultural and religious practices are continuous with those of Tibet; and Tibeto-Burman-speaking ethnic populations with independent religious traditions influenced to various degrees by Indic and Tibetan practices.

In the second half of the eighteenth century, Indo-Nepali under the leadership of Prithvi Narayan Shah consolidated Nepal, conquering the Kathmandu Valley in 1769. The consolidation required an ideology that organized ethnic diversity, and those in power drew largely on Hindu caste ideology in formulating an integrative legal and administrative culture. Initially Nepal was ruled as a divine-right Hindu monarchy by the Shah royalty, whose power was usurped by Rana royalty in the mid-nineteenth century. The Ranas effectively ruled Nepal as hereditary prime ministers until 1950, when they were ousted and the Shah monarchy reestablished. In 1990 a "people's movement" led to the establishment of a constitutional Hindu monarchy. Political order, however, was undermined by a Maoist insurgency that began in 1996 and by the massacre of most of the royal family in 2001. In late 2002 the new king, Gyanendra, dissolved the elected parliament and appointed an interim prime minister, heightening the instability of the political situation and precipitating a power struggle between the king, the Maoists, and a coalition of political parties.

A Nepalese boy wears the traditional costume and makeup while participating in the Gaijatra *ritual.* AP/WIDE WORLD PHOTOS.

RELIGIOUS TOLERANCE The 1992 constitution granted freedom of worship to all Nepali citizens but also established Nepal as a Hindu monarchy. The constitution bans proselytization. Although discrimination against low castes and non-Hindus continues, Nepali of all religious persuasions have historically been comparatively tolerant, and syncretic practices reflecting the amalgamation of Hindu, Buddhist, and indigenous forms are evidence of a relatively open and tolerant religious scene. Hindu nationalism and intolerance, which has been on the rise in neighboring India, has yet to have a major impact in Nepal.

Major Religions

HINDUISM

BUDDHISM

HINDUISM

DATE OF ORIGIN before fifth century C.E.

NUMBER OF FOLLOWERS 21 million

HISTORY Inscriptions from as early as the fifth century C.E. indicate that the most important ruling dynasties in what is now Nepal were ecumenical and nonsectarian in their support of both Hindu and Buddhist practice. Following Muslim incursions into North India in the thirteenth century C.E., a significant number of Indian Hindus migrated into what is now Nepal. Sectors of this population came to dominate the then largely non-Hindu population of the central Himalayas in the late eighteenth century, declaring the newly consolidated Nepal "a pure Hindu country." The politically dominant groups actively encouraged Hindu practice and institutions throughout the nineteenth and twentieth centuries. Early on, the Hindu rulers banned the killing of cows and enforced respect for Brahman priests among the indigenous Tibeto-Burman-speaking groups. During the nineteenth century the high-caste rulers made the Hindu rituals of Dasain the national rites of Nepal, and most sectors of the population, except those closest to Tibet, adapted these sacrificial rituals for local practice.

Hinduism also gained substantial support early on from the rulers of the Newar, the ethnic group that formed the majority population of the city-states of the Kathmandu Valley. The Malla rulers (fourteenth through eighteenth century C.E.) enforced caste rules, built grand Hindu temples, instituted Hindu rituals of state, and patronized Brahman priests, even though at the time many of the Newar were Buddhist. Contemporary developments in Nepali Hinduism reflect the changing religious aspirations of a burgeoning middle class, coupled with a greater cultural identification with India that has been facilitated by media and travel. As Hinduism in Nepal has become increasingly allied with the wider politics of the subcontinent, non-Hindu ethnic organizations in the country have exhorted their members to stop observing Hindu rituals.

EARLY AND MODERN LEADERS Hindu practice in Nepal is not centrally organized, and identifying leaders recognized by broad sectors of the population would be impossible. The king and the royal guru, or spiritual adviser, are important, as are the chief Brahman priests at principal temples and pilgrimage sites.

MAJOR THEOLOGIANS AND AUTHORS The two most significant Nepali Hindu scholars are Bhanu Bhakta Acharya (1872–1936), best known for translating the Hindu epic *Ramayana* into colloquial Nepali, and Yogi Naraharinath (1911–2003), a saint and scholar who was the most important Hindu leader in Nepal during the twentieth century.

HOUSES OF WORSHIP AND HOLY PLACES The most important sacred place in Nepal is the Pashupatinath temple in Kathmandu, which houses an image of Shiva. Closely associated with Pashupatinath is a temple to Guhyesvari, a form of the goddess Durga and the consort of Shiva. Although Shiva is the most important Hindu divinity in Nepal, there are also sites sacred to Vishnu, especially at Changu Narayan and Buddhanilkantha (Jalasyana Narayan). Manifestations of Durga are also focal points for worship, including the temple of Taleju in Kathmandu, where annual royal sacrifices occur during Dasain, the national festival. Outside the Kathmandu Valley, the most important pilgrimage site is Gosainkund. Among a host of other divinities, Nepali give special attention to Ganesh, whose image can be found everywhere, both in independent shrines in homes and neighborhoods and in the temples of other divinities. Shrines or sacred sites of one form or another are found almost everywhere in both rural and urban Nepal, and much of daily worship focuses on these local sites.

WHAT IS SACRED? Nepali imbue all unusual features of their mountainous landscape with sacred significance. Rivers—especially the confluences of rivers—are thought to be particularly sacred and, by definition, purifying. Salagrams, fossils of ammonoids (an extinct group of mollusks) found in the upper reaches of the Kali Gandaki River, are worshiped as iconic manifestations of Vishnu. Cows are sacred in Nepal because they are associated with Brahmans and symbolize the Hindu state and the historical ascendancy of high-caste Hindus. Sacred rhesus monkeys are found in huge numbers at temple complexes like Pashupatinath and Swayambhunath. Hindus link *tulsi,* an herb similar to basil, to Vishnu, and it is not uncommon to find *tulsi* plants growing in special shrines outside Hindu homes. The most sacred part of a house is the hearth room, which is kept especially pure and which only immediate family members are usually allowed to enter.

HOLIDAYS AND FESTIVALS Dates of all holidays and festivals are calculated according to the Vikram Sambat, the Hindu calendar and official calendar of Nepal. Dasain, the most important festival, falls in the Nepali month of September-October. The 10-day festival focuses on the goddess Durga. Dasain is followed in Kartick (October-November) by Tihar, which includes worship of Lakshmi, the goddess of wealth, as well as the recognition of cows, bullocks, and dogs. Of particular social significance is the blessing of brothers (*bhai tika*) during a ritual exchange in which sisters provide blessings and brothers offer gifts in return. Shiva Ratri, or the night of Shiva, occurs in February-March at Pashupatinath temple. In July-August Hindus celebrate Janai Purne, during which all high-caste men replace their sacred threads. Other festivals in the Kathmandu Valley of special significance to urban Newar, both Hindu and Buddhist, include the processions of chariots with images of red Matsyendranath and white Matsyendranath, which occur in the cities of Patan (April-May) and Kathmandu (December-January), respectively. Gai Jatra (Cow Festival), another distinctively Newar festival, honors the recent dead with processions of cows and dancers in August-September. Also in August-September, the festival of Indra Jatra celebrates, with the divinity Indra, one of the most important living goddesses in the Kathmandu Valley, Kumari, who blesses the king of Nepal during the festival.

MODE OF DRESS Men of the highest Nepali castes wear sacred threads, which are generally covered with other clothing.

DIETARY PRACTICE Although dietary restrictions are easing among cosmopolitan sectors of society, many conservative Hindus in Nepal will take cooked rice only from those of the same, or of a higher, caste. Foods that are parched or cooked in oil or butter are shared more widely and are the foods of festive occasions. High castes will not accept water from untouchables. Many high-caste Brahman families are vegetarian. Hindus cannot eat beef under any circumstances, and high castes will not eat domestic pork, though some will eat wild boar.

RITUALS The elementary ritual act of Hindus in Nepal is the performance of *puja,* or offerings to divinities. *Puja* ranges from simple offerings made to representations of divinities in households to elaborate spectacles in large temples. Some divinities, especially goddesses, require blood sacrifices. In return for offerings, divinities confer blessings or protection (*prasad*), usually in the form of a portion of the offerings. Householders can make offerings on their own, but on important occasions or in major temples, Brahman priests act as intermediaries.

RITES OF PASSAGE The rites of passage for higher-caste Hindus in Nepal begin at birth, when mother and child are purified over an 11-day period. Parents name the child in a ceremony on the 11th day. The next rite occurs at the first rice feeding, at the age of five months for girls and six months for boys. High-caste boys in Nepal go through an initiation known as *bartaman,* which usually occurs just before marriage but can be performed much earlier. It is during this ritual that they receive the sacred thread. At menarche high-caste girls from traditional families must go into seclusion in a dark room for 12 days, at the end of which time they are purified. The most auspicious and socially extensive rite of passage is marriage, which includes feasting for the friends and family of the bride and groom. The death of an individual brings pollution to immediate kin and patrilineal relatives for a period of 13 days, though principal mourners observe restrictions for a year. Hindus cremate corpses, usually at the edge of a river.

MEMBERSHIP Hindus in Nepal do not proselytize, and conversion by people outside the caste system is virtually impossible. Historically, however, Hindus have encouraged recognition of Hindu divinities and rituals by all Nepalis.

SOCIAL JUSTICE Although Hindu foundations in Nepal often support charitable activities, and some monasteries (*ashrams*) have become refuges for the dispossessed, Hinduism remains linked with the inequalities of the caste system. Despite the fact that social activists regularly work against caste discrimination, they generally do not do so as members of Hindu organizations.

SOCIAL ASPECTS Caste inequality was an essential part of Nepalese society for centuries, and higher-caste Hindus continue to hold most influential positions in society, despite the leveling of the caste hierarchy. Women are subject to restrictions because their relative purity reflects on their natal families while they remain unmarried and on their husband's once they are married. A first marriage is referred to as "gift of a virgin," and chastity before marriage is carefully guarded. Hindu families are patrilineal, and men have formal authority over the family. Women, however, wield considerable informal power in the home, especially as they gain status in their husband's household after bearing male children. Higher castes do not allow widows to remarry. Nevertheless, Hindu women in Nepal are generally considered less restricted than in India.

POLITICAL IMPACT Throughout its history the state of Nepal has encouraged Hindu institutions and practices, and Hindu caste ideology was used to bring organization to Nepal's ethnic diversity. Even after the "people's movement" of 1990 and the establishment of democratic forms of government, Nepal officially remained a Hindu monarchy.

CONTROVERSIAL ISSUES Buddhist communities, and ethnic groups who refuse to define themselves as Hindu or Buddhist, have opposed the official designation of Nepal as a Hindu state and have called for boycotts of the Hindu national festival.

CULTURAL IMPACT Especially in Kathmandu, Nepalese examples of Hindu art, which are usually associated with temples, rival the finest art found anywhere in South Asia. Although nationalist sentiment has linked the development of Nepali-language literature with a nineteenth-century Nepali version of the famous Hindu epic *Ramayana,* most literature in Nepali is of a secular bent.

BUDDHISM

DATE OF ORIGIN before sixth century C.E.

NUMBER OF FOLLOWERS 2.8 million

HISTORY Gautama Buddha, the historical Buddha, was born in what is now Nepal in 563 B.C.E. Scholars project that early forms of Buddhism were likely practiced within Nepal from the time of the Buddha. The religion was well established there by the sixth century C.E., at which time Mahayana Buddhism appeared in India. Sectors of the Newar community, an important urban ethnic population, continue to practice Mahayana Buddhism. Later, Vajrayana, or Tantric, Buddhism also took hold among the Newar and has remained integral to Buddhist practice in Nepal.

Tibetan Buddhism began to have a serious impact in Nepal beginning with the introduction of Vajrayana forms of Buddhism in Tibet during the reign of Songtsen Gampo in the seventh century. Scholars hypothesize that Tibetans were key supporters of Buddhist sites in Nepal by the thirteenth century and that they gained additional support from indigenous Tibeto-Burman-speaking populations. Tibetan forms of Buddhism strongly influenced the religious life of the latter for the next 500 years.

Following China's occupation of Tibet and assumption of direct administration in 1959, large numbers of Tibetans fled to India and Nepal. Many took up residence around the great stupa at Bauddhanath in Nepal. Modern developments of note include the introduction of Theravada Buddhism in Nepal, especially among the Newar, in the 1930s. Also, the Sherpa and related groups have converted many of their monasteries from noncelibate to celibate practice. Finally, Tibeto-Burman-speaking groups like the Gurung and Tamang have begun to assert their identity as Buddhists more forcefully in Hindu Nepal.

EARLY AND MODERN LEADERS Early leaders of Buddhism are impossible to identify clearly from the historical record. They are associated with the founding of particular monasteries or monastic communities, which number in the hundreds in Nepal. Most contemporary Tibetan Buddhists in Nepal, especially Tibetan immigrants, hold the Dalai Lama in high esteem. Other Buddhists identify their leaders according to sect or ethnic community.

MAJOR THEOLOGIANS AND AUTHORS Buddhist practice in Nepal remains relatively decentralized. Identifying key leaders and theologians recognized by all Nepalese Buddhists is impossible because each of the thousands of communities across the country finds its leaders among local practitioners.

HOUSES OF WORSHIP AND HOLY PLACES The most important Buddhist sites in the Kathmandu Valley are the stupas and associated monasteries at Bauddhanath and Swayambhunath. Probably the most significant monastery and temple for the Newar Buddhists of Patan is Kwa Bahah. The Sherpa region of Solu Khumbu boasts several large monasteries, the most famous of which is Tengboche. Large monastic communities and important temples are also found in the Mustang district north and west of Kathmandu. Lumbini, the birthplace of the Buddha, lies in the southern Terai plains of Nepal and has become a Buddhist pilgrimage site in recent decades.

WHAT IS SACRED? Buddhists in Nepal have linked local geography to Buddhist mythology, and outstanding features of the landscape and nature are thus sacred. Relics associated with high incarnate lamas are held in reverence and sometimes entombed in stupas, which are themselves objects of veneration. The Buddhist word, including mantras as well as sacred texts, is powerful and sacred, whether printed in the canon or etched into the face of a rock.

HOLIDAYS AND FESTIVALS The cycles of Buddhist holidays and festivals in Nepal are determined independently by the traditions of different ethnic groups, each of which has unique focal festivals. Universally recognized by Buddhists, and a national holiday as well, is Buddha Jayanti, which celebrates the Buddha's birth, enlightenment, and death. Tamang and Tibetan Buddhists celebrate a festival of lights in December-January that commemorates the mythic completion of the Bauddhanath stupa. For Tibetan communities and some Tibeto-Burman communities, Lhosar, the Tibetan New Year celebration, has become an increasingly important festival. Sherpas of the northeastern district of Solu Khumbu are known for their monastic dance dramas called Mani Rimdu. In addition to celebrating Buddha Jayanti, Newar Buddhists in the Kathmandu Valley celebrate two grand chariot festivals focused on Karunamaya Matsyendranath (the bodhisattva Avalokitesvara).

MODE OF DRESS Buddhist monks in Nepal wear red robes and shave their heads. The married monks of the Newar, Tamang, Gurung, and other Buddhist ethnic groups don special habits for the performance of rituals.

DIETARY PRACTICE Newar Buddhists are divided into castes and follow dietary rules similar to those of Hindus. Clean castes will not accept water from untouchable castes. Higher castes will take water only from other higher castes, and they will not accept cooked rice from castes lower than their own. The sharing of such items as liquor and tobacco across caste boundaries is also highly restricted. Other Buddhists in Nepal are less concerned with purity.

RITUALS Major rituals for all Buddhists in Nepal include offerings to the divinities and Buddhas and prayers both at temples and monasteries and at home. Monks make such offerings and prayers on a daily basis. Laypersons do so on important dates of the ritual calendar. The Buddhist laity tends to be most interested in the worldly benefits of worship. Tibetan Buddhist laypersons, for instance, participate in rituals in order to receive blessings of power, long life, and good fortune. Most Buddhists make regular pilgrimages to major shrines and temples, sharing pilgrimage destinations with Hindus. Many pilgrimages have only local or regional significance, but others, such as the pilgrimages to Gosainkund and Muktinath, attract Buddhist and Hindu pilgrims from throughout Nepal.

RITES OF PASSAGE Newar, Tamang, Gurung, Thakali, and other Tibeto-Burman-speaking Buddhist populations follow, more or less, the same rites of passage as Hindus—but with a different emphasis. Most observe rites of purification at birth, at the first rice feeding, at marriage, and at death. High-caste Buddhist Newar boys are initiated into a monastery in a rite that parallels the Hindu *bartaman.* Some, like the western Tamang, observe a first haircut for boys at the age of three. Among the Tibeto-Burman and culturally Tibetan populations of Nepal, death rites stand out as those having the most extensive social ramifications, whereas marriage is the most important rite of passage among Hindus.

MEMBERSHIP Buddhists do not proselytize, but Buddhism, being a universalizing religion, welcomes converts.

SOCIAL JUSTICE Buddhists in Nepal do not have a history of social activism in alleviating poverty and injustice. Nevertheless, Buddhism has become the religion of many disadvantaged ethnic groups in Nepal.

SOCIAL ASPECTS Buddhist doctrine is not directly oriented toward the regulation of family or gender relations. With the exception of the Newar, Tibetan and Tibeto-Burman populations of Nepal allow women greater freedom than do Hindu populations, and they are not concerned about purity and pollution in ways that make women symbolically vulnerable.

POLITICAL IMPACT Historically Buddhism was extremely important in regional politics, but for centuries it has not had an impact on the Nepal nation-state. Within Buddhist communities high-ranking Buddhist functionaries are politically important because they are associated with and patronized by the most influential individuals in the community. Buddhism has become a significant factor in the nation's identity politics, with ethnic associations of Tibeto-Burman-speaking groups, for example, invoking their Buddhist identity in opposition to the dominant Hindu population.

CONTROVERSIAL ISSUES Buddhists in Nepal do not involve themselves in controversy concerning social issues, except in their demand for respect for the Buddha and the Buddhist religion. Most recent controversies have focused on international filmmakers shooting in Nepal who have represented the Buddha in ways that Buddhists find offensive. The filming of both *Little Buddha* (1993) and *Hollywood Buddha* (2004) met with protests.

CULTURAL IMPACT The main cultural impact of Buddhism in Nepal has been in the visual arts. Painting, especially in the Tibetan tradition, has been almost exclusively associated with Buddhist iconography. Newar metalworkers are world-renowned for the production of religious sculptures and statuary.

Other Religions

Most significant among other religious practices in Nepal is shamanism. Shamans or specialists in possession can be found practicing in every community. Most Hindu villagers regularly engage specialists in possession for propitiatory or exorcistic rituals. All Tibeto-Burman-speaking hill groups also employ shamans. Shamans among the Tibeto-Burman-speaking populations perform such services as capturing lost shadow-souls, propitiating household divinities, attaining revelatory visions, divining the future, exorcizing evils, and rejuvenating the life force. Shamans also lead pilgrimages to sacred sites.

Shamanism per se does not constitute a separate religion in Nepali communities; rather, it is a fully integrated part of the complex, nondoctrinal ritual systems found among most ethnic groups in Nepal. Although shamanism is declining in some communities, like the Sherpa, and among the middle classes of Kathmandu and other urban areas, it continues to be a vital force in village ritual life.

Small communities of Muslims have lived in Nepal for centuries. Some urban Muslims trace their families' origins in Nepal back to the days when the country was an important trade center. Nepali from disadvantaged ethnic groups have converted to Christianity in significant numbers during the past 30 years. Tiny communities of Sikhs, Jains, and Bahá'ís have migrated from India.

David H. Holmberg

See Also Vol. I: *Buddhism, Hinduism*

Bibliography

Bennett, Lynn. *Dangerous Wives and Sacred Sisters: Social and Symbolic Roles of High-Caste Women in Nepal.* New York: Columbia University Press, 1983.

Gellner, David N. *Monk, Householder, and Tantric Priest: Newar Buddhism and Its Hierarchy of Ritual.* Cambridge; New York: Cambridge University Press, 1992.

Hitchcock, John T., and Rex L. Jones, eds. *Spirit Possession in the Nepal Himalayas.* New Delhi: Vikas Publishing House, 1976.

Holmberg, David H. *Order in Paradox: Myth, Ritual, and Exchange among Nepal's Tamang.* Ithaca, New York: Cornell University Press, 1989.

Levi, Robert I. *Mesocosm: Hinduism and the Organization of a Traditional Newar City in Nepal.* Berkeley: University of California Press, 1990.

Maskarinec, Gregory G. *The Rulings of the Night: An Ethnography of Nepalese Shaman Oral Texts.* Madison, Wis.: University of Wisconsin Press, 1995.

Ortner, Sherry B. *High Religion: A Cultural and Political History of Sherpa Buddhism.* Princeton, N.J.: Princeton University Press, 1989.

Slusser, Mary Shepherd. *Nepal Mandala: A Cultural Study of the Kathmandu Valley.* Princeton, New Jersey: Princeton University Press, 1982.

Toffin, Gérard. *Le Palais et le temple: La Fonction royale dans la vallée du Népal.* Paris: CNRS Éditions, 1993.

Netherlands

POPULATION 16,259,300

ROMAN CATHOLIC 31 percent

PROTESTANT 21 percent

MUSLIM 5.3 percent

OTHER 2.7 percent

NONRELIGIOUS 40 percent

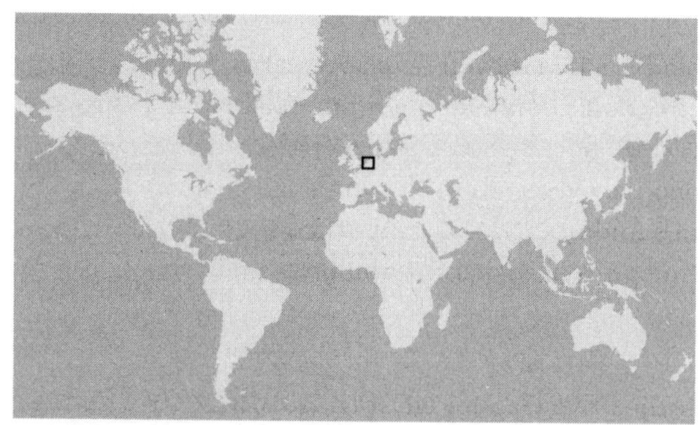

Country Overview

INTRODUCTION The Netherlands, a small and densely populated country in western Europe, belongs to the most secularized part of the world. It is bordered by Belgium to the south, Germany to the east, and the North Sea to the north and west.

Although Christianity is still the main religion in the Netherlands, the Christian churches (both Roman Catholic and Protestant) have suffered major losses in membership during the past century. Islam has become the second largest religion, but it is almost exclusively the religion of immigrants from such Mediterranean countries as Turkey and Morocco, as well as from the former Dutch colony of Surinam. Other religions in the Netherlands include Judaism, Hinduism, and Buddhism. A large and still growing group consists of those who do not adhere to any religious group or organization.

RELIGIOUS TOLERANCE The Netherlands has a long tradition of religious tolerance. The Union of Utrecht (1579) declared individuals free to choose their own religion. For centuries the Dutch Reformed Church (Gereformeerde Kerk) was the privileged church, but other denominations were allowed to perform their worship services. The Dutch Republic was a refuge for religious and political dissidents from abroad, including such groups as Jews and Huguenots, as well as such noted individuals as Baruch de Spinoza (1632–77) and René Descartes (1596–1650). In 1796 the Dutch National Assembly declared all religions to be equal. In the 1848 constitution state and church were formally separated, and the freedom of religious organization was acknowledged. The contemporary growth of Islam in Dutch society has made the issue of religious tolerance important again.

Major Religion

CHRISTIANITY

DATE OF ORIGIN Seventh century C.E.

NUMBER OF FOLLOWERS 8.5 million

HISTORY Before Christianity arrived in western Europe, tribes such as the Frisians and Batavians had their own gods and sacred places. The first evidence of Christian presence in the Low Countries (the region now comprising the Netherlands, Belgium, and Luxembourg) was a church built in Maastricht in the fourth century during the rule of the Roman Empire, but Christianization on a larger scale did not begin before the end of the seventh century. Anglo-Saxon missionaries Saint Willibrord (658?–739) and Saint Boniface (c. 675–754) tried to convert the Frisians by founding churches and monasteries and destroying pagan shrines. About a century later the Low Countries were more or less Christianized, although under the Christian surface pagan beliefs and rites continued to exist, some until the present day. From the twelfth century onward, monasteries of various orders, including Benedictines, Norbertines, Cistercians, Franciscans, and Dominicans, contributed to the religious and economic development of the Low Countries. The lay movement of Geert Groote's (1340–84) *devotio moderna* (modern devotion), or the Brethren and Sisters of the Common Life, and Thomas à Kempis's *Imitation of Christ* (1418), both of which emphasized personal piety and asceticism, were influential in the fifteenth and sixteenth centuries.

Dutch Roman Catholics carry the remains of the holy Willibrord during a celebration of the restoration of the episcopacy. After centuries of absence, the Roman Catholic Church reestablished the episcopal hierarchy in the Netherlands in 1853. © AFP/CORBIS.

The sixteenth-century Reformation initially brought Lutheranism and Anabaptism to the Netherlands. In 1566 outbursts of iconoclasm took place in many local churches. In the southern part of the Low Countries (what is modern Belgium), the majority remained Catholic. Those who joined the Lutherans and Calvinists were persecuted by Spanish occupiers and, with few exceptions, fled to the northern provinces. During the Dutch Revolt against the Spanish government (1568–1648), the Calvinists eventually took power, though they were still a minority. Within the young Dutch Republic, a federation of seven relatively autonomous provinces, the Dutch Reformed Church became the privileged church. Public functions were reserved exclusively for members of this church. Other denominations were tolerated but were denied a public role and were often compelled to build clandestine churches. Contradictions between orthodox and moderate Protestants occasionally led to political and theological clashes. At the famous Synod of Dordt (1618–19), which settled the supremacy of Calvinist Orthodoxy for a long time, a severe conflict broke out between followers of Jacobus Arminius (1560–1609), who stressed the free will of individuals to accept or reject God's grace, and ultraorthodox Calvinists, who believed that, even before Creation, God had decided who would be saved and who would be damned. The Arminians were expelled from the synod and formed the small dissenting church of the Remonstrant Brotherhood.

Within the Dutch Reformed Church a form of Pietist Calvinism developed during the seventeenth and eighteenth centuries called the Nadere Reformatie (Second Reformation), which, at the start of the twenty-first century, still claimed a profound influence in the right wing of the Dutch Reformed Church and other orthodox Reformed denominations. In 1796, strongly influenced by the French Revolution, the radical National Assembly declared all churches to be equal. In practice, however, the dominance of the Dutch Reformed Church continued.

In 1815 the Netherlands became a monarchy. King William I tried to consolidate the state influence upon the Dutch Reformed Church, changing its structure from a bottom-up organization to a top-down organization. Following the reorganization, the name of the church became Nederlandse Hervormde Kerk. Unease about the authoritarian structure and the dominance of theologically liberal ideas led to the small but influential

Reveil (Revival) movement (1825–55), which was popular among Protestant members of the aristocracy, and the Separation movement (1834), which formed a loose gathering of free churches in the northern part of the country. The persecution of members of these separated churches brought minister A.C. van Raalte and his followers to immigrate in 1847 to the United States, where they settled in Michigan, Iowa, and Illinois.

The 1848 constitution allowed all denominations to arrange their organization as they preferred. After centuries of absence, the Roman Catholic Church reestablished the episcopal hierarchy in the Netherlands (1853), which was followed by a period of emancipation and bloom under the leadership of Herman Schaepman (1844–1903). The neo-Calvinist Doleantie (Plaint) movement of theologian and politician Abraham Kuyper (1837–1920) broke away from the Dutch Reformed Church and founded the Reformed Churches in The Netherlands (Gereformeerde Kerken in Nederland, 1886), which were generally more strict than the larger Dutch Reformed Church. Combining Calvinist orthodoxy with the use of modern mass media and organizational techniques, Kuyper transformed the small Anti-Revolutionary Party into a modern democratic political party. He also established the newspaper *De Standaard* and the Free University.

The struggle of Roman Catholics and neo-Calvinists for power and emancipation led to the so-called period of pillarization (c. 1880–1965), in which almost all sectors of public and private life—politics, media, education, trade unions, health care, marriage—were organized along religious or political dividing lines, with each group forming a pillar of society on its own. This period came to an end with the advance of the welfare state, television, and youth culture in the post–World War II decades. The Dutch ecumenical movement, seeking closer relations between Catholics and Protestants, was at its peak during the 1960s and 1970s. At the same time, Roman Catholic and Protestant churches began to lose members and influence at a high rate. At present only some remnants of the formerly "pillarized" Dutch society are visible. For example, Protestant and Catholic groups formed the Christian Democratic Party in 1980, and the Dutch broadcasting system includes a Catholic, a mainstream Protestant, and an Evangelical broadcasting organization.

From 1961 onward the Dutch Reformed Church, the Reformed Churches in the Netherlands, and the Lutheran Church, together totaling 2.5 million members, were engaged in a long-term and complicated unification process, which finally resulted in the foundation of the Protestant Church in the Netherlands in 2004. This church loses about 75,000 members every year. More orthodox Reformed denominations show stability or modest growth in membership, in part because more new members are born into Reformed churches than are lost through death. Evangelical and Pentecostal groups have a certain appeal to members of the established Protestant churches. Elements of evangelicalism, such as music, worship styles, and personal devotion, continue to be taken over by several Reformed denominations, which were always greatly shaped by Calvinist beliefs and practices.

In the 1960s a strong movement away from conservatism toward ultraliberalism began among Dutch Roman Catholics. This liberal movement started among a new generation of Roman Catholic intellectuals who, seeking to integrate into the broader society, no longer wanted to solely follow the Roman Catholic doctrines. For example, some priests wanted to abolish celibacy. Several times the Vatican intervened to bring the Dutch Catholic Church closer to Rome through, among other things, the appointment of conservative bishops and the calling of a special Dutch bishop synod at the Vatican in 1980. Bishops have protested since against liberal norms and values in Dutch society, but at the local level many clerics and lay persons have continued to plead for an open and ecumenical Catholicism. Ecumenical cooperation with Protestants is stronger at the local level than at the national level. Church involvement is relatively low among Roman Catholics. At the start of the twenty-first century, the Roman Catholic Church in the Netherlands, still claiming to have about 5 million adherents, was losing 55,000 members every year. Surveys showed that, with respect to norms and values, it was difficult to tell Catholics apart from those with no religious affiliation. Despite modern mobility and the process of church decline, Catholic influences were nevertheless still visible in the southern provinces of Brabant and Limburg at the beginning of the twenty-first century.

EARLY AND MODERN LEADERS Prince William of Orange (1533–84) is considered the father of the Dutch Fatherland. He started as stadtholder (governor) of the provinces of Holland, Utrecht, and Zeeland under Spanish King Philip II; later, when the regime of Philip became harsh and oppressive, William led the resistance movement. Born in a German Lutheran family and raised a Catholic at the court of King Charles V, William was initially not outspoken in religious affairs but became a moderate Calvinist in 1573 after a long period of hesitation. He sought the unity of Dutch Catholics, Lutherans, and Calvinists in the struggle for freedom from the Spanish. In 1581 the seven northern provinces of the Low Countries declared themselves independent from the Spanish king as the Republic of the Seven United Netherlands. They chose William as their first stadtholder. After several attacks upon his life, he was killed by a French assassin. His name lives on in the Dutch national anthem "Wilhelmus," both a political and religious song, which describes William as a highly religious freedom fighter who is still loyal to the Spanish king.

Theologian and politician Abraham Kuyper organized the neo-Calvinist movement in the late nineteenth century and was the first Calvinist prime minister (1901–05). Kuyper's influence has been evident through the twenty-first century, especially in churches that were founded by Dutch emigrants. Priest, poet, and statesman Herman Schaepman was an eloquent champion of the Roman Catholic emancipation movement. He was a great advocate for the cooperation of Catholics and Protestants against liberalism.

MAJOR THEOLOGIANS AND AUTHORS Thomas à Kempis, member of the medieval Modern Devotion movement of Geert Groote, wrote *Imitation of Christ,* one of the most popular spiritual books of Christian time. Erasmus of Rotterdam (1466–1536), the great Renaissance humanist scholar, published the first text-critical edition of the Greek New Testament. Arminius, a dissident professor of theology within the Dutch Reformed Church, propagated the doctrine that God has given man the choice to accept or reject Him. This doctrine, Arminianism, became popular in international revival movements such as Methodism, Baptism, and Evangelicalism.

Edward Schillebeeckx (born in 1914), a Flemish Dominican priest, is one of the most influential contemporary Roman Catholic theologians. He has contributed strongly to the worldwide renewal movement within the Catholic Church after the Second Vatican Council (1962–65). Huub Oosterhuis (born in 1933), author of many songs and prayers, is the most influential contemporary Christian poet. Harry Kuitert (born in 1924) was raised in the Kuyperian Reformed churches. In his theological career he attacked many of the cherished beliefs and dogmas of Reformed and other Christians.

HOUSES OF WORSHIP AND HOLY PLACES As in other countries where Christianity is or has been dominant, churches in the Netherlands are the most important houses of worship. Some of the more famous churches include the Reformed Westerkerk and the Catholic Dominicuskerk in Amsterdam; the Reformed Kloosterkerk in the Hague; the Reformed Domkerk in Utrecht; the Reformed Nieuwe Kerk in Delft, where Prince William of Orange and other members of the Royal House of Orange are buried; and the Catholic Saint Janskathedraal in Den Bosch. The Nieuwe Kerk on the Dam in Amsterdam is used only on special occasions, such as royal weddings.

There are about 650 places of Catholic pilgrimage in the Netherlands, of which Amsterdam is one of the most famous. Every year thousands of believers walk silently in the night through the old inner city, commemorating the Medieval Miracle of Amsterdam. In 1345 a devout Catholic man was very ill and threw up the Sacred Host he had received from the priest. The Sacred Host then was thrown into the fire but did not burn. Soon pilgrims came to the house of the sick man seeking cure and celebration.

WHAT IS SACRED? The Dutch Republic originated out of a struggle against Spanish oppression. Several times in its history, the Dutch have had to suffer under the occupation of foreign powers, most recently the German occupation during World War II (1940–45). These were traumatic experiences for the Dutch. Therefore, the notion of sacredness is often connected to general concepts such as freedom, tolerance, equality, and independence, in which politics, ethics, and religion flow together. The origins of the Dutch Reformed Church coincide with the birth of the Dutch nation. This church has long considered itself to be "God's plantation on Dutch soil."

HOLIDAYS AND FESTIVALS The traditional Christian holidays, such as Christmas, Easter, Ascension, and Whitsuntide, remain official holidays in contemporary times. A minority goes to church on these days. In the Netherlands Christmas is celebrated as in other European countries; however, the tradition of giving presents is more connected to the popular *Sinterklaasfeest* (Saint Nicholas Eve) on 5 December, a tradition that dates back to medieval times.

MODE OF DRESS Dress is not commonly associated with Christian religion in the Netherlands. In very orthodox Reformed churches, however, women are expected to wear hats and long gowns or skirts during worship and long hair all the time. Men dress appropriately and are rarely seen wearing baseball caps or displaying tattoos, piercings, or long hair.

DIETARY PRACTICES Dutch Christians generally have no specific dietary practices. The Roman Catholic habit of fasting in the weeks before Easter has almost disappeared.

RITUALS About one in six Netherlanders attends church on Sundays. At the start of the twenty-first century, the percentage of Roman Catholics who visited church on a regular basis was 22 percent, while among mainstream Protestants the number was 46 percent. The smaller Orthodox Calvinist denominations have maintained very high rates of church attendance. In some of these churches Canaan (Tale Kanaäns), which is the language of the 1637 Dutch Bible translation, Statenvertaling, mixed with Pietist Calvinist expressions of the seventeenth- and eighteenth-century movement Nadere Reformatie, is still spoken. Not seldomly a minister will start weeping when he preaches about eternal salvation and damnation.

RITES OF PASSAGE In the Roman Catholic Church and most of the Protestant denominations, child baptism is the rule. Mennonites, Evangelicals, and Pentecostals prefer adult baptism after a public confession of faith. Roman Catholic youngsters go through a confirmation ceremony at the age of twelve. Protestants are expected to give a public confession of faith in their adolescence after a lengthy period of confirmation classes. A minority of those who are baptized in the mainstream Protestant denominations will eventually be confirmed. In many local Protestant churches, children are allowed to take part in the Lord's Supper. Wedding and funeral services are generally held apart from the Sunday service.

MEMBERSHIP Those who are baptized within Protestant or Catholic churches are considered to be a member of these denominations unless they have deliberately had their names removed from the membership lists. The percentage of church members who consider themselves as belonging to the church, however, is much lower than official percentages. The former Catholic and Protestant pillars (divisions by religious affiliations) have lost many of their defensive and emancipatory functions, and the mainstream churches have lost hold of their members, both socially and ideologically. Based upon the extrapolation of trends, especially among the younger generations, it is predicted that within 20 years only 25 percent of the Dutch population will consider itself to belong to one of the Christian churches.

SOCIAL JUSTICE For centuries the Christian churches have struggled against poverty and have contributed to education and social justice in Dutch society. The Dutch Council of Churches, in which the Roman Catholic Church and many Protestant denominations are represented, periodically stands up for neglected or maltreated groups in society.

SOCIAL ASPECTS After a period of resistance, some mainstream Protestant churches in the Netherlands have more or less accepted the equality of other forms of cohabitation than the traditional family. In these churches gay marriages can receive blessing. The Roman Catholic Church and the smaller Orthodox Protestant denominations are strongly opposed to gay marriages and forms of cohabitation without marriage. Female pastors are an accepted phenomenon only in the mainstream Protestant churches.

POLITICAL IMPACT Churches have little or no direct influence upon politics, but Christian political parties, trade unions, and mass media still have an impact. During most of the twentieth century, Christian parties, both Catholic and Protestant, were represented in coalition cabinets. In 2002, after eight years of opposition, the Christian Democrats—a fusion of former Catholic and Protestant parties—returned to power. Jan Peter Balkenende, elected prime minister in 2002, is a typical descendant of the Kuyperian Reformed tradition.

CONTROVERSIAL ISSUES In spite of the separation of state and church, confessional schools are subsidized as equally as public schools. About two-thirds of Dutch elementary and secondary schools have a Protestant or Catholic identity. Adversaries argue that subsidizing both confessional and public schools is expensive and outdated. Advocates of state subsidies appeal to the constitutional right of Christians and others to organize their own schools.

In 1918 ultraorthodox Calvinists founded Staatkundig Gereformeerde Partij (Political Reformed

Party), a political party with strictly theocratic ideals. This small party has maintained representation in the Dutch Parliament, and at the start of the twenty-first century it still excluded women from membership. In 2001 the United Nations Convention on the Elimination of All Forms of Discrimination against Women (CEDAW) condemned the Dutch state for tolerating the exclusive policy of this party.

Conservative Protestants and Catholics have unsuccessfully protested against the Abortion Law (1981), the Equal Rights Law (1994), and the Euthanasia Law (2000).

CULTURAL IMPACT Paintings by Rembrandt and his seventeenth-century contemporaries show an appetite for biblical themes. The famous Dutch painter Vincent van Gogh (1853—90) started his career as an evangelist among Belgian miners. The abstract paintings of Piet Mondrian (1872–1944), another well-known Dutch painter, are said to reflect the soberness and asceticism of the Calvinist milieu in which he grew up. The magnificent 1637 translation of the Bible into Dutch (Statenvertaling) has influenced and shaped the Dutch language for many generations.

Modern Dutch painters, musicians, and writers sometimes deal with religious and biblical themes, most often from an independent, outsider position. Contemporary writers often represent Dutch liberalism and individual freedom in their works. Popular novelists such as Jan Wolkers (born in 1925) and Maarten 't Hart (born in 1944) wrote of breaking away from a strict orthodox Reformed environment. Novelist A.F.Th. van der Heijden (born in 1951) wrote of similar circumstances regarding his Catholic background. Gerard Reve (born in 1923), another well-known post–World War II novelist, was converted to a personal kind of Catholicism after being raised in an atheist and Communist family.

Other Religions

The People's Census of 1960 showed that only 0.01 percent of the Dutch population was Muslim. This soon changed. Young men from Muslim countries around the Mediterranean Sea, including Morocco and Turkey, moved to the Netherlands to fill the gaps in industrial jobs during the 1960s and 1970s. At the time nobody could foresee that they would stay in the Netherlands permanently and that their families would join them. After the Declaration of Independence of the former Dutch colony of Surinam in 1975, many Muslims and Hindus, descendants of Indian and Javan contract laborers, immigrated to the Netherlands. During the late twentieth century, many refugees from Muslim countries in Africa and Asia found asylum in the Netherlands. Compared with those of native Dutch families, Muslim birth rates are much higher. The fastest growing religion in the Netherlands, Islam accounted for 5.3 percent of the population at the beginning of the twenty-first century. The influx of Muslims has led to a growing number of mosques. There is some discussion about the official acknowledgment of Muslim holidays. Efforts to found Muslim political parties have failed, mainly because of different ethnic origins, but Muslims have entered the existing political parties, including Social Democrats, Radical Left, Liberals, Conservative Liberals, and even the Christian Democrats.

As Muslims began to represent a potential force in Dutch society, the proverbial Dutch tolerance was tested. Such questions as whether Orthodox Muslim women should be allowed to wear headscarves (*burqas* or *niqaabs*) at work, whether imams (Shiite leaders) should have the right to call for jihad (strive, struggle) against Western civilization in their sermons, or whether cultural background can be an extenuating circumstance when a young Muslim kills his sister because she has besmirched the honor of the family prompted vigorous debates about cultural integration of Muslims in Dutch society. Additionally, Islam in the Netherlands is—both in religious and ethnic respects—far from unified. Some experts predict the development of a liberal type of Islam typical of the Dutch tendency.

By the end of the sixteenth century, many Jews from eastern Europe, Spain, and Portugal had found refuge in the Dutch Republic. They lived predominantly in Amsterdam but moved to other places, as well. After the Holocaust, the number of Dutch Jews had decreased by 70 percent. In modern times a minority of Jews in the Netherlands have been active members of one of the Jewish denominations.

Immigrants from Surinam and various Asian countries have founded Hindu or Buddhist organizations during the last decades. Temples and meditation centers can be found in various Dutch cities. Eastern religions also hold a certain attraction to "unchurched" native Dutch individuals.

Hijme C. Stoffels

See Also Vol. I: *Christianity, Islam, Judaism, Reformed Christianity, Roman Catholicism*

Bibliography

Coleman, J.A. *The Evolution of Dutch Catholicism, 1958–1974.* Berkeley: University of California Press, 1978.

Dekker, G., J. de Hart, and J. Peters. *God in Nederland, 1966–1996.* Amsterdam: Anthos, 1997.

Felling, A., J. Peters, and O. Schreuder. *Dutch Religion: The Religious Consciousness of the Netherlands after the Cultural Revolution.* Nijmegen: Instituut voor Toegepaste Sociale Wetenschappen, 1991.

Israel, J. *The Dutch Republic: Its Rise, Greatness, and Fall.* Oxford: Clarendon Press, 1995.

Lijphart, A. *The Politics of Accommodation: Pluralism and Democracy in the Netherlands.* 2nd ed. Berkeley: University of California Press, 1975.

Rooden, P. van. "Long-Term Religious Developments in the Netherlands, Ca. 1750–2000." In *The Decline of Christendom in Western Europe, 1750–2000.* Edited by H. McLeod and W. Ustorf, 113–29. Cambridge: Cambridge University Press, 2002.

New Zealand

POPULATION 3,908,037

ANGLICAN 17 percent

PROTESTANT 21 percent

ROMAN CATHOLIC 15 percent

MAORI CHRISTIAN (RATANA AND RINGATU) 1.5 percent

OTHER CHRISTIAN 5 percent

BUDDHIST 1 percent

HINDU 1 percent

ISLAM .5 percent

OTHER 1 percent

NONRELIGIOUS 37 percent

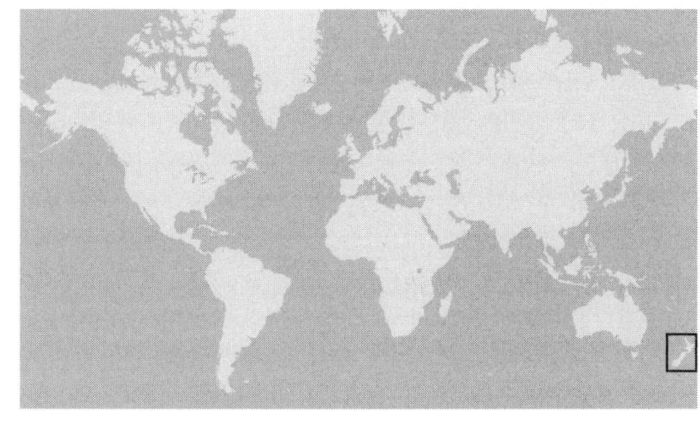

Country Overview

INTRODUCTION New Zealand consists of two major islands, North and South, located deep in the southern Pacific Ocean almost a thousand miles east of Australia. The climate ranges from semitropical in the far north of the North Island to cool and temperate in the far south of the South Island. The Polynesian ancestors of the Maori people first settled the country in the thirteenth century C.E. After fleeting visits by Dutch explorer Abel Tasman in the seventeenth century and Captain James Cook in the late eighteenth century, organized British settlement began in 1840. By this time many of the country's Maori had adopted Christianity. English and Scottish Protestants, mainly Anglican and Presbyterian, and a smaller group of Irish Catholics dominated the main waves of settlement from the United Kingdom. Most colonists were from lower middle class or working class backgrounds, and they came in search of a better life. They sought to establish an egalitarian society with opportunity for all that no class or church could dominate. Religiously tolerant New Zealanders elected two freethinkers as premier of the country before 1890, and in 1893 New Zealand became the first country in the world to give women the right to vote.

Weekly churchgoing, which peaked in the late nineteenth century at around 30 percent of the population, slowly declined during the twentieth century and more rapidly from the mid-1960s. At the beginning of the twenty-first century, approximately 8 to 10 percent of the population regularly attended church services. By that time secular New Zealanders professing no religion or objecting to state a religious preference made up more than one-third of the population. Asian immigration burgeoned in the late twentieth century, introducing small but growing numbers of Hindus, Muslims, Sikhs, Confucians, Buddhists, and Asian Christians into the country.

A Maori man stands inside a house of worship built for the famous Maori religious leader, Te Kooti Arikirangi Te Turuki. Te Kooti created the rituals, prayers, and hymns of his Ringatu Church. © MACDUFF EVERTON/CORBIS.

RELIGIOUS TOLERANCE The British crown and Maori Christian chiefs signed the Treaty of Waitangi in 1840. In return for ceding sovereignty, the treaty guaranteed Maori authority over their lands, forests, fisheries, and other treasured possessions. Maori were given all the rights and privileges of British subjects. The treaty also guaranteed religious liberty. Although the crown subsequently breached the treaty, it has remained the basis for the compensation processes occurring sporadically since the 1880s and more systematically since 1975 and for affirming partnership between Pakeha (that is, non-Maori) and Maori today. Biculturalism remains very important in contemporary New Zealand.

No state church took root in New Zealand. The country prided itself on its reputation as an egalitarian, religiously tolerant, and socially progressive democracy. Ethnoreligious minorities—Irish Roman Catholics, Maori prophets, and the Chinese—sometimes suffered discrimination and injustice at the hands of a state that they saw as all too faithfully reflecting the attitudes of the British Protestant majority.

Major Religion

CHRISTIANITY

DATE OF ORIGIN 1769 C.E.

NUMBER OF FOLLOWERS 2.3 million

HISTORY The French explorer Jean de Surville's Dominican chaplain celebrated the first Roman Catholic mass in Doubtless Bay in 1769. Anglican missionary Reverend Samuel Marsden held the first Protestant service in 1814. During the bloody intertribal Musket Wars of the 1820s, many Maori began to question traditional beliefs. The new way of peace, literacy, and Christianity preached by the missionaries attracted thousands of Maori to Anglican, Methodist, and, from 1838, Roman Catholic mission stations. Most of the country's 100,000 Maori inhabitants embraced Christianity during the 1830s and 1840s. Following the signing of the Treaty of Waitangi in 1840, British settlers arrived in growing numbers. About half the incoming settlers were English, mostly Anglican; one-quarter Scottish, mostly Presbyterian; and about one-fifth Irish, mostly Roman Catholic.

The first Anglican bishop, George Selwyn (1809–78), sought to protect Maori rights and welfare while giving the colony's Anglican church more independence and the laity more say than in England. In 1925 the Anglican Synod agreed to found an autonomous Maori diocese. Not until 1978, however, was the bishop of Aotearoa given full status and a diocese. Penelope Jamieson became the first woman diocesan Anglican bishop in the world when she was appointed bishop of Dunedin in 1990. During the 1990s the Anglican Church reorganized itself into three *tikanga,* or cultural streams—Maori, Pacific Island, and Pakeha—to give effective voice to its Maori and Pacific Island members.

Protestant settlers arrived in growing numbers from 1840. Scottish Free Church Presbyterians dominated the Otago settlement launched in 1848 in the southeast of the South Island. English Anglicans led the Canterbury settlement, established in 1850. Evangelical Protestants championed the great social crusades, including temperance and prohibition, Bible-in-Schools, and woman suffrage, that burgeoned between 1880 and 1920.

Roman Catholicism developed with the arrival of the newly appointed Vicar of Oceania, Bishop Pompallier, in 1838. He directed the Catholic Maori mission, dominated by priests from the Society of Mary. This mission enjoyed modest success. After 1840, however, a growing influx of Irish Catholic settlers began to preoccupy the hierarchy. The first Maori priest, Wiremu Te Awhitu, was ordained in 1944. Catholic adherence and attendance rates held up into the 1980s, while Anglican, Presbyterian, and Methodist numbers steadily declined. By the 1990s, however, Catholic numbers also began to decline, a process that has continued in the twenty-first century.

Pentecostalism arrived with English faith healer Smith Wigglesworth's mission in Wellington in 1922. The Pentecostal Church in New Zealand was established in 1924, the Assemblies of God in 1927, and the Apostolic Church in 1932. Numerous new Pentecostal or charismatic churches have been founded since the 1970s.

Following the land wars of the 1860s, Maori Christians, reading and interpreting the Maori Bible (a translation of the King James version), launched a series of independent movements led by Maori prophets. The Ringatu movement, led by warrior-prophet Te Kooti Arikirangi Te Turuki (c. 1830–93), grew out of the East Coast wars of the late 1860s. After a series of military victories against the colonial militia and Maori enemies, Te Kooti created the rituals, prayers, and hymns of his Ringatu Church, which appealed to many in the Rongowhakaata, Ngati Maru, and Tuhoe tribes. Tahupotiki Wiremu Ratana (1870–1939), a farmer turned faith healer, founded one of the most important and enduring Maori churches. His Ratana Church, established in 1925, attracted many detribalized Maori, especially in the central North Island. Ratana embraced the religion of Jehovah and repudiated various traditional Maori beliefs and practices. The church adopted Maori and European symbols, including the *patu* (club) and *whetu marama* (five-pointed star). As Jesus was sent to the Jews, adherents believed, Ratana was sent to the Maori people. Ratana also launched a political campaign that eventually succeeded in placing members of the Ratana Church on all four of the parliamentary seats specially reserved for the Maori. By 1950 20 percent of Maori belonged to the Ratana Church. At the start of the twenty-first century, the Ratana Church remained influential in some Maori communities.

EARLY AND MODERN LEADERS George Selwyn played a key role in establishing the Anglican Church in New Zealand and became the country's first Anglican primate. Selwyn reshaped the church to give the laity more say, championed Maori rights and welfare during the colonial period, and founded the Melanesian Mission. Sir Paul Reeves, the first Maori Anglican primate, became New Zealand's first Maori governor general in 1985 and represented the worldwide Anglican Communion at the United Nations in 1991.

After the land wars of the 1860s, Maori prophet Te Whiti O Rongomai (died in 1907) established a Maori Christian community in the 1870s at the village of Parihaka in the Taranaki province of the North Island. Blending traditional Maori values with New Testament teachings, Te Whiti instructed his followers in peaceful resistance as a means to disrupt the government's attempts to take over land, which, he insisted, belonged to his people. In 1881 government officials arrested and imprisoned without trial Te Whiti and many of his followers.

MAJOR THEOLOGIANS AND AUTHORS James K. Baxter (1926–72), a Catholic convert from a Presbyterian background, won fame during the second half of the twentieth century as a poet, prophet, and lay theologian. Baxter set out to befriend the poor and marginalized, especially Maori, and to liberate New Zealanders from puritanical moralism.

As a Presbyterian professor of Old Testament at the Theological Hall, Knox College, Lloyd Geering gained notoriety during a heresy trial in the 1960s for publicly expressing liberal Protestant views on the resurrection of Christ. He has published widely, including such works as *God in the New World*, *Faith's New Age*, and *Christianity without God*, growing increasingly secular in outlook after becoming Foundation Professor of Religious Studies at Victoria University, Wellington, in 1971.

HOUSES OF WORSHIP AND HOLY PLACES Rangiatea Anglican Church at Otaki, originally built by Maori Christians in the mid-nineteenth century, synthesized traditional Maori and European artistic and architectural styles. The church was noted for its large wooden poles carved in traditional Maori style, as well as tukutuku panels woven with Maori patterns and motifs. When the church was destroyed by fire in 1995, hundreds of people, Pakeha as well as Maori, donated money to rebuild it.

War memorials dot the country, commemorating New Zealanders who gave their lives during World War I and II. These memorials regularly attract pilgrims. Christian crosses appear discreetly, reflecting the community's determination to avoid sectarian quarrels.

WHAT IS SACRED? Popular Christianity treats war memorials as sacred sites. Many New Zealanders consider the Treaty of Waitangi a sacred, though not religious, document.

HOLIDAYS AND FESTIVALS Anzac Day, on which New Zealanders remember soldiers who lost their lives fighting at Gallipoli during World War I, remains a major holy day. Large crowds assemble for the Anzac Day Dawn Parade in towns and cities across the country, and many attend church services.

MODE OF DRESS New Zealand Christians dress much like everyone else in the country. In Auckland, the largest Polynesian city in the world, Samoan Christians dress entirely in white for church on White Sunday. This annual event, held in October, commemorates the arrival in Samoa of John Williams, a London missionary, in 1830.

DIETARY PRACTICES Few churches restrict the dietary practices of members. Some Pentecostal groups encourage prayer and fasting. Seventh-day Adventists observe their church's dietary restrictions, such as abstaining from meat, coffee, and other stimulants. After the Second Vatican Council (1962–65), fasting before Mass and avoiding meat on Fridays dwindled amongst Catholics.

RITUALS Until the 1970s sending children to Sunday school functioned as the central ritual of popular Protestantism. A far greater proportion of New Zealand parents sent their children to Sunday school than attended church themselves. Anzac Day, when New Zealanders solemnly gather at dawn parades and church services conducted by Christian ministers to remember their war dead, remains the most popular ritual of the nation's quasi-Christian civil religion. Maori Christianity has in some ways come to function as the country's *de facto* civic spirituality. At *marae* (meeting houses) and on public ceremonial occasions, Maori clergy and lay Christians regularly offer *karakia* (prayers). Many Pakeha, including nonchurchgoers, respect such occasions.

RITES OF PASSAGE Though declining in popularity since the 1960s, Christian rites of passage—baptisms, weddings, and funerals—remain widely observed. Maori Christian funerals (*tangi*), normally lasting several days, bring friends, family (*whanau*), subtribe (*hapu*), and the wider community together at *marae.* Often presided over by ministers of several denominations, these funerals blend Christian with older, traditional elements, such as the ritual keening of senior women.

MEMBERSHIP The three largest Protestant churches—Anglican, Presbyterian, and Methodist—largely eschewed evangelization and steadily declined in relation to a growing population, especially since the 1960s, as their congregations aged. Maori Christian membership and attendance rates have been declining at about the same rate as Protestant Pakeha. Catholic membership held up longer than in the mainline Protestant churches but began to decline in the 1980s.

Pentecostals, offering dynamic experiential and expressive religion in a contemporary musical style, have steadily grown, often by attracting people from mainline denominations. By 1982, with weekly attendance rates above 40,000, the Pentecostal worshiping community approached the number of regular participants in Presbyterian churches and eclipsed those attending Baptist or Methodist churches.

SOCIAL JUSTICE In the years that followed the signing of the Treaty of Waitangi in 1840, church leaders often protested the crown's failure to uphold its treaty obligations. Bishop Selwyn, for example, publicly protested a British proposal of 1846 to treat all unused Maori land as wasteland that the government could take. Again, in 1860 Selwyn and most Anglican clergy and missionaries condemned the government's decision to buy disputed Maori land in Taranaki, plunging the colony into war. In the 1980s and 1990s, the Anglican, Methodist, and

Presbyterian churches renewed their commitments to the principles of the treaty and to biculturalism by giving greater recognition and autonomy to their Maori members.

SOCIAL ASPECTS The mainline Protestant churches have cautiously endorsed more liberal social attitudes and government legislation concerning marriage and family since the 1970s. For example, liberal Protestant church leaders endorsed abortion law reform in the 1970s, and in the 1980s they favored decriminalizing homosexual acts between consenting adults. The Catholic Church, smaller evangelical churches, and many charismatics and Pentecostals have taken more conservative positions on such issues. The Catholic bishops have regularly taken strong stands on social issues concerning work and unemployment.

POLITICAL IMPACT From the 1930s until the 1990s, the Ratana Church's alliance with the Labour Party encouraged the support of most Maori. Beginning in the 1990s New Zealand First, led by Winston Peters, a populist Maori member of Parliament, helped splinter the Maori vote.

Most lay Christians work through long established centrist political parties. After New Zealand embraced a proportional representation electoral system in the 1990s, small, explicitly Christian parties, such as Christian Heritage, Christian Democrats, and Future New Zealand, emerged.

CONTROVERSIAL ISSUES Beginning in 1877 government funding of private, mostly Catholic schools provoked heated debate. The 1975 Private Schools Integration Act, which integrated private schools into the state education system with full funding, largely resolved the debate. During the late twentieth century proposals to legalize abortion and prostitution and to ordain homosexuals as ministers have excited fierce debate within the Christian churches and society.

CULTURAL IMPACT In a predominantly Protestant culture, the Catholic minority has contributed an unusual number of writers and artists, such as the poet James K. Baxter, whose poetry is sometimes infused with Christian mythology, and historian and biographer Michael King, whose works express liberal Catholic viewpoints. For a small country New Zealand boasts a remarkable number of hymn and songwriters, such as the Methodist Colin Gibson and charismatics David and Dale Garratt.

Other Religions

From the beginning of white settlement, New Zealand attracted groups that practiced religions other than the Protestantism and Catholicism of the vast British and Irish majority. Heterodox sects and cults such as spiritualism, theosophy, and freethought thrived within the settler community. Lebanese Christians, both Catholic and Maronite, arrived in the late nineteenth century. A tiny Jewish minority, often playing prominent roles in local and national politics, business, and culture, also established residence from the beginning of white settlement. Chinese gold miners, practicing Confucianism, Buddhism, and Chinese folk religions, arrived seeking gold in the 1860s. From the 1880s until World War II, however, the government pursued a policy aimed to exclude Asians. Only in the 1980s did the state, under economic pressure to pursue Asian investment and trading opportunities, open up immigration policy. Growing numbers of Asian immigrants took to New Zealand their distinctive religious traditions, including Hinduism, Islam, Sikhism, Buddhism, Confucianism, Shinto, and Christianity. By the early twenty-first century, Asian New Zealanders, making up approximately 6 percent of the total population, eclipsed Pacific Islanders as the second largest ethnic minority group after Maori, which totaled approximately 15 percent. Asian immigrants have encountered some racial and religious prejudice.

John Stenhouse

See Also Vol. 1: *Anglicanism/Episcopalianism, Roman Catholicism*

Bibliography

Adhar, R., and J. Stenhouse. *God and Government: The New Zealand Experience.* Dunedin: University of Otago Press, 2000.

Breward, I. *A History of the Churches in Australasia.* Oxford: Oxford University Press, 2001.

Colless, B., and P. Donovan, eds. *Religion in New Zealand Society.* Palmerston North: Dunmore, 1985.

Darragh, Neil. "Contextual Theology in Aotearoa New Zealand." In *Asian Christian Theologies.* Edited by John England et al., 541–98. Maryknoll, N.Y.: Orbis Books, 2002.

Davidson, Allan. *Christianity in Aotearoa: A History of Church and Society in New Zealand.* Wellington: The New Zealand Education for Ministry Board, 1991.

Davidson, Allan, and Peter J. Lineham. *Transplanted Christianity: Documents Illustrating Aspects of New Zealand Church History.* 3rd ed. Palmerston North: Department of History, Massey University, 1995.

Donovan, P., ed. *Religions of New Zealanders.* Palmerston North: Dunmore Press, 1990.

King, M. *The Penguin History of New Zealand.* Auckland: Penguin, 2003.

———, ed. *Tihe Mauri Ora: Aspects of Maoritanga.* Wellington: Methuen, 1978.

Nicaragua

POPULATION 5,023,818

ROMAN CATHOLIC 75.9 percent

PROTESTANT 18.7 percent

JEHOVAH'S WITNESS 1.4 percent

OTHER 4.0 percent

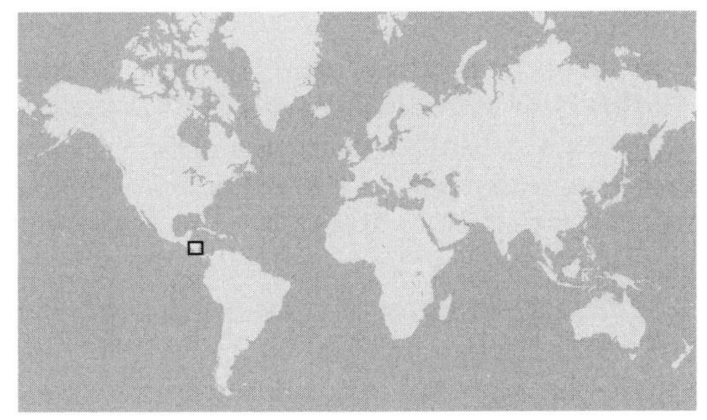

Country Overview

INTRODUCTION Nicaragua, with an area of 50,446 square miles, is the largest Central American country. It is bounded by the Pacific Ocean on the west and the Caribbean Sea on the east. Tropical forests make up more than one third of its territory. The capital, Managua, is located on the shores of Lake Nicaragua. Various mountain ranges, with a number of active volcanoes, run through the country. Many communities are notably isolated; hence their congregations are highly autonomous.

The Roman Catholic Church entered Nicaragua with the Spanish colonists in 1522 and was a part of the colonial administration until the country achieved independence in 1821. The first Protestant missionaries traveled to Nicaragua in the mid-nineteenth century. In 1963, 96 percent of the population had considered itself Roman Catholic. By 2000 the percentage had decreased to almost 76 percent. At the national level, however, the Roman Catholic Church has remained the dominant religious group and exercises considerable political influence.

Many Nicaraguans are practicing members of two churches or are registered at multiple churches while actually visiting only one. These double affiliations make it difficult to compile accurate statistics about religious practices.

RELIGIOUS TOLERANCE During the Spanish colonial era the Roman Catholic Church was part of the government administration. After Nicaragua gained independence from Spain, its first constitution (1826) proclaimed Roman Catholicism as the state religion. The liberal revolution of General José Santos Zelaya in 1893 marked the beginning of the Catholic Church's separation from the Nicaraguan state. The subsequent Nicaraguan constitutions contained provisions to guarantee religious freedom for all. As a result of the efforts of progressive Catholics and Protestants who were involved in the left-wing Sandinista government (1979–90), religious tolerance has been stronger since the 1980s.

Although Roman Catholicism has not been the official religion since 1894, the Nicaraguan state has maintained a privileged position for the church, which is exempted from taxes and which has received many financial benefits. The cathedral in Managua, for in-

A man paints his son as part of the Santo Domingo holiday. The Roman Catholic fiestas in August celebrating Santo Domingo, the patron saint of Managua, are the largest in scale and participation. © AFP/CORBIS.

stance, was paid for in part by the government in the 1990s. Various Protestant organizations have challenged this situation. In the polarized religious climate little ecumenical cooperation exists.

Major Religion

ROMAN CATHOLICISM

DATE OF ORIGIN 1522 C.E.
NUMBER OF FOLLOWERS 3.8 million

HISTORY In 1522 Roman Catholic evangelization efforts in Nicaragua started on the Atlantic coast. During the Spanish colonial era the Catholic Church formed an almost inseparable part of the government administration. Evangelization on the Pacific coast began in 1689. The country became a full ecclesiastical province in 1912.

In the 1940s the international Catholic Action movement was introduced to Nicaragua to propagate orthodox Catholicism, to increase lay participation in hierarchy-controlled organizations, and to ward off Protestant missionaries. In the 1960s the Nicaraguan bishops remained conservative, but a small group of clergy was eager to play a more active role in promoting social change.

After a long U.S. military intervention the Somoza family ruled Nicaragua from 1937 to 1979. In 1979 Sandinista guerrillas, aided by progressive Catholics and Protestants, defeated the national guard and took over the government. In the Nicaraguan Catholic Church there have been intense political divisions between the conservative hierarchy and the left-wing progressive clergy and lay leaders (the so-called popular church).

EARLY AND MODERN LEADERS For more than 30 years the main Roman Catholic leader in Nicaragua has been Miguel Obando y Bravo, who was appointed archbishop of Managua in 1970. Throughout the 1970s he moved the church away from supporting the brutally repressive and corrupt Somoza regime. Nevertheless, under his leadership the church hierarchy remained closely allied with the upper and middle classes. Obando y Bravo frequently clashed with the left-wing Sandinista government and rebuked priests who were actively involved in it. He was made a cardinal in 1985.

MAJOR THEOLOGIANS AND AUTHORS Ernesto Cardenal (born in 1925) has published numerous critically acclaimed poems and essays and various theological studies. He became a priest in 1965 and founded a community, Nuestra Señora de Solentiname (Our Lady of Solentiname), on a small island in Lake Nicaragua, where poor farmers learned to apply the gospel to their own lives. He became involved in the guerrilla movement against the Somoza regime in the 1970s. After the Sandinista military victory he was appointed minister of culture. The Catholic hierarchy threatened with sanctions all priests who were active in the Sandinista government, and Cardenal was thus reprimanded several times. Pope John Paul II personally admonished Cardenal by lifting a rebuking finger to him at the Managua airport in 1983.

HOUSES OF WORSHIP AND HOLY PLACES The central Catholic building in Nicaragua is the cathedral on the Plaza de la República in Managua. The original cathedral was destroyed in an earthquake in 1972, and a new cathedral was finished in the 1990s. Many colonial-style churches can be found in León and Granada.

WHAT IS SACRED? La Purísima (the Most Pure Lady, which is a reference to the Virgin Mary) is the patron saint of Nicaragua and, as such, is a powerful symbol for the country's Roman Catholics. A statue of la Purísima, also known as la Virgen del Trono (the Virgin of the Throne), was reportedly taken to Nicaragua in 1567 by Pedro de Ahumada, the younger brother of Saint Teresa of Avila. It is kept in a shrine at the Basílica de Nuestra Señora de la Inmaculada Concepción (Basilica of Our Lady of the Immaculate Conception) in El Viejo. Other popular patron saints in Nicaragua are San Sebastián (Saint Sebastian), Santiago (Saint James the Greater), and Santo Domingo (Saint Dominic).

HOLIDAYS AND FESTIVALS The main Catholic holidays in Nicaragua are Christmas (*Navidad*) and the Holy Week (*Semana Santa*) during Easter (*Pascua*). These have a profoundly national character; the entire country closes down for about a week for each holiday.

Each town and city in Nicaragua has annual celebrations (*fiestas patronales*) for its patron saints. These usually take the form of elaborate processions and mock battles in which masked figures satirize the Spanish conquerors. Well-known patron saint's days include those in honor of San Sebastián in January and in honor of Santiago in July.

Wealthy Catholics celebrate the fiesta of la Purísima in December by giving gifts (drinks, sweets, fruits, or toys) to friends and neighbors and by paying for lavish fireworks displays. The fiestas in August celebrating Santo Domingo, the patron saint of Managua, are the largest in scale and participation.

MODE OF DRESS The dress code for annual celebrations and Sunday Mass is quite formal in urban areas. Men generally wear dark trousers, light shirts, and ties. Women wear skirts, blouses, and dresses in modest colors. The mode of dress is less formal in rural areas.

DIETARY PRACTICES There are no particular dietary practices observed by Roman Catholics in Nicaragua.

RITUALS On Sunday all Catholics are supposed to participate in the celebration of Mass, but only about 10–20 percent of all Nicaraguan Catholics actually do. Other important rituals are the annual feasts of the patron saints and a few national pilgrimages, such as to the basilica in El Viejo.

RITES OF PASSAGE The baptism ceremony, performed a few weeks after birth, is an important social event. First Communion takes place at age eight, when young boys and girls are dressed nicely for the first time that they will be allowed to partake in the sacrament. Boys usually wear dark trousers, light shirts, and ties; girls wear dresses in pastel colors. The importance of going to confession has decreased since the 1960s, although some clergy members have been trying to revitalize the practice. Upper-class Catholics with good clergy contacts are the most likely candidates to be administered the last sacrament on their deathbeds.

MEMBERSHIP Because many Catholics left the church in the 1970s and 1980s to become active in Protestant churches, the main objective of the Roman Catholic Church in Nicaragua has been to retain its members. In 1957 the church started a radio station, Radio Católica. Cardinal Obando y Bravo personally funded a second radio transmitter, Radio Estrella del Mar, in 1995. Its prime objective is evangelization, both among Catholics and among Protestants. The church gets much exposure on the three national television stations. The Catholic Church in Nicaragua also has a strong and well-organized presence on the Internet.

SOCIAL JUSTICE During the Sandinista era (1979–90) the Nicaraguan bishops stressed respect for human rights. Since 1990 church leaders have emphasized the importance of education for the poor.

SOCIAL ASPECTS The Roman Catholic Church in Nicaragua is staunchly pro-family, and its family morals are highly conservative. Premarital sex is discouraged, the use of contraceptives is strictly prohibited, and divorce is forbidden. Sexual fidelity is expected of both men and women. The church is a powerful lobbying group against abortion, birth control, divorce, and euthanasia.

POLITICAL IMPACT Since its days as a colonial administrative power, the Catholic Church in Nicaragua has been deeply involved in the country's politics. Until the 1930s the church formed political alliances with conservative governments against the perceived threats of economic liberalism and anticlericalism. In the 1940s and 1950s the church's concern was combating communism and Protestantism. The Social Christian Party was formed in 1957.

As the Somoza regime became increasingly corrupt and repressive in the 1960s, the Catholic hierarchy gradually distanced itself from it, finally rejecting it in the

1970s. Throughout the 1970s the Nicaraguan bishops criticized the regime and the social situation. The church distrusted the leftist ideas of the Sandinista rebels, however, and it did not openly support the Sandinistas until 2 June 1979, six weeks before their final military victory.

After the Sandinistas took power, their relations with the church became strained. The conflict was essentially a political power struggle over the control of Catholics. On one side, progressive Catholics (the lower classes, left-wing intellectuals, priests, friars, and lay leaders) sympathized with the reformist ideas of the Sandinistas. On the other side, the conservative church hierarchy wanted to control its progressive priests and to avoid divisions within the church. With the support of Pope John Paul II the Nicaraguan church marginalized Catholics who supported the Sandinistas, disciplining priests and expelling lay leaders.

Since the 1970s the main division in the Roman Catholic Church in Nicaragua has been between the official church and the popular church. The latter consists of base communities (local groups in which poor people learn to discuss the Bible to reflect upon their own experiences with poverty and injustice) and other lay groups, and it emphasizes devotion to saints. The popular church was reported to be highly active in the 1980s, in part because the poorer sectors were disappointed by the official clergy's backing of the Somoza dictatorship. The 1990 elections marked a new political era of neoliberal governments that protected the interests of the Roman Catholic Church.

CONTROVERSIAL ISSUES There is a wide gap between the official opinions of the church and the actual practices of Roman Catholics in Nicaragua. Abortion, birth control, euthanasia, and divorce are all forbidden by the Catholic Church. However, 50 percent of all sexually active women in Nicaragua use contraceptives. Abortion is illegal but is clandestinely practiced in private clinics. The occurrence of divorce is hard to measure, since many Nicaraguans live together in common union without being officially married in the church.

CULTURAL IMPACT The major cultural impact of Roman Catholicism in Nicaragua has been on architecture, art (especially painting), and poetry (for example, the work of Ernesto Cardenal). The Sandinista government strongly supported the arts (literature, painting, pottery, theater, music, and crafts) through the Ministry of Culture, which was headed by Cardenal for many years.

Other Religions

The first infringement on the Catholic religious monopoly in Nicaragua was the arrival of the Moravian Church in 1849. It converted many members of the black and Miskito Indian populations on the Caribbean coast. After 1900 U.S. missionaries from the Central American Mission, from the older Protestant churches (Adventist and Lutheran), and from the new Pentecostal churches (such as the Assembly of God) further undermined the Catholic stronghold in Nicaragua.

The first period of Protestantism in Nicaragua, roughly until 1965, was characterized by institution-building by missionaries. In the late 1960s the first boom of Protestant churches took place, aided by the high number of missionaries, social turmoil, and the successful In-Depth Evangelization campaigns. The 1980s were the second Protestant boom period. Protestant membership growth continued at high rates until 1990, when about 15 percent of the Nicaraguan population considered itself Protestant.

The 1965–90 Protestant growth explosion in Nicaragua was actually a Pentecostal boom. Pentecostalism had become the religion of the urban poor, especially in Managua. A few possible factors in the Pentecostal boom were intensive evangelization, the emotional appeal of Pentecostalist practices (faith healing, speaking in tongues, singing, and swaying), and dissatisfaction with Catholicism. Since the 1960s the Pentecostal churches, originally led by foreign (mostly U.S.) missionaries, have increasingly come under the leadership of Nicaraguans. Unlike the Roman Catholic Church, many Pentecostal (and Protestant) churches had a good relationship with the Sandinista government after it deposed the Somoza regime in 1979.

In the 1990s the Brazilian-based *iglesias de los cines* (cinema-churches) became a religious phenomenon in Nicaragua. They lure members away from other churches by renting cinemas on Sundays to demonstrate spectacular faith healings.

Henri Gooren

See Also Vol. I: *Christianity, Lutheranism, Pentecostalism, Seventh-day Adventist Church, Roman Catholicism*

Bibliography

Barrett, David B., George T. Kurian, and Todd M. Johnson. *World Christian Encyclopedia: A Comparative Survey of Churches and Religions in the Modern World.* 2nd ed. 2 vols. Oxford: Oxford University Press, 2001.

Hawley, Susan. "Protestantism and Indigenous Mobilisation: The Moravian Church among the Miskitu Indians of Nicaragua." *Journal of Latin American Studies* 29, no. 1 (1997): 111–29.

Johnstone, Patrick, and Jason Mandryk. *Operation World.* Carlisle, Calif.: Paternoster Publishing/WEC, 2001.

Samandú, Luis. *Revisión de tendencies en el evangelismo actual en Nicaragua.* Zeist, Netherlands: ICCO, November 2001.

Williams, Philip J. *The Catholic Church and Politics in Nicaragua and Costa Rica.* London: Macmillan, 1989.

———. "The Catholic Hierarchy in the Nicaraguan Revolution." *Journal of Latin American Studies* 17 (1985): 341–69.

Niger

POPULATION 10,639,744

MUSLIM 86 percent

AFRICAN INDIGENOUS BELIEFS 13 percent

CHRISTIAN AND OTHER 1 percent

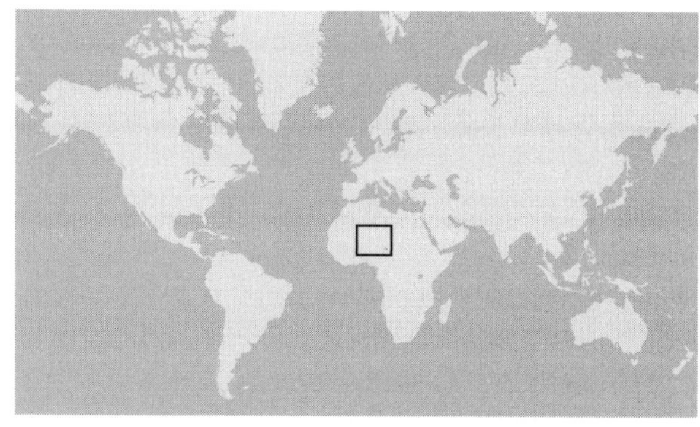

Country Overview

INTRODUCTION Located in West Africa, the Republic of Niger is bordered by seven countries: to the north by Algeria and Libya, to the east by Chad, to the south by Nigeria, to the southwest by Benin and Burkina Faso, and to the west by Mali. Although Niger is the largest country by area in the region, 80 percent of its land is desert. The rest consists of savannas. Garden farms occupy the land along the Niger River in the southwestern portion of the country. Niger is one of the world's poorest countries, and more than 40 percent of the country's budget consists of foreign aid and gifts.

Of the many ethnic groups in the country, the Hausa are the largest, representing more than half the population. The Songhai, Zarma, and Dendi together make up roughly 20 percent of the population; the Tamajeq and the Fulani, about 10 percent each; and the Kanuri, about 5 percent. About 2 percent of the population are Arabs.

The majority of Nigerois are Muslim. They belong to the Malikite school, one of the four schools of law in Sunni Islam, which is based on the teachings of Malik ibn Anas (died in 795). Islam came to Niger from North Africa in the tenth and eleventh centuries. As in much of the rest of West Africa, Islam was first embraced by the aristocracy and people in cities. It was only in the nineteenth century that Islam made great gains in Niger, advancing into rural areas. In Niger Islam has incorporated various African indigenous beliefs, though strong efforts are being made, through the establishment of Islamic cultural centers and universities, to move the country toward a purer form of Islam.

Despite the small percentage of Christians (Catholic and Protestant) in Niger, Christianity has a long history in the country. It began in the seventh century, when Christian Berbers, driven out of North Africa by Muslims, migrated to Niger. Over time descendants of these early Christian migrants melted into the general population, adopting the beliefs and practices of other peoples. Christianity did not reappear in the country until the late nineteenth century, when the French introduced Roman Catholicism.

RELIGIOUS TOLERANCE Relations between Christians and Muslims in Niger are generally good, and conversions from Islam to Christianity are allowed. There are friendly contacts between individuals and official groups representing the two religions. For example, on the 50th anniversary of the Catholic Church in Niger (19 January 1998), Sheikh Abubakar Hassim of Kiota congratulated Bishop Guy Romano of Niamey, sending a message of friendship to him. Even so, incidents of intolerance and intimidation have occurred. In the mid-1990s Muslim fundamentalists tore down posters promoting condom use and family planning.

Muslims have shown a great openness to Christian messages, although few have converted. The Christian radio station ELWA (Eternal Love Winning Africa) has a considerable Muslim audience. In addition, a number of Fulani, who are predominantly Muslim, have become Christians as a result of contact with Christian famine-relief workers in the Sahel area.

Nigerois dance with palm leaves at celebrations commemorating the birth of Mohammed. Mawlid al-Nabi, Mohammed's birthday, is celebrated as a public holiday in Niger. © TIZIANA AND GIANNI BALDIZZONE/ CORBIS.

Major Religion

SUNNI ISLAM

DATE OF ORIGIN 1000 C.E.
NUMBER OF FOLLOWERS 9.2 million

HISTORY Islam came to Niger in the tenth and eleventh centuries from North Africa by way of neighboring West African countries. For centuries merchants were Islam's primary representatives in the region. The ruling elites embraced the religion as an aid in the administration of their territories, providing a means of unifying Niger's varied ethnic populations.

In the early nineteenth century Islam was spread beyond the elites by Usman dan Fodio (1754–1817), a Fulani cleric. Having once served at the court of the Hausa kingdom of Gobir, he declared a jihad in 1804 to defend the more strictly Islamic community he had established within the kingdom. Leading to Islamic control of the region, the jihad brought concepts of rule and administration that have persisted to the present day. In particular, the Shariah (Islamic law) provided a common system of moral law that would apply not only to the smallest village courts but also to the presidential palace. As Islam became the dominant religion in the area, it helped unite the Nigerois under a common religious identity and through shared social and cultural practices.

In 1922, after trying for more than two decades to bring the region under their control, the French established a colony in Niger. The French administration was aided by a number of Nigerois religious leaders who also wielded political power, for political rule in Nigerois societies was never exclusively secular. Despite this cooperation, some Nigerois sought independence from France and saw the Fulani jihad as a precedent for a common, religious-based movement. After Niger became an independent country in August 1960, Hamani Diori (1916–89) was elected president. Diori became the virtual dictator of Niger, and ethnic rivalry predominated over Islamic unity as his fellow Zarma came to treat the state as their communal property. The military removed Diori from office in 1974, and Niger subsequently experienced further coups and assassinations.

EARLY AND MODERN LEADERS The territorial conquests of Sonni Ali (died in 1492), head of the Songhai Empire, helped the spread of Islam in the region, as had further expansion of Songhai territories under Askia Muhammad I (died in 1528). In the early nineteenth century, the leaders of the Islamic jihad in West Africa, including Usman dan Fodio, helped introduce Islam to the masses of Niger.

This nineteenth-century jihad led to the rise of various Islamic political centers in Niger. Unfortunately these new powers had little desire to follow the precepts of Islam concerning social justice. In addition to spreading Islam, the jihad encouraged slavery as a means of dealing with the many prisoners taken during the fighting. Slavery was also used in establishing new states, such as Damagaram (now Zinder), where Tanimu (emir 1841–43 and 1851–84) and his heirs were able to keep their autonomy in the midst of rapid political change in the Sahel area.

Other leaders included the Hausa emirs (*sarki*), who were theocratic rulers of their states, and Tuareg nobles, considered Islamic scholars and leaders. Zarma chiefs were chosen not only for their aristocratic descent but also for their spiritual powers. These powers, however, were never exclusively Islamic; rather, Islam displayed a syncretic genius in incorporating traditional spiritual powers into its faith. Local spirits had to be appeased, and leaders gained their power through their ability to placate the spirits. In turn, people became attached to their leaders largely on spiritual grounds, which strengthened political and economic ties.

MAJOR THEOLOGIANS AND AUTHORS There have been no major Muslim theologians or religious authors in Niger.

HOUSES OF WORSHIP AND HOLY PLACES The major mosque in Niger is in the capital, Niamey. The mosque in Yaama, built by local villagers using mud bricks, is considered one of the world's great mosques because of its innovative use of traditional materials. Mosques in Niger are equipped with loudspeakers, which are used to broadcast the word of Islam.

WHAT IS SACRED? Muslims in Niger hold the same views concerning the sacred as Muslims elsewhere. Many also follow traditional practices, such as offering sacrifices to spirits, and recognize within them sacred elements. Because these "pagan" practices are prohibited by Islam, they are mainly done in secret.

HOLIDAYS AND FESTIVALS Muslims in Niger generally observe the month of Ramadan, fasting each day until sundown. The main Islamic feasts—Id al-Fitr (marking the end of Ramadan) and Tabaske, or Id al-Adha (Feast of the Sacrifice)—can last up to 10 days in various regions of Niger. Many Nigerois Muslims observe Christmas, at least as a secular holiday, and various local holidays are tied to Islamic practice. Friday, the Muslim Sabbath, is considered a sacred day. Other Muslim holidays recognized in Niger include Mawlid al-Nabi, the Prophet Muhammad's birthday, and *al-isra wa-l-miraj,* the anniversary of the Prophet's journey to Jerusalem and his ascension to heaven.

MODE OF DRESS Nigerois Muslims tend to dress like other West African Muslims. Men typically wear long robes and turbans (or skullcaps), which is also the style of Muslim men in northern Nigeria. Others have modernized their dress, wearing Western trousers and a caftan (with a head covering) in a manner similar to that of Yoruba Muslims in western Nigeria. Women in Niger usually wear a wraparound skirt, called a *pagne,* with a matching blouse and headscarf. Men and some women dress in white for Friday afternoon prayer at the mosque.

DIETARY PRACTICES The dietary practices of Muslims in Niger are similar to those of Muslims elsewhere. They are not supposed to eat pork or drink alcohol. Some also refrain from smoking tobacco as a religious practice. Animals slaughtered for meat must be killed in the manner stipulated by Islamic law. Meat, moreover, is cooked thoroughly so that blood is not part of the meal; the eating of any blood product is prohibited.

RITUALS Muslims in Niger generally follow the same Islamic rituals found elsewhere in the world. Friday afternoon is the time for religious services, which men and women attend separately. Huge crowds gather in Niamey, the capital, to listen to the reading of the Koran and to hear imams explain its meaning.

Nigerois Muslims hold naming ceremonies for boys and purification ceremonies for women who have just given birth. Weddings are usually arranged by the families of the bride and groom. The local imam officiates at the marriage ceremony. Sometimes proxy marriages (in which one of the participants is absent) take place; in these instances, the bride and groom sign a marriage contract.

Burial of a deceased Nigerois Muslim should take place within a day of death. A widow must be secluded after the death of her husband. She generally refrains from contact with members of her village for a specified period—usually four months, with local variations. A widow must refrain from sexual intercourse during the *iddat* (also *idda*), or waiting period, which must be completed before she can remarry. A pregnant widow must wait until after the delivery of her child and purification to remarry.

Although all Nigerois Muslims belong to the Malakite branch of Sunni Islam, there are variations in ritual practice, some coinciding with membership in one of the mystical Sufi brotherhoods, each of which has its own secrets and rituals. Divisions within Nigerois Islam also follow ethnic, regional, and social lines. Many rural Hausa rituals are only superficially Muslim, combining local traditional practices with Islamic ones. Belief in traditional spirits persists, and rituals involving these spirits, such as sacrificial offerings, are still common. Such rituals tend to be conducted by family members, though specialists are needed to perform the rituals for curing illness. Some Muslims also follow forms of sorcery and "soul eating," which aid practitioners in dealing with the stresses of their personal lives and the tensions that result from change.

RITES OF PASSAGE Islamic men go through several rites of passage in Niger. Circumcision and naming ceremonies are the earliest such rites. When a boy becomes a man, around the age of 13, he is permitted to wear the *babban riga,* a long robe. The birth of her first child and first son mark important milestones in a Muslim woman's life. Marriage is an important rite of passage for both women and men.

MEMBERSHIP Muslims in Niger actively seek converts to the faith. They use television, radio, and the Internet to attract people to Islam. They also use traditional methods of evangelization, going to villages and using loudspeakers mounted on trucks or in mosques as they preach and read the Koran.

Of the Sufi brotherhoods found in Niger, the Tijaniyya has the largest membership. The Qadiriyya and the Sanusiyya also have significant followings in the country. The competition for members among the brotherhoods has led to conflicts among their *mallams* (leaders trained in religious law), as well as violence.

SOCIAL JUSTICE Muslims in Niger have a strong sense of social justice. Members of the faith are directed to give to charity, to provide aid to fellow Muslims, to seek justice in relationships, and to work toward peace. Historically in Niger there has been a great deal of tolerance toward members of other faiths, and the government has worked hard to continue that tradition. Islamic leaders in Niger have willingly cooperated in this effort.

SOCIAL ASPECTS Muslims in Niger are opposed to abortion and birth control. Divorce is easy for men, and difficult for women, to obtain. The father is the undisputed head of the family, and after a divorce weaned children stay with their father. Despite these restrictions, the Shariah, or Islamic law, is not part of the official code in Niger (as it is in a number of states in neighboring Nigeria).

POLITICAL IMPACT Islam has been a major political force in Niger since its arrival in the Middle Ages, and became even more so after the Fulani jihad of the early nineteenth century. In contemporary Niger there are some who support a stricter adherence to orthodox Islam and who believe that an Islamic state would solve the country's problems, such as poverty, corruption, immorality, and Western secular influence on society. Advocates of an Islamic state see hope in Niger's extreme poverty, given the appeal of fundamentalist Islam in other impoverished countries. Nevertheless, the government of Niger has discouraged those who wish to set up an Islamic republic, and Nigerois Muslims tend to get along well with their Christian neighbors.

CONTROVERSIAL ISSUES Muslims in Niger tend to take conservative stands on marriage, the role of women, and other social issues. They are against birth control and abortion, and they favor the dominance of men in marriage. Men can obtain divorces easily, while women cannot. There is no stigma attached to the education of women, however, and women do play a role in the political life of Niger.

Prior to the military government of Ibrahim Baré Maïnassara (1996–99), there were riots in which Muslim fundamentalists stoned women who dressed in a manner they considered inappropriate. Although some underlying unrest has persisted, greater tolerance and a spirit of compromise have been shown. For example, Nigerois women no longer wear miniskirts publicly, but they are able to hold important government positions. Women from other African countries wear veils and gloves in public, but foreigners are allowed to consume alcohol openly.

CULTURAL IMPACT Islam has strongly influenced Niger's music, art, and architecture. Notable is the

Yaama Mosque, built of handmade mud bricks, which is one of the world's most beautiful mosques. Because Islam discourages the depiction of the human form in art of any kind, decorative art has flourished in Niger. The Hausa are known for their beautiful embroidered robes of indigo dyed cloth, which reflect the influence of Islamic traditions of dress.

Other Religions

The French brought Catholicism to the country in the late nineteenth century, and a number of Catholics remain, especially in the urban areas. The connection to the French has brought prestige to Catholicism, and relations between the Catholic bishop and Muslim leaders have been good.

Protestants, Mormons, and especially evangelical Christians have also been active in Niger. Mormons from the United States have increased their proselytizing efforts, traveling in pairs in neat black suits. Their persistence has earned them a respectful hearing, and they are known for their unfailing goodwill and courtesy. The Christian holidays of Christmas and Easter are public holidays in Niger.

African indigenous beliefs, mixed or unmixed with Islam, remain a force in Niger, exerting a strong hold on most people in the country, regardless of their ostensible religion or position in life. Central to this tradition are various spirits, each of whom is believed to perform a particular function. Various spirit ceremonies performed by traditionalists are also attended by Muslims, albeit quietly. Traditionalists, along with Muslims and Christians, have continued to use sorcery and other forms of magic. Sorcery, a ritualistic form of magic, is found especially in the city of Zinder, where it is used to help people cope with problems in daily life.

Other religions found in Niger include the Bahai faith, Hinduism, and Judaism, but their numbers are small.

Frank A. Salamone

See Also Vol. I: *African Indigenous Beliefs, Islam, Sunnism*

Bibliography

Baum, Robert M. *Shrines of the Slave Trade: Diola Religion and Society in Precolonial Senegambia.* New York: Oxford University Press, 1999.

Faulkingham, Ralph H. *The Spirits and Their Cousins: Some Aspects of Belief, Ritual, and Social Organization in a Rural Hausa Village in Niger.* Amherst: University of Massachusetts Department of Anthropology, 1975.

Glazier, Stephen D., ed. *Anthropology of Religion: A Handbook.* Westport, Conn.: Praeger, 1999.

Greenberg, Joseph. *The Influence of Islam on a Sudanese Religion.* New York: J.J. Augustin, 1947.

Kilaini, Method. "Ecumenism in a Multi-Religious Context." *The Ecumenical Review* 53, no. 3 (2001): 357.

Parrinder, Geoffrey. *African Traditional Religion.* London: Hutchinson's University Library, 1954.

Stoller, Paul, and Cheryl Olkes. *In Sorcery's Shadow: A Memoir of Apprenticeship among the Songhay of Niger.* Chicago: University of Chicago Press, 1987.

Nigeria

POPULATION 129,934,911

MUSLIM 50 percent

CHRISTIAN 40 percent

TRADITIONAL 10 percent

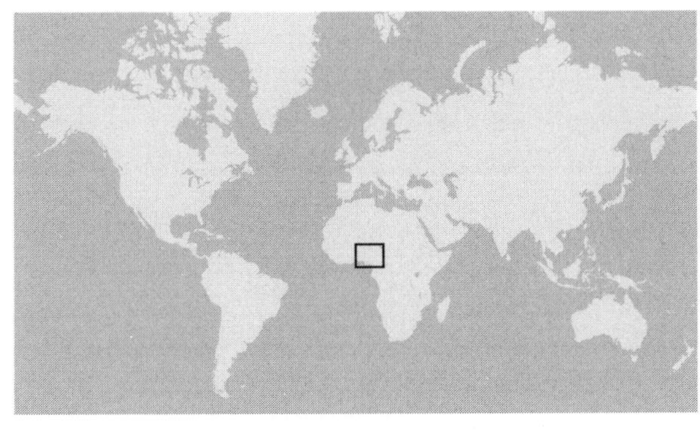

Country Overview

INTRODUCTION The Federal Republic of Nigeria, located in western Africa, is the most populous country on the continent. It is bordered to the south by the Gulf of Guinea, to the east by Cameroon, to the northeast and north by Chad and Niger, and to the west by Benin.

Nigeria is a country of striking geographic, ethnic, and religious diversity that, over the decades, has been a source of its strength as well as its weakness. According to ethnographers, its ethnic groups number between 250 and 400. The three largest are the Hausa-Fulani in the north, the Yoruba in the southwest, and the Ibo (Igbo) in the east. Other groups include the Kanuri, Edo, Tiv, Nupe, Ibibio, and Ijaw. The religious composition of the country—as well as the tumultuous relations today among the three major faiths (traditionalism, Islam, and Christianity)—is the result of several influences, including migrations over the centuries, beginning perhaps around 300 B.C.E.; the impact of the slave trade (fifteenth to nineteenth centuries); and the imposition of British colonial rule, spearheaded by the Royal Niger Company, between 1861 (when Lagos was annexed as a colony) to 1914 (the date marking the unification of the Northern and Southern Nigerian protectorates).

Even before its independence from Britain on 1 October 1960, Nigeria had a difficult religious environment. Northern Nigeria, Islamized since the eleventh century and unified culturally by a religious war waged by the Fulani from 1804 to 1808, hesitated to join Southern Nigeria and Lagos as a unified country. Northern Nigeria feared the loss of political and religious autonomy to its more Western-educated and Christianized neighbors. Today Nigeria continues to be an unstable country threatened by military coups and religious disharmony, despite its substantial economic resources, democratic elections, and powerful position within the Economic Community of West African States (ECOWAS), the Organization of Petroleum Exporting Countries (OPEC), the African Union (AU), and the Commonwealth of Nations.

RELIGIOUS TOLERANCE The 1999 Nigerian constitution guarantees religious freedom. The Islamic northern states, however, have slowly introduced various codes of the Shari'ah (Islamic law) and have attempted to impose them over every citizen in Northern Nigeria, which has led to chaos. The federal government has been unable

Young Muslim and Christian girls line up at the start of a lesson at the main secondary school for girls. About 40 percent of the Nigerian pupils are Christians and wear their traditional headdress, while 60 percent are Muslims and wear the Islamic hijab (headscarf). © AFP/CORBIS.

or unwilling to resolve the situation. As a result of fighting between Muslims, Christians, and traditionalists, as well as infighting among Muslims and Christians, tens of thousands have been killed since the mid-1960s.

Major Religions

ISLAM

CHRISTIANITY

ISLAM

DATE OF ORIGIN Eleventh century C.E.
NUMBER OF FOLLOWERS 65 million

HISTORY Islam initially came to Northern Nigeria from North Africa in the eleventh century through the proselytizing efforts of merchants and traders along the Trans-Saharan caravan routes. As in most of West Africa, Islam in Nigeria, beginning with the Kanem-Bornu and the Hausa states, was initially an urban phenomenon, becoming the religion of the Hausa elite and the royal palace dwellers. Once the kings and chiefs had embraced the new faith, the populations felt pressured to follow suit because becoming a Muslim meant higher social status, greater business and economic opportunities, and interaction with an international community of Muslims strategically placed in the Middle East and having a long history of intellectual and economic achievements. By the sixteenth century Islam was flourishing in the north. The west and east, later to be part of Nigeria, resisted the political encroachment of the northern emirs, who tried not only to gain converts to Islam but also to incorporate the new faithful in a political system based on the laws of Islam and Middle Eastern traditions; the latter effort was seen in the spread of Arab culture and the Arabic language in prayer and education.

The resistence to Islam, especially by the Yoruba and Ibo, led to increased tensions in the area, as did the perception by Muslims that their faith was not being practiced in its pure North African form, which proscribed such traditional beliefs and practices as ancestor veneration, the spiritual power of images (sculpture, masques, charms, and amulets), and consultation of traditional healers and charlatans. In 1804 a Fulani Muslim leader, Usuman Dan Fodio, declared a jihad, or holy war, against all Hausa states that did not practice pure Islam (beginning at Nupe and then across the Niger River) to convert what the Muslims called the "pagans"—those who were not Muslim or who did not practice pure Islam. By 1808 Dan Fodio had achieved his goals and placed emirs at the head of Hausa-Fulani theocratic states, of which the emirate of Sokoto was supreme. Dan Fodio's army and followers were unable to convert the Yoruba in the "middle belt," as well as in the southwest, except for a few pockets, and the east. Thus, the north became predominantly Muslim, and most of the southwest and the east became fertile ground for Anglican and Roman Catholic missionary work, respectively. In the north Muslim brotherhoods, such as the Qaddiryia and the Tijanyia, were active in promoting Islam. From 1861 to 1914 Nigeria, consisting of the colony of Lagos and the Northern Nigeria and Southern Nigeria protectorates, was administered separately by the British, who allowed the north to maintain most of its political, social, and religious traditions as long as it paid taxes and did not obstruct the trade routes and the exercise of minimal colonial activity, such as visits by colonial officers and the establishment of administrative buildings, schools, and hospitals. Missionary work in the north was proscribed by the British.

The different approaches of the British toward Lagos, Northern Nigeria, and Southern Nigeria had several consequences, including the division of the future nation along religious lines; the creation of educational disparity, resulting in more Western-educated Christian and traditional ethnic groups in the southwest and east; and, in Northern Nigeria, a subtle resistance to independence and a tendency toward viewing its own leaders as the natural inheritors of the colonial state, even if that entailed the use of force. Thus, most of the military coups in Nigeria have been engineered by northerners, and the country's religious violence has been a result of the exclusion of non-Muslims in the north from major civil and military responsibilities, the continuous imposition of the Shari'ah in the 12 northern Muslim states, and efforts by Muslims to establish an Islamic Supreme Court with jurisdiction over any litigation that involves Islamic issues.

After Nigeria's independence from Britain in 1960, religion continued to be a divisive issue. During Nigeria's civil war (Biafran War, 1967–70), for example, conflicts between the Hausa and Ibo led to the killing of Ibo Christians in the north. Beginning in 2000 thousands of people died from interethnic and religious violence in Plateau State and other parts of the country. In Yelwa, one of the middle belt towns where neither Muslims nor Christians predominate, more than 600 Fulani Muslims and non-Muslim Tarok died in fighting with Christians in May 2004.

Intrareligious harmony, especially among Christians, has been explicitly courted through an ecumenic movement called the Christian Association of Nigeria (CAN), established in 1976. Yet the same cannot be said of Islam and Christianity and between Islam and traditionalism, most notably in the north. Indeed, CAN was established not only to unite Christians but to fight the intrusion of Islam in government affairs, the introduction of Shari'ah codes into the legal system, and what is perceived by non-Muslims as a backdoor effort by Muslims to make Nigeria a member of the Organization of the Islamic Conference.

Although some Nigerian Muslims, especially the young, supported the Islamic militant terrorist attacks in the United States on 11 September 2001, there is little evidence that the fundamentalist movement, openly advocating violence against the West, has taken root in the country. The feared Maitatsine Kano cult of the 1970s and 1980s, which claimed to have divine revelation superseding that of the prophet Muhammad, attracted large, rural, poverty-stricken masses, in the process causing violent intra-Muslim confrontations. Its impact has, however, subsided, and the sect is no longer a threat to Islam or other religions in the country.

EARLY AND MODERN LEADERS Religious and military leader Usuman Dan Fodio (1754–1817) unified the system of government and the laws of the Hausa-Fulani states. As the emir of Sokoto, he ensured that the states followed Islamic law and recognized his authority as supreme. The early nationalist leaders—Sir Ahmadu Bello (1910–66) of Sokoto, grandson of Dan Fodio and premier of Northern Nigeria in 1954, and Sir Abubakar Tafawa Balewa (1928–66), teacher, member of the Northern People's Congress, and Nigeria's first prime minister—are fondly remembered by many Nigerians, including Christians and traditionalists. Nigeria's Muslim spiritual leader is the Sultan of Sokoto, a position held by Alhadji Mohammad Maccido at the beginning of the twenty-first century.

MAJOR THEOLGIANS AND AUTHORS Muslim scholar Imam Alhadji Abubakar (1911–81) of Kagora was educated in Europe and was distinguished as a newspaper editor, one of the founders of the Northern People's Congress, and a member of the Northern House of Assembly and the Nigerian House of Representatives. He also wrote short stories and a novel in Hausa, his native language.

HOUSES OF WORSHIP AND HOLY PLACES The mosque is the only house of worship and the main holy place among Muslim Nigerians, even though people pray in their homes and during community activities. These events, such as meetings and celebrations, almost always begin and end with prayers to Allah. Cemeteries are respected as holy places.

Mecca is the most sacred of all places of worship. Thus, each Nigerian Muslim aspires to make a pilgrimage to it at least once in his or her lifetime. The trip to Mecca is so popular among wealthy politicians and businesspeople that the term *hajj* (pilgrimage to Mecca) is often used to refer to any successful trader and businessperson.

WHAT IS SACRED? In addition to mosques, the Koran and Islam's traditional written sources are sacred to all Muslims, including Nigerian Muslims.

HOLIDAYS AND FESTIVALS Nigerian Muslims celebrate the birth of the prophet Muhammad, the beginning and end of the fasting month of Ramadan, and the day three months after returning from the *hajj*.

MODE OF DRESS The customary Muslim dress code stresses the importance of never showing parts of the body, especially those of women, that might arouse the viewer. In accordance with this code, Nigerian Muslim men wear the usual Muslim boubou, a long garment that reaches to their feet, with a white or red cap that is wound with a white cloth (sign of pilgrimage to Mecca). Women wear a dress down to their feet, sometimes with a head veil. Those women who have made the *hajj* wear a white robe.

DIETARY PRACTICES Except for abstinence from pork, camels, and horses, Nigerian Muslims observe no specific dietary practices. Nigerian Muslims, as is the case with every devout Muslim in the world, fast during Ramadan. Even though many Nigerian Muslims do not observe it, drinking alcohol was forbidden in 2004, and so was smoking. The state of Kano banned alcohol sales in hotels and bars, normally owned by Christians, and imposed a heavy fine of 50,000 *naira* for each offense, angering the area's businesspeople.

RITUALS Apart from Friday prayers and the observance of the five pillars of Islam—*shahadah* (profession of faith), *salat* (prayer in the morning and at midday, sunset, midnight, and dawn), *zakat* (alms to the poor), *ruza* (fasting during the month of Ramadan), and hajj—no significant rituals occur among Nigerian Muslims. Naming and circumcision for both male and female children normally occur eight days after birth and are important occasions celebrated by the immediate family and relatives.

RITES OF PASSAGE For Nigerian Muslims birth (followed by infant naming and circumcision), weddings, and funerals are important rites of passage, all of which are accompanied by prayers to Allah and by visits from relatives and elaborate meals. Funerals are not as elaborate as those for Christians and traditionalists. The deceased is washed and covered with perfumed clothes, shown to the praying mourners, and buried.

MEMBERSHIP As a proselytizing religion, Islam in Nigeria uses its ulama (religious leaders or scholars), brotherhoods, politicians, converts, and compulsory almsgiving to gain new members. Newspaper ads, television appearances, and radio programs have attracted prospective converts. Conversion to Islam is affirmed by a bath symbolizing the purification of one's soul, submission to Allah, and acceptance of the Prophet's place in the Islamic faith. Today, however, Islam in Nigeria relies primarily on the household offspring who automatically increase the number of the faithful; for this reason Nigerian Muslim women are expected to marry early and bear many children.

SOCIAL JUSTICE Apart from Islamic teaching about the equality of people before Allah and the giving of alms to the poor, nothing special distinguishes Islam from other religions that promote human rights and educational opportunities for all Nigerians. Nigerian Muslims insist on the adoption of the Shari'ah (Islamic law), which imposes severe punishment for adultery (stoning), stealing (cutting off one's arm), and drinking (flogging). In addition, gambling, changing one's religion (a capital offense), and the mixing of men and women in mosque and classroom seating are punished by fines, stigmatization, and beatings.

SOCIAL ASPECTS Nigerian Muslims forbid premarital sex and favor large families. According to Islamic belief, men may have up to four wives, and Nigerian Muslims frequently uphold this tradition. Although remaining single is tolerated, Muslims expect their children, especially females, to marry, and most do so at an early age.

Theoretically women are equal to men, but they do not participate in political decisions, do not hold high positions in religion, and have strictly defined roles in society, with household and agricultural chores being their most common obligations. Inheritance and divorce favor men. A notable case of discrimination against women occurred in 2003 when Amina Lawal, a single Muslim woman who bore a child after her divorce, received the death sentence by stoning. In that case there was such an international outcry that a higher court declared the Muslim court's decision unconstitutional, and the woman's life was spared. Men, on the other hand, can do whatever they wish following dissolution of matrimony.

POLITICAL IMPACT Because of their greater population and their traditional view that religion and state are inseparable, every political position of importance in the north is held by a Muslim. Since 1966 most of Nigeria's military leaders have been northern Muslims, and so have been the members of the Federal House and Senate representing the northern states. Muslims, like Christians, have overwhelmingly voted for presidential candidates of their own religion and ethnic group.

CONTOVERSIAL ISSUES Believing in the sanctity of life and the need for a large family, which guarantees the survival of the lineage and of Islam, Nigerian Islamic tradition and teaching reject abortion and artificial means of preventing conception, except when the life of the mother is at stake. Muslims in Nigeria are opposed to the use of condoms for HIV/AIDS prevention and preach total abstinence. In January 2001 Ibrahim Umar Kabo, leader of Kano's State Islamic Council, forbade Muslims from attending an AIDS seminar sponsored by the U.S. Agency for International Development and Johns Hopkins University, claiming that it would contribute to sexual promiscuity. In regard to other health matters, Muslims in Nigeria have forbidden their children from being inoculated against polio, arguing that it is harmful and anti-Islamic, thus slowing the eradication of this infectious and crippling disease in Nigeria and Africa as a whole.

CULTURAL IMPACT The impact of Islam in Northern Nigeria has been enormous. Northerners, in fact, see themselves primarily as Muslims rather than Nigerians. Arabic and the Hausa language are preferred over English, and many favor Islamic over Western education. Mosques, such as the one in Lagos, and other buildings, such as the emir's palace in Sokoto and the sultans' residences in the north, reflect Islamic Middle Eastern architectural style. Northern Nigerians are ambivalent about music, especially from the West, with its perceived titillating, sexist, and violent message.

CHRISTIANITY

DATE OF ORIGIN 1472
NUMBER OF FOLLOWERS 52 million

HISTORY Christianity initially entered Nigeria from the coast of the Gulf of Guinea. Portuguese seamen and merchants and Roman Catholic priests landed in Lagos and the Kingdom of Benin in 1472, and there is evidence that, by 1515, several Catholic churches and schools had been established, including some at the royal palace of Benin. Until the nineteenth century, however, the focus on the slave trade in the region impeded the spread of Christianity in Nigeria. Christian evangelization resumed when former slaves returned from Brazil in 1848, determined to Christianize the area by reintroducing the Catholic Church, or the *ijo aguda,* as the Nigerians called it. It was not until 1868, however, that Catholic missionaries resumed in earnest their work in Lagos and the eastern part of Nigeria.

The Church Missionary Society (CMS), or the Anglican Church of Nigeria, moved into Nigeria from Sierra Leone in 1841 through the pioneering work of Rev. J.F. Schön and Bishop Samuel Ajayi Crowther. This Protestant missionary work was reinforced in 1842 and 1843, when Henry Townsend and two Yoruba former slaves, Andrew Whilhelm and John McCormack, traveled to Badagry, Lagos State, and Abeokuta, Ogun State, where they built schools and churches. By 1858 Rev. Crowther had reached Onitsha, Anambra State, and Yoruba territory in the Niger River delta. During the 1890s some African-American churches also made several inroads into Nigeria. The Apostolic Church appeared in Nigeria in 1931. Most of the now popular Pentecostal churches, or "prosperity churches" (so called because of the theme of prosperity in their preaching), entered the country during the 1970s and have continued to grow at the expense of the Catholic and Anglican churches, especially in the southeast. Presbyterians began their missionary work in the Ibibio Niger Delta in the early 1900s, followed after 1945 by the Brethren, Jehovah's Witnesses, and Seventh-day Adventists.

By the eve of independence in 1960, the religious lines in Nigeria had been drawn: The Hausa-Fulani in the north were predominantly Muslim; the Yoruba in the southwest, predominantly Protestant (Anglican and Methodist); and the Ibo in the southeast predominantly Roman Catholic, while the small denominations found adherents in both the southwest and the southeast. In the process several breakaway syncretic Christian churches, including those from Yoruba land that were called *aladura,* emerged. Their major distinguishing feature has been the emphasis on free cultural expression during services. The breakaway syncretic churches and small denominational churches include the Brethren Church of Nigeria, Church of the Lord (*aladura*) in Lagos, Lutheran Church of Christ in Nigeria, Methodist Church, Nigerian Baptist Convention, Presbyterian

Church of Nigeria, Deeper Life Ministries, Redeemed Church of God, Living Church Chapel, Rhema Chapel, Christ Chapel, New Covenant Church, Mountain on Fire Ministry, Celestial Church of Christ (*aladura*), and Cherubim and Seraphim Church (*aladura*). Today independent Christian churches are constantly emerging, mainly in the south, and are allowed to function freely as long as they obtain an official permit.

EARLY AND MODERN LEADERS It is impossible to single out each of the celebrated leaders in the history of Nigeria's Christianity. The Anglicans remember Bishop Samuel Ajayi Crowther (1809–91), a missionary and explorer and the first African (Yoruba) Anglican bishop. Another celebrated early Anglican leader is Dr. Majola Agbebi (1860–1917), a teacher who worked with all Christian denominations and who in 1903 founded his own church. He also served as the editor of four Nigerian newspapers. At the start of the twenty-first century the Anglicans' best-known leader was Ven. Samuel B. Akinola, the denomination's secretary-general in Lagos.

One of the earliest and best-remembered Catholic missionaries in Nigeria was Father Louis J. Ward (1872–1935), who was ordained as a priest in 1903 and immediately thereafter was sent to Ogboli-Onitsha, Nigeria. He was later transferred to Calabar. He worked tirelessly for 18 years in Nigeria and died from poor health in the United States. Today the Catholic Church has more than 36 bishops, notable among whom are the archbishop emeritus of Onitsha, Rev. Albert Kanene Obiefuna, and Rev. John O. Onaijekan, who for many years has served as president of the Catholic Bishops' Conference. Cardinal Francis Arinze (born in 1932), who was educated in Nigeria and Rome, was ordained as archbishop of Onitsha in 1967 and was made a cardinal in 1985. Arinze became the second Nigerian cardinal, and he is the most visible cleric in the Nigerian Catholic Church. A well-known theologian, Arinze resides in Rome, where he is a member of the Sacred Congregation for the Evangelization of the Peoples. His name has been floated in discussions of candidates for the papacy.

Presbyterians remember Rev. Hope Masterton Waddel of Jamaica, who was sent to Calabar in 1846. He initiated the building of churches and schools and successfully fought against the killing of slaves after the death of a chief or king. He also helped end the practice of murdering twins, whose birth was considered unnatural. W.F. Kumuyi (born in 1941) is the acclaimed founder of the Deeper Life Ministries in Nigeria and a university professor. The Apostolic Church prides itself on its founder, Apostle Joseph Ayo Babalola (1904–59), one of the most publicized Christian healers in West Africa and the founder of the Teacher Training College at Efon Alaye, Ondo State.

MAJOR AUTHORS AND THEOLOGIANS Cardinal Francis Arinze, a renowned theologian in the Catholic Church, has written numerous books, including *Sacrifice in Ibo Religion* (1970), *Meeting Other Believers* (1997), and *Religions for Peace* (2002). The Anglican theologian Rt. Rev. Joseph Abiodun (born in 1929) received training in Nigeria and England and was ordained as a bishop in 1988. He is known as an articulate defender of democratic principles in Nigeria. The Anglican bishop Samuel Ajayi Crowther, who translated the Bible from English to his native Yoruba language, is also considered a theologian. Among lay people the novelist Chinua Achebe (born in1930) is likely the most renowned of the Nigerian Christian writers, even though his writings are not complimentary of missionary work in Nigeria.

HOUSES OF WORSHIP AND HOLY PLACES Apart from the various churches and chapels (some are elaborate, while others are simply made out of straw and mud) and cemeteries, no Christian holy places or places of pilgrimage exist in Nigeria. Those who can afford it go to Rome or the Holy Land.

WHAT IS SACRED? Objects related to worship and God, such as medallions, miniature crosses, the Bible, holy water, priestly robes, and saintly images (sculptures and paintings), are sacred. The tradition of associating certain objects with the divine is found almost exclusively among the Catholics. For Nigerian Christians no animal or plant is sacred.

HOLIDAYS AND FESTIVALS All Christians celebrate Christmas; Boxing Day (6 December), considered the ideal day for weddings; Easter Sunday; and Easter Monday. Sundays are days of rest, even though Nigerians sometimes work as hard on holy days and Sundays as on weekdays.

MODE OF DRESS Western styles have not supplanted traditional dress in Nigeria. For worship Christians may wear either the traditional long robe, which is folded around the shoulders, and a cap or Western clothing. Consequently, Christians are hardly distinguishable from the traditionalists.

DIETARY PRACTICES Nigerian Christians have no dietary restrictions, except that the consumption of horse meat is forbidden. Fasting and abstinence, even among Catholics, have become matters of individual choice. Moderation in drinking is stressed, yet many Nigerian Christians drink heavily. Seventh-day Adventists are forbidden to eat pork.

RITUALS Most Christian Nigerians still take going to church on Sunday and holy days seriously and dress well for these occasions. Many in the major denominations go on retreats in the mountains or hills or in designated secluded places not only to renew and strengthen their faith but also to counter the successful advance of the Pentecostal and Apostolic church movement in the country.

Christian weddings and funerals are important. The ceremonies themselves are quite elaborate and, at times, long, punctuated with church services and prayers. The process leading to each ceremony seems to have acquired increased importance. For example, weddings are preceded by bride wealth negotiations, guest selection, and examination of the family history of the spouse-to-be. Before a funeral the coffin selection, the embalmment, the wake, and decisions about how, when, and where the deceased is to be buried must take place. As an accompaniment to both rituals, however, excessive eating and drinking are common, especially if the families involved are wealthy. Christian weddings in Abuja (the new capital), especially among the oldest Christian families in the country, are known for attracting even the most distant relatives and Christian acquaintances.

RITES OF PASSAGE For Christians in Nigeria, cyclical rites rejuvenate the church, provide new membership, and make Christian life interesting and meaningful. At baptism the child is given a Christian name; at first Communion he becomes a fully participating member of the community; and at confirmation he becomes a defender of his faith. Matrimony proves the maturity of the participants. With ordination to the priesthood, deaconate, or ministry, the participant affirms a lifelong commitment to God.

MEMBERSHIP Even though proselytizing is allowed, most membership recruitment is done not by campaigning door-to-door but informally, through household tradition, one-on-one conversations, exemplary living, and advertisements of churches and worship services on the radio, in newspapers, and on the Internet, if affordable. People are also inclined to join a congregation through the church choir. As the church has become more Africanized, foreign missionary work has decreased considerably. In fact, the abundance of priests and ministers in Nigeria is such that Nigerians are asked to serve as missionaries in other parts of Africa and, informally, in Europe and in the United States.

SOCIAL JUSTICE The post-independence Christian church in Nigeria has always been the defender of human rights and justice, whether the governments have been civilian or military. One of the best- known church leaders who has continued to speak fearlessly against government human rights abuses, national corruption, disrespect for democratic principles, and the effort to Islamize or desecularize the state is Rev. Anthony Okogie, the Catholic archbishop of Lagos since 1973. Christians have also been vocal agents against the introduction of Shari'ah laws in the north, which they see as being opposed to individual conscience, as the laws call for the punishment of such acts as religious conversion and a woman's giving birth after a legal and religious divorce. Although Nigeria has never been a socialist state, many church schools were taken over by the government prior to the 1990s. At the start of the twenty-first century the church began to recapture its important role in education by running schools where education was free and discipline was stressed.

SOCIAL ASPECTS Whether they live in rural or urban areas, Nigerian Christians still prefer large families and maintain strong bonds with kin. Many Christians question the church hierarchy's stance against polygyny, and the success of the Pentecostal and Apostolic congregations has been partly based on their covert support of polygynous relationships. Many Christians also question priestly celibacy in the Catholic Church because, in the Nigerian spiritual context, marriage and procreation are divine attributes.

POLITICAL IMPACT The political impact of Christianity in Nigeria cannot be underestimated, even though many of the top political and military leaders have been Muslims. Nigeria's president, Olusegun Obasanjo, who was elected in 1999 and reelected in 2003, is a born-again Christian. Christians have prevented the Islamization of the federal republic and have established dozens of civil societies, many of which are based on Christian principles. Today most of those serving in the federal government are Christians, not just because of their Christian upbringing but also due to their Western education.

CONTROVERSIAL ISSUES Nigerian Christians are modern in outlook. Even though they favor large families, they tolerate abortion. The ecclesiastical hierarchy does not oppose the use of such contraceptives as condoms as protection against HIV/AIDS transmission. Divorce is common, and divorcées are no longer shunned. In principle, a woman's role in ecclesiastical life is not restricted in Nigeria, even though the major denominations still find it difficult to treat women as equal to men. In the syncretic and smaller denominations, women may be pastors, deaconesses, prophets, and healers. They are allowed to direct church boards and often lead prayers and conduct services. Women have also been the founders of many of the country's new churches.

CULTURAL IMPACT For many Nigerians, being Western-educated has also meant being a Christian. Missionaries trained teachers, catechists, and interpreters; introduced Euro-Christian music still heard today in Sunday worship; translated the Bible and religious (and secular) literature; and built churches, such as the sumptuous Catholic basilicas in Lagos and Onitsha and the Anglican Saint Peter's Cathedral at Arim in Ibadan. All Christian churches still reflect Christian traditions and values in their crosses, imagery, and seating arrangements. Notwithstanding its lure—most notably in the past—as a symbol of high social status and as a source of educational opportunities, the church has been unable to make Nigerians turn against their cultural traditions of language, attire, art, and folklore, which explains why many Christians still cling to such practices as ancestor veneration and the consultation of traditional healers.

Other Religions

Traditionalists, who account for about 10 percent of the Nigerian population, worship in the ways of their forefathers, who settled in the area as early as 200 B.C.E., as indicated by artifacts of the Nok culture of Western Nigeria. Ethnographers and anthropologists admit that Nigeria has one of the most comprehensive religious structures in Sub-Saharan Africa. It is also assumed that the major Bantu migration that started in Nigeria and Cameroon around 800 to 1000 C.E. influenced the nature of virtually every traditional religion in Sub-Saharan Africa. Moreover, the religion of the Yoruba in West Nigeria has had a far-reaching influence on religions of the New World (Santeria and vodou), a result of the blending of Yoruban religious tenets and the teachings of Christianity among the slave population. Of the various religious traditions of Nigeria, that of the Yoruba in the southwest has received the most attention from Western scholars.

Nigeria's traditional religion entails a complex belief system that posits the existence of a Supreme Being (called *Olorun* or *Olodumare* among the Yoruba), the sole creator of humankind and the universe, who is assisted by powerful spirits (labeled lesser deities by Western scholars), some of whom are anthropomorphically conceived as being male or female. Thus, there is the *orixá* (also *orisha;* spirit or deity) of the earth and fertility, the wind, warfare, fire, rain, and thunderstorms and lightning. In sum, each element and force in the universe is attributed to an *orixá.* Humans function as priests, seers, and healers and may serve as mediators between *Olodumare* and the worshipers. In this comprehensive religious system, ancestors, or the "living-dead," play a prominent role as guardians of the community's values and mores and may appear in visions, dreams, or in a newborn child.

In contrast to indigenous religions in many parts of Africa, Nigeria's traditional religion has maintained recognizable major shrines, such as the Yoruba Osogbo shrine along the Osun River, where pilgrims offer sacrifices, pray, consult an oracle, or heed a divine call to become devout believers or priests or priestesses. Several forests have been designated as sacred or evil (*ajo ofia* in Yoruba), and evildoers and those who have broken long-held taboos are dumped in the *ajo ofia* to slowly die a painful death. Also, in contrast to other parts of the continent, in Nigeria traditionalists have few taboos or sacred animals. Thus, only the camel (among some people) and the dog (among all people) may not be eaten, except when the latter is offered as a sacrifice. Pregnant women are forbidden to consume salty plants and vegetables. Interestingly, among the Yoruba, a dog, a chicken, or a goat that is offered in sacrifice to the Supreme Being or the spirits must be white in color.

Ethnic groups in Nigeria observe several elaborate rites, the most common being the initiation ceremonies. These include male and female circumcision and the incision of ethnic marks (most notably among the Yoruba), both of which usually take place shortly after birth. The festival of the yam (*ogiyan*) is held at the beginning of the planting and the harvest seasons. The masquerade festival (*egungun* among the Oyo people of Ibadan, for example) is a major traditionalist holiday designed to get answers from judges or cultural experts hidden behind the masks. During *egungun* participants pray for the health of children and their success in life, and the festival also commemorates the brief return of dead ancestors to ensure that the living inhabitants and their relatives are doing well on earth. Most of these festivals are accompanied by music, dance, libations to ancestors, eating, and drinking, which at times makes it almost impossible to differentiate the secular from the religious. Perhaps the most elaborate and lively festivals occur among the Urhobo of the Niger Delta. Each year hundreds of people gather to witness the verbal fighting and performance competition among the different clans. Each clan has a hero—an acknowledged poet, storyteller, orator, or someone who knows the opposing clan's or spokesperson's weaknesses—who insults and humiliates opponents with words. The Urhobo adopted this peaceful method of "beating" the enemy through words and performance after growing tired of interclan warfare.

In Nigeria every traditional ethnic group maintains secret societies that have both secular and religious purposes. These societies participate in ceremonies (such as offering sacrifices to God, the spirits, or the ancestors; partaking of a special meal; or pouring a libation) that take place during child naming (usually on the ninth day of the infant's life), weddings, and funerals. Funerals may take several days and may be reenacted for the benefit of those family members who missed the burial. For days after a man has died, his widow—or widows, if he had more than one wife—may carry on loud conversations with her deceased husband.

Traditionalists hold that life is sacrosanct. They ascribe greater value to the community than the individual; thus, fairness is a required virtue of every community. The evil act of an individual affects the whole community and its leaders. In this context, justice must be rendered by appropriately compensating the offended individual and atoning for the community as a whole through sacrifice, libation, and restitution.

Traditional religion in Nigeria disapproves of the Western practices of abortion and contraception, including the use of condoms to prevent HIV/AIDS, and upholds the need for a large family. Women, lest they be accused of being prostitutes, may not drink, smoke, use vulgar language, or advocate the use of artificial means to prevent pregnancy (except naturally spaced conception). For social and economic reasons, polygyny is the right of every man who can afford to formally marry more than one wife. Divorce is still hard to obtain because it involves families (at times clans) and restitution of all or part of the bridewealth.

Traditional religion's membership is guaranteed by households in which children are raised with the expectation that they will adopt their parents' belief system. Thus, proselytizing or missionary work among Nigerian traditionalists has never been practiced, even though the presence of traditional priests is common. In this social milieu, while their roles are ascribed and mostly revolve around household chores, farming, and socializing children, women, especially among the Yoruba and Ibo, hold important positions in the religious domain as priestesses, officials, and leaders. Some serve as fortunetellers, counselors, advisers, healers, and litigators. Yet, notwithstanding this "liberal" treatment of women, those undergoing their menstrual period are forbidden to touch sacred objects and may not officiate at community worship for at least seven days. In addition, it is taboo for a man to have intercourse with a woman at the time of her menstruation. Twins, who in the distant past were killed at birth by certain ethnic groups, are still not completely welcome as they are considered to be abnormal and a bad omen. It is believed that, in contrast to an animal, a human being should give birth to only one child.

Even though Islam and Christianity are expanding at the expense of traditionalism, the political and cultural impact of traditionalism is considerable in Nigeria. Muslim and Christian politicians court traditional priests and healers, both to attract votes through them and to secure their help in predicting and influencing their political fortunes. That some traditional beliefs and practices are upheld by even Christians and Muslims educated in the West attests to the power of traditional religion, which informs both the spiritual and secular lives of Nigerians, whatever their professed faith. While in today's Christian churches, the tendency has been to revert to African dance, language, and songs, with offerings at the altar that are in tune with African farming tradition and festivals, traditionalists are attempting to modernize themselves by wearing Western attire and building shrines of cement and zinc (considered to be a European metal). In addition, their healers are working with medical doctors, nurses, and community health care professionals and leaders. The well-known syncretic congregation of Chief G.O.K. Onyioha in Ibo land (called Godism), the Ogboni Fraternity, and the Erosia National Church in Yoruba land and among the Edo people all represent attempts to modernize traditional religion and ensure its survival and acceptance by other religious groups in the country.

Mario J. Azevedo

See Also Vol. I: *Christianity, Islam, African Traditional Religions*

Bibliography

Ayandele, E.A. *The Missionary Impact on Modern Nigeria: A Political and Social Analysis.* London: Longman, 1996.

Caldwell, Barbara. *Muslim Hausa Women in Nigeria.* London: Longman, 1981.

Enwerem, I.M. *Dangerous Awakening: The Politicization of Religion in Nigeria.* Ibadan, Nigeria: FRA, 1996.

Esposito, John L., ed. *The Oxford History of Islam.* New York: Oxford University Press, 2000.

Gilland, Dean L. *African Religion Meets Islam: Religious Change in Northern Nigeria.* Lanham, Md: UPA, 1986.

Levtzion, Nehemia, and Randall L. Powells, eds. *The History of Islam in Africa.* Athens: Ohio University Press, 2000.

Metz, Helen Chapin. *Nigeria: A Country Study.* Washington, DC: Government Printing Office, 1992.

Ojo, M.A. "The Charismatic Movements in Nigeria Today." *International Bulletin of Missionary Research,* 19, no. 3 (1995): 114–18.

Olajubu, Oyeronke. *Women in the Yoruba Religious Sphere.* New York: State University of New York Press, 2003.

Olaniyan, Richard. *In the Service of God: The Catholic Church in Oyo Diocese, 1884–1994.* Ile-Ife: Bateman Awolowo University Press, 1994.

Oyewole, Anthony, and John Lucas. *Historical Dictionary of Nigeria.* Lanham, Md: Scarecrow Press, 2000.

Peel, J.D.Y. *Religious Encounter and the Making of the Yoruba.* Bloomington: Indiana University Press, 2000.

Peel, John D.Y. *Aladura: A Religious Movement among the Yoruba.* London: Oxford University Press, 1968.

Rasmussen, Lissi. *Christian-Muslim Relations in Africa: The Case of Northern Nigeria and Tanzania Compared.* London: British Academic Press, 1983.

North Korea

POPULATION 22,224,195

JUCHE between 20.0 and 70.0 percent

CHEONDOGYO, BUDDHIST, PROTESTANT, ROMAN CATHOLIC, FOLK RELIGIONIST LESS THAN 0.2 percent

NONRELIGIOUS between 20.0 and 70.0 percent

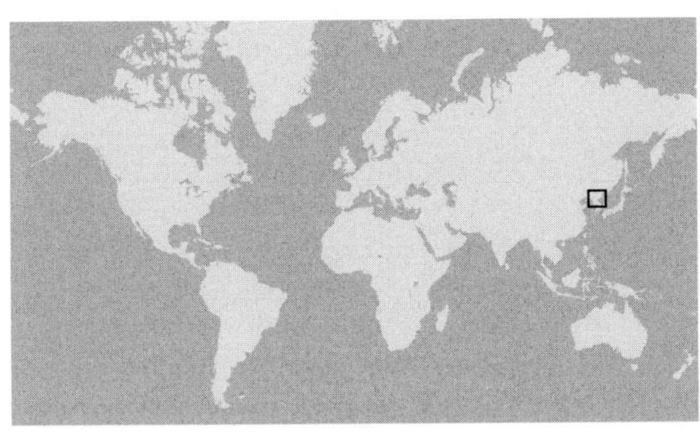

Country Overview

INTRODUCTION Known officially as the Democratic People's Republic of Korea, North Korea occupies the northern half of a peninsula that juts out of northeastern China toward southern Japan. Before North Korea was separated from South Korea in 1945, it was home to a vibrant and pluralistic religious culture. More than half of all the Christians on the Korean Peninsula lived in what is now North Korea. Cheondogyo, a religion founded in Korea in the nineteenth century, had more than twice as many believers in the northern half of the peninsula than in the south. Buddhism, on the other hand, was much stronger in the south. Nevertheless, there were at least 400 Buddhist temples and about 1,600 monks north of Seoul before 1945.

Though there are still a few Christians, Buddhists, and followers of Cheondogyo in North Korea, they are far outnumbered by believers in Juche, a political philosophy with religious overtones promoted by the Communist government of the north. The exact percentage of the North Korean population that believes in Juche is unclear. Close to 20 percent of the population are members of the Korea Worker's Party, which is open only to believers in Juche. Because the government heavily promotes Juche in schools and the media, outside observers assume that more than half of nonparty members may believe in Juche as well.

Government proselytizing of Juche would not have been so successful if Juche had not provided answers to the sorts of questions Koreans have traditionally asked religions to answer. For example, Juche has provided its own moral code emphasizing loyalty and obedience to the government and the ruling party to ensure that North Koreans do not have to turn to Christianity, Buddhism, or Cheondogyo for guidance on how to behave. It has depicted its founder, Kim Il Sung, as a paragon of wisdom and virtue, portraying him as superior in every way to Jesus, Buddha, and any other revered founder of a religion so that North Koreans do not have to look any farther than Kim to find someone to revere and to model their lives after. And Juche has created its own rituals so that North Koreans do not need to enter

North Korean citizens pray during a memorial service for North Korean founder Kim Il Sung at the Kumsusan Memorial Palace. The site has been transformed into a mausoleum preserving his embalmed body and is now described by North Korea as the sacred temple of Juche. AP/WIDE WORLD PHOTOS/ NORTH KOREA CENTRAL NEWS AGENCY.

a Buddhist temple or a Christian or Cheondogyo church to join with others in communal displays of veneration for a power greater than themselves.

RELIGIOUS TOLERANCE Article 68 of the constitution of the Democratic People's Republic of Korea states, "Citizens have freedom of religious belief." That same article adds, "No one may use religion as a means by which to drag in foreign powers or to destroy the state or social order." The North Korean government has used that second statement to legitimize its strict control of all religious activities within its borders. Moreover, the North Korean government adopted Juche as its official ideology, stating in article 3 of its constitution that Juche ideology is "the guiding principle of its actions," making Juche the equivalent of an official religion.

Major Religion

JUCHE

DATE OF ORIGIN 1960s C.E.
NUMBER OF FOLLOWERS 4–16 million

HISTORY North Korea first appears in historical records in 108 B.C.E., when China established an outpost in what is now the North Korean capital of Pyongyang. The Manchurian kingdom of Goguryeo overran Pyongyang in 313 C.E. and a century later, in 427, moved its capital there from southern Manchuria. The Goguryeo court, which controlled northern Korea until 668, borrowed Buddhism from China and made it the official religion. After 668 most of northern Korea came under the control of another Manchuria-based kingdom, Parhae (698–926), which was also influenced by Buddhism from China. When Parhae fell, the north Korean portion of its territory was absorbed by Goryeo (935–1392), the first kingdom to bring almost all of the Korean Peninsula under one government.

Goryeo adopted Buddhism as its official religion but also sponsored rituals honoring local deities and promoted Confucian scholarship. The Joseon dynasty (1392–1910), which replaced Goryeo, withdrew official support from Buddhism and folk religion and made Confucianism the official ideology of the country instead. When Confucianism was challenged by the birth of a Roman Catholic church in Korea in 1784 and the rise of Donghak (now called Cheondogyo), Korea's first indigenous organized religion, in 1860, the Joseon government responded with bloody persecutions. By the time the first Protestant missionaries arrived in Korea in the 1880s, however, the Joseon dynasty had grown too weak to engage in any more religious violence.

Japan absorbed Korea into its colonial empire in 1910, ending the reign of Confucianism. When Japan was forced off the Korean Peninsula in 1945, the peninsula was split in two for the first time in almost 1,000 years. Since September 1948 there have been two competing Korean governments: The non-Communist Republic of Korea has controlled the southern half of the peninsula, and the Democratic People's Republic of Korea has controlled the north. Since 1948 Buddhism, Confucianism, Christianity, and Cheondogyo have declined in North Korea and have largely been replaced by Juche. The Communist government of North Korea strictly controls any religious activity outside of the official state ideology of Juche.

The North Korean leader Kim Il Sung first used the term *juche* (self-reliance) in a formal speech in 1955. Initially he used the term to indicate that North Korea was an independent Communist country and would let neither China nor Russia control it. By 1965, however, Kim Il Sung was presenting Juche as a new ideology, a product of his uniquely Korean genius that superseded the traditional Marxism-Leninism that had been the official ideology of North Korea. The constitution of North Korea was revised in 1972 to show that Juche was now "the guiding principle of its [the country's] actions."

In the 1970s and 1980s Kim Jong Il, the son and future heir of Kim Il Sung, began elaborating on the implications of a philosophy of self-reliance for understanding the place of humanity in the universe. Kim Jong Il explained that traditional Marxist materialism slights the unique position of human beings. Human beings, and only human beings, possess consciousness, creativity, and autonomy, giving them not only the power but also the duty to dominate everything else in the universe and remake the world to better fit human needs.

Kim also explained that Juche philosophy, which he began to call Kimilsungism, recognizes that human beings exist only within societies. Because social relationships define human existence, human beings will continue to exist even after their individual physical lives end, as long as their society continues to exist. Because Juche is an immortal philosophy, all those who hold fast to Juche philosophy and unite around a Juche-led organization under the guidance of a leader who embodies Juche will enjoy an eternal sociopolitical life.

Though the leaders of North Korea have never claimed explicitly that Juche is a religion, it clearly has come to function as such in the lives of those who believe in it. Juche followers believe in the tenets of Juche with the same religious fervor as that displayed by followers of other religions, and they have the same expectation that their faith will be rewarded with immortality. Juche provides explanations of the meaning of life as comprehensive as those provided by other religions. Juche has commandments as obligatory and as wide-ranging as the moral codes of other religions. Juche has rituals that allow its followers to display respect for their founder with the same solemnity shown by followers of other religions when they worship their gods. And even though Juche denies the existence of gods, Juche writings have begun to refer to both Kim Il Sung and Kim Jong Il with language that in other contexts would be interpreted as a reference to a supernatural being.

The emphasis Juche ideology places on the leader's importance led to a growing apotheosis of Kim Il Sung from the 1970s onward. Already in 1967 he was being hailed as the father of the nation, and his mother was hailed as the mother of the Korean race. In 1972 a 20-meter high bronze statue of Kim was unveiled in Pyongyang; it has been a site for ritual displays of loyalty to Kim and his Juche philosophy ever since. Ten years later, in 1982, North Korea used more than 25,000 slabs of white granite to erect the Tower of the Juche Idea, which, at 170 meters, is slightly taller than the Washington Monument. Three years after Kim's death in 1994, the Tower of the Juche Idea was joined by a new granite tower, the Tower of Immortality, which proclaims, in golden letters stretching down its 92 meters, "The great leader Comrade Kim Il Sung will always be with us." Also in 1997 North Koreans changed the way they name the years starting with the year Kim Il Sung was born. Under this new Juche calendar the year of Kim's birth, 1912, became Juche 1, and 1997 became Juche 86.

After Kim Jong Il replaced his father as the actual head of the North Korean government (though the North Korean constitution states that Kim Il Sung remains the eternal president of the country, and the chairman of the parliament is the official head of state), he, too, was elevated far above the status of ordinary mortals. North Koreans are told that on the night Kim Jong Il was born, three stars suddenly appeared in the sky above his birthplace, and in subsequent years his birthdays have been marked by such supernatural events as the appearance of double rainbows above that same site. Kim Jong Il's purported birthplace, a log cabin on Korea's highest mountain, Mount Paekdu, has joined Kim Il Sung's birthplace in Pyongyang as a sacred site visited by pilgrims and newlyweds. Moreover, North Korean media have quoted Juche advocates calling Kim Jong Il "the only savior in the world" and even *hanul-nim,* an indigenous Korean term for the Supreme Being.

The moral code of Juche reflects this emphasis on a godlike leader, using terms that resonate with overtones of Confucianism. When Kim Il Sung was alive, North Koreans were told that they could be truly happy only when their hearts were filled with filial love for him. After his death North Koreans were frequently reminded that the moral principles of the Korean people find their highest expression in a person's absolute loyalty to Kim Il Sung. Though the North Korean government denies that Juche is a religion, the Juche promise of immortality and the language that Juche devotees use to talk about the two Kims make it difficult to deny that Juche functions as a religion for millions of North Koreans.

EARLY AND MODERN LEADERS Kim Il Sung (1912–94) is considered the founder of Juche thought, given that the Korean term *juche* was not widely used until he began using it to refer to his policy of political and economic self-reliance. Moreover, it was Kim Il Sung who had North Korea officially adopt Juche as its "monolithic ideological system." It is his son, Kim Jong Il (born in 1942), however, who is credited with clarifying the implications of his father's ideas in order to provide a comprehensive explanation of the role of human beings in the cosmos, including a promise of sociopolitical immortality for individuals. Kim Jong Il also expanded the range of Juche thought to encompass cultural performances, such as drama, dance, and music. His most influential philosophical essays are "On the Juche Idea," "On Some Questions in Understanding the Juche Philosophy," and "On Correctly Understanding the Originality of Kimilsungism."

MAJOR THEOLOGIANS AND AUTHORS Scholars outside of North Korea recognize Hwang Jang Yeop as the person who turned Juche ideology into a full-fledged philosophy. He authored many of the articles attributed to Kim Il Sung and Kim Jong Il. Before he defected to South Korea in 1997, Hwang had served as president of Kimilsung University, speaker of the Supreme People's Assembly (North Korea's parliament), and secretary of the ruling Worker's Party Central Committee. Hwang, who had majored in philosophy at Moscow University in the late 1940s, claims that in 1967 Kim Il Sung asked him to ghostwrite articles on Juche philosophy to be published under Kim's name. Later Hwang headed a research institute for Juche philosophy in the Organization and Guidance Department of the Worker's Party Central Committee. Hwang claims he defected because, among other reasons, Kim Jong Il had distorted Juche thought by placing too much emphasis on the role of a supreme leader.

HOUSES OF WORSHIP AND HOLY PLACES Because the North Korean government claims that Juche is not a religion, it erects no houses of worship in the usual sense. Students and millions of other North Koreans, however, have made pilgrimages to Mount Paekdu (on North Korea's border with China) to show their respect for Kim Il Sung, Kim Jong Il, and their Juche philosophy. These pilgrimages include visits to such sacred places as the alleged site of Kim Il Sung's headquarters during his struggle against Japanese colonial rule and the log cabin where Kim Jong Il is said to have been born. Foreign visitors to Pyongyang are expected to join North Koreans in paying their respect at various sacred sites around that capital city. Of particular importance are Kim Il Sung's birthplace at Mangyongdae as well as the Kumsusan Memorial Palace, which has been transformed into a mausoleum preserving the embalmed body of Kim Il Sung and is now described by North Korea as the sacred temple of Juche.

WHAT IS SACRED? North Koreans pay special reverence to two flowers: the Kimilsungia (developed in Indonesia in 1975) and the Kimjongilia (developed in Japan in 1988). Both are cultivated in special greenhouses so that devout Juche followers can pay homage on such special occasions as Kim Il Sung's birthday (15 April) and Kim Jong Il's birthday (16 February).

Pilgrims to Mount Paekdu trek to various trees around Kim Il Sung's pre-1945 mountain headquarters, which, it was announced in 1987, still bear slogans carved more than 50 years ago praising Kim Il Sung and Kim Jong Il. Typical slogans found on those trees include "Lodestar General Kim Il Sung, born of heaven" and "The bright star of Paekdu [Kim Jong Il] has appeared over our land."

South Korean sources report that North Korea has more than 35,000 statues of Kim Il Sung, before which devotees bow to show respect and loyalty. As of 2003 no statues of Kim Jong Il have been reported.

HOLIDAYS AND FESTIVALS The period from 16 February (Kim Jong Il's birthda) through 15 April (Kim Il Sung's birthday) is called the Loyalty Festival Period, the most festive period of the year in North Korea. Public celebrations are held throughout the country on the first and last days of this festival period, and in between, students are asked to demonstrate their loyalty by hiking in groups to sacred sites. Reflecting the Juche belief that Kim Il Sung was a sun providing light for all humankind, 15 April has been renamed Sun's Day.

The North Korean government has also preserved such traditional folk holidays as the Autumn Harvest Moon Festival (in the ninth month of the lunar calendar) and Cold Rice Day (in the fourth lunar month). Koreans traditionally visited their immediate ancestor's graves at the time of the Autumn Harvest Moon Festival and on Cold Rice Day. Now they are also expected to lay a bouquet of flowers before a statue of Kim Il Sung as part of the holiday festivities.

MODE OF DRESS No special articles of clothing serve to identify a Juche believer, with one exception. When Kim Il Sung was alive, loyal North Koreans pinned to the left side of their chests a badge with Kim Il Sung's picture on it. That badge can now be replaced by a badge with Kim Jong Il's picture on it. The size of the badge indicates the rank of the badge wearer. The larger the badge, the higher the party or government rank of the person wearing the badge. Nonbelievers are not supposed to wear either of the badges.

DIETARY PRACTICES There are no special dietary practices for followers of Juche.

RITUALS Given that North Korea claims that Juche is not a religion, it has no formal worship services or prayers. Juche believers, however, are encouraged to bow before statues of Kim Il Sung and to place flowers before them every year on the anniversary of his birth. North Koreans are also encouraged to visit such sacred sites as Kim Il Sung's birthplace and Mount Paekdu, which is officially described as sacred to the Korean nation.

Moreover, North Koreans are mobilized in large numbers for "mass games" on special occasions, such as the birthdays of Kim Il Sung and Kim Jong Il. These mass games involve thousands of people marching and dancing in unison to express their love for their country and their loyalty to its leader.

RITES OF PASSAGE There are no Juche clergy to preside over weddings or funerals. When a couple marries, they both swear their loyalty to Kim Il Sung and Kim Jong Il. After the brief wedding ceremony the newlyweds are expected to visit a nearby statue of Kim Il Sung, place some flowers in front of it, and then have their picture taken with the statue in the background. At a funeral it is common for mourners to cry out, "Though this body is deceased, the spirit of the revolution still lives."

MEMBERSHIP Compulsory classes on Juche thought are part of the curriculum at every level in the North Korean school system, from elementary school through university. North Korea has also attempted to promote Juche thought overseas. In 1988 it founded the International Seminar on the Juche Idea, which has headquarters in Tokyo but claims to have branches in more than 100 countries. Every year since 1988 such seminars have been held at various locations around the globe. North Korea also distributes booklets on Juche thought in Japanese, English, French, German, Spanish, Arabic, Russian, and Chinese.

SOCIAL JUSTICE North Korea claims that a society governed by Juche thought will eliminate poverty, provide education for everyone who wants it, and protect human rights. The Juche concept of human rights, however, focuses more on national autonomy than on individual liberty. Juche education teaches students Juche ideology rather than how to think independently and critically. And the elimination of poverty by Juche thought in North Korea has been defined as equal access to whatever health care, housing, and educational facilities are available, whether or not individuals have any discretionary income. North Korea, therefore, criticizes societies that do not follow its Juche ideology as lacking true human rights, failing to provide a proper education, and masking poverty with an abundance of consumer goods.

SOCIAL ASPECTS The family, rather than the individual, is the basic unit of North Korean society, just as it was in Confucian times. North Korea also maintains the Confucian stress on such familial virtues as filial piety. Unlike Confucianism, however, Juche holds that loyalty to the paternalistic leader of the country takes precedence over filial obedience to a biological parent.

In another departure from the Confucian past, men are not allowed to have more than one wife. Divorce is frowned upon today almost as much as it was in the past (except for cases of divorce from someone who is politically tainted). Moreover, though the Juche constitution of 1972 says that "women hold equal social status and rights with men," North Korea remains a patriarchal society, with men occupying the vast majority of the most powerful posts in government.

POLITICAL IMPACT Given that Juche is enshrined in the North Korean constitution as its official ideology, it dominates political discourse. Moreover, because the words of Kim Il Sung, and increasingly the words of Kim Jong Il, are treated as sacred writ, it is tantamount to sacrilege to propose any major changes to government policies introduced in those writings. Significant political or economic reform is therefore difficult, if not impossible, to achieve. In addition, North Korea's relations with other nations are problematic because North Korea expects foreigners who visit Pyongyang, including official representatives of foreign governments, to participate in ritual displays of respect for Kim Il Sung, the founder of Juche thought.

CONTROVERSIAL ISSUES Perhaps the most controversial aspect of Juche is the insistence that human existence has meaning only within a sociopolitical community centered on one supreme leader, to whom all owe undying loyalty. Almost as controversial is the Confucian legacy of respect for hereditary status, which has allowed Kim Jong Il to succeed his father as the only one with the proper bloodline to correctly understand and interpret Juche thought.

Juche thought per se takes no explicit position on issues controversial in other religious traditions, such as birth control or abortion. Juche writings frequently stress the importance of motherhood, and a woman who is still unmarried at middle age is viewed as abnormal. Kim Il Sung called for "making all women communist mothers and fine communist educators for the next generation."

CULTURAL IMPACT Juche has impacted North Korean culture in a couple of ways. First, because Juche began as an assertion of Korean autonomy, North Korean music, drama, dance, literature, and art are supposed to draw more on Korean aesthetic traditions than on foreign models. That means, for example, that Juche music is performed with modified traditional musical instruments in addition to such imported instruments as pianos. Second, the dominance of Juche thought means that all cultural productions must preach Juche ideals. Kim Jong Il's comment on drama is typical of what he has written about dance, music, literature, and cinema as well. He wrote that drama must inspire "the people of our times with the Juche outlook that man is the master of the world" and that it "plays the decisive role in transforming the world."

Other Religions

Until 1945 the major difference between northern and southern Korea was that Koreans in the north were more likely to be a Christian or an adherent of Cheondogyo (an indigenous new Korean religion) than were Koreans in the south. In fact, before 1945 almost 60 percent of Korea's Protestants and 50 percent of Korea's Roman Catholics lived in what is now North Korea, as did more than 70 percent of Cheondogyo believers, even though the population of the northern half of the peninsula was much less than the population of the south. Buddhism and shamanism, on the other hand, were underrepresented in the north. Only about a third of Korea's shamans, and less than 15 percent of Korea's Buddhists, lived in the north. Nevertheless, it is estimated that there were a total of 400,000 north Koreans with a religious affiliation in 1945.

That changed with the founding of the Democratic People's Republic of Korea in 1948. Under pressure from their Communist government to renounce existing religions, almost all of those in the north who had regularly participated in religious activity either fled south or abandoned any public display of their religious beliefs. The result was a sharp drop in the number of people willing to be recognized as religious to less than 40,000.

Cheondogyo (Religion of the Heavenly Way) is the strongest surviving non-Juche religious organization in North Korea. Founded in 1860 as Donghak (Eastern Learning), Cheondogyo is the oldest of Korea's indigenous new religions. Constructed from local Confucian, shamanistic, Roman Catholic, Buddhist, and Taoist elements, Cheondogyo has no links with foreign religious organizations and thus has been viewed more favorably by Communist authorities than have "imported" religions, such as Buddhism and Christianity. Moreover, Cheondogyo is identified with the Donghak peasant rebellion against the Joseon dynasty in 1894, giving it the image of a religion for the oppressed masses. The official Cheondoist Association boasts 15,000 members and 800 meeting halls, and a Cheondogyo political party, the Cheong'u (Young Friends) Party, fills several seats in the North Korean parliament as a junior partner to the ruling Worker's Party. Twice in recent years, in 1986 and again in 1997, leaders of Cheondogyo in the south have been drawn by the greater visibility of Cheondogyo in the north to defect and assume leadership positions in both the Cheondoist Association and the North Korean government. The Cheondoist Association has tried to establish links with another new religion in the south, Daejonggyo, which worships Dangun, the legendary ancestor of the Korean people. Given that there are no representatives of Daejonggyo in the north, the Cheondoist Association has since 1995 been leading the rituals honoring Dangun at the site of what North Koreans claim to be Dangun's tomb.

Buddhists in North Korea are represented by the Korean Buddhist Federation, which claims to have about 10,000 members, served by some 300 monks working in approximately 70 temples. There do not appear to be any major doctrinal differences between Buddhists in North Korea and those in South Korea. Unlike the majority of monks in South Korea, however, monks in North Korea are married and do not shave their heads. Moreover, their clerical robes resemble those worn when Korea was under Japanese colonial rule and are quite different in both color and style from the clerical garb favored by South Korean monks these days. Another major difference between Buddhism in South Korea and Buddhism in North Korea is that there are no nuns in the Korean Buddhist Federation, though there are thousands of nuns in South Korea.

Buddhism is permitted an institutional presence in Juche-dominated North Korea because of the contributions Buddhism has made over the centuries to Korean culture. Buddhist temples in North Korea are maintained primarily as manifestations of the architectural and artistic accomplishments of the Korean people in centuries past, not as sites for worship and religious ritual today. Moreover, the North Korean government in 1988 printed a 25-volume vernacular translation of the Korean Tripitaka to call attention to Korea's history of scholarly achievements, not to promote belief in Buddhism. Another reason the government allows the Korean Buddhist Federation to exist is that monks sometimes provide a useful channel for interaction with Buddhist believers in South Korea and elsewhere.

The same diplomatic benefits North Korea gains from its monks provides the rationale for two official Christian organizations. The Korean Catholic Association has fewer than 5,000 active members. It only has one church, in Pyongyang, and it is still waiting for a resident priest. Nevertheless, Korean Catholics have occasionally been dispatched overseas to explain the policies of the North Korean government to Catholics outside the country. The Korean Christian Federation has served the same purpose with Protestant communities. There are two Protestant churches in Pyongyang, serving a total membership of approximately 10,000. This small community has generated enough interest overseas to attract visits from such prominent Christian leaders as Billy Graham, who visited Pyongyang twice and, in 1992, preached at the Catholic church and at one of the Protestant churches.

Unlike Protestant Christianity in South Korea and most other countries, there are no competing denominations within North Korea's Protestant community. All Protestants in North Korea belong to the same denomination, the Korean Christian Federation. The doctrinal and ritual differences that separated Presbyterians and Methodists before 1945 have disappeared from public view.

Just as invisible is the folk religion that was the dominant religious orientation of the entire Korean Peninsula before 1945. Shamans are the ritual specialists in the folk religion, as well as being its most visible manifestation. Before 1945 shamans in the northern half of the Korean Peninsula were more conspicuous, though fewer in number, than those in the south because northern shamans tended to go into a trance and become possessed by spirits of gods and ancestors during a ritual, while most southern shamans did not. Now, though shamanism thrives in South Korea, no shamans are allowed to perform their rituals in North Korea. Despite the official ban on shamans and the animistic folk religion in which they are embedded, South Korean sources report that the extreme economic hardships endured by North Koreans for most of the 1990s stimulated a revival of folk religious practices, particularly shamanic fortune-telling. There have been no reports in the North Korean press to substantiate such claims, however. The beliefs, and even some of the practices, of Korea's centuries-old folk religion probably survive in North Korea's villages and possibly even its cities. Nevertheless, with no official shaman or folk religion association in North Korea, it is impossible to estimate how many believers and practitioners there are today.

Donald L. Baker

See Also Vol. I: *Buddhism, Christianity, Confucianism*

Bibliography

Kang, Wi Jo. "Christianity in North Korea and Its Future in Relation to Christianity and the Politics of South Korea." In *Christ and Caesar in Modern Korea: A History of Christianity and Politics,* 155–63. Albany: State University of New York Press, 1997.

Kim Il Sung. *Works.* Pyongyang: Foreign Languages Pub. House, 1980.

Kim Il Sung Encyclopedia. New Delhi: Vishwanath, 1992.

Kim Jong Il. *Selected Works.* Pyongyang: Foreign Languages Pub. House, 1992.

Park, Han S. *North Korea: Ideology, Politics, Economy.* Englewood Cliffs, N.J.: Prentice Hall, 1996.

———. *North Korea: The Politics of Unconventional Wisdom.* Boulder, Colo.: Lynne Rienner Publishers, 2002.

Sinbeopt'a. "A Study of Buddhism in North Korea in the Late Twentieth Century: An Investigation of Juche Ideology and Traditional Buddhist Thought in Korea." In *Pukhan pulgyo yeon'gu,* 361–503. Seoul: Minjoksa, 2000.

Norway

POPULATION 4,525,116

EVANGELICAL LUTHERAN 86 percent

OTHER PROTESTANT 2 percent

ROMAN CATHOLIC 1 percent

OTHER RELIGIONS (INCLUDING MUSLIM, JEWISH, BUDDHIST) 2 percent

NONE 9 percent

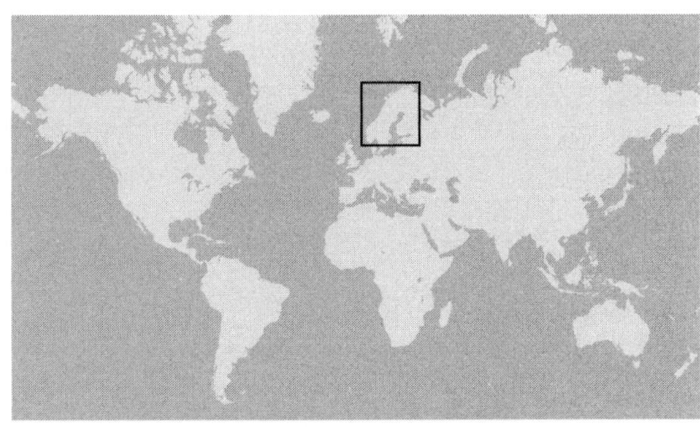

Country Overview

INTRODUCTION The Kingdom of Norway is located on the western side of the rugged, mountainous Scandinavian Peninsula. It is bordered by the Norwegian and North Seas to the west, the Barents Sea to the north, and Sweden, Finland, and Russia to the east.

Norway came to Christianity rather late compared with much of the rest of Europe. Late in the Viking Age (c. 800–1050 C.E.), Anglo-Saxon Christian missionaries struggled to convert the residents from their belief in Norse gods. King Olav I (reigned 995–c. 1000), a Viking who embraced Christianity while in England, returned to Norway to Christianize his subjects. King Olav II (reigned 1015–30), later canonized Saint Olav, consolidated the whole of Norway into a single realm and converted the population to Christianity, by force when necessary, toward the end of the Viking Age. Some elements of the Norse religion persisted until Roman Catholicism established a more secure foothold.

The kingdom, weakened by economic decline and by the Black Death (1349), united with Denmark under one king in 1380. This union continued until 1814. Roman Catholicism remained the religion of the realm until, by royal decree, the Danish king imposed the Lutheran Reformation in 1537. The Evangelical Lutheran Church became the state church, with the king as constitutional head.

Norway experienced a Pietistic movement during the eighteenth century and a popular, or laymen's, revival during the nineteenth century. Lutheranism in Norway often has had two centers of activity: the state church and the revival movement. After some initial conflict with the church administration, the revivalists were integrated into the state church. Norway is also home to a smaller number of other Protestant denominations, Catholics, Jews, Muslims, and humanists.

RELIGIOUS TOLERANCE Religious freedom in Norway is constitutionally guaranteed. Citizens are considered members of the state church unless they officially join another religious community or decline state church membership. The church is supported jointly by funds

A wooden stave church in Heddal, Norway. The approximately 30 surviving medieval wooden stave churches, the oldest of which was constructed in 1070, are architecturally the most striking church buildings in Norway. © CHARLES & JOSETTE LENARS/CORBIS.

from national and local governments. Other registered faith communities can receive state and local government funding in proportion to their membership. An ecumenical Council for Religious and Life Stance Communities provides representation and a voice for a wide range of religious communities.

Major Religion

EVANGELICAL LUTHERANISM

DATE OF ORIGIN 1537 C.E.
NUMBER OF FOLLOWERS 3.9 million

HISTORY The Evangelical Lutheran Church was founded in 1537, when King Christian III of Denmark-Norway imposed the Lutheran Reformation. It became an autonomous state church when Norway declared its freedom from Denmark in 1814. Attacked that year by Sweden, Norway was united with Sweden until achieving total independence in 1905.

The nineteenth century was marked by several popular religious awakenings inspired by Hans Nielsen Hauge (1771–1824), who began preaching and writing in 1796. Between 1804 and 1814 Hauge was imprisoned several times for violating the Conventicle Act, which prohibited laymen from preaching the gospel, an activity reserved for the clergy. Hauge's laymen's movement triumphed, after his death, with the repeal of the Conventicle Act in 1842, allowing greater freedom for lay preachers. Despite the tension with the rationalist clergy, Hauge recommended against leaving the state church. In the 1850s–60s Professor Gisle Johnson inspired another popular awakening.

In the next decade the debate over lay preaching continued, and in 1884 lay preachers were allowed to use church premises in addition to the laymen's prayer houses. The lay movement also established a theological training college in competition with the state university's theological department. Pressured by this Pietistic movement, the church also faced attack from secular cultural leaders who challenged many of its beliefs. The church was further democratized with the introduction of local parish councils in 1920, diocesan councils in 1933, the National Council in 1969, and diocesan synods and the General Synod in 1984. An eight-member Sami Church Council was established in 1992 to deal with church matters for Norway's indigenous minority community.

EARLY AND MODERN LEADERS Hans Nielsen Hauge inspired an important nineteenth-century laymen's revival movement that challenged the exclusive authority of the clergy. The Bishop's Conference, an official body since 1934, has provided much of the church leadership. Eivind Berggrav, appointed bishop of Oslo in 1937, was instrumental in the church's resistance to the German occupation during World War II. Bishop of Oslo Gunnar Stålsett became spiritual adviser to the royal family beginning in the 1990s.

MAJOR THEOLOGIANS AND AUTHORS Among Norway's internationally known twentieth-century theologians are Sigmund Mowinckel, Einar Molland, Thorleif Boman, Ragnar Leivestad, and Jacob Jervell. Nationally

Kristian Schjelderup, Eivind Berggrav, and Per Lønning stimulated discussion of the role of the twentieth-century church, while during the first half of the century J.C. Heuch and Ole Hallesby defended the core ideas of the revival movement. Among authors who challenged the church's contemporary teaching was Philip Houm, who first shook the establishment with a critical book of theology in 1965.

HOUSES OF WORSHIP AND HOLY PLACES Each of the 1,300 parishes has a church building belonging to the state church. Many parishes also have meeting or prayer houses that serve revivalist groups, such as the Inner Mission. Architecturally the most striking church buildings are the approximately 30 surviving medieval wooden stave churches, the oldest of which was constructed in 1070. Trondheim's Nidaros Cathedral, the destination for medieval pilgrims visiting the shrine of Saint Olav, Norway's patron saint, is historically the most significant of Norway's cathedrals.

WHAT IS SACRED? According to the constitution, Evangelical Lutheranism is the state church, and the person of the king is inviolable, his office is for life, and he is the (highest) chief of both the state and the church. The sacraments celebrated in the church ritual are sacred.

HOLIDAYS AND FESTIVALS Evangelical Lutherans recognize the same holidays as other Christians in Norway. Public or religious holidays, celebrated with church services, are New Year's Day, Epiphany, Shrove Tuesday, Palm Sunday, Maundy Thursday, Good Friday, Easter Sunday and Monday, Whit Sunday and Monday, Constitution Day (17 May), Saint Olav's Day (29 July), Christmas Day, and Boxing Day (26 December). Christmas Eve church services often attract church members who attend services only once or twice a year.

MODE OF DRESS At Sunday church services the pastor wears a seasonal liturgical stole, while the congregation wears "Sunday best" clothes, such as suits and ties for men and dresses for women. The colorful *bunad,* derived from regional peasant or folk costumes, is considered proper attire at rites of passage, such as baptisms and weddings, and for secular holidays.

DIETARY PRACTICES The Evangelical Lutheran Church has no food taboos, but some special foods are associated with particular religious holidays. In southern Norway lutefisk, prepared by soaking cod in lye water, is the traditional Christmas dish. Salted ribs of mutton are traditional in western Norway. In other regions roast pork or pork ribs with sauerkraut are preferred for Christmas meals.

RITUALS Sunday services in the Evangelical Lutheran Church normally follow this sequence: an organ prelude, a hymn appropriate to the church calendar, the confession of sin, the *kyrie* (a prayer in the Mass for God's mercy), the prayer for the day, the first lesson (from the Old or New Testament), a hymn of praise, the second lesson, the confession of faith, a hymn, the sermon by the pastor, a hymn, the Lord's Prayer, Communion, a prayer of thanksgiving, a closing hymn, the benediction, and an organ postlude. Church members celebrate the Eucharist, or Communion.

RITES OF PASSAGE Life progress is marked by a combination of sacred and secular celebrations. Baptism signifies a child's acceptance into the Evangelical Lutheran Church. Close family, friends, and godparents attend the ceremony, performed by a pastor. Confirmation, which until 1912 was mandatory for citizens, is the culmination of months of preparation and marks the acceptance by young persons, ages 14–20, of the principles of Lutheranism. Civil confirmations are available for those who do not wish church affiliation. Youths often acquire a *bunad,* or folk costume, at confirmation. Church weddings are the norm. Wedding guests often choose to wear their national costumes. Approximately 94 percent of deaths are marked by church funerals.

MEMBERSHIP While 86 percent of Norwegians belong to the state church, only about 10 percent of the members regularly attend services. The church and associated Lutheran organizations are active in both domestic evangelism and foreign missions. Organizations such as the Norwegian Mission Society, the Norwegian Lutheran Mission, and the Norwegian Santal Mission in India support approximately 800 foreign missionary and aid workers. In addition, the Lutheran Mission to Seamen has established facilities in foreign ports for seamen from Norway's large merchant navy.

SOCIAL JUSTICE Norwegian Church Aid, now an ecumenical organization, is Norway's largest nongovernmental development agency and supports aid and assistance programs in less-developed countries. Church leaders have played an active role, both domestically and internationally, in human rights and social issues. Gunnar Stålsett, bishop of Oslo, has served on the Nobel Peace Prize Committee.

SOCIAL ASPECTS Church weddings are the norm, although secular weddings are not uncommon. Church members are required to bring up their children in the Evangelical Lutheran Church. Godparents, usually selected at the time of baptism, are charged with caring for the child and bringing him or her up in the church in case the parents are unable to do so. Religion and moral issues are part of the school curriculum.

POLITICAL IMPACT The Lutheran state church has been at the center of many political controversies related to the increased democratization of the church. Political parties have increasingly favored loosening the ties between church and state. While Norway has been socially liberal, the church has emphasized the importance of a Christian-based morality.

CONTROVERSIAL ISSUES Following the disestablishment of Sweden's state church in 2000, the movement for separating church and state in Norway has grown. Opinion polls in 2002 revealed for the first time that more than half the sampled population favored disestablishing the state church.

Women have been seeking a greater role in the church. Women pastors were first permitted by an act of the Storting (parliament) in 1938 and were first ordained as state church ministers in 1961. The first woman bishop was appointed in 1993. In 2001 the National Council of the Church of Norway concluded that adoption of children by same-sex partners was permissible. The appointment of gay clergy has created heated controversy within the church community.

CULTURAL IMPACT Much of Norway's literature and art is influenced by the historic struggles within Lutheranism. The nineteenth-century laymen's movement produced religious poetry, tracts, and hymns. In the 1880s the novels of Alexander Kielland (1849–1906) attacked the church obliquely with negative portrayals of clergy. Bjørnstjerne Bjørnson (1832–1910), who won the Nobel Prize in Literature in 1903, struggled with religious themes in his plays and novels, moving from a conventionally religious stance to a more secular perspective late in his career. Norway's greatest playwright, Henrik Ibsen (1828–1906), followed a similar trajectory in his treatment of religion.

Other Religions

Norway is increasingly a multireligious society. The Oslo Declaration on Freedom of Religion or Belief was officially signed by an interfaith coalition of 25 religious groups on 8 November 2001.

One of the largest independent Protestant denominations is the Evangelical Lutheran Free Church of Norway, with approximately 22,000 members. The Norwegian Baptist Union was established in 1845 after the Storting enacted a law guaranteeing religious freedom. Baptist missionaries from England and the United States helped organize the denomination, which currently numbers approximately 10,000. Norwegian Baptists established a theological seminary in 1910 and have supported missionary work abroad since 1920. Originating in a nineteenth-century religious awakening, the Pentecostal movement, with approximately 45,000 members, supports missionaries abroad. In 1998 the Pentecostal Church began assisting foreign refugees and asylum seekers in the Oslo area. Other smaller Protestant denominations include the United Methodist Church, with 14,000 members; Jehovah's Witnesses, with 8,000 members; and the Church of England, with 1,600 members.

Most of the approximately 44,000 adherents of the Roman Catholic Church in Norway were born abroad. Although Catholic practices were banned with the Reformation in 1537, small groups of Catholics continued to practice their faith quietly. Catholics currently worship in three church districts, centered in Oslo, Trondheim, and Tromsø.

Norway's first Jewish community, composed of immigrants from Poland and Lithuania, organized in 1892. Centered in Oslo and Trondheim, the community grew to about 2,000 in the 1930s. During World War II the Nazi occupiers of Norway sent 750 Jews to Auschwitz. Only 25 lived to return to Norway. The small community of Orthodox Jews, which grew after an influx of several hundred refugees from Hungary in 1947, currently numbers about 1,000.

Muslims, originating from the Balkans, South Asia, and Africa, constitute less than 2 percent of the Norwegian population and are concentrated around Oslo

Fjord. Approximately 75 percent of Norwegian Muslims are registered members of a Muslim association. In contrast with the highly organized Muslim population, only about 50 percent of Norway's 14,000 Buddhists have registered as members of Buddhist organizations. With 60,000 members, the Norwegian Humanist Association claims to be the largest humanist organization in the world in proportion to the national population.

The indigenous Sami of northern Norway number between 30,000 and 75,000. While many Sami are active members of the Lutheran Church, traditionally the Sami had spiritual leaders who, in addition to providing moral and religious guidance, were specialists in folk medicine.

Douglas D. Caulkins

See Also Vol. 1: *Christianity, Lutheranism*

Bibliography

Mathiesen, Thomas, and Otto Hauglin. "Religion." In *Norwegian Society.* Edited by Natalie Rogoff Ramsoy, 226–59. Oslo: Universitetsforlaget, 1974.

Molland, Einar. *Church Life in Norway: 1800–1950.* Translated by Harris Kaasa. Westport, Conn.: Greenwood Press, 1957.

Stenius, Henrik. "The Good Life Is a Life of Conformity: The Impact of the Lutheran Tradition on Nordic Political Culture." In *The Cultural Construction of Norden.* Edited by O. Sorensen and Bo Straath, 161–71. Oslo: Scandinavian University Press, 1997.

Thorkildsen, Dag. "Religious Identity and Nordic Identity." In *The Cultural Construction of Norden.* Edited by O. Sorensen and Bo Straath, 138–60. Oslo: Scandinavian University Press, 1997.

Oman

POPULATION 2,497,000

IBADI ISLAM 75 percent

OTHER (SUNNI AND SHIA ISLAM; HINDU) 25 percent

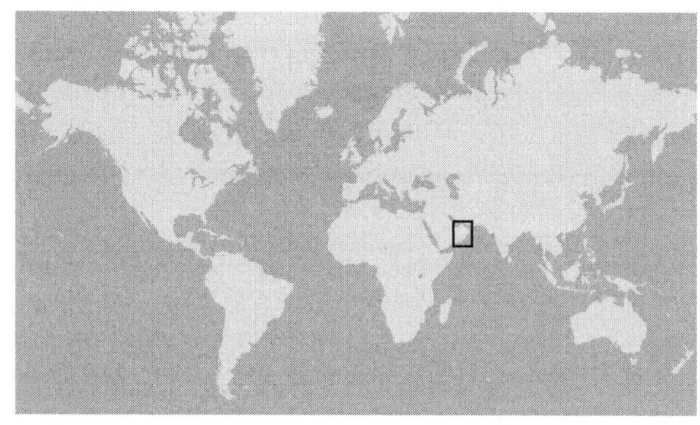

Country Overview

INTRODUCTION Historically, politically, and geographically, Oman is the most isolated part of Arabia. Bordering to the west are the United Arab Emirates, Saudi Arabia, and Yemen. The desert of the Empty Quarter serves as a land barrier to the north, but a 1,700-kilometer coastline along the Persian Gulf and the Indian Ocean enabled Oman to develop into a major maritime power until the nineteenth century. The mountainous interior, a stronghold of Ibadi Islam, is distinct from the more cosmopolitan culture of the coast. The southwestern region of Dhofar is culturally linked with the Hadramawt desert valley of southeastern Yemen and follows the Shafii legal school of Sunni Islam.

The Azd tribe of Oman voluntarily embraced Islam in 627 during the lifetime of the Prophet Mohammad. Azdis from Oman participated in the early Islamic conquests and settled in large numbers in the southern Iraqi garrison city of Basra, where they were prominent opponents of the Umayyad dynasty (661–750). One byproduct of this opposition was the founding of the Ibadi sect, which spread rapidly through Oman. A main focus of Ibadism is the establishment of a government headed by a just "imam," a political and military leader and religious authority, selected by the leading men of the community for his piety. The struggle to establish and maintain such an imamate colors Omani history.

The majority of Omanis are Ibadi Muslims, with Sunni and Shiite Muslims, as well as Hindus, making up the rest of the population. The Hindus and many of the Shiites, especially the followers of the Agha Khan, are Indian immigrants. Ibadis are entirely Omani Arabs; Sunnis are particularly concentrated in the southwestern region of Dhofar; the Shiites are found mainly on the coast.

Omani society is essentially tribal. From the eighteenth century until recent decades, conflicts between two tribal federations—the Ghafiris, claiming north Arabian ancestry, and the Hinawis, claiming south Arabian ancestry—played an important part in Omani politics.

Arabic is the national language of Oman, but there are some small tribes thought to have lived in Oman before the Arabs, and they speak their own unique languages. These are the Qara ("Jibalis"), Mahra, Shera, and Batahira of the south; the Harasis of southeastern corner of the Empty Quarter; and the Kumazara of the Masandam peninsula.

RELIGIOUS TOLERANCE Islam is the official religion of Oman, and Ibadi scholarship and the study of the Ibadi heritage are actively promoted by the government of Sultan Qabus ibn Said. Nonetheless, Ibadis are known for their religious tolerance, and non-Ibadi Muslims are active at all levels of society and government. Hindus and Christians are free to build houses of worship and practice their religion.

Major Religion

IBADI ISLAM

DATE OF ORIGIN 700 C.E.
NUMBER OF FOLLOWERS 1,873,000

HISTORY Jabir ibn Zayd, who originally came from Nizwa in Oman, was a prominent Ibadi leader in Basra in the seventh and early eighth centuries. He was exiled to southern Arabia around 700 C.E. and brought Ibadism to Oman, the only country where Ibadis form a majority. Oman's isolation led to its being favored as a base of Ibadi operations against the Umayyad caliphate by Jabir's successor, Abu Ubayda Muslim ibn Abi Karima.

Ibadism emerged from the Khariji sect, which broke with the main body of Muslims in 657 because they believed Muslim political leaders had failed to follow Islamic law and so should be considered apostates deserving death. The Khawarij (Kharijites) believed that any unrepentant, sinning Muslim ceased to be a believer. Such a person could be killed, his wives and children enslaved, and his property plundered. Whereas the Sunnis claimed that political leadership should be given to a member of the Prophet's tribe, the Quraysh, and the Shiites believed it must be given to the Prophet's cousin Ali and his descendants, the Khawarij said that the most pious person should be selected leader without regard to lineage. The Khawarij withdrew from the rest of the Muslim community and declared war against it. Eventually this form of Kharijism died out.

Ibadis share with the Khawarij rigorous moral standards for leaders, but they refrain from condemning sinning Muslims as apostates. Sinning Ibadi Muslims and non-Ibadi Muslims are to be seen not as *kuffar shirk,* or unbelieving polytheists, but as *kuffar nima,* people who are ungrateful for God's blessings. One should avoid "friendship" (*wilaya*) with such people, but this is really an inner attitude of "dissociation" (*baraa*), not overt hostility or avoidance of social contact. Ibadis strongly condemn Khariji violence toward Muslims of other sects, but they agree with them regarding the stipulations for leadership. A leader must be chosen on the basis of piety, and if he is unjust, he must be removed from power.

The British Prince of Wales shares a meal with Omani Muslims during Id al-Fitr, *the feast that ends the month-long fast of Ramadan."* AP/WIDE WORLD PHOTOS.

The first Ibadi imamate in Oman, established in 749, lasted only two years. The second imamate, established in 793, lasted 100 years. The collapse of the second imamate led to the first theoretical formulations of the nature of the Ibadi imamate. Centuries of political struggles yielded to the 500-year rule of the Nabahina in the twelfth century. The Portuguese arrived in the Persian Gulf in 1507 and seized a number of coastal towns of Oman, including Muscat, in order to control the strait of Hormuz. Their dominion was challenged by both internal rebellion and Ottoman attacks, but the Portuguese retained control of some cities until the mid-seventeenth century, and their forts can still be seen.

A new Ibadi imamate emerged with the founding of the Yarubi dynasty in 1615, which extended Omani rule in the Persian Gulf and East Africa. In 1753 power passed to the Bu Saidi dynasty, which continues to rule in Oman. Despite the theoretical separation of the imamate from considerations of lineage, imams have, in fact, typically been selected along dynastic lines or because of their descent from earlier imams. After 1804 the Bu Saidi rulers of Oman ceased to call themselves imams, and Ibadi centers in the al-Jabal al-Akhdar ("Green Mountain") region generally regarded these sultans as hostile to their religious principles.

Sayyid Said ibn Sultan (ruled 1806–56) transferred the capital of Oman to the East African island of Zanzibar in 1832. In the nineteenth century Zanzibar became a major center of Islamic scholarship. Omani settlements in East Africa resulted in the growth of Ibadi populations there, which diminished in strength due to conversion to Sunni Islam and, finally, the Zanzibar revolution of 1964. After Sayyid Said's death the domains of Zanzibar and Oman were divided among his sons.

In 1868 an Ibadi imamate movement, led by the great scholar Said ibn Khalfan al-Khalili, succeeded in overthrowing Sultan Salim and installing his cousin Azzan ibn Qays as imam. This imamate was overthrown by British power in early 1871, and Turki ibn Said was installed as sultan. A new imamate movement in 1913 succeeded in capturing the mountainous interior of Oman but not in overthrowing the sultan. In 1920 the British-facilitated Treaty of Sib recognized the separation of the domains of the sultan from the domains of the imam. This separation continued until December 1955, when all of Oman was united under the rule of Sultan Said ibn Taymur, who was replaced in a palace coup in 1970 by his son, the current sultan, Qabus ibn Said.

EARLY AND MODERN LEADERS The first imam in Oman was al-Julanda ibn Masud (ruled c. 748–50). Al-Warith ibn Kab al-Kharusi (ruled 795–808) was the first imam of the important clan of Bani Kharus and the first of many imams to take his oath of allegiance in the town of Nizwa, which for centuries was the most important center of Ibadi scholarship and fervor. Imam al-Salt ibn Malik was forcibly removed from the imamate in 886 after a reign of more than 35 years by the scholar Musa ibn Musa ibn Ali al-Anbari, who replaced him with Rashid ibn al-Nazr. Al-Salt's deposition caused great turmoil and discord between the scholars of Nizwa and those of Rustaq. Rashid was in turn replaced in 890 by Azzan ibn Tamim al-Kharusi, but turmoil continued until 893, when Muhammad ibn Nur, acting on behalf of the Abbasid Caliph, al-Mutadid, invaded Oman, killed the imam, and subjected the people of Nizwa to plunder, tortures, and humiliation.

In the tenth century Oman was ravaged by the sectarian Qaramita (Carmathians), and civil war ensued. The next political leader of note was imam Nasir ibn Malik, founder of the Yarubi dynasty in 1624, which expelled Portuguese and Persians from Oman and heralded a new period of Omani expansion. The great leaders of the Bu Saidi dynasty in Oman include its founder, Ahmad ibn Said (1749–83) and his grandson, Said ibn Sultan (1806–56).

MAJOR THEOLOGIANS AND AUTHORS The written collection of hadith (Muhammad's sayings and deeds) that forms the backbone of Ibadi law is by the eighth-century scholar al-Rabi ibn Habib, who was originally from the Batina region of Oman, studied in Basra, and returned to Oman late in life. An important early theoretical discussion of the imamate is by the ninth-century scholar al-Salt ibn Khamis al-Kharusi al-Bahlawi ("Abu l-Muaththir"). Writings by Ibadis from North Africa—the Mzab valley of Algeria, the Tunisian island of Jerba, and the Jabal Nafus region of Libya—are used along with Omani writings. Perhaps the most influential Omani scholar is the tenth-century Abu Said al-Kudami, who elaborated the doctrines of friendship (*wilaya*) and dissociation (*baraa*) and their implications for the imamate.

The early nineteenth century brought a period of renewed scholarship, with such eminent figures as Abu Nabhan Jaid ibn Khamis al-Kharusi (1734–1822) and his son Nasir (1778–1847), who emigrated to Zanzibar in 1831 with Sayyid Said. Nasir's students included Jumayyil ibn Khalfan al-Sadi, author of *Qamus al-sharia,* a 90-volume compendium of Ibadi teaching that is only partially published, and Said ibn Khalfan al-Khalili, leader of the successful imamate movement of 1868–71. The Ibadi "renaissance" extended to the North African Ibadi community, where the most important scholar was the Algerian Muhammad ibn Yusuf Atfayyish (Atfiyash), whose brother visited Oman and whose works were published in Zanzibar. Likewise, Ibadis in North Africa read works by Omani scholars of the nineteenth century. Nur al-Din Abdallah ibn Humayd al-Salimi (1869–1914) is the most influential of all of

Oman's modern scholars. A prolific author in law, theology, and history, he led the imamate movement of 1913.

Notable contemporary scholars include Salim ibn Hamad al-Harithi, mufti in the town of Mudhayrib, Sharqiyya province, as well as the Grand Mufti, Ahmad ibn Hamad al-Khalili. Originally from the island of Pemba in Zanzibar, the Grand Mufti has led the transformation of Ibadism toward rapprochement with Sunni Islam.

HOUSES OF WORSHIP AND HOLY PLACES There are nearly ten thousand mosques in Oman. Traditional mosques in Oman had neither domes nor minarets. They were simple structures of mud and plaster with wooden beams and doors. Some mosques have old inscriptions recording important events. Mosques are built inside the forts found throughout Oman. Smaller mosques are sometimes built far from habitation as places of solitary devotion, and there are also small mosques for women.

Until the 1970s Ibadis in Oman did not gather for the Friday congregational prayer, believing this should be done only in traditional capital cities like Nizwa in the presence of a just Ibadi imam. Sultan Qabus decreed that Friday congregational prayer be observed in all towns. Places of prayer are also set aside specifically for the two feast-day prayers that end Ramadan (the Islamic month of fasting) and the *Hajj* (the pilgrimage to Mecca).

In recent years mosques with domes, minarets, and beautiful inlaid decorations have been built. The most important is the Sultan Qabus Grand Mosque, opened in the Bawshar district of Muscat on 4 May 2001. With a space of 4,160,000 square meters, it can accommodate six thousand men in the main prayer room and seven hundred women in a separate room.

Ibadi Muslims do not build shrines to honor holy individuals, as do Sunni and Shiite Muslims. Consequently, saint's shrines are found only in the Sunni Dhofar region; these include the tomb in Mirbat of Muhammad ibn Ali ibn Alawi (d. 1161) and the purported tomb of Job in the mountains overlooking Salala.

WHAT IS SACRED? Omanis do not venerate plants, animals, or relics, although certain plants and parts of animals may be used for traditional healing, along with verses and the various names of Allah found in the Koran, the holy book of Islam. The Koran is sacred and may be recited in its entirety in a formal gathering to thank God for good fortune or to ensure continued good fortune.

HOLIDAYS AND FESTIVALS Muslims celebrate two main feasts: *Id al-Fitr,* which ends the month-long fast of Ramadan, and *Id al-Adha,* the sacrifice at the end of the Hajj. Both feasts are celebrated over a four-day period with special foods and include elaborate sword dances, singing, and firing of guns. In the non-Ibadi coastal areas, there is more dancing and playing of musical instruments. The Prophet's birthday and ascension through the heavens are also commemorated.

MODE OF DRESS Ibadi Islam does not dictate the mode of dress among Omani men. All Omani men dress similarly, regardless of their religious or political status. They wear the *dishdasha,* an ankle-length white robe with long sleeves and no collar and with a tassel hanging from the right side of the neckline. Traditionally men wore a belt with a dagger (*khanjar*) that had an ornate, decorated sheath; men still wear this on formal occasions. On their heads they wear either a *kumma,* an embroidered flat-topped brimless cap, or a *massar,* a square cloth of cotton or wool with ornate patterns, which is folded into a triangle and tucked in like a turban. Non-Omanis may not wear Omani men's dress. Traditionally men did not trim or shave their beards, but today most do. Head hair is short.

Islamic law requires women to cover all of their body except their face and hands, but aside from that, women's dress varies according to region in Oman. It is often very colorful. Women in Muscat commonly wear baggy trousers gathered at the ankle, over which they drape a large tunic of the same pattern. In the Green Mountain region women wear tighter, heavier embroidered pants and tunics. Outdoors women usually wear a black overgarment (*abaya*) and headscarf. Traditionally they wore face or nose masks, but today these are seen mainly among the Bedouin women.

DIETARY PRACTICES There are no Islamic dietary practices that are distinctive to Oman. Omanis follow the Islamic law that prohibits consumption of pork and alcohol and requires that animals be slaughtered in Islamic fashion. Rice is the foundation of most Omani meals, to which meat or fish is added. Dates, the main agricultural product, are much loved and come in many varieties.

RITUALS Ibadi ritual practices do not differ significantly from those of Sunni Muslims: five daily prayers, with extra prayers at night during Ramadan, fasting during Ramadan, and participation in the pilgrimage to Mecca. Men usually pray in the mosque, while women pray at home. Traditionally Ibadi scholars were divided over the permissibility of performing the Friday congregational noon prayer under the reign of any but a just imam, but it is now normative for all Muslim townsmen to attend. Unlike Sunnis, Ibadis keep their arms down at their sides during the Koran recitation in *salat* and do not say *amin* ("amen") after the recitation of the *Fatiha* (the opening chapter of the Koran).

Nearly all Omanis marry. Islamic law allows a man to have up to four wives concurrently, although some Muslim countries have enforced stipulations to limit polygamy, and Tunisia and Turkey have outlawed it altogether. Polygamy is legal in Oman, but it is not common. Most marriages are arranged by family members, and customarily cousins are preferred over other candidates. As in Muslim societies in general, marriage is a civil contract accomplished through signing a contract before witnesses and payment of the *mahr,* a gift that theoretically goes to the bride, though in practice it often goes to her father. The secular features of weddings include festivities lasting several days, during which men and women celebrate separately. Weddings in the Ibadi interior are far less lavish than those of many Arab countries, or even of the Omani coast, and do not include display of the bloody sheet as proof of virginity, in contrast with many traditional Arab societies.

Omani burial customs do not differ from common Muslim custom. As soon as a person has died, the body is washed, perfumed, and prepared for burial, which should take place in daylight within 24 hours. There is no embalming. The body is wrapped in a white cotton shroud and buried in a shallow grave with unmarked stones noting the position of head and feet; the body is aligned north/south and turned on its side in the direction of Mecca. A close male relative or religious figure leads a prayer on behalf of the dead, and the congregation recites the *Fatiha.* The period of mourning and consolation varies in length, depending on the age, sex, and status of the deceased. When a man dies, his widow goes into mourning for a period of four months and ten days, after which she performs a ritual bath and returns to normal life.

RITES OF PASSAGE There are no Islamic rites of passage that are unique to Oman. Boys are circumcised, but this ritual is not accompanied by great ceremony and may be done any time before puberty.

MEMBERSHIP Ibadis are not particularly known for their missionary zeal, although they are pleased when non-Muslims embrace Islam. Most Ibadis today do not ascribe much importance to the differences between Ibadism and Sunni Islam. Ibadis and Sunnis pray together, intermarry, and share burial grounds. However, a strong distinction is maintained between them and the Shiites, with whom they do not pray or intermarry.

SOCIAL JUSTICE Islamic teaching is very concerned with social justice, especially the care of the poor, orphans, and widows. Thanks to its oil revenues, Oman today is largely free of dire poverty. Nonetheless, charitable endowments and giving are highly valued both culturally and religiously. It is traditional to be especially generous with the less fortunate on the two feast days, and a portion of the animal sacrificed at the end of the Hajj must be shared with the poor.

Until the accession of Sultan Qabus to the throne in 1970, modernization was severely restricted in Oman. There were very few schools, roads, or hospitals. Sultan Qabus embarked on a rapid program of modernization, including the building of schools, hospitals, roads, and other infrastructural developments.

SOCIAL ASPECTS Oman stands out among the countries of the Middle East for the cultural value placed on extreme politeness and self-control. There is a lack of open interpersonal conflict, and social conduct is marked by pervasive civility and tact. Divorce is rare because of the need to avoid the social entanglements that would ensue. Even co-wives who share a house feel pressured to present an appearance of harmony. Emotions are not expressed openly. Outright correction of others, even children, is rare, although all acts are scrutinized; individuals internalize the need for self-control. Behavior that is felt to be morally and personally repugnant, such as homosexual prostitution, is tolerated without any show of indignation. The Omani code of "honor," unlike most of the Middle East, precludes public expressions of one's worth or violence in defense of honor.

For Muslims, marriage is a sacred duty. Formerly, betrothals and weddings were made about the time of puberty, but in the cities many young people postpone marriage until they have completed their education.

Women in towns or villages were traditionally secluded and until recently were rarely educated beyond Koran schools for children. Today both girls and boys go to school in large numbers, although education is not compulsory; the sexes are taught separately. Classes at Sultan Qabus University, opened in 1986, are coeducational, although the library is partially segregated by sex, and cross-gender socializing is banned. Initially all fields were open to women, but in the early 1990s women were barred from the College of Engineering because engineering was seen as incompatible with cultural norms for women. By 1994 women comprised 20 percent of the government work force, mostly in education and health. A significant number of women were employed in the banking and hotel sectors, and about 1,500 women owned their own businesses. Many middle- and upper-class women are professionals, serving as lawyers, doctors, dentists, engineers, bankers, and university professors. The overwhelming majority of women are unpaid agricultural workers and are not counted in labor statistics, which place the percentage of women in the labor force at 8.6 percent.

As in most Arab countries, Omani men and women socialize separately. In Muscat today, however, families often socialize together, walking, picnicking, or playing soccer on the beach.

POLITICAL IMPACT Ibadi Islam is actively promoted by the Omani government but in a manner that largely removes its sectarian dimensions and its traditional emphasis on the need to establish a just imamate. Islamic prayers and sermons often accompany public and military ceremonies, but politically sensitive issues are largely avoided. Preachers in mosques are under government surveillance and must adhere to parameters set by the government. There is little evidence of religiously fueled political opposition in Oman, although an alleged plot against the regime in 1994 was said to have been led by "Muslim militants," some of whom were sentenced to death, although the sultan later pardoned them.

CONTROVERSIAL ISSUES The most controversial issue in the Muslim world today is the role of women in society. The Basic Law of November 1996 declares Islam the official state religion and the Shariah (Islamic law) "the basis for legislation." Although codes have been adopted on commercial, criminal, labor, and tax matters, personal status remains unlegislated, so Islamic law is in effect: Husbands control their wive's ability to work and travel, and they hold unilateral rights to divorce; children belong to the husband's family, so a mother may lose them if she is divorced. The government bans socializing between women and unrelated men.

Sultan Qabus strongly promotes the education and economic participation of women in Omani society, but women are often encouraged to enter fields like social work and teaching, which are seen as consistent with traditional, nurturing female roles. A Directorate General of Women and Child Affairs, established in 1984, supervises the creation of branches of the Omani Women's Association, which teaches women literacy, hygiene, cooking, and housekeeping and provides nurseries.

Social identity is often dictated by tribal membership. In the past, tribal tensions and warfare were a constant feature of Omani society. Although this is no longer the case, the sultan must maintain a balance in his patronage of various tribes.

CULTURAL IMPACT Ibadi religious practice favors simplicity and lack of ostentation. This has been reflected in the plain designs of traditional Ibadi mosques, although recent mosques sponsored by Sultan Qabus are elaborate, ornate monuments to power in the manner of other Muslim royalties. These newer mosques feature soaring minarets, domes, and elaborate inlaid geometric designs and arabesques, all features avoided in the past, although artistic representations of people or animals are still avoided.

Of all artistic endeavors, poetry is by far the most culturally valued and pervasive; traditional Muslim texts were often written in the form of poetry for easy memorization, and poems of a more literary character overwhelmingly express religious and political sentiments rather than love, in contrast to most Arab countries. Ibadis have not developed religiously oriented music, and in general singing, music, and dancing are culturally associated with the descendants of African slaves, although others might enjoy hearing it. There is a royal symphony orchestra, but it plays the classical music of the West. Popular Arab music of Egypt and other countries does not seem to play an important role in Omani cultural life.

Other Religions

The most prominent religious minorities in Oman are Sunni and Shiite Muslims, as well as Hindus. Sunnis and Shiites observe the same holidays as Ibadis, although Shiites also commemorate the martyrdom of Husayn (*Ashura*) in the first month of the lunar calendar. The Shiites have their own mosques and houses of assembly.

Sultan Qabus donated land to build three Hindu temples in the Muscat area and provided them with a cremation ground, despite Muslim aversion to cremation. Hindus celebrate their own festivals, such as *Ganapathi,* the birthday of the elephant-headed god Ganesh, and *Diwali,* the five-day festival of lights that marks the Hindu New Year. Hindus were the first non-Muslims to be accorded Omani citizenship, and some Indian Christians have also been naturalized. There are also at least eight churches serving Christians in Oman, who are all expatriates.

Valerie Hoffman

See Also Vol. I: *Hinduism, Islam, Shiism, Sunnism*

Bibliography

Allen, Calvin H., Jr., and W. Lynn Rigsbee II. *Oman under Qaboos: From Coup to Constitution, 1970–1996.* London and Portland, Ore.: Frank Cass, 2000.

Barth, Fredrik. *Sohar: Culture and Society in an Omani Town.* Baltimore and London: The Johns Hopkins University Press, 1983.

Chatty, Dawn. "Women Working in Oman: Individual Choice and Cultural Constraints." *International Journal of Middle East Studies* 32 (2000): 214–54.

Eickelman, Christine. *Women and Community in Oman.* New York: New York University Press, 1984.

Hoffman, Valerie J. "Ibadi Islam: An Introduction." Islamic Studies, Islam, Arabic, and Religion. University of Georgia. 25 June 2004. http://www.uga.edu/islam/ibadis.html.

Ochs, Peter J. *Maverick Guide to Oman.* Gretna, La.: Pelican Publishing, 1998.

Riphenburg, Carol J. *Oman: Political Development in a Changing World.* Westport, Conn., and London: Praeger, 1998.

Wikan, Unni. *Behind the Veil in Arabia: Women in Oman.* Baltimore and London: The Johns Hopkins University Press, 1982.

Wilkinson, John C. *The Imamate Tradition of Oman.* Cambridge, London, and New York: Cambridge University Press, 1987.

———. *Water and Tribal Settlement in South-East Arabia: A Study of the Aflaj of Oman.* Oxford: Clarendon Press, 1977.

Pakistan

POPULATION 147,663,429

SUNNI MUSLIM 81 percent

SHIA MUSLIM 15 percent

HINDU 2.02 percent

CHRISTIAN 1.63 percent

OTHER.35 percent

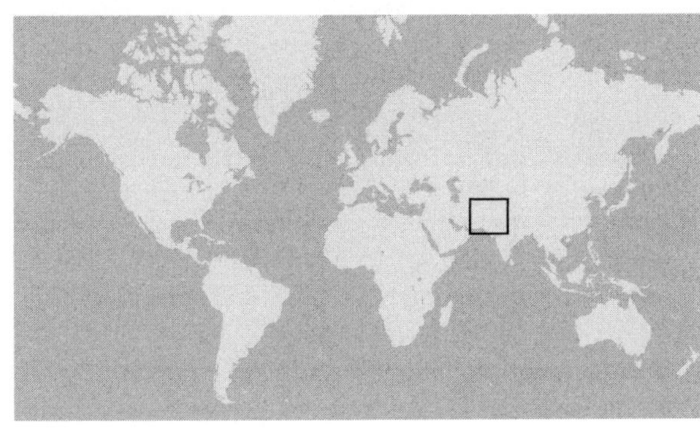

Country Overview

INTRODUCTION Pakistan came into existence in 1947, when India, ruled by the British, was granted independence and partitioned into two countries: Pakistan, as a haven for Muslims living all across the Indian subcontinent; and India, which was overwhelmingly Hindu. It is for this reason that Islam is at the center of Pakistan's national identity and deeply intertwined in Pakistani political discourse. The country adopted its current name, the Islamic Republic of Pakistan, in 1956. Pakistan borders India to the east, Iran to the west, Afghanistan to the northwest, China to the northeast, and the Arabian Sea to the south. An eastern wing of Pakistan, located northeast of India, succeeded in 1971 and became Bangladesh.

In Urdu the word "Pakistan" means "land of the pure," and the name was used to set Pakistanis apart from the Hindus in India. The founder of Pakistan, Muhammad Ali Jinnah (1876–1948), instituted a secular state, stressed the separation of religion and politics, and made provisions for the free expression of other faiths. In 1973, under Zulfikar Ali Bhutto (president, 1971–77; prime minister, 1973–77), Pakistan was declared an Islamic state in a new constitution, opening the way toward Islamization. The military dictator General Mohammad Zia ul-Haq (1924–88) toppled Bhutto in 1977 and governed as president from 1978 to 1988. In an effort to court the support of the Islamic parties, Zia ul-Haq instituted constitutional amendments that implemented draconian blasphemy laws and established Shariah (Islamic law) courts and Hudood punishments. Such punishments, said by some Muslim jurists to be derived from the Koran and the *sunnah,* or the tradition of the Prophet Muhammad, include stoning to death for adultery and amputation of hands for theft.

At the beginning of the twenty-first century, it was estimated that 96 percent of the country's population was Muslim; most were Sunni, with a smaller percentage following Shiite Muslim beliefs. The remainder of the population was composed of Christians, Hindus, Ahmadiyya, Zikris, Bahais, Zoroastrians (called Parsis), Buddhists, and Sikhs. Small populations, such as the Kalasha in Chitral, maintain indigenous, shamanistic beliefs.

Sunni Muslims offer prayer over victims killed by a Shiite Muslim gunman. Tensions between the two groups can often lead to violence. AP/WIDE WORLD PHOTOS.

RELIGIOUS TOLERANCE Although Pakistan is an ethnically and religiously diverse country, legislation gives absolute preeminence to Sunni Islam. Zia ul-Haq's Blasphemy Laws, enacted in 1979, stipulate death or life imprisonment for anyone who "by imputation, innuendo, or insinuation, directly or indirectly" defiles the Koran or the name of the Prophet Muhammad or who commits any other act of blasphemy. Any statement or action by religious minorities that seems offensive to a Sunni male can be deemed blasphemous. The testimony of a single Sunni male is grounds for arrest and prosecution. Bail is denied for those held on blasphemy charges. Religious minorities and women are prohibited by law from instigating blasphemy cases. The vagueness of the charge leaves the law open to abuse and facilitates numerous false accusations. Pressure by religious extremists upon the judiciary practically ensures that plaintiffs will not receive a fair hearing. Often defendants are killed prior to court hearings. Reflecting the extreme atmosphere of religious intolerance and sectarian violence in Pakistan, those acquitted by the courts have been murdered by extremists or have been forced to flee the country.

Major Religion

SUNNI ISLAM

DATE OF ORIGIN Eighth century C.E.
NUMBER OF FOLLOWERS 120 million

HISTORY Islam arrived in the Indian subcontinent as early as 712 C.E. following Arab conquests on the coast of Sindh (in southern Pakistan). It was not until the eleventh century, when Turkish forces of the Ghaznavid dynasty (962–1186 C.E.) spread from Afghanistan to northern India, that Islam became a significant influence. Sufi orders established in India helped continue the dissemination of Islam in the region. By 1206 Delhi became the capital of the Muslim sultanate, and it remained so until 1526, when another Muslim dynasty, the Mughuls, supplanted the Muslim sultanate. With the rise of the Mughal Empire during the sixteenth century, Islam became fully entrenched in the subcontinent.

European control over India began in 1600 with the founding of the British East India Company, which steadily acquired governmental authority until 1858, when the British Crown assumed full authority over the subcontinent with the establishment of the British Raj (1858–1947). During the nineteenth century colonial rule ignited a debate among Sunni Muslims over two different interpretations of Islam. One group favored a moderate form that was tolerant of religious diversity and stressed modern education and accommodation to a world dominated by Western powers. A second group espoused a puritanical interpretation of Islam that viewed accommodation to Western influences as counter to the faith and to the unity and strength of the Islamic community, or *ummah*. The latter was associated with Deobandi Islam, a Sunni movement that took its name from the town of Deoband (north of New Delhi), where the first Deobandi school, *Dar-ul-uloom* (House of Learning), was founded in 1867.

After gaining independence from Great Britain in 1947, the Indian subcontinent was partitioned into two countries, based on the principle that Muslims and Hindus constituted separate nations. Pakistan was formed as the homeland of Indian Muslims. This partition, proposed by the Muslim educator, jurist, and reformer Sayyid Ahmad Khan (1817–98), led to violence between Hindus and Muslims, costing the lives of more than half a million people, dislocating several million others, and creating lasting animosities between India and Pakistan. Despite the migration of Muslims into the newly formed Pakistan, more Muslims remained in Indian territories in Punjab, Bengal, and Kashmir, creating regional hot spots of sectarian violence inside India.

Pakistan's founder Muhammad Ali Jinnah was committed to a progressive, democratic, secular state; however, because of the rise of powerful, fundamentalist religious parties, his vision did not survive his death. The Jamaat-i-Islami (Islamic Society), founded by noted Sunni theologian Maulana Abdul Ala Mawdudi (1903–79), emerged as the leading fundamentalist party. The objective of the Jamaat-i-Islami was to transform Pakistan into an unequivocally Islamic theocracy based upon Shariah with Islam as the ideology overriding ethnic identities, linguistic differences, and regional political allegiances. When East Pakistan declared independence as Bangladesh in 1971, Pakistani Islamic parties developed an even more radical fundamentalist stance to deter deviation from the strictest interpretation of Islam.

Two other factors contributed to the radicalization of Sunni Pakistan. First, there was the perceived threat of Ayatollah Ruhollah Khomeini (1900?–89), who in 1979 toppled the neighboring, secular government of the Shah of Iran and established a revolutionary Shiite government. Second, there was the Afghan resistance movement, backed by the United States and Saudi Arabia, which opposed the Soviet invasion of neighboring Afghanistan in 1979. This movement was portrayed by the Americans as a jihad (struggle, or holy war) against the Soviets, and Pakistan served as the hub and staging ground for the war. With the arrival of thousands of militant Muslims from around the world eager to fight the atheistic Soviet military forces, Pakistanis were exposed to radical Islamic ideologies.

In 1979 General Zia ul-Haq established the Federal Shariah Court, which was given wide discretionary powers to implement Hudood ordinances and blasphemy laws. It also established separate seats in the National Assembly for Muslims and non-Muslims; the 207 ordinary districts were reserved for Muslims, and non-Muslims could vote only for the 10 additional seats set aside for them. Zia ul-Haq became the patron of the fundamentalist Deobandi and Wahhabi movements, influenced Ahle Hadith political party. He also facilitated the Islamization of the Pakistani military and the Inter-Services Intelligence Agency (ISI), an organization that controlled Pakistan's foreign policy and supported Islamic insurgency in the Indian state of Kashmir, with the goal of incorporating Kashmir, with its Muslim majority, into Pakistan. Overall, Zia ul-Haq's Islamization policies not only had wide social impact in Pakistan but also attracted considerable foreign funding and led to the establishment of a militant Islamic infrastructure that was still in operation at the start of the twenty-first century.

EARLY AND MODERN LEADERS Muhammad Iqbal (1877–1938) was a noted philosopher, poet, political leader, and advocate for an independent homeland for India's Muslims. Mohammad Ali Jinnah was the founder of Pakistan and first governor-general of the Dominion of Pakistan (the official name of Pakistan from 1947 to 1956).

Ayub Khan assumed power as chief martial law administrator in 1958 during a time of political unrest and shortly declared himself president (1958–69). He undertook the reorganization of Pakistan's administrative bureaucracy and instituted economic reform. Muhammad Yahya Khan, a protégé of Ayub who was appointed to assume control of the country's administration during a period of political unrest, became president (1969–71) after forcing Ayub Khan to resign in March 1969. Zulfikar Ali Bhutto, an Oxford educated lawyer and highly popular figure, came to power when Yahya Khan's position became untenable after the breakaway of East Pakistan as independent Bangladesh. Bhutto served as president of Pakistan (1971–73) and prime minister (1973–77). During Bhutto's tenure Pakistan was declared an Islamic state with the adoption of the Pakistan Constitution (1973). He was overthrown in a military coup in 1977 and executed in 1979 by General Zia ul-Haq. General Zia ul-Haq, appointed by Zulfikar Ali Bhutto as lieutenant general in 1975 and chief of army staff in 1976, assumed power in 1977, when he overthrew his benefactor and became president (1978–88). To consolidate his political power, strengthen Pakistan's failing economy, and begin the Islamization of the country and the military force, Zia ul-Haq took advantage of the flow of arms and cash subsidies coming into Pakistan from the United States and Saudi Arabia for the jihad against the Soviets in Afghanistan. Zia ul-Haq died in a mysterious airplane crash in 1988.

Prime Minister Benazir Bhutto (1988–90; 1993–96), the Harvard and Oxford educated daughter of Zulfikar Ali Bhutto, was the first female leader of any Muslim country. She became the head of her father's Pakistan People's Party after his death and emerged as a leading political figure in Pakistan after Zia ul-Haq's death in 1988; on 1 December 1988 she was elected prime minister, heading a coalition government. In 1990 President Ghulam Ishaq Khan dismissed Bhutto's government on charges of corruption. In 1993 Bhutto was again elected prime minister but was removed from office in 1996 under charges of corruption, as well as economic and administrative mismanagement.

Nawaz Sharif became prime minister in November 1990. He passed the Shariat Bill, which stipulated the Koran and *sunnah* as national law, as well as attempting to introduce free-market reform and economic growth. He lost his office to Bhutto in 1993 but was prime minister again from 1997 until 1999, when he was toppled by General Pervez Musharraf. Musharraf, who had been appointed head of the military by Nawaz Sharif in 1998, was involved in the military invasion of Indian Kashmir in 1999 that nearly led to war between India and Pakistan. Angry over being forced to retreat by orders of Sharif, Musharraf overthrew him and assumed power in 1999. Musharraf declared himself president in 2001 for an indefinite period.

MAJOR THEOLOGIANS AND AUTHORS Muhammad Iqbal, one of Pakistan's noted authors, is also considered the spiritual founder of Pakistan. An important intellectual, Iqbal was a champion of freedom and author of many books of poetry in Persian and Urdu, as well as treatises on Sunni Islam. His famous works include *The Secrets of the Self* (1915), a long spiritual philosophical poem, and *Javid-nama* (1934), a poem written in response to Dante's *Divine Comedy.*

Maulana Abdul Ala Mawdudi, founder of the Jamaat-i-Islami political party, is one of Pakistan's most important Sunni theologians and is known for his work *Towards Understanding Islam* (1980). Mawdudi sought to establish a truly Islamic society in which every facet of human existence, not just the spiritual domain of life, was subordinated to the moral principles set forth by God. He rejected Western ideals of secularism (the separation of religion and politics), commingling of the sexes, nationalism, and democracy as contrary to Islam and the principal cause of the decadence of Muslim society. These Western ideals, he argued, were based upon *jahiliyaa,* or ignorance, and are to be rejected. Writers such as Mawdudi viewed nationalism as a road to the cult of the nation, democracy as a dictatorship by the majority, and secularism, which eschews God's sovereignty over everything, as atheism. Therefore, any Muslim who upholds the ideals of Western nationalism, democracy, or secularism is in reality eschewing Islam, renouncing God, and guilty of apostasy. Mawdudi's ideas had a considerable impact upon radical Muslims throughout the Arab world, including the Taliban, who ruled Afghanistan from 1996 to 2001.

HOUSES OF WORSHIP AND HOLY PLACES The massive King Faisal Mosque in Islamabad, begun in 1976 and completed in 1986, was paid for by donations from King Faisal of Saudi Arabia. Following his death in a plane crash in 1988, General Zia ul-Haq was buried on the grounds of the King Faisal Mosque. His tomb is treated like a religious shrine where devotees come to pray and place flowers. Other famous Sunni mosques include the Badshahi and Wazir Khan mosques in Lahore, the Tooba Mosque in Karachi, and the Shahjehani Mosque in Thatta.

WHAT IS SACRED? The Koran and other icons and symbols of Islam are considered sacred objects by Pakistanis. For example, the Muslim profession of faith, *la-illaha illa Allah wa-Muhammad rasul Allah* ("There is no god but Allah, and Muhammad is the prophet of Allah"), appears in calligraphy on the walls of mosques and on the Pakistani flag. The graves of sayyids (Islamic leaders), Sufi saints, and religious martyrs are also treated as sacred places, though the attitude of Sunni Muslims toward such local customs varies. Those associated with the puritanical Deobandi movement and the Wahhabi Ahle Hadith consider accommodation to local customs and all deviations from the strictest interpretation of Islam as heretical, while those associated with the Barelvi school, influenced by Sufi mysticism, are more tolerant to indigenous customs.

HOLIDAYS AND FESTIVALS Sunni Muslims in Pakistan celebrate the principal Muslim religious festivals, such as Id-i-Ramadan, or Chhoti Id (Eid al-Fitr), when people fast from dawn until sunset; Bari Id, or Id Qurban, when those who are able slaughter an animal and distribute the meat to the poor; and Id-i-Mawlud, when people attend special gatherings at mosques to hear stories of the Prophet's life and take part in street processions singing praises of Muhammad. The religious festival of Shab-i-Barat (on the fourteenth day of the eighth month of the Muslim calendar) is held to remember deceased family members; food is given to the poor, and children celebrate with fireworks. The birthday of Ali Jinnah coincides with Christmas, and on this day Sunni Muslims and Pakistani Christians hold celebrations. Both Muslims and Christians wear new, brightly colored clothes and visit friends and relatives.

In February Pakistanis in the Punjab, including Muslims, celebrate Basant, "The Festival of Kites," which marks the advent of spring. At this time the skies over Punjabi cities such as Lahore, Faisalabad, and Rawalpindi teem with multicolored kites. Although it has traditionally been a secular event, in recent years Islamists have attempted to ban the Basant by condemning it as a Hindu festival.

MODE OF DRESS Pakistani Muslims dress modestly in accordance with Islamic values, although their particular mode of dress is distinctive to Pakistan and neighboring Afghanistan. In general, Pakistani men and women wear the traditional *shalwar-kameez,* a loose shirt that extends down to the knees and that is worn over loose baggy pants. Many men wear vests and coats over their *shalwar-kameez.* Turbans, *qaraquli* hats, and *patti* caps are worn by men as well. Women's attire consists of the *shalwar-kameez* and *dupatta,* or scarf, for the head. In some areas, such as the North-West Frontier Province, women wear the all-enveloping *burka,* or veil; however, in cities like Karachi, Lahore, and Islamabad they generally put on only a headscarf and go unveiled. Women in the Punjab and Sindh regions often wear the Indian sari. Students, some government officials, and members of the educated elite often wear western style clothing.

DIETARY PRACTICES Pakistani Muslims abide by Islamic dietary practices that prohibit pork, the flesh of meat-eating land animals and birds, and alcoholic beverages. The consumption of alcohol was banned under Zulfikar Ali Bhutto in 1976 as part of his effort to win over Islamic political parties, although non-Muslims were allowed to produce or purchase it by permit. Alcohol is available at the luxury hotels in the major cities that cater to foreign travelers, and many Pakistani Muslims do consume alcohol despite restrictions, purchasing it covertly from hotels. During the month of Ramadan, Pakistani Muslims fast in accordance with Islamic tradition.

RITUALS In general, there are no Islamic rituals that are distinctive to Pakistan. The veneration of shrines, sayyids, and *pirs* (holy men) varies depending on whether a particular community espouses the puritanical Deobandi and Ahle Hadith traditions or the more moderate Barelvi. As is celebrated throughout India and Afghanistan, Pakistani Muslims observe Shab-i-Barat (in recognition of deceased family members) by giving food to the poor, reading the Koran, and saying prayers.

RITES OF PASSAGE Sunni Muslims in Pakistan observe a number of Islamic life cycle rituals concerning birth, male circumcision, matrimony, and death. While there are certain regional variations, these rituals share similarities throughout the country. The birth of children is celebrated with the gathering of relatives and feasting. A mullah is summoned to whisper "Allah-u-Akbar" ("God is great") into the child's ear, establishing its Muslim identity. According to the *sunnah,* boys are circumcised before they reach puberty, with the ritual signifying a transition from childhood to manhood. In more recent times, however, infants are circumcised in the hospital or at home after birth. Failure to perform circumcision is considered an act of blasphemy under Pakistani law. There are no comparable Islamic puberty rites for girls.

Traditionally marriages are arranged. Typically under Islamic law a dowry, called *mehr,* is paid by the groom to the bride's family. During the wedding ceremony the couple exchanges vows while a Koran is held over the bride's head. A mullah issues the marriage certificate, or *nikanamah,* in the presence of the family members and guests. Islam permits the practice of polygyny, whereby a man may have up to four wives at the same time. Under Pakistani law the husband is required to inform his existing wife or wives of his intentions to marry again.

Sunni Muslims in Pakistan observe Islamic burial rites under the supervision of a mullah. Relatives of the same sex wash the body and place a shroud over it. The mullah recites funeral, or *jinazah,* prayers. The body is then taken to the burial grounds and placed in a grave facing Mecca. Only Muslims may engage in the burial rites of Muslims, and only men attend funerals, regardless of whether the deceased is male or female.

MEMBERSHIP The Pakistani constitution enacted in 1973 has empowered the state with the authority to define the religion of its citizens. For example, the Ahmadiyya were declared non-Muslims by the government, even though members of this group consider themselves to be Muslims and perform rites that are similar to those of the Sunni. As a result of their non-Muslim status, the Ahmadiyya are not allowed to express their beliefs in public without being charged with blasphemy. The Pakistani state also imposed an exclusionary definition of Islam, giving absolute preeminence to Sunni Islam. The law prohibits all other religious groups from proselytizing. Since the 1980s well-organized Sunni proselytising movements, such as the Tableeghi Jamaat, that are closely linked with the puritanical Deobandi school have been actively working to gain converts for their Islamist ideology. The thousands of Ahle Hadith and Deobandi *madrasahs* (Islamic religious schools), where many of the Taliban were taught and given military training, actively proselytize in an effort to acquire militant Islamic recruits.

SOCIAL JUSTICE According to Islam, moral principles are preordained by God and must be obeyed—they cannot be shaped according to ballot counts. As such, social justice is not compatible with the democratic principle of majority rule. Therefore, social justice is restricted to those who abide by God's law. This has posed significant problems in Pakistan. For example, under General Zia ul-Haq, *zakat,* the Islamic charity to the poor, was automatically deducted from bank accounts by the government and allocated solely to Sunni religious projects, such as the *madrasahs*.

Similarly, Pakistan's blasphemy laws privilege Sunni Islam above all other religious beliefs and serve as the legal basis for discrimination, victimization, and persecution of Shiites and non-Muslims. There are no measures in place to protect the civil and political rights of Shiites and non-Muslims who fall outside the boundaries of the *ummah* (Islamic community), as defined by Sunni ideologues in Pakistan. Also, under the prevailing Islamic legal system, civil rights for women are severely restricted. There are high rates of domestic violence against women, who have no judicial protection or redress. Under Pakistan's Hudood ordinances, marital rape is acceptable, and no distinction is made between forced and consensual sex.

SOCIAL ASPECTS Sunni Muslims in Pakistan follow Islamic marriage practice, which involves the *nikah,* a contractual agreement made before witnesses that symbolizes the legal union between the couple. Muslim marriage signifies the union not only of the husband and wife but also of their entire families. Pakistani Muslims are prohibited from marrying members of other religious or ethnic groups.

Relations within the family follow traditional Islamic values. The father is responsible for family's economic needs and for protecting the women in the family. The mother attends to domestic affairs and cares for the children. Sunni women observe *purdah,* or seclusion from males not part of their immediate kin.

POLITICAL IMPACT Pakistan was created in the name of religion, and since its founding in 1947, Islam has served as its ideological basis. Zulfikar Ali Bhutto's 1973 constitution declared Pakistan an Islamic state and opened the way to Islamization under Zia ul-Haq, which was in part a reaction to the Ayatollah Khomeini's 1979 revolution in neighboring Iran.

This Islamization was greatly amplified during the Soviet occupation of Afghanistan (1979–89), when Pakistan became the conduit through which massive amounts of weapons and cash were funneled from the United States, Saudi Arabia, and other Arab countries to the so-called mujahideen, or Islamic guerrilla fighters, who fought Soviet troops. According to an explicit understanding between the Central Intelligence Agency (CIA) and Pakistan's Inter-Services Intelligence Agency, aid was directed to Islamic rather than moderate Afghan nationalist political parties. Radical Muslims, brought to Pakistan from over fifty countries for training and indoctrination, were provided logistical support and linked together in a transnational network and militant Islamic infrastructure. Pakistan became the nexus of militant Islamic radicalism.

Deobandi and Ahle Hadith *madrasahs*, or religious schools, set up along the Afghan frontier produced large numbers of militant Islamic radicals, one manifestation of which was the rise of the Taliban in Afghanistan in the last decade of the twentieth century. As a result, Pakistan has become one of the fulcrums of transnational radical Islamism, a movement that is at odds with nationalism, modernity, and democratic ideals. In Pakistan radical Islam poses an internal security threat to the state and is at the root of much of the sectarian and anti-foreign violence in the country.

CONTROVERSIAL ISSUES In addition to human rights abuses and the absence of religious freedom, there are two major controversial issues concerning religion in Pakistan. First, it is estimated that 20,000 Taliban and 5,000 members of al-Qaeda (an international terrorist organization) driven out of Afghanistan in 2001 found refuge among the powerful militant Islamic groups in Pakistan. Entrenched in a network of mosques and *madrasahs* and supported by an extensive militant infrastructure established during the Afghan war with the Soviet Union, the militants have dominated Islamic discourse in Pakistan and have threatened to undermine state authority. The militants do not represent the majority of Pakistani Muslims, who aspire for a truly democratic society and want to live in peace.

Second, the radicalized *madrasahs* themselves have been controversial in Pakistan. It is estimated that the country has 40,000 such schools with more than 3 million students. Many of these schools teach radical Islam that is derived from Wahhabi and Deobandi precepts, which emphasize hatred of the West and martyrdom through suicide bombings and permit violence against non-Muslim or non-Sunni Muslim civilians. These schools helped produce the Taliban in the 1990s and at the start of the twenty-first century were still training students for operations in Kashmir, Afghanistan, and former Soviet Central Asia.

A related issue for Pakistani Muslims was the government's cooperation with the United States and its "war on terror" during the first few years of the twenty-first century. The Pakistani government was reluctant to intervene with religious institutions, including *madrasahs*, as such moves could be perceived as an attack on Islam itself. For this reason, efforts at controlling the *madrasahs* were more or less symbolic in nature.

CULTURAL IMPACT The Pakistani government supports the arts and humanities, in part through the Pakistan National Council of Arts, which oversees the National Gallery and the National Music and Dance Center. These institutions hold regular exhibitions and performances. Art is one area in which religion does not play a significant role so long as proper Islam decorum is kept (women, for example, must dress properly, and sexual content is forbidden). The Sufi orders are known for a special category of devotional music called *Qawwali,* which involves vocal chanting of words from the prophets, as well as tributes to God.

Other Religions

Pakistan is an ethnolinguistically and culturally diverse country. In addition to the majority Sunni Muslims, there are Shia Muslims (Shiites), Christians, Hindus, Sikhs, Jains, Bahais, Buddhists, Zoroastrians, Ahmadiyya (Ahmadis), Zikris of Baluchistan, and the Kalasha of Chitral.

The Shiites represent approximately 15 percent of the total population of Pakistan. They are divided into two major groups: the Imami and the less numerous Ismaili (also called Agha Khani after their spiritual leader). This division, as with the rift between Sunnis and Shiites, resulted from a disagreement over the true successors of Muhammad. Other Shiite groups in Pakistan include the Bohras, Dawoodis, and Khoja.

Pakistani Shiites generally live in the cities of Quetta, Peshawar, Karachi, and Hydarabad and in the northern regions of Gilgit and Hunza. The major Shiite religious observance is Ashura, which falls on the tenth day of Muharram (the first month of the Islamic year). Ashura marks the start of 40 days of mourning over the death of Shiite leader Husayn ibn Ali and his companions at Karbala in 680 C.E. To commemorate this event, men and boys take to the streets in processions, pounding their chests and striking their backs with chains tipped with blades. In Pakistan Shia and Sunni tensions become particularly acute during this time, often resulting in riots. Chhelum marks the fortieth day after Ashura, and it, too, is observed by Shiite processions. Following Zia ul-Haq's Islamization policies, sectarian tensions between Shia and Sunni Muslims escalated dramatically. By the early twenty-first century there was an increasing number of assassinations of prominent Shiite leaders and bombings of Shiite mosques by Sunni militant groups, such as the Laskhar-i-Jahangvi, an offshoot of Jamiat-i-Ulama-i-Islam (Society of Learned Islamists).

The majority of Pakistani Christians are either Roman Catholic or mainline Protestant, although many other denominations, such as Seventh-day Adventists and United Presbyterian Church of Pakistan, are represented as well. Christianity was introduced by missionaries during the European colonial period beginning in the eighteenth century. Most Pakistani Christians live in large cities, such as Bahawalpur, Hydarabad, Lahore, Rawalpindi, Quetta, and Peshawar, and they have their own churches with Pakistani and Western clerics. Pakistani Christians celebrate Christmas and Easter. During the late 1990s and the beginning of the twenty-first century, Pakistani Christians became the targets of considerable sectarian violence at the hands of militant Muslims, principally as a response to the United State's war on Islamic terrorists, which was depicted by radicals inside Pakistan as a war on Islam.

Most Pakistani Hindus live in Sindh, the southeastern province that borders India. Since the inception of Pakistan, the political and economical status of the Hindu population has been marginalized. Hindus celebrate the religious festivals of Diwali and Holi at the Shalimar Gardens in Lahore. Having been subject to retaliation and outright attacks by Islamists, especially during periods of heightened tensions between Pakistan and India, Pakistani Hindus have attempted to maintain a low profile.

The Muslim group Ahmadiyya, founded by Mirza Ghulam Ahmad (c. 1839–1908), has many followers in the town of Rabwah in the Punjab, where the movement originated in 1889. Other followers live in Sindh. The Ahmadiyya are divided into two groups: the Qadiani, who are named after the birthplace of the founder and who claim that Ahmad was a recipient of divine revelation and a prophet (*nabi*); and the Lahori group, who accept Ahmad as an Islamic reformer rather than a messiah. As early as 1953 the group became a target of Sunni agitation. In 1974, to appease radical Muslims, Zulfikar Ali Bhutto legally declared the Ahmadiyya non-Muslims, depriving them of their right to worship. According to the 1973 constitution, the Ahmadiyya are subject to prosecution for blasphemy should they refer to themselves as Muslims, recite the oath *kalima shahada,* call their places of worship mosques, perform the call to prayer, recite verses of the Koran in public, or even use the traditional Islamic greeting "salam alaikum" in public. The Ahmadiyya leadership and many of its practitioners left Pakistan after their classification as non-Muslims. Those who remained have been the most frequent targets of the blasphemy laws.

Guru Nanak (1469–1539), a native of what is now Pakistani Punjab, founded Sikhism after receiving divine revelations. Some scholars consider Sikhism to be a syncretic religion, merging elements of Hinduism and Sufi Islam, although some practitioners consider it to belong to the Hindu religious tradition. Still others see it as a distinct religious tradition based on direct revelation from God. In Pakistan Sikhs live mainly in the Punjab province, but some Sikh communities are also found in the North-West Frontier Province, whose members have ties with Sikhs across the border in Afghanistan. The Sikh community regularly holds ceremonial gatherings at sacred sites in the Punjab. The Panja Sahib Shrine in the town of Hasan Abdal near Rawalpindi is associated with a scared rock bearing the hand imprint of Guru Nanak. Sikh pilgrims from around the world come here during a mid-April holiday called Baisakhi. Unlike the Christians, Hindus, and Ahmadiyya, the Sikhs, who have been well organized and have had strong social support networks, have not been targets of religious hate crimes.

The Parsis are followers of the ancient religion Zoroastrianism, which was founded by the Persian prophet Zoroaster in the sixth century B.C.E. They worship the deity Ahura Mazda. Their ancestors migrated to the Indian subcontinent from Persia during the eighth century C.E. to escape Muslim persecution. Parsis mainly live in the cities Karachi and Lahore, with smaller numbers in Islamabad and Peshawar. The main Parsi religious festival is in August, when followers celebrate the New Year and pray for the dead. As is the case with Sikhs, the Parsis have not been targets of religious hate crimes in Pakistan.

The Kalasha are an indigenous population in Chitral who are culturally associated with the people of Nuristan, who live across the border in Afghanistan. The Afghan ruler Amir Abdul Rahman Khan forcibly converted the Nuristani to Islam during the nineteenth century, but the Kalasha have maintained a shamanistic religion and have retained their distinct ethnolinguistic identity. Despite their relative isolation, they have not escaped the notice of the Islamists and have been under continual cultural pressure to convert to Islam.

The Zikris ("those who recite the name of God") are an Islamic group in Makran in the province of Baluchistan. They subscribe to the main tenets of Islam but consider the fifteenth-century Sufi teacher Sayyid Muhammad Jaunpuri (1443–1505) as the Mahdi, or messiah. Their central ritual, which they refer to as the hajj, takes place on the 27th day of Ramadan, when supplicants perform a pilgrimage to Koh-i-Murad, a mountain in Turbat where their prophet made an appearance before vanishing into Afghanistan. In recent years there has been an intensified campaign by the Jamiat-i-Ulama-i-Islam to declare the Zikris non-Muslims.

Homayun Sidky

See Also Vol. I: *Islam, Shiism, Sunnism*

Bibliography

Amnesty International, *Pakistan: Blasphemy Laws Should be Abolished,* 2001, ASA 33/023/2001.

Amnesty International, *Pakistan: Insufficient Protection of Religious Minorities,* 2001, ASA 33/008/2001.

International Religious Freedom Report. *Pakistan.* Bureau of Democracy, Human Rights, and Labor, 2002.

Malik, Iftikhar. *Religious Minorities in Pakistan.* London: Minority Rights Group International, 2002.

Mehta, Mandavi, and Teresita Schaffer. *Islam in Pakistan: Unity and Contradiction.* Washington, D.C.: CSIS Report, 2002.

Nasr, Seyyed Vali Reza. *The Vanguard of the Islamic Revolution: The Jama'at-i Islami of Pakistan.* Berkeley: University of California Press, 1994.

Rashid, Ahmed. "Pakistan and the Taliban." In *Fundamentalism Reborn: Afghanistan and the Taliban.* Edited by William Maley, 72–89. New York: New York University Press, 2001.

Palau

POPULATION 19,700

ROMAN CATHOLIC 42 percent

EVANGELICAL 22 percent

MODEKNGEI 9 percent

SEVENTH-DAY ADVENTIST 6 percent

OTHER 6 percent

UNKNOWN OR NO RELIGIOUS AFFILIATION 15 percent

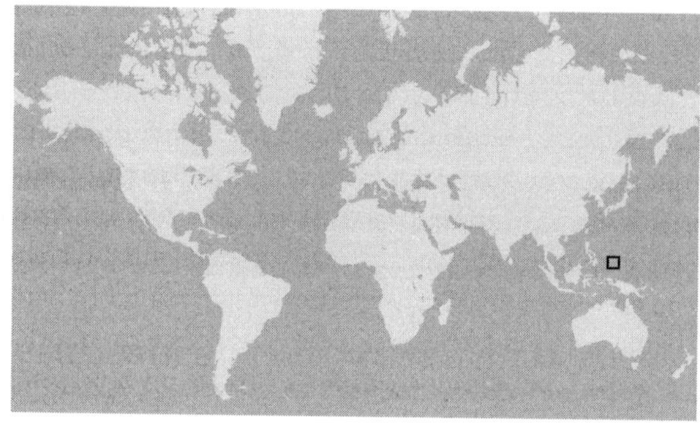

Country Overview

INTRODUCTION The Republic of Palau, an archipelago in the western Pacific Ocean, lies east of the Philippines and north of Papua New Guinea. After centuries of contact and trade with Western powers—as well as direct rule by Spain, Germany, Japan, and the United States—Palau became an independent country in free association with United States in 1994. The United States agreed to be responsible for Palau's defense and to assist it financially.

Prior to European contact in 1521 C.E., Palauans viewed their islands as a complete and closed universe that had been formed from the body of a fallen giant. Local gods created the forests and reefs to protect the giant's body, and people were thought to have come out of the body. Palau's first contact with Christianity was in 1710, when a Spanish explorer, Francisco Padilla, came upon Sonsorol, about 200 miles southwest of the main cluster of islands. Two Spanish priests were left there, but real religious conversion did not occur until 1891.

After Spain lost the Spanish-American War in 1899, they sold Palau to Germany. German administrators continued to allow Catholic priests to travel to Palau and build churches and schools. During World War I Japan took over Palau; they developed the islands until 1945, when the United States defeated the Japanese in World War II.

Palau remained under U.S. administration until 1994, when it achieved independence. Today the nation has a wide variety of religious practices. The major religion is Christianity; the Roman Catholic Church has the largest membership, followed by Evangelical (Protestant) churches, Seventh-day Adventists, Jehovah Witnesses, Church of Jesus Christ of Latter-day Saints, Victory Chapel, Assembly of God, Liebenzell Mission, and a Baptist church. Modekngei is the only religion rooted in the traditional religions of Palau, where each village had its own god or gods and their own customs of worship and prohibitions. Modekngei became an organized religion during the Japanese administration and has been a part of Palau culture and society ever since.

RELIGIOUS TOLERANCE The constitution of Palau promotes individual freedom of worship. There is no state-sponsored religion, and small Christian groups and churches, as well as other faiths, are able to spread their message without hindrance from the government or other churches. The government provides financial assistance to private religious schools, though members of any faith may request this support.

Major Religion

ROMAN CATHOLICISM

DATE OF ORIGIN 1891 C.E.
NUMBER OF FOLLOWERS 8,300

HISTORY The Spanish government became active in the Pacific Islands in 1521 C.E., when the explorer Ferdinand Magellan sailed to Guam. From 1522 to 1885, however, Spain focused most of its attention on Guam, Saipan (one of the Northern Marianas Islands), and the Philippines. Spanish Catholic missionaries attempted to convert the other islands of the Carolines with no real success. After continuous political conflicts between Germany, Britain, and Spain, the pope declared in 1885 that Spain had the right of control to the Caroline Islands (which included Palau) and the Marianas Islands. In 1891 Spanish Capuchin missionaries began converting Palauans to Christianity, starting with the highest clan members.

After Spain lost the Spanish-American War in 1899, it sold Palau, the other Carolines, and the Marianas Islands (except Guam, which became a U.S. territory) to Germany. Spanish missionaries were allowed to remain in Palau and operate schools during the German administration, but by 1906 the last of the Spanish had left the islands. In 1907 a number of German priests of the Capuchin order arrived in Palau; two years later Franciscan nuns arrived from Germany to run a girls' school on the island of Koror. By 1911 two Franciscan sisters had taken charge of a school in Melekeok on Babelthaup, an island north of Koror.

Germany's main focus was economic development of copra and phosphate; it continued to allow the Catholic missionaries to work with the local population. At this time the only schools in Palau were those run by the Catholic missionaries, and the Palauans' desire for education facilitated conversion to Catholicism. Other Catholic schools were opened in Aimeliik, Airai, and Angaur.

A religious house in Koror, Palau. Palau's first contact with Christianity was in 1710 when a Spanish explorer dropped off two priests near the main cluster of islands. © RICHARD A. COOKE/CORBIS.

In 1914 Japan seized the phosphate mine and radio stations on Angaur, ending the German administration. Like the Germans, the Japanese were interested more in economic than in spiritual development. They allowed the churches to continue, but by 1915 all German missionaries had been forced out of Palau. They were replaced by Spanish Catholic missionaries in 1921. As the Japanese administration continued to focus on the economic development of Palau (through agriculture, aquaculture, and phosphate and bauxite mines), the population of Japanese in Palau increased, and by 1940 they had outnumbered the Palauans. The Japanese prohibited religious schools. After 1929 the Catholic

Church had to compete with Evangelicals for membership. Despite these challenges, the Catholic Church in Palau continued to develop and grow slowly and steadily.

In 1945 the United States Naval administration took control of Japanese possessions in the Pacific. The major impact of the U.S. administration has been the influence of a social ideology in which freedom of expression and freedom of worship are important values, as evidenced by the opening of new Catholic churches and schools and the growth of Palau's older churches. Beginning in the 1990s an increasing number of Filipinos immigrated to Palau, adding another facet to the Catholic community there.

EARLY AND MODERN LEADERS Felix Yaoch (ordained in 1968; died in 2002) was the first Jesuit priest from Palau. Working in Palau and throughout Micronesia, he helped to develop the faith of the people in these regions.

MAJOR THEOLOGIANS AND AUTHORS Most of the church leaders in Palau have been more interested in working with individuals and society than in writing what would be considered major theological material. The German priest Salvador Walleser (1874–1946) arrived in Palau in 1907, and by 1913 he had published the first Palauan grammar, as well as a Palauan-German dictionary. Walleser was appointed the first bishop of the Vicariate of the Carolines and Marianas in 1912. Since the 1970s Father Francis Hezel, an American Jesuit priest based in Micronesia, has written about the social conditions of the islands.

HOUSES OF WORSHIP AND HOLY PLACES In Palau there is one major Catholic church, Sacred Heart Church on Koror, which is where the majority of Palauans worship. When it opened in 1935, it was one of the only cement buildings on Koror. Many smaller churches are located throughout Palau.

WHAT IS SACRED? Catholics in Palau have developed a strong devotion to the saints and to relics that might be deemed sacred. The Catholic Church in Palau, however, has been emphasizing the life, death, and resurrection of Jesus Christ as the most sacred element of the faith.

HOLIDAYS AND FESTIVALS Palaun Catholics follow the liturgical calendar of the Catholic Church; the major holidays are Ash Wednesday, Good Friday, Easter, and Christmas. In Palau the first week of February is considered Catholic week and is celebrated by the Catholic schools.

MODE OF DRESS All people in Palau, whether they belong to a church or not, follow the Western style of dress.

DIETARY PRACTICES The only dietary practice that Catholics observe in Palau is fasting during Lent.

RITUALS The major Catholic ritual practiced in Palau is Sunday Mass. For Catholics in Palau, rituals sometimes involve a combination of Catholic and indigenous traditions. Funerals, for example, might include traditional practices, a church ceremony, or both.

RITES OF PASSAGE There are no known rites of passage that are distinctive to Palauan Catholics.

MEMBERSHIP The Catholic schools in Palau play a role in seeking and retaining members. In addition, the church uses the media to spread its message. The Catholic Church has aired weekly radio programs since the 1960s, and in 1986 a group of Catholics began producing video documentaries on religious themes.

SOCIAL JUSTICE The Catholic Church in Palau has united with other churches to protest the government's policies on certain problems, specifically gambling, prostitution, and alcohol and drug use.

SOCIAL ASPECTS Despite the Catholic Church's opposition to abortion and birth control as forms of family planning, the church in Palau has not taken a strong public stance on these issues. Birth control is widely practiced in Palau, even by Catholics. Abortion is available, though its legal status remains unclear.

POLITICAL IMPACT Although church teachings might affect the political views of its members, the Catholic Church has no overt influence on Palauan politics or lawmakers. The church has been and is separate from the government.

CONTROVERSIAL ISSUES The church has not involved itself in any major controversial issue except gambling, which is illegal in Palau. Church members have protested the government's attempts to legalize it.

CULTURAL IMPACT Gospel songs—performed during services, on special celebrations for the church, and for national holidays—have had a major impact on Palauan music. The Catholic Church has also influenced literature in Palau, most notably through the early German and Spanish missionaries' work in creating a Palauan writing system and producing the first written materials in Palauan.

Other Religions

A key development during the Japanese administration (1914–45) was the organization of the Modekngei Society in 1918 as a traditional religious response to foreign missionaries—and specifically to the Japanese government's treatment of Palauans. Modekngei, as a revived form of the islands' indigenous religion, worships Palauan ancestral gods. The Japanese allowed Christianity and Modekngei to continue under their administration, but by 1926 they had introduced Buddhism and Shintoism to the islands. Modekngei, with nearly 2,000 members, continues to be a part of Palauan society.

During their administration of the islands the Japanese allowed non-Catholic Christians to come to Palau. The first Protestant (Evangelical) missionaries arrived in Palau from the German Liebenzell Mission in 1929 and established a church. They found many of their converts among the Modekngei adherents and Catholics. After World War II the Liebenzell missionaries established two Christian high schools (one for boys and one for girls) in Palau. Today they are administered by the Palauan Evangelical Church. The Pacific Islands Bible College, based in Chuuk and Guam, also trains church leaders in Palau. The Evangelical Church in Koror runs a kindergarten program (which includes Bible instruction) to prepare students for elementary school.

The other older churches in Palau are Seventh-day Adventists, Jehovah Witnesses, and the Church of Jesus Christ of Latter-day Saints. Since 1993 Palau has seen the development of additional Christian churches, including Victory Chapel, Assembly of God, and Baptist churches. These groups have established their own churches or places of worship; for them the church and cemeteries might be considered holy or sacred. The Seventh-day Adventists and the High Adventure Ministries (a radio evangelistic organization founded in Lebanon in 1979) operate their own radio stations in Palau.

Since the end of the twentieth century there have been Muslims practicing in Palau; these are mainly foreign laborers from Bangladesh and Nepal. The Muslim community has begun worshiping more openly, but as of 2004 Muslims had not yet built a mosque in Palau.

Palau also has a small number of Bahais and individuals who practice Buddhism, Hinduism, and Shinto.

Tutii Chilton

See Also Vol. I: *Christianity, Evangelical Movement, Roman Catholicism*

Bibliography

Adams, William Hampton, and Florencio Gibbons, eds. *Palau Ethnography.* Vol. 1, *Rechuodel,* by the Palau Society of Historians. San Francisco, Calif.: U.S. National Park Service, 1997.

Borofsky, Robert, ed. *Remembrance of Pacific Pasts.* Honolulu: University of Hawai'i Press, 2000.

Davis, James E., and Diane Hart. *Government of Palau: A Nation that Honors Its Traditions.* Koror: The Ministry of Education, 2002.

Hezel, Francis X. "The Catholic Church in Palau." 4 October 2004. http://www.micsem.org/pubs/books/catholic/palau.

Hezel, Francis X., and M.L. Berg, eds. *Micronesia: Winds of Change.* Saipan: Omnibus Program for Social Studies–Cultural Heritage, 1979.

Hijikata, Hisakatsu. *Gods and Religion in Palau.* Translated and edited by Hisashi Endo. Tokyo: Sasakawa Peace Foundation, 1995.

———. *Myths and Legends of Palau.* Translated and edited by Hisashi Endo. Tokyo: Sasakawa Peace Foundation, 1996.

———. *Society and Life in Palau.* Translated and edited by Hisashi Endo. Tokyo: Sasakawa Peace Foundation, 1993.

Parmentier, Richard J. *The Sacred Remains: Myth, History, and Polity in Belau.* Chicago: University of Chicago Press, 1987.

Rechebei, Elizabeth D., and Samuel F. McPhetres. *History of Palau: Heritage of an Emerging Nation.* Koror: Ministry of Education, 1997.

Panama

POPULATION 2,882,329
ROMAN CATHOLIC 78 percent
PROTESTANT 12 percent
MUSLIM 4.4 percent
BAHAI 1.2 percent
BUDDHIST 0.8 percent
INDIGENOUS 0.7 percent
OTHER 2.9 percent

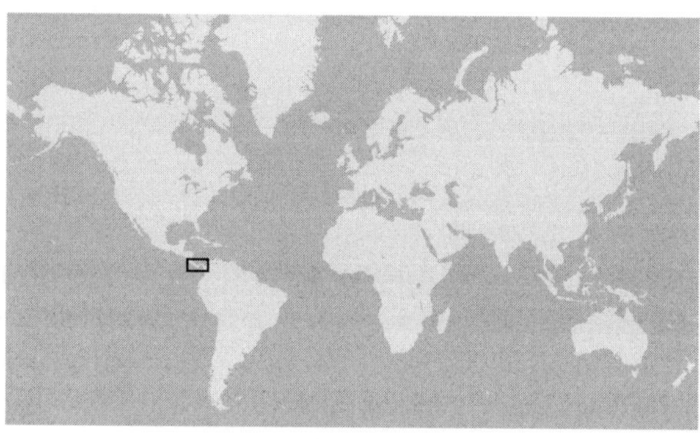

Country Overview

INTRODUCTION The Republic of Panama, bordered by the Caribbean to the north and the Pacific Ocean to the south, is an isthmus connecting Central and South America. To the west is Costa Rica, and to the east is Colombia.

Almost all Panamanians claim some religious affiliation, the majority as Roman Catholics. The second largest group consists of Protestants, mostly evangelicals. The construction of the Panama Canal, opened in 1914, and the country's role in international trade have resulted in the arrival of people of other religions, including Bahais, Buddhists, Hindus, Muslims, Jews, and Sikhs.

After achieving independence from Colombia in 1903, Panama established a constitutional democracy. Its civilian government was overthrown in 1968 by a military coup, and for 20 years Panama was run by a military junta led by generals Omar Torrijos (1968–81) and Manuel Noriega (1983–89).

RELIGIOUS TOLERANCE Although Panama's constitution does not designate the Roman Catholic Church as the country's official religion, it recognizes Roman Catholicism as "the religion of the majority of Panamanians." The archbishop of Panama enjoys privileges usually reserved for government officials, and Catholicism is taught in public schools, although the classes are not mandatory. The constitution guarantees freedom of religion, as long as "Christian morality and order" are respected; allows religious organizations to own property; bars clergy from public office, except in the areas of social welfare, public instruction, and scientific research; and prohibits discrimination in employment based on religion.

The Panamanian Ecumenical Committee includes Roman Catholics and mainstream Protestants. The Institute for Ecumenism and Society sponsors dialogues between Christians, members of other religions, and humanists. There have been no reports of religious prisoners or detainees.

Major Religion

ROMAN CATHOLICISM

DATE OF ORIGIN 1513 C.E.

NUMBER OF FOLLOWERS 2.2 million

HISTORY In 1510 the Spanish established Santa María de la Antigua del Darién, the first European city on the mainland of the Americas, and in 1513 Darién became the first diocese. After the cathedral Nuestra Señora de la Asunción de Panamá was established on the Pacific coast in 1519, the territory became the Diocese of Panama. In 1925 it became an archdiocese and metropolitan.

During the colonial period the church enjoyed a close relationship with the government, gaining wealth through tithes and land ownership. The bishop's authority, received from the Spanish crown, in effect made him vice governor. Panama's cathedral featured gold and silver crucifixes, candelabra, ornate vestments, and carved cedar altars and shrines. Robed religious brotherhoods formed elaborate processions through Panama City. Following independence from Colombia in 1903, Panama rejected the 1887 Colombian concordat with the Vatican, favoring instead the separation of church and state. The obligation to pay the church for confiscated property was repudiated, cemeteries were laicized, and education increasingly came under state control and was secularized.

During the twentieth century the majority of the country's priests were foreign born, mainly Spanish. With few native-born church leaders to take strong political stands, anticlericalism did not develop in Panama as it did in other Latin American countries. From 1960 to 1990 the church's relation to politics changed, as concern over social issues increased and conflicts with the government arose.

EARLY AND MODERN LEADERS In 1514 Juan de Quevedo, the first bishop of Darién (1514–19), led Franciscans to convert the indigenous peoples. The second bishop, Vicente Peraza (1520–26), led the Dominicans. Jesuits had arrived by the mid-sixteenth century, augmenting their numbers with native-born members, including theologian Pedro Ignacio de Cáceres, educator Juan Antonio Giraldo, and missionary and martyr Agustín Hurtado.

Contemporary leaders include Archbishop Marcos Gregorio McGrath, C.S.C. (1924–2000), secretary general of the Council of Latin American Bishops (1966–68), proponent of liberation theology, and supporter of Panama's claim to sovereignty over the canal. Rómulo Emiliani Sánchez, bishop of Darién (1988–2002), received international recognition for his commitment to peace and justice and for his service to the poor. His ministry focused on agricultural cooperatives, education, health, and the use of radio, television, and the Internet to spread the church's message. José Dimas Cedeño Delgado was appointed archbishop of Panama in 1994.

Catholics crawl on their knees toward the Church of San Felipe where the statue of the Black Christ is kept. This is one of the most popular processions in Panama. © REUTERS NEWMEDIA INC./CORBIS.

MAJOR THEOLOGIANS AND AUTHORS Writers from the colonial period who provided good descriptions of the era include the Dominican general Adriano Ufelde de Santo Tomás, a noted evangelist, and Don Juan Sacedo, *maestre escuela* (school master) and deputy of the Holy Cross in Panama.

Among twentieth-century Panamanian theologians, Marcos McGrath has been the most influential nationally and internationally. He founded the theological journal *Teología y Vida* (Theology and Life), and during the Second Vatican Council he served on the committee that produced the document *Gaudium et Spes* ("Joys and Hopes"). Catholic theology from the perspective of Panama's indigenous people has been articulated by Aiban Wagua, a Kuna Indian ordained as a Roman Catholic priest in 1975. Crescenciano Vásquez S. has written from the perspective of people of African and indigenous ancestry. Miguel Angel Picard Ami has addressed the issue of the church and agrarian reform, and

Nestor Jaen, the issue of spirituality, resistance, and liberation.

HOUSES OF WORSHIP AND HOLY PLACES Among the most noted churches are the Metropolitan Cathedral of the Archdiocese of Panama (Panama City); the National Shrine of the Immaculate Heart of Mary (Panama City); the Church of San José, renowned for its golden altar (Panama City); and the Church of San Felipe, with its statue of the Black Christ (Portobelo).

WHAT IS SACRED? In Panama churches are sacred places, saints are an important part of the cultural landscape, and the celebration of the Eucharist is the church's most sacred ritual. In 1999 Santa María de la Antigua was proclaimed as patron saint of the archdiocese of Panama, and in 2000 she was made patron saint of the Republic of Panama. In 1999 the country was dedicated to the Immaculate Heart of Mary.

HOLIDAYS AND FESTIVALS Among the major festivals are Carnaval, starting the weekend before Ash Wednesday (in Panama City and elsewhere, especially in Las Tablas); Feast of Jesus the Nazarene, 8–12 March (in Atalaya); Holy Week (in Pesé); Feast of Santa Librada, 20 July (in Las Tablas); Feast of the Virgen de las Mercedes, 24 September (in Guararé); and the Feast of the Black Christ, the week of 21 October (in Portobelo).

MODE OF DRESS Panamanians generally wear modern Western clothing to church. When religion combines with folk festivals, however, traditional attire is worn: for women, the *pollera,* an intricately embroidered full-length white dress and matching blouse of Spanish origin; for men, an embroidered long-sleeve shirt, calf-high trousers, and a straw hat.

DIETARY PRACTICES The diet of most Roman Catholics in Panama is based on economic circumstances and availability rather than religious prescriptions. *Sancocho,* a chicken soup with vegetables accompanied by white rice, is the country's national dish and is served on major holidays and special occasions.

RITUALS Devout Catholics in Panama take seriously their religious duties, including Mass, confession, and holy days of obligation. Special rituals, such as processions during Holy Week and at other times, attract large numbers of Panamanian Catholics, regardless of their level of devotion. One of the most popular processions occurs during the pilgrimage made for the Feast of the Black Christ in Portobelo. Pilgrims arrive at the Church of San Felipe, where the statue is kept. Many wear purple (the color of Christ's robe), some arrive on their knees, and others carry crosses to make requests or to give thanks for miracles granted through the Black Christ. Christian rituals can take on a decidedly Panamanian character, especially in the countryside. In many places Easter Eve is celebrated with a dance; following Easter Sunday Mass, people hold a wake for Judas (the disciple who betrayed Christ) and burn a straw effigy of him.

RITES OF PASSAGE In Panama baptism is almost universal, incorporating the child into the Catholic Church and a particular family. As a part of this rite the selection of the child's godparents (*padrinos*) creates a web of fictive kin involving not only the child and godparents but the parents and godparents as *compadres.*

In the folkloric *campesino* wedding, the couple, dressed in traditional clothing, is married in the church, and then family and friends parade them through town on horseback. The last rites of the church are administered even to individuals who have not regularly participated in the church's other rituals.

MEMBERSHIP The number of Catholic priests in Panama grew from 224 in 1966 to 396 in 2000. The church maintains kindergartens, primary and secondary schools, and the Pontifical University of Santa María la Antigua, established in 1965. Catholic and missionary efforts include Panama's Knights of Columbus, the ecclesial movement Apóstoles de la Palabra (Apostles of the Word), and La Fundación para el Apoyo de la Nueva Evangelización y la Solidaridad en la Fe Cristiana (Pro-Fe) [Foundation in Support of New Evangelization and Solidarity in Christian Faith (For the Faith)]. The Catholic Church's communications network includes Internet sites, radio stations, television, and the weekly newspaper *Panorama Católico.*

SOCIAL JUSTICE In 1962 a small group of priests and nuns from Chicago began work in San Miguelito, a district composed of urban poor and recent rural immigrants to Panama City. The San Miguelito Mission is an early example of the practice of liberation theology through the formation of Christian base communities. The mission's main church, Cristo Redentor, opened in

1965 with a mural behind the altar portraying Jesus as a Panamanian *campesino* (country person) and a Mass that incorporated traditional Panamanian music and instruments. By 1980 the mission, with its 53 parishes and base communities, had been terminated because of controversy over the liturgy, vocal opposition in San Miguelito to the military government, and accusations by the military that the mission's priests were CIA agents.

From 1967 to 1971 Father Hector Gallego worked in impoverished rural communities around Santa Fé, Veraguas. Gallego, committed to liberation theology, helped organize and direct *campesino* cooperatives, but he drew criticism from the local elite and attracted the attention of the military government. In 1971 he was abducted from home. His disappearance, and that of others during the years of military rule, led to the establishment of a truth commission in 2000. At a special Mass in Panama City's Metropolitan Cathedral in 2002, the commission delivered its report documenting the fate of 110 murdered and disappeared individuals.

SOCIAL ASPECTS Marriage is one of Catholicism's seven sacraments, and among Panamanian Catholics it ideally binds a couple for life. Nevertheless, for many Panamanians marriage is consensual, and a formal marriage ceremony represents the culmination of a couple's life together and economic success. Formally constituted marriage with a church wedding at the start of a relationship is the rule for the urban elite and middle class as well as for prosperous rural families.

Kinship is a major factor in Panamanian social life. While men may be sexually active outside of marriage, women are expected to be faithful and dedicated to home and family. The Christian Family Movement, begun in 1977 by Archbishop McGrath, celebrates an annual Family Week to promote marriage and family values. During the folklore festival in Guararé the church sponsors a novena (nine days of prayer) dedicated to the Virgen de las Mercedes (the Virgin Mary), a model for the Christian family.

POLITICAL IMPACT In 1987 the Crusada Civilista Nacional (CCN), a coalition of more than 100 business, civic, and religious groups, organized antigovernment demonstrations calling for the resignation of Manuel Noriega as head of Panama's army and de facto head of the country. Catholic priests were frequently present at CCN rallies, and Masses became focal points for some CCN activities. During this period of unrest the Vatican Embassy became a safe haven for politicians, including Guillermo Endara and Noriega.

CONTROVERSIAL ISSUES In 1996 Panama was the site of the church's First International Conference in Defense of Life and the Family, which promoted chastity, natural family planning, the right of parents to be the primary educators of their children, respect for life, and post-abortion reconciliation. Despite opposition from the Catholic Church and antiabortion groups, Panama's Legislative Assembly passed and the president signed the United Nations Convention on the Elimination of All Forms of Discrimination Against Women. Abortion remains illegal in Panama, however.

CULTURAL IMPACT In Panama many observances of Catholic feasts and saint's days combine religious rituals with popular and folk traditions—especially music, dress, and dance—reinforcing the national culture. The best-known celebration is Carnaval, held on the four days leading up to Ash Wednesday. The Feast of the Virgen de las Mercedes (24 September), also known as the Feria de la Mejorana (a small guitar played in rural areas to accompany singing and dancing), takes place in Guararé and is the country's largest folkloric festival. The Feast of Santa Librada in Las Tablas offers elaborate displays of traditional clothing, and the Feast of Corpus Christi in Villa de los Santos includes dramas with dancers representing angels, devils, and legendary spirits. A Passion play performed on Good Friday is a part of the traditions in Pesé.

During the colonial period elaborate places of worship were constructed, such as the Church of San Francisco de Veraguas (in 1727), where indigenous images and symbols were woven into the baroque art and architecture. The Museum of Colonial Religious Art (in Panama City) is housed in the building that was erected in 1678 for the Santo Domingo Church and Convent.

Other Religions

Panama's Protestants are mostly evangelical. The largest denominations, in terms of number of congregations and members, are Assemblies of God, Seventh-day Adventist, Foursquare Gospel, Church of God (Cleveland), and Baptist. Many operate their own Bible schools and seminaries and have missions in the indigenous areas. There are also congregations of mainstream churches, including Episcopal, Methodist, and Lutheran. All spread their messages by radio, television, print, and Internet sites.

Muslims are largely concentrated in Panama City and Colon, with smaller groups in Aguadulce and David. The first Muslims on the isthmus were among the African slaves. Muslims from the Middle East, India, and Pakistan arrived in the late nineteenth and early twentieth centuries and formed the Sunni Indo-Pakistan Muslim Society, later known as the Panama Muslim Mission. There are five *masjids* (mosques) in the country. The Center for Islamic Research and Studies publishes a newsletter and presents lectures.

Most of the Jewish population lives in Panama City, but they also live in Colon and David. There has been a recent influx of Jewish immigrants, including more than 1,000 Israelis. The first synagogue (Reform) was established in 1876. The Orthodox have one Ashkenazic congregation and two Sephardic congregations, the largest with a mikvah (ritual bath) on the premises. Panama City has two Jewish high schools, a Hebrew cultural center, a Jewish sports club, and a kosher supermarket. There have been two Jewish presidents.

Panama has two Hindu temples and one ISKON (International Society for Krishna Consciousness) temple. Sikhs, who went to Panama during the construction of the Panama Canal, have a *gurdwara* (temple) in Panama City. The Bahai temple for South America, the Mormon Temple, and two Buddhist centers are also located in Panama City. Since 1989 the group Serapis Bey of Panama has offered courses on New Thought and the metaphysical teachings of the Ascended Masters.

Claude Jacobs

See Also Vol. 1: *Christianity, Roman Catholicism, Seventh-day Adventist Church*

Bibliography

Biesanz, John, and Mavis Biesanz. *The People of Panama.* New York: Columbia University Press, 1955.

Bravo, Francisco. *The Parish of San Miguelito in Panama.* Cuernavaca, Mexico: Centro Intercultural de Documentación, 1966.

Hedrick, Basil Calvin. *Historical Dictionary of Panama.* Lanham, Md.: Scarecrow Press, 1970.

Rudolf, Gloria. *Panama's Poor: Victims, Agents, and Historymakers.* Gainesville: University Press of Florida, 1999.

Papua New Guinea

POPULATION 5,172,033

ROMAN CATHOLIC 27.1 percent

EVANGELICAL LUTHERAN 19.5 percent

UNITED CHURCH 11.5 percent

SEVENTH-DAY ADVENTIST 10.1 percent

PENTECOSTAL 8.6 percent

EVANGELICAL ALLIANCE 5.2 percent

ANGLICAN 3.2 percent

BAPTIST 2.5 percent

OTHER CHRISTIAN 8.1 percent

JEHOVAH'S WITNESS 0.4 percent

MORMON 0.4 percent

OTHER RELIGION (BUDDHIST, MUSLIM, ETC.) 0.3 percent

BAHAI 0.3 percent

NOT STATED 2.0 percent

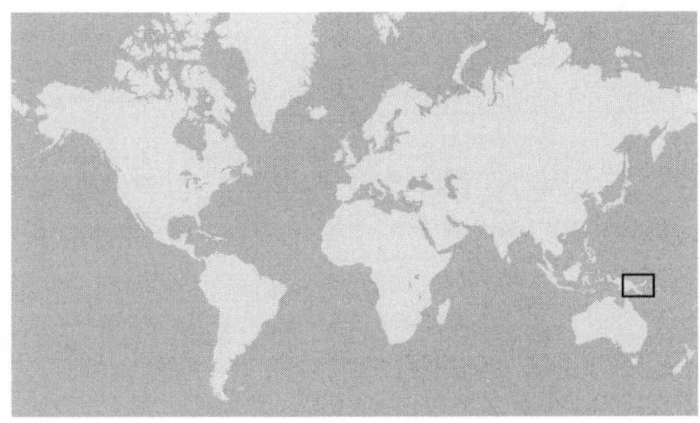

Country Overview

INTRODUCTION The Independent State of Papua New Guinea, comprising the eastern half of New Guinea and a number of smaller islands in the southwestern Pacific Ocean, lies east of Indonesia and north of Australia. According to archaeological sources the region that is now Papua New Guinea has been inhabited for more than 40,000 years. There have been various migrations to the area from Southeast Asia, resulting in a cultural complexity that is evidenced by the more than 800 languages spoken in Papua New Guinea.

Although Europeans made a brief landing on New Guinea in the 1520s, and the British first attempted to start a colony there in 1793, it was not until the 1880s and 1890s that colonial administrations were established on the island, with the Dutch occupying the western portion; the Germans, the northeast; and the British, the southeast. During the same period Christian missionary groups from the colonizing nations also began to establish themselves in these areas and on nearby islands. Nevertheless, another 40 to 50 years passed before outsiders penetrated the Highlands of the interior, the most densely populated portion of the island. Australia assumed control of British New Guinea in 1906 and of German New Guinea in 1921. Full independence was granted to the areas under Australian control in 1975.

Beginning in the mid-nineteenth century Christianity was introduced in the islands that came to make up Papua New Guinea, and during the following decades it spread throughout the region. Today 96 percent of all Papua New Guineans identify themselves as Chris-

Men of the Gogodala tribe paddle a canoe with a decorative bow that represents their ancestors. Traditional religious practices form an underlying stratum in the faith of many Christians. © CHARLES & JOSETTE LENARS/ CORBIS.

tian, and 75 percent of the country's youth claim to attend church services weekly. Protestants make up almost 70 percent of the population, while about 27 percent of people identify themselves as Roman Catholic. Traditional religious practices, which include the veneration of ancestors and rituals for maintaining relationships with life-giving powers, continue and form an underlying stratum in the faith of many Christians. Small numbers of adherents of other religions are also found in Papua New Guinea.

RELIGIOUS TOLERANCE Papua New Guinea's constitution guarantees freedom of conscience, thought, and religion. There have been calls to make Christianity the official religion and thereby limit the activities of members of other faiths, such as Muslims. Such moves have been opposed by the principal Christian churches, however, in the name of freedom of religion.

In practice, relations between the various Christian subgroups have not always been characterized by tolerance. Some groups with more fundamentalist orientations deny that Catholics, Anglicans, and others from mainline churches are indeed Christian. A number of new religious movements and Pentecostal churches—which offer livelier worship services and healing rituals—are growing at the expense of the older, established churches.

Major Religion

CHRISTIANITY

DATE OF ORIGIN 1847 C.E.
NUMBER OF FOLLOWERS 4.9 million

HISTORY From the mid-nineteenth to the early twentieth century missionaries introduced Christianity to various parts of what is now Papua New Guinea. Roman Catholic missionaries from France landed on Muyua (Woodlark Island) in 1847. Although the surviving members of the mission left the island only eight years later, the Catholic effort was renewed by German and French members of the Missionaries of the Sacred Heart of Jesus on New Britain in 1882 and on New Guinea in 1884, by German representatives of the Society of the Divine Word along the northern New Guinea coast in 1896, and by French missionaries of the Society of Mary on Bougainville in 1901. In 1871 missionaries from the nondenominational London Missionary Society landed on New Guinea's southern coast. Wesleyan Methodists went to the Duke of York Islands in 1875, Lutherans arrived in Finschafen in 1886 and Madang in 1887, and Anglicans landed at Dogura in 1891. Seventh-day Adventists from Australia arrived in Papua (formerly British New Guinea) in 1908, and the German Liebenzeller Evangelical Mission entered the Admiralty Islands in 1914. The United Church in Papua New Guinea (originally called the United Church in Papua New Guinea and Solomon Islands) was formed in 1968, the result of a merger of the churches that grew from two missions—the London Missionary Society and Australasian Methodist Church—and some associated congregrations. Since the mid-twentieth century many of the Christian churches have become localized, drawing their leaders from among Papua New Guineans instead of foreign missionaries, with the result that Christianity has become accepted as a part of everyday life.

EARLY AND MODERN LEADERS In different parts of Papua New Guinea people still reminisce about the first Christian missionaries to land in their midst. For example, Lutherans around Morobe remember Johann Flierl (1858–1947) and Christian Keysser (1877–1961). Flierl is considered the father of the Lutheran mission in Papua New Guinea, and Keysser, who was instrumental in publishing a dictionary of the indigenous Kate language in 1925, was known for his deep respect for the indigenous culture.

Bishop Louis Vangeke (1904–82), the son of a well-known sorcerer, was the first native Papua New Guinean to become a Roman Catholic priest. When Vangeke returned to Papua New Guinea in 1937 after completing his studies in Madagascar, his presence challenged the colonial authorities, whose strict regime forbade Papuan men to drink alcohol, wear shirts, or be in Port Moresby after dark—all of which were required of Vangeke as a Catholic priest.

Bishop Sione Kami (died in 1999), a Tongan Methodist who ministered in Papua New Guinea from 1968 until 1994, was instrumental in fostering ecumenical cooperation. He was one of the many Pacific Islander evangelists and missionaries who helped establish Christianity in Papua New Guinea. Other well-known Christian leaders include the Catholic archbishop Peter Korunku and Anglican archbishop George Ambo (born in 1922). Prominent contemporary leaders include the retired Anglican bishop David Hand, the Lutheran bishop Wesley Kigasung (born in 1951), the United Church moderator Samson Lowa, the Assemblies of God pastor Joseph Walters, and the Catholic archbishop Brian Barnes (born in 1933). These leaders have been active both within Papua New Guinea and in international bodies.

MAJOR THEOLOGIANS AND AUTHORS While the number of publications by indigenous authors has grown as Papua New Guinea continues its transition from an oral to a written tradition, the country has not produced a major Christian theologian. Nevertheless, the Christian influence is apparent in the writings of several prominent authors. The philosopher and politician Bernard Narokobi is well known for his book *The Melanesian Way: Total Cosmic Vision of Life* (1980), which blends elements of the traditional Melanesian worldview and Christianity. Similarly, Simeon Namunu (died 2002), who served as a United Church bishop, wrote about traditional beliefs from a Christian perspective. Former government minister Anthony Siaguru has been explicitly Christian in his regular political commentaries in the press, in which he often addresses corruption and the need for transparency. In his many books the respected writer and statesman Paulias Matane has often dealt with secular themes from a Christian viewpoint.

HOUSES OF WORSHIP AND HOLY PLACES One of the best-known houses of worship in Papua New Guinea is the imposing Norman-Romanesque Anglican Cathedral, which was built in the 1930s on an isolated plateau at Dogura. Sione Kami Memorial Church, in Port Moresby, was named for the United Church missionary and bishop.

In general, holy places in Papua New Guinea are associated with particular denominations or cultural groups. Rakunai village in East New Britain, for example, is the original burial place of Peter To Rot, a lay catechist killed by Japanese soldiers in 1945, who became the first Papua New Guinean to be beatified by the Roman Catholic Church. The chapel and surrounding springs there have become a focus for pilgrims. There is also a popular pilgrimage each year to Maria Helpim, a small Catholic shrine at Guyaba village near Madang.

Other holy places are associated with the arrival of early missionaries. These include Yule Island on the South Papuan coast, where a chapel commemorates the landing of the first Sacred Heart missionaries in 1885; Simbang, near Finschafen, the site of the first Lutheran mission station; and Kaieta beach, near Dogura, where the first Anglican missionaries landed. A *modawa* tree that sprouted from a corner post of the original Anglican mission house in Dogura has come to symbolize the survival and growth of the church in Papua New Guinea.

WHAT IS SACRED? The traditional Melanesian religious worldview, with its integration of the sacred and secular, continues to influence contemporary Papua New Guinean Christians in their perception of the sacred. While they consider the Bible to be sacred as the word of God, some, including many Catholics, consider statues and other devotional objects—most of them imported from the Philippines—and practices to be equally sacred. Papua New Guineans also tend not to separate church and state. For example, priests can run for office, and they have been elected to the National Parliament, and at one time there was a cross on the roof of the House of Assembly in Port Moresby.

Cemeteries are treated with a combination of reverence and fear, as are bones and other body parts of the dead. Some people have sought to retrieve the bones of ancestors held in overseas museums. Traditional totemic beliefs continue to be held by many Christians in Papua New Guinea; thus, they do not kill or eat animals, birds, or fish with which they have a totemic relationship.

HOLIDAYS AND FESTIVALS Papua New Guinea follows a Christian calendar, with public holidays at Christmas and Easter. Two of the country's six additional official holidays—Good Friday and Easter Monday—are associated with the observance of Easter. Major holidays may be marked by sporting or cultural events; however, aside from church services, there are few public religious celebrations. In some towns a cross is carried through the streets on Good Friday.

MODE OF DRESS Most members of Catholic and Anglican orders, particularly women, wear religious habits similar to those worn in Western countries. Some ministers of other churches—the Lutheran Church, for example—wear a clerical collar on formal occasions. Many male pastors in the United Church wear a wraparound cloth called a *sulu* instead of trousers. Some conservative Christian groups encourage a white shirt and tie for men and long skirts for women. For most people in Papua New Guinea, however, dress is not determined by religious affiliation but varies according to the altitude, the demands of work, and whether one lives in a rural or urban environment.

Churches differ in their views of traditional Papua New Guinean dress. Some consider it obscene, while others encourage its use on special occasions, including formal worship services. A long blouse commonly worn by Papua New Guinean women was originally introduced by missionaries.

DIETARY PRACTICES In general, dietary practices in Papua New Guinea depend more on the regional availability of food than on religious beliefs. The Seventh-day Adventist's proscription against eating pork has added significance in Papua New Guinea, where pigs are of great importance in traditional life and ritual. Catholics, like their fellows elsewhere, are expected to fast during Lent and to abstain from meat on Ash Wednesday and on Fridays during Lent, but few adhere strictly to these requirements. Some Christians follow indigenous cultural taboos prohibiting the eating of birds, fish, or other animals with which their tribes have totemic relationships. The chewing of betel nuts, which contain stimulants, is prohibited by some churches.

RITUALS Rituals in Papua New Guinea are often associated with life stages, such as a first birthday, marriage, and death. Many of these rituals have changed, reflecting the joint influence of Christianity and traditional beliefs. For example, traditional rituals associated with the purification of woman following childbirth and for strengthening the child might be combined with a Christian baptism.

Christian rituals in Papua New Guinea often retain a foreign aspect. Some Pentecostal pastors stress the Bible and preaching in conducting services, copying the manner of televangelists, while priests and pastors in sacrament-oriented churches tend to follow universal practices in their worship services, with translation into a local language being the major concession to the surrounding culture. There have been some attempts to integrate the Christian faith and indigenous culture—in reconciliation ceremonies between tribes that have been at war, for example—but such efforts are more the exception than the rule.

In Papua New Guinea, particularly in the Highlands, politics takes on a ritual or cultic aspect, with candidates often portraying themselves as "God-fearing" savior figures. Accordingly, candidates may be presented with tokens of honor—flowers, for example—or carried on people's shoulders during recruitment campaigns. A pastor is often invited to open campaign meetings with a prayer, and music may be provided by youth from a local church playing instruments provided by the candidate. A feast for the candidate's supporters typically follows.

RITES OF PASSAGE Traditional initiation rites for men have been discouraged by some churches, and the Christian rites of baptism, first Communion, and confirmation now function as the rites of passage to a new way of life. The most significant traditional initiation rite for women was marriage. This is still the case, though many couples delay or avoid Christian marriage ceremonies. There have been attempts to incorporate some forms of the traditional initiation rites within Christian religious practices. For example, an extended retreat into the forest for purification and instruction may precede the Christian confirmation rite.

People normally become members of a Christian community through baptism, either as children or adults. Some churches emphasize a private moment of conversion involving a personal commitment to Christ, with baptism being merely the outward sign of this prior commitment. Baptism in Papua New Guinea is often a public event that is usually performed in a dammed-up stream.

Funerary rites were traditionally perceived to constitute an initiation into a new life with a different role in the community. The deceased have gone to live in the place of the dead, but they could be summoned to aid the living by giving advice or by helping to kill or injure enemies. Traditional beliefs hold that the spirit of a dead person must be buried with the body, requiring relatives of anyone who dies far from home to retrieve the spirit, as well as the body, of the deceased. This and other practices indicate that Christianity has had little influence on traditional mortuary practices. For Papua New Guinean Christians, the mourning period tends to be curtailed, and some churches encourage the celebration of a funerary feast while an elderly person is still alive, thus precluding the traditional festivities associated with the spirit of the dead that would normally take place upon the person's death.

MEMBERSHIP Local churches have sought growth through traditional missionary activities, such as preaching and social work. One method commonly used to attract new members, particularly youth, is to offer them education in a church-run school or to offer to pay their fees at schools run by other churches or the state. There have also been renewed efforts at church "planting"—that is, starting a new church with a small group of people—and ministering to backsliders on the part of evangelical preachers.

SOCIAL JUSTICE The mainline churches—Catholic, Lutheran, United, and Anglican—are major providers of health and educational services in Papua New Guinea. Church agencies provide 50 percent of health services in rural areas and 45 percent of such services throughout the country. Only in 1985 did state school enrollments rise higher than those of the mission schools. With the average number of years of formal education at less than three, churches have pushed for universal education and vocational training.

By lobbying the government, holding public meetings, and offering shelter and counseling services, the Christian churches have addressed such issues as bribery and corruption, domestic violence, alcoholism, and gambling. Another recurrent issue is the plight of indigenous people from West Papua (Irian Jaya) who have fled to Papua New Guinea to escape the Indonesian military. The churches provide services for the refugees, and religious leaders have spoken out against government plans to repatriate them.

In addition to their formal social service programs, the mainline churches issue statements about injustice through the Papua New Guinea Council of Churches and sometimes air social justice issues through the *Wantok* newspaper, a publication of the Word Publishing Company, which is jointly owned by the Catholic, Lutheran, Anglican, and United churches. The Salvation Army also takes a leading role in addressing social issues.

SOCIAL ASPECTS The churches strongly emphasize marriage and the family, though only a minority of couples take Christian marriage vows. Although marriages were traditionally arranged by the families of the bride and groom, churches have supported the trend toward young men and women choosing their own spouses.

Faith is integrated into most areas of social life in Papua New Guinea. Social occasions, including all sessions of parliament and most public gatherings, normally begin with a prayer. At the village level churches offer the only formally organized activities for youth, including sports.

POLITICAL IMPACT Papua New Guinea's government is a secular democracy. Nevertheless, the preamble to the country's constitution pledges citizens "to guard and pass on to those who come after us our noble traditions and the Christian principles that are ours now." Church-based political parties have had little success in Papua New Guinea. Still, most politicians see it as an advantage to be regarded as a "God-fearing" Christian.

The Catholic Bishops Conference of Papua New Guinea and Solomon Islands is at times an outspoken critic of the government, taking public officials to task on such issues as corruption and the introduction of gambling machines. With the churches providing about half the health and educational services in the country, the bishops have the power to influence government policy in those areas.

CONTROVERSIAL ISSUES The most controversial issues affecting Christian churches in Papua New Guinea are clergymen's becoming politicians and fragmentation among the churches. John Momis (born in 1942), at the time a Catholic priest, took a leading role in the creation of the country's constitution, and several priests and pastors, including Momis, have been elected to the National Parliament, much to the consternation of bishops and other church leaders, who have published statements prohibiting their priests from standing in national elections, on pain of suspension from public pastoral and priestly duties.

Prior to World War II there were just seven denominational groups working in Papua New Guinea: Anglicans, Congregationalists, Evangelicals, Lutherans, Methodists, Catholics, and Seventh-day Adventists. After the war representatives of many other denominations and interdenominational groups—including the Baptists, Assemblies of God, South Seas Evangelical Mission, Christian Brethren, Australian Church of Christ, Swiss Evangelical Brotherhood Mission, Nazarene Mission, Apostolic Church Mission, and New Tribes Mission—began to arrive. Prominent among the Pentecostal missions were the Four Square Gospel Church, the Christian Revival Crusade, and the Swedish Pentecostal "Philadelphia" Church. By the early 21st century almost 90 church organizations held work permits from the Papua New Guinean government. This has often led to fragmentation and competition among the different church groups.

CULTURAL IMPACT Early Christian missionaries introduced the written word, printing facilities, and the work of translation to the indigenous peoples of Papua New Guinea. Hosea Linge (died in 1973), who in 1932 became the first Papua New Guinean to publish a book, and Alice Wedega (1905–87), the first woman to hold a seat in the country's National Parliament, have explained in their writings the inevitable transition from the oral tradition to the written tradition. The Christian churches have covertly supported the notion that Papua New Guinean writers have a moral obligation to act as their society's conscience. For example, the autobiographical works of such authors as Albert Maori Kiki (born in 1931), Vincent Eri (born in 1936), and Michael Somare (born in 1936) asserted the value of traditional culture against the impositions of the West. Later writers, including the journalist Frank Senge Kolma (born in 1963), have addressed political issues and criticized social, political, and economic injustices.

Traditionally, decoration of the human body was the principal art form in Papua New Guinea, and this form has been accepted and adapted by some churches. Traditional graphics and carvings have been used in the decoration of some churches, including the Catholic cathedral in Port Moresby. Christianity has also had a negative impact on traditional art, however. Many churches, for example, seeing a link between traditional art and what they regard as satanic spirits, have supported the destruction of the *tambaran* (spirit) houses, which were important sources of artwork.

Most Christian religious music in Papua New Guinea is imported. The *Praise* program on the country's one national television channel airs music mostly from Polynesia. Introduced by early Methodist missionaries, *peroveta,* or prophet, songs blending Melanesian and Polynesian themes continue to be popular.

Other Religions

The Australian nursing sister Violet Hoehnke introduced the Bahai faith into Papua New Guinea while working on Manus Island in 1954. Apelis Mazakmat, the first native-born Bahai, spread the faith to the island of New Ireland and beyond, and traveling teachers took it to New Guinea. Numbering more than 15,000, Bahais are now found throughout the country. With their policies of tolerance and obedience to the government, they form an unobtrusive but growing presence in Papua New Guinean society.

Mahayana Buddhism was officially introduced into Papua New Guinea in 1996 by a Taiwanese Buddhist monk, Fo Kuang Shang, who went to minister in the Buddhist Centre in Port Moresby at the invitation of Buddhist workers from China and Malaysia who wanted a religious teacher and guide. There are fewer than 1,000 Buddhists in Papua New Guinea, and all are foreign-born. They are found in the main cities and in other areas where there are expatriate workers. They perform charitable work and run a preschool.

Islam was formally registered as a religious organization in Papua New Guinea in 1983. Like Buddhism, it was first taken to the country by expatriate workers, but it has since been accepted by some Papua New Guineans. Most Muslims in Papua New Guinea follow the Shafi'iyah school of the Sunni branch of Islam. There is a group of Ahmadia Muslims in Kimbe, West New Britain, but their movement is not accepted by other Muslims. Most Muslims live in Port Moresby, where there is a mosque, and in Simbu Province in the Highlands. Muslim's belief in one, unseen God is acceptable to Papua New Guineans, and traditional menstrual taboos bear similarities to those of Islam. Food restrictions, however, especially the prohibition against eating pork, tend to separate Muslims from mainstream Papua New Guinean society.

There are about 500 Hindus in Papua New Guinea. All are expatriate workers, and most come from India, Nepal, Fiji, and Australia. They gather in small groups to celebrate such Hindu festivals as the Diwali festival of lights. Through the Satya Sai Centre in Port Moresby, they collect funds and work in cooperation with the Catholic Missionary Sisters of Charity to help the needy.

Judaism is limited to a small number of foreign delegates and expatriate workers—fewer than 100—who practice their faith privately. There are no known Papua New Guinean Jews.

Any reference to indigenous religion in general is problematic because of the diversity of cultures in Papua New Guinea. Moreover, indigenous religion in Papua New Guinea is dynamic, and the development of new forms has intensified since contact with modern civilizations was established.

The Papua New Guinean philosopher Bernard Narokobi, stressing the holistic character of the traditional Melanesian worldview, has written that "for [Melanesians] . . . an experience, or experience in general, is a total encounter of the living person with the universe that is alive and explosive." According to this view a person is born into a cosmic spiritual order, and many of life's tasks are devoted to the maintenance and promotion of that order. Departure from it most likely leads to misfortune for oneself or one's children.

Indigenous rituals in Papua New Guinea range from large communal events like pig-killing ceremonies to personal rites like spells. The aim of such practices is to influence relationships between people and between humans and the spirit world, with the intention of maintaining the well-being of both the individual and the community. Dancing, gardening, the slaughter of animals, and sexual activity are woven together through rich symbolism and artistic display to form a unity in both economic and religious life. As the religious historian Ennio Mantovani has written, "The link between the garden, the womb and the tomb is obvious in everyday life and in religious life."

A particular form of logic lies behind much traditional ritual. By this logic, which the historian Garry Trompf calls the "logic of retribution," revenge killings, prodigious acts of kindness, and intricate explanations of events like sickness and death are integrated in the Melanesian understanding of the give-and-take that motivates beings, both human and spiritual.

With most Papua New Guineans professing to be Christian, indigenous religious rites have become less frequent and less obvious; however, the worldview underlying traditional ritual continues to influence people's lives. For example, belief in the power of the spirits of the dead remains a source of fear, and in some areas accusations of witchcraft as the cause of death have increased. In addition, so-called cargo cults have continued to appear, incited by the visions or dreams of prophets who claim knowledge of secret sources of wealth and well-being. Some scholars view these cults and other new indigenous religious movements as ways of seeking salvation in Melanesian terms.

Melanesian indigenous religion is also influential in Papua New Guinean contemporary art, including drama and graphic art. Groups like the Raun Raun Theatre perform throughout Papua New Guinea and internationally, dramatizing traditional myths and integrating traditional Melanesian spirituality in critiques of present-day realities. A homogenized indigenous artistic style has been used in the decoration of such modern buildings as the House of Assembly in Port Moresby. Attempts to incorporate traditional art in modern building projects have stirred controversy, however, when they were perceived to tamper with the religious meanings of the art forms.

Philip Gibbs

See Also Vol. I: *Christianity, Lutheranism, Roman Catholicism*

Bibliography

Aerts, Theo. *Christianity in Melanesia.* Port Moresby: University of Papua New Guinea Press, 1998.

Herdt, Gilbert H., ed. *Rituals of Manhood: Male Initiation in Papua New Guinea.* Berkeley: University of California Press, 1982.

Irwin, Geoffrey. *The Prehistoric Exploration and Colonisation of the Pacific.* New York: Cambridge University Press, 1992.

MacDonald, Mary. "Magic, Medicine and Sorcery." In *An Introduction to Melanesian Religions,* Point Series No. 6. Edited by Ennio Mantovani. Goroka, Papua New Guinea: Melanesian Institute, 1984.

Mantovani, Ennio. "Comparative Analysis of Cultures and Religions." In *An Introduction to Melanesian Religions,* Point Series No. 6. Edited by Ennio Mantovani. Goroka, Papua New Guinea: Melanesian Institute, 1984.

Narokobi, Bernard. "What Is Religious Experience for a Melanesian?" In *Living Theology in Melanesia: A Reader,* Point Series No. 8. Edited by John D'Arcy May. Goroka, Papua New Guinea: Melanesian Institute, 1985.

Pech, Rufus. "The Acts of the Apostles in Papua New Guinea and Solomon Islands." In *An Introduction to Ministry in Melanesia,* Point Series No. 7. Edited by B. Schwarz. Goroka, Papua New Guinea: Melanesian Institute, 1985.

Siaguru, Anthony. *In-House in Papua New Guinea with Anthony Siaguru.* Canberra: Asia Pacific Press, 2001.

Trompf, G.W. *Melanesian Religion.* Cambridge: Cambridge University Press, 1991.

———. *Payback: The Logic of Retribution in Melanesian Religions.* Cambridge: Cambridge University Press, 1994.

Zocca, F., and N. de Groot. *Young Melanesian Project: Data Analysis,* Point Series No. 21. Goroka, Papua New Guinea: Melanesian Institute, 1997.

Paraguay

POPULATION 5,884,491

ROMAN CATHOLIC 89.5 percent

PROTESTANT 6.0 percent

OTHER 2.0 percent

NONRELIGIOUS 2.5 percent

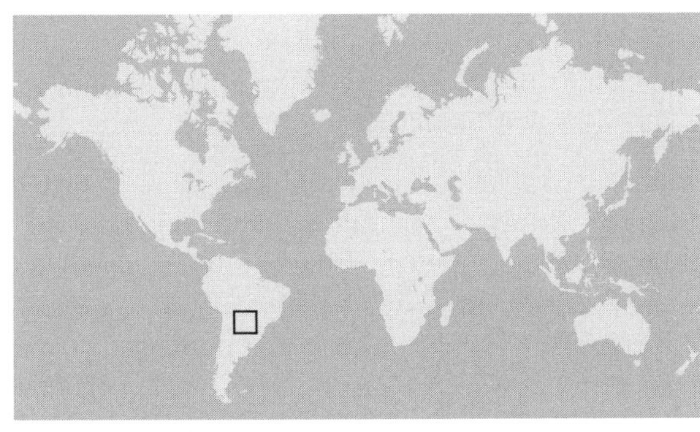

Country Overview

INTRODUCTION The Republic of Paraguay, located in South America, is a landlocked country of 157,048 square miles (406,752 square kilometers). It is bordered by Bolivia to the north and northwest; Argentina to the south, southeast, and west; and Brazil to the northeast and east.

Spanish conquistador Juan de Salazar and his company of soldiers and colonists founded Fort Asunción in 1537 as part of a campaign to subdue and colonize an estimated 200,000 Amerindians, principally the Tupi-Guaraní. Within 20 years of its founding, Asunción boasted a Spanish population of 1,500, a Roman Catholic cathedral, a textile mill, and the beginning of the livestock industry. For more than two centuries Asunción was a principal center of Spanish influence in the Río de la Plata basin.

In 1811 Paraguay declared its independence from Spain and from the newly independent government in Buenos Aires. The country's first president, Dr. José Gaspar Rodríguez de Francia, established a dictatorship that lasted from 1811 to 1840. Catholicism was the only religion allowed, but the regime was anticlerical. Rodríguez de Francia's next two successors ruled as dictators, abusing their power and weakening the country. Throughout the late nineteenth century and through the mid-twentieth century, Paraguay was led by numerous unsuccessful presidents. Gen. Alfredo Stroessner Matiauda came to power in 1954 and ruled ruthlessly until overthrown by a military coup in 1989, which provided an opening for democracy. Despite a marked increase in political infighting since then, the nation has held relatively free and regular presidential elections through the beginning of the twenty-first century.

From the 1870s to the present, Paraguay has experienced considerable social progress, mainly due to the arrival of waves of immigrants from Argentina, Italy, Germany, France, Spain, the Middle East, and North America. Some of these early immigrants were members of Protestant congregations before their arrival in Paraguay. During the 1930s and after World War II, Japanese Shinto and Buddhist immigrants arrived and settled in agricultural colonies near Asunción and Encarnación. In the early 1970s thousands of Brazilians began migrating to Paraguay, mainly because of the availability of

Catholic families honor their deceased loved ones during the Day of the Dead in a cemetery in Paraguay. AP/WIDE WORLD PHOTOS.

cheap land; by the early 1990s an estimated 300,000 to 350,000 Brazilians, most of whom were Catholics or followers of spiritist religions (Candomblé and Umbanda), lived in the eastern border region. Also during the 1970s an estimated 30,000 to 50,000 immigrants (mainly Buddhists) from Korea, Hong Kong, and Taiwan began arriving in Paraguay. Many of these immigrant groups brought their own religious traditions with them, enriching the religious diversity of Paraguay.

RELIGIOUS TOLERANCE The Constitution of 1993 provides for freedom of religion for all persons. The government generally respects this right in practice and does not tolerate its abuse, either by governmental or private organizations. The constitution and other laws prohibit discrimination on the basis of religion. All religious groups must be registered with the Ministry of Education and Culture; however, the government imposes no controls on these groups, and many informal religious organizations exist.

Major Religion

ROMAN CATHOLICISM

DATE OF ORIGIN 1537 C.E.
NUMBER OF FOLLOWERS 5.3 million

HISTORY Prior to the arrival of Roman Catholic missionaries in 1537, the Amerindians of the region that is now Paraguay practiced animism. In 1547 the Bishopric of Our Lady of Asunción was created through a papal decree, but the first Catholic bishop did not preside within the diocese until 1556. After 1588 Jesuit and Franciscan priests began working among the Indians along various rivers, including areas now part of surrounding nations.

In order to gain converts the Jesuits recognized the importance of protecting the Indians from Spanish and Portuguese enslavement. From 1609 to 1767 the Jesuits established and maintained missions among the Guaraní and other tribes in the upper Plata River region, where the natives were settled in a system of communal towns called *reducciones* under Jesuit administration.

The Treaty of Madrid in 1750 transferred the territory occupied by seven Jesuit-Guaraní missions, located east of the Uruguay River, from Spain to Portugal. Although Spain, at least officially, no longer permitted slavery, this inhumane practice was legal in the Portuguese territories. Shortly thereafter the Spanish rulers ordered the missions to be disbanded, and Pope Clement XIV suppressed the Jesuits, forcing the missionaries to abandon their work in approximately 100 *reducciones* in the Americas, including those in Paraguay. In 1754, however, the Guaraní Indians and a few dissident Jesuits refused to abide by the order to disband the missions and created a short-lived rebellion that was cruelly put down by the Spanish authorities.

Following the Jesuit's formal expulsion from the Americas in 1767 by Spain's King Charles III, many of the Paraguayan Indians were captured and sold into slavery and became part of mestizo (mixed European and Indian ancestry) society. After 1767 the spiritual administration of the Jesuit *reducciones* was transferred to the Franciscans and other religious orders, while the public administration was given to Spanish and Portuguese civil officials.

Throughout the nineteenth century relations between church and state were poor. The state attempted to hold power over both the bishop and the clergy. President José Gaspar Rodríguez de Francia, although advancing a secular state, was extremely anticlerical and resorted to violent measures to suppress the church. After Rodríguez de Francia died in 1840, Carlos Antonio López came to power and ruled despotically from 1841 to 1862. After his death in 1862, he was followed in power by his son, Francisco Solano López, who ruled until 1870. President Francisco Solano López secretly recruited priests to gain information about insurrection among the people. The second López was also responsible for plunging his weak nation into a savage and bloody war against the combined military forces of Argentina, Uruguay, and Brazil. In the War of the Triple Alliance (1865–70), about two-thirds of Paraguay's adult males were killed, and much of its territory was lost to the victors. Church-state relations worsened after the government executed the bishop of Asunción, Manuel Antonio Palacio, during the War of the Triple Alliance. When the war ended, there were only 55 priests left in the whole country, and there was no bishop for 11 years.

Between 1870 and 1954 there were 40 presidents in Paraguay, most of whom were jailed, exiled, or murdered before they completed their terms of office. The conservative Colorado Party, founded in 1887, ruled the country from its founding until the 1904 Revolution, when the Liberal Party seized power and ruled with only a brief interruption until 1940. The Colorado Party dominated the political life of the country beginning in 1946. In 1954 Gen. Alfredo Stroessner Matiauda led a military coup and took control of the government. Beginning in the late 1950s the bishops and priests were frequently at odds with the national government. Confrontations began with individual priests who preached sermons calling for political freedom and social justice. The political and human rights activities of the clergy and various lay groups, such as Catholic Action, pushed the church hierarchy to make increasingly critical statements about the regime of President Stroessner.

In 1988, a national election year, Pope John Paul II visited Paraguay. Although the government was reluctant to allow the pope to convene with representatives from opposition political parties, labor, and community groups, the visit was ultimately sanctioned. Pope John Paul II noted the importance of church involvement in Paraguayan society. Observers saw the pope's visit as supporting the Paraguayan Catholic Church's encouragement of a shift from dictatorship to democracy. On 3 February 1989 a new stage of Paraguayan history began with the overthrow of the Stroessner regime and a transition to democratic rule under the continuing leadership of the conservative Colorado Party.

EARLY AND MODERN LEADERS Msgr. Juan Sinforiano Bogarín, who was bishop of Asunción from 1895 to 1930 and became archbishop (1930–49) after the post was created, and Msgr. Aníbal Mena Porta, archbishop from 1949 to 1969, were key figures in the establishment of the Paraguayan Catholic Church. Both hoped to establish a church that would act as an intermediary among the various contenders for political power in Paraguay. Msgr. Ismael Blas Rolón Silvero served as archbishop from 1970 to 1989 and was followed by Msgr. Felipe Santiago Benitez Avalos (1989–2002). Contemporary archbishops have stressed the importance of respecting human rights, strengthening democracy, and encouraging political dialogue among all social sectors.

MAJOR THEOLOGIANS AND AUTHORS Bible scholar José Luis Caravias has worked with the Christian Agrarian Leagues since the 1960s; he was the principal editor of *Vivir como Hermanos* (Live as Brothers), published in 1971, which is one of the most important documents produced in Paraguay by proponents of liberation theology, a socially and politically progressive Latin American Catholic movement.

HOUSES OF WORSHIP AND HOLY PLACES In Caacupé, a city in eastern Paraguay, devotees make an annual pilgrimage on 8 December to the shrine of the Virgin of Caacupé. Jesuit *reducciones,* including those found in La Trinidad, San Ignacio Guazú, and Santa María, continue to be significant sites of Catholic influence.

WHAT IS SACRED? Most Catholic churches in Paraguay have a variety of statues of Mary, Jesus, the Apostles, and other saints, which are revered and maintained by the faithful and used for special occasions, such as processions during Christmas and Holy Week.

HOLIDAYS AND FESTIVALS Together with Immaculate Conception Day (8 December), the most important religious holidays are Lent and Holy Week. The religious center of Caacupé is the most important site for Immaculate Conception Day. Another prominent religious celebration is San Blas Day, which honors the patron saint of Paraguay on 3 February. Christmas is more of a family holiday than a religious one, although special activities are planned, such as pageants and parades.

MODE OF DRESS There is no special dress code for Catholics in Paraguay.

DIETARY PRACTICES Many Paraguayan Catholics still fast or refrain from eating meat during Lent, as is common among most Catholics all over the world.

RITUALS Since colonial times Catholicism has been an essential component of Paraguayan social life. In the mid-twentieth century active participation in the rites of the church, such as confession and the Mass, was more common among upper- and middle-income groups and among women more so than men. By the beginning of the twenty-first century, the number of Catholics who practiced the traditional rites of the church had diminished.

RITES OF PASSAGE In Paraguay Catholic ritual marks the important transitions in life: baptism, first Communion, confirmation, marriage, and last rites. Many poor couples, however, cannot afford a church wedding and forego this ritual for a civil ceremony, or they decide to live together without the benefit of a ceremony.

MEMBERSHIP For many Paraguayans affiliation with the Roman Catholic Church is more of a social obligation than a moral and spiritual commitment, with less than 20 percent of Catholics regularly attending Mass. Religious nominalism is dominant in Paraguay, and the Catholic clergy is doing little to revitalize the church.

SOCIAL JUSTICE During the 1960s students and faculty at the Catholic University of Our Lady of Asunción expressed antiregime sentiment. Some of the worker organizations that arose from this period sponsored literacy programs, welfare activities, and various types of cooperatives. In addition, beginning in the 1960s progressive Catholics operated a news magazine and radio station, both of which were critical of the government's repressive measures.

SOCIAL ASPECTS Traditionally religious devotion in Paraguay is a sphere of activity dominated by women and children. Until the 1960s the Roman Catholic Church and popular Catholic religiosity dominated the social life of Paraguay. As elsewhere, however, a large gap has emerged between the official teachings of the church and the people regarding marriage and family life. A growing number of couples now choose civil rather than religious weddings. In addition, there has been an increase in the number of children born to single mothers, in the use of unauthorized methods of birth control, and in the divorce rate.

POLITICAL IMPACT Throughout the 1970s and 1980s Catholic Church authorities criticized the absence of political freedom in Paraguay and the government's human rights abuses. In response to criticism the government expelled foreign-born clergy and intermittently closed the Catholic University of Our Lady of Asunción, the Catholic news magazine *Comunidad,* and the Catholic radio station. The archbishop of Asunción, Msgr. Ismael Blas Rolón Silvero, excommunicated several leading government officials and refused, along with other clergy, to participate in major civic and religious celebrations.

At the Catholic Bishops Conference of Paraguay in the early 1990s, 14 bishops signed a pronouncement entitled "One Constitution for Our Nation." In this document the Catholic Church of Paraguay gave unconditional support to establish a new era of religious liberty in the nation, which began with congressional approval of a new constitution in February 1993.

CONTROVERSIAL ISSUES Since the 1970s a growing number of Paraguayan Catholics have been discontent with the church's official policy regarding birth control, divorce, remarriage, abortion, the role of women in the church, obligatory celibacy for priests and nuns, the absolute authority of the pope and the bishops, and the lack of lay participation in decision making within the church. The ongoing tension between conservatives, moderates, and liberals over the church's social priorities, its internal management, and the need for renewal and modernization are areas of social and religious conflict.

CULTURAL IMPACT During the colonial period Guaraní Indians crafted decorative wooden and stone statues and altarpieces for churches in Jesuit *reducciones.* These distinctive works of art attract visitors from around the world. In general, however, Catholicism did not have a strong impact on art, literature, and music, which are more secular than religious.

Other Religions

The Protestant movement entered Paraguay in the nineteenth century with the arrival of agents of the American Bible Society (1856) and missionaries of the Methodist Episcopal Church (1886), the Church of England or Anglicans (1886), and the German Lutherans (1893). During the early twentieth century dozens of other Protestant groups appeared among the growing immigrant population or as the result of missionary endeavors from Europe and North America. Prior to the 1950s the total Protestant population in Paraguay was less than 10,000, but it had grown to about 311,000, or an estimated 6 percent of the total population, in 2002. Approximately 35 percent of all Protestants in Paraguay are Pentecostals. Non-Pentecostals, totaling 65 percent of all Protestants, include, among others, Adventists, Anglicans, Baptists, Lutherans, and Mennonites.

Included in the non-Pentecostal category are at least 25 Mennonite denominations with approximately 70,000 adherents, most of whom live in 17 agricultural colonies scattered across northern and eastern Paraguay. Whereas other Protestant immigrants, regardless of their cultural heritage, have largely assimilated to the dominant Paraguayan Hispanic culture, the Mennonites have remained a culturally distinct social group, maintaining many of the characteristics of nineteenth-century rural European and North American society and retaining the use of their original language—Plautdietsch, or Low German. Since the 1920s the government has allowed the Mennonites to create their own agricultural colonies; maintain their cultural traditions; manage their own educational, medical, social, and financial institutions; freely practice their religion; and be exempt from military service.

Other religious groups were estimated at 2 percent of the population in 2002. These include the Russian Orthodox Church and a variety of non-Protestant Christian groups—the Church of Jesus Christ of Latter-day Saints (Mormons), Jehovah's Witnesses, People of God Church (unique to Paraguay), Universal Church of the Kingdom of God (from Brazil), and Voice of the Chief Cornerstone Church (from Puerto Rico), among others.

A variety of non-Christian religions, such as Judaism, Islam, and the Baha'i faith, are present, especially among immigrants from the Middle East. Also represented are Asian religions from India, China, Korea, and Japan, including Hindu, Buddhist, and Shinto groups. Elements of precolonial animistic Amerindian religions continue to exist, especially in the western region of Chaco; 17 tribal groups total about 60,000 people. Also present are new religious movements from Brazil and Argentina, such as Ancient Wisdom (Rosicrucians, Gnostics, and New Acropolis Cultural Centers) and Magic-Spiritualist-Psychic-New Age groups, such as Candomblé, Umbanda, Basilio Scientific School, Spiritualist Centers, and Unification Church of Rev. Sun Myung Moon, among others.

Clifton L. Holland

See Also Vol. 1: *Christianity, Roman Catholicism*

Bibliography

Brierly, Peter. *World Churches Handbook.* London: Christian Research, 1997.

Herring, Hubert. *A History of Latin America from the Beginnings to the Present.* 3rd ed. New York: Alfred A. Knopf, 1968.

Plett, Rodolfo. *El Protestantismo en el Paraguay.* Asunción: FLET, 1987.

PROLADES-RITA official website. 13 Sept. 2004. http://www.prolades.com.

U.S. Department of the Army. *Area Handbook for Paraguay.* Washington, D.C., 1992.

U.S. Department of State. Bureau of Democracy, Human Rights, and Labor. *International Religious Freedom Report 2003: Paraguay.* Washington, D.C., 2003.

Peru

POPULATION 27,949,639

ROMAN CATHOLIC 90 percent

PROTESTANT (ANGLICAN, METHODIST, EVANGELICAL CHRISTIAN) 8 percent

OTHER 2 percent

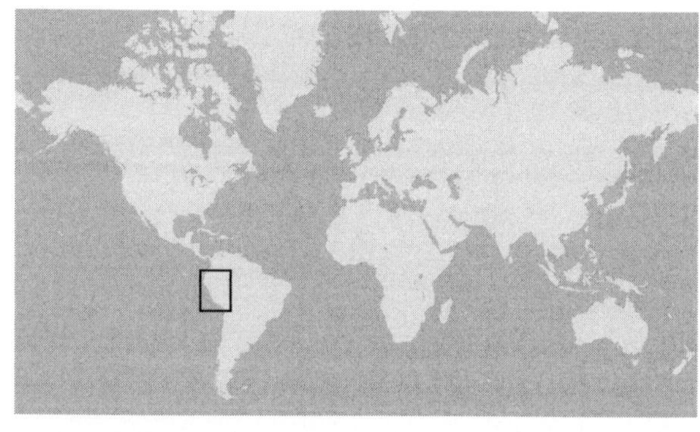

Country Overview

INTRODUCTION Peru, bordering the Pacific Ocean, is located in the western part of South America between Chile and Ecuador. The complex geography of Peru is reflected in the native Andean concept of *huaca,* which refers to anything imbued with supernatural power. Notable features of the landscape—from mountain crags to stones—are seen as having this power. This conception of sacred geography continues today, centuries after the introduction of Catholicism.

The earliest centralized state to develop in the region was that of Chavín, which flourished between 950 B.C.E. and 450 B.C.E. It served as a center for an influential priesthood, which spread a distinctive ritual and artistic style. After its decline a number of localized cultures, including the Gallinazo, Mochica, Paracas, Nazca, and Chimú, developed on the coast and in the highlands.

The great Inca civilization arose from the Quechua people in the thirteenth century. From the fifteenth century the Incan ruler was worshiped as the God of the Sun and wielded absolute political and spiritual authority. The priests of the Inca empire oversaw a complex ceremonial calendar that reflected the agricultural preoccupations of Andean life.

After Francisco Pizarro and the Spanish arrived in the sixteenth century, Catholicism was imposed on the native population, and the religious rituals and artifacts of the indigenous groups were suppressed or destroyed. Although Catholicism is by far the dominant religion in Peru today, pan-Andean, pre-Christian elements of religious cosmology persist. For example, the feasts and dances associated with the summer and winter solstices have their parallels with the Christianized indigenous groups in Peru. In addition, Protestantism and Mormonism are growing rapidly among the poor residents of urban areas as well as among indigenous groups.

RELIGIOUS TOLERANCE After Peru's independence from Spain in the nineteenth century, the Roman Catholic Church was declared the official church of the state. This was a result of the church's influence over members of the constitutional conventions, a factor that ultimately outweighed the liberator's ideological preference for separation of church and state. Catholicism is no longer the official religion of Peru, but the church continues to enjoy a special privilege in relation to the state.

Protestantism began making a significant appearance in Peru in the nineteenth century, mainly through the presence of British diplomats and merchants, who practiced their faith in private and lived in relative peace with their Catholic neighbors. By the mid-nineteenth century the Catholic clergy had become less tolerant, but Peru's liberal factions made additional attempts to ensure religious freedom for Protestants and members of other religions, an effort that continues today.

Catholic devotees participate in a procession to celebrate the day of the Lord of the Miracles. The festival is based upon an image of the crucified Christ that was created in 1651 by an anonymous artist. AP/WIDE WORLD PHOTOS.

Major Religion

ROMAN CATHOLICISM

DATE OF ORIGIN 1531 C.E.
NUMBER OF FOLLOWERS 26 million

HISTORY The Spanish, led by Francisco Pizarro, arrived in Peru in 1531. Members of Roman Catholic religious orders went to the region shortly thereafter; these included Dominicans, Franciscans, and Mercederians by 1550, Augustinians in 1551, and Jesuits in 1568. For much of its history the church in Peru largely collaborated with the oligarchy, aligning itself with the *hacendados,* or large landowners. This began to change in the 1950s and 1960s with the arrival of Maryknoll priests in Puno, the Second Vatican Council, the meeting in Medellin of the Latin American Conference of Bishops, and the rise of liberation theology. The combined effect of these events was to distance the church from the ruling classes and to encourage its identification with the poor and marginalized. Yet by the 1980s a counterreaction had begun, instigated by more conservative elements within the institutional church, particularly in association with the Opus Dei movement.

EARLY AND MODERN LEADERS Roman Catholic friars went to Peru in the sixteenth century to spread Christianity to the native peoples. They took two types of religious figures with them; there were humanists such as Garcilaso de la Vega, who advanced the idea of native religious dignity, and zealots such as Viceroy Francisco de Toledo, who advocated the destruction of "idolatry."

The contemporary Catholic Church in Peru is faced with a somewhat similar dichotomy between conservatives and liberals. In 1992, 6 of Peru's 18 bishops were members of the highly conservative Opus Dei movement. The number seems to be increasing, for on 18 January 2002, *The National Reporter* wrote, "Observers believe Cipriani [Cardinal Juan Luis Cipriani of Lima, Peru] became the first Opus Dei cardinal in February 2001 in part because of the high concentration of Opus Dei bishops in Peru. Cipriani said there are three Peruvian bishops who are full members, and four to five more who belong to the Society of Holy Cross." On the other hand, Peru is also the home of Gustavo Gutierrez, the priest who introduced left-wing liberation theology to Latin America in his 1973 book *A Theology of Liberation.*

MAJOR THEOLOGIANS AND AUTHORS During the colonial era the writer and poet Garcilaso de la Vega, the son of a Spaniard and an Incan princess, produced works—such as *Comentarios reales* ("Royal Commentaries")—that asserted the validity of Incan religion and ways of life. At the same time, anti-idolatry campaigns were waged, led by such clerics as Pablo de Arriaga, who described them in detail in his *The Extirpation of Idolatries in Peru* (1621).

For many years the church ministered primarily to the *hacendados,* or large landowners, but this began to change in the mid-twentieth century, culminating in 1973 with the publication of Gustavo Gutierrez's *A Theology of Liberation.* Liberation theology, a movement arising from the modernizing and liberalizing climate of the Second Vatican Council, focuses specifically on the plight of the poor. A central component of liberation theology involves the formation of *Comunidades Eclesiasticas de Base,* or Christian Base Communities.

HOUSES OF WORSHIP AND HOLY PLACES Each village, town, and city in Peru has its own church, with a patron saint or religious figure who is celebrated annually. Throughout much of Peru's history and into the present day, however, the institutional church has been centered in the capital city of Lima. It is the center of church activities, which take place at the eastern edge of the Plaza de Armas. It is from this central square that all points in Peru are measured. In addition, native Andean conceptions of the sacredness of topographical features persist and have become intertwined with Christianity.

WHAT IS SACRED? In the fifteenth century, in addition to shrines in Tiahuanaco (situated in modern-day Bolivia) and other locations erected to such high deities as Viracocha, local topographical features (such as rocks and lakes) were considered sacred by different cults. In areas with strong native populations, Andean cosmology is mixed with Roman Catholicism, particularly in terms of animistic beliefs about spirits that inhabit the natural landscape. These spirits include *apus* (spirits of mountains, lakes, and other natural sites) and *naupa machus* (ancient ancestors); they reside in objects and locations known as *huacas.* The Spanish Catholic Church used syncretism to convert the native population, substituting Catholic saints for local deities and transforming local shrines into ones dedicated to Christianity. Thus, the Christian God was superimposed on Inca celestial deities such as the sun, while the Virgin Mary came to represent the spirits inhabiting nature.

The combination of forced conversion to Christianity and the lack of priestly involvement with large portions of the Peruvian (and especially the native Peruvian) population led to a personalization and localization of elements of Catholicism. For example, a tree that naturally resembled a cross might be dressed in a priestly cloth and venerated as both a Christian and a native Andean sacred symbol. In the more Hispanicized coastal areas of Peru, people follow pan-Catholic religious practices more closely, with an emphasis on venerating patron saints, manifestations of Christ, and the crucifix.

HOLIDAYS AND FESTIVALS Each village or town in Peru typically has its own annual patron-saint festival. This can be an expensive and labor-intensive affair, with *mayordomos* (festival sponsors) and, frequently, a *hermanadad* (brotherhood) taking part in organizing and funding the festival. The major festival in Peru is that of the Señor de los Milagros (Lord of the Miracles) in October. The cult of the Señor de los Milagros has its origin in the colonial-era exclusion of blacks and Native Americans from mainstream religious life in Lima. Slaves had created a chapel for themselves, on which an anonymous artist in 1651 painted an image of the crucified Christ that survived a huge earthquake a few years later. This formed the basis of the annual festival.

In the heavily native Andean town of Cuzco, the feast of Corpus Christi is celebrated as nowhere else in Latin America. Because the Catholic Corpus Christi festival occurs at the same time of year as the Inca June solstice, known as Inti Raymi, and the Andean harvest festivals, the Catholic festival has become closely linked with Inti Raymi in contemporary Peru. The association between the two continues today in Cuzco. Another Christian festival with clear pre-Christian elements is that of Qoyllur Rit'i (celebrated shortly before the feast of Corpus Christi), during which Peruvians travel to Mount Ausangate, near Cuzco, to venerate a boulder believed to be the site of an apparition of Jesus Christ. At this festival both local *apus* (spirits of natural sites) and Christ are honored.

Other special occasions that mix pre-Christian and Catholic beliefs and practices include the feasts of All Saints (1 November) and All Souls (2 November), during which families prepare offerings of food, drink, and cigarettes for their ancestors. Further evidence of the "Andeanization" of Christianity in parts of Peru is the relative lack, in different parts of the country, of festival attention to Easter, the climactic event in European Christianity.

Many of the specifically Peruvian Catholic festivals relate to natural disasters such as earthquakes, resulting in the veneration of "disaster saints" in a manner combining Catholic and Andean spiritual concerns. One of these "disaster saints" is the Señor de los Temblores (Lord of the Earthquakes), who serves as patron of Cuzco and who commemorates a great earthquake in 1650. Similarly, in Huanchaco, near Trujillo on the northern coast, the Virgen del Perpetuo Socorro (Virgin of Perpetual Help) is celebrated in commemoration of an earthquake in 1619.

MODE OF DRESS Members of the Catholic laity in Peru generally do not have a special mode of dress, with the exception of those garments worn for participation in specific festival processions. For example, during the Camino de la Cruz (Way of the Cross), held annually on Good Friday, participants acting out the roles of Pontius Pilate or the Virgin Mary typically dress in imitation of popular images of these figures. Additionally, during the Corpus Christi procession in heavily native Andean Cuzco, participants dress in native Andean costume.

For members of religious orders, particularly missionary nuns, the heat and relative scarcity of car transportation has resulted in the adoption of habits more suitable to the generally hot environment of Peru.

DIETARY PRACTICES Like Catholics in other countries, Peruvians follow basic Vatican II guidelines regarding abstention from meat on Fridays during Lent and fasting. For Catholics who continue to follow pre–Vatican II directives out of habit or preference, this may mean eating fish every Friday rather than only on Fridays during Lent. In addition, certain dietary practices are customary during particular feast days. For example, in the northern department of Piura it is traditional to not eat breakfast on Good Friday and, instead, to eat a large midday meal with up to seven courses. One dish customarily eaten in Peru at Easter is *malarrabia,* made with mashed plantains and accompanied by cheese and olives.

RITUALS When the Spanish went to Peru in the sixteenth century, there were four main kinds of religious devotion popularly practiced on the Iberian peninsula: pilgrimage to shrines of Mary, pilgrimage to shrines of Jesus Christ, veneration of saintly relics, and veneration of images of various saints. Of these, only pilgrimage to shrines devoted to Mary and Jesus were to become significant practices in Peru.

In addition to Catholic practices followed in other countries (such as attending Mass and participating in the sacraments), there are several distinctive Peruvian Catholic rituals. Most notably, virtually every village, town, and city has its own church, patron saint, and feast days. These play a vital role in the social life of the area. In particular, the patronal festivals associated with each locality are celebrated with varying degrees of pomp and splendor, and in agricultural areas they frequently correspond with harvest times. Many of Peru's coastal areas are generally Roman Catholic in religious practice, while in the highland towns and villages precolonial rituals intended to influence the fertility of the land have been preserved alongside Catholic rituals. Such Andean religious rites revolve around *despachos,* or dispatches to the nature spirits (*apus* and Pachamama, or Earth Mother). This entails making offerings of *aswa* (corn beer, also called *chicha*), animals such as llamas, bundles of maize, or coca and animal fat. Rituals involving animals are often tied to the Christian festival calendar; alpacas are involved in the Christmas celebration, sheep during the Carnaval season, and lambs on the feast of San Juan in June.

Public institutions also have patronal saints and festivals. For example, the military's patron saint is the Virgen de las Mercedes (Virgin of Ransoms), and her feast day is celebrated throughout Peru. Because geographical isolation and prejudice have prevented many Peruvians from participating fully in the institutional church, localities have historically developed their own versions of Christianity led by lay religious leaders. Peruvian Catholicism thus took on its own character, resulting in specific Catholic devotions, such as the veneration of the crucifix in a procession called Taita Mayo, or Father May (on 3 May), and taking down hilltop crosses to be blessed before re-erecting them on 14 September.

RITES OF PASSAGE Rites of passage are celebrated in Peru as in other Catholic countries and are frequently tied to the sacraments. A birth is marked by a *bautismo,* or baptism; initiation, by a wedding or entrance into religious life; and death, by a wake and funeral. The life cycle of an individual is marked by fiestas, the preparation and expense for which can be enormous. This may cause a delay in receiving a sacrament—as, for example, when a family needs to save for as long as two years before they can afford to throw a lavish party for a child. When the party can be thrown, the child can be baptized. Similarly, when a family member dies, the onus is traditionally on the bereaved family to offer food and drink to the community for a period of nine nights, during which formal *luto,* or mourning, is observed. A rationale of reciprocity underlies these customs, for the family offering food or entertainment for a baptism or wake can expect to be invited to their neighbor's celebrations in the near future.

MEMBERSHIP During the colonial era the *encomienda* system operated to spread Christianity to the native population. Adopted in 1503, this system obligated indigenous peoples to supply labor and tribute to *encomenderos* (colonists who were usually large landowners) in return for protection and education in Christianity. In practice, however, the *encomienda* system more closely resembled slavery and was not eliminated until the late eighteenth century. In many ways the similar *hacendado* (large landowner) system persisted in the northern coastal area until the 1970s. Native American resistance to this system during the 1560s took the form of a millenarian religious revival in Huamanga known as Taki Onqoy (dancing sickness), which preached rejection of Spanish culture and religion. Adherents experienced seizures, danced convulsively, and fell to the ground, while leaders claimed to be messengers from the native deities.

The combination of the colonial-era church's strategy of syncretism and the church's inability to effectively minister to much of the population in remote areas has resulted in a largely syncretic form of Catholicism in Peru. During the 1970s the Christian Base Community movement (influenced by liberation theology) sought to revitalize parish life in Latin America, including Peru. Nuns, priests, and lay leaders went to the formerly neglected rural areas to prepare residents to be lay leaders in their home parishes.

SOCIAL JUSTICE Although elements of the official Catholic Church hierarchy in Peru are staunchly conservative, at the grassroots level the church has been highly activist in organizing the populace in the form of neighborhood associations, self-improvement groups, and mother's clubs. Church organizations such as Caritas and Catholic Relief Services are active in Peru. By providing food to the poor, Caritas in particular played a vital role in the 1990s during President Fujimori's "shock stabilization" plan (to stabilize inflation and create revenue).

An important factor in the mobilization of church activists for the cause of social justice was the theology of liberation advocated by Gustavo Gutierrez, for whom Christian salvation was intimately tied to human liberation. According to liberation theology, sin had both individual and collective dimensions, and therefore in order to fully spread and live the gospel, the church needed to align itself more actively with the political struggles of the poor and disenfranchised. Centros de Educación Popular (Popular Education Centers) were opened by church advocates of liberation theology to provide materials and resources to aid activists in their efforts to organize the populace. Overall, nuns and priests increased their political and social involvement in Peru during the 1970s and 1980s.

SOCIAL ASPECTS Family life among Peruvian Catholics is enriched by participation in fiestas organized around the sacraments and the rites of passage. In addition, a distinctive aspect of Peruvian Catholicism at the local level is the tradition of *compadrazgo*, or the relationship between parent and godparent. This form of ritual coparenthood has important economic and social, as well as religious, components. Catholics in a number of countries follow the tradition of naming godparents for children, with an emphasis on the godparent offering spiritual and temporal guidance and support for the godchild. In Peru, however, the relationship between the parents and godparents (*compadres*, or coparents) is highlighted as well, in order to extend the network of fictive kin that can be called upon for support.

POLITICAL IMPACT Until the nineteenth century the Catholic Church and the Peruvian state were closely connected. The church was an arm of the state with significant financial assets, and it wielded significant influence in the areas of education and social welfare. Since Peru achieved independence in the nineteenth century, however, the church has lost primary control over such vital realms as education and marriage. While the Catholic Church is no longer the official religion of Peru (due in large part to a 1979 constitutional revision), it continues to hold a privileged position in relation to the state and is entitled to government cooperation. Church and state ritual are closely intertwined, linking political events with Holy Week and saint's festivals. It is notable, in this respect, that the presidential inauguration involves a High Mass in the Lima cathedral.

By the 1960s and 1970s the church and state had come into renewed and sometimes volatile conflict as the military-controlled government endangered civil liberties, thrusting the church into the position of advocate for the marginalized. Church-state relations were particularly difficult during Fujimori's presidency in the 1990s, starting with the election period, when conservative bishops unofficially tried to undermine Fujimori's candidacy, and continuing as a result of concerns about human rights abuses and the issue of birth control.

CONTROVERSIAL ISSUES Controversy in the Peruvian Catholic Church today results from tension between liberals and conservatives. Unlike other Latin American countries (such as Brazil, which has a church that can be described as liberal and critical of the Vatican, or Colombia, where the church generally adheres to Vatican policies), the Peruvian church has both orientations. Debated issues include the role of women in the church and the pros and cons of capitalist industrialization. In the 1980s, in particular, liberation-theology Catholics were accused of collusion with guerrilla terrorists who were tied to the emergence of the Shining Path in 1980 and of the Tupac Amaru movement in 1984. These accusations were never officially substantiated, however, and terrorist groups killed liberals as well as conservatives.

CULTURAL IMPACT During the colonial era the Cuzquena, or Cuzco, school of painting flourished. Native Andeans were required to create copies of European religious art for colonial churches, and the result was a distinctive artistic style that combined the baroque with indigenous elements and the use of bright colors and gold. Today in Peru the devotional art known as *retablos* is a popular form of folk art. These are three-dimensional representations of scenes, often religious, made from potato paste and painted bright colors.

Other Religions

Protestantism has spread rapidly in Peru since the 1970s. The first Anglican church was founded in Lima in 1849, and the first Methodist missionary arrived from the United States in 1877. During this period Joseph Lancaster, an English preacher, opened schools in Peru, and the Regions Beyond Missionary Society was founded.

There are two types of Protestantism in Latin America: mainline Protestant churches and evangelical groups. Mainline denominations include the Methodist or the Lutheran churches (originally established as the result of foreign immigration or early missionary activity). The evangelical groups, whose adherents are called Evangelistas, are primarily committed to spreading the gospel and promoting a Bible-centered religious ideology. In addition, approximately one quarter of Peru's non-Catholics are Mormons. Evangelical Christianity has been popular at the grassroots level and was a major factor in Fujimori's successful 1990 presidential campaign.

Since World War II Protestant groups have continued their struggle for acceptance and equality in Peru, particularly in relation to the government. One point of contention was a Peruvian law that mandated religion classes at all schools. In the postwar years this led to criticisms from the ministry of education that Protestant schools were failing to teach Catholicism. A breakthrough occurred in 1956, when minister of education Jorge Basadre eliminated the rule.

Pentecostals are the most prominent group of evangelical Christians in Peru today. The popularity of Pentecostalism may be attributed to the desire for greater participation in church life, less ritualized forms of worship, and the massive urban growth since the 1970s that has left people stranded in unfamiliar environments and in need of the support system that evangelical religion provides.

Another growing religion of note is the Bahai faith, one of the few non-Christian religions in Peru. The Bahai community in Peru has distinguished itself by its efforts to promote religious understanding and interfaith collaboration. A letter written by the Universal House of Justice (the governing body of the Bahai faith) calling for an elimination of religious intolerance played a role in the establishment in 2002 of a Directorate of Interfaith Affairs in Peru.

Natalie M. Underberg

See Also Vol. 1: *Christianity, Evangelical Movement, Pentecostalism, Roman Catholicism*

Bibliography

Dean, Carolyn. *Inka Bodies and the Body of Christ: Corpus Christi in Colonial Cuzco, Peru.* Durham, N.C., and London: Duke University Press, 1999.

Dobyns, Henry, and Paul Doughty. *Peru: A Cultural History.* New York: Oxford University Press, 1976.

Fleet, Michael, and Brian Smith. *The Catholic Church and Democracy in Chile and Peru.* Notre Dame, Ind.: University of Notre Dame Press, 1997.

Lehmann, David. *Struggle for the Spirit: Religious Transformation and Popular Culture in Brazil and Latin America.* Cambridge: Polity Press, 1996.

MacCormack, Sabine. *Religion in the Andes: Vision and Inspiration in Early Colonial Peru.* Princeton, N.J.: Princeton University Press, 1991.

Sallnow, Michael. *Pilgrims of the Andes: Regional Cults in Cusco.* Washington, D.C.: Smithsonian Institution Press, 1987.

Sigmund, Paul, ed. *Religious Freedom and Evangelization in Latin America: The Challenge of Religious Pluralism.* Maryknoll, N.Y.: Orbis Books, 1999.

Philippines

POPULATION 84,525,639

ROMAN CATHOLIC 80 percent

PROTESTANT 10 percent

MUSLIM 5 percent

OTHER 5 percent

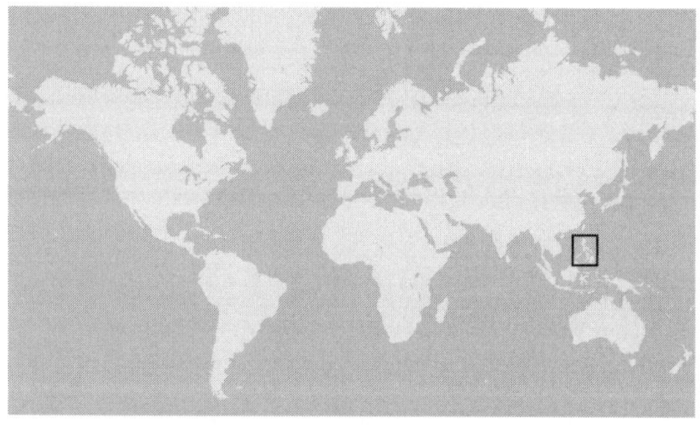

Country Overview

INTRODUCTION The Republic of the Philippines consists of 7,100 islands (of which 2,773 are named), with a total land area of 115,707 square miles. It is located a little above the equator in Southeast Asia. Because it is close to China, it has a strategic geographical location. It also sits at the crossroads of world trade routes in the region. The archipelago has rich natural resources such as forests, energy resources, mines yielding gold and other minerals, fisheries, and abundant plant and animal life. It has fertile soil capable of producing large crops of rice, corn, coconut, hemp, tobacco, and other agricultural products. This is why foreign powers were interested in colonizing the islands during various eras. The Philippines acquired their Christian heritage from Spain and the United States. It is the only predominantly Christian nation in Asia.

More than 60 percent of Asia's Christian population lives in the Philippines, and their numbers have been growing at an increasing rate. There are approximately 11 million non-Catholic Christians practicing in more than 350 organizations, most of which operate under the umbrella organization of the National Council of Churches in the Philippines. The largest denominations in this group include the charismatic Philippines for Jesus movement and the Protestant Iglesia ni Cristo.

Islam is an older presence than Christianity, and the largest religious minority group is the Sunni Muslim population. Muslims live in Mindanao and the Sulu islands but have migrated to other provinces.

RELIGIOUS TOLERANCE Before the colonization of the Philippines by Spain (1565–1898) and by the United States (1898–1946), the local people were widely reputed to be tolerant of other religions. In precolonial times there was a significant amount of interreligious dialogue and exchange among the peoples of Asia. The early islanders were variously influenced by Hinduism, Buddhism, Taoism, Confucianism, and Islam. The Spanish, however, changed this dynamic when they took to the Philippines the Roman Catholic Church, which was instrumental in setting up colonial rule over the islands. The close working relationship between the state and the Roman Catholic Church was dismantled by the American colonial regime, which introduced Protestant Christianity and a new government mandate, the separation of church and state.

The Black Nazarene, a 200 year-old, life-size statue of Christ, is carried through congested downtown Manila by thousands of barefoot devotees, mostly men. This Roman Catholic celebration is one of the largest in the Philippines. AP/WIDE WORLD PHOTOS.

Today religious freedom in the Philippines is guaranteed by the constitution. The contemporary disagreement between the Muslim peoples of the southern islands and the federal government is not so much about religion as it is about political goals.

Major Religion

ROMAN CATHOLICISM

DATE OF ORIGIN 1568 C.E.
NUMBER OF FOLLOWERS 67.6 million

HISTORY Roman Catholicism was taken to the Philippines by Spanish colonizers and friars in the sixteenth century. Since then it has been the most dominant religion in the land. It has influenced the social, political, and economic development of the nation. Filipino nationalists have used the language of Christianity to express their own struggles for liberation from colonial rule by Spain (1565–1898) and the United States (1898–1946).

The Philippine churches, especially the Roman Catholic Church, played pivotal roles in the events that led to the end of the Marcos dictatorship (1966–86). Filipino nationalists and religious leaders used Vatican II social teachings to galvanize the nation into the "People's Power" revolution, which peacefully ousted the corrupt dictator, Ferdinand Marcos, from power in 1986.

EARLY AND MODERN LEADERS The historical roots of the nationalist movement against Marcos's martial law regime stem from the 1896 Philippine revolution against Spain. By that time an organized nationalist movement—led by liberal Roman Catholic clergy, professionals, and a group of students—had gained a strong following. A local uprising in Cavite in 1872 provoked the Spanish to react aggressively. Three Filipino priests—Jose Burgos, Mariano Gomez, and Jacinto Zamora—were garroted after being convicted of inspiring subversion. Their deaths galvanized the Filipino fight for liberation from oppressive governments.

Three Catholic revolutionary heroes were Jose Rizal, Andres Bonifacio, and Emilio Aguinaldo. Rizal led the Propaganda movement to promote equality for Filipinos. Bonifacio led the secret Katipunan (a revolutionary secret society) movement, which advocated armed insurrection, and Aguinaldo led the Philippine revolution for independence that defeated the Spanish in 1898. The Katipunan organized a major revolt in 1896. Many revolutionaries were captured and executed, including the pacifist Rizal, who was killed by a firing squad.

Benigno S. "Ninoy" Aquino, Jr. became a national hero in the Philippines for sacrificing his life to fight the Marcos regime. On 21 August 1983 the former senator Aquino returned from a three-year exile in the United States to run for president against Ferdinand Marcos. On his arrival at Manila International Airport (now known as Aquino International Airport), Aquino was arrested and assassinated on the spot by one of Marcos's soldiers, who had been sent to "guard" him. His brutal assassination led nationalist and church leaders to organize the People's Power movement.

It was the call of the archbishop of Manila, Jaime Cardinal Sin, in February 1986, that prompted thousands of Filipinos to surround Camp Crame and Camp Aguinaldo in support of a small military revolt against Marcos that forced him into exile.

MAJOR THEOLOGIANS AND AUTHORS Several major contemporary theologians have achieved notoriety for writing about the relationship between the Christian churches and Philippine nationalism. Father Wilfredo Fabros and Father John Schumacher wrote about the involvement of the Roman Catholic Church in the revolution for a free Philippines. Mariano Apilado and Oscar Suarez have written about the Protestant role in the revolutionary struggle against colonial rule in the Philippines. Edicio de la Torre, who was imprisoned under the Marcos military regime for his involvement in the nationalist movement for liberation, invented the term "theologies of struggle," which is the Philippine expression for liberation theology. Father Karl Gaspar was also jailed under the Marcos dictatorship. His books on theologies of struggle are based on his missionary work in some of the poorest of the poor communities in the southern Philippines. Reynaldo Ileto wrote about popular religious protests in the national revolutionary movement against colonialism.

HOUSES OF WORSHIP AND HOLY PLACES In the Philippines the Roman Catholic house of worship is the church, which is usually situated in the center of a town. Among the most popular churches in the Philippines are the Church of the Black Nazarene, located in Quiapo, Manila, and the Santo Nino Church in Cebu City in the central Philippines. Sites where miracles have taken place draw large crowds on Sundays and feast days. For example, every 9 January at Quiapo in Manila, the Black Nazarene, a 200 year-old, life-size statue of Christ, is carried through congested downtown Manila by thousands of barefoot devotees, mostly men. This celebration is one of the largest in the Philippines. It has roots in Mexico, where a priest bought the statue before taking it to Manila in 1606. The statue has been at the Quiapo church since 1787.

WHAT IS SACRED? Since precolonial times in the Philippines religious leaders have been powerful figures. Their charisma derived from their holiness, which was constantly on display and reenacted in state-sponsored rituals. Heirlooms and amulets associated with these figures were—and still are—considered especially powerful, and they are believed to protect those to whose care they are entrusted.

Priests, nuns, and ministers are so highly respected in the Philippines that requests from them are taken as mandates. Because of their influence over the population, they are courted by politicians and business leaders. A family considers having a son or daughter with a religious career to be an honor. Friendships with clerics and nuns are highly valued.

Sites and religious objects associated with miracles are believed to be sacred. An example is Santo Nino Church in Cebu City, where a miraculous statue of the Christ child is housed.

HOLIDAYS AND FESTIVALS Easter is the most important Christian observance in the Philippines. On Easter weekend entire Christian areas are shut down from noon on Holy Thursday until the morning of Black Saturday, which is so called because the world is mourning Jesus, who was crucified the day before. International flights continue to operate, and hospitals are open, but restaurants, shops, national television broadcasts, and church services stop, and transportation is sparse. Special events take place on Good Friday. There are religious processions, such as parades of statues of saints throughout communities.

Another national holiday in the Philippines is All Saint's Day (1 November), set aside to commemorate the dead. Families gather at the cemetery where their ancestors are buried to hold a 24-hour vigil. They place candles and flowers on the graves. Food is shared, and prayers are offered for the souls of deceased relatives and friends.

Every Christian village has a patron saint. On the saint's anniversary day villagers prepare a lavish feast. At dawn and dusk they parade the statue of the saint around the village while chanting the rosary and singing religious hymns.

MODE OF DRESS Roman Catholics in the Philippines dress in modest Western fashions. Traditionally, women covered their heads when attending church services. This custom is no longer practiced by the younger generations. Many orders of nuns in the Philippines continue to wear their religious habits in public. Missionary and diocesan priests, however, wear their holy garbs primarily when performing sacred ceremonies and religious services. Otherwise they wear Western clothes that are indistinguishable from those worn by any other Filipino man.

DIETARY PRACTICES The diet of most Filipino Catholics is not based on religious practice. During religious celebrations such as town fiestas held in honor of patron saints or during a house blessing, *lechon* (a suckling pig that is slowly roasted until the skin forms a hard brown crust) is served. Strips of the skin with the fat attached are considered the best pieces. The importance of the host and of the occasion is measured by the amount of *lechon* served. Blood drained from the pig is used to make *dinuguan* (blood porridge). For festive meals Filipinos prepare numerous other specialty dishes, such as *pancit,* a noodle-based mix of baby shrimp and thinly diced vegetables, and desserts such as sticky rice, which is boiled in sweet coconut milk and wrapped in banana leaves.

Tuba (gin distilled from coconut juice) and beer are available for men and are sometimes accompanied by *balut,* a duck egg with an embryo.

RITUALS Most Roman Catholic rituals were introduced to the Philippines by the Spanish. The Lenten season, beginning with Ash Wednesday and ending on Easter Sunday, is a solemn period. During this time all joyous festivities are suspended. People chant the *pason* (Christ's Passion) or attend the *ceraculo,* a religious play portraying the life, suffering, and crucifixion of Christ.

When a Catholic Filipino dies, a 24-hour rosary vigil is held at the deceased person's home, after which the body is escorted to the cemetery. The tradition is for mourners to walk behind the coffin. For six weeks after the death family members wear mourning garb. This may consist of black clothes or of a black pin worn on the blouse or shirt. The mourning ritual ends after one year, at which time a meal or party is provided by family members and close friends at the gravesite to commemorate the deceased.

RITES OF PASSAGE The baptismal ceremony marks an infant's or converted Christian's first rite of passage into the Roman Catholic faith. In the Philippines it is customary for parents to arrange for their infant to have up to five sets of godparents at this ceremony. Godparents are perceived to be part of the family, as they are expected to provide added social security for the child throughout his or her life.

Marriage is the most important rite of passage in the Philippines. It sanctifies parenthood and provides a stable environment in which to nurture and educate children into the ways of the group. Philippine marriages involve not only two people in love but also the bonding of two families.

Because poverty is widespread and the middle class has been disappearing in the Philippines, many Filipinos migrate and work abroad to support their families back home. Transnational families now are commonplace in the Philippines. Even across great distances many of the traditional Catholic rites of passage continue to be enacted inside the context of the Filipino family.

MEMBERSHIP Most Roman Catholics in the Philippines acquire their religious affiliation at birth.

SOCIAL JUSTICE The reformist ideas of Vatican II and other international Catholic and ecumenical convocations have had a profound effect on the Philippine churches. Progressive church leaders, Catholic and Protestant alike, have stressed the need to improve the political and socioeconomic conditions of the poor, while working for a more justice-oriented and environmentally concerned society. In the particular context of the Catholic Church's commitment to fostering human development in all of its social, cultural, economic, educational, aesthetic, and political aspects, progressive church members and clergy have acted as protectors of the ideals of democracy, while defending human rights, social justice, and freedom in the name of the Gospel.

SOCIAL ASPECTS Members born outside of the faith have converted for various reasons, including for the purposes of marrying a Catholic and raising their children to be Catholics. Divorce is not allowed for members of the Roman Catholic Church. Members may, however, have their marriages officially annulled if the conditions for a valid marriage were not there in the first place. In this case they are allowed to remarry in the church.

POLITICAL IMPACT The separation of church and state has never been fully implemented in the Philippines. For example, the Catholic Church exerts a strong influence on some state legislation. The church lobbied against the divorce law in 1987, and the congress and senate did not approve it. The Catholic and Protestant churches have been influential in terms of grassroots democratization movements. They have organized people for resistance, especially against Ferdinand Marcos's dictatorship (1972–86) and in speaking up for human rights.

CONTROVERSIAL ISSUES Church leaders committed to working for social justice have come into conflict with the Philippine government, for example, the Marcos dictatorship, over human rights issues.

Because of the HIV and AIDS epidemic, artificial forms of contraception are another issue of contention between the Roman Catholic Church and the state in the Philippines. While the state promotes family planning and the use of condoms, the only method of birth control that has been officially approved by the church hierarchy is the rhythm method.

CULTURAL IMPACT Music, art, and literature in the Philippines are largely based on oral folklore traditions, the influence of the church, and Spanish and American colonialism. During the early years of the Spanish colonial regime, most literary, musical, and artistic expressions in the Philippines were religious. For example, a popular subject matter that was sung and performed in religious theatrical plays was the *pason* (Passion), the story of Christ's sufferings and his death on the cross.

During the mid-nineteenth century the Spanish colonizers allowed some members of the middle class (mostly men) to gain a university level education. As the middle class became educated, Filipino literature flourished. The greatest historical literature came out of the movement for independence from Spain (1565–1898) and the United States (1898–1946). Jose Rizal's novels, written at the turn of the twentieth century to counter Spanish colonialism, continue to inspire modern Filipino nationalism.

Other Religions

American Protestant missionaries came to the Philippines at the turn of the twentieth century and found a people fighting for political independence and religious reforms. Since these missionaries represented various denominational groupings, they saw a need to promote harmonious working relationships and eventual unity among the different Protestant Church groups. As early as 1900 the missionaries organized an alliance to encourage greater denominational cooperation. This movement led to the development of the Evangelical Union, which set up territorial division groups among the members in the country. Filipino converts were brought into the Evangelical Union, which represented the combined coalition of most Protestant churches, and as early as 1923, a Filipino scholar and educator, Jorge Bocobo, was elected to its top leadership.

In a few years the growing Filipino churches sought greater control of organizational and ministerial responsibilities. Since the churches had begun to come under Filipino leadership, one of the church commissions recommended the formation of a council that would represent the churches rather than the missions. In 1929 an organization called the National Christian Council replaced the Evangelical Union and brought the various church-related agencies, churches, and missions together into one ecumenical body. Since Philippine independence in 1946, the National Christian Council (also called the National Council of Churches) has become entirely a Filipino endeavor. It continues to play an important role in the national ecumenical movement for greater social equity, justice, and peace.

In 1902 the Philippine Independent Church, also known as the Aglipayan Church, was organized in a reaction against the Spanish clergy's control of the Roman Catholic Church. The cofounders of the church were Isabelo de los Reyes y Florentino, an author, activist, and senator who was imprisoned during the revolution for criticizing the Spanish colonial regime, and Gregorio Aglipay y Labayan, a Philippine Roman Catholic priest who was excommunicated in 1899 for participating in the Philippine independence movement. In 1903 Aglipay accepted de los Reyes's request that he serve as the supreme bishop of the new church, a position Aglipay held until his death in 1940.

The Philippine Independent Church continues to follow Roman Catholic forms of worship, although its doctrine has been strongly influenced by Unitarianism. A schism developed in 1946, and a Unitarian faction left the church. Under Isabelo de los Reyes, Jr. (elected bishop in 1946), the church adopted in 1947 a new declaration of faith and articles of religion that were Trinitarian. The Protestant Episcopal Church in the United States consecrated three bishops of the Philippine Independent Church in 1948, and the two churches entered into close association. In 1961 the church was accepted into full communion with the Church of England and the Old Catholic churches.

There are approximately 4 million Muslims in the Philippines. Muslims are concentrated in the southern part of the country, on the island of Mindanao and on the Sulu archipelago. They are distinguished from Christian Filipinos not only by their profession of Islam but also by their evasion of more than 300 years of Spanish colonial domination. Although the Spanish consolidated their control of the northern and central Philippines, they never completely subdued the Muslim south. Muslim Filipinos are separated from each other by language differences and geographical distances. They have been divided into five major groups: Hanon, Tausig, Maguindanao, Samal, and Badjao. In 1968 the National Moro Liberation Front, a Muslim separatist movement, emerged in a struggle for self-determination for Philippine Muslims.

Hinduism and Buddhism are not widespread in the Philippines. Although these religions were carried to the Philippines by travelers as early the fifth century, many Hindus and Buddhists later converted to Islam or Christianity.

In 1938 in Solano, Nueva Vizcaya (a small town in northern Luzon), Felix Maddela became the first Filipino Bahai (after reading one of the pamphlets left in the library in Manila by an American Bahai traveler, Louie Mathews). A community was soon formed that included members of Maddela's family. They elected their first Local Spiritual Assembly, which became incorporated in 1946.

In 1957 the Regional Spiritual Assembly of the Bahais of Southeast Asia was elected at a convention held in Jakarta, Indonesia, with the Philippine delegate, Orlando D. Maddela, in attendance. In 1967 Mashid Ighani arrived in the Philippines and settled in Baguio as the first Iranian student pioneer. Many more Iranian youths followed and enrolled in universities all over the country. The Bahai campus crusade was instrumental in opening up many new areas for the teaching of the Bahai faith.

In 2000 there were approximately 229,500 Bahais in the Philippines, a great increase from 67,500 in 1970. They scattered in thousands of localities. Whenever there are nine adult Bahais in a *barangay* (village), they may officially form a Local Spiritual Assembly, the highest governing local administrative body. There are more than 150 Local Spiritual Assemblies elected only during Ridvan (21 April, the anniversary of Bahaullah's proclamation in Baghdad) of each year.

Bahais in the Philippines come from almost all kinds of religious backgrounds, classes, and strata of society. Members have found in their faith a common ground for fostering principles of the oneness of humankind and the elimination of prejudice.

Other Philippine religious faiths include the ancient animist beliefs and practices of the upland hill tribes of northern Luzon, Palawan, Mindoro, and Mindanao. These indigenous uplanders have a traditional concept that the universe consists of five areas: the Earth, the Skyworld, the Underworld, the Upstream area, and the Downstream area. The Skyworld is geomorphic and is occupied by a creator-god and some other high gods. Many of the great adventures of the gods take place in this cosmic space. The other areas of the cosmos have their own characteristics. The first order of deities consists of high gods. The second group is considered to be the spirits of dead ancestors and relatives. The third group consists of mythological creatures and culture heroes who once were human but whose origins are too ancient to trace. Spirits are also thought to inhabit forests, riverbanks, brooks, swamps, pathways, and large trees.

Kathleen M. Nadeau

See Also Vol. I: *Bahai Faith, Christianity, Evangelical Movement, Islam, Roman Catholicism*

Bibliography

Apilado, Mariano. *Revolutionary Spirituality: A Study of the Protestant Role in the American Colonial Rule of the Philippines, 1898–1928.* Quezon City, Philippines: New Day Publications, 1999.

De la Costa, Horacio, S.J. *The Jesuits in the Philippines, 1581–1768.* Cambridge, Mass.: Harvard University Press, 1961.

Fabros, Wilfredo. *The Church and Its Social Involvement in the Philippines, 1930–1972.* Quezon City, Philippines: Ateneo de Manila Press, 1988.

Junker, Laura Lee. *Raiding, Trading, and Feasting: The Political Economy of Philippine Chiefdoms.* Honolulu: University of Hawai'i Press, 1999

Nadeau, Kathleen. *Liberation Theology in the Philippines: Faith in a Revolution.* Westport, Conn.: Praeger Publications, 2002.

Schumacher, John N. *Revolutionary Clergy: The Filipino Clergy and the Nationalist Movement, 1850–1903.* Quezon City, Philippines: Ateneo de Manila Press, 1981.

Suarez, Oscar. *Protestantism and Authoritarian Politics: The Politics of Repression and the Future of Ecumenical Witness in the Philippines.* Quezon City, Philippines: New Day Publications, 1999.

Youngblood, Robert. *Marcos against the Church: Economic Development and Political Repression in the Philippines.* Ithaca, N.Y.: Cornell University Press, 1990.

Poland

POPULATION 38,634,000

ROMAN CATHOLIC 93 percent

OTHER CATHOLIC 0.5 percent

ORTHODOX CHRISTIAN 1.3 percent

NONRELIGIOUS 4 percent

OTHER 1.2 percent

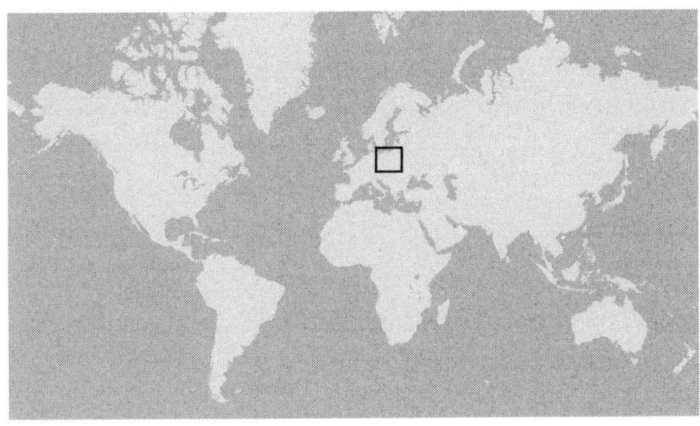

Country Overview

INTRODUCTION The Republic of Poland is located in Central Europe to the east of Germany; it is bordered on the north by the Baltic Sea and Russia and on the south by the Czech Republic and Slovakia. Most of the people in the country are Polish; minorities include Ukrainians, Germans, and Belarusians.

Religion has been highly significant in Polish history. The Catholic Church is the largest religious organization in Poland and has been closely connected to both the statehood and culture of the country for more than a thousand years. The Christianization of Poland began in 966, when the Polish dukes received baptism from the Bohemian monarchy. This enabled the dukes to make connections with Christian rulers and protected the country against German hegemony. The date is widely recognized as the beginning of the Polish state.

There are four rites in the Catholic Church in Poland: Roman Catholic (by far the largest with nearly 36 million members), Byzantine-Ukrainian, Byzantine-Slavic, and Armenian. The last three are in formal union with Roman Catholic Church. There are also three Old Catholic churches (separated from the church in Rome). A majority of Polish Roman Catholics (72 percent) are so-called "passive churchgoers."

The Polish Autocephalous Orthodox Church is the second-largest registered religious group, with about half a million laypersons. Protestantism, the third-largest branch of Christianity in Poland, is divided into a dozen or so denominations, including the Augsburg-Evangelical (Lutheran) Church, the United Pentecostal Church, and the Seventh-day Adventist Church. There is a sizeable number of Jehovah's Witnesses in Poland and relatively small numbers of Muslims, Jews, and practitioners of Eastern religions, such as Buddhism and Hinduism.

RELIGIOUS TOLERANCE Poland is a secular state, neutral in matters of religion and convictions. It does not have an official religion, and the constitution grants freedom of religion. The constitution also maintains that religion may be taught in schools, provided that doing so does not infringe upon any person's religious freedom.

One of the best known Catholic shrines in Poland is the Marian shrine of Jasna Góra in the city of Czestochowa. It is recognized as the spiritual heart of the country and is treated as the national shrine. © DAVE G. HOUSER/CORBIS.

Major Religion

ROMAN CATHOLICISM

DATE OF ORIGIN 966 C.E.

NUMBER OF FOLLOWERS 36 million

HISTORY In Poland there are seven churches based on Catholic tradition. The biggest, with almost 36 million members, is the Roman Catholic Church. The Byzantine-Ukrainian (123,000 adherents), Byzantine-Slavic (300 adherents), and Armenian (8,000 adherents) churches are in formal union with Roman Catholic Church, accepting the pope's primacy in matters of church jurisdiction. The other three are so-called Old Catholic churches.

The beginning of Christianity (and the Roman Catholic Church) in Poland is closely connected with the state's formation. In 966 Prince Mieszko accepted Christianity for his state. The clergymen who subsequently Christianized the people codified the Polish language into a written form. In the years 999 and 1000 the first archdiocese was founded by Boleslav I, the first king of Poland, who continued the support of Christianity. In 1207 Leszek the White placed Poland under the Holy See, positioning the state into the system of the vassal kingdoms of the Roman Catholic Church.

In 1384 Jadwiga—daughter of Louis the Hungarian (ruled Poland 1370–82)—ascended the throne. The assembly of ruling magnates arranged her marriage to Jagiello, the pagan ruler of Lithuania. Lithuanians had to convert to Christianity and become part of the Polish kingdom. In 1386 Jagiello was baptized and became King Ladislaus of Poland. This arrangement (called the Union of Krewo), concluded in 1385, provided the Polish church with vast opportunities for extending the Catholic Church. It also led in 1410 to a battle between the Teutonic Knights (a religious order that sought to claim eastern Lithuania) and the Polish-Lithuanian-Ruthenian army. The Knights were defeated, and their order was permanently weakened.

In the sixteenth-century the Protestant Reformation did not affect Poland as greatly as it did Germany, and the majority of the Polish population remained Catholic. Two centuries later, in the eighteenth century, Poland fell under the dominance of Russia. Prussia and Austria also took advantage of Poland's internal power struggles to divide up the country's territory in three stages. The third partition (1795) wiped Poland from the map of Europe, but the Roman Catholic Church preserved Polish national identity. Because of this Catholicism has become closely connected with the social and cultural definitions of "Polish traits."

Poland lost one-fifth of its population during the Second World War. More than 2,000 members of the Catholic clergy were killed. In postwar Poland the Communist authorities promoted an atheistic society; nevertheless, the church began to reconstruct religious life and the church administration. In 1944 the concordat between Poland and the Vatican was invalidated because of the Vatican's war policy, under which some jurisdictions of the Polish church were handed over to the Roman Catholic Church in Germany.

During the Communist regime in Poland (1945–89) the Roman Catholic Church was accused of having a hostile policy toward the government that was influenced by the Vatican and Western governments. In the post-Communist state (after 1989) the church has served as a significant agent of social change.

EARLY AND MODERN LEADERS One of the most important leaders of the Catholic Church in Poland was Cardinal August Hlond (1881–1948). He played a significant role in creating the framework of a free Polish state. Another noteworthy person in modern Polish Catholic history was Prince Adam Sapieha (1867–1951), an archbishop who was raised to the rank of cardinal in 1946. During World War II he cooperated with the Polish government in exile (which was recognized by the Allied governments), and he stood up for persecuted members of society during the Communist era.

Bishop Stefan Wyszynski (1901–81) was nominated primate of Poland in 1948. He was a skillful politician and was able to negotiate with the Communists. Under his administration the church founded seminaries, church courts, charities, sacral buildings, and convents. He was raised to the rank of cardinal in 1952. Wyszynski was imprisoned in 1953, following his condemnation of the Communist government. He was freed in 1956, but relations remained tense.

On 16 October 1978 the cardinals of the Roman Catholic Church chose the first non-Italian pope in more than 400 years. The archbishop of Kraków, Karol Józef Wojtyla (born in 1920), became known as Pope John Paul II. As pope he continued to apply the decisions of Vatican II and placed special emphasis on Marian devotion. He opposed the imposition of martial law in Poland (1981) and supported—prior to the collapse of Communism—the Solidarity movement, a labor union that was an important element of Polish civic society. In 1981 Józef Glemp (born in 1929) was elected primate of Poland. In the same year he was a mediator between the Communist state and the Solidarity movement.

MAJOR THEOLOGIANS AND AUTHORS Polish theologians are not widely known outside the country, and their impact on Catholic discourse in Poland is not substantial. One exception is Karol Józef Wojtyla (Pope John Paul II), whose writings influenced the theology of the Catholic Church worldwide.

In 1997 Bishop Kazimierz Romaniuk (born in 1927) published the first Polish translation of the Bible by a single translator. He has also written many books on biblical sciences. Waclaw Hryniewicz (born in 1936), a theologian and priest, has served as director of the Ecumenical Institute at the Catholic University in Lublin. Another influential Polish theologian was Franciszek Blachnicki (1921–87), a priest and social activist who, in 1954, founded the youth movement Ruch Oazowy (the Oasis movement, from 1976 known as Ruch Swiatlo-Zycie, or the Light-Life movement). Blachnicki is a candidate for beatification. One of the most important contemporary Polish philosophers was Józef Tischner (1931–2000). In 1980 he was appointed a chaplain to the Solidarity movement. He was a great moral authority and a well-known figure in Polish public life.

HOUSES OF WORSHIP AND HOLY PLACES As in the whole Roman Catholic Church, the Catholic house of worship in Poland is the church. Sanctuaries are also important to Polish devotees and are traditional destinations of pilgrimages; most are devoted to the Mother of God. The best-known sanctuaries are those in Lichen, Gniezno, Warsaw, Niepokalanow, Czestochowa, Góra Swietej Anny, Piekary Slaskie, Kraków-Lagiewniki, and Kalwaria Zebrzydowska.

WHAT IS SACRED? A distinctive characteristic of Polish Catholicism is devotees' strong attachment to holy sites. One of the best-known sites, the Marian shrine of Jasna Góra, is in the city of Czestochowa in southern Poland. It is recognized as the spiritual heart of the country and is treated as the national shrine.

Another phenomenon is not connected with things or places but with a unique way of reasoning and acting—the so-called "miracular religiosity" that develops in areas where, according to popular belief, wonders happen. For example, there are sanctuaries with a statue of Virgin Mary that is said to weep blood. To some extent, these miracles shape people's opinions, social attitudes, religious practices, and ways of life.

HOLIDAYS AND FESTIVALS In Poland some of the Catholic Church's holidays (Easter Monday, Corpus Christi, Assumption of the Virgin Mary, All Saints' Day, and Saint Stephen's Day) are recognized as national holidays. In general, there are no differences in the way Polish Catholics celebrate religious holidays compared with Catholics in other European countries. In traditional Catholic communities (mainly in the rural and provincial areas of Poland), however, religious holidays and festivals have a more profound influence and meaning in people's lives.

The most popular practices connected with religious festivals are sharing of *oplatek* (Christmas wafer), blessing of food in church, blessing of a candle on Candlemas Day and lighting it at the bedside of a dying person, blessing of palms and herbs in church, and taking part in a Corpus Christi procession.

MODE OF DRESS In Poland there is no distinctive mode of dress among Catholic laypeople. Only in the most traditional parishes (in villages and small towns) are there culturally defined requirements that women not wear trousers during religious services. Wearing a holy medal (pendant with a picture of the Holy Mother) or a small cross or crucifix is common. Often devotees wear rosary rings on their fingers, a practice connected with Marian devotion.

DIETARY PRACTICES The majority of Polish Catholics observe, to some extent, the Roman Catholic Church's formal regulations regarding fasting and abstaining. In Poland religious fasting is understood as temporary restrictions in food consumption, specifically, the abstaining from eating meat (fish is allowed, however) and alcohol; it usually allows one meal a day. There are several kinds of fasts. The rigorous or strict fast is obligatory during the fast days of Ash Wednesday and Good Friday (only one full meal per day and in reduced quantity). Poles also observe a strict fast on Christmas Eve, abstaining from eating during the day and then participating in an evening meal. Restrictions in meal consumption are also obligatory on Fridays, but less than a third of Polish Catholics observe this practice.

RITUALS Most Catholic rituals in Poland are connected with religious services. As in the entire Roman Catholic Church, there is a Holy Mass. In Poland recipients usually receive the Holy Communion while kneeling. Almost half of Poles participate in weekly masses, religious meetings, and services. About every year six to seven million Polish devotees participate in pilgrimages. Another common religious ritual is the procession. In modern Poland processions have retained their various regional characteristics.

Much Catholic practice in Poland may be characterized as folk religiosity, which is strongly rooted in Polish culture and focuses more on the devotee's sentiments than on Catholic doctrine. Such religiosity (especially in traditional areas) is based on ceremony and tradition rather than on conscious participation. Folk religiosity is often connected with irregular religious practice, negligence of sacraments, and lack of religious education.

As a result of the changes in the Polish sociocultural milieu since 1989, religious rituals have been in a transitory phase. Some folk customs connected with religious rituals continue to be supported, but others have been omitted. Particularly notable has been the disappearance of annual customs characterized by regionalism, folklore, and magic.

RITES OF PASSAGE In the Polish Roman Catholic Church rites of passage include baptism, first Communion, confirmation, wedding, and funeral. There are no noticeable dissimilarities with those of the church in general. Polish children are usually baptized as infants. There are also rituals of adult initiation (baptism), but these ceremonies are not highly visible. Since 1990, when religion lessons were reintroduced to Polish schools, the preparation for the sacraments of first Communion and confirmation has usually taken place in primary and secondary schools. The first Communion is typically introduced when a Pole is about 8 years old, and confirmation is achieved when she or he is about 15 years old.

MEMBERSHIP Catholicism is the culturally dominant religion in Poland, and membership is mainly determined by birth. Catholic parents have a religious duty to bring up their children within the Catholic religion.

SOCIAL JUSTICE Many Roman Catholic clergy in Poland are regularly involved in working among the poor. There are numerous Catholic institutions and nonprofit organizations involved in charity, education, and human rights. The best-known Catholic charity organization is Caritas Polska, which seeks to help the poor and underprivileged through fund-raising, providing relief to the needy, and education. Other social justice activities are support for children, youths, and poor families; healthcare; care for the aged and terminally ill; support for migrants; and helping the unemployed find jobs.

SOCIAL ASPECTS Marriage and family are highly respected institutions in Poland. As a result of the political and economical transformations since 1989, the Polish family has become less traditional. The number of divorces has increased, the number of new marriages has decreased, and the birthrate has been declining. Nevertheless, Catholics continue to perceive family as a source of support for individuals.

POLITICAL IMPACT After the fall of the Communist government in 1989, Poles strongly approved of the church's involvement in sociopolitical matters. In the early 1990s, however, the church began to present political and social pressures and demands. For example, in the parliamentary elections of 1991 the church declared its neutrality, but it soon started its own moral and political campaign. This resulted in a change in social attitudes toward the church.

Poles in general and part of the church hierarchy do not accept the church's interference in political affairs; many interpret it as compromising the state's nonreligious character. According to this view, parliament spends too much time debating ideological issues, such as abortion, divorce, religious education, and the presence of Christian values in the media. Those who defend the church's political involvement view it as a necessary consequence of pulling the church into the realities of social life.

CONTROVERSIAL ISSUES One issue that has been controversial for Polish Catholics is the place of religious education in the public school system. In 1990 the government—reacting to pressure from the Polish bishops—restored religious education in public schools. After this the Polish public's support for the church began to erode.

The church's involvement in politics is the major divisive issue among Polish Catholics. Alongside the political transformations of 1989, full diplomatic relations with the Vatican were restored. Many aspects of the concordat (agreement between the Vatican and Poland) were criticized, especially its definition of state-church relationships. For instance, it enabled priests to serve as public officials and enforced the sacredness of Catholic cemeteries (which entailed refusal of burial to non-Catholics).

CULTURAL IMPACT Catholic values and traits can be found in almost all spheres of Polish national culture, both historical and contemporary. For instance, in the late fifteenth century the great German artist Veit Stoss (in Polish, Wit Stwosz) created renowned sculptures and carvings for Polish Catholic churches. A school of sixteenth-century Polish composers (including Mikolaj Gomolka) produced notable church music. Today Polish traditional religious art continues to affect both folk art and high art.

There are many contemporary examples of Catholic cultural influence in Poland. The most visible spheres are Catholic publishing activity, architecture, and Christian music. There are several influential publishing houses in Poland that put out books concerned primarily with Catholic religious, theological, philosophical, and cultural ideas.

An interesting example of transformations in Polish sacral architecture is the Catholic sanctuary in the village of Lichen. Originally a nineteenth-century shrine to Mary, since the 1960s it has been expanded into a complex containing religious buildings, paintings, sculptures, and monuments. The images at Lichen—which include patriotic as well as religious and moralizing motifs—reflect the folk religiosity that is embraced by the pilgrims who travel to the site. In 1994 construction began on an immense basilica (the largest church in Poland) at Lichen.

Since 1989 the Catholic Church in Poland has organized Christian music festivals and concerts, and there are a number of well-known Christian music groups.

Other Religions

In 1989 the bill on the freedom of belief and worship was introduced in Poland. It initiated a mass registration of religious movements and communities. Until this law took effect, hardly 30 religious groups were active in the country. Today Poland has about 150 officially registered churches, religious denominations, and other religious groups; there are also more than 150 unregistered religious groups.

Orthodox Christianity (Polish Autocephalous Orthodox Church), with about 500,000 members, is Poland's second-largest religion. Most Orthodox Christians in Poland are members of the Belarusian minority in the eastern part of the country and of the Ukrainian minority in southeastern districts. The largest Protestant denomination in Poland is Evangelical Augsburg (Lutheran) Church; it has about 87,000 adherents, many of whom have German ethnic roots. The next-largest churches are the United Pentecostal Church and the Seventh-day Adventist Church.

After the fall of the Communist regime in 1989, there were more opportunities for public social activities in Poland, and many new religious movements emerged and developed. Although membership in these movements has increased, the actual number of members is not substantial.

Almost all new religious movements in Poland, even those of Eastern origin, arrived from western Europe or the United States. The best known of these are the Science of Identity Institute (also called Chaitanya Mission), the International Society for Krishna Consciousness, The Family, the Bahai faith, and the Unification Church. There are also groups with a native Polish origin, including Evangelical Congregation-Jerusalem (which has as its main aim evangelization), Panmonistic Congregation (a nondogmatic and nonceremonial confession), and Association of the Native Faith (whose aim is to spread proto-Polish customs and ceremonies as well as to celebrate native holidays).

There is a sizable population (127,000) of Jehovah's Witnesses in the country. Other religious groups operating in Poland include the Muslim Religious Union, the Union of Jewish Religious Communities, and the Karaite Religious Board (the Karaites are an ethnic minority of Turkic origin). There are a number of organizations related to Eastern religions, including Buddhist groups and practices that draw upon Hindu traditions.

The Jewish community in Poland is rather small (about 5,000 members), but the presence of Jews in Polish history is remarkable. In the past Poland was home to the largest concentration of Jews in Europe, and it was the most important center of Jewish culture. There were more than 3,500,000 Jews in Poland in 1939, the year that Germany began its attack on Poland and World War II began. About 100,000 Jewish soldiers were in the Polish Army at the beginning of the war; many received the highest combat distinctions. Of the nearly 9 million Jews who lived in Europe before the Holocaust, 6 million perished as a result of Nazi genocide. During the war 3 million Jews died in Poland. Most of them were Polish; there are no precise records of how many Polish Jews were deported or fled the country.

Pawel Zalecki

See Also Vol. I: *Christianity*

Bibliography

Borowik, Irena. "The Roman Catholic Church in the Process of Democratic Transformation: The Case of Poland." *Social Compass* 49, no. 2 (2002): 239–52.

Borowik, Irena, and Przemyslaw Jablonski, eds. *The Future of Religion: East and West.* Kraków: NOMOS Publishing House, 1995.

Casanova, José. "Poland: From Church of the Nation to Civil Society." In *Public Religions in Modern World.* Chicago: University of Chicago Press, 1994.

Johnston, Hank, and Jozef Figa. "The Church and Political Opposition: Comparative Perspectives on Mobilization against Authoritarian Regimes." *Journal for the Scientific Study of Religion* 27, no. 1 (1988): 32–47.

Kloczowski, Jerzy. *A History of Polish Christianity.* New York: Cambridge University Press, 2000.

Monticone, Ronald C. *The Catholic Church in Communist Poland, 1945–1985: Forty Years of Church-State Relations.* New York: Columbia University Press, 1986.

Stachura, Peter D. *Poland in the Twentieth Century.* New York: St. Martin's Press, 1999.

Szajkowski, Bogdan. *Next to God—Poland: Politics and Religion in Contemporary Poland.* New York: St. Martin's Press, 1983.

Zalecki, Pawel. "How the Polish Roman Catholic Church's Representatives Explain Decline of the Positive Estimations of the Church's Public Activities." *Slovak Sociological Review* 35, no. 6 (2003): 533–56.

———. "The Roman Catholic Church in Poland as both Dominant and Minority Group." In *Dominant Culture as a*

Foreign Culture: Dominant Groups in the Eyes of Minorities. Edited by Janusz Mucha. New York: East European Monographs and Columbia University Press, 1999.

Portugal

POPULATION 10,084,245

ROMAN CATHOLIC 89 percent

PROTESTANT 4 percent

OTHER CHRISTIAN 3 percent

OTHER 1 percent

NONE 3 percent

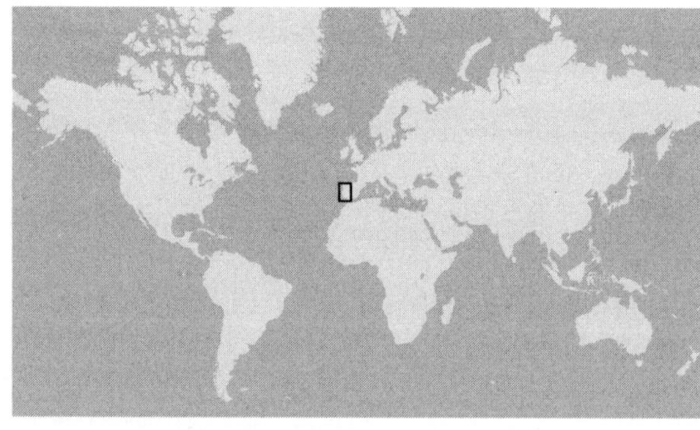

Country Overview

INTRODUCTION The Portuguese Republic, located on the Iberian Peninsula in southwestern Europe, is bordered by the Atlantic Ocean on the south and west and by Spain on the north and east. The archipelagos of the Azores and of Madeira, in the Atlantic, are part of Portugal. The capital and largest city is Lisbon.

Portugal shares the Iberian Peninsula with Spain, and the early histories of the countries were parallel. The Romans conquered the peninsula in 202 B.C.E., and Christianity was introduced in the first century C.E. Roman control collapsed during the early fifth century when the Visigoths, Germanic invaders from central and northern Europe, overran the area. In 711 armies of Muslims (Moors) from North Africa conquered most of the peninsula. Portugal established its independence during the Reconquista (Reconquest), as Christian armies retook the peninsula from the Moors. In 1139 Henry of Burgundy, who became known as Afonso Henriques, was appointed count of Portucalense (Portugal), a vassal of the Castilian king. Portugal won independence from Castile, and Spain recognized Portugal's independence in 1143. The Moors were driven from Lisbon in 1147, and the armies of Afonso III drove them from the southern province of Algarve in 1249, thereby consolidating Portugal as a Roman Catholic country.

Beginning in the fifteenth century, Portuguese navigators explored Africa, Asia, and South America, and Portugal established a vast network of colonies. In general, however, the sixteenth and seventeenth centuries began a period of decline in the empire. During the Thirty Year's War (1620–50) trade with other nations was cut off, and the Dutch attacked Portugal's colonies to obtain access to their commercial products. Although the Dutch were driven from the colony of Brazil in 1654, most of Portugal's Asian colonies were permanently lost, and the country was never again a world power. Nonetheless, Portugal had a profound cultural and religious influence on those parts of the world it had colonized, particularly Brazil.

During the twentieth century there were almost continuous struggles in Portugal between conservatives and liberals and, later, socialists and Marxists. A republican government was established in 1910, and in 1911 the monarchy was abolished. Up to this time Roman Catholicism had been the state religion, although other religions were tolerated as long as they were not practiced in a building having the exterior form of a church. After the long dictatorship of Antonio de Oliviera Salazar (1932–68), democracy was gradually restored.

RELIGIOUS TOLERANCE The 1976 constitution established freedom of religion, and the government generally respects the right in practice. The Religious Freedom Act of 2001 created a legislative framework for religious organizations that have been established in Portugal for more than 30 years or those recognized internationally for at least 60 years. The act provides recognized religious organizations with benefits previously reserved for the Roman Catholic Church, including tax-exempt status and chaplain visits to prisons and hospitals.

People pray at the Shrine of Fátima. Millions of Roman Catholics make the annual pilgrimage to the shrine to pray at the spot where they believe the Virgin Mary appeared to three peasant children in 1917. AP/WIDE WORLD PHOTOS.

Major Religion

ROMAN CATHOLICISM

DATE OF ORIGIN First century C.E.
NUMBER OF FOLLOWERS 9 million

HISTORY Most of the Iberian Peninsula was Christianized during the first century C.E. In the fourth century the Diocese of Lisbon was established, as were those of Braga and Porto in northern Portugal and Évora in the south-central region. The Visigoths, who conquered the peninsula in the early fifth century, were initially Arian Christians, denying the divinity of Jesus, but the Iberians followed the orthodox position of Rome. After 589 the Portuguese adhered to the Roman Catholic faith.

With the establishment of Portugal in 1139, church and state were united in a long and mutually beneficial relationship. King Afonso Henriques (ruled 1139–85) declared Portugal a vassal state of the Vatican and granted the church vast lands and privileges. The church became the nation's largest landholder, and for a time its power came to rival that of the nobles, the military, and even the monarchy. With papal approval, however, the monarch named the country's bishops.

During the reign of King Afonso II (1211–23) there began a religious revival. The Franciscans, invited to Portugal by the king's sister, won the affection of the people, but they were not received with cordiality by the secular clergy and by other orders, which saw their financial interests threatened. At Oporto, for example, the bishop ordered the Franciscans out of town and sacked and burned their convent, but many citizens sided with the Franciscans, who were later able to return. The Franciscan Order soon spread over the countryside, where wealthy citizens built convents for them, members of the royal family selected their churches as burial places, and the popes bestowed bishoprics on their friars and assigned them important missions. The Dominicans also entered Portugal in the early thirteenth century, in 1217. By virtue of their austere morals, poverty, and humility, they received a welcome second only to that given the Franciscans. The Society of Jesus (Jesuits), which entered Portugal in 1540, was placed in charge of public education during the late sixteenth century.

During the early fourteenth century the so-called Theory of the Three Ages, originally formulated by Joachim de Fiore (1132–1202), began to permeate Portuguese thought. The theory proclaimed the imminent rise of an Age of the Holy Ghost, to be followed by ages of the Father and of the Son. The idea of an Empire of the Holy Ghost reemerged throughout Portuguese history as a mystical concept, especially under the guise of the Fifth Empire as proclaimed in Sebastianism. The disappearance of King Sebastian at the Battle of Alcazar-Kebir in Morocco in 1578 resulted in the usurpation of the throne by King Philip II of Spain. During this period the belief spread among the Portuguese that King Sebastian had not died but was alive and would return to reclaim his throne, reestablish Portugal's independence, and lead the nation into an age of grandeur, called the Fifth Empire. This messianic expectation fostered the emergence of diviners, fake kings, and prophets. Thus, Sebastianism and the Fifth Empire, which foresaw a glorious future for the nation, became a mystical foundation for Portuguese identity.

Reformer Sebastião Joseph Carvalho, Marquês de Pombal, who was the de facto ruler of Portugal from 1750 to 1777, expelled the Jesuits in 1759. The Office of the Holy Inquisition, established in Portugal in 1536 under King John III, was not abolished until 1821, as a consequence of the liberal revolution of 1820. The national archives hold records of an estimated 40,000 inquisitorial processes. In contrast to Spain, however, Catholicism in Portugal was less harsh and more humanized.

The liberal movement of the 1820s and 1830s was not favorable toward the Catholic Church. In 1834 the government prohibited male religious orders, auctioned off many church properties, and abolished a number of holidays and festivals. The First Republic (1910–26), which was inspired by the Freemasons, dissolved the concordat with the Vatican and separated church and state. The new government seized church properties and secularized public education, while prohibiting the ringing of church bells, the wearing of clerical garb in public, and the celebration of many religious festivals.

The right-wing military coup of 1926, which initiated 48 years of dictatorship, most of them under Antonio de Oliviera Salazar, restored many privileges to the Catholic Church. In 1929 male religious orders were allowed to return, and in 1940 a new concordat was signed with the Vatican. The state reintroduced religious instruction in the public schools, Catholic clergy regained the right to celebrate marriages, and the church retook control of many of its assets, including convents, monasteries, and schools.

EARLY AND MODERN LEADERS Saint Anthony of Padua (1195–1231), the patron saint of Portugal, was baptized Fernando Bulhom, the heir to a noble title and lands. He entered a monastery at age 15 and became a biblical scholar, theologian, missionary, and popular preacher serving the Franciscan Order in Portugal, Morocco, France, and Italy, where he died. He took the name Anthony after the church where he had first lived as a Franciscan and the name Padua from the place in Italy he chose as his home after he began preaching. In a time of feuds, vendettas, and wars, Anthony preached peace, saying, "No more war; no more hatred and bloodshed, but peace. God wills it."

Isabel de Portugal (c. 1271–1336), the daughter of King Peter III of Aragon and the wife of King Dinis of Portugal, was named for Saint Elizabeth of Hungary, her great-aunt. Known as the Holy Queen, she was canonized in 1625. She is mainly venerated in the Church of Santa Clara in Coimbra, where her silver mausoleum is located. During her festival the city is largely closed to automobiles while it hosts a procession that includes hundreds of mostly rural women dressed as the Holy Queen, with a robe and a crown.

José da Cruz Policarpo (born in 1936) was ordained a priest in 1961, appointed a bishop in 1978, named patriarch (archbishop) of Lisbon in 1998, and made a cardinal in 2001.

MAJOR THEOLOGIANS AND AUTHORS Perhaps the most important Portuguese theologian was Bartholomew of Braga (1514–90). Born Bartholomew Fernandez at Verdela, near Lisbon, he entered the Dominican Order in 1527 and was ordained in 1529. He taught philosophy in the monastery at Lisbon and then for some 20 years taught theology in various houses of his order. He received a master's degree at Salamanca in 1551. In 1558 he accepted appointment to the archiepiscopal See of Braga, for which he had been chosen by Queen Catherine, and in 1559 he received episcopal consecration. In 1561 Bartholomew took part in the Council of Trent, where he was highly esteemed for his theological learning and the holiness of his life and where he exercised great influence in the discussions, particularly those on the reform of ecclesiastical life. He returned to his see in 1564, and in 1566 he held a provincial synod in which decrees were passed for the restoration of ecclesiastical discipline and the elevation of the moral life of the clergy and people. The archbishop then devoted himself to the tasks of carrying out the reforms of the Council of Trent and the decrees of his provincial synod. In 1582 he received permission to resign his see, and he withdrew to the monastery at Viana. He was declared venerable in 1845 by Pope Gregory XVI.

José Régio (1901–69) and Miguel Torga (1907–95) are among modern Portuguese writers who have developed religious themes.

HOUSES OF WORSHIP AND HOLY PLACES The village of Fátima, located in west-central Portugal, has one of the world's best-known Marian shrines. Although the town had no significance in ancient times, in 1917 a series of apparitions of the Virgin Mary were allegedly witnessed by three young children. Soon thousands of pilgrims began flocking to the site, in an isolated ravine called Cova da Iria, where a chapel was built in honor of the Virgin of Fátima. In 1930 the Vatican authenticated the apparitions and approved the building of the Sanctuary of Our Lady of Fátima, paid for by donations from around the world.

Santo António à Sé is the church in Lisbon that honors Portugal's patron saint, Anthony of Padua. The stone walls of his underground shrine bear hundreds of written statements of endearment and thanksgiving in a host of languages. The present church, built in 1812, was financed by alms collected by the children of Lisbon.

WHAT IS SACRED? The concept of what is sacred among Roman Catholics in Portugal is in keeping with similar beliefs in other Catholic countries. There are numerous shrines and sacred places, including caves and grottos, rivers, lakes, lagoons, hills, mountains, and crossroads. Many of these were sacred for the earliest inhabitants, even before Roman colonization and the introduction of Christianity, but they were later clothed with Catholic symbols and renamed in honor of the Virgin Mary, Christ, or a saint.

HOLIDAYS AND FESTIVALS Religious festivals abound in Portugal. Every June millions of Roman Catholics, most of them women, flock to Fátima to pray at the spot where they believe the Virgin Mary appeared to three peasant children in 1917. Some go to pay homage to what they believe is the Mother of God, some to ask the Virgin of Fáima for a special favor, such as physical healing, and others to carry out a promise made. Once they arrive at the Sanctuary of Our Lady of Fátima, many pilgrims walk across the large square on their knees to show that they are true believers.

The eve of the feast of Saint Anthony of Padua, on 12 June, is marked by a costume parade on Avenida da Liberdade (Liberty Avenue) in Lisbon. Bonfires are built along the route, and people cook meals, with grilled sardines and sangria being popular. On 13 June, the feast day itself, many couples marry. The town hall traditionally sponsors the weddings of poor couples and provides a reception. In 2001, for example, more than 2,000 of these so-called brides of Saint Anthony were wed at the town hall.

Each village and region in Portugal has its own patron saint and annual festival. Among the most popular saints are Isabel, Eulalia of Barcelona, Eulalia of Mérida, Catarina, Quiteria, Anne, Mary Magdalene, John the Baptist, Macarias, Bartholomew, and Matthew, all considered as intermediaries with a remote and inaccessible God. During the traditional annual festival the local priest and a group of parishioners parade through the streets, carrying a float with the image of the patron saint, accompanied by floral decorations and music, and during the weekend there often are special activities that include carnivals, banquets, concerts, and sporting events.

MODE OF DRESS In keeping with local Roman Catholic traditions, women in Portugal dress conservatively, including covering their heads in church. This is especially true of older women. Members of religious orders, for both men and women, wear traditional vestments.

DIETARY PRACTICES In general there are no special dietary practices among Roman Catholics in Portugal.

RITUALS Popular religiosity in Portugal includes a blending of motifs from pre-Christian traditions with Roman Catholic rituals and the cults of the saints. The church has tolerated and sometimes encouraged such forms of religiosity as a way of maintaining adherence to Catholicism. Church officials, however, have prohibited other aspects of folk religion, such as witchcraft, magic, and sorcery. Nonetheless, particularly in the isolated villages of northern Portugal, belief in the evil eye, witches, evil spirits, and werewolves has continued to be widespread. Although church authorities disapprove of these ancient practices, they seem powerless to do much about them.

RITES OF PASSAGE The traditional Roman Catholic rites of passage of baptism, first Communion, confirmation, marriage, and last rites are practiced in Portugal, although less today than in previous generations.

MEMBERSHIP Although 89 percent of all Portuguese claim adherence to the Roman Catholic Church, less than 30 percent participate in weekly church observances. There are striking regional differences, with a higher percentage in the north attending Mass regularly than in the south. Nationwide, attendance at Mass is lower in the cities and larger towns than in rural areas. In general, the bulk of the people present at Mass are the elderly, women, and children taken by their parents or grandparents. Little is done by church officials to convert non-Catholics, and there has been an erosion of Catholics to Protestant denominations and other religions or to no religion at all.

SOCIAL JUSTICE In general, the Roman Catholic Church in Portugal follows Vatican policy regarding the promotion of education, the reduction of poverty, support for human rights, and the condemnation of racial, ethnic, religious, and gender discrimination.

SOCIAL ASPECTS Until the 1960s the Roman Catholic Church and popular Catholic religiosity dominated the social life of Portugal. As elsewhere, however, a large gap has emerged between the teachings of the church and the people regarding marriage and family life. A growing number of couples choose civil rather than religious weddings. In addition, there has been an increase in the number of children born to single mothers, in the use of unauthorized methods of birth control, and in the divorce rate.

POLITICAL IMPACT During much of the modern period, the Roman Catholic Church, along with the army and the economic elite, was the most powerful institution in Portugal. Historically, military, economic, governmental, and Catholic influences were closely intertwined. The church was unable, however, to prevent adoption of the constitution of 1976, which formally separated church and state, and it could not block legislation that liberalized laws on abortion and divorce. By the early 1990s the Catholic Church had lost its former preeminence in Portugal.

CONTROVERSIAL ISSUES Most Portuguese consider themselves Roman Catholic in a vaguely religious and cultural sense, even though they disagree with church policy on birth control, abortion, divorce, and the role of women in church and society. Homosexuality has remained controversial both within the church and in society generally, where today there is greater acknowledgment as well as tolerance of its practice among consenting adults.

CULTURAL IMPACT Perhaps the greatest influence of Roman Catholicism on the arts in Portugal has been in architecture. Portugal's proximity to Santiago de Compostela in Spain and to the pilgrim routes from the east that converged there was an important factor in bringing, first, Romanesque and, later, Gothic architecture to the country. The period between 1300 and 1500 saw the full flowering of the Portuguese Gothic style. Almost every town in Portugal has a Roman Catholic church on the main square or on a hilltop overlooking it. Many were built in the sixteenth century, at the height of the colonial period.

In keeping with their austere philosophies, the first modern churches built by the mendicant orders in Portugal were of the utmost simplicity and almost completely devoid of decoration. As the carving of such architectural features as capitals and portals became more elaborate, however, figurative sculpture gained a foothold. Many of the early sculptors were French, but in time workshops were established that also used local artists and craftsmen. Reflecting the character of the religion in Portugal, the faces depicted on the statues of Catholic saints are complacent, calm, and pleasant, in contrast to the painful and anguished faces of those in Spain.

Other Religions

There are a number of other religious groups in Portugal, although in many cases their numbers are small. The Lusitanian Church of Portugal was formed in 1871 as the result of a schism within the Roman Catholic Church when traditionalists rejected declarations of the First Vatican Council. Today this small movement is affiliated with the Anglican Communion. Since 2000 considerable numbers of eastern Europeans, including many Eastern Orthodox, have emigrated to Portugal. There are parishes of the Greek Orthodox Church and the Russian Orthodox Church.

Among the largest Protestant denominations in Portugal are Assemblies of God; Manna Christian Church; Seventh-day Adventist Church; Evangelical Methodist Church; New Apostolic Church; Portuguese Baptist Convention; Evangelical Christian Brethren; Christian Congregation in Portugal, which originated in Brazil; Anglican Church; and Evangelical Presbyterian Church. Most have only a few thousand members. Non-Protestant Christian groups include Jehovah's Witnesses; the Church of Jesus Christ of Latter-day Saints (Mormons); the Universal Church of the Kingdom of

God (Igreja Universal do Reino de Deus), founded in Brazil; and the Light of the World Church, which originated in Guadalajara, Mexico.

There is a small Jewish community, though many of its members are foreigners. The Lisbon government has provided matching funds for the restoration of the city's historic nineteenth-century synagogue. Portugal's Muslim community consists of immigrants from former colonies in southern Africa and workers from North Africa, mainly Morocco. The Lisbon government has provided matching funds for the construction of the first mosque. There also is a small Hindu community, which traces its origins to South Asians who emigrated from Portuguese-speaking areas of Africa and from the former colony of Goa in India. Among other groups in Portugal are those with spiritualist beliefs, including Candomblé and Umbanda, the syncretistic religions of African and Roman Catholic origin from Brazil. There are also small numbers of Baha'is, Buddhists, Taoists, Hindus, and ancient wisdom-psychic-New Age groups, such as the Church of Scientology, Federation of Spiritists, Raelians, Rosacrucians, Gnostics, Martinista Order, and Theolosophical Society. About 3 percent of the population is agnostic, atheist, or without a religious preference.

Clifton L. Holland

See Also Vol. I: *Roman Catholicism*

Bibliography

Brierly, Peter, ed. *World Churches Handbook.* London: Christian Research, 1997.

Catholic Encyclopedia, s.v. "Portugal." 13 Sept. 2004. http://www.newadvent.org/cathen/12297a.htm.

Herring, Hurbert. "The Iberian Background." Chap. 3 in *A History of Latin America, from the Beginnings to the Present.* 3rd ed. New York: Alfred A. Knopf, 1968.

Huertas Riveras, Pilar, Jesús de Miguel y del Ángel, and Antonio Sánchez Rodríguez. *La Inquisición: Tribunal contra los delitos de fe.* Madrid: Editorial LIBSA, 2003.

Payne, Stanley G. *A History of Spain and Portugal.* Library of Iberian Resources Online. 13 Sept. 2004. http://libro.uca.edu/payne1/payne7.htm.

U.S. Department of State. *International Religious Freedom Report 2003: Portugal.* Washington, D.C.: Bureau of Democracy, Human Rights, and Labor, 2003.

Qatar

POPULATION 793,341

MUSLIM (PREDOMINANTLY SUNNI WITH SOME SHIITE) 92 to 95 percent

OTHER (CHRISTIAN, HINDU, BAHAI) 5 to 8 percent

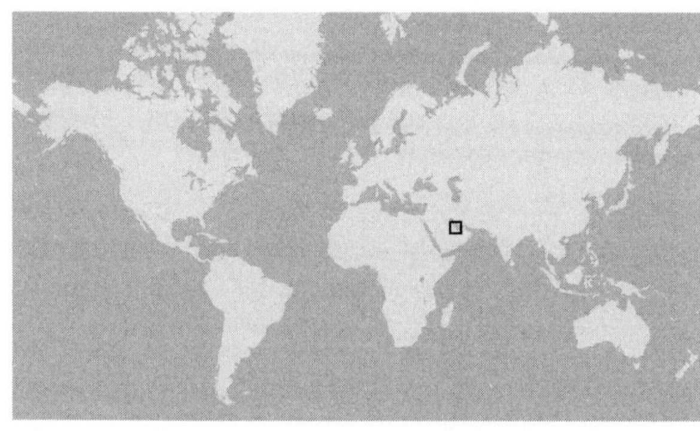

Country Overview

INTRODUCTION The State of Qatar, located on a small peninsula in the Persian Gulf, shares a border with two countries to the south: Saudi Arabia, the birthplace of Islam, and the United Arab Emirates. About 26 percent of Qatar's total population are citizens. The rest are foreign workers (mostly Sunni Muslims, with a minority of Shiite Muslims, Christians, Hindus, and Bahais). No official census data exists concerning numbers of believers.

Most of Qatar's indigenous population professes Wahhabism, a form of the literalist Hanbali school of Sunni Islam (modeled after the teachings of the eighteenth-century reformer Muhammad ibn Abd al-Wahhab). Qatari's religious preference has historically been shaped by their Saudi neighbors, who are Wahhabi Muslims. Within Qatar's indigenous population is also a small Shiite minority, originating from southern Iran. The Christian community, comprising Catholic, Orthodox, Anglican, and Protestant denominations, is a blend of Filipinos, Arabs, Indians, Europeans, and Americans. The Hindu community is primarily Indian, while the Bahai community is mostly Iranian.

RELIGIOUS TOLERANCE Islam is the official state religion of Qatar. As in Saudi Arabia, Wahhabism not only constitutes Qatar's social fabric but also dictates its form of government. The Ministry of Islamic Affairs oversees the construction of mosques and supervision of clerics and Koranic education. While the Wahhabi state limits public displays of worship by non-Muslims in the foreign community, they are allowed to practice discreetly in private. There are strict penalties for proselytizing to Muslims.

There has been a trend toward more religious freedom for Christians. The government justifies these allowances by stating that the Koran conveys special status to Christians as People of the Book. Hindus are not accorded such privileges because the government does not find a precedent for allowing a polytheistic religion to practice.

Major Religion

ISLAM

DATE OF ORIGIN Seventh century C.E.
NUMBER OF FOLLOWERS 610,000

HISTORY Originating in Arabia as a political force in 622, Islam was adopted in the Arabian Gulf shortly thereafter and has remained a powerful force ever since. From the mid-seventh century Islam spread along the maritime trade routes. Later, Islamic practice was strongly influenced by the teachings of Muhammad ibn Abd al-Wahhab (1703–92).

Qatar was a British protectorate until 1971, when it adopted a provisional constitution declaring Qatar an Arab nation with Islam as its official religion and the Shariah as the basis of its legal code. Since 1995 Sheikh Hamad ibn Khalifa al-Thani has provided progressive political leadership for the country. His policies, along with abundant oil revenues and the development of a modern infrastructure, have had a moderating effect on the expression of Qatari Wahhabism. Results of this include increased freedom of the press and the 1996 establishment of the Qatari satellite television station Aljazeera, one of the most influential independent media sources in the Middle East and the Islamic world. Important changes in the political process include provisions that allowed women to vote and run for office during the first election of the country's Central Municipal Council in 1999.

EARLY AND MODERN LEADERS During the 1750s the al-Thani family (from the Nejd in present-day Saudi Arabia) settled in the area. In 1766 the al-Khalifa family moved into Qatar from Kuwait. These two families largely influenced Qatar's religio-political development. By the mid-1850s the al-Thani family gained political control, and Sheikh Muhammad al-Thani was declared the emir. As of the early twenty-first century, the al-Thanis remain in control of Qatar.

In 1972 Khalifa ibn Hamad al-Thani became emir of Qatar. The emir, while exercising absolute power within the guidelines of Islamic jurisprudence, rules through consensus, seeking guidance from leading citizens who are part of an appointed advisory council. Khalifa's son Hamad wrested power from him in a 1995 palace coup.

MAJOR THEOLOGIANS AND AUTHORS Islamic theology in Qatar has been dominated by the teachings of Muhammad ibn Abd al-Wahhab (1703–92), who studied Hanbali law, the strictest of Islamic legal schools, which requires the literal interpretation of the Koran and the hadith (the reports of Muhammad's sayings and deeds). Wahhabism provided the al-Thanis with the ideological justification for their political resistance to the authority of the non-Wahhabi al-Khalifa family, who were seeking to expand their influence in Qatar.

HOUSES OF WORSHIP AND HOLY PLACES Among the 260 mosques in Doha (Qatar's capital) is the country's largest, the Grand Mosque, distinctive for its many domes. The Abu Bakir al-Siddiq and the Umar bin-Al Khattab mosques, also in Doha, are known for their mixture of traditional Arab and modern architecture.

WHAT IS SACRED? Wahhabism bans the worship of sacred trees or the veneration of the tombs and holy relics of saints or religious martyrs. Readings of the Koran, considered both a sacred object and a sacred text, are thought to drive away *jinni* (spirit beings), cure diseases, and ward off the evil eye.

HOLIDAYS AND FESTIVALS The celebration of Islamic holidays in Qatar does not differ significantly from that found elsewhere in the Islamic world. Qataris observe holiday festivities based on the lunar calendar; the dates are determined according to local sightings of various stages of the moon. The month of Ramadan is a major religious observance when Qataris fast, sunrise to sunset. Id al-Fitr, celebrated at the conclusion of Ramadan, marks the return of ordinary routines. Id al-Adha marks the close of the hajj (pilgrimage to Mecca). During this time families ritually sacrifice sheep, which are then distributed among the poor in the community.

MODE OF DRESS Muslim women in Qatar adhere to a strict code of modest dress when in public. They wear a black *abaya,* a floor-length flowing silky cloak that covers the head. A veil covers most of the face (except the eyes). Young women may opt for a *tarha* (headscarf), which will cover their hair; they may or may not wear a veil to cover their face. They may also wear *abaya*s fashionably adorned with brightly colored embroidered hems.

Qatari men wear a *thoub,* a traditional long shirt that covers a loose pair of pants. They also wear a white headdress, called a *gutrah,* which is held in place by an *agal,* a black band, which surrounds the top of the head.

DIETARY PRACTICES Aside from observing Muslim dietary rules, Muslims in Qatar do not follow any distinctive dietary practices.

RITUALS There are no distinctive ritual obligations among Muslims in Qatar.

RITES OF PASSAGE Qataris observe Muslim life cycle rituals, including celebrations at birth, circumcisions, weddings, and funerals. All Muslim male children are required to be circumcised. There is some variation in when this is performed. In modern times it is done quickly at the medical center where the child was born. Traditionally it was done when the child was older, signifying a puberty rite. Female circumcision rites, once widespread among the tribes of Qatar, were performed on girls before they reached puberty, usually between the ages of seven and nine. The government has discouraged the practice of female circumcision, and it has almost totally disappeared.

MEMBERSHIP The practice of Islam by foreign workers conveys distinct employment and legal advantages. For instance, only Muslims may hold high-ranking positions in the Qatari government and military, and only Muslims are allowed to bring cases in the Shariah courts to settle civil claims. While there are no reported cases of the government forcing individuals to convert to Islam, there are incentives for conversion. For instance, prisoners who memorize the Koran may have their sentences reduced. Although non-Muslims may convert to Islam, it is considered apostasy for a Qatari to adopt another faith, a crime with severe penalties.

SOCIAL JUSTICE As part of their *zakat* (almsgiving) obligation (to which all Qataris adhere), people contribute money to charity organizations that provide assistance to needy women, the physically handicapped, and children's services, such as orphanages. Since 1990 the Qatari government has promoted education for women as a means to eradicate illiteracy among this segment of the population, as well as to encourage more women to join the workforce.

SOCIAL ASPECTS Islam impinges on life in Qatar in many ways. Marriage is a partnership in which each spouse assumes certain roles. Women bear and raise children and manage the domestic affairs of the household. They are expected to fulfill these obligations even if they have careers outside the home. Men have the duty to act as heads of the household and provide their families with sustenance.

POLITICAL IMPACT Wahhabism enabled the ruling al-Thani family to legitimize their aspirations for political authority, resisting the efforts of the non-Wahhabi al-Khalifa family to establish a political power base in Qatar. It has also provided the judicial basis for both criminal and civil jurisprudence.

CONTROVERSIAL ISSUES Emir Khalifa ibn Hamad al-Thani and his son Hamad have been confronted with the difficult task of reconciling tribal values and traditions with modernity. Tension has existed between the Wahhabi requirement of spirituality and asceticism and the changes brought about by forces of modernization, including the influx of Western and foreign ideas and the materialism associated with the great wealth derived from Qatar's oil revenues.

The status of Qatari women is better than that of women elsewhere in the Arab Islamic world because women can vote, run for governmental office, and enter various professions, such as law and medicine. Social customs, however, temper these freedoms. For example, while pay scales are equal for women and men, much inequality and discrimination occur in the workplace.

CULTURAL IMPACT Because Islam prohibits engraving or drawing the images of humans or animals, artistic expression takes the form of poetry and song. These restrictions have not prevented the elaboration of handicrafts, especially weaving, for which Qatar was once famous.

Other Religions

About 74 percent of the total number of people living in Qatar are temporary guest workers from both Muslim and non-Muslim countries. Qatar's citizenship restrictions have the goal of ensuring the cultural integrity of the country's tribal population. As a means of minimizing the visibility of non-Muslims, the state prohibits them from conducting public services or building their own houses of worship. Missionary work is strictly prohibited, and heavy penalties exist for those trying to convert Muslims in Qatar.

There has been a move to differentiate between non-Muslims regarded as People of the Book, such as Christians, and those who practice faiths not recognized in the Koran, such as Hindus. On the grounds that the Koran stipulates tolerance toward People of the Book, the government has allowed private gatherings to celebrate Christian holidays. Qatar seems to show a greater degree of religious tolerance, mitigated as it is, in comparison with Saudi Arabia and other Gulf states.

Deborah S. Akers

See Also Vol. I: *Islam, Shiism, Sunnism*

Bibliography

Abu Saud, Abeer. *Qatari Women, Past and Present.* New York: Longman, 1984.

Anscombe, Frederick F. *The Ottoman Gulf: The Creation of Kuwait, Saudi Arabia, and Qatar.* New York: Columbia University Press, 1997.

Country Profile: Bahrain, Qatar, 1991–92. London: Economist Intelligence Unit, 1991.

Ferdinand, Klaus. *Bedouins of Qatar.* New York: Thames and Hudson, 1993.

Metz, Helen Chapin, ed. *Qatar: A Country Study.* Washington: GPO for the Library of Congress, 1993.

Zahlan, Rosemarie Said. *The Creation of Qatar.* London: Croom Helm, 1979.

Republic of the Congo

POPULATION 2,958,448

CHRISTIAN 50 percent

AFRICAN TRADITIONAL RELIGIONS 48 percent

MUSLIM 0.8 percent

OTHER 1.2 percent

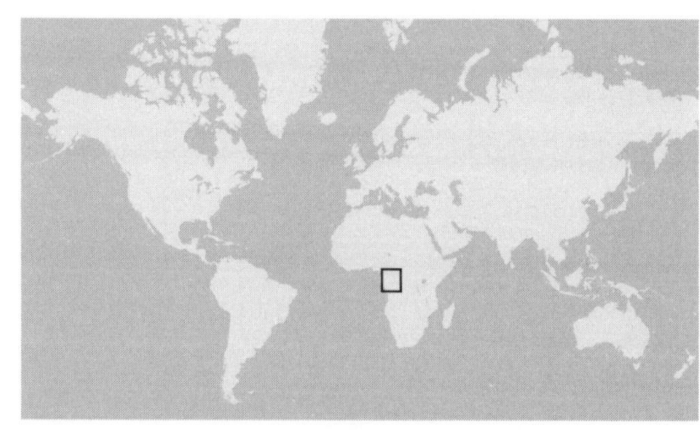

Country Overview

INTRODUCTION The Republic of the Congo, a West Central African nation on the Atlantic Ocean, borders Gabon, Cameroon, the Central African Republic, the Democratic Republic of the Congo (DRC; formerly Zaire), and Angola. Topographically, from southwest to northeast, the country includes a relatively treeless coastal plain, an escarpment, a vast plateau region, and then an expansive lowland. While the DRC was a former Belgian colony, Congo (then Moyen, or Middle, Congo) was colonized by France. The main ethnic groupings are the Kongo (nearly 50 percent of the population; they live in the southwest), Teke (about 17 percent; most grow cassava and bananas), Mboshi (about 12 percent; they live in the northwest and are mainly traders, farmers, and fishermen), and Sangha (in the northeast; farmers and fishermen on the edge of the rain forest). At least 70 percent of the population lives in Brazzaville (the capital), Pointe-Noir (the sea port), or along the rail line between them, where there is industry and agriculture.

About half Congo's population is Christian; most of these are Roman Catholic. The Congolese Catholic Church comprises one archdiocese, five dioceses, and an apostolic prefecture (under the authority of one of the dioceses). Among Protestant groups, the Église Évangélique du Congo is the largest denomination. Founded by Presbyterians, it has been autonomous since 1961 and has 105 parishes, a theological seminary, and some 150,000 members.

While Christian missions made inroads into traditional religious belief systems, they failed to eradicate deeply held faith in intermediary deities, ancestor veneration, and magic. Many Congolese have faith concurrently in elements of Christianity and traditional religions. Messianic groups (formalized syncretic movements combining elements of Christianity with traditional religion and, often, political ideals, founded by Africans), including Matsouanism (Amilcalism), Anzimba, Ndjobi, and Kimbanguism (Kakism or N'Gounzism), account for a small but politically prominent number of Congolese.

About 50 mosques in Brazzaville and Pointe Noir serve a Muslim community of mainly of West and North African origin.

RELIGIOUS TOLERANCE There is no state religion in Congo. The right to practice any religion is guaranteed in the constitution, approved in January 2002; before that the Fundamental Act provided these freedoms. Various Congolese governments, however, have intermittently banned or persecuted certain religious groups for their political orientation or in retaliation for uprisings that have occurred, and in 1963 President Alphonse Massamba-Debat nationalized the private schools, causing friction with the Catholic Church. Many have since been returned to the church.

Nongovernmental religious intolerance has at times jeopardized the safety of priests, pastors, and the laity in Congo. In 1965 radical youth gangs under the instruction of the ruling party attempted to eradicate traditional religious practices and to suppress the Matsouanism movement. During two civil wars in the 1990s, private militias and renegade soldiers assassinated Protestant and Catholic clergy and looted and destroyed church property and parishioners' homes. Matsouanism was linked to political opposition and armed insurrection in the Pool region (adjacent to the Malebo Pool on the Congo River in Brazzaville) in 1998–99.

A visit by Pope John Paul II in May 1980, during which he celebrated Mass before an estimated 400,000 faithful in Brazzaville, gave the Catholic Church new life in the Republic of the Congo. © VITTORIANO RASTELLI/CORBIS.

Major Religions

CHRISTIANITY

AFRICAN TRADITIONAL RELIGIONS

CHRISTIANITY

DATE OF ORIGIN c. 1500 C.E.

NUMBER OF FOLLOWERS 1.5 million

HISTORY Portuguese explorers brought Christianity to Congo. Diego Cao landed at the mouth of the Congo River in 1484 and found the king of the Kongo (the Mani Kongo) in charge of several feudal states extending north from present-day Angola across the lower DRC into southern Congo. Influenced by the conversion of the Mani Kongo Affonso I (1506–43), the kingdom's elite embraced Christianity and changed the name of their capital from Mbanza Kongo to Sao Salvador. Christianity spread through the kingdom, and in 1521 Sao Salvador was promoted to an episcopal see (seat of power) led by a Congolese bishop.

In 1663 Portuguese missionaries founded the first Catholic mission at Loango, and French missionaries spread Christianity to the hinterlands in the 1880s. Swedish missionaries founded the first Protestant mission in 1909 near Kinkala. Under French colonial rule (1875–1960), Catholic missionaries promulgated a *mission civilisatrice* (civilizing mission), which sought to evangelize and socialize Congolese through Western-style schooling. Until the mid-1950s, high school education was only available at two Catholic seminaries.

In the 1930s and 1940s Congolese from all classes and ethnicities protested against French rule and religion and generated messianic groups throughout the south. These groups were Christian and monotheistic but retained traditional beliefs, such as polygamy, and advocated a return to African roots.

The influence of the Catholic Church was regarded with some suspicion after independence from France in 1960. Influential Catholic leaders were exiled or driven underground. A visit by Pope John Paul II in May 1980, during which he celebrated Mass before an estimated 400,000 faithful in Brazzaville, gave the Catholic Church new life. The pope subsequently encouraged further Africanization of the Congolese Catholic Church.

The Église Évangélique du Congo, the Salvation Army, and the Catholic, Kimbanguist, Lutheran, and Greek Orthodox churches have joined to form the Ecumenical Council of Christian Churches in Congo.

EARLY AND MODERN LEADERS Affonso I (a Kongo king) first welcomed Portuguese explorers and missionaries, converted to Christianity, established diplomatic relations with Portugal and the Vatican, and sent his son Henri Kinu Mbemba and other young nobles to Rome and Portugal for a Catholic education. Under his leadership the Church of the Holy Cross was built in Sao Salvador around 1510.

Theophile M'bemba (1917–71) was appointed the first Congolese archbishop of Brazzaville in June 1969. He is credited with decolonizing the Congolese Catholic Church by appointing African clergy and allowing Congolese musical forms and dance into the liturgy.

Cardinal Emile Biayenda (1927–77) also participated in the Africanization of the church. He studied in missionary schools and was the first Congolese elevated to cardinal. He was abducted and killed during a military insurrection minutes after meeting with President Marien Ngoabi, who was also killed. Although never proven, it was widely rumored that Denis Sassou-Nguesso (who later became president) was behind both murders.

MAJOR THEOLOGIANS AND AUTHORS Fulbert Youlou (1917–72), Congo's first president, authored a book on Matsouanism, a movement founded by André Grénard Matsoua that combined Catholicism with indigenous religious beliefs. Youlou, whose name means "heaven" in Lari (the language of the Lari ethnic group of the Pool region), was trained in Catholic mission schools and ordained as a priest in 1946. Forbidden by church superiors to use his pulpit for political purposes, he traded on the mystical appeal of Matsoua among the Lari and became his successor.

HOUSES OF WORSHIP AND HOLY PLACES Affonso I built churches in Sao Salvador in the early 1500s, including the town's most important church, Sao Salvador. He also honored the traditional resting place for kings near the town's sacred woods with the construction of the Our Lady of Victories Church in 1526. Congo has five Catholic cathedrals, one in each of the five dioceses.

WHAT IS SACRED? Congolese Christians consider the Bible and the sacraments of baptism, confirmation, marriage, Eucharist, ordination, anointing of the sick, and reconciliation sacred. They also venerate saints, praying to them, remembering and celebrating them on their feast days, sometimes taking a saint's name, and fasting, fund-raising, and making local pilgrimages in the name of a saint.

HOLIDAYS AND FESTIVALS Christmas, Ascension, and Pentecost are celebrated as national holidays. Christmas Mass is often held near midnight on 24 December and is followed by feasting and dancing until early morning. Congolese Catholics celebrate Holy Week the week preceding Easter with special masses on Thursday and Saturday. On Saturday followers decorate the churches with flowers in anticipation of the resurrection of Christ. Converts are baptized into the church at a Saturday night mass. On Easter Sunday Congolese Christians welcome family and friends into their homes for a sumptuous meal of chicken, rice, beer, and palm wine.

MODE OF DRESS Christian mores decree it unacceptable for women to wear shorts, short skirts, or jeans in public. Women and sometimes men belonging to the same church may wear clothing with the same pattern or design to services or church functions. In the 1980s many Catholics wore African prints commemorating the pope's visit.

DIETARY PRACTICES Congolese Catholics do not eat meat on Fridays, especially during Lent, in memory of Christ's suffering and death on the cross. The interdiction typically causes little disruption because of the relatively high price of meat. During Lent many Catholics deprive themselves of a favorite food and donate the savings to charity. Protestants generally observe no dietary restrictions other than a ban on alcohol, but members of the Church of Jesus Christ of Latter-day Saints do not drink caffeinated beverages, and Seventh Day-Adventists do not eat meat.

RITUALS Like Catholics worldwide, Congolese Catholics sprinkle holy water, light candles, and burn incense during the Mass. To add local meaning to European symbols, the Catholic Church in Congo has made some highly visible reforms, including using African drums and instrumentation during the liturgy; singing original African hymns; dancing around the altar; making offerings of fruit, cassava, and local produce; and praying to ancestors.

Rituals of the Mass are also performed during baptism and marriage. A Congolese church wedding is typically a major affair similar to its European counterpart. In Congolese society, however, weddings unite clans and families in a larger sense. Prior to the church ceremony the families of the bride and groom negotiate *la dote* (the bride price), which the groom's family pays to the bride's in the form of goats, bolts of cloth, Coleman lanterns, and other desirable objects.

When ill or dying, Catholics may request the sacrament of anointing of the sick, which is intended to uplift the spirit and, if necessary, speed it on its way to heaven. A mass is said for the deceased; relatives may also attempt to ascertain who or what was the cause of the death and to assign blame for it, a holdover from traditional Congolese religious practices.

RITES OF PASSAGE Believing in the connectedness of the unborn, the living, and the dead, Congolese Catholics celebrate three fundamental rites of passage in the life cycle: baptisms, marriages, and funerals. Each includes a sacrament and substantial involvement on the part of the church. Baptisms are performed within two weeks of birth. The sprinkling of water symbolizes not only the parents' commitment to providing a Christian upbringing but also protection for the newborn from evil spirits, sorcery, and other harm.

Before getting married, a Catholic couple undergoes a period of domestic education conducted by elders in the family and the church. The bride is assumed to be a virgin, and the couple may be asked on the morning after the wedding whether the consummation was successful, including whether blood was evident as proof of virginity. Nonvirginity is sufficient reason to annul a marriage and remit the bride price.

Passage from life to death is accorded great significance, especially among the Bakongo, who have elaborate funerals and set up prominent tombstones. Both Christians and non-Christians in rural areas traditionally construct homelike tombs into which they place furniture, personal objects, and the corpse, dressed and positioned to recall his or her vocation. People living in the cities have these tombs constructed in their home villages.

MEMBERSHIP The Catholic Church maintains and expands church membership through baptism. Catholic missions in Congo emphasize schooling and ministering to the needs of the faithful over evangelizing.

Congolese Protestants pursue with great vigor the biblical injunction to evangelize. Proselytizing is a requirement for Jehovah's Witnesses and members of the Church of Jesus Christ of Latter-day Saints. The Protestant Église Évangélique du Congo has expanded its membership since taking a more charismatic approach to its ministry in 1947 that emphasizes spiritual gifts such as vocations, prophesying, visions, and healing through the laying on of hands. The popularity of this shift is seen in people's devotion to faith-based television and radio programming and crusades featuring world-class evangelists.

SOCIAL JUSTICE Christian exhortations to treat others as one would be treated, to be meek in spirit, to help the sick and downtrodden, to seek justice, and to minimize wealth and worldly pursuits for spiritual gain fit well with traditional Congolese attitudes, which require obligation to one's family, clan, community, and ethnic group. Family members who attain wealth share with less fortunate family members, and people with jobs in cities are expected to accommodate family and friends from their home villages for long periods of time.

A number of Catholic structures have historically promoted social justice in Congo, including the Justice and Peace Commission, the St. Vincent de Paul Society, and regular giving to social justice causes through tithes and offerings. The powerful Catholic labor union federation, an umbrella organization linked to European labor unions, protected the rights of individual workers until the government banned it in 1963.

Among Protestants the Église Évangélique du Congo administers several health clinics, maternity wards, pharmacies, and a rural public health project the covers 30 villages. Nearly all the churches have joined the national campaign to fight HIV and AIDS.

SOCIAL ASPECTS Christianity introduced new family values to Congo. French Christian missions encouraged the schooling of girls, job and skills training for women, the pivotal role of fathers in bringing up children, and monogamy. The effects have been huge, raising the status of women and girls, who have acquired rights nearly equal to those of men. Polygyny has not ceased but is practiced less than before, especially by Western-educated people and faithful Christians.

POLITICAL IMPACT Relations between the Catholic Church and the government have improved since the 1963 discord over privatizing mission schools, and many politically conscious Congolese have used Catholic missions and schools as an avenue of upward mobility. Most of Congo's leaders in the decolonization period were products of mission schools and carried the church's influence with them into politics. Abbé Fulbert Youlou was one of 150-odd students trained in Catholic seminaries during the interwar years. Youlou formed a political party, the Democratic Union for the Protection of African Interest, and was elected mayor of Brazzaville in November 1956, becoming the first African mayor in French Equatorial Africa. He was later the first elected prime minister of Congo and, in November 1959, the president of the republic. In the immediate postindependence period the Catholic federation of labor unions opposed President Youlou's labor policies and successfully deposed him. The church's weekly newspaper, *La Semaine,* has appeared regularly since preindependence and has exerted influence on government policies.

CONTROVERSIAL ISSUES Many Congolese Catholics only partially observe the church's unyielding position on matters such as polygamy, divorce, birth control, and abortion. The church has had many disciplinary problems because of these practices and has attempted through education and awareness-building to reduce them.

CULTURAL IMPACT In Congo, Christianity introduced new instruments and such musical styles as hymn music and the Latin-based music of the Mass. Mission schools were the first places where Congolese children learned to read and write. The introduction of literacy made possible the translation of the Scriptures and religious materials into Congolese languages; it also introduced a new literary genre, as storytellers put pen to paper. Congo has since produced many great Francophone authors, among them Sony Labou Tansi, a novelist and playwright who died from complications of AIDS in 1995. In modern Congolese art the most ubiquitous Christian symbol is the crucifix, sculpted from wood, chiseled in stone, or made from gold.

Christianity historically had a negative impact on Congolese art and performance. Catholic and Protestant missionaries burned ceremonial masks, amulets, statuettes, and fetishes, without which Congolese could no longer perform religious ceremonies and dances.

AFRICAN TRADITIONAL RELIGIONS

DATE OF ORIGIN Unknown

NUMBER OF FOLLOWERS 1.4 million

HISTORY The dates and origins of African traditional religions in Congo are unknown, but most have certainly evolved over several millennia. Traditional practices have proven far more resilient in rural areas of Congo, where they have been less subjected to Christian, colonial, and urban influences.

The basic tenets of Congolese traditional religion hinge on spirits and animated elements in the cosmos, including the Supreme Being (Nzambi), lesser spirits, and nature spirits. The eastern Kongo groups living near the Congo River believe the dead (especially those who lived relatively important lives) have the most access to Nzambi (God), followed by clan heads and elders; those of lowest social status have the least access. The western Kongo groups believe the dead must die a second death before they can make contact with Nzambi.

A Congolese creation myth among the Bakongo people of lower Congo holds that in the beginning the supreme being, Nzambe, presided over a dark world covered by water. He brought the world into existence by spilling the cosmos of stars and planets out of his mouth, and he created human beings and animals in a like manner. The story reflects possible Christian influence from contact with missionaries after the fifteenth century.

EARLY AND MODERN LEADERS Patriarchal heads of lineages, chiefs, witch doctors, diviners, sorcerers, and fetishers, as professional practitioners of religion, all provide decentralized leadership in Congolese traditional religions. Healers use amulets and medicines to get the spirits to act favorably toward human needs. Diviners determine whether someone's illness or bad fortune was caused by witchcraft, sorcerers, ancestral spirits, or gods. Sorcerers and fetishers manipulate outcomes, which often cause harm to innocent victims, through medicines, spells, and rituals. Chiefs formerly acted as intermediaries between clan members and ancestral spirits, and they alone had the power to make offerings or to pray to ancestors. They were also responsible for ensuring that the traditions handed down from the ancestors were obeyed. As the state has gained in influence relative to traditional holders of power, the chiefs' secular and religious authority has declined.

MAJOR THEOLOGIANS AND AUTHORS Congolese traditional religions have no written theology. Among the eastern Kongo peoples religion is passed down by the clan or lineage chief, who keeps a sacred basket of relics (such as the hair and nails of former chiefs and albinos, who are believed to be reincarnated chiefs) in an ancestral hut. Practitioners honor the sacred basket by bringing such offerings as palm wine or bananas. The chief or lineage head is the medium through which the living can contact the dead.

HOUSES OF WORSHIP AND HOLY PLACES The chief of a clan carries out traditional religious practices in the privacy of the ancestral hut in his compound. Healing and divining ceremonies, spells, incantations, and other rituals are practiced either in the compound or in spaces in the forest.

WHAT IS SACRED? Traditional African belief systems are based on a cosmic oneness of being. No distinction exists between the sacred and the secular, and humans relate to the divine through contact with nature. Adherents believe in a supreme being who is distant and unapproachable, but their veneration centers on ancestor spirits and animate and inanimate intermediary deities found in nature, such as trees, plants, rocks, and sky, animal, and bird totems. Religious leaders may call on spirits for any occasion, particularly for births and deaths and at seedtime and harvest. Relics passed down from ancestors to clan or lineage chiefs are sacred.

HOLIDAYS AND FESTIVALS Each year at the beginning of the dry season, practitioners of traditional religions in Congo hold solemn ceremonies, often in the family cemetery, to give thanks for the rains and the growing season. They may sacrifice a chicken or goat as an offering. They celebrate Christmas, Ascension, and Pentecost in a secular sense as national holidays.

MODE OF DRESS Congolese women have their own traditional African dress, which consists of three or four pieces of cloth—a head scarf, a tailored blouse, and two pieces of wrap-around cloth called *pagnes* (like sarongs)—cut from the same colorful pattern. Unmarried women wear one wrap-around instead of two. Women may not wear shorts, short skirts, or jeans in public.

DIETARY PRACTICES Followers of traditional belief systems in Congo generally observe no dietary restrictions, although taboos prohibit or require consumption of certain foods and drinks during pivotal events such as pregnancy or mourning the death of a kinsman. Dietary taboos include those against eating pork, meat from animals that die natural deaths or that are killed by strangling, and fish without scales (eating catfish would be taboo).

RITUALS Under the guidance of the supreme being, the spirits are believed to control health, fertility, and prosperity. Traditionalists observe various rituals, especially for pregnancy, birth, marriage, and death, in an attempt to influence the spirit world for good. Congolese fathers may perform purification rituals during and after the birth of a child. In some social circles when a young couple expresses its desire to marry, the boy's maternal uncle offers palm wine to the girl's maternal kin on successive visits. The recipients indicate their acceptance of the overture by drinking the wine. The marriage agreed upon, the groom's family pays the bride price in cloth, animals, and lamps.

RITES OF PASSAGE Performing rituals and teaching taboos are especially important in marking rites of passage, giving individuals a sense of belonging to a clan or lineage. Birth, adolescence, marriage, and death were formerly occasions for elaborate rituals involving the invocation of spirits and exchanges of gifts. Urbanization and modernization have made these practices less common and less elaborate where they persist.

Initiation rites for adolescents mark their passage to adulthood. Girls live together in one house, have their bodies painted and adorned with necklaces and bracelets, and attend special nighttime dances to meet possible future husbands. Among the Yombe, a Kongo subgroup in the south, initiation takes place after the marriage proposal is made. Circumcision is an important rite for boys among the Kongo; some Kongo groups require it before marriage, when boys are near or entering puberty. Girls are not circumcised among Congolese ethnic groups.

In rural areas Congolese families mourn the loss of a head of household for a long period. Widows may mourn anywhere from a month to the rest of their lives, depending on their piety, the village customs, and the ethnic group of the family. Some customs require widows to grieve by shaving their heads, dressing in rags, bathing infrequently, and even begging for crumbs from the tables of relatives.

MEMBERSHIP Indoctrination takes place during initiation ceremonies. Proselytizing is uncommon since most adherents follow in the footsteps of their parents and relatives.

SOCIAL JUSTICE Congolese traditional beliefs favor social equalizing and obligation to one's family, clan, community, and ethnic group. Adherents are expected to help those in extreme poverty—their own family members before members of their extended families, and members of their ethnic group before others. Extreme prosperity beyond the norm risks accusations of sorcery or threats of being subjected to sorcery. Traditional hospitality requires urbanites to host rural extended family—a phenomenon so pervasive that it has been referred to as "family parasitism."

SOCIAL ASPECTS Congolese widely practice polygyny for reasons of status as well as humanitarian concern: Having many wives and children is a sign of wealth, and in a society with no social safety net, it is also a means of supporting widows, orphans, and oneself in old age. Divorce is common in Congo. Rural traditionalists resist change, particularly interventions that discourage polygyny and encourage family planning and the use of contraceptives. Urbanized Congolese, influenced by Christianity and Western education, no longer consider polygyny desirable or practical. Men often cannot support more than one wife in a city.

POLITICAL IMPACT Indigenous religion has had little observable political impact in Congo. However, heads of state have probably hired traditional fetishers for protection from black magic, evil, and perceived enemies and have probably consulted oracles and diviners before making important decisions.

CONTROVERSIAL ISSUES Controversy has most often erupted where tradition clashed with the modern and rural with urban. Youth's and women's roles, for example, have changed as they have received formal education, but sometimes their espousal of nontraditional beliefs has led to accusations of sorcery by less literate elders.

Controversy surrounds the accepted philosophy in traditional groups that nothing happens without reason. If someone falls ill without explanation or cure, loses money inexplicably, suffers a spate of bad luck, or dies before old age, blame must be assigned and justice meted out. Traditionalists engage diviners, who use magic to explain causality, seek retribution for misfortune, punish evildoers, and protect against the vicissitudes of nature. What typically follows is a witch hunt mired in jealousy and speculation. Congolese society condemns both witches (whose powers are thought to operate at night, outside their bodies, and without their knowledge) and sorcerers (*ndoki,* who employ medicines, spells, and rituals) to punishment or death, because they cause innocent victims to suffer. Specialized diviners (*nganga ngombo*) may determine that a person is a witch, but conviction is unlikely without physical evidence. The colonial administration outlawed the use of proof poison, formerly used to determine whether someone accused of witchcraft was guilty. Postindependence governments have continued the ban, which has probably driven the use of proof poison underground.

CULTURAL IMPACT Traditionalists design masks, amulets, statuettes, and fetishes for religious ceremonies and dances. These ritual objects are believed to carry social, cultural, and religious power. After Christian missionaries destroyed many of the antiquities in this art, Western values brought in a commercial dimension; much of what is produced today is for the tourist market.

Other Religions

Christian missionary activity in Moyen-Congo between World Wars I and II gave rise to some 80 politico-messianic syncretic movements throughout Congo that have left indelible political and social marks on the country. These groups share certain characteristics, one of which is the goal (similar to that of Roman Catholic and Protestant missions) of destroying fetishes (*nkisi*). Also, their founders usually claimed to have had visions leading them to a political or religious calling. Members of these groups attend their own churches regularly and sometimes hold rallies, retreats, and mass-based events much like their Christian counterparts. Adherents may attend conventional churches to baptize their children.

Simon Kimbangu (1889–1951), a Christian convert born in the Belgian Congo who had a vision calling him to heal the sick, generated anticolonial sentiment among the Lari on both sides of the Congo River. In 1918 Kimbangu proclaimed himself a prophet and the son of God. He borrowed the rituals of baptism and confession from Christian practices and the cult of the ancestors from African traditional religion. Kimbanguism (also known as Kakism, a reference to the khaki cloth worn by followers in Congo) spread rapidly among Protestants, but the disapproval of the missionaries, combined with attempts by the civil authorities to suppress the movement, caused followers to break away from the mainstream Christian churches. Kimbanguism went underground, where it grew to become the largest independent African religion on the continent, recognized by both Congo governments and accepted into the World Council of Churches in 1969. Because Kimbangu stressed the biblical passages that gave the oppressed the right to revolt, the Belgian police arrested him in 1921, and he died a martyr in a Katanga prison 30 years later.

André Grénard Matsoua (1899–1942), a former Catholic catechist, founded a nonreligious association in 1927 for education, mutual aid, and equality of status with French citizens that developed into a political movement known as Amicalism, later renamed Matsouanism. The movement took root among the Lari peoples in the Pool region. Unlike Kimbangu, Matsoua had little intention of founding a religion, but he also became a martyred divinity after he died in prison. By the late 1960s Matsouanists had been absorbed into Kimbanguism. In the 1992–93 elections, however, Bernard Kolélas cast himself as a neo-Matsouanist disciple to curry favor with the Lari electorate and proved that the movement still had political importance. Many Lari have not accepted the reality of Matsoua's death. His statue towers above their administrative capital at Kinkala.

Many other political figures have used messianic groups as stepping-stones to power. In the late 1940s Fulbert Youlou imitated Matsoua, successfully laid claim to his mantle of political leadership, and became the country's first president. President Joachim Yhomby Opango (born in 1939; in office 1977–1979) claimed to be a prophet of the Anzimba movement. In 2003 President Sassou-Nguesso established Matsouanist chapters throughout the country, hoping to cash in on the latent popular support for Matsoua.

Historically messianic groups have been relatively small and localized, but their size a matter of speculation. The Matsouanists are thought to number no more than a few hundred and may never have numbered more than a few thousand. The Lassy Zerpherinists, who are politically salient in the Kouilou and Niari regions of southern and southwestern Congo, have managed to assemble crowds as large as twenty thousand. The Kimbanguists and Ngouzistes appear the largest, with between five and twenty thousand or more adherents. Over the past 30 years the numbers of all messianic groups have declined. Observers attribute this erosion partly to the failure of the founding generations to impart their faith firmly among succeeding generations and partly to the strength of the Catholic Church in Congo.

The Muslim community in Congo is relatively small, comprising some 25,000 to 50,000 people. Most of them are immigrants from North and West Africa working in the urban centers in commerce, including the clothing trade. Their specialty is the cloth that women use for making *pagnes* (sarongs). The Jehovah's Witnesses and the Church of Jesus Christ of Latter-day Saints have estimated memberships of fewer than 5,000 in Congo. The Bahai faith is also represented.

Robert Groelsema

See Also Vol. I: *African Traditional Religions, Christianity*

Bibliography

Africa South of the Sahara 2003: The Republic of the Congo. 32nd ed. London: Europa Publications, 2003.

Anderson, Efraim. *Churches at the Grass-roots: Study in Congo-Brazzaville.* London: Lutterworth, 1968.

———. *Messianic Popular Movements in the Lower Congo.* Uppsala: Almqvist and Wiksell; New York: W.S. Heinman, 1958.

Decalo, Samuel, Virginia Thompson, and Richard Adloff. *Historical Dictionary of Congo.* Vol. 69 of *African Historical Dictionaries.* Lanham, Md., and London: The Scarecrow Press, 1996.

MacGaffey, Wyatt. *Modern Kongo Prophets: Religion in a Plural Society.* Bloomington: University of Indiana Press, 1983.

———. *Religion and Society in Central Africa.* Chicago: University of Chicago Press, 1986.

McDonald, Gordon C., et al. *Area Handbook for People's Republic of the Congo (Congo Brazzaville).* Area Handbook Series. Washington, D.C.: U.S. Government Printing Office, 1971.

Youlou, Fulbert. *Le Matsouanisme.* Brazzaville: Imprimerie Centrale, 1955.

Romania

POPULATION 22,317,730

ORTHODOX CHURCH 86.7 percent

ROMAN CATHOLIC 4.7 percent

REFORMED 3.2 percent

PENTECOSTAL 1.5 percent

GREEK CATHOLIC 0.9 percent

BAPTIST 0.6 percent

SEVENTH-DAY ADVENTIST 0.4 percent

UNITARIAN 0.3 percent

MUSLIM 0.3 percent

CHRISTIAN OF OLD RITE 0.2 percent

CHRISTIAN ACCORDING TO THE GOSPELS 0.2 percent

OTHER 1.0 percent

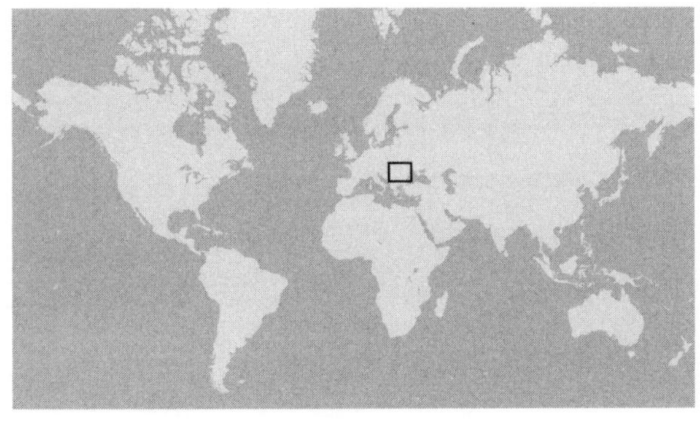

Country Overview

INTRODUCTION Romania is situated on the Balkan Peninsula. The country is bounded by Ukraine, Moldova, Hungary, Serbia, Bulgaria, and the Black Sea. Christianity was established in the present Romanian territory from the third century C.E.

The church is considered by some to have been the most important cultural institution and a key factor in preserving the national identity even when different parts of Romanian lands were subsequently under Ottoman, Polish, Habsburg, and Russian suzerainty. In Transylvania, Habsburg domination replaced Ottoman suzerainty at the end of the seventeenth century, and part of the Romanian population accepted unification with the Roman Catholic Church.

The Romanian principalities of Moldavia and Walachia united in 1859, and according to the constitution of 1866, Romania was declared the official name of the country. Independence was declared in 1877, with Romania becoming a kingdom in 1881, although the union of all Romanian territories was achieved only in 1918. At that time the Orthodox Church and the Greek Catholic Church were considered national churches. During World War II a large number of Jews were deported or exterminated, and in the first years of the communist regime most of the remaining Jews emigrated. After 1944 the church was gradually removed from state life—the Greek Catholic Church was banned, and repressive policies started against all Christian confessions. After 1989 religious freedom was completely reestablished.

Patriarch Teoctist Arăpaşu kisses a holy cup held by Orthodox Ecumenical Patriarch Bartholomew I. Patriarch Teoctist, head of the Romanian Orthodox church, continues to promote unity among churches. AP/WIDE WORLD PHOTOS.

According to a nationwide poll conducted in November–December 2001, 88 percent of citizens say that the Romanian Orthodox Church is the institution they trust most, this result classifying Romania among the highest-ranked nations in Eastern Europe regarding trust in religious institutions. Of those polled, 1 percent said they go to church on a daily basis, 10 percent go to church several times per week, 35 percent go several times per month, 38 percent attend services once a month or less, and 16 percent do not go to church at all.

RELIGIOUS TOLERANCE At present in Romania there are 15 religious denominations officially acknowledged and upwards of 120 religious associations. The state also materially supports religious organizations, providing money for religious staff, for the building of new abodes, and for the conservation and restoration of valuable assets of national heritage.

Since 1989 some Romanian politicians have criticized anti-Semitism, racism, and xenophobia in official declarations, but there are still signs of intolerance, both among politicians and the general public, toward some ethnic and religious communities. On 13 March 2002 the government issued two decrees: one banning fascist, racist, or xenophobic organizations and symbols, and the other prohibiting the encouragement of a cult of personality of war criminals.

Major Religion

ROMANIAN ORTHODOX CHURCH

DATE OF ORIGIN Third century C.E.

NUMBER OF FOLLOWERS 19.3 million

HISTORY Christianity entered this region during Roman occupation in the second and third centuries, and according to tradition the Apostle Andrew preached in Dobruja, the ancient Scythia Minor. The early spread of Christianity coincided with the formation of the Romanian people, with the core religious vocabulary in Romanian having Latin origin. From 500 to 1000 C.E. Romanian Christianity was preserved in popular forms without a well-organized clerical hierarchy. After the Slavs established themselves in the region, however, the church became organized, and the Slavonic language replaced Latin, becoming the official language of the church, with many terms relating to church hierarchy deriving from it.

The Romanians are the only Latin people of the Orthodox faith with Slavonic as their cultural and liturgical language. During the Middle Ages the creation of the voivodeships (provinces) of Walachia and Moldavia led to metropolitanates (sees of metropolitan bishops) having religious and political ties to Byzantium. Thus, in 1359 the metropolitan see of Walachia was established, being granted authority over the Orthodox Romanians in Transylvania, and in 1401 a metropolitan see was established in Moldavia. In 1360 the first Romanian archpriest known by name was mentioned in a document in Transylvania, but the Orthodox faith was subjected to Catholic and Protestant proselytism. Consequently Orthodoxy became a means of preserving traditions, as well as a means of preserving ethnic and linguistic identity.

In 1885 the ecumenical patriarch of Constantinople recognized the Romanian Orthodox Church as autocephalous (independent of external authority). After the unification of Romanian lands in 1918 and national reorganization of the church, the metropolitan of Walachia was raised to the rank of patriarch of the Romanian

Orthodox Church on 25 February 1925. The first patriarch, Miron Cristea, was enthroned in 1925. He was followed by patriarchs Nicodim Munteanu (1939–48), Justinian Marina (1948–77), Justin Moisescu (1977–86), and Teoctist Arăpaşu (from 16 November 1986).

EARLY AND MODERN LEADERS Religious leaders have played a role at different times in the development of the politico-historical life of Walachia, Moldavia, and Transylvania and, subsequently, in the modern Romanian state. As simple monks, they advised their contemporary rulers (Daniil Sihastrul was a saint and the main adviser of Stephen the Great [1457–1504]) or conducted uprisings against the invaders. They sometimes used the power of diplomacy to gain religious rights for Romanians during different occupations (Andrei Şaguna [1809–73], metropolitan of the Romanian Orthodox Church in Transylvania, reorganized the church, making it one of the leading forces in the national movement) or even engaged in active roles in political life (the patriarch Miron Cristea was a member of the regency council in 1930). Patriarch Justinian Marina continued the ecumenical work of his predecessors, with the Romanian Orthodox Church becoming a member of the European Council of Churches (1959) and the World Council of Churches (1961). Patriarch Iustin Moisescu intensified ecumenical contacts, and the present patriarch, Teoctist Arăpaşu, maintains the same principles in this field.

MAJOR THEOLOGIANS AND AUTHORS Saint John Casian (360–435) established two monasteries in Marsilia (France) and is considered one of the founders of monasticism in western Europe. Dionisius Exiguus (460–545) laid the foundations for the present chronological system, counting years starting from the birth of Christ (that is, the Christian era).

Metropolitans Varlaam (1672–79), Dosoftei, the first great Romanian poet (1671–86), and Antim Ivireanul (died in 1716) and bishop Melchisedec Ştefănescu (1864–92) had major roles in Romanian culture.

Contemporary Romanian theologians distinguished through their works and ecumenical activity include Ioan Coman, Liviu Stan, Nicolae Chiţescu, Emilian Vasilescu, Nicolae Balca, Ene Branişte, Ioan Rămureanu, Mircea Chialda, Nicolae Lungu, and Teodor Bodogae.

One of Europe's most outstanding theologians is Dumitru Stăniloae (1903–93), who wrote nearly 1,300 titles, including treaties, commentaries, and translations. His most important work, *Orthodox Dogmatic Theology*, introduced Orthodox theology into the ecumenical debate.

HOUSES OF WORSHIP AND HOLY PLACES Orthodox churches are built to represent the universe. The interior of an Orthodox church is divided into three parts: the narthex, representing the world in which mankind is called to repentance; the nave, being the place of the assembled church, which includes both the living and the departed; and the sanctuary, which represents the throne of God with the Lord himself invisibly present there.

The sixteenth and seventeenth centuries signify the climax of Romanian medieval art. Five monasteries in northern Moldavia (Suceviţa, Moldoviţa, Humor, Arbore, and the most famous monastery, Voroneţ, with its original blue) are the most important ensembles of monuments with exterior mural paintings in Europe and are under UNESCO patronage. Images represent scenes from the Bible and major events in the lives of Christian saints.

Also worth mentioning are the monasteries of Dealu, Curtea de Argeş (the greatest achievement of post-Byzantine art), Dragomirna, Secu, Căldăruşani, Hurezi, Văcăreşti, Văratec, and Sihăstria, as well as the churches at Potlogi and Mogoşoaia.

WHAT IS SACRED? In the Romanian Orthodox Church there are similar sacred elements to those in all other Orthodox churches. Thus, the words of the Holy Scriptures and Holy Tradition are sacred and cannot be changed. The Holy Scripture comprises the writings of both the New and the Old Testaments. The Holy Tradition includes writings, teachings, and acts of the apostles, saints, martyrs, and church fathers; liturgical and sacramental traditions from throughout the ages; and the decisions of the ecumenical councils.

In liturgical life there are different objects that help the community to perform ceremonies. In addition, icons and relics are venerated. This veneration, according to the decisions and canons of the Seventh Ecumenical Council (787), relates not to the sacred images but to their prototypes or to the persons whom they represent.

HOLIDAYS AND FESTIVALS The church calendar begins on 1 September and ends on 31 August. On each day, the church celebrates at least one saint or a major religious event. Several major feasts are observed annually, and of these Easter is the most important. The other major feast days are the Nativity of the Virgin Mary (8 September), the Exaltation of the Holy Cross (14 September), the Presentation of the Virgin Mary in the Temple (21 November), Christmas—Nativity of Jesus Christ (25 December), Epiphany—the Baptism of Christ (6 January), Annunciation (25 March), the feast of Saint George (23 April), the feast of Saints Helen and Constantine (21 May), Palm Sunday (the Sunday before Easter), Ascension (40 days after Easter), Pentecost (50 days after Easter), the Transfiguration of Christ (6 August), and the Dormition of the Virgin Mary (15 August).

MODE OF DRESS Liturgical vestments have many decorative and symbolic purposes. For example, the stole symbolizes the direct relationship between the material and the divine world. Used by priests at all important ceremonies, it represents the spiritual power Christ gave to the apostles and, through them, to all bishops and priests.

Everyday clothes ought to be clean and modest. Clothing that is suggestive or may distract from the church ceremony and interfere with concentration and attention to prayer is not allowed. According to the words of the Bible, there should be a distinction between men's and women's clothing, which should be particular to each sex. At religious ceremonies women are not allowed to wear trousers, short skirts, or skin-tight dresses and should cover the head as a sign of humility. Moreover, men are supposed to dress modestly, being forbidden to wear women's clothes, T-shirts, or shorts. In different parts of Romania, especially in rural regions of Moldavia and Transylvania, people wear their traditional folk clothes on major religious occasions or even for Sunday Mass.

DIETARY PRACTICES As in all other Orthodox churches, fasting is an important factor in Christian life, not simply a set of dietary laws or legalistic requirements. Fasting is accompanied by prayer and almsgiving as a spiritual aid in disciplining the body and the soul. In Orthodox tradition fasting involves abstaining from meat, fish, dairy, eggs, wine, and olive oil; eating a smaller quantity of food; and even eating fewer meals.

There are four main periods of fasting during the year: the Great Fast (Lent) begins seven weeks before the Resurrection; the Fast of the Apostles starts on the Monday eight days after Pentecost and ends on 28 June; the Dormition Fast lasts two weeks, from 1 to 14 August; and the Nativity Fast lasts 40 days, from 15 November to 24 December. In addition, all Wednesdays and Fridays—and, in some monasteries, Mondays as well—are fast days. Other fast days include the day before Epiphany (5 January), the day of the Beheading of John the Forerunner (29 August), and the day of the Exaltation of the Cross (14 September).

RITUALS Romanian Orthodox rituals are the same as those of other Orthodox churches. The main features of worship are unaccompanied chanting during religious ceremonies and standing or kneeling as default posture for private or public worship.

Because sacred time is an essential element of Orthodox worship, there are different Christian prayers according to the specific times of day (services called hours). The most important religious service is the Divine Liturgy (Eucharist, Mass, or Holy Communion). The most frequently used prayers are Our Father and the Creed but also the repetitions of the Jesus prayer—"Lord Jesus Christ, Son of God, have mercy on me the sinner"—invoking trust and obedience from God.

The main pilgrimages in the Romanian Orthodox Church are to monasteries and to saint's relics during their annual celebration, such as Saint Pious Parascheva (14 October) in Iasi and Saint Dimitrie (28 October) in Bucharest.

RITES OF PASSAGE Christian life should be seen as a unity, as a single and great sacrament. The Romanian Orthodox Church, as all Orthodox churches, has seven sacraments: baptism, confirmation, Holy Eucharist, confession, ordination, marriage, and holy unction.

Baptism is the door through which someone enters into the church. Confirmation is the completion of baptism. In the sacrament of the Holy Eucharist, with the bread and wine, the faithful partake of the very Body and the very Blood of Jesus Christ for remission of sins and eternal life. In the sacrament of confession, Jesus Christ, the founder of the sacrament, through the confessor, forgives the sins committed after baptism by the person who confesses his sins and sincerely repents of them. In the sacrament of ordination through prayer and the laying-on of hands by a bishop, divine grace comes down on the ordained enabling him to be a minister. In marriage divine grace sanctifies the union of husband and wife. In the sacrament of holy unction the sick person is anointed with sanctified oil, and divine grace heals his bodily and spiritual ills.

MEMBERSHIP Church membership is open to any person, regardless of age, who receives the sacrament of baptism. According to Orthodox doctrine, members of the church are members of Christ's mystical body, and through the sacraments they receive God's grace. Membership involves regular attendance at divine services and the receiving of sacraments engaging their personal lives according to Christ's commandments.

According to official doctrine the Romanian Orthodox Church does not proselytize. Its pastoral methods are based on the direct contact of ministers with members of the local communities concerning their lives and religious needs. The church has different publications and theological magazines, and it benefits from exposure and airtime on national radio and television, but a presence on the Internet is not well developed except in the Romanian religious diaspora.

SOCIAL JUSTICE Despite the economic difficulties facing not only the Romanian Orthodox Church but also the whole country, the church after 1989 reestablished charitable associations helping orphans and old or handicapped people and granting religious assistance in hospitals, orphanages, and homes for the elderly or conscripts. New units of theological education were also opened, such as the Faculties of Theology in Iasi and Cluj-Napoca; new high school seminaries in Roman, Galaţi, Alba Iulia, and Suceava; and the Monastery of Agapia (for girls).

SOCIAL ASPECTS The social doctrine of the Romanian Orthodox Church is the same as in other Orthodox churches. Marital union in the Orthodox Church is compared to the union between Christ and the Church. Marriage has a sacramental character and is an act of devotion in front of God and the community. The church allows divorce only in cases of fornication, death (of husband or wife), desertion, cruelty, or incompatibility; remarriage is allowed only two times. In the Orthodox Church marriage between first and second cousins and between persons who have the same godparents is forbidden. Mixed marriages (between Orthodox and non-Orthodox) are allowed only if they are performed according to Orthodox rites and if the couple agrees to bring their children up in the Orthodox faith.

POLITICAL IMPACT The highest authority of the Romanian Orthodox Church, for all the dogmatic and canonical problems, is the Holy Synod. It consists of the patriarch and the appointed hierarchy (metropolitans, archbishops, bishops, and vicars). The executive representative body of the Holy Synod is the National Church Council.

Since 1994 the Romanian Orthodox Church has wished to be recognized by the Romanian government as the National Church of Romania. Even if the church is not involved officially in politics, in practice Romanian authorities consider it as such, and therefore, it enjoys a political influence.

CONTROVERSIAL ISSUES The Romanian Orthodox Church does not agree with the use of contraceptives for birth control. A strong trend, however, has recently developed that supports the position that this question should be left to the discretion of each individual couple in consultation with their confessor or spiritual father. Abortion is considered murder, being allowed only in the case of therapeutic abortion when the life of the mother is endangered.

The church considers homosexual orientation as a disorder and disease, and therefore views homosexual actions as sinful and destructive.

CULTURAL IMPACT In the Middle Ages the Romanian Orthodox Church was the main cultural institution printing the first books in Romanian and circulating manuscripts throughout the region. The first printing houses functioned in monasteries or diocesan seats, and the first secondary schools (the College at the Monastery of the Three Holy Hierarchs in Iasi) and schools of higher education (the Academy of Saint Sava in Bucharest) were set up under their auspices.

In all big monasteries remarkable artistic activity developed, such as making icons, vestments and liturgical vessels, embroideries, and wood sculptures.

The Romanian Orthodox Church also helped other Christian churches, especially those under Ottoman rule, by printing books in Greek, Arabic, and Gruzian and granting relief aid to other churches in eastern and southeastern Europe and the Near East. Donations supported other churches in the fight for their own national culture and independence.

Other Religions

Regarding the relationship with other religions after 1989, the Romanian Orthodox Church has repeatedly criticized the "aggressive proselytizing" of Protestant, neo-Protestant, and different religious groups, describing them as sects. The actions of these groups are perceived as attempts to convert Romanian Orthodox Church members. Moreover, minority religious groups allege that the Orthodox clergy have provoked isolated mob incidents; for example, the Seventh-day Adventist Church has reported such events in Botoşani and Galaţi. The major Protestant church is the Reformed Church of Romania, which came into being in 1554. Most of its members belong to the Hungarian minority in Romania. The first Baptists in Romania date back to 1856 and the first Pentecostals to 1922.

The Romanian government reestablished diplomatic relations with the Vatican in 1990. The Roman Catholic Church in Romania has 12 dioceses according to three types of rites: six Roman Catholic dioceses, five Greek Catholic dioceses, and one Ordinariat of Armenian Catholics. On 7–9 May 1999 Pope John Paul II made a historic visit to Romania, his first visit to a major Orthodox country.

Relations between the Greek Catholic Church and the Orthodox Church are tense because of the controversy over property restitution of former cathedrals and district churches that now belong to the Orthodox Church. In 1948, when the Greek Catholic Church was banned, it had 2,600 churches for its 1,664,000 faithful (on average, one church for every 640 worshipers). At the beginning of the twenty-first century it had 350 churches (150 taken from the Orthodox—according to the State Secretariat for Religious Denominations, the Greek Catholics claim that they have received only 143 such properties—and 200 new constructions) for its 230,000 faithful (on average, one church for every 660 worshipers). A 1990 government decree called for the creation of a Joint Orthodox and Greek Catholic Committee at a national level to decide the fate of churches that had belonged to the Greek Catholic Church before 1948. This committee met six times until 2003 but did not manage to end the dispute.

Another religion with an important role in Romania's history is Judaism. According to the official census of 1930, the ethnic structure of Romania did not differ from other countries in the region where ethnic minorities represented an important proportion of the population. At that time Romania, with 13 million inhabitants, had 750,000 Jews; the preliminary results of the 2002 census reported there to be only 6,179 Jews (the Jewish Community Federation states that it has approximately 12,000 members). Most Jews were deported during World War II or emigrated in the first years of communism. Since 1989 the Jewish community has received 42 buildings by government decree.

Lucian N. Leustean

See Also Vol. I: *Christianity, Eastern Orthodoxy, Eastern Rite Churches, Judaism*

Bibliography

Bria, Ion. *The Sense of Ecumenical Tradition: The Ecumenical Vision and Witness of the Orthodox.* Geneva: World Council of Churches, 1991.

Bransea, Nicolae I., and Stefan Lonita. *Religious Life in Romania.* Buchaersti: Editura Paideia, 1999.

Păcurariu, Mircea. *Istoria Bisericii Ortodoxe Române.* Bucharest: EIBMBOR, 1992.

Popescu, Dumitru. *Ortodoxie şi Catolicism—Dialog şi reconciliere.* Bucharest: România Creştină, 1999.

Stăniloae, Dumitru. *Comunitate şi spiritualitate în liturghia ortodoxă.* Craiova, Romania: Mitropolia Olteniei, 1986.

———. *The Experience of God: Orthodox Dogmatic Theology.* Translated by Ioan Ioniţă and Robert Barringer. Brookline, Mass.: Holy Cross Orthodox Press, 1994.

———. *Theology and the Church.* Translated by Robert Barringer. Crestwood, N.Y.: St. Vladimir's Seminary Press, 1980.

Stebbing, Nicolas. *Bearers of the Spirit: Spiritual Fatherhood in Romanian Orthodoxy.* Kalamazoo, Mich.: Cistercian Publications, 2003.

Russia

POPULATION 144,978,573

ORTHODOX CHRISTIAN 33.0–40.0 percent

MUSLIM 8.0–10.0 percent

BUDDHIST 0.7 percent

JEWISH 0.7 percent

PROTESTANT 0.7 percent

ROMAN CATHOLIC 0.2 percent

OTHER LESS THAN 1.0 percent

NONRELIGIOUS 46.7–55.7 percent

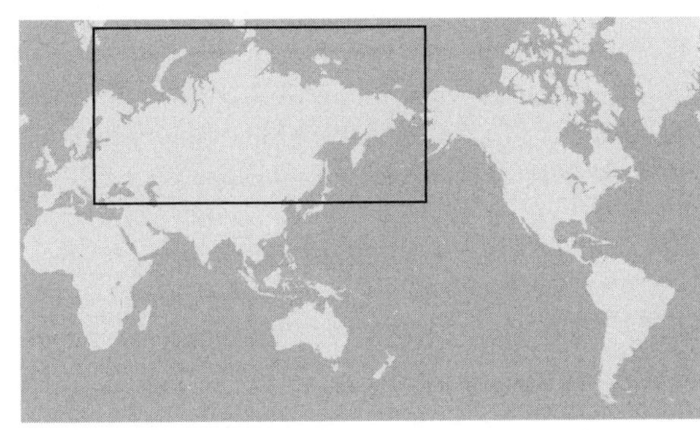

Country Overview

INTRODUCTION The Russian Federation, which includes parts of eastern Europe and northern Asia, is the world's largest country by area. Its population is the sixth largest in the world. Although Russians are the dominant group, the country's population is estimated to include more than 150 nationalities. As a result, a great diversity of religions is found among the peoples of Russia. In 2002, for example, there were more than 20,000 religious organizations belonging to 67 separate faiths registered with government judicial bodies.

Historically each of the indigenous peoples and groups of Russia professed its own religion, which was thus confined to specific regions, although over time the religious diversity within regions has tended to increase. In its Orthodox form Christianity became the religion of the central European part of Russia, beginning in the tenth century C.E. In ethnic terms Russians are the largest Orthodox group. Islam began to penetrate the territory of present-day Russia as early as the seventh century. Muslims in Russia are found mainly in the Volga region, the Caucasus, the Ural Mountains, and Siberia. The principal Muslim groups are the peoples of the Caucasus, including the Chechen, Ingush, Nogai, and Adygei, and the Tatars and the Bashkirs. Buddhism has been professed in Asian parts of Russia since the sixteenth century, but there are no wholly Buddhist groups of peoples in the country. For example, Buddhism is the religion of only a half of the Kalmyks and Tuvinians, a third of the Buryats, and a quarter of the Altaians.

Because legislation prohibits asking citizens to state their religious affiliation, there is no official statistical data about religious membership in Russia. The only methods for estimating the number of believers are, first, the number of religious organizations registered with state judicial bodies and, second, the results of sociological polls.

RELIGIOUS TOLERANCE Russia is a secular country, with religious bodies separate from the state and equal

A Russian Orthodox priest baptizes a young girl in the Moskva River. Christening is one of the seven sacraments recognized by the Russian Orthodox Church. © AFP/CORBIS.

before the law. The Russian constitution and the federal law On Freedom of Conscience and Religious Associations (1997) guarantee Russian citizens the right to freedom of conscience. The 1997 law does, however, recognize Orthodoxy as being closely linked to Russian identity throughout history. According to legislation on religious affairs, the state is to support religious organizations financially, materially, and in other ways in teaching general subjects at the educational institutions they run and in repairing their houses of worship. In addition, the state grants tax privileges to religious organizations.

There is no open religious conflict in Russia. Tensions do exist, however, between the Orthodox Church, on the one hand, and the Roman Catholic and some Protestant churches, on the other.

Major Religion

RUSSIAN ORTHODOX CHURCH

DATE OF ORIGIN Tenth century C.E.
NUMBER OF FOLLOWERS 48–58 million

HISTORY Orthodoxy is the largest confession in Russia and has a special role in the history of the country and in the development of its culture. The Russian Orthodox Church came into being in the late tenth century, when Byzantine Christianity was adopted as the state religion. The church was initially headed by a metropolitan who was a subordinate of the patriarch of Constantinople. At first his residence was in Kiev and then, beginning in 1299, in Vladimir and later, after 1328, in Moscow. The Russian Orthodox Church officially became independent of the Constantinople patriarchate in 1589, at which time the Russian patriarchate was formed. Although patriarchs were formally appointed by church assemblies, the final say belonged to the tsar, who was proclaimed the Vicarius Christi (Vicar of Christ). The only cleric of the Russian Orthodox Church who tried to make the church superior to secular authorities was the patriarch Nikon (1605–81), who carried out reforms in the second half of the seventeenth century, correcting prayer books to make them conform to the Greek original and adjusting church rites to the Greek traditions. His reforms led to a schism in the church, with his opponents forming the Old Ritual Church.

In 1700 Peter the Great abolished the patriarchate, and in 1721 the Spiritual Collegium, later transformed into the Holy Synod, was founded to govern the Russian Orthodox Church. The chief procurator of the Holy Synod, who was appointed by the tsar from among laymen, was the actual head of the church. Before the Revolution of 1917 the Russian Orthodox Church was considered a part of the state machinery. The church underwent a deep crisis on the eve of the revolution, however. Grigory Rasputin, a favorite of the last tsar, Nicholas II, gained a decisive say in religious affairs, and the population became progressively alienated from the church.

After the Bolsheviks came to power in 1917, the Russian Orthodox Church found itself on the verge of destruction. The church was formally separated from the state, and government authorities pursued a policy of forced atheism. A church assembly in 1917 restored the institution of the patriarchy, but when Patriarch Tikhon died in 1925, the Communist authorities prohibited the election of a successor. In 1927 the metropolitan Sergii, who was acting patriarch at the time, was forced to issue a declaration in support of the Soviet government. Nonetheless, up to 1943 the Communist leaders continued a policy of overt repression of the Orthodox Church. During World War II, however, Joseph Stalin deemed it advantageous to use the church as a symbol of the succession of two empires—that is, of tsarist Russia and of the Soviet Union. He also used the church for patriotic purposes: to build a common Russian front against German invasion. Many hierarchs and priests were released from jail, and government authorities allowed the clergy to convene an assembly and to elect a new patriarch, Aleksii I (Simanskii). At the same time, all of the church's activities were controlled by the Council for the Affairs of the Russian Orthodox Church, which was formed by the government.

No significant changes took place in the relations between the Russian Orthodox Church and the Soviet state after 1943. The church remained under the full control of the state and, to preserve itself, supported the authority of the Communist regime. In the early 1960s, however, when the Communist Party and the Soviet government were headed by Nikita Khrushchev, oppression of the church increased. Not until 1991, with the collapse of the Communist regime, did the period of oppression and discrimination end.

EARLY AND MODERN LEADERS The Russian Orthodox Church has had a number of eminent historical leaders. One of the earliest was Filipp (1507–69), the metropolitan of Moscow and of all Rus (Russia), who openly opposed the terrors of Ivan the Terrible and who was killed on the tsar's order. Filipp was later canonized. When Nikon (1605–81), the patriarch of Moscow and of all Rus, tried to rescue the church from the direct control of the tsarist authorities, he was deprived of his orders and exiled. Feofan Prokopovich (1681–1736), archbishop of Novgorod, was a prominent state and church figure. A pamphleteer during the reforms of Peter the Great, he became an advocate of Russia's development on a Western model. Patriarch Tikhon (1865–1925) opposed Soviet power and the separation of the church from the state, but he recognized the Communist regime in 1923. Nonetheless, he was kept under house arrest until the end of his life. He also was later canonized. Nikodim (1929–78), the metropolitan of Leningrad and Novgorod, advocated dialogue between the Russian Orthodox Church and other confessions, especially the Roman Catholic Church. The most influential contemporary leaders of the Russian Orthodox Church are the patriarch Aleksii II (born in 1929) and Kirill (born in 1946), the metropolitan of Smolensk and the head of foreign church relations of the Moscow patriarchate.

MAJOR THEOLOGIANS AND AUTHORS Among important theologians and writers of the Russian Orthodox Church, Iosif of Volok (1440–1515) was a renowned polemicist who advocated that churches be richly decorated and that monasteries own land. He developed the doctrine of the theocratic nature of the power of the grand prince of Moscow, or the tsar, and criticized the heretical movements of the time. He was canonized after his death. Nil of Sora (c.1433–1508), known for his sermons, was an expert in theological literature who advocated reforms in monasticism. In his view the purpose of the monastic life was internal self-perfection rather than mortification of the flesh, and he considered correspondence between the Scriptures and reason a necessary part of good conduct. He believed that the church should not possess wealth, and he opposed luxury generally. He also was known for demonstrating a degree of religious tolerance. The monk Filofei of Pskov (sixteenth century) created the idea of Moscow as the so-called Third Rome in order to substantiate the tsar's claims to ecumenical authority and as the heir and legal successor to the Eastern, or Byzantine, Empire. Platon (Piotr Georgievuch) Levshin (1737–1812), a metropolitan of Moscow, was known as a writer and preacher. Filaret (1783–1867), another metropolitan of Moscow, wrote the catechism of the Russian Orthodox Church and translated biblical texts. He was a brilliant homilist, and a collection of his sermons was translated into English and French while he was still living. The Russian Orthodox seminaries Saint Sergius, in Paris, and Saint Vladimir, in Crestwood, New York, have produced a number of eminent theologians, including Alexander Schmemann (1921–83) and John Meyendorff (1926–92).

HOUSES OF WORSHIP AND HOLY PLACES There are a number of revered churches and holy places of the Russian Orthodox Church, including several monasteries. The Troitse-Sergieva monastery near Moscow, the spiritual center of the Russian Orthodox Church, was founded in the 1340s. It is the home of the Moscow Spiritual Academy and of a seminary, and its principal sacred articles are the relics of its founder, Sergii of Radonezh. The Valaam monastery, in the northwest of Russia, was founded in the fourteenth century or earlier. The relics of the monks Sergii and German are preserved there. The Optina monastery, in the Kaluga oblast of central Russia, was founded in the late fourteenth or early fifteenth century. It was especially revered in the nineteenth century because of its elderly spiritual advisers, who lived in special cells near the fence and who were deemed to be endowed with a special bliss. The Russian writer Fyodor Dostoyevsky described the spiritual advisers in his novel *The Brothers Karamazov.* The Aleksandro-Nevskaya monastery in Saint Petersburg was founded in the eighteenth century.

Significant churches in Russia include the complex within the walls of the Kremlin in Moscow, built from the fifteenth to the seventeenth centuries. Christ the Savior, in Moscow, is the largest cathedral in Russia. It was built in the nineteenth century, blown up during the Soviet period, and restored in 1997. All Russian Orthodox Church buildings have richly decorated interiors.

WHAT IS SACRED? The dogmas and beliefs of the Russian Orthodox Church do not differ in important ways from those of other Orthodox churches. The church recognizes both the Scriptures and the so-called Sacred Tradition, the writings of the fathers of the church. Only the decisions of the first seven ecumenical councils—those before the Schism of 1054—are recognized, however. In addition to the Holy Trinity, Russian Orthodox venerate Mary (known as the Mother of God), angels, saints, and relics. One of the traditions is communication with God and saints through icons.

HOLIDAYS AND FESTIVALS There are 12 principal festivals in the Russian Orthodox Church, the most important being Easter. The second most important holiday is Christmas. Most Russians who designate themselves as Orthodox Christians celebrate religious holidays as merely cultural observances, however. Only 2 or 3 percent of Orthodox Christians in Russia keep the fasts before holidays.

MODE OF DRESS The dress of the clergy in the Russian Orthodox Church, especially that of its supreme hierarchs, was inherited from the Byzantine church. The vestments are luxurious, made of velvet and brocade in bright colors such as red, green, yellow, and blue, and featuring gold and numerous precious stones. Monks and nuns, on the other hand, wear modest black garments. Although there are no dress restrictions for laypersons, women must cover their heads in church, and they also are discouraged from using makeup and wearing short skirts, pants, or garments of bright colors.

DIETARY PRACTICES In the Russian Orthodox Church, Easter, Christmas, Saint Peter's Day, and Assumption are preceded by fasts, when believers refrain from consuming meat, milk, eggs, and sometimes even fish. The longest and strictest fast is the seven weeks of Lent, before Easter. In addition, all Wednesdays and Fridays, except those of Easter week, are days of fasting. The clergy may exempt sick and elderly persons, travelers, and some other believers from fasting. Only a very small percentage of the Orthodox observe the fasts, however.

RITUALS The rituals of the Russian Orthodox worship service, which were inherited from the Byzantine church, are sophisticated and solemn. Worship is accompanied by burning candles and incense and by choral singing, with the use of musical instruments prohibited. The service is prolonged, and worshipers stand. The language of the service is Church Slavonic, which is not intelligible to most worshipers. Sermons, however, are given in Russian and in other local languages. The Russian Orthodox Church recognizes seven sacraments: christening, or baptism; chrismation; Communion; confession; marriage; ordination; and holy unction, the sacrament for dangerously ill persons but also used for the sick generally and sometimes performed preventively. Only clerics are entitled to perform the services and sacraments.

While the liturgies and other public services are celebrated in churches, private services may be celebrated in homes. The most widespread private services are prayers for health and offices for the dead.

RITES OF PASSAGE Any person who has undergone christening is considered to be Orthodox, and thus this rite is central to the Russian Orthodox Church. Christening usually is done in infancy by a priest, but if a child's life is in danger, the infant may be christened by a layman. The rite is normally performed in churches, although on special occasions it may be done in the home. Christening begins with a prayer said by the priest, who then makes signs of the cross on the infant's head, ears, hands, legs, chest, and shoulders with anointing oil and immerses the infant in the baptismal font three times. As guarantors of the child's faith, the godfather and godmother are present during the rite. The infant is then arrayed in white clothes, which are preserved as a relic.

MEMBERSHIP The membership of the Russian Orthodox Church may be divided into laypersons and the clergy. The laity consists of everyone who has been christened and who undertakes confession and receives Communion at least once a year. Polls show that as many as 40 percent of the people of Russia consider themselves Orthodox, but only 2.5 to 3 percent are active believers who observe church discipline. Most of those who call themselves Orthodox are ignorant of the principal dogmas of the church, do not take part in church life, and do not observe religious rituals.

The clerical hierarchy consists of three levels. Deacons take part in public and private services and assist priests in performing the sacraments. Priests perform all of the sacraments except for the ordination of bishops. Bishops, who include archbishops, metropolitans, and the patriarch, are entitled to perform all of the sacraments. All bishops are considered to be equal in their dignity as priests. The Russian Orthodox Church is headed by the patriarch, who is elected from among the bishops by an assembly. He governs the church together with the Holy Synod, which consists of bishops, and the assembly, in which both clergy and laymen take part.

There are numerous Orthodox monasteries and convents in Russia. Only men can become priests, however. The clergy is divided into two categories, black (monks) and white (married clerics). Only monks can become bishops.

Historically the missionary activity of the Russian Orthodox Church was aimed at a rural population that was mostly uneducated. The contemporary church, however, must function in an urbanized and well-educated industrial society, which requires different approaches, and the church has found itself unprepared for the situation. In the 1990s people began returning to the church, not because of missionary activities but because they were seeking new values to replace socialist ideology.

Several factors have hindered the ability of the Russian Orthodox Church to expand. With only limited experience functioning as an independent body, the church has continued to strive for close relations with Russian state authorities. It thus tends to depend on administrative support from the state, and many of its hierarchs seek a privileged status over other religions. In addition, the church finds it difficult to recruit new members. For one thing the language of the services is archaic. For another the Slavophilism, and hence the anti-Western stance, of many active believers and clerics—the position, for example, of *Russkij Dom,* an Orthodox monthly—makes the church unattractive to young people. Many Russians also find unappealing the strict adherence to ritual and the critical attitude of Orthodox hierarchs toward modernist social trends.

SOCIAL JUSTICE The document "Fundamentals of the Social Conception of the Russian Orthodox Church" (2000) states the official position on important social problems. It proclaims that the church should protect the poor and advocates a just distribution of the products of labor. The document warns society against the striving for material wealth and declares that a person's economic status cannot in itself be treated as a sign of God's favor or disfavor. With respect to the secular nature of education in Russia, the document denounces the monopoly of a materialistic outlook and declares that the purpose of the church should be to assist schools in the upbringing of children. In fact, to the detriment of other religions, the church looks for preferential access to educational institutions. The church insists on the compulsory study of what is called "Orthodox culture" by schoolchildren of all confessions, thus demonstrating its intention to gain a monopoly over other ideologies in influence with students.

SOCIAL ASPECTS The Russian Orthodox Church denounces conjugal infidelity, and divorce is considered a sin. The church recognizes the exclusive social role of the family. Orthodox ideology condemns belittling the social importance of motherhood and fatherhood in comparison with parent's success in their work. The church opposes women's neglect of their roles as mothers and wives.

POLITICAL IMPACT Historically the Russian Orthodox Church has been connected to the power of the state and has been dependent on it. With only a few exceptions, it has not held an independent position in the political and social life of Russia. After the collapse of the

Soviet Union, Russian authorities tried to gain ideological support from the church. There has been a tendency, however, for active believers to support the Communist Party, which tries to connect patriotism with Orthodox ideology and with extreme anti-Western, especially anti-American, sentiments. During the conflict in Kosovo at the end of the 1990s, for example, anti-American feelings were grounded by nationalists and communists in the fact that Yugoslavia was an Orthodox country.

CONTROVERSIAL ISSUES The Russian Orthodox Church denounces homosexual relations and other forms of alternative sexual orientations, as well as extramarital intercourse and prostitution. It opposes sexual education as taught in the schools, which presents premarital sex as a normal practice and which does not reject nontraditional sexual orientations. The church considers abortion and the decision not to have children to be sins. It denounces the donation of sexual cells to infertile couples on the grounds that this impairs the integrity of the personality and violates the exclusiveness of marital relations through the invasion of a third party. The church considers the cloning of humans to be unacceptable, but it does not oppose the cloning of isolated cells and tissues. The church denounces the use of tissues and organs of human fetuses in medicine.

CULTURAL IMPACT Historically Orthodoxy has had a strong impact on Russian cultural life. Such eminent composers as Dmitri Stephanovich Bortnyansky, Mikhail Ivanovich Glinka, and Pyotr Ilich Tchaikovsky created music for singing in church. The influence of Orthodoxy on the Russian visual arts is exemplified in the icon paintings of Andrey Rublyov and others and by the frescoes found in churches. Its influence on fiction is most pronounced in the novels of the nineteenth-century writer Fyodor Dostoyevsky.

After the process of Westernization began in the early eighteenth century, the role of Orthodoxy in Russian culture began to weaken, and religious forms of culture were replaced by secular ones. In contemporary times, in spite of the state's support, the impact of Orthodoxy on Russian culture is insignificant.

Other Religions

There are Orthodox churches in Russia outside the jurisdiction of the Russian Orthodox Church. One is the Russian Free Orthodox Church, which seceded from the Russian Orthodox Church in 1991. Another is the True, or Catacomb, Orthodox Church, which was founded in 1927 by believers who opposed the reconciliation between the Russian Orthodox Church and the Communist regime. There also are Old Ritualists of various sects, which emerged as a result of the rejection of the reforms of the patriarch Nikon in the late seventeenth century.

There are some 1 million active members of Protestant communities in Russia. Unlike Orthodox parishes, the membership of Protestant groups is determined by a special procedure that includes baptism and a formal application to join. More than 90 percent of Protestants in the country are ethnic Russians. Protestant churches attract young people by offering sermons in the local language, and they are active in supplying social services and aid to such institutions as hospitals and jails. There are more than 20 Protestant educational institutions in Russia.

The activities of the Roman Catholic Church in Russia are complicated by its conflict with the Russian Orthodox Church, which accuses Catholics of striving to increase their membership through missionary activities among the Orthodox. The top Orthodox hierarchs have categorically opposed visits by the pope to Russia. Roman Catholics have four educational institutions in the country.

There are between 11 and 15 million Muslims in Russia. Muslims do not have a single organization in Russia, and there are more than 50 spiritual directorates and centers throughout the country. The most important regional associations are the Central Spiritual Directorate of Muslims, in Ufa, and the Council of Muftis of Russia, in Moscow. There are some 50 Muslim educational institutions in Russia.

Most Muslims in Russia are Sunni. Wahhabism, a fundamentalist movement, is widespread in northern Caucasia, mainly in Chechnya. Many of the Azerbaijanis who live in Russia profess Shiism. The Islamic faith in Russia has grown rapidly, tripling in the decade after 1992, and there has been an increase in those participating actively in religious life. Large numbers of Muslims in Russia are migrant laborers, which has brought them into contact with people of other faiths. This has made relations between Islam and other religions an important factor in Russian life.

Small religious minorities with historical roots in Russia include Jews and Buddhists. Judaism has been present in Russia since the eighth century C.E. During the twentieth century the numbers of Jews in Russia decreased because of emigration to other countries, including Israel. Most Jewish religious organizations are registered in Moscow and Saint Petersburg, but there is no single spiritual center. Jews have one educational institution in Russia. Likewise, the Russian Buddhist community has no single spiritual center. There are three Buddhist educational institutions in the country.

The religious groups that emerged in Russia in contemporary times may be divided into those of Russian and of foreign origins. The most influential associations of local origin are those based on pagan beliefs and the Last Testament Church. The latter was found by Vissarion (Sergei Torop; born in 1961), a militiaman who proclaimed himself God's Messiah and God's Son. He took his mission to be that of acquainting people with what he called the Last Testament from the Father, consisting of 61 commandments. The most numerous and rapidly growing organizations of foreign origin have been the Jehovah's Witnesses, the Society of Krishna's Consciousness, and Mun's Reunion Church.

Larissa Andreeva

See Also Vol. I: *Christianity, Islam, Eastern Orthodoxy, Sunnism*

Bibliography

Anderson, John. *Religion, State, and Politics in the Soviet Union and Succesor States, 1953–1993.* Cambridge: Cambridge University Press, 1994.

Cheremnykh, Grigori Grigorievich. *Svoboda sovesti v Rossiiskoi Federatsii.* Moscow: Manuskript, 1996.

Ellis, Jane. *The Russian Orthodox Church: Triumphalism and Defensiveness.* Basingstoke, N.Y.: Macmillan Press, 1996.

Fennell, John. *A History of the Russian Church to 1448.* London and New York: Addison-Wesley, 1995.

Kotiranta, Matti., ed. *Religious Transition in Russia.* Helsinki: Aleksanteri Institute, 2000.

Nielsen, Niels Christian. *Christianity after Communism: Social, Political, and Cultural Struggle in Russia.* Boulder, Colo.: Westview Press, 1994.

Novye religioznye kul'ty, dvizheniya i organizatsii v Rossii. Moscow: Izdatel'stvo Rossijskoj Akademii Gosudarstvennoj Sluzhby, 1998.

Pravoslavie: Vekhi istorii. Moscow: Politizdat, 1986.

Pravoslavnaya tserkov': Sovremennye eresi i sekty. Saint Petersburg: Pravoslavnaya Ru's, 1995.

Religii narodov sovremennoi Rossii. Moscow: Respublika, 1999.

Religiya, svoboda sovesti, gosudarstvenno-tserkovnye otnosheniya v Rossii. Moscow: Izdatel'stvo Rossijskoj Akademii Gosudarstvennoj Sluzhby, 1996.

Rwanda

POPULATION 7,398,074

ROMAN CATHOLIC 65 percent

AFRICAN TRADITIONAL RELIGIONS 23 percent

PROTESTANT 10 percent

MUSLIM 1 percent

OTHER 1 percent

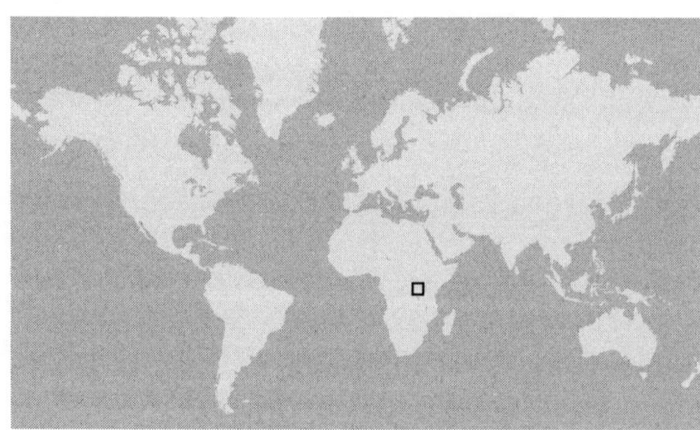

Country Overview

INTRODUCTION The Rwandese Republic, located in Central Africa, is surrounded by the Democratic Republic of the Congo, Uganda, Tanzania, and Burundi. The land is green and hilly. In pre-colonial times Rwanda was a land of migration: cattle-herders (called Tutsi) and cultivators (Hutu) displaced the original inhabitants, who were hunter-gatherers (Twa). The group's indigenous religions emphasized rituals to benefit these occupations. The Tutsi and Hutu together created an *ubwiru* (centralized ruling institution) based on Hutu monarchical symbols, including the ideas of a divine kingship, a sacred fire, royal drums, agricultural rituals, and royal burial customs. The *ubwiru* operated through a clan system; 14 major and many minor clans included members of all three occupational groups (Tutsi, Hutu, and Twa). Clan members sought protection from enemies, paying their patrons (clan leaders, who were cattle owners) in cattle or produce. Cattle remained the central symbol of prosperity; cattle owners could raise armies and became important in the royal courts.

By 1899, when Rwanda and Burundi were incorporated into German East Africa, their centralized monarchies had operated for centuries. In Rwanda a *mwami* (king) ruled a state dominated politically by a Tutsi clan, the Nyiginya. Belgian forces occupied Rwanda after World War I and administered it from 1920 on as part of the Ruanda-Urundi territory, prompting a massive conversion to Christianity.

By the 1950s an independence movement had coalesced, led by Hutu intellectuals and supported by some missionaries. Simultaneously in 1957 the Hutu published the Bahutu Manifesto, and the bishops of Burundi and Rwanda published a joint declaration asserting themselves as spokespersons for social justice. The government and monarchy's domination by Tutsi spawned accusations of racial discrimination, and Rwandans previously united through religious practices divided into "ethnicities" along occupational lines. When the *mwami* died in 1959 and Tutsi Jean-Baptiste Ndahindurwa was proclaimed the new *mwami,* the Rwandan state dissolved into anarchy. A peasant revolt spread through the country, and the Catholic missions became sanctuaries for Tutsi. In July 1961 Belgium granted Rwanda's independence. The first president,

Grégoire Kayibanda, was a member of the Parti de L'Émancipation du Peuple Hutu (Hutu People's Emancipation Party, formerly called Parmehutu).

The majority of Rwandan Christians are Roman Catholic. Most Protestants are Anglican. Other Christian groups include Baptists and hundreds of small independent evangelical churches that combined claim 250,000 followers. A limited number of Seventh-day Adventists and Baha'is and a small community of Muslim traders also exist.

RELIGIOUS TOLERANCE The indigenous monarchical system reinforced by the Belgian colonial administration was abolished at independence, promoting greater religious tolerance in Rwanda. The 1991 Constitution and the new 2003 Constitution prepared by the administration of President Paul Kagame (former leader of the Rwanda Patriotic Front) mandate religious tolerance in accordance with international and human rights legislation. Public schools offer Christian moral education and private mission schools support religious tolerance.

Major Religion

ROMAN CATHOLICISM

DATE OF ORIGIN 1900 C.E.
NUMBER OF FOLLOWERS 4.8 million

HISTORY In 1899 Monsignor Jean-Joseph Hirth of the White Fathers (Society of Missionaries of Africa) entered Rwanda accompanied by a small army of 150 porters, Sukuma guards, and Ganda auxiliaries. After a difficult visit the *mwami* (royal) court agreed that the missionaries should live among the Hutus and not at court. The first mission was finally located at Save station, 20 kilometers from the capital, Nyanza. The work of the White Father's Ganda catechists progressed rapidly. When the Belgians took over Rwanda after World War I, education was given to the missionaries, who trained clerks and petty officers for the colonial administration. The Tutsi became interested in European systems of education and Catholicism in general. In 1930 1,934 out of the total Tutsi population of 9,014 were baptized.

In 1931 the Belgians and the White Fathers deposed the Rwandan king Musinga and gave the throne to his son, Rudahigwa (Mutara IV), a Catholic catechumen. The subsequent impossibility of opposing Catholicism, along with the advantages of literacy for court functionaries, secured a massive conversion to Christianity by the king's elite group and the Tutsis in general. African religions went into rapid decline. The White Fathers also converted hundreds of Hutu, who saw the missionaries as protectors. Catholicism became the state religion, and the White Fathers took roles in leadership and government. Though only a quarter of Rwandans were Catholic, they held more political sway, economic resources, and positions in the Belgian administration.

A woman rests against the bullet-ridden wall of a church in Rwanda. Many important religious leaders, as well as hundreds of priests, nuns, catechists, and lay leaders, died during the 1994 genocide. © LANGEVIN JACQUES/CORBIS SYGMA.

Catholicism continued to dominate the country for 30 years following independence. The White Fathers saw the 1994 genocide as a complete failure of Catholicism, however, and most expatriate missionaries left. As soon as the Rwandan Patriotic Front assumed control of the country, Catholic religious practices took on a central role in a difficult period of reconciliation and nation building.

EARLY AND MODERN LEADERS Monsignor Jean-Joseph Hirth was central to the White Fathers missionary enterprise in Rwanda. Born in Alsace in 1854, he was trained in French seminaries and ordained in 1878. He accompanied the first White Fathers into Central Africa. Hirth survived persecution in Uganda and in 1890 was consecrated Vicar Apostolic of the Nyanza Méridional region, which extended from Kilimanjaro to Rwanda and included German East Africa. Part of the initial missionary expedition to Rwanda in February 1900, Hirth negotiated the first mission stations with the royal court, aided by his ability to speak German with the Kaiser's colonial officers. His directives to the newly arrived missionaries were central to the growth of Catholicism in Rwanda. He helped them avoid the manipulation of local chiefs, emphasized better neophytes over large numbers of newly baptized Christians, and started an educational system that later nurtured all Rwanda's major leaders. Hirth's enthusiasm created a Hutu church within a Tutsi kingdom in the first period of Catholic expansion, but most of the archbishops that followed accommodated the Tutsi dominance, creating a major division in the church. The first Rwandan bishop, Monseignor Aloys Bigirumwami (born in 1904), was consecrated bishop of Nuyndo in 1959.

Many important religious leaders, as well as hundreds of priests, nuns, catechists, and lay leaders, died during the 1994 genocide. Among them was Father Chrysologue Mahame SJ, born in Kibeho, the first Rwandese Jesuit. Father Mahame studied theology at Eagenhoven in Belgium and was ordained in 1961. In 1992 he founded the human rights organization Association des Volontaires de la Paix (Association of Volunteers for Peace) and served as an intermediary between the government and the Rwanda Patriotic Front. He was 67 when he was killed at the Center Christus in Kigale, where he was religious superior. Father Patrick Gahizi SJ, ordained in 1984 and superior of the Jesuit students at the University of Butare, was imprisoned in 1990 after the war broke out. He was 48 when he was killed at the same retreat center.

MAJOR THEOLOGIANS AND AUTHORS During the colonial period Rwanda produced a number of Catholic theologians and intellectuals, both Tutsi and Hutu, who pushed for systematic reflection on the role of the indigenous clergy in Rwanda and the Catholic mission in Africa. By the 1930s Rwanda was seen as a Catholic kingdom where court historians and theologians had enormous influence.

Among these theologians, Père A. Pagès proposed in 1933 that the Tutsi had come from Christian stock living on the Ethiopian border. He advocated building a Christian kingdom based on Coptic Christianity. In 1939 Chanoine de Lacger wrote about the historical Tutsi feudal system, describing it as if it were part of an African Old Testament. The best-known Rwandan author was Abbé Alexis Kagame, a court historian who belonged to a family of *ubwiru* and had access to unique royal materials. In his writings from 1938 to 1966, Kagame gave cultural and historical justifications for church and state relations under Tutsi control.

Other writers, including Jan Vansina (published in 1962) and M. D'Hertefelt (published in 1971), have challenged the primacy of the court historians. As a result, all theologians, Tutsi and Hutu, had to choose between two Catholic models, one hierarchical and another egalitarian. As ethnic tensions increased, however, most Rwandan theologians operated through religious centers in Kinshasa, Zaire (formerly the Belgian Congo, now the Democratic Republic of the Congo), and were later absorbed into larger debates about African theology and enculturation.

HOUSES OF WORSHIP AND HOLY PLACES Churches tend to be large, accommodating two thousand people at a time. The dioceses of Kigale, Butare, Byumba, Cyangugu, Gikongoro, Kabgayi, Kibungo, Nyundo, and Ruhengeri have churches large enough to be considered cathedrals. Most churches in rural areas are built on hills apart from concentrations of houses or huts. In areas where people were killed during the 1994 genocide, churches still have human remains within them.

WHAT IS SACRED Rwandan Catholics see all human life as sacred, because every person has a soul created by God. In traditional Rwandan society this sacredness is expressed and lived through the family, where children are brought up to understand the ongoing process of life and death as creative and fertile. Because community life and good relations with others are also central to their concept of the sacred, Rwandans attend rites of passage related to the birth and death of kin, friends, and members of their social networks.

HOLIDAYS AND FESTIVALS Public holidays that reflect the Catholic liturgical year include Good Friday, Easter Sunday, the Ascension of the Virgin Mary (15 August), the Solemnity of All Saints (1 November), and Christmas Day. Christmas and Easter are the largest festivals. The Solemnity of All Saints, a popular holiday, is closely linked with the 2 November remembrance of dead relatives. Families visit the graves of their loved ones and take part in the parish Eucharist, which can be celebrated three times that day.

MODE OF DRESS Most Catholics in Rwanda have adopted European dress, reflecting the Belgian influence during the colonial period. The majority of the population relies on second-hand clothes of European origin. The clergy use clerical dress and altar boys wear the standard red or white tunics introduced during colonial times.

DIETARY PRACTICES Rwandan Catholics in good health abstain from meat on Fridays during Lent and on Good Friday.

RITUALS The Eucharist is celebrated in churches, many gathering thousands of people every Sunday. Prayer groups meet in huts or outside spaces to read the Bible. Most Rwandan Catholics pray daily with their families, at schools, and at community gatherings. People also gather to pray daily at the many graves marked by white crosses that appeared after the 1994 genocide.

RITES OF PASSAGE Rwandan Catholic and traditional values converge in the treatment of birth, marriage, fertility, and death. Infant baptism, the first rite of passage and the introduction into social life, is the norm in Catholic families. Adults are sometimes baptized as well. Marriage, which traditionally incorporates couples into new families and social roles, is not just a ceremony but a process. Marriage arrangements, visits, and the payment of the dowry sometimes take years, and the celebration of the sacrament in the church is the culmination of the process. Because procreation and fertility are central to African values, a marriage is only considered socially stable when the first child is born.

Funerals are large, well-attended events in Rwanda. Employers customarily give a leave of absence to office workers who must attend a funeral, and relatives of the deceased may travel long distances. Funerals are treated as a celebration of life, particularly if there are descendants to continue the family life experienced by the deceased.

MEMBERSHIP Baptized children usually belong to the same church as their parents throughout their lives. Because indigenous traditions were disturbed during the 1994 genocide, the number of Catholics has increased. The large number of single parents and orphans, also a result of the genocide, has translated into greater membership in the church and has led to attempts at reconciliation at the level of local parishes and communities. Most local congregations rely on economic support from abroad; financial contributions from members are very small.

SOCIAL JUSTICE Rwandan Catholics have traditionally accepted poverty as a fact of life. Colonial Catholic missionarie's belief in a divinely ordered society matched the traditional understanding that the king had access to all resources and lives. Riches were a gift from God to the righteous. Hutu members of the Catholic Church challenged this order at the time of independence. Catholic communities now accept some social obligations toward the poor, orphans, and others in need.

Since the 1994 genocide and within the new social order suggested by Kagame's administration, Rwandan Catholics have become a driving force in the search for social justice. Many take part in networks for justice and peace, including women's movements for peace and commissions to establish truth and reconciliation modeled on the South African experience after the end of apartheid.

SOCIAL ASPECTS The most important social moment for Rwandan Catholics, marriage is usually a commitment involving large extended families. Although individuals sometimes marry without the consent of extended family, in most cases two families enter into an obligation that includes payments in kind or in cattle for the transferal of a daughter to her husband's family. Within marriage the husband provides for the family, and the wife cares for the children, the household, and older family members. Women also have a social obligation to provide descendants for their Catholic families, which are aligned by ethnicity and clan membership. A woman who cannot bear children poses a strain on social relations that may lead to the dissolution of her marriage.

POLITICAL IMPACT The 2003 Rwandan constitution provides for a secular government and protects citizens from ethnic or religious discrimination. Rwandan political parties have never been constituted along religious lines, but because of the large Catholic majority, the voice and opinions of the bishops exercise some influence, particularly in the ongoing process of reconciliation. Their position was weakened, however, after accusations that some bishops aided perpetrators of the genocide.

CONTROVERSIAL ISSUES Ethnic divisions and tribalism are still endemic among religious practitioners in Rwanda. Though Catholicism might have acted as a unifying force in the country, not only did Catholics fail to prevent the 1994 genocide but some of them were even involved in planning, supporting, and enacting the killings.

Polygamy remains a challenge for the Catholic Church. Because fertility is a valued cultural norm, Rwandan Catholics follow the church's ban on condoms and other contraceptive devices, despite the massive spread of HIV and AIDS through heterosexual relations.

CULTURAL IMPACT Historically the Rwandan Catholic Church imported European art, including liturgical vestments, ritual objects, statues, and paintings. Since independence Rwandans have been part of the Christian enculturation movement supported by African bishops. Rwandan theologians have reflected more deeply on the relationship between faith and culture and have encouraged artists to depict gospel scenes and texts in an African fashion. Rwanda remains behind in such indigenous creations, however, owing to years of ethnic divisions that have kept Hutu and Tutsi artists and musicians from being effectively promoted and supported.

Other Religions

Indigenous religious practices—particularly Hutu and Twa, whose rituals centered on land and ethnicity—lost meaning during the 1994 genocide, when adherents were displaced from land and separated from community. Most foreign missionaries left the country, and ethnic reconciliation and nation building since the genocide have taken little account of religion; therefore, large numbers of Rwandans still believe in influencing the divine through rainmakers and healers without the means of having the rituals performed, and active membership in indigenous religions has decreased, especially among young people working in urban areas. In rural areas traditional beliefs and the cult of ancestral spirits are still integral to daily life, though practitioners often attend Christian churches.

Rwandan traditionalists historically believed in a high god, Imana, who communicated with the living through lesser gods, the ancestors, and the monarch. After the end of the Rwandan monarchy, which had enacted rituals on behalf of all Rwandans, local members of secret or religious societies continued performing rituals of symbolic communication with the supernatural world, particularly with the ancestral heroes, the Kubandwa. Two major religious societies are the Lyangombe in central and southern Rwanda and the Nyabingi in northern Rwanda.

Most Rwandan villages have a Kubandwa priest, a traditional healer who combines the skills of a medical doctor and a priest to cure sick people affected by spirits. Traditionalists believe that illness is caused by social rupture, either with the living or the dead. Neglect of the dead can expose the living to evil spirits that come out of burial grounds near the villages. Cures involve herbal medicines and rituals that connect the living with their dead ancestors.

The Anglican Church Missionary Society (CMS) arrived in northeastern Rwanda in 1930 and challenged the Hutu support for the White Fathers, capitalizing on the view of Catholicism as the religion of the powerful and their patrons. Their mission in Rwanda represented one of the most evangelical wings of the Anglican Church, and their preaching on conversion, the Holy Spirit, and the public confession of sins quickly attracted adherents of traditional religions, who found in Anglicanism confirmation of their belief in spirits and witchcraft. At the Rwanda-Uganda border, a region that had produced Nyabingi prophetesses, indigenous shamans called their people to the Sunday service of the CMS. In 1937, however, the Abaka (converts, or "those who shine with the power of the Holy Spirit") started criticizing the missionarie's lifestyle, saying they were spreading evil, and led witch hunts against them. In 1942 the Abaka movement was finally outlawed in most places because of its calls for violence. Much later CMS missionaries spread Anglicanism in Rwanda with greater success, and the Church of the Province of Rwanda, established in 1992, now has nine dioceses with their own bishops and priests. Other evangelical groups such as the Église de la Restauration (Church of the Restoration) and the Église Baptiste (Baptist Church) are still growing in northern Rwanda.

Muslims are present within the western Roman Catholic diocese of Cyangugu and the northern diocese of Nyundo. Islam has grown through immigration and the financial input of rich Arab countries, and the past few years have seen attempts to form an Islamic Party. Most Rwandan Muslims speak Swahili. The Baha'i faith has also secured a number of converts throughout Rwanda.

Mario I. Aguilar

See Also Vol. I: *African Traditional Religions, Islam, Protestantism*

Bibliography

Aguilar, Mario I. *The Rwanda Genocide and the Call To Deepen Christianity in Africa.* Eldoret: AMECEA Gaba Publications, 1998.

Chrétien, Jean-Pierre. *Rwanda: Les Médias du Génocide.* Paris: Karthala, 1995.

Gravel, Pierre. *Remera: A Community in Eastern Rwanda.* The Hague: Mouton, 1968.

Khan, Shaharyar M. *The Shallow Graves of Rwanda.* London: I.B. Tauris, 2000.

Lemarchand, René. *Rwanda and Burundi.* London: Pall Mall Press, 1970.

Linden, Ian with Jane Linden. *Church and Revolution in Rwanda.* Manchester and New York: Manchester University Press and Africana Publishing Company, 1977.

Louis, Roger. *Ruanda-Urundi 1884–1919.* Oxford: Clarendon Press, 1963.

Malkki, Liisa. *Purity and Exile: Violence, Memory and National Cosmology among Hutu Refugees in Tanzania.* Chicago: University of Chicago Press, 1995.

Maquet, Jacques. *The Premise of Inequality.* London: Oxford University Press for the International African Institute, 1961.

Newbury, Catherine M. *The Cohesion of Oppression: Clientship and Ethnicity in Rwanda 1860–1960.* New York: Columbia University Press, 1988.

Pottier, Johan. *Re-imagining Rwanda: Conflict, Survival and Disinformation in the Late Twentieth Century.* Cambridge and New York: Cambridge University Press, 2002.

Prunier, Gérard. *The Rwanda Crisis 1959–1994: History of a Genocide.* London: Hurst, 1997.

Reyntjens, Filip. *L'Afrique des Grands Lacs en Crise. Rwanda, Burundi 1988–1994.* Paris: Karthala, 1994.

Saint Kitts and Nevis

POPULATION 38,736

ANGLICAN 27.5 percent

METHODIST 25.3 percent

MORAVIAN 7.3 percent

ROMAN CATHOLIC 6.9 percent

PENTECOSTAL 5.5 percent

CHURCH OF GOD 4.3 percent

BAPTIST 3.9 percent

SEVENTH-DAY ADVENTIST 3.5 percent

WESLEYAN HOLINESS 2.7 percent

BRETHREN 1.8 percent

RASTAFARIAN 0.7 percent

HINDU 0.4 percent

SALVATION ARMY 0.1 percent

MUSLIM 0.1 percent

OTHER 4.1 percent

UNDESIGNATED 5.9 percent

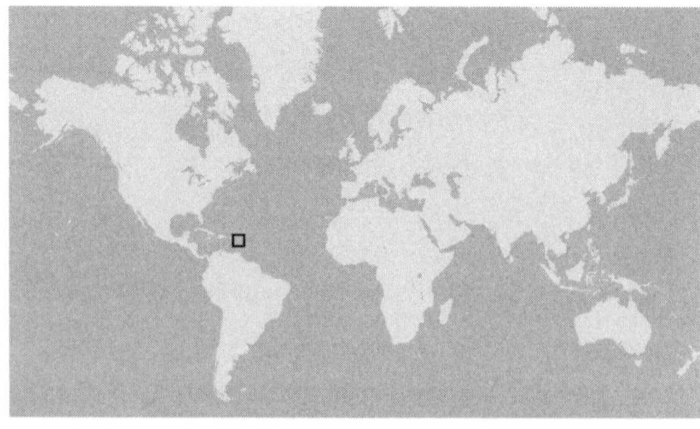

Country Overview

INTRODUCTION Saint Kitts and Nevis are two islands of the Lesser Antilles in the eastern Caribbean Sea. Separated by a narrow channel, they occupy 104 square miles. Previously British colonies (1871–1956), the two islands, together with neighboring Anguilla, were part of the West Indies Federation from 1958 to 1962. The Federation of Saint Kitts and Nevis became an independent nation on 19 September 1983. Since independence considerable political tension has existed between the two islands, with Nevis continuously asserting its constitutional right to secede from the federation. The 1998 plebiscite on secession was narrowly unsuccessful.

Christopher Columbus landed on Saint Kitts in 1493, accompanied by a number of Roman Catholic clergymen who were intended to serve as missionaries. During bloody wars in the seventeenth century, Saint Kitts shifted from Spanish to French to English domination. In the end Catholicism was effectively wiped out on the island, and it was not until the nineteenth century that the denomination was "revived from its ashes." By 1791 England had taken full control of the island with the help of Anglican clergy. The Roman Catholic and Anglican religions erased all vestiges of indigenous faiths on the islands.

Initially practiced by English settlers and indentured white servants, Anglicanism changed in its nature and practice by the middle of the seventeenth century, when sugar plantations began to flourish and West African slave labor was introduced. Before the end of the century, there was a shift in attitudes toward the saving of souls, culminating in the founding of the Society for the Propagation of the Gospel in Foreign Parts, whose purpose was to Christianize slaves and indigenous peoples in the colonies.

By the mid-1700s there were 10 times as many blacks as whites in Saint Kitts. As word of the atrocities of slavery spread throughout Europe, missionaries from other Protestant denominations traveled to the Caribbean. In 1777 two missionaries from the Moravian Church arrived in Saint Kitts to start a mission that still survives. In 1787 the Methodists began their missionary work in Saint Kitts. In strong contrast to the Anglicans, who remained dominant in the islands, Methodists, Moravians, and, before the end of the century, Baptists reached out explicitly to slaves and free blacks.

At least 20 denominations are active in contemporary Saint Kitts and Nevis.

RELIGIOUS TOLERANCE Freedom of religion is a constitutional provision, and the government of Saint Kitts and Nevis generally respects this right in practice. Historically the federation's citizens have been tolerant of all faiths.

Major Religions

ANGLICANISM

METHODISM

ANGLICANISM

DATE OF ORIGIN 1623 C.E.

NUMBER OF FOLLOWERS 10,650

HISTORY Anglicanism came to Saint Kitts on 28 January 1623, when Sir Thomas Warner arrived from England. With Warner was the English clergyman John Featley, who set up what was perhaps the first Anglican parish in the British West Indies in Old Road, the first town built on Saint Kitts.

The Society for the Propagation of the Gospel in Foreign Parts was responsible for supplying clergy to the islands. Even so, ecclesiastical appointments were handled by the colonial governor and were linked with appointments to civil service posts. Thus, the clergy served as state chaplains to English officials and planters. Anglican outreach to the majority slave population did not begin until 1796, when the first Anglican catechist and teachers arrived in Saint Kitts. They built schools and published religious literature, Bibles, and prayer books. With the abolition of slavery in 1834, the church played a significant role in reconstruction, increasing its efforts to spread the gospel and educate former slaves. Through education grants provided by the British government, 30,000 pounds annually went toward missionary work among freed slaves. Today the church is fully integrated and under the leadership of an indigenous, predominantly black clergy.

Grave markers line the foreground of St. Thomas's Anglican Church, located in Saint Kitts and Nevis. AP/WIDE WORLD PHOTOS.

In 1870 the British parliament began its campaign to disestablish the Anglican Church. Left to organize themselves and find their own financing, the churches sought to form an alliance of dioceses. Thus, an ecclesiastical council, the Provincial Synod, was founded in the West Indies in 1873. At that time, few dioceses had been established in the region, but by 1959 the synod had become fully representative, with members from the dioceses of Jamaica, Barbados, Antigua and Guyana, Nassau and the Bahamas, Trinidad and Tobago, Honduras (now Belize), and the Windward Islands. The synod consists of the House of Bishops, the House of Clergy, and the House of Laity. Two representatives from each diocese attend each of the latter two houses. As part of the diocese of Barbados, Saint Kitts and Nevis has been represented in the synod since it was founded in 1873.

EARLY AND MODERN LEADERS John Featley is considered the father of Anglicanism in Saint Kitts and

Nevis. Daniel Gatewood Davis became the first creole to be ordained as a priest on Saint Kitts. Thomas Cottle, a president of Nevis, built Saint Mark's Chapel of Ease on his estate in 1824 so that his family and slaves could worship together there. Rector James Ramsey championed the abolition of slavery in the islands. Rudolph Smithen was the first native Nevisian to be appointed rector in the parish of Saint George in Basseterre, the capital. He was also the first native to become an archdeacon and has been assigned to the diocese of Antigua since 2003.

The Reverend Verna Morgan was the first Nevisian woman to be ordained as a deacon. The Reverend Yvette Bagnall, the first Kittitian woman to be ordained as a deacon (2004), has been assigned to Saint George's parish in Basseterre. Canon Alston Percival, a native of Saint Kitts, is the superintendent of Anglican clergy in Nevis and also chairs the Christian Council on that island.

MAJOR THEOLOGIANS AND AUTHORS Saint Kitts and Nevis has produced no major Anglican theologians or authors.

HOUSES OF WORSHIP AND HOLY PLACES There are 11 Anglican churches on Saint Kitts and 5 on Nevis. The seventeenth-century structures that remain are of particular interest. One of these, Saint James Windward Church in Nevis is known for the black Madonna in its sanctuary. The church is also one of three Anglican churches in the Caribbean to display a black crucifix. Built in 1643, Saint Thomas's Lowland Church is the oldest church on Nevis and the first Anglican church built in the Caribbean.

The history of the British and French struggles in the country is reflected in Saint George's Church in Basseterre. The French built this church, originally known as Notre Dame, in 1670. In 1706 the British burned it to the ground, only to rebuild it four years later. The church was rebuilt three more times; the present structure is the result of the 1869 restoration.

WHAT IS SACRED The Holy Eucharist is the most sacred of all things in the Anglican Church. Also deemed sacred are vessels for the Eucharist, as well as the ormbry (ambry), the cabinet that houses the vessels. The altar is considered holy, as is the Blessed Mother. Ultimately, all church buildings are held sacred.

HOLIDAYS/FESTIVALS Anglican holy days in Saint Kitts and Nevis include Christmas, Good Friday, Easter, Pentecost, Ash Wednesday, All Saint's Day, and All Soul's Day. The festivals of patron saints are observed in the parishes. Special observances during Lent include midweek services and retreats. Thanksgiving festivals associated with the harvest are celebrated annually.

MODE OF DRESS Traditionally, Anglican clergy wore cassocks in public. Vestments included a surplice and, depending on the rank of the individual, a mortarboard. This attire is now reserved for High Mass and other formal occasions. The choir, acolytes, and sexton still don traditional robes. Worshipers tend to reserve their finery for Sunday services. Modern dress is acceptable, and casual wear is worn for weekday services and meetings.

DIETARY PRACTICES In general, Anglicans in Saint Kitts and Nevis observe no special dietary restrictions. Many Anglicans fast and abstain from meat and alcohol during Lent.

RITUALS Anglicanism in Saint Kitts and Nevis has remained highly structured and liturgical, observing all the strict traditions of the Church of England. The form of worship is more interactive than is typical, however, and may include such Caribbean embellishments as the singing of evangelical-style choruses before or during the liturgical Mass or a sermon with a call-and-response format. Feast days are appropriately observed, as are all other sacraments and celebrations.

RITES OF PASSAGE In addition to the major rites of passage (infant baptism, first Communion, and confirmation), marriage and the burial of the dead may be considered rites of passage in Anglican churches in the federation.

MEMBERSHIP Membership is gained through baptism and confirmation. Each church welcomes any person professing Christianity and expressing a desire for fellowship with that particular congregation. Traditional missionary work is on the decline, but evangelization is by no means dormant. Churches often broadcast their Sunday services. The spirit of ecumenism is strongly encouraged.

SOCIAL JUSTICE Social justice has become an integral part of the operation of the Anglican Church in Saint

Kitts and Nevis. The Mother's Union is charged with the development of the whole family. The Anglican Young People's Association (AYPA) has also been active as an agent of social justice for youth of both sexes. The Brethren of Saint Andrew, a men's organization, engages in philanthropic work in the parishes. Canon Alston Percival, rector of the parishes of Saint George and Saint John in Nevis, established a home for senior citizens in Gingerland. In addition, he has been an active advocate for the young and disenfranchised of the island.

SOCIAL ASPECTS While there are no longer any Anglican schools in the islands, the churches have remained active in the religious education of youth in Sunday schools. Members of church organizations regularly visit the sick and disabled, both at home and in hospitals; they reach out to the needy in society; and they fight for good morals among all citizens.

POLITICAL IMPACT During much of the colonial period church and state were inextricable, with the Anglican leadership playing a leading role in the administration of the islands. With disestablishment, the tie between church and state was officially broken, though in practice it remained firm for a considerable period. Although still regarded as the "state church" by some, the Anglican Church no longer holds any special political authority.

CONTROVERSIAL ISSUES The Anglican Church in Saint Kitts and Nevis has accepted the ordination of women to the priesthood. The ordination of nonabstaining homosexuals has caused a great deal of debate within the church. Archbishop Drexel Gomez of the Province of the West Indies has maintained that such ordinations are a clear departure from the Anglican consensus as expressed at the 1998 Lambeth Bishop's Conference. The church has firmly opposed same-sex marriage.

CULTURAL IMPACT All aspects of life in the islands were affected by the segregationist prescriptions of the white English elites (including Anglican leaders) who controlled the islands during the greater part of their history. These traditions have completely eroded, however, and since the middle of the twentieth century, the African elements of the culture, which were previously strictly suppressed, have risen in importance and respectability.

METHODISM

DATE OF ORIGIN 1787 C.E.

NUMBER OF FOLLOWERS 9,800

HISTORY Methodism was introduced in Saint Kitts in 1787 by the Reverend Thomas Coke, the first Methodist bishop and a friend of John Wesley, Methodism's founder. Introduced in Nevis in 1789, Methodism attracted large followings on both islands because of the wide appeal of its message to the disadvantaged, mostly black populations. Through the centuries, Methodists maintained their commitment to proselytization; in addition, they provided education for members and children in both day and Sunday schools. Although the Methodist Church has remained prominent, it experienced its peak between the second half of the nineteenth century and the first half of the twentieth. Since then there has been a marked decline in membership on both islands, due in no small part to the influx of newer denominations from North America.

EARLY AND MODERN LEADERS Until the mid-twentieth century Methodist ministers in Saint Kitts and Nevis traditionally came from England or the larger Caribbean islands. Among contemporary leaders is the Reverend Franklin Manners, a native Nevisian and the superintendent minister in Basseterre, who in 2003 completed a double term as president of the Methodist Conference in the Caribbean and the Americas. The head of the church in Nevis is the Reverend Moreland Williams. Methodism's strong lay leaders have included Sir Probyn Inniss, the first governor-general of the federation.

MAJOR THEOLOGIANS AND AUTHORS No major Methodist theologians have originated in Saint Kitts and Nevis.

HOUSES OF WORSHIP AND HOLY PLACES There are 10 Methodist congregations in Saint Kitts and 7 in Nevis. The church buildings themselves are regarded as holy places, and the cemeteries attached to them are treated with reverence.

WHAT IS SACRED Methodists regard Holy Communion as sacred. The altar, at which Communion is served, is also deemed sacred, as is the pulpit. Methodists, like all Christians, venerate the cross, though not with the same degree of fervor as in some denominations.

HOLIDAYS/FESTIVALS Methodists in Saint Kitts and Nevis celebrate Christmas, Good Friday, Easter, and Pentecost. Other major annual festivals include a harvest thanksgiving service and a week of so-called missionary meetings, which consists of fund-raising activities rather than missionary work. The church also recognizes such celebrations as Mother's Day and Father's Day.

MODE OF DRESS Methodist clergy usually don the traditional cassock and surplice for Sunday worship as well as for weddings, funerals, and baptisms. In modern times, however, it has not been unusual for them to wear business attire, even during Sunday services. Church choirs usually wear robes on all formal occasions. Worshipers wear relatively elaborate, if conservative, attire for Sunday services; however, for other events everyday attire is acceptable.

DIETARY PRACTICES Methodists in Saint Kitts and Nevis observe no particular dietary restrictions. Abstinence from alcohol is preached though not necessarily practiced.

RITUALS The practice of Methodism has traditionally been simple though highly liturgical and structured. Modern-day worshipers have sometimes attempted to emulate more charismatic denominations, but, in general, services are orderly and relatively conservative. Weddings and funerals are equally liturgical and ritualistic but vary in the degree of embellishment.

After Sunday worship, class meetings, which are at the very core of Methodist practice, provide the opportunity for spiritual fellowship. Prayer fellowship is also an integral aspect of Methodism in Saint Kitts and Nevis.

RITES OF PASSAGE Methodist rites of passage include baptism and confirmation. Candidates for confirmation must first undergo a prescribed period of study and indoctrination.

MEMBERSHIP Efforts to expand the Methodist membership are ongoing. The old-fashioned open-air meetings still take place, though usually in rural rather than urban settings. Churches on both islands broadcast their Sunday services via radio and television.

SOCIAL JUSTICE Education for all has been a major plank of Methodism in Saint Kitts and Nevis. Methodists have also conducted special services for the poor, a vibrant prison ministry, advocacy for indigents, and regular visits to the sick at home and in hospitals. They operate a private elementary school in Saint Kitts, where enrollment is open to children of any denomination.

SOCIAL ASPECTS The church heavily influences the behavior of the inhabitants of the islands. In both form and style, the religion is highly conservative, and temperance is its hallmark.

POLITICAL IMPACT The political impact of the Methodist Church in the islands has been minimal. In the debate over the secession of Nevis from the federation, the church has advocated less drastic methods of settling the differences between the two islands.

CONTROVERSIAL ISSUES Methodism in Saint Kitts and Nevis has tended toward a more conservative approach to such controversial issues as abortion and birth control. At the same time, the church advocates the judicious use of birth control, especially since some contraceptive devices aid in the containment of sexually transmitted diseases. Divorce is tolerated as a last resort in resolving marital problems, and the church will marry divorced persons. From its earliest beginnings, and certainly during the last 50 years, women have played an active part in the church. The ordination of women to full ministry has been widely endorsed by both clergy and laity.

CULTURAL IMPACT Methodism has had a profound impact on the culture of the two islands—regrettably, one that has been more negative than positive. Having derived from what was essentially a slave society and having its own conservative bent, it gave rise to a cultural malaise that persisted well into the modern era. In the case of the Methodists, striving for rewards in heaven did not lead to the deep exploration of creativity, pleasure, and enjoyment of the here and now.

Other Religions

The Moravian Church came to Saint Kitts in the late eighteenth century from Germany, where its adherents practiced a strict, fundamentalist Protestant faith. In Saint Kitts the Moravians set to work to convert the slaves, openly embracing them and building churches, establishing schools, and looking after their health needs. Modern economic constraints forced the church to turn over its schools to the government, but it has remained active in the development of the youth of the island. There are four Moravian churches in contemporary Saint Kitts but none in Nevis.

The Roman Catholic Church was the first European church introduced in Saint Kitts and Nevis. There are, however, no accounts of this church ever having taken root until Capuchin friars arrived from France in 1623. Destroyed during the political turbulence of the mid-seventeenth century, Roman Catholicism did not revive in Saint Kitts until the arrival of Portuguese immigrants in 1846. It has since flourished in Saint Kitts, though it did not reach Nevis until 1947. The church offers a wide variety of social services. For more than 100 years it has operated a convent school on Saint Kitts offering primary and secondary education. Roman Catholic churches on both islands conduct the Mass in Spanish for growing populations of Spanish-speaking immigrants from the Dominican Republic.

The Wesleyan Holiness Church, a denomination that broke away from Methodism, is the oldest fundamentalist denomination on the islands. The Brethren, a group that apparently evolved from the United Brethren (as the Moravian Church was also known), have been on the islands for about 60 years. Pentecostals, Baptist splinter groups, and the Church of God came to the islands in the mid-twentieth century from North America. These groups have all made major inroads in the memberships of the established churches in the islands.

The Seventh-day Adventists are one of the fastest-growing religious groups in the islands. Aggressive proselytization has attracted large numbers to their folds.

As 95 percent of the population of the islands is of African origin, it is not surprising to see the influence of African-derived religions there. The best-known and most influential of these is obeah, a West Indian form of black magic. Other African-derived religious influences can be found in such cultural activities as the Christmas Masquerades, which feature musicians and dancers in elaborate costumes. The Masquerades, which include elements of both African and European (especially French) dance, can be traced back to the time of slavery, when slaves were permitted to celebrate the sugarcane harvest.

Other religious groups on the islands include Rastafarians, Hindus, Muslims, and Bahá'ís. Most are immigrants, or the descendants of immigrants, from other Caribbean islands.

Rhonda Johnson and Olivia Edgecomb-Howell

See Also Vol. I: *Anglicanism, Christianity, Methodism*

Bibliography

The Anglican Communion Official Website: http://www.anglicancommunion.org

The Church in the Province of the West Indies: http://www.thebahamas.net/cpwi/

Cross, F.L., ed. *The Oxford Dictionary of the Christian Church.* 3rd ed. Oxford; New York: Oxford University Press, 1997.

Kremser, Manfred. "African-Derived Religions in St. Kitts and Nevis." In *Encyclopedia of African and African-American Religions,* edited by Stephen D. Glazier, pp. 321–23. New York: Routledge, 2001.

Official Site of the Nevis Tourism Authority: http://www.nevisisland.com/Index.htm

Peters, Melvin K.H. "Caribbean." In *The Encyclopedia of Protestantism,* edited by Hans Hillerbrand. 4 vols. New York: Routledge, 2004.

Robinson, Lisa Clayton. "St. Kitts and Nevis." In *Africana: The Encyclopedia of the African and African American Experience,* edited by Kwame Anthony Appiah and Henry Louis Gates, Jr., pp. 1781–84. New York: Basic Civitas Books, 1999.

St. Kitts and Nevis Demography Digest 2002: http://www.caricomstats.org/Files/Publications/kitspub/demodigest/Introduction.htm

St. Kitts and Nevis Statistical Review 2002: http://www.caricomstats.org/Files/Publications/kitspub/statsreview/Intro.htm

U.S. Department of State: International Religious Freedom Report 2002: St. Kitts and Nevis: http://www.state.gov/g/drl/rls/irf/2002/14056.htm

Saint Lucia

POPULATION 160,145

ROMAN CATHOLIC 79 percent

SEVENTH-DAY ADVENTIST 7 percent

PENTECOSTALIST 3 percent

ANGLICAN 2 percent

OTHER 9 percent

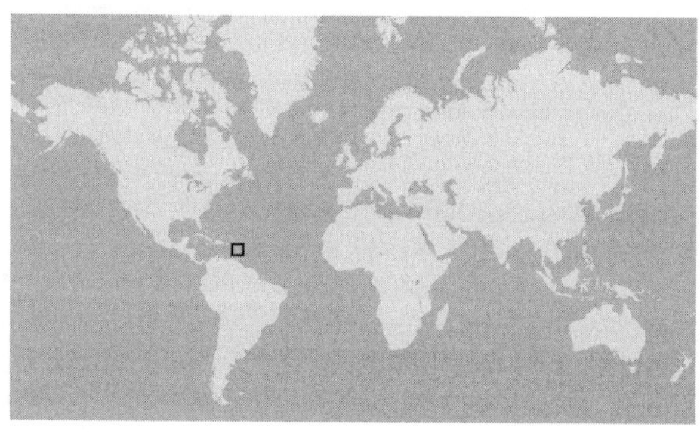

Country Overview

INTRODUCTION Saint Lucia is a small, mountainous island of volcanic origin situated between the islands of Martinique and Saint Vincent. The majority of its citizens are black; there are small minority populations of whites and East Indians. Saint Lucia's economy is primarily based on bananas grown for export to Europe. Additional economic activities include cash crop production of coconuts, tourism, subsistence farming, and fishing.

When Europeans first arrived in the region, Saint Lucia was inhabited by Caribs, indigenous migrants from South America who colonized much of the Lesser Antilles. Fifteenth- and sixteenth-century Spanish colonists deliberately overlooked Saint Lucia because of its small size and rugged terrain. The British twice attempted to settle on the island in the early seventeenth century but were thwarted by illness and hostility from the resident Caribs. The French established the first successful European settlement in 1650. The island alternated between French and British control fourteen times before finally becoming British in 1814. In 1979 Saint Lucia became independent and is a parliamentary democracy within the British Commonwealth. Because of slavery, disease introduced by foreigners, and violent encounters with Europeans, only small populations of Caribs survive today on Dominica and Saint Vincent. None remain on Saint Lucia.

Catholicism, introduced by French settlers, is the religion of the majority of Saint Lucians. Though Saint Lucia was last controlled by the British, Anglicans have always constituted a minority population. The introduction of various Protestant sects beginning in the late nineteenth century has led to declining membership in both the Catholic and Anglican Churches. Traditional African beliefs systems were introduced by slaves brought to the island beginning in the seventeenth century and by African immigrants who arrived after emancipation in 1834. Some of these beliefs, possibly combined with those of the original indigenous population, persist today in a fragmented fashion alongside mainstream religions and are often practiced by individuals who categorize themselves as Catholic or Protestant.

RELIGIOUS TOLERANCE Saint Lucia has no official state religion, and the government supports religious freedom. The Saint Lucia Christian Council is part of an ecumenical movement that has periodically worked to foster a spirit of tolerance and cooperation between various churches. Occasional tension arises among members of various religious groups. In 2000 two Rastafarian men attacked Catholic worshipers in the Castries cathedral, setting several on fire (two later died) as well as desecrating the altar. The attackers were sentenced to death by hanging.

Saint Lucian girls celebrate their first Communion. Groups of children who train for their first Communion together often remain lifelong friends. © BOB KRIST/CORBIS.

Major Religion

ROMAN CATHOLICISM

DATE OF ORIGIN 1650 C.E.
NUMBER OF FOLLOWERS 126,500

HISTORY Seventeenth-century French settlers brought Catholicism to Saint Lucia. Irish and possibly Scottish Catholics fleeing religious persecution in Britain and emigrating from other Caribbean colonies bolstered their numbers. Saint Lucia's first documented Catholic mass was conducted in 1719 by Father Suffret de Villeneuve. Traveling French priests, who ministered to the spiritual needs of Catholic colonists, met with limited success in their attempts to convert Caribs. By the eighteenth century Saint Lucia acquired resident parish priests. The island's Catholicism was never significantly challenged by any Protestant denomination, partly because the French controlled Saint Lucia for the longest uninterrupted period and partly because the French arrived in larger numbers than the British, who wanted the island more for strategic purposes than for settlement.

The Archdiocese of Castries was established on Saint Lucia in 1974. It has associated dioceses on Dominica, Grenada, Carriacou, Petit Martinique, Antigua, Barbuda, Saint Kitts-Nevis, Montserrat, Anguilla, the British Virgin Islands, and Saint Vincent and the Grenadines.

Since the 1960s the Roman Catholic Church has experienced a steady decline in membership, from approximately 92 percent of the total population in 1960 to 79 percent at the 2001 census. The influx of various evangelical Protestant sects beginning in the 1960s has contributed to the decline.

EARLY AND MODERN LEADERS In the seventeenth century religious missionaries and priests traveling with French military units served Saint Lucian Catholics. Some of the better-known Catholic missionaries were Père Jean Baptiste Labat (1663–1738), Père Jean Baptiste du Tertre (1610–87), and Father Breton (1609–79). The priests sought to minister to the spiritual needs of the surviving indigenous people as well as Catholic colonists. Du Tertre, who arrived on Saint Lucia in 1666, learned the Carib language in order to preach to the indigenous population more effectively. Archbishops for the Archdiocese of Castries have included Charles Gachet (1911–84), Patrick Webster (1924–89), and Kelvin Edward Felix (born in 1933).

MAJOR THEOLOGIANS AND AUTHORS Although the missionary efforts of seventeenth- and eighteenth-century priests were largely unsuccessful, some of them did produce valuable descriptions of Carib society, including language dictionaries. Father Breton wrote the *Dictionnaire caraibe-franÿois* (*Carib-French Dictionary*). In 1956 the Reverend C. Jesse wrote *Outlines of Saint Lucia's History*; updated editions are published regularly.

HOUSES OF WORSHIP AND HOLY PLACES The Cathedral of the Immaculate Conception in Castries, built in 1897, has a striking interior, with murals covering the wooden walls. More than twenty parishes have their own Catholic churches.

WHAT IS SACRED? Like Catholics worldwide, Saint Lucian Catholics consider crosses, altars, churches, and saints sacred.

HOLIDAYS AND FESTIVALS Easter is the primary holiday for Saint Lucian Catholics. In observation of Lent they limit festive occasions, abstain from particular foods, and attend services more frequently. Holy Week precedes Easter Sunday. On Good Friday Saint Lucian Catholics eat special foods, such as *akwa,* a fish entrée, and *pain d'espices,* a small oval cookie made with ginger.

During Corpus Christi in May or June, church members carry platforms holding statues of the Virgin Mary through the streets of towns. In November there are two Catholic holidays of particular importance to St. Lucians: All Souls Day, or Fet Le Mo (Celebrate the Dead), marked by visiting the graves of ancestors, cleaning cemeteries, and burning candles at home; and Saint Cecilia's Day, celebrated with a music festival. On 13 December Catholics honor Saint Lucia (or Saint Lucy), the patron saint of the island, with a procession of lights, traditional music and other cultural activities, and a feast. The midnight mass on Christmas draws the largest attendance of the year. Catholics also observe Whitsuntide (Pentecost) in May or June, as well as the feasts of Saint Rose de Lima (August) and Saint Margaret Alacoque (October), flower festivals that last for several days with masses, street parades, and parties with lavish banquets.

MODE OF DRESS Saint Lucian Catholics, like non-Catholics in the country, dress in Western-style clothing.

DIETARY PRACTICES During Lent many Saint Lucian Catholics limit or eliminate consumption of alcohol and meat.

RITUALS Every June in Saint Lucia Catholics bless their fishing boats, which they festively decorate. Also called Fèt Péchè (Fisherman's Feast), the ritual includes a special mass for the fishermen; thanksgivings to the fishermen's patron saints, Peter and Paul; and lavish feasting.

RITES OF PASSAGE At Saint Lucian christenings an infant is introduced to the church community, blessed by a priest, and given godparents charged with helping to raise him. Groups of children who train for first Communion together often remain lifetime friends. Weddings are celebrated with a church service and Communion. Funerals are community events with a special religious service held in the name of the deceased. Friends often provide gifts of food, candles, and liquor for the reception.

MEMBERSHIP Because of steadily declining membership, Saint Lucia's Catholic Church has attempted to increase community interest. Since the Vatican II reforms in 1965, it has conducted Mass in English, recruited clergy from the local population, and expanded the responsibilities of laypeople.

SOCIAL JUSTICE The Catholic Church on Saint Lucia promotes the well-being of the community at large through the construction and staffing of schools, hospitals, nursing homes, and orphanages. Until the 1960s the church provided most of the primary and the only secondary education on the island, the latter in Castries at Saint Mary's College (for boys, established by Father Louis Tapon in 1890) and Saint Joseph's Convent School (for girls). Saint Jude's Hospital in Vieux Fort, managed by a convent until 2003, is considered one of the best in the country. The Catholic Church oversees the Ozanam shelter for homeless men, a youth group that promotes healthy outdoor activities, the Centre for Adolescent Rehabilitation and Education for disadvantaged youth in Castries, and the Marian Home for the Aged, among other organizations.

In 2003 the Archdiocese of Castries sponsored a conference on strategies to fight the spread of AIDS in the country and region. The conference endorsed a plan used in Uganda that emphasized sexual abstinence and fidelity in marriage.

SOCIAL ASPECTS On Saint Lucia, as elsewhere in the Caribbean, Catholic couples often marry after several years of cohabitation, sometimes after having had several children, because of the expense of a wedding. Unions formalized by a religious marriage ceremony are accorded higher prestige in the church community.

POLITICAL IMPACT Saint Lucian Catholics have periodically tried to influence government decisions on such issues as education, family planning, and abortion. When the government legalized abortion in 2003, Catholics staged pro-life (antiabortion) rallies and gathered more than 9,000 signatures on a petition criticizing the decision as immoral. The Catholic Church's media outlets on the island, the *Catholic Chronicle* and the Catholic Television Broadcasting Service, allow the church to publicize its point of view on various topics.

CONTROVERSIAL ISSUES Saint Lucian Catholics see premarital sex, modern methods of birth control, and abortion as immoral. Despite the church's stance, unmarried Catholic couples live and raise families together out of practical necessity, and the island's Planned Parenthood association has disseminated information about family planning since the 1960s.

CULTURAL IMPACT The Saint Lucian Catholic Church contributes to the arts largely through the influence of its private primary and secondary schools on the island. Two alumni of Saint Mary's College in Castries went on to become Nobel laureates: Sir Arthur Lewis for economics in 1979 and the Honorable Derek Walcott for literature in 1992.

Other Religions

Seventh-day Adventists came to the Caribbean in the late nineteenth century. Their membership on Saint Lucia increased substantially in the 1960s and 1970s, when a number of other North American evangelical Protestant groups, including the Pentecostals, arrived in the region. Both groups have steadily gained in popularity, partly because of their vision of a more egalitarian society and a growing disillusionment with the perceived status quo of the Catholic Church.

The British brought Anglicanism to Saint Lucia during the colonial period. The Holy Trinity Church in Castries and Christchurch in Soufrière serve Anglicans, whose historically small numbers are in decline. The Anglican Church runs an infant school and a few primary schools. Other Protestant groups that operate in Saint Lucia include Methodists, Presbyterians, Baptists, Church of God, and Jehovah's Witnesses. The first Methodist and Presbyterian ministers arrived on Saint Lucia in the 1880s. The Methodists, who are active but have never attained significant membership, also established a few private primary schools.

Rastafarianism, which came from Jamaica to Saint Lucia in the early 1970s, has grown quickly in urban areas, primarily among young black males who view it as a vehicle for protest against the traditional power structure. Rastafarians seek to promote public awareness of and pride in the African heritage of the majority of citizens on Saint Lucia, regardless of religious denomination.

Saint Lucia has a small population of East Indians. Mostly Hindu, they have abandoned many of their traditional cultural practices, including religion.

Informal beliefs in the spirit world, many if not all African-based, coexist with public religious beliefs. People in the northern part of the island perform a ceremony, called the Kélé, to honor and express gratitude to particular deities (Shango, for example). The ritual was apparently brought to Saint Lucia by migrant African laborers in the mid- to late nineteenth century.

Kathryn A. Hudepohl

See Also Vol. I: *Roman Catholicism*

Bibliography

Bisnauth, Dale. *History of Religions in the Caribbean.* Trenton, N.J.: Africa World Press, 1996.

Brathwaite, Joan, ed. *Handbook of Churches in the Caribbean.* Barbados: Christian Action for Development in the Caribbean, 1973.

Folk Research Centre (FRC). *A Cultural Calendar of Saint Lucia.* Saint Lucia: FRC, 1992.

———. *Cultural Education Resource Kit: Religion and Spirit Power in Saint Lucia.* Saint Lucia: FRC, 1992.

Greenleaf, Floyd. *The Seventh-day Adventist Church in Latin America and the Caribbean.* 2 vols. Berrien Springs, Mich.: Andrews University Press, 1992.

Harmsen, Jolien. *Sugar, Slavery and Settlement: A Social History of Vieux Fort Saint Lucia from the Amerindians to the Present.* Saint Lucia: Saint Lucia National Trust, 1999.

Jesse, Reverend C. *Outlines of Saint Lucia's History.* Saint Lucia: The Saint Lucia Archaeological and Historical Society, 1994.

Kremser, Manfred, and Karl R. Wernhart, eds. *Research in Ethnography and Ethnohistory of Saint Lucia.* Horn-Wien, Austria: Verlag Ferdinand Berger and Sšhne, 1986.

Saint Vincent and the Grenadines

POPULATION 116,394

ANGLICAN 17.75 percent

PENTECOSTAL 17.6 percent

METHODIST 10.9 percent

SEVENTH-DAY ADVENTIST 10.2 percent

SPIRITUAL BAPTIST 9.95 percent

ROMAN CATHOLIC 7.45 percent

OTHER (CHURCH OF JESUS CHRIST OF LATTER-DAY SAINTS, HINDU, JEHOVAH'S WITNESS, BAHAI, AND THOSE WITH NO RELIGIOUS AFFILIATION) 26.15 percent

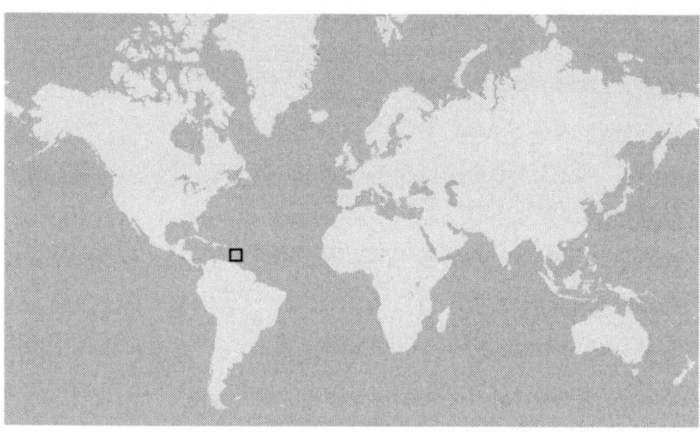

Country Overview

INTRODUCTION Saint Vincent and the Grenadines, an island group in the eastern Caribbean, lies between Saint Lucia to the north and Grenada to the south. The total land area is just 150 square miles (388 square kilometers), 90 percent of which is on the island of Saint Vincent. The other islands, known as the Grenadines, include Mustique, Baliceaux, Canouan, Petit Mustique, Bequia, Union Island, and Mayreau. The islands are mountainous, rising in Saint Vincent to over 4,000 feet. Approximately 66 percent of Vincentians are blacks, 19 percent are of mixed race, 6 percent are East Indian, 2 percent are Amerindian Caribs, and 7 percent are of other ethnicities.

The original inhabitants of Saint Vincent were Caribs, Amerindians who migrated northward from South America looking for new land and in pursuit of their weaker rivals, the Arawaks. French settlers arrived about 1650, probably from Martinique, bringing Catholicism to the island. Because it produced large quantities of sugar, the Caribbean region was of great importance to European powers and was featured in many of their conflicts for dominance, including various wars between France and Britain. Saint Vincent passed into British hands at the 1763 Peace of Paris. With the British came Anglicanism, Methodism, and other Protestant groups, and Roman Catholic growth was somewhat arrested. The indigenous people survived for some time but were not integrated into the society. By the time of British occupation, slaves from Africa had begun to constitute a substantial portion of the population. Saint Vincent and the Grenadines remained a British colony until they negotiated their independence from Britain in 1979.

Except for some seven thousand people who have no religious affiliation, the population claims to be Christian. The preliminary census data for 2001 lists 12 Christian denominations on Saint Vincent and the

Grenadines. Some newer denominations (the Church of God, evangelicals, Pentecostals, and Seventh-day Adventists), more aggressive in their approach to evangelization than the older denominations, have made substantial inroads and claim more than ten thousand adherents. Between 1980 and 2000 Anglicans, Roman Catholics, and Methodists declined by 20 to 40 percent.

RELIGIOUS TOLERANCE Freedom of religious expression is guaranteed under the constitution of 1979. The variety of religious groups is reflected in the country's ecumenical Council of Churches, which includes Anglicans, Roman Catholics, Methodists, and others. For the most part Christian and non-Christian groups, as well as groups that may be called only marginally religious, such as the Rastafarians, coexist peacefully.

Some churches require members to separate themselves from other Christian bodies. For example, one report, issued by Baptists, lamented the strong inroads ecumenism was making into Saint Vincent's religious life and asserted that more Baptist churches, especially in the interior and on the Grenadine islands, might remedy the situation.

Anglicans worship at a church service in Saint Vincent. Like Anglicans elsewhere, Vincentian Anglicans hold as sacred their place of worship and the sacraments of the church. © TIM THOMPSON/CORBIS.

Major Religion

ANGLICANISM

DATE OF ORIGIN Late 1770s C.E.
NUMBER OF FOLLOWERS 20,700

HISTORY Anglican work began on Saint Vincent in the late eighteenth century, when British occupiers arrived after the Peace of Paris. The church originally formed part of the diocese of Barbados and the Leeward Islands, established in 1824. In 1878 the Vincentian Anglicans became part of the newly established diocese of the Windward Islands, administered originally by the Bishop of Barbados. The island's first full-time Anglican bishop was appointed in 1927. Since the 1960s Anglicans have moved purposefully toward a local ministry, and church leadership has included a number of people born in the region. The church has also made efforts to respond to the challenges of the region and the era.

EARLY AND MODERN LEADERS The Most Reverend Cuthbert Woodroffe (born in 1918), former bishop of the Windward Islands and archbishop of the West Indies, was the first native of the Windward Islands to hold such high offices. He was succeeded by the Right Reverend Sehon Goodridge, appointed bishop of the Windward Islands in 1994. A graduate of Codrington College, where he also served as principal, Goodgridge went on to head the Simon of Cyrene Theological Institute in London, where he was elected bishop.

MAJOR THEOLOGIANS AND AUTHORS The Anglican Church of Saint Vincent has produced no theologians of note. Bishop Goodridge published a book on the first bishop of Barbados, William Hart Coleridge, and articles on liberation theology, development, human rights, and peace.

HOUSES OF WORSHIP AND HOLY PLACES The main Anglican church of Saint Vincent and the Grenadines, Saint George's Cathedral in Kingstown, was completed and dedicated in 1820. The island has some 20 other Anglican churches.

WHAT IS SACRED? Like Anglicans elsewhere, Vincentian Anglicans hold their place of worship and the sacraments of the church to be sacred.

HOLIDAYS AND FESTIVALS Vincentian Anglicans celebrate Christmas day, Good Friday, Easter Monday, and Whit Monday, and the government recognizes them as public holidays.

A particularly Vincentian celebration called the Nine Mornings—originally Catholic but now celebrated by other Christians, including Anglicans—is held during the nine days before Christmas. According to tradition, the Nine Mornings originated in the 1920s when Father Carlos Verbeke (a Dominican priest in charge of St. Mary's cathedral from 1919 to 1957) started celebrating a novena in the early morning hours instead of at midday, perhaps to take advantage of the people being already in the streets. Novenas, long customary in the Roman Catholic Church, are a devotion that is practiced over nine consecutive days as an act of thanksgiving or penitence.

The Nine Mornings may also be the continuation and expansion of a tradition of merriment that dates back to the 1870s, when rival bands from different villages paraded in the streets of Kingstown. Over the years the celebration has incorporated a variety of practices, including worship on Christmas itself and various thanksgivings for relief from hurricane, volcanic eruption, or other disasters. People also decorate houses, churches, and commercial buildings. The celebrations now coincide with the nine shopping days before Christmas, a testimony to the increasing commercialization of the festival.

MODE OF DRESS Anglicans on Saint Vincent and the Grenadines are expected to dressed appropriately for worship. Choir members, acolytes, and others officiating in the sanctuary are often robed. For the Eucharist ordained ministers wear specific robes (in the colors of the various seasons of the Christian year). Anglican clergy wear "choir" dress—a cassock, surplice, scarf (long and black, similar to a stole), and academic hood—for morning and evening prayer services. Before the 1970s Anglican clergy were required to wear clerical dress in public, but guidelines have become more relaxed.

DIETARY PRACTICES The only dietary rule for Anglicans on the islands is that of moderation, since eating too much is regarded as a sin (gluttony). The Anglican Church does encourage moderate fasting during Lent and sometimes generally on Wednesdays and Fridays.

RITUALS Eucharistic rituals on Saint Vincent vary from the simple to the elaborate. More elaborate services involve processions, the use of incense at various points, and much ceremony in moving from one part of the service to another. Good Friday liturgies are characterized by the veneration of the cross and Easter by the blessing of the paschal candle and the renewal of baptismal vows.

RITES OF PASSAGE The Anglican Church practices infant baptism. In most churches water is poured on the head of the infant or adult. Confirmation takes place at age 12 or older. Whereas baptisms, marriages, and funerals were formerly separate services, it is increasingly the custom that such services take place within the context of the Eucharist; thus, nuptial and requiem masses are common.

MEMBERSHIP The Anglican Church is not aggressive in seeking new members, a complacency that survives from a time when it was virtually the state church. Membership has declined significantly with the aging of the congregations and the rise of newer denominations.

SOCIAL JUSTICE In addition to its 25 congregations, the Anglicans administer five primary schools and three secondary schools in Saint Vincent and Bequia. Because the government is unable to provide for all the educational needs of its citizens, the church still has work to do in this area.

SOCIAL ASPECTS The Anglican Church on Saint Vincent and the Grenadines has begun to relax its views on nontraditional family arrangements. For many years the church (like all Anglican churches in the West Indies) declined to remarry divorced persons, viewing such marriages as improper while the divorced partner was still alive. Since 1977, however, remarriage is allowed, though only under specific conditions determined by the bishop.

Common-law unions on Saint Vincent go back two or more centuries to the period when enslaved Africans were not permitted to contract marriages. Though the Anglican Church waged a long battle against common-law unions, it has had to come to terms with the growing social recognition and acceptance of the practice. The Anglican Mother's Union, which formerly did not admit unmarried mothers, has started to do so with the church's approval. Not all the organization's members agree with this change, despite their group's name and the preponderance of unwed mothers in the region.

POLITICAL IMPACT Members of the Anglican Church have served as judges, senators, and politicians in Saint Vincent. Once a lay preacher at the cathedral was simultaneously a government minister. The Anglican Church's views on marriage have been expressed in sermons, and Bishop Goodridge spoke out against the ordination of a homosexual priest as a bishop in the Untied States.

CONTROVERSIAL ISSUES There is some controversy on Saint Vincent and the Grenadines over the ordination of women. While the Anglicans and Methodists ordain women, the Roman Catholics do not. The Anglican Church is permissive in the matter, and the final decision rests with the local bishop. Only one priest of the diocese has disagreed to the extent of severing his association with the Anglican Church and entering the Roman Catholic Church.

CULTURAL IMPACT Most of the existing Anglican churches on Saint Vincent and the Grenadines are European-style in architecture and old. With its own rich tradition of music, the Anglican Church never really attempted to include Caribbean music in the liturgy, though this has begun to change. Ecclesiastical authorities of the Anglican Province of the West Indies has mandated that its Commission on Liturgy and Music undertake to prepare a hymnal incorporating Caribbean music.

Other Religions

The beginnings of Pentecostalism in Saint Vincent are undocumented. Its growth has been rapid. From 3,941 adherents in 1980, church membership grew to over 11,000 in 1991 and 18,708 in 2001. The Pentecostals practice believer's baptism, meaning that one can be baptized only after the profession of faith. Pentecostals usually perform baptisms by immersion in the sea. As part of their belief in gifts of the Spirit, they also practice speaking in tongues—languages unknown even to the speaker and requiring an interpreter. Vincentian Pentecostals are inclined to break off from the main church for various reasons to start other "cells."

Methodism came to Saint Vincent in 1787 when Thomas Coke, an English missionary on the way to North America, was shipwrecked in Antigua. Coke visited Saint Vincent before completing his journey. The Methodists were given a warm welcome at first, but along with other dissenters of Anglicanism, they came to be viewed suspiciously by slave society. The Methodist Church resumed its growth after emancipation but declined as the nineteenth century wore on. The arrival of new denominations from North America since the 1980s has furthered that decline.

The Seventh-day Adventists began their work in Saint Vincent in 1901. Their first place of worship was a former Presbyterian Church building. The Vincentian Seventh-day Adventists are part of the Eastern Caribbean Conference of the Seventh-day Adventists and have experienced tremendous growth—enough to have 32 church buildings of their own. A major part of their success stems from their social programs. They administer three primary schools, a primary health care facility, and a dental clinic. The Seventh-day Adventists practice believer's baptism, usually administered in the sea. Members are not allowed to drink anything alcoholic or to eat pork.

Originally known as "Shakers," the Spiritual Baptists began work in Saint Vincent in the late nineteenth century, perhaps as early as 1870. The church drew its leadership and adherents from among the lower classes, and its growth attracted adverse notice, inspiring efforts to suppress it. Vincentian Spiritual Baptists worshiped noisily, often in the open air, ringing handbells, pouring water at the four corners of any buildings used for worship, and singing loudly, which earned them the nickname "Shouters." They were accused of practicing obeah, or witchcraft. Their activity was made illegal in 1912 by an ordinance that was not repealed until 1965. The group then began to attract adherents from the middle classes, and a government minister was said to have become a member. Gradually the islands became more open-minded toward new religions, leading to a greater respect for the church, which in turn encouraged its growth. Spiritual Baptists have Holy Week and Easter rituals similar to the those of the Anglicans, but the Baptist's are often more elaborate and include outdoor processions with ringing bells. Ministers wear clothing similar to that of Anglican and Catholic priests for worship. Spiritual Baptists usually perform baptisms by immersion in the sea.

French settlers brought Roman Catholicism to Saint Vincent in the mid-seventeenth century. Though the church's growth slowed after the arrival of the British, it made gains during the twentieth century. Historically part of the joint diocese of Bridgetown-Kingstown, the Saint Vincent Catholic Church became separate in 1989, forming the diocese of Kingstown. There are six parishes, and the church also administers five preschools, three primary schools, and three secondary schools.

The Church of Jesus Christ of Latter-day Saints (Mormons) is working to establish itself on Saint Vincent and the Grenadines. Young Mormon men, required to do a period of missionary work before going to college, come to the islands from the United States and work for a year or two before moving on.

Saint Vincent has small communities of Hindus, Jehovah's Witnesses, and Bahais, the latter two going from place to place to communicate their message.

Noel Titus

See Also Vol. I: *Anglicanism/Episcopalianism, Christianity, Pentecostalism*

Bibliography

Adams, Edgar. *Nine Mornings.* Kingstown: Edgar Adams Publishing, 1998.

———. *People on the Move.* London: Edgar Adams Publishing, 2002.

Flannery, Austin, ed. *Vatican Council II: The Conciliar and Post Conciliar Documents.* Northport, N.Y.: Costello Publishing Company, 1975.

Henney, Jeannette. "Spirit Possession and Trance in Saint Vincent." In *Trance, Healing, and Hallucination.* New York: John Wiley and Sons, 1974; Malabar, Fla.: Robert E. Krieger Publishing Company, 1982.

Simpson, G.E. *Black Religions in the New World.* New York: Columbia University Press, 1978.

Samoa

POPULATION 178,631

CONGREGATIONALIST 34.7 percent

ROMAN CATHOLIC 19.7 percent

METHODIST 15.0 percent

MORMON 12.7 percent

OTHER 17.9 percent

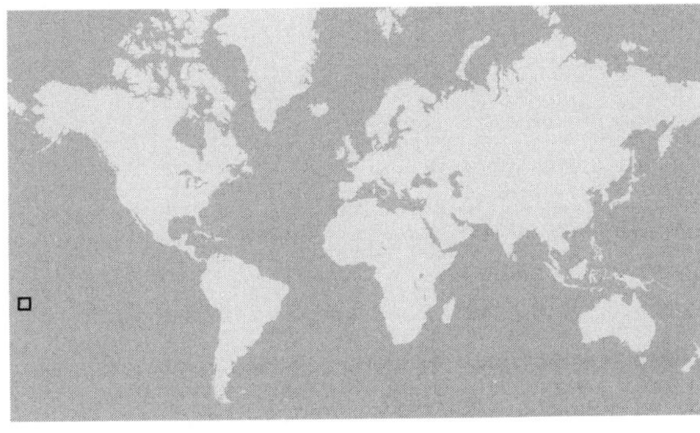

Country Overview

INTRODUCTION The Independent State of Samoa is part of the Samoa Islands, which lie on an east-west axis in the South Pacific Ocean. The western part of the group, with a total land area of 1,130 square miles, forms the Independent State of Samoa (formerly called Western Samoa), while the eastern part forms the U.S. territory of American Samoa.

Originally settled by Polynesians, the islands came under European influence (and later European control) in the late eighteenth century. They became independent in 1962.

Before 1830 Samoans practiced an animistic form of religion. The arrival of English Evangelical missionaries in 1830 marked the beginning of modernization in the Samoan islands. Thousands of Samoans forsook their ancient religion and converted to Christianity, whose God was generally perceived to be stronger than the traditional gods. By 1860 practically the entire population of about 45,000 had changed their allegiance to Christianity, with only a few pockets of animists remaining. Today Samoa is almost 100 percent Christian.

As it did in ancient times, religion continues to play a central role in Samoan life; little is done without recourse to religious influence. For while the gods have changed in name, traditional religious practices, such as evening family prayers, continue under Christianity. In addition to their religious functions and the moral power that they command in Samoan society, the major Christian groups have had a deep impact on the country's educational system.

RELIGIOUS TOLERANCE Samoa is a Christian nation, "founded on God," according to the preamble of the country's constitution. A provision in the constitution, however, provides for the freedom of expression and religion. There have been no religious wars in Samoa, apart from rivalries for membership between the various Christian sects. Since the 1960s these groups have been drawn closer to one another through joint efforts, including the translation of a common Samoan Bible and the formation of ecumenical bodies such as the National Council of Churches.

Children line up to enter a Congregationalist church on White Sunday. On White Sunday Samoans from 3 to 19 years of age sing religious songs and perform religious dramas in the churches. © ANDERS RYMAN/CORBIS.

Major Religion

CONGREGATIONAL CHRISTIAN CHURCH IN SAMOA

DATE OF ORIGIN 1830 C.E.

NUMBER OF FOLLOWERS 62,000

HISTORY The Congregational Christian Church in Samoa is the largest religious group in the country. It is a product of the late-18th-century Evangelical movement in England. The prime object of this movement was to spread the gospel to those parts of the world, including Oceania, that did not have access to it. A mission body called the London Missionary Society (LMS) was formed in London in the 1790s. It was a nondenominational group made up of members from various Protestant churches in England, though it was later to be dominated by Congregationalists. One of its earliest mission fields was Oceania, to which the first group of missionaries was sent at the turn of the eighteenth century.

The LMS proselytized in the Society Islands for 30 years before sending two missionaries, John Williams and Charles Barff, to Samoa in 1830. The arrival of six more LMS missionaries in 1836 intensified Samoan conversion and education. The missionaries created an orthography based on a modified version of the Roman alphabet; this became the basis for developing literacy among the converts. They also enabled the establishment of many mission schools, where reading and writing were taught. In 1845 the Malua Theological College was established to train native teachers. From this college hundreds of Samoan teachers went forth to spread the gospel in various parts of western Polynesia and Melanesia.

In 1961 the church in Samoa changed its name from LMS to Ekalesia Faapotopotoga Kerisiano I Samoa (Congregational Christian Church in Samoa). In addition, Samoan teachers were no longer to be called *faifeau Samoa* (Samoan pastors), but reverend, on an equal footing with their European counterparts. Finally, beginning in 1962 the Samoan church became independent of the parent body, while continuing to maintain close ties to it.

From that date Samoan elder pastors (*faifeau toeaina*) replaced European missionaries at the district level. The European presence became restricted mainly to the staff of the Malua Theological College, but even there, a Samoan pastor, Rev. Mila Sapolu, was finally appointed principal in the late 1960s. The Samoan church also started to send graduates of Malua Theological College overseas for more advanced training.

The highest governing body of the church is the Annual Church Conference, held in May of each year. The top church officials are the conference chairman, vice chairman, general secretary, and treasurer. Of its committees the Committee of Elders is generally regarded as the most powerful.

EARLY AND MODERN LEADERS The evangelization of the Samoan islands was largely a group effort by the London Missionary Society, but several names stand out in the nineteenth century, namely John Williams and Charles Barff. They arrived in Samoa in 1830 and were responsible for laying the groundwork for the large-scale missionary work that followed in other parts of the Pacific. Samoan leaders since the 1960s include Rev. Vavae Toma, Rev. Mila Sapolu and Rev. Oka Fauolo (former principals of Malua Theological College), and Rev. Sulufaiga Samasoni, who has served as both the chairman and vice chairman of the Annual Church Conference.

MAJOR THEOLOGIANS AND AUTHORS The Congregational Christian Church in Samoa subscribes to Congregational theology, especially with respect to the central role of the local congregation in administration and in other aspects of church life. Those who have written on Congregationalist ideas in Samoa include Rev. Mila Sapolu, Rev. Oka Fauolo, and Rev. Otele Perelini (who was appointed principal of the Malua Theological College in 1994).

Outstanding authors include Rev. Sulufaiga Samasoni, who has published a number of popular sermons, including the best-selling book *O Le Lupe I Vao Ese* (1998; "The Pigeon in Strange Lands").

HOUSES OF WORSHIP AND HOLY PLACES Practically every village in Samoa has a Congregational church. All churches are highly esteemed by the people, and almost all are constructed in European style. Among the Congregationalists no particular church is regarded as more important than another, but certain religious sites inspire deep awe. These include Sapapalii, Savaii, where the first Evangelical missionaries set foot on Samoan soil. Another site is Malua, Upolu, the location of the theological college.

WHAT IS SACRED? Churches, rather than any particular physical site or monument, are the main sacred sites for Samoan Congregationalists. The church generally follows traditional Samoan beliefs with respect to the sacredness of relationships between brothers and sisters (the *feagaiga* system) and especially between people and their gods. The *feagaiga* system particularly affects the church's pastors, because it pertains to their relationships with their congregations. As *feagaiga,* pastors and their children are regarded as sacred, and the congregation owes them certain duties—for example, material support and protection.

HOLIDAYS AND FESTIVALS The main holidays and festivals are those in the Christian calendar (for example, Easter and Christmas). Other important dates are the Annual Church Conference, which attracts Samoan Congregationalists from all over the world in May, and White Sunday, dedicated to the young people, in October. On White Sunday Samoans from three to 19 years of age sing religious songs and perform religious dramas in the churches. After these performances their families treat them to lavish feasts.

MODE OF DRESS The men's mode of dress for Sunday services and ceremonial occasions is a Western suit, usually white; a *lavalava* (wraparound) or *ie faitaga* (a more formal version of the *lavalava*) is normally worn instead of trousers. Sunday dress for women consists of a white dress, white *lavalava,* and white hat. The color white is associated with purity of heart, innocence, and redemption; this symbolism was probably introduced by the early missionaries. At other times daily wear is less formal for all genders.

DIETARY PRACTICES Congregationalist dietary practices in Samoa are marked by periods of fasting, which can last from a half-day to a full day (sunrise to sunset). Such fasts are resorted to for various reasons, such as penance, divine favors, and spiritual awareness.

RITUALS The main Samoan Congregationalist rituals are associated with baptisms, weddings, funerals, and house dedications. These occasions are generally accompanied by other cultural activities, such as gift exchanges involving food, cash, and *'ie Toga,* intricately woven mats (the most valuable form of traditional goods used for exchange ceremonies among Samoans).

RITES OF PASSAGE Rites of passage for Samoan Congregationalists include baptisms (usually performed in infancy or childhood), becoming an official member of the congregation, and rites for the dying. Becoming a congregation member imposes certain religious duties on a person, such as the obligation to lead a proper Christian life. As the member makes progress and demonstrates his or her ability to practice the rules and serve the needs of the church, he or she may be inducted as a deacon. Further competence may result in a deacon becoming an assistant pastor (*aoao fesoasoani*). For the truly ambitious the next step might be to study for the ministry at Malua Theological College.

MEMBERSHIP In Samoa people become members of the Congregationalist Church by birth to current members or through conversion. They are expected to undergo a period of socialization and education within the church system in preparation for their responsibilities as members. At the end of this probationary period they are formally inducted into the church.

The Congregationalist Church no longer deliberately proselytizes within Samoa, but it is deeply involved in sending missionaries to other mission fields, mainly in the West Indies and in Africa.

SOCIAL JUSTICE The Congregational Christian Church in Samoa has been dedicated not only to the development of the spiritual lives of its members but also to their social, economic, and political advancement. In general, however, the church's lasting effect has been in the area of education. From the 1830s until the end of the twentieth century, education for most Samoans was provided by the pastor's village schools.

SOCIAL ASPECTS The Congregationalist Church has always been allied with traditional Samoan society. Thus, the church supports core Samoan values, beliefs, and practices, provided these do not conflict with Christian teachings (for example, the church has prohibitions against revenge and polygamy).

POLITICAL IMPACT During its first 30 years in Samoa the Congregationalist Church adopted a neutralist stance in political affairs. From the 1860s to the late 1890s, however, it became increasingly embroiled in political matters. It sought, for instance, to promote its own candidates for the kingship of the Samoan islands. After Samoa gained independence in 1962, the church again exerted immense influence on state affairs, mainly because several politicians occupied important posts in the Annual Church Conference.

CONTROVERSIAL ISSUES The very conservative Committee of Elders largely controls church policies and theological dogma. These, therefore, are traditional and serve to uphold the status quo. The newer graduates of the Congregational theological colleges tend to be more liberal and innovative. Church leaders have increasingly expressed concern about the introduction of religious groups such as Muslims and Hindus to Samoa.

CULTURAL IMPACT The church's cultural impact on music, art, and literature is generally a conservative one. For instance, in matters of church music, the official line is that the old tunes should be preferred over the new ones. In art, however, the church has made a valuable contribution through the establishment of the Leulumoega Fou Art School, headed by Italian artist Ernesto Coter. It is the only such school in the country. The church's contribution to literature is relatively modest, consisting of translations of books to Samoan and the writings of several pastors, including Rev. Sulufaiga Samasoni.

Other Religions

Catholicism was introduced to Samoa by the order of Marists, founded in France in the nineteenth century. Their missionary efforts in Oceania were first concentrated in French Polynesia and Wallis and Futuna, all of which later became French colonial possessions. Soon after their arrival in Samoa in 1845, the French missionaries obtained the patronage of one of the most powerful Samoan chiefs, Mataafa Fagamanu. French influence was felt in the Samoan Catholic Church up to the time of Samoan independence in 1962.

In 1968 a Samoan, Pio Taofinuu, finally succeeded to the bishopric; he presided over the Diocese of Samoa and Tokelau (districts that had been defined as vicariates until 1966). In 1973 he was elevated to the College of Cardinals. Another major landmark in the history of the Samoan Catholic Church was the establishment of the Diocese of Samoa-Pago Pago in 1982. A Maryknoll priest, Father Quinn Weitzell, was named its first bishop. At the same time the Holy See created the Archdiocese of Samoa-Apia and Tokelau, with Cardinal Pio as its first archbishop.

In 1987 Tokelau was separated from the Samoa-Apia archdiocese and became a part of the Wellington archdiocese of New Zealand, in keeping with Tokelauan's status as New Zealand citizens. After 35 years as bishop and archbishop of Samoa, Cardinal Pio stepped down to be replaced by Father Alapati Mataeliga in 2002.

In Samoa the most distinctive feature of Catholicism is the indigenized version of the Mass. It is conducted in the Samoan language, and it incorporates Samoan rituals such as the *ifoga* (a ceremonial act of penitence). The Mass also prominently features traditional symbols in the form of the national dress and fine mats, as well as traditional songs. The indigenization of the Mass is in keeping with the ritualistic changes recommended by the Second Vatican Council.

In 1835 the first European Wesleyan (Methodist) missionary, Rev. Peter Turner, and several Tongan teachers arrived in Samoa. The following year Turner was joined by Matthew Wilson. They preached and printed religious books in Tongan, which was easier for Samoans to understand than Tahitian (the original language used by missionaries).

The Wesleyan's success was short-lived because of a dispute over jurisdiction with the Congregationalists. The matter was finally resolved in favor of the Congregationalists, and Turner's group left Samoa in 1839. The Tongan Wesleyans, under the leadership of their king, Taufaahau Tupou George, continued to sponsor Wesleyan missionary activities in Samoa.

Wesleyan aspirations in Samoa were revived in 1857, when the New South Wales Wesleyan Conference of Australia took the Samoan mission under its wing as a circuit of the Australian Synod and sent Rev. Martin Dyson to reorganize it. The dynamic George Brown followed him in 1860, and from then on the Wesleyan Church in Samoa (called the Lotu Toga) continued to grow. The Lotu Toga became independent of its Australian parent body in 1963, though close ties have been maintained. It has its own Annual General Conference, under which there are 12 synods. Like the Congregationalists and the Catholics, the Methodists operate primary and secondary schools in Samoa.

The first Mormon (or Latter-day Saints) missionaries to the Samoan islands—Kimo Pelio and Samuela Manoa—traveled there from Hawaii in 1863. They were followed by Joseph Dean, who sailed to the eastern island of Aunuu in 1888. By then the infant church had 35 baptismal members, six church leaders, and nine missionaries. The Mormon message was carried to Western Samoa in 1889, when Dean and other missionaries sailed to Apia. They constructed a mission home in Fagalii, which served as the base from which Mormon missionaries spread their message to other parts of Samoa.

By 1900, 20 Mormon branches had been established on Upolu Island—12 on Tutuila, and eight on Savaii. From Samoa the mission work was carried to other Pacific islands, such as Tonga, Fiji, the Cook Islands, and Niue. The Mormon Church has been one of the fastest-growing religious groups in Samoa, and in the Pacific generally.

There are a number of other churches in Samoa, among the larger the Assembly of God and the Seventh-day Adventist. Smaller groups include the Worship Centre, the Congregational Church of Jesus, Jehovah's Witnesses, the Full Gospel Church, Nazarenes, and the Voice of Christ. There are a small number of Bahais and members of Aoga Tusi Paia (Bible schools that act as churches, insofar as they have followers and teachers).

Unasa L.F. Va'a

See Also Vol. I: *Christianity, Latter-day Saints, Methodism, Reformed Christianity, Roman Catholicism*

Bibliography

Davidson, J.W. *Samoa Mo Samoa: The Emergence of the Independent State of Western Samoa.* Melbourne: Oxford University Press, 1967.

Garrett, John. "The Conflict Between the London Missionary Society and the Wesleyan Methodists in Nineteenth-Century Samoa." *Journal of Pacific History* 9 (1974): 65–80.

Gilson, R.P. *Samoa 1830 to 1900: The Politics of a Multi-Cultural Community.* Melbourne: Oxford University Press, 1970.

Hamilton, Andrew. "Nineteenth-Century French Missionaries and Fa'a Samoa." *Journal of Pacific History* 33, no. 2 (1998): 163–77.

Harris, R.C. *Samoa Apia Mission History.* Apia: Samoa Apia Mission, 1983.

Meleisea, Malama. *The Making of Modern Samoa: Traditional Authority and Colonial Administration in the History of Western Samoa.* Suva, Fiji: Institute of Pacific Studies, University of the South Pacific, 1987.

Tiffany, Sharon W. "The Politics of Denominational Organization in Samoa." In *Mission, Church, and Sect in Oceania.* Edited by James A. Boutilier, Daniel T. Hughes, and Sharon W. Tiffany. Lanham, Md.: University Press of America, 1984.

Va'a, L.F. "The Parables of a Samoan Divine." M.A. thesis, Australian National University, 1986.

———. *Saili Matagi: A Study of Samoan Migrants in Australia.* Suva, Fiji: Institute of Pacific Studies, University of the South Pacific, 2001.

San Marino

POPULATION 27,730

ROMAN CATHOLIC 99 percent

OTHER 1 percent

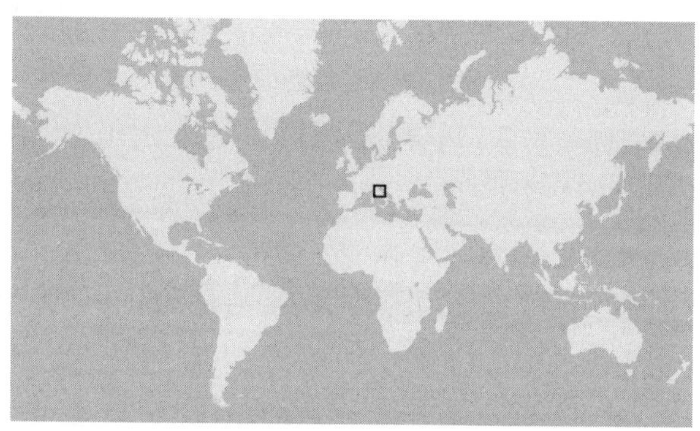

Country Overview

INTRODUCTION The Republic of San Marino is the third smallest independent state in Europe. It is situated in central Italy (between the regions of Emilia-Romagna and Marche) and covers a total area of 24 square miles. In the middle of the country stands Mount Titano.

The San Marino parliament consists of the Grand and General Council (Consiglio Grande e Generale), with 60 representatives. Two captains regent, who are elected every six months, act as heads of state. The State Congress is the executive organ and is made up of 10 members. Catholics make up almost the whole of the population.

RELIGIOUS TOLERANCE In the "Declaration of Citizen's Rights and Principles of the San Marino Government" (1978), the state guarantees freedom of meeting and association, and expression of thought, conscience, and worship.

Major Religion

ROMAN CATHOLICISM

DATE OF ORIGIN 301 C.E.

NUMBER OF FOLLOWERS 27,500

HISTORY Saint Marino, the founder of the country, was a stonemason from Dalmatia. In 301 C.E. he established on Mount Titano a community of Christians fleeing religious persecution by the Emperor Diocletian. Until the tenth century the population ruled itself. At the beginning of the eleventh century the state was governed by the Arengo, an assembly of heads of families, which drew up statutes and laws based upon democratic principles. In the fourteenth century the Arengo was replaced by the Grand and General Council.

San Marino became known as a republic and reached its present size in 1462. The history of this small state has predominately been one of freedom and independence, even if San Marino has had to defend itself from external threats on several occasions. There have been just brief military occupations, such as those of Cesare Borgia in 1503 and Cardinal Alberoni in 1739. In the latter case, independence was regained through the intervention of Pope Clement XII, who restored San Marino to its people's government on 5 February 1740.

The Republic of San Marino is part of the Diocese of San Marino-Montefeltro. In 1977, at the suggestion of Pope Paul VI, the name of the diocese was changed from Montefeltro to San Marino-Montefeltro, and some parishes were redistributed to adjoining dioceses. The bishopric had been at the fortress of San Leo until 1569, when it was transferred to the town of Pennabilli. Among the most important religious events in the history of San Marino were the papal visits by Julius II in 1506 and John Paul II in 1982.

EARLY AND MODERN LEADERS Captain Regent Antonio Onofri has been called the *Padre della patria* (Father of our native land). In 1796 Napoleon offered San Marino support to widen its territory, but Onofri refused the offer because he believed that expansion and French interference would pose a threat to San Marino's freedom and independence. In 1948 Federico Bigi founded the Christian Democratic Party of San Marino. He also represented San Marino as a judge at the European Court of Human Rights. Another important figure was Giovanni Galassi, ambassador for San Marino (beginning in 1980) and deacon of ambassadors at the Holy See (beginning in 1998).

MAJOR THEOLOGIANS AND AUTHORS Giovanni Bertoldi (died in 1445), a Franciscan friar and theologian born in San Marino, became bishop of Fermo. He made a translation into Latin and a commentary on Dante's *Divine Comedy,* which he presented to the bishops reunited at the Council of Constance (1413–18). Thanks to this Latin translation Dante's work began to circulate in Germany.

Another notable theologian was Valerio Maccioni (died in 1676). A member of the Theological College of Padua, he was an advisor to the duke of Brunswick and to the bishop of Morocco.

Among important figures of contemporary Catholicism is Father Ciro Benedettini (born in Serravalle in 1946), who edited *Eco di San Gabriele,* a Catholic magazine. In 1995 he became vice director of the press office of the Holy See.

HOUSES OF WORSHIP AND HOLY PLACES The Basilica of San Marino, built in the mid-nineteenth century on the site of an ancient parish church, is the most significant place of worship in the country. Pope John Paul II visited it in 1982. Other churches of note are those of San Francesco and San Quirino, as well as the church of San Michele Arcangelo at Domagnano, built in 1542.

WHAT IS SACRED? In San Marino the Catholic faith takes on the same form as in other western European countries, especially Italy. Devotion must be remembered to the founder saint, whose relics are housed in the Basilica of San Marino. At Baldasserona is the Sacellum of the Saint, a natural cave where Saint Marino first found refuge. It is a popular site for pilgrims to visit.

HOLIDAYS AND FESTIVALS The two most significant Catholic feast days are those of Saint Agatha and of Saint Marino. On the Feast of Saint Agatha (co-patron saint of the state), which takes place on 5 February, there is a procession from the town of Borgo Maggiore to the city of San Marino. The independence that was regained in 1740 is also commemorated on this day. Saint Marino, patron saint of the Republic, is celebrated on 3 September. After a High Mass in the Basilica of San Marino, large crowds take part in a procession through the streets of the city, displaying the relics of the saint. In the afternoon there are great town festivities that end with the *Palio delle Balestre Grandi,* a crossbow competition. In San Marino the Feast of Corpus Domini is a state holiday.

MODE OF DRESS In San Marino Catholics do not dress differently from other citizens. Priests and other religious figures follow general Vatican regulations.

DIETARY PRACTICES The Catholic Church does not envisage any special food restrictions for its members. There are only a few days during the year when the church recommends fasting and abstinence from meat.

RITUALS At the Basilica of San Marino there are celebrations for the anniversary of the Arengo, the Militia Feast Day (25 March), and the election and installation (1 April and 1 October) of the captains regent. For baptisms and weddings a church celebration is usually followed by feasting and banquets.

RITES OF PASSAGE Major moments of transition in San Marinese life have traditionally been marked by Roman Catholic ritual.

MEMBERSHIP In San Marino in the late twentieth century, there emerged Catholic lay movements with the purposes of drawing lapsed Catholics back to the faith and missionizing among the unbaptized. The most common are Communion and Liberation, the Neocatechumenal Way, and the Renewal Charismatic Catholic.

SOCIAL JUSTICE There are no Catholic schools in San Marino, but San Marinese Catholics are particularly active in state schools. Among the teachers at nursery schools there are always 12 nuns. Catholic teaching is compulsory in all schools, although a student may ask to be exonerated.

SOCIAL ASPECTS San Marino has a divorce law, but abortion is illegal. In 1997 article 274 of the penal code condemning homosexuality was suppressed. The Diocese of San Marino-Montefeltro has been attempting to respond to threats to the Christian concept of family. For example, in 1993 a movement called *Coppie in cammino* (Couples on the Path) was established by a group of married and betrothed couples seeking to use Christian experience to address marital issues.

POLITICAL IMPACT Catholicism has always had an indirect impact on public life in San Marino. The most important case is the presence of a San Marino Christian Democratic Party, founded immediately after World War II.

CONTROVERSIAL ISSUES One of the most hotly debated ethical subjects in San Marino is a proposed law in favor of abortion rights, which some citizens and political figures advocate. A project that many Catholics are against is the building of a casino on San Marino's territory.

CULTURAL IMPACT Catholicism has had an important cultural role in San Marino. Local artists have drawn their inspiration from religious subjects and have created works for the main places of worship in the Republic. They are not well known outside of their country, with the exception of Maestro Menetto, an architect and stonecutter of the fourteenth century, and Antonio Orafo, who was such a highly esteemed goldsmith during the Renaissance that he became goldsmith of the Holy See. On national television every Saturday there is a slot dedicated to the Sunday gospel, and there are often special programs on religious subjects.

Other Religions

In San Marino there are also, even if not in significant numbers, Jehovah's Witnesses and Muslims. Because of the country's small size, there are no mosques.

Lorenza Gattamorta

See Also Vol. 1: *Roman Catholicism*

Bibliography

Balducci, Cristiana. *Geografie e agiografia: Analisi della Vita Sancti Marini e ipotesi sulla libertas perpetua.* San Marino: Edizioni del Titano, 1998.

Carrick, Noel. *San Marino.* New York: Chelsea House, 1988.

Centro di documentazione della Biblioteca di Stato della Repubblica di San Marino, ed. *Storia illustrata della Repubblica di San Marino.* 3 vols. San Marino: AIEP, 1985.

Edwards, Adrian, and Chris Michaelides. *San Marino.* Oxford: Clio, 1996.

Foresti, Fabio. *Quella nostra sancta libertà: Lingue storia e società nella Repubblica di San Marino.* San Marino: AIEP, 1998.

Guardigli, Pier Paolo. *Terre e torri: Per una storia economica e sociale della Repubblica di San Marino.* San Marino: Edizioni del Titano, 1992.

Rossi, G., ed. *A Short History of San Marino.* San Marino: C.N. Packett, 1979.

São Tomé and Príncipe

POPULATION 170,372

ROMAN CATHOLIC 89.5 percent

OTHER CHRISTIAN 6.3 percent

BAHAI 2.1 percent

AFRICAN TRADITIONAL 1.1 percent

NONRELIGIOUS 1 percent

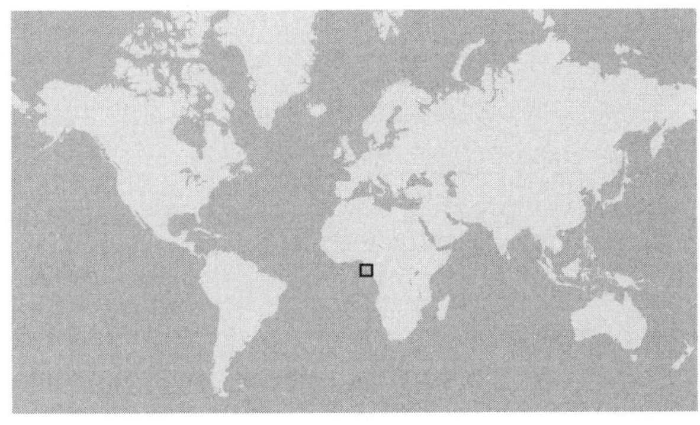

Country Overview

INTRODUCTION The Democratic Republic of São Tomé and Príncipe consists of two small islands in the Gulf of Guinea off the coast of west central Africa. Their total land area is 386 square miles. Uninhabited at the time of their discovery by Portuguese mariners in the 1470s, São Tomé and Príncipe bears the mark of five hundred years of Portuguese colonial rule. The distinctive creole society, language, and culture of the islands are the product of importations of slaves from the African mainland, as well as smaller migrations from Portugal, including expelled "New Christians" (converted Jews), civil and political criminals from Portuguese African colonies, and planter-settlers.

The Roman Catholic Church has been present in São Tomé and Príncipe since the end of the fifteenth century. Catholic clerics participated actively in the slave trade and factional struggles that characterized the early colonial history. Because the islands were far from Portugal, their society and culture developed for long periods of time in isolation from Lisbon and Rome.

São Tomé and Príncipe gained political independence in 1975. In 2000 more than three-quarters of the population was Roman Catholic. Adherents of other religions include Evangelical Protestants and Seventh-day Adventists, a handful of Jehovah's Witnesses, a growing number of Bahais, and followers of African traditional religions.

RELIGIOUS TOLERANCE Freedom of religion in São Tomé and Príncipe is guaranteed by the 1990 constitution and upheld by the government. Religious organizations must register with the government, but no group is denied registration, nor is any unregistered group restricted.

Major Religion

ROMAN CATHOLICISM

DATE OF ORIGIN 1499 C.E.

NUMBER OF FOLLOWERS 152,000

HISTORY The history of Roman Catholicism in São Tomé and Príncipe is inextricably linked to Portuguese colonial expansion and the Atlantic slave trade. By the late fifteenth century Portugal sought to convert the islands into sugar-producing colonies based on slave labor. By 1504 the first church and slave plantations had been established. In the sixteenth century São Tomé prospered through sugar production and the slave trade. The early history of Catholicism in São Tomé was complicated by a number of factors, including high mortality rates, departures of priests for the mainland, active involvement by priests in the slave trade, and political tensions between colonists and Portugal and between competing factions on the islands. Nonetheless, by 1534 São Tomé was named the seat of an enormous new diocese that stretched from Cape Palmas (in present-day Liberia) to the Cape of Good Hope. No bishop resided in the islands, however, until the 1550s. These years were characterized by ideological and power struggles between local priests, planters, and slave traders, as well as outside bishops and clerics sent from Portugal. In 1612 much of the territory of the diocese was lost to the new apostolic administration of Mozambique.

With the rise of the Brazilian sugar economy and the waning of Portuguese control of the slave trade in the seventeenth century, the economic fortunes of the islands diminished. The Catholic clergy continued to play a prominent role in political affairs, even during periods of relative isolation from Portugal. For long periods in the eighteenth and nineteenth centuries, the church was run entirely by local clergy. In the nineteenth century the economy was revived with the introduction of coffee and cocoa. Portugal officially abolished slavery in 1875 but replaced it with a highly exploitative plantation economy that depended on contract labor from other Portuguese colonies, including Angola, Mozambique, and Cape Verde.

During five centuries of Portuguese intervention, a complex, hierarchical society arose based on a number of sociocultural groups: *filhos da terra* (sons of the land), who descended from mixed unions of slaves and slave owners; *Angolares,* descendants of fugitive slaves; *forros,* descendants of freed slaves; *serviçais* and *tongas,* contract laborers who worked on the coffee and cocoa plantations; and finally descendents of Portuguese. After independence in 1975 São Tomé and Príncipe adopted a secular Marxist ideology for a time, but this did not weaken Catholic or other Christian religious practices.

EARLY AND MODERN LEADERS Although not the first bishop appointed to the diocese of São Tomé, Gaspar Cão, who served from 1554 until his death circa 1572, was the first bishop to reside in the islands. A Portuguese-born Augustinian professor of theology, Cão struggled to enforce civil and ecclesiastical laws, to provide some protection and religious instruction to slaves, to fight prostitution, and to impose observance of Sunday as a holy day.

In the eighteenth century Father Manual do Rosário Pinto, a black priest from São Tomé and one of the most powerful men on the island, was archdeacon of the diocese, counselor to the governor, and a close ally to Bishop João de Sahagum. Pinto fought against mixed-race clergy who discriminated against black clerics.

MAJOR THEOLOGIANS AND AUTHORS São Tomé and Príncipe does not seem to have produced major theologians, but a number of priests and missionaries have written on the history and religious life of the islands. In 1734 Father Manuel do Rosário Pinto published *History of São Tomé,* a valuable text that covered the first two-and-a half centuries of Portuguese presence. In contemporary times António Ambrósio, a missionary on the islands from 1963 to 1973, drew on published and archival church materials in his 1983 *Contributions towards the History of São Tomé and Príncipe.*

HOUSES OF WORSHIP AND HOLY PLACES Augustinian missionaries built the first church in São Tomé, Nossa Senhora da Graça, in 1504. This church later became the cathedral for the diocese of São Tomé and still stands.

WHAT IS SACRED? Roman Catholicism is the dominant religion on the islands, but continual influxes of African laborers over the centuries have shaped this Portuguese-African creole culture. Qualities of Catholic and African belief systems combine in supernatural beings. For example, Sum d'Océ (Lord of the Heavens) is both the Christian creator and the controller of wealth and people. A number of island churches are also devoted to Mary, *a senhora Mãe de Deus* (our Lady Mother of God). In the early twentieth century plantation laborers built tiny chapels in which they placed rough-cut crosses surrounded by African charms.

HOLIDAYS AND FESTIVALS The people of São Tomé and Príncipe are deeply religious but depart in certain ways from Catholic orthodoxy. Major Christian holidays are celebrated, and individual communities hold festivals on the day of their patron saint. Baptisms, festivals, processions, funeral masses, and mourning ceremonies are crucial. At the same time, however, Sunday Mass and Communion are less central to religious practice.

MODE OF DRESS Catholics in São Tomé and Príncipe do not dress distinctively. Western-style clothing predominates.

DIETARY PRACTICES With the exception of standard Catholic Lenten dietary restrictions, which include abstinence from meat on Fridays and fasting on Ash Wednesday and Good Friday, there do not appear to be specific Catholic dietary practices in São Tomé and Príncipe.

RITUALS In addition to the Mass and Catholic sacraments, a number of adaptations involving music, dance, and processions are also practiced. Individual towns throughout the islands celebrate their patron saint's day by holding festivals that combine religious ceremonies, traditional cuisine, music, and performances.

RITES OF PASSAGE In São Tomé and Príncipe baptisms, funerals, and mourning practices are important. Church marriages, however, rarely occur.

MEMBERSHIP Beginning in the fifteenth century Catholic missionaries sought to convert and instruct slaves. By the time Portuguese colonial missionaries arrived in 1878, São Tomeans had been Catholics for almost four centuries. During the plantation era in the nineteenth and twentieth centuries, little effort was made to evangelize the usually non-Christian contract laborers imported from the African mainland. Because of a long Catholic tradition on the islands, membership today is derived primarily within families rather than from proselytizing.

SOCIAL JUSTICE During the early slave era in São Tomé and Príncipe, Catholic clerics both participated in the slave trade and sought to provide religious instruction, hospital care, and schooling to win souls and mitigate suffering. During the cocoa and coffee plantation period, priests performed Mass, baptisms, and marriages on the plantations but did not seem to have challenged the harsh working and living conditions of contract laborers. The main challenge to colonial era oppression seems to have come from secular intellectuals trained in Europe. Today São Tomean society remains permeated by inequality, including sexual inequality. The Catholic Church has continued to sponsor education and health care while denouncing political irregularities and corruption that have benefited certain politicians in the country.

SOCIAL ASPECTS Despite Catholic views about marriage as a sacrament, few São Tomeans either desire or can afford the major expense of a church wedding. In practice both men and women tend to have multiple liaisons in their lives, and polygamy is prevalent. While formally opposed to polygamy and childbirth out of wedlock, the church accommodates these practices. Mothers frequently shoulder the economic burden of supporting children and running households in polygamous unions.

POLITICAL IMPACT During the early centuries missionary and local priests played an active and sometimes leading role in the factional struggles that characterized political life in São Tomé and Príncipe. During the plantation period of the nineteenth and twentieth centuries, the Catholic Church did not dispute the dominant plantation owners. Since independence in 1975 the church has been run primarily by expatriate priests who have not played an official political role.

CONTROVERSIAL ISSUES São Tomé and Príncipe inherited pre-independence Portuguese laws prohibiting abortion, which reflected Catholic condemnation of the procedure. Abortion was, nonetheless, permitted to save the life of the woman. In practice abortion policies are more liberal; abortion is allowed for medical reasons and in cases of rape, incest, or fetal impairment. Although the country has a strong Catholic orientation, birth control is practiced. Divorce is frequent in spite of Catholic interdictions against it.

CULTURAL IMPACT The devil, angels, and the Virgin Mary have been incorporated into an elaborate traditional dance, *danca congo,* which entails drumming, colorful costumes, and the enactment of old folk tales. Another art form, *tchiloli,* draws on a sixteenth-century Portuguese play honoring the Christian King Charlemagne. Another play from the Charlemagne cycle, *Auto da Floripes* (Drama of Floripes), is performed in Príncipe on the feast day of Saint Lawrence. The elaborate spectacle reenacts battles between the Christians and Moors.

Other Religions

The presence of Protestant and independent Christian denominations in São Tomé and Príncipe has grown, particularly since the 1930s, when an exiled Angolan Christian initiated the Evangelical Church and Portuguese Seventh-day Adventists began missionary efforts. Today Seventh-day Adventists have six churches on São Tomé and one on Príncipe. Membership in the Assemblies of God and, particularly, the New Apostolic Church has increased significantly since independence. In 1990 Brazilian missionaries with the interdenominational "Youth with a Mission" began proselytizing.

Since the 1970s the number of Bahais has grown rapidly through conversion. In 1995 there were 18 local spiritual assemblies.

In the popular creole culture of São Tomé and Príncipe, both Christian and African beliefs and practices are evident. Beliefs in witchcraft and sorcery are widely held. African ancestors, *Nén ké Mu* (the dead), provide protection for their descendants and receive offerings of food, wine, and clothing.

John Cinnamon

See Also Vol. I: *Roman Catholicism*

Bibliography

Garfield, Robert. *A History of São Tomé Island 1470–1655: The Key to Guinea.* San Francisco: Mellen Research University Press, 1992.

Hodges, Tony, and M.D. Newitt. *São Tomé and Príncipe: From Plantation Colony to Microstate.* Boulder, Colo.: Westview, 1988.

Shaw, Caroline, comp. *São Tomé and Príncipe.* World Bibliographic Series. Oxford: Clio Press, 1994.

Tenreiro, Francisco. *A Ilha de São Tomé.* Lisbon: Memórias da Junta de Investigações do Ultramar, 1961.

Saudi Arabia

POPULATION 23,513,330

SUNNI MUSLIM 95.5 to 96.5 percent

SHIA MUSLIM 1 to 2 percent

CHRISTIAN 2.5 percent

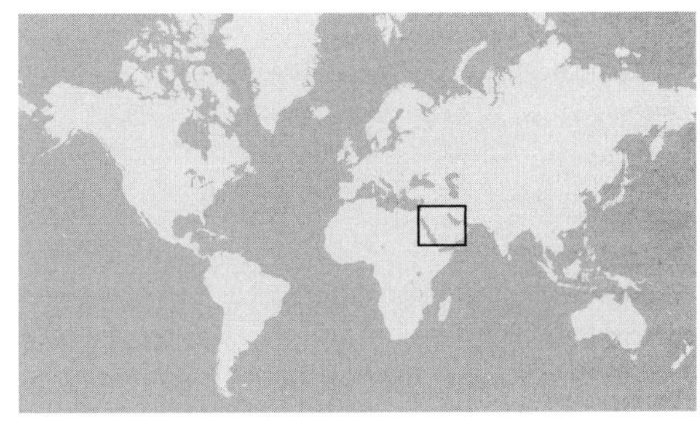

Country Overview

INTRODUCTION The Kingdom of Saudi Arabia is located in the Arabian Peninsula in southwest Asia. It borders Jordan, Iraq, and Kuwait to the north; the United Arab Emirates, Qatar, and the Arabian Gulf to the east; Yemen and Oman to the south; and the Red Sea to the west. One of the leading oil-producing Gulf States, Saudi Arabia is a desert country with mountainous areas, particularly in the southeast, and no permanent rivers or lakes. Except in the Asir Province, which gets significant precipitation, human settlements are confined to oases and areas with natural water sources.

The indigenous population, comprised of many Bedouin clans, traditionally herded camels, sheep, and goats, though some were farmers or urban merchants. After the advent of Islam in 622 C.E., pilgrims came from throughout the Islamic world and stayed, forming a diverse ethnic population in the western provinces, such as the Hejaz, now a cosmopolitan region. The central region of Nejd, historically less open to outside influences, is more religiously conservative and strict.

Saudi Arabia is the birthplace of Islam and the home of Islam's two holy cities, Mecca and Medina, where every year millions of devout pilgrims come to pray and take part in the *hajj* (pilgrimage). The Saudi state has its origins in a mid-eighteenth-century alliance between Mohammad ibn Saud, a local Nejdi prince, and Mohammad ibn Abd al-Wahhab, a Muslim religious reformer, who consolidated religious and political power in the region. In 1932 King Abdul Aziz ibn Saud established Saudi Arabia as an Islamic state ruled under Islamic law, and the great majority of its inhabitants are Sunni Muslims.

A Shia Muslim minority (estimated at between two hundred and four hundred thousand) lives primarily in the oil-rich Eastern Province, concentrated in the oases of Qatif and al-Hasa. Other religious minorities exist among the country's foreign contract laborers, which, like most Gulf States, Saudi Arabia relies heavily on. This transient work force, about one-fifth of the population, is mostly made up of Indians (1.4 million), Bangladeshis (1 million), Pakistanis (900,000), Filipinos (800,000), and British and Americans (70,000). While no official census data exists for the religious or sectarian affiliations of these people, the majority are Sunni and Shia Muslims, with the remaining minority non-Muslims.

The K'abah, the holiest shrine in Islam, is in the central courtyard of the Grand Mosque, the Haram, in Mecca. AP/WIDE WORLD PHOTOS.

RELIGIOUS TOLERANCE The Saudis regard the kingdom not only as the cradle of Islam but also as a preserve for Islam created by the prophet Muhammad, making it the most holy of territories where the public practice of no other religion is permitted. Sunni Islam is the only officially recognized religion in Saudi Arabia. Non-Muslims are permitted to practice in private, but they may not publish or distribute religious texts or proselytize in any way. The same restrictions apply to Shiites. The Sunni Saudis reject the central Shia premise of a divinely appointed leadership and consider a number of Shiite rituals polytheistic and therefore sinful. In the eastern part of the country, however, Shiites are allowed their own mosques where they may practice their religion.

The government's Committee for the Propagation of Virtue and Prevention of Vice, run by *mutawwiin* (state volunteers), enforces universal public compliance with Islamic codes of behavior. The duties of the *mutawwiin,* include ensuring that shops close during prayer times; policing daytime restrictions on public eating, smoking, and drinking during Ramadan; and enforcing the injunction that women dress modestly in public. *Iqamas* (government-issued identification cards that foreigners carry) indicate the bearer's religious orientation.

Major Religion

SUNNI ISLAM

DATE OF ORIGIN 622 C.E.

NUMBER OF FOLLOWERS 20.6 million

HISTORY Islam originated in Arabia in the early seventh century when Muhammad (c. 570–632 C.E.), a Meccan merchant from the Quraysh tribe, received a series of revelations from God through the angel Gabriel. By the time of his death, Muhammad had consolidated the secular and spiritual leadership of Arabia. Islam encompassed all aspects of life, recognizing no distinction between religion and state.

After Muhammad's death, his Meccan and Medinan supporters spontaneously elected his companion, Abu Bakr (c. 573–634 C.E.), upon whom the title *khalifat rasul Allah,* or "successor of the messenger of God," was bestowed. The caliph served as head of state, supreme judge, leader in public worship, and military commander. In less than a year the message of Islam had spread to most of the peninsula. All non-Muslims were required to convert, except Jews and Christians, who were deemed *ahl al-kitaab,* literally "People of the Book," or followers of other sacred texts revealed by God. They were, however, required to accept the supremacy of Muslim rule and pay a special tax.

The Umayyids, who ruled the peninsula from 661 to 750 C.E., moved the seat of the caliphate to Damascus. Nonetheless, Arabia continued to derive importance as the birthplace of the Prophet and the location of the holy cities of Mecca and Medina, which still drew the devout, as well as bringing prestige to those who ruled the area.

In 1750 Mohammad ibn Saud and Mohammad ibn Abd al-Wahhab joined forces to create a new religio-political movement. The Saud family became the political head of the region, while Mohammad ibn Abd al-Wahhab and his descendants, the Al ash-Shaykh, oversaw matters of faith. The alliance paved the way for King Abdul Aziz ibn Saud's formation of the Islamic state of Saudi Arabia in 1932, which gave the government responsibility for the collective moral ordering of society.

EARLY AND MODERN LEADERS Saudi Arabia's principle historical figure is King Abdul Aziz ibn Saud (c. 1880–1953), founder of the modern-day Saudi state. Ibn Saud ruled according to the teachings of Mohammad ibn Abd al-Wahhab and assumed the role of the preserver of the tenets of Islam. He convinced the devout that devices such as telegraphs, telephones, and automobiles could be used to spread Islam. In doing so, he modernized the country and centralized and stabilized the power of the state.

King Faisal ibn Abdul Aziz (reigned 1964–75) instituted other modernization programs, established a body of fundamental laws, organized a consultative council, abolished slavery, and expanded educational opportunities, especially by offering schooling for girls.

MAJOR THEOLOGIANS AND AUTHORS The teachings of Mohammad ibn Abd al-Wahhab (1703–92) have dominated Islamic theology in Saudi Arabia. Mohammad ibn Abd al-Wahhab studied Hanbali law, the strictest of Islamic legal schools, which requires the literal interpretation of the Koran and the hadith (traditions of the Prophet). He rejected anything that compromised strict monotheism and regarded the association of any object with God as *shirk,* a heinous sin and a form of polytheism. Among questionable acts he included praying to saints, visiting tombs, and venerating trees and rocks. Innovation or the introduction of any new or foreign ideology is *bida'*, a violation of God's oneness. To avoid both *shirk* and *bida'*, Mohammad ibn Abd al-Wahhab advocated returning to the ways of the Prophet with strict adherence to the Koran and hadith.

Mohammad ibn Abd al-Wahhab emphasized *tawhiid*, or the uniqueness of God, who deserved the absolute devotion of his followers. Mohammad ibn Abd al-Wahhab's teachings are known as *ad dawa wa tawhiid*, "the call to unity," and his followers refer to themselves as *ahl at tawhiid*, "the people of unity," or *muwahhidun* ("unitarians"). Western scholars refer to the form of Islam practiced in Saudi Arabia as Wahhabi, but adherents rarely use this term, calling the movement Salafiyyah instead.

Through the twentieth and early twenty-first century, Shaykh Abd al-Aziz Ibn Baz, as well as his colleagues Salih b. Fawzan al-Fawzan and Abdallah Jabrin, have largely been responsible for the preservation of the Wahhabi legacy in the face of numerous challenges brought about by globalization and the spread of Western lifestyles and values.

HOUSES OF WORSHIP AND HOLY PLACES One of the most important holy sites in Saudi Arabia is Mecca's al-Masjid al-Haram, the Grand Mosque of Sanctuary the Haram. The Al-Mataf is a marble pavement around the mosque's inner sanctuary, and the Kaaba, the holiest shrine in Islam, is in the central courtyard of the mosque. The sacred well of Zamzam is located in the mosque as well.

Medina, second only to Mecca as a pilgrimage city, is home to the Prophet's Mosque. According to tradition, Muhammad built the mosque himself as a prototype for all subsequent mosques. The Prophet is buried inside the mosque, as are Abu Bakr and Umar, the first two caliphs.

WHAT IS SACRED? The Saudi Arabian notion of sacredness is complex. Wahhabi Islam adheres to the strictest interpretation of the Koran and stresses the absolute uniqueness and oneness (unity) of Allah. For this reason it forbids worshiping any object, personage, or locality as sacred. This construal of sacredness, however, raises certain dilemmas. For example, to refer to the kingdom as a sacred land would raise objections, despite the fact that it is considered a preserve of Islam that must be guarded against the intrusion of Western values, modernity, and other non-Muslim influences. Similarly, to refer to sites such as Mecca and Medina as sacred would evoke protest, and yet these are holy cities and centers for pilgrimage that possess great significance in the history of Islam. The Koran is considered sacred, not as an object but because therein reside the words of the one God.

HOLIDAYS AND FESTIVALS The principal officially observed Muslim religious festivals in Saudi Arabia are Ramadan, when people fast between sunrise and sunset, and Id al-Fitr, celebrated at the end of Ramadan, when people give gold coins and new clothes to children in the family. At Id al-Adha, held at the end of the hajj, Saudis ritually sacrifice a sheep, camel, or goat and distribute the meat to the poor in the community.

MODE OF DRESS Saudi Muslims are conservative and adhere to traditional dress codes. Women wear a black *abaya*, a long, flowing, silky cloak that covers the head and drapes over the body to the ground. In urban settings most women wear a black cloth that covers their face completely. In the surrounding countryside women may wear a face cover that leaves the eyes exposed. Both types of veils are similar to those worn by women throughout the Arabian Gulf, with minor modifications. Some young women, however, wear just a *tarha*, a head scarf that covers their hair, and no veil. *Abayas* with embroidered trim have become fashionable among the younger generation, who often add such fashion accessories as Western-style designer shoes and purses.

Saudi men wear a *thoub* (a traditional long shirt) and a *gutra* (a white headdress) or a *shimagh* (a red-and-white checkered head covering). An *'iqal*, a black band that encircles the top of the head, holds the gutra in place. On formal occasions men wear a *mashlah*, a long, flowing, gauzy cloak trimmed with gold embroidery, on top of their *thoub*.

DIETARY PRACTICES Like Muslims in other countries, Saudi Muslims refrain from eating pork and observe fasting days. Saudi Arabia is one of the few Muslim countries that has completely banned not only the consumption of alcohol but also its importation into the country. Non-Muslims cannot buy alcoholic beverages in specialty stores as they can in some other Arab states.

RITUALS Saudi Arabian Muslims practice the same rituals as Muslims worldwide, including *shahadah* (profession of the faith), *salat* (prayer five times daily), *zakat* (gifts of alms to the poor), *sawm* (a fast during the month of Ramadan), and *hajj* to Mecca.

RITES OF PASSAGE Within a shared Islamic tradition, Saudi life cycle rituals vary considerably between rural and urban populations and between the indigenous Bedouin Arabs and different Muslim immigrant groups who came to the peninsula later. Births are joyous occasions sometimes celebrated with animal sacrifice. Traditionally the mother and her newborn baby are secluded from the gaze of strangers for 40 days after the birth. On the seventh day, the child is named in a ceremony called the *tasmia,* which marks the formation of the child's Muslim identity. Family members hug the child and whisper *"allahu akbar"* ("God is great") in its ear. All Saudi Muslim boys are circumcised, but the age of the initiate and the elaborateness of the ceremony varies among different groups. Learning to recite the Koran is another important childhood rite, indicating the child's full participation in the Islamic community.

Most Saudi marriages are arranged, and villagers and urban dwellers alike have elaborate prenuptial rituals in which the families of the bride and groom participate. The marriage contract is signed during a special ceremony officiated by a sheikh (a respected elder).

After a death the body is prepared quickly and is buried as soon as possible in an unmarked grave. Saudis do not visit the graves of their deceased relatives. A sheikh recites the Koran at the mosque as part of the burial sermon.

MEMBERSHIP Muslims do not actively proselytize in Saudi Arabia because all Saudis are Muslim. There are inducements, however, for members of the foreign population or of other Muslim groups (such as the Shia) to convert to Sunni Islam. For example, Saudi employers hire Muslims over non-Muslims, and foreign workers who convert obtain other employment and legal advantages more easily than those who are not Muslims.

Saudi patrons are keen to spread Islam overseas. Toward this end they have funded the construction of new mosques and *madrasahs* (Islamic religious schools) throughout the Islamic world. These efforts have been more cautious since the terrorist attacks in the United States on 11 September, 2001, however; the adverse attention from the Western media and the pressure from American politicians concerned by the direct involvement of so many Saudi nationals in the attacks have prompted the Saudi government to pay closer attention to the Islamists inside Saudi Arabia and to address questions concerning Saudi internal security.

SOCIAL JUSTICE All Saudis attempt to fulfill their Islamic duty to the poor and needy through *al-zakat,* or obligatory almsgiving. Saudi Muslims have organized a number of charities to provide services to needy Muslims around the world. Since the 2001 terrorist attacks in the United States, however, allegations that Saudi-sponsored charities had connections to terrorist organizations have brought such activities under both Saudi and international scrutiny.

SOCIAL ASPECTS Modern Saudi families deviate little from traditional Islamic social mores and obligations. In marriage the husband is head of the household and chief provider, and the wife is the family's caretaker and household manager. Although women are encouraged to pursue professions in medicine, education, and business, they are still expected to meet all their family obligations while maintaining their professional life. Under Shari'ah (Islamic law) women are not permitted to petition for divorce, but informal channels enable women to obtain divorces: The woman returns to her paternal household, and her family exerts pressure on the husband to grant a divorce. Birth control is readily available over the counter; abortion, however, is strictly forbidden.

POLITICAL IMPACT Because Islam is the political as well as the spiritual basis of the state, it has had enormous political impact in Saudi Arabia. Shari'ah is the law of the land. King Fahd bin Abdul Aziz, who has ruled Saudi Arabia since 1982, adopted the title Guardian of the Two Holy Mosques, emphasizing the spiritual legitimacy of his political role. The ulama (religious leaders) also wield considerable political influence: Legislation is based on their legal opinions and rulings.

In November 1979 Saudi Sunni militants occupied the Grand Mosque in Mecca in the country's first modern Muslim fundamentalist uprising. The militants denounced the government for corruption and immorality and called for its overthrow. Since then King Fahd's government has relied on religion to legitimize its activities, obtaining *fatwas* (religious decrees) from the ulama for support.

Religious intolerance has also increased. For decades Christians among the foreign work force have held discreet services inside compounds and private homes without disturbance. In the 1990s, after the first Gulf War, religious conservatives among the ulama in Saudi Arabia pressured the government for more repressive measures against non-Muslims, targeting Indian and Southeast Asian Christian communities more often than European or American Christians. *Mutawwiin* (state volunteers) cracked down on non-Muslims, breaking up privately held religious services and detaining and deporting a number of people.

CONTROVERSIAL ISSUES Saudi monarchs have had to balance the requirements of modernity and the expansion of political, economic, and educational programs with the concerns of a conservative Islamic base. The second Gulf War, a weak economy that cannot provide jobs for a growing population, and the perception of greed and corruption among the Saudi royal family have led to an increase in regional and sectarian resentments and Islamic radicalism. Salafi (the ultrafundamentalist element of Islam in Saudi Arabia; Muslims who long for a return to the kind of pristine Islamic society that Muhammad established) and other conservatives have urged a return to a strict form of government, one incompatible with Western democratic ideals and tending toward anti-American feeling. Moderates stress the need for greater democracy, gender equality, and individual human rights. Members of the royal family are divided in their views on this issue and are under pressure from American demands to curb the influence of the conservatives.

Another controversial issue that is highly publicized in the Western media is gender inequality. Women are excluded from professions that would require them to work in public or alongside male coworkers. Saudi women work in such fields as girl's education, family medicine, and dentistry; in business and banking they are assigned to offices that serve only women. Women are also prohibited from driving automobiles. This curtails women's movement and poses many problems, and there is considerable discussion in Saudi society about ways to do away with the regulation.

CULTURAL IMPACT Islam has had a considerable impact on all aspects of Saudi culture. Restrictions imposed on imagery have resulted in an emphasis on poetry and oral narrative. Many Saudis enthusiastically recite poems and listen to oral narratives about Bedouin tribal culture and important historical events. On special public occasions, Bedouin tribesmen engage in sword dances to the accompaniment of beating drums. Women dance, too, but usually in the privacy of their own homes and only in the company of other women.

Islamic religious calligraphy has developed into a highly refined art form in Saudi Arabia. Some of the finest examples of such calligraphy appear in the classical manuscripts and the many resplendent copies of the Koran.

The impact of Islam is clearly evident in architecture. The mosque in Medina, said to have been built by Muhammad himself, has served as the prototype for all other mosques in the Islamic world. The Arabian mosque includes a large courtyard and an enclosed sanctuary, with arcades supporting the roof, and usually has minarets in the corners. Walls, domes, and ceilings are covered with geometric and floral forms and stylized Arabic script on glazed tiles.

Saudi Arabia has no movie theaters, but videotapes are widely available for private viewing. Before such videotapes are marketed, however, local distributors must check their content and censor them to meet the government's moral criteria. Government television channels air not only local productions but also programs from elsewhere in the Arab world and the West; most programs are censored for content. Globalization has brought Western culture, music, and movies to Saudi Arabia, and these have particularly influenced the younger generation. Many families have satellite television access and are able to receive all varieties of uncensored programming direct from broadcasters around the world. Similarly, the Internet and E-mail provide Saudis access to a wide range of information and software programs that are not available through local outlets. Conservatives, who view the intrusion of Western ideas and arts with suspicion, are openly critical of the changes brought about by the information revolution.

Other Religions

Sizable communities of guest workers in Saudi Arabia, most engaged in temporary contract jobs, are Christian. While these communities retain their own ethnic and cultural affiliations, they may not practice their religions publicly or build houses of worship, such as churches or temples. Moreover, they must abide by the Islamic codes of behavior while in public. Christians hold services in private homes. Proselytization by non–Sunni Muslims is a criminal offense.

Like the majority of Saudis, Shia Muslim communities celebrate Eid al-Adha (the Feast of the Sacrifice) and Eid al-Fitr (the end of Ramadan). In the eastern city of Qatif and the southern region of Najran, where a small number of Ismailis Shias (members of a Shia subgroup) live, Shiites may also observe their own holy day of Ashura, commemorating the martyrdom of the Prophet's grandson, Husayn, but they are banned from performing the passion plays and holding the public marches and displays of self-flagellation that accompany Ashura elsewhere.

Deborah S. Akers

See Also Vol. I: *Islam, Shiism, Sunnism*

Bibliography

Doran, Michael Scott. "The Saudi Paradox." *Foreign Affairs* 83, no. 1 (2004): 35–51.

Doumato, Eleanor Abdella. *Getting God's Ear: Women, Islam, and Healing in Saudi Arabia and the Gulf.* New York: Columbia University Press, 2000.

Esposito, John L. "Political Islam and Gulf Security." In *Political Islam.* Edited by John L. Esposito. Boulder, Colo.: Lynne Reinner Press, 1997.

Habib, John. *Ibn Saud's Warriors of Islam.* Leiden: E.J. Brill, 1978.

al-Juhany, Uwaidah. *Najd before the Salafi Reform Movement: Social, Political, and Religious Conditions during the Three Centuries Preceding the Rise of the Saudi State.* Reading, England: Ithaca Press, 2002.

al-Rasheed, Munerah. *Politics in an Arabian Oasis: The Rashidi Tribal Dynasty.* London: I.B. Tauris, 1991.

Rentz, George. "Al-Arab Djazirat." In *Encyclopedia of Islam.* Edited by B. Lewis. Leiden: E.J. Brill, 1978.

al-Yassini, Ayman. *Religion and the State in the Kingdom of Saudi Arabia.* Boulder, Colo.: Westview Press, 1982.

Senegal

POPULATION 10,589,571

MUSLIM 94 percent

ROMAN CATHOLIC 4.9 percent

AFRICAN TRADITIONAL RELIGIONS 1 percent

PROTESTANT 0.1 percent

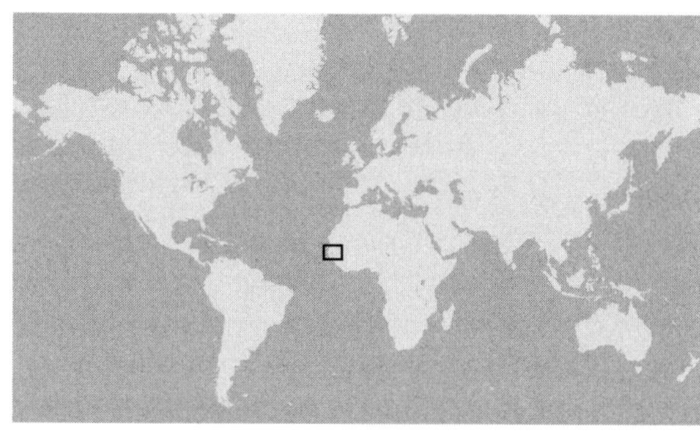

Country Overview

INTRODUCTION Situated on the Atlantic coast of West Africa, with its northern border in the Sahel (the region at the edge of the Sahara), the Republic of Senegal has historically bridged the Arab culture of North Africa and the cultural traditions of the South. The country has witnessed continuous migrations from prehistory to the present and has been a "melting pot" for many different ethnic groups: Wolof, Sereer, Pulaar, Manden, Joola, Basari, Baynuk, Manjak, and (since the beginning of the twentieth century) Lebanese.

Surrounded by Mauritania (to the north), Mali (to the east), and Guinea and Guinea-Bissau (to the south), Senegal is characterized by tropical rainforest in the south, grass and shrub savanna across a central band, and short-grass steppe in the north. Although its economy is largely agricultural, Senegal is a becoming increasingly urban: 47 percent of the population lives in cities, half of that in the capital city of Dakar.

The large majority of Senegalese are Sunni Muslims. North African Berbers converted to Islam in the eighth century, and by the ninth century Berbers on the north shore of the Senegal River had also become Muslim, bringing Islam into Senegal. In the middle of the fifteenth century, Portuguese navigators visited Senegal's coast and created such trading centers as Saint-Louis (established in 1659) in the north and Gorée, on an island near the capital city of Dakar. Controlled in turn by the Portuguese, Dutch, British, and French, these centers became important ports in the transatlantic slave trade; Gorée, the last stop on their route to the Americas, was "the door of no return" for many enslaved Africans. European contact brought Christianity to the region, but opposition to the subsequent French colonization (the French colonial administration took over in 1885) prompted an accelerated and massive conversion to Islam.

Few Senegalese identify themselves as adherents of traditional African religions. Alin Sitoe Jatta (died in 1943), a woman priest and prophet of the ancient Joola belief system, was a prominent figure during the colonial period and has become a Senegalese symbol of both the spirituality of ancient religions and the resistance to French colonial rule. She was arrested by the French administration and reportedly died during deportation.

Since independence from France in 1960, Senegal has been a multiparty democratic republic. Lèopold Sèdar Senghor, the first Senegalese president (served 1960–1980), was a Catholic; Abdou Diouf, the second president (served 1980–2000), and President Abdoulaye Wade, who defeated Diouf in 2000, are both Muslims.

RELIGIOUS TOLERANCE After it became independent from France in 1960, Senegal adopted a constitution proclaiming the secularity of the state, a principle that has survived all constitutional changes. In particular, the constitution stipulates that no political party may be based on a religious or ethnic platform.

Major Religion

ISLAM

DATE OF ORIGIN Ninth century C.E.
NUMBER OF FOLLOWERS 9.9 million

HISTORY Islam reached northern Senegal around the ninth century. The king of Tekrûr (a territory in the valley of the Senegal River) converted to Islam and by the time of his death in 1040 had adopted Muslim law for his kingdom. Also early in the eleventh century the Almoravids militarily imposed an orthodox and puritanical Islam on the Berber tribes and the populations living in the Sahelian region of West Africa. This campaign accelerated conversions to the new faith. As Islam spread southward, Wolof and Pulaar scholars founded learning centers that flourished, disseminating Islamic knowledge and practices.

At the end of the eighteenth century and throughout the nineteenth century, French colonialism brought about the collapse of traditional Senegalese kingdoms and the disruption of their social order. The Senegalese people were moved to follow the religious leadership of local Senegalese masters known as *shaykhs* or *seriñ* (*ceerno*), who headed Sufi mystical orders. These orders provided converts with the social structure of an organized fraternity, some education in the Muslim religion, and a religious center where periodical gatherings took place.

Senegalese Muslims belong to the Sufi brotherhoods (or mystical paths) known as the Qadiriyya (the path of Abd al Qadir Jîlânî, who died in the eleventh century in Baghdad), the Tijjaniyya (the path of Abul Abbass Ahmad al-Tijjanî, who died in 1815 in Fez, Morocco), the Muridiyya, and the Laayeen. The latter two orders are among Senegal's contributions to Sufism. The Tijjaniyya is the most important order in Senegal; its several branches are under the leadership of different religious families. Of the four systems of interpreting Muslim Law (the Maliki, the Hanafi, the Shafiíi, and the Hanbali), all founded in the ninth century by Arab scholars, Senegalese Muslims follow the Maliki.

Senegalese Muslims belonging to the brotherhood of the Muridiyya wait to enter a mausoleum in Touba, Senegal. AP/WIDE WORLD PHOTOS.

EARLY AND MODERN LEADERS The Kunti religious family, who came originally from Mauritania, provides leadership for the Qadiriyya Sufi order. The center for the order in Senegal is the village of Ndiassane.

El Hadj Malick Sy (1855–1922), the founder of the main branch of the Tijjaniyya order, settled in Tivaouane in 1902. The Senegalese city became the center of the order, and many Tijjani Muslims make pilgrimages to visit Malick Sy's shrine. Abdullahi Niasse, another Tijjani master, settled in Kaolack, the hub of the colonial peanut economy, which became the center of Niasse's branch of the order. The descendants of Malick Sy and Niasse are still the main leaders and religious authorities of the Tijjaniyya order.

The *shaykh* Ahmadu Bamba Mbacke (1853–1927) created his own path, recognizing the Prophet as his only spiritual master. He founded the Muridiyya order and called himself Khadimou Rasûl, "servant of the

Prophet." He also founded the city of Touba and began building a great mosque there, later finished by his sons and successors at the head of the order. The French administration suspected Bamba of preparing for a religious war against colonial rule and arrested him in 1895, deporting him to Gabon. Members of the Muridiyya order all over Senegal, especially those in Touba, commemorate the date of his return in 1902 every year in a celebration known in Wolof as the Magal. The shrine of Bamba, located in the mosque, is now the spiritual center of Touba. The city has become the second largest in Senegal after Dakar.

Seydinâ Limamu Laye (1843–1909), founder of the Laayeen movement, declared himself the promised Mahdi, the expected Messiah of some Muslim traditions. Limamu Laye won most of his followers from among Lebu fishermen in the Dakar area and from the traditional village of Yoff, now incorporated in the town of Dakar and the Layeen order's historical and spiritual center.

MAJOR THEOLOGIANS AND AUTHORS Senegal's main Muslim theologians are the founders of the four Sufi orders. They most often passed on their ethical, theological, and mystical teachings in poetry, as the form is easier to memorize. Thus, references are often made in Senegalese Islam to the *khassaids* (an Arabic word for poems adopted in local languages) of these *shaykhs*—for example, "Masalik al-Jinan" (The Path to Paradise) by Bamba or "Nuniyya" (a poem named after the Arabic letter "nun") by Malick Sy.

HOUSES OF WORSHIP AND HOLY PLACES Senegal has many mosques, the most important being the Great Mosque in Dakar (built in Moroccan style) and the mosques in Touba and Tivaouane, considered the main houses of worship for the Muridiyya and the Tijjaniyya Sufi orders. Followers of the orders also often visit the shrines of Bamba, Malick Sy, and their deceased descendants in these same cities.

WHAT IS SACRED? Senegalese Muslims consider Mecca the only sacred place. Every year about five thousand Senegalese go there on pilgrimage, one of the five obligations of Islam. Before or after the pilgrimage, they often visit the city of Medina, home of the Prophet's shrine and, along with Jerusalem, a holy place for the Islamic faith.

HOLIDAYS AND FESTIVALS Like Muslims around the world, Senegalese Muslims celebrate Id al-Adha, commemorating Abraham's sacrifice of a ram in place of his son, and Id al-Fitr, marking the end of Ramadan, the holy month of fasting. Senegalese Muslims also celebrate holidays more specific to Sufi Islam. The Mawlûd (Id al-Mawlid), the anniversary of the Prophet's birthday, is honored in a celebration known as the Gamu that involves religious chants around the country, especially in the religious centers of the different Sufi orders. The most important Gamu is celebrated by the Tijjani in Tivaouane. The Muridiyya order celebrates the Magal, the return of the order's founder from exile, as its own specific holiday, and the Laayeen commemorate the "call" of their founder every year.

MODE OF DRESS Senegalese Muslims have adopted the boubou, a large, long robe that is often embroidered, especially the women's boubous. Men sometimes wear hats and women wear headscarves that match their boubous. Senegalese Muslims feel the headscarves satisfy the Islamic requirement of modest dress; Senegalese women do not usually wear veils.

DIETARY PRACTICES Like Muslims worldwide, Senegalese Muslims refrain from eating pork and drinking alcohol and only eat meat butchered according to Islamic halal practices.

RITUALS Muslims in Senegal pray five times a day facing east toward Mecca, like Muslims elsewhere.

RITES OF PASSAGE Senegalese Muslims circumcise male children when they are seven or younger. Certain ethnic groups, such as the Pulaar and the Manden, believe female circumcision to have significance in Islam, but the majority of Senegalese do not follow the practice. Senegalese feminist movements, human rights nongovernmental organizations, and activists against female circumcision, backed by some international pressure, pushed for a ban on the practice. In 1999 the parliament voted to ban it, and the government signed the ban into law.

MEMBERSHIP Membership in Islam in Senegal, as elsewhere in the Muslim world, is determined by a profession of faith: "There is no God but God, and Muhammad is His prophet." The formula by which one is accepted into a given Sufi order varies, but the meaning is the same: The marabout confers membership on the disciple and gives him the blessings attached to that membership.

SOCIAL JUSTICE In Senegal the egalitarian message of Islam has led to the questioning of certain traditional hierarchies that define caste systems among many different ethnic groups. The castes have always corresponded to traditional division of labor: Smiths or people whose ancestors were smiths form a caste, as do weavers, woodcutters, griots (storytellers and musical entertainers who serve as keepers of the knowledge of history and genealogies), and others. The Laayeen Sufi order has addressed the issue of equality most directly—for example, by encouraging intercaste marriages.

SOCIAL ASPECTS In Senegal a secular legal system coexists with Islamic customs concerning marriage, divorce, and inheritance. Muslims generally follow Muslim law in these matters. Afterward the secular legal system records the decisions made according to Muslim Law.

POLITICAL IMPACT Islam is a strong presence in the public sphere in Senegal. In the same way the colonial administration had to come to terms with the Sufi orders and try to gain their support, successive Senegalese governments since independence from France in 1960 have made an art of attending to Muslim needs and concerns. The state cannot ignore religion, and the Sufi orders in Senegal, not being fundamentalist, do not advocate Islam in place of secularism. Two of the three presidents of the republic since independence have been Muslim.

CONTROVERSIAL ISSUES A controversy over the Family Code, established in 1972 with the objective of defining the legal framework for marriages, divorces, parental responsibility, and inheritance, has challenged secularism in Senegal. Some Muslim groups complain that the code, which encourages the trend toward ending polygamy, goes against the prescriptions of Islam; they call for the state to refrain from introducing legislation in family matters that could conflict with Islamic law. Other Muslim groups—intellectuals and women's groups in particular—insist that the government should improve existing legislation to mandate equality of roles and responsibilities between men and women. These groups argue that since the dawn of Islam in the seventh century, the ultimate aim of the Islamic faith has been to dramatically improve the situation of women through a progressive interpretation of religious law.

CULTURAL IMPACT Islam in Senegal has inspired the development of important learning centers called *daara.* Islamization has also aided in the development of Senegalese languages as literary languages. In the Pulaar, Manden, and Wolof languages, Arabic script was used to capture a rich oral tradition as literature. Sufi praise-poetry, often chanted, is the most pervasive literary genre.

Islam has also had an impact on popular painting. *Suweer* (from the French *sous verre,* meaning "under glass"), the art of reverse painting on glass, was imported from the Middle-Eastern regions of the Islamic world to illustrate the religious imagery of the Senegalese people. Senegalese artists use the technique to portray those they venerate as saints, such as Ahmad al-Tijjanî, Shaykh Ahmadu Bamba, and El Hadj Malick Sy.

Other Religions

Though a small minority of 519,000, Senegalese Catholics have a vibrant community and a dynamic church. The Portuguese brought Catholicism to Senegal in the middle of the fifteenth century. As the cities of Saint-Louis and Gorée developed during the seventeenth and eighteenth centuries, a population of *signares* (from the Portuguese *senhora,* the name given to African women married to European men) and people of mixed race became socially important. Christian by their association with the Europeans, they constituted the core of the non-European Christian community. At the end of the nineteenth and throughout the twentieth century, vigorous evangelization led to important conversions in the regions inhabited by the Sereer and the Joola ethnic groups.

Though often perceived as an expression of European colonialism and cultural imperialism, the Senegalese Catholic Church has been engaged, since the country's independence from France in 1960, in "Africanizing" its message in the progressive and more pluralistic spirit of the Second Vatican Council (1962–65). In 1962 Pope John XXIII elected Monseigneur Hyacinthe Thiandoum (born in 1921), a native Senegalese, to replace Monseigneur Marcel Lefebvre, a French citizen, as metropolitan archbishop of Dakar. In 1976 Monseigneur Thiandoum was made cardinal priest. The gospel has been translated into and is often preached in local languages, while church choirs sing traditional Senegalese music and chants. Catholic religious music also makes use of Senegalese modes of movement and hand clapping and such local instruments as the tam-tam, kora (a kind of harp), and *balafon* (an African xylophone).

The state observes Christian holidays, including Christmas, Easter, and All Saints Day, as public holidays. Every year since 1888 thousands of Senegalese Catholics have made a pilgrimage on the Monday of Pentecost to a famous Marian shrine in the village of Poponguine, where they gather to address prayers to the Black Virgin, also known as Our Lady of Deliverance.

Protestants number a mere 10,000 in Senegal. Missionaries, mostly from France, brought Protestantism to Senegal around 1861.

Senegalese who declare themselves followers of traditional African religions number 100,000 or fewer. The date of origin of local religions is unknown. Ethnological evidence indicates connections between Senegalese beliefs and cosmogonies that existed in ancient Egypt. Senegalese indigenous religions posit the existence of one supreme being, as well as a chain of being that connects the living to their dead ancestors, who acquire the status of protective spirits, called *tuur* in Wolof and *pangol* in Sereer. These religions mainly resulted in egalitarian societies, with a diffuse authority and no centralization.

Because of the fairly ancient presence of Islam and the mass conversion to Sufi orders, ancient African religions in contemporary Senegal are rapidly disappearing as religions, though certain practices connected with them survive. Among first-generation converts to Christianity or Islam, traditional practices sometimes persist—for example, ancient healing methods using herbs, exorcisms (known as *ndëpp* in Wolof), and incantations, often accompanied by sacrifices of bulls or rams to the *tuur,* to ask for a propitious rainy season. Traditional healers and soothsayers known as *saltige* remain influential even among the Christianized or Islamized Sereer.

Christian and Muslim Joola still practice male circumcision as a rite of initiation and still honor a particular sacred wood where the ancient rites are performed. Most indigenous religions have a period of ritual initiation, when youth are taught to become accomplished men and women who live in harmony with their society. Besides the sacred wood, other natural places serve traditional religions as places of worship—for example, certain trees (the baobab in particular) and certain beaches where sacrifices are performed to honor the spirits living in the ocean.

Souleymane Bachir Diagne

See Also Vol. 1: *Islam, Sunnism*

Bibliography

Baum, Robert Martin. *Shrines of the Slave Trade: Diola Religion and Society in Precolonial Senegambia.* New York: Oxford University Press, 1999.

Cruise O'Brien, Donal. *Saints and Politicians: Essays on the Organization of an Islamic Brotherhood.* Cambridge: Cambridge University Press, 1975.

Diop, Momar Coumba, ed. *Senegal: Essays in Statecraft.* Dakar: Codesria, 1999.

Linares, Olga F. *Power, Prayer, and Production: The Jola of Casamance, Senegal.* New York: Cambridge University Press, 1992.

Peter, Mark. *The Wild Bull and the Sacred Forest: Form, Meaning, and Change in Senegambian Initiation Masks.* New York: Cambridge University Press, 1992.

Robinson, David. *The Holy War of Umar Tal: The Western Sudan in the Mid-nineteenth Century.* Oxford: Clarendon Press, 1988.

———. *Paths of Accommodation: Muslim Societies and French Colonial Authorities in Senegal and Mauritania, 1880–1920.* Athens: Ohio University Press; Oxford: James Currey, 2000.

Westerlund, David, and Eva Evers Rosander, eds. *African Islam and Islam in Africa: Encounters between Sufis and Islamists.* London: Hurst and Company, 1997.

Serbia and Montenegro

POPULATION 10,656,929

SERBIAN ORTHODOX CHURCH 68 percent

MUSLIM 20 percent

ROMAN CATHOLIC 5 percent

PROTESTANT 2 percent

OTHER 5 percent

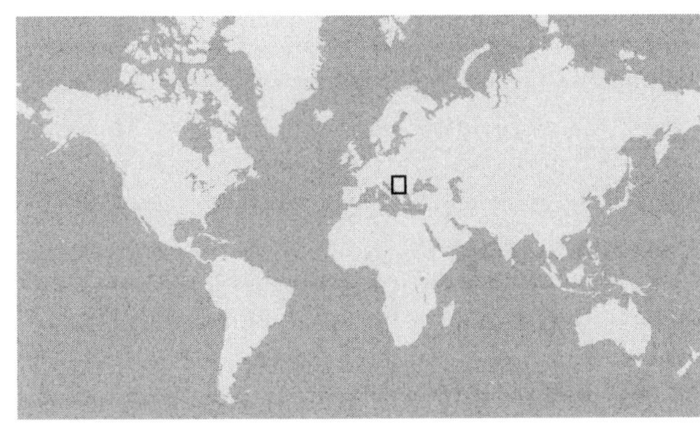

Country Overview

INTRODUCTION Serbia and Montenegro, a country in southeastern Europe, was created in 2003 from the eastern part of the former Yugoslavia. At the country's southwestern tip is the Adriatic Sea, while surrounding the remaining border are seven other countries: Bosnia and Herzegovina, as well as Croatia, to the west; Hungary to the north; Romania to the northeast; Bulgaria to the east; and Macedonia and Albania to the south.

In a relatively short period of time, from 1918 to 2003, the region was politically transformed several times. The Kingdom of Serbs, Croats, and Slovenes was established in 1918, and its successor, the Kingdom of Yugoslavia, existed from 1929 until its collapse in 1941. The socialist state of the Federal People's Republic of Yugoslavia was formed in 1943 and was officially proclaimed with a constitution in 1946. This state was renamed the Socialist Federal Republic of Yugoslavia in 1963 and existed until just after the fall of the Soviet Union in 1991. The Federal Republic of Yugoslavia, which consisted of the Republic of Serbia and the Republic of Montenegro, lasted from 1992 until 2003, when it was renamed Serbia and Montenegro. Within this union Serbians accounted for a larger percentage of the population than Montenegrins. Although a census of all the territory of Serbia and Montenegro had not been conducted as of 2003, the population was estimated to be 10,656,929.

Serbia and Montenegro bears three main religious traditions: Orthodox Christianity, prevalent throughout the country; Islam, concentrated in the southern regions; and Roman Catholicism, concentrated in the northern regions. The Serbian Orthodox Church has significantly influenced the development of Serbian and Montenegrin national identity and the history of the country.

Islam arrived in Serbia as a result of Ottoman conquest in the fourteenth century. Following the introduction of Islam into the region, intense antagonism developed between Christians and Muslims, which has marked the country, especially the predominantly Muslim Kosovo region, in modern times. Since the beginning of the twentieth century, population growth among Muslims has been high, while Christian populations have diminished, especially after World War II. Be-

A woman is baptized by an Orthodox priest in Montenegro. Since 1990 a great number of adults have been baptized in church. © BOJAN BRECELJ/CORBIS.

tween 1990 and 1995 separatist tendencies grew stronger, pushing Yugoslavia into civil war. During the conflict, it is estimated that nearly 800 Serbian Orthodox parishes, monasteries, churches, and chapels were damaged or destroyed. Additionally, 300 mosques and other Islamic sacred buildings were destroyed or damaged in Kosovo alone during 1998 and 1999.

RELIGIOUS TOLERANCE Officially Serbia and Montenegro is a secular state that guarantees freedom of worship and prohibits any religious discrimination. In the 1990s, as Serbia and Montenegro moved away from a state bias toward atheism, allowing religion to become more prominent, disparate religious communities have been challenged to remain tolerant of one another. Further, although individual freedom is respected, people are expected to remain faithful to their birth religion. Converting to another religion is considered treason. As an extension of the Orthodox Church, the Serbian Orthodox Church maintains that unity among various Christian groups can be established if all return to the Orthodox tradition.

Major Religion

SERBIAN ORTHODOX CHURCH

DATE OF ORIGIN 1219 C.E.

NUMBER OF FOLLOWERS 7.2 million

HISTORY The conversion of Serbians from the Old Slavic religion to Christianity took place between the seventh and eighth centuries, following the influences of Rome and Constantinople. This conversion was accelerated by brothers Saint Cyril (c. 827–69 C.E.) and Saint Methodius (c. 825–84 C.E.), and their disciples, who translated Christian religious services from Greek into the Old Slavic language. During the early ninth century, Serbs marked the border zone between the Byzantine and Roman spheres of influence.

The Serbian Orthodox Church was established in 1219 when Saint Sava (c. 1176–c. 1236) was consecrated the first archbishop (1219–35). From that period until the Turkish conquest in 1389 and the collapse of Serbia in 1459, the Serbian Orthodox Church flourished within the Byzantine cultural circle, influencing every aspect of life and serving to uphold Serbian cultural and spiritual heritage. At the same time, an independent branch of the Serbian Orthodox Church existed in the Austrian Empire. Following Turkish rule in 1459, the Serbian patriarch was abolished, though in 1557 it was reestablished in Peć, only to be abolished again in 1766 when the church came under the control of the patriarch of Constantinople. In 1879, after the creation of an independent Serbian state, an autocephalous (ecclesiastically independent) Serbian Orthodox Church was created in the kingdom of Serbia. The title of patriarch was renewed in 1920, uniting the church under one head (with residence in Belgrade) and embracing all Orthodox Christians in the Kingdom of Serbs, Croats, and Slovenes. The new patriarch was Dimitrije Pavlović (reigned 1920–30).

Between World War I and World War II, the Serbian Orthodox Church was the state church. During the Second World War hundreds of thousands of Orthodox Serbs were killed in concentration camps. Among those imprisoned were Orthodox clergy, including Partriarch Gavrilo Dožić. Following Allied and Soviet liberation in 1944, the country came under atheistic Communist rule, and efforts were made to destroy religion. Serbian Patriarch Pavle, the former bishop of Raška and Prizren, was elected at the end of 1990 and presided over the Serbian Orthodox Church throughout the disintegration of Yugoslavia and during the civil war and its aftermath. At the beginning of the twenty-first century, the Serbian Orthodox Church had 39 dioceses in Serbia and in the diaspora.

EARLY AND MODERN LEADERS In 1219 Rastko Nemanjić, known as Saint Sava, became the first archbishop of the Serbian Orthodox Church, and he is considered to be its greatest leader. In addition to establishing the national Serbian Orthodox Church, Saint Sava instituted the so-called Serbian *slava,* a custom honoring a family patron saint. This tradition served as a reminder of Serbian national identity throughout the five centuries of Turkish rule, and it helped to preserve faith throughout a half century of atheistic Communist rule. Saint Sava is also highly regarded for his writings, which many consider to be seminal works of medieval Serbian literature.

Patriarch Macarius (reigned 1557–70) is celebrated as the reorganizer of the Serbian patriarchate under the Turks. Metropolitan Mihajlo Jovanović (1859–98) of Belgrade initiated liturgical unification. Patriarch Dimitrije Pavlović, who served as metropolitan from 1905 to 1920, became the first patriarch of the united Serbian Orthodox Church, presiding from 1920 to 1930. Patriarch Pavle Stojčević became patriarch in 1990. Pavle's special concern has been peace and reconciliation among the people of Serbia and Montenegro.

MAJOR THEOLOGIANS AND AUTHORS Saint Sava initiated the development of a Serbian national literature and was the author of *The Life of Saint Simeon.* At the Resava Monastery secular ruler Stefan Lazarević (1377–1427) established the Resava school for translating and copying texts into Serbian. In 1791 Stefan Stratimirović (1757–1836) founded a theological seminary in Sremski Karlovci. Serbian theologians of the nineteenth century include Metropolitan Mihailo, who wrote *The History of the Serbian Church,* and Bishop Nikodim Milaš (1845–1955), author of books on church canon law. Twentieth-century theologians include Bishop Nikolaj Velimirović, who is noted for his sermons and poetry, and Archimandrite Justin Popović, who is recognized for his dogmatics and theological philosophy. The most influential contemporary theologians are Serb bishops and metropolitans who have tried to restore the power of the Serbian Orthodox Church in society.

HOUSES OF WORSHIP AND HOLY PLACES Serbian Orthodox churches are highly ornamental and are decorated with gold, silver, precious stones, and polished marble in multiple colors, as well as icons and crosses. Like other Eastern Orthodox churches, the iconostasis, or partition that separates the altar from the nave of the church, has three doors.

Studenica Monastery, built in the twelfth century (1183–91), is an important monastery in Serbia. Chilandar Monastery, which was built in 1198, is located in Mount Athos, an independent Orthodox Christian territory situated in what is modern Greece. Chilander Monastery has served as a center of Serbian literary, cultural, and educational work for centuries. Monastery Manasija, known originally as Resava, was built from 1406 to 1418; it is covered in frescoes and is an important church in the Moravian school of architecture. Ostrog, a seventeenth-century monastery built in a stone cave in Montenegro, is a pilgrimage site. Saint George's Church in Oplenac, which was built in 1912, is decorated with elaborate mosaics.

WHAT IS SACRED? In the beginning of the thirteenth century, the Serbian Orthodox Church established its own cult of saints and canonization dates. One of the earliest Serbian saints was the father of Saint Sava, Stefan Nemanja (reigned c. 1167–96), who organized the first Serbian state in the beginning of the twelfth century and founded Chilandar Monastery at Mount Athos.

Throughout its history the holy Council of Bishops has established a list of 54 Serbian saints whose liturgical services are contained in the book *Serbicon.* Orthodox adherents demonstrate their commitment to the saints by worshiping their images or relics.

HOLIDAYS AND FESTIVALS Significant Christian holidays are celebrated in the Serbian Orthodox Church. Most of the dates of observance are different, because the Serbian Church observes the Julian calendar. Each day in the Serbian Church is dedicated to a saint or a holy event, and, thus, there is a religious service for every day of the year. Additionally, each month has a liturgical book that contains specific services for every day of that month. All local churches in Serbia and Montenegro have their own special feast day called Church Patron's Day (*crkvena slava*). Each Serbian Orthodox family celebrates its holy protector, such as Archangel Michael, Saint Nicholas, Saint John the Baptist, or Saint George. Since time immemorial family members and relatives have come together to attend the cutting of the *slava* bread and to enjoy the festive meal.

MODE OF DRESS The Serbian Orthodox Church has preserved the style and form of the old liturgical vestments of Orthodox Christianity that date back to Byzantine times. Priest's vestments differ according to rank, and they reflect the hierarchical structure of the church. When the Turks occupied Serbian and Montenegrin areas in the fifteenth century, bishops served as lay Orthodox Christian rulers and dressed accordingly, wearing a *sakos,* or ruler's robe, and a *mitre,* or ruler's crown.

Contemporary practitioners are expected to dress with proper solemnity for church. Men go bareheaded, and women cover their heads and refrain from wearing makeup. It is not suitable to wear jeans, slippers, short skirts, or trousers or to have bare arms.

DIETARY PRACTICES Fasting in conjunction with some feast days is important in the Serbian Orthodox Church. Usually limited to water, vegetable oil, and fish, the fast involves abstention from such foods as meat, milk, and eggs. The church prescribes four seasons of fast per year (lasting several days or weeks): Lent, Mary's fast, Advent, and Peter's fast. Strict followers also are expected to fast every Wednesday and Friday. Traditionally, prior to taking Holy Communion, an adherent was expected to fast on water for seven days and prepare all food for the fast with water and no fat.

RITUALS *Slava,* a day devoted to worshiping the guardians and helpers of Serbian homes, churches, families, and towns, is the greatest annual holiday among Serbs and a specific feature of Serbian Orthodoxy. The rituals associated with this holiday date back to pre-Christian times, originating from family cults in the Old Slavic religion. As Serbia became Christianized, Saint Sava reformed the ritual, replacing the Serb's pagan gods with Christian saints.

During the *slava* ceremony, the parish priest, or the host of the household in special circumstances, performs the rite of cutting the *slava* bread and consecrating corn, which is a symbol of resurrection. After the priest cuts the bread crosswise and pours wine over it, all members of the household participate in turning the bread around and singing. Then the priest, along with the host, breaks the bread. Traditionally *slava* has been connected with rituals honoring the souls of departed family members.

As is common with other Eastern Orthodox churches, eucharistic rites are an essential part of the Serbian Orthodox Church. Celebrated on Sunday and on certain holidays, the Eucharist helps bind the community of followers.

RITES OF PASSAGE Before Communist rule, birth, marriage, and death records were kept by religious communities. In 1945 record books were taken away from the churches and given to the city councils. Since 1990, however, a great number of adults have been baptized in church, and couples have been increasingly married in church.

In Serbia and Montenegro the funeral rite is almost always performed by a priest. The memory rite, which is the service for the departed, takes place in a church or at a cemetery forty days after death, a half a year later, and a year later. Funeral rituals differ substantially from village to village and represent local traditions.

MEMBERSHIP The Serbian Orthodox Church is a national church to which membership is conferred by birth. The missionary purpose of the church has been to return Serbs to the faith and traditions of their ancestors, as well as to strengthen the faith of its nominal adherents. Most monasteries and churches maintain websites. The greatest missionary accomplishment of the Serbian Orthodox Church has been the reinstatement of catechism in public schools in 2001.

SOCIAL JUSTICE Traditionally the Serbian Orthodox Church has viewed poverty and suffering as a means toward reaching salvation. Through the centuries, monasteries, which were built by Serbian rulers and princes, have served as refuges in which monks, who have taken a vow of poverty, could follow a Christian ascetic life dedicated to learning and social work. In the past monasteries have had hospitals, orphanages, and schools for the poor, although no such social institutions existed in monasteries at the beginning of the twenty-first century.

SOCIAL ASPECTS The Serbian Orthodox Church aligns itself with the greater Eastern Orthodox Church on issues of marriage and family. The formation of a family through the sacrament of marriage is seen as an event influencing the destiny of both the couple and the church as an institution. Although the church encourages marriage as God's command, it also recommends monastic life as a particular path to serve God. A priest is allowed to marry but cannot marry a widow or a divorced woman, nor can a priest marry a second time. Bishops never marry, but widowers may become bishops or even patriarchs. Serbian Orthodox women serve traditional roles. Although women can study theology, they are not allowed to become priests, and they are forbidden to go behind the iconostasis in churches or to visit Mount Athos.

POLITICAL IMPACT While the government of Serbia and Montenegro is ostensibly secular, in practice the Serbian Orthodox Church has an overwhelming presence in national politics, and the church has acted to preserve Serbian national identity through its language and cultural heritage. As some Serbs embraced Islam between the fourteenth and nineteenth centuries, they essentially lost their Serbian national identity and became Bosniacs.

CONTROVERSIAL ISSUES The Serbian Orthodox Church forbids premarital sex. Abortion and contraception are frowned upon; however, in practice the church does not forbid abortions or punish those who have them. Homosexuality is considered a sin, and marriage between a homosexual couple or adoption by a homosexual couple is taboo.

CULTURAL IMPACT The impact of the Serbian Orthodox Church on Serbian culture began in the ninth century with the translations of Greek texts by the brothers Saint Cyril and Saint Methodius, who invented the Old Slavic alphabet *Glagoljica* and the Cyrillic alphabet. The most famous example of Serbian literature is the twelfth-century work Miroslavljev's Gospel, which includes the gospel readings for Sundays and holidays. Miroslavljev's Gospel was preserved in the Chilandar Monastery until 1896, when King Aleksandar Obrenovic received the work as a gift from Serbian monks, and it was later moved to the National Museum in Belgrade.

Serbian architecture can be classified according to three main styles: Rascian (twelfth century), Serbian-Byzantine (late thirteenth to fourteenth century), and Moravian (late fourteenth to mid-fifteenth century). Medieval Serbian monasteries and churches represent the greatest feats of Serbian architecture. The Temple of Saint Sava in Belgrade, which was finished in 2004, is the most impressive contemporary church building.

The music of the Serbian Orthodox Church developed through the centuries and is entirely vocal, differentiating it from secular music. Prominent Serbian Orthodox Church composers include Kornelije Stanković (1831–65) and Stevan Mokranjac (1856–1914).

Other Religions

Like the former Yugoslavia, Serbia and Montenegro is a state union of many nations and many religions. Within Serbia and Montenegro more than fifty religious communities are registered, reflecting the influences of both Western and Eastern traditions.

Having defeated the Serbian army on the Marica River in 1371, the Turks increased their presence in Serbia. Serbia was defeated in the Battle of Kosovo in 1389 and at Smederovo in 1459, after which the country succumbed to Turkish occupation. During Ottoman rule part of the Serbian Orthodox population converted to Islam. This conversion was, in principle, voluntary but not without various forms of pressure, as the Turks gave special privileges to Muslims. Between Serbia's independence from the Turks in the nineteenth century and the First World War, Islam was accepted in Serbia but held inferior status to Orthodoxy. During the twentieth century social changes, ethnic divisions, and wars divided the religious communities. With the disintegration of Yugoslavia in the 1990s, religious communities were divided further by the newly formed borders of Serbia and Montenegro.

At the start of the twenty-first century, the total number of Muslims in Serbia and Montenegro was estimated at more than two million. Except for those in Sandžak, the majority are of Albanian descent. Religious practices among Muslims in Serbia and Montenegro are similar to those in neighboring Bosnia and Herzegovina.

In the pre-Ottoman period there was significant correspondence between Orthodoxy and Roman Catholicism. Stefan Nemanja, the founder of Serbia's Nemanjic dynasty, and his son Saint Sava, the founder of the Serbian Orthodox Church, were baptized Roman Catholics. Until the time of Emperor Stephen Dusan (Dušan Silni; reigned 1331–55), Serbian rulers were crowned in Rome and maintained communication with the Vatican. Cultural relations flourished between Orthodox and Catholic denominations during this time, as both groups used the same Slavic liturgical language, as well as the *Glagoljica* and Cyrillic alphabets. Not until the fall of the Ottoman Empire did significant regional differences arise between Orthodox and Catholic churches in what became Serbia and Montenegro.

At the beginning of the twenty-first century, there were approximately 500,000 Roman Catholics in Serbia and Montenegro and about 65,000 Catholics in Kosovo, most of whom were Albanians. Catechization takes place at the church in the form of Sunday schools and sacraments.

Protestant Christianity began to spread into the northern Serbian province of Vojvodina in the 1550s.

Lutherans and Reformed Protestants were the first Protestant groups to appear as colonists in the late eighteenth century. They were organized among the ethnic Germans, Hungarians, and Slovaks and gained only occasional ethnic Serbian members. The largest Protestant congregations in modern Serbia and Montenegro still include the Slovak Lutheran Evangelical Church, with 40,000 members, and the Reformed Church, whose 16,000 members are mostly of Hungarian, Slovakian, and, to a much lesser extent, German ancestry. Although Lutherans and Reformed were the first Protestant groups in the area, the Christian Nazarene Community was the first Protestant organization to spread among the ethnic Serbian population. This congregation, however, began to decline in membership after World War I. The largest Protestant community in Serbia and Montenegro not organized according to ethnicity is the Seventh-day Adventist Church, which first arrived in Vojvodina in 1890. It has built over 200 churches, and by the twenty-first century the Seventh-day Adventist Church reported 20,000 members. Followers of other smaller churches and communities include Baptists, Pentecostals, and Brethren.

Zorica Kuburić

See Also Vol. I: *Christianity, Eastern Orthodoxy, Islam, Roman Catholicism*

Bibliography

Birviš, Aleksandar. "Obstacles to Dialogue from a Protestant Perspective." In *God in Russia, the Challenge of Freedom.* Edited by Aharon Linzey and Ken Kaisch. Lanham, Md.: University Press of America, 1999.

Bjelajac, Branko. *Protestantism u Srbiji.* Belgrade: Alfa and Omega, 2003.

Bremer, Tomas. "Role of the Church in a Pluralist Society." In *Democracy and Religion.* Edited by Goran Bašić and Silvo Devetak. Belgrade: ERC/ISCOMET, 2003.

Hussey, Joan. *The Orthodox Church in the Byzantine Empire.* Oxford: Clarendon Press, 1990.

"Savremena administracija." In *Enciklopedija pravoslavlja.* Edited by Dimitrije Kalezić. Belgrade: Savremena administracija, 2002.

Slijepčevic, Djoko. *Istorija Srpske Pravoslavne Crkve.* Belgrade: Beogradski izdavačko-grafički zavod, 1991.

Seychelles

POPULATION 80,600

CHRISTIANITY 95.9 percent

OTHER 4.1 percent

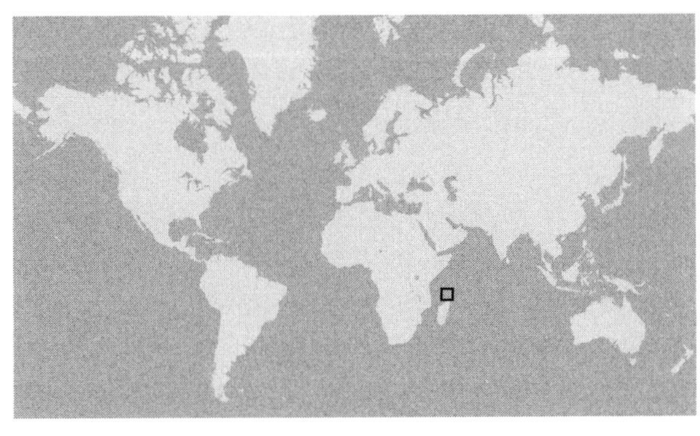

Country Overview

INTRODUCTION The Republic of Seychelles is a group of 86 small islands in the Indian Ocean about 700 miles northeast of Madagascar. Its land area is only 176 square miles (455 square kilometers). About half the islands are coral, while the other half are granite and mountainous.

The Seychelles are one of the most Christianized countries in the world. Catholics make up 86.6 percent of the population, Anglicans 6.8 percent, and other Christian groups 2.5 percent. Hindus, Buddhists, Muslims, and members of the Bahai faith account for the rest. Although not formally represented, African traditional beliefs are widely held. Pentacostals, Seventh-day Adventists, and Assemblies of God are among the fasting-growing churches.

Named for a controller-general of finance under Louis XV of France, the Seychelles were first settled by French planters around 1771 and were under French rule until ceded to Great Britain in 1814 as part of the Treaty of Paris. Saddled with islands they did not want to administer, the British left them in French hands. In 1903, however, the Seychelles became a British Crown Colony; it obtained its independence in 1976. Trade attracted Chinese to the islands, and after slavery was abolished in 1835, the Malabards from Mauritius and India arrived.

The population is 99 percent ethnically homogeneous of European, African, and Asian ancestry and speaks a Creole language based on French and African languages (with some Hindi and Malagasy words). English is the second official language, and French is the third.

RELIGIOUS TOLERANCE The Seychelle's constitution prohibits state identification with any one religion and provides for freedom of worship. Both the government and the population display a spirit of tolerance for different faiths. In May 2000, however, following criticism of a government policy that granted paid leave to members of the Bahai faith on their holy days (President France-Albert René's wife was Bahai), the government announced that civil servants of all faiths would receive paid leave on their holy days. The government also grants tax privileges to registered religious organizations and provides program time to different faiths on the national radio broadcasting service.

A Catholic bishop blesses the congregation during a ceremony in the Seychelles. © ZEN ICKNOW/CORBIS.

Major Religion

CHRISTIANITY

DATE OF ORIGIN 1768 C.E.

NUMBER OF FOLLOWERS 77,300

HISTORY Christianity in the Seychelles dates to the arrival of French Roman Catholic planters around 1770. During the 1830s the Church of England waged a half-hearted campaign to establish Protestantism in the islands, but these efforts had little effect. Nonetheless, the British government refused or ignored settler requests for a Catholic priest. In March 1851 a Savoyard Capuchin priest, Father Léon des Avanchers from Aden, arrived unannounced in Mahé, sparking a great revival among Catholics. Because Catholic baptisms and weddings were perceived as a threat, the British civil commissioner denied him the right to stay on the islands, citing his non-British status. Des Avanchers petitioned everyone, from his ecclesiastical superiors to Queen Victoria, and returned two years later.

Inspired by Des Avanchers, schools and churches were built across the archipelago, and until the government acquired mission schools in 1944, missionaries took charge of education. The colonial government continued to subsidize parochial schools, and it used public funds to pay for schools run by Catholic brothers and nuns—a source of anxiety among British taxpayers, especially Anglicans. As social consciousness increased in the 1950s and 1960s, criticism of missionaries and the colonial government intensified. Reflecting Catholic dominance in the country, a majority of government ministers have been Catholic since the Seychelles gained independence in 1976.

EARLY AND MODERN LEADERS Seychellois regard Father Léon des Avanchers as the founder of the Catholic Mission in the Seychelles. In the 1950s Archdeacon Charles A. Roach of the Anglican Church championed the poor and spoke out against the neglect and abuses by the colonial government. The Catholic bishop of Port Victoria, the Right Reverend Xavier Baronnet, and the Anglican bishop of Seychelles, the Right Reverend French Chang-Him, presently exercise religious leadership.

MAJOR THEOLOGIANS AND AUTHORS There are no major Seychellois theologians or Christian authors.

HOUSES OF WORSHIP AND HOLY PLACES Hundreds of churches dot the Seychelles. The Roman Catholic Cathedral of the Immaculate Conception opened in Victoria in 1862. The Anglican cathedral in Victoria is St. Paul's Pro-Cathedral, completed in 1859. Churches constructed in the nineteenth century from wood have gradually been replaced by concrete and masonry.

WHAT IS SACRED? Although interpretations of the scriptures vary according to faith and church, Christians profess their belief in the Christian Bible of the Old and New Testaments, which they hold to be divinely inspired, holy, and sacred. Catholics venerate saints, and the celebration of the sacraments is sacred for both Catholics and Protestants.

HOLIDAYS AND FESTIVALS The government recognizes Good Friday, Easter Sunday, the Fête Dieu (Corpus Christi), Assumption Day (15 August), All Saint's Day (1 November), the Day of the Immaculate Conception (8 December), and Christmas Day (25 December). On holidays, families typically attend Mass, which is often followed by an outing to the beach.

MODE OF DRESS Religion does not influence everyday dress in the Seychelles. Church festivals, baptisms, confirmations, weddings, and funerals—even Mass—require a level of grooming and style not generally practiced in the West. Women buy new clothes for church-related events, where status-conscious Seychellois show off their Western-style dresses, shoes, hats, and handbags.

DIETARY PRACTICES Catholics in the Seychelles observe no dietary restrictions other than avoiding meat on Fridays, especially during Lent. Some Protestants avoid alcohol, and Seventh-day Adventists do not eat meat.

RITUALS Seychellois Catholics observe the same rituals as do Catholics elsewhere, including the Eucharist (Communion) and six other Catholic sacraments. Weddings confer status on Seychellois Christians, especially where social mobility is possible by "marrying up." Common are lavish weddings and receptions, which involve renting grand villas and hiring buses to convey friends and relatives to the location. Men often miss the church ceremony while they prepare to receive the guests.

Recognizing that not all Seychellois can afford expensive rituals, the Catholic Church offers three funeral packages. The high-end package includes ringing bells three times, singing, organ music, and a homily, as well as broadcasting the news to all. For a more modest outlay, bells are rung twice, with much less show. A bare-bones funeral is free and consists of a single bell rung eleven times. Few people attend cheap funerals for fear of losing status.

RITES OF PASSAGE As with Christians in other countries, rites of passage in the Seychelles are organized around birth, baptism, confirmation, marriage, and funerals. Ideally many distinguished invitees will witness the rites in an auspicious church setting, where social status is assured.

MEMBERSHIP In the Seychelles the Catholic Church has taken a measured approach to retaining members and cultivating new ones through its institutions, rites, and rituals. Its weekly newspaper, *Echo des Iles,* has a circulation of 2,800 and maintains a bias toward the ruling party. The government reciprocates by having weekly radio broadcasts of the Catholic Mass and Anglican services, each on alternate weeks. The Far East Broadcasting Association (FEBA) produces nondenominational Christian radio programming.

SOCIAL JUSTICE Since independence Catholics and Protestants alike have become more concerned about alleviating poverty and protecting human rights. Christian churches have in part followed the lead of the Reverend Charles A. Roach, an Anglican who in the 1950s denounced low wages, inadequate housing, poor education standards, and bad administration. Until the year 2000, however, there were no human rights organizations in the country other than the Catholic Church's Justice and Peace Commission.

SOCIAL ASPECTS The Catholic Church in Seychelles, as elsewhere, considers the marriage of a man and woman holy and the family unit sacred. Every year 1 August is celebrated as family day to remember the holy family of Mary, Joseph, and Jesus. In light of this belief, the church in the Seychelles has taken a rather dim view of the low prevalence of marriages in the country. Among established households in 1967, for example, only 47 percent married in the church. The Catholic Church still considers these unmarried couples, or *ménages,* more as circumstantial than intentional, and it has become more cognizant of the psychological, socioeconomic, and religious reasons that Seychellois do not marry.

POLITICAL IMPACT Although the administration of France-Albert René (in power since 1977) and the country's political parties are ostensibly secular, historically the Catholic and Anglican churches have had important influences on political affairs. The Catholic newspaper still has a pro-government bias, and the Reverend Wavel Ramkalawan, a Protestant minister, has led the political opposition. Ramkalawan accused the government of favoring the Bahai faith because of a $164,000 grant in 1999 to build a Bahai temple. The government responded that $192,000 of the national budget is available to assist faiths. In the past Anglican, Hindu, and Roman Catholic faiths all benefited from government grants. The government also provides 15 minutes of airtime on state radio to Muslims and Hindus on Fridays and 15 minutes to the Bahai and Seventh-day Adventists on Saturdays.

CONTROVERSIAL ISSUES Catholic Church leaders have lamented what they consider to be low morality in Seychellois society—thefts, drinking, domestic violence, and promiscuity. In 1998 75 percent of births were out of wedlock, and 13 percent of births occurred to women under 20 years of age. Many Seychellois men have concubines, and impoverished young women willingly accept these relationships either for financial reasons or for lack of a better alternative.

Because many Seychellois live together without being married, they are excluded from the sacraments. Discrete wedding ceremonies after Sunday morning Mass have in part remedied this, but weddings in the Seychelles are often meant for show. Some priests have urged the church to develop policies and pastoral activities that prepare young people for marriage and that encourage unmarried couples to regularize their relationship so that they can be brought into full communion with the sacraments. One priest-advocate suggested that unmarried couples leading otherwise exemplary lives be allowed to partake of the sacraments while waiting to consecrate their common law marriage.

CULTURAL IMPACT Christianity has influenced church architecture, which, with its transepts, arches, bell towers, and gable motifs, is reminiscent of church architecture on the European continent and in the British Isles. Christian symbols, such as crucifixes and chalices, have a more local stamp and are carved out of teak.

The Christianity of a bygone era has also left its mark on music, dance, and social customs. Besides historic church hymns, music and dance at formal parties and wedding receptions recall eighteenth-century France and the social mores of that time. At these parties boys and girls are segregated, with boys sitting on one side and girls on the other. They choose dance partners under the supervision of the chaperones. A popular dance called *contredanse* blends waltz and polka and was introduced by the earliest French colonists to the islands. *Contredanse* has its origins in the court of Louis XIV.

Other Religions

About 4 percent of the population identifies itself as non-Christian. There is a small Chinese Buddhist community dating to at least 1940, when a pagoda served both as a temple and as a club meetinghouse for members. Similarly, there are a small number of Hindus, mainly among the Indian population, which accounts for approximately 1 percent of Seychelle's population. It is also estimated that a few hundred Muslims live on the islands, some of whom trace their origins to the Arab and Swahili traders of coastal East Africa.

African traditional religion was brought to the Seychelles colony from East Africa. Missionary accounts record that slaves, having received little Christian instruction, practiced voodoo and other forms of magic, using fetishes, charms, amulets, gris-gris, and medicinal powders. No doubt they also observed other forms of African religion involving the veneration of ancestors, worship of animate and inanimate deities found in nature, and ritual invocation of spirits for planting, harvesting, fertility, and prosperity.

Despite the disapproval of Christian clergy, sorcery and witchcraft are deeply embedded in the island's cosmology. Indeed, most Seychellois see little inconsistency between their Christian orthodoxy and their belief in magic. It is not unusual for people to consult a witch doctor—known as a *bonhomme de bois* or a *bonne femme de bois*—for fortune-telling and to ward off enemies. Soothsayers use their powers, real or imagined, to cast spells, chase away evil spirits, heal, and bring good fortune. Their trade is made more believable through the practice of secret rituals and incantations.

Robert Groelsema

See Also Vol. 1: *Christianity*

Bibliography

Africa South of the Sahara 2003. London: Europa, 2003.

Benedict, Burton. "The Equality of the Sexes in the Seychelles." In *Social Organization: Essays Presented to Raymond Firth.* Edited by Maurice Freedman. London: Frank Cass, 1967, 43–64.

Bennet, George. *Seychelles.* Vol. 153 of *World Bibliographical Series.* Oxford: Clio, 1993.

Bradley, John T. *The History of the Seychelles.* Victoria, Seychelles: Clarion, 1940.

Hoarau, Gabriel. "Mariage et Concubinage aux Seychelles." In *Mariage et Sacrement de Mariage.* Edited by Pierre De Locht. Paris: Le Centurion, 1970, 43–57.

Roach, Charles A. *The Seychelles Story.* London: UDC, 1960.

Sierra Leone

POPULATION 5,614,743

MUSLIM 60 percent

AFRICAN TRADITIONAL RELIGION 30 percent

CHRISTIAN 10 percent

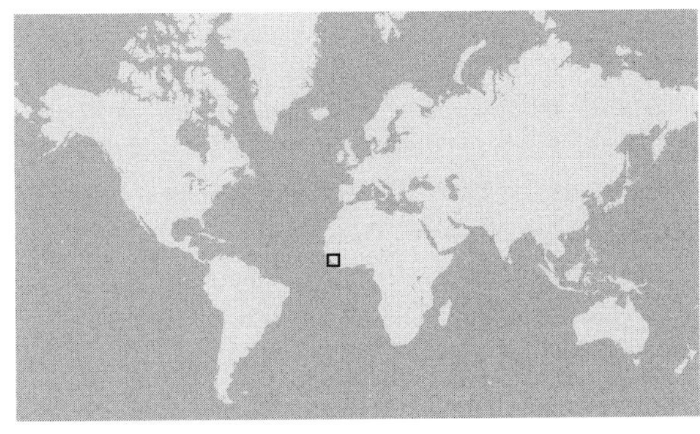

Country Overview

INTRODUCTION The Republic of Sierra Leone is a small West African country between Guinea and Liberia. Mountains in the east slope down to an upland plateau, wooded hills, and an Atlantic Coastal belt of mangrove swamps. About two-thirds of the inhabitants are subsistence farmers, but diamond mining provides the main hard currency. The Mende and Temne, the largest of the 18 principal ethnic groups, account for 60 percent of the population. Mende is spoken in the south, Temne in the north, and a literate minority speaks English (the official language). Ninety-five percent of the population also speak Krio, an English-based Creole.

Muslim traders and clerics brought Islam to northern Sierra Leone in the thirteenth century. Most Sierra Leonean Muslims are Sunnis, though some 10,000 Lebanese traders are Shiites. Portuguese explorers introduced Christianity on the mountainous, 25-mile-long Sierra Leone peninsula in 1462. Father Baltasar Barreira (1531–1612), a Catholic Jesuit priest, recommended that England and America settle freed slaves there. In 1787 a British Protestant abolitionist, Granville Sharp, established a settlement on the peninsula for 400 "black poor" from the London streets. Freed slaves from the American colonies and escaped slaves living in Jamaica joined them. In 1807 the British government, which had outlawed slavery in all its territories, took over the colony; nearly half of the 3,000 settlers had succumbed to disease and other threats. Over the next few decades the British navy patrolled the Atlantic for slave ships, and by 1836 it had resettled 55,000 freed slaves (called "recaptives") in the colony.

Known as the Krios (Creoles), the settlers formed a culture separate from that of the mainland and dominated by the Anglican and Methodist churches. The Krios replaced the foreign clergy by 1861 and named a recaptive, Samuel A. Crowther, the first Anglican bishop in 1864. In 1896 the British established a protectorate over the rest of present-day Sierra Leone. Independence came peacefully in 1961. An 11-year civil war (1991–2002) displaced many people, blurring the north/Muslim–south/Christian divide. Christians—mostly Creoles—have disproportionately influenced Sierra Leonean society owing to their prominence under colonial rule. Ahmed Tejan Kabbah, an ethnic Malinke/Mandingo and a Muslim, became president in 1996.

Devil Dancers in grass costumes perform for the queen and Prince Phillip in the interior of Sierra Leone. © BETTMANN/CORBIS.

Many Sierra Leonean Muslims and Christians retain such traditional African religious practices as ancestor veneration and belief in magic, evil spirits, and witchcraft. Some even belong to indigenous secret societies, or mystery cults, known as Poro ("laws of the ancestors"; for men) and Sande (Bundu, in Temne; for women).

RELIGIOUS TOLERANCE Religion bridges ethnic boundaries in Sierra Leone and has never caused major conflict. A few colonial governors tried to halt the spread of Islam in the 1800s. Christian missionaries discouraged membership in traditional secret societies and demonized traditional initiation masks. Orthodox Muslims were more accepting of certain indigenous practices: Some built mosques on sacred forest groves to derive an added holiness, which traditionalists found sacrilegious and intrusive. The minority Islamic Ahmadiyya sect also resents practices like these; it has made public its intention to rid West African Islam of its indigenous beliefs. During the civil war the Inter-Religious Council, a coalition of Muslim and Christian leaders, brought people of different faiths together to advance peace and to rehabilitate child soldiers and other war victims.

The 1991 constitution provides for freedom of religion, which the government respects and enforces. Religious instruction is allowed in public schools, but pupils may choose whether to attend classes oriented toward Islam or Christianity.

Major Religions

ISLAM

AFRICAN TRADITIONAL RELIGION

ISLAM

DATE OF ORIGIN thirteenth century C.E.
NUMBER OF FOLLOWERS 3.4 million

HISTORY Islam became established in Sierra Leone between the thirteenth and seventeenth centuries, during the time of the Mali and Songhai empires. In the eighteenth century, as a result of the Fouta Djallon jihad in Guinea, Sierra Leone took part in a greater Islamic revival in the subregion. The nineteenth century saw the arrival of substantial numbers of Muslims known as Aku—resettled Africans who were strongly influenced by the Yoruba culture—originally from Nigeria and other parts of West Africa and captured from departing slave ships. Large numbers of Muslim migrants also arrived from the Guinean towns of Kankan, Timbo, and Tuba to work as landlords, merchants, craftsmen, political organizers, clerics, and educators.

A strong solidarity network, effective political and social organization, and the establishment of Islamic schools that taught Arabic, the Koran, and Islamic culture helped consolidate the faith in Sierra Leone. Muslim associations and nongovernmental organizations flourished. The Sierra Leone Muslim Congress was founded in 1932 and the Kankaylay—the Sierra Leone Muslim Men and Women's Association—in 1942.

Islam has been a religion of prestige in Sierra Leone, owing to the large number of conquerors, chiefs, rulers, businesspeople, teachers, and scholars who have embraced the Muslim faith across ethnic groups. Since World War II it has been the fastest growing religion in the country, in part because it is unencumbered by colonial baggage and because it has been propagated by black Africans. Though historically most Muslims lived in the north, the greatest concentrations are now in commercial centers, such as Makeni, Bo, and Freetown, which offer commerce, jobs, and Muslim associations. Local mosques, *madrasahs* (Islamic schools), Koran classes, Islamic youth and women's associations, Islamic lantern clubs (youth associations that organize parades with floats, lanterns, music, songs, and dance), and countless village and town associations (*jama'ahs*) offer social and religious networks outside the family to Muslims in Sierra Leone.

EARLY AND MODERN LEADERS In the early 1700s Fodé Mamudu Katibi Turé helped found a political federation called the Kingdom of Moriah, which welcomed the Yansane, Fofana, Sise, Silla, and other Mande (Mandingo or Malinke) families who were devout, zealous Muslims. In the latter part of the 1700s, Fula Mansa migrated from the Fouta Djallon in Guinea (where he had been a political leader) and established similar conditions for the propagation of the faith in Yoni country among the Temne.

In 1930 Kontorfilli Haidara (c. 1890–1931), a radical Susu Muslim missionary from French Guinea, threatened to kill all those in his district who would not convert to Islam. In 1931 he led a short-lived tax revolt against the colonial government and was killed by the Royal West African Frontier Force. The Fula (Fulani) community in Freetown benefited greatly from the philanthropic efforts of Al-Haji Omaru (c. 1851–1931), a Fula trading agent for a French company and headman of the Fula migrant community. Omaru pressured the government to open a school for sons of Fula residents in Freetown and built a mosque on Jenkins Street.

Dr. E.W. Blyden (1832–1912)—an immigrant from the Caribbean, a scholar, an educator, and a leading pan-Africanist—opened a private Arabic-English school in the Fourah Bay district of Freetown in 1887. Probably a Christian, he was critical of Christian racial discrimination and was sympathetic to Islam. Appointed state director of Muhammadan Education in 1901, he promoted and oversaw the establishment of six government-funded *madrasahs* in Freetown and directed a program aimed at replacing Christian *madrasah* teachers with Muslims.

MAJOR THEOLOGIANS AND AUTHORS The Sierra Leonean Muslim scholar and philosopher Mohamed Sanussi was known for his library of Islamic works by West African authors. In 1872 British Governor John Pope Hennessey appointed him official government Arabic writer in charge of correspondence with chiefs in the interior. Kisimi Kamara (c. 1890–1962), another Arabic scholar, is credited with having invented the Mende syllabary (written characters representing syllables), the KiKaKu, around 1921. Sheikh Jibril Sesay, a great scholar of law and theology, took leadership roles in several progressive Islamic organizations and served as General Secretary of the Muslim Congress for 11 years. He became the chief imam of the main Temne mosque in Freetown in the 1950s and was made a member of the Freetown city council in 1957. He is credited with helping modernize Islamic institutions.

HOUSES OF WORSHIP AND HOLY PLACES Sierra Leonean Muslims may say their daily prayers almost anywhere, but the mosque serves as the house of worship and a place for Friday prayers. The principal Temne mosque in Freetown is the Jami al-Jalil ("jami" means the place where Muslims gather for Friday prayer). Malinke villages in northern Sierra Leone have simple mosques—thatch-roofed cylindrical huts, with a hole in the roof allowing for calls to prayers.

WHAT IS SACRED? Muslims in Sierra Leone accept the Koran as the divinely inspired word of Allah revealed to Islam's last and greatest prophet. Words and texts from the Koran written on prayer recitation boards in washable ink are thought to have supernatural power, imparting protection and good health. The water used to wash the boards may be captured in a bowl and consumed or used to rinse the body. The month of Ramadan is also sacred, because the first revelation of the Koran reportedly occurred during this month.

HOLIDAYS AND FESTIVALS Sierra Leonean Muslims celebrate three Islamic holidays: the birthday of the Prophet (Maulid-al-nabi), Tabaski (Id-al-adha, commemorating the sparing of Abraham's son Ishmael on the altar), and the end of Ramadan (Id-al-fitr). The dates of these feasts are set according to the Islamic lunar calendar. Hunters' societies and popular carnival clubs, which have names like Paddle and Firestone, hold masquerades on all three occasions. Ramadan, the month-long Muslim fast, ends with prayer celebrations in mosques and open fields, followed by feasting, gifts, and visits to family and friends. The night before Id al-fitr, lantern parades fill the streets, featuring truck-sized floats and portable lanterns of various designs. The lanterns and floats are judged competitively by Islamic and government officials. Although in 1994 the Supreme Islamic Council proclaimed that the lantern parades had nothing to do with Islam and advised that they be moved from that night, they draw huge crowds and are broadcast live on national radio.

MODE OF DRESS Muslims in Sierra Leone wear the traditional Islamic robes popular throughout West Africa, but they have also adopted Western-style clothing. Women may wear long, translucent gowns made from *gara,* a locally dyed fabric, over pieces of colorful, wraparound cotton cloth (*lappas*), sometimes with head scarves. Men wear loose-fitting shirts over trousers, sometimes of matching material. On prayer days and special occasions, men and women dress elegantly in *grand boubous*: flowing robes worn over matching pants. Boubous may be very expensive, depending on the quality of cloth, the pattern, and the intricacy of the embroidery.

DIETARY PRACTICES The diet of most Muslims in Sierra Leone is based on regional availability, not religious prescription, but devout Muslims do not drink alcohol or eat pork. Food is taken with the right hand only from a shared platter, and a bowl of water is made available for washing hands before and after the meal.

RITUALS Sierra Leonean Muslims observe the five core Islamic rituals: professing the name of and attributing all to Allah, praying five times daily, fasting during the holy month of Ramadan, giving alms to the poor, and, if possible, making a pilgrimage to Mecca.

RITES OF PASSAGE Muslims in Sierra Leone mark four life transitions—birth, puberty, marriage, and death. Seven days after the birth of a child, families hold a naming ceremony during which the marabout (the village religious leader) leads prayers, shaves the infant's head, and announces the name of the child for the first time.

Puberty rites are extremely important, but school calendars and the demands of urban lifestyles have made them less elaborate. Performed at five-year intervals for groups of boys and girls between the ages of 6 and 13, the rites include circumcision. Human rights groups increasingly oppose the practice of clitoridectomy.

Historically marriage was important in forming political and trade alliances, and it is still a significant way to strengthen ties between lineages. A girl may be betrothed at birth to a boy of 12 years old or less. Prior to the marriage the families must negotiate the bride-price, which the groom's family may pay in installments over as many as seven years.

An imam leads prayers after a eulogy to ask for forgiveness for the dead person. Mortuary ceremonies may be held throughout the 45-day judgment period to pray for and support the deceased in a hoped-for passage into paradise.

MEMBERSHIP Membership in the Islamic faith is expanded in Sierra Leone through baptisms, *madrasahs*, conversions, and Muslim institutions. Since the 1970s there has been an upsurge of missionary zeal, in part due to proselytizing Ahmadiyya missionaries and their schools, as well as to a multitude of informal and formal Sunni Muslim missionary organizations, such as the Sierra Leone Muslim Reformation Society, the Muslim Brotherhood Mission, the Pilgrims' Association, and the Muslim Congress.

SOCIAL JUSTICE Owing to weak state institutions and state collapse in the 1990s, Shari'ah (Islamic law) governs many domestic issues in Sierra Leone. Rural exodus has spread Shari'ah to urban areas throughout the country. Islamic jurists across Sierra Leone apply Shari'ah to personal and communal matters, including divorce, child custody, inheritance, theft, and curses.

Sierra Leone's Muslims are expected to give alms to the poor. In colonial times during Ramadan, Alhaji Momodu Allie, a Muslim Fula entrepreneur noted for his wealth as a landlord, waived the rents and provided tenants with sugar, rice, onions, and other staples. The African Muslims' Agency, funded with Kuwaiti money, distributes rice for Muslim feast days to needy Muslims.

Since 1970 many Muslim associations have sprung up with the purpose of soliciting government funds and funds from outside the country to build schools and mosques, recruit foreign teachers, and send students abroad. Islamic education is funded by both state and private sources.

SOCIAL ASPECTS Polygyny is legal in Sierra Leone, but while multiple wives may be an asset in a subsistence economy, they are a financial burden in an urban environment. In addition bride-prices are expensive, and Islamic law requires that each wife be treated equally. Only the more prosperous men are polygamous, and professionals tend to prefer monogamous marriages, but they may have concubines and extramarital affairs. The Ahmadiyya sect condemns large-scale polygyny.

Muslims in Sierra Leone are socially conservative and send their daughters to traditional Sande or Bundu camps, because these schools teach girls housekeeping and child raising. In some ethnic groups, such as the Mende, the importance of matrilineal ties raises women's status. In urban areas women's traders associations and other organizations, such as the United Muslim Women's Organization in the town of Bo, offer women mutual help, protect their financial interests, and overall raise their status. Most domestic affairs, however, including issues related to women and children, are governed by customary and Islamic law rather than English law.

POLITICAL IMPACT Islam has had a significant impact on political forms in Sierra Leone. Arabic titles in current use, such as *almamy* (headmen, or village chiefs), *alkali* (deputies), and *santigi* (political leaders of middle rank), testify to historical influence. Headmen rely on Islamic advisers, courts use Shari'ah law, and such Muslim organizations as the Supreme Islamic Council (formed in 1969 and 1970) have a collaborative relationship with the government. Leaders of the Muslim Congress, Muslim Brotherhood, Islamic-Arabic Institute, and United Muslim Institute have held government posts and have obtained government funding for building mosques and *madrasahs* and for organizing pilgrimages to Mecca. Senior government members have used their connections to obtain government and foreign funding for propagating Islam. Sierra Leone is a member of the Organization of the Islamic Conference, which supports the Palestine Liberation Organization.

Sierra Leone has no national Islamic political party, but at independence Muslim leaders were instrumental in forming the Sierra Leone People's Party and the All People's Congress. The Islamic lantern clubs used songs to lampoon the excesses of the corrupt political regime of former President Joseph Saidu Momoh (in office from 1985–92), which led to a ban on the clubs from 1988 to 1992.

CONTROVERSIAL ISSUES Since 1937 efforts by zealous members of the missionary Pakistani Ahmadiyya sect (whose adherents believe their founder, Mirza Ghulam Ahmad, is the promised Messiah) to convert other Muslims to their creed has generated much tension. Some Ahmadiyya Muslims have adopted militantly anti-Christian and antitraditional attitudes.

The influx of petrodollars from Iran, Libya, and Saudi Arabia for *madrasahs* and other Islamic organizations since 1973, as well as the international community's concern about the spread of radical Islamic beliefs in Africa since the terrorist attacks on the United States on September 11, 2001, has increased speculation about possible links between Sierra Leoneon Islamic groups and international terrorism. The government had already criticized Islamic nongovernmental organizations for fund-raising overseas without its involvement; in 1987 it created the Federation of Sierra Leonean Muslim Organizations in 1987 to control these activities.

CULTURAL IMPACT African artisan castes and Islam have coexisted for many years. The Mande and Fula griot (musician-entertainer) castes perform Islamic religious music to eulogize the deceased and traditional songs recounting the epics and glories of past empires. Leather workers cover neatly folded, thread-wrapped papers bearing Koranic lines (chosen by a cleric) with strips of leather, usually black, to make amulets. They may decorate these simple but elegantly shaped round, rectangular, and triangular leather forms with painted or stamped designs. Muslims believe that wearing these amulets protects them from harm and brings luck in money and love.

AFRICAN TRADITIONAL RELIGION

DATE OF ORIGIN c. 200 C.E.

NUMBER OF FOLLOWERS 1.7 million

HISTORY The traditional religious practices that exist in Sierra Leone were likely brought into the area by migrating ethnic groups, such as the Mende, around 200 C.E. The first Portuguese explorers of the area found traditional religion in place in the late fifteenth century, and in the sixteenth century the Portuguese were the first outsiders to observe the importance of the traditional secret societies.

African traditional religion is widespread, though it is strongest in villages and rural areas where Islam and Christianity have penetrated less. The Poro and Sande secret societies are prevalent throughout West Africa's coastal rain forest, including in Sierra Leone. Islam opposes the secret societies, and membership tends to be stronger where Islam is weak. Not all traditionalists belong to the societies, but they are significant in the political, social, and religious life of many of Sierra Leone's ethnic groups. The secret societies' main purpose is to engage the spirit world by means of performing rituals in the sacred forests (groves) where traditional leaders (ancestors) are buried. Sacrifices and initiations access the power of ancestral spirits, solicit their protection from evil, and ask for their assistance in the social welfare and important life matters of the community, such as good health, sufficient rain, and abundant harvest.

EARLY AND MODERN LEADERS In Sierra Leone the leaders of the various branches of the Poro and Sande secret societies lay down rules that govern headmen of villages, clan and lineage heads, diviners and fortunetellers, and traditional doctors. High-ranking elders who gain seniority, learn the esoteric secrets, and pay substantial fees may eventually reach the inner circle of leadership in the secret societies. These elite leaders, whose identity is never revealed, generally belong to high-ranking families, but that need not be the case. Leadership is hierarchical and exchanges take place between and among leaders of the various societies.

MAJOR THEOLOGIANS AND AUTHORS Traditional doctrine is unwritten; it is learned and practiced by heads of families and clans and handed down from generation to generation. Diviners, traditional doctors, and fortune tellers are employed to determine the causes of evil, of the death of babies, and of otherwise unexplainable events. Because people believe in witches—good and evil—and witchcraft, these religious practitioners may also be solicited to provide charms, amulets, and medicines for protection.

HOUSES OF WORSHIP AND HOLY PLACES The Sierra Leonean secret societies maintain clearings in what they consider sacred forests for religious ceremonies, such as initiation and puberty rites. Kissi villages feature a sacred *tungo* (a shelter without walls) that contains an altar and the graves of ancestors or stones taken from where the ancestors were buried. Individual families may keep shrines in the privacy of an ancestral hut or compound to remember and appease ancestors.

WHAT IS SACRED? Ceremonial masks worn for religious events are thought to embody the ancestors and other spirits and are considered sacred by traditionalists in Sierra Leone. Spirits are believed to live in sacred groves in the forest where Poro leaders are buried and where sacrifices and initiations take place. The Baga are governed by an initiation society called Simo, which means "sacred." Some ceramic vessels are sacred and may be used to store medicinal plants and herbs used in rituals.

HOLIDAYS AND FESTIVALS In rural areas Sierra Leonean villagers hold ceremonial feasts following the harvest and after initiations that include dancing, drumming, and the pouring of libations. Freetown residents, whatever their religion, participate in such annual traditional celebrations as the hunters' society masquerades and the lantern parades. The large, intricate floats decorated with candles and lanterns and carrying masked figures who sing and dance embody a mixture of Islamic, Christian, and traditional beliefs.

MODE OF DRESS Sierra Leonean villagers tend to dress simply and to go barefoot or wear plastic sandals. Some traditionalist men wear shirts made from four- to six-inch-wide strips of cotton sewn together to make "country cloth"; others wear Western shirts or undershirts with shorts or long pants. Many men wear Muslim-style shirts (with cut-outs at the neck rather than buttons) over their pants, and some wear the long Muslim gowns. Women wear the typical wrap-around skirt and blouse.

DIETARY PRACTICES Traditional religion in Sierra Leone prohibits adherents from eating animals and plants identified with their totem group. Totems are animals and sometimes plants that have appeared to people in miraculous ways, providing assistance to their ethnic group, and henceforth occupy a mystical and sacred relationship with the group. Totems among various clans of the Kono people, for example, are leopards, tortoises, goats, pigs, catfish, and bush yams. It is believed that harm will befall members of the totem group if they eat or kill their totem.

RITUALS The Poro and Sande secret societies are responsible for conducting all rites and rituals. The societies are secret in the sense that beliefs and practices are not shared with nonmembers, members of the opposite sex, or uninitiated children. Initiation rituals take place at puberty. When performing official functions, cult leaders wear masks representing a spirit or a cult object, which might be something that symbolizes fertility, health, prosperity, or abundant harvest.

RITES OF PASSAGE Sierra Leonean traditionalists see the rites of passage—birth, puberty, marriage, and death—as a continuum linking the unborn with the ancestors. When a baby is about three weeks old (so its survival is more assured), a naming ceremony signals its official birth. Among the Kono, parents bring the child out in public, whisper its name in its ear, and parade the child about to receive gifts.

Initiation is the most important rite, administered by leaders of the secret societies in sacred groves. The purpose is to introduce adolescents into the mysteries of life, ensure that they conform to traditions, and offer them practical skills to equip them for adulthood. Sande initiates, for example, learn housekeeping skills. All initiates are circumcised as a sign that they are ready for adulthood. To fit in with modern lifestyles, the period of initiation has been reduced from several months to a few weeks. During the Poro secret society initiation rite of the Mende, the boys are forced onto the ground, and their backs are cut with razors. The resulting scars mark the teeth of the Poro spirit that consumes the boys. The "newborn" initiates reemerge from the bush with a new social status. In theory, initiation is a prerequisite for marriage, but not everyone chooses to do it.

Marriages may be arranged shortly after a child's birth. A middle-aged man can request the hand of a newborn baby girl by presenting gifts to the parents, with the understanding that the girl may refuse the marriage when she comes of age. Members of the same clan may not marry; indeed, marriages serve to strengthen relations between different clans.

In some local vernaculars the word for death means "life goes out," signifying that the spirit leaves the body for another world. Burials are usually held the same day or the next morning., but chiefs are buried secretly in the night by Poro members. A period of weeping is usually followed by feasting and dancing. Members of the family may pour a mixture of rice powder and water (to provide the soul sustenance on its journey) on the grave and dance around it.

MEMBERSHIP Sierra Leoneans are members of traditional religion by virtue of belonging to a kinship group that includes the unborn, the living, and the dead. Full membership in the Poro and Sande secret societies requires initiation, however, without which a person remains outside the community. Membership offers spiritual fulfillment and sometimes the possession of medicinal secrets considered a potent force for good or evil. Since the societies cross ethnic lines, members gain opportunities to form alliances with, trade with, marry into, and be accepted into other ethnic groups. The societies contribute greatly to solidarity among their members and offer status to individuals, especially those who advance to senior ranks. People may become active members of several secret societies at the same time.

SOCIAL JUSTICE In traditional communities in Sierra Leone, the social welfare of the individual depends primarily on immediate family and relatives and to a lesser extent on the wider kinship group. Urbanites are expected to provide shelter and food for extended periods to family and members of their ethnic group or secret society who move to the city for education or employment. People who live at a great distance from their village form mutual aid societies and hometown and village associations, pooling their resources as insurance to be used for marriages, naming ceremonies, hospitalization, funerals, or repairing damage from floods or fires. Urban settlers also contribute to such community development projects as classrooms, health clinics, bridges, and wells.

SOCIAL ASPECTS The lineage—the congregation of ancestors around whom a cult is built—is central to traditional religion in Sierra Leone. Membership in the lineage entails rights, obligations, and duties defined by tradition and handed down by elders and secret society leaders; included is a sense of reciprocity among ethnic group members, respect for elders, and obedience to community rules regarding land tenure, protection of the environment, and marriage. Rights accumulate with age and seniority, and elders have special powers and duties to interpret and enforce rules and traditions and to resolve disputes between group members. Because of historical conquest and subjugation, Mandingo and Fula societies are highly stratified by occupational clans and social position.

Marriages cement social contracts between lineages. The Temne are related to each other through common patrilineal descent from a male ancestor, while the Mende trace their lineage through both matrilineal and patrilineal ties. In the Mende, Sherbro, Krim, Vai, and Gallinas ethnic groups, where matrilineal ties are important and powerful female secret societies exist, women have considerable independence in conducting their affairs.

POLITICAL IMPACT Peace treaties, trade pacts, and political marriages are formed between clans and lineages of different tribes or ethnic groups as a channel for interethnic communication.

The relationship between the Poro secret society and political leadership in Sierra Leone is not publicized, due to the secrecy of Poro, but it is widely assumed that the two overlap significantly. Mende chiefs are always members of Poro but are rarely the Poro heads, and the highest-ranking Poro leaders are seldom top government officials. Poro membership is thought to enhance the managing of public affairs, and a chief without the support of the Poro is ineffective. The Sande secret society offers women solidarity and political empowerment. Women traditionalists have held cabinet posts, have been delegates to the United Nations, and have advised presidents and military leaders.

CONTROVERSIAL ISSUES Modernization has caused social disruption and controversy in Sierra Leone's traditional community. Urban migration by men and youth and the changes brought about by telecommunications, a cash economy, secular state political authority and public bureaucracy, elitist professions and lifestyles, modern schooling, transformation in the chieftaincy, and emphasis on the individual instead of the community have posed new threats to traditional religion. Migrants return to their villages with new ideas that question the structure of the family, reliance on community, and obedience to community elders.

CULTURAL IMPACT Traditional religion, expressed through the secret societies, has influenced many art forms, notably the sculpture of Sande helmet masks, which embody the *Sowo,* the guardian spirit. Designed to fit over female dancers' heads, the masks are worn only by women and are their exclusive property—a practice unique to the subregion (Sierra Leone, Liberia, and Guinea). The masks are carved with elaborate rows of braided hair, high foreheads, small noses and mouths, and large multiple neck rings; strands of raffia are tied to the base of the helmet. These features are a stylized image of female physical and spiritual perfection. In other arts such as pottery or leatherworking, the products may be more than objects, their capacities extending into metaphysical realms, having economic, social, and spiritual value.

Other Religions

Christians make up a small but influential portion of the population of Sierra Leone. The Portuguese introduced Catholicism to the area in 1462, and the Jesuit Father Barreira began proselytizing in 1605. Catholics now make up approximately 3 percent of the total population and have established a number of primary and secondary schools. Protestant missions were launched in Sierra Leone at the end of the eighteenth century. When the British outlawed slavery in all its colonies, British antislavery patrol ships on the Atlantic Ocean took thousands of slaves to Freetown. The Krio (Creole) language developed there among freed slaves who learned English but recollected their various mother tongues. A famous episode in missionary history occurred in 1839, when captives on a Spanish slave ship off Cuba, the *Amistad,* mutinied and sailed to Long Island. The U.S. Supreme Court eventually declared the slaves free, and representatives of the American Missionary Association helped resettle them in Sierra Leone. The small missionary outpost they established eventually became the Sierra Leone Annual Conference of the United Methodist Church.

The Church Mission Society (CMS) made the most ambitious effort to convert the Sierra Leonean hinterland and peninsula. In addition to building schools and churches, CMS founded Fourah Bay College (now the University of Sierra Leone) in 1827, one of Africa's most prestigious institutions of higher learning in that century. Graduates include Sierra Leoneans Samuel Adjai (Ajayi) Crowther (1809–91), the forerunner of Nigerian evangelism, and Sierra Leone's first prime minister, Sir Milton Margai (1895–1964), who was a Methodist. His half-brother and successor, Albert Margai (1910–80), was Roman Catholic and was educated at St. Edward's Secondary School in Freetown. Virtually all Sierra Leone's independence-era political leaders were trained in missionary schools. Despite this Christianity made comparatively few colonial- and independence-era converts in the country because of its unpopular assault on African norms and values.

Among early Christian church leaders in Sierra Leone were Boston King (born c. 1760), a black loyalist from South Carolina who escaped to Nova Scotia and traveled to Sierra Leone and England as a Methodist missionary; and Reverend Joseph Claudius May (1845–1902), the principal of a leading Sierra Leonean Protestant grammar school and editor of the *Methodist Herald* from 1882 to 1888. Along with Dr. E.W. Blyden, May cofounded the *Sierra Leone Weekly News,* the most widely read newspaper in the country of its time. Reverend Ethelred Nathaniel Jones (1884–1954), who took the name Laminah Sankoh after 1920, was a radical churchman, educator, and political advocate. A leading proponent of unifying the peninsular Colony with the Protectorate (most Krios resisted this move), he started a daily newspaper (the *African Vanguard*) and helped found the Sierra Leone People's Party in 1949. He also espoused the creation of an authentic African church, to be called the "People's Church," that would be Christian in outlook but free of Western accretions.

Christian missions have been most successful in urban areas, where Sierra Leoneans appreciate their schools and medical facilities and where traditional influence is weaker. Christian theology—with its emphasis on monogamy, the individual, and abstinence from alcohol and its condemnation of secret societies—has not been popular in Sierra Leone, but some people have found ways to reconcile Christian teachings with African beliefs. Such African syncretist churches as the God of Our Light Church, founded in Ghana, and the Church of the Lord (Aladura), which originated in Nigeria, maintain the essence of the Gospel but add faith healing, African rituals, and African liturgy to it.

Robert Groelsema

See Also Vol. I: *African Traditional Religion, Islam*

Bibliography

Africa South of the Sahara 2004. The Republic of Sierra Leone. 33rd ed. London: Europa Publications, 2003.

"Creoles of Sierra Leone." In *Worldmark Encyclopedia of Cultures and Daily Life.* Vol. 1, *Africa.* Farmington Hills, Mich.: The Gale Group, 1998.

Foray, Cyril P. *Historical Dictionary of Sierra Leone.* From *African Historical Dictionaries.* Metuchen, N.J.: The Scarecrow Press, 1977.

Frank, Barbara E. *Mande Potters and Leatherworkers: Art and Heritage in West Africa.* Washington D.C. and London: Smithsonian Institution Press, 1998.

Jalloh, Alusine, and David E. Skinner, eds. *Islam and Trade in Sierra Leone.* Trenton, N.J.: Africa World Press, 1997.

Kaplan, Irving, et al. *Area Handbook for Sierra Leone.* Area Handbook Series. Foreign Area Studies of the American University. Washington, D.C.: U.S. Government Printing Office, 1976.

"Malinke." In *Worldmark Encyclopedia of Cultures and Daily Life.* Vol. 1: *Africa.* Farmington Hills, Mich.: The Gale Group, 1998.

U.S. Department of State. *International Religious Freedom Report 2003: Sierra Leone.* [Online] Available at http://www.state.gov/g/drl/rls/hrrpt/2003/27750.htm (Accessed October 2004).

Singapore

POPULATION 3.2 million

BUDDHIST 42.5 percent

MUSLIM 15 percent

NONRELIGIOUS 15 percent

CHRISTIAN 14.5 percent

TAOIST 8.5 percent

HINDU 4 percent

OTHER 0.5 percent

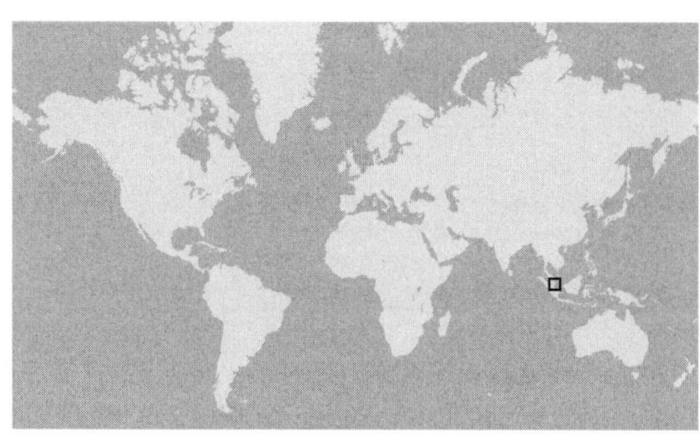

Country Overview

INTRODUCTION Situated just north of the equator in Southeast Asia, the Republic of Singapore consists of Singapore Island, which measures a mere 26 miles by 14 miles, and about 50 smaller, largely uninhabited islands. Singapore straddles one of the world's most important shipping lanes, the Strait of Malacca, which separates the country from the Indonesian island of Sumatra to the west. To the north of Singapore Island, beyond the narrow Johore Strait, is Malaysia.

Established in 1819 as a British trading center, Singapore began the process of devolving from Britain in the 1950s, and after a brief and unsuccessful union with neighboring Malaysia, the country became fully independent in 1965. The People's Action Party has maintained political power since 1959.

Because most Singaporeans are descended from Chinese, Malay, and Indian laborers who were imported to support Britain's economic power, the range of cultural and religious diversity in the country is striking. While Chinese constitute the majority of the population (76.8 percent), they have historically been further divided by dialect group, the dominant one being Hokkien, followed by Teochew, Cantonese, and Hakka. English is the official language of Singapore, though Mandarin is now the most common language spoken at home among ethnic Chinese. Other languages spoken include Malay and Tamil, the principal language of Singapore's Indian community.

Religion is closely linked to ethnicity in Singapore, with the widest range of religious practices found in the ethnic Chinese community. Because of the historical mixing of Buddhism and Taoism in Singapore, it is sometimes difficult to separate the two as distinct religions. Both Taoism and the practice of Chinese Buddhism are in turn strongly influenced by Confucian teachings, and, indeed, one can argue that Confucianism is the unofficial state religion of Singapore. To the extent that Prime Minister Goh Chok Tong and other Singaporean political leaders have fashioned themselves as Confucian *junzi* (men of learning, talent, and virtue), Singapore's political landscape has largely been informed by Confucian values.

In the country's remaining ethnic groups, religion is almost inextricably linked to ethnicity. Most ethnic Malays (13.9 percent of the population) are Muslim, while the majority of Indians (7.9 percent of the population) practice Hinduism (though there are significant numbers who practice Islam and a smaller number of Sikhs).

RELIGIOUS TOLERANCE Freedom of religion is guaranteed in Article 15 of Singapore's constitution, and Singapore has a relatively strong tradition of religious tolerance as long as religious groups scrupulously avoid politics. The Jehovah's Witnesses have been banned since 1972 on the grounds that its members refused to participate in compulsory military service, and the Unification Church has been prohibited since 1982, presumably because of the perception that its intense proselytizing has the potential to challenge the country's political and social order.

A woman lights incense at the altar of a temple. For many Buddhists in Singapore, ritual practice is centered around altars in the home, at business establishments, or in temples. © ADAM WOOLFITT/CORBIS.

Major Religion

BUDDHISM

DATE OF ORIGIN c. 1820 C.E.
NUMBER OF FOLLOWERS 1.35 million

HISTORY The history of Buddhism in Singapore began with the syncretic religious practices of the Chinese who immigrated to Singapore between the mid-nineteenth and early twentieth centuries; the vast majority practiced a uniquely Chinese blend of Taoist, Confucian, and Buddhist traditions. The earliest Taoist temples in Singapore, constructed in the nineteenth century by Chinese immigrants, contained Taoist deities, Confucian masters, and statues of the many manifestations of the Buddha. In Chinese Mahayana Buddhism a wide range of gods are venerated and worshiped, including not only the Gautama Buddha and numerous bodhisattvas but also Taoist deities and revered Confucian teachers. Thus, the Chinese practice of Buddhism in Singapore has always been considerably more eclectic than that found in India or Thailand, where the Theravada school of Buddhism prevails.

During the 1980s and 1990s a combination of social factors, driven primarily by education and language policy, resulted in a new, reformed form of Buddhism that has replaced Taoism as Singapore's most popular religion. Some Singaporean Buddhist temples now offer a range of activities that mirror the social and outreach functions of many Christian churches, creating a sense that Buddhism is part of a unified religious community. Whereas many traditional Chinese temples reflected syncretic practices that cut through religious lines, reform Buddhism in Singapore has stressed that which is distinctly Buddhist, while encouraging the application of religious teachings to real-life situations. Thus, Buddhism has come to be seen as an increasingly practical and worldly religion, especially among the young, contributing to its remarkable surge in popularity.

EARLY AND MODERN LEADERS Buddhist temples in Singapore have traditionally been autonomous, without a centralized body or a common practice from which religious leaders could emerge. It was Singapore's politicians, more than any single Buddhist leader, who created the conditions under which Buddhism could flourish—through the promotion of language and education policies favoring the development of a more "modern" and streamlined Buddhism, which has come to replace traditional Chinese religious practices.

MAJOR THEOLOGIANS AND AUTHORS Even with the growth of a more highly organized, reformed Buddhism in Singapore, major indigenous theologians and authors have yet to emerge.

HOUSES OF WORSHIP AND HOLY PLACES Singapore possesses dozens of significant Buddhist centers, temples, and associations representing the Theravada and Mahayana branches of Buddhism. The Siong Lim Temple, completed in 1908, is Singapore's oldest Buddhist temple. Other important temples include the Thai-style Theravada Buddhist temple Sakya Muni Buddha Gaya (Temple of a Thousand Lights) and the modern Kong Meng San Phor Kark See Temple.

WHAT IS SACRED? To a Singaporean Buddhist, statues of the Buddha and his bodhisattvas are considered sacred, and many homes and businesses contain altars devoted to the Buddha, to Taoist and traditional Chinese deities, and to Confucian masters. One of the most venerated gods in the region is Guanyin, a female manifestation of the bodhisattva of compassion.

HOLIDAYS AND FESTIVALS The principal Buddhist holiday, Vesak Day, celebrates the birth and enlightenment of the Buddha and falls on the full moon in the month of Vesakha (April/May). Devotees visit temples and perform acts of generosity and kindness, and the day concludes with candlelit processions in the streets.

MODE OF DRESS There is no mode of dress specified by Buddhist practice in Singapore, though the country's Buddhist monks—virtually all of whom hail from other countries—wear robes appropriate to their order.

DIETARY PRACTICES Although some Singaporean Buddhists are vegetarian, the vast majority are not, because pork, chicken, and seafood are integral elements in Singaporean Chinese cooking.

RITUALS For many Buddhists in Singapore ritual practice is centered around altars in the home, at business establishments, or in temples where devotees may light joss sticks and prostrate themselves before a particular deity. Young, educated Singaporean Buddhists who do not speak dialects are more likely to avail themselves of practices that are relatively new to Singapore (such as meditation classes and dharma talks offered by masters of Tibetan tantric traditions) or to attend regular Sunday services. Many of these services follow a structure that is similar to that found in Christian churches, complete with Buddhist-themed hymns and readings and the active participation of those attending the service.

RITES OF PASSAGE Buddhism does not tend to mark rites of passage in the same formal manner as other religions. The practice of encouraging young men to serve as novice monks for periods of months or years, common in Thailand, is not present in Singapore, and most Buddhist monks in Singapore have been trained outside the country.

MEMBERSHIP An entire generation of Singaporeans has received instruction in a more modern, doctrine-driven, and ethically based form of Buddhism through the Religious Knowledge curriculum offered in the country's secondary schools. This factor may be largely responsible for the significant increase in the number of individuals who identify themselves as practitioners of Buddhism compared with just a generation ago.

SOCIAL JUSTICE Singapore's government has made it clear that religion cannot cross into politics, citing the potential for social unrest in a region characterized by enormous religious diversity. Many Buddhist temples and organizations feature an outreach component to those who are poor, sick, old, or disabled, while avoiding more overtly political forms of social activism.

SOCIAL ASPECTS Singaporean Buddhists have traditionally valued marriage, both to ensure the continuation of the family line and to guarantee that ancestors are venerated. Though economic prosperity has reduced family size and raised the marriage age—especially among the educated—there is tremendous pressure to marry. Newer, reform Buddhist temples and organizations offer a wider range of opportunities for young men and women to meet and socialize than had been the case in traditional Chinese temples. Singapore has an increasingly visible gay and lesbian community that is largely ignored by organized religion, though Buddhism does not condemn homosexuality.

POLITICAL IMPACT Under the 1990 Maintenance of Religious Harmony Act, Singapore's government has the power to restrain leaders and members of religious groups from engaging in politics, from creating "ill-will" between religious groups, and from engaging in subversive activities. Given these prohibitions, it is hardly surprising that religion has no direct impact on the country's political life. Few of the country's politicians are Buddhist, and a disproportionate number of those who occupy high positions in government are Christian.

CONTROVERSIAL ISSUES Buddhists have steered clear of controversial issues, especially because Singapore's government has placed strong curbs on religious speech that strays into the realm of politics. Singaporean women have free access to both birth control and abortion, rights that religious groups have not sought to rescind.

CULTURAL IMPACT Buddhism has had little impact on the performing arts in Singapore, and religion is not a common theme in the regional forms of *jingju* (Chinese opera) popular with many dialect-speaking Singaporeans. The impact of Buddhism is more clearly evident in temple architecture, though traditional Chinese temples are more influenced by Chinese cultural and design precepts than Buddhist ones.

Other Religions

The overwhelming majority of Singapore's ethnic Malay community practices Islam, a religion that constitutes an inseparable component of their cultural identity. In addition, a quarter of Singapore's Indian population is Muslim. Singapore's Geylang Serai neighborhood comes alive after nightfall during Ramadan, as Malays flock to the area for a *pasar malam* (night market) offering an array of goods, conversation, and an abundance of food to break the daylong fast. Hari Raya Puasa marks the end of the fasting period and involves paying respects to one's elders, resolving conflicts, and asking for forgiveness.

A form of Shariah law is administered by the Islamic Religious Council of Singapore (MUIS), a quasi-governmental organization that regulates matters such as inheritance, marriage, and divorce for Muslim Singaporeans. Under Shariah law Muslim men are permitted to practice polygamy, but this is relatively rare in Singapore. Muslim women are free to wear the traditional headscarf or the more concealing chador, but girls are required to keep their heads uncovered at government-run schools.

Though it is considered sacrilegious, some Singaporean Muslims engage in *keramat* worship, a practice that involves venerating the graves of important historical figures. Offerings in the form of bananas, stones tied to strings, or glutinous rice are made at a number of significant sites in Singapore.

Christians represent less than 15 percent of the total population, and the majority of these are Protestant, while approximately one-third are Roman Catholic. Pentecostal forms of Protestantism have become increasing popular and appear poised for continued growth. All the major Christian groups are present, and services are held in English, Mandarin, and Chinese dialects. Christianity has increasingly become the religion of educated, English-speaking, upwardly mobile Chinese Singaporeans.

British colonials took Protestant denominations and the Catholic Church to Singapore, building three especially noteworthy structures in the mid-nineteenth century: the Armenian Church, designed by noted architect George Coleman; Saint Andrew's Cathedral, designed in the Gothic Revival style; and the Cathedral of the Good Shepherd, Singapore's first permanent Catholic church.

Many Singaporean Chinese celebrate Christmas regardless of their religion, though the holiday's public face is more commercial than religious. Christian Singaporeans tend to celebrate it much as Western Christians do, with special worship services, the exchange of gifts, and visits to family and friends. Special services are also held in many Christian churches for Chinese New Year.

In 1987 the government arrested and detained 22 social activists, many of whom were influenced by the Liberation Theology movement within the Catholic Church; the government claimed that they had sought to overthrow the government and turn Singapore into a Marxist state. The detainees were all eventually released, but since then Christian groups in Singapore have carefully steered clear of politics.

Though there was a decline in the number of Singaporean Taoists during the 1980s and 1990s, the religion is more significant in the Chinese community than its relatively small numbers suggest. Taoist deities sit alongside the Buddha and portraits of ancestors on many family altars, and many older Singaporeans practice a fusion religion that brings together elements of Taoism, Buddhism, and Confucianism. Noteworthy Taoist temples include the Thaian Hock Keng Temple, which has been an important site for Singapore's Hokkien-speaking immigrants since the early days of settlement, and the Tua Peh Kong Temple on Kusu Island, a popular pilgrimage spot that is much visited during the ninth lunar month.

While Confucianism is not a recognized religion for census purposes, Singapore is a center for neo-Confucian thought, and former prime minister Lee Kuan Yew has been active in the International Confucian Association. Singapore's principal Chinese holidays reflect traditional Confucian values more than overtly religious ones. The country's principal holiday is Chinese New Year, which marks the beginning of the lunar new year (January/February). The festival culminates on the eve and the first two days of the new year, during which time Chinese families come together to convey greetings, exchange *hong bao* (money packets in red envelopes), and offer respect to their elders. Other significant Chinese holidays include the Ching Ming Festival, when homage is paid to one's ancestors; the Dragon Boat Festival, which commemorates the death of the Chinese poet-scholar Qu Yuan; and the Hungry Ghost's Festival, when offerings are put out to appease the spirits of the dead.

Singapore's sizable Hindu community is almost exclusively composed of ethnic Indians, most of whom are descendants of laborers taken to Singapore by the British in the nineteenth and early twentieth centuries. The country's oldest Hindu temple, the Sri Mariamman Temple, was once used as a temporary residence for new immigrants; it serves as an important center for Tamil culture. The Sri Thandayuthapani Temple (also known as Chettiar's Hindu Temple), completed in 1860 and significantly restored since that time, is one of the grandest and most opulent Hindu temples in the region.

The most important purely religious Hindu rite is Thaipusam, held in the Tamil month of *Thai* (January/February). For this rite, devotees, often with their skin pierced by metal skewers, carry a load-bearing pole known as a *kavadi* through the streets to honor a vow made to the Lord Subramaniam. This procession—especially popular among working-class, Tamil-speaking Hindus—ends when the worshiper deposits an offering attached to his *kavadi* inside the Sri Thandayuthapani Temple. Thimithi, a ritual in which devotees of the goddess Draupadi walk on burning coals at the Sri Mariamman Temple, falls in the Tamil month of Aipasi (October/November). Also falling in Aipasi, the holiday of Deepavali cuts across all Hindu ethnic and caste lines. With this festival the defeat of the demon Narakasura by the Lord Krishna, and the victory of light over darkness, are commemorated by the lighting of lamps and massive public lighting displays in Singapore's Little India neighborhood.

Spirit mediums and individuals with powers of divination and the gift of healing have also historically been relied upon for their services, not only in the Chinese community but also among the Malay, who refer to such individuals as *bomoh.* Though spirit mediums have largely disappeared from the Chinese temples since the 1950s, it is not uncommon to find someone capable of reading tossed joss sticks or practicing other forms of divination within the temple grounds for a fee. Today spirit mediums, healers, and *bomoh* work largely from private residences, and clients are referred through word-of-mouth.

William Peterson

See Also Vol. 1: *Buddhism, Christianity, Confucianism, Hinduism, Islam, Mahayana Buddhism, Theravada Buddhism*

Bibliography

Clammer, John. "Religious Pluralism and Chinese Beliefs in Singapore." In *Chinese Beliefs and Practices in Southeast Asia.* Edited by Cheu Hock Tong. Selangor, Malaysia: Pelandunk Publications, 1993.

———. *The Sociology of Singapore Religion: Studies in Christianity and Chinese Culture.* Singapore: Chopmen Publishers, 1991.

Kuo, Eddie C.Y. *Religion in Singapore.* Singapore: Singapore National Printers, 1995.

Leow Bee Goek. *Census of Population 2000: Education, Language and Religion.* Singapore: Singapore Department of Statistics, 2001.

Tamney, Joseph B., and Linda Hsueh-Ling Chiang. *Modernization, Globalization, and Confucianism in Chinese Societies.* Westport, Conn.: Praeger, 2002.

Tham Seong Chee. *Religion and Modernization: A Study of Changing Rituals among Singapore's Chinese, Malays and Indians.* Singapore: UNESCO, 1985.

Zuraihan Bte Isahak. *Cultural Practice versus Religious Injunctions: A Study of Keramat Worship in Singapore.* Singapore: National University of Singapore, 1995.

Slovakia

POPULATION 5,422,366

ROMAN CATHOLIC 68.9 percent

EVANGELICAL (LUTHERAN) 6.9 percent

GREEK CATHOLIC 4.1 percent

REFORMED 2.0 percent

NOT AFFILIATED 13.0 percent

OTHER 5.1 percent

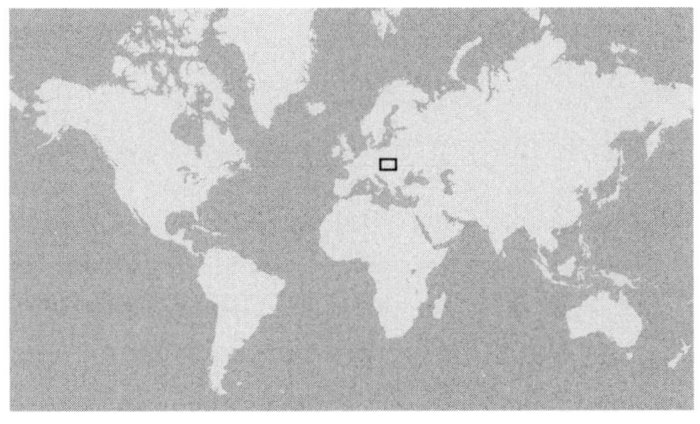

Country Overview

INTRODUCTION Located in central Europe, the Slovak Republic is bordered by Poland and the Czech Republic to the north, Austria to the west, Hungary to the south, and Ukraine to the east. Since the eighth and ninth centuries Christianity has played a crucial role in the history and culture of Slovakia, and it continues to form an integral part of Slovak national identity.

Formerly part of Hungary, Slovakia became a constituent republic of Czechoslovakia in 1918. Between 1948 and 1989 it was ruled by a Communist regime, which systematically tried to eliminate religion from the country. The independent Slovak Republic was created in 1993 after the "velvet" dissolution of Czechoslovakia. According to the 2001 census, more than 83 percent of the population is Christian.

RELIGIOUS TOLERANCE Historically in Slovakia there has been mutual toleration among religious groups. For centuries the Slovaks have lived in central Europe together with the Czechs, Austrians, and Hungarians. It was religion that united these nations in a multinational monarchy, Austria-Hungary, from 1867 to 1918. Today signs of ecumenism in Slovakia include the activities of the Ecumenical Council of Churches, as well as occasional common prayers and a search for shared pursuits among various denominations. Religious radicalism and fundamentalism have no tradition in Slovakia, nor do they exist today.

Major Religion

ROMAN CATHOLICISM

DATE OF ORIGIN Eighth–ninth century C.E.

NUMBER OF FOLLOWERS 3.7 million

HISTORY The first Christian church in what is now Slovakia was consecrated in 828. In 880 the first bishopric in the area was established in the city of Nitra. The Christian missionaries who went there were mainly Franks, but there were also Irish-Scottish and Italian

Located in Bratislava, St. Martin's Cathedral is the most renowned Catholic church in Slovakia. For centuries it was used for the coronation ceremonies of the Habsburg monarchy. © WOLFGANG KAEHLER/CORBIS.

missions. An important date was 863, when Saints Cyril and Methodius, the Macedonian-born "Apostles of the Slavs," went to the Great Moravian Empire (which included the territory of Slovakia). They and their pupils not only translated the Bible and the liturgy but also created original works in the Slavic language.

In 885 Pope Stephen V—acting under the influence of the Bavarian clergy—prohibited the use of the Slavic liturgy. As a result, the Great Moravian duke Svätopluk expelled the pupils of Saints Cyril and Methodius from his empire. This act had profound historical consequences, as it meant the integration of the Slavs into the Western, Latin culture. The terms Christian, Western, and Catholic started to be used as equivalents in this area. The further institutionalization of Christianity in the area was facilitated by constructing a network of churches and other sacral architecture, mainly during the twelfth century.

In the sixteenth century the territory was divided as a result of the Protestant Reformation. People of Slovak and German origin became mostly affiliated with the Evangelical Church of the Augsburg Confession. Hungarians turned mainly to Calvinism. In the seventeenth century, after the Counter-Reformation, many people—especially those in the northern and western parts of present-day Slovakia—returned to the Roman Catholic Church; Greek Catholicism took hold in eastern Slovakia.

By the early eighteenth century members of the Catholic clergy had been instrumental in creating a Slovak national identity. Since 1977 Slovakia has constituted an ecclesiastical province within the Catholic Church, and since 1995 there have been two church provinces in Slovakia: Bratislava-Trnava and Košice.

EARLY AND MODERN LEADERS In the past Slovak Catholic leaders were notable for their involvement in cultural and educational development. Anton Bernolák (1762–1813), for example, was a Catholic priest who codified the first official version of the Slovak language. There are two well-known Slovak cardinals: Jozef

Tomko (born in 1924) and Ján Chryzostom Korec (born in 1924).

MAJOR THEOLOGIANS AND AUTHORS An author who profoundly influenced Catholic intellectual thought in Slovakia was Ladislav Hanus (1907–94); his work in the fields of theology, philosophy, and sacral architecture was inspired by twentieth-century theologian Romano Guardini. In 1940 Jozef Spirko published an important history of the Catholic Church and its presence in Slovakia. The work of Cardinal Ján Chryzostom Korec is devoted mainly to the history of the Catholic Church in Slovakia, especially during the Communist period.

HOUSES OF WORSHIP AND HOLY PLACES In Slovakia the houses of worship and holy places of the Roman Catholic Church are churches, chapels, crucifixes, calvaries, sanctuaries, and icons of the Virgin Mary. These sacral buildings and objects are dispersed throughout the country. Of special importance are places of pilgrimages connected with the Virgin Mary. The best known of these is Šaštín-Stráže, a small town with the National Basilica of the Virgin Mary of the Seven Sorrows. Other important Marian pilgrimage places are churches in the towns of Levoča, Mariánka, Staré Hory, Nitra, Lutina, and Rajecká Lesná (with the popular handmade wooden crèche). The most renowned Catholic church in Slovakia is Saint Martin's Cathedral (Dóm svätého Martina) in Bratislava, a Gothic church that for centuries was used for the coronation ceremonies of the Habsburg monarchy.

WHAT IS SACRED? In Slovakia sacred status is attributed to houses of worship and holy places and to the great feasts of the Roman Catholic Church. See the sections immediately above and below this one.

HOLIDAYS AND FESTIVALS Religious celebrations and official state holidays often overlap. There are 14 state holidays in Slovakia, and nine of them are Christian feasts: Epiphany (6 January), Good Friday, Easter Monday, All Saint's Day (1 November), Christmas Eve (24 December), Nativity of the Lord (25 December), Saint Stephen's Day (26 December), Our Lady of the Seven Sorrows (the patron of Slovakia, 15 September), and Saints Cyril and Methodius the Apostles (5 July). The last two holidays are specifically Slovak Christian feasts.

There are also the following holy days of obligation: Virgin Mary, Mother of God (1 January), Ascension of the Lord (the 40th day after Easter), Most Holy Body and Blood of Christ (Thursday after the Sunday of the Most Holy Trinity), Saints Peter and Paul the Apostles (29 June), Assumption of Virgin Mary (15 August), and the Feast of the Immaculate Conception (8 December). There are special feasts connected with the patron saints of local churches or parishes.

MODE OF DRESS There is no distinctive mode of dress for Catholics in Slovakia. The Catholic clergy in Slovakia wears the attire prescribed by the general rules of the church.

DIETARY PRACTICES In Slovakia church regulations concerning Lent were strictly observed until the 1950s, but today compliance with them varies. It is thought that most Catholics in Slovakia observe at least the abstinence from meat on Ash Wednesday and Good Friday.

RITUALS Catholics in Slovakia perform worship services in accordance with church regulations. Attendance on Sundays and on other holy days of obligation was, until the 1950s, observed by a large majority of Catholics. The participation decreased substantially during the Communist regime. Today approximately one-third of the Catholics attend services regularly (i.e., on Sundays and on other holy days of obligation), and about one-fifth do not attend church at all.

Before the Communist period, prayer rituals formed a common part of everyday life, both private and public (e.g., in schools and hospitals). During the Communist regime prayers were restricted to the private sphere, and this arrangement has remained in practice.

Pilgrimages, especially Marian, have a long tradition in Slovakia, and there are more than 30 places of pilgrimage. Šaštín and Levoča are of national importance. In addition, Slovaks go on pilgrimages abroad, mainly to Poland, Austria, Italy, Spain, and the Holy Land.

RITES OF PASSAGE The rites of passage for Slovak Catholics correspond with the seven sacraments of the church: baptism, confirmation, Holy Eucharist, penance, anointing of the sick, holy orders, and matrimony. While the lives of most Catholics were structured by these religious ceremonies before the 1950s, the Communist regime altered this practice, promoting at first dual ceremonies (religious and civil) and then strictly civil ones. After the fall of Communism there was a renaissance of religious ceremonies (such as baptisms, church weddings, and church funerals).

MEMBERSHIP The sacrament of Baptism is the means of initiation into the Catholic Church in Slovakia as elsewhere. After the fall of Communism in 1989, the church began to use the media—radio, television, and the Internet—to spread its message. The Slovak clergy and members of religious orders participate in missions in many countries.

SOCIAL JUSTICE In Slovakia the church is involved in social justice issues, especially education, poverty, and human rights. It focuses on work in hospitals, nursing wards, orphanages, and homeless shelters; it also works with convicts, single mothers, and members of the minority Roma community.

The Slovak Catholic Charity is an independent organization that pursues primarily social and charitable activities. There are more than 100 Catholic schools in Slovakia, including primary and secondary schools as well as universities, and there are also special and vocational educational institutions. The church issues official statements on questions of social justice and human rights through the pastoral letters of the Slovak Bishop's Conference, which emphasize individual responsibility.

SOCIAL ASPECTS Marriage and raising children remain two of the main priorities declared by Slovak Catholics, in particular by the church hierarchy and by many Catholic lay associations. In 2001 Slovakia for the first time had more deaths than births in its population. The regions with the highest birthrates, such as Orava, had the highest percentage of Catholics.

POLITICAL IMPACT Because of Slovakia's location in central Europe, it has been involved in various religious wars of Europe. During World War II representatives of the Catholic clergy held key positions in the Slovak Republic, which collaborated with Germany. The church also played a political role during the destruction of Communism in the 1980s; the need for social change during this period was articulated primarily by Catholics.

Today the church does not openly engage in politics, though its statements and views can have political implications. In general, Catholics in Slovakia do not support left-wing parties.

CONTROVERSIAL ISSUES The most sensitive issue for Catholics in Slovakia has been abortion, especially since the government adopted a liberal abortion statute in 1988. The constitutionality of the statute has been questioned, and Slovak Catholics, although not completely uniform in their views, have generally opposed the statute. Another controversial issue, for both the Catholic and Evangelical churches, is whether shops should be forbidden to open on Sundays and on other Christian feasts. Most Catholics have been in favor of keeping the shops open.

CULTURAL IMPACT In Slovakia the cultural impact of the Catholic Church and its members has been substantial in literature, music, art, and especially architecture. There is a wide range of sacral buildings all over the Slovak territory. Saints Cyril and Methodius created original works in the Slavic language, and their texts are considered literary treasures of the early Middle Ages. The Virgin Mary, the saints, and Biblical stories have found their way into the work of many artists. The influence of the church on traditional everyday and folk culture, though visible, has been gradually overcome by secularism.

Other Religions

In addition to Roman Catholicism, the major Christian churches in Slovakia include the Greek Catholic Church, the Evangelical Church of the Augsburg Confession (Lutheran), and the Reformed Christian Church (Calvinist). Membership in the remaining faiths was, according to the 2001 census, less than 1 percent of the population.

Jews have lived in Slovakia since the early Middle Ages. Prior to the World War II they formed about 3.5 percent of the population, but during the Nazi era most perished in the Holocaust. Today Jews in Slovakia are represented by the Central Union of Jewish Religious Communities.

The Greek Catholic Church is affiliated with the Roman Catholic Church. Its roots in the area go back to Saint Cyril and Saint Methodius, who introduced the Byzantine (Eastern) rites to the Slovak territory in 863. Cyril and Methodius translated the liturgy into the Slavic language, and this Slavonic liturgy is used to this day by Byzantine-rite Slavs. The Greek Catholic Church was founded through the Uzhorod Union in 1646, when

Byzantine Christians were reunited with Rome. In Slovakia it had just one bishopric, which was abolished in 1950 by the Communists, who forced Greek Catholics to join the Orthodox Church. In 1968 Greek Catholics were again allowed union with Rome, but the church began to develop freely only after 1990, when it was partially compensated for the wrongs perpetrated against it by the government. The Greek Catholic Church in Slovakia currently forms an independent church province with a hierarchical structure; its head is a residential bishop, nominated by the pope. The bishop is a member of the Bishop's Conference of Slovakia. Greek Catholics mainly live in eastern Slovakia.

The Evangelicals (Lutherans) represent, after the Catholics, the second largest religious group in Slovakia. Its history in Slovakia dates back to the first half of the sixteenth century. In Hungary (of which Slovakia was a part until 1918) the organizational structure of the Evangelical church took form following the Žilina Synod in 1610. Evangelicals were later aided by the Toleration Patent of 1781, which allowed the free development of churches in Hungary. In 1919 the Evangelical Church of the Augsburg Confession in Slovakia—with a democratic ecclesiastical organization and administration—proclaimed independence from what was then the Evangelical Church of Hungary. Its clergy and scholars contributed to a large extent to the cultural, educational, and national revival of the Slovaks during the nineteenth century, laying down the ideological and political foundation of the modern Slovak nation.

Calvinism spread in the region mainly among those of Hungarian origin. In 1918–21 the Reformed Christian Church emerged in Slovakia as an autonomous Calvinist body. Its highest authority is the Synod, with a bishop and the curator-general (a layman) at its head. The church is a member of the World Reformed Alliance and the World Council of Churches. The Reformed Christian Church is the only church in Slovakia in which ethnic Hungarians form a majority.

The Orthodox Church (also referred to as the Eastern Church) began in Slovakia in 1924, when Russian emigrants founded an Orthodox monastery in Ladomírová. The Communist government forcibly added Greek Catholics to the church following the so-called Prešov Ecclesiastical Congress in 1950. After 1968, when Greek Catholics were allowed to reunite with Rome, the Orthodox Church pursued negotiations with the Greek Catholic Church for the settlement of property claims. The Orthodox Church in Slovakia forms part of an independent church with its headquarters in Prague. It has two eparchies (dioceses) in Slovakia, which are made up of various ecclesiastical communities and other bodies.

In Slovakia there are also members of the Church of the Old Catholics, which was founded after the First Vatican Council (1870). Old Catholics split from the Roman Catholic Church because they rejected the council's doctrine of papal infallibility. The church's international center is in Utrecht, The Netherlands. It began to create its organizational structure in Slovakia only after World War I.

The Baptist Church, which is of Anglo-American origin, entered Slovakia in the 1860s, and the first Baptist community was founded in 1888. Methodism from the United States reached Slovakia in the 1920s and spread among those of Czech ethnicity. Also from the United States, Seventh-day Adventists appeared in Slovakia after the First World War, but their activities were not legalized until 1956. The Church of the Brethren was established in Slovakia in 1924 under the influence of the American Missionary Society.

Other religious groups in Slovakia include the Plymouth Brethren, founded in 1840 by an Anglican priest, J.N. Darby, and legalized in Slovakia in 1956; the Apostolic Church, a Protestant religious society legalized in Slovakia in 1969; and the Jehovah's Witnesses, registered in the Slovak Republic since 1993. In addition, there are many communities of nontraditional beliefs; these are associated with Christianity, Eastern traditions, or occultism. Their forms and activities vary significantly.

Adela Kvasničková

See Also Vol. I: *Christianity, Eastern Rite Churches, Lutheranism, Roman Catholicism*

Bibliography

Henderson, Karen. *Slovakia: Escape from Invisibility.* London and New York: Routledge, 2002.

Kirschbaum, Stanislav J. *A History of Slovakia: The Struggle for Survival.* New York: St. Martin's Press, 1995.

Poláčik, Š., ed. *Atlas cirkví, náboženských spoločností a religiozity Slovenska.* Bratislava: Chronos, 2000.

Sčítanie obyvatelov, domov a bytov 2001. Bratislava: Statistical Office of the Slovak Republic, 2001.

Toma, Peter A., and Dušan Kováč. *Slovakia: From Samo to Dzurinda.* Stanford, Calif.: Hoover Institution Press, 2001.

Slovenia

POPULATION 1,964,000

ROMAN CATHOLIC 57.8 percent

REFUSED TO ANSWER 15.7 percent

ATHEIST 10.1 percent

UNKNOWN 7.1 percent

NONCONFESSIONAL BELIEVERS 3.5 percent

MUSLIM 2.4 percent

ORTHODOX 2.3 percent

PROTESTANT 0.9 percent

OTHER 0.2 percent

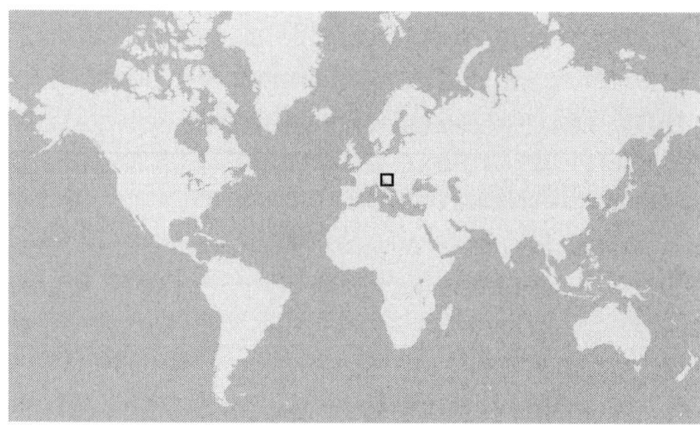

Country Overview

INTRODUCTION The Republic of Slovenia, a Central European country, is bordered by Italy to the west, Austria to the north, Hungary to the northeast, and Croatia to the south and southeast. The coast of the Gulf of Venice is a small part of its western border. The first organized Slovene state was the Duchy of Carantania (630–745 C.E.). In 745 Borut, duke of Carantania, accepted Christianity in order to receive support from Bavaria. Carantania politically came under the Bavarian and the Frankish reign. The Habsburgs began to rule the region in the thirteenth and fourteenth centuries, continuing to do so until the end of the First World War (1918).

Slovenes became part of the multinational and multireligious Kingdom of Serbs, Croats, and Slovenes (renamed Yugoslavia in 1929), which was Catholic in the north, Orthodox in the south, and partly Muslim in Bosnia and Herzegovina, Kosovo, and Macedonia. During the Second World War Germany invaded Yugoslavia (1941), partitioning it and annexing northern Slovenia. Josip Broz Tito of the Communist Party of Yugoslavia led the struggle against the occupation. By 1945 Tito had consolidated Communist control of Yugoslavia; during the Communist years the state promoted an atheistic ideology, which was intolerant toward religion.

After Tito's death (1980) political and cultural movements for democratization in Yugoslavia arose and caused the fall of Communism and the dissolution of the state. Slovenia seceded from Yugoslavia in 1991, and the following year the independent state of Slovenia was recognized internationally. An era of political democratization and religious freedom began.

The majority of Slovenes are Catholic. A small number of Slovenes adhere to Protestantism, which has been in Slovenia since the sixteenth century. Most Muslims and Orthodox Christians in Slovenia migrated there from Bosnia and Serbia when Slovenia was part of Yugoslavia. The number of new religious groups has been growing since the 1980s.

RELIGIOUS TOLERANCE The Communist government (1945–90) implemented a constitutional separation of church and state. Religious believers were excluded from higher political and leadership positions until 1990. The constitution of Slovenia (1991) preserves the separation of state and religious entities, and the state has guaranteed the equal rights of religious communities and the free profession of faith. Nevertheless, there have been reports of intolerance toward Orthodox and Muslims.

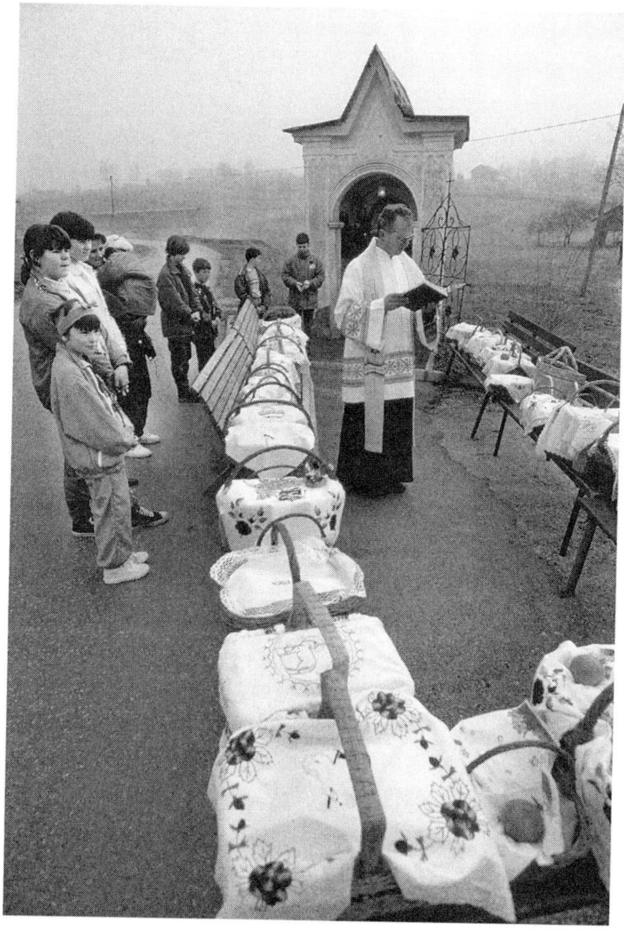

A priest blesses baskets of Easter breakfast food in Moravee, Slovenia. © BOJAN BRECELJ/CORBIS.

Major Religion

ROMAN CATHOLICISM

DATE OF ORIGIN 745 C.E.
NUMBER OF FOLLOWERS 1.1 million

HISTORY Christianity has existed in Slovenian territory since the first century C.E., when the region was part of the Roman Empire. During the seventh and eighth centuries missionaries from Salzburg (now in Austria) and Aquiliea (in modern-day Italy) introduced Christianity to Slovenes. Christianity was officially established in 745 C.E., when Borut, duke of Carantania, converted as a condition of receiving Bavarian protection against invaders from the east. Saints Cyril and Methodius from Macedonia, known as the Apostles of the Slavs, arrived in the region in 866. They translated the scriptures and liturgical texts into the Slavic language, and a written Slavic culture began. In the tenth and eleventh centuries a network of parishes was formed. Numerous monasteries were built in the twelfth century, and the first two dioceses were established in 1228 and 1461.

In 1525 Protestant teachings started to spread throughout Europe. In reaction, the Catholic Church implemented the Counter-Reformation. In Slovenia this Catholic renewal led to a flourishing of religious life, particularly pilgrimages. Fraternal and monastic organizations multiplied. In the eighteenth century, by the imperial reforms of Maria Theresa (1717–80) and Emperor Joseph II (1741–90), numerous new parishes were established, but a great number of monasteries were closed.

The greatest challenge for the Catholic Church in Slovenia was the victory of the Communist Revolution and its regime (1945). Many priests were killed, and others (together with many thousands of laypeople) emigrated to avoid the Communist persecutions. More than 200 priests were imprisoned. Church property was expropriated, and all church schools were closed. The Communist regime intended to destroy the church, and when this proved unsuccessful, they tried to marginalize it socially.

From the end of the 1960s a softening occurred on the part of the state, and the Slovenian Catholic Church was able to reorganize itself. After Slovenia's independence the church gained more freedom, but it was faced with the challenge of negotiating with the new state and was limited by its uncertain economic situation. The Slovenian Bishops' Conference was established in 1993.

EARLY AND MODERN LEADERS In its early history Slovenia had neither its own nobility nor military and political leaders; consequently, the role of religious leaders became more significant. Bishop Tomaz Hren was one of the leaders of the Slovenian Counter-Reformation in the late sixteenth and early seventeenth centuries. Bishop Alojzij Wolf (1824–59) published a new translation of the Bible and founded a school for boys. Bishop Anton Martin Slomsek (1800–62) was a poet and writer who supported Slovenian national revival. He promoted education, and by reorganizing his diocese he influenced the later establishment of the national boundaries. In 1999 he was beatified, becoming the first Slovenian saint.

Before the Second World War there were some significant Slovenian priests, including Anton Korosec (1872–1940) in politics and Janez Evangelist Krek (1865–1917) in the social field. During the years of Communism the bishops were the only public authorities not subordinated to the Communist state.

MAJOR THEOLOGIANS AND AUTHORS Franc Grivec (1878–1963), ecclesiologist, developed the idea of Christian universality and of the brotherhood of the Eastern and Western Christians, blazing the trail for the church's ecumenism. Ales Usenicnik (1868–1952), a theologian and philosopher, defended the Christian faith against atheism and liberalism. The poet and theology professor Vladimir Truhlar (1912–77) researched the intertwining of religion with aesthetics.

HOUSES OF WORSHIP AND HOLY PLACES Slovenia has a large number of churches, which are typically located on hilltops. A great number are pilgrimage destinations, and they are often dedicated to the Mother of God. The main pilgrimage center is the Basilica of Our Lady of Mercy in Brezje. Crosses and small chapels are common and are usually situated along roads or near homes. These are often signs of thanksgiving or remembrance of the deceased and have been decreasingly used for prayer.

WHAT IS SACRED? Popular Catholicism venerates religious signs—above all, the images of the cross, Mary, and the saints. In their homes believers often keep religious images that have been blessed. After the Communist era it became common to perform rites of blessing for new roads, bridges, schools, and houses.

HOLIDAYS AND FESTIVALS In Slovenia Christmas is the most popular holiday for Catholics. After the fall of Communism it was recognized as a labor and school holiday. Before Lent there is widespread merriment known as Carnival, but this has lost its religious dimension. After the Communist era the Feast of the Assumption (Mary's ascent into heaven; 15 August) was established as a state holiday, and it became popular to celebrate it with pilgrimages. On the Catholic All Saints' Day (1 November), called Remembrance Day, people visit relatives' graves.

MODE OF DRESS Slovenian Catholics do not have a particular mode of dress for their daily life or for Sundays and holidays. Children usually wear special dress to receive the sacraments of first Communion and confirmation. For more significant religious events, a minority of Catholics dress in traditional national costumes. After the period of Communism ended, it was again possible for priests, monks, and nuns to wear their official uniforms in public.

DIETARY PRACTICES Catholic fasting rules require a strict fast and abstinence for Ash Wednesday and Good Friday. Meat is forbidden, and only one full meal a day is allowed. Most of the faithful in Slovenia fulfill this obligation. Many older Catholics in Slovenia also observe meatless Friday, which was a common practice in the past.

RITUALS The central Catholic ritual is the Mass. Although the Communist regime frequently hindered liturgy (it did not permit ritual outside of the church; sports and other activities were organized during the time of the Mass), attendance at Sunday Mass was significantly higher in the past. Now only about one-fifth of Slovenian Catholics attend Sunday Mass.

RITES OF PASSAGE In Slovenia major life transitions have traditionally been marked by Roman Catholic rituals. The rate of participation in such rituals is much higher than for ordinary church worship. The Communist authorities introduced socialist rituals, often as attempts to replace the Catholic rites of passage. The civil rite of marriage was obligatory; the Catholic wedding ceremony could only be done afterward. Interest in church weddings has been increasing in Slovenia. The most solemn rite of passage is priest ordination. When a newly ordained priest celebrates Mass in his home parish for the first time, hundreds of guests honor the occasion with a banquet.

MEMBERSHIP Eighty percent of the Slovenian population have formally been church members through baptism, but in the 2002 census only 57.8 percent of Slovenians reported being Catholics. Mostly they are baptized as infants, but some parents leave this decision to their children. To avoid nominal membership, the church has begun to request the parents' religious preparation for this rite. The church has become the subject of general critical observation in Slovenia. There has also been a rise in the number of nonconfessional believers (people who are believers but who belong to no religion), which may be linked to the decrease in the number of Catholics.

SOCIAL JUSTICE At the beginning of the Communist regime the church was not allowed to speak out on societal issues. In the 1970s the Catholic Church took action against the discrimination of citizens on the basis of religious beliefs. The church also opposed the state's use of the educational system to promote atheism.

In 1985 the church's Commission for Justice and Peace was established. It has prepared statements related to all socially relevant questions, including constitutional changes, respect for human rights, and justice for victims executed during and after the revolution (many of whom remain buried in hidden crevasses).

SOCIAL ASPECTS The Catholic Church in Slovenia supports the traditional form of the family. It is against pluralizing family forms, which would provide same-sex unions with the same rights as married couples.

POLITICAL IMPACT Before the Second World War the Catholic Church influenced politics in Slovenia primarily through the pro-clerical political parties, thereby intensifying polarization between the clerical and liberal camps. Throughout the Communist era the presence and ordinary work of the church was viewed as an alternative to the state's ideology. By educating young Christians, the church helped bring about Communism's demise. The church supported Slovenia's incorporation into the European Union, which was finalized in 2004.

CONTROVERSIAL ISSUES Many antagonisms remain between the state and the church in Slovenia. From the church's point of view, liberalism contains many elements of atheistic Communism; the liberal side accuses the church of striving for wealth and political power. Because of the church's opposition to abortion, contraception, euthanasia, artificial insemination without the father's role, and institutionalizing same-sex unions, it has been accused of destructive conservatism. The church's aspiration for religious education in public schools has been a highly controversial issue.

CULTURAL IMPACT The oldest known Slovenian—and also Slavic—text written in the Latin alphabet is *Brizinski spomeniki* (tenth century; "Freising Monuments"), a collection of documents containing sermons and liturgical texts. In the eighteenth and nineteenth centuries literary figures included the Catholic priests Marko Pohlin (1735–1801), Jurij Japelj (1744–1807), and Franc Serafin Metelko (1789–1860). In the twentieth century the priests Franc Saleski Finzgar (1871–1962) and Franc Ksaver Mesko (1874–1962), among others, developed strong literary activities.

Christianity has inspired the poetry and literature of many Slovenian writers, including the poet France Preseren (1800–49) and the novelist Ivan Cankar (1876–1918). In the fine arts most of the Catholic cultural heritage is represented by sacral art, the oldest example being the late-fifteenth-century "Danse Macabre" (dance of death) frescoes in the Holy Trinity Church in Hrastovilje, in the region of Istria. Churches are the oldest and most prominent cultural monuments in Slovenia. The sacral works of Joze Plecnik (1872–1957), a Slovenian architect, are of international importance.

Other Religions

In Slovenia there are 34 religious groups registered in addition to the Catholic Church. The beginnings of the Protestant movement in Slovenia go back to the sixteenth century. Slovenian representatives of the Protestant Reformation included Primoz Trubar (1508–86) and Jurij Dalmatin (1547–89). Trubar published the first printed books in the Slovenian language in 1550, and Dalmatin prepared a complete translation of the Bible (published in 1584).

In the Counter-Reformation period (sixteenth and seventeenth centuries) the Protestant Church in Slovenia was suppressed, except for two parishes. After the Proclamation of Tolerance was issued in 1781, the parishes were gradually reestablished. Today the Protestant Church of Slovenia belongs to the Augsburg denomination.

In Slovenia Muslim and Orthodox Christian religious communities are the most populous after Catholicism. These communities largely migrated from Bosnia and Serbia when they, along with Slovenia, were part of Yugoslavia. In 1967 an Islamic religious community was established. There are plans to build a mosque in the capital, Ljubljana. The Orthodox believers are organized in nine parishes.

There have been Jewish communities in Slovenia since at least the twelfth century. In 1941 the Shoah (Holocaust) began in Slovenia. The vast majority of Jews—about 4,500— perished in extermination camps. Since 1976 the Slovenian Jewish community has been registered as an official religion; there are only about 100 members today.

Since the 1990s religious communities that developed from Buddhism and Hinduism have spread to Slovenia. They include the International Society for Krishna Consciousness, the Baha'i faith, and the United Church. New Age groups have also appeared in Slovenia.

Vinko Potocnik

See Also Vol. I: *Christianity, Roman Catholicism*

Bibliography

Alexander, Stella. *Church and State in Yugoslavia since 1945.* New York: Cambridge University Press, 1973.

Flere, Sergej, and Marko Kersevan. *Religija in sodobna druzba.* Ljubljana: Znanstveno in publicisticno sredisce, 1995.

Ramet, Sabrina P. *Balkan Babel : The Disintegration of Yugoslavia from the Death of Tito to the War for Kosovo.* 3rd. ed. Boulder, Colo.: Westview Press, 1999.

Roter, Zdenko, and Marko Kersevan. *Vera in nevera v Sloveniji, 1968–1978.* Maribor: Obzorja, 1982.

Sturm, Lovro, ed. *Cerkev in drzava.* Ljubljana: Nova revija, 2000.

Tomka, Miklós, et al. *Religion und Kirchen in Ost(Mittel)Europa: Ungarn, Litauen, Slowenien.* Ostfildern: Schwabenverlag, 1999.

Tomka, Miklós, and Paul Michael Zulehner, eds. *Religion during and after Communism.* London: SCM Press, 2000.

Solomon Islands

POPULATION 490,000

ANGLICAN 34 percent

ROMAN CATHOLIC 19 percent

SOUTH SEA EVANGELICAL (BAPTIST) 17 percent

UNITED CHURCH OF PAPUA NEW GUINEA AND THE SOLOMON ISLANDS 11 percent

SEVENTH-DAY ADVENTIST 10 percent

OTHER PROTESTANT 5 percent

TRADITIONALIST 4 percent

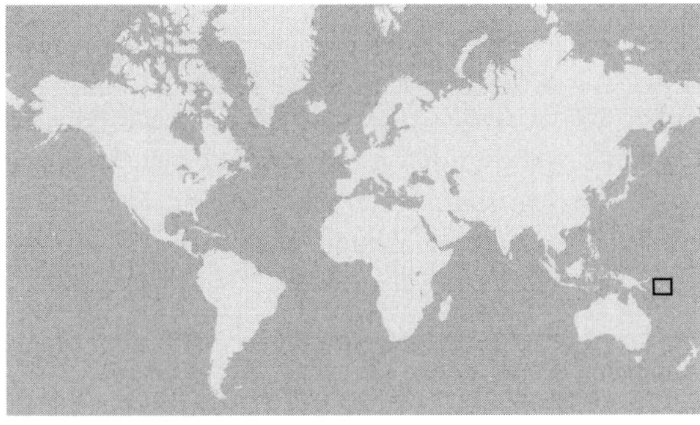

Country Overview

INTRODUCTION The Solomon Islands, an island archipelago in the southwestern Pacific Ocean, lies just east of Papua New Guinea. Its main islands include Choiseul, New Georgia, Santa Isabel, Malaita, Guadalcanal, and Makira (or San Cristobal). The inhabitants are nearly all Melanesians, but some are western Polynesians.

As a result of missionary work since the mid-nineteenth century, the islands are almost exclusively Christian. The geographical distribution of denominations derives from an interchurch agreement in 1880. Guadalcanal is mainly Anglican and Catholic; on Malaita the South Sea Evangelical Church is concentrated in the north, while Anglicans are more widely spread. In the remaining larger islands the United Church (formerly the Methodists) is strong in the west, as are the Adventists, and Anglicans predominate in the central west and the east. Traditional customs remain strong in the country's 90 indigenous culture areas, and in some pockets traditional religion persists.

RELIGIOUS TOLERANCE The constitution affirms freedom of religion. Interchurch relations are cordial, even if larger groupings have a history of mistrusting smaller Protestantism denominations (such as Adventism) and independent movements. In the case of serious conflict (such as the civil war at the turn of the twenty-first century), tribal principles of revenge are readily invoked to justify armed action, and the Bible is often used to support such actions.

Major Religion

CHRISTIANITY

DATE OF ORIGIN 1857 C.E.

NUMBER OF FOLLOWERS 470,000

Skulls of tribal chiefs and warriors rest in a sacred burial site in the Solomon Islands. The skulls date back to the tribal battles at the turn of the twentieth century. © AFP/CORBIS.

HISTORY When missionaries first arrived in the 1840s, Solomon Islanders had a reputation for fierce fighting (and even headhunting). The most dangerous area was to the west. The eastern islands appeared more promising, and after French Marist failures (1847–48), the Anglican Melanesian Mission had a serious impact there by 1857. After Britain took full colonial protection over the Solomons in 1893, other missions established themselves. French Marists arrived again in 1898, Australian Methodists in 1902, a branch of the Queensland Kanaka Mission (later the South Sea Evangelical Mission) in 1904, and the Seventh-day Adventists in 1914. In 1926 the Anglicans added New Guinea to their Melanesian diocese.

World War II affected the Solomons in 1942–43 when Japan invaded the islands, but the Japanese were repelled by Allied forces, and the threat to church growth was removed. Anticolonial sentiments followed the war, and the Solomons achieved independence in 1978, only to experience a civil war (1998–2003) that polarized inhabitants of Malaita and Guadalcanal.

EARLY AND MODERN LEADERS Anglican George Selwyn (foundation bishop of New Zealand from 1841) founded the Melanesian Mission in 1849, and John Coleridge Patteson became the first bishop of Melanesia in 1861. The latter's death in 1871 at the hands of Nukapu Islanders (who had taken him to be a labor recruiter, or "slaver") spurred the first serious attempts by colonial governments in Australia and New Zealand to curtail forcible-labor recruiting in the islands.

Two early Solomonese Anglican leaders were George Sarawia (c. 1860–1901), the first indigenous priest, and Ini Kopuria (c. 1900–45), founder of the Melanesian Brothers. New Zealand Methodist missionary John Goldie stands out for his vociferous stance against trader's handling of local people. A Methodist Choiseulese, Leslie Boseto, was later to become the best-known moderator of the United Church (1973–80). Silas Eto, called the Holy Mama (1905–84), founded the separatist Christian Fellowship Church (CFC) on New Georgia.

MAJOR THEOLOGIANS AND AUTHORS English Anglican missionary Robert Codrington (1830–1922) wrote the first general work on Melanesian cultures. The first Solomonese writer was deacon Clement Marau (1858–c. 1910); a Banks Islander, he wrote an autobiographical account of his evangelistic work on Ulawa in the eastern Solomons.

HOUSES OF WORSHIP AND HOLY PLACES Of the churches in the Solomon Islands, the Siota Cathedral on Small Nggela Island receives the most pilgrims. Others of interest are the Catholic Holy Cross Cathedral in Honiara; Anglican village churches on San Cristobal, which are traditionally timber-framed and decorated; and, on New Georgia, churches with unusual iconography combining Roviana and Wesleyan motifs (built by the independent CFC).

WHAT IS SACRED? For most Solomonese the best-known sacred place is the martyr's memorial at Nipwa on the Polynesian reef island of Nukapu. This marks Bishop Patteson's death in 1871, discussed above under EARLY AND MODERN LEADERS. In pre-Christian tradition the notion of *mana* denoted sacred things and power, and it continues to be used to indicate dynamism both in the exertion of authority and in the events of life. People with remarkable gifts of leadership can have the term applied to them.

HOLIDAYS AND FESTIVALS Apart from Independence Day and Liberation Day, the major Solomons holidays reflect Christian, especially Anglican, practice. These include Easter, Whit Sunday, Queen's Birthday, and Christmas (which is followed by National Thanksgiving Day on 26 December). The most colorful church celebrations connect tradition and church—for instance, when the arrival of the first missionaries is celebrated on a given island.

MODE OF DRESS In leaving behind traditional attire for Western dress, the Solomons reflect the same massive shift experienced everywhere in Melanesia over the last hundred years. Little distinguishes the Solomonese dress, except in the case of the indigenous Anglican brotherhoods and sisterhoods. The Melanesian Brothers wear black shirts and shorts with a white sash and black waistcloth, symbolizing the light of Christ shining in the midst of "heathen" darkness.

DIETARY PRACTICES In the Solomon Islands pigs are the most highly prized domesticated animal, and pork is consumed in both traditional rites and at many church celebrations (except among the Seventh-day Adventists, for whom pork and coastal crabs are forbidden). Yams and taro are used in both customary and modern Christian festive practices.

RITUALS Christian worship often appears artificially Western in this Melanesian context. Few distinctively Solomonese Christian rituals have developed, except in terms of charismatic phenomena and music. South Sea Evangelicals of North Malaita experienced a "revival" in the 1970s; it involved collective experience of the Holy Spirit, healing miracles, indigenous interpretations of the Bible, and prayers and dreams in the Spirit.

"Spiritistic activity" had already marked the independent CFC on New Georgia. When Silas Eto (the Holy Mama) broke from Methodism (1950–60s), the phenomenon of *taturu* (collective ecstasy and seizures during worship) was taken as the legitimating sign of a new ecclesial identity. A centerpiece in CFC worship is singing hymns to brass band music; the hymns invoke the Holy Mama as "the fourth man" (or aspect) of the Trinity. Eto encouraged people to pray in the open air before lines of strings made of traditional material while visualizing God (instead of certain spirits, as in the old times).

RITES OF PASSAGE In a country where traditional initiations were by ordeals, the display of sacred objects in rituals, and a severe instilling of tribal rules, the Christian churches have few equivalents. The Christian ceremony of confirmation looks tame by comparison. Sometimes dramas are enacted to mark the seriousness of the transition to Christian life.

MEMBERSHIP Nominalism—the willing attachment to a church, yet with little involvement—is a common problem. Christianity has come to express "the new life" and a new identity, but many old pressures (to enact revenge for deaths, for example) have not died. Efforts to encourage stronger involvement in the practice of the Christian faith have been most obvious on Malaita, with the South Sea Evangelical Church revival in the 1970s and the "Practical Holiness" movements that began in the 1990s. Members of the Practical Holiness movements identify themselves as Israelites, fly an Israeli flag, and sometimes accept circumcision.

SOCIAL JUSTICE The churches have a strong tradition of medical and educational services and social welfare in the Solomon Islands. The Melanesian Brotherhood has helped the poor and acted for peace—monitoring the relinquishment of firearms (2002) in the civil war and opposing the Guadalcanal-based warlord Harold Keke (2003), who had fought to drive Malaitians from the island. The churches have fostered special respect toward women and children and have sponsored sporting competitions as substitutes for armed violence.

SOCIAL ASPECTS Christianity has significantly changed marriage and family life in the Solomons. Traditional polygyny has virtually ceased. Infanticide is proscribed by both the churches and state. Compact village units have replaced dispersed hamlets in the bush and the separation of the men in cult houses for ritual and warrior functions; more nuclear families now sleep under the same roofs. Social policies to limit the number of children in families for the sake of women's health are given some support from church leadership, but they have been resisted by most males (who oppose the use of birth-control methods).

POLITICAL IMPACT The Christian churches have had a crucial impact on Solomonese political life. Both the parliamentary and the public service elite typically appeal to a Christian basis for their activities. Political advantage can accrue to political leaders through their denominational connections.

CONTROVERSIAL ISSUES Revenge wars against enemies were expressions of group energy central to precolonial religious life in the Solomons, and the pull of warrior tradition continues. The "Christian peace" is always fragile because of the temptation to solve disputes by a show of force; those resorting to old manners are often called "skin Christians." The recent civil war has brought this controversial issue to a head. It is a challenge to the churches to help secure a lasting peace and the handing in of weapons.

CULTURAL IMPACT Traditional religious practice remains intact only in a few pockets of the Solomon Islands, yet the distinctiveness of most cultures has been retained. Dances, designs, languages, and food-presentation ceremonies have their place (albeit adapted) in church community-building, as well as in activities that promote a new national identity.

Introduced music styles include European hymns and choruses. Indigenous chants have been adapted for Christian praise, sometimes, especially in the west, with panpipes. Grassroots compositions have been promoted—as part of South Sea Evangelical revivalism, for instance, or as nationally disseminated string-band "spiritual songs." Churches often have art works that reflect traditional styles (for example, wooden Catholic crucifixes and designs on church facades).

Other Religions

Truly indigenous religious ritual is rare in the Solomon Islands. The isolated Kwaio of Malaita propitiate their ancestors and various local spirits through the sacrifice of pigs, the quest for prestige (*mana*) as gift-givers, and the observance of *tabus* (ancestral prohibitions passed down especially at initiations). In most areas churches have replaced ancestral shrines as centers for managing the fears and vexations arising from the old spirit world. Select traditional dances serve only to remind of the old days or are performed in modern competitions.

Since 1957 there has been one successful attempt to revive traditional lifeways: the Moro movement (which takes its name from its founder) in southern and western areas of Guadalcanal. They require that people live without Western clothes, Western food, and buildings. In the Moro movement there are signs of a collective hope that, through keeping the old ways, the ancestors will send untold riches.

Garry W. Trompf

See Also Vol. I: *Anglicanism/Episcopalianism, Christianity, Evangelical Movement, Roman Catholicism, Seventh-day Adventist Church*

Bibliography

Bennett, Judith A. *Wealth of the Solomons: A History of a Pacific Archipelago, 1800–1978.* Honolulu: University of Hawai'i Press, 1987.

Davenport, William, and Gülbün Çoker. "The Moro Movement of Guadalcanal, British Solomon Islands Protectorate." *Journal of the Polynesian Society* 76 (1967): 123–75.

Griffiths, Allison. *Fire in the Islands: The Acts of the Holy Spirit in the Solomons.* Wheaton, Ill.: Harold Shaw Publishers, 1977.

Hilliard, David L. *God's Gentlemen: A History of the Melanesian Mission, 1849–1942.* Brisbane: University of Queensland Press, 1978.

Keesing, Roger Martin. *Kwaio Religion: The Living and Dead in a Solomon Island Society.* New York: Columbia University Press, 1982.

Somalia

POPULATION 7,753,310

SUNNI MUSLIM 99.96 percent

CHRISTIAN 0.04 percent

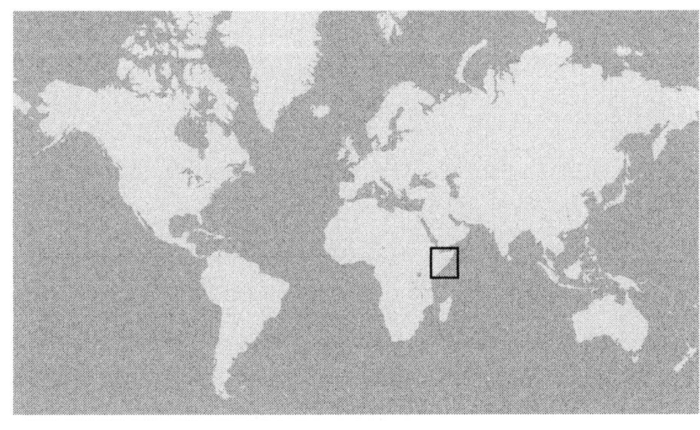

Country Overview

INTRODUCTION Somalia, one of the most Islamic countries in Africa, lies at the extreme east coast of the continent in an area called the Horn of Africa. To the north is the Gulf of Aden, and to the east and south are the Indian Ocean. Inland it borders Djibouti to the northwest, Ethiopia to the west, and Kenya to the southwest. Somalia is unique because it is the only monoethnic African nation-state. Somalis are united by culture, language, religion, and a common ancestor (Samaal); however, they are still divided politically between various ethnic subgroups.

Modern Somalia, which is largely a creation of European powers, has tried without much success to create a centralized authority through the armed forces and a civilian bureaucracy. The majority of Somalis maintain ethnic loyalty that gives greater political and emotional allegiance to traditional lineages. The Daarood, Dir, Isaaq, Hawiye, Digil, and Rahanwayn remain the major ethnic subgroups and are scattered throughout the country. Another group, the Somali Bantu (Muslim descendants of slaves considered by the majority of the population to be culturally inferior), continue to experience discrimination.

In general, Somalis are intensely religious, with more than 99 percent of the population professing to be Sunni Muslim. Islam, the country's official religion, is thus a significant social and political force. The arrival of European Christian missionaries in the early nineteenth century and the close proximity of Somalia to Ethiopia—one of the strongest Christian countries in Africa—did not divert the devotion of the majority of the Somalis from Islam to Christianity. In contemporary Somalia, Christianity is the religion of only a small percentage of the population, chiefly Western expatriates.

RELIGIOUS TOLERANCE In Somalia, where an overwhelming majority of the population practices Islam, religious tolerance has been more an ideological than a practical concern. In the past the government only tacitly tolerated the practice of non-Islamic faiths, and in some areas proselytizing by non-Muslim groups has been illegal. Islam, on the other hand, has enjoyed unparalleled support from the government, and its political role in Somalia has acquired an unquestioned legitimacy.

Although Somalia has not had a functioning central government since 1991, Islamic leaders have assumed the role of legal authorities in some regions. In these

Young girls listen to their teacher in a classroom in Hargeisa, Somalia. AP/WIDE WORLD PHOTOS.

areas new provisions have been established to promote and protect the rights of all religious communities, which had led to a greater social recognition of these rights. This recognition, moreover, has helped to ensure freedom of worship and to minimize religious discrimination and extremism. Many Somalis believe religious tolerance, as expressed by the Western ideas of legal equality and human rights, is consistent with traditional Somali legal practice and values.

Major Religion

ISLAM

DATE OF ORIGIN seventh century C.E.
NUMBER OF FOLLOWERS 7.7 million

HISTORY Arabian culture is enshrined in the rich traditions of the Somali people. It is believed that the remote ancestors of the Somalis came from Saudi Arabia and were likely kinsmen to the founder of Islam, the prophet Muhammad. The Somalis have occupied their present location, known as the Horn of Africa, since 100 C.E. Historically the medieval Arabs called the Somalis Berberi, but members of the proto-Sam, the indigenous ethnic population who came to occupy the Somali Peninsula, were known as the Samaale, or Samaal (a reference to the mythical ancestral figure of the main Somali clan families), which led to the name Somalia.

Somalis adopted the Islamic religion by the late ninth or early tenth century. It is possible that Islam was taken to Somalia in the seventh century by early followers of the prophet Muhammad who sought refuge from persecution in Mecca or in the late eighth century through contacts with the Persian and Arab merchants and seamen who founded settlements along Somali coastlines. Mogadishu, which later became the postcolonial capital, was founded by Arab traders and was one of the earliest seaports. Following the acceptance of Islam, the culture of the Somalis became intertwined with their faith, and religion became the foundation and dominant feature of their culture, as well as the mark of their identity as a people. Most Somalis still trace their history to the time when Islamic religion spread among them.

It is thought that in the late sixteenth and early seventeenth centuries the Somalis migrated to the fertile land along the Jubba and Shabeele rivers and the plain between the rivers. In the arid highlands of the northeast, the northern Somalis cultivated boswellia and commiphora trees, which became the sources of frankincense and myrrh, for which Somalia has been known since ancient times. In the middle of the seventeenth century the Somalis formed an alliance with the Bantu-speaking people to cultivate land, adopting their vocabularies in agriculture and civil discourse. The Somalis in the north then acquired the notoriety of being warlike and lawless, while the southern Somalis regarded themselves as peaceful.

In the nineteenth century Europeans began penetrating Somalia, and by 1887 Great Britain established British Somaliland, a protectorate in northern Somalia. By 1889 Italy had established control of southern Somalia, creating Italian Somaliland. The imperial partitioning of Somalia exacerbated the division between the north and south.

Although in 1960 Somalia gained independence, with its northern and southern halves united, it continued to experience political uncertainty. In 1969 a military coup, led by Muhammad Siad Barre, took over the country. Aligned with the Soviet Union, the government proposed a new "scientific socialism," a plan for economic, social, and political change that challenged the privileged position of Islam in Somali public life. According to Siad Barre, religious leaders were to avoid political involvement. In January 1991, after having lost the support of the Soviet Union, the military regime collapsed, resulting in a state of anarchy and a loss of effective central government. Within months the United Nations sent peacekeeping forces to restore order, and the United States joined the peacekeeping forces in December 1992. By 1995, though order had not been reestablished, the United Nations had withdrawn its forces, leaving the country still contested by various warlords and other factions.

After the ouster of Siad Barre in 1991, Islam regained its prominence in Somalia, and the popularity of fundamentalist Muslim movements, as well as conservative Islamic schools, increased. Active amid the political instability were competing Islamic groups, including Al-Islah, seeking a revival of Islam in line with the modern world, and al-Ittihad al-Islami, a militant Muslim group that aimed to establish an Islamic state in Somalia.

EARLY AND MODERN LEADERS One of the most celebrated Islamic leaders in Somalia was Sheikh Ibrahim Hassan Jebro, who acquired land in southern Somalia along the Jubba River in 1819 and established a religious center, which constituted the first religious community (*jamaa*) in Somalia's history. Sheikh Awes Muhammad Baraawi (d. 1909) spread the teachings of the Qadiriyah, one of the most prominent Sufi Islamic orders in Somalia. He wrote devotional poetry in Arabic and even attempted without appreciable success to translate traditional hymns from Arabic into Somali.

Also important in Somalia was Sheikh Abdirrahman Abdullah of Mogadishu, who stressed Islamic mysticism and was popular in Islamic communities in the 1930s. His tomb, conspicuously placed in Mogadishu, has become a pilgrimage center for his devoted followers who have continued to circulate his writings.

MAJOR THEOLOGIANS AND AUTHORS The Somali Islamic identity is reflected through poetry; however, until the twentieth century the Somali language was not written down. Poems circulated largely by word of mouth, and those judged the best were carefully transmitted from one generation to the next through a dynamic oral tradition.

One of the most famous Somali Muslim poets is Muhammad ibn 'Abd Allah Hasan (1864–1920). At the beginning of the twentieth century he led a 20-year guerrilla campaign against the British and Italian colonial occupation of Somalia. It was for his distaste of colonialism that the British nicknamed him "Mad Mullah." Hasan, whose works have been passed down through oral tradition, remains one of the most respected Muslim authors and poets of the Somali people.

HOUSES OF WORSHIP AND HOLY PLACES In Somalia the common house of worship is the mosque. For Sunni Muslims the mosque has also served as a place where devoted young boys learn to memorize portions of the Holy Koran and acquire a basic religious education.

To help pay for their sons' Islamic education, some parents lavish Islamic teachers with gifts, and as a result the students are allowed to move from one mosque to another in Muslim communities. Students do not leave their families permanently, and as adults they often return to their communities to become teachers. Although this practice has diminished throughout Africa as people have increasingly moved to cities, it is more prevalent in Somalia than elsewhere on the continent.

WHAT IS SACRED? Most Somali Muslims regard all life as sacred, reflecting their faith in the Koran. Many also draw from African traditions and cosmological systems, and they see their traditional understanding of life as consistent with Islamic teachings.

HOLIDAYS AND FESTIVALS Like Muslims throughout the world, Somalis celebrate two major religious festivals. The first, known as Id al-Adha, is the "Great Feast" that commemorates God's testing of Abraham by commanding him to sacrifice his son Isma'il. The second, called Id al-Fitr, marks the end of fasting during Ramadan (the lunar month when, according to tradition, the prophet Muhammad received his initial revelations in 610 C.E.). From dawn to dusk during Ramadan, Muslims in Somalia abstain from food, alcohol, and sex. At the end of the fasting period, family members come from near and far to feast and exchange gifts in a celebration that can last for three days.

MODE OF DRESS Unlike many Muslim women in the Arab world, Somali women have never gone veiled from head to toe, nor have they segregated themselves from male society, although they do wear a headscarf. Muslim men do not dress distinctively in Somalia.

DIETARY PRACTICES Somalis, like most Muslims in the world, abstain from pork and follow strict dietary practices during Ramadan. During Ramadan Somalis abstain from tobacco, alcohol, and sexual relations from dawn until sunset.

RITUALS In Somalia Muslims often follow Islamic requirements for ritual purity. For example, washing after contact with unclean substances, such as a dead body, is required to maintain Islamic purity. These requirements are more likely to be observed by settled than by nomadic Somalis.

RITES OF PASSAGE In Somalia, to mark the passage from childhood to the community of adults, all Muslim boys undergo circumcision at approximately 5 years old. Female Muslim children are circumcised between the ages of 8 and 11. Males, however, are not yet adults until marriage, which signifies entrance into full adulthood and higher status in the community. Preparations for Islamic marriage involve great expenditures of both time and money. Marriage is not a sacrament but a civil contract, and it is an alliance between two extended Somali Muslim families.

MEMBERSHIP Because more than 99 percent of the Somali population is Muslim, proselytizing is seen as largely unnecessary. Devout Somali Muslims and nominal Muslims who value the title of *Alhaji* (for men) or *Hadjia* (for women) often take the pilgrimage (*hajj*) to Mecca to enhance their Islamic membership status or personal prestige in the community.

SOCIAL JUSTICE Somalia was politically fractured during the 1970s and 1980s, partly because social divisions between northern and southern Somalis persisted under Siad Barre's military administration. In an effort to suppress unrest, he unleashed a reign of terror against the Majeerteen, Hawiye, and Isaaq tribal groups in the 1980s. At the time Islam was not seen as a powerful unifying force for civil liberty. Despite the revolutionary regime's intention of stamping out ethnic loyalties and promoting a spirit of nationalism, the advancement of social justice was not high on its agenda. Attempts to remove Siad Barre from office by junior army officers in the 1970s and 1980s failed, further eroding any hope for social justice. In reaction to these failed attempts, Siad Barre became more desperate and took to harsher methods to quell opposing groups. Opposition leaders were tried and executed or sentenced to long prison terms.

Among the current challenges in Somalia remain the restoration of internal order, strengthening the positions of traditional leaders, moving Somalis away from clan loyalties toward common national objectives, and eliminating widespread unemployment, social strife, poverty, and occasional drought. The government is trying to mobilize Islamic communities to address these problems.

SOCIAL ASPECTS The family counts above all else among Somali Muslims. Although the nuclear family exists in Somalia, it is also common for two related Muslim men to live with their wives and children under the same roof. Islam, which condones polygamy, has lent support to the traditional African practice of one man having multiple wives.

Settled Somalis generally cultivate land and educate their children in Koranic schools. Among nomadic Somalis, women usually look after the livestock, while men care for the camels, which are the source of meat and milk, as well as an object of prestige and beauty. Because livestock must be moved to suitable grazing locations with the changing of seasons, nomadic husbands provide their wives with separate houses that can be easily taken up and relocated. Nomadic Somalis must keep close ties to their families, as family support is essential during migrations.

In Somalia most Muslim men have lived traditional lives as warriors and herders, and they consider these roles more noble than sedimentary life. The Digil and Rahanwayn tribes in Somalia are derogatorily called *Sab*, meaning "ignoble," because of the perception that they have lowered themselves by their reliance on farming and sedentary agrarian life.

POLITICAL IMPACT Islam is thoroughly wedded to Somali political life. It is expected, for example, that political leaders be practicing Muslims. In the 1970s, when the government introduced new measures to protect the rights of women, many Islamic community leaders quoted the Koran to voice opposition.

Islam forms an important element in the political identity of Somalia. After independence in 1960, all Somalis started referring to one another as *jaalle*, an indication of Islamic brotherhood. Every Somali was a *jaalle*, or comrade, regardless of hereditary affiliation or tribal lineage. With the loss of central political authority in 1991, Islam remained a powerful unifying force in the country.

CONTROVERSIAL ISSUES Somali women live according to a code of strict decorum, but unlike most Muslim women in the Arab world, they have never worn the traditional all-enveloping veil, nor have they been segregated from male society. Under Somali customary law, women were under legal protection of males, either fathers or husbands. This changed in 1975 when the Supreme Revolutionary Council (SRC) and the Council of Ministers gave equal rights to Somali women in several areas, including inheritance. This move led to protests by some Islamic leaders and generated inflammatory debates throughout the country. In the south some feared the new family law would undermine the basic structure of Islamic society. By 1990, however, increasing numbers of females were attending secondary schools and universities, and six women had been elected members of the People's Assembly.

Female virginity among Muslims is traditionally safeguarded by the controversial method of infibulation, the surgical joining of the lips of the vulva, carried out between the age of 8 and 11. Because of strong opposition from Western and Western-educated Somalis, this practice has begun to fade.

CULTURAL IMPACT Islam regularly features in architecture, paintings, and other arts in Somalia. It also plays a major role in the literary life of Somalis. For example, even when the government introduced the Roman alphabet in the 1970s to promote literacy, the Arabic script remained the choice of most Islamic leaders in the discussion of literacy.

Somalia is known for its rich poetic tradition, though prior to 1973 no written Somali language existed. Poetry and storytelling were conveyed through oral tradition. Many early Somali poets were also religious leaders whose works appeared in Arabic.

Other Religions

During the colonial period missionaries entered Somalia, and a tiny Christian community emerged, mostly in the south. Christians, however, were viewed as outsiders, and in the 1970s the government nationalized church property and banned missionary work. In the 1990s, when the country fell into anarchy, much of the Christian community fled the country.

Today, of the country's 7.7 million people, only a few thousand are Christian, and many of these are Western expatriates. Remaining church buildings are in poor repair. Somali Christians sometimes worship on Friday to avoid association with foreign Christianity. Christians have also been the target of militant Muslims. In 2003 Annalena Tonneli, an Italian nun, was murdered in front of a hospital she founded.

Caleb O. Oladipo

See Also Vol. I: *Islam, Sunnism*

Bibliography

Besteman, Catherine. *Unraveling Somalia.* Philadelphia: University of Pennsylvania Press, 1999.

Cassanelli, Lee Vincent. *The Shaping of Somali Society: Reconstructing the History of a Pastoral People, 1600—1900.* Philadelphia: Pennsylvania University Press, 1982.

Cerulli, Enrico. *Somalia: Scritti vari editi ed inediti.* 3 vols. Rome: Istituto Poligrafico della Stato, 1957—64.

Hess, Robert L. *Italian Colonialism in Somalia.* Chicago: University of Chicago Press, 1966.

Jardine, Douglas J. *The Mad Mullah of Somaliland.* London: Jenkins, 1923; reprint, New York: Negro University Press, 1969.

Laitin, David D. *Politics, Language, and Thought: The Somali Experience.* Chicago: University of Chicago Press, 1977.

Lewis, I. M. *Islam in Tropical Africa.* 2nd ed. Bloomington: Indiana University Press, 1980.

Samatar, Ahmed I., ed. *The Somali Challenge: From Catastrophe to Renewal?* Boulder, Colo: Lynne Rienner Publishers, 1994.

Samatar, Said S. *Oral Poetry and Somali Nationalism: The Case of Sayyid Mahammad Abdille Hasan.* Cambridge: Cambridge University Press, 1982.

South Africa

POPULATION 43,647,658

CHRISTIAN 74.1 percent

TRADITIONAL 18.3 percent

MUSLIM 1.4 percent

HINDU 1.3 percent

JEWISH 0.2 percent

OTHER 4.7 percent

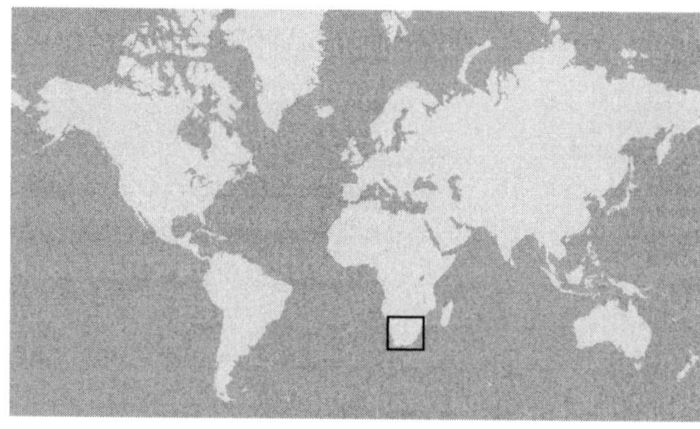

Country Overview

INTRODUCTION The Republic of South Africa, the most developed country in sub-Saharan Africa, lies at the extreme southern tip of the continent. Historically South Africa has had six major ethnic groups—Khoisan, Bantu-speaking Negroid, Nguni, descendants of European settlers, Coloured (people of mixed race), and Asian (largely of Indian origin). In addition, there are 11 official languages—Sedepi, Sesotho, Setswana, siSwati, Tshivenda, Xitsonga, Afrikaans, English, isiNdebele, IsiXhosa, and isiZulu.

In the 1990s South Africa, the last white-ruled nation-state in Africa, shifted relatively peacefully from apartheid and the threat of civil war to a true democracy. Freedom is protected by the constitution and by a number of bodies designed to restrict the power of the government. The greatest challenges remaining in South Africa are to eliminate widespread unemployment, poverty, and HIV/AIDS; to mobilize religious communities to address these problems; and to strengthen national unity. The new government has made determined attempts to improve the lives of all South Africans.

South Africans are intensely religious, and their faiths can be characterized as comprehensive and broad. Virtually 80 percent of the population professes some kind of faith in a recognized world religion. Christians of various denominations are by far the largest religious group. A significant social force, religious practice in South Africa cannot be completely understood apart from its geographical, ideological, political, cultural, and historical context.

Before the arrival of European missionaries in about 1488 C.E., South Africans were followers of African traditional religions, and approximately 8 million members of the indigenous population continue to practice them. Other religions in South Africa include Islam (from 1658), Hinduism (from 1857), and Judaism (beginning before 1669).

While there clearly has been a major Christianization of black South Africa, so too has there been a significant Africanization of Christianity, to the extent that it is probably inaccurate to consider the European-derived mainline churches as the "mainstream" denominations. The African Initiated Churches, the Pentecostal churches, and the evangelical churches have become central to Christianity in South Africa. In terms of demographics they may be viewed as the mainstream Christian churches.

Perhaps one of the most important developments of the Christian faith in the twentieth century was its transition in Africa from a white, European-dominated religion to a vibrant, black-majority religion rooted in African idioms and cultures. At the same time, it became engaged in the struggle against white social, political, and ecclesiastical domination.

RELIGIOUS TOLERANCE Under apartheid the government tacitly tolerated the practice of non-Christian religions. Christianity, especially the Nederduitse Gereformeerde Kerk (Dutch Reformed Church, or DRC), enjoyed unparalleled support from the government. As the church of the government, the DRC had a powerful political role in South Africa and gave unquestioned legitimacy to apartheid.

In the last three decades of the twentieth century, however, a new interfaith union of Christians, Muslims, Hindus, Jews, and secularists surfaced at the funerals of victims of state brutality. This ecumenical movement established unprecedented common moral foundations and a platform from which to oppose apartheid. Because apartheid was a common enemy, there was a decline in religious particularity and a greater emphasis on religious humanism and universalism. Out of the wreckage of apartheid a new South Africa, with initiatives for interfaith dialogue, has emerged.

In May 1996 the parliament approved a constitution that provided for the establishment of a commission to promote and protect the rights of all religious and linguistic communities. South Africa thus became a secular state. The constitution guarantees freedom of worship and prohibits discrimination on the basis of religion.

Young girls, having just been confirmed, surround Archbishop Desmond Tutu outside of a South African church. Tutu is one of the most celebrated Christian leaders in South Africa. © DAVID TURNLEY/CORBIS.

Major Religion

CHRISTIANITY

DATE OF ORIGIN 1488 C.E.

NUMBER OF FOLLOWERS 32.7 million

HISTORY For at least 500 years Christianity has been a dominant religion in South Africa. With 14.3 million members, the mainline churches are by far the largest Christian groups. Mainline religious bodies include the Anglican, Methodist, Lutheran, Presbyterian, United Congregational, Roman Catholic, Dutch Reformed, Baptist, and Greek Orthodox churches. South Africa also has a large number of evangelical and Pentecostal churches, and approximately 12 million South Africans are members of African Initiated Churches (AICs).

The history of the church in South Africa is set not only against a background of relentless European settlement and conquest, and of African resistance, but also against powerful international economic and political forces aimed at enriching Europeans and their white surrogates. As an established religion of European powers, Christianity migrated with Portuguese explorers when they entered South Africa in the late fifteenth century. It was further established in the seventeenth century by missionaries from Portugal, Spain, and the Netherlands.

The Dutch set up the first permanent coastal trading practices in 1652, although with no interest in settling in South Africa. In the nineteenth century mainline churches were initially established along the coasts of South Africa, but they took root elsewhere after the discovery of gold and diamonds in the mainland. They are similar to European churches and are identical with regard to architecture and liturgy.

If the arrival of missionaries in the seventeenth and eighteenth centuries represented the "first conversion" of South Africans to Christianity, the creation of the AICs (beginning in the late nineteenth century) represented the "second conversion." They are not radically different from the mainline denominations, but many of their church activities are unique. All the traditions that European missionaries taught Africans to discard as evil—such as traditional dancing and drumming—were revived as legitimate mediums of Christian worship in the AICs. Their liveliness is a new development in liturgy. There is a deep-rooted sense of common humanity and moral responsibility, and there are no officially authorized gender roles; women have played a major role as innovators in the AICs.

Because the apartheid government denied the majority black population a homeland in this life, most AICs in South Africa claim "Zion" to be their homeland and are thus called Zionists. There are more than 4,500 different Zionist groups. Their distinctive elements of worship include dreams, visions, healing, and the experience of the Holy Spirit.

While the AIC movement represents distinct African ideas, the Pentecostal/charismatic movement in South Africa is part of a global Christian phenomenon. In South Africa Pentecostalism was disseminated through the social networks created by Zionist groups. It is of little surprise, therefore, that they share many spiritual characteristics. One of the unique features of Pentecostalism in South Africa is its transdenominational character. Its members have interactions with members of other religious bodies, both Christians and non-Christians.

EARLY AND MODERN LEADERS One of the most celebrated Christian leaders in South Africa is the former Anglican archbishop of Cape Town, the Most Reverend Desmond M. Tutu. He was succeeded in 1996 by another important church leader, the Most Reverend Njongonkulu Winston Hugh Ndungane. Bishop Edward Lekganyane is the leader of one of the largest South African religious groups, the Zion Christian Church in Zion City, Moria. It was founded in 1910 and has almost 4 million members.

Isaiah Shembe was considered something of a "Black Messiah" in South Africa. He was the founder of the Zulu Zionist movement, and in 1911 he started the Nazareth Baptist Church in Kwa Mashu, near Durban. In 1920 Shembe composed what is regarded as an authentic Zulu Christian liturgy.

MAJOR THEOLOGIANS AND AUTHORS Perhaps the most important modern theologian of the Dutch Reformed Church was Beyers Naudé. He was one of the leaders of the Broederbond, or the "Band of Afrikaner Brothers," an organization established in 1918 that admitted only whites. The Broederbond was widely believed to be the éminence grise guiding the apartheid policies of the nationalist government that had come to power in 1948. A peaceful protest against pass laws in Sharpeville in 1960 triggered a massacre of civilians by police. This incident led Naudé to reject apartheid as unjust. In 1963 he was part of a group that established the Christian Institute, a nonracial ecumenical body; Naudé served as its first director, and through the institute's journal, *Pro Veritate,* he wrote extensively to oppose apartheid on theological grounds. The government subjected Naudé to bitter attacks and harassment. His persistent opposition to apartheid was a blow to the Dutch Reformed Church.

Other Christian leaders include Allan Boesak, an antiapartheid activist theologian, and Frank Chikane, who was a pastor in the Apostolic Faith Mission before he became an antiapartheid campaigner. He was the first director of the Institute for Contextual Theology and later became the general secretary of the South African Council of Churches. National Christian leaders also include Father Albert Nolan, Bishop Simeon Nkoane, and Wolfram Kistner.

One important author is Alan Paton, whose classic antiapartheid novel *Cry, the Beloved Country* (1958) centers on a young black man and his father, who is a minister. Another author who wrote on religious and political issues was Steve Biko. In 1977 he was tortured and died while in police custody for opposing apartheid. His book *I Write What I Like* (1978) was published posthumously. Other theologians and authors include David Bosch, James Cochrane, Bonganjalo Goba, John de Gruchy, Jocelyn Hellig, Jim Kiernan, Louise Kretzschmar, Klaus Nürnberger, G.C. Oosthuizen, Martin Prozesky, and Charles Villa-Vicencio.

HOUSES OF WORSHIP AND HOLY PLACES In South Africa, as in other places, the common house of Christian worship is the church. For the mainline denominations the church served another function during apartheid, becoming a place where funerals were conducted for the victims of police brutality and state-sponsored killings.

Because Pentecostalism has no need for church buildings or trained clergy, many Pentecostal churches have been established in the backyards of leader's homes or in abandoned public buildings.

WHAT IS SACRED? The spirits of traditional African cosmological systems continue to play a significant role in South African Christian consciousness. Many Christians in South Africa have also retained the traditional belief that an offense against a fellow human being leads to problems such as misfortune and illness. It is partly for this reason that human life is considered especially sacred.

HOLIDAYS AND FESTIVALS The most popular Christian holidays in South Africa are Christmas and Easter. Children typically receive new clothes for the holidays, and worship services are well attended. Christmas is not marked by an exchange of gifts; believers congregate for meals and fellowship. Schools are usually closed approximately two weeks before Christmas, while an extended weekend marks the Easter holiday.

MODE OF DRESS Protestant Christians in South Africa do not have a particular mode of dress. African Initiated Church (AIC) members wear white robes to church and do not wear shoes during worship or religious activities. Perhaps this is in reference to the command Moses received from God to take off his shoes because he was on holy ground.

DIETARY PRACTICES The AICs have embraced a Leviticus-style sensitivity to diet. Because they believe that a healthy body is the only body suitable to be the "temple of the Holy Spirit," Zionists forbid the intake of harmful substances. The use of traditional Zulu medicine is also strictly forbidden. Pentecostalists avoid drinking alcohol.

Many South African Catholics restrict themselves to eating only fish after sunset on Fridays, and some do not eat meat at all on weekends. The mainline churches have no specific regulations for dietary practices. During Lent, however, many Christians in the mainline churches prepare for Easter by fasting and devoting their religious activities to penitence. At Easter most South African Christians customarily eat fish and hot cross buns.

RITUALS In South Africa all Christian babies are christened. The AICs practice baptism by immersion, which can be done in running waters or at a beach. For Pentecostalists "baptism in the Holy Spirit," the ability to speak in tongues, is the most important qualification for leadership in the church.

Because members of the AICs believe that dancing links the physical world with the supernatural world, they often incorporate traditional dancing into their worship services. This is an important example of cross-fertilization between the Christian faith and the traditional African religious worldview.

RITES OF PASSAGE Baptism is an important rite of passage for most South African Christians in the mainline churches. This is done upon a profession of faith. Converts to the AICs are largely adults who are troubled by misfortune. Upon baptism members eschew all worldly pursuits and cultivate a semi-ascetic approach to life that stresses diligence, sobriety, frugality, and saving. These churches also emphasize principles of shared responsibility and mutual support. This impetus to give for the common good is called *ubuntu.*

For most South African Christians the 21st birthday is considered the beginning of adulthood and is marked by a worship service in the church. The person celebrating the birthday is called to the front of the church to face the congregation as several of its members congratulate and admonish him or her.

MEMBERSHIP It appears that the leadership of the mainline churches are generally unwilling to ordain Africans as pastors, or reluctant to give them full responsibility in financial matters or to admit them as equals. The Reformed Church and a number of other churches in South Africa, however, have been traditionally open to ordaining black ministers. This is partly for pragmatic reasons, because the church continues to grow rapidly among the indigenous black population in South Africa. The years of study in theological institutions, however, and the strict ethical standards required of ministers in Christian denominations have exacerbated the modern shortfall of Christian ministers. As the AICs continue to multiply, they are making attempts to restructure ministerial formation in ways that are consistent with African vitality and inner strength.

The missionary-related churches proselytize, but the AICs draw membership either from family members or indiscriminately from other Christian denominations.

Pentecostalism has grown rapidly in South Africa, partly because it is free from missionary supervision and also because it has welcomed Africanization. Features that are regarded as typically African, such as the warmth and dignity of the people and a strong sense of community, are central to the South African Pentecostal experience. The mainline churches have lost members to the Pentecostal churches not only because of the success of the latter's indigenous definition of Christianity but also because they have adapted well to the demographic shift from rural to urban centers. Most mainline churches find it difficult to adapt to the trend of urbanization. Further, the poor in big cities prefer churches that are organized in, and oriented toward, small groups and that can thus identify with members at a grassroots level, address their existential needs, and help them deal with their day-to-day lives.

SOCIAL JUSTICE The nation was terribly fractured under apartheid, and beneath the thin veneer of a new South Africa filled with endless opportunities, political and social divisions persist. Christianity has been a unifying factor in South African society. In reaction to the killings and state brutality under apartheid, the various religious groups and communities united for the promotion of social justice. The main civil rights activities in South Africa in the 1980s and early 1990s were protest marches, political rallies, and funeral services for victims of state brutality. Out of the problems of the 1980s, there emerged a South Africa with a multiple religious heritage—Christianity, Islam, Hinduism, Judaism, and African traditional religions—with all groups vying for social justice.

The AICs are distinguished by their remarkable goals; not only do they aim to reorganize an unjust society but they also endeavor to mend the lives of individuals who have suffered under apartheid. They attempt to salvage individual members by supporting them economically, emotionally, socially, and spiritually.

SOCIAL ASPECTS Many aspects of Christian social life in South Africa are rooted in traditional culture. Marriage is important, and it carries both religious and social meanings. A refusal to marry is tantamount to remaining in a permanent state of adolescence. A marriage is not so much between two individuals as it is an alliance of two extended families. The husband's family is required to pay *lobola,* or bride-price. This may be in the form of movable goods or money.

While sex within marriage has a strong cultural tradition in South Africa, sexual experience is little talked about. Women are expected to take care of the children, manage the household expenses, prepare food, and perform all other domestic duties. Men are required to provide financial and emotional support. Among certain indigenous groups the family is defined so broadly that it includes those who have died and those who have yet to be born. Overall, however, modern South Africans often highlight the Christian meaning of the family and its social aspects.

In a society that was notoriously segregated by race under apartheid, Pentecostalism represented empowerment for blacks and gave them an alternative way to reorder their lives. Social life for Pentecostalists is organized around church meetings and the nuclear family, where members learn self-discipline and a puritan work ethic.

POLITICAL IMPACT The control of the Cape passed from the Dutch to the British in about 1806. This opened the way for a steady influx of English-speaking Christians with their own division into churches (including Anglican, Methodist, Presbyterian, Congregational, Catholic, and Baptist). In due course this exacerbated the fragmentation of black South Africans, who had aligned themselves according to the Christian denominations they had inherited from Europeans. Opportunistic politicians in South Africa exploited the situation, taking measures that eventually resulted in insidious subjugation and racial segregation.

It took the church the latter half of the twentieth century to unite in order to confront the unjust system of apartheid. Mainline churches in South Africa carefully weighed the Dutch Reformed Church's unholy alliance with the apartheid government against the positive, liberating resources black Christians had found in Christianity. As many churches tried to preserve their own institutions, they became complicit in the injustices.

CONTROVERSIAL ISSUES The chief controversial issue of Christianity in South Africa is the great racial, linguistic, and cultural heterogeneity of its people. Classification by race continues to exert a strong influence on social life and religion, despite the modern constitutional prohibition on racial discrimination. For example, the view that blacks are intellectually inferior to other racial groups persists.

The South African churches that displaced the missionary churches have been more radical and have used Christian ideology and institutions to wage an assault on white control. Nothing has demonstrated this more forcefully than the Truth and Reconciliation Commission (TRC) hearings. In 1996 President Nelson Mandela—the first nonwhite president of South Africa, who crafted the country's transition to full democracy—appointed Archbishop Desmond M. Tutu to head the commission. Its purpose was to grant amnesty to those who had committed politically motivated crimes under apartheid if they came forward to testify truthfully and to face the victims or their families. The TRC revealed near Pretoria a special police base, Vlakplaas, where government agents had secretly murdered hundreds in order to silence opposition to apartheid. The commission's approach has been criticized, however. Some believe that the political criminals should be prosecuted, not granted amnesty, while others view the TRC as a witch hunt.

The AICs have also struggled to address many controversial issues, such as polygyny, birth control, abortion, divorce, traditional African chieftaincy, and the role of women in modern South Africa. Leaders of AICs view the Bible as the authority on controversial issues. In defense of polygyny, for example, church leaders have often stated that the Bible does not mention a sin called polygyny but does tell of those who sinned by divorcing their wives and thereafter taking other wives.

CULTURAL IMPACT Christianity has deeply affected South African culture, particularly music and literary traditions. Traditional Zulu dance and performing arts, for example, have embraced Christian themes. Contemporary artists who have been involved in gospel music include Lucky Dube, Rebecca Malope, the Soldiers of the Cross singers, and the Joyous Celebration group.

Respected modern South African writers include Peter Abrahams, W.P.B. Botha, Dennis Brutus, J.M. Coetzee, Modikwe Dikobe, Nadine Gordimer, Rayda Jacobs, Steve Jacobs, Alex La Guma, and R.L. Peteni. Many of their literary works are reactions against apartheid, and some are saturated with Christian images.

Other Religions

In addition to blending with Christianity, African traditional religion has survived in its own right among more than 18 percent of the South African population.

The indigenous people of South Africa believed in a supernatural entity whose existence affects the cosmos. Traditionally the activities of the Supreme Being have been associated with natural phenomena such as lightning and thunderstorms. The material and social well-being of the people is the main focus of traditional religion, and the causes of misfortune have been regularly linked to human actions rather than to the involvement of the Supreme Being. Therefore, the active features of traditional religions are human agents who provide theories of causation regarding deprivation, illness, misfortune, and distress.

Diviners in South Africa are religious specialists who communicate the wishes of the Supreme Being to the people. They can be men or women, and they undergo a period of ritual isolation for the purpose of training. Diviners are also equipped to diagnose the causes of misfortune and to determine its origin in ancestral and human relationships. Because it is believed that there is a spiritual component to healing, herbalists are also important in traditional religion. The roles of the diviners and herbalists are mutually dependent.

Some scholars have suggested that when Africans convert from traditional religions to Christianity they find a familiar terrain of religious consciousness. This may be because African religious thought—with its ancestors, diviners, herbalists, sorcerers, and witches—has a compelling affinity with that of the biblical religions, which include spiritual agents such as angels and prophets. Thus, the unveiling of a tombstone after burial, for example, can be both an African and a Christian rite. Certain elements, such as ritualistic dancing and the veneration of ancestral spirits, have been deeply incorporated into Christianity, while others combine imperfectly and uneasily with Christian teachings. As a result of the attenuated form of traditional religious beliefs within Christianity, black South Africans have a formidable range of religious resources to draw upon as they order their existences.

Jan van Riebeeck of the Dutch East India Company went to South Africa in 1652, and the first Muslims arrived approximately six years later. Called *mardyckers*, they were employed as mercenaries to protect the Dutch colonists from the Africans.

In South Africa the mosque has a dual role, serving as a place of worship and providing space for social and political gatherings. The first mosque in the country was built in about 1804 on Dorp Street in the Cape. Some of the most beautiful mosques in South Africa are in Kwa Zulu Natal. They were built by Indian Muslims whose ancestors had migrated to South Africa in the 1850s to work as indentured laborers in the sugarcane fields of Natal.

In South Africa, as in many areas of colonial Africa, there are seven fundamental teachings that underpin Islamic political ideology: (1) understanding the article of faith, (2) praying five times a day, (3) learning and remembering God, (4) serving and honoring fellow Muslims, (5) being sincere in intention, (6) avoiding idleness, and (7) doing evangelical work. Most of the ulama and other Islamic scholars in South Africa are trained in the Middle East. A synthesis of Southeast Asian Islam and elements of indigenous cultures has modified the practice of Islam in South Africa. It has also given South African Islam a significant cultural flexibility and adaptability; Islam and Christianity coexist more amicably in South Africa than in other countries.

Popular Islamic rituals in South Africa include the use of *azimat* (talismans and amulets to word off evil spirits), the communal celebration of the Prophet Muhammad's birthday (*milad,* or *mawlud*), and occasional collective prayers to bless the dead. The distinction between the Sufis (Islamic mystics) and the Sunnis and Shiites (the two principal branches of Islam) is not as strong in South Africa as it is elsewhere.

The Islamic religion symbolizes more in South Africa than it does in other African countries. It implies a new language, a new concept of law and government, and new standards of dress and architecture. This is partly because Islam, which teaches freedom and equality of the races, was seen as an alternative to the oppressive system of apartheid. Muslims do not discriminate on the basis of race, and white devotees participate regularly along with Indian, Coloured, and black members at Islamic functions. The egalitarian spirit of Islam has been an important factor in its growth in South Africa. Although the Muslim population is relatively small (approximately 1.4 percent of the population), Islamic teachings have had a profound influence on South African society, and Muslims have played key roles in dismantling apartheid and reconstructing the country. Christian efforts to convert Muslims in South Africa have been largely unsuccessful.

The South African Hindu community, with more than half a million members, is the third largest in the world. This is because the largest Indian population outside India is found in South Africa. In 1857 a labor shortage in the sugar industry in Natal led the South African government to import indentured laborers from India. Approximately 90 percent of the workers were Hindus from the Tamil- and Telugu-speaking communities of the southern Indian state of Madras (now Tamil Nadu). Eighty percent of South African Indians live in Kwa Zulu Natal, making Natal a bastion of Hinduism. A broad religious tradition, Hinduism contains a great variety of cultural, philosophical, and religious elements that are at least 4,000 years old. In South Africa, however, the word "Hinduism" is not used to describe the religion. Devoted followers prefer the term *sanathana dharma* (the eternal way).

Despite miserable working conditions on the sugar estates, the Hindu workers demonstrated their religious commitments by building small shrines and temples. The oldest is the Equefa Perumalsami Temple near Umzinto (a coastal resort in Kwa Zulu Natal), built in 1864. Today South Africa has four main strains of Hinduism: Sanathana, Arya Samaj, neo-Vedanta, and Hare Krishna. The last three are often collectively referred to as neo-Hinduism or Reformed Hinduism. Sanathana emphasizes the practical and ritual dimensions of Hinduism, whereas the others highlight its precepts. Minor differences regarding details of worship, rituals, social customs, and what is sacred continue to exist between these branches of Hinduism, but all South African Hindus believe in an unending process of reincarnation governed by karma. Most Hindu places of worship in South Africa are adorned with the symbol of Divine Reality, conceptualized in three forms as the so-called Trimurti, consisting of Brahma (the creator), Vishnu (the preserver), and Shiva (the destroyer). Brahma is seldom worshiped (even in India), and there are no Brahma temples in South Africa.

Perhaps the most important feature of Hinduism in South Africa is the importance of dharma (duty and moral obligation). This includes such principles as truthfulness, living a pure life, forgiveness, self-control, goodwill, generosity, and protecting all living beings. South African Hindus observe a number of religious festivals, including Christian and Muslim religious celebrations. Because of the influences of Christian education and the broader South African culture, the caste system that is associated with Hinduism in India has eroded in South Africa.

The most celebrated Gujarati Hindu in South Africa was Mahatma Gandhi, who arrived in Natal in 1893 and spent approximately 20 years there. A month after his arrival he became embroiled in South Africa's political problems when he was evicted from a first-class train compartment at the Pietermaritzburg train station. In 1894 the Natal Indian Congress was founded, and Gandhi served as its first secretary. It was in South Africa that he developed his philosophy of nonviolent resistance against injustice.

Another unique element in the South African religious fabric is Judaism. The Jews of South Africa, who are culturally Europeans, view themselves as no less South African than the Zulus. At the end of World War II only the United States surpassed South Africa as the destination of European Jewish immigrants. Most South African Jews are descendants of Lithuanian immigrants who fled the anti-Semitic persecutions under Soviet-controlled Lithuania. For this reason the South African Jewish community is one of the most organized Jewish communities in the world. South African Jews, however, are by no means a homogeneous population. For example, Zionism is an integral part of Jewish life in South Africa, having both strong support and opposition. The majority of South African Jews are labeled "unobservant orthodox," partly because many do not observe the precepts of Orthodox Judaism in dietary matters. Johannesburg is the center of Jewish religious life, but Cape Town remains an important locus because early Jews in South Africa first settled there.

It can be argued that, although Cecil Rhodes, an imperialist Englishman, was responsible for opening South Africa to mineral wealth, the Jews of South Africa were the ones who created the financial institutions to sustain the wealth. Jews played vital roles in the South African deep-level mining industry and in the financial systems that raised capital to support it. Such Jewish businessmen as Alfred Beit, Barney Barnato, Louis Cohen, Lionel Phillips, Julius Wehrner, Solly Joel, Adolf Goertz, George Albu, and Abe Bailey are remembered for transforming South Africa from a rural agrarian economy into the world's most vibrant and largest mining economy.

Caleb O. Oladipo

See Also Vol. I: *African Traditional Religions, Anglicanism/Episcopalianism, Baptist Tradition, Christianity, Hinduism, Islam, Judaism, Lutheranism, Methodism, Reformed Christianity, Roman Catholicism*

Bibliography

Arkin, A.J., K.P. Magyar, and G.J. Pillay, eds. *The Indian South Africans: A Contemporary Profile.* Durban: Owen Burgess, 1989.

Bradlow, Frank R., and Margaret Cairns. *The Early Cape Muslims.* Cape Town: A.A. Balkema, 1978.

Chidester, David. *Religions in South Africa.* London and New York: Routledge, 1992.

Cochrane, James, John de Gruchy, and Stephen Martin, eds. *Facing the Truth: South African Faith Communities and the Truth and Reconciliation Commission.* Cape Town: David Philip Publishers, 1999.

Prozesky, Martin, and John de Gruchy, eds. *Living Faiths in South Africa.* Cape Town and Johannesburg: David Philip, 1995.

Saron, Gustav, and Louis Hotz, eds. *The Jews in South Africa: A History.* Cape Town: Oxford University Press, 1955.

Sundkler, B.G.M. *Bantu Prophets in South Africa.* Cape Town: Oxford University Press, 1961.

Thomas, David. *Christ Divided: Liberation, Ecumenism, and Race in South Africa.* Pretoria: University of South Africa Press, 2002.

Villa-Vicencio, Charles. *A Theology of Reconstruction: Nation-Building and Human Rights.* Cambridge: Cambridge University Press, 1992.

———. *Trapped in Apartheid: A Socio-Theological History of the English-Speaking Churches.* Maryknoll, N.Y.: Orbis Books, 1988.

South Korea

POPULATION 48,324,000

CHRISTIAN 24.2 percent

BUDDHIST 23.3 percent

CONFUCIANIST 1.0 percent

SHAMANIST 1.0 percent

WONBULGYO 0.3 percent

CHEONDOGYO 0.2 percent

OTHER RELIGIONS (INCLUDING DAEJONGGYO, TAOIST, EASTERN ORTHODOX CHRISTIAN, MUSLIM, JEHOVAH'S WITNESS, MORMON, JEONDOGWAN, UNIFICATION CHURCH, SOKA GAKKAI, AND TENRIKYO) 3.0 percent

NONRELIGIOUS 47.0 percent

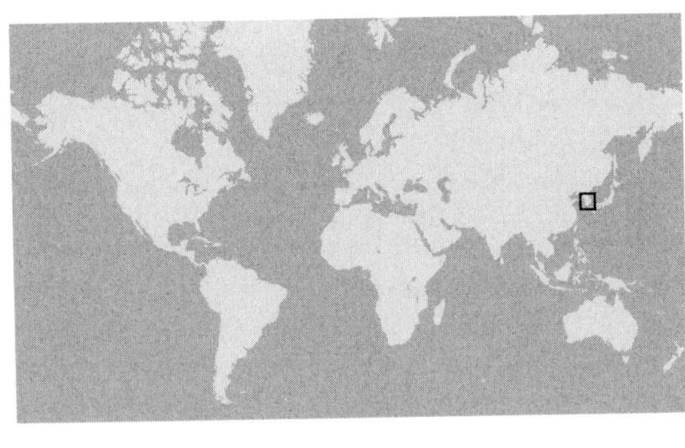

Country Overview

INTRODUCTION South Korea occupies the southern half of the Korean Peninsula, which juts out of northeastern China. It is surrounded by the Yellow Sea to the west and the Sea of Japan to the east. Lying just east and southeast, respectively, are the Japanese islands of Honshu and Kyushu.

Following World War II the Korean Peninsula was divided along the 38th parallel into an initially Soviet-occupied northern zone and U.S.-occupied southern zone. In 1948 two ideologically opposed governments were formed: the Republic of Korea (South Korea) and the Democratic People's Republic of Korea (North Korea).

South Korea is among the most religiously diverse countries in East Asia, although roughly half of the population claims to be nonreligious. Despite the introduction of foreign religions, such as Buddhism and Christianity, older practices of animism, geomancy, and shamanism have survived with a remarkable resilience.

Buddhist governments dominated Korea from the 370s to the 1390s. At the end of the fourteenth century the last such government was overthrown by the Joseon dynasty (1392–1910), which declared Confucianism to be the official state creed for the next five centuries. Confucianist power, however, neither eliminated Buddhism nor successfully prevented Roman Catholicism from entering Korea in the eighteenth century, with Protestantism following a century later.

South Korea's four principal religions are Christianity, Buddhism, Confucianism, and shamanism. The total number of Christians and Buddhists together—47.5 percent of the population—is slightly higher than the number of nonreligious. Of the Christian population, about three-quarters are Protestant and the rest are Roman Catholic. There are 18 different Buddhist sects. Smaller religious groups include Wonbulgyo, Cheondogyo, Daejonggyo, and Tongilgyo (Unification Church), as well as Islam, Jehovah's Witnesses, Mormonism, Tenrikyo, and Soka Gakkai. New religions have drawn largely on traditional and Christian elements, resulting in diverse views. Multiple denominational affiliations are not uncommon among all groups.

RELIGIOUS TOLERANCE South Korea has guaranteed religious freedom since 1898. But while religious discrimination has been largely minor throughout the twentieth century, shamanism has historically been associated with the lowest social classes; the remnants of such stigmatization are still visible today. There were an estimated 300 new religions in South Korea during the 1980s, though many were minor and temporary phenomena.

Buddhist nuns pray during festivities celebrating the Buddha's birthday. In 1975 the South Korean government declared the Buddha's birthday a national holiday. © CHRIS LISLE/CORBIS.

Major Religions

CHRISTIANITY

BUDDHISM

CHRISTIANITY

DATE OF ORIGIN Late Seventeenth century C.E.

NUMBER OF FOLLOWERS 11.7 million

HISTORY Korea's earliest contact with Christianity occurred during the Japanese invasion of 1592, when Catholic Japanese soldiers "converted" Korean captives. Of more lasting significance, the Jesuit writings of Matteo Ricci reached Korea via China during the seventeenth century. The first Catholic missionary arrived in 1794, with Protestant missionaries following in the 1880s. Ricci's theological writings, heavily informed by physics and mathematics, were of particular interest to the scholarly circle Silhak (Practical Learning). Silhak consisted of *yangban* (aristocratic) reformers who pressed for sociocultural change, technological development, and openness to the outside world. Joseon dynasty authorities tried to halt the new religion's progress by arguing that Christianity was intolerant of other religions and that it eschewed ancestor devotion, which was highly regarded by Confucianism.

After 1885 both Roman Catholicism and Protestantism engaged in considerable missionary activity. After the initial establishment of both churches was completed about 1910, Korean Christianity began serving congregations according to the specific needs of their region and social circumstances. While Protestants achieved greater prominence in the early twentieth century by establishing numerous educational and medical institutions, the Catholic Church in the ensuing years was able to gain converts by providing the populace with similar services.

During the Japanese occupation (1910–45) the Roman Catholic Church largely pursued a policy of nonconfrontation; however, after the Japanese attacked Pearl Harbor, foreign Catholic authorities were expelled and replaced by Koreans chosen by the Japanese. During the Korean War (1950–53) Protestant churches were instrumental in providing relief aid and establishing international child-adoption programs. Leaders of both denominations spoke out against South Korea's military regimes in the 1960s–80s.

EARLY AND MODERN LEADERS Yi Seung-Hun, a Joseon diplomat in Beijing, returned home a baptized

Catholic in 1784. His teachings formed the basis of the early Catholic movement. Protestant missionary work gained momentum in the late 1880s through the efforts of American Presbyterian and Methodist missionaries, such as Horace Allen, Henry Appenzeller, and Horace Underwood. In 1896 Protestant reformers Yun Chi-Ho (1865–1945) and So Chae-Pil (1866–1951) founded *The Independent,* Korea's first Christian newspaper, advocating a modern society based on Christian principles.

Christians formed the core of the independence movement (1896–1945), with Lee Seung-Hoon, Ahn Chang-Ho, Dr. Philip Jaisohn, and Yun Chi-Ho the most prominent leaders. South Korea's dictatorship era (1960s–80s) also gave rise to opposition leaders within the various churches, most notably Presbyterians Pak Hyong-Gyu and Mun Ik-Whan and Catholics Bishop Chi Hak-Sun and Cardinal Stephen Kim. Syngman Rhee, a Methodist with an American education, became the first president of the Republic of Korea.

MAJOR THEOLOGIANS AND AUTHORS In the early 1880s Anglican missionary John Ross and Methodist Henry Loomis oversaw the Hangeul (Korean) translation of the New Testament, a task carried out by Lee Ung-Chang, Baik Hong-Joon, Kim Jin-Ki, Lee Sung-Ha, and Lee Soo-Chung. The use of Hangeul was crucial for the survival of Christianity in southern Korea. From about the 1890s through the 1930s, Revs. Horace Underwood and Henry Appenzeller introduced translations of American faith books and founded several Protestant magazines that were distributed through the Jesus Tract Society.

During the 1930s Protestant editors, such as Chun Young-Taik, launched the native magazines *New Life, Real Life, Living Well,* and others. Among the first native Presbyterian ministers, Kil Sun-Ju deserves mention for his inspiring sermons. Kil's theological writings include commentaries on Romans, cross-religious comparisons, and meditations. Native Korean theologies have emerged since the height of the 1980s antiregime movement, with the Minjung theology among the most influential.

HOUSES OF WORSHIP AND HOLY PLACES Central Seoul's Gothic-style Myeongdong Cathedral, erected during the 1890s, is the oldest and one of the largest Roman Catholic structures in East Asia. It has played an important role in national independence movements, providing refuge for political dissidents and hosting union rallies and demonstrations during the final battles against military regimes in the 1980s. Among the largest churches in the world, the Full Gospel Church on Yoido Island (Seoul) claims a membership exceeding 700,000.

The common practice of *kidowon* (to go pray) represents an interesting blend of Buddhist and Christian culture. While there are no specific holy places of Christian devotion other than churches, *kidowon* is a function in which a person or group may hike into nature in search of places that may lend power to their prayers, fasts, or study of the scriptures. Some churches may have special *kidowon* prayer halls located in a beautiful natural surrounding, or individual members may see a special place in nature as their personal variety of *kidowon.*

WHAT IS SACRED? Besides such universal Christian symbols as the cross, the Bible, and the rosary, some unique Korean elements deserve mention. South Korean Christians often carry their Bibles everywhere: to weekly Bible circles, to Sunday worship, and on public transportation. A used, worn Bible can reflect the divine value a person has attached to it. South Korean devotion to Christianity is also reflected in the countless illuminated Christian crosses on churches or housetops in villages, towns, and cities. Great significance is also attached to liturgical or service music.

HOLIDAYS AND FESTIVALS The most significant Christian holidays in South Korea are Easter, Pentecost, Christmas, and the traditional Lunar New Year. The latter, called *seollal,* is observed on 1 January with a midnight candle prayer intended to express hope for the new year. Depending on each congregation's culture, various festive days may be reserved for picnics, outings, sports and games days, prayer hikes, and discipleship training.

MODE OF DRESS Christianization has been an important catalyst of modernization in South Korea. Donning Western suits became a symbol of progress and modernity following the decline of the Joseon dynasty (1392–1910). Western missionaries encouraged the outward change of clothes as proof of inward renewal and a break with the superstitions of the past. Some Presbyterian women wear a white traditional Korean dress (*hanbok*) during Pentecost.

DIETARY PRACTICES Christian dietary practices in South Korea do not deviate significantly from the culinary norm. Because *tteok* (special rice cakes) are sometimes shared as offerings during Confucian ancestor worship, Christians may consume *tteok* only when it has been prepared separately from that used in the Confucian rituals. Food taboos for Christians may extend to foods that come from Buddhist temples and shamanistic rituals.

RITUALS South Korean Christians commonly say grace before eating in restaurants, in dining halls, or even on trains. On Seoul's many university campuses students often lean onto each other in spontaneous prayer. House prayer meetings are also common; many Christians will undertake long commutes to take part in a prestigious home prayer group.

There is a taboo among Christians concerning the practice of bowing to shrines or ancestors. Christians may remedy tense family situations, however, by praying for their deceased, a practice seeming to represent a compromise between Confucian reverence and Christian proscription of idolatry.

RITES OF PASSAGE Korean forms of Christian rites of passage include all or parts of the following for laity: Holy Communion, confession, baptism and anabaptism, marriage and funeral rites, and the Eucharist or Lord's Supper. For clergy the following rites remain important: candidacy, affirmation, and ordination. Wedding and funeral ceremonies are conducted with both traditional and modern elements. Many Christians still embrace important traditional Korean rites of passage, such as *tteol* (first birthday) and *hwangap* (60th birthday) celebrations.

MEMBERSHIP Membership in Protestant denominations has risen enormously in South Korea since the Korean War (1950–53). There are many Anglo- and Korean-American missionaries in South Korea, in addition to many native Korean proselytizers. Based on the long, thriving presence of American missionaries in the country, Protestantism is almost synonymous with "American religion." Catholics are less fervent about seeking converts.

An extensive global network of Korean missions has evolved to attend to the needs of Korean diaspora communities worldwide. While many missionaries serve within South Korea, increasing numbers of South Korean missionaries from various denominations currently serve in other parts of the globe, including eastern Europe and Africa.

SOCIAL JUSTICE South Korean Christians see a strong link between the Gospel and reforms in education, economics, and health care. Today liberal-minded Protestants are active in such causes as advocating women's rights, protesting against abortion of female babies, eliminating prejudice toward the physically and mentally challenged, combating discrimination against orphans and children from non-Korean backgrounds, and overcoming the clannish tradition of extending kindness only to family and friends. Christian-sponsored organizations have played an important role in reorganizing an agrarian society into an urban society and in easing industrialization pains by supporting union movements.

The situation for South Korean women benefited most significantly from the introduction of Christianity. Organizations such as the Women's Friendship Meeting, the Korean YWCA, and the Women's Christian Moderation Meeting became instrumental in the crusade against such nineteenth-century plights as concubinage and female confinement in the inner rooms of family residences (*anbang*). These Protestant women's groups, the members of which were called "progressive foxes" by the conservative establishment, battled strong resistance from Confucian-based favoritism toward males. Especially challenging was the task of convincing parents of the value of girl's education. This challenge proved easier with lower-class families than with Confucianist aristocratic *yangban* families. Along with Korean's "will to greatness" (as explained by Carter J. Eckert), Christianity offered what the country long had been ready to take on—namely, more humanity, more social mobility, more equality, more democracy, and more education. Institutions of higher education established by Christian churches include the Protestant universities of Yonsei and Ehwa and their Catholic counterparts at Sogang and Hyosung.

SOCIAL ASPECTS South Korean Christian's views of marriage and family largely receive definition from both Christianity and Confucianism. Despite women's liberation emanating from Christianity, Confucian values of family continuity in harmony, male authority, and filial piety remain strong even in the modern nuclear family. Although divorce is frowned upon considerably, divorce rates are on the rise.

POLITICAL IMPACT The sociocultural progress that entered Korea with Christianity's arrival also fueled the political fervor that drove the independence movement. Many Christians in contemporary South Korea, such as long-time opposition leader and president Kim Dae-Jung (served 1998–2003), a Catholic, have been outspoken advocates of human rights and critics of oppressive government. Many leaders maintain memberships in Protestant churches, and the rate of Catholics and Protestants in the parliament is high.

CONTROVERSIAL ISSUES A recent controversy has revolved around the defacing of traditional religious and national symbols—such as images of Korea's mythical founder, Dangun—which have been interpreted by some Christian leaders as idolatrous. Such incidents have caused a reorientation toward Eastern religions by many Koreans wary of Christian agitation. Another increasingly pressing issue is the tension between Christians and Buddhists. During the second half of the 1990s, there were more than 20 arson assaults on Buddhist temples, for which Protestant extremist groups claimed responsibility. Despite public apologies by liberal Protestant leaders, the attacks persisted.

Because of a broad traditional acceptance, abortion of female children is not addressed comprehensively enough even by Christian churches. This practice is still widely upheld by the older, and especially male, sector of society.

CULTURAL IMPACT Christianity, as part of a broader Western influence, has throughout the twentieth century led South Korea to new approaches in faith, ethics, and education, as well as in music, literature, and art. Even so, South Koreans have put a distinct Korean spin on their work, appropriating Western ideas and forms and placing them into indigenous contexts. Minjung art, for example, a form of political art that emerged out of South Korea's movement for democracy, combined Western-based values and ideas with Korean images and political concerns.

BUDDHISM

DATE OF ORIGIN 372 C.E.

NUMBER OF FOLLOWERS 11.3 million

HISTORY The Chinese monk Shuntao introduced Mahayana Buddhism to the kingdom of Goguryeo in 372 C.E. Buddhist teachers introduced Koreans to Chinese methods of agriculture, architecture, lunar calendrics, and writing, while the Korean aristocracy appropriated the Buddhist Avatamsaka (*hwaeom,* meaning all things and people have their fixed place within the harmony of the universe) doctrine to support their autocratic rule. Mahayana (accepting diverse kinds of people with varying beliefs) ritual practice was acknowledged to be superior, though not contradictory, to that of shamanism, and its spiritual success beckoned leaders to maintain it as a reliable nation-protection religion.

Buddhism became a state-sponsored faith during the Unified Silla (668–935) and Goryeo (935–1392) periods. Monasteries received huge landholdings, on which they were expected to build temples and pagodas. The world's most extensive scriptures, hewn into woodblocks, were crafted. Only one, the Tripitaka Koreana (from the thirteenth century), survived.

The assets used to enrich Buddhist culture exhausted the country's economy and ultimately led to the state's demise toward the end of the Goryeo period. With the establishment of the Joseon dynasty (1392–1910), Buddhism lost its central role in Korean society and was relegated to remote monastic estates, on which taxes were now levied. During the twelfth century the contemplative Seon Buddhism (Zen in Japan) began to spread, deemphasizing textual study (Kyo) and encouraging meditation as the true means of attaining "worldlessness." Following the Hideyoshi invasions (1592–1604), Buddhism improved its standing among the Joseon because 5,000 monks had joined the fight against the invaders.

At the end of the Joseon dynasty, Japanese colonists used the distinctively Eastern aspects of Buddhism to counter Christianity's increasing influence. This period's legacy is the Taego order. Unwilling to be seen in accord with Japan, however, many Buddhists kept a low profile until liberation (1945). After the Korean War (1950–53) Buddhist monks gradually reclaimed their presence in the cities by instituting socioreligious centers. Since then Buddhism has grown considerably by adapting creatively to modern needs, allowing it to compete with Christianity for members.

EARLY AND MODERN LEADERS Ilyeon (1206–89) was among the first monks to write national history from a Buddhist perspective. He recorded native Goryeo poetry, documented the nation's early years, and provided the earliest written account of Dangun, Korea's mythical founder. Other notable monks included Weonhyo (617–86) and Jinul (1158–1210). Jinul added a disciplinary ethos to Buddhism that resonated with military and Confucian rulers, clearing the path for Seon (Zen) masters Sosan (1520–1604) and Sa-Myeong (1544–1610), who lent monk troops to the Joseon defense against Hideyoshi. Noteworthy twentieth-century Buddhists include Han Yong-Un, a fierce challenger of celibacy and one of only two Buddhist signers of the 1 March 1919 independence declaration, and Ko Un, a writer-activist who protested the military dictatorships of the 1970s–80s.

MAJOR THEOLOGIANS AND AUTHORS Weonhyo (617–86) exerted a powerful influence on early Korean Buddhism. His ideas about a unified "Pure Land," while invoking expectations of a paradise, formed a this-worldly viewpoint that appealed to converts. Uicheon (1055–1101) and Jinul (1158–1210), both syncretists, worked to unify the two major branches of Kyo and Seon (Zen).

During the 1970s–80s progressive monks founded Minjung Buddhism, allying themselves with the masses in the struggle against dictatorship. They justified their prodemocratic activism against conservative fellow clergy by claiming that the bodhisattva tradition called for resistance against tyranny.

HOUSES OF WORSHIP AND HOLY PLACES Sanshin, a mountain god of shamanistic origin, is unique to Korean Buddhism. A shrine in his honor can be found on a mountain above most major temples. It usually features a white-bearded old man, a tiger, and a pine tree (symbolizing spirituality, strength, and longevity, respectively). Among the most spectacular of South Korea's temples or holy sites are the Bulguk temple, Seokguram grotto, Pongdeok bell, and Haein temple (housing the Tripitaka Koreana, the world's oldest, most complete Buddhist scripture). Today these temples and shrines serve as residences for nuns and monks, places of prayer, destinations for pilgrimages, and tourist attractions. Private sites of Buddhist worship also exist, in the form of apartments, houses, rooftops, backyards, and business shrines.

WHAT IS SACRED? The three sacred foundations of South Korean Buddhism are the Buddha himself, an extensive body of sutras (scriptures), and a clergy of right-living and -thinking. In practice this translates into meditation, a study of the sutras, and a search for inspiration. Kwaneum (goddess of mercy), Korea's most popular bodhisattva (enlightened being), is unique only to that country.

HOLIDAYS AND FESTIVALS In 1975 the South Korean government declared Buddha's birthday a national holiday. The elaborate festivities on this (lunar) day in April include Bathing the Buddha ceremonies, followed by congratulatory speeches, lectures, displays of paper lanterns, the issuing of merit certificates for sponsors, purification and prayer sessions, and concerts. Buddhists might conclude this day with an extensive family feast honoring the Buddha. After dark many Buddhists visit the thousands of lighted lotus lanterns around a monastery. Buddha's birthday is also an important day for offering alms.

MODE OF DRESS Both nuns and monks are easily spotted in city crowds in their long gray robes, pointed straw hats, and emblematic knapsacks. Around the wrist they typically wear a Buddhist rosary, which may have either 18 beads, symbolizing the Buddha's original 18 disciples, or 108 beads, representing humankind's 108 delusions.

Religious dress code is almost exclusively restricted to the ordained. Inside a monastery different dress codes distinguish different levels of ordination. For example, a probationary candidate (*haengja*) is given a used robe, which he wears during the months of his postulancy. During this time he must not wear any formal robe (*changsam*) or any festively dyed cloak (*kasa*). Upon ordination a *haengja* is given a regular robe, a pair of baggy gray pants with leggings, and the traditional outer jacket. He is now addressed as an ordained novice (*sami*). For travel, or in the cold season, monks wear a thick cotton coat. A fully ordained monk wears a large, dark brown *kasa*. Summer clothing may consist of a light polyester *changsam*. A monk who has disrobed (renounced his commitment) surrenders his formal robes to the monastery and returns to secular life. Various full festive regalia are required for ritual specialists, public speakers, and performers during major celebrations.

DIETARY PRACTICES South Korean Buddhists usually adhere to the strict Mahayana dietary requirements of vegetarianism (no meat, eggs, fish, or dairy products). By maintaining these rules, Korean monasteries have become a protector of culinary traditions in rural areas, although the traditional peasant diet allows for meat. Monastic food taboos include alcohol and even garlic and onions, as they are seen as aphrodisiacs.

RITUALS Buddhist ritual practice flourished during the Goryeo dynasty (935–1392). Most rituals were intended to protect the nation from evil or solve serious problems. Others prepared the living and the dead for nirvana or pacified the spirits of the seas, skies, earth, and underworld. Chants and recitals were for purification, exorcism, offerings, and benedictions. Ritual activity declined sharply at the end of the Goryeo era and became largely deemphasized during the Joseon dynasty (1392–1910).

Life for observing Buddhists is imbued with daily and annual rituals. Most are simple, such as the burning of incense to ward off evil. Some of the few salient rituals in Seon (Zen) practice are the regular commemoration rituals—on the first of each lunar month—for former monastic leaders.

Each shrine in a monastery receives a short, simple service. After cleaning the shrines and filling their water vessels, monks place rice offerings on the altar, recalling the Buddha's habit of eating one major daily meal. These rituals are important only for ceremonial specialists, while the majority of monks are primarily interested in honing their meditative skills or performing chores. Also important is Enlightenment Day (usually in early January), during which Buddha's complete, perfect self-realization experience is reenacted.

RITES OF PASSAGE During the Bodhisattva Precepts Ceremony adult laity are confirmed or reconfirmed in their faith. They receive an ordination certificate, along with a touch to the forearm with a glowing incense stick. This symbolic endurance of pain signifies bodily detachment, while the certificate reminds worshipers to keep the 10 Buddhist precepts (e.g., not to kill, steal, or lie and to refrain from sex and alcohol).

In monasteries rites mark the stages of monkhood. Specific rites exist for young monks as they gain further acceptance into the order, with different robes marking each stage. According to Robert Buswell in *The Zen Monastic Experience: Buddhist Practice in Contemporary Korea,* most monks view ritual as a "minor part" of their lives and place greater emphasis on Seon (Zen) Buddhist practice—namely, the search for enlightenment.

MEMBERSHIP Since the 1970s Buddhism has attempted to adapt to modernity, printing a vernacular "Buddhist Bible" and distributing updated versions of Buddhist chants, folk songs, and borrowed Christian hymnals with texts from Buddhist scriptures. In the cities monks have formed proselytizing centers, many sponsored by lay auxiliary associations. With a greater overall presence in society, Buddhist membership grew from 700,000 in 1962 to more than 11 million in 1991.

Lay Buddhist organizations today are shouldering major responsibilities in proselytizing. Buril Hoe (Buddha Sun Society), for example, sponsors many socioreligious functions, including services, lectures, ceremonies, music sessions, vegetarian feasts, and site pilgrimages. Especially important has been the society's efforts to allow laity to directly communicate with clergy, from the lowest to the highest ranks. This new relationship provides mutual awareness of needs and mutual benefits in the strengthening of Buddhism.

Based on a 1997 survey, most Buddhists claim to be at ease with their religion because it does not appear as demanding as Christianity, and worshipers freely admit their lack of absolute devotion to their faith. They donate sizable sums of money only twice a year (during major festivities), and about 55 percent of Buddhists never read the scriptures. Most followers are women, while church leadership is overwhelmingly recruited from a monastic male elite.

SOCIAL JUSTICE Peacefulness, tolerance, loving compassion, and ecumenical spirit, all prominent in South Korean society today, can largely be credited to the enduring presence of Buddhism. These virtues helped clear the path for contemporary religious tolerance and diversity in Korea. There has been a long-standing critique that meditation and detachment foster ignorance of modern ills in society. In today's South Korea, with its highly educated citizenry, social responsibility has become obligatory for any prominent religious organization. Following centuries of internal tensions, Seon (Zen) Buddhism has, since the late 1960s, developed a renewed image of social involvement. The difficult events of the 1950s–80s prompted Buddhist clerics to take a more active role in pushing for the country's democratization.

SOCIAL ASPECTS Korean Buddhists see their faith largely as a higher protection mechanism that reaches where modern economic securities still cannot advance—namely, the well-being and happiness of the family. This includes educational and professional success, a peaceful earthly life from pregnancy to the funeral bier, and an assurance of heavenly life upon reaching the state of nirvana.

POLITICAL IMPACT Aside from its influence on peace, the political impact of Buddhism is hard to measure, because it focuses so intently on the search for self-actualization. Only today, with so much emphasis on measurable success, has Buddhism expressed its values more prominently. In recent decades Buddhist political activism has helped guide the search for democracy, a modern Korean identity, and environmental protection. Patience and goodwill are needed when it comes to unification with North Korea, and Buddhism has been consistently vocal in its demands for the peaceful unification of the country. Korean Buddhism passed an important test during the 1980s when it supported the politically oriented Minjung Bulgyeo (Buddhism for the masses) by lending its social values and worldview to the cause of democratization.

CONTROVERSIAL ISSUES The age-old preference toward male children prevails in South Korean society. Only recently has the dark side of this practice—namely, abortion of female children—been confronted by religious organizations. From within Buddhism the Venerable Seongdeok, a nun from Unmun temple, and the Venerable Seok Myogak, a monk from Bulguk temple, have spearheaded the organization of self-help groups for young women who have been pressured to abort female fetuses. Venerable Seongdeok has also openly criticized the Jogye order for investing too much of its revenue in building maintenance instead of allocating funds to women's support groups.

Another recurring issue has been the question of whether a broader curriculum—one including Buddhist cultural history, comparative philosophy, and English—should be taught to young monks in training. Buddhist leaders such as Cheong Pyeong-Jo, a professor at Dongguk University, South Korea's leading Buddhist institution of higher education, have supported the modernization of monastic education.

Perhaps the most controversial issue for Buddhists has been the recent arson attacks (more than 20 during the second half of the 1990s) on Buddhist sites and verbal assaults on Buddhist believers. In hope of remedying deteriorating relations between Buddhists and Christians and preventing further violence, several Buddhist associations have organized dialogues between the two groups.

CULTURAL IMPACT Outstanding examples of Buddhist architecture, sculpture, and painting draw large crowds to South Korean temples and museums, many of which are included on UNESCO's World Heritage List. Among them are the Haein temple near Daegu, featuring the Buddhist scriptures of the Tripitaka Koreana, along with its depository Janggyeon Panjeon (fifteenth century). The Seokguram grotto and Bulguk temple (both eighth century), near the city of Gyeongju, are also regarded by South Koreans as important cultural assets.

Buddhist sculpture claimed a central role in South Korean fine arts from the fourth century until the end of the Goryeo dynasty (935–1392). Buddhist thought also influenced the national literature through the popular *hyangga* style of poetry, reflecting the sublime poetic spirit of the Unified Silla period (668–935).

Other Religions

Ancient Eurasian migrants probably introduced early forms of shamanism to the Korean Peninsula. Its earliest influence can be traced to legends surrounding Korea's mythical founder, Dangun, dating back almost 5,000 years. South Korean shamanism worships three major spirits: the mountain spirit Sanshin (usually depicted as an old man with a tiger at his feet), Dokseong (a recluse), and Chilseong (the Big Dipper). It also acknowledges thousands of lesser spirits that reside in natural objects, such as rocks, trees, and streams. Shamanism, having no established temples or scriptures, sets up shrines in homes, backyards, and businesses. It is relatively free of orthodox structure and has a dualistic worldview in which body and soul are separate entities. This view allows for souls or spirits to enter a living body by way of a "physical possession."

Most Korean shamans (*mudang*) are women. A *mudang* acts as an intermediary between the living and the spiritual world. She is believed to be capable of averting bad luck, curing sickness, and assuring favorable passage from this world to the next. *Mudang* are also believed to resolve lingering conflicts between the living and the dead. While a few wealthy *mudang* may operate from a

Seoul office suite, most work from their houses or apartments. Their regular healing services include focused listening followed by judicious suggestions for better or healthier living. The consultation usually concludes with a brief touching of a specifically selected stone, commonly called the Stone Grandmother.

Mudang will also perform elaborate *kut* ceremonies sponsored by families wishing to communicate with their deceased. In addition, these ceremonies may be used for opening new office buildings or christening ships. *Kut* rituals involve one or two fellow *mudang,* musicians, and assistants who prepare food, decorate the altar, and help the *mudang* change dresses. There are 12 stages of ritual performance, during each of which the *mudang* wears a different ceremonial dress. In recent decades public performances of *kut* have enjoyed increasing popularity. The emphasis is almost exclusively on entertainment.

Records from the Three Kingdoms period (c. 37 B.C.E.–668 C.E.) reveal the earliest influence of Confucian ideas. The Unified Silla government (668–935) sent delegations of scholars to Tang China to study Confucian institutions and to record their observations. For the Goryeo dynasty (935–1392) Buddhism served as an "otherworldly" state religion, while Confucianism formed the "this-worldly" philosophical foundation of its power. After the Joseon dynasty (1392–1910) supplanted the Goryeo kingdom, almost everything related to Buddhist lavishness was eradicated, and the Joseon embraced Confucianism as the official state ideology. The Joseon developed a Confucian value system, reinforced by education, protocol, and civil administration. Monarchs encouraged the erection of stone-tablet monuments to historic figures who had lived according to Confucian precepts, and royal scholars published these brave people's stories as collected essays of prominent men (*munjip*).

After liberation from Japanese occupation in 1945, Confucianism as a religion began to become publicly invisible. However, it established itself as a strong moral-philosophical backbone for the entire nation. Confucianism's presence in South Korea today shines through most consistently in attitudes toward education, wherever new forms of Confucianism are emerging. Many modern-day South Koreans arrange for a Confucian-style funeral of their deceased or perform regular annual ceremonies of ancestor worship. Families of high status maintain their own cemeteries where elders are worshiped.

Wonbulgyo, or Won Buddhism, was established in 1916 by Chungbin Pak (1891–1943), later called Sotaesan Taejongsa (Great Ancient Teacher). It combines traditional Buddhist teachings with a concern for social reform and environmental conservation. Sotaesan founded the Won order with the goal of ushering all humans from the state of suffering into earthly paradise. He held that humans had become slaves to materialism, which obstructed the attainment of enlightenment. Won Buddhism's objective is the truth of Irwon (one circle). Based on the tenet of Irwon, Won Buddhists offer respect to anybody they meet, any work they do, and any object they handle. Won Buddhists performed selfless relief work for war refugees following liberation (1945) and during and after the Korean War (1950–53). Today they have a quarter million members and envision one global religious community.

Cheondogyo (Religion of the Heavenly Way) is a blend of shamanistic, Confucian, Buddhist, Taoist, and Roman Catholic elements. Originally called the Donghak movement, it is regarded as Korea's first important syncretic religion. It was founded in 1860 by Choe Jeu (1824–64) in reaction to foreign Christian religions and encroaching modernity. Choe, a landed aristocrat, claimed that God (Haneullim) had told him to preach all-encompassing renewal to the world. His four basic teachings are as follows: (1) There is complete unity between humans and God; (2) the mind of a human being is a replica of God's mind; (3) service to fellow humans represents service to God; and (4) all human beings are equal, regardless of social status or class.

The Joseon government came to fear Choe and his ideal that humans are their own gods, and executed him as a heretic in 1864. By then, however, Choe had acquired a number of followers, who were already disseminating his ideas in written form. Donghak spread among Korea's poor and eventually caused the largest peasant insurrection in Korean history, the Donghak uprisings of 1894, which led to the Sino-Japanese War in 1895. In the 1970s–80s the Donghak movement received renewed interest among members of the influential Minjung movement.

Daejonggyo (Great Religion of Dangun), founded by Na Cheol and Oh Hyeok in 1909, revolved around Korea's legendary founder, Dangun. By realigning Koreans with Dangun, Daejonggyo encouraged the purification and unity of the national spirit. Na Cheol saw the belief in Dangun and his line of descendants as the only way to save the nation from Japanese hegemony. Daejonggyo became a major resource for recruits and funds for the anti-Japanese struggle. Na Cheol retired as a high priest of the religion in 1916 and committed ritual suicide, becoming a martyr of both Daejonggyo and the independence movement. Today Daejonggyo claims about a quarter million followers in South Korea. It has its own temples, shrines, and schools and publishes the sacred writings of the Dangun Bible.

Jeondogwan (the Evangelical Church) was founded by Pak Tae-Seon, who was expelled from the Presbyterian Church in the 1950s for heresy. By 1972 his following numbered as high as 700,000, many of whom lived in Jeondogwan communes.

The Holy Spirit Association for the Unification of the World Christianity, or Unification Church (Tongilgyo), was founded by Moon Son-Myong in 1954 with the goal of Korean and, ultimately, global unification. During the 1970s the Unification Church had several hundred thousand members worldwide. Moon claimed that God had appointed him as a messiah to unify all people into one family, governed by himself.

Soka Gakkai (Value Creation Society), or Jangga Hakhoe in Korean, a popular religious organization in low-income areas of major cities, originated as a radical society of followers of the thirteenth-century Japanese monk Nichiren Shoshu. It comprises Buddhist, Shinto, and Christian elements distilled into a simple doctrine of optimism, faith healing, and strong leadership, with the ultimate goal of world leadership. The lore of Nichiren Shoshu spread in Korea in the early 1960s. By 1969 Soka Gakkai's membership had expanded to 30,000 households. Although the government initially banned the religion, in 1965 the group won a lawsuit under the country's religious freedom laws.

Today the group has many international chapters, organized into Soka Gakkai International, with about 80,000 members in South Korea. The faithful are expected to chant daily, donate money, and recruit new members. Soka Gakkai is involved in multiple businesses and finance corporations. Former members created the worldwide Soka Gakkai Victims Association, which in 1995 counted about 10,000 members.

Tenrikyo, a new religion from Japan, is fast growing in Korea and around the world. Some research indicates that in South Korea there are between 500,000 and 600,000 members, who congregate in about 150 groups. Their faith is based on Jiba, the source of all blessings, which includes the search for world harmony, balance of body and mind, altruism, self-correction, and, mainly, a joyous life. Tenrikyo emphasizes proselytizing so others may find access to the joyous life.

Michael C. Reinschmidt

See Also Vol. I: *Buddhism, Confucianism, Christianity, Mahayana Buddhism, Reformed Christianity*

Bibliography

Buswell, Robert E. *The Zen Monastic Experience: Buddhist Practice in Contemporary Korea.* Princeton, N.J.: Princeton University Press, 1992.

Clark, Donald N. *Christianity in Modern Korea.* Lanham, Md.: University Press of America, 1986.

Eckert, Carter J. "Korea's Transition to Modernity: A Will to Greatness." In *Historical Perspectives on Contemporary East Asia.* Edited by Merle Goldman and Andrew Gordon, 119–54. Cambridge, Mass.: Harvard University Press, 2000.

Grayson, James H. *Korea: A Religious History.* Rev. ed. London and New York: Routledge, 2002.

Harvey, Youngsook Kim. *Six Korean Women: The Socialization of Shamans.* Saint Paul, Minn.: West Publishing Company, 1979.

Janelli, Dawnhee, and Roger Janelli. *Ancestor Worship and Korean Society.* Stanford, Calif.: Stanford University Press, 1982.

Kang, Wi-Jo. *Religion and Politics in Korea under the Japanese Rule.* Lewiston, N.Y.: E. Mellen Press, 1986.

Kendall, Laurel. *Shamans, Housewives, and Other Restless Spirits: Women in Korean Ritual Life.* Honolulu: University of Hawai'i Press, 1985.

Kendall, Laurel, and Griffin Dix, eds. *Religion and Ritual in Korean Society.* Berkeley, Calif.: Institute of East Asian Studies, 1986.

Koo, John H., and Andrew C. Nahm. *An Introduction to Korean Culture.* Elizabeth, N.J.: Hollym, 1997.

Lee, Kwan-Jo. *Search for Nirvana: Korean Monk's Lives.* Seoul: International Publishing House, 1982.

Pai, Hyung-Il. *Constructing "Korean" Origins: A Critical Review of Archaeology, Historiography, and Racial Myth in Korean State-Formation Theories.* Cambridge, Mass.: Harvard University Press, 1999.

Paik, George. *The History of Protestant Missions in Korea, 1832–1910.* 1929. Reprint, Seoul: Yonsei University Press, 1970.

Spain

POPULATION 40,077,100

ROMAN CATHOLIC 82.1 percent

OTHER 2.0 percent

NONE 14.6 percent

UNKNOWN 1.3 percent

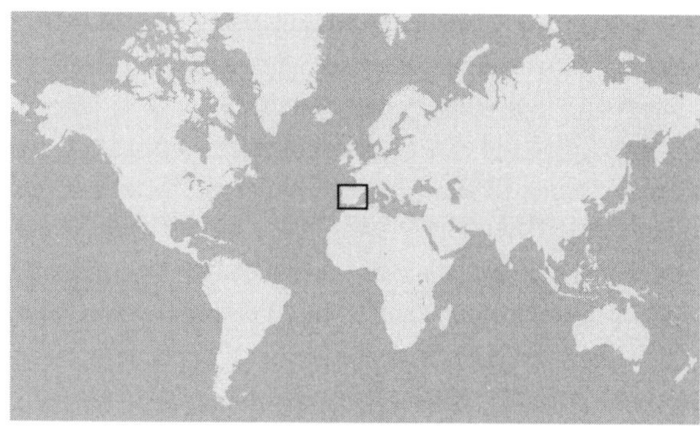

Country Overview

INTRODUCTION The Kingdom of Spain, located on the Iberian Peninsula in southwestern Europe, is bordered by the Atlantic Ocean, France, and Andorra to the north, the Mediterranean Sea to the east, the Mediterranean Sea and Gibraltar to the south, and Portugal and the Atlantic Ocean to the west. Mountains and rivers separate the peninsula into distinct regions, which helps to explain the divisive regionalism that has marked its history. The Canary Islands and Balearic Islands, as well as the cities of Ceuta and Melilla in North Africa, are part of Spain. Madrid is the capital and largest city.

By the beginning of the Christian era, the Iberian Peninsula was incorporated into the Roman Empire. After the collapse of the empire early in the fifth century, the Visigoths, Germanic invaders from central and northern Europe, swept onto the peninsula. The Visigoths ruled until 711 C.E., when Muslim armies from North Africa conquered most of the peninsula. During their rule of almost eight centuries, the Muslims (Moors) exerted a profound influence on cultural and economic life. Most Moors were expelled by 1492, which is considered the beginning of the modern Spanish state, and by 1512 the unification of Spain as a Roman Catholic country was complete.

Because of the immense wealth derived from its American colonies, Spain was the most powerful nation in Europe during the sixteenth century. A series of long, costly wars and revolts led to a steady decline of Spanish power, however. Political controversies consumed the country during the eighteenth and nineteenth centuries. There were wars over the issue of succession to the throne and a struggle between monarchists and republicans. The monarchy was briefly ousted during the First Republic (1873–74). At the same time, Spain began to loose its colonies, either by revolt or war, but not before it had exerted an enormous cultural and religious influence on them.

The Second Republic (1931–36) was dominated by political polarization that culminated in an electoral victory by the leftist Popular Front. Pressures from all sides, coupled with unchecked violence, led to the outbreak of the Spanish Civil War in 1936. This bloody conflict, which pitted brother against brother and priests against Marxists, ended in 1939 with the victory of the traditionalist General Francisco Franco, who ruled Spain as a military dictator until his death in

1975. A new constitution, adopted by referendum in 1978, established a parliamentary monarchy.

RELIGIOUS TOLERANCE From the mid-1400s to 1967 the Roman Catholic Church dominated religious life in Spain, with no other religious groups allowed to exist openly. Persecution during the Spanish Inquisition (1478–1835) forced adherents of other religions to flee, convert to Catholicism, or go underground. Although a measure of religious tolerance was introduced with the establishment of the First Republic in 1873–74, religious freedom did not exist until the 1967 Law of Religious Freedom established a legal basis for non-Catholic organizations.

The 1978 Spanish constitution provides for freedom of religion, which is generally respected in practice. Further protection is provided by the Organic Law of Religious Liberty (1980), in support of religious minorities. Although there is no official state religion, the Catholic Church enjoys privileges that are not available to other religious groups, including tax exemptions.

Catholic nuns wait for the arrival of Pope John Paul II. The Roman Catholic Church in Spain generally follows the Vatican in matters of social policy. AP/WIDE WORLD PHOTOS.

Major Religion

ROMAN CATHOLICISM

DATE OF ORIGIN First century C.E.
NUMBER OF FOLLOWERS 32.9 million

HISTORY Christianity entered Spain as early as the first century C.E. Ancient tradition affirms that James the Elder, one of the 12 apostles of Jesus, was the first to evangelize the Iberian Peninsula. This became the basis for the development during the Middle Ages of the Way of Saint James, or Camino de Santiago, as a pilgrimage route from France to the Santiago de Compostela Church in Galicia. The first diocese in Spain was established at Toledo in the first century, and the first bishop was Saint Eugenius, a Roman priest.

The Visigoths, who conquered the Iberian Peninsula early in the fifth century, adhered to the Arian version of Christianity, which held that Christ was not divine, while the Iberians followed the orthodox position of the Roman Catholic Church. In 589, during the Third Council of Toledo, Reccared, the Visigoth king in Toledo, formally renounced his views and pledged loyalty to the bishop of Rome. The religious unity established by the council was the basis of the fusion of the Visigoths and Hispano-Romans that produced the modern Spanish nation. During the seventh century the Catholic Church prospered in Spain and made significant contributions to the development of Spanish culture, particularly through the influence of Saint Isidore of Seville (560–636), an ecclesiastic and scholar.

Infighting between various Visigoth rulers, however, created discord, which prepared the way for the invasion of Muslims (Moors) from North Africa in 711. Muslim rule was tolerant, and Christians who had fled to the northern mountains were invited to return to their homes. The Moors showed little zeal for converting Christians and Jews to Islam, they did not impose unbearable taxes, and the three societies lived in relative peace. By the mid-thirteenth century, however, the Moors had been forced to retreat to the mountainous kingdom of Granada in southern Spain.

During this period of prosperity, the Catholic Church shared in the triumphs of the Christian kingdoms of Castile and Aragon. Great cathedrals and monasteries were built with generous endowments, and the clergy grew powerful and their privileges were enlarged. The energy and devotion of the missionary orders—the French Benedictines and Cistercians from the ninth to twelfth centuries, followed by the Franciscans and the Dominicans in the thirteenth century—strengthened the role of the church. The Dominicans, founded by the Spaniard Domingo de Guzmán (Saint Dominic) in 1219, became the chief protagonists of learning in Europe, whereas the Franciscans were skillful in spreading the faith among the people.

The marriage in 1469 of King Ferdinand of Aragon and Queen Isabella of Castile led to the establishment of a unified Catholic kingdom in Spain. In 1492 the monarchs conquered the Moorish kingdom of Granada and expelled those Jews who would not convert to Christianity, estimated at between 70,000 and 100,000, followed in 1502 by the expulsion of the remaining Muslims. The wealth confiscated from the departing Jews enabled Ferdinand and Isabella to finance the voyages of the Genoese navigator Christopher Columbus and to evangelize the newly discovered American territories that became part of their kingdom. The expulsion of the Jews and Muslims, followed by the condemnation, persecution, and expulsion of the Protestants after 1521, was part of a crusade to make Catholicism an essential component of Spanish identity. Thus ended the brief period of the Enlightenment in Spain—the University of Salamanca had been one of the first and foremost European universities—and the beginning of a dark period of purging heresy and humanistic freethinking.

In 1478, with papal approval, the monarchs had established the Office of the Holy Inquisition as state policy. The purpose was to defend the Catholic faith and to root out heresies, including the influences of Jews, Muslims, Protestants, blasphemers, bigamists, practitioners of witchcraft, and those committing acts against the Inquisition. In the quest to maintain the purity of the Catholic faith and to protect its members, offenders could be detained, imprisoned, tortured, and killed. It was not until 1835 that the tribunals of the Inquisition were finally abolished in Spain.

The Catholic Church not only dominated religious life in Spain but also exported the faith through the missionary endeavors of its religious orders, especially in Latin America. Its close relationship with the state allowed the church to receive financial support for its maintenance and expansion into the Spanish colonies in the Americas and allowed its religious orders to become heavily involved in social services at home, including schools, hospitals, and welfare. The reformist policies of liberal governments during the First (1873–74) and Second (1931–36) Republics, however, clashed with the conservative forces of the monarchy and the church, which ended in violent confrontation during the Spanish Civil War (1936–39).

During the dictatorship of General Francisco Franco (1939–75), Spain again became a confessional state, and until the 1960s the government supported the Catholic Church financially. One consequence of this policy was intolerance of other religions, although adherents were allowed to worship in private. From 1953 until 1967 Spain had a concordat with the Vatican ensuring that Catholicism was an important part of state policy and providing legitimacy to the dictatorship. Nonetheless, the first move toward religious tolerance by Franco's government was encouraged by the Catholic Church as part of the modernization process advocated by the Second Vatican Council. This opening produced the 1967 Law of Religious Freedom, under which other religious groups acquired legal status.

During the 1980s, however, the Roman Catholic Church in Spain showed signs of becoming more conservative. After decades as a minority in the Spanish hierarchy, conservative bishops reasserted their influence and began to wrestle power from liberals. This ideological shift was accompanied by a decline in the influence of the church, partly as a result of the modernization of the Second Vatican Council. One indicator of this trend was the decline in the number of men and women in the priesthood and in religious orders and the decline in the number of seminarians.

An opinion poll by the Center for Sociological Research in 1985 revealed that, although outwardly devoted Catholics, Spaniards were actually the most skeptical believers in Western Christianity on matters of dogma. Only 37 percent believed in the infallibility of the pope, 40 percent in the existence of hell, 41 percent in the resurrection of the dead, 46 percent in the existence of an eternal soul and in the virginity of Mary, 50 percent in the existence of heaven, 56 percent in Jesus Christ as God, and 59 percent in the creation of the world by God.

EARLY AND MODERN LEADERS Iñigo López de Loyola (1491–1556), who later took the name Ignatius, was the son of a nobleman in the Basque region. He was wounded in 1521 while fighting for Spain against the French. Recovering from his wounds, he read religious books, was converted, fasted, and did penance and works of charity. He then studied for the priesthood, became a scholar, wrote the work *Spiritual Exercises,* and in 1540 founded the Society of Jesus (Jesuits), which became the largest Catholic order in the world.

San Juan de Ávila (1500–69), known as the Apostle of Andalusia, is the patron saint of the secular clergy of Spain. He was born into a rich family, but when his parents died, he gave his wealth to the poor and spent three years in prayer and meditation. He became a priest and studied philosophy and theology at the University of Alcalá. His life was mainly spent serving the people of Andalusia, where he gained a reputation as an excellent preacher. He was canonized in 1970.

Saint Teresa of Avila (1515–82) was a mystic and reformer of the Carmelite Order. Known for frequent visions and ecstatic experiences, she founded the Sisters of the Barefoot Carmelites, whose discipline required great self-sacrifice, and established convents and monasteries. San Juan de la Cruz (1542–91) was another well-known Spanish mystic. Born Juan Yepes in a humble family in Fontiveros, he entered the Carmelite Fathers at the age of 21 and was ordained a priest in 1567. When a new convent was established at Salamanca, he was named rector and became known as Fray Juan de la Cruz. The author of many books and poems on Catholic spirituality, he was a friend and colleague of Saint Teresa of Avila.

The priest Josemaría Escrivá de Balaguer (1902–75) founded the influential and controversial lay organization Opus Dei (God's Work) in 1928. He was beautified in 1992 and declared a saint in 2002.

MAJOR THEOLOGIANS AND AUTHORS Melchor Cano (1509–66), who was born in Pastrana, studied theology in Valladolid and in Rome. He became a Dominican monk in Salamanca and later became a professor and founded a school of thought known as "fundamental theology." Francisco Suárez (1548–1617), a member of the Jesuits, was an author and a professor of philosophy, canon law, and theology in Spain and Italy. He is considered one of Spain's greatest philosophers and theologians. The most important Spanish Catholic philosopher of the nineteenth century was Jaime Luciano Balmes (1810–48), a priest and philosopher who wrote many articles defending Catholicism against Protestantism.

In modern times Casiano Floristán (born in 1926) was professor of pastoral theology at the Pontifical University of Salamanca and editorial director of the *Nuevo Diccionario de Pastoral,* published in 2002. Jorge Loring (born in 1922), a Jesuit, was raised in Barcelona and Madrid. Ordained to the priesthood at the age of 33, he became identified with a traditionalist, pre-Vatican II perspective. He has written several books, including *Para Salvarte.* Juan José Tamayo-Acosta (born in 1941) is secretary of the Juan XXIII Association of Theologians and a professor at the University of Valencia. A specialist on liberation theology and the philosophy of religion, he is a prolific writer who has published more than 1,000 articles and 30 books, including *Nuevo Paradigma Teológica.*

HOUSES OF WORSHIP AND HOLY PLACES The antiquity of Roman Catholicism in Spain means that there are many ancient churches, monasteries, and shrines. One of the most sacred is the Cathedral of Our Lady of the Pilar, the patron of Spain, in Zaragoza, which marks the site of the first recorded Marian apparition in Europe. According to Catholic tradition, the apostle James the Elder spent the years following the crucifixion of Jesus preaching in Spain. He allegedly arrived in Zaragoza in 40 C.E. and had a vision of Mary, who instructed him to build a church. The chapel that was constructed became a regional center for the conversion of pagans. Other holy places include his tomb (rediscovered in 813 or 838), known as Santiago de Compostela and located in Galicia, and the shrine (since 890) of the Black Virgin of Montserrat, near Barcelona, which is one of the most popular pilgrimage sites in Spain.

WHAT IS SACRED? In Spain there are numerous shrines and places that are sacred for Roman Catholics. Among these are caves and grottos, rivers, lakes and lagoons, hills and mountains, and even crossroads. Many such places were sacred to the inhabitants of the peninsula long before the introduction of Christianity, and it was only later that they were renamed in honor of Christ, the Virgin Mary, or a saint. The most popular devotion of Spaniards is to the Virgin Mary.

HOLIDAYS AND FESTIVALS National religious holidays in Spain include Epiphany (6 January); Holy Thursday, Good Friday, and Easter; Assumption of the Virgin Mary (15 August); All Saint's Day (1 November); Immaculate Conception Day (8 December); and Christmas (25 December). Many communities celebrate local religious holidays, such as the days of their patron saints. Although not an official holiday, 12 October is celebrated as Día de la Hispanidad (Colombus Day) and Our Lady of the Pilar Day. The festival of the apostle James the Elder is celebrated on 9 November.

Roman Catholic festivals in Spain are celebrated with church functions that include a solemn Mass, music, and a sermon, besides processions and pilgrimages. Some processions, such as those surrounding the festivities of Holy Week in Seville, have become widely known.

MODE OF DRESS Roman Catholic women in Spain have traditionally dressed conservatively, although this practice has diminished over time. As in other Catholic countries, the tradition of covering the head in church is still practiced. Many of the religious orders now allow members to wear regular street clothes in public.

DIETARY PRACTICES Spanish Catholics observe no dietary practices different from Roman Catholics worldwide. The variations in diet that exist are explained by local customs and practices within the various ethnolinguistic regions.

RITUALS One of the unusual Roman Catholic rituals in Spain is that of the flagellants who march in Holy Week processions and beat themselves on their backs with a short whip. This is an ancient form of penitence and sharing in the sufferings of Jesus, who endured beatings by Roman soldiers as he walked to the hill of Golgotha, outside Jerusalem, where he was crucified. The practice began in the Middle Ages in Europe, notably in Italy, Germany, France, and Spain, and spread to Spanish colonies in the Americas and to the Philippine Islands, where it is still observed.

RITES OF PASSAGE Roman Catholics in Spain observe the traditional rites of passage of baptism, first Communion, confirmation, marriage, and last rites. Fewer Catholics observe these rites today, however, than in previous generations.

MEMBERSHIP Since the 1970s there has been a gradual decline in Roman Catholic affiliation in Spain. According to a poll in 2002, only about 82 percent of the population claims to be Roman Catholic, of whom just 19 percent attend Mass regularly. Despite various efforts of the clergy to increase church attendance, many Spaniards no longer identify with the Catholic Church.

SOCIAL JUSTICE The Roman Catholic Church in Spain follows the general policies of the Vatican on matters of social policy. These include promoting education and reducing poverty, as well as support for human rights and condemnation of discrimination based on race, ethnicity, religion, or gender.

SOCIAL ASPECTS Until the 1960s the Roman Catholic Church and popular religiosity dominated the social life of Spain. Several forces, however, have brought fundamental changes to the role of the church in society. For example, there has been a marked improvement in the economic situation of a majority of Spaniards, which has made society more materialistic. In addition, there has been a demographic shift from rural to urban areas, where the church has less influence over the opinions and values of its members. The archdioceses of Madrid and Barcelona have the lowest percentages of Catholics in Spain.

Thus, in the past several decades a gap has emerged between the church and the general population, particularly on issues of marriage and the family, and the role of the church in weddings, family planning, and related issues has greatly diminished. Couples increasingly are married in civil rather than religious ceremonies, and the divorce rate has risen, as has the number of children born to unmarried women. Many couples use unauthorized methods of birth control.

POLITICAL IMPACT The Roman Catholic Church was traditionally aligned with the political right in Spain and dictated its preferences to its congregants. This situation changed during the right-wing dictatorship of General Francisco Franco (1939–75), however, when many Catholics reacted against the government's abuse of power and its restrictions on human rights. Some resented the support given by the church to the dictatorship. With Franco's death in 1975, the long tradition of mutual support between church and state weakened, and it ended in 1978 with the adoption of a new constitution that forbade the establishment of a state religion.

Today the Catholic Church plays only a minor role in Spanish politics, mainly by exerting its influence on the conservative parties that are more prone to respect Catholic tradition and authority. It thus had less influence under the Socialist government of Felipe González Márquez (1982–96) than under José María Aznar López (1996–2004) and the center-right Popular Party.

CONTROVERSIAL ISSUES Although church and state have been separate since 1978, Roman Catholicism continues to have a special place in Spanish society. Most Spaniards consider themselves Catholic, even if only in a vague sense, but they often disagree with church policy on such matters as birth control, abortion, divorce, and the role of women in both society and the church. As in other countries, the issue of homosexuality is controversial within the church, although in society generally it is more acknowledged and tolerated than in the past. Officially the Catholic Church prohibits those who have taken a voluntary oath of celibacy from homosexual, as well as heterosexual, acts.

CULTURAL IMPACT During its 2,000-year history on the Iberian Peninsula, the Roman Catholic Church has had a profound influence on the arts in Spain, particularly on architecture and the visual arts and on literature, and the influence appears as well in Hispanic culture in the Americas. The presence of religious art in every Catholic church in every town and village of the Spanish-speaking world bears testimony to this fact. During the medieval period especially, Spain produced many excellent architects, sculptors, and painters, and their work can often be seen in churches and other religious buildings. The importance of the Spanish language and of Spanish literature is universally recognized, and among Spanish authors there have been many notable Catholic writers. These include, during the Middle Ages, San Juan de Ávila and Saint Teresa of Avila and, among contemporary writers, Jorge Loring and Juan José Tamayo.

In popular festivals in Spain, religious observances hold an equal place with secular diversions. The morning is often devoted to magnificent church functions and the afternoon to dances, bullfights, and other secular amusements, which are carried on into the night. Although the character of the popular diversions may vary by region, the religious activities tend to be uniform.

Other Religions

Only about 2 percent of the population of Spain consists of followers of religions other than Roman Catholicism. These include Judaism, Islam, and Protestantism, as well as non-Christian religions.

From the late fifteenth century, after the Inquisition had begun, to about 1920, there were virtually no Jews living in Spain. Today there is a small Jewish population. Likewise, from the time the Moorish kingdom of Granada fell to the Christians in 1492 to the early twentieth century, there were few Muslims. Today, however, Spain has a significant community of Muslims, many of whom are migrants from North Africa.

Although Martin Luther and other sixteenth-century reformers had followers in the country, the development of the Protestant Reformation in Spain was impeded by the Inquisition. In the late nineteenth century Protestants began to appear once again. The Spanish Reformed Episcopal Church and the Spanish Reformed Church (later Spanish Evangelical Church) were founded in 1868, and the Congregationalists of the Ibero-Evangelical Union was founded in 1890. There also are small numbers of non-Protestant Christian groups in Spain, including Jehovah's Witnesses and the Church of Jesus Christ of Latter-day Saints (Mormons).

Some 100 non-Christian groups are known to exist in Spain, roughly half of which have been classified as "satanic." Most of these are located in Madrid and Barcelona. Older non-Christian groups include the Theosophical Society (1889), Gnostic Church of Jules Doinel (1895), and Ordo Templi Orientis (1919). The majority of such groups, however, have been established since 1970, following approval of the Law of Religious Freedom in 1967. Spain also has members of the Bahai faith, as well as small numbers of Hindus and Buddhists.

In a 2002 poll 14.6 percent declared that they had no religious affiliation. Of these, 10.2 percent were agnostics, and 4.4 percent were atheists.

Clifton L. Holland

See Also Vol. I: *Roman Catholicism*

Bibliography

Brierly, Peter, ed. *World Churches Handbook.* London: Christian Research, 1997.

Herren, Ricardo. "Los Españoles, menos religiosos que nadie." *Cambio,* 21 January 1985, 74–78.

Herring, Hurbert. "The Iberian Background." Chapter 3 in *A History of Latin America, from the Beginnings to the Present.* 3rd ed. New York: Alfred A. Knopf, 1968.

Huertas Riveras, Pilar, Jesús de Miguel y del Ángel, and Antonio Sánchez Rodríguez. *La Inquisición: Tribunal contra los delitos de fe.* Madrid: Editorial LIBSA, 2003.

Payne, Stanley G. *A History of Spain and Portugal.* Library of Iberian Resources Online. 14 Sept. 2004. http://libro.uca.edu/payne1/payne7.htm.

PROLADES-RITA official website. 14 Sept. 2004. http://www.prolades.com.

U.S. Department of State. *International Religious Freedom Report 2003: Spain.* Washington, D.C.: Bureau of Democracy, Human Rights, and Labor, 2003.

Sri Lanka

POPULATION 19,576,783

BUDDHIST 69 percent

HINDU 15 percent

CHRISTIAN 8 percent

MUSLIM 7 percent

OTHER 1 percent

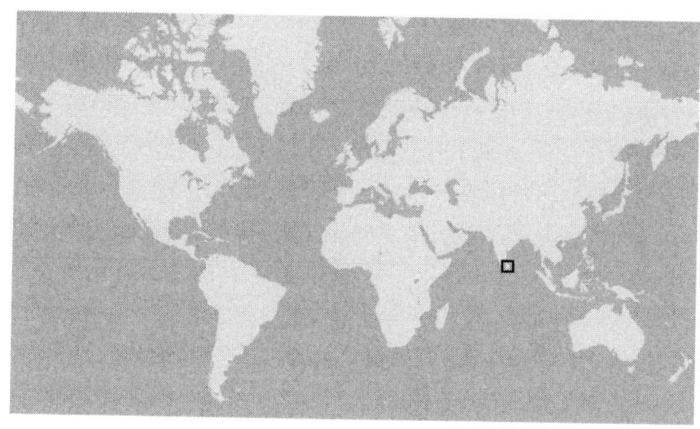

Country Overview

INTRODUCTION Sri Lanka (officially known as the Democratic Socialist Republic of Sri Lanka, formerly known to the colonial world as Ceylon, and known by its Sinhala name, Lanka, throughout history) is the island nation found just off the southern tip of India.

By about the third century B.C.E. Buddhist laity had begun to dedicate meditation retreats for Buddhist monks. A line of kingship supportive of Buddhist monks, who would later establish the orthodox Mahavihara tradition of Theravada Buddhism, gained political hegemony by the middle of the third century B.C.E. Over the next 13 centuries the capital city of Anuradhapura developed spectacularly into a thriving cosmopolitan city and international center of learning.

By the last half of the first millennium C.E., three major monastic sects (the orthodox Theravada Mahavihara and the more doctrinally eclectic Abhyagiriya and Jetavana) were headquartered in Anuradhapura and dominated cultural, social, economic, and political life throughout the country until the collapse of Anuradhapura, which was brought about by invasions from south India in the tenth century C.E. These invasions abetted the introduction of Hindu forms of religious practice in Sri Lanka.

Meanwhile, Arab Muslim traders began to frequent the island from as early as the eighth century C.E., taking with them versions of Islam current in the locales of their origins. Over the centuries many other Muslims migrated to Sri Lanka from south India and Malaysia.

In the sixteenth century C.E. the Portuguese arrived with colonial designs and their militant Roman Catholicism. The Dutch, who succeeded the Portuguese, were ousted by the British. The British eliminated the last of the Lankan Buddhist kings in 1815 and revolutionized the political system before ceding independence in 1948.

RELIGIOUS TOLERANCE Degrees of religious tolerance and intolerance have ebbed and flowed historically. But a dominant trait of Sinhala Buddhist culture has been its extraordinary pliability and inclusiveness. For example, the penchant for toleration and inclusiveness is signaled by a remarkable irony of history that occurred in the middle of the eighteenth century, when the

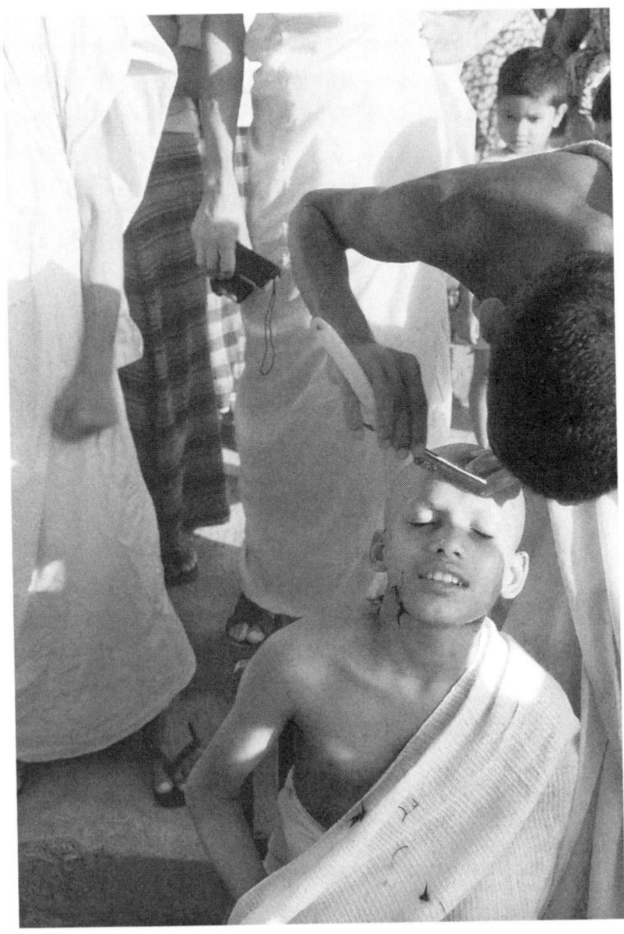

A young Sri Lankan Buddhist initiate's head is shaved during a ceremony. Sri Lanka is home to the oldest continuing Buddhist civilization in the world, dating back some 2,300 years. © TIM PAGE/CORBIS.

Kandyan king Kirti Sri Rajasimha (reigned 1752–81), ethnically a Tamil in origins, provided protection and sustenance to Sinhala Catholics in his kingdom after they fled the low country from Protestant Dutch oppression. Here, a Tamil Buddhist king protected one type of Christian from another. Muslims and Hindus were also thoroughly integrated into the social fabric of the Kandyan kingdoms (fifteenth through eighteenth century). Late medieval Sinhala literature and contemporary forms of popular religious practice are replete with evidence of this remarkable inclusiveness. The Sinhala Kotte kingdom (fifteenth and sixteenth centuries) also witnessed extraordinary degrees of religious toleration and cultural conflations between Hindu and Buddhist communities. Periods of intolerance historically were almost always the by-product of political invasion or machination. Imperial invasions from south India in the tenth and thirteenth centuries destroyed Buddhist monastic infrastructures on the island. Portuguese militancy led to the wanton desecration of many, if not most, Hindu and Buddhist places of worship in the south and west. More recently, following the Sinhala violence against Tamil people in 1983, Sri Lanka's protracted ethnic conflict has been portrayed by some, especially in the Western media, as a religious conflict. While it was clearly not motivated by Buddhist causes, some of the more strident sections of the Sinhala population have appealed to a Buddhist sense of historical ownership of the island as a rationale for the need to defend the political unity of the island on the one hand and to purge popular aspects of religious culture on the other in order to regain a perceived original pristine purity of Theravada Buddhism.

Major Religion

THERAVADA BUDDHISM

DATE OF ORIGIN Third century B.C.E.
NUMBER OF FOLLOWERS 13 million

HISTORY Sri Lanka is home to the oldest continuing Buddhist civilization in the world, dating back some 2,300 years. Although forms of Mahayana Buddhism were practiced in medieval Sri Lanka, especially from the eighth through the eleventh century, the predominant form of the religion that has been sustained is the Theravada (way of the elders), self-styled as conservative in nature and purporting to represent the original teachings of the Buddha (Tipitaka) as preserved in the Pali Tipitaka and its commentaries. Theravada claims an unbroken lineage of teaching from the time of the Buddha's formation of the monastic sangha to the present day.

The chronicles aver that a son (Mahinda) and a daughter (Sanghamitta) of the great third century B.C.E. Indian emperor Ashoka arrived on the island at this time to convert the Lankan king, Devanampiya Tissa, to the Buddha's dharma and to establish the Buddhist order of monks and nuns in the newly consecrated capital city of Anuradhapura. Sanghamitta is said to have brought with her a sapling of the original bodhi tree under which the Buddha had gained enlightenment. The same tree, one of the world's oldest, continues to be venerated by Sinhala Buddhists in Sri Lanka to this day as a symbol of the Buddha's dharma.

According to monastic histories, the teachings of the Buddha were first committed to writing in the first century B.C.E.. Subsequently monastic controversies of two types began to assail the unity of the sangha (monastic community) in the early Common Era centuries: (1) doctrinal arguments over the nature of the Buddha (supramundane or not) and (2) arguments over the monastic vocation (whether the path of the Buddha's dharma is best pursued through mediation in isolated forest hermitages or through acquiring wisdom by scholarly learning in a village, a context in which the laity might also be better served).

After the demise of the Anuradhapura civilization (third century B.C.E. through tenth century C.E.), wherein the Mahavihara monastery had flourished as a bastion of the Theravada, and following the reestablishment of Sinhala kingship at Polonnaruva in the twelfth century under Parakramabahu I, the Buddhist sangha throughout the country was thereafter unified "under one umbrella," although the community of nuns (*bhikkhunisangha*) was not reestablished at that time. From this reestablished base of Theravada Buddhist monasticism in which the institution enjoyed lavish royal patronage, an orthodox form of Buddhism stressing the progressive path of *sila* (morality), *prajna* (wisdom), and *samadhi* (meditation) spread to Pagan (Myanmar [Burma]) and from there to northern Thailand, Laos, and Cambodia by the thirteenth and fourteenth centuries to become the normative form of religion in mainland Southeast Asia to this day. In Sri Lanka, Theravada's historical condition has stood in reflexive relationship to the health of Lankan kingship—that is, whenever the kingship atrophied, so did the health of the religion, as the king was its chief patron. Monastic and temple culture flourished especially during the reigns of Parakramabahu I in Polonnaruva (twelfth century), Parakramabahu II in Dambadeniya (thirteenth century), Parakramabahu VI in Kotte (fifteenth century), and Kirti Sri Rajasimha in Kandy (eighteenth century). Following the disestablishment of Lankan kingship by the British in 1815, the religion atrophied until the closing decades of the nineteenth century, from which time it has reemerged as a vital force in Sri Lanka's cultural regeneration and the rise of nationalist politics.

EARLY AND MODERN LEADERS After decades of passive resistance to the Christian missionary efforts in the early to mid-eighteenth century, a small coterie of determined Buddhist monks, including Potuvila Indajoti, Kahave Nanananda, Mohottivatte Gunananda, and Valigama Sumangala, began to respond aggressively to the Christian missionary challenge by publishing a series of pamphlets defending the Buddhist tradition on philosophical grounds. Mohottivatte is especially well remembered for his stirring two-day debate with a Sinhalese Wesleyan minister at Panadura in 1873 amidst crowds of 5,000 to 10,000 people, an event that, in retrospect, may have marked the beginning of modern Sinhala Buddhist nationalism.

In 1880 the American theosophist Henry Steele Olcott (1832–1907) arrived on the island, capitalized on the momentum initiated by these Buddhist monks and galvanized the efforts of supportive Buddhist laity by establishing modern curricula at many newly founded Buddhist schools, organizing the liturgical calendar of public Buddhist holidays (the full-moon Poya Day observances), and disseminating widely in print his *Buddhist Catechism.* One of Olcott's early followers was Anagarika Dharmapala (1864–1933), who wrote the voluminous *Return to Righteousness* and founded the Mahabodhi Society in an effort to promulgate Buddhist values based on morality and honest, diligent work within the everyday lives of lay Buddhists. Dharmapala also enlisted international support for his campaign to regain Buddhist control over holy places of pilgrimage in India associated with the birth, first sermon, enlightenment, and final *nibbana* (nirvana) of the Buddha. Since the late nineteenth century the *mahanayakas* (chief prelates) of the Malvatta and Asgiriya chapters of the Siyam Nikaya in Kandy (heirs to the Mahavihara traditions in Anuradhapura) and the *mahanayakas* of the Ramanna and Amarapura Nikayas have served as important monastic spokesmen for the various Sinhala Theravada sects of the sangha. Since the 1990s the reformist Venerable Gangodawila Soma Thero of Colombo, an outspoken social and political critic representing Sinhala nationalist fears and aspirations, has become a well-known, influential, and controversial television personality.

MAJOR THEOLOGIANS AND AUTHORS The most important figure for defining Theravada orthodoxy (correct doctrine) and orthopraxy (correct practice) has been the monastic Indian commentator Buddhaghosa (fifth century C.E.), whose *Visuddhimagga,* among other works, remains the classic Theravada formulation of the path of dharma based on the cultivation of morality, wisdom, and meditation leading to the experience of *nibbana* (nirvana). The fifteenth-century *gamavasi* (village monk) Sri Rahula, a gifted linguist and aesthetician with a wide-ranging intellect, extended the scope of Buddhist monastic religious culture in numerous ways, as seen in his composition of several lyrical poetic tracts in which popular practices such as veneration of deities, the incantation of mantras, and other apotropaic practices were valorized. The eighteenth-century reformist monk Saranamkara reestablished the primacy of moral practice and deepened the practice of monastic learning through literary excellence in the Sinhala vernacular.

HOUSES OF WORSHIP AND HOLY PLACES There are 16 sacred places of pilgrimage often depicted within the visual liturgy of temple and cave paintings dating to the eighteenth century. Each of these 16 is associated with events depicted in the monastic chronicle *Mahavamsa,* in which three purported visits of the Buddha to Lanka took place following his enlightenment experience. The sapling of the original bodhi tree brought to Anuradhapura in the third century B.C.E. is also one of the holiest sacred places of pilgrimage on the island, as is Sri Pada (Adam's Peak), where the footprint of the Buddha is said to be embossed in stone. The shrines to the deities Kataragama Deviyo (also known as Skanda or Murugan, among others) in the deep south and east of Sri Lanka and Aluthnuvara Deviyo (also known as Dadimunda or Devata Bandara) in the Kandyan highlands attract thousands of pilgrims with petitions not for religious salvation but rather for more mundane reasons having to do with the alleviation of suffering (*dukkha*). Kalaniya Rajamahavihara, just northeast of Colombo, constructed on a site where the Buddha is said to have settled an ancient dispute between rival indigenous or mythical kings, and Devinuvara (the most southern point in Sri Lanka and therefore of the Indian subcontinent), where Vishnu is venerated, are also important sites of sacrality for Sri Lankan Buddhists, along with Mahiyangana in the east-central part of the country, where the Buddha is said to have first appeared in Lanka in the process of expelling *yakkha*s (demons) thereby rendering Lanka fit for the spread of his dharma.

WHAT IS SACRED? Relics of the Buddha are enshrined at holy sites throughout Sri Lanka to commemorate his ancient hallowing presence. Of these sacred relics, the Dalada Maligava (Temple of the Tooth Relic) in Kandy remains the holiest, insofar as the Dalada has been the veritable symbol of Sinhala Buddhist people since at least the Polonnaruva period (eleventh through thirteenth century). Until the British disestablished the last Lankan king in 1815, possession of and care for the Dalada was incumbent upon Lankan royalty. In turn, the presence of the Dalada legitimated a sovereign's reign.

HOLIDAYS AND FESTIVALS Major public holidays and festivals occur on full-moon Poya Days. Poya Days provide opportunities for the laity to visit the local temple and to practice *sil* (observing the fivefold morality of abstaining from causing injury, from falsehood, from improper sex, from taking intoxicants, or from taking anything that is not given), in addition to practicing meditation, hearing sermons, and, in general, engaging in the monastic life for a day. The most popular *poya* celebration, the Asala Perahera, occurs in July–August in the old royal capital of Kandy when the Dalada of the Buddha and the insignia of the national guardian deities (Natha, Vishnu, Pattini, and Kataragama) are taken out from the sanctum sanctorum of their respective shrines, mounted on sacralized elephants, and processed through the streets of Kandy for a period of 10 nights. During the same time at the southern shrine of Kataragama, thousands of pilgrims perform often radical forms of body-piercing asceticism to express their devotion to this increasingly popular deity. Vesak Poya, usually held in May, celebrates the Buddha's birth, enlightenment, and *parinibbana* (final spiritual attainment at death). Colorful displays of lanterns adorn the homes of laity and commercial establishments, while white-clad young women sing *bhakti gee* (devotional songs) from mobile platforms mounted on trucks or in ensembles at public spaces in cities. *Pandal*s, which are popular pictorial displays of Jatakas (birth stories of the Buddha), are capped by spectacularly lighted Buddha images and erected in many small towns and in major cities. Poson Poya, held in June, with the major events taking place in Anuradhapura and nearby Mahintale, where Ashoka's son, Mahinda (third century B.C.E.), is said to have first preached the Buddha's dharma in Lanka, celebrates the introduction of Buddhism to the island with more than a million people in attendance each year. Kathina, held at the end of the rain retreat season when monks are given new robes for the year, is an important merit-making occasion for the laity. Other major holidays include the celebration of the New Year on 12–13 April and extending for several days thereafter during which the first meal, first bath, first visit, first work, and so forth are ritually enacted.

MODE OF DRESS Buddhist monks, whether fully ordained or not, wear an orange or burnt-orange colored robe at all times. *Dasa sil matas or sil maniyos* (precept-holding lay women who have achieved a "nun's" status in the eyes of many) may wear yellow or orange robes. Laity who observe *sil* on Poya Days or who participate in any formal ritual occasion wear white shirts, white sarongs, or white saris.

DIETARY PRACTICES Contrary to what many in the West believe, there are no absolute dietary restrictions for Buddhists. Many do follow a vegetarian diet on moral grounds (ahimsa), however, and some will not eat pork recalling the Mahaparinibbana Sutta's account of how the Buddha fell ill during his last meal from eating pork. In Sri Lanka rice with various curries is consumed copiously, but monks and "nuns" refrain, in accordance with the Vinaya monastic rules, from eating solids after noon.

RITUALS Ancient monastic rites continue to be observed within the sangha. The Patimokkha, observed every two weeks at the new and full moon, consists of a collective recitation and affirmation of the 227 rules of monastic discipline as these have been preserved in the Vinaya Pitaka to ensure the community's moral purity. Monks also continue to chant *pirith* (Sanskrit, *paritta*) sutras, a form of blessing the laity, to offer protection and purification on a variety of occasions that need to be made auspicious. *Bana* (sermons) are regularly preached at the temple on Poya Days or on occasions when monks have been invited into the homes or neighborhoods of the laity for special events. *Upasampada* is a ritual performed during the month of Vesak (May) to ordain novice monks into the sangha. Buddha *puja* (worship of the Buddha) is usually performed at least twice a day in most Buddhist temples. Meditation is left to the discretion of the individual monk. *Pindapata* (morning alms rounds for food), which is practiced by Theravada monks in Myanmar (Burma), Thailand, Laos, and Cambodia, is rarely carried out in Sri Lanka. Laity regularly offer food to the monks of the temple as a means of gaining merit and also offer flowers and incense to the Buddha during Buddha *puja,* observe *sil* on Poya Days (as explained above under HOLIDAYS AND FESTIVALS), and undertake pilgrimages to specific sacred places at specific times throughout the calendar year. *Peraharas* (public processions), *pujas* (worship ceremonies) for deities at their shrines (*devalayas*), and, less frequently, rites of exorcism and sorcery are also part of lay religious life.

RITES OF PASSAGE *Upasampada* (as explained above under RITUALS) and funerals (cremations) are the only formal rites of passages observed in the sangha. At the cremation of a famous monk, an orange (robe colored) paper hut may be constructed over the body and the funeral pyre before incineration. Often, solemn testimonies are read and passages from the Pali scriptures distributed throughout the congregation before the pyre is lit. There is no specific Buddhist marriage ceremony per se in Sinhala Buddhist culture, though the trappings and symbols of Sinhala culture are found increasingly at the hotel venues marking middle-class Sinhala marriages. But marriage is not a sacrament. Funerals for laity are preceded by a three- or four-day period of visitation at the deceased's home, where the body lies in an open coffin. Food is not prepared in the house of the deceased for a seven-day period that ends with the ritual chanting of scriptures by monks and a merit transfer rite performed by the departed's kin for the benefit of the deceased. Merit-making and commemorative rites are performed as well on the occasions marking the end of three months and on each annual anniversary thereafter. Infant rites usually begin at three months, when children are taken to *devalayas* (shrines) to receive the blessing and protection of the gods. At puberty young women traditionally were isolated in a special room for the duration of their first menstruation, though this custom has atrophied in recent generations, particularly among the urban population.

MEMBERSHIP Though the origins of Buddhism in Sri Lanka are linked to the missionary efforts of Ashoka, Theravada Buddhism, throughout its long history, has been decidedly nonmissionary and not evangelical in nature. Moreover, for most of its history Buddhists have coexisted peacefully with Hindus, Muslims, or Christians. Buddhism is a major index for Sinhala ethnicity in Sri Lanka. One is either born into a Buddhist family or elects, on the basis of personal motivations, to become a Buddhist. In Sri Lanka there has been little in the way of active proselytization. During the past few decades, however, some monks and laity have organized missions with the support of wealthy expatriates to take the dharma to the West. Modern technology has abetted this process. In addition to international information centers now established in Colombo, websites are ubiquitous on the Internet.

SOCIAL JUSTICE Buddhism often has been portrayed in the West as a mystical or otherworldly tradition. But early on Buddhist kingship was legitimated by a rich mythology that stressed the moral justice administered by a righteous king (*cakravartin*) who conquered by moral example rather than by force. Ashoka's rule of dharma became a paradigm for all Theravada-inclined kings to emulate, the physical and social well-being of the people being the paramount responsibility of the ruler. Since the disestablishment of kingship and the resurgence of indigenous culture and nationalism in the late nineteenth century, Buddhist concepts of morality have frequently fused with more secularly oriented initiatives to alleviate the suffering (*dukkha*) of the people. The Sigalovada Sutta is a good text illustrating the importance of social relations. In that text the Buddha puts forward the view that instead of cultivating important relations with the deities of the cardinal directions, Buddhists should concentrate on honoring and cultivating relationships with their parents, children, teachers, employers, and so forth. Sarvodaya, a Buddhist-inspired nongovernmental organization founded in 1958 by a schoolteacher, A.T. Ariyaratne, aimed at uplifting village life through the alleviation of poverty, the promotion of sanitation and sustainable development, and the education of rural youth, remains an excellent example of how Buddhist values promote social justice in contemporary Sri Lanka. Though suicide is clearly condemned within Buddhist thought, Sri Lanka has one of the highest suicide rates in the world.

SOCIAL ASPECTS The nuclear and extended family remains the most powerful social unit in Sinhala Buddhist society. The sustained cohesion of the extended family is a consequence of how faithful most Sri Lankans are to the ritual life of the family, including New Year's observances, funerals, and weddings. Most marriages are arranged by weighing such factors as caste, religion, economy, and horoscope. Children frequently live with parents into their late 20s and early 30s, and parents can often rely upon children to care for them in their old age. Many Buddhists systematically practice family planning, a feature that has led some conservative elements within the community to worry about future population trends in relation to birth rates among Muslims and Catholics. Divorces are rare, though not as rare as among Muslims and Hindus.

POLITICAL IMPACT Religion has become a distinctive marker of ethnic identity in Sri Lanka. Before the colonial incursions Sri Lanka was predominantly a political culture dominated by Buddhist kingship, values, and ideals. The introduction of democracy following independence in 1948 served to heighten awareness of the island's various ethnic identities as politicians searched for ways to generate affinities with the electorate. In 1956 the Sri Lanka Freedom Party candidate for prime minister, S.W.R.D. Bandaranaike, who had only recently converted from Anglican Protestant Christianity to Buddhism, swept to power on a platform of "Sinhala only" and "Buddhism as religion of the state." Since that moment religion has been a powerful factor in the dynamics of national politics, creating a modest measure of cohesion among Sinhala Buddhists but also fostering fragmentation in the nation as a whole. While Buddhism was never made the official state religion, it has enjoyed a special status in the country's successive constitutions. Official preference for the Sinhala language and Buddhism by the majoritarian, Sinhala-dominated postindependence governments has led to various strains of alienation between the Sinhalese Buddhist and Tamil Hindu, Muslim, and Christian communities, devolving finally into a mounting civil war along ethnic lines since 1983.

CONTROVERSIAL ISSUES The politicization of Buddhism and the rise of various militant Buddhist sections of Sri Lankan society is probably the most controversial issue current in Sinhala society. Various dimensions of the issue have raged in public debates, but the political involvement of monks advocating political positions from the extreme left to the extreme right has raised the old question about the appropriate vocation of Buddhist monasticism. Those favoring political involvement have interpreted the Buddha's teaching to "wander for the welfare of many" as a mandate to be politically and economically involved. Others have championed the view that the vocation of the monk is best served by the vocation of meditation and ritual performance. Reintroducing the ordaining of women to become full-fledged *bhikkhunis* (nuns) has also been controversial. After the establishment of many *aramayas* (retreats) for renouncing laywomen ascetics throughout the twentieth century, a few Sinhalese women have now taken the higher ordination in Sri Lanka, thereby ending a period of more than a thousand years in which the *bhikkhunisangha* (community of nuns) was absent.

CULTURAL IMPACT The substance of virtually all Sinhala literature and art before the nineteenth century was

Buddhist in nature, almost all of it penned or painted by Buddhist monks or religiously inspired laity. Buddhism remains an important theme in contemporary fiction as well. Premodern Sinhala prose was based substantially on Pali sources (Jatakas, *vamsas*, sutras, and so forth), while temple and cave paintings represented the extended lives of Buddha within the mythology of the Buddhist cosmos. While Buddhist monks eschewed music, with the exception of chanting, the evolution of dance and music were the by-products of ritual observances (*peraharas* [public processions] and *sokari* and *kohomba kankariya* dramas) performed by the Buddhist laity.

Other Religions

The number of publicly observed holidays in Sri Lanka is 28, the largest number of any country in the world. Almost all public holidays are religious observances, eight of them non-Buddhist. Their official observance is testimony to the fact that Sri Lanka is a truly multireligious country. In addition to the Buddhist Poya Days, national patriotic days, and New Year's observances, the following religious holidays are also publicly observed: Thai-pongal in January; Mahasivaratri in February–March; Dipavali in October–November for Hindus; the Hajj, Ramadan, and Muhammad's birthday according to the shifting lunar calendar for Muslims; and Good Friday in March–April and Christmas in December for Christians. Because of the large number of holidays, it is impossible to live in Sri Lanka without becoming aware of the profoundly variegated religious roots and publicly recognized religious sentiments in Sri Lankan society—religion saturates Sri Lankan social life. Nevertheless, it is also surprising to learn how many Sri Lankans are almost totally ignorant about the basic beliefs and rites of traditions other than their own. In part this is a function of how religion is taught in public schools: Buddhists learn from Buddhists, Christians from Christians, Hindus from Hindus. Therefore, there is never a discussion of other religions, nor is there any type of developed discourse for talking about religion generically.

Historically Hindu practices have exercised a profound impact on the religious culture of Sri Lanka, even within the specific context of popular forms of Sinhala Buddhist ritual practice. Indeed, from the fourteenth century C.E., images of deities of Hindu origins (especially Vishnu) have been worshiped alongside the image of the Buddha within Buddhist halls of worship. Moreover, the fact that the goddess Pattini and the gods Vishnu, Kataragama, and Natha (originally Avalokitesvara) are regarded as the highest and national guardian deities of the Sinhala pantheon indicates how Sinhala Buddhist religious culture has incorporated and transformed the major trajectories of religion (Sakta, Vaishnava, Saivite, and Mahayana Buddhist) prevalent in the history of south Indian religious culture. Increasingly the liturgical rites constitutive of worshiping these "Buddhist" deities in Sri Lanka reflect the influence of temple-based bhakti (devotional) Hindu practice. Hindu holy men, such as Sai Baba, also attract a considerable following among Sinhala Buddhists in Sri Lanka.

At the same time, Hindu ritual and devotional practices within the Sri Lankan Tamil cultural context do not show many signs of assimilation from the Sinhala side. Religious practices among Sri Lankan Tamils do not seem to vary in many significant ways from the forms of Hindu practice found in the Indian state of Tamil Nadu. And it does not seem to be the case that militant forms of Hindu nationalism that arose in the 1980s and 1990s in India have exercised great influence upon the Tamil cause to establish an independent state of Eelam in Sri Lanka's north and east.

During Sri Lanka's protracted civil war of the late twentieth century, the Christian community on the island fragmented along ethnic lines. The Roman Catholic Church has been especially affected in this regard. For example, the National Seminary in Ampitiya, located just outside of Kandy, has become almost exclusively Sinhala, while some Tamil priests in the north and east of the island have actively promoted the separatist agenda of Eelam, rationalizing their activities by appealing to tracts of liberation theology.

In the closing decades of the twentieth century, the Muslim community experienced fundamental changes because of international and national religious and political dynamics. The spread of Sunni-based conservative practice from the Middle East has contributed to a homogenization process among Sri Lanka's Muslims. Local practices related to the idiosyncratic character of religion in Sri Lanka are increasingly eschewed by Muslim religious leaders in an effort to establish greater orthodoxy throughout the community. Muslim children are increasingly educated exclusively at Koranic-based schools or within the context of international schools, thus leading them to experience, in their youths, further separation from Hindu and Sinhala children. During the past 20 years Muslim females have begun to wear burkhas to cover their heads in public, further marking their identities as distinctively Muslim. At the same time, the civil war in the country has exacerbated relations between Tamils and Muslims. In the early 1990s Muslims were expelled from the northern region of the country by Tamil militants, and several episodes of communal violence between Muslims and Tamils, especially in eastern regions of the island, have created serious tensions. Muslims have also clashed periodically with Sinhalas in Colombo and in the Kandyan highlands, mostly over economic issues. Within the current context of political negotiations to settle the civil war, the Muslim community is demanding political representation separate from the Sinhala and Tamil communities in order to help secure a degree of autonomy within the possibility of a new federal political state.

The Vadda community, indigenous inhabitants of the island who have lived traditionally as hunters and gatherers, are nearly in a state of cultural extinction. They survive in waning pockets of wilderness in the island's east-central regions. Many of their myths and rites have been absorbed into late medieval popular Sinhala folklore, but their cultural survival, especially in a future likely to include more intensified rural economic development, remains questionable at best.

John C. Holt

See Also Vol. I: *Buddhism, Hinduism, Theravada Buddhism*

Bibliography

Bartholomeusz, Tessa. *Women under the Bo Tree.* Cambridge: Cambridge University Press, 1994.

Bond, George. *The Buddhist Revival in Sri Lanka.* Columbia: University of South Carolina Press, 1988.

Carrithers, Michael. *The Forest Monks of Sri Lanka.* Delhi: Oxford University Press, 1983.

Gombrich, Richard. *Buddhist Precept and Practice.* Delhi: Motilal Banarsidass, 1989.

Gombrich, Richard, and Gananath Obeyesekere. *Buddhism Transformed.* Princeton, N.J.: Princeton University Press, 1988.

Gunawardana, R.A.L.H. *Robe and Plough.* Tucson: University of Arizona Press, 1979.

Holt, John Clifford. *Buddha in the Crown.* New York: Oxford University Press, 1991.

———. *The Religious World of Kirti Sri.* New York: Oxford University Press, 1996.

King, Winston. *Theravada Meditation.* University Park: Pennsylvania State University Press, 1980.

Malalgoda, Kitsiri. *Buddhism in Sinhalese Society, 1750–1900.* Berkeley: University of California Press, 1976.

Obeyesekere, Gananath. *The Cult of the Goddess Pattini.* Chicago: University of Chicago Press, 1983.

Seneviratne, H.L. *Rituals of the Kandyan State.* Cambridge: Cambridge University Press, 1978.

———. *The Work of Kings.* Chicago: University of Chicago Press, 1999.

Tambiah, S.J. *Buddhism Betrayed.* Chicago: University of Chicago Press, 1992.

Sudan

POPULATION 37,090,298

MUSLIM 70 percent

AFRICAN TRADITIONAL RELIGIONS 18–20 percent

CHRISTIAN 10–12 percent

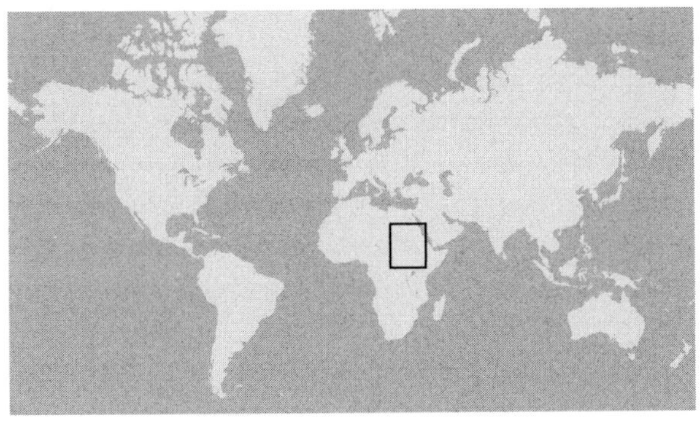

Country Overview

INTRODUCTION With an area of 967,491 square miles, the Republic of the Sudan is the largest country in Africa. It borders Libya and Egypt to the north; the Red Sea, Eritrea, and Ethiopia to the east; Kenya, Uganda, and the Democratic Republic of the Congo to the south; and the Central African Republic and Chad to the west.

The country is characterized by a flat plain, with the Darfur Highlands on the west and the Red Sea Hills in the east. The Sudan has an extremely warm climate, and the northern quarter is part of the Sahara. Grasslands prevail in the central section, while the south, where there is more abundant rainfall, is covered with shrubs, broadleaf trees, and grass. The Red Sea Hills have extensive savannahs of euphorbia.

The Sudan is primarily an agricultural country. Livestock rearing is particularly important, and a considerable portion of those dependent upon it are semi- or fully nomadic. Major crops include cotton, sugarcane, sorghum, sesame, and gum arabic.

Perhaps the dominant geographical feature of The Sudan is the valley of the Nile River, which passes through the entire country, dividing into the Blue and the White Niles at Khartoum, the capital. The Blue Nile, which contributes the great bulk of water to the main Nile, originates in Ethiopia, and the White Nile, in passing through the southern part of the Sudan, expands into an enormous swampland. It was along the main Nile that early Christian kingdoms arose. Perhaps the southern geography helped to inhibit the spread of Islam to the south and preserve the traditional indigenous religions.

Since the mid-1980s the Sudan has suffered from civil war between the northerners and the southerners. It is partly for this reason that the population and the numbers of religious adherents are only estimates and approximations.

RELIGIOUS TOLERANCE The Sudan is sharply divided between the northern two-thirds, where Sunni Islam prevails, and a southern third, where the population adheres primarily to indigenous religions and Christianity. Put simply, the north and the south are different worlds, initially joined together by forces of British imperialism.

Muslims of the Sufi sect pray outside of a mosque in Omduran, Sudan. Members of the Sufi sect have exerted a considerable influence on Sudanese social affairs. AP/WIDE WORLD PHOTOS.

Largely because they were earlier subjected to Muslim Arab slaving activity, a great many southerners are suspicious of northerners, while northerners sometimes look down upon southerners.

Since independence in 1956 power has been vested in the Muslim northerners. The situation has not, therefore, lent itself to religious tolerance. Jaafar Nimayri, who ruled the Sudan between 1969 and 1985, attempted to impose Shariah, or Islamic law, upon all Sudanese, and the present regime considers itself to be an Islamic state. Such situations impose difficulties upon the non-Muslims, including the extensive Christian missionizing efforts in the south. It should be noted that Muslim-Christian relations were not improved during the colonial period when the British reserved the south for Christian missionizing and placed the educational system in the hands of missionaries in order to create a substantial Christian community. If the contemporary Muslim state is not particularly tolerant of non-Muslims, it is also the case that Christian missionaries are not so tolerant of non-Christians.

Major Religion

ISLAM

DATE OF ORIGIN 641 C.E.

NUMBER OF FOLLOWERS 26 million

HISTORY The spread of Islam over the northern two-thirds of what is now the Sudan was a slow process. Initial contact with Muslims dated from 641 C.E., but in the early centuries of the Muslim religion there was no attempt to convert the Sudanese. One problem was the existence of Monophysite Christian kingdoms along the main Sudanese Nile. These existed beginning in the fifth century but over the course of time began to decline. The last survived until the fifteenth century.

Particularly by the thirteenth century there commenced a more vigorous Islamization process. Arab pastoralists began crossing the Red Sea and gradually percolating inland, while others descended from the north. Arab merchants and traders spread throughout the north of the country and intermarried with the local population, rearing their young as Muslims. Sufi orders were a major missionizing force, especially with the appearance of the Funj kingdom.

In the west the rulers of Darfur embraced Islam in about 1200, and the region gradually became Islamized. The Funj kingdom, dominated by an indigenous Arabized Muslim population, arose in the early sixteenth century, with its center in Sennar. The Funj rulers encouraged Muslim scholars to settle in the country, and they established Koranic schools, while Sufi mystics established religious orders. Thus, the Gezira and central Sudan were soon converted, although it was not until the eighteenth century that Islam became the religion of the entire north. It is from these mystics and scholars that there arose a number of holy families who have exerted a considerable influence on Sudanese social affairs.

Turkish rule prevailed over most of the Sudan from 1821 to 1881, and it eventually provoked opposition from the Sudanese in the form of a religious reform movement, the Mahdiyya, led by Muhammad Ahmad Abdallah, who proclaimed himself to be the Mahdi (guided one). A Mahdist state was maintained until 1898, when it was overthrown by the British, who essentially made the country a colony under the name Anglo-Egyptian Sudan. In 1956 Sudan was given independence as a parliamentary democracy. This, however, lasted only two years, when it was followed by a military dictatorship that in turn was succeeded by a return to parliamentary rule. This also lasted only a short time, to be replaced by yet another dictatorship, followed by a short span of parliamentary rule once again from 1986 to 1989, when yet another military rule was instituted with a strong emphasis on a rigidly conservative and aggressive Islam.

EARLY AND MODERN LEADERS Khalifa Abdallahi Muhammad (1846–99) was the successor to Muhammad Ahmad Abdallah in the leadership of the Mahdist state in the Sudan from 1885 to 1898. Direct descendants of Al Mahdi have periodically had major leadership roles in the independent republic. Abd Al Rahman Al Mahdi led the Mahdist movement until his death in 1959, and Sadiq Al Mahdi (born in 1935) twice served as prime minister (1966–67 and 1986–89) under a parliamentary regime.

Ismail Al Azhari (1902–69) was prime minister from 1954 to 1956, during which time he led the country to independence, and from 1965 to 1969 he was president of the republic. He was the most prominent of the more secularly oriented politicians of the democratic regimes in the Sudan. Hassan Al Turabi has been the primary figure in the development of the country's Islamist movement. He was the intellectual power behind General Umar Hassan Al Bashir, who took power in 1989, until he had a falling-out with the general, for which he was arrested in 2001.

MAJOR THEOLOGIANS AND AUTHORS In the early nineteenth century Muhammad Al Nur Dayf Allah compiled a collection of biographies on 260 Sudanese scholars and saints, known as "Tabaqat Wad Dayf Allah." Without doubt the most prominent Sudanese religious figure, however, was Muhammad Ahmad Abdallah (1844–85), who proclaimed himself Al Mahdi, the "guided one," and who led the northern Sudan in a revolt that overthrew Turkish rule in 1881 and established in its place his conception of an Islamic society. The movement represents one of the first revolts in Africa against colonial rule. Ali Al Mirghani (1878–1968), for years the leader of the Mirghaniyya, a religious brotherhood, was another major religious leader in the Sudan. Mahmud Muhammad Taha (1909–85) wrote extensively on religion and politics in the Sudan and the Middle East. His views on Islamic thought were regarded as a political threat, and he was executed for alleged apostasy.

HOUSES OF WORSHIP AND HOLY PLACES The mosques and tombs associated with Muhammad Ahmad Abdallah, in Omdurman, and with Ali Al Mirghani, in Khartoum North, are the most impressive. The Sudan is an overwhelmingly rural society, however, and the mosques and saint's tombs in the villages and small towns are simple. In rural areas few mosques have minarets, and in some areas they consist merely of an open space marked off by stones.

WHAT IS SACRED? In the Sudan the greatest importance is given to the tombs of holy men. In various parts of the country belief in the holiness of certain entities, which are quite unorthodox, have been retained. Thus, along the main Nile there is a sanctity attributed to the river. Among Nilotic Arabs women have a spirit possession cult (*zar*). The women also preserve a number of complex non-Islamic rituals related to childbirth and marriage, although these have begun to disappear. At least until modern times, in Darfur, in the west, the Fur and Zaghawa offered sacrifices to sacred stones and revered certain places as holy.

HOLIDAYS AND FESTIVALS As elsewhere in the Sunni Muslim world, the major religious festivities in The Sudan are the Great Feast (Al Id Al Kbir), at the end of the pilgrimage to Mecca (hajj); the Little Feast (Al Id Al Sughayar), at the end of Ramadan; and the prophet Muhammad's birthday. The various Sufi religious orders conduct services in connection with the anniversaries of the deaths of their founders, and they also have regular weekly services. Tombs of saints are visited, and there prayers are offered and vows are made or offerings are given for a vow fulfilled.

MODE OF DRESS In general, Sudanese Muslims dress in fashions tied to the Islamic tradition—that is, they emphasize covering most of the body. Among the Nile Arabs men dress in ankle-length shirts (*jallabiya*), and they wear a skullcap covered with a turban. Moustaches are common. Many Beja men retain their distinctive bushy, fuzzy hairstyle, heavily anointed with butter, and finely braided hair, a style that dates to pharaonic times, is common among Arab women along the Nile. Women wear long garments, and when they are outdoors, they often wear a wrap (*thoub*) around the head and upper body that also sometimes covers the lower part of the face. In rural areas, however, when a woman is working outside, she does not cover herself so completely. Henna is widely applied by women, especially to the hands and feet.

Religious officials in the Sudan are distinguished by the *abaya* (robe) and by beards. Few Sudanese have been attracted to Western-style dress since their own attire is much cooler.

DIETARY PRACTICES Sudanese Muslims follow Islamic rules regarding food and drink, although some disregard the prohibition against alcohol. In the central Sudan homemade beer (*marsa*) may be purchased at houses flying white flags, and in the communities of the main Nile alcohol distilled from dates or sorghum is consumed, especially on the occasion of weddings. Under the prevailing Islamist regime it is likely that these activities have at least been curtailed, particularly since total abstinence has been an important feature of official Muslim practice.

RITUALS The Arabs and Nubians of the Nile appear to be fairly faithful performers of the *salat,* the ritual prayer that all Muslims are expected to perform five times each day. Friday noon is a time for a congregational prayer, and usually at the same time the prayer leader (imam) delivers a sermon. A moderately high proportion of Sudanese apparently make the pilgrimage to Mecca. In some communities there are pilgrimage societies, in which members contribute funds so that each year one or more persons may go on the pilgrimage. Nomadic pastoralists in the Sudan are less observant of Muslim rituals than are sedentary people.

As with a number of Muslim countries, the various Sufi religious brotherhoods (singular, *tariqa*) are of considerable significance in both Sudanese religion and politics. The regular services of these organizations entail the singing of hymns, the recitation of litanies, and a *dhikr,* in which there is repetition of a ritual phrase accompanied by bodily movements to induce a state of spiritual ecstasy. Hyperventilation and self-hypnosis are involved. Rituals are also held in connection with a burial. Recitation of the Koran is common at funerals, and when people see family members for the first time after a death, they recite the *fatihah,* or opening chapter of the Koran, as a way of offering condolences. This is followed with an embrace.

RITES OF PASSAGE The birth of a child in the Sudan is surrounded with a number of rituals, which are observed over several days. Between the ages of 5 and 10, boys are circumcised, and girls have the operation of infibulation. It is believed, incorrectly, that infibulation inhibits sexual desire in women. While some commentators have sought to identify infibulation with Islam, it must be emphasized that the operation is actually not in accord with Islamic or Sudanese law but rather is an ancient pre-Islamic practice that today has become less common in the major cities, if not in the countryside. A 2003 law declared infibulation un-Islamic and illegal. It was once also common among many of the Arab people to perform scarification on the cheeks of young children, but since the mid-twentieth century this has been largely discontinued.

Marriages, which are largely arranged affairs and often between cousins, involve payment of bride wealth by the family of the groom. Weddings are accompanied by elaborate festivities that may last for days. Because of infibulation, it is sometimes necessary to call upon a midwife to open the bride's vagina surgically so that intercourse is possible.

During a funeral there is ritual mourning by the women, Koran recitation, and the sharing of food.

MEMBERSHIP Sudanese Muslims belong to the Sunni branch of Islam and generally adhere to the Maliki school of religious law (*madhhab*). A Muslim is born into the faith as a member of the religious community, although a person may, of course, also convert to Islam. Sunni Islam is loosely structured and is primarily a lay religion, in that an individual is not dependent upon any special class of persons to achieve salvation. Nonetheless, a number of holy families, invariably associated with the founder of a Sufi religious brotherhood or with the Mahdiyya, exert a great deal of influence in both religious affairs and politics. Many of the ulama (religious scholars) are derived from them.

Each mosque has an imam, or prayer leader, who is selected from residents of the community. The amount of religious training of an imam varies widely. Islam is taught in the public schools, and there are innumerable village-sponsored Koran schools. In these the emphasis is upon teaching children, usually all boys, to memorize the Koran. Missionary activity is carried on in the non-Muslim parts of the Sudan mostly in an informal manner, particularly by merchants and traders who move into an area and spread the religion by the public example of their ritual behavior.

SOCIAL JUSTICE Muslims in the Sudan, as elsewhere, are obligated to give assistance to the poor and needy as the third of the Five Pillars of the faith. There is a traditional system of charitable endowments (singular, *waqf;* plural, *awqaf*) that support hospitals, schools, mosques, and holy families. In the contemporary period there has been an expansion of Islamic banks that seek to avoid interest, which is prohibited by Islam. While Islam recognizes the right of private property, it also accepts the right of the state to interfere in the economy when it is for the public benefit.

SOCIAL ASPECTS The Sudanese family is the cornerstone of the social order. Especially in rural areas the family is often of an extended pattern, and among Nile Arabs the senior male occasionally resides with his married daughters and their immediate families. Senior women who are grandmothers have a considerable amount of power, and the practice of mother-in-law avoidance, in which the son-in-law does not look at, touch, or speak to his mother-in-law, is still to be found. Polygyny is not uncommon, and a man may have two wives dwelling in two different households. Divorce, too, is common, but only a husband may undertake such proceedings.

Tribal organization is widespread in the Sudan, and even where a group no longer has any formal organization or significant function, individuals still identify themselves with the tribal name. The enslavement of southerners by northern Muslims has apparently had some recurrence since the 1980s.

POLITICAL IMPACT Islam remains a powerful political force in Sudanese society. Some of the religious brotherhoods and the Mahdiyya have even been organized as political parties, although they are outlawed. The present regime is Islamist in that it aims to institute its interpretation of Shariah, or Islamic law, throughout the Sudan.

CONTROVERSIAL ISSUES The most controversial issue in the present-day Sudan is the application of Shariah, or Islamic law. The non-Muslim population obviously has misgivings about this, but liberal-minded Muslims do as well. They are concerned particularly about how the law is interpreted by the ruling powers, and if it is to be applied, they would like to see it interpreted in a modern light. In general, Sudanese Muslims are a tolerant and broad-minded people. The prevailing Islamist regime has been imposed by force and is not universally favored among Muslims, let alone the non-Muslim minority.

CULTURAL IMPACT Muslim religious architecture in the Sudan reflects not only Islamic but also African tradition, as, for example, in the domes of saint's tombs, which have a peculiarly Sudanese character. The music of the religious brotherhoods is a major contribution to Sudanese life, as are their litanies and the biographies of holy men. Hymns follow the Arabic style.

Other Religions

Perhaps 7 million Sudanese follow one of several indigenous religions. These are found predominantly in the southern third of the country, although in the past few decades there has been a large migration of adherents to the Khartoum-Omdurman urban area. The Dinka ethnic community comprises the largest of these people—some 4 million—followed by the Nuba, who are made up of several related groups. The Nuer, Azande, and Bari also make up large populations, well over 500,000 for each. Indigenous religions have lost considerable ground in the past century to Christian missionizing activity, but much less so to Islamization.

While each indigenous religion is associated with a specific ethnic community, most share a number of common beliefs and practices. They have a belief in a supernatural substance, which may be manifested as a supreme god and at the same time as separate individual spirits found in natural phenomena and in ancestors. Thus, ancestor worship is common. The supreme god is often held to be a distant entity, and prayers and sacrifices are more frequently directed to the individual spirits. The Dinka, however, frequently address their supreme god. While the Nuer also have a belief in a supreme being, they have no name specifically for this; the name is the same as that for all supernatural entities. The Shilluk, in addition to having a divine hero-god, Nyikang, also regard their king as a divine being, but he has no real authority today since this is assumed by the government. In sharp contrast to the Shilluk, the Dinka and Nuer have an acephalous social order, in which there is no centralized authority and leadership is weak.

Throughout the south cattle are sacred. The Dinka and Nuer name their animals, and each man has special oxen closely associated with him. Cattle serve as the supreme sacrifice in religious activities, and cow barns function as shrines and gathering places. In their barns the Dinka keep sacred spears, which are identified with the chief of the spear, who is essentially a rainmaker.

Rainmakers are important religious functionaries throughout the south. The Nuer have leopard skin chiefs who are empowered to curse and to mediate disputes. Among the Azande any misfortune is seen as the result of witchcraft, and the belief that witchcraft is an inherited characteristic is widespread. Diviners are common, especially for the diagnosis of witchcraft. Occasionally there have appeared prophets who are believed to be possessed of special spiritual powers and so have a certain sanctity, although this is often a sanctity to be feared. Among the Nuba there is a similar notion; it is believed a person may be possessed of a spirit that has a will of its own and so may act as it sees fit. A person so possessed may act as an exorcist, a rainmaker, and a curer of disease.

Neither circumcision nor infibulation is practiced by the southern people of the Sudan, but there are various forms of scarification. The Dinka and Nuer, for instance, cut several lines across the forehead of adolescent boys as an adult initiation rite. Marriage entails a payment made by the groom's family to that of the bride. The fundamental form of social organization is a segmentary lineage system, in which an ethnic group is divided into clans and clans into lineages, with descent reckoned through the male line.

One dramatic difference between the north and south is in dress. Nudity prevails among the Dinka and Nuer, and other groups wear only a minimum of attire. This can be highly disconcerting to Muslims and conservative Christians.

The Christian community, which is overwhelmingly confined to the south, numbers around 4 million. Some 2,250,000 are Roman Catholics, more than 1 million are members of the Episcopal Church of the Sudan (affiliated with the Anglican Communion), and perhaps 750,000 are in one or another of a half dozen Protestant bodies. The Coptic Church has a few thousand adherents who are of Egyptian origin, and there are also a few in the related Ethiopian church who are Ethiopian immigrants. Christian missionizing began in the Sudan in 1898 and has been directed almost exclusively at those who adhere to indigenous religions. It is carried on by all of the Christian bodies except for the Coptic and Ethiopian. It is from the Christian community that the leaders of the southern Sudanese separatist movement have been drawn.

Harold B. Barclay

See Also Vol. I: *African Indigenous Beliefs, Christianity, Islam*

Bibliography

Barclay, Harold B. *Buurri al Lamaab: A Suburban Village in the Sudan.* Ithaca, N.Y.: Cornell University Press, 1964.

———. "The Nile Valley." In *The Central Middle East.* Edited by Louise E. Sweet. New Haven, Conn.: Human Relations Area File, 1971.

———. "Sudan." In *On the Frontier of Islam.* Edited by Carlo Caldarola. Berlin: Mouton, 1982.

Boddy, Janice. *Wombs and Alien Spirits.* Madison: University of Wisconsin Press, 1989.

Deng, Francis M. *The Dinka of the Sudan.* New York: Holt, Rinehart, and Winston, 1972.

Evans-Pritchard, E.E. *The Divine Kingship of the Shilluk of the Nilotic Sudan.* Cambridge: Cambridge University Press, 1948.

———. *Nuer Religion.* Oxford: Clarendon Press, 1956.

———. *Witchcraft, Oracle, and Magic among the Azande.* Oxford: Clarendon Press, 1937.

Hasan, Yusif Fadl. *The Arabs in the Sudan: From the Seventh to the Early Sixteenth Century.* Edinburgh: Edinburgh University Press, 1967.

Hillelson, S. "The Tabaqat Wad Dayf Allah: Studies in the Lives of the Scholars and Saints." *Sudan Notes and Records* 6, no. 2 (1923): 190–230.

Holt, P.M. *The Mahdist State in the Sudan, 1881–1898: A Study of Its Origins, Development, and Overthrow.* 2nd ed. Oxford: Clarendon Press, 1970.

———. *A Modern History of the Sudan from the Funj Sultanate to the Present Day.* London: Weidenfeld and Nicolson, 1961.

Lienhardt, Godfrey. *Divinity and Experience: The Religion of the Dinka.* Oxford: Clarendon Press, 1961.

MacMichael, H.A. *A History of the Arabs in the Sudan.* 2 vols. Cambridge: Cambridge University Press, 1922.

McHugh, Neil. *Holymen of the Blue Nile: The Making of an Arab Islamic Community in the Nilotic Sudan, 1500–1850.* Evanston, Ill.: Northwestern University Press, 1994.

Nadel, S.F. *The Nuba.* Oxford: Oxford University Press, 1947.

Nordenstam, Tore. *Sudanese Ethics.* Uppsala: Scandinavian Institute of African Studies, 1968.

Seligman, C.G., and Brenda Z. Seligman. *Pagan Tribes of the Nilotic Sudan.* London: Routledge, 1932.

Trimingham, J. Spencer. *Islam in the Sudan.* Oxford: Oxford University Press, 1949.

Suriname

POPULATION 436,494

HINDU 27.4 percent

PROTESTANT 25.2 percent

ROMAN CATHOLIC 22.8 percent

MUSLIM 19.6 percent

OTHER 5 percent

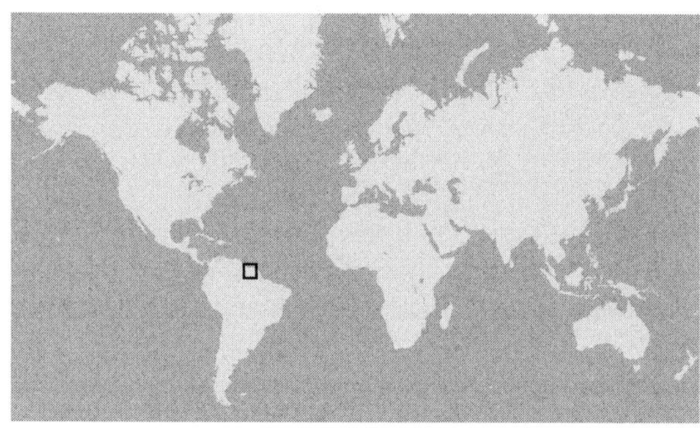

Country Overview

INTRODUCTION The Republic of Suriname is located on the northern coast of South America between Guyana and French Guiana. The territory was originally inhabited by Arawak peoples (c. 3000 B.C.E.) and later by Carib peoples.

Portuguese Roman Catholic missionaries introduced Christianity to the region after the Treaty of Tordesillas (1494 C.E.) gave it to Portugal. Spain officially claimed the territory in 1593; however, it was not until 1650 that the first Europeans settled there, starting with the British. In 1667 the Dutch assumed control of the territory, and it became a colony known as Dutch Guiana. During the Dutch and English colonial periods, forced manual labor was provided first by Native Americans, after 1640 by Africans, and after 1863 (when slavery was abolished in the colony) by a series of indentured laborers from the Dutch East Indies (now Indonesia), Portugal, and South Asia.

Today the population of Suriname is composed of many ethnic and religious groups. The largest ethnic group, forming 37 percent of the population, are descendants of immigrants from India; in Suriname they have come to be called Hindustanis or East Indians. They are predominantly Hindu; a minority is Muslim. Creoles (31 percent) are people of mixed African and European ancestry; they are largely Christian, though some are practitioners of a syncretic religion called Winti. Javanese (15 percent) are descendants of immigrants from Indonesia and largely practice Islam. The Maroons (about 10 percent) are descended from African slaves who fled the plantations in the 1660s and took refuge in the forests. Most practice a distinctly Maroon, African-influenced religion. There are also Native Americans and descendants of Dutch, Chinese, Portuguese, and Lebanese immigrants. Following independence in 1975, about a third of Suriname's population left the country for the Netherlands to take advantage of their Dutch citizenship.

RELIGIOUS TOLERANCE The constitution provides for freedom of religion and allows all the various faiths to worship freely. There is no state or dominant religion, and foreign religious workers face no special government restrictions. The constitution prohibits racial and religious discrimination. There is an interreligious council, composed of representatives from various religious groups, that arranges ecumenical activities.

Major Religions

HINDUISM

PROTESTANTISM

HINDUISM

DATE OF ORIGIN 1873 C.E.

NUMBER OF FOLLOWERS 120,000

HISTORY After the final abolition of slavery by the Dutch in 1863 C.E., plantation owners in the colony were faced with a shortage of manual labor. Consequently, the Dutch colonial authorities approved the importation of indentured servants from India between 1873 and 1916. These immigrants were referred to as Hindustanis (rather than "Indians," which is what the Native Americans were called).

The majority of the Hindustani immigrants were Hindu (a smaller number were Muslim). They were from various parts of India and had different linguistic, cultural, and religious traditions. Nevertheless, their ethnic identity was based on a British colonial concept of "Mother India," which they considered the place of origin of their common traditions. Some of them eventually returned to India, but those who remained in Suriname, with their descendants, developed into a community. The Hindustanis' various languages (including Hindi and Urdu), along with elements of Dutch and English, combined and evolved into an informal language called Sarnami Hindi.

The Hindus took the Indian caste system with them to Suriname, but eventually it underwent many modifications. The majority of the immigrants were members of the lower castes who entered Suriname as contract laborers; some of them were of the higher castes and arrived on their own as nonagricultural workers.

Although the Hindu organizations in Suriname have a primarily religious orientation, they also have a cultural dimension. For instance, language is an important element of ethnic identity. Beginning in the 1950s the Hindu community in Suriname made efforts to revive Hindi in an attempt to recover their ethnic heritage. Several religious and cultural organizations have played an important role in this revitalization process. Today about 27 percent of Suriname's population claims Hinduism as their religion.

EARLY AND MODERN LEADERS After indentured servants began arriving in Suriname in 1873, Hindu pundits helped maintain traditional practices among the Indian community. In the late twentieth century the most prominent Hindu leader in Suriname was probably Nanan Panday, chairman of Sanatana Dharma (the "eternal religion" of orthodox believers), the country's largest Hindu group.

MAJOR THEOLOGIANS AND AUTHORS Suriname has not produced any major Hindu religious authors.

HOUSES OF WORSHIP AND HOLY PLACES There are nearly 220 Hindu temples (*mandirs*) in Suriname. The oldest temple, constructed in the late nineteenth century, is a Sivalay (dedicated to the worship of Shiva) in the Saramacca district. The temple was renovated in 2003; Hindu leaders hoped that this would serve as a stimulus to the Hindu community to recover their cultural roots.

WHAT IS SACRED? Many Hindustanis in Suriname observe traditional Hindu religious beliefs and practices, including reverence for sacred books, images (statues and paintings), dances, songs, and temples.

HOLIDAYS AND FESTIVALS Held in November, Divali (the Festival of Lights) is a celebration of the triumph of good over evil and Lord Rama's return from exile. During Divali it is customary to light *diyas* (coconut oil lamps) at home and to organize illuminations in public places. Holi, or Phagwah (the Hindu spring festival), is held in March or April; people celebrate by throwing brightly colored powder on each other and holding a ceremonial burning of the demon Holika. Navaratri (literally meaning "nine nights") is one of the biggest celebrations of Hindus in Suriname; it is celebrated twice yearly (April/May and September/October). In Suriname it is chiefly a women's festival, as Navaratri honors the goddesses Sarasvati, Lakshmi, and Durga.

MODE OF DRESS One of the ways that Hindus in Suriname assert their cultural identity is by wearing on special occasions the traditional dress of India, such as the sari for women and the pyjama (loose pants) and kurta (a long, loose shirt) for men.

DIETARY PRACTICES Many Hindus in Suriname observe Hindu dietary practices, which vary widely. According to some estimates, about 10 percent of Surinamese Hindus practice vegetarianism.

RITUALS Although in Hinduism there is no specific time for visiting a temple, among Hindus in Suriname it is customary to do so on Sunday mornings, a practice that has probably been influenced by Christianity.

RITES OF PASSAGE Many Hindus in Suriname practice traditional Hindu rites of passage, such as *jatakarma,* the birth ceremony, which is performed before the umbilical cord is cut, and *namakarana,* the naming ceremony that takes place 10 days after the child's birth. Hindu weddings in Suriname are extravagant, including exquisite costumes, special ceremonies, and a huge feast.

MEMBERSHIP Hinduism in Suriname is limited largely to the immigrants from South Asia and their descendants, and there are no efforts to gain converts.

SOCIAL JUSTICE Among Surinamese Hindus social justice activities have generally centered on overcoming discrimination through establishing a strong cultural identity. Because they occupied agricultural jobs vacated by freed slaves, contract laborers from India were placed at a low level of the social order. Although these immigrants had previously identified themselves according to their region in India and not as "Indians," they developed a new consciousness as "Hindustanis" based on their shared cultural and religious values. By the mid-twentieth century the Hindustani community had been shaped into a significant force in Surinamese society.

SOCIAL ASPECTS The pressure to maintain traditional marriage and family values is strong among the Hindu community in Suriname, but intermarriage with other ethnic groups has resulted in an shifting of those values.

POLITICAL IMPACT The Hindustanis were disfranchised politically until 1927, when those born in Suriname were granted Dutch citizenship, opening the door for political participation. Since the 1950s the United Hindu Party (later called the Progressive Reform Party) has represented the social and political aspirations of the Hindustani community (including both Hindus and Muslims) in Suriname.

CONTROVERSIAL ISSUES Despite the fact that the Hindustani community has largely gained equality in Suriname, ethnic conflict continues to create social, religious, and political tensions in Surinam.

CULTURAL IMPACT The majority of Hindustanis in Suriname have retained the traditions, language, and beliefs of India. Music, dance, art, and literature are important for maintaining cultural cohesion. The Indian Cultural Center, located in Paramaribo, provides instruction in classical Hindu music, dance, yoga, and the Hindi language. Two popular television channels in Suriname, Trishul and RBNM, broadcast Hindi programs.

PROTESTANTISM

DATE OF ORIGIN 1735 C.E.
NUMBER OF FOLLOWERS 110,000

HISTORY The Protestant movement in Suriname is composed of about 20 denominations, the oldest of which is the Dutch Reformed Church (now called the Reformed Church in Suriname), founded in 1668 C.E. In the beginning it was a church for the Dutch colonists, and most church activities took place in Paramaribo and around the various plantations in the countryside. Until the 1850s it was a Dutch-speaking church and existed almost exclusively for the elite class. After the 1850s this denomination opened itself to non-Dutch members and to the African slaves.

The German Moravian Brethren arrived in 1735 to work with Amerindians, and after 1830 they worked with African plantation slaves. These lay missionaries were successful in establishing many local congregations among the non-Dutch (including the slave population). Today the Moravian Church is the largest Protestant denomination in Suriname.

The Dutch Evangelical Lutherans arrived in 1741, mainly to serve the small white population of plantation owners, administrative officials, and merchants. The Church of England (Anglicans) arrived during the British occupation of 1799–1816 to serve English colonists and other international residents.

Most of the other Protestant groups in Suriname arrived after World War II, mainly from the United States, to serve the general population. These included the Pilgrim Holiness Church (now the Wesleyan Church) in 1945; Seventh-day Adventists, 1945; the West Indies Mission, 1954; the Assemblies of God, 1959; Southern Baptists, 1971; the Church of God, 1982; the Church of the Nazarene, 1984; Mennonites, 1985; the Orthodox Presbyterian Church, 1987; the Christian and Missionary Alliance, 1987; and the Church of God of Prophecy, 1992.

EARLY AND MODERN LEADERS The Moravian Church is divided into autonomous provinces, each of which is administered by a committee of elders. Suriname is one of these provinces, and in 1999 Brother Hesdie Zamuel was elected its chairman.

MAJOR THEOLOGIANS AND AUTHORS Suriname has not produced any major Protestant theologians. The Moravians operate a theological seminary in Paramaribo.

HOUSES OF WORSHIP AND HOLY PLACES The central Reformed Church building in Paramaribo has special historical significance. It serves as the auditorium of the University of Suriname, and it was there that the first president of the country took the oath of office when Suriname became an independent state in 1975.

WHAT IS SACRED? As elsewhere, the Protestant movement in Surinam does not consider particular objects or places to be sacred.

HOLIDAYS AND FESTIVALS There are no holidays or festivals that are unique to Protestants in Suriname.

MODE OF DRESS There are no special dress codes among Surinamese Protestants.

DIETARY PRACTICES Seventh-day Adventists are vegetarians. They are the only Protestants in Suriname that have special dietary practices.

RITUALS Each denomination has its own special traditions and rituals. The Lutherans, Anglicans, Presbyterians and Reformed, Methodists, and Moravians have a liturgical form of worship in Suriname, whereas the majority of other Protestant groups are less formal and more spontaneous in worship and practice.

RITES OF PASSAGE Among the country's various Protestant denominations, there are no rites of passage that are specific to Suriname.

MEMBERSHIP Despite the growth of new evangelical groups in Suriname after World War II, the Moravian Church continues to be the largest Protestant denomination (10 percent of the total population). The Evangelical Lutherans often focus on gaining and retaining members among the youth of Suriname. The evangelistic activities of the Adventists and the Pentecostals include street preaching, house-to-house visitations, and the use of radio, television, and literature.

SOCIAL JUSTICE Traditionally the Dutch Reformed Church, the Lutherans, and the Anglicans have mainly served the small white population (plantation owners, administrative officials, and merchants) in Suriname, whereas the Moravians, Methodists, and Baptists have predominantly served the former slave population, the Creole population (people of mixed African and European ancestry), and the Amerindian groups. The latter is true of the various evangelical groups that arrived in Suriname after 1945. The Evangelical Lutherans offer various social services for the poor, including an outreach program in a housing project in Paramaribo.

SOCIAL ASPECTS Most Protestants in Suriname maintain conservative marriage and family values, according to which the husband is expected to work and provide for the family, and the wife's main duty is to run the household and raise children.

POLITICAL IMPACT The older liturgical denominations in Suriname (Reformed, Lutheran, and Anglican) have historically supported the political concerns of the upper class, whereas the denominations in the "Free Church" tradition have defended the human and civil rights of the middle and lower classes.

CONTROVERSIAL ISSUES Protestant churches in Suriname have not tended to focus on controversial issues. Women in Suriname are typically marginalized in public and political life, and the Protestant churches have usually not made efforts to address this problem. The Evangelical Lutherans in Suriname, however, ordain women, and the first woman to be elected president of a Lutheran church was Ilse Labadie (elected in 1986; died in 1999) of Suriname.

CULTURAL IMPACT The Protestant movement has not widely affected the music, art, and literature of Suriname.

Other Religions

Two Roman Catholic priests from the Netherlands settled in the colony in 1817 C.E. and established the Prefecture Apostolic of Dutch Guyana-Suriname, and soon the Catholic Church had a large following among the general population. In 1852 the Vicariate Apostolic of Dutch Guiana, with its seat at Paramaribo, was established as the center of Catholic authority in the region, and in 1958 it became the Diocese of Paramaribo.

Prior to independence in 1975 most of the religious schools in Suriname were operated by the Catholic Church and were often subsidized by the government. Consequently, the church played an important role in the socialization process by providing religious and moral instruction to a diverse range of ethnic groups. After World War II the Catholic Church was influential in preparing leaders of the nationalist movement. Catholic social thought has continued to affect Surinamese political life. As a result of its role in public education, Catholicism has had a significant influence on many aspects of Surinamese life, including music, the arts, and literature. It has especially affected the culture of the Creole and Maroon populations. Today almost a quarter of the total population is Roman Catholic. There has been a serious decline in the quality of pastoral care given to the Catholic community as a result of the reduction in the number of Catholic priests since 1966.

A minority of the laborers who were imported to Suriname from South Asia (now India, Pakistan, and Bangladesh) beginning in 1873—subsequently called Hindustanis—were Muslim. In 1890 Muslim immigrants also began to arrive from Java, Indonesia, where they had been recruited as indentured laborers to work on sugar plantations. Like the Hindustanis who had come before them, the Javanese immigrant laborers were placed at the bottom of the socioeconomic hierarchy. The plantation owners maintained their control over the labor force by enforcing the physical isolation of the Javanese during the period of their "indentured servitude" status, which also isolated them culturally. After the closure of many of the plantations during the 1930s, the Javanese began to establish themselves as small-scale farmers, living close together in family units or villages in rural areas, where they maintained their culture, language, and religious practices.

The majority of both Hindustani and Javanese Muslims in Suriname are Sunnis. Most villages have two mosques, which represent two groups within the Islamic community: the East prayers (which is more oriented toward an Arabic version of Islam; they understand Mecca to be to the east, and their mosques are oriented accordingly) and the West prayers (which preserves traditional Javanese culture; they pray to Mecca in the west, because this was the tradition in Java). The Javanese practice of Islam in Suriname is syncretic, because in Java Islam was historically blended with native beliefs and elements of Hinduism and Buddhism.

Mosques in Suriname are led by a *maulana,* who also functions as a traditional healer. When important events happen, there is always a sacrificial meal in which only the men take part. The *dukun* is a traditional healer in Javanese communities; her principal task is to serve as a midwife and to prepare natural medicines. All Muslims in Suriname, like Muslims everywhere, celebrate two official religious holidays, Id al-Fitr (marking the end of the Ramadan fast) and Id al-Adha (the feast of the sacrifice, a four-day event that concludes the annual pilgrimage rituals). Few Javanese Muslims in Suriname have converted to other religions. The Ahmadiyya movement (a Sufi, or mystical, order founded in India in the 1890s) has a small following in Suriname, as does the Bazuin of God movement.

Most Javanese in Suriname continue to work in agricultural occupations and are further behind other major ethnic groups in achieving upward social mobility. Although this traditional ethnic division of labor has broken down since the end of World War II and the achievement of independence (1975), the Javanese in Suriname are struggling to rise out of poverty and to achieve greater equality of opportunity. The Javanese community has developed into a significant political force, officially represented by the Indonesian Peasant's Party.

The Maroons are the descendants of escaped African slaves who settled in the dense tropical forests. They live in relative isolation and are grouped in five major tribes (Saramacca, Ndjuka, Matawai, Aluku, and Paramacca). Most Maroons continue to practice the religious traditions of their African ancestors; this involves a belief in a pantheon of deities and in nature spirits and ancestral spirits. Many Maroons have converted to

Christianity, but even those who have done so typically tend to retain their traditional religious practices, blending them with Christian beliefs and rituals.

Some of the Creoles (people of mixed African and European ancestry) practice Winti, a syncretistic religion combining African, Native American, Javanese, and European (including Jewish) elements. Winti is similar in some ways to Condomblé in Brazil, Santeria in Cuba, and Vodou in Haiti.

The Jewish community in Suriname dates to the arrival (in the mid-seventeenth century C.E.) of Jews from Europe (many via Brazil), who were followed a short time later by a group of Jews from England. Today there are two synagogues in Paramaribo, which serve a Jewish community estimated at 700 people. The wooden Sedek Ve Shalom, built in the 1730s, is perhaps the oldest synagogue in the Americas. It is adjacent to a mosque, a testament to the country's tradition of tolerance. The other synagogue, Neve Shalom (nineteenth century), is notable for its sand floor.

In the 1850s contract laborers from China and the Madeira islands were taken to Suriname. After World War I a new wave of Chinese (largely Buddhist), Lebanese (Muslim and Eastern Orthodox Christians), and Portuguese (mainly Madeira islanders who were Roman Catholic) immigrants arrived in Suriname. Portuguese-speaking Roman Catholic migrants from neighboring Brazil also settled in the country.

Since World War II a large number of faiths have established missionary programs throughout the country. These include church groups from the United States (most of which are Baptist-affiliated), Jehovah's Witnesses, and Mormons. Today in Suriname there are also members of the International Society for Krishna Consciousness (Hare Krishnas), Rastafarians, small groups of Baha'i, several groups of Druids (nature religion), and at least one group affiliated with the Ancient and Mystical Order Rosae Crucis.

Clifton L. Holland

See Also Vol. I: *Christianity, Hinduism, Protestantism, Roman Catholicism*

Bibliography

Beatty, Noelle B. *Suriname.* Philadelphia: Chelsea House Publishers, 1997.

Brierly, Peter, ed. *World Churches Handbook.* London: Christian Research, 1997.

Hoefte, Rosemarijn. *In Place of Slavery: A Social History of British Indian and Javanese Laborers in Suriname.* Gainesville: University Press of Florida, 1998.

Hoefte, Rosemarijn, and Peter Meel, eds. *Twentieth-Century Suriname: Continuities and Discontinuities in a New World Society.* Kingston, Jamaica: Randle Publishers, 2001.

Price, Richard, and Sally Price, eds. *Stedman's Surinam: Life in an Eighteenth-Century Slave Society.* Baltimore: Johns Hopkins University Press, 1992.

www.saxakali.com/indocarib/sojourner7a.htm (Gautam, Mohan K., "The Construction of the Indian Image in Surinam")

Swaziland

POPULATION 1,123,605

CHRISTIAN 66 percent

SWAZI TRADITIONAL RELIGION 33 percent

OTHER (BAHA'I AND MUSLIM) 1 percent

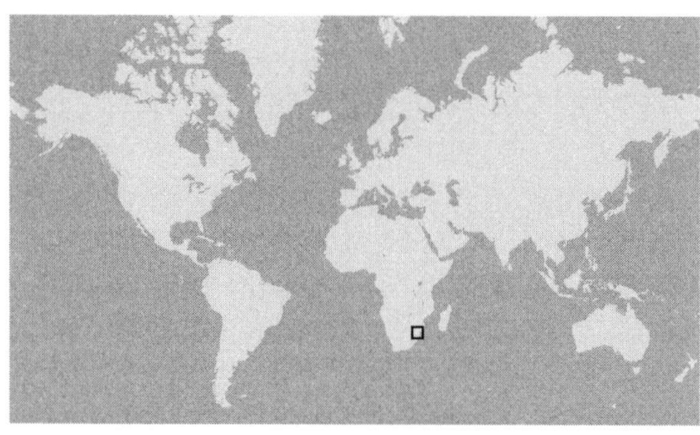

Country Overview

INTRODUCTION The Kingdom of Swaziland, a small, landlocked country in southern Africa, shares its eastern border with Mozambique and its northern, western, and southern borders with South Africa. The terrain consists of mountains and hills with some sloping plains. Subsistence farming occupies more than 80 percent of the inhabitants, though only 10 percent of the land is arable, and drought is a chronic problem. About 90 percent of Swaziland's imports come from South Africa, and nearly 75 percent of its exports go there. Mbabane is the capital, though Lobamba is the royal and legislative center.

Founded by King Sobhuza I (Somhlolo; ruled from 1818–36), a leader of the Dlamini ruling clan, and consolidated by King Mswati II (ruled from 1839–65), after whom the Swazi were named, Swaziland is ruled by dual monarchs, the king and his mother (the senior queen), who are recognized not only as heads of state but as symbols and representatives of Swazi culture, religion, and national identity.

Western missionary evangelism (which began in 1845) and British colonial rule (1903–68) greatly undermined the sovereignty and influence of the Swazi monarchy, who nevertheless welcomed European and American Christian missionaries into the country and permitted them to evangelize freely among the Swazi. Although they commended Christianity to the Swazi, most of whom converted, the king and queen mother resisted formal conversion. They retained the roles of high priest and priestess of Swazi religion but by 1937 had added new roles as patrons and defenders of Swazi Indigenous Churches.

When Swaziland regained its political independence in 1968, it adopted a democratic, British-style constitutional monarchy in which the king and queen played merely ceremonial roles. In 1973, however, King Sobhuza II (1921–82) repealed the liberal constitution on the grounds that it was incompatible with the Swazi way of life and that it engendered hostility, bitterness, and social unrest in the country. The nonparty Tinkhundla system of government introduced in 1978 gives the monarchy supreme legislative, executive, and judicial powers. Many Swazi have openly criticized the system through civil disobedience, mass demonstrations, public statements, pastoral letters and sermons, and boycotts of national elections and other state-sponsored commissions.

Swaziland is home to a small number of Muslims and members of the Baha'i faith.

RELIGIOUS TOLERANCE The 1968 Swazi Constitution provides for freedom of belief, worship, and membership. Relations between the state and religions have been complex and inconsistent, however. The state might enjoin all Swazi to participate in indigenous rituals and simultaneously urge all Swazi to attend specific Christian ceremonies. Only Christian churches are allowed to proselytize over national radio and television stations, and Christian prayers are said in public schools and offices and at national ceremonies. Opponents of absolute monarchical rule have enjoyed the covert and overt ideological support of the older mission churches—the Catholic, Anglican, Lutheran, and Methodist Churches.

King Mswati III of Swaziland wears a feather headdress during his coronation ceremony. © REUTERS NEWMEDIA INC./CORBIS.

Major Religions

CHRISTIANITY

SWAZI TRADITIONAL RELIGION

CHRISTIANITY

DATE OF ORIGIN 1845
NUMBER OF FOLLOWERS 742,000

HISTORY The first Christian mission station in Swaziland was established by the Methodist Church in 1845 at the invitation of King Mswati II. Because of the diplomatic, nonviolent policy of the Swazi monarchy toward Europeans in general, Christian mission churches had flooded the country by 1900, each with its own following of Swazi converts. The main Christian missions with permanent stations included the Anglican Mission (1860), the Lutheran Church (1887), the South African General Mission (1890), the Scandinavian Evangelical Alliance (1894), the Church of the Nazarene (1910), and the Roman Catholic Church (1914).

By 1907 Europeans owned close to 66 percent of Swaziland. Commoners and women, especially, turned to missionaries and mission stations for social, economic, and political support. Thus, the missionaries, with the help of the British colonial administration, tacitly compromised the position of the monarchs by taking over their role as landowners, leaders, benefactors, employers, educators, and religious advisors to the Swazi.

The country's geographical proximity to South Africa, where African Indigenous Christianity is strong, explains the religion's rapid growth in Swaziland. Cross-fertilization between indigenous Swazi religion and Christianity, though weakening Swazi religion, has also helped it survive.

EARLY AND MODERN LEADERS Dr. David Hynd (1899–1991), a founder-missionary and medical doctor, is the historical leader of evangelical Christianity in Swaziland. Under the auspices of the Church of the Nazarene (established in 1910), Hynd contributed to the creation of numerous churches and several mission stations in the country, placing the Church of the Nazarene and other Swazi evangelical churches at the head of influential nongovernmental organizations that spearheaded social development. In 1912 Hynd founded the Swaziland Conference of Churches (SCC), an association of conservative evangelical churches that combine an otherworldly and individualistic piety with a negative attitude toward traditional Swazi beliefs and traditions.

Bishop Stephen Mavimbela (1860–1948), a leader of the indigenous Swazi Christian Church in Zion, was the first vice-president of the League of African Churches in Swaziland (LACS), an association of African independent churches formed in 1937 whose main patrons are the king and queen mother. Mavimbela helped promote a distinctively African Christianity unequivocally identified with the dominant values, beliefs, and traditions relating to Swazi culture and the institution of sacred kingship. LACS was the antithesis of the colonial evangelism pioneered by Hynd.

Catholic Bishop Ambrose Mandlenkosi Zwane (1932–80) was the first president of the Council of Swaziland Churches (CSC), an association of ecumenical churches (including the Catholic, Anglican, Methodist, and Lutheran Churches) that broke away from the SCC in 1975 because of conflicts over doctrinal, moral, and political issues. Zwane helped form a vibrant nongovernmental organization that has focused on socioeconomic progress and other political concerns, including advocacy for women's rights.

MAJOR THEOLOGIANS AND AUTHORS Bishop Zwane, one of the few influential Swazi Christian theologians whose writings were compiled in a book, supported the inherent dignity of every human being. He believed that the mandate of the Church was to protect humanity from unjust laws and social structures, evil customs, and oppressive religious practices, and he fought for social justice in Church and society. A committed and practicing ecumenist, Zwane was described as "a man for all people."

HOUSES OF WORSHIP AND HOLY PLACES Christian denominations belonging to the SCC and the CSC worship in permanent church buildings. Most of the churches belonging to LACS hold worship services at the residence of the pastor or bishop. Made of cement bricks and corrugated iron sheets, these house-churches accommodate small-scale Christian communities at the local level. Church leaders identify worship locations by hanging out sashes in the official colors of the church uniforms worn by the members.

WHAT IS SACRED? Most Swazi Christians revere the Bible, the Holy Cross, church buildings and cathedrals, the altar, portraits and sculptures of Jesus Christ, clerical attire, and church uniforms.

HOLIDAYS AND FESTIVALS During the Good Friday Festival, founded in 1937 by leaders of African Indigenous Churches in consultation with King Sobhuza II, Swazis celebrate Easter with the king, the queen mother, and the nation at large at the queen mother's residence at Ludzidzini, the ritual capital of Swaziland. The evangelicals' Somhlolo Festival of Praise, founded in 1987, celebrates King Somhlolo's success in bringing Christianity to Swaziland. Swazi royalty and government representatives actively participate each July at a celebration hosted by the queen mother.

MODE OF DRESS Many Christian denominations have designed special church attire for their members. Some of the older mission churches—the Methodist, Anglican, and Catholic Churches and the Church of the Nazarene—require all or some of their full (baptized) members to wear church uniform on special occasions. During the annual Easter Convention, for example, male Methodists must wear a black blazer, a black tie, and black shoes; a white shirt; a red waistcoat; and gray trousers. Women wear a red jacket with a white collar; a black skirt, black shoes, and black stockings; and a white cap.

Swazi African Indigenous Churches require full members to wear church attire at all times. Church regalia is considered sacred: It is dedicated to God and must be blessed by the clergy prior to use. Male attire includes a blue or green coat with a woolen belt, a white shirt, and white trousers. Women wear a white dress, a blue or green apron and woolen belt, and a white or blue-green head scarf. Male members of the "Red-gown" Zionists wear a gown of yellow and either maroon or red, a woolen yellow and red sash on the forehead, and khaki or dark trousers. Women wear a red or yellow dress with a yellow woolen belt, as well as a scarf of red and either green or yellow.

DIETARY PRACTICES Swazi Christianity does not prescribe a particular diet, but many Christian celebrations involve the slaughtering of cattle, goats, and chickens to feed the congregations.

RITUALS Besides baptism, the Eucharist, and the Sunday worship service, there are four main rituals common among Christian in Swaziland.

Imvuselelo, or revival worship services, attract multitudes of Christians from different denominations. Prevalent in conservative evangelical churches and normally held in a church every evening for a week, these services are intended to rekindle and revitalize Christian piety and to win new converts to the church. The revivals are led by prominent and articulate preachers (many of them faith healers) from southern African countries, including South Africa, Zimbabwe, Zambia, and Kenya. A typical revival service is characterized by singing, a passionate sermon, an altar call, prayers for forgiveness of sins, and healings accomplished through the laying on of hands.

An Umlindzelo, or a funeral night vigil, is an interdenominational worship service held in honour of the deceased. Since funeral rites normally take place at around 6 A.M., it has become customary for the bereaved family to arrange an all-night prayer service for the mourners, many of whom may have traveled long distances to attend. Mourners at a night vigil gather in a tent pitched in the deceased's family compound and are served maize meal porridge and meat from a cow or ox slaughtered for the occasion. A lengthy worship follows, during which people sing and extol the virtues (especially the Christian commitments) of the deceased. The service ends at dawn, when a formal funeral service begins, normally conducted by an ordained minister. A celebratory meal follows the burial rites.

Inkonzo Yentsaba (literally, "the Service on the Mountain"), or the Women's Prayer Service for Rain, is an interdenominational worship held in late September or early October at the Swazi National Church, situated next the queen mother's residence. During the two-day ceremony women from different regions of the country embark on a period of sustained fasting and prayer, beseeching God to provide rain and fertility in the coming year.

Lunchtime prayer sessions normally take place at selected government offices or other convenient open spaces in urban centers. Groups of Christians, mostly Pentecostal women, gather to sing and praise the Lord; to proclaim a gospel of individual salvation, material prosperity, peace of mind, and contentment regardless of one's Christian affiliation; and to draw new converts.

RITES OF PASSAGE The ecumenical churches in Swaziland mark the birth of a child through infant baptism, while conservative evangelical churches dedicate the child to God at a special Sunday service. The child is received as God's gift, and the congregation is enjoined to provide life-long moral and spiritual support to him or her. Puberty is celebrated through adult baptism in conservative evangelical churches, while ecumenical churches celebrate the rite of confirmation. Concurrent with the transition from childhood to responsible adulthood, the Christian in both cases must affirm a commitment to Christ and the church publicly. At a Christian wedding ceremony, conducted by an ordained clergy and witnessed by the given Christian church, the groom and the bride make a public promise to lead their married lives in conformity with Christian teachings. The wedding usually ends with a celebratory meal. Though most Swazi Christians fear and resent death, the Christian funeral ritual is meant to celebrate the final liberation of the soul from worldly problems, including want, sickness, and death.

MEMBERSHIP Christianity in Swaziland has always sought to convert all persons belonging to other religions. With the establishment of a state-controlled radio broadcasting service in the 1960s and a state-run television channel in the 1980s, both of which allocate ample air-time to Christian programs and exclude the newer religions, the Christian faith has gradually assumed the status of a traditional religion to many Swazi. Most Christian churches use radio, television, and the press to spread their influence.

SOCIAL JUSTICE Conversion to Christianity in Swaziland was historically linked to a good education, a professional career, a good income, and an awareness of basic human rights. Swazi Christianity has pioneered the ideal of universal education, and most Christian churches (including Swazi Indigenous Churches) support education as a means of alleviating poverty. The Anglican and Catholic Churches have established permanent organizations and institutions to help the needy, including vocational schools, refugee centers, and homes for people with AIDS. Almost one-third of Swaziland's adult population is infected with HIV.

SOCIAL ASPECTS Most Christian churches in Swaziland oppose divorce and support marriage as a life-long, monogamous commitment between a man and woman. The churches frown on homosexuality, which is illegal in Swaziland. All denominations condemn sexual activity outside of marriage. Christians are expected to procreate, and the prevention of pregnancy is regarded as ungodly. The mainline churches proscribe the use of pills, condoms, and abortion as contraceptives. Children are regarded as gifts from God to be nurtured and cared for.

POLITICAL IMPACT The overwhelming majority of those who have held important, responsible political positions in Swaziland have been educated and trained in Church-sponsored schools and colleges. Graduates from mission-run schools tend to espouse social justice, democracy, and the protection and promotion of basic human rights. The Ngwane National Liberation Congress, the oldest political organization in the country and one of the most influential, has been supported mainly by graduates from mission schools. It and the People's United Democratic Movement are led by members of the older ecumenical churches—Catholic, Anglican, and Methodist. The two parties have challenged the legitimacy of the monarchy's power over parliament, the cabinet, and the judiciary. They advocate a return to the 1968 Independence constitution that restricted the monarchy's role.

CONTROVERSIAL ISSUES The doctrine of divine kingship presupposes that the dual monarchs are patrons of all established religions in the country, including Christianity. The Catholic, Anglican, Lutheran, and Methodist churches have challenged this presumed royal authority by not sending delegates to national Christian conventions and ceremonies in which the monarchy assumed the role of Christian leaders.

The most controversial subject among Swazi Christians is the relationship between Christianity and certain aspects of Swazi culture and religion seen as inimical to Christian faith and practice. Most if not all evangelical churches belonging to the SCC see ancestral veneration, consultation of diviners and herbalists, participation in national royal rituals, polygyny, and cumbersome mourning customs and taboos that limit the freedom of widows as problematic. Overt and systematic condemnation of traditional practices, however, may be interpreted as a castigation of the sacred monarchy itself, because the monarchy embodies and promotes Swazi indigenous religion. The liberal, indigenous, and independent churches want to support Swazi indigenous beliefs, values, and rituals that promote the common good, provided they do not compromise the Christian faith.

CULTURAL IMPACT Christianity's impact on Swazi architecture can be seen in various church buildings, both rural and urban. Styles include simple rectangular brick houses with corrugated iron roofs, small and large medieval-style stone buildings, and modern, spacious churches and cathedrals. Paintings of Christ and his disciples decorate many Swazi homes. Popular Christian literature, especially vernacular copies of the Bible, can also be found in the average Swazi home.

Swazi Christian churches, especially conservative evangelical churches, have contributed above all to the development and proliferation of popular Christian music. Many Swazi enjoy gospel music at concerts, fund-raising functions, and music festivals. The abundance of newly released cassettes, compact discs, and videos by Swazi and South African gospel artists attests to gospel's vitality as an industry.

SWAZI TRADITIONAL RELIGION

DATE OF ORIGIN c. 1800 C.E.
NUMBER OF FOLLOWERS 371,000

HISTORY Swazi religion is made up of several religious traditions drawn from the main clans and ethnic groups (including Tonga, Nguni, and Sotho) that merged to form the Swazi nation in the nineteenth century. A synthesis of Nguni and Tonga kingship traditions gave rise to a unique idea of sacred kingship, in which dual monarchs (the king and his mother, a tradition borrowed from the Sotho) function as both secular and sacred personages.

The first Swazi king, Sobhuza I (Somhlolo), assumed such religious duties as the national priesthood (the dual monarchs serve as intermediaries between the Swazi and the ancestors, relaying messages and prayers and receiving dreams and guidance) and the prestigious job of rainmaking (before the Swazi state existed, rainmaking was the preserve of the Mnisi and Magagula clans).

The core values of Swazi religion include ancestral veneration, protection of virginity before marriage, chastity, polygamy, permanence of marriage, resourcefulness, altruism, respect for seniority, obedience to civil authorities, patriotism, and life after death. The ancestors (*emadloti*) have power and influence over the living, promoting the good of their relatives and regulating their behavior. In their invisible spiritual world the ancestors retain their earthly gender, rank, status, and obligations; thus family ancestors are expected to protect the earthly interests of their kin, while royal ancestors guard the interests of the nation, including security, peace, and progress.

EARLY AND MODERN LEADERS All former Swazi kings, queen mothers, and queen regents are historical leaders of Swazi religion. The most prominent include King Sobhuza I (ruled from 1818–36), King Mswati II (ruled from 1839–65), Queen Regent Gwamile (ruled from 1889–1921), King Sobhuza II (ruled from 1921–82), Queen Mother Lomawa (ruled from 1921–38), Queen Mother Ntombi (began rule in 1984), and King Mswati III (began rule in 1986).

King Sobhuza II successfully affirmed and defended Swazi traditional religion while welcoming education, Christianity, and other beneficial elements of modernity. An astute conservative leader, he firmly believed in the viability of cultural and religious pluralism. The governor of Ludzidzini Royal Capital Residence, Jim Gama (took office in 2001), who works closely with the queen mother and serves as the country's prime minister, is also a prominent contemporary leader of Swazi religion.

MAJOR THEOLOGIANS AND AUTHORS Dr. J.S.M Matsebula, a Swazi historian, highlighted the impact of the ancestral cult and sacred kingship on the foreign policy of the kingdom during and after the colonial era. He contended that the country's policy toward European colonialists was shaped by a dream King Somhlolo had about the arrival of Europeans in Swaziland. Interpreted primarily as a warning emanating from the royal ancestors, the dream advised Somhlolo to welcome the Europeans and accept their knowledge but receive their money with caution. Somhlolo warned the Swazi against fighting the Europeans, saying resistance would lead to annihilation. Swazi rulers and politicians took Somhlolo's advice seriously and used the dream to justify nonviolence, tolerance, and peaceful coexistence with European traders, farmers, missionaries, and colonial administrators.

HOUSES OF WORSHIP AND HOLY PLACES The Sibaya, or cattle byre (pen), is the most prominent feature of an average traditional homestead and is constructed on its eastern boundary. The family Sibaya is the sacred social space in which Swazi communicate with their ancestors; also, a marriage is only valid after certain rituals are performed in the groom's family cattle byre. The royal cattle byre at the queen mother's residence is a national shrine used to invoke the royal ancestors. All major Swazi national rituals and crucial meetings take place at the Ludzidzini royal cattle pen.

The KaGogo (ancestral hut; literally "grandmother's hut") is the central sacred space in every homestead. Family ancestors are affectionately called boGoGo-Mkhulu (great grandmothers), regardless of their sex. A distinctive, thatched-roofed hut, the KaGogo is reserved for a variety of family rituals, including birth rituals, thanksgiving feasts in honor of the ancestors, and crucial family and clan meetings. The national ancestral hut (the Indlunkhulu, or "great hut") at the queen mother's residence is used for such national rituals as the Incwala ritual of kingship.

The *emadliza* (family graveyard), historically part of the homestead but situated a distance from the main huts, is also treated with reverence. The graves are laid out according to seniority, status, and blood relations. Family members visit the graveyard to pray, report, or submit family concerns, requests, or complaints to the ancestors. Community cemeteries have replaced most family graveyards because of space limitations and modern pressures, but their sacredness remains intact. Royal graveyards, usually caves in sacred mountains, are visited only by members of the royal family.

WHAT IS SACRED? The favorite sacrificial animal in Swazi religion is the goat, slaughtered to solicit the blessings of family ancestors. White goats are sacrificed in gratitude for good luck and success; black goats are used to ask for alleviation of misfortune or when in mourning; and variegated goats are used for a variety of occasions, including thanksgiving feasts to honor the ancestors, marriage ceremonies, diviners' graduation ceremonies, healing rituals, and funerals.

During such national ceremonies as the Incwala, cattle from a sacred sacrificial herd (the Imfukwana; many live and roam around the sacred Mdzimba mountains) are offered to the ancestors. Preparations for the Incwala also include construction of the temporary Inhlambelo Shrine inside the royal cattle byre using the *lusekwane,* a sacred evergreen shrub with leafy branches. During the ceremony a number of strong young men capture and kill a semiwild Inkunzi Lemnyama (viewed as a sacred black bull; actually a black ox selected from the sacred herd) with their bare hands for ritual use in the shrine.

HOLIDAYS AND FESTIVALS In the mid-1800s King Mswati II transformed a traditional celebration of the first fruits of summer into the Incwala ritual of sacred kingship. A solemn, elaborate, month-long thanksgiving ceremony and festival held in December to coincide with the summer solstice, the Incwala solicits the blessings of the national ancestors on the king and the harvest. All Swazi are expected to participate in the dance, wearing their indigenous Incwala attire. The main actors are members of Swazi royalty, male regimental groups (*emabutfo*) representing all key regions of the country, and the king, who is ritually fortified and strengthened on behalf of the nation. He ushers in the new year by biting the first fruits of the summer harvest.

The Umhlanga (Reed Dance) is a four-day ceremony held in August or September. To pay tribute to the queen mother, approximately 5,000 young, unmarried women from all regions of the country walk about 40 kilometers to collect fresh reeds, carry the heavy bundles to Ludzidzini, deliver them to the queen mother to use as a windbreak, and sing and dance before her, the king, and more than 10,000 spectators. On behalf of the nation, the king demonstrates his appreciation by performing a giya dance and placing his cow shield before each regimental group. The festival promotes such dominant cultural values as virginity, resourcefulness, social responsibility, and loyalty to the monarchy.

The Butimba (royal hunt) is a winter festival held in July or August each year (depending on the availability of game) at Hlane Game Reserve, the country's biggest animal park and reserve. After petitioning the ancestors to guide, protect, and bestow good fortune on them, the *emabutfo* march about one hundred kilometers in three days to reach the game park. The men are armed with special fighting sticks and spears, while the King and his guests (usually including the Zulu King, Zwelithini) hunt with rifles. The spoils of the day—*imphalas* (bucks), *tinyatsi* (buffalo), *timpunzi* (antelope), and *tingongoni* (gnu)—are displayed near the king's residence. The climax of each day takes place after sunset: A celebration dance is performed, with the king taking the lead in singing special hunting songs. The regiments are fed on roasted beef from royal cattle slaughtered for the occasion. On the final day of the hunt, the wild meat is distributed to all the regiments present.

In February the Buganu (marula wine) Festival celebrates the year's first sample of *buganu,* a seasonal traditional brew made from wild *buganu* (marula fruit), and gives thanks to the ancestors for good rains and a bountiful fruit harvest. The *lutsango,* the nation's women's regiment, presents large quantities of fresh wine to the king and queen mother, who receive them on behalf of the nation and make brief speeches, enjoining the nation to take pride in their cherished traditions. The celebrants (thousands of both male and female regiments) are served with wine and meat from royal cattle. A program of song and traditional dance builds to a climax when the queens join in and the queen mother presents her own dance.

MODE OF DRESS Swazi married males dancing in the Incwala ceremony must wear an *umdada* (leopard-skin) skirt, a heavy *sigeja* shawl made of numerous oxtails, a single oxtail tied to the right wrist, an oxtail armband over the left arm, a fighting stick, a *siblangu* (cow shield), and an *inyoni* crown of black bird feathers. Young unmarried males attired specifically to fight the Incwala sacred bull wear a penis cap and loin skins made of antelope or buck. For the Butimba (royal hunt) the traditional regiments wear special hunting regalia: loin skins, a goat-skin sash (used to carry numerous boxes of matches), and, above the forehead, a ball of woven black and brown speckled bird feathers.

The ceremonial attire for women consists of orange, red, or blue *umhelwane* cloths wrapped over a black leather skirt. The women carry long staffs made of bamboo or grass. For the Umhlanga (Reed Dance) the young unmarried women wear *tindlamu* (ceremonial short beaded skirts decorated with fringe and buttons), anklets, bracelets, necklaces, and colorful sashes with wool streamers. Red wool means the girl is betrothed; blue wool means she has no lover yet.

DIETARY PRACTICES Each clan in Swaziland has distinctive religious taboos and traditions relating to food. The Dlamini ruling clan prohibits the eating of black sheep, while the Matsenjwa clan (a large commoner clan) forbids goat meat. Taboos prohibit newly married women from eating such popular foods as *emasi* (yogurt made from fermented sour milk). Women may not eat meat from a cow's head, including the coveted tongue. No Swazi may harvest any home-grown vegetables before the Incwala harvest festival takes place. Every major ritual that involves invoking the ancestors requires slaughtering domestic animals (chicken, goats, and cattle) and brewing indigenous beer from maize (the staple food), and everyone is expected to eat and drink.

RITUALS *Kuphahla,* or invoking the ancestors, is the most common and basic religious practice in Swazi religion. All major rituals begin and end with such an invocation, and the ancestors' response comes in various forms, including good rains, plentiful harvests, good fortune, good health, and general material blessings. The rituals vary according to purpose and may include personal prayer, thanksgiving, a complaint or protest, an annual family party, an urgent requisition, or a communal petition.

RITES OF PASSAGE The scripture and social teachings of Swazi religion are embedded in the four main rites of passage that occur at birth, puberty, marriage, and death. Rituals at these stages affirm and inculcate Swazi traditional knowledge, beliefs, and values.

The puberty and royal funeral rites practiced in Swazi religion are distinctive to Swaziland. Unlike in other neighboring southern Bantu societies, where puberty rites are regulated by local religious functionaries and often involve male and female circumcision, in Swaziland these rites are seen as royal and national ceremonies in which teenage girls and boys pay tribute to the nation through the king and queen mother. The Umhlanga (Reed Dance) trains girls to serve and be loyal and responsible to the monarchy. The Lusekwane (Shrub Rite), held at the beginning of the Incwala, trains boys to be courageous, morally upright (avoiding sexual relations with married women), and loyal to the king. Youth are taught to see themselves as life-long allies in the service of the king, the queen mother, and the country.

The funeral rites for close members of the Swazi royalty are unique, as the deceased are laid to rest not underground but in selected sacred caves and mountains. While commoners are buried in coffins, royalty are interred in fresh, black cow skins in a seated position with provisions of goat meat and beer to take with them into the afterlife. The Swazi believe the royal burial sites are sacred and that royal ancestors become national ancestors, but commoners may not participate in royal funeral rituals or visit the sacred royal caves.

MEMBERSHIP Membership in Swazi religion is attained at birth, and the individual is nurtured into the religion through socialization at family, clan, community, and national levels. Nobody is constrained to convert to Swazi religion except through marriage (for women) and naturalization (for foreigners who pledge their allegiance to Swaziland). Thousands of Swazi follow Swazi religion privately, outwardly professing themselves Christians. Swazi religion is promoted through royal rituals and ceremonies (including royal weddings and funerals and national celebrations) that embody and affirm the dominant values, beliefs, and traditions cherished by the Swazi nation.

SOCIAL JUSTICE Like many Bantu ethnic religions, Swazi religion advocates the holistic socioethical value of *buntfu,* or humanness characterized by caring, fellowship, sharing, and generosity. Its equivalent concepts in other world religions are unconditional love (Christianity), ultimate goodness (Confucianism), and desireless action (Hinduism). Swazi religion promotes the values held by many conservative Swazi and has no specific social teachings on human and civil rights.

SOCIAL ASPECTS Swazi religion affirms two vital principles about marriage and family: that marriage is irrevocable and that a polygamous marriage and family is the norm. A public ceremony involving family and the wider community seals the marriage as a permanent contract between the groom and bride. At a typical marriage ceremony the bride stabs the ground inside the groom's family's cattle byre, signifying her consent to the marriage and formally ratifying it in the presence of the ancestors of the groom's family.

That the Swazi marriage is typically polygamous is demonstrated through other conditions of marriage, such as the *lobola,* or bride price. Along with the required number of cows, the groom expects the bride's family to provide an *inhlanti* (girl) to accompany the bride to her new home. Later the *inhlanti* invariably marries the groom as a cowife in the polygamous family.

POLITICAL IMPACT Swazi religion has promoted national and ethnic solidarity through royal ceremonies and festivals, which foster strong ties among the commoners, as well as mutual collaboration and fraternal relations between the commoners and the aristocrats (the chiefs, princes and princesses, and the national councilors that advise the king and queen mother).

CONTROVERSIAL ISSUES Institutionalized sexism in Swazi religion has caused controversy among the Swazi people. Boys are valued more than girls, and women have been viewed as inferior to men. Traditional marital rights make the husband the principal administrator of the family estate, holding any property in trust on behalf of his wife and children, and an unmarried woman cannot own land except provisionally, on behalf of a minor male child. Widows must obey mourning taboos, including ritual isolation that severely restricts income-generating activities outside the home for anywhere from six months to two years. Traditional arranged marriages, which require the wife to live with or near the husband's family, allow the relatives of a deceased husband to control the estate of the deceased.

Polygamy has given rise to other controversies. Modern Swazi women have expressed concern that polygamy compromises their conjugal rights and inadvertently promotes adultery on the part of the cowives. Women in polygamous families have also been more susceptible to infection by the HIV virus.

CULTURAL IMPACT Swazi religion has promoted art, music, dance, and environmental values. The colorful ceremonial attire, the songs composed and sung and the dances performed by ritual participants, and the sacred objects and artifacts used in healing ceremonies have collectively contributed to the development of a distinctive Swazi art and performing style. Swazi religion promotes the preservation of the sacred fauna and flora, as well as an appreciation of caves, mountains, springs, rainfall, hurricanes, the ocean, the moon, and the sun.

Other Religions

Islam was introduced into Swaziland in 1963 by Muslim migrant workers from Malawi. Not until 1972 was it firmly established with the full consent of the Swazi monarchy. Since then Islam has spread gradually, and many Swazi who reside in urban areas have embraced the faith. Less that 45 percent of Muslims in Swaziland are Swazi nationals, however, and Islam is still generally perceived as a foreign religion. Muslims have not been permitted to spread their faith through the state-controlled radio station and television channel.

The Baha'i faith was established in Swaziland through the pioneering work of an American family led by John and Valera Allen. The Allens arrived in the country in 1954 and attained their initial converts, school teachers of Matsapha National High School, the same year. The Allen family was later introduced to the king, who welcomed them and granted them permission to preach and spread their religion. The royal consent inspired many Swazi—including prominent princes and princesses—to embrace the Baha'i faith. Its focus on the unity of humankind and its inclusive and tolerant attitude toward other religions have attracted many converts. The Baha'is in Swaziland are known above all for their contribution to national progress through the establishment of reputable educational institutions open to all Swazi. Like Islam, however, the Baha'i faith has not taken root among the average Swazi. It appeals largely to the educated classes in urban areas.

Hebron Ndlovu

See Also Vol. 1: *African Traditional Religions, Christianity*

Bibliography

Hall, James. *Umlungu in Paradise: The Anthology.* Mbabane, Swaziland: Websters, 1998.

Kasenene, P. *Religion in Swaziland.* Braamfontein, Johannesburg: Skottaville Press, 1994.

Kuper, H. *The Swazi: A South African Kingdom.* 2nd ed. New York: Holt, 1986.

Matsebula, J.S.M. *A History of Swaziland.* 3rd ed. Cape Town: Longman, 1987.

Ndlovu, H.L. "The Autonomy of African Traditional Religions: The Case of Swazi Religion." *UNISWA Research Journal* 12 (1998): pp. 69–77.

Sundkler, B.G.M. *Zulu Zion and Some Swazi Zionists.* London: University Press, 1976.

Sweden

POPULATION 8,876,744

CHURCH OF SWEDEN 84 percent

OTHER CHRISTIAN 5.2 percent

ISLAM 2 percent

OTHER 8.8 percent

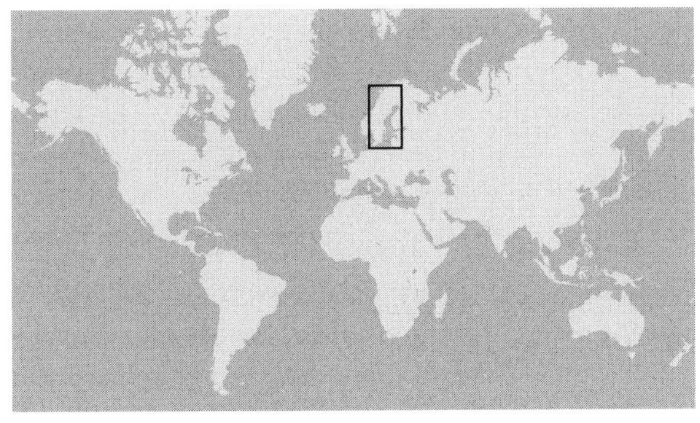

Country Overview

INTRODUCTION The Kingdom of Sweden, which shares the Scandinavian Peninsula with Norway in the north of Europe, has enjoyed a period of considerable material prosperity for much of the past century. Despite the presence of Christianity since the ninth century C.E., Sweden has a reputation for being one of the most secularized countries on earth. Most of the population, however, has retained membership in the Church of Sweden, and the majority of the people look to the church to organize such rites of passage as baptisms, marriages, and funerals. Levels of religious practice are generally lower in urban areas and higher in parts of the country, such as the west coast and the north, that experienced evangelical revivals in the nineteenth century. While Protestant Christianity long enjoyed a relative monopoly within a country that, until the post–World War II period, was ethnically quite homogeneous, increased levels of immigration have led to a diversification of the religious environment, with Catholicism and Islam gaining a higher profile in the latter half of the twentieth century.

RELIGIOUS TOLERANCE According to church law instituted in 1686, all Swedes were required to confess the Lutheran faith, although from 1782 Jews were allowed to settle in the country without converting to Christianity. During the nineteenth century freedom of religion increased, and this period saw the initial emergence of the "free," or nonconformist, churches. Full freedom of religion, however, was not legally instituted until 1951. Since then all members of the population have had the right to choose whether or not to belong to any religious body. Until 1996 membership in the Church of Sweden had been conferred by birth—that is, through citizenship—provided that one parent was a member, but subsequently it could be acquired only through baptism or special application. Church and state were formally separated at the end of the twentieth century.

Major Religion

CHURCH OF SWEDEN

DATE OF ORIGIN Ninth century C.E.

NUMBER OF FOLLOWERS 7.5 million

For the festival of Saint Lucia on December 13, young girls wear white dresses and carry lighted candles on their heads during a special ceremony in remembrance of the saint. © VANDER ZWALM DAN/CORBIS SYGMA.

HISTORY The first Christian missionaries arrived in Sweden in the ninth and tenth centuries, but paganism remained strong for two or three centuries afterward. A French Benedictine monk by the name of Ansgar was, in 829, possibly the first to preach the Christian gospel in Sweden. Sweden was one of the last European countries to accept Christianity, however, and the complete conversion of Sweden was hampered in part by the division of the country into independently run provinces. The first monarch to be baptized was Olof Skötkonung, in around 1000, and the town of Uppsala became the seat of the archbishop in 1164. Church and state were united soon thereafter.

The Reformation took place during the reign of King Gustav Vasa, who led a revolt against the confederation of Nordic countries originally established during the fourteenth century. After he was crowned king of Sweden in 1523, he became the head of the Swedish state church, established on Lutheran principles. In 1527 Vasa declared the Church of Sweden independent from the Roman Catholic Church and confiscated its property, and in 1530 he broke off all relations with the pope. Although the New Testament had been translated into Swedish earlier, the first fully Swedish Bible was published in 1541. The marriage between church and state became so strong that it took an act of Parliament to change the prayer book, while bishops were chosen by the cabinet. For much of its history, the Church of Sweden remained unchallenged by other religious constituencies, but in the nineteenth century free churches emerged as an important part of the so-called folk, or popular, movements (also including the Worker's and Teetotal movements), which played a key part in the rapid transition of Sweden from an agricultural to an industrial society. Women became eligible for ordination in 1958, and the first female candidates were admitted to the priesthood in 1960.

EARLY AND MODERN LEADERS Saint Bridget (Birgitta), who was active during the fourteenth century and who was canonized in 1391, was one of the great religious figures of the Middle Ages in Sweden. She founded an order of monks and nuns known as Birgitinorden (Ordo Sanctissimi Salvatoris, or the Order of the Most Blessed Savior) in Vadstena. The order of monks was dissolved after the Reformation, in 1595, whereas the order of nuns lasted until 1959 and was then revived in the 1960s. Saint Bridgit's fourth child, Saint Catherine, accompanied her mother on trips to Rome and the Holy Land.

King Gustav Vasa's efforts to secure the Reformation in Sweden were supported by two brothers, Olavus and Laurentius Petri, who had been influenced by Martin Luther and other reformers on the Continent. Laurentius Petri was consecrated the first Swedish Lutheran archbishop in Uppsala in 1531. Much later, ecumenism in Sweden was promoted by Archbishop Nathan Söderblom (1866–1931), who emphasized the idea that the Roman Catholic and Evangelical Lutheran faiths were part of the same Church. For this and other work Söderblom won the Nobel Prize for Peace in 1930.

MAJOR THEOLOGIANS AND AUTHORS In 1526 Olavus Petri published the first hymn book in Swedish as well as the first Swedish translation of the New Testament. Paul Petter Waldenström (1838–1917), editor of *The Pietist,* helped to formulate a strict sense of the church as an association of true believers, and in 1878 a group of his followers founded the Svenska Missionsförbundet (Swedish Covenant Mission Church), one of the most important of the free churches. Nathan Söderblom was professor of the history of religion at the University of Uppsala, and in his work he stressed revelation as an ongoing process, not limited to the apostolic age. Einar Billing (1871–1939), also a professor at Uppsala, helped to develop the notion of a folk church, embracing all people within the parish system and thus opposing the more exclusive membership policies of free church congregations. Bengt Sundkler (1909–95), who was ordained in the Church of Sweden in 1936, became a celebrated academic specializing in African church history. He served as a missionary in Africa and later as the first Bishop of Tanzania. Lewi Pethrus (1884–1974) was not only the dominant personality in the emergent Swedish Pentecostal movement but also an internationally known figure, among other things through his hosting of the European Pentecostal Conference in Stockholm in 1939.

HOUSES OF WORSHIP AND HOLY PLACES Uppsala Cathedral is the largest church in Scandinavia. It contains the relics of King Erik Jedvardsson, who was killed in a battle with Danish troops in 1160. After a fire in Uppsala at the beginning of the eighteenth century, the cathedral was rebuilt in baroque style, with a new altar and pulpit. In the latter part of the nineteenth century the cathedral was restored according to High Gothic principles. In 1989 Uppsala Cathedral hosted an ecumenical service incorporating the first-ever visit from a pope (John Paul II), while at a service in the cathedral in 1997 Christina Odenberg was ordained as the first female bishop in Sweden. Among other buildings sacred to Christianity, the first cathedral in Lund was built in the eleventh century, while the present building dates from the 1100s. Saint Bridget's relics are preserved in the cloister church of her monastery at Vadstena, another site that was a destination for Pope John Paul II on his visit in 1989.

WHAT IS SACRED? Much of what is held sacred in Sweden can be predicted from the broadly Christian background of the country and from the important role of the Church of Sweden in its history. Given the strongly secular nature of modern Sweden, however, other elements have tended to arise as substitutes for the traditional role of religion in national life. One particularly significant feature of Swedish culture, and to some extent of internal and external stereotypes of the country, is a devotion to nature that may sometimes approach the spiritual. Although the majority of Sweden is urban, there are some 600,000 country cottages throughout the nation of between 8 and 9 million inhabitants, a statistic that indicates the great love of natural settings.

HOLIDAYS AND FESTIVALS The celebration of midsummer is particularly marked in Sweden, a country in which daylight is of relatively short duration throughout the winter. Possibly for similar reasons, the feast of Saint Lucia (December 13) has become a national festival. Lucia was a fourth-century Sicilian saint whose feast day is said to mark the return of the sun and whose name itself means "light." The day also commemorates the beginning of the Christmas celebration, and candlelight parades are common. Each year the privilege of crowning Stockholm's so-called Lucy bride, who impersonates the saint, is granted to the winner of the Nobel Prize for Literature.

MODE OF DRESS Modes of dress in Sweden are generally not determined on religious grounds but are characteristic of Western societies as a whole. For the festival of Saint Lucia on December 13, however, some young girls wear white dresses and carry lighted candles on their heads during a special ceremony in remembrance of the saint. Lucia herself is said to have used such candles when taking food to persecuted Christians who were reduced to hiding in dark tunnels.

DIETARY PRACTICES For the most part tradition rather than religious practice determines the Swedish diet. Coffee, mulled wine, ginger biscuits, and traditionally shaped breads are served for the festival of Saint Lucia, while saffron-colored dough is held to symbolize the fact that the sun will soon return. The Christmas meal on December 24 traditionally consists of the Swedish smorgasbord (*smörgåsbord*), which incorporates ham, jellied pig's feet, pickled fish, and rice porridge.

RITUALS Communion remains common in Swedish churches, and the new *Book of Worship* for the Church of Sweden, in use from the 1980s, has aimed to encourage a richer eucharistic liturgy. Minimal attendance at weekly services contrasts with much higher levels of participation in baptisms, confirmation, weddings, and funerals, as well as for Advent Sunday, Christmas, and Easter. Around three-quarters of all children are baptized, and 9 out of 10 funeral services are performed under the auspices of the church. The use of older Evangelical Lutheran churches for weddings is known even among free church members.

RITES OF PASSAGE The meaning of baptism in the Church of Sweden has been transformed, given that since 1996 it has been the primary means of gaining membership in the church. In this way the Church of Sweden has moved toward the practices of the free churches. Whereas the Church of Sweden has continued to practice infant baptism, however, many of the latter insist on adult, or at least noninfant, baptism and on a public confession of faith in order to ensure that membership is acquired as a conscious decision on the part of the believer. The Church of Sweden continues to have the legal authority, and the primary responsibility, for burial services and the upkeep of cemeteries.

MEMBERSHIP Since the Church of Sweden lost its status as the state religion, baptism has become a criterion of membership, and the church has instituted a program of evangelization. It is intended that every parent belonging to the church be contacted by the local parish for information about membership rules and baptism. The Church of Sweden has not been as effective, however, as some of the free churches in using mass media for evangelization or in maintaining contact among members. Pentecostalists, for example, with only about 90,000 members in the country, have deployed a daily newspaper, *Dagen,* as well as radio and television broadcasts within and beyond Sweden. A newer charismatic movement, allied to the prosperity churches of the United States and centered on the Livets Ord (Word of Life) ministry in Uppsala, has used satellite broadcasts and the Internet to evangelize globally. The Church of Sweden, on the other hand, has tended to rely on more personal methods of recruitment.

Within the Church of Sweden, the Evangeliska Fosterlands-Stiftelsen (National Evangelical Organization) is a semi-independent, lay-oriented organization with around 20,000 members that was founded in 1856. Apart from worship services held by local groups, it is particularly concerned with mission work both within Sweden and abroad in such areas as Africa and India.

SOCIAL JUSTICE Founded in 1992, the Sveriges Kristna Råd (Christian Council of Sweden) functions as the main ecumenical body of Christian churches in the country. Among its main areas of work is social ethics. Partly as a result of the initiatives of Nathan Söderblom, churches have been active within the peace movement, and the Life and Peace Institute was founded in Uppsala in 1985. In 1998 the government published a report that assessed the needs of persons leaving the so-called New Religious Movements, such as Scientology and the Unification Church, with special attention paid to children.

SOCIAL ASPECTS Viewed by international standards, the Church of Sweden developed a liberal stance in the late twentieth century toward family roles and marriage. The role of female priests has remained controversial in some quarters, but women have been ordained within the church since 1960. The free churches, however, have traditionally adopted stricter views on women's roles, personal morality, and the use of alcohol. Sweden has a partnership law that allows homosexuals to marry, and the Church of Sweden has a blessing ceremony for such couples.

POLITICAL IMPACT The merging of political and religious power has been important at various points in Swedish history, although the two have come to operate relatively independently. King Gustav Vasa's movement of national liberation was catalyzed in part by the decision of Christian II of Denmark, king of the Nordic Union, to depose two bishops in Stockholm. Vasa later became head of the Church of Sweden. The state church remained in charge of keeping civil records from the seventeenth century until 1991, when the function was handed over to the government. Christian Democrats are represented in Parliament, but they remain a small party.

CONTROVERSIAL ISSUES Over the past two centuries controversial issues have included women priests and the right of denominations to exist independently of the Church of Sweden. In the late twentieth century the actions of the New Religious Movements (like Scientology and Hare Krishna) began to cause concern within and beyond Christian circles, although such movements have remained small. Concerns were expressed regarding their proselytizing, and in particular their potential influence over youth. Particularly during the 1980s, the emergence of prosperity-oriented charismatic churches, such as the Word of Life in Uppsala, was highly controversial. These groups were perceived to be aggressive, foreign to the spirit of accommodation among Swedish churches, and intent on promulgating unorthodox views on material and physical well-being.

CULTURAL IMPACT Swedish churches have provided important forums for music, and despite the Reformed character of the Church of Sweden, many buildings contain pictorial art. Sigtuna, founded as the first Christian town in Sweden, contains much of Swedish religious history in its art and architecture. Rune stones commemorating the dead in ancient carved script survive from the Viking period of a thousand years ago, as do some of the oldest churches in the country. Odensala church from the thirteenth century is well known for its medieval wall paintings, commemorating scenes from the Bible. Religious themes of guilt and loss of spirituality have been important in the highly influential films of Swedish director Ingmar Bergman.

Other Religions

The Muslim community in Sweden has perhaps 100,000 active believers and a broader total affiliation of around 250,000. The majority of its members are immigrants from Turkey, the Middle East, and the former Yugoslavia. Mosques have been built throughout the country. The Jewish community in Sweden has been longer established, and there are about 18,000 Jews in the country, of whom less than half belong to synagogues. There are some 3,000–4,000 Buddhists and about the same number of Hindus. Jehovah's Witnesses and Mormons (Church of Jesus Christ of Latter-day Saints) began to establish themselves in Sweden at the time the traditional Swedish nonconformist churches emerged—during the latter half of the nineteenth century and in the early twentieth century. Perhaps the most important of the nonconformist churches is the Swedish Covenant Mission Church, which is particularly active in rural areas. With the Baptist Church, it has built a theological college at Lindingö.

Since the 1960s the Roman Catholic Church has grown in Sweden, mainly as a result of immigration from southern Europe and Latin America, and it has come to have around 160,000 members. The Orthodox Church has approximately 100,000 members, the main national groups being Greek, Serbian, Syrian, Romanian, Estonian, and Finnish.

Simon Coleman

See Also Vol. I: *Christianity, Lutheranism*

Bibliography

Coleman, Simon. "Conservative Protestantism and the World Order: The Faith Movement in the United States and Sweden." *Sociology of Religion* 54, no. 4 (1993): 353–73.

———. *The Globalisation of Charismatic Christianity: Spreading the Gospel of Prosperity.* Cambridge: Cambridge University Press, 2000.

Ekman, Ann-Kristin. "Community, Carnival and Campaign: Expressions of Belonging in a Swedish Region." *Stockholm Studies in Social Anthropology.* Stockholm: University of Stockholm, 1991.

Frykman, J., and O. Löfgren. *Culture Builders: A Historical Anthropology of Middle-class Life.* New Brunswick, N.J.: Rutgers University Press, 1987.

Lindquist, Galina. "Shamanic Performances on the Urban Scene: Neo-Shamanism in Contemporary Sweden." *Stockholm Studies in Social Anthropology.* Stockholm: University of Stockholm, 1997.

Milner, D. *Sweden: Social Democracy in Practice.* Oxford: Oxford University Press, 1990.

Stromberg, Peter. *Symbols of Community: The Cultural System of a Swedish Church.* Tucson: Arizona University Press, 1986.

Switzerland

POPULATION 7,301,994

CHRISTIAN 79.3 percent

MUSLIM 4.3 percent

HINDU 0.4 percent

BUDDHIST 0.3 percent

JEWISH 0.2 percent

OTHER 0.1 percent

NONRELIGIOUS 11.1 percent

NO INDICATION 4.3 percent

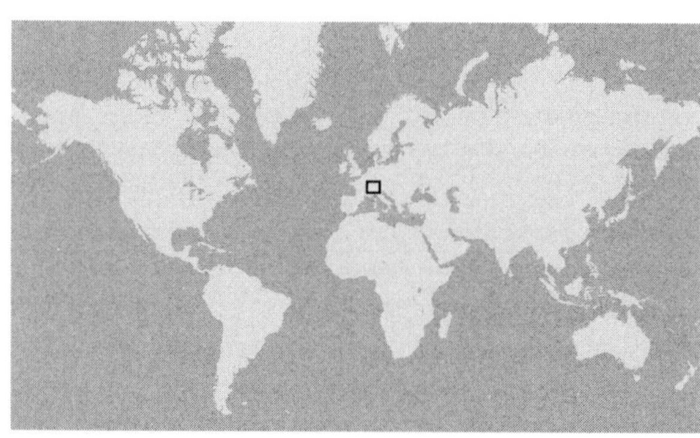

Country Overview

INTRODUCTION Surrounded by Germany, Liechtenstein, Austria, Italy, and France, the Swiss Confederation is among the smallest but richest countries of western Europe. It consists of 26 cantons (of which six are half-cantons). The capital is Bern. Switzerland is a multicultural country with four national languages—French, German, Italian, and Romansh.

About 20 percent of Switzerland's 7.3 million inhabitants are not of Swiss nationality. Of Switzerland's Christians (Swiss-born and foreigners), nearly 53 percent are Roman Catholic and 43 percent are Reformed (Protestant), with the rest belonging to some other, smaller Christian denomination (for example, Protestant free churches, Orthodox Christian Church, or Christ Catholic Church).

The foundations of what is now called Switzerland were laid in the thirteenth century as a federation of rural areas (Landschaften) and cities. In the following centuries several other areas and cities joined this federation. The rural areas were governed democratically; aristocracy or guilds governed the cities. This democratic element in Swiss history is exceptional in comparison to most other European countries. The Protestant Reformation, begun in the sixteenth century, was especially strong in Switzerland because many city councils saw it as an opportunity to decide religious matters themselves. Switzerland as a state was founded in 1848. It was designed to be a liberal, federal state. Because of its liberal foundations (based on individual and economic freedom), its relatively early industrialization, and the fact that it was able to avoid participating in both world wars, Switzerland today enjoys high levels of personal income and social security. This has several important consequences for religion. Secularization is growing rapidly, as in comparable European countries, and Switzerland is an attractive destination for immigrants and asylum seekers. Because immigrants increasingly are from non-Christian countries, Switzerland is becoming more and more multireligious.

RELIGIOUS TOLERANCE The Swiss constitution guarantees freedom of worship and prohibits discrimination on the grounds of religion. Laws concerning religious groups vary in different cantons. In most cantons only three denominations (Reformed, Roman Catholic, and Christ Catholic churches) are recognized as public institutions, which gives them certain privileges (for example, the possibility to raise a church tax or to teach in schools). These privileges are considered by some to be a form of discrimination.

While the many stereotypes of the two large denominations (Reformed and Roman Catholic) have in the last decades virtually vanished in Swiss society, certain prejudice exists against non-Christian religions. Xenophobia focuses especially on Islam. Because 88.3 percent of Muslims do not have Swiss nationality, they are subject to restrictive laws for foreigners. It is also common for people to hold stereotypes of and feel much prejudice toward Hindu gurus and religious groups. Anti-Semitism is forbidden by law and is not tolerated in public, although on a more latent level attitudes toward Jews are sometimes unfavorable. While anti-Semitism on religious grounds seems to be waning, a new anti-Zionism is rising. One cause is disagreement over how Israel has handled conflict with the Palestinians; another is the pressure Jewish groups put on Swiss banks in the 1990s concerning their behavior (hiding deposits of Holocaust victims) during and after World War II.

The most important place of pilgrimage for Swiss Catholics is the internationally renowned monastery at Einsiedeln (canton of Schwyz), which was founded in the tenth century. © PAUL ALMASY/CORBIS.

Major Religion

CHRISTIANITY

DATE OF ORIGIN Fourth century C.E.
NUMBER OF FOLLOWERS 5.8 million

HISTORY The first signs of Christianity in Switzerland date back to the fourth century C.E. The area that today makes up western Switzerland was Christianized during the sixth century; the Christianization of the Alamans in the east took place in the following centuries.

In 612 the Irish monk Gallus settled in Switzerland, leading to the foundation (in 720) of the monastery of Saint Gallen, which gave its name to the city and canton of Saint Gallen. At the beginning of the sixteenth century, Huldrych Zwingli (1484–1531), a priest at the Grossmünster in Zurich, brought the Reformation to Switzerland and gave birth to the Reformed Church (to be distinguished from the Lutheran Church). Several other cities (for example, Basel, Bern, Lausanne, and Neuchâtel) followed Zwingli's Reformation. In 1536 the French-born reformer John Calvin (1509–64) started to preach in Geneva. His teaching had a worldwide impact. As a consequence of the Reformation in Zurich, the Anabaptist movement under the leadership of Konrad Grebel (1498–1526) was born. The Anabaptists were fiercely persecuted yet had important historical consequences. Many emigrated to the United States. The Reformation was largely an affair of the cities and the areas they dominated. Rural areas remained Catholic and were able to fortify their beliefs and their attachment to Rome during the counter-Reformation. Reformed cities and Catholic rural areas of the Swiss federation were to be locked in a constant state of tension during the following centuries, leading sometimes to war. On the whole, however, the fact that it was a biconfessional federation was accepted.

After the era of the Enlightenment and Pietism, the Swiss federation was shaken in 1847 by yet another confessional war (Sonderbundskrieg), which the Reformed and liberal cities won. This led in 1848 to the birth of the (liberal) Swiss Federal State. Because the Catholics had lost the Sonderbundskrieg in 1847, and as the Swiss Federal State was hostile toward several aspects of Catholicism, the Catholics withdrew and built a sort of subsociety with institutions just for themselves. In 1875 the Christ Catholic Church split from the Roman Catholic Church in reaction to the First Vatican Council.

After the two world wars the relationship between Protestants and Catholics improved. This was largely because of the democratic dynamics of the Swiss Federal State and the Second Vatican Council (1962–65). Since World War II the differences between Protestants and Catholics seem to be vanishing. Similarly, the differences between the "positive," "liberal," and "religious-social" movements inside Protestantism are declining. In both the Protestant and Catholic churches traditional belief, service attendance, and unquestioned denominational identity are waning. On the other hand, there is a relative rise in Evangelical free churches, Catholic movements, new religious movements, and people with no religious affiliation.

EARLY AND MODERN LEADERS The most important early religious leader was Niklaus von Flüe (1417–87). He was an eremite with political influence who was able to bring peace to the Swiss federation at the time.

The major leaders of the Protestant Reformation in Switzerland were Huldrych Zwingli (1484–1531), Heinrich Bullinger (1504–75), and John Calvin (1509–64). Zwingli, influenced by scholasticism and the views of Erasmus, began in 1522 to discard whatever could not be legitimized biblically. Saint's images, monasteries, processions, sacred music, Catholic confirmation, and the order of the Mass: All of this was abolished on Zwingli's recommendation. In addition, Communion was given much less importance than the sermon and was now held only four times a year. Especially important was Zwingli's symbolic view of Communion: Bread and wine were to be understood only as symbols of the body and blood of Christ. On this he had an unresolvable dispute with Martin Luther, who argued that the body and blood of Christ were actually present in Communion. Bullinger, a friend and successor of Zwingli's in Zurich, was of international importance in the development of European Protestantism. One of his many achievements was that, together with Calvin, he managed to reconcile Zwinglianism and Calvinism.

Calvin went to Geneva in 1536 and soon started to reform the church. In his view the public life of the cities (politics, economy, education), as well as the private lives of the citizens, had to be reorganized in a way prescribed by the Bible. Individuals who would not accept this order ("sinners") would be admonished and excluded from Communion or punished more severely still. Calvin's Geneva became the center of the second wave of the Reformation in Europe.

An important leader on the Pietist and Evangelical side was German-born Christian Friedrich Spittler (1782–1867). He founded many missionary and social institutions, among them the Pilgermission Saint Chrischona in Basel.

MAJOR THEOLOGIANS AND AUTHORS The major authors of the Protestant Reformation in Switzerland—Huldrych Zwingli (1484–1531), Heinrich Bullinger (1504–75), and John Calvin (1509–64)—were also considered important religious leaders (see also above under EARLY AND MODERN LEADERS). Important works of Zwingli are his *67 Schlussreden* and *Commentarius de vera et falsa religione.* Bullinger is famous for his *Confessio Helvetica Posterior.* The centerpiece of Calvin's written work is *Institutio christianae religionis,* the most important book of the dogmatics of the Reformation. One of Calvin's central theological claims was his belief in predestination; that is, men were saved by the grace of God and could themselves do nothing about it. Good works, therefore, could not influence the choice of God; they were, however, necessary, to glorify him.

One of the most important writers of the Enlightenment was Swiss-born Jean-Jacques Rousseau (1712–78), who was influential throughout Europe. He thought that religion was a matter of "natural emotion." In modernity mention should be made of Alois Emanuel Biedermann (1819–85), on the Protestant side, who was the leading figure of theological liberalism in the Reformed Church—a current that is still strong in Swiss theological thinking today. Karl Barth (1886–1968), who reacted to New Protestantism and theological liberalism by founding dialectical theology together with others (for example, Friedrich Gogarten and Rudolf Bultmann), is one of the most important theologians of Protestantism. As a professor of theology in Germany, he was cofounder of Germany's Bekennende Kirche (Confessing Church) and had to re-emigrate to Switzerland in 1935 because of his resistance to the Nazis. The leading thought of his theology was that a person's knowledge of God depends completely on the initiative of God. God is thus imagined to be totally sovereign and superior. A modern Swiss theologian on the Catholic side was Hans-Urs von Balthasar (1905–88), a friend of Barth's who observed culture and Christianity and took an overall ecumenical stance.

HOUSES OF WORSHIP AND HOLY PLACES Swiss Protestantism is reluctant to give too much importance to churches or so-called holy places. For historical reasons, however, mention should be made of the two churches where the most prominent reformers taught: the Grossmünster in Zurich (Huldrych Zwingli) and the Cathédrale Saint Pierre in Geneva (John Calvin).

On the Catholic side there are several places of pilgrimage. The most important one is the internationally renowned monastery at Einsiedeln (canton of Schwyz), which was founded in the tenth century and where believers worship especially a statue of a black Madonna. The Jakobsweg—a way of pilgrimage to Santiago de Compostela—leads through Einsiedeln. Another important place of pilgrimage is Flüeli Ranft in the canton of Obwalden, which is where Saint Niklaus von Flüe (Brother Klaus) lived in the fifteenth century. A third noteworthy place is the monastery of Saint Gallen, founded in the seventh century and famous for its vast library of antique books.

WHAT IS SACRED? In Christianity it is traditionally God, Jesus Christ, and the Holy Ghost who are considered sacred, as well as anything that is in close contact with this Trinitarian God. In modern Switzerland different things are considered sacred, depending on the group of Christians. In the Catholic Church the tradition of veneration of the saints is still to be found, with Einsiedeln as the most important place of pilgrimage. In contrast the Reformed Church, following Huldrych Zwingli and John Calvin, has abandoned the veneration of the saints, their pictures, and relics as nonbiblical. Among those in the Evangelical free churches, a kind of sacredness is found in the Christian way of life.

HOLIDAYS AND FESTIVALS Whereas the Roman Catholic Church in Switzerland officially follows its complex structure of the church year with a large number of different saints, feasts, and special occasions, the Reformed Church only celebrates the main Christian events (Christmas, Easter, Pentecost, and Ascension), with a few additional holidays. Depending on whether Roman Catholic or Reformed tradition is followed, different holidays are respected in different cantons. The important Christian holidays are the rare occasions on which the Catholic and Reformed churches are full of worshipers, because going to religious service is perceived by many as being part of the holiday. In Swiss society Christmas is regarded as the most important Christian holiday by far, but more for its popular rites (for example, Christmas tree, calendars, and Christmas presents) than its Christian rites.

MODE OF DRESS In today's Switzerland modern clothing is prominent, as in all other countries of western Europe. While there is neither a type of clothing that is especially Christian nor one that is especially Swiss, attire that is too "worldly" (for example, short skirts or body piercings) is often not tolerated in strict Christian groups.

DIETARY PRACTICES The one important dietary practice in Christianity is the ascetic rite of fasting, which was adopted from Judaism. Traditionally fasting is expected on a Friday. Only a minority of Roman Catholics in modern Switzerland adhere to fasting rules. Those who do increasingly see fasting not only as an act of penitence but also as one of social, medical, or political importance. Indeed, many see it as an act of solidarity with the poor in this world. The Reformed Church traditionally does not place much importance on fasting. Huldrych Zwingli, in fact, started his Reformation by beginning a dispute on fasting with the Catholic Church. In the Reformed Church today, however, fasting seems to be gaining in importance.

RITUALS The central activity in both the Reformed and the Roman Catholic churches remains the religious service, although it is frequented less and less. Only 5.1 percent of Protestant and 13.9 percent of Roman Catholic members go to church every Sunday. Some 82.2 percent go to service every Sunday in the Protestant free churches.

RITES OF PASSAGE Baptism, confirmation, and first Communion represent a person's passage toward being a full Christian. In modern Switzerland child baptism is common in both the Reformed and the Roman Catholic churches. In the Protestant free churches baptism of adults is more common, often presupposing a confession of faith. Some 96.4 percent of all Christians living in Switzerland claim to be baptized, with only a small minority baptized as adults. Confirmation (Firmung) in the Roman Catholic Church is administered at the age of 12 or 13. A new movement in the Catholic Church promotes confirmation after the age of 17 or 18. Catholic Church confirmation is considered to be a sacrament. Confirmation in the Reformed Church is preceded by confirmation classes of normally one or two years and is usually performed at the age of 15 or 16. It is not a sacrament but is regarded as a means of giving the individual enough knowledge to be a full Christian and as an act of public worship for the individual. Communion is practiced in Roman Catholicism at every mass. First Communion, which has to be preceded by confession in Switzerland, is taken at the age of 9 or 10. In the Reformed Church, Communion is performed less often; the frequency varies (in the Zwingli tradition Communion took place only four times a year). Children and adults who have not been baptized are now often allowed to take Communion in the Reformed Church.

Two further rites of passage are marriage and funerals. In modern Switzerland marriage is a matter of civil right. Marriage in a church can follow but is not necessary. The number of married individuals in Switzerland is dropping, and the percentage of Christian marriages among marriages in general is also falling. There is also a trend toward new, personalized elements in Christian marriages, where, for example, spouses recite speeches or poems they have selected during the ceremony. Church funerals are still much the norm. Here, too, is a trend toward deinstitutionalization and individualization. The number of nonchurch rituals in which, for example, a member of the family says a few words in commemoration of the deceased is rising.

MEMBERSHIP Most Swiss are born into one of the two large churches (Roman Catholic or Reformed). Little religious knowledge is handed down to the new generations, and to many people their membership has little meaning. This leads to considerable disaffiliation (an advantage of which is not having to pay the church tax). For theological as well as financial and legitimating reasons, the Roman Catholic and Reformed churches draw no clear boundaries between members and nonmembers. Instead the churches are open to anybody wishing to join their activities, and they try to propagate religious dialogue and refrain from internal mission. Thus, they can argue that they provide a service to the whole society, which means they should continue to be subsidized by the state. The exact opposite can be found in the Protestant free churches and certain Catholic movements. These groups normally accept only members who have experienced a personal "conversion" and who act according to a fairly strict moral code. Such groups are therefore much more closed and are usually active when it comes to missionary activities.

SOCIAL JUSTICE Although the Swiss churches helped refugees that managed to get into the country in World War II, they stayed mostly silent regarding the persecution and murder of the Jews in Germany and the restrictive Swiss policy of admission for Jewish refugees. In modern Switzerland several Reformed and Roman Catholic organizations focus on helping the country's needy and on development in poor countries. Especially important are the efforts for aiding immigrants and asylum seekers. The Protestant free churches also work to improve social justice; in contrast to the large churches, however, they combine it more clearly with the idea of mission for their type of Christianity.

SOCIAL ASPECTS Among Reformed Protestants and Roman Catholics interconfessional marriage has risen steadily since the 1960s. Whereas previously it was generally socially undesirable to marry a person belonging to a different confession, today it does not really matter if one's partner shares the same faith or even belongs to a religion at all. Marriages to spouses of non-Christian religions, such as Islam, are, however, still seen as problematic.

POLITICAL IMPACT Historically the antagonism between the Reformed Church and the Roman Catholic Church was central to politics, resulting in several wars throughout the centuries. In modern Switzerland, however, the differences between the two denominations have almost no political importance.

Cantons differ from one another concerning the way they regulate religion. Total separation of church and state exists in some cantons (for example, Geneva and Neuchâtel), while close links between the state and officially recognized religions (usually the Reformed

Church and the Roman Catholic Church) exist in other cantons (for example, Vaud and Zurich). In cantons where church and state are closely associated, a recurring political question is whether the situation should be changed; in these areas some have proposed total separation of church and state, while others would like to expand official recognition (along with the designation as "public institution") to additional religious groups.

There is one important political party with explicit Roman Catholic roots: the Christliche Volkspartei. While the party has emancipated itself on an ideological level from political Catholicism, its electorate remains mainly Catholic. Therefore, secularization seems to be undermining the basis of this party.

CONTROVERSIAL ISSUES While in earlier days controversial issues in Swiss Christianity revolved around the antagonism of the two leading denominations (for example, concerning mixed marriages, acceptance of baptism, and acceptance of Catholic bishops), the controversies that modern Swiss Christians are involved in have totally changed. Mainstream Christians and churches often have humanitarian goals and speak out for immigrants and asylum seekers who suffer from the sometimes severe governmental policy. Their antagonists are the political right and extreme right. Evangelical Christians (often organized in free churches) and Christians from the traditional Catholic side, on the other hand, initiate debates on themes such as homosexuality or abortion. Their opponents are left-wing parties, homosexual pressure groups, and women's rights groups.

CULTURAL IMPACT In the earlier stages of European societies, religion, music, and art were much intertwined. A process of functional differentiation then separated the various subsystems of society. In modern Switzerland this process seems to have been almost totally completed. Religion seems to have only a minor impact on contemporary music, art, or literature. An exception to the rule is the writer Friedrich Dürrenmatt (1921–90), who received an honorary doctorate from a theological faculty (Zurich) for the theological themes treated in his books.

Other Religions

The number of people in Switzerland affiliated with Islam has risen steadily since 1980, when Islam accounted for 0.9 percent of the population. Muslims in Switzerland can be divided into five different groups: (1) manual laborers who emigrated mainly from the former Yugoslavia and Turkey in the 1970s and 1980s (plus their children—that is, the second generation of Muslims, often born in Switzerland); (2) asylum seekers from Turkey (often Kurds), Iran, or Lebanon; (3) Muslim businesspeople or officials of international organizations; (4) immigrants (often students) from the Maghreb (Morocco, Algeria, and Tunisia); and (5) Swiss converts. The first two groups account for more than 75 percent of the Muslim presence in Switzerland. In 2000 some 56.3 percent of Muslims in Switzerland were from the former Yugoslavia and 20.2 percent of Muslims were Turks; most were Sunnites, followed by much smaller numbers of Shiites, Alawites, and others.

There is a certain lack of tolerance toward Muslims in modern Switzerland concerning both their legal and social status. Most mosques are not easily recognized from the outside; they are located in houses or office buildings that have been rebuilt to fit the needs of the respective communities. In Switzerland only two large mosques are easily recognizable as such: one in Zurich (built in 1963 and belonging to the Ahmadayyia movement) and one in Geneva (built in 1978 and financed by Saudi Arabia). Muslims have encountered certain problems in the practice of their religion—for example, no time off for daily prayers or Islamic feasts, prohibition of ritual slaughter, and little acceptance of the headscarf. One of the biggest problems is that Muslims have been unable to bury their dead in Switzerland in correct Muslim fashion, having received no land for a Muslim cemetery. Swiss society is slowly getting accustomed to these peculiarities of Islamic religion and culture, however, and solutions are increasingly being found. Because of their social characteristics and legal status, most Muslims in Switzerland belong to the lower class, having few political rights. With the increasing growth and age of the Muslim community and with the appearance of the second generation, a political conscience is emerging among Muslims, who are increasingly demanding their rights.

Of the Hindus living in Switzerland, 81.8 percent are from Sri Lanka (Tamils), 7.6 percent are from India, and 7.5 percent are Swiss. Hinduism in Switzerland is a relatively recent phenomenon. In the first half of the twentieth century, scarcely a Hindu group was to be found; theosophists, however, already showed a lively interest in the "new" religious faith. Contemporary

Hindu presence is chiefly the result of three factors: First, there was important immigration of Tamils, mainly as asylum seekers, in the 1990s. Second, Hindu gurus have been able to build small groups of followers (often of Swiss nationality); this process started in the 1950s and has continued, with important names being, for example, Paramahansa Yogananda, Swami Sivananda, and Satya Sai Baba. Most groups went to Switzerland in the 1970s. Third, the teaching of Yoga, often without going into the spiritual background of the technique, has been quite successful. The first Swiss school of Yoga was opened in 1948 in Zurich by Selvarajan Yesudian. Today there exist in Switzerland hundreds of Yoga groups and several professional Yoga schools that train Yoga teachers. Tolerance of Hinduism in Switzerland varies depending on the kind of Hinduism. Tamil immigrants are relatively well respected, yet their religious affiliation is not even known to most Swiss. Yoga as a "healthy activity" is not subject to intolerance (except from certain Evangelical Christians who may have some reservations).

Of Switzerland's Buddhist population, slightly more than half are of Swiss nationality and the rest are foreign-born (mainly immigrants or asylum seekers), mostly from Thailand, Vietnam, China, Cambodia, or Japan. Important Buddhist places in Switzerland include the Rabten Choeling Institute for Higher Tibetan Studies (Mont Pèlerin, near Lausanne), the Haus der Besinnung (Dicken, canton of Saint Gallen), and the Theravada cloister in Kandersteg (canton of Bern). Buddhism was introduced to Switzerland in 1910 when German-born Buddhist monk Nyanatiloka (Anton W.F. Gueth) went to live in Switzerland for two years. In 1942 Max Ladner founded the Buddhistische Gemeinschaft Zürich and published the Buddhist magazine *Einsicht.* A breakthrough occurred in the late 1960s–70s when a large number of Buddhist centers were opened. Buddhism is found mostly in urban areas.

The percentage of Jews in Switzerland has been continuously diminishing since the 1920s. The reason for this decrease is mainly the rising number of mixed marriages (Jews and non-Jews) and the "defection" (from Judaism) of these couple's children. Jews have lived in Switzerland as far back as Roman times. In the Middle Ages (especially after the plague in 1348) Jews were accused of and persecuted for poisoning the wells. After 1766 Jews were allowed to settle only in Surbtal, a valley in the canton of Aargau, and they had to wait until 1866 to receive rights equal to those of non-Jewish Swiss citizens. In the nineteenth century Jews from Surbtal, Germany, and France (especially Alsace) settled in the bigger cities of Switzerland. At the end of the nineteenth century Jewish refugees (some 4,000 to 5,000) emigrated from Russia and Poland, and in the 1950s–60s Jews emigrated from Northern Africa.

In Switzerland there are four distinguishable Jewish subgroups—orthodox, conservative, liberal, and reformed—who have in varying degrees adapted to modernization. About 15 percent of Switzerland's Jewish people belong to the orthodox group. Half of Switzerland's Jewish population attend synagogue only on a family occasion or never at all. About three-quarters of Jewish households are located in or near Switzerland's four largest cities—Zurich, Geneva, Basel, and Bern—where, consequently, most synagogues are also to be found. One of the biggest problems Jews face in Switzerland is that they are not allowed to slaughter animals the way their religion prescribes.

In Switzerland, just as in similar Western countries, there are various new religious movements, many having a Hindu or Buddhist background. Other new religious movements have roots in Scientology, Rosicrucianism, the Unification Church, Raëlianism, and so on. Their numbers are generally modest, contrasting with the (mostly critical) attention they get in the media (less than 0.1 percent of the population belong to such groups). Few of these groups were founded in Switzerland. The most important exception is the spiritist movement Orden Fiat Lux, which was founded by Uriella (Erika Bertschinger) in 1980 in Zurich. Another Swiss example is the Saint Michaelsvereinigung in Dozwil (canton of Thurgau), a movement with a Catholic background founded by Paul Kuhn, who was believed to be the reincarnation of the Apostle Paul. Considering the size and cultural impact, the most important group might well be the Anthroposophical Movement (founded by the German Rudolf Steiner). The worst reputation was gained by the Ordre du Temple Solaire, based in Switzerland and Canada. This group's leaders organized the collective murder and suicide of its members in 1993.

Switzerland's new religious movements (both of Eastern and Western background) are in part surrounded by the cultic milieu, a social system consisting of individuals with a similar worldview (including, for example, concepts of psychic energy, reincarnation, vegetarianism, or ecology and encompassing such diverse elements as astrology, Oriental wisdom, parapsychology, or flying saucers). Interestingly both Hinduism and Buddhism are perceived by many as belonging to this milieu. Cultic seekers explore different products or practices, moving between one therapy and the next or from one guru to the next. It is not easy to determine the size of the cultic milieu. In a recent survey 4 percent of people living in Switzerland claim to be attracted to New Age, which is almost a synonym of cultic milieu. The cultic milieu in Switzerland is visible as a result of the numerous esoteric bookshops, an esoteric fair (Lebenskraft, which takes place in Zurich every March), and two esoteric magazines (*Recto-Verseau* and *Spuren*).

The number of people without any religious affiliation has risen steadily, from 1.1 percent of the population in 1980 to more than 10 percent in 2000, with numbers especially high in the cantons of Basel and Geneva. These people are mostly those who have left one of the two large Christian churches (Roman Catholic or Reformed). Reasons for this exodus include no subjective feeling of membership, no subjective faith, a critical attitude toward church positions on public issues, and the wish to avoid church tax. People with no religious affiliation are mostly young, highly educated, and on the political left. Despite their assertion that they are without affiliation, they are among the most interested when it comes to products or therapies from the cultic milieu.

Jörg Stolz

See Also Vol. 1: *Christianity*

Bibliography

Altermatt, Urs. *Katholizismus und Moderne.* Zurich: Benziger Verlag, 1989.

Baumann, Christoph Peter, and Christian J. Jäggi. *Muslime unter uns: Islam in der Schweiz.* Lucerne: Rex, 1991.

Baumann, Martin. "Geschichte und Gegenwart des Buddhismus in der Schweiz." *Zeitschrift für Missionswissenschaft und Religionswissenschaft* 82, no. 4 (1998): 255–80.

Bedouelle, Guy, and François Walter. *Histoire religieuse de la Suisse: La présence catholique.* Paris: Les Editions du CERF, 2000.

Campiche, Roland J., and Alfred Dubach, et al. *Croire en Suisse(s).* Lausanne: Editions l'Age d'Homme, 1992.

Eggenberger, Oswald. *Die Kirchen, Sondergruppen und religiösen Vereinigungen: Ein Handbuch.* 6th ed. Zurich: TVZ, 1994.

Kupfer, Claude, and Ralph Weingarten. *Zwischen Ausgrenzung und Integration: Geschichte und Gegenwart der Jüdinnen und Juden in der Schweiz.* Zurich: Sabe, 1999.

Mayer, Jean-François. *Les Nouvelles voies spirituelles: Enquête sur la religiosité parallèle en Suisse.* Lausanne: Editions L'Age d'Homme, 1993.

———. "'Our Terrestrial Journey Is Coming to an End': The Last Voyage of the Solar Temple." *Nova Religio: The Journal of Alternative and Emergent Religions* 2, no. 2 (1999): 172–96.

McDowell, Christopher. *A Tamil Asylum Diaspora: Sri Lankan Migration, Settlement and Politics in Switzerland.* Providence, R.I.: Berghahn Books, 1996.

Stolz, Fritz. "Religion in Switzerland." In *Switzerland Inside Out.* Edited by Lydia Lehmann, 221–40. Zurich: Swiss-Japanese Chamber of Commerce, 1998.

Stolz, Jörg. "Evangelicalism and Milieu Theory." In *Les Dynamiques européennes de l'évangélisme.* Edited by Roland J. Campiche, 74–96. Lausanne: ORS, 2001.

Syria

POPULATION 17,155,814

SUNNI MUSLIM 74 percent

ALAWITE 12 percent

CHRISTIAN 10 percent

DRUZE 3 percent

OTHER 1 percent

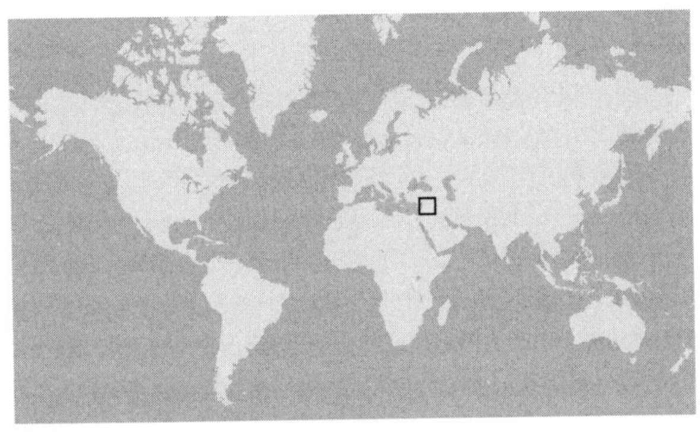

Country Overview

INTRODUCTION The Syrian Arab Republic comprises only a small portion of the area historically referred to as Syria, or Bilad al-Sham, which included (in addition to present-day Syria) Lebanon, Israel, Jordan, and part of Turkey. From the earliest times Syria has formed a crossroads of military and trade routes between the Mediterranean Sea and Mesopotamia, as well as being the object of invasion and occupation by powerful kingdoms, empires, and dynasties, which provides part of the explanation for the geographic distribution and close-knit character of Syria's religious minorities. Contemporary Syria is a small, developing, middle-income country with a diverse landscape, consisting of a narrow Mediterranean coast extending between Lebanon and Turkey, paralleled by several mountain ranges, and with semiarid and desert plateau to the east. Also bordering Syria are Iraq, Jordan, and Israel.

Although almost three-quarters of the inhabitants of present-day Syria are Sunni Muslim, the area has been and remains home to diverse religious groups, including several branches of Shiite Islam (Alawite, Druze, Ismailite, and Twelver Shiite); Jews, who migrated to the area in the thirteenth century B.C.E.; and Yazidis, predominantly Kurdish-speaking adherents to an ancient and heterodox religion that arrived in Syria from Iraq in the fifteenth and sixteenth centuries.

Christianity in Syria dates back to the apostolic age, which ended about 70 C.E. Christians became the majority population in Syria at some point after the administrative center of the Roman world shifted from Rome to Byzantium in the fourth century, contributing to Christianity's spread throughout the region. Christianity did not become a minority in Syria until perhaps as late as the thirteenth century.

RELIGIOUS TOLERANCE Although the Syrian constitution of 1973 specifies that the president must be Muslim, article 35 proclaims that the state respects all religions and the freedom to hold any religious rites, provided they do not disturb the public order. Religious groups are subject to their respective religious laws on marriage, divorce, child custody, and inheritance.

While religious rights are generally respected by the government in practice, Alawites currently possess power and position in the military and security apparatus (police, secret police, civilian intelligence) considerably disproportionate to their percentage in the population, which may place non-Alawi individuals and religious groups at a disadvantage in relation to other civil and political rights. All religions are subject to registration and monitoring by the government, and in 1964 Jehovah's Witnesses were banned from the country for being a Zionist organization, though such actions seem to be undertaken for political rather than religious reasons. Unlike most other Muslim-majority countries, Syria has not banned proselytizing, though groups that proselytize have been prosecuted for inciting religious hatred. Jews are the only religious minority group whose religion both exempts them from military service and is noted on their identity cards and passports.

A Syrian vendor arranges sweets at his shop in downtown Damascus. Sweets sales rise as Muslims prepare for Id al-Fitr, a three-day feast at the end of Ramadan that is celebrated as a public holiday in Syria. AP/WIDE WORLD PHOTOS.

Major Religion

SUNNI ISLAM

DATE OF ORIGIN 634–41 C.E.
NUMBER OF FOLLOWERS 12.7 million

HISTORY When Muslims conquered Syria in the middle of the seventh century, most of the population was Christian and would remain so until Christians became a minority no later than the thirteenth century. After Damascus became the capital of the first imperial Islamic caliphate, the Umayyad (661–750), conversion to Islam increased. Conversion continued after the Abbasid dynasty (750–1258) overthrew the Umayyad caliphate and moved the political center from Syria to Iraq. In succeeding centuries the caliphate lost its hold, and Syrian rule passed among various competing Muslim dynasties.

Late in the eleventh century European Christian Crusaders established military states in Syria. They were expelled by the Sunni Ayyubids, led by Saladin, in the latter half of the twelfth century. In the thirteenth century the Mamluks took power. Sultan Salim I conquered Syria in 1516, beginning what would be 400 years of Ottoman rule, sustained by their claim to be ruling in accordance with Islam and by their incorporation of Syria's Islamic institutions, symbols, and religious scholars (ulamas).

In 1918 a parliamentary government was established in Damascus, and in 1920 an independent Arab Kingdom of Syria was established under King Faysal of the Hashemite family. Faysal's rule over Syria was brief, and the country soon came under French mandate, which lasted until Syria declared its independence in 1946. The early years of independence were marked by political maneuvering and military coups, which eventually brought Arab nationalist and socialist elements to power. After a short-lived union with Egypt in 1958, creating the United Arab Republic, Syria seceded, reestablishing itself as the Syrian Arab Republic.

In 1963 the Baath Party seized control with a power base consisting of a coalition of social and religious forces (namely Alawite, Druze, and Ismailite) previously dominated by the majority Sunni urban leadership and espousing a socialist, secularist ideology. Hafiz al-Asad assumed the office of president in 1970, becoming the first non-Sunnite in modern Syrian history to hold that position. Asad died in 2000 and was succeeded by his son, Bashar.

The most visible opposition the Asad regime has faced has come from Sunni fundamentalists. The branch of the Muslim Brotherhood that was formed in Syria in 1945 under the leadership of Mustafa al-Sabai engaged in a number of violent clashes with the government throughout the 1960s and 1970s. Association with the Muslim Brotherhood was made a capital offense in 1980.

EARLY AND MODERN LEADERS In the tenth century Sayf al-Dawla founded the Hamadanid dynasty of Aleppo. He was famous for his patronage of the greatest

Muslim intellectuals of the time, including classic Arab poet al-Mutanabbi and Islamic philosopher al-Farabi.

The beginning of Muslim reunification and the first victories against the Crusaders began in Syria under Zangi, ruler of Aleppo and Mosul. Zangi's son Nureddin succeeded him as ruler of northern Syria and took control of Damascus. In addition to fortifying the city's defenses, Nureddin patronized its Sunni religious and educational institutions. Saladin, the most famous Muslim warrior of this period, began his career in the service of first Zangi and then Nureddin, whom he eventually succeeded as ruler of a Muslim state that at the time stretched from the Libyan Desert to the Tigris River Valley.

In contemporary Syria, official Sunni Islam has been represented by Shaykh Ahmad Muhammad Amin Kuftaru (born in 1915), a man with Kurdish lineage who in 1964 became grand mufti of Syria as well as the head of both the Supreme Council of Fatwa and the Supreme Council of Waqf (religious endowments). Shaykh Kuftaru, leader of the Naqshabandi Sufi order (which traces its lineage back to Abu Bakr, the first caliph), is known for his emphasis on religious tolerance and interfaith understanding. Shaykh Kuftaru was propelled into the international limelight in 2001 when he greeted Pope John Paul II at the Umayyad Mosque in Damascus during what was the first visit by the head of the Roman Catholic Church to a Muslim place of worship.

Another important contemporary religious figure is Shaykh Muhammad Said Ramadan al-Buti (born in 1929). Like Shaykh Kuftaru, Shaykh al-Buti is of Kurdish origin, but unlike the former, he represents the more traditionalist, non-Sufi current in Sunni Islam, which remains strong in Syria. He has been a significant force in popularizing an orthodox interpretation of Islamic law and ideals in Syrian society.

MAJOR THEOLOGIANS AND AUTHORS The most famous Syrian theologian is Taqiy al-Din Ahmad Ibn Taymiyya (1263–1328), a scholar of the Hanbali school of jurisprudence who advocated a doctrine of conservative reformism, stressing the need for communal solidarity and a strict adherence to the Koran and authentic *sunnah* (example of the Prophet Muhammad). The Hanbali school remains the predominant source of law in the religious courts in Syria. Ibn Taymiyya was also a staunch critic of all forms of Sufism. He remains a lasting influence on contemporary Wahhabi and Salafi Islamist movements.

HOUSES OF WORSHIP AND HOLY PLACES Like other Muslims, Syrian Muslims worship in the mosque (*masjid,* or *jamaa*). The most historically important mosque in Syria is the Umayyad Mosque in Damascus, founded in 706 C.E. on a religious site dating back to about 1000 B.C.E. The current structure encompasses an earlier Aramaean structure, a Roman temple to Jupiter, and a Byzantine church, and it holds a reliquary said to bear the head of Saint John the Baptist. Another Umayyad mosque, referred to as the Great Mosque, lies in Aleppo and was completed in 717 by the same Umayyad caliph, Khalid ibn al-Walid, who had earlier constructed the Umayyad Mosque in Damascus. The Takiyya Mosque complex, another important mosque in Damascus, was built over a period of six years (beginning in 1554) at the order of Süleyman the Magnificent and according to the design of the Ottoman's most brilliant architect, Sinan.

WHAT IS SACRED? Syrian Sunni Muslims do not hold any animals, plants, or relics sacred. Certain religious sites in Syria, however, hold particular significance for Muslims. Damascus is considered by many Sunnites to be the fourth holiest city (after Mecca, Medina, and Jerusalem) because of its central role in Islamic history and numerous mentions in the Koran. Similarly, the Umayyad Mosque in Damascus is considered by many Sunni Muslims to be the fourth holiest mosque (after the Grand Mosque in Mecca, the Mosque of the Prophet in Medina, and the Dome of the Rock in Jerusalem). It is believed that Jesus will descend at a white minaret, called the Minaret of Jesus, in the Umayyad Mosque to begin the holy campaign against the Antichrist.

HOLIDAYS AND FESTIVALS Syrian government offices, banks, and post offices and all Muslim-run businesses are closed on Fridays in recognition of the Muslim day of prayer. Of the other 11 public holidays in Syria, four are Muslim. Muslim holidays follow the Islamic calendar, which is lunar. The Muslim New Year (Ras al-Sana al-Hajira) is celebrated in a relatively low-key manner in Syria on the first day of the first Islamic month (Muharram). The birth of the Prophet Muhammad (Mawlid al-Nabi), celebrated on the 12th day of the third Islamic month (Rabi al-Awal), is a festive holiday in Syria, with chanters reciting verses from the Koran and a narrative of Muhammad's life and the streets alight with celebrations.

The ninth Islamic month, Ramadan, is celebrated by fasting during the day and a large family meal that breaks the fast after sunset. Only the Breaking of the Fast (Id al-Fitr), a three-day feast at the end of Ramadan, is celebrated as a public holiday, with many Syrians staying up all night, visiting family members, eating sweets, and wearing new clothes. It is also customary for children to often receive gifts of money from their uncles during Id al-Fitr and be treated to carnival-type rides and fireworks.

The Feast of the Sacrifice (Id al-Adha), commemorating both the end of the hajj (pilgrimage to Mecca) and the willingness of Abraham to sacrifice his son to God, is celebrated in the 12th Islamic month (Zoul Hajja) by slaughtering a sheep and distributing its meat among family, friends, and the poor. Syrians also refer to the holiday as Id al-Kabir (the Great Feast), or Qurban Bayram (from Turkish).

MODE OF DRESS Syrian mode of dress is often determined more by other forms of identity—such as ethnicity and locality—than by religion. Syrian Sunnites include Kurds, Bedouins, Turks, and Palestinian refugees, who each have distinct styles of traditional dress. Sunni city dwellers tend to dress differently than rural villagers, and most Syrian villages have their own style of dress, as well as a favored fabric, weave, stitch, and color of cloth. Western dress has mixed with and, in some cases, supplanted traditional styles.

DIETARY PRACTICES Most Syrian Muslims heed religious prescriptions prohibiting them from drinking alcohol and eating pork; pigs are considered unclean in Islam. Permitted animals (all animals except pigs and carnivorous animals) are slaughtered according to Islamic rites in order to be suitable for consumption (halal foods are those sanctioned by Islamic law).

RITUALS Public prayer is widely practiced by Syrian Sunni Muslim men, particularly in rural areas. The Friday noon prayers are the most important public prayer and provide the occasion for sermons by religious leaders. Women attend public worship at the mosque less often than men, and when they do attend, they are segregated in the mosque. More commonly women pray at their home or gather at the homes of other women for prayer and study. Since the 1980s Sunni women, many of whom are affiliated with Sufi orders, have increasingly sought lessons or study sessions not only in private homes but also in mosques and schools. Within the space of these female gatherings, Sunni women have played a key role in advancing women's religious education, as well as transmitting religious knowledge in Syrian society.

Weddings are major social events in Syria. Festivities involve dancing, singing, and feasting that lasts most of the night.

A death in a Sunni family is followed by three days of mourning and visits from friends, relatives, and neighbors. The corpse must be washed, wrapped in a simple plain cloth, and buried facing Mecca within 24 hours. Women relatives of the deceased wear black, sometimes for many months after the death.

RITES OF PASSAGE The typical Syrian understanding of a Muslim life cycle involves birth, naming, circumcision, marriage, parenting, and death.

MEMBERSHIP In Syria, Muslim children are considered to inherit the religion of their father upon birth. Conversion to Islam is undertaken by simply reciting the *shahadah* (Islamic declaration of faith): "There is no god apart from God, and Muhammad is the Messenger of God." Conversion from Islam to another religion is rare because it is officially forbidden by Islamic law.

SOCIAL JUSTICE *Zakat* (almsgiving) is widely understood as a method of redistributing wealth in the community and is considered one of the Five Pillars of Islam. Traditionally every middle- and upper-class Muslim must give 2.5 percent of what they possess to the poor. Almsgiving in Syria has become a more private matter, with Muslims giving alms to poor neighbors during Ramadan or those with means contributing properties to support religious and charitable activities or institutions.

SOCIAL ASPECTS Although arranged marriages are still common among Sunni Muslims in Syria, especially in villages and among the Bedouins, most Sunni Muslims have some say in choosing their partner. The parents of both partners, however, must agree to the marriage. Before the wedding the groom usually pays a bride-price (*majr*) to the bride's family. Although polygamy is legal for Muslims in Syria, it is not widely practiced. It is unusual for Syrians to divorce.

POLITICAL IMPACT The Syrian constitution, adopted in 1973, requires that the president be Muslim but does not make Islam the state religion, nor does it require that the president be Sunni Muslim. Islamic jurisprudence is stated as the main source of legislation, but the judicial system in Syria remains an amalgam of Ottoman, French, and Islamic laws, with civil and criminal courts, military courts, and the security courts, as well as religious courts, which adjudicate matters of personal and family law, such as divorce and inheritance.

No Islamist political parties are recognized by the Syrian government. The Syrian Muslim Brotherhood currently operates in exile in Jordan and Yemen.

CONTROVERSIAL ISSUES Sociopolitical conflict in Syria has both sectarian and economic aspects. Traditionally the eminent and influential class comprised Sunni landowners and merchants, but with the consolidation of the state economy under successive Baathist governments, sociopolitical power shifted from the traditional commercial bourgeoisies to the dominant state bourgeoisies, including the armed forces, where religious minorities—primarily the Alawites but also to some extent Druze and Ismailites—are more proportionately represented.

Many conservative Sunnites regard the Alawites as heretics to Islam. The Syrian Muslim Brotherhood, which has instituted activities against the Baath Party, has tended to be led by Sunni clerics and scholars, and its rank and file consists largely of young Sunni bourgeois or urban poor. Currently, however, the group does not form a formidable opposition to the Baath regime.

CULTURAL IMPACT Because Islam is thought to forbid the depiction of human and animal forms, visual art in Syria is concentrated in intricate abstract geometric and floral designs and calligraphy. This art form is seen in Syrian wood-, metal-, and glassworks and, most commonly, in architecture. The Umayyad Mosque in Damascus is considered one of the finest examples of Islamic art, owing to its numerous finely crafted mosaics, woodworks, and other decorations.

Other Religions

There are a significant number of non-Sunni Muslim groups in Syria. These include various offshoots of Shiism—Alawites, Ismailites, and Druze—as well as Christians, Jews, and Tazidis.

Currently the Alawites (also known as the Nusariyyins), found almost entirely in Syria, are the country's most influential religious group. Their origins can be traced to the 11th Shiite imam, al-Hasan al-Askari (died in 873), and his pupil Muhammad Ibn Nusayr (died in 868). The Alawites believe in a sort of trinity where Ali, the first Shiite imam and fourth Sunni caliph, is the "Meaning"; Muhammad, whom Ali created of his own light, is the "Name"; and Salman, an early Shiite saint, is the "Gate"—thus placing Ali in an exalted, deified position and hence the name Alawite, or "followers of Ali." Alawites celebrate some Islamic and some Christian holidays. Although they have been in the territory that is now known as Syria for a very long time, they only came to the powerful position they now hold after Hafiz al-Asad became the first Alawite head of state in 1971 and brought other Alawites into key positions. Asad, like many other Alawites, had used the military to gain an education and social status and eventually used that same institution, along with the Baath party, to gain political power. The Alawites, numbering about 2.1 million in 2002, have traditionally occupied the mountainous ranges along the coast, known as the Jabal al-Nusariyya, and form the majority population of the Latakia province. Syrian Alawites are divided into four tribal confederations: Kalbiyya, Khayatin, Haddadin, and Matawira.

Syria also has about 200,000 followers of the Ismaili faith, primarily residing south of Salamiyah on land granted to them by Abdul Hamid II, sultan of the Ottoman Empire from 1876 to 1909. The Ismailites believe there are two imams, one visible and one hidden, the latter of whom will return to lead the faithful. The Syrian Ismailites belong to the Misari branch, which recognizes the Aga Khan as its head.

The Druze, an offshoot of Ismaili Shiism that first appeared in the tenth century, form a small minority concentrated in the Jabal Druze area, a rugged mountainous region in southwestern Syria. The Druze have a tradition of keeping their doctrine and ritual secret in order to escape persecution. Although the Druze see themselves as a successor to all three main monotheistic religions, they believe that rituals and ceremonies have caused Jews, Christians, and Muslims to turn aside from pure faith. They do not observe Muslim rituals such as fasting or pilgrimage, and their meeting for religious instruction and prayer is Thursday rather than Friday and does not take place in mosques.

Christianity formed the majority of the population throughout much of Syria's history and can trace its original liturgical language to the Syriac dialect of Arabic spoken at the northern Syrian town of Edessa. The dialect is still spoken in a few Syrian towns and remains in use in Syrian Orthodox churches. Today Christians still constitute about 10 percent of the population. Forming the largest groups are the Orthodox denominations, including the Greek Orthodox, whose leader has been the "Patriarch of Antioch and All the East" since 1342; the Syrian Orthodox, or Jacobite; and the Armenian Orthodox, or Gregorian. There are also five Uniate denominations, which are Eastern churches in communion with the Roman Catholic Church but that retain their own distinctive liturgies. Listed in descending order of numbers, they are Greek Catholic, Armenian Catholic, Syrian Catholic, Chaldean Catholic, and Maronite. There are also a few Protestant Christian communities.

Jews may constitute the oldest monotheistic religious community in Syria, claiming 2,500 years of history there. With the creation of the state of Israel and the lifting of government restrictions on emigration, however, their numbers have dwindled to about 500 in Syria, primarily in Damascus and Aleppo.

Michaelle Browers

See Also Vol. 1: *Christianity, Islam, Shiism, Sunnism*

Bibliography

Abd-Allah, Umar F. *The Islamic Struggle in Syria.* Berkeley, Calif.: Mizan Press, 1983.

Böttcher, Annabelle. "Islamic Teaching among Sunni Women in Syria." In *Everyday Life in the Muslim Middle East.* Edited by Donna Lee Bowen and Evelyn A. Early, 290–99. Bloomington: Indiana University Press, 2001.

———. *Official Sunni and Shii Islam in Syria.* San Domenico, Italy: European University Institute, 2002.

Christmann, Andreas. "Islamic Scholar and Religious Leader: Shaikh Muhammad Said Ramadan al-Buti." In *Islam and Modernity: Muslim Intellectuals Respond.* Edited by John Cooper, Ronald Nettler, and Mohamed Mahmoud, 57–81. London: I.B. Tauris, 1998.

Commins, David. *The Historical Dictionary of Syria.* Lanham, Md.: Scarecrow Press, 1996.

Khuri, Fuad I. "The Alawis of Syria: Religious Ideology and Organization." In *Syria: Society, Culture, and Polity.* Edited by Richard T. Antoun and Donald Quataert, 49–61. Albany: State University of New York Press, 1991.

Taiwan

POPULATION 22,603,001

CHINESE RELIGION (BUDDHIST, TAOIST, CONFUCIAN, AND CHINESE FOLK RELIGION) 89.1 percent

I-KUAN TAO 3.9 percent

PROTESTANT 2.6 percent

ROMAN CATHOLIC 1.3 percent

OTHER 3.1 percent

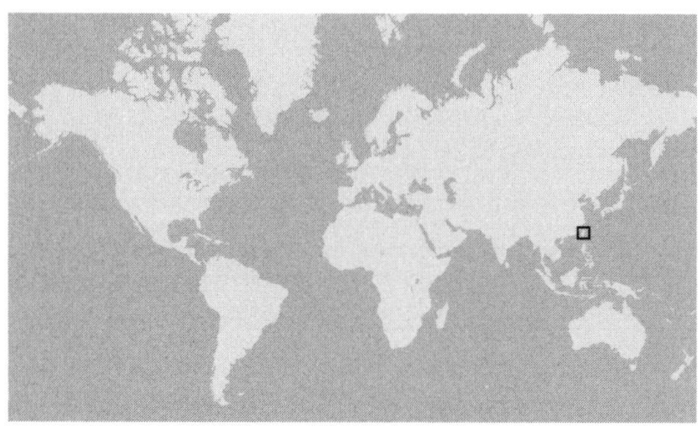

Country Overview

INTRODUCTION Taiwan is an island located nearly 100 miles from the southeast coast of mainland China. It is bordered on the south by the Bashi Channel; on the north by the East China Sea; on the east by the Pacific Ocean; and on the west by the Taiwan Strait, which separates Taiwan from mainland China. In addition to the main island, the Taiwanese government (called the Republic of China) has jurisdiction over the P'eng-hu, Quemoy, and Matsu archipelagos and about 20 other remote islets.

From the end of the sixteenth century C.E. to the beginning of the seventeenth, the first Europeans (such as Portuguese, Dutch, and Spaniards) went to the island; the latter two introduced Protestant Christianity and Roman Catholicism, respectively. Though Taiwan was known to the Chinese as early as the third century C.E., significant Chinese settlement did not take place until the seventeenth century, when Ming-dynasty loyalists used the island as a center of opposition to the Manchu (Ch'ing) regime that had taken control of the mainland. In 1683 part of the island fell to the Ch'ing and subsequently was incorporated into Fukien province. Buddhism, Taoism, and Confucianism arrived on the island with the Chinese.

Taiwan remained under Chinese control until 1895, when it was ceded to Japan as a consequence of the Sino-Japanese War. It remained a part of the Japanese empire until 1945, when Taiwan was returned to the Chinese Nationalist government. After its defeat by the communists in 1949, the Nationalist government, led by Chiang Kai-shek and the Kuo-min Tang (KMT), fled to Taiwan, taking with it 1.5 million refugees, among whom were many Taoist priests and Buddhist monks and nuns; they contributed significantly to the development of Taiwanese religion. The KMT remained the dominant political force in Taiwan until 2000, when Ch'en Shui-pian, a member of the opposition Democratic Progressive Party (DPP), was elected president.

Most Taiwanese today engage in a combination of practices associated with Buddhism, Taoism, Confucianism, and Chinese folk religion. Christians comprise a small but significant portion of the population, with the vast majority being Protestant and the rest Roman Catholic. Finally, there are a large number of Taiwanese who are adherents of new religious movements such as I-kuan Tao, T'ien-ti, and Hsüan-yüan Chiao.

RELIGIOUS TOLERANCE Taiwan's constitution protects religious freedom. Authorities generally uphold this protection and are intolerant of its abuse. Relations among the various religious communities are typically friendly. A number of private organizations and institutions, such as the World Religions Museum (established in 2001 by the Buddhist monk Master Hsin Tao), encourage mutual understanding, tolerance, and respect among followers of different religions.

A man lights incense in the Lung-Shan Temple in Taipi, Taiwan. People from all over Taiwan go to the temple to worship numerous deities. © BOHEMIAN NOMAD PICTUREMAKERS/CORBIS.

Major Religion

CHINESE RELIGION

DATE OF ORIGIN Seventeenth century C.E.
NUMBER OF FOLLOWERS 20 million

HISTORY In the seventeenth century C.E. Chinese immigrants to Taiwan often took with them images of deities from local temples associated with Buddhism, Taoism, and popular Chinese folk religion; this practice allowed them to maintain connection with their homeland. In Taiwan they then established associations and constructed temples for the veneration of these deities. As immigrants settled in subethnic groups on the island, such temples became centers of religious, political, and social life, forming the foundations of Chinese religion in Taiwan.

During the Japanese occupation (1895–1945) the colonial government occasionally limited popular religious expression by destroying local temples and burning their images. More commonly, however, Japanese officials attempted to control Chinese religiosity by supplanting Taiwanese religion with Japanese Buddhism and Shintoism. The number of Shinto temples built during this time increased significantly, and many Taiwanese Buddhist associations and temples felt inclined to align themselves officially with Japanese Buddhist organizations in order to avoid persecution. In 1949, after its defeat in the Chinese civil war, the Kuo-min Tang government fled to Taiwan, along with approximately one and a half million refugees, including Buddhist monks, Taoist priests, and Christian missionaries.

Since Chinese contact Taiwanese people have adhered to beliefs and rituals that derive principally from four Chinese traditions: Buddhism, Taoism, Confucianism, and folk religion. Today, with the exception of folk religion, these traditions operate as distinct organized religions. The majority of people, however, practice aspects of all of them throughout their lives, often regarding each tradition as serving specific ritual functions. The Taiwanese generally believe that Buddhist monks conduct funerals; Taoist priests perform marriage ceremonies; folk ritual specialists aid in the propitiation of ghosts; and Confucian principles guide family relationships. Because Chinese traditions serve as the basis of Taiwanese religiosity, it is therefore appropriate to refer to the major religion in Taiwan as Chinese religion.

EARLY AND MODERN LEADERS Many important figures have shaped the course of Taiwanese religion. For example, Chang En-p'u (1904–69), the 63rd patriarch of Celestial Master Taoism, established the Taiwan Taoist Society in 1951 in order to unify Taoist groups on the island and to encourage the development of Taoism throughout Taiwan. Likewise, modern Buddhist leaders, such as Master Sheng-yen (born in 1930) and Master Hsing-yün (born in 1927), have created two of the most influential Buddhist centers in Taiwan: Dharma Drum Mountain (Fa Ku Shan) and the Buddha's Light Mountain (Fo Guang Shan), respectively. They have built monastic centers, academic institutions, and lay organizations that offer opportunities for people to study meditation, chanting, and Buddhist doctrine.

One of the most popular personalities in modern Taiwan is Master Cheng Yen (born in 1937), a Buddhist nun who in 1966 founded the Buddhist Compassion Relief Foundation (Tzu-Chi), a charitable organization comprised mainly of lay volunteers. It provides services for the poor, such as health care and financial assistance. The group has been responsible for constructing hospitals and medical clinics, supplying disaster relief, and offering educational opportunities to people all over the world.

MAJOR THEOLOGIANS AND AUTHORS The scholar-monk Master Yin-shun (born in 1906) was possibly the most influential Buddhist thinker in twentieth-century Taiwan. Many scholars and practitioners regard his interpretations of Buddhist concepts and his commentaries on Buddhist texts as authoritative. He has authored treatises on Buddhist practice and doctrine, perhaps the most widely read of which is *Ch'eng fo chih Tao* (1960; *The Way to Buddhahood*).

Yin-shun is well known for his "humanistic Buddhism" (*jen-chien fo-chiao*), which emphasizes the relevance of Buddhism to people living in the modern world and discourages the focus on the cycle of death and rebirth and on birth into Pure Lands (paradise-like places where practitioners reside until they attain enlightenment) so characteristic of early to mid-twentieth-century Chinese Buddhism. His efforts to make the tradition pertinent to human beings living in this world have deeply influenced contemporary Buddhist figures such as Sheng-yen, Hsing-yün, and Cheng Yen (all three of whom are discussed above under EARLY AND MODERN LEADERS)—giving rise to the emphasis in their teachings on issues of social justice and environmental ethics.

HOUSES OF WORSHIP AND HOLY PLACES The primary places of worship in Taiwan are temples and shrines. Some are exclusively Buddhist (for example, Master Sheng-yen's Nung-Ch'an Temple in Pei-t'ou, outside of Taipei, and Master Hsing-yün's Fo Guang Shan Temple in Kao-hsiung) or Taoist (for instance, Chih-nan Temple in Taipei), but many are a synthesis of Buddhism, Taoism, Confucianism, and folk religion and contain images and icons from all of these traditions. Perhaps the best-known example of the latter type is Lung-shan (Dragon Mountain) Temple in Taipei. The temple was originally constructed in 1738 for the worship of Kuan-yin, the bodhisattva of mercy. Today, however, people from all over Taiwan go to the temple to worship numerous deities in addition to Kuan-yin, including the folk deities Ma-tsu (the goddess of the sea, who sailors petition for protection) and Kuan Kung (the god of war and commerce, who believers seek out for the increase of wealth and prosperity). In temples and shrines one can experience the sacred through such practices as prayer, meditation, and study.

WHAT IS SACRED? Much of the religious devotion in Taiwan focuses on Buddhas, bodhisattvas, Taoist gods, and folk deities. Because many adherents believe that these beings actually inhere in their physical representations, images of these figures are treated with particular respect and reverence. Perhaps the two most widely recognized and venerated beings are the bodhisattva Kuan-yin (Avalokitesvara) and the goddess Ma-tsu. Kuan-yin is often referred to as the bodhisattva of compassion and mercy. People pray to her for comfort in times of distress and for a safe childbirth or healing. Ma-tsu, a goddess associated with the sea, is petitioned by sailors seeking her protection during their voyages. She is also recognized and venerated by Taiwanese in general as a goddess of compassion and love who protects them in times of danger.

HOLIDAYS AND FESTIVALS There are many holidays and festivals associated with the religious practices and beliefs of the Taiwanese people. Some are related to specific religious traditions such as Buddhism, Taoism, and Confucianism; others are associated with temples that venerate certain folk deities; and many, reflecting the nature of Taiwanese religiosity in general, combine customs and practices from a variety of religious contexts, synthesizing elements from Confucianism, Taoism, Buddhism, and folk religion. The following examples are only two of the many holidays and festivals celebrated in Taiwan.

The Ghost Festival is celebrated on the 15th day of the 7th lunar month to honor the spirits of the deceased, who are let out of the underworld once a year to experience the pleasures of the living. Traditionally, families in China offered newly harvested grain to departed ancestors. In Taiwan an elaborate table of wine and meat and perhaps a slaughtered pig or sheep are offered to ancestors and to the ghosts of those who have no living family.

During Tomb-sweeping Day, occurring in April, people visit the family grave sites in order to worship their ancestors. Family members clean the graves, weed the surrounding area, and repair any damage to the tomb. They also light incense and pray to the deceased as well as engage in a ritual known as "securing paper," during which golden paper functioning as money is placed on the tomb for the ancestors to use in the spirit world.

MODE OF DRESS People in Taiwan are encouraged to dress modestly in temples. Buddhist monks and nuns in Taiwan typically shave their heads and wear robes. Some Buddhist lay practitioners wear robes for certain ceremonies but change into their regular clothes after the ceremony is completed. Similarly, Taoist priests only don their vestments when conducting rituals. Otherwise, they live and dress like the majority of Taiwanese.

DIETARY PRACTICES In Taiwan the Buddhist clergy strictly adheres to a vegetarian diet that also excludes the ingestion of the five types of pungent roots (onions, chives, leeks, scallions, and garlic). Lay Buddhists are encouraged to eat at least one vegetarian meal a day or, alternatively, to eat only vegetarian meals once a week. In Taoism, during certain rituals and ceremonies, such as new temple dedications, both the priest and the laity engage in purification fasts. For other Taoist celebrations the community shares in an elaborate feast. The general rule, however, is that, outside of feast days, meals should be frugal and based primarily on grains.

RITUALS Ritual practice in Taiwan can occur in both individual and communal contexts. Many people go to temples of all types to pray and offer incense for various needs (such as healing, safety, and business success) or to seek advice from mediums, who channel a deity's guidance in either written or spoken form. Buddhist temples and associations offer practitioners opportunities to learn and practice meditation and chanting in groups or as individuals. The Taoist tradition conducts an elaborate ritual known as the celebration of cosmic/community renewal; this is performed when a new temple is consecrated or an old one renovated. While pilgrimage to temples has always been a way for people to express their religious piety, the practice has been occurring more frequently, especially in light of modern conveniences, such as touring buses that can take people to more than one temple in a day and dormitories constructed to accommodate overnight stays.

RITES OF PASSAGE Traditionally, Buddhism, Taoism, and folk religion have attended to the life-cycle rituals of the family in Taiwan. Modernization and medical science, however, have divested these traditions of their influence in life-transition periods such as pregnancy, childbirth, and adolescence.

Yet when it comes to the performance of funeral rites and matters surrounding death and ancestor worship, the Taiwanese continue to seek advice from both Taoism and Buddhism, considering religion to have authority in issues regarding the afterlife. They often request Buddhist monks and Taoist priests to conduct wedding services.

MEMBERSHIP Though many temples and religious associations draw membership from the local communities they serve, some Buddhist and Taoist organizations actively seek a wider constituency. They provide opportunities for religious instruction by means of books, tapes, and websites. They offer classes for the study of doctrine and practice, run youth and study camps, and build religious institutes and universities. Some, such as the Fo Guang Shan Buddhist monastic order, actively proselytize—not only in Taiwan but also in other parts of the world. They have established temples and centers in many of the major cities of the United States and Europe, and they even have a Buddhist university in California.

SOCIAL JUSTICE Along with "humanized Buddhism" is an increasing emphasis in Taiwan on a socially engaged Buddhism—that is, a Buddhism that specifically and pragmatically addresses social and environmental problems, including issues of social justice (such as poverty, education, and health care). Master Cheng Yen's Buddhist Compassion Relief Foundation actively works to overcome the great disparity between the rich and the poor by offering financial aid, housing, medical assistance, and vocational training to those in need. The group also places importance on education and has constructed a nursing school, a medical school, and a university. Other religious organizations likewise address these issues. The Cultural Institute (a Taoist organization), for instance, has a school, provides health care, and participates in a variety of social welfare projects.

SOCIAL ASPECTS Family and marriage are valued in most religious contexts in Taiwan. Many groups, whether Buddhist, Taoist, or a synthesis of both, stress the cultivation of strong and healthy relationships between family members. Even Buddhist groups that maintain a monastic tradition and have historically regarded human relationships as potential sources of attachment and suffering perform wedding ceremonies during which couples are encouraged to love and care for one another. Moreover, in regards to family and marriage, characteristically Confucian language appears in the rhetoric of many religious groups in Taiwan; for instance, they discuss the importance of filial piety, family loyalty, maintaining family harmony, respecting elders, and caring for children.

POLITICAL IMPACT From 1952 to 1989 the Buddhist Association of the Republic of China (BAROC) was the exclusive representative of Buddhism in Taiwan. Its function was to communicate the directive of the ruling Kuo-min Tang party to its lay and monastic followers and in turn transmit the concerns of the Buddhist community to the government. After 1989 the BAROC lost this favored status.

Other groups, such as Master Hsing-yün's Fo Guang Shan, pursued political interests. They endorsed candidates (such as 1996 presidential candidate Chen Li Pan) and organized protest movements against governmental policies that they considered unjust. Other groups, such as the Buddhist Compassion Relief Foundation, avoid political involvement, prohibiting members from participating in politics. They argue that adherents should focus on Buddhist practice and charitable activities. Finally, because both Buddhist and Taoist organizations represent a significant portion of the population, the political leadership actively maintains good relationships with them, making special visits to their centers and seeking endorsements from their leadership.

CONTROVERSIAL ISSUES Abortion is a controversial issue (although it is not as politically charged in Taiwan as in the United States). It is contested by both Confucian principles—namely, those that emphasize the importance of having heirs for the patrilineage—and Buddhist moral guidelines that discourage the harming of life. Despite such opposition, abortion was made legal in Taiwan in 1985. Its practice has given rise to a concern among many Taiwanese people, especially women, for the welfare of the ghosts of aborted fetuses and the conditions of their afterlife. This concern has resulted in the performance of highly controversial fetus-ghost appeasement ceremonies, which are purported to help the spirit of the fetus move on to its next life. These services are not offered by any particular religious tradition; Buddhist monks, Taoist priests, and other religious specialists often perform the ritual.

CULTURAL IMPACT Buddhist and Taoist organizations in Taiwan continue to build temples and shrines in the traditional architectural style (noted for its curved roofs, bold colors, balance, and symmetry), though some, like the Buddhist Compassion Relief Foundation, prefer a more modern look, reflecting perhaps the principles of a "humanistic Buddhism." Traditional Taiwanese folk arts, such as woodcarving, continue to be influenced by Buddhism and Taoism, especially in the making, decorating, and painting of icons. Finally, many groups representing both religions have preserved traditional temple music in their rituals, while others have incorporated more contemporary styles, taking pride in creating choirs and sponsoring orchestras.

Other Religions

In addition to Buddhism, Taoism, and Confucianism, Taiwan is home to a variety of other religious traditions. Catholicism, a variety of Protestant Christian groups, and Islam all have a significant following. Moreover, over the course of the twentieth century there was a rise in the number of new sectarian, often syncretistic religions.

One such religious movement is I-kuan Tao (Way of Unity), which teaches that the Way (Tao) is the essence of all the religions and philosophies of the world. It combines the basic teachings of Buddhism, Taoism, Confucianism, Christianity, and Islam, while strongly reasserting the traditional Chinese attitudes regarding family relationships advocated by the Confucian tradition, namely filial piety, loyalty, and respect. Adherents do not dress differently from the majority of Taiwanese, but they are encouraged, out of compassion for all living beings, to become vegetarians.

In 1930 Shi Zueng and Shih Mu founded I-kuan Tao in Shanghai, China. They fled to Taiwan in 1949 to avoid the Communist revolution. Despite persecution by the Taiwanese government in its early years, the movement has grown quickly, claiming today to be the third largest religion in Taiwan, with 2 million members, 200 temples for worship, and 15,000 family shrines. The movement is socially focused: It runs a number of nursing homes, hospitals, medical clinics, and nursery schools. Moreover, it engages in disaster relief efforts and provides financial assistance for those who cannot otherwise afford an education.

Protestant Christianity was taken to Taiwan by the Dutch in the early seventeenth century. Roman Catholicism, brought by the Spanish, followed soon afterward. Today other Christian groups in Taiwan include the Presbyterian, True Jesus, Mormon, Baptist, Lutheran, Seventh-day Adventist, and Episcopalian churches as well as Jehovah's Witnesses.

Muslims were among the groups that fled the mainland with the Nationalist government in 1949. Beginning in the 1980s additional Muslims immigrated to the country from Indonchina. A number of mosques have since been built in Taiwan.

Scott Hurley

See Also Vol. 1: *Buddhism, Taoism*

Bibliography

Clart, Philip, and Charles Jones, eds. *Religion in Modern Taiwan: Tradition and Innovation in a Changing Society.* Honolulu: University of Hawai'i Press, 2003.

Huang, Chien-yu Julia, and Robert P. Weller. "Merit and Mothering: Women and Social Welfare in Taiwanese Buddhism." *Journal of Asian Studies* 57, no. 2 (1998): 379–96.

Jones, Charles B. *Buddhism in Taiwan: Religion and the State, 1660–1990.* Honolulu: University of Hawai'i Press, 1999.

Kohn, Livia. *Daoism and Chinese Culture.* Cambridge: Three Pines Press, 2001.

Moskowitz, Marc L. *The Haunting Fetus: Abortion, Sexuality, and the Spirit World in Taiwan.* Honolulu: University of Hawai'i Press, 2001.

Nagata, Judith. "The Globalisation of Buddhism and the Emergence of Religious Civil Society: The Case of the Taiwanese Fo Kuang Shan Movement in Asia and the West." *Communal/Plural* 7, no. 2 (1999): 231–48.

Rubinstein, Murray A., ed. *Taiwan: A New History.* New York: M.E. Scharpe, 1999.

Schipper, Kristofer. *The Taoist Body.* Translated by Karen C. Duval. Berkeley: University of California Press, 1993.

Weller, Robert P. "Living at the Edge: Religion, Capitalism, and the End of the Nation-State in Taiwan." *Public Culture* 12, no. 2 (2000): 477–98.

Tajikistan

POPULATION 6,719,567

ISLAM 95 percent

OTHER 5 percent

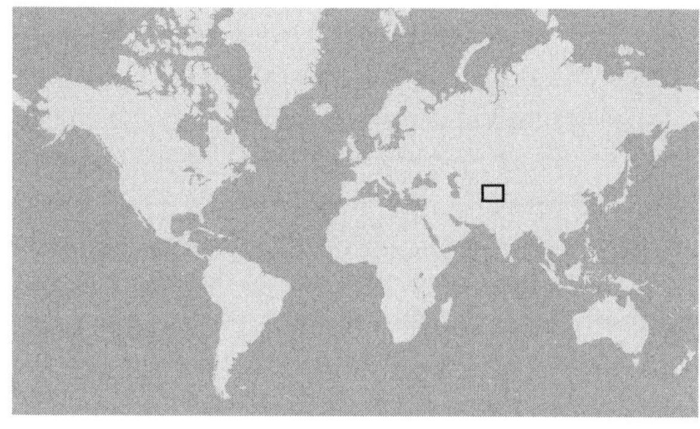

Country Overview

INTRODUCTION Located in the mountainous region of Central Asia, the Republic of Tajikistan shares borders with China, Afghanistan, Uzbekistan, and Kyrgyzstan. Linguistically and anthropologically, Tajiks, like Iranians and Afghans, are a Persian-speaking, Indo-European indigenous people, distinct from their predominantly Turkic neighbors.

Although Islam bears a long history in this region, it was not the first religion to be adopted by the local population. From the last centuries before the Christian Era through the first few centuries C.E., the leading religion of the area was Zoroastrianism. Founded by the prophet Zoroaster, Zoroastrianism is recognized as one of the earliest religions to espouse a monotheistic philosophy. At the same time, Hellenistic beliefs, Nestorian Christianity, Buddhism, and other faiths proved influential among the area's inhabitants. In the seventh century C.E., however, the region's invasion by Islamic forces resulted in the total elimination of any other faiths but Islam.

The Russian colonial period, which began in the 1860s, lasted until the Soviets completely incorporated Tajikistan into the U.S.S.R. in the 1920s. With the collapse of Communism, Tajikistan declared independence in 1991, but it was immediately beset by civil war that lasted until 1997, when a national reconciliation was initiated. Tajikistan is the only country in all of Central Asia where a religious party (the Islamic Revival Party) legally exists and holds a few seats in parliament.

There are other religions in modern Tajikistan. After centuries of being the second-largest religious confession in the region, Judaism was greatly reduced in the late twentieth century. Russian Orthodox, Bahais, Jehovah's Witnesses, Korean Protestants, and other religious groups have adherents in Tajikistan.

RELIGIOUS TOLERANCE Because no other religion has ever posed a challenge to Islam in the region, religious tolerance toward minorities has historically been positive. Judaism and Orthodox Christianity were tolerated in large cities until the Soviet era.

Religious tolerance is also observed within Islam in Tajikistan. Historically the Shiite Muslim minority in Tajikistan has lived in the Badakshan province. Approximately 150,000 residents belong to the Isma'ili sect of Islam and receive support from the international Isma'ili community. The Isma'ilite's geographic remoteness and small number have contributed to their peaceful coexistence with majority Muslims in Tajikistan.

The constitution of the Republic of Tajikistan declares the separation of religion and state, and the government strictly follows the policy of secularism. The law prohibits campaigning in mosques and other such uses of religion in politics. Nonetheless, government and pro-Islamic activists sometimes institute unofficial discrimination against nontraditional groups.

Major Religion

ISLAM

DATE OF ORIGIN Seventh century C.E.
NUMBER OF FOLLOWERS 6 million

HISTORY For the last 1,300 years the territory of Tajikistan has been part of the Muslim world, and Sunni Islam has been the dominant religion in the country. Islam was established in the region in the seventh century C.E., when Arab forces conquered Central Asia. In the ninth and tenth centuries the Tajiks were ruled by the Persian Samanid dynasty. Much of the region came under Turkish control in the early eleventh century.

As in other Islamic countries, Islam served as a civil and criminal code in Tajikistan until the 1920s, when the country became part of the Soviet empire. For the following 70 years of Communist rule, the practice of Islam was drastically diminished. During the first decade of the Soviet era most of the mosques were destroyed, and religious schools were banned. Beginning in early 1930s Tajiks were restricted in their religious practices, and Islam was relegated to a minimal role in the daily lives of the people.

The antireligious policy of the Communist era detached the nation from any normal experience of Islam. As a result of this policy, the population preserved only the most basic religious customs. For decades any curriculum that might contain Islamic concepts was prohibited. In addition to the fact that religious literature was eliminated from public life, the alphabet in which those books were written was changed twice, causing later generations to experience overall illiteracy in religious studies.

The collapse of the Soviet Union and Tajikistan's declaration of independence in 1991 made possible a revival of Islam. Although the majority of the population was only modestly interested, the number of mosques and prayers increased, and both Islamic education and pilgrimages to holy lands became freely permitted.

Ram's horns, an Islamic symbol of strength, appear as grave markers in a cemetery in Tajikistan. The collapse of the Soviet Union and Tajikistan's declaration of independence in 1991 made possible a revival of Islam.

Tajik Muslims recognize all of the basic values of Islam and do not diverge conceptually from the majority of the Muslim world. Tajikistan espouses the Hanafi school of law and a relatively moderate interpretation of Islam, and it rejects some of the more restrictive approaches to the religion.

EARLY AND MODERN LEADERS Qazi Akbar Turajonzoda was the spiritual leader of Tajikistan's Islamic opposition during the civil war in the early 1990s. In 1998 the peace agreements allotted government positions to the opposition, and Turajonzoda was appointed first deputy prime minister of Tajikistan. Mufti Amonullo Negmatzoda became the spiritual leader of the Tajik Muslims in 1996.

MAJOR THEOLOGIANS AND AUTHORS Tajiks affiliate themselves with a broad Persian literature, including theological authors. Nasser Khisrav, who lived and was buried in Tajikistan 1,000 years ago, is one of the legendary scholars of Shiite Islam's Isma'ili concept.

The philosopher Ahmad Donish (1826–97) was the most influential Tajik thinker of the nineteenth and early twentieth centuries. He sought to reform society by adopting modern forms of education and government. Donish inspired many authors in the tradition of Jadidism, a Sunni Muslim reform movement.

HOUSES OF WORSHIP AND HOLY PLACES Ordinary mosques, which have proliferated since the 1990s, serve as the main houses of worship for the majority of religious Tajik people. Traditionally only males attend mosques. Mosques in Tajikistan can serve as funeral homes and guesthouses, depending on the need. In Tajikistan the local interpretation of Islam and the influence of regional culture allows people to believe in numerous sacred places (predominantly the graves of famous people) in Tajikistan as well as in neighboring countries.

WHAT IS SACRED? Muslims in Tajikistan respect all sacred subjects prescribed by the Koran. The Koran, mosque, and holy graves are the main sacred objects in Tajikistan.

HOLIDAYS AND FESTIVALS After independence (1991) Tajikistan restored the celebration of traditional Islamic holidays. Today Tajikistan celebrates two major Islamic holidays, Ramadan (Tajiks call it Ramazohn) and Id al-Adha (the Day of Sacrifice; Tajiks call it Qurbon). These are observed as national holidays. Distinct from Muslims in other countries, Tajiks often observe these holidays by visiting family graves.

MODE OF DRESS Tajiks dress mainly according to European style. The most familiar accessories of the Islamic code, head coverings for women, were prohibited during the Soviet era, and few women in Tajikistan have returned to wearing them. Shawls or local types of head scarves are, however, prescribed for Muslim women at religious ceremonies. Men wear traditional hats while attending mosques and funerals. Turbans may occasionally be seen but only on elderly villagers.

DIETARY PRACTICES There are no Islamic dietary practices that are distinctive to Tajikistan. Fasting during Ramadan is prescribed for every Muslim but is not strictly practiced by the majority in Tajikistan.

RITUALS For years Soviet authorities prohibited the hajj (pilgrimage to Mecca). Since the 1990s the number of Tajiks who perform the hajj has risen significantly. One popular ritual in Tajikistan is pilgrimages to *mazars* (shrines that are often the site of a saint's tomb). This tradition has been traced to pre-Islamic practices. Strict Islamic rules apply to death in Tajikistan: The dead person must be buried before sunset or as soon as all ceremonies are over. Thereafter the family mourning period traditionally continues for one year.

RITES OF PASSAGE Although any child born into a Muslim family is considered Muslim, it is a ritual practice for a mullah or other respected man to chant a few verses from the Koran into the ear of the newborn child. Circumcision is strictly recommended for boys. Parents administer it when a boy is three to five years old. Girls are never circumcised in Tajikistan, and the practice is unheard of anywhere in the region.

MEMBERSHIP The vast majority of Tajiks consider themselves Muslims more by heritage than by religion, while some derive their Muslim identity both from their heritage and faith. Most Islamic values are respected as part of local tradition and custom; people do not receive a thorough education in Islamic studies. All Islamic activists in Tajikistan, including the Islamic Revival Party and local clerics, have been making concentrated efforts to increase the number of their followers. Some Muslim groups from Saudi Arabia and other Middle Eastern countries have proselytized in Tajikistan. The country has several Islamic publications, such as the newspaper of the Islamic Revival Party.

SOCIAL JUSTICE In the aftermath of Soviet-imposed socialism, Tajikistan has been experiencing a difficult transition to a capitalist system. The reforms sponsored by international institutions are often compromised by corruption, drug trafficking, and other factors. The influence of conservative religious attitudes on the people, especially in rural areas, has stimulated the emergence of radical Islamic cells.

SOCIAL ASPECTS Married Tajik women have more rights than women in other Islamic countries. They are expected to focus on motherhood and child rearing but can work, study, and participate in public activities. A woman must obtain permission from her family in order to pursue a career. Arranged marriages are widespread in Tajikistan but are not a strict requirement for the majority. Although the law prohibits polygamy, second marriages for men have regained popularity. As in the rest of Muslim world, Tajik families prefer to have boys rather than girls.

POLITICAL IMPACT Tajikistan's government is ostensibly secular. Today the Islamic opposition that led the antigovernment forces during the civil war (1992–95) is less influential and prefers not to challenge the government in the political sphere. The fear of an extremely restrictive clerical regime has diminished people's support for religious movements such as the Islamic Revival Party. The majority of Tajikistan supports a secular approach to statehood.

The main Islamic institution in Tajikistan is the *muftiyat,* chaired by the mufti, who acts as the official representative of Tajik Muslims. His role is to serve the common needs of Muslims and to provide ceremonial assistance in religious customs. The secular government and other provisions limit the authority of the *muftiyat.* Moreover, according to Islam in Tajikistan, no absolute religious leader can be elected or appointed.

CONTROVERSIAL ISSUES Although it is traditionally a Muslim-populated region, Tajikistan considers itself an Eastern European nation, and the majority prefers a European way of life. The incumbent government has implemented a strategy of sustaining moderate Islam as a general religion and continues to promote an active secularism overall in the country. Nevertheless, both the Islamic Revival Party and prohibited extremist Islamic groups such as Hizb-ut-Tahrir seek to gain greater Islamic influence.

CULTURAL IMPACT Unlike strict Islamic states, Tajikistan has demonstrated a keen interest in painting, sculpture, and other genres of fine art, and it offers schools and training facilities for their study. Sufi Muslims have influenced culture in Tajikistan, notably in the art of carpet weaving, an important form of artistic expression.

Other Religions

Most Christians in Tajikistan are Russian Orthodox. During the Soviet era large numbers of indigenous people and ethnic Russians immigrated to Tajikistan, taking with them other forms of Christianity, including Roman Catholicism, Lutheranism, Baptism, and Adventism. After independence (1991) these denominations shrank significantly, but newer missionaries, including Jehovah's Witnesses, have begun to operate in some towns, boosting the number of converts to Christianity.

Judaism has existed in the region since the Middle Ages. A large number of Jews fled Tajikistan during the civil war of the 1990s many settled in Israel. There are small numbers of Bahais, Zoroastrians, and Hare Krishnas in Tajikistan. Most members of these groups live in large cities. Pre-Islamic religious practices continue to make up part of Tajik domestic rituals.

Karim Khodjibaev

See Also Vol. 1: *Islam*

Bibliography

Fathi, Habiba. "Otines: The Unknown Women Clerics of Central Asian Islam." *Central Asian Survey* 16, no. 1 (1997): 27–43.

Tadjbakhsh, Shahrbanou. "Between Lenin and Allah: Women and Ideology in Tajikistan." In *Women in Muslim Societies: Diversity within Unity.* Edited by Herbert L. Bodman and Nayereh Tohidi. Boulder, Colo.: Lynne Rienner Publishers, 1998.

Tett, Gillian. "'Guardians of the Faith?': Gender and Religion in an (ex) Soviet Tajik Village." In *Muslim Women's Choices.* Edited by Camillia Fawzi El-Solh and Judy Mabro. Oxford: Berg, 1994.

Tanzania

POPULATION 37,187,939

CHRISTIAN 40 percent

MUSLIM 39 percent

AFRICAN TRADITIONAL RELIGIONS 20 percent

OTHER (HINDU, SIKH) 1 percent

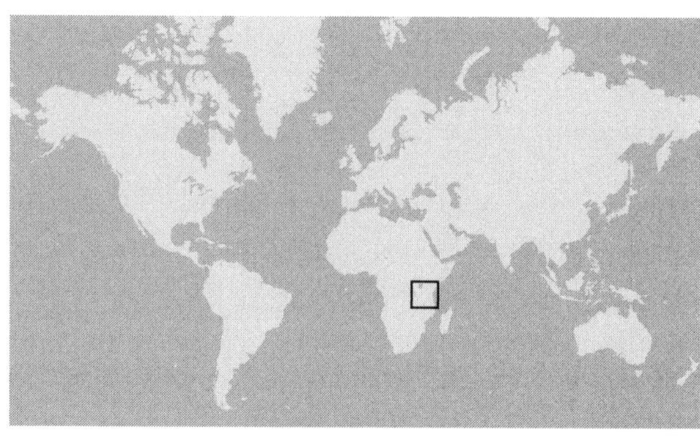

Country Overview

INTRODUCTION Tanzania lies on the East African coast, just south of the equator. It shares borders with Kenya, Mozambique, Malawi, Zambia, the Democratic Republic of the Congo, Rwanda, Burundi, and Uganda. The Tanzanian mainland is dominated by vast plains and plateaus and contains numerous lakes, including Lake Tanganyika, one of the world's deepest. Kilimanjaro, Africa's highest mountain, rises in the northeast near the border with Kenya. Tanzania's territory also includes several coastal islands, the largest of which are Mafia, Pemba, and Zanzibar. In 1964 Zanzibar, Pemba, and other islands joined the mainland state of Tanganyika to form the United Republic of Tanzania.

Tanzanians were a highly spiritual people before the arrival of the world's major religions, and they continue to be so, as is exemplified by the contemporary situation in the country. The churches on the predominantly Christian mainland (the former Tanganyika) and the mosques on the islands of Zanzibar and Pemba, where the population is 99 percent Muslim, overflow with the faithful on a regular basis. These local representations of Islam and Christianity are also extremely dynamic, engendering both syncretic and new forms of spiritual expression. Those who have not converted to either Islam or Christianity are steadfast in maintaining and practicing their traditional beliefs.

To some extent Tanzania's religious communities also foster social isolation. Interethnic marriage is common, particularly among the groups that make up the mainland's Bantu-speaking majority, but mixed religious unions are rare. From a broader perspective religion can also be seen as a potentially destabilizing force in Tanzania. This aspect was obscured in the past by a fixation on the presumed evils of "tribalism," which turned out to be largely a fiction of the colonial system and discourse. The divisiveness implied by the term never materialized, but in 2001 there were violent demonstrations by some Islamic residents of Zanzibar and Pemba advocating secession from the multireligious mainland. These repressed outbursts led to exile in neighboring countries for some Muslim leaders and suggest that religion has the power to incite and mobilize segments of the Tanzanian population in opposition to state policies. These communities of true believers pose the real threat to the federated nation as now constituted. A delicate peace has been maintained by a constitutional arrangement that has always allowed for a separate president for Zanzibar.

RELIGIOUS TOLERANCE The Tanzanian constitution allows for religious freedom, and this position has been realized in practice, despite the existence of religious tensions. Government policy also prohibits discrimination on religious grounds. There is legislation prohibiting political campaigns in places of worship and the publication and circulation of material considered inflammatory. Separation of church and state is not complete. Religious organizations are required to register with the Ministry of Home Affairs, for example, and Islamic law applies in civil and domestic matters concerning the Muslim populations of Pemba and Zanzibar.

Muslim passengers kneel in prayer upon their approach to the island of Zanzibar. In 2001 there were violent demonstrations by some Islamic residents of Zanzibar advocating secession from Tanzania. © ALISON WRIGHT/CORBIS.

Major Religions

CHRISTIANITY

ISLAM

AFRICAN INDIGENOUS BELIEFS

CHRISTIANITY

DATE OF ORIGIN c. 1840 C.E.
NUMBER OF FOLLOWERS 14.9 million

HISTORY The Eastern African littoral, part of which was to become coastal Tanganyika in the nineteenth century, was known to Mediterranean seafarers as long ago as the first century C.E., as indicated in the Greek document *The Periplus of the Erythrean Sea.* Meaningful European contact with this Swahili coast was not established until the early sixteenth century, with the arrival of the Portuguese in the city-state of Kilwa and on the Kenyan seaboard to the north. This initial incursion had little religious impact on the already deeply rooted Muslim communities in the area. Christianity did not reach the traditional communities of the interior until the arrival of such nineteenth-century explorers as Richard Burton (1821–90), John Hanning Speke (1827–64), David Livingstone (1813–73), and Henry Morton Stanley (1841–1904), as well as some more politically active German agents. By the end of the century European forays had resulted in the establishment of the German colony of Tanganyika on the mainland and a British protectorate on the islands of Zanzibar. (After World War I Tanganyika also came under British control as a British League of Nations mandate.) These historic events initiated the vigorous spread of Christianity to the now more exposed interior. The various Christian missionary groups on the mainland soon worked out agreements that allowed each uncontested access to a different area for the purposes of proselytization. Such efforts were restricted on the island of Zanzibar for the sake of administrative peace. By the time the Republic of Tanganyika declared its independence in 1961, the majority of its people subscribed to Christianity.

EARLY AND MODERN LEADERS Because most of the initial figures in the Christian movement in Tanzania were Europeans, it is not possible to speak of indigenous Christian leaders. Foreign missionary organizations included, from Germany, the Lutheran Berlin Mission Society, the Leipzig Mission Society, and the Moravians; from England, the Anglican Universities Mission and the Anglican Church Missionary Society; and from France, the Catholic Holy Ghost Fathers. By the end of the twentieth century the hierarchies of all Christian denominations represented in Tanzania had been Africanized. During the process the Catholic Church also Africanized the past to some extent by canonizing indigenous East African saints. Contemporary church leaders in Tanzania include the Evangelical Lutheran bishop Samson Mushemba; Donald Leo Mtetemela, the Anglican archbishop and primate of Tanzania; and Cardinal Polycarp Pengo (born in 1944), the archbishop of Dar es Salaam since 1992.

MAJOR THEOLOGIANS AND AUTHORS Although there have been many articulate and literate Christian leaders from every denomination in Tanzania, it is not possible to identify any who have had an influence on Christian theology in general. This situation might well change if and when indigenous leaders of separatist Christian churches become more articulate in representing a regional African perspective.

HOUSES OF WORSHIP AND HOLY PLACES Upon their arrival in Tanzania, German Lutheran missionaries began to build a cathedral in the colonial capital, Dar es Salaam. At the same time the Anglicans built a massive cathedral on the site of the former slave market in Zanzibar town. (The eradication of slave trading from the area had provided the British with a Christian rationale for their protectorate.) Both stone structures still stand today, while more modest places of worship dot the countryside. No community of Christians in Tanzania would feel worthy without such gathering sites.

WHAT IS SACRED? There are no notions of the sacred among Tanzanian Christians that are distinct from those of orthodox Christianity. Belief in the soul and in an afterlife, the nature of which is determined by the moral worth of a person's life in this world, is central to the belief system of Tanzanian Christians.

HOLIDAYS AND FESTIVALS Because Christian religious holidays tend to coincide with seasonal changes celebrated by pre-Christian societies in the Northern Hemisphere, some of them have less significance in tropical Tanzania. This discordance is particularly evident at Christmas, which is more an expression of industrialized consumerism in many parts of the world than it is a holy day. As celebrated in Tanzania, Christmas has more to do with spiritual reflection than with the exchange of consumer goods. Easter is of greater importance to Tanzanian Christians. Sunday for most Christians—Saturday for Seventh-day Adventists—is recognized as a day of rest, church attendance, and separation from normal activities.

MODE OF DRESS Christians in Tanzania usually wear Western dress.

DIETARY PRACTICES Although pork is not prohibited, many Tanzanian Christians avoid eating it, with the usual explanation that it is unclean.

RITUALS Tanzanian Christians engage in the usual Christian sacramental rituals from birth to death, with the exception of matrimony. Church weddings often take place after years of cohabitation because of the expenses involved in getting married. These financial burdens often combine the traditional bridewealth exchange with the expenses that accompany contemporary weddings. The amount of wealth required is usually beyond the reach of the average young male, who must bear both fiscal responsibilities.

RITES OF PASSAGE Christian rites of passage in Tanzania coincide with the Christian life-cycle rituals that are typically marked by sacraments. They are generally orthodox ceremonies, except for marriage rites, which often include some local customs. The addition of indigenous cultural elements to the marriage ceremony is determined by the customary principle of descent. For example, in a patrilineal society such as is the norm in Tanzania, the groom offers bridewealth to the bride's family, and his kin carry out a symbolic capture of the bride before the wedding. Both actions express the loss of the young woman by her own kin group.

MEMBERSHIP Membership in a Christian church in Tanzania requires either conversion, which has become increasingly rare, or baptism. Continued membership in a congregation entails active participation in church affairs, both religious and social. Contributions to the general welfare are also expected at church services, even if they are in the form of fruits of the land.

SOCIAL JUSTICE There is a well-defined emphasis among Tanzanian Christians on helping less fortunate members of the community. This inclination, which is more an expression of tradition than of Christian ideals, is usually referred to as the "economy of affection." Its informal economic arrangements involve the distribution of individual wealth among family and other kin.

Not to engage in this system would signal a rupture with the community and create a social stigma.

SOCIAL ASPECTS Christian churches have done little to challenge the patriarchal nature of most traditional Tanzanian social practices, such as male-only inheritance customs, and Christianity has weakened the structure of matrilineal societies. The latter, though not matriarchal, did place a greater emphasis on gender equality.

POLITICAL IMPACT Although Tanzania's government and political parties are secular, organized religion represents a challenge to the federation of Tanganyika and Zanzibar. As the mainland contains both the majority of the population and the majority of Christians, while the island population is almost entirely Muslim, political and economic tensions between the two areas have led to expressions of Muslim political dissent.

CONTROVERSIAL ISSUES The educational, economic, and political advantages that accrued to the Christian community as the result of colonialism have been a sensitive issue since Tanzania achieved independence. Tourism, important to the mainland economy and relatively insignificant but more noticeable on Zanzibar, is another point of contention. Island residents take issue with the presumed corrupting Western Christian influence of this activity on their Islamic culture.

CULTURAL IMPACT Indigenous artistic expression, particularly in music, has been adapted to Christian rituals. On the other hand, dance, which was and continues to be an integral feature of Tanzanian artistic culture, has been deemphasized and finds scant room in Christian expression.

ISLAM

DATE OF ORIGIN Seventh–thirteenth century
NUMBER OF FOLLOWERS 14.5 million

HISTORY According to some Arabic documents, pre-Islamic Arab urban trading communities on the East African coast—from Somalia in the north to Mozambique in the south—accepted the new faith emanating from the Arabian Peninsula before the end of the seventh century. Although this assertion is debatable, the chronology suggests that some sections of coastal Tanzania, such as the southern town of Kilwa, are among the oldest Muslim communities in the world. It is more certain that, as a result of increased cultural contact with the Arab and Persian Islamic world, most of the Tanganyikan littoral was predominantly Sunni Muslim by the thirteenth century. Although large expanses of the hinterland still remained untouched by Islam, by the eighteenth century some interior trading station communities as far west as the present-day Congo had become Islamic. The establishment of European colonialism in the late nineteenth century allowed for the spread of Islam to the interior. (There was also a small influx of Indian Muslims later during the period of the British Mandate.) This incursion of European culture also provided, however, a strong alternative to Islam, which no longer necessarily conveyed political and economic superiority. The result was the development of a multireligious mainland, where the Islamic faith was less influential.

EARLY AND MODERN LEADERS That the ancient roots of Islam were in Tanzania's coastal region meant that the identities of the merchants, traders, and *walimu* (teachers) who spread the faith became lost during the colonial period. In the initial stages of colonial rule there was a revival of Islam in response to external European influences. At the coastal mainland settlement of Bagamoyo, letters claiming that the Day of Judgment was near, which were said to have originated in Mecca, called for a rejection of European values. The message was circulated by Abu Bakr bin Taha, an influential *mwalimu* and imam (prayer leader), who achieved some notoriety as a result. At the same time, the Qadiriyya brotherhood was brought to Zanzibar from Mecca by Sheikh Husein bin Abdallah, and another Qadiriyya branch from Somalia was introduced, led by Uways bin Muhammad. Devotion to saints, although not unknown on Zanzibar, is less common than in other parts of the Muslim world, which is one reason for the relative dearth of information on religious figures there.

MAJOR THEOLOGIANS AND AUTHORS Although the area that is now Tanzania has ancient Islamic roots and a centuries-old Arabic literate tradition, it has not produced a major religious authority.

HOUSES OF WORSHIP AND HOLY PLACES The usual Muslim place of worship in Tanzania is the mosque—or *mskiti* in Swahili, a language with a strong association with Islam owing to its being the language of Tanzania's coast. Despite the relative poverty of Muslims in comparison with Christians, particularly on the mainland, each and every Muslim community endeavors to erect a place of worship, even if it is made with only the simplest natural materials.

WHAT IS SACRED? There are no local notions of the sacred that are distinct from those of Islamic orthodoxy.

HOLIDAYS AND FESTIVALS Tanzanian Muslims recognize and, ideally, abide by the orthodox liturgical calendar, which includes observing the Ramadan fast and the feast at its conclusion, Id al-Fitr. On Id al-Fitr a congregational prayer is followed by familial or domestic celebrations initiating the month of Shaban.

MODE OF DRESS As European dress is associated with Christianity in Tanzania, Arabic couture is associated with Tanzanian Islam. For men this may entail a long shirtlike garment, which is usually worn over another shirt, as well as trousers. Alternatively, men may don a piece of cloth called a *kanzu,* which is wrapped around the waist and worn with a shirt. A cap called a *kofía* is worn as a de rigueur symbol of the faith. For women on Zanzibar and the coast, the public costume may be a dramatic black garment, referred to as a *buibui* (Swahili for "spider"), that covers the body from head to toe, with slits for the eyes. Other women may wrap themselves in a series of colorful *kanzu*s, with one covering the head and part of the face.

DIETARY PRACTICES The abstention from pork among Tanzanian Muslims is total and unproblematic. It was unlikely to have been considered fit for consumption before conversion and is avoided by most Tanzanians, whatever their religion. The enjoined total abstinence from alcohol, particularly locally brewed products, is more difficult to achieve for many. Some varieties of the local beverage, concocted from grains and bananas, have been considered almost synonymous with food itself.

RITUALS Islamic rituals surrounding birth, male circumcision, marriage, and death are all conducted in accordance with the Shari'ah (Islamic law). Marriages are usually arranged by the senior males of the families involved and include the offer of bridewealth by the groom to the wife's family. The woman's consent is required, but in practice she usually has little control over the situation.

RITES OF PASSAGE Muslim rites that mark life changes, which center around the mosque and family, have replaced traditional celebrations of the life cycle.

MEMBERSHIP Becoming a member of the community, or *jamaa,* is an essential aspect of Tanzanian Islam. This status is achieved through birth or conversion and maintained by vigilant practice that is monitored by others. In a country like Tanzania, where there were some traditional differences of belief and custom, adherence to Islam provided people with a set of common expectations and practices. Adherents of Islam, a proselytizing religion, continue to try to convert practitioners of traditional religion in Tanzania.

SOCIAL JUSTICE All members of the Islamic community in Tanzania, regardless of ethnic background, are considered equal, and the tradition of almsgiving ensures that wealth, however little there is, is shared to some extent.

SOCIAL ASPECTS Reflecting its roots in the Arabian Peninsula, Tanzanian Islam reinforces local patriarchal principles regulating descent, marriage, and gender relations.

POLITICAL IMPACT As is to be expected in a country where one federal component is associated with Christianity and the other with Islam, religion has become a matter for consideration and management in the national political arena. Muslims have found themselves relatively handicapped in both political and economic affairs in the four decades since Tanzania achieved independence. The potentially explosive nature of this situation has been kept in check by a secular constitution and a de facto sharing of power.

CONTROVERSIAL ISSUES As in other parts of Africa where it is still practiced, female circumcision, or genital mutilation, is a contentious issue in Tanzania. The practice has been erroneously associated with Islam, though it actually antedates the arrival of Islam in Tanzania. Moreover, Islam does not call for the circumcision of females, and it has not been practiced on the country's Muslim coast or islands. Although legally banned, female circumcision is still engaged in by Muslim, Christian, and traditional groups in the interior, which suggests it is an indigenous cultural trait and not a religious ritual. The fact that Christian missionaries railed against the practice while Muslims ignored or condoned it as a secular matter has led to some of the confusion with regard to its origins.

CULTURAL IMPACT Arab and Islamic influences were obvious in Tanzanian literature and poetic style for centuries before the penetration of European culture. They also figured significantly in the development of the East African language and culture known as Swahili, which prevails in Tanzania. Household and some public architecture in Tanzania also reflects Arabic influence. The music and dance of Tanzanian Muslim groups still conveys more of an indigenous African flavor.

AFRICAN INDIGENOUS BELIEFS

DATE OF ORIGIN Unknown
NUMBER OF FOLLOWERS 7.4 million

HISTORY The original population of scattered hunter-gatherers in what is now Tanzania, whose surviving artworks indicate spiritual concerns, was joined about 800 years ago by Bantu-speaking agriculturalists, who filtered into the area incrementally until they formed the vast majority of the population. This Bantu incursion was followed in turn by the arrival of Cushitic-speaking agro-pastoralists from the northeast a few centuries later. Finally, after another century or two, Nilotic-speaking pastoralists who originated in the southern Sudan made their presence known in the region. These groups brought with them distinct languages and somewhat varying religious conceptions, which influenced those of other groups over time. Descriptions of these original religious experiences as paganism, totemism, animism, or polytheism indicates little more than an inclination for classification linked to a profound ignorance of these traditional systems of thought.

Notions about witches, sorcerers, and other evil and benign spirits and figures abounded among the Bantu peoples. These ideas were more a feature of a general cosmology than a religion. The indigenous theologies all recognized a high God and Creator—with a variety of manifestations—who was not as imminent or personal as the God of Judaism, Christianity, or Islam. Indeed, it was often thought that this figure had little or no interest in mundane affairs. In some instances the dead were recognized as being relevant to their living descendants, though they were not necessarily worshiped. People communicated with all representatives of the supernatural world—God and ancestors—through ritual and sacrifice as well as collective and individual prayer.

After the arrival of Islam and Christianity, the vast majority of indigenous peoples in Tanzania joined one of the two new religious groups. The main exceptions were the Masai and other pastoral peoples, who managed to hold onto to their religious ideas and indigenous cultural system in general. The Masai's conservatism has been made possible by their pastoral mode of production, which has protected them from having to adapt completely to the demands of industrial capitalism. The Masai represent traditional religion in Tanzania in its purest form and will be the focus of much of what follows.

EARLY AND MODERN LEADERS Many indigenous mainland groups in Tanzania recognized heroes with supernatural abilities, who figured in origin myths but were distinct from the Creator. With the advent of written language, the situation changed, for the actions of new heroes could now be recorded for posterity. As European influence expanded in Tanzania in the late nineteenth and early twentieth centuries, some traditional leaders rose up against the violence of the initial German colonial administration. The Maji Maji (Water Water) revolt of 1905–07, a reaction against colonialism and cultural imperialism that also opposed Christian missionaries and Arab traders, was led by the prophet Kinjikitile Ngwale (died in 1905), who claimed to be possessed by the spirit of a regional deity. Kinjikitile also proclaimed to his many followers that supernatural medicine he had received had the power to turn bullets into water, thus giving the movement its name. The Maji Maji revolt quickly spread and almost succeeded in forcing the Germans off the mainland entirely before it was subdued with enormous loss of native life. The revolt marked the end of resistance to European influence.

Among contemporary Masai, who have largely ignored rather than resisted European influence, ritual leaders for vast areas, who are called *loibon,* continue to hold sway at religious ceremonies.

MAJOR THEOLOGIANS AND AUTHORS Some Masai have engaged the larger world in different arenas, with considerable success. One of them, Tepilit Ole Saitoti (born in 1949), has given some attention to the Masai religion in his writings about his life.

HOUSES OF WORSHIP AND HOLY PLACES Among the Bantu peoples both local and regional shrines to ancestors and deities were common. These sites, which were sometimes maintained by priests, functioned as places of prayer and ritual, including animal sacrifice. For the Masai there are no specific places set aside for worship on a permanent basis. The homestead occupied by one or two adult males and their wives, children, and cattle, however, can be legitimately considered a religious space at times of daily prayer. These supplications take place at dawn and dusk, with the senior males of the settlement officiating. In addition, temporary settlements called *manyata* are constructed for grander rituals involving large groups of males who are entering a new stage in the life cycle.

WHAT IS SACRED? For the Masai cattle are conceived of as sacred in a delicate and subtle way. Although not worshiped—or even revered in ordinary settings—these animals can be sanctified at important religious ceremonies. In this state cattle, who were once heavenly creatures, become the primary means of communicating with God (Enkai), who provided the Masai with cattle as a means of subsistence. This relationship among humans, cattle, and God is consistent with the Masai's referring to themselves as "people of the cattle." Other indigenous peoples also have engaged in animal sacrifice, but the sacral nature of the beast itself was not as pronounced as in Masai rituals.

HOLIDAYS AND FESTIVALS The primary holidays for many traditional mainland groups have to do with the passage of males through the life cycle, usually beginning with circumcision, which takes place before or at the onset of puberty. In the past this event was also usually recognized later at a major collective ceremony. For females the procedure—if it took place at all—was more of a local and individual occasion. For groups that did not practice male circumcision, there was usually some other collective coming-of-age ceremony.

MODE OF DRESS For male and female Masai traditional attire is a cloak, tied at the shoulder, that reaches to the knees. The few Masai who have converted to Christianity or Islam have altered their dress accordingly, wearing Western or Arabian garb as a sign of their religious affiliation.

DIETARY PRACTICES Pastoralists generally avoid any meat except that which comes from their herds, which may include some sheep and goats in addition to cattle, which have the highest cultural and symbolic value. One of the latter is slaughtered as a sacrificial offering to God at every major ceremony.

RITUALS Male circumcision was a traditional ritual of some significance for many mainland Bantu peoples. Some of these groups may have adopted the custom from the Masai or other pastoral people. For most Bantu groups birth, marriage, and death were also significant cultural, if not ritual, occasions. For the Masai and others like them male circumcision is still a major occasion, as are other progressive moments in the male life cycle. Birth, marriage, and death, however, have little or no ritual significance.

RITES OF PASSAGE Among the Masai female circumcision is carried out on an individual basis after the naming ceremony and after the onset of puberty. The event involves a local celebration and a feast hosted by the homestead. The young woman remains secluded after the procedure and enters into an arranged marriage with a senior male shortly thereafter. At that point she moves to her husband's household, which may include other wives.

For a boy circumcision is followed by his moving from the natal community to a specially built village called a *manyat,* which is inhabited by other males who have recently had a similar experience. From here the young men roam the countryside in small groups in search of food from other homesteads. Eventually, a collective rite of passage called *eunoto,* which takes place about every seven years, is held. At the conclusion of this ceremony involving animal sacrifices and blessings, the boys are recognized collectively as members of an age grade called *moran* (warrior). These *ilmurran* may not marry until they become elders some years later at another elaborate and even more important ceremony called *olon'esher.* At this point they are recognized as adults who are able to marry, raise families, and establish their own homesteads. In all the Masai perform six rituals that accompany young men's development from the *moran* stage to that of elder.

After death, which ideally should take place outside of the homestead to avoid pollution of the home, the body is left above ground some distance away for scavengers to consume. Although there may be individual and collective grieving, this emotional response is maintained in silence, and the death and the name of the deceased are no longer mentioned.

MEMBERSHIP Ideally participation in what would best be called a ritual community was the result of birth. There were great consistencies of culture among the Bantu peoples, however, who recognized similar myths, deities, shrines, and rituals, and this led to collective practices among them. Male circumcision, for example, was a regional activity, as one Bantu group would follow another across the countryside in organizing this rite.

SOCIAL JUSTICE The redistribution system referred to as the "economy of affection," which enjoined the sharing of resources among kith and kin, was an ideal of traditional Bantu societies. The failure to abide by this arrangement could result in accusations of witchcraft, which was seen as the epitome of antisocial behavior. Pastoralists who lack this belief in witchcraft, however, are only slightly less given to redistribution. The significance of cattle—particularly as bridewealth and as a woman's means of sustaining her own children in a polygynous homestead—may underlie the pastoralist's inclination to redistribute wealth.

SOCIAL ASPECTS Chiefs were rare among indigenous peoples prior to colonization. Male elders and religious leaders were usually responsible for maintaining order through mediation and conducting communal rituals. The imposed system of chiefdoms was abolished when Tanzania became independent, but traditional ritual figures still have considerable influence in some ethnic groups, particularly in times of stress.

POLITICAL IMPACT Although in Tanzania there is no association between religion and the state, or between religion and political parties, the traditional pastoral peoples have at times been the victims of unofficial discrimination by agents of the state. This has been due in part to their unwillingness to adopt either Islam or Christianity and to reactions against pastoral expansion and conquest in the precolonial period.

CONTROVERSIAL ISSUES The continuing practice of female circumcision by the Masai and other groups is a delicate matter. Although illegal, the procedure is still carried out regularly, and the government has looked the other way. The role of women in general in Tanzania thus remains debatable, particularly in a country that has espoused socialist principles throughout most of its existence.

CULTURAL IMPACT A few indigenous groups in Tanzania have been known for their wood-carving traditions. The most famous of these are the Makonde people, who include expressions of good and evil creatures in their works. Music and dance, which are universal in Tanzania, continue to have a secular flavor.

Other Religions

There are small groups of Hindus and Sikhs in mainland cities who migrated to Tanzania during the British colonial period, primarily as low-level civil servants or traders. Many emigrated after the country became independent because the new government abolished private religious schools in the name of socialist democracy. (Such schools have since become permissible again.) Temples were unaffected by the legislation, so those Sikhs and Hindus who remained have continued to form viable religious communities that are characterized by a high degree of endogamy and traditional religious orthodoxy.

William Arens

See Also Vol. I: *African Traditional Religions, Christianity, Islam*

Bibliography

Arens, W. "Islam and Christianity in Sub-Saharan Africa." *Cahiers d'Études africaines* 15 (1975): 443–56.

Århem, Kaj. *Ethnographic Puzzles: Essays on Social Organization, Symbolism and Change.* London: Athlone Press, 2000.

Iliffe, John. *A Modern History of Tanganyika.* Cambridge: Cambridge University Press, 1979.

Lewis, I.M., ed. *Islam in Tropical Africa.* London: Oxford University Press, 1966.

Saitoti, Tepilit Ole. *The Worlds of a Maasai Warrior: An Autobiography.* Berkeley and Los Angeles: University of California Press, 1986.

Spear, Thomas, and Isaria N. Kimambo, eds. *East African Expressions of Christianity.* Oxford: James Currey, 1999.

Trimingham, J. Spencer. *Islam in East Africa.* Oxford: Clarendon Press, 1964.

Thailand

POPULATION 62,354,402

BUDDHIST 90.0 percent

MUSLIM 3.0 percent

CHRISTIAN 0.5 percent

HINDU 0.1 percent

OTHER 6.4 percent

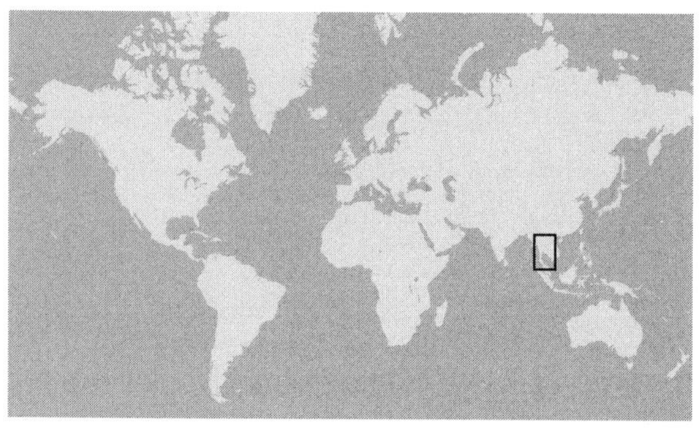

Country Overview

INTRODUCTION Situated along the southeastern rim of continental Asia, the Kingdom of Thailand is bordered by four countries: Myanmar to the west, Laos and Cambodia to the east, and Malaysia to the south. Its southern peninsular region is flanked to the east by the Gulf of Thailand and to the west by the Andaman Sea and the Strait of Malacca. Much of Thailand is economically undeveloped. Its climate is tropical, its terrain is mountainous, and rivers have traditionally provided the most common travel routes through the country. Thailand's port cities lured traders from India, whose ships also took Buddhist missionaries to Thailand.

Theravada Buddhism, which originated about 2,000 years ago in Thailand, has some 56 million followers there. Animism, which has the second largest following, is practiced by indigenous tribal peoples as well as by tribal refugees from neighboring countries. Thai-speaking Muslims live mainly in the Bangkok region, but Malay-speaking Thai Muslims are found predominantly in southern Thailand on the Malay Peninsula, an area that was formerly a Malayan sultanate. Other religions in Thailand are Christianity, which first appeared in the seventeenth century, and Hinduism, which dates back nearly 2,000 years.

Unlike neighboring mainland Southeast Asian countries, Thailand was never a European colony, and the Thai do not blame the West for debasing local culture and religion. As a result, Thai Buddhist monks do not call for a revival of the past and may pursue Western secular knowledge. The modern Thai state has used the sangha (community of Buddhist monks) to legitimize its authority, but it has not done so to promote a national ideology.

RELIGIOUS TOLERANCE Although Buddhism is popularly viewed as the national religion, Thai society maintains a secular tolerance of other religions, thereby reflecting a Buddhist emphasis on the responsibility of individuals to make their own moral choices. For example, although Christian converts in southern Thailand were drawn mainly from the ethnic Chinese and Vietnamese rather than Thai populations, the Thai elite have customarily enrolled their children in Christian schools. This has enabled Thai Christians to assume important posts in the military, in commerce, in the government bureaucracy, and at universities. In northern Thailand, where many tribal peoples have converted to Christianity, divisions between Thai Buddhists and tribal Christians are more informed by ethnic, as opposed to religious, grounds. Malay-speaking Muslims often do profess an alienation from Thai society, but a major reason for this may be seen in the fact that they face limited educational opportunities, since Thai is the language of instruction.

Monks line up to receive food from a Thai Buddhist. A chief means of merit-making for women is to offer food and alms to monks. Thai Buddhists view such activities as another aspect of a mother's role as nurturer. © KEVIN R. MORRIS/CORBIS.

Major Religion

THERAVADA BUDDHISM

DATE OF ORIGIN First century C.E.

NUMBER OF FOLLOWERS 56 million

HISTORY Before the thirteenth century the territory of Thailand was divided between two Theravada Buddhist kingdoms: the Mon's Dvaravati kingdom in the north and the Khmer in the south. Thai-speaking people may have begun to migrate as early as the seventh century from the region of southern China to what is now Thailand, where they were strongly influenced by the Hindu-Buddhist Khmer and the Buddhist Mon.

The first independent Thai kingdom was Sukhothai, which was a flourishing center of Buddhist civilization during the thirteenth and fourteenth centuries. Ram Kamheng, Sukhothai's third king, erected a pillar in 1292 written in the script he devised for the Thai language, declaring, among other things, his and his people's devotion to Buddhism. A sect of Buddhism new to Southeast Asia, Sinhalese Theravada Buddhism, was introduced to southern Thailand and came to exert a strong influence on Sukhothai art, architecture, and religion. Sukhothai kings established close ties with Sinhalese Buddhism and Sri Lanka (Ceylon). Monks from Sukhothai sought teachings from Sinhalese Buddhist masters, were reordained in the Sinhala tradition, and returned to establish Sinhalese Buddhism in Sukhothai. Ram Kamheng's son and successor, Lo Tai (c. 1299–1346), was known as Dharmaraja (king of dharma) because of his devotion to Buddhism.

Lo Tai's son, Lu Tai, was a Buddhist scholar who became Dharmaraja II in 1347. He dramatized the close relationship between the king and the sangha by undergoing ordination as a monk to become a "world renouncer" and then returning to his throne to reassume the role of "world conqueror," or king. The Sukhothai representation of the relationship between the throne and the sangha can also be seen in the plan of the city of Sukhothai. The palace was located close to the city's main temple. These buildings were surrounded by a series of concentric walls, symbolizing the idea that the king and the temple formed a duality at the center of the cosmos. The city plan also gave rise to a categorical distinction between city-dwelling and forest-dwelling monks.

Another Thai kingdom, Lan Na, and its capital, Chiang Mai, emerged during the thirteenth century in northern Thailand. Lan Na was itself a center for Theravada Buddhist culture and the dissemination of Theravada Buddhism to other regions of Thailand. Lan Na was part of the Burman empire from the sixteenth to the nineteenth century.

The Ayutthaya kingdom (1351–1767) eventually unified much of present-day Thailand and was referred to by its neighbors as Siam. The Siamese capture of Angkor resulted in their assimilation of aspects of Khmer culture and the Hindu practices of the Khmer royal cult. The rulers of Ayutthaya, nonetheless, continued to be staunch supporters of Theravada Buddhism and sent Buddhist missions to Sri Lanka. The Ayutthayan era came to an end in 1767 when the Burmese attacked and captured the royal family. The military leader Taksin rebuffed the Burmese invasion and located his new capital at Thon Buri, near Bangkok.

The first king of the Chakri dynasty, Rama I, who reigned from 1782 to 1809, directed himself to restoring the heritage of the former Ayutthaya kingdom. He assigned learned monks the task of recording and editing the *Traipitok* (in the Pali language, *Tipitika*) and expelled members of the sangha who violated disciplinary rules or endorsed Taksin's claims to be a bodhisattva (a future buddha). Rama IV (Mongkut), who reigned from 1851 to 1868, was previously a monk himself and promoted attention to textual knowledge, monastic discipline, and the elimination of noncanonical rituals in his efforts to purify Buddhism. He founded the Thammayut sect, which was to become the model for Buddhist reform during the reign of Chulalongkorn (Rama V). Chulalongkorn's younger brother, Prince Vajirañana, had entered the monastic order and become head of the Thammayut sect. Prince Vajirañana developed a standard system of monastic education to help unify Thailand's sangha into a Thammayut order.

In 1902 Chulalongkorn instituted the Sangha Act, establishing the sangha as a unified body under a supreme patriarch who would be appointed by the king. Under this act only monks who were authorized by the supreme patriarch could ordain new monks, and those entering the monastic order were required to register with the sangha authorities. Resistance to the Sangha Act on the part of a revered northern Thai monk eventually led to the monk's recognition of the sangha authoritie's control over monastic ordination in exchange for their permitting the continuation of the traditional ritual practices of northern Thai Buddhists. The royal promotion of a unified sangha and standardized monastic curriculum laid the foundation for Buddhist nationalism. The Sangha Act of 1941, prompted by the transformation of an absolute monarchy into a constitutional monarchy in 1932, regulated the sangha's expenditures, limited monastic political activity, and democratized monastic authority. A third Sangha Act was put forth in 1963 by Thailand's Prime Minister Sarit to reverse some of the reforms of 1932. The 1963 act eliminated the democratic features of the previous act—powerful ecclesiastical organizations—and centralized monastic power in a supreme patriarch.

Contemporary Buddhist practice in Thailand incorporates the growing popularity of the meditation taught by the forest monastic schools and also the development of reform movements that promote either unconventional meditation techniques, puritanism, or ecological awareness and social justice.

EARLY AND MODERN LEADERS Mongkut (Rama IV; 1804–68), who emphasized the importance of orthodoxy in such matters as ordination rituals, the creation of ritual space, the wearing of robes, and the pronunciation of the Pali language, founded a movement that became known as Thammayut, meaning "those who follow the law." He raised the standard of monastic education, established a printing press to disseminate Pali texts, and strove to purify the canon. Mongkut is credited with reviving intellectual and scholarly interest among Thailand's sangha.

At the beginning of the twentieth century the forest monk tradition was revived by Phra Ajaan Mun Bhuridatta Mahathera (1870–1949), who was revered as a great meditation master, teacher, and perfected saint, and his teacher, Phra Ajaan Sao Kantasilo Mahathera (1861–1941). Contemporary Buddhist leaders who may be associated with *araññavasi* (rural and forest-dwelling monks) include Bodhiraksa, the leader of the controversial Santi Asoke sect, which advocates strict vegetarianism, refusal of monetary donations, and a simple lifestyle. Another such leader is Sulak Sivaraksa (born in 1933), who has actively campaigned and been persecuted for his promotion of a socially engaged Buddhism that fosters grassroots movements and rural development projects that are based on principles of Buddhist ethics.

A modern sect in the *gamavasi* (city monk) tradition emerged in the 1970s when Metanando (born in 1956), Dhammajayo (born in 1944), and Phadet Pongswardi (born in 1941) developed Dhammakaya teachings into an institutionalized, urban-oriented movement. The Dhammakaya meditation techniques are unorthodox and controversial.

MAJOR THEOLOGIANS AND AUTHORS The major contemporary theologians of Theravada Buddhism in Thailand are not part of the sangha establishment and, therefore, have often been controversial. Phra Ajaan Mun Bhuridatta Mahathera, who revived the forest monk tradition, believed that salvation lay with practicing, rather than studying, the scriptures. Phra Ajaan Lee

Dhammadharo Mahathera (1907–61) authored many commentaries and introduced the forest monk tradition to urban Thai society. Buddhadhasa Bhikku (1906–93) began to gain renown in the 1950s for his teachings and writings on how Buddhists can cultivate moral behavior and attain salvation while living in, as opposed to escaping from, worldly existence. Since the 1970s Caokhun Rajavaramuni (born in 1939) has produced major scholarly works that locate the bases for ethical responsibility and social justice in the Buddhist scriptures.

HOUSES OF WORSHIP AND HOLY PLACES A house of worship in Thailand is known as a *wat,* the term for a building complex including a monastery, temple, and *chedi* (stupa). Wat That Phanom Chedi, Wat Phra Singh, and Wat Phra That Doi Suthep are 3 of 12 shrines that are particularly sacred because they are reputed to have been visited by the Buddha or to contain his relics. Each of these shrines is associated with one of the years of the 12-year cycle. On their birthdays and 12-year anniversaries, pilgrims visit the particular shrine associated with their birth year. The Phra Pathom Chedi Ratchaworawiharn, the tallest *chedi* in Thailand, built to commemorate the arrival of Buddhist missionaries from India in the third century B.C.E., is among the most popular pilgrimage sites. Other particularly noteworthy pilgrimage destinations include Wat Phra Kaew in Bangkok, which houses the Emerald Buddha; Wat Pho in Bangkok, which encloses the reclining Buddha; the Phra Puddhabat temple in Suraburi province, which is associated with the most important of the Buddha's footprint relics in Thailand; and Wat Phra Maha That Woramaha Wihan, situated in southern Thailand and purported to have been transported from Sri Lanka 2,000 years ago. Caves and rock formations associated with the Buddha's journeys are also significant pilgrimage destinations.

The foundation pillar of the city of Bangkok is surrounded by a shrine dedicated to guardian deities and is revered as a guardian deity itself. The pillar and the guardian deities receive offerings from the daily crowds who seek favors.

WHAT IS SACRED? In Thailand amulets may represent images of the Buddha or of various types of animals and beings. If sacralized by monks, amulets become repositories of spiritual power. Amulets that have been blessed by forest saints are the most highly valued. Laypeople believe that the spiritual power of the monks is transmitted to the possessor of the amulet and will ensure the success of the owner's ventures.

Certain images of the Buddha are credited with extraordinary powers. Thai kings have attributed their victories in battle, the legitimacy of their reign, and the protection of their territory to four of Thailand's most famous statues: the Sinhala Buddha, the Jinasīha Buddha, the Jinarāja Buddha, and the Emerald Buddha. King Rama I brought the Emerald Buddha from Laos, installed it as the protector of the Thai kingdom, and officiated at seasonal ceremonies when the statue's clothing and ornaments were changed. The Emerald Buddha is said to ensure prosperity when the rulers observe virtuous conduct but to move itself to a better location should the ruler not be righteous.

Following the cremation of kings of the Chakri dynasty, bone fragments found in the ashes became sacred relics that legitimated the authority of successive monarchs. Some of the bone fragments were given to the former king's children to be worn in gold lockets, and the remaining fragments were encased in a gold container and conveyed to the palace.

HOLIDAYS AND FESTIVALS The timing of major *wat,* or temple, ceremonies is closely interlinked with the rice agricultural cycle. The Songkran Festival, held over three days in April, at the end of the dry season, celebrates the traditional New Year and includes such events as the bathing of Buddha images, demonstrating respect for elders by pouring scented water over their hands, and visiting temples and offering food to monks. Wisaka Bucha, which occurs as rains begin and fields are ploughed, marks the day of the birth, enlightenment, and death of the Buddha. Asarna Bucha commemorates the Buddha's first sermon after attaining enlightenment. The following day is observed as Buddhist Lent Day, the start of the three-month rain retreat for monks. At the conclusion of Buddhist Lent, rains will have ceased and rice will be maturing. The ceremony held at this time, Bun Kathin, marks the emergence of monks and novices from their rain retreat and is the occasion for monks and novices to receive collective offerings of robes and gifts. Following this ceremony many monks and novices resume a lay life. Makha Bucha, held at harvest time in the third lunar month, honors the occasion of one of the Buddha's most important sermons.

MODE OF DRESS Traditional dress for Buddhist women in central and southern Thailand consists of a *pasin,* a long skirt or sarong typically made of silk, and a long- or short-sleeved silk blouse, which may be adorned with a sash on formal occasions. Buddhist men wear trousers and a long- or short-sleeved shirt with a high, uncollared neck. On formal occasions men tie cummerbunds about their waists.

White robes are worn by nuns and novices. White clothing is also worn by the laity to symbolize their upholding of the eight precepts or ethical guidelines (*pancha shila*) on Buddhist holidays. Laymen residing at forest monasteries wear white pants and shirts, and laywomen, white shirts and black skirts. Monks generally wear yellow robes made of pieces of cloth stitched together, but forest monks wear robes of a dark brown color.

DIETARY PRACTICES Although Thai monks may observe a strict vegetarian diet, Theravada Buddhism does not prescribe vegetarianism.

RITUALS Worship practices include offerings, prayer, and physical prostration to a physical or mental image of the Buddha or to his relics enshrined in a pagoda. Prayer consists of the recitation of memorized chants in the Pali language, which is unknown to most of the laity. Many who have had no monastic training, however, know the appropriate context for a particular chant. Sermons, which have been translated into Thai, are standardized texts delivered during calendrical temple festivals or Buddhist Lent.

Meditation is not taught at most of Thailand's *wat,* and most monks do not practice it. Some *wat,* however, may harbor individual monks who have become meditation masters and who attract large followings of disciples, many of them laypersons. Forest hermitages, on the other hand, are renowned for their focus on meditation.

On the morning of a Thai Buddhist wedding, the couple offers food to monks to receive their blessing. During the wedding ceremony, monks recite Buddhist scriptures. The couple offers their respect to senior relatives, who bind the couple's hands together with a sacred white cord or a garland of flowers. This action represents the binding of the couple's spirit essence and, therefore, good fortune for the marriage. Another monk or a senior relative conveys blessings to the couple by pouring water over their hands.

Thai Buddhist funeral rituals enable merit-making for the living but are directed toward the fate of the *winjan,* the soul that takes rebirth. Shortly after a death the corpse must be cleaned and dressed by relatives. Water is poured on the hands of the deceased to pay respect. The corpse's head must point to the west, the direction of death, and a number of articles used by the deceased are placed by the head of the corpse for the deceased to take with him or her to the cemetery. Monks arrive to generate merit for the deceased and to reconstitute the bodily elements, the mind, and the soul, which are scattered at death. Once the corpse is removed from the house, precautions are taken to prevent the *winjan* from finding its way back. Puffed rice, symbolizing the belief that the *winjan* will not be reborn as the same person, is strewn along the path to the cemetery. The coffin is circumambulated three times in a counterclockwise direction around the funeral pyre.

On the day following the cremation, rituals are performed to purify the *winjan* and direct it to its next rebirth. This involves, among other rites, collecting the bones from the ashes, placing them in a pot, and washing them with scented water. Monks lead the funeral procession and officiate at the cremation and the dispatching of the *winjan.* In the case of accidental death the body must be buried as opposed to cremated to protect the living from the possibility that the *winjan* has become a dangerous ghost. The burial is conducted quickly, without ritual elaboration. Once the deceased is buried, monks are invited to recite prayers for three nights and conduct rituals to transfer merit to the deceased and protect the living. After several months or years the corpse is considered safe to disinter and cremate. Following this the bones are processed according to the rites of normal funerals.

RITES OF PASSAGE Thai Buddhists engage in several important ritual complexes that are not performed by Buddhist monks. Rituals to retrieve or secure the *khwan* (a kind of spiritual essence or secondary soul) are associated with rites of passage and officiated by lay elders. For example, a "soul retrieval" ritual is performed for the *khwan* of a pregnant woman and her fetus, for monks about to enter their Lenten season retreat, for people about to depart on or return from long journeys, for young men joining or leaving military service, for illness or for recovering from illness, and for counteracting bad luck. In villages, khwan ceremonies are performed at marriages to ensure marital stability.

Novicehood or monkhood may constitute a rite of passage in itself for Thai males, since the roles of novice or monk may be assumed for short durations. Thai males are expected to undergo one or both of these monastic initiations in order to make merit for their parents or relatives. Ordination ceremonies occur just prior to the Lenten season. The candidate for monkhood is referred to as a *nag* (from the Sanskrit *naga,* a water spirit associated with fertility and rain), symbolizing the virility and secular life the monk will renounce. A *sukhwan* ritual is performed the day prior to the ordination ceremony to give the initiate confidence to assume his new status. At the completion of his ordination, the new monk pours water, which symbolizes the transfer of the merit he has acquired to his parents and relatives. They, in turn, may pour water to transfer the merit they have just received to their ancestors. Monks who decide to return to secular life undergo a derobing ceremony.

MEMBERSHIP Buddhist missionaries are encouraged in Thailand and have been active in Thailand's tribal regions as well as in the West. The emergence of Thai Buddhist missions in the West grew from Phra Ajaan Chah, a noted forest monk, who established a *wat* in 1975 to accommodate his many Western disciples. He set up a sangha in England, which became a branch monastery of his Thai *wat* in 1979, and more branch monasteries emerged in succeeding years in Europe, Australia, and New Zealand. Other forest monks established monasteries in England and the United States. Buddhist websites, used to recruit new members, began to appear in the 1990s.

SOCIAL JUSTICE As a national monastic organization, the sangha has come under public criticism for its refusal to address organizational reform and social justice issues. On the local level, however, several influential Thai monks have endeavored to promote human rights and counter drug abuse, economic exploitation, and environmental degradation by introducing agricultural and environmental reforms to create self-sustaining communities that are oriented toward Buddhist ethics.

In northern Thailand several monks have established hospices for AIDS patients and participated in projects to educate villagers about HIV transmission and AIDS. The Sangha Metta (Compassionate Monks) Project was initiated in 1998 by a lay Buddhist teacher to train monks and nuns as educators in the prevention and social management of AIDS. The abbots of many *wats,* however, do not permit monks to assist AIDS patients within the *wat* compounds, and monks following the forest monk schools of the northeast have no contact with AIDS patients.

SOCIAL ASPECTS Ideally every Thai Buddhist male should take the vows of monkhood for however short the period. Experiencing monkhood is believed to instill an enduring moral sense in a man. Women desire to marry such men, and a girlfriend is likely to be the first person to greet a young man departing from the monastery and his monastic life at the end of a Buddhist Lenten season. Entering the monastery enables a man to create significant merit for his parents, who typically sponsor his monastic initiation. During his first year in the monastery, a monk generates merit for his mother. Should he remain longer, he earns merit for both parents.

A chief means of merit-making for women is to offer food and alms to monks. Thai Buddhists view such activities as another aspect of a mother's role as nurturer.

POLITICAL IMPACT Since the sangha was established as a national institution in 1902, the state has used it to legitimize the state's authority. Monks performed Buddhist rituals at official state functions, taught in state-sponsored schools, and, during a time of unrest in the 1960s, were dispatched as missionaries to tribal areas. One of the sangha's concerns was the relative success of Christian missionaries in tribal regions. By the 1970s, however, some distinguished monks chose not to serve the state's interests and supported student and labor groups that were engaged in confrontations with the government. Other monks during this time advocated the killing of communists.

The revitalization of the forest monk tradition, as a tradition distinct from the sangha hierarchy, in the 1950s and 1960s initially inspired state suspicion that the forest monks might constitute a communist movement, but in the 1970s the royal family's public support of masters of the forest monk tradition transformed the government's perspective. This continued a longstanding Thai royal tradition to lay claim to the legitimacy of their rule by supporting a purified sangha. The state has not, however, used the sangha to promote a national ideology.

CONTROVERSIAL ISSUES Although women in Thailand can become nuns, they continue to be excluded from higher ranks in the Buddhist hierarchy and are popularly perceived as unlikely to attain salvation. Public attention has been drawn recently to sexual misconduct on the part of monks.

CULTURAL IMPACT Buddhists in Thailand introduced several innovative gestures in Buddhist images. During the ninth century the Mon created standing images of the Buddha displaying the teaching gesture with both hands and images of the Buddha riding on a mythical animal. Bronze sculptures of long-limbed walking Buddhas, which had been exceedingly rare in Buddhist cultures, were characteristic of the Sukhothai period (mid-thirteenth to mid-fifteenth century). King Rama III's desire to systematize Buddhist iconography gave rise to three interpretations of the Buddha's gesture of reassurance. The modern trend in Thailand has been to adopt a naturalistic style of Buddha image.

Sukhothai architecture was influenced by Khmer, Mon, Burmese, and Sinhalese styles, but the Thai developed a distinct type of building that placed a small stupa on top of a Khmer-like conical tower set into a Burmese-style temple foundation. The structure, referred to as a "temple containing a great relic," was situated in the center of the ancient cities of the Sukhothai kingdom.

One genre of folk theater, the *lakon jatri,* enacts the story of the Buddha's birth.

Other Religions

Thai villagers subscribe to guardian spirit cults. Spirits (*phii*) are believed to be responsible for rain and agricultural fertility but also for affliction. Ancestral spirits retaliate against moral infringements by their living descendants by causing illness. Such illnesses are typically diagnosed by mediums, who are often women, and treated by placating the spirit. Malevolent spirits, on the other hand, are believed to take possession of their victims and must be addressed by exorcists.

Several nationwide festivals honor non-Buddhist deities or spirits. For example, the Loy Krathong Festival honors the water goddess and is held on the full-moon night of the 12th lunar month. People float lotus-shaped offerings on rivers, lakes, or ponds to pay their respect to the life-giving power of water and to apologize for polluting it. The Rocket Festival, held in northeastern Thailand in May, propitiates a swamp spirit and village guardian spirits to ensure rain for the agricultural season.

During the ninth to thirteenth centuries the Khmer empire expanded to include about half of what is modern Thailand, bringing the Thai into close contact with a Hindu-influenced Khmer civilization. The Thai subsequently incorporated Hindu elements into court rituals, their performing arts, and literature. The king of Ayutthaya, following his conquest of the Khmer, adopted, among other Khmer Hindu practices, the cult of the *devaraja,* or god-king. The influence of Hindu ritual on the Thai royal court is continued in modern Thai royal ceremonies. Ten Brahman priests are associated with the current royal household and attend the single Brahman temple in Bangkok. Their responsibilities include officiating at the king's coronation, the king's birthday, the Ploughing Ceremony (a brahmanical ritual marking the beginning of the rice-growing season), the seasonal changing of the Emerald Buddha statue's attire, and the celebration of Siva's annual return to earth.

The first Christian missionaries in Thailand were Jesuits visiting the court of Ayutthaya in the seventeenth century, but Christianity was not to have a noticeable presence in Thailand until a greater influx of Christian missionaries was permitted in the nineteenth century. Most of Thailand's 312,000 Christians are Catholic.

Marcia Calkowski

See Also Vol. I: *Buddhism, Theravada Buddhism*

Bibliography

Ekachai, Sanitsuda. *Keeping the Faith.* Bangkok: Post Books, 2001.

Gosling, Betty. *Sukhothai: Its History, Culture, and Art.* Singapore: Oxford University Press, 1991.

Keyes, Charles F. *Thailand: Buddhist Kingdom as Modern Nation-State.* Boulder, Colo.: Westview Press, 1987.

Le May, Reginald. *A Concise History of Buddhist Art in Siam.* 2nd ed. Rutland, Vt.: Charles E. Tuttle, 1962.

Ringis, Rita. *Thai Temples and Temple Murals.* Singapore: Oxford University Press, 1990.

Tambiah, Stanley J. *Buddhism and the Spirit Cults in North-east Thailand.* New York: Cambridge University Press, 1970.

———. *The Buddhist Saints of the Forest and the Cult of Amulets.* New York: Cambridge University Press, 1984.

———. *World Conqueror and World Renouncer.* New York: Cambridge University Press, 1976.

Wyatt, David K. *Thailand: A Short History.* New Haven: Yale University Press, 1984.

Togo

POPULATION 5,285,501

VODUN (VOODOO) 27 percent

ROMAN CATHOLIC 24 percent

SUNNI MUSLIM 12 percent

PROTESTANT 8 percent

AFRICAN INDEPENDENT CHURCHES 1 percent

OTHER AFRICAN INDIGENOUS RELIGIONS 28 percent

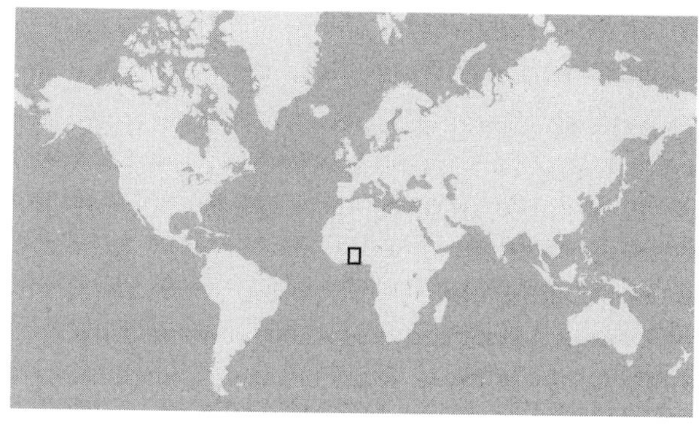

Country Overview

INTRODUCTION The Republic of Togo (République-Togolaise), situated along the Gulf of Guinea, borders Ghana to the west, Burkina Faso to the north, and Benin to the east. One of West Africa's most ethnically and religiously diverse countries, Togo is home to some 40 ethnic groups, most of which adhere to indigenous religious practices, including Vodun (Voodoo), a polytheistic, eclectic, and dynamic faith practiced among the Ewe and related ethnic groups in southern Togo.

Islam, the most prominent monotheistic religion in northern and central Togo, was introduced in the seventeenth century and is widespread among the Tsokosi, Kotokoli, Tchamba, Bariba, Fulani, Hausa, Bisa, and Dagomba. Its practice in Togo is highly syncretic and often includes the use of traditional healing methods.

German Protestants, the first successful European missionaries in Togo, arrived in 1847 and began proselytizing in the southern and coastal regions. Germany took control of the area, calling it Togoland, in 1884. After German forces surrendered to the colonial armies of Britain and France during World War I, Togoland was divided. The western section was annexed to the British Gold Coast; the eastern half, under French colonial control, became Togo. French missionaries introduced Catholicism, which displaced Protestantism as the main imported religion. At the end of World War II the United Nations invited the Ewe to vote on their political affiliation. Because the Gold Coast (to be renamed Ghana) was poised to gain independence from Britain, the Ewe under the British protectorate voted overwhelmingly to remain under British rule. The French pressured the Togolese Ewe not to participate in the measure, and the group thus is still divided by a national border. Togo became independent from France in 1960.

Togo's religious landscape is often described by its own intellectual elite as "50 percent monotheistic and 100 percent animistic," referring to the plurality of beliefs that coexist there. Inspired by former president Mobutu Sese Seko of the Democratic Republic of

The patriarch of a Temberma family offers a rooster in sacrifice for each of his family members and ancestors at an alter by his tata (sod house). © LUCILLE REYBOZ/CORBIS.

Congo (formerly Zaire), Togo's president Gnassingbe Eyadéma (born in 1935 in Kabye territory) instituted a policy of authenticity in the 1970s aimed at promoting indigenous religious practices and African identity. As a result, independent African churches appeared only toward the end of the century and have had difficulty establishing themselves. Political discontent with Eyadéma's regime in the late 1990s, however, has contributed to religious diversification, and several Pentecostal churches and new Protestant missions, many of them American, have been founded since then. Their impact remains limited.

According to official statistics, Vodun is represented by 27 percent of the population. The true percentage is probably higher, as adherence to Christianity overlaps with involvement in Vodun religion without the latter officially being declared.

RELIGIOUS TOLERANCE The Togolese government officially recognizes Roman Catholicism, Protestantism, and Islam, although none is declared a state religion. Initially most mainstream Christian churches were openly intolerant of indigenous religious forms, but the Africanization of Christianity has decreased the antagonism between the Church and local populations. Churches that once required of their members a total allegiance to Christianity now tolerate cultural practices considered part of African identity, although syncretism is not encouraged. Clashes have been reported between members of independent churches and Vodun adherents, who perceive the independent churches as neocolonial Christian proselytizers and feel that the Africanization of Christian practices depletes indigenous traditions and usurps important local identity symbols.

Togo's diversity of ethnic groups has allowed a high degree of religious tolerance among indigenous practitioners. Some practices, such as Vodun, stretch across ethnic boundaries, but more often an individual's specific indigenous religion is an ethnic marker, and proselytizing across ethnic boundaries is rare. Mixed marital unions, especially in urban centers, tend to promote adherence to Christianity or Islam alongside local religions.

Major Religions

CHRISTIANITY

VODUN

CHRISTIANITY

DATE OF ORIGIN 1847 (Protestantism) and 1922 (Catholicism)

NUMBER OF FOLLOWERS 1.72 million

HISTORY Portuguese Jesuit missionaries attempted to introduce Catholicism in southern Togo in the fifteenth century, and British and French evangelists followed in the sixteenth century, but the opposition from local populations led to insurrections each time. The German Bremen (Presbyterian) mission, established in southeastern Togoland in the mid-nineteenth century, had one of its seats in Atakpame in Ewe territory. When German Togoland was divided between Britain and France in 1922, the Bremen Mission in French-controlled Togo was renamed the Ewe Church and, later, the Église Evangélique Presbytérienne du Togo. The church fought for survival after the departure of the German missionaries. Many of the Bremen missions were taken over by French Catholic priests, and Catholicism supplanted Protestantism as the major Christian denomination in Togo. The Wesleyan Methodist Missionary Society retained a foothold in Aného. Catholicism expanded to the north, and in 1937 a new order was established in Sokodé. Catholicism became an important factor in regions such as Niamtougou, Siou, Bombouaka, Dapaong, Kandée, and Yadée.

African clergy have now replaced the French hierarchy in the Togolese Catholic Church. Catholicism is mostly practiced among the Mina in southern Togo, while Protestantism is widespread among the Chakosi (Tyokosi, Tsokosi), Mahi (Maxi), and Hwla (Xwla) in the southwest.

EARLY AND MODERN LEADERS Monseigneur Jean-Marie Cessou, one of the founders of the Catholic church in Togo, established Catholic missions in the 1920s on the sites left behind by the Germans. He also expanded the Catholic faith beyond the southern regions, establishing churches in the southeast and farther north. In 1937 Monseigneur Joseph Strebler (1892–1984) took over leadership of the church founded by Cessou in Sokodé. Monseigneur Philippe Fanoko Kossi Kpodzro (born in 1930) has served as the archbishop of Lomé and the leader of the Catholic Church in Togo since 1992.

Among Protestants, Pastor Bergi, a Swiss missionary working for the Bremen mission, retained his position in Lomé until 1921, enabling him to transfer his responsibilities to the local clergy of the Église Evhé.

MAJOR THEOLOGIANS AND AUTHORS Pastor Henry of the Wesleyan Methodist Missionary Society translated the Bible into the Mina language.

HOUSES OF WORSHIP AND HOLY PLACES The main Catholic church in Togo is in the center of Lomé. The dioceses of Atakpame in central Togo and Afagnan in the southeast are also major Catholic centers.

WHAT IS SACRED? The sacraments of baptism and the Eucharist are among the most important and sacred aspects of Catholic Christianity in Togo. Such sacraments as (monogamous) marriage may distinguish Catholics and Protestants from non-Christians, but not all Christians adhere to these.

HOLIDAYS AND FESTIVALS Togolese Christian holidays and festivals are celebrated according to the Christian calendar. Some, such as Christmas and the New Year, are official public holidays. Religious leaders make a point of inviting each other across denominations on holidays, demonstrating Togo's tolerance toward religious pluralism.

MODE OF DRESS The Catholic church advocates no particular dress code, but Sunday Mass is an important social occasion, and men often wear their Sunday best, while women put on their most striking, colorful, tailor-made dresses. Adherents of mainstream Christianity demonstrate their "modern" way of life by eschewing African dress on such occasions, a tendency that has prompted many of the newer independent churches to call for a greater acceptance of African identity among their congregations.

DIETARY PRACTICES Catholics abide by dietary rules associated with religious fasts. The Catholic and Protestant clergy denounce indigenous religions' use of libations and the consumption of meat from sacrificial animals, and they encourage their congregations to abandon such practices.

RITUALS The rituals of baptism, marriage, and death, carried out as in other parts of the Christian world, are among the most important markers of Togolese mainstream Christianity. For Roman Catholics the celebration of the Mass acts as an important acknowledgment of faith.

RITES OF PASSAGE In Togolese Christianity baptism, weddings, funerals, and other rites of passage declare adherents' membership in a wider religious context. Thus, celebrations follow universal rather than local patterns.

MEMBERSHIP The spread of Christianity in Togo depends on the churches' proselytizing activities. Catholicism relies on catechism (instruction) rather than the sacrament of baptism for its propagation. Catechists—often village-based preachers not officially ordained by the clergy—teach the basic tenets of Christianity in the local language. Often married and with children, the lay preachers are perceived by most as ordinary Togolese, whereas the celibate clergy are seen as living lives far removed from African reality. The Catholic Church mainly proselytizes in the south, where most Christians are found, leaving the north to the influence of Islam.

SOCIAL JUSTICE The advent of Christianity and its establishment of schools and other educational institutions fundamentally altered Togo's cultural landscape. Many educational institutions continue their activities under the aegis of the Church. The Church also focuses on alleviating poverty and establishing medical centers and hospitals. The Italian Catholic Mission in Afagnan runs one of the largest and best equipped hospitals in Togo, providing primary health care alongside advanced surgical facilities. Many Ewe in the region, however, view their work with suspicion, fearing that conversion will be expected in exchange for health care.

Since the 1990s the Roman Catholic Church of Togo has more openly championed social justice and human rights, though the clergy try to steer clear of open political debate and activity.

SOCIAL ASPECTS The Christian denominations insist, officially at least, on the importance of monogamy. The Catholic Church does not promote the use of contraception and advocates the moral virtues of chastity, faithfulness, and abstinence in its discourse on how to combat the spread of HIV and AIDS.

POLITICAL IMPACT In the postindependence context of President Eyadéma's one-party rule (representing the Rassemblement du Peuple Togolais, "the Rally of the Togolese People," which came to power in a military coup in 1967), the Catholic Church's championing of human rights can be seen as a major political statement. Monseigneur Kpodzro, the archbishop of Lomé, was invited to head the national assembly in charge of the democratization process, established in the aftermath of violent riots that destabilized Eyadéma's hegemony on power in 1990. Because he found his loyalty compromised, the archbishop resigned shortly after his nomination. Though Christianity—particularly Catholicism—represents the religion of Togo's intellectual elite, it sometimes challenges the authority of these same groups.

CONTROVERSIAL ISSUES The Protestant and Catholic advocacy of monogamy has stirred controversy among members and nonmembers who consider such a directive a colonial import disruptive to African values. In actuality the church has long taken a pragmatic view on the issue, often turning a blind eye to the polygynous marriages of its members: Many Christians are officially married once in church (often in the city) and enter into other marital unions in traditional ceremonies affirmed through local indigenous religious authorities. Most members of mainstream denominations do not seek to alter the official stance of the Church, while many members of independent churches, in their quest to Africanize Christianity, advocate with some controversy that polygyny be introduced into the faith. Since 1991 the Catholic Church and the major Protestant denominations have seen their authority challenged by the establishment of a number of independent churches, which have questioned mainstream Christianity's legitimacy and authenticity.

CULTURAL IMPACT Although the Roman Catholic Church originally delivered its sermons in Latin, the Protestant missions translated the Bible into Mina and Ewe as early as the late eighteenth century. The Catholic Church contributed to the spread of the French language as the lingua franca of Togo, and French and Latin still prevail within Togolese Catholicism.

Catholic and Protestant missionaries viewed traditional dancing and music with unforgiving eyes and attempted to stem such cultural practices. Christianity's impact has included the construction of churches across the capital and in other big cities, such as Sokodé and Kpalimé. The main Catholic church in Togoville is a prime example of colonial architecture, and its historical stained-glass windows vividly depict the suffering of early African martyrs.

VODUN

DATE OF ORIGIN sixteenth century C.E.

NUMBER OF FOLLOWERS 1.4 million

HISTORY Vodun religion is practiced in southern Togo among the Ewe and related ethnic groups—the Aja, Mina, Watchi, and Guen—who make up 40 percent of the population. Vodun's origins are difficult to establish, but groups to the east of Togo—the Fon of Benin and the Yoruba in Nigeria—practice similar religions. In the eighth century the first migrants arrived from the east, from Ile-Ife in Yoruba territory. Further migration occurred in the twelfth and thirteenth centuries. The historical towns of Tado and Notse (Notsie) became important political, economic, and religious centers and are believed to have played key roles in the establishment of Vodun in Togo. Notse's period of glory as the capital of the Ewe kingdom came to an abrupt end in the early seventeenth century, prompting a massive exodus of its population. The dispersion of Notse greatly contributed to the spread of religious practices to new territories. The Vodun religion in Togo has also been strongly influenced by migrations from the west and has incorporated many features present in the religious practices of western neighbors, such as the Anlo, Ga, and Akan of Ghana.

Vodun has been shaped as much by its local historical past as by the role it played in the Ewe experience of colonialism and slavery. The tacit resistance of local populations made Ewe territory difficult to penetrate by early missionaries, who preferred to settle where Vodun religion was not so strong. The influence of Christians who did stay in the region was modified by Vodun. The massive and forced migrations of the slave trade brought Vodun religion to the New World, where it is widely established in Haiti, Brazil, Cuba, and the southern United States. It has recently become part of the urban religious landscape of New York City.

Characterized by its polytheistic structure, Vodun religion accommodates a vast proliferation of deities (Vodun), each responsible for particular natural territories, animals, or illnesses. Vodun Anyigbato is the patron of the earth and is connected to the outbreak of illnesses, such as smallpox. Vodun Hevieso rules over thunder and lightning, is represented by rifles and iron rods, and is said to inflict the injuries caused by warfare. The worship of a particular Vodun runs in families and may be passed on from one generation to the next. Vodun may be forgotten then reintroduced for worship several decades later. What then appears to be an individual choice of deity can be governed by historical ties involving the group as a whole.

Shrines to Vodun are erected on behalf of the clans, and priests and priestesses tend the shrines in order to legitimate the presence of deities in the community. Many Vodun shrines are also associated with female secret societies, or possession cults, which invoke the deities through prayers. The Vodun are said to descend upon the devotees, possessing them and using them as mouthpieces to communicate the gods' intentions and desires. The secret societies celebrate female attributes, such as childbirth, menstruation, and matrifiliation (inheritance in the female line). Adherence to possession cults is most often hereditary (though new adepts may be selected by the god) and is generally passed on in the female line, from grandmother to granddaughter. A few men are included in the secret societies; they also inherit membership in the matriline (from a maternal grandmother). Unlike their female counterparts, all male devotees have to be born within the enclosure of the shrine. These men are allowed to sacrifice animals, an action prohibited to the female devotees. Priests and priestesses achieve their status by advancing through the ranks of the secret society after initiation.

EARLY AND MODERN LEADERS The leadership of Vodun shrines is kept within the clans that founded them and is passed from one generation to the next, generally patrilineally. Most shrines are associated with groups of worshipers rather than individuals, and the worship itself focuses on the personality and attributes of the gods and the clans rather than on the priests or priestesses. Yet the skills of a particular priest or priestess in healing practices or as a mediator in possession rituals may be acknowledged and praised far and wide. The shrines are a microcosm of the collective history of a particular settlement, a history that is perpetually in the making, so that new names of leaders are continually added to commemorative celebrations.

MAJOR THEOLOGIANS AND AUTHORS Every shrine leader is considered a theologian of Vodun, but the divinities themselves stand at the center of the religion.

HOUSES OF WORSHIP AND HOLY PLACES The historic Togolese towns of Notse and Vogan continue to play an important role in Vodun religion. Vodun originated in Notse, where annual rituals are held to celebrate them and bring together large congregations of followers. Vogan is the most important contemporaneous center for the celebration of Vodun, home to the most powerful shrines, the strongest congregations, and the most flamboyant possession rituals in Togo.

Every compound includes a shrine that shelters the clan's Vodun, and every village also has larger shrines for collective worship. There are also sacred forests and other sites, such as wild trees, termite mounds, and mountains, where Vodun are said to dwell.

WHAT IS SACRED? Togolese Vodun practitioners view as sacred various features of the environment: animals, plants, the sea, rivers, and natural phenomena, such as thunder, lightning, and falling meteorites. Mami Wata (also present in other parts of West Africa), goddess of wealth, financial fortune, ships, and seafaring, inhabits the sea, while Toxosu is guardian of rivers and inland waterways. The python, crocodile, chameleon, leopard, owl, and parrot hold special positions as physical manifestations of deities on earth and are thus themselves deified. Vodun also focuses on illnesses and their cure, often deifying certain conditions, such as the birth of twins and such "abnormalities" as albino children or those with Down's syndrome. These individuals are believed to be particularly close to the gods and have shrines erected on their behalf to demonstrate this link.

HOLIDAYS AND FESTIVALS Each Vodun is associated with a particular day of the week, when its name and identity are celebrated and when work is prohibited. Followers of a god must abide by specific codes of conduct and dress and adhere to taboos pertaining to food and abstinence from sexual intercourse on the god's designated day of the week.

Yearly festivals celebrate the foundation of the shrine of some deities. The effigy of the Vodun is taken out of the shrine, protected by a shroud so as not to be seen by the uninitiated, and given plant and animal concoctions to renew its powers and strengthen its association with its guardian. These ceremonies are often associated with acts of possession celebrating communion between the deity and its human followers.

MODE OF DRESS Togolese Vodun initiates and devotees use simple pieces of cloth to cover the midriff, leaving their chests bare. Clothing in the color triad of red, black, and white plays a prominent part in marking the different stages of ritual and the status of those involved. In ceremonial and everyday contexts cult leaders often dress in white. During initiation those who are "coming out" wear different colors of cloth during different stages of the ceremony; the neophytes dress in red at the beginning, are wrapped in a white shroud during one of the ceremonial acts, and appear in expensive everyday multicolored cloth at the end, marking their reintegration into society.

DIETARY PRACTICES Adherents of Vodun follow dietary prescriptions and prohibitions made by the deities themselves; in the process of setting taboos, priests and priestesses generally follow historical precedent. The Vodun generally prohibit the consumption of dog meat, as dogs are deemed to attract evil powers, but some Vodun (those included in the category of gorovodu, for example) may condone eating dog meat on specific occasions.

RITUALS The Vodun are at the center of many rituals. Some, such as initiation rituals marking the adherence of new recruits to secret societies, are held on a regular basis. Others occur only when necessary, such as healing rituals staged to ward off sudden or recurring illnesses; the rituals involve imploring divine blessings. When evil spirits or witchcraft need to be purged from a household or village, a dog is often sacrificed and the carcass left at a crossroads to attract the spirits away from inhabited areas.

Trance, experienced through possession by one or several Vodun, is also part of ritual practice. Initial experiences of possession may occur at random, but after initiation most occur on organized ritual occasions.

RITES OF PASSAGE The most dramatic rite of passage marks initiation into the secret societies (possession cults). The mostly female devotees learn to communicate with the gods and become receptacles for their spirits during possession. An initiate's new status elevates her to being the mouthpiece of the gods she embodies when possessed. She will have to abide by the taboos set by the god; others will have to tread carefully around her so as not to upset the deity. An important and often collective ritual that mobilizes all the households of the selected devotees marks the end of the initiation. The coming out ceremonies last for several days.

The performance of a ritual called *axoafa* is vital for the inclusion of an individual in the Ewe (or related) community and is a requirement for subsequent involvement in Vodun. Usually performed before a child is five, as soon as the danger of infant mortality has passed, the ritual is generally a family affair, gathering the parents, the child, and one or two grandparents. It also involves divination; consulting the oracle Afa (the deity of divination) reveals the child's destiny and life path. The child has its head shaved and is given personal advice and protective amulets. Afa divination affirms one's personal identity as an independent being and one's individual destiny and place in the cosmological order. Many Christians appeal to Afa divination without practicing Vodun.

MEMBERSHIP All members of the Ewe, Aja, Mina, Watchi, and Guen are included in the Vodun religious community. Many believe in Vodun without actively participating in religious practices. Vodun and affiliation to a shrine may become relevant when one experiences prolonged illness or misfortune, infertility, disrupted social relationships, repeated or violent deaths in the family, and the like. Membership in the secret societies is elective and requires active involvement. Because this membership is hereditary, new adepts in the female line continuously replace deceased members. Initial possession can visit one who has been selected to replace a deceased ancestress or to a new adept, whose initiation then marks the beginning of a new line of devotees. Illness and misfortune can also act as markers.

SOCIAL JUSTICE Vodun are strongly connected with Ewe morality—with notions of good and evil and with the establishment of moral codes of conduct that enhance commonality, as well as individual and collective good fortune. Devotion and worship should lead to prosperity and health. Vodun is also a system of law: Judicial matters are regularly brought to the arbitration of Vodun in order to safeguard morality. Theft, adultery, land disputes, division of property, and inheritance fall under the jurisdiction of Vodun (the protagonists may choose whether to consult the Vodun or the state courts of law).

SOCIAL ASPECTS Vodun is a highly egalitarian religion in which male and female reinforce one another in achieving the perfect representation of creation on earth. Male and female attributes are symmetrically represented in every shrine and in everyday social life. All Vodun deities operate in male and female pairs, and all households have both a male and female head. Although Ewe Vodun communities have a division of labor where men and women are allocated specific tasks (women clear the fields, while men sow and harvest them; women fetch water, and men hunt), men and women can perform tasks allocated to the other gender. Wealth is inherited in the cognatic line: women inherit their mother's wealth, while men inherit their father's.

Unlike Christianity and Islam, Vodun religion does not regulate such social institutions as the family and marriage. Marriage follows specific ritual practices that do not require the involvement of Vodun.

POLITICAL IMPACT Vodun priests are usually prohibited from officiating as kings or chiefs or holding openly political positions. Chiefs have to be approved for office, however, by the blessing of Vodun. This is done through divination: Influential priests consult the deities to confirm the choice of leaders made by humans.

Vodun has provided a powerful yet muted idiom of resistance to political authority, including colonial rule. Vodun's critical voice is often reflected in rituals of spirit possession; ridiculing political leaders, former colonial masters, and other figures of authority is a common feature of these rituals.

CONTROVERSIAL ISSUES Influenced by early missionaries, Christians often depict Vodun religion as evil, sometimes viewing it as a direct manifestation of the devil. Independent churches trying to establish themselves in southern Togo have experienced antagonism from Vodun congregations, who often perceive the discourse held by the new churches as a continuation of earlier colonial attitudes. The new churches condemn Vodun adherents for their "primitive" beliefs.

CULTURAL IMPACT Vodun permeates the lives of most inhabitants of southern Togo. Clay or concrete effigies of gods are displayed in the streets of the capital, Lomé, and along village paths. To boost business, the traders in the market in Lomé perform rituals outside their shops. The market of Bê is internationally renowned as one of the largest juju (charms or amulets made of animal and herbal concoctions) markets in West Africa. Vodun ritual ceremonies known nationally and internationally feature in folkloristic representations, tourist brochures, popular films, and other media in Togo. Many Vodun priests and priestesses have websites that display their gods, skills, and achievements.

Vodun has also influenced Western popular culture. The term "voodoo" is used to describe dark religious practices that involve zombies and little dolls laden with pins and sacrificial blood. The Rolling Stones titled one of their albums *Voodoo Lounge*, a "Voodoo Doll Kit" for the office is being sold to alleviate the stresses of modern life, and websites offer their services in sending anonymous curses to friends and enemies.

Other Religions

Kabye is Togo's second largest ethnic group, claiming 15 per cent of the population. The fact that President Eyadéma is a Kabye further enhances the group's status. The image of the Kabye wrestler and warrior stands as an icon of resistance to colonial rule. The Kabye are nationally and internationally renowned for their male initiation rituals, particularly for the warrior-like behavior encouraged by the ritual itself and promoted by the cultural authorities in charge of popularizing

Togo's traditional image. Unlike among the Ewe, Kabye male initiation is more elaborate than its female counterpart. When they are around 15 years old, boys begin their initiation by undergoing the *afalaa,* a ceremony that separates them from the female sphere by dramatically removing them from their homesteads. Four further steps take place over the next 10 years or so, including a long period of actual exile from the community. The cycle follows a gradual symbolic and pragmatic passage from childhood to adulthood, enabling the boy to marry, head a family, find work, and become involved in politics. Heavy Kabye migrations to urban centers of Togo and other countries over the past four or five decades have changed the character of the initiation. The first and last stages have become more important and are more heavily celebrated than before.

Kabye girls see their initiation as marking a change of status rather than a fundamentally altered gender identity. It announces their eligibility to marry. Generally completed over the course of a year, the initiation includes two stages. The first is marked by her fiancé's official invitation to marriage: He submits to the elders' authority, and she accepts or refuses. The second—her removal (through abduction) to her future husband's compound—occurs half a year to a year later. The lapse of time allows her to prepare for married life through instruction by female elders. It also allows for the bond to be broken if the parties consider it an incompatible union. Her abduction marks both parties' introduction to married life. The girl is physically removed, through the use of symbolic force and mock violence, from her compound. She is carried away under a blanket, all the while protesting loudly at her treatment. The abduction publicly declares the young man's commitment to his bride-to-be. Her family, usually well aware of the identity of the abductor, goes looking for her the next day, demanding her return to her parents' homestead. By putting up a fight and antagonizing her relatives, the young man signals his serious intentions and his suitability as a husband.

Independent estimates of the number of Muslims in Togo range from 500,000 to 1 million, depending on the source; the Islamic congregations put the figure at 50 percent of the total population (just as the number of Christians may be inflated by the Church). Islam is among Togo's fastest growing religions due to proselytism by resident Muslims and outsiders (Saudi Arabia and the Libyan Jamahirya have financed the building of several mosques and Islamic schools).

Islam was first introduced in northern Togo in the seventeenth century as a religion of the privileged. The first wave of conversion to Islam occurred among the Tsokosi aristocracy. The elevated status of this group was maintained through limited proselytism. In the eighteenth century various outside groups influenced the Tem in the north, and in the latter half of the century the Tidjanya Brotherhood was introduced by El Hadj al-Hassani Traore. Islam was able to flourish and expand in the northern territories during early German colonial rule through the signing of a treaty in 1907 that banned Christian missionaries from the region. In exchange Muslim leaders put large contingents of mercenaries at the Germans' disposal, to be used to fight the war against the French and British.

Though Togo's Muslim community is ethnically, culturally, and economically diverse, the most deprived groups, particularly in cities, gravitate toward Islam as a healing cult. The use of amulets containing Koranic verses and other protective texts is common, as are other practices that incorporate local medicines. Islam's representation as a religion seeking to spread social justice and fairness contributes to its expansion. Major cities and towns within and outside northern Togo have mosques; Lomé has some 30 to 40 mosques that attract local Muslims and migrants from Nigeria, Côte d'Ivoire, and Burkina Faso. Some Islamic festivals, such as Tabaski, are public holidays.

The Togolese government has long discouraged the establishment of independent churches, though an American-based denomination, the Assembly of God, was allowed in the 1940s by ecclesiastical decree to build a church and proselytize in Dapaong and subsequently in Mango (1950) and Bassar (1951). Political upheavals in the early 1990s lead to a diversification of the religious landscape, and many independent churches from Ghana, Benin, and Nigeria have established small congregations in Togo. The independent churches remain limited in number. Since 1991 the Togolese government has officially recognized around a hundred minor religious groups, most of them offshoots of the Protestant faiths.

Nadia Lovell

See Also Vol. 1: *Africian Traditional Religions, Roman Catholicism*

Bibliography

Cornevin, R. *Le Togo: Des origines à nos jours.* Paris: Académie des Sciences d'Outre-Mer, 1988.

Debrunner, H. *A Church between Colonial Powers.* London: Lutterworth Press, 1965.

Decalo, S. *Historical Dictionary of Togo.* London: The Scarecrow Press, 1996.

Delval, R. *Les Musulmans au Togo.* Paris: Publications Orientalistes de France, 1980.

Lovell, N. *Cord of Blood: Possession and the Making of Vodun.* London and Sterling: Pluto Press, 2002.

Piot, C. *Remotely Global: Village Modernity in West Africa.* Chicago and London: University of Chicago Press, 1999.

Rosenthal, J. *Possession, Ecstasy and Law in Ewe Voodoo.* Charlottesville and London: University Press of Virginia, 1998.

Toulabor, C. *Le Togo sous Eyadéma.* Paris: Éditions Karthala, 1986.

Tonga

POPULATION 106,137

FREE WESLEYAN CHURCH 35 percent

ROMAN CATHOLIC 15 percent

MORMON 15 percent

FREE CHURCH OF TONGA 10 percent

CHURCH OF TONGA 6 percent

SEVENTH-DAY ADVENTIST 4 percent

TOKAIKOLO FELLOWSHIP 3 percent

ASSEMBLIES OF GOD 2 percent

OTHER 10 percent

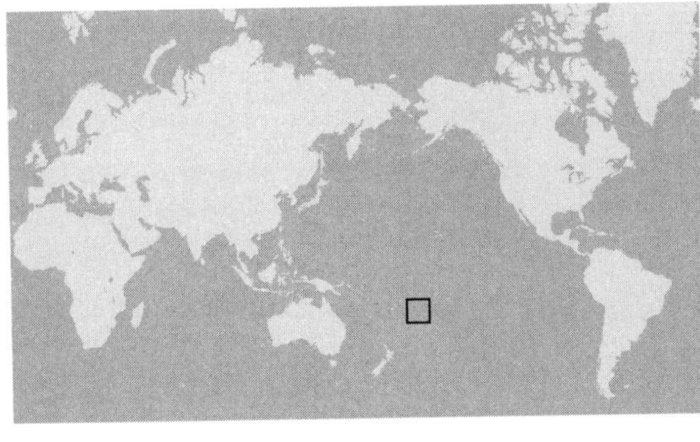

Country Overview

INTRODUCTION The Kingdom of Tonga is an archipelago of more than 150 islands in the Pacific Ocean. It lies between Samoa to northeast, New Zealand to the southwest, and Fiji to the west. A British protectorate from 1905 to 1970, Tonga has nonetheless maintained considerable independence from European colonial powers and has fostered its indigenous cultural traditions and lifestyles.

Before Western contact and the arrival of Christianity, the Tongan people adhered to a religious system that had much in common with other Polynesian religions found in Samoa, Hawaii, and elsewhere in the Pacific. At the center of this religion was a belief in a pantheon of gods, the concept of mana as the supernatural force creating good fortune and prosperity, and a system of taboo restrictions, known as *tapu,* meant to ensure balance and prosperity.

English missionaries arrived in 1826, and by the middle of the nineteenth century nearly all Tongans were converted to Christianity. Tonga was politically centralized into a monarchy. The rapid political unification of the Tongan islands led to a conversion of most of the people to Wesleyan Christianity, excluding a few chiefly factions who, in opposition to the new king, converted to the newly arrived Catholic Church. Christian converts, whether Wesleyan or Catholic, did not discard all aspects of indigenous religion. In fact, in the mid-nineteenth century Tongans began to integrate Christianity into traditional practices and belief.

Religious groups with memberships of less than 1 percent of the population include the Free Constitutional Church, the Anglican Church, Gospel Chapels, the Salvation Army, the Jehovah's Witnesses, the Church of Christ, and the New Apostolic Church. There are also small numbers of Bahais, and Muslims.

RELIGIOUS TOLERANCE Christian and non-Christian religious groups are free to practice their religion in the kingdom. Nevertheless, Christianity dominates the culture, as revealed by a weekly round of choir practices, worship services, organizational meetings, and feasts that fill the lives of a majority of Tongans. Tonga has restrictive laws concerning certain activities (such as swimming, shopping, and farming) on Sundays, when Tongans tend to turn their full attention to religious worship.

Major Religion

FREE WESLEYAN CHURCH

DATE OF ORIGIN 1826 C.E.
NUMBER OF FOLLOWERS 37,000

HISTORY The Free Wesleyan Church traces its historical heritage to the arrival of the first Wesleyan missionaries from England in 1826. The Tongan-led religious revival of 1834 was particularly important for establishing the new religion. This was followed by a religious civil war (1835–40) between the newly converted Christians and those still adhering strongly to the Tongan religion. The Christian faction, led by Chief Taufa'ahau (died in 1893), won, and Taufa'ahau (King George Tupou I) became the king of the new Tongan monarchy in 1862. By the late 1860s the monarchy had created its own legal code, and the new church had created Tupou College, an institution for the training of Tongan ministers.

In 1880 King George Tupou I declared the Wesleyan mission membership to be independent of the mission and established the independent Free Church. The vast majority of Wesleyan Tongans moved membership from the mission Wesleyan church to the Free Church. In 1924 Queen Salote made a largely successful attempt to reconcile these two Wesleyan groups and unite them into one new church, the Free Wesleyan Church. The union was not entirely successful, however, and some Tongans remained in the Free Church. In 1926 the Free Church lost a portion of its membership to the newly formed Free Church of Tonga.

In the 1970s a movement called the Tokaikolo Fellowship, or Maamafo'ou (New Light), characterized by calls for spiritual renewal, led to the departure of several thousand members from the Free Wesleyan Church.

The princess of Tonga leaves the main church in Nuku'alofa after her marriage. Marriage is an important rite of passage in Tonga. © AFP/CORBIS.

This initiated a period of membership loss to rival denominations and of internal reform of the church. Since the 1970s more emphasis has been placed on women and youth. Women were given the right to become ordained clergy, and additional youth programs were created. The establishment of congregations overseas (for example, in Los Angeles, Auckland, and Honolulu) has greatly widened the denomination's sphere of influence.

EARLY AND MODERN LEADERS The Free Wesleyan Church, similar to other denominations in Tonga, promotes great honor and respect for the *faifekau,* or minister. From the beginning of Christianity in Tonga, young Tongans have aspired to the position of minister. Because of the educational, social, and religious opportunities offered to the clergy, ministers came to hold a place of honor in Tongan society formerly reserved for the chiefs.

Queen Salote (1900–65) is noteworthy for her successful efforts to unite the majority of Wesleyans into one church and for her celebration of the unity of Tongan culture and Christianity. Rev. Sione 'Amanaki Havea (died in 2000) made significant contributions as president of the Free Wesleyan Church and as head of the Pacific Theological College in Suva, Fiji.

MAJOR THEOLOGIANS AND AUTHORS Figures of historical note include Rev. J.E. Moulton (active in the late nineteenth and early twentieth centuries), who helped found and nurture Tupou College, the initial mission school; Rev. Sione Latukefu (1927–95), the author of the book *Church and State in Tonga* (1974); and Amanaki Havea (died in 2000), theologian and greatly respected president of the Free Wesleyan Church in the latter part of the twentieth century.

HOUSES OF WORSHIP AND HOLY PLACES In any Tongan village the church is the most elaborate building, and the Free Wesleyan Church buildings are some of the oldest and largest in the kingdom. Of particular note is the main church in Nuku'alofa, which serves the royal family. Cemeteries are areas of great importance, and each congregation spends time maintaining its cemetery.

WHAT IS SACRED? The Sabbath day (Sunday) is the most visibly sacred aspect of worship in the Free Wesleyan Church. Work, sport, and leisure are set aside so that the whole day may be spent in worship. Rugby fields are empty, stores are closed, and only tourists are found at beaches, while Tongans of every religious denomination, including the Free Wesleyan Church, turn their attention to a full schedule of church activities, starting with the predawn church bells summoning the very devout to early morning devotions and ending with evening worship or choir performance. In the Free Wesleyan Church the main Sunday morning worship hour includes hymns sung by the choir, lengthy prayers, and a sermon.

HOLIDAYS AND FESTIVALS Tongans, particularly those belonging to the Free Wesleyan Church, celebrate with feasting. The importance of the feast goes back to the beginning of Tongan culture, and the Free Wesleyan Church is noteworthy for its feasts held in conjunction with Christian holidays (such as Christmas and Easter), important times of spiritual emphasis, and annual church conferences. The New Year is particularly important for marking spiritual renewal, and during that holiday Free Wesleyan congregational members take turns hosting feasts for ministers, local dignitaries, and honored guests.

MODE OF DRESS The Free Wesleyan Church is noteworthy for showing respect for God and country through special forms of dress. Free Wesleyan men, in accordance with Tongan tradition, wear Western-style dress shirts and, instead of trousers, the Tongan style of lavalava (a rectangular cloth resembling a skirt, common in Polynesia), known as a *tupenu.* A hand-crafted mat, known as a *ta'ovala,* is wrapped around the waist and over the *tupenu;* it is the most important sign of religious respect. Free Wesleyan women show their respect by wearing a decorative belt or waistband known as a *kiekie.*

DIETARY PRACTICES Drinking kava (water mixed with the pounded root of the *Piper methysticum* plant) was central to pre-Christian religious ritual on the islands and was largely under the domain of chiefly elites and the priests. In the Free Wesleyan Church kava drinking for the male elders has been incorporated into the Sunday worship routine, occurring before the main church service. While kava is banned by some of the newer church groups, such as the Assemblies of God and the Adventists, kava-drinking parties are important social events.

Also of note is the Sunday main meal that occurs after the morning church service. The Free Wesleyan Church, as a strong supporter of cultural traditions, is noteworthy for its insistence on traditional foods for the meal—such as taro root and taro leaves, fish, and yams—which are cooked in the traditional underground oven, the *'umu.*

RITUALS The Free Wesleyan Church makes feasting a central activity and puts much effort into a round of feasting on such occasions as New Year's Day, Palm Sunday, and the church's annual weeklong conference. In addition, the church service itself has its formalities of language, dress, and procedure. For example, kava drinking by male elders before the service can also take on a ritualistic form, as names and titles are called out, kava is served in a particular order, and seating follows rules of social hierarchy.

RITES OF PASSAGE Important rites of passage for Tongan Wesleyans include first birthdays, women's 21st birthdays, weddings, and funerals. The Wesleyan Church is a great champion of such traditions, and most of its members mark rites of passage with feasts, speeches, and resource distribution (gift giving in which participants are rewarded for their attendance), particularly of fine mats made from pandanus (a plant similar to a palm) and tapa cloth made from mulberry bark. On these occasions the biggest pigs are slaughtered and, along with the largest yams, cooked in an *'umu* (underground oven).

Of all the church groups in Tonga, the Free Wesleyan Church is the most prominent in its maintenance of funeral rituals. In the pre-Christian era and through the nineteenth century, the task of aiding the transition into the afterlife would take days, weeks, and even months. Today the funeral process is more limited, but the Free Wesleyan Church encourages the local congregation, and even the whole community, to take part in all-night vigils, kava drinking, choir singing, feasting, and burial rituals.

MEMBERSHIP In contrast to some of the religious groups that are newer to Tonga, the Free Wesleyan Church is not notably evangelical, but the church is determined to remain the pillar of Christian institutions in the modern monarchy. The Free Wesleyan Church claims most of the nation's elite members (including the king, a majority of the nobility, and a great many members of the business community).

SOCIAL JUSTICE The Free Wesleyan Church plays a central role in the ecumenical movement within Tonga and the wider Pacific and has been active in discussion of basic issues of poverty, education, and human rights. The church's high level of commitment to education is reflected in the continued strength of its education system, from preschools to theological seminaries.

SOCIAL ASPECTS The Free Wesleyan Church is well known in Tonga for valuing the extended family (*famili*), kin group (*kainga*), and congregation (*kaingalotu*). Sermons, speeches at family-sponsored church feasts, and conversations around the kava circle continually emphasize the importance of such social ties. Similar to many other religious groups in Tonga, the Free Wesleyan Church works hard to ensure that the activities of the local congregation consume most of the time and energy of its families and that congregational life and family life are mutually supportive.

POLITICAL IMPACT The Free Wesleyan Church has generally had a conservative influence on the nation and has given considerable support for the preservation of pre-Christian traditions. In addition, the church has provided much support for the political system of the nobility, the monarchy, and the government. At the same time, the church has allowed for discussion of Western-influenced ideas of modernity and grassroots political movements, some of them pro-democracy.

CONTROVERSIAL ISSUES Controversial issues such as abortion, divorce, and spousal abuse continue to cause concern for the church leadership in Tonga, and the church has generally taken a cautious stand on such matters. The allowance and even encouragement of women as members of the clergy, a matter of grave concern for conservatives, indicates some willingness on the part of the church to address current issues.

CULTURAL IMPACT The Free Wesleyan Church, as a patron and supporter of traditional dance, poetry, art, and music, continues to be a force for cultural vitality. The church has also influenced Tongan culture by introducing Western hymns and church architecture.

Other Religions

By the mid-twentieth century the religious landscape of Tonga included three different Wesleyan-derived denominations, the Catholic Church, and groups such as the Mormons and the Seventh-day Adventists.

The Catholic Church has been important for Tongan culture as a vital repository and sanctuary for many traditions of art, music, poetry, and drama. These traditions were preserved within Tongan Catholicism because the Catholic chiefly factions maintained the traditional ways to a greater extent than converts to the king's Wesleyan Christianity. Since the 1980s the Tongan Catholic leadership has played a key role in addressing social issues of health, education, and social welfare for Tongan society.

The Latter-day Saints (Mormons) are distinctive in Tonga for allowing and sponsoring Western-style social dances (which entail relaxing the traditional Tongan rules of brother-sister avoidance). More generally, the Mormon investment in Western-style education, particularly as exemplified in the large secondary school Liahona, has encouraged the learning of English and American culture. Indeed, the Mormons are one of the strongest forces for cultural and religious change in Tonga. The Seventh-day Adventists and the Assemblies of God are similarly noted in Tonga for the ways in which they encourage American ideas of religion and culture among its membership. This can be seen in their use of American music, American English, and American forms of dress, among other things.

In the last quarter of the twentieth century, indigenous religious movements—such as that of the Tokaikolo Christian Fellowship, a breakaway movement from the Free Wesleyan Church in 1978—and locally organized groups such as the Pentecostal Church (Assemblies of God) have fostered discussion about the use of Tongan religious practices among some of the well-established, more "traditional" Christian denominations.

At the beginning of the twenty-first century, small Christian groups (including the Jehovah's Witnesses, the Salvation Army, the Church of Christ, and Gospel Chapels) were a modest presence in the kingdom. In Tonga there are also fledgling groups of Bahai and a small group of Muslims.

Ernest Olson

See Also Vol. I: *Christianity, Latter-day Saints, Roman Catholicism*

Bibliography

Addo, Ping-Ann. "God's Kingdom in Auckland: Tongan Christian Dress and the Expression of Duty." In *Clothing the Pacific.* Edited by Chloë Colchester. New York: Berg, 2003.

Barker, John. *Christianity in Oceania.* Lanham, Md.: University Press of America, 1990.

Ernst, Manfred. *Winds of Change.* Suva: Pacific Conference of Churches, 1994.

Finau, Makisi, Teruro Ieuti, and Jione Langi. *Island Churches: Challenge and Change.* Suva: Institute of Pacific Studies of the University of the South Pacific, 1992.

Forman, Charles. *The Island Churches of the Pacific.* Maryknoll, N.Y.: Orbis Books, 1982.

Gordon, Tamar G. *Inventing Mormon Identity in Tonga.* Ph.D. diss., University of California at Berkeley, 1988.

Latukefu, Sione. *Church and State in Tonga.* Canberra: Australian National University Press, 1974.

Olson, Ernest. "Signs of Conversion, Spirit of Commitment: The Pentecostal Church in the Kingdom of Tonga." *Journal of Ritual Studies* 15, no. 2 (2001): 13–26.

Van der Grijp, Paul. "Travelling Gods and Nasty Spirits: Ancient Religious Representations and Missionization in Tonga (Polynesia)." *Paideuma Mitteilungen zur Kulturkunde* 48 (2002): 243–60.

Trinidad and Tobago

POPULATION 1,298,000

ROMAN CATHOLIC 29.4 percent

HINDU 23.8 percent

ANGLICAN 10.9 percent

MUSLIM 5.8 percent

PRESBYTERIAN 3.4 percent

OTHER 26.7 percent

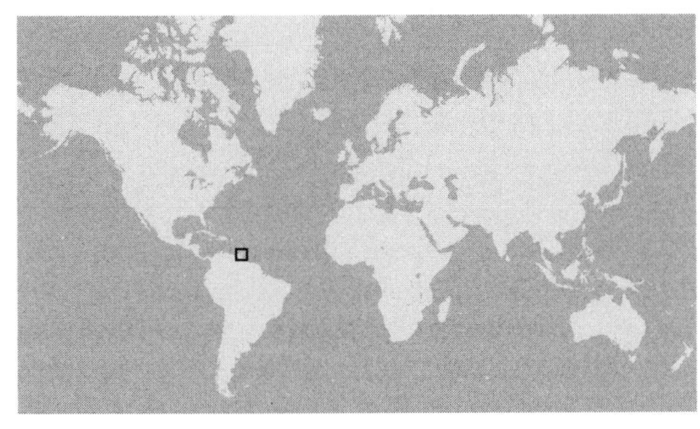

Country Overview

INTRODUCTION The Republic of Trinidad and Tobago, located seven miles north of Venezuela, comprises two islands at the southernmost tip of the Caribbean archipelago. At 1,980 square miles, the country is about one and a half times the size of Rhode Island. Three mountain ranges cross Trinidad, the larger of the two islands, in an east-west orientation. Parts of both its east and west coasts are swampy.

In 1498 Christopher Columbus glimpsed three mountains on the Northern Range of the larger island. He claimed the island for Spain, naming it Trinidad after the Holy Trinity. Although little developed by Spain, Trinidad was given its first European identity by Spanish settlement. In 1793, at the invitation of the Spanish, French Catholic planters and their enslaved Africans set up sugar and cocoa plantations on the island. By thus developing it, Spain had hoped to stave off continuing encroachments by the British. In 1797, however, the British captured Trinidad, which was formally relinquished to them in 1802.

Roman Catholicism was the religion of the Spanish and the early French settlers. With the British came Protestantism, as well as the English language. Slavery was abolished in 1834, but until then enslaved Africans from West and Central Africa brought with them their indigenous religions, particularly (but not exclusively) from the Yoruba and Dahomey traditions. In 1845 the British brought to Trinidad indentured laborers from India to work the plantations. These laborers were primarily Hindu, but there were significant numbers of Muslims as well. Other indentured populations who migrated to Trinidad include Portuguese from Madeira (Roman Catholic) and Chinese, largely from southern China, who brought their own indigenous religions. Throughout the nineteenth century additional labor migrants came to the islands, notably Christian Syrian-Lebanese merchants and Venezuelan workers headed for cocoa plantations, most of whom were Roman Catholic. Because colonial rule was British until Trinidad and Tobago's independence in 1962, Protestantism, particularly the Anglican Church, has been very influential, despite the fact that Roman Catholics have always outnumbered Protestants.

Mourners gather to witness the cremation ceremony of a Hindu pandit. The official Hindu cremation site is located near the Caroni River. © ADAM WOOLFITT/CORBIS.

Until the nineteenth century Tobago was distinct from Trinidad. It was claimed by various European colonizers and was developed for plantation production. Although it now forms a republic with Trinidad, Tobago has historically never been as culturally, ethnically, or religiously heterogeneous. Its population is predominantly of African descent, the majority of whom are Roman Catholic.

RELIGIOUS TOLERANCE In the early part of the nineteenth century animosity between Britain and France fostered tension between Trinidad's Protestants and Roman Catholics. Particular areas of contention were religious representation in government and government policy favoring Protestants. Social bias also existed against Trinidadian African-based religions, such as Orisha, and laws supporting this bias attempted to discourage their growth and public expression. By the late twentieth century, however, changes in the country's social and cultural life, as well as its legal system, led to reduced discrimination.

Present-day Trinidad and Tobago is a parliamentary democracy. Religious tolerance is not only encouraged but is part of a national ideology of tolerance and harmony.

Major Religion

ROMAN CATHOLICISM

DATE OF ORIGIN Sixteenth century C.E.
NUMBER OF FOLLOWERS 382,000

HISTORY After Columbus visited Trinidad in 1498, the Spanish colonized the island, bringing with them Roman Catholicism. From the sixteenth century the Spanish placed indigenous Amerindian inhabitants into missions governed by the Spanish colonial authority and administered by Roman Catholic priests. During the next three centuries Roman Catholicism became further embedded within the society as the French, Irish, German, and Portuguese settled in Trinidad and Tobago.

In 1783 Spain issued a *Cedula de Poblacion,* an invitation to other Catholic colonists (particularly the French) in the Caribbean region and elsewhere to settle in Trinidad and bring their enslaved African labor to work land granted by Spanish authorities. This population movement into Trinidad increased significantly the numbers of Catholics but also deepened French cultural and linguistic influences on Trinidadian society, many of which are still evident. These settlers became the foundation of a significant sector of the local elite still known as French Creoles. The number of Roman Catholic and other immigrants from Europe diminished gradually during the eighteenth and nineteenth centuries (particularly after such regional events as the Haitian Revolution and emancipation), yet the population of Roman Catholics expanded through migration from other parts of the region and from religious conversion.

EARLY AND MODERN LEADERS The archdiocese of Port of Spain was established in 1850. Richard Patrick Smith was the first archbishop, serving just two years. Archbishop Anthony Pantin, head of the Port of Spain archdiocese from 1968 to 2000, was beloved as "the people's priest." For decades he participated in building the nation of Trinidad and Tobago. He was a founding member of the Inter-Religious Organization (ILO) and established the Mary Care Center home for pregnant, unmarried teens. Archbishop Pantin was succeeded by Archbishop Edward Joseph Gilbert.

MAJOR THEOLOGIANS AND AUTHORS Although there have been locally important Roman Catholic leaders in Trinidad and Tobago, there have been no major Roman Catholic theologians and authors.

HOUSES OF WORSHIP AND HOLY PLACES In the capital city, Port of Spain, the Holy Trinity Cathedral is an important place of worship. Further east, in the hills of the Northern Range Mountains, is the Abbey of Mount Saint Benedict; still active, it was built in 1912, making it one of the oldest monasteries in the region. The Church of La Divina Pastora, in the southwestern town of Siparia, has at least since the mid-nineteenth century been an annual pilgrimage site for devotees of *La Divina Pastora* (Divine Shepherdess), who embodies both the Virgin Mary and Kali Mai, a goddess in the Hindu pantheon.

WHAT IS SACRED? In general Roman Catholics in Trinidad and Tobago do not differ from Roman Catholics elsewhere in what they consider sacred. One distinctive sacred object, however, was discovered probably late in the eighteenth century. This object is a small, wooden, carved statue of *La Divina Pastora.* Housed in a church in the town of Siparia, she has been revered by both Roman Catholics and Hindus throughout Trinidad. She is counted among the Black Madonnas in the Americas.

HOLIDAYS AND FESTIVALS The Festival of Sipari Mai, held on Maundy (Holy) Thursday and Good Friday, can be counted as a Roman Catholic event, despite its commemoration of a dual persona: the Virgin Mary (Catholicism) and Kali Mai (Hinduism). The festival, typical of Marian devotion elsewhere in the Roman Catholic world, includes a recitation of the rosary, praying for Mary's intercession, a religious procession carrying her statue (*La Divina Pastora*), and eucharistic Liturgies devoted to Marian themes, such as motherhood.

MODE OF DRESS The church does not influence the mode of dress in Trinidad and Tobago. Adherents of Roman Catholicism are not distinguishable from the populace as a whole, all of whom wear Western dress.

DIETARY PRACTICES Roman Catholics in Trinidad and Tobago observe the same dietary rules as Roman Catholics in other countries. Some do not eat meat on Fridays, and many observant Roman Catholics forego some food for the duration of Lent.

RITUALS In Trinidad and Tobago Roman Catholics attend Mass and may observe saint's days. They may also participate in funeral wakes, although they are not necessarily Roman Catholic events in Trinidad and Tobago. While the country is not officially Roman Catholic, some saints are prominent. In Tobago, for example, the annual Fishermen's Festival is held on Saint Peter's Day (2 July), as Saint Peter is the patron saint of fishermen.

RITES OF PASSAGE Roman Catholics in Trinidad and Tobago participate in the traditional rites of Roman Catholicism, such as baptism and confirmation. The Rite of Christian Initiation for Adults (RCIA), a Catholic program found throughout the world, runs a lengthy process of initiation into the church, which includes baptisms. RCIA is particularly active in Trinidad and Tobago, in part because of the diversity of religions in the country.

MEMBERSHIP Beginning in the sixteenth century there was an active conversion effort on the part of Roman Catholic priests, most of whom came from abroad, notably Europe. Since the 1970s Trinidad and Tobago, like many other nations, has experienced the rise of Protestant evangelical religions. In response the Roman Catholic Church has concentrated on its congregations and shored up local charities, as well as its association with regional and international charitable organizations.

SOCIAL JUSTICE Roman Catholicism in Trinidad and Tobago has always been committed to education, and some of the oldest and best schools are Catholic—for example, Saint Mary's College and Saint Joseph's Convent, where, until 1870, instruction was in French. The church in Trinidad and Tobago has a large and important social justice commission, staffed by social justice professionals, that is active in working with the government on issues such as reforming the prison system and reducing poverty.

SOCIAL ASPECTS Marriage and the family among Roman Catholics in Trinidad and Tobago reflect the same principles, and challenges to those principles, as in other parts of the Roman Catholic world. Marriage is considered sacred and permanent, and these are the goals of Roman Catholics. Divorce and children born out of wedlock are also part of marriage and family patterns in Trinidad and Tobago. The cultural notions of respectability, which include Roman Catholic (as well as other religion's) ideals, have different impacts, expressions, and values based on class (socioeconomic) membership.

POLITICAL IMPACT The government of Trinidad and Tobago is secular. When it was a British colony, however, especially in the early to mid-nineteenth century, there were tensions between the governing Protestants (notably Anglicans) and the more populous Roman Catholics, including the local French Creole elite. Religious policy was the major area of conflict, particularly as it affected resources for education and the authority of priests. By the end of the nineteenth century these tensions had abated, with the concerted efforts of colonial governors bringing about equitable representation of both religions. These tensions continued to diminish as the English (Protestant) and French Creoles (Roman Catholic) began to emphasize their common heritage, while a growing, educated Afro-Trinidadian middle class increasingly moved toward twentieth-century political leadership. Today the church is viewed as an inclusive, nonpartisan body.

CONTROVERSIAL ISSUES The controversial issues that typify Roman Catholicism elsewhere in the world—such as abortion and divorce—are also subjects of discussion among church members in Trinidad and Tobago.

CULTURAL IMPACT In Trinidad and Tobago Roman Catholicism has historically been associated with Spanish and French cultural traditions and with such syncretic religions as Orisha, which mixes European Catholic and African indigenous traditions in its belief and practice. An influx of Venezuelan immigrant laborers, likely Roman Catholic, who came to work on cocoa estates in the late nineteenth century, brought with them a style of folk Christmas music and dance known as *parang,*, which is performed annually.

Other Religions

Slavery was abolished in British Caribbean colonies in 1834. In May 1845 the British brought Hindu, as well as Muslim, indentured laborers from India to Trinidad to work on sugar plantations. Indians continued to arrive, in decreasing numbers, until the end of the indenture practice in 1917.

Hinduism has played a central role among Indians in Trinidad and Tobago. On plantations, in village communities, and in urban areas, it has served as a basis for social organization, identity formation, and political ideology. The principle of caste and its attendant notions of purity, however, could not be maintained under plantation labor conditions. As a result, caste became a more fluid category, one more applicable to an individual's or a family's social status than to an ascribed structural position in the society. Caste is therefore no longer sacred among the Hindus of Trinidad and Tobago.

Hinduism in Trinidad and Tobago, as elsewhere, has gradually become more unified and homogeneous in belief and practice, giving rise to forms of religious orthodoxy. Hindu educators and missionaries (for example, Arya Samaj reformists) visited Trinidad and Tobago throughout the nineteenth and twentieth centuries, at times contributing to local debate about the practice of Hinduism and the relationship between India and its diaspora. After the partition of India and Pakistan in 1947, there were tensions between Hindus and Muslims in Trinidad and Tobago, but the prevailing sentiment among them was consistent with the national ideology of harmony and tolerance, as well as with the value they put on their mutual history of emigration. In 1946 the colonial government legalized Hindu marriages, which was a major step toward the equal participation and representation of Hindus in Trinidad and Tobago.

Hindu leadership in the country has been provided by various Hindu religious organizations, including the Sanatan Dharma Maha Sabha, which was established by an act of parliament in 1952. Many local, regional, and national Hindu leaders are known as pandits (Hindu learned men). Pandits are sometimes associated with specific *mandirs* (houses of worship), and they may be trained abroad or self-educated. Most Hindus place great importance on their early ancestors in Trinidad, who maintained the religion under the oppressive conditions of indenture and, later, in the face of economic and political inequality.

From the mid-nineteenth century to the present time, Hindus in Trinidad and Tobago have worn a combination of traditional clothes. These include the dhoti (loincloth) among men, as well as *shalwar-kamiz* (pants with a long shirt) and saris among women. As Hindus became increasingly assimilated into mainstream culture, they donned Western garb, notably dresses for women and shirts and pants for men. By the mid-twentieth century women stopped wearing elaborate silver and gold jewelry on their arms, hands, and faces. As upward social mobility became a reality for an increasing number of Hindus, religious and cultural identity were again symbolized by traditional dress, though only in particular contexts—notably ritual events, including *pujas*, and cultural performances, such as dance and music concerts.

The most common ritual among Hindus in Trinidad and Tobago is the *puja*: devotional prayers honoring particular deities or commemorating certain events, such as marriages or deaths. Also common are the *yagya* and *bhagwat* rituals, which, held over a consecutive period of days and nights, demonstrate reverence to deities through prayers, music (such as the harmonium), singing, offerings, and interpretations of scripture by pandits. The official Hindu cremation site is located near the Caroni River, and the river is where many Hindu rituals are held.

Hinduism has strongly influenced the arts—song, dance, and music—in Trinidad and Tobago. There are several radio programs that focus on Indian culture, broadcasting, for example, Hindu bhajans (songs of worship). Hindu cultural themes have also found their way into calypsos and carnival costumes, occasionally inspiring controversy. Trinidad and Tobago is the native country of novelist V.S. Naipaul, a Hindu, who won the Nobel Prize in Literature in 2001.

Protestantism was brought to Trinidad and Tobago by British colonizers and settlers. Anglicanism, the most significant early form of Protestantism, was initially represented among the British ruling elite, though it spread among the working and middle classes throughout the nineteenth and twentieth centuries. Beginning in the mid-twentieth century, proselytization by evangelical and Pentecostal missionaries (coming primarily from North America) increased, gaining momentum particularly among the working and middle classes. These "small church" forms of Protestantism have continued to be important in Trinidad and Tobago, as they have in much of the Caribbean and Latin America. In 1868 Canadian Presbyterian missionaries arrived in Trinidad to minister to the Indian indentured laborers. Presbyterianism has since had a dramatic impact on the Indo-Trinidadian population, notably in formal education. Indo-Trinidadians have become clergy, teachers, and principals of Presbyterian schools, and some of the most highly regarded schools in Trinidad and Tobago today are Presbyterian.

Although only 5.8 percent of the country's population is Muslim, the impact of Islam has been significant, and Islamic practices contribute to the national character of Trinidad and Tobago. Dotting the landscape are numerous *masjids* (mosques)—some humble, serving small communities and local villages, and others grand, built as centers of learning and worship for the larger populations of towns and cities. Included among Trinidad and Tobago's public holidays is Id al-Fitr (marking the end of the Islamic month of Ramadan), which is celebrated by congregational prayers and social visiting. Historically Indo-Trinidadian Muslim religious organizations, such as the ASJA (Anjuman Sumnat-ul Jamaat) and TML (Trinidad Muslim League), have played an important role in the political and cultural life of the country, working, for example, for the state sanctioning of Muslim marriages (achieved in 1936). Trinidad and Tobago is the only place in the Caribbean where the Muslim festival Muharram has occurred each year since the arrival of Indian Muslims. Locally known as "Hosay" (after Hussein, one of the martyred grandsons of the prophet Muhammed mourned in the festival), it provides a distinctive contribution to the national culture. Traditionally expressed as a dignified march of mourners parading large taziyas, or representations of the martyr's tombs, Hosay has stimulated public debate among Muslims, as well as non-Muslims, about how the event should be observed and whether it should continue, given questions about its Islamic authenticity and concern about inappropriate revelry by onlookers. Also important in the country are Afro-Trinidadian Muslims, represented in very small numbers in the nineteenth century among enslaved and free Africans, but in the later twentieth century an increasing number of Afro-Trinidadians embraced Islam. Afro-Trinidadian Muslims have been a notable voice calling for political and social equality in Trinidad and Tobago. In July 1990 the Jamaat al Muslimeen, a Muslim group composed mostly of Afro-Trinidadians, attempted a government coup.

Rastafarians form a small percentage of the population. Although they look to the Bible for guidance, they have reinterpreted it, following, for example, the prophecy of Marcus Garvey (1887–1940), who wrote, "Look to Africa for the crowning of a Black King, he shall be the Redeemer." Rastafarians identified Haile Selassie I (1892–1975), the Ethiopian emperor once known as Ras (Prince) Tafari, as their Messiah. They also believe that Babylon, both symbolically and literally, refers to places where black people have been enslaved and people in general have been oppressed, and that Zion is where the oppression and predatory relationships of Babylon do not exist. Historically concentrated among impoverished Afro-Trinidadian and Afro-Tobagonian populations, these communities have by and large faced the disapproval of mainstream society and governmental institutions.

Orisha is a traditional form of religious worship in West Africa. In Trinidad and Tobago, however, it is a syncretic religion, melding West African, Catholic, Hindu, Protestant, and Kabbalah elements. Its practitioners are from various ethnic groups and classes. Important Orisha practices include the veneration of a pantheon of deities and regularly occurring ritual feasts in honor of a deity, which may include singing, drumming, and spirit possession. Historically outlawed in Trinidad and Tobago, Orisha was officially recognized by the government in 1999.

Aisha Khan

See Also Vol. I: *Christianity, Roman Catholicism; Hinduism*

Bibliography

Brereton, Bridget. *A History of Modern Trinidad, 1783–1962.* London: Heinemann, 1981.

Houk, James. *Spirits, Blood, and Drums.* Philadelphia: Temple University Press, 1995.

Khan, Aisha. *Callaloo Nation: Idioms of Race and Religious Identity among South Asians in Trinidad.* Durham, N.C.: Duke University Press, 2004.

———. "Juthaa in Trinidad: Food, Pollution, and Hierarchy in a Caribbean Diaspora Community." *American Ethnologist* 21, no. 2 (1994): 245–69.

Klass, Morton. *East Indians in Trinidad: A Study of Cultural Persistence.* New York: Columbia University Press, 1961.

———. *Singing with Sai Baba: The Politics of Revitalization in Trinidad.* Boulder, Colo.: Westview, 1991.

Munasinghe, Viranjini. *Callaloo or Tossed Salad? The Cultural Politics of Identity in Trinidad.* Ithaca, N.Y.: Cornell University Press, 2001.

Schwartz, Barton. "The Failure of Caste in Trinidad." In *Caste in Overseas Indian Communities.* Edited by Barton Schwartz. San Francisco: Chandler Publishing, 1967.

Tinker, Hugh. *The Banyan Tree: Overseas Emigrants from India, Pakistan, and Bangladesh.* New York: Oxford University Press, 1977.

Vertovec, Steven. *The Hindu Diaspora.* London and New York: Routledge, 2000.

———. *Hindu Trinidad.* London: Macmillan, 1992.

Wood, Donald. *Trinidad in Transition: The Years After Slavery.* London: Oxford University Press, 1968.

Tunisia

POPULATION 9,815,644

MUSLIM 99.7 percent

OTHER 0.3 percent

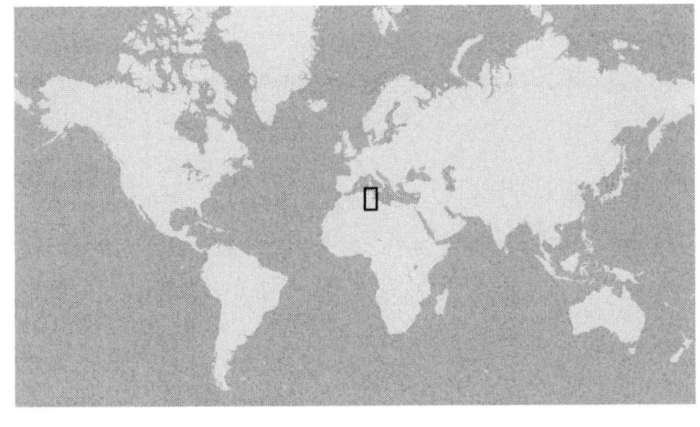

Country Overview

INTRODUCTION The Tunisian Republic, a small country of 63,200 square miles, is located on the Mediterranean coast of North Africa. Except in the southwestern corner, where desert prevails, Tunisia has a mild Mediterranean climate. The countryside is hilly in the north, but in the east it is rather flat. Less than a quarter of the population is engaged in agriculture, whereas in the mid-twentieth century more than half were farmers. Since then tourism and manufacturing have become of considerable importance. Compared with other Africans and Middle Easterners, Tunisians are economically well off, and one does not find enormous extremes of wealth in the country.

Early on, Tunisia was inhabited by the ancestors of modern-day Berbers, but in the twelfth century B.C.E. the area was settled by Phoenicians, who built the Carthaginian empire. This was eventually conquered by the Romans and, then, inherited by the Byzantines. By the seventh century C.E., Tunisia had been conquered by Arab Muslims. Along with a conversion to Islam came the adoption of the Arabic language and customs. Over the course of more than 12 centuries thereafter, Tunisia was ruled by a succession of Muslim dynasties. France established colonial control in 1881 and inaugurated a protectorate, which was replaced in 1956 by an independent republic with Habib Bourguiba as president.

RELIGIOUS TOLERANCE Tunisia is almost entirely Muslim, with less than 1 percent of the population Christian, Jewish, Bahai, or without religion. Except for the small minority of Ibadi, Muslims in Tunisia are Sunnis of the Maliki Madhhab, or school of law. While Islam is the official religion, theoretically there is religious freedom, although it exists within very prescribed limits. The state has been highly repressive of so-called fundamentalist Islamists, and there are hundreds of political prisoners in jails, many for religious reasons. Even Islam is free only so long as it contributes to the benefit of the state, and Muslim officials are subordinate to the government. Christian missionaries seeking to proselytize are expelled from the country.

Tunisian mourners gather at the cemetery of the Great Mosque of Kairouan. The mosque is the oldest in North Africa, having originally been constructed in the seventh century. © BERNARD AND CATHERINE DESJEUX/CORBIS.

Major Religion

SUNNI ISLAM

DATE OF ORIGIN 647 C.E.
NUMBER OF FOLLOWERS 9.8 million

HISTORY The most important religious event in Tunisian history was the conquest by Arab Muslims and the rather rapid Islamization of the country in the seventh century. A much reduced Christian community lasted for several centuries until finally becoming extinct, while a Jewish community has survived. Although ostensibly under Umayyad and then Abbasid rule initially, a major portion of Tunisia was part of a Kharijite domain during the eighth and ninth centuries. By 800 C.E. much of the country had come under the rule of Aghlabid emirs, who were officially subject to the Abbasids but in reality were independent. In the tenth century the Fatimids, Ismaili Shiites who spread eastward and conquered Egypt in 972, prevailed. There followed other short-lived Sunni dynasties until Hafsid rule in 1236, which lasted for 300 years and then was replaced by the Ottoman Turks. In 1881 Muslim authority ended in favor of French administration. The French introduced secular rule, which was maintained to some extent after independence in 1956.

EARLY AND MODERN LEADERS Abul Hasan Al Shadhili (1196–1258) taught in Tunis after studying Sufism (Islamic mysticism) in various localities and before eventually moving to Egypt. During his life he taught a ritual discipline that, following his death, was used by followers as the basis for the Shadhiliyya *tariqa,* or Sufi brotherhood, one of the most noted of such organizations. In modern times mention may be made of Rashid Ghannoushi (born in 1942), who became a leader in the movement to establish a conservative Islamic state in Tunisia. He formed the Nahda (Awakening, or Renaissance) movement, which was suppressed by the government.

MAJOR THEOLOGIANS AND AUTHORS The greatest of all Tunisian Arabs and probably the first true sociologist was Abd Al Rahman Ibn Khaldun (1332–1406). He served under several North African rulers and for a time was the grand *qadi* (chief Islamic judge) of Cairo. His *Muqaddimah* was an empirical investigation of the rise and fall of civilizations and proposed a cyclical theory of history.

HOUSES OF WORSHIP AND HOLY PLACES There are several ancient mosques in Tunisia, the most important being the Zituna Mosque in Tunis, which dates from the ninth century, and the Great Mosque of Kairouan, which is the oldest mosque in North Africa, having originally been constructed in the seventh century. Hundreds of white domed tombs of holy men (*walis*) dot the Tunisian countryside.

WHAT IS SACRED? In Tunisia the greatest sanctity is ascribed to mosques and to the tombs of holy men. In ancient times there also were sacred trees, graves, wells, and caves. Although some sacred trees and caves have persisted, they are invariably disguised as the burial places of Muslim holy men.

HOLIDAYS AND FESTIVALS The three major religious feasts characteristic of Sunni Islam are celebrated throughout Tunisia. The Great Feast of Islam (al Id al Kbir), which occurs during the month of Zul Hijja, commemorates the occasion on which the prophet Abraham was alleged to have offered his son, Ismail, as a sacrifice before God bade him take a lamb instead. Thus, on this occasion each man is expected to sacrifice a sheep and to distribute most of the meat to others. The pilgrimage to Mecca is often carried out in conjunction with the feast. The Little Feast (al Id al Sughayar) ends the fast of the month of Ramadan, and like the Great Feast it entails the sacrifice of an animal and the distribution of meat. Both feasts commence with communal prayers in the mosque. The third major religious festival is the occasion of the Prophet's birthday, which occurs on the 12th of Rab al Awwal, the third Muslim month.

Festivals are also held in connection with the numerous local holy men. These saints, who may have claimed descent from the Prophet, were often the founders of villages, and they are invariably identified as leaders in a Sufi brotherhood. Their tombs are the object of visitations, where prayers may be recited and where a person may make a vow or give an offering for a vow fulfilled. Weekly meetings of the Sufi brotherhood associated with the holy man, as well as annual celebrations of his life, are also held in the vicinity of the tomb.

MODE OF DRESS Islam ordains modesty in dress and personal appearance, and this especially applies to women. Thus, in Tunisia the customary attire for women has traditionally been a long dress, and when a woman goes into public places, she wears a white or black head shawl held together with the teeth. Beginning in the late twentieth century, there was an increase in more complete veiling by conservative Muslims. Western-style apparel has also become common and prevails in the major cities.

If a mosque in Tunisia has a formal prayer leader (imam), he dresses in a conservative fashion, in a long gown and a turban and with a full beard. As elsewhere in the Muslim world, a man entering a mosque is expected to wear a garment that covers his body at least to the knees and the elbows. He should also wear a head cover and remove his street shoes. Even more than women, however, men have adopted Western clothing, although the more traditional dress of long gowns, skull caps, and turbans remains widespread.

DIETARY PRACTICES Tunisians observe Muslim rules regarding food. Therefore, they avoid pork and any meat not processed by recognized Muslim rules of slaughter. Some Tunisians argue that the wild boar, which is found in the northeast, is not prohibited. Most Tunisians also avoid alcoholic beverages, although the upper class is less observant of this rule. Further, as a result of French influence, grapes are raised in Tunisia and used for making wine.

RITUALS As elsewhere, each Muslim in Tunisia is obligated to observe a highly formalized prayer (*salat*) five times each day following ritual ablutions. The prayers may be performed in any place, except that the ground should be ritually pure. All prayer times are announced by a *muadhdhin* (muezzin), traditionally from a minaret or from the front door of a mosque. In contemporary times, however, there has been increasing use of recordings broadcast over a loudspeaker. Friday noon is a time for congregational prayer at a mosque, following which there is a sermon preached by a mosque official. Observance of the *salat* is by no means universal in Tunisia, and this is especially true for women. Attendance at the Friday service includes a distinct minority invariably composed only of men.

Another important ritual is either a pilgrimage to Mecca or a lesser pilgrimage to a saint's tomb. At the latter the pilgrim often sacrifices an animal and distributes the meat. The different Sufi brotherhoods hold regular meetings at which hymns in praise of the Prophet and the founder of the organization are sung. A *dhikr*, in which a ritual phrase is repeated, accompanied by bodily movements, is performed with the aim of elevating the believer into a state of spiritual ecstasy.

Brief religious rituals may also be held on a number of different occasions. In addition to funerals, these include beginning a meal, leaving a house, opening a business, contracting a marriage, or greeting a friend after a long absence. Recitation of the Koran is common before the beginning of Friday services at mosques and also at funerals.

RITES OF PASSAGE Important rites of passage for Tunisian Muslims concern birth, the circumcision of boys, marriage, and funerals. All have the common features of offering food and drink and of feasting. Except for funerals, they also entail the giving of gifts and often music and dancing. Reciprocity is a characteristic of all such ceremonies. Relatives and guests contribute to the support of the celebration and expect the recipient to assist them on similar occasions.

Tunisian marriages involve a payment of bride wealth by the family of the groom to that of the bride.

This does not mean, however, that the wife is purchased. Most of the money is used to help pay for the wedding celebration and for buying items for the new household. The climax of any wedding is to show the bloodied sheet of the wedding bed as proof of the bride's virginity. Unlike some other parts of Africa, neither clitoridectomy nor infibulation is practiced in Tunisia.

MEMBERSHIP Islam in Tunisia is loosely organized. Most religious affairs are conducted by lay members, and congregations have considerable input in the management of mosques. Large mosques in major Tunisian cities have professional preachers, although villagers rely on lay members with a special interest in religion to conduct services. The most important figures in the religious system are the learned scholars of the sacred law, collectively referred to as the ulama. The state appoints one of their number as the grand mufti, whose role is to advise on religious issues and to render opinions on problems that may be submitted to him, but his opinions, which are called *fatwas*, are not considered infallible.

Perhaps the only true missionary activity in Tunisia is conducted by conservative Muslims who seek to introduce Islamic law as they interpret it and to create an Islamic state. Islam is taught in the public schools, but there is a prohibition against attempting to convert individuals from one religion to another. There are radio broadcasts of recitations of the Koran and of sermons, and a few Koranic schools remain.

SOCIAL JUSTICE Islam teaches the obligation to assist the poor and the needy, with the third of the Five Pillars of Islam requiring the believer to give alms, which is observed in Tunisia. This also implies support for hospitals, mosques, and schools. A traditional system of charitable endowments (*habus*) has been nationalized in Tunisia. The Koran teaches honesty and fairness and prohibits gambling, dealing in futures, and the taking of interest. Thus, as in other parts of the Muslim world, there are Islamic banks in Tunisia that seek to avoid charging interest. Islam has always supported state interference in the economy when it is believed to be for the public benefit and at the same time has favored individual enterprise.

SOCIAL ASPECTS In Tunisia, as in Islam generally, the family is held to be the central structure of human society, and religious authorities maintain that religion is the preserver of the family. Modern Tunisian law prohibits the practice of polygyny, which Islamic law tolerates. In Tunisia marriage is conceived as a secular contract that may be terminated for any number of reasons. Traditionally it was only the husband who had the right to divorce, but since, independence laws have been enacted giving the courts the power to regulate divorce.

POLITICAL IMPACT It is clear that religious institutions in Tunisia no longer exert as much influence as they did in the past. While Islam remains the state religion, numerous regulations have been enacted that run counter to Muslim teaching. In addition to such matters as polygyny and divorce, the government has also imposed regulations controlling mosques and their operation and has sought to discourage the fast of Ramadan, which is probably the most widely observed of Muslim obligations. While Islam is part of the school curriculum, the government officially claims that "public education teaches the value of tolerance, peace, and moderation inherent in Islam."

In contrast, there has been a rise in a conservative, fundamentalist orientation that stresses the full application of the interpretation of Shariah, or Muslim law. Thus, even if Tunisians are not always observant of the pillars of the faith, they continue to identify closely with Islam.

CONTROVERSIAL ISSUES Family planning has been part of governmental policy since independence, and Tunisia has liberal regulations regarding abortion. The Tunisian ulama have endorsed the government's policy on family planning, although opposition to it comes from the fundamentalist Muslims. A personal status law has greatly expanded the freedom of women, but they continue to have no role in leading religious services.

CULTURAL IMPACT The most significant impact of religion on art forms in Tunisia, as elsewhere in the Muslim world, has been in architecture, both in the design of mosques and of saint's tombs. Islam in general frowns upon dance, music, and the theater, although the Sufi brotherhoods have introduced numerous hymns, and some consider the bodily movements of the *dhikr* to be a dance form. Islam prohibits the re-creation of the human form in sculpture and painting and has directed the artistic impulse to the elaboration of calligraphy.

Other Religions

The largest religious minority in Tunisia is the Ibadi sect of Islam, which is the last surviving branch of the Kharijites. They are the remnant of those who formed the Kharijite realm in Tunisia during the eighth and ninth centuries. Some 45,000 are found on the island of Jerba, where they are actually members of a subsect of Ibadi known as the Wahhabi (not to be confused with the Wahhabi of Saudi Arabia). While Ibadi law differs little from the Maliki, the group is intensely conservative, prohibiting jewelry, tobacco, music, dance, theater, the cult of saints, and Sufi brotherhoods. Their mosques are noticeable for their plainness. The Ibadi do not recognize as truly Muslim anyone who does not practice all of the obligations of the religion, and they have held that the leadership of the community may be invested in any upright practicing Muslim provided that he is elected by the faithful. Further, the Ibadi believe that any leader who does not follow all of the requirements of the religion must be deposed.

The Christian minority in Tunisia consists overwhelmingly of European residents and includes about 5,000 Roman Catholics and 1,000 Protestants. Before independence there were more than 100,000 Christians, mostly French residents. The Jewish community is ancient, dating from the first century C.E. Whereas in the mid-twentieth century there were 60,000 Jews, by the end of the century there remained only about 2,000. The Tunisian government subsidizes the Jewish community. The largest non-Muslim minority are those who profess no religion, numbering between 10,000 and 20,000.

Harold B. Barclay

See Also Vol. I: *Islam, Sunnism*

Bibliography

Abu Zahra, Nadia. *Sidi Ameur, A Tunisian Village.* London: Ithaca Press, 1982.

Abun Nasr, Jamil M. *A History of the Maghrib in the Islamic Period.* Cambridge: Cambridge University Press, 1987.

Anderson, Lisa. *The State and Social Transformation in Tunisia and Libya, 1830–1980.* Princeton, N.J.: Princeton University Press, 1986.

Bosworth, C.E., E. Van Denzel, B. Lewis, and C. Pellat, eds. *The Encyclopaedia of Islam.* Leiden: E.J. Brill, 1999.

Bouhdiba, Abdelwahab. *La sexualité en Islam.* Paris: Presses Universitaires de France, 1975.

Duvignaud, Jean. *Change at Shebika.* London: Penguin, 1970.

Hejaiej, Monia. *Behind Closed Doors: Oral Narratives in Tunis.* New Brunswick, N.J.: Rutgers University Press, 1996.

Ibn Khaldun. *The Muqaddimah: An Introduction to History.* Princeton, N.J.: Princeton University Press, 1974.

Laroui, Abdallah. *The History of the Maghrib.* Princeton, N.J.: Princeton University Press, 1977.

Salem, N. Habib. *Bourguiba, Islam and the Creation of Modern Tunisia.* London: Croom Helm, 1985.

Valensi, Lucette. *Tunisian Peasants in the Eighteenth and Nineteenth Centuries.* Cambridge: Cambridge University Press, 1985.

Turkey

POPULATION 67,308,928

SUNNI MUSLIM 84 percent

ALEVI AND OTHER MUSLIM 15 percent

OTHER (ARMENIAN APOSTOLIC, CHALDEAN, GREEK CATHOLIC, JACOBITE, JEWISH, PROTESTANT, ORTHODOX CHRISTIAN, ROMAN CATHOLIC) 1 percent

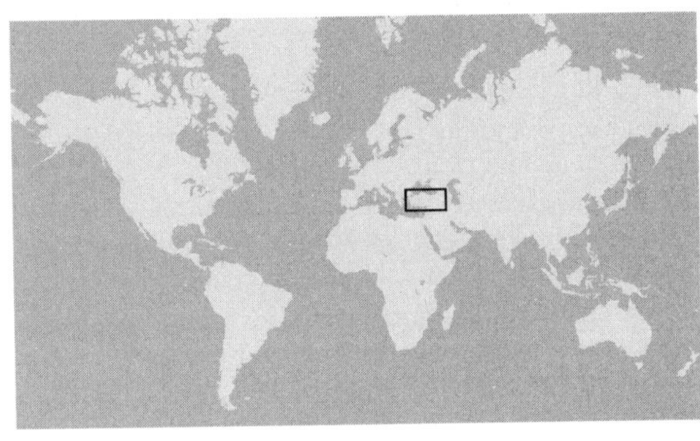

Country Overview

INTRODUCTION The Republic of Turkey was formed after the collapse of the Ottoman Empire in 1923. Geographically its lands lie mostly in Anatolia, or Asia Minor, with an extension into Thrace in the southeastern Balkan Peninsula.

The Ottoman Empire was religiously more mixed than is present-day Turkey, containing substantial Armenian and Greek Orthodox and Jewish communities as well as smaller, more unusual groups, such as the Yezidis and the Zoroastrians. Each of these minority groups, however, have experienced a significant decrease in numbers—albeit under different circumstances—during the last hundred years. Mutual conflict, deportation, and unrest in the late nineteenth and early twentieth centuries led to the almost complete disappearance of the Armenians. After the formation of the Turkish republic, a population exchange was arranged whereby almost the entire Greek Orthodox population in Anatolia was repatriated to Greece. Most of Turkey's Jewish population has gradually emigrated, primarily to Israel but also farther afield. The Yezidis and Zoroastrians, whose absolute numbers were always small, have also emigrated, often to Europe. As a result of these changes, Turkey's population has become almost entirely Muslim. Sunnis make up the large majority of Turkish Muslims, though there is also a significant heterodox minority known as Alevis.

RELIGIOUS TOLERANCE The Turkish republic is constitutionally both secular and democratic. The years since its founding, however, have seen great social upheaval, one consequence of which is that the early republican vision of the separation of personal religious choice from state activity has slowly given way to extensive state-supported teaching of Sunni Islam. Accompanied as it has been by a wider revival of political Islam, this shift has meant that, in some cases, skeptics, those who have lapsed in their faith, and those who practice other religions or unusual forms of Islam have experienced a significant decline in tolerance.

Major Religion

SUNNI ISLAM

DATE OF ORIGIN 1453 C.E., with the Ottoman capture of Constantinople

NUMBER OF FOLLOWERS More than 56 million

HISTORY The Republic of Turkey's first president, Kemal Atatürk (1881–1938), completed a long-standing trend toward secularization that had already been present, although in a much more tentative form, in the late Ottoman period. He initiated a series of reforms through the Republican People's Party: abolition of the Caliphate and the Shariah courts in 1924; adoption of Western dress (the so-called hat law) and the Gregorian calendar in 1925; the abolition of the *tariqas* (Sufi mystical brotherhoods), also in 1925; adoption of the Swiss civil code in 1926; and conversion from the Arabic script to the Latin alphabet in 1928. The secularist movement was continued by Ismet Inönü (1884–1973) after Atatürk's death. Following the introduction of democracy and the first free elections in 1950, the reforms were partially reversed by the populist prime minister Adnan Menderes (1899–1961), whose term marked the beginning of a period during which Islam was slowly reintroduced—albeit not without protest—to public life. In 2002 an Islamic political party gained a majority in the Grand National Assembly for the first time.

Mevlevis, who are known in the West as the Whirling Dervishes, dance in the Mevlana dance hall. The Mevlana's tomb is a significant site of pilgrimage. AP/WIDE WORLD PHOTOS.

EARLY AND MODERN LEADERS Throughout its later history the Ottoman Empire gradually became more influenced by Sunni Islam. This historical inclination remains in contemporary Turkey, so that Muhammad has eclipsed Ali, the Prophet's son-in-law and founder of the Shiite sect, in importance in popular orthodox thought. Islamic leadership also has often been associated in Turkey with military victory, and in recent times the resurgent Islamic mass movement has stressed such leading Ottoman figures as Sultan Mehmed Fatih, the Ottoman conqueror of Istanbul, to great effect. The long-standing formal exclusion of religion from public life in the republic has meant that only lately have explicitly religious political leaders emerged. Important among these are Necmettin Erbakan (born in 1926), who has led several political parties founded upon Islam since the 1970s, and Tayyip Erdoğan (born in 1954), the head of the Islamically oriented Justice and Development Party and prime minister beginning in March 2003. Erdoğan has emerged as the contemporary leader of the Islamic movement in Turkey.

MAJOR THEOLOGIANS AND AUTHORS Secularism has tended to cause a bifurcation of commentaries on religion in Turkey. Authors like Ethem Fiğlali (born in 1937), who have been convinced by the republican secularist message, have written widely on the relationship between laicism and piety, stressing the opportunity that a believer may gain to communicate directly with God if obstacles (such as a powerful clergy) between the worshiped and the worshiper are removed. Influenced by the philosophical arguments underlying the French Revolution, Fiğlali and others emphasize the distinction between the pious self and the rationally organized external world of science and knowledge. Contrariwise, there have been a number of authors who have stressed the potential for Islam's becoming reconciled with modernity. Such was the argument of the philosopher, scholar, and immensely popular writer Said-i Nursi (1877–1960), whose adherents in contemporary Turkey still number about 3 million. Nursi abjured violence and contended that conditions would be right for the return of Islamic law at some time in the future. Until then, his followers believe, it behooves them to study, play a full part in scientific and technological advances, and seek their anticipation in revelations in the Koran. Later interpreters of Said-i Nursi, such as Fethullah Gülen (born in 1938), have themselves gained large followings.

HOUSES OF WORSHIP AND HOLY PLACES Besides Mecca the imperial Ottoman mosques of Istanbul remain the central symbol of Islamic worship for Turkey's Sunni population. Chief among these is Hagia Sophia, the massive Byzantine structure converted to a mosque immediately after the conquest of Istanbul. Now a state museum, it remains a profound source of controversy, with activists calling for it to be made available again for prayer services on a regular basis. Other key monuments include the tomb of Muhammad's standard bearer, which lies at the head of the Golden Horn; the mosque of Ahmed I, known in the West as the Blue Mosque; and the Süleymaniye mosque complex, which sits gracefully on the horizon overlooking the city. While the early republicans closed down the *tariqas* and the tombs associated with their founders, many of these tombs remain significant places of pilgrimage. The most important is the Mevlana complex in Konya, the home of the Mevlevis, who are known in the West as the Whirling Dervishes, after their turning dance. Each year the Mevlana's tomb is visited by more than a million supplicants, many of whom seek a particular favor or reward through the intercession of the saint who lies there.

WHAT IS SACRED? Mosques and the Koran are widely respected and cared for throughout the country. Many tombs are also regarded as sacred by virtue of the bones of the saints buried in them. Additional relics from the lives of saints may be placed in the tombs. Although the practice is frowned upon by purists, people all over Anatolia tie little scraps of cloth to trees or bushes near saint's tombs in the belief that this will aid them in adversity or sickness. Sometimes the sense of the sacred extends to such natural objects as springs, trees, and mountains and to sites associated with Christianity, particularly those where a Christian saint is believed to be buried. The complex of holy places around Ephesus and the house of the Virgin Mary, which are visited by both Christians and Muslims, are examples of this. Throughout Anatolia there is a marked reluctance to disturb graves, whether they are ostensibly Muslim or not.

HOLIDAYS AND FESTIVALS Although it is the day of prayers, Friday is not usually a holiday in Turkey, which operates according to the European working week. Public holidays do mark the Feast of Sacrifice (*qurban bayram*) and the conclusion of the Ramadan fast. Ramadan itself is celebrated throughout the month, not just with special foods but also with the hanging of bright lights on the mosques, special publications, and religious broadcasts on television. The Ramadan celebration has gained in importance in popular media and mass culture in parallel with the rise of the Islamist movement. In Istanbul a large, "traditional" Ramadan fair held in the Byzantine hippodrome in Sultan Ahmed offers Ottoman foods and soft drinks throughout the night, along with such entertainment as roundabouts and music. These two festivals remain the most significant in Turkey, though some people observe other holy days in the Islamic calendar, particularly the four Kandil nights. It is also increasingly common to have Christmas trees in the home, or in public places, during December, as well as parties on New Year's Day. Occasionally during this time images of Father Christmas, known as Noel Baba, may also be seen.

MODE OF DRESS The secular republic required that almost all indications of religious status be removed from people's clothing. This meant that the fine gradations between different ranks of clergy and brotherhood followers were no longer apparent in everyday attire. It is regarded as appropriate from the religious point of view, however, for both men and women to dress somberly and to protect the body from public gaze. In effect this usually means a jacket, shirt, and trousers for men. Men consider it an Islamic custom to wear a mustache or, if a man is a religious activist or perhaps simply particularly pious, a beard. Men who attend the mosque regularly may wear a round cap without a peak, loose trousers, and overshoes over lighter, leather inner shoes. The officially appointed mosque leader, or imam, is permitted to wear a white prayer cap. Women, particularly those from a rural background, may wear a headscarf. A woman who belongs to a brotherhood may wear an enveloping black garment known as a *çadýr.* Since the late twentieth century it has become increasingly common for women who are associated with the Islamic movement to wear a turban, which in this case is a large scarf that covers the head entirely and falls down to a loose-fitting long coat. Still more recently an Islamic fashion movement has arisen that attempts to offer attractive, patterned designs that are nevertheless compatible with Islamic mores.

DIETARY PRACTICES Most Turks usually avoid pork and eat *halal* (permissible under Islamic law) meat. Turkish cuisine is extremely rich, and various foods have become associated with Ramadan, including certain milk puddings (*güllaç*), *pide* bread, and fruit sugar drinks, or *şerbet.* Alcohol is found fairly commonly throughout Anatolia. While alcohol consumption is a subject of debate, it is often held that the Prophet forbade wine but not raki, a strong distilled drink flavored with aniseed. Nevertheless, activist movements regard any form of alcohol with distaste, and there have been increasing attempts to prohibit its sale. So far these efforts have been most successful in small and medium-sized communities, though bars have also been closed down in Istanbul.

RITUALS Rituals and religious practice in Turkey are centered upon the Five Pillars of Islam. Within Turkish Sunni Islam, however, it is usual to observe only four of the pillars: the affirmation of faith in the one God, prayer, fasting, and the pilgrimage to Mecca. The fifth, paying alms, is less regularly observed. It is widely held that it is possible—even laudable—to pray anywhere. For this reason attendance at a mosque is not required. Nevertheless, there is substantial attendance for the Friday prayers and on religious festival days. The majority of women do not attend prayers at a mosque, though the larger structures may have a separate area marked out for their use. Funerals are usually begun by the mosque, and the body is then taken to the cemetery. Burial is considered a practice of the Islamic faith, and cremation is considered inappropriate. While a secular form of the marriage ceremony is obligatory in order to officially register a marriage, it is very common for an imam to be asked to perform a short ceremony (*nikah*) prior to the official wedding.

Although frowned upon officially, there is in Turkey a large body of what is called by skeptics "superstitious" lore, or sorcery (*büyücülük*). The contents of this lore range from healing practices to prayers and incantations and include instruction in fortune-telling, divination, and casting spells or curses to appeal to magical entities. While many theologians and other religious representatives deplore these practices, those who follow them justify them in part by claiming that supernatural entities are mentioned in the Koran.

RITES OF PASSAGE Individual rites of passage vary according to gender. It is regarded as necessary for a man to be circumcised, and while circumcision may take place at any age, the operation is usually carried out at around eight or nine years of age. The event may be celebrated with a party or festival if the boy's family is wealthy or with a parade of cars around the streets, with the boy dressed in an Ottoman soldier's uniform. After the age of 40, or when a man feels that he has reached maturity, he may go on the pilgrimage to Mecca to cleanse himself. After his return he is likely to consciously avoid reprehensible acts, and he may permit his beard to grow.

For women the most significant rite of passage is likely to be marriage, which is held to be a sacred bond and an auspicious step to take from the religious point of view. Marriage is followed in importance by the birth of a woman's first child. On reaching maturity a person of either sex may increasingly wish to engage in acts of charity, such as donating a mosque to the community, thus building up credit in his or her favor before death and judgment at the hands of God.

MEMBERSHIP The secular inclination of the early Turkish republic was strengthened by a conviction that religion was responsible for the gradual degradation of Ottoman power, the loss of territory, and the Empire's ultimate economic collapse. Partly for this reason modern Turkey long avoided in its international dealings any suggestion of religious activism and attempted to suppress those who wished to take such a line. At the level of the individual, however, secularization was only partially successful. To be Muslim remained an essential personal attribute for most of the population, and within this context orthodox or Sunni expansion continued—and even gained strength—throughout the country, thus helping to create a somewhat uniform national ethic. After 1950, when Adnan Menderes came to power, this personalized piety began to be reflected politically in increased public funds for the creation of specialist religious high schools known as *imam-hatip,* official tolerance being extended toward certain *tariqas,* and an expanded role for the state-led Directorate of Religious Affairs. The subsequent re-Islamification of the government and body politic has meant that internal pressure to maintain a stricter religious orthodoxy has continued, and it is possible that this will affect Turkish foreign policy in the future.

SOCIAL JUSTICE There is a long tradition of charitable activity within Turkish Islam, ranging from building mosque complexes that include schools and kitchens to helping individuals in distress. This charitable inclination is reflected in the establishment of trusts, called *vakýfs,* that are run by the government or by private boards. Often nongovernmental organizations oversee these trusts alongside official bodies, providing an opportunity for charity under government auspices. For example, the Directorate of Religious Affairs, the public body responsible for overseeing the appropriate conduct of religion in the country, has associated with it the largest private charitable organization, the Diyanet Vakfý, which distributes religious literature, hands out food to the needy, and pays for circumcisions for those who could not otherwise afford them.

SOCIAL ASPECTS The moral side of religion, *ahlak,* has received sustained attention during the republican period in Turkey. Translated broadly the term *ahlak* conveys the idea that it is against the precepts of religion to force another into any particular path or to steal, exploit, lie, or cheat in any way. Appropriate moral behavior also includes fidelity to husband or wife and family. Abortion is widespread, and legal, though it is held by some to be inauspicious from the strictly religious point of view. While divorce is permitted, it is avoided whenever possible. This approach has contributed to the strength of the nuclear family in Turkey, which remains one of the country's most identifiable social attributes.

POLITICAL IMPACT Although it is difficult to be precise, certainly less than half the Sunni orthodox population has accepted the republican precept that the state should not support religion. The consequence of this is that any political party that favors Islam is assured of more votes in Turkey than one that does not. This simple fact of electoral mechanics has profoundly shaped Turkey's democratic landscape and has led to the gradual reintroduction of Islam into political life. Internationally Turkey has pursued a policy of neutrality with regard to its immediate neighbors, though it has intervened where it has perceived a threat to a Muslim minority. Examples of such intervention include Turkey's involvement in the establishment of a Turkish state on the island of Cyprus and the Turkish government's readiness to act as a broker in the Bosnian conflict of the 1990s.

CONTROVERSIAL ISSUES Within Turkish orthodox Islam the single most controversial issue remains the secular constitution of the republic. This in turn raises the issue of whether an overtly Islamic political party may hold office and whether the state should be providing religious education in its schools (and, if so, of what sort). There is a host of additional related issues that are continuously discussed. These range from the legitimacy of organ transplantation to the use of the Turkish language in prayer and in Koranic readings. Other important points at issue are the wearing of headscarves inside government and civil services buildings, such as schools or the parliament building; the amount of money that should be spent by the state in general on religious activities; the number and construction of mosques; the electronic amplification of the call to prayer; and, from a more philosophical point of view, the relationship between science, revelation, and the Koran.

CULTURAL IMPACT The cultural impact of Sunni Islam in Turkey has been profound, affecting diet, dress, manners, morals, and ceremony. The pattern of religious architecture that became a symbol of the Ottoman Empire remains a strong feature of Turkish life. In literature and art, and in the country's museums, the modernist tone of the republic, which has come slightly more to the fore, gives a greater emphasis to the Anatolian roots of Turkish culture. In effect, Islam and the republic represent the two ends of Turkey's cultural spectrum. People at one end of this spectrum choose a religiously orthodox lifestyle, self-consciously avoiding those aspects of Turkish culture that are problematic from a religious perspective. Others, especially those in the larger cities, may cultivate a more republican approach, attempting to avoid recourse to a life controlled by Islam. Still others manage to follow a mixture of these two approaches, drawing from one or the other at different points in their life or as their convictions evolve and change. The existence of this broad spectrum means that, while life in Turkish villages and small towns may often appear rather uniform, a far greater variety of lifestyles prevails in the cities.

Other Religions

Although Turkey is predominantly Islamic, there are many interpretations and variants of Islam within the country. Many of these different approaches are associated with the *tariqas. Tariqas* themselves vary from being supporters of a more strongly orthodox republic, such as the Naqshbandis, to being of a more mystical bent, like the Bektashis. Theoretically proscribed at the outset of the republic, the *tariqas* have come to be tolerated or, depending on the political context of the day, even encouraged.

The Alevis are the largest subgroup within Turkish Islam, making up roughly 15 percent of the total population. Strongly influenced by an esoteric interpretation of the Muslim faith, many Alevis call themselves Bektashis. Markedly heterodox in their orientation, they stress the way of their own *tariqa* over that of the Five Pillars. For this reason, Alevis rarely attend the mosques in their communities. Instead, they attend their own collective ceremonies, which are held under the auspices of hereditary holy men known variously as *dede* (grandfather), *pir* (leader), or *baba* (literally, father). These ceremonies (*cem*) provide an opportunity to worship together, face to face, and, at the same time, a forum for resolving disputes within the community. Indeed, worship may not take place unless all within the room are at peace with one another. Should there be a disagreement, it is resolved under the leadership of the *dede*, or the disputants are asked to leave the room.

There are a number of elements within the Alevi interpretation of Islam that make it problematic from the orthodox point of view. In the collective ceremonies men and women worship together. The ceremonies are held primarily in Turkish, rather than in Arabic. The interpretations of the *dedes* are often accompanied by the song of a an *aşýk*, or minstrel, who plays a double-stringed instrument known as the *saz* or *bağlama*. The ceremony culminates in a dance called a *sema*. The *dedes* are held to be qualitatively closer to God than others because they or their forebears were given the ability to perform miracles (*keramet*). All these aspects of Alevi's worship go against an orthodox view that insists upon the separation of the sexes, the equality of all men in the eyes of God, and the avoidance of music and dance as sinful.

Perhaps most controversial of all are the emphasis that the Alevi creed places on Ali and the associated hint of Shiism in their religious practice. The collective ceremony itself is a celebration of the twelve duties assigned by Allah to Ali to mark his being given the secrets of existence. The Alevis believe that Ali, Muhammad, and God are an indivisible trinity in which Ali has an equal place as a reflection of divine glory. Within their songs the Alevis often call upon Ali and affirm that they are on "his" road. While Alevis may fast during Ramadan, they are also likely to respect the Shiite days of commemoration during the month of Muharram.

The Alevi's emphasis on mystical quietism tinged with Shiism is sometimes described by comparative scholars as having similarities to the beliefs of other religious minorities in the Middle East, such as the Ali-Haq in Iraq or the Druze in Lebanon and Israel. Throughout the history of the republic, however, the Alevis themselves have not sought to identify themselves as Shiites but rather with the secular tenets of the republic. Politically they have expressed this secular orientation by voting for the Republican People's Party and by strongly supporting the staunchly secularist prime minister, Bülent Ecevit, in the late 1990s. This has led to a partial identification of the left with Alevilik, a fusion particularly noticeable in the music and songs of Turkey's social democratic movement.

Throughout the 1980s, and increasingly in the 1990s, there was something of an Alevi revival. Fueled by a growing sense of vulnerability, the Alevis have increasingly moved to reaffirm their distinctive religious practice via the Internet and an explosion in publications concerning their history, traditions, and religion. Ultimately distinctions between Sunnis and Alevis may come into sharper focus in the Turkish republic, which could lead to a grave societal split along religious lines. Such a development would mark a transformation of religious sensibility within a country that has long attempted to minimize such distinctions.

Although in absolute terms the number of non-Islamic minorities is now extremely low, questions surrounding other religions remain a marked feature of intellectual and political life in Turkey. Church buildings are not prominent in themselves, but there remain functioning embassy and consulate churches in the centers of Ankara and Istanbul. Istanbul is also the seat of the Orthodox Patriarch. Attempts to practice other faiths in Turkey (or unusual modern variations, like the feminist Mother Goddess movement, centered on the neolithic excavations at Çatalhöyük) are treated as political, as well as religious, matters and are received coolly at best. The free practice of Christianity in Turkey is likely to become problematic in the future, and as relations intensify with Europe it may also become a source of awkwardness in the sphere of international relations.

David Shankland

See Also Vol. I: *Islam, Sunnism*

Bibliography

Andrews, Peter A., ed. *Ethnic Groups in the Republic of Turkey.* 2nd ed. Wiesbaden, Germany: L. Reichert, 2002.

Bruinessen, Martin van. *Agha, Shaikh, and State: The Social and Political Structures of Kurdistan.* London and Atlantic Highlands, N.J.: Zed Books, 1992.

Delaney, Carol. *The Seed and the Soil: Gender and Cosmology in Turkish Village Society.* Berkeley: University of California Press, 1991.

Hasluck, F.W. *Christianity and Islam among the Sultans.* Edited by Margaret M. Hasluck. 2 vols. Oxford: Clarendon, 1929.

Lewis, Bernard. *The Emergence of Modern Turkey.* London and New York: Oxford University Press, 1961.

Mardin, Şerif. *Religion and Social Change in Modern Turkey: The Case of Bediüzzaman Said Nursi.* Albany: State University of New York Press, 1989.

Meeker, Michael E. *A Nation of Empire: The Ottoman Legacy of Turkish Modernity.* Berkeley: University of California Press, 2002.

Özdemir, Adil, and Kenneth Frank. *Visible Islam in Modern Turkey.* New York: St. Martin's Press, 2000.

Shankland, David. *Islam and Society in Turkey.* Huntington, England: Eothen Press, 1999.

Stirling, Paul. "Religious Change in Republican Turkey." *Middle East Journal* 12 (1958): 395–408.

Tapper, Richard, ed. *Islam in Modern Turkey: Religion, Politics, and Literature in a Secular State.* London and New York: I.B. Tauris, 1991.

White, Jenny B. *Islamist Mobilization in Turkey: A Study in Vernacular Politics.* Seattle: University of Washington Press, 2002.

Turkmenistan

POPULATION 4,688,963

SUNNI MUSLIM 89 percent

EASTERN ORTHODOX 9 percent

OTHER 2 percent

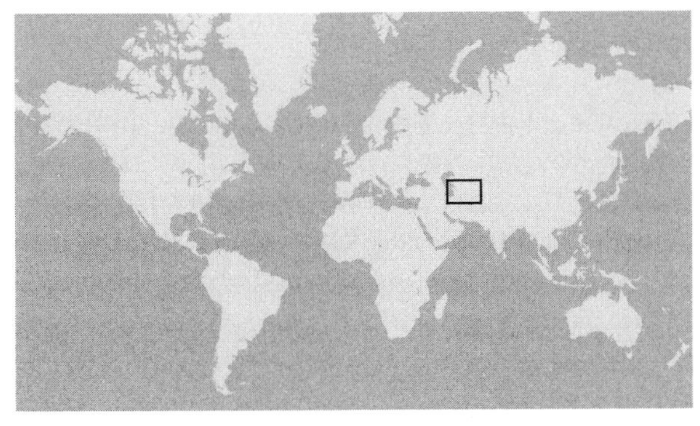

Country Overview

INTRODUCTION Turkmenistan, a desert country in southwestern Central Asia, borders Afghanistan and Iran to the south, Uzbekistan to the east and northeast, Kazakhstan to the northwest, and the Caspian Sea to the west. For millennia it was the home of agriculturists and pastoral nomads. Arab invaders brought Islam to the area during the seventh and eighth centuries C.E., and by the tenth century most Turkmen had converted to Islam.

In 1884 Turkmenistan (then Turkmenia) became a colony of Tsarist Russia. The Tsar's military administration built a railway, allowed a massive migration of Christian Orthodox Russians into the newly subjugated territories, and displaced the indigenous ruling elite. Russian policies were hostile to Islam and generated considerable opposition from the Turkmen. By 1920 the Soviets had occupied Turkmenistan and installed Communist administrators, declaring it the Turkmen Soviet Socialist Republic in 1925. The Bolsheviks outlawed religion, shut down mosques, and banned child marriages, polygyny, *waqf* (religious endowments), bride wealth, and the Arabic script. These measures and Joseph Stalin's oppressive forced settlement and collectivization policies sparked a nationalist rebellion, which Stalin crushed in 1932, executing thousands of Turkmen political and religious leaders.

Turkmenistan declared independence from the Soviet Union in 1991. Saparmurat Niyazov, the country's former Communist First Secretary and a member of the Democratic Party of Turkmenistan, was elected President in 1992. A Muslim in name, he has forced the main opposition activists out of the country and runs one of the most autocratic governments in Central Asia, with no independent media and severe restrictions on all religious activities.

RELIGIOUS TOLERANCE The majority of Turkmen are Sunni Muslims. Historically Turkmen society has been fairly tolerant of other religious faiths. The constitution stipulates freedom of religion, but religious organizations must register and prove a minimum membership of 500 citizens of at least 18 years of age living in the same location. Only Sunni Muslim and Russian Orthodox Christian groups have managed to register. Nonregistered groups are forbidden to meet, distribute religious literature, establish houses of worship, proselytize, or even conduct services in private homes. No one

A mosque under construction in Turkmenistan. Mosque attendance is low, even though the total number of mosques in the country increased from four in 1986 to over 300 in 2002. © DAVID SAMUEL ROBBINS/CORBIS.

may publish or import religious literature; violators may face criminal prosecution and lose their homes. The KNB (National Security Committee), successor of the KGB, monitors religious activities and punishes offenders.

Major Religion

ISLAM

DATE OF ORIGIN Tenth century C.E.

NUMBER OF FOLLOWERS 4.2 million

HISTORY Sufi *shaykhs* claiming descent from Muhammad, the first caliphs (Muhammad's designated successors), important saints, and wandering dervishes spread Islam throughout Turkmenistan during the tenth century. The Turkmen tribal system, with its strong emphasis on genealogical relationships, lent itself to the Islamic tradition of venerating the descendants of the Prophet. "Islamizer" *shaykhs* often became the patron saints of particular Turkmen tribes and clans.

Turkmenistan's conquest and colonization by Tsarist Russia and the Soviets isolated Turkmen from the rest of the Islamic world. The Soviets attempted to eradicate religion; they undermined Islamic identity and unity in the region by creating the Central Asian Soviet republics according to ethnicity. A system of Islamic Spiritual Directorates maintained an official Islam compatible with Soviet Marxist doctrines. Local mullahs (Islamic leaders) were permitted to operate only if they registered with the government and adhered to official restrictions on religious practice. The people generally discredited those mullahs who complied and looked elsewhere for spiritual guidance. In 1928 the Soviets banned Islamic *zakat* (alms) and pilgrimages to Mecca and began shutting down mosques.

Soviet repression and Islam's introduction through miracle-working saints and dervishes rather than through the mosque and the learned written tradition resulted in an unofficial, folk practice rather than a formal observance of the Five Pillars. Turkmen Islam centers on the veneration of saints and pilgrimages to their shrines, called *mazar,* and other holy places. Revered Sufi leaders with syncretistic beliefs have assumed the role of the mullahs, acting as religious guides and counselors, healers, and dispensers of charms and amulets. Since independence long-standing pre-Islamic shamanistic practices and ancestral worship have revived among rural Turkmen, who view Islam not in terms of piety but as an aspect of their national identity. Mosque attendance is low, even though the total number of mosques in the country increased from four in 1986 to over 300 in 2002 (many built with funds from Kuwait and Saudi Arabia).

EARLY AND MODERN LEADERS Muhammad Junaid Khan (1860–1938), a member of the Yomud tribe, united the various Turkmen tribes in 1916 to defeat the Russian army. He established an independent political base in Khiva but was overthrown by the Soviets in 1920.

Saparmurat Niyazov, who the Turkmen parliament declared president for life in 1999, transformed himself into a Muslim leader by making the hajj to Mecca in 1992, an act unprecedented for a communist party chief. Referring to himself as *Türkmanbashi* (Father and Chief of all Turkmen), Niyazov has built a personality cult unrivaled in Central Asia, naming buildings, streets, cities, and even months of the year after himself. His birthplace has been transformed into a shrine, and his statues and images are everywhere. Niyazov has written a national spiritual guide called the *Rukhnama* (Ruhnama, or Book of the Soul) and has made it compulsory reading in all public schools. Supporters have proclaimed Niyazov a prophet.

MAJOR THEOLOGIANS AND AUTHORS The spiritual writings and poetry of Mahtum Quli Azadi-oghli (1733–90) encouraged the emergence of a Turkmen nationalistic consciousness. In the early twentieth century Abdulhekim Qulmuhammed-oghli (died 1937), a member of the Basmachi politico-religious resistance, and Berdi Kerbabay-oghli (1897–1974) formed the Turkmen literary society. The emergence of a cadre of Muslim nationalist scholars brought about a new period of intellectual life in Turkmenistan. Most of these scholars perished, along with the bulk of the Muslim clergy, during Stalin's 1930s purges.

Sufi *shaykhs*, revered for their sacred pedigrees and their miraculous shamanistic powers, oversee life cycle rituals and act as mediators in disputes between clans. The nomadic tribesmen believe the *shaykhs* can cure sickness, ward off evil spirits and the evil eye, and perform other magical feats. They belong to *ovlyads* (*övlat,* or honored groups) and live in small numbers among various Turkmen tribes. Tribes lacking *ovlyads* are generally held in low esteem.

HOUSES OF WORSHIP AND HOLY PLACES Local communities must obtain a government permit to build a mosque and must pay the building and maintenance costs themselves. The state supports the major mosques. President Saparmurat Niyazov plans to make a national religious pilgrimage site of Saparmurat-Khodji mosque at Gšk Tepe, where Turkmen freedom fighters dealt the Russians a major defeat in 1879.

Turkmen also worship at shrines associated with natural objects, rock formations, caves, and trees; the graves of saints and martyrs; and localities visited by cultural heroes or where miraculous events transpired. Muslims visit Paraw Bibi in western Turkmenistan seeking fertility and cures for mental illnesses. The mosque-shrine complex of Khoja Yusup Baba near Merv is the interment place of the Sufi teacher Yusuf Hamadani (1048–1140), whose disciples developed the Naqshbandi and Yasavi Sufi orders. Said to have great miraculous powers, Khoja Yusup is considered so important by the Turkmen that two pilgrimages there are deemed the equivalent of one visit to Mecca.

WHAT IS SACRED? Particularly sacred to Turkmen Muslims are the Koran, places associated with miraculous events, and the graves of *shaykhs* and religious martyrs. Cemeteries often develop around the graves of such holy personages, who acquire the status of *gonambashi* (chief of the cemetery).

HOLIDAYS AND FESTIVALS Turkmen celebrate the main Islamic holidays and festivals, including Ramazan (Ramadan) Bayram (Id al-Fitr), which marks the end of Ramadan, and Kurban Bayram (Id al-Adha, or Feast of the Sacrifice), when households slaughter an animal and share the meat with relatives and the poor. Rukhnama Day, observed on 12 September, is a public holiday celebrating the completion of President Niyazov's book, the *Rukhnama.*

MODE OF DRESS Traditional Islamic Turkmen dress includes shaggy sheepskin hats, baggy pantaloons, knee-high boots, a shirt with an embroidered collar, and a thick silk jacket. The embroidery is based on traditional designs, some of which are intended to ward off evil influences. Men also wear triangle-shaped cloths or leather protective amulets containing verses from the Koran. Women wear brightly colored, ankle-length dresses with decorated sleeves and collars over trousers with embroidery at the ankles. Younger women wear silk belts, woven socks, and knee-guards. Women also wear headscarves, tall hats, silver head ornaments, and bracelets and brooches set with semiprecious stones. Women do not wear face veils.

DIETARY PRACTICES Russian immigrants introduced pork into Turkmenistan, and some Turkmen eat it despite the Muslim interdiction. Turkmen also consume wine, beer, and vodka despite the Islamic prohibition.

RITUALS Pilgrimages to shrines, increasingly popular since independence, include circumambulating burial sites and making *hudaiyoli* (offerings of food). Some Turkmen Muslims pray five times a day. Turkmen are now permitted to make the pilgrimage to Mecca, but Niyazov limits the number of individuals who can go and sends them with a government escort. Few Turkmen aspire to go.

Everyday ritual behaviors include cupping the hands and stroking the face (an expression of thanks to Allah) after every meal and when passing a shrine. When Turkmen discuss important events, they use the term *mashallah,* "as God has willed it."

RITES OF PASSAGE For a period of 40 days (called *chila*), Turkmen shield their newborn children from the gaze of strangers to protect them from the "evil eye," keeping the Koran near the cradle as an additional safeguard. At the end of *chila,* mother and newborn child undergo a special purification bath.

Mullahs perform circumcisions, weddings, and funerals. Boys are circumcised according to the *sunnah* (examples set by the Prophet) at the age of ten or eleven, attended only by close family members. Turkmen marriages involve music, dancing, and a considerable degree of festivity. A *kalym* (customary bride price) is paid to the bride's family. *Aksakals* (village elders) set the date of the wedding according to astrological signs, after which the families place flowers on the graves of ancestors to ensure good fortune. According to Islamic tradition, women may not take part in a burial. The bereaved family holds commemorative feasts on the seventh and fortieth days after the death and at the end of one year. On the anniversary of the death, they make sacrificial offerings, either slaughtering an animal or distributing bread and sweets to neighbors.

MEMBERSHIP Through the Gengish (Council for Religious Affairs, which controls mosque and church funds) and the KNB, the state imposes parameters on Islamic membership drives and discourages religious leaders from proselytizing.

SOCIAL JUSTICE Devout Turkmen Muslims believe that, according to the Koran and Islamic tradition, every individual has rights to life, sustenance, work, justice, freedom of religious expression, ownership of property, protection of body and offspring, honor and dignity, and practicing his or her talents among other members of the *ummah,* the universal community of Muslims. Turkmen make no distinction between secular and spiritual dimensions of life. Niyazov's Soviet-model political structure, however, has created an environment incompatible with social justice, heavily curtailing Muslim's expression of their social ideals and raising an international outcry over human rights abuses.

SOCIAL ASPECTS Islamic values and Turkmen customary laws and values, or *adat,* often operate together in matters of marriage, family life, deference to ones parents and elders, property rights and inheritance, and tribal and clan identities. Tribal affiliations and kinship are the basis of family organization and play a role in the arranging of marriages in rural areas. During the Soviet period many Turkmen women entered the work force, altering traditional family relations and gender roles that assigned women to the domestic sphere and men to a public one. Former Soviet restrictions on Islamic practice (bans on the veil, polygyny, and child marriages, for example) have permanently impacted Turkmen social customs.

POLITICAL IMPACT Following the country's independence from the Soviet Union, Islam experienced a brief resurgence in Turkmenistan, but the newly elected government quickly clamped down on religious expression. Niyazov maintains strict control of the official aspects of the religion: The Gengish (established in 1994) oversees the appointment of all Muslim clerics and requires them to report regularly. In 1997 the government banned mosque-based religious teachings by imams and closed the Zamakhshari Madrasa, a center of Islamic education in Dashoguz. The Theological Faculty at Turkmen State University in Ashgabat is the only legal religious educational institution, and the number of clerical students there has been restricted to 20 a year.

Because Turkmenistan is an Islamic society with a secular political apparatus, the state has found it expedient to incorporate the metaphors of Islam into the official political rhetoric and to emphasize the Muslim credentials of politicians such as President Niyazov. Niyazov has successfully protected Turkmenistan from the spread of Islamic extremism on the same grounds as he has non-Islamic belief systems—that it might contribute to civil instability and threaten his regime.

CONTROVERSIAL ISSUES Devout Turkmen Muslims are uneasy over Niyazov's efforts to promulgate his quasi-religious personality cult and vision of religiosity, which is an odd blend of Turkmen nationalism, moral aphorisms, poetic couplets, fatherly advice, snippets from the Koran and Islamic lore, and personal aggrandizement, encapsulated in the *Rukhnama.* Claiming divine inspiration from Allah, Niyazov touts the tome as equal to the Koran. Devout practitioners find such efforts markedly un-Islamic. Several Muslim clerics have refused to exalt the *Rukhnama* and have been dismissed.

CULTURAL IMPACT Islam's impact on the traditionally nomadic and seminomadic Turkmen culture was milder than on their urban-dwelling and agricultural neighbors, the Afghans, Persians, and Uzbeks. A merged Islamic-Turkic cultural identity persisted during the Russian and Soviet occupations primarily through Islamic poetry, literature, and architecture. Famous Muslim Turkmen poets include Mammetveli Kemine (1770–1840) and Mollanepes (1810–62). An important aspect of Turkmen heritage, *dastans* (traditional epic tales) sung by performers called *bagshi* combine elements of ancient Turkish culture and Islamic values. One famous *dastan* is "Goroglu," which consists of over 200 verses and relates the heroic struggle of one man against unjust rulers. The embroidery on Turkmen clothing also reinforces Turkmen identity. The state, which both sponsors and monitors the arts, encourages artists to promote the emergent national identity using both Islamic heritage and indigenous culture.

Other Religions

A small number of Shia Muslims live along the border between Turkmenistan and the predominantly Shia Iran. The religious practices of Turkmen Shia are not politicized, and Sunni Muslims do not perceive the Shia as a threat. Niyazov has a great distaste for the Shia, however, and has banned them from worshiping in public and establishing mosques.

Most Turkmen Christians, the majority of them Russian immigrants who arrived during the Soviet period, belong to the officially recognized Russian (Eastern) Orthodox Church, which has 11 churches, 5 priests, and no seminaries in Turkmenistan. Russian Orthodox Christians are permitted to worship in a limited number of registered venues.

Other churches and religious groups represented in Turkmenistan include Pentecostal Christian, Roman Catholic, Jehovah's Witness, Seventh-Day Adventist, Baptist, Bahai, and Hare Krishna. The government views these with hostility as "foreign" religions that do not belong in Turkmenistan and has attempted to restrict and even eradicate them.

Homayun Sidky

See Also Vol. 1: *Christianity, Eastern Orthodoxy, Islam, Sunnism*

Bibliography

Amnesty International. *Turkmenistan: January to December 2002.* London: Amnesty International, 2003.

Basilov, V.N. "Honor Groups in Traditional Turkmen Society." In *Islam in Tribal Societies: From the Atlas to the Indus.* Edited by A. Ahmed and D. Hart. London: Routledge and Kegan Paul, 1984.

Blackwell, Carole. *Tradition and Society in Turkmenistan: Gender, Oral Culture and Song.* Surrey, England: Curzon Press, 2001.

Curtis, Glenn E., ed. *Turkmenistan: A Country Study.* Washington, D.C.: Federal Research Division, Library of Congress, 1996.

International Religious Freedom Report. Released by the Bureau of Democracy, Human Rights and Labor. Washington, D.C.: U.S. State Department, 2003.

Lewis, David. *After Atheism: Religion and Ethnicity in Russia and Central Asia.* Surrey, England: Curzon Press, 2000.

Tyson, David. "Shrine Pilgrimage in Turkmenistan as a Means to Understand Islam among the Turkmen." *Central Asian Monitor* 1 (1997): 15–32.

Tuvalu

POPULATION 11,146

TUVALU CHRISTIAN CHURCH 92 percent

SEVENTH-DAY ADVENTIST 2.4 percent

BAHAI 1.8 percent

JEHOVAH'S WITNESS 1.3 percent

ROMAN CATHOLIC 0.5 percent

OTHER 2 percent

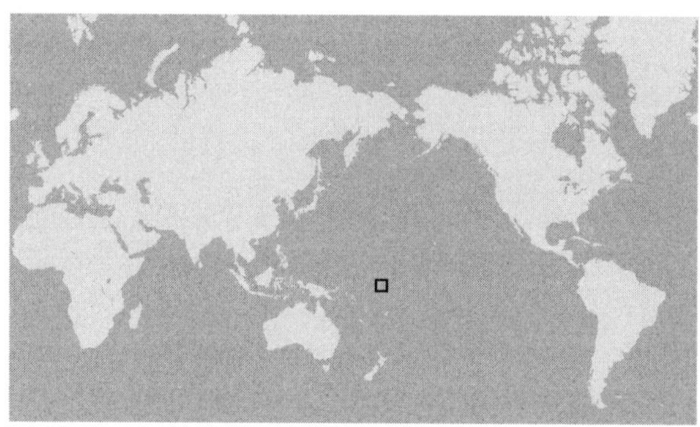

Country Overview

INTRODUCTION The nation of Tuvalu, part of the Polynesian archipelago in the southwest Pacific Ocean, consists of nine islands in a chain 360 miles long. The total area of these low-lying, coral reef islands is only 9.4 square miles. No point on the islands is more than 15 feet above sea level. Its main crop is coconuts, and its main resource is fishing.

The pre-Christian religion of these islands, formerly known as the Ellice Islands, was suppressed in the late 1800s, though elements may remain in the everyday Christianity that now dominates Tuvaluan identity. The national motto is "Tuvalu mo te Atua," or "Tuvalu and the Almighty." The Tuvaluans see themselves as highly Christian.

RELIGIOUS TOLERANCE The constitution of Tuvalu enshrines tolerance, but new faiths cannot proselytize unless they have existing adherents in the country. The Tuvalu Christian Church is effectively an established (official state) church and has a considerable degree of influence over government policy. While there is some diversity in the capital (on Funafuti Atoll), on the outer islands the church is so dominant that other denominations struggle. Religious conformity reflects a strong communal ethos.

Major Religion

TUVALU CHRISTIAN CHURCH

DATE OF ORIGIN 1861 C.E.
NUMBER OF FOLLOWERS 10,300

HISTORY The Tuvalu Christian Church emerged from the London Missionary Society (LMS), established in 1795. Initially a hybrid Protestant organization, the LMS by the 1860s derived its theological impetus from Congregationalism.

In Tuvalu evidence of Christian practices dates back at least to the 1850s. The arrival of true Christianity, however, occurred in 1861, when Elekana, a LMS deacon from the Cook Islands, shipwrecked on Nukulaelae Atoll. Elekana found a people eager to become literate and open to change their religion. He alerted the LMS in Samoa, but the establishment of a system of churches was delayed until 1865, when the LMS installed Elekana and several Samoan teachers in the southern islands group of Tuvalu.

Under the LMS local Tuvalu churches were linked to a network of sister churches and missions in Kiribati (formerly the Gilbert Islands), Tokelau, and Samoa. Foreign influence in the area strengthened in 1892, when the British established the Gilbert and Ellice Islands Protectorate, in 1916 becoming a British colony. Nevertheless, the church remained powerful and gradually acquired a more Tuvaluan character, separating from its Samoan equivalent in 1958. In 1975 the Ellice Islanders voted overwhelmingly for political separation from the Micronesian Gilbertese, leading to Tuvalu's self-government and then full independence in 1978.

EARLY AND MODERN LEADERS Until the 1950s most pastors and their wives were Samoan. Some achieved great influence and prestige during long-term residence in Tuvalu, but the pastor's power was always constrained by local deacons and lay preachers.

The transition to church independence and reduced external control helped Tuvalu create a local cadre of young, dynamic church leaders who were involved in administration, reorganization, youth affairs, publicity, external relations, and Bible translation. The Tuvaluan New Testament appeared in 1978 and the complete Bible in 1986, finally replacing the Samoan Scriptures. One of the most dynamic leaders of the postindependence era was the Reverend Alovaka Maui, general secretary of the Tuvalu Christian Church from 1977 until his early death in 1982.

MAJOR THEOLOGIANS AND AUTHORS Although there are no major theologians or religious authors from Tuvalu, some Tuvaluan pastors and pastoral applicants have written theses at the Pacific Theological College in Suva, Fiji, or at other colleges in New Zealand and elsewhere. Several of these studies rethink Christian theology in a Tuvaluan context.

HOUSES OF WORSHIP AND HOLY PLACES Churches are considered the holiest places in Tuvalu. There is at least one on every island, with several serving the much larger and more diverse population on Funafuti. Memorials mark missionary events on some islands, including the site of Elekana's arrival at Nukulaelae.

WHAT IS SACRED? The Christian God, called Te Atua in Tuvalu, is considered the most sacred being in the universe, followed closely by Jesus Christ. Tuvaluans sometimes ascribe mystical power to the Scriptures, and this belief may extend to using the Bible in unsanctioned personal rituals, for which bottles of coconut oil may also be deployed.

Tuvaluans manifest a fervor for the religious power of society. They place great stress on consensus and community, enhancing these by rituals and displays of religious unity.

HOLIDAYS AND FESTIVALS In Tuvalu, as elsewhere, Sunday is the main day of worship for mainstream Christian denominations, though services are also held at other times. Members of the Tuvalu Christian Church attend special services to celebrate the main Christian festivals of Christmas and Easter. There is often a church service on New Year's Eve as well.

MODE OF DRESS Religion does not influence dress on Tuvalu. Churchgoers are expected to dress respectably, but there is no standardized attire. Everyday wear for men commonly includes a good shirt and *sulu* (sarong), but trousers are also acceptable, as are T-shirts, though without inappropriate slogans. Women wear long dresses and tunics. Bright colors are permitted for both sexes. Shoes and sandals are becoming more popular, and they may be worn in church; previously all footwear had to be left outside.

DIETARY PRACTICES There are no dietary restrictions followed by members by the Tuvalu Christian Church. Seventh-day Adventists abstain from pork, a favorite feast food in Tuvalu, which sometimes creates tensions with the majority community of the Tuvalu Christian Church.

RITUALS The main Sunday service begins at 9:00 A.M., and another service, with a much lower attendance, starts at 3:00 P.M.. Services usually include prayers, one or more collective Bible readings, hymns, and a sermon, followed by notices. Each congregation holds a monthly Communion service for the *ekalesia,* adult members of the church in good standing.

Families are also expected to conduct *lotus*, or services, in the early morning, though many do not, and at 7:00 P.M. before the evening meal, which almost all do. On outer islands the evening *lotu* is still strictly enforced. On Funafuti, however, people walk or drive during *lotu* without incurring serious penalties other than social disapproval.

RITES OF PASSAGE Marriage in the Tuvalu Christian Church is marked by a church ceremony, including one or more couples, preceded by separate processions of brides, grooms, and their supporters and followed by dancing, singing, and feasting, sometimes over several days.

After a death a church bell often tolls, and a group of mourners attends the corpse, singing and praying during an all-night vigil. A full church funeral usually takes place on the day of death or the next day. Different islands have different burial practices. On some islands the dead are laid to rest in village cemeteries, while on others they are placed in family plots near houses or on the grounds of the family home.

MEMBERSHIP Confirmation and admittance to full membership of the *ekalesia* typically occurs after a childhood spent attending church or Sunday school and a period of Bible study in the *kau talavou,* or church youth group. Adults may be expelled from the *ekalesia* for transgressions such as adultery or drunkenness, but they may be readmitted after further study and good behavior.

SOCIAL JUSTICE Social justice in a Western sense is not a major concern of the Tuvalu Christian Church.

SOCIAL ASPECTS Church leaders often express views concerning marriage, family, sexuality, and gender roles. The church encourages engaged couples to seek counseling from their pastor, who at the wedding feast is likely to urge them to live harmoniously as a Christian couple. Some pastors have conservative views on conjugal matters; others are somewhat more liberal.

Formerly the church had a dominant role in education, with pastors and their wives providing much of the primary schooling; later the colonial administration took over education. By the early 1900s the church ran advanced schools for the separate training of boys and girls. Primary schools are now virtually all run by the government, as is the main secondary school on Vaitupu, though pastors and church officials do work there. The Tuvalu Christian Church sometimes resurrects the idea of church secondary schools, but such ventures suffer from lack of funding.

Some gender liberalization has occurred in Tuvalu, with women receiving theological training and administrative employment but not in village pastorates. Women's committees have long been involved in health and economic development issues but are now less identified with the church and more with local government.

POLITICAL IMPACT Pastors and other church leaders do not dictate people's political views, though the church does have considerable informal influence, and parliamentary candidates benefit from *ekalesia* membership. Pastors have held political office in the past, but leaders now tend to emerge from the educated secular elite.

Pastors are still widely accorded special powers and responsibilities to uphold community well-being and may intervene in fights with impunity. The village has to compensate them for injuries or accidents.

CONTROVERSIAL ISSUES The Tuvalu Christian Church has relatively conservative views on divorce and abortion, but it is liberal concerning birth control, an issue made more important by the country's problems with population growth. Pre- or extramarital sexual relations are frowned on, but liberal church leaders recognize the need to educate people about HIV/AIDS and other sexually transmitted diseases. Controversy continues over whether ordained women can become pastors in village congregations, whether minority religions should have equivalent status, and whether pastors should have the automatic right to sit in *maneapas*, or village meetinghouses.

CULTURAL IMPACT In Tuvalu the standard local dance form, called *faatele,* is not religious as such, but its sung lyrics often contain religious themes. Performances by church choirs are popular in Tuvalu.

Virtually no printed Tuvaluan literature exists other than government publications, Scriptures, and a church newsletter. Craftspeople concentrate on weaving pandanus mats or carving canoes and other wooden artifacts, and they are not inspired by religion to any great extent. Village churches, especially those on the outer islands, are usually the grandest buildings and feature religiously significant designs and decoration.

Other Religions

It is estimated that 8 percent of the population of Tuvalu are members of minority faiths. Some two-thirds of these live on Funafuti, where the majority of people are employed in government and in small- and medium-sized businesses. These relatively well-off Tuvaluans undermine loyalty to the Tuvalu Christian Church, which expects large financial commitments from its members.

On Funafuti Seventh-day Adventists, Bahais, Jehovah's Witnesses, and Roman Catholics all have compounds with places of worship, school buildings, and other facilities. Bahais place emphasis on primary education and offer it without obligation to children of other faiths. Some families take advantage of overseas educational opportunities offered by churches like the Seventh-day Adventist. There are also a small number of adherents of Ahmadiyya, an Islamic sect; their number is unknown, though the Koran has been translated into Tuvaluan.

Michael Goldsmith

See Also Vol. 1: *Christianity*

Bibliography

Besnier, Niko. "Christianity, Authority, and Personhood: Sermonic Discourse on Nukulaelae Atoll." *Journal of the Polynesian Society* 103, no. 4 (1994): 339–78.

Goldsmith, Michael. "Alovaka Maui: Defender of the Faith." In *The Covenant Makers: Islander Missionaries in the Pacific.* Edited by Doug Munro and Andrew Thornley. Suva, Fiji: Pacific Theological College, Institute of Pacific Studies; University of the South Pacific, 1996.

Goldsmith, Michael, and Doug Munro. *The Accidental Missionary: Tales of Elekana.* Christchurch: University of Canterbury, Macmillan Brown Centre for Pacific Studies, 2002.

———. "Conversion and Church Formation in Tuvalu." *Journal of Pacific History* 27, no. 1 (1992): 44–54.

Koch, Gerd. *Songs of Tuvalu.* Translated by Guy Slatter. Suva, Fiji: University of the South Pacific, Institute of Pacific Studies, 2000.

Kofe, Laumua. "Old-Time Religion" and "Palagi and Pastors." In *Tuvalu—A History.* Edited by Hugh Laracy. Suva, Fiji: University of the South Pacific, Institute of Pacific Studies and Extension Services; Funafuti: Ministry of Social Services, Government of Tuvalu, 1983.

Munro, Doug. "The Humble Ieremia: A Samoan Pastor in Tuvalu, 1880–1890." *Pacific Journal of Theology* 2, no. 23 (2000): 40–48.

———. "Kirisome and Tema: Samoan Pastors in the Ellice Islands." In *More Pacific Islands Portraits.* Edited by Deryck Scarr. Canberra: Australian National University Press, 1978.

———. "Samoan Pastors in Tuvalu, 1865–1899." In *The Covenant Makers: Islander Missionaries in the Pacific.* Edited by Doug Munro and Andrew Thornley. Suva, Fiji: University of the South Pacific, Pacific Theological College and Institute of Pacific Studies, 1996.

Uganda

POPULATION 24,699,073

CHRISTIAN 78 percent

MUSLIM 9 percent

AFRICAN INDIGENOUS BELIEFS 8 percent

AFRICAN INDEPENDENT CHURCHES 4 percent

OTHER 1 percent

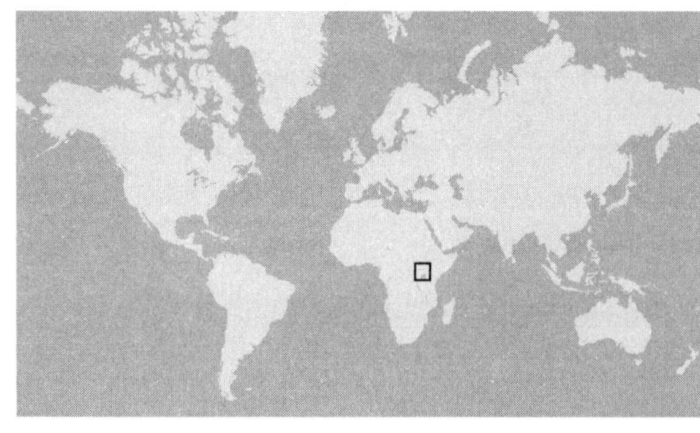

Country Overview

INTRODUCTION Situated in East Africa, the Republic of Uganda is a country of savannas and plains surrounded by mountain ranges. It is bordered by Tanzania and Rwanda to the south, the Democratic Republic of the Congo to the west, the Sudan to the north, and Kenya to the east. Lake Victoria extends across its southeastern corner. Uganda became independent from Britain in 1962 and a republic in 1963. During the country's colonial history a massive conversion to Christianity took place, so that today Christians make up the large majority of the population.

In 1877 Anglicanism arrived with the first colonial explorers at the court of the kingdom of Buganda. They were followed two years later by Catholic missionaries. The advantages of literacy for court functionaries, and the sympathies of the king of Buganda, secured a massive conversion to Christianity by the king's elite group. Anglicanism was initially considered the official colonial and state religion, but a large number of conversions to Catholicism, supported by foreign missionaries, followed within the next few years. With an even number of Anglicans and Catholics, Christians in contemporary Uganda have a population of more than 19 million.

Other Christian groups in Uganda include Greek Orthodox and several African Independent Churches. Orthodox Christians started a community in Uganda after a Greek Orthodox priest baptized a member of the Anglican Church in 1929. The number of Orthodox Christians has remained small, however, with membership at 50,000 in 1995.

Religion shapes the social and political involvement of most Ugandans, whose political party affiliations are related to their religious affiliations. African indigenous religions are not very strong in Uganda; they are most prevalent in the precolonial kingdoms of Buganda, Toro, Ankole, and Bunyoro. A small percentage of Ugandans are Muslim. Muslims are found mainly among ethnic groups and families from the Sudan. Islam has had greater impact in neighboring countries, such as Tanzania and Kenya, than in Uganda. One percent of Ugandans follow a variety of other religious traditions, such as the Bahai faith (with about 1,000 members), or consider themselves "born-again" Christians.

RELIGIOUS TOLERANCE Despite postcolonial political turmoil, Uganda has experienced a broad religious tolerance, which in 1993 was built into its constitution. Since the 1993 constitutional reforms local monarchies have once again been considered part of public life. For example, in March 1993 Ronald Metebi became king of the Baganda 26 years after the abolition of the monarchy in Buganda, and monarchs were also reinstated in the kingdoms of Toro and Bunyoro. Although the restoration of the monarchy was rejected in Ankole (the region of Yoweri Museveni, president of Uganda since 1986), most Ugandans recognize that the old kingdoms played a central part in restoring democracy and in securing ongoing religious tolerance.

Since the 1990s there has been religious tension between Anglicans and Catholics within the Ugandan government. While President Museveni does not actively take part in one of the major Christian traditions, he considers himself a Christian and has respected the privileged status that was granted to Anglicans by the colonial administration and the British Commonwealth. Among top civil servants, there are many more Anglicans than Catholics, and it has been pointed out that Museveni has given much larger gifts to newly appointed Anglican bishops than to new Catholic bishops. Nevertheless, such differences exist within a system of religious tolerance, one in which Museveni's wife has proclaimed herself a born-again Christian.

Despite the generally high level of religious tolerance, in northern Uganda guerrilla movements have formed along religious lines. For example, in 1986 Alice Auma—claiming to be led by Lakwena, a local Christian spirit—organized an army, armed with sticks and stones, to fight the central government. Assuming the name Alice Lakwena, she said her Holy Spirit Movement was a necessary cleansing of sin and a means of establishing a close unity with nature. In 1987 her followers were violently crushed by the Ugandan government. Other movements, however, such as the Lord's Resistance Army, have continued to be active in the northern territories, out of the army's reach, and all have claimed to be led by Lakwena.

Pope Paul VI dedicates the Basilica of the Ugandan Martyrs in July 1969. It was there in 1886 that 26 Christians were tortured and executed for refusing to renounce their faith. © BETTMANN/CORBIS.

Major Religion

CHRISTIANITY

DATE OF ORIGIN 1877 C.E.

NUMBER OF FOLLOWERS 19.3 million

HISTORY When Portuguese explorers visited parts of the East African coast during the sixteenth century, territories within Uganda remained inaccessible to them. At that time immigrants from southeastern Sudan founded the kingdom of Bunyoro, and a century later the kingdom of Buganda became the most centralized and powerful in the region.

Christianity in Uganda began with contacts between Europeans and Kabaka (King) Mutesa I of Buganda (died in 1884). In 1862 Mutesa admitted British explorers John Hanning Speke and James Grant into his kingdom. In 1874 American journalist Henry Morton Stanley visited the kingdom and was surprised by Mutesa's interest in Christianity. After the arrival of Stanley's letter to the *Daily Telegraph* (15 November 1875), Anglican missionaries of the Church Missionary Society reached Buganda in 1877. The Catholic White Fathers followed two years later and made an impact on the kabaka's court, particularly through discussions of the importance of literacy. Mutesa never committed himself to any creed, though he allowed his young court members to become Muslim or Christian, Anglican or Catholic. The Arabs resented his refusal to be circumcised, and the Christian missionaries could not baptize him because he rejected the idea of monogamy and remained a polygamist all his life.

In 1884 Mutesa was succeeded by his son Mwanga, who, while puzzled by the constant fights between Anglicans and Catholics, allowed Christian and Muslim missionaries to live close to the king's court and to engage its members in discussions about religion and politics. He became weary of the missionaries' influence over young Christians (known as readers, or *abasomi*), who, in his opinion, had agreed to the missionaries' request to leave their old ways and had rejected traditional religion, actions that many considered rebellious. As a consequence Mwanga requested that all Christian converts renounce their faith. Since many did not comply, he ordered that 200 of them be killed. Those killed later became known as the Ugandan Martyrs, the largest group having been killed at the Namugongo Hills on 3 June 1886.

Earlier, in October 1885, Mwanga had ordered the killing of the new Anglican bishop of Eastern Equatorial Africa, James Hannington, because the bishop was entering the kingdom in order to take up his headquarters in Kampala by a route that took him through the neighboring kingdom of Busoga, and that appeared surreptitious. Mwanga presumed evil intentions and ordered his soldiers to kill the bishop.

In 1888, as Mwanga tried to reduce the religious group's influence, he was deposed by a coalition of Muslims and Protestants. When the coalition collapsed, the Muslims appointed a new kabaka, and the Christian missionaries had to leave the kingdom. In 1889 Ugandan Catholics and Protestants overthrew the Muslims and reinstated Kabaka Mwanga under tight control by the local chiefs.

By 1892 Catholics and Protestants in Uganda had declared war on each other, and the Church Missionary Society lobbied the British government, requesting an intervention by the British crown in Uganda. In the same year Captain Frederick (later Lord) Lugard arrived in Uganda to make arrangements for the British East Africa Company to take control of the country. Lugard sided with the Anglicans, who became part of the official colonial enterprise. It was clear that he perceived the White Fathers, who were mostly French, as foreigners. By this time Anglicans were already known as Bangereza (English), while Catholics were identified as Bafaranza (French). Their rivalry would continue over the years and would shape later political developments within Uganda.

In 1894 the Uganda British Protectorate was set up, and two years later the kingdoms of Bunyoro, Toro, Ankole, and Busoga were incorporated into the protectorate. Several years later northern territories along the Nile became part of the protectorate, and by 1919 Britain had taken possession of most of the territories that are part of contemporary Uganda. The British relied on the cooperation of the Baganda for all annexations that required negotiations with local authorities.

European Anglican and Catholic missionaries now had access to all of the territories, and a steady conversion of the Ugandan population to Christianity took place. The administration relied on the missions for schools and hospitals; it was only in the 1950s that the British administration opened government schools. The colonial expansion created tensions along religious and ethnic lines. On the one hand, those who attended school became Anglicans or Catholics; on the other hand, the Baganda became close allies of the colonial government and increased their territories, as well as the distrust in which they were held by other kingdoms and ethnic groups.

By the 1950s political parties in Uganda had amalgamated support for independence along religious and ethnic lines. Thus, the political movement known as the Uganda National Congress was formed in 1952. In 1954 the Catholics established the Democratic Party in order to balance the political drive of the Anglicans. In 1960 the Uganda National Congress joined the Uganda People's Congress party, led by Milton Obote (born in 1924), which represented a movement toward independence along official lines and which had secured Anglican support within the political sphere. Within this political spectrum the Baganda, who opposed a wider Uganda (with Buganda as one territory among many), formed their own party, the Kabaka Yeka (King Alone), which sought to preserve Buganda's political autonomy. In the first elections before independence, the Baganda supported the Uganda People's Congress, which won the elections. Uganda became independent in October

1962, with Milton Obote as prime minister. By 1963 Uganda had become a republic, with Mutesa II (1924–69), the Bugandan kabaka, as president.

After independence Buganda's position within the new country, and relations between Anglicans and Catholics, were the sources of most political tension and governmental concern. In February 1966, following the escalation of the conflict over Buganda's central role in Uganda, Obote staged a military coup against Mutesa II, who fled into exile. By April Obote had appointed himself president, and in 1967 he abolished the four kingdoms, bringing Buganda under the Ugandan central administration. By 1969 Obote had abolished all opposition parties, thus reinforcing the central role of the Anglican Church within Uganda.

In 1971 Idi Amin staged a military coup against Obote and took over the government. Some religious leaders, such as Catholic bishop Adrian Ddungu, of Masaka, publicly welcomed the change, suggesting that they had had enough of Obote's Anglicanism and socialism. Despite support from some Christian quarters, Amin tried to expand Muslim influences within Uganda. Saudi Arabian donors provided the funds for a Muslim center in Uganda; however, most of the money disappeared before Amin could fulfill his aspirations of fostering Islam within Uganda. In 1973 and 1977 Amin outlawed all churches except the Anglican Church of Uganda, the Catholic Church, and the Orthodox Church. By 1976 violence between Muslims and Christians had erupted in Ankole, and the cardinal and Anglican archbishop Janani Luwum met to discuss the ever-increasing violence in the country. Amin became weary of the religious leader's power within Uganda and crushed all who criticized the lack of democracy (rather than the violence) in the country, particularly Catholic individuals. After an assassination attempt against Amin on 25 January 1977, Archbishop Luwum's house was raided. Following conversations with the cardinal, the Anglicans wrote a letter to Amin protesting the national situation. On 16 February Archbishop Luwum was murdered.

After a failed attempt to annex the Kagera Salient in Tanzania in 1979, Amin was defeated by the Tanzanian Army and the rebel movement led by the Ugandan National Liberation Army. In elections in 1980 Obote returned to power under accusations of electoral fraud. In 1985 a military coup ended Obote's government, and a military council seized power. In the following year, however, Yoweri Museveni's National Resistance Army took over Kampala, dissolved the military council, and formed a government, inviting all guerrilla movements that had participated in deposing Obote to be part of the new administration.

Museveni called for local elections in 1989 and set up a review of the constitution. By 1993 the kings of Buganda, Toro, Bunyoro, and Soga were reinstated, and a draft constitution was published. Following his "non-party movement," which embraced all Ugandans regardless of religion or ethnicity, Museveni won the 1996 presidential elections with 70 percent of the total vote. His government has helped make Uganda a progressive model of a pluralistic society in which the Christian churches still play a fundamental role.

EARLY AND MODERN LEADERS Most of the political figures remembered by Ugandans were clergymen who faced the difficulties of speaking out against the regimes of Milton Obote and Idi Amin. For example, when Kabaka Mutesa II had to flee Uganda to avoid arrest by government forces, he entrusted the Buganda kingdom and its peoples to Anglican bishop Dunstan Nsubuga and Catholic archbishop Cardinal Emmanuel Nsubuga.

During Amin's regime Janani Luwum, the Anglican archbishop of Uganda, won the love of many Ugandans as he denounced Amin's genocidal policies. Elected archbishop in 1974, Luwum was from the land of the Acholi people, who supplied the backbone of Obote's army, and was thus distrusted by Amin and his administration. After an attempt on Amin's life in January 1977, which was probably carried out by guerrilla opponents and rebel soldiers, Luwum was arrested and killed by the Ugandan Army. While his sealed coffin was sent to his native village, 4,500 people gathered in Kampala for a memorial service at a grave that had been prepared for Luwum next to that of Bishop James Hannington, who was killed by Kabaka Mwanga of Buganda in 1885. Another 10,000 people gathered in Nairobi, Kenya, to honor the memory of Luwum. As the Church of Uganda celebrated the 100th anniversary of the arrival of the Christian gospel in June 1977, 25,000 people celebrated the courage of Luwum in Kampala. The date of his death, 16 February, is remembered in the calendar of the Church of Uganda as Janani Luwum Day, a day as important as that of such Christian martyrs as Bishop James Hannington and the Ugandan Martyrs of 1886. Luwum's successor, Silvanus Wani, was from the Nile Region, as was Amin, and while most Anglican bishops had to flee for their lives, Wani managed to prevent any further harm to the churches or the local population. His statement "Do not bring politics into the Church but take the Church into politics" became famous.

MAJOR THEOLOGIANS AND AUTHORS At independence Uganda boasted one of the best colleges in Africa, Makerere College, where hundreds of students prepared for public life and a few for further studies in Europe and the United States. The number of students decreased during the political turmoil that followed Milton Obote's first term in office. The Anglican and Catholic Churches maintained vibrant seminaries for the training of priests throughout these difficulties times, however. Some of these institutions have become well known outside Africa and have made an impact in research on religion and politics during the administration of Yoweri Museveni. For example, John Waliggo, a Catholic priest and scholar, has influenced political research on ethical management and the ethics of religion within a pluralistic society. A historian trained at Cambridge University, Waliggo has lectured at the National Seminary and served as the general secretary of the Ugandan Constitutional Commission (1989–93). With the founding of the Ugandan Martyrs University in 1993, he became involved in research on religion, ethics, politics, and corruption in African business and governmental institutions. Other religious scholars, such as theologian Peter Mpagi, have researched Baganda traditional rites and their relation to Christian liturgy. Mpagi's book *African Christian Theology in the Contemporary Context* (2002) has had an enormous influence on church schools and Christian communities.

HOUSES OF WORSHIP AND HOLY PLACES Uganda's largest Christian shrine is the Basilica of the Ugandan Martyrs in the hills of Namugongo, Kampala. It was there, on 3 June 1886, that a number of newly converted Christians, 22 of them Catholic, were tortured and executed on the orders of the Bugandan kabaka, Mwanga. The 22 Catholic martyrs were beatified by Pope Benedict XV in 1920 and were subsequently canonized (recognized as saints and examples for other Christians) by Pope Paul VI on 18 October 1964. The basilica was dedicated by Pope Paul VI on his visit to Uganda in July 1969. The shrine, a modern structure based on traditional Bugandan architecture (*kasiisira*), was completed and dedicated in 1975. Famous pilgrims to Namugongo have included Archbishop Robert Runcie of Canterbury (January 1984) and Pope John Paul II (February 1993).

WHAT IS SACRED? For Christians in Uganda, as elsewhere, all human life is sacred because every person has a soul created by God. Such sacredness is expressed and lived through the family, in which children are brought up in the context of an ongoing process of life and death, a process understood as creative and fertile in traditional Ugandan society. It is in ideas about fertility, birth, and death that Christian values and Ugandan traditional religious values converge. Christianity upholds the sanctity of marriage and holds that human life begins at the moment of conception, while at the same time it values those who are old and infirm as they prepare for their passage into another life.

HOLIDAYS AND FESTIVALS Public holidays in Uganda reflect an inclusive political society, one in which Christian festivals are important. Christian holidays that are celebrated as public holidays include Christmas Day, Good Friday, and Easter Monday. The Christian Feast of the Ugandan Martyrs, on 3 June, however, has become central to Ugandan identity and historical remembrance. The main celebrations take place at the Basilica of the Ugandan Martyrs in Namugongo.

MODE OF DRESS Most Christians in Uganda adopted European dress because of British influence during the colonial period. While more affluent citizens can afford suits and ties or flowery European dresses with hats for weddings and major festivals, most of the population wears secondhand clothing of European origin. Among the clergy, clerical dress—a white cassock—is widely used, and altar boys wear the standard red or white tunics that were introduced during the expansion of colonial Christian practices.

DIETARY PRACTICES Ugandan Anglicans and Catholics in good health abstain from meat on Fridays during Lent, including Good Friday. Some people are forced to practice vegetarianism because of lack of resources, though most Ugandans prefer either beef or fish, depending on the geographical area where they were raised. Chicken is the most common food in the villages, where, occasionally, goats and sheep are also eaten.

RITUALS For Ugandan Christians Christmas and Easter are the largest festivals, while Good Friday, also a national holiday, occupies a central place in the Christian calendar. The Eucharist tends to be celebrated on weekdays in houses located in Christian neighborhoods, while large celebrations take place in central parishes on Sundays. Prayer groups that meet in houses to read the Bible are common, and most Ugandan Christians pray daily with their families, at school, and in community gatherings.

RITES OF PASSAGE In a country where the average life expectancy is 39 years, baptism, the first Christian rite of passage, marks an individual's passing into social life. Infant baptism is the norm in Christian families, though there are a small number of adult baptisms every year.

The second rite of passage is marriage. Christians visit churches before they start their married life. Traditionally marriage was a process of incorporation into new families and new social roles, and it is still understood as a process rather than as a ceremony. Marriage arrangements, visits between the families involved, and bridewealth payments (made by the husband to the family of the bride) can take years, and the ritual exchange of vows at the church is only the culmination of a long process. Procreation and fertility are central African values; thus, a marriage is considered socially stable only after the couple's first child has been born.

The third rite of passage consists of biological death and the subsequent funeral. Funerals are large and well-attended events in Uganda; relatives of the deceased often come from afar to attend the services. It is customary to give a leave of absence to office workers who have to attend a funeral. Funerals are perceived as celebrations of life, particularly if there are descendants who will continue the family life experienced by the deceased.

MEMBERSHIP Both the Anglican and Catholic Churches use missionary drives to increase their memberships and to sharpen the intensity of their follower's religious practices. Since freedom of expression was restored in the 1990s, radio, the press, and the Internet have been used to promote knowledge of the Christian faith in Uganda. As most Christians in the country are members of the Anglican Church of Uganda or the Catholic Church, financial contributions have been expected of them in order to support the administration of parishes and the drives for increasing membership. As the number of indigenous clergy has increased, membership growth has been stressed as a means of making the clergy self-sufficient and of ending the reliance of local churches on foreign funds, missionary contributions, and local collections. Uganda does not have a tax on religion, and most church members expect their contributions to be nontaxable.

SOCIAL JUSTICE Ugandan Christians have traditionally accepted poverty as a fact of life. Colonial Christian missionaries believed that the social order was divinely given and that Christians fit within this established order. In accordance with the Old Testament, riches were seen as gifts from God to those who were righteous. This view matched the traditional understanding that the king had access to all resources and lives. African independence movements and fresh indigenous theologies produced at the time of Uganda's independence challenged these assumptions. Further, their disastrous political situation under the regimes of Milton Obote and Idi Amin raised questions among Christians about society, politics, and political office.

Christians in contemporary Uganda have become a driving force in the search for justice within the new social order provided by Yoweri Museveni's administration. The Catholic bishop's Justice and Peace Commission has encouraged all Christian communities to study poverty and injustice and to be active in helping the poor and destitute, and many people do participate in community service to benefit the needy, orphans, and strangers. In a country hit hard by the AIDS pandemic, the Christian communities have asked difficult questions about the state's care for those affected by the disease and have sought better policies for the redistribution of wealth, resources, and goods.

Uganda has one of the largest educational systems in Africa, with schools supported by the Christian churches—mainly the Anglican Church of Uganda and the Catholic Church. Both churches have maintained colleges of higher education, seminaries, and teacher training colleges.

SOCIAL ASPECTS Marriage represents the most important social moment within all the religious traditions of Uganda. For Christians marriage represents the culmination of a social process that usually involves the extended families on both sides. Although in contemporary Uganda some people have become engaged and married without the consent of their extended families, the families usually enter into a social obligation. That obligation has included bridewealth, payments in kind or in cattle made by the husband's family to the family of the bride. While men are supposed to provide for their families, women are responsible for the care of children, the household, and older members of the family. Furthermore, women are obligated to provide descendants to Christian families (which are aligned by ethnicity, clan membership, and other alliances). Although Christianity does not allow divorce after a religious marriage, a woman's inability to bear children poses a strain to relations between her and her relatives and can lead to the annulment of the marriage.

POLITICAL IMPACT Uganda's constitution provides for a secular government and protects Christians from any discrimination. The country's political parties are identified with the major Christian traditions. For example, Catholics have influenced political developments through the Democratic Party of Uganda (DP), and Protestants have identified themselves with the Uganda People's Congress (UPC).

CONTROVERSIAL ISSUES Ethnic and tribal loyalties are still endemic among religious practitioners in Uganda. Moreover, each political ruler has favored a particular ethnic group, including Yoweri Museveni, whose regime has seemed closer to groups in the south. Anglican archbishops have been chosen primarily because of their ability to work closely with the current ruler and to assure the survival of Christian communities in extremely difficult and violent times. The most controversial issue, however, has been the position of the Baganda within Christianity. Christianity is a central component of Bagandan identity, and the Baganda, forming a majority of the Anglican and Catholic communities, have tried to control both.

Polygamy remains a challenge for the Christian churches in Uganda, and the churches still do not accept abortion or divorce. The use of condoms and other contraceptives devices is condemned by the Catholic Church. There is a massive spread of HIV and AIDS through heterosexual relations, and a dispute as how to combat it.

CULTURAL IMPACT Traditionally Christian churches in Uganda imported European art so that liturgical vestments, ritual objects, statues, and paintings could be made to resemble those of Europe. Since independence Ugandans have been part of the Christian inculturation movement supported by the Conference of East African Bishops (AMECEA). Within this movement theologians have fostered a deeper reflection on the relation between faith and culture and have encouraged artists to depict gospel scenes and texts in an African fashion. Most prominent among such works have been paintings and statues of the Ugandan Martyrs, which have remained central in the art and literature supported by the Christian churches and have made a lasting impact on Ugandan society as a whole.

Other Religions

Despite the self-confessed Christian majority in Uganda, most Ugandans respect the traditional religious practices associated with the major ethnic groups and their kingdoms—that is, Buganda, Ankole, and Toro. It can be said that most members of the Church of Uganda or the Catholic Church at one point or another have taken part in traditional religious practices. These practices involve a closer relation to nature and belief in indigenous spirits and the existence of a "high god." Among the groups who rely on cattle for their living, the high god orders the world and is the creator of everything. Indigenous African religions within Uganda stress the sacredness of life, encouraging values of fertility and community within a large, extended family (in which polygamous marriages exist). Reverence for the sacredness of life is expressed through giving birth to many children. The values of community and good relations with others are also central to the traditional conception of the sacred, and large numbers of Ugandans attend rites of passage related to the births and deaths of kin, friends, and other members of their social networks. Spirit possession is common, and the ancestors seem to return often to trouble the living and to request offerings and ceremonies in their honor.

Evangelical Christian churches were not encouraged by the colonial administration and were distrusted by Milton Obote and Idi Amin. Small numbers of evangelical Christians can be found in Uganda, however, because of migration and intermarriage with members of those churches in Kenya and Tanzania. Evangelical Christians do not take an active part in the political life of Uganda and preach a spiritualistic Christianity.

Islam continues its growth through migration and with the help of financial input from rich Arab countries. It does not, however, form part of the central religious identity of Uganda and its peoples. Moreover, conflicts in neighboring Sudan have increased public concern about Islam and its possible impact on Ugandan society. Muslims in Uganda pray and celebrate their festivals in mosques. Their holidays include Id al-Adha (Feast of the Sacrifice) in February, which lasts from 2 to 10 days, and the largest Muslim festival, Id al-Fitr, which marks the end of the month of fasting, Ramadan, in the latter part of the year. The dates for both festivals are set according to local sightings of various phases of the moon during the lunar calendar year. Muslims pray at the mosque five times a day and visit the mosque for naming ceremonies, weddings, and funerals. They gather for fasting, prayers, and the evening meal during the month of Ramadan. Islam accepts the possibility of divorce and the dissolution of marriage because of a wife's failure to conceive a child. Muslims founded their own university at Mbale in 1988.

Mario I. Aguilar

See Also Vol. I: *African Indigenous Beliefs, Anglicanism/ Episcopalianism, Christianity, Islam, Roman Catholicism*

Bibliography

Gifford, Paul. *African Christianity: Its Public Role.* London: Hurst and Company, 1998.

Gifford, Paul, ed. *The Christian Churches and the Democratisation of Africa.* Leiden: E.J. Brill, 1995.

Hansen, Holger Bernt, and Michael Twaddle, eds. *From Chaos to Order: The Politics of Constitution-Making in Uganda.* London: James Currey, 1994.

———. *Religion and Politics in East Africa: The Period since Independence.* London: James Currey, 1995.

———. *Uganda Now: Between Decay and Development.* London: James Currey, 1988.

Hastings, Adrian. *African Catholicism: Essays in Discovery.* London: SCM, 1989.

———. *African Christianity: An Essay in Interpretation.* London: Geoffrey Chapman, 1976.

———. *The Church in Africa, 1450–1950.* Oxford: Oxford University Press, 1994.

———. *A History of African Christianity, 1950–1975.* Cambridge; New York: Cambridge University Press, 1979.

Peel, J.D.Y. "Conversion and Tradition in Two African Societies: Ijebu and Buganda." *Past and Present* 77 (1977): 108–41.

Pirouet, M. Louise. *Black Evangelists: The Spread of Christianity in Uganda, 1891–1914.* London: Rex Collings, 1978.

Soghayroun, Ibrahim El Zein. *The Sudanese Muslim Factor in Uganda.* Khartoum: Khartoum University Press, 1981.

Taylor, John V. *The Growth of the Church in Buganda: An Attempt at Understanding.* London: SCM, 1958.

Tourigny, Yves. *So Abundant a Harvest: The Catholic Church in Uganda, 1879–1979.* London: Darton, Longman, and Todd, 1979.

Tuma, A.D. Tom, and Phares Mutibwa, eds. *A Century of Christianity in Uganda, 1877–1977: A Historical Appraisal of the Development of the Uganda Church over the Last One Hundred Years.*. Nairobi: Uzima Press, 1978.

Ward, Kevin. "'Obedient Rebel's—The Relationship between the Early 'Balokole' and the Church of Uganda: The Mukono Crisis of 1941." *Journal of Religion in Africa* 19 (1989): 195–227.

Wrigley, Christopher. *Kingship and State: The Buganda Dynasty.* Cambridge: Cambridge University Press, 1996.

Ukraine

POPULATION 48,396,470

EASTERN ORTHODOX CHRISTIAN 61 percent

GREEK CATHOLIC 8 percent

PROTESTANT 3 percent

ROMAN CATHOLIC 1 percent

MUSLIM 1 percent

JEWISH 0.6 percent

SLAVIC (UKRAINIAN) PAGAN 0.2 percent

HINDU, BUDDHIST, AND PRACTITIONERS OF OTHER EASTERN RELIGIONS 0.1 percent

OTHER 0.1 percent

NONAFFILIATED 25 percent

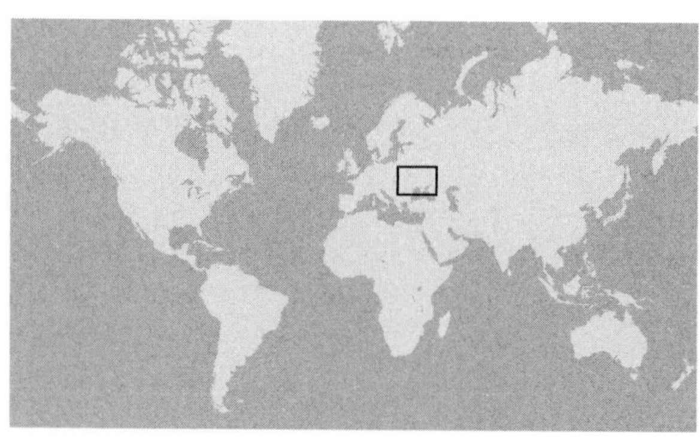

Country Overview

INTRODUCTION Located in eastern Europe, Ukraine is one of the largest countries on the continent, both in size and population. It is bordered to the north by Belarus, to the northeast and east by Russia, to the south by the Sea of Azov and the Black Sea, to the southwest by Moldova and Romania, and to the west by Hungary, Slovakia, and Poland.

Lasting from the eighth until the thirteenth century, Kievan Rus, with its capital at Kiev, was the first and most influential Ukrainian state. It lost its independence in the fourteenth century as a result of the Mongol-Tatar invasion from the east and Polish conquests in the west. Since that time Ukraine or some parts of it have been incorporated into neighboring states—the Polish-Lithuanian Commonwealth, Russia, Austria-Hungary, Germany, Romania, Czechoslovakia, Hungary, and the Soviet Union. The religious policies of all these countries were quite different, and they supported different, sometimes opposite, confessional groups within Ukrainian society.

Ukrainians made a serious attempt to obtain independence in the seventeenth century under the leadership of Bohdan Khemel'nyt'skyj. Their efforts were more successful at the beginning of the twentieth century, when Ukraine was independent for almost four years (1917–20). In 1920 Ukraine's territory was again occupied and divided between the Soviet Union, Poland, Czechoslovakia, and Romania. Those portions of Ukraine that had been divided among Poland, Czechoslovakia, and Romania were incorporated into the Soviet Union in 1939 and 1940, according to the secret protocols of the German-Soviet Nonagression Pact. With the disintegration of the Soviet Union, Ukraine was the first country after the Baltic states to declare its independence in 1991.

Since the pre-Christian period the territory of present-day Ukraine has been under the influence of different cultures, religions, even civilizations. Before the baptism of the Kievan Rus in 988, local Slavic tribes had practiced polytheistic forms of paganism. After accepting Christianity in its Byzantine form, ancient Ukraine became a monoconfessional state (that is, a state with only one dominating religion) and remained so for six centuries. After 1596, when many Ukrainians accepted union with the Roman Catholic Church, Ukrainian society was divided into two main confessional groups. The majority were adherents of Eastern Orthodoxy, and the largest minority belonged to the Uniate Church, which became known officially as the Greek Catholic Church in the eighteenth century. Contemporary Ukrainian Protestantism has an uninterrupted history that extends back to the last decade of the nineteenth century.

RELIGIOUS TOLERANCE The state law on freedom of conscience and religious organizations, adopted in 1991, guarantees the right of Ukrainian citizens to confess any religion. All religions enjoy equal status and privileges. Despite the existence of this liberal law, serious tensions exist between the Greek Catholic and Orthodox churches, as well as between different jurisdictions of the Orthodox church. These tensions have emerged since 1989 with the liberalization of religious and political life in Ukraine.

Major Religion

EASTERN ORTHODOXY

DATE OF ORIGIN 988 C.E.
NUMBER OF FOLLOWERS 29.5 million

HISTORY From the baptism of the Kievan Rus in 988 until 1686, the Kievan metropoly (church province uniting several dioceses) was under the jurisdiction of the Ecumenical Patriarchate of Constantinople. Due to the distance between the metropoly and the church center, however, relations between the Kievan church and Constantinople were almost purely formal, and the Kievan metropoly enjoyed considerable autonomy. This autonomy led to the emergence of several specific features of Ukrainian Orthodoxy, including a high level of lay participation in church life, the dominance of informal types of spiritual expression, the election of clergy of all levels, and an openness to the influences of Western spirituality.

Clergy members walk in front of Saint Sophia Cathedral. Built in 1037, Saint Sophia became the most important and popular cathedral in Ukraine. © ALAIN NOGUES/CORBIS SYGMA.

In 1448 several northern dioceses, then within the territory of the Grand Principality of Moscow, declared their complete independence and started to develop their own identity, which later became the basis of the Russian Orthodox Church. (After the loss of Ukrainian statehood in the fourteenth century, Kiev and the majority of the dioceses became part of the Polish-Lithuanian Commonwealth.) In 1686 the Kievan metropoly, having been removed from the jurisdiction of the patriarch of Constantinople, was incorporated into the Russian church. Subsequently, during the eighteenth and nineteenth centuries, the majority of features specific to Ukrainian Orthodoxy were abolished according to the policies of the Russian state and church.

The idea of creating an autocephalous (independent) Orthodox Church in Ukraine appeared at the beginning of the twentieth century. Although there have been several relatively successful attempts to forge church jurisdictions in Ukraine that were independent from the Moscow patriarchate (the Ukrainian Autocephalous Orthodox Church [1921 through January 1930, 1942–44, and since 1989] and the Ukrainian Orthodox Church under the Patriarchate of Kiev [since 1992]), the Orthodox jurisdiction under the supervision of the Patriarchate of Moscow still remains primary in Ukraine. This church is led by Metropolitan Volodymyr Sabodan (born in 1935) and has 10,384 parishes in 36 dioceses. The Orthodox Church of the Patriarchate of Kiev has 3,395 parishes in 31 dioceses and is led by Patriarch Filaret Denysenko (born in 1929). Metropolitan Mephodij Kudriakov (born in 1949) is the head of the Ukrainian Autocephalous Orthodox Church, which has 1,156 parishes in 12 dioceses.

EARLY AND MODERN LEADERS Many Ukrainian national leaders have been important figures in the country's Orthodox Church. In 988 Great Prince Volodymyr (died in 1015) baptized his country. Volodymyr's successor, Prince Jaroslav the Wise (978–1054), completed improvements to the organizational structure of the church and founded Ukraine's first monasteries and schools. After the majority of bishops established the Uniate Church in 1596, the Ukrainian hetman (military and political leader) Petro Sahajdachnyj (died in 1622) restored the hierarchy of the Orthodox Church in Ukraine in 1620 with the help of Theophanus, patriarch of Jerusalem.

Dominated by the antireligious Soviet Union for many years, the clergy and certain intellectuals became the real leaders and ideologists of the church in Ukraine. Among the most famous figures of this period were Filaret Denysenko, metropolitan of Kiev and Galicia (since 1966) and patriarch of Kiev and the whole of Rus-Ukraine (since 1995); Theodosij (1926–2001), bishop of Poltava, the author of several appeals to the Soviet government about religious persecution in the country; and the writer Yevhen Sverstiuk (born in 1928), a political dissident, church polemist, and strong advocate of autocephaly for Ukrainian Orthodoxy.

MAJOR THEOLOGIANS AND AUTHORS In the middle of the eleventh century, Illarion, the first Slav to become Kievan metropolitan, authored *The Word about Law and Blessing,* the first church treatise written in Ukraine. The monks of the Kiev–Cave Monastery, which was founded in the mid-eleventh century, started the practice of writing church chronicles (*litopysy*).

During the early seventeenth century, the golden age of the Ukrainian theological tradition, Petro Mohyla (1596–1647), the metropolitan of Kiev, wrote the first catechism in the history of the Byzantine tradition for all of Eastern Orthodoxy. Mohyla also prepared *Trebnyk* (The Book of Needs), still the most complete compilation of texts of church services for all occasions. In the early eighteenth century the metropolitan Dymytrij Rostovskyj (1651–1709) wrote *Chetji Mineji,* the most complete collection of stories about the lives of the saints. The most important Ukrainian theologian of the twentieth century was the metropolitan Illarion Ohienko (1882–1972), who completed the most popular translation of the Bible into Ukrainian (1962) and contributed many works to the fields of church history, dogma, patristics (the study of the works and lives of the church fathers), and language.

HOUSES OF WORSHIP AND HOLY PLACES Built in 1037, Saint Sophia became the most important and popular cathedral in Ukraine. Two Ukrainian monasteries are particularly famous: the Kiev–Cave *lavra* (monastery of the first rank) and the Pochajiv *lavra,* founded in Western Ukraine by Saint Iov of Pochajiv (1551–1651). Other famous holy sites include places where sacred signs have appeared, springs of holy water, and *pustyni,* or places where famous monks found personal solitude.

WHAT IS SACRED? The relics of saints are among the most sacred objects in the Ukrainian Orthodox tradition. They are kept in special boxes (*rakas*) in famous churches and cathedrals, which have become popular pilgrimage sites. In several places relics are kept in the caves and underground churches where the saints lived and served. Among the most famous relics in Ukraine are those of Saint Barbara (died in 306), which arrived in Kiev in the twelfth century; Saint Makarij of Kiev, metropolitan from 1495 to 1497; the saints Anthony (died in 1073) and Theodosij (1036–74) in the Kiev–Cave *lavra;* and the saints Iov of Pochajiv and Amphilokhij (1894–1971) in the Pochajiv *lavra.*

The most important sacred icons in the Ukrainian tradition are *Vladimirskaya Theotocos* (now in Russia but originally from the Kiev environs), *God's Mother of Pochajiv,* and *God's Mother of the Kiev–Cave Lavra.* Especially in the western part of Ukraine, the tradition of installing crosses at crossroads and near important places, hills, and churches is still widespread.

HOLIDAYS AND FESTIVALS Easter is more important and bears a deeper tradition of celebration in eastern Ukraine. Christmas is more important in western dioceses because of the Western Catholic influence there. Easter, Christmas, and the Holy Trinity (Pentecost) are state holidays as well. Historically two different holidays devoted to Saint Nicholas (in December and May) were unique to the Ukrainian Orthodox tradition, but now they are also celebrated in Russia. Ukrainians are particularly fervent about the Protection of the Mother of God in October, a holiday of less importance in other Orthodox traditions.

In Ukraine many Christian holidays are connected with the practice of consecrating. Common throughout the country is the tradition of consecrating water on Epiphany in January and apples and other fruits for the Feast of the Transfiguration in August. Some traditions of consecrating, however, are dominant in particular regions: In western Ukraine candles are consecrated on Presentation in February and flower wreathes on Dormition of the Virgin Mary in August; in eastern Ukraine flowers are consecrated for the Feast of the Maccabean Martyrs in August.

MODE OF DRESS Ukrainian Orthodoxy does not require laypeople to follow a specific dress code. Women are expected to wear handkerchiefs, long skirts, and long-sleeved shirts during church ceremonies, but these are not mandatory.

Orthodox clergy in the northern, central, eastern, and southern parts of Ukraine dress mainly according to the tradition of the Russian Church. Clergy from the western part of the country (Galicia) are accustomed to the simpler Greek style of dress, which has been preserved in the region partly because the clergy of the Greek Catholic church wear the same vestments. In some cases attire for western Ukrainian Orthodox clergy reflects the influence of the Catholic tradition. Classical Greek clerical headgear (instead of the Russian type) is also becoming more popular.

DIETARY PRACTICES Ukrainian Orthodoxy's only dietary restrictions are connected with the highly popular practice of fasting. Any meat, fish, or other animal products—such as milk, eggs, and butter—and alcoholic drinks are completely prohibited during fasting periods. Almost all Wednesdays and Fridays are fasting days. Besides one-day fasts, there is the system of long-term fasts, which is shared by all Orthodox traditions. But the Great Lent, or the Great Fast, which begins 48 days before Easter, and the fast before the Dormition of the Virgin Mary (from 14 to 27 August, according to the Gregorian calendar) are particularly important and are strictly observed in the Ukrainian tradition.

RITUALS Among the three types of liturgies used in Ukrainian Orthodoxy, the Liturgy of Saint John Chrysostom is the most frequently delivered in Ukraine. The Liturgy of Saint Basil the Great is delivered only during fasting periods and on the saint's day itself. The Liturgy of Saint George is delivered only on Wednesdays and Fridays during Lent.

The Ukrainian Orthodox Church holds special evening worship—Vsenichne Bdinnia (All-night Vigil)—every Saturday and on the eves of big holidays. Ukrainian Orthodoxy accepted the Western tradition of commemorating the *pasiji* (passion) of Christ, which originated in the seventeenth century. Also, Orthodox dioceses in Galicia have borrowed from the neighboring Catholic communities the tradition of holding everyday evening services in May, with special prayers and sermons in the name of the Virgin Mary.

RITES OF PASSAGE The Orthodox Church in Ukraine recognizes that a child becomes conscious and responsible for his or her own life at age seven. Thereafter, the child is expected to confess and take Communion regularly.

Ukrainian Orthodoxy holds that special services and rituals for the dead—on the first, third, ninth, and fortieth days after death—are important for the deceased's life after death. These services involve bringing homemade bread and sweets to church.

MEMBERSHIP According to tradition, anyone born in the territory dominated by the Ukrainian Orthodox Church automatically belongs to the church. Nevertheless, while church officials have estimated that there are no less than 40 million Orthodox in Ukraine, in fact only 61 percent of the population (29.5 million) have declared their Orthodox beliefs, and active adherents make up an even smaller percentage. Indeed, although Sunday liturgy, the main service, is considered obligatory for church members, only an estimated 17 percent of Orthodox Christians in Ukraine attend church services at least twice per month. In concert with the Russian Orthodox Church, Ukrainian Orthodoxy vigorously opposes other confessional influences, especially the widening influence of Protestantism and its growing number of adherents, as well as the proselytizing efforts of the Roman Catholic Church.

Various branches of the Orthodox Church have founded more than 100 newspapers in Ukraine. They also maintain websites, and many broadcast religious programs on local and national television. Some dioceses also have their own websites.

SOCIAL JUSTICE At the beginning of 2000 the two main Orthodox jurisdictions in Ukraine—the Patriarchate of Kiev and the Ukrainian Orthodox Church under the jurisdiction of the Patriarchate of Moscow—adopted new social doctrines, in which the discussion of poverty, education, and human rights figured prominently. No serious distinctions exist between the respective doctrines. In response to the urgent problem of poverty during Ukraine's transition to a market economy, which has been most pronounced among less educated and older people (who make up the majority of church adherents), many Orthodox institutions have started to organize food centers, modest financial assistance, the distribution of aid from abroad, and other systems of help for the poorest people. Secondary education is obligatory and free in Ukraine, but churches have begun to develop their own educational systems through a network of Sunday schools and primary and higher theological institutions, which are mainly for the preparation of future clergy.

Although the Orthodox Church in Ukraine has fought for the rights and resources of its own followers, at the same time it has advocated limiting certain rights of adherents of others religions. For example, it has urged the state to be more strict in the registration of new religious groups and organizations, to restrict the activities of foreign missionaries, and to emphasize the state's official recognition of the unique role of Orthodoxy in the historical development of the country.

SOCIAL ASPECTS As pre-Christian paganism lacked strict concepts of monogamy and permanent family, the Christianization of the Kievan Rus in the tenth and eleventh centuries was critical to the appearance and confirmation of family values in Ukraine. In present-day Ukraine the church strictly opposes divorce, abortion, and anything it sees as detrimental to family values. In general the idea of the family as the smallest church, or "home church," is increasingly popular in Ukraine.

POLITICAL IMPACT Orthodoxy has been closely intertwined with politics since the Christianization of the Kievan Rus. When Ukraine lost its independent statehood in the fourteenth century, Eastern Orthodoxy became for many centuries an essential aspect of Ukrainian national identity. Indeed, religious differences were one of the most important aspects of the tension between Orthodox Ukrainians and Catholic Poles in the seventeenth and eighteenth centuries. Conversely, Ukraine's religious sympathies with Russia contributed to its reunion with the Moscow State in 1654.

Following the establishment of an independent Ukrainian state between 1917 and 1920, autocephalous jurisdictions emerged within Ukrainian Orthodoxy, and in 1918 the state decreed the autocephaly of the Ukrainian Church. Later, Ukrainian anti-Communist opposition was marked by the closeness between political and religious movements. Furthermore, the revivals of the Ukrainian state and the autocephalous Orthodox Church paralleled each other during the late 1980s and early 1990s.

In contemporary Ukraine a number of progovernmental and Communist parties, as well as formal and informal political lobbies, are ready to accept—at least in part—the Russian model of state-church relations, which emphasizes the unique role of one church organization, the Orthodoxy. Also, two officially registered "fractions," or groups, of deputies who support the Orthodox Church exist in the Ukrainian parliament, though they have different orientations. One gives legislative support to the autocephalous Ukrainian Church and its recognition by other churches; the other supports that branch of the Orthodox Church which is in canonical union with the Moscow Patriarchate.

CONTROVERSIAL ISSUES The most controversial issue in contemporary Ukrainian Orthodoxy surrounds the persistent division between its three branches (even while the majority of the Ukrainian population supports their unification). This lack of internal unity is a significant factor in the continued refusal of other Orthodox churches to recognize the independent Ukrainian Orthodoxy as a canonical and autocephalous church, an end that is widely desired by the Ukrainian people. From 1998 to 2001 the Ecumenical Patriarchate of Constantinople attempted to help resolve the problem by unifying at least two autocephalous church branches, but the effort was abandoned when the Patriarchate of Moscow threatened to suspend its liturgical communication with the Ecumenical Patriarchate.

CULTURAL IMPACT The cultural development of Ukraine bears an essential connection with the Orthodox tradition. Church authors—monks and members of the church hierarchy—created the first written texts during the ancient period. Later, monasteries became the main places of mass education and of preserving the cultural heritage. Almost all branches of Ukrainian culture have started or have made significant achievements in direct connection with the spiritual sphere: painting with the tradition of icons, architecture with the building of churches, music with the religious tradition of polyphonic singing, and literature with the works of church writers.

Other Religions

Concentrated mainly in the western regions of Galicia and Transcarpathia, the second largest religious community in Ukraine is that of the Ukrainian Greek Catholics, also known as the Ukrainian Uniate Church. This church was established in 1596 at the Council of Brest, when five of seven bishops of the Kievan metropoly declared their unity with Rome. Through this unification, the Kievan bishops sought to attain equal rights with the Roman Catholic bishops and to secure certain political and juridical privileges, including the right to take part in the state parliament, or *sejm,* and to receive essential financial support from the king and the state.

Although the Greek Catholic Church was later banned by the Russian Empire, in western Ukraine it gained support from the Polish-Lithuanian Commonwealth and remained intact when Galicia, which had been annexed by Poland in the fourteenth century, became part of the Austrian-Hungarian Empire in 1772. After enduring a period of complete prohibition during the post–World War II Soviet era, the church experienced a revival in 1989. Over the next 15 years it reestablished its tradition and structures and once again became a vital part of religious life in western Ukraine, building its own network of social services, charitable organizations, and evangelical programs. The contemporary Greek Catholic Church comprises 3,340 parishes and more than 3,000 clergymen, and it enjoys the strong support of the Vatican and other Catholic organizations abroad. Archbishop Liubomyr Huzar (born in 1933) of Lviv was elected head of the church in 2000 and appointed cardinal in 2001.

Roman Catholicism has traditionally been identified with national minorities in Ukraine—Poles, Slovaks, and Hungarians, for example. Roman Catholicism emerged in Ukraine in the twelfth century, when the first Dominican monasteries were founded there. Although some conversion of Orthodox Ukrainians ensued, many resisted the new teachings. The contemporary Roman Catholic Church in Ukraine unites seven dioceses with 863 parishes and more than 1,100 clergymen. Marjan Javorsky (born in 1926), the archbishop of the Roman Catholic Church in Lviv, became a cardinal in 1997 (officially announced in 2001), making the city the only one in the world where two Catholic cardinals coexist.

Protestants form Ukraine's third largest religious group. Protestantism was first introduced in Ukraine in the sixteenth and seventeenth centuries. Facing strong opposition from Cossacks and state prohibitions, however, Protestantism was completely destroyed in the second half of the seventeenth century and did not reappear in Ukraine until the mid-nineteenth century, when it was reestablished through the missionary efforts of German Baptists. By the beginning of the twentieth century approximately 5 percent of Ukrainians were Baptists. According to the number of adherents, the Baptist Church of Ukraine is the largest Baptist body in Europe. In the twentieth century Pentecostal, Adventist, and Jehovah's Witness movements also developed in different regions of Ukraine. No less than 3 percent of the Ukrainian population now confesses various Protestant denominations.

Judaism originated in Ukraine in the tenth century. In the fifteenth and sixteenth centuries western European Jews immigrated to Ukraine through Poland in significant numbers, establishing settlements—almost 80 towns—throughout most of the country. Ukraine is the birthplace of the Hasidic movement, which was founded in the eighteenth century by Baal Shem-Tov (1700–60), who was born in eastern Galicia.

Ukraine became notorious for several massacres of the Jewish population that occurred within its borders. These took place in the mid-seventeenth century, during the war for independence; in the second part of eighteenth century, during several peasant insurrections; at the beginning of the twentieth century, during anti-Jewish pogroms organized by Russian nationalistic organizations; and during the Holocaust of World War II. During the latter conflict more than 100,000 Jews were killed in Kiev alone, at a site called Babi Yar.

After mass emigration at the end of the 1970s and during the post-Communist period, fewer than 200,000

Jews remain in Ukraine. They have created 230 communities—including Hasidic, Progressive, and Messianic types—and several dozen Jewish organizations.

Islam in Ukraine is concentrated in the Crimean peninsula, where a strong Crimean Tatar Muslim community of 400,000 people exists. The traditional local ethnic group of Turkic origin, the Crimean Tatars finally accepted Islam as a national religion in the fourteenth century under the khan Uzbek. In 1944 the Crimean Tatars were completely deported from their motherland to Middle Asia by Josef Stalin's Soviet regime, having been unjustly accused of cooperating with Nazi occupiers during World War II. They began to return to Crimea in the late 1980s. Their return has caused some ethnic and religious conflicts with the ethnic Russian majority on the peninsula.

The beginning of the 1990s saw the revival of specific forms of Ukrainian neopaganism, which is based on the ideas of traditional, pre-Christian Ukrainian paganism. Two main branches represent contemporary Ukrainian paganism: The Native Ukrainian National Faith has based its ideas of reformed paganism on the book *Maga vira* (1979), by Leo Sylenko (born in 1932), developing monotheistic ideas and establishing an aggressive attitude toward Christianity; the Native Belief has continued a polytheistic tradition, substantiated in the works of Volodymyr Shajan (1908–74). In all, 70 pagan communities are active in contemporary Ukraine.

The 1990s also witnessed the development of new religious movements in Ukraine. Notable among these has been the Great White Brotherhood, which originated at the beginning of the decade. The Great White Brotherhood gained attention because of the mass spreading of the movement (even abroad) and its attempts to forecast the end of the world in 1993. Still, new religious movements have remained marginal, and their activities are subject to mass public opposition.

Andrij Yurash

See Also Vol. 1: *Christianity, Eastern Orthodoxy*

Bibliography

Biddulph, Howard L. "Religious Liberty and the Ukrainian State: Nationalism versus Equal Protection." *Brigham Young University Law Review* no. 2 (1995): 321–46.

Blazejovskyj, Dmytro. *Hierarchy of the Kyivan Church (861–1990).* Rome: Universitas Catholica Ucrainorum Clementis Papae, 1990.

Filipovych, L.O. "Role of Religion for the Ukrainian Nationalism." In *Nacionalismo en Europa, nacionalismo en Galicia: la religión como elemento impulsor de la ideológia nacionalista,* 167–78. La Coruña, Spain: Universidade la Coruña, 1998.

Kolodny, Anatolij. *Religion and Church in the Democratic Ukraine.* Kiev, 2000.

Millenium of Christianity in Ukraine: A Symposium. Ottawa, Ontario, Canada: Saint Paul University, 1987.

Yelensky, Victor. "The Ukrainian Church and State in the Post-Communist Era." In *Church-State Relations in Central and Eastern Europe.* Edited by Irena Borowik, 136–52. Krakow: Nomos, 1999.

Yurash, Andrew. "Religion as a Non-Traditional Component of the National Security Problem: The Ukrainian Pattern." In *Church-State Relations in Central and Eastern Europe.* Edited by Irena Borowik, 221–35. Krakow: Nomos, 1999.

Yurash, Andrij. "Essential Macroconfessional Processes in Modern Ukraine." *Geneza-Expert* no. 1 (1996): 35–40.

United Arab Emirates

POPULATION 2,445,989

SUNNI MUSLIM 80 percent

SHIITE MUSLIM 16 percent

OTHER 4 percent

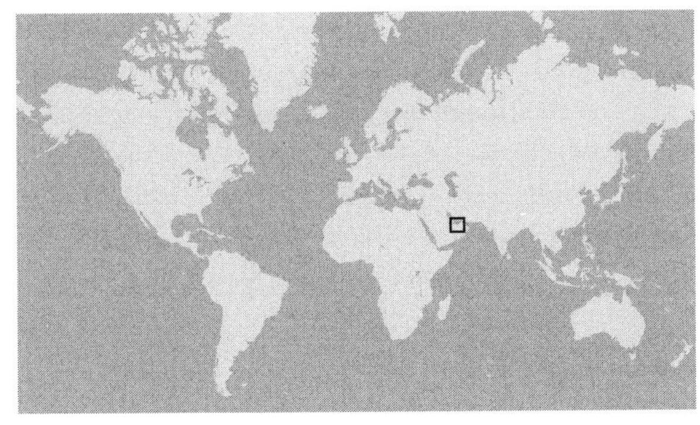

Country Overview

INTRODUCTION The United Arab Emirates, founded in 1971, is a federation of seven emirates (Abu Dhabi, Ajman, Dubai, al-Fujayrah, Ras al-Khaymah, Sharjah, and Umm al-Qaywayn) lying along the eastern coast of the Arabian Peninsula. It is bordered by Oman and the Gulf of Oman to the east, Saudi Arabia to the south and west, Qatar to the northwest, and the Persian Gulf to the north. The capital is Abu Dahbi town.

The population consists of four social and cultural groups: the Shihu and Habus peoples in the mountainous regions of the north, the lowland peoples living on the plains, the polyglot of workers and immigrants living in the major cities, and the tribal peoples connected by lineage to the old Arabian tribes. A major oil producer, the country has a fast growing Arab and non-Arab expatriate population, with indigenous peoples now making up a minority of less than 20 percent.

The vast majority of Muslims in the United Arab Emirates follow the Sunni branch of Islam. Compared with other Persian Gulf states, the country is relatively liberal and open.

RELIGIOUS TOLERANCE Although Islam is the official religion of the United Arab Emirates, the government pursues a policy of tolerance toward other religions. Foreign clergy are allowed to minister to foreign populations, and non-Muslim groups—Christians, Hindus, and Sikhs—are permitted to engage in private charitable activities and to send their children to private schools. These groups are not supported financially by the state, however. Relationships among people of different cultural backgrounds are governed by interpretations of the Koran and the hadith (traditions of the Prophet Muhammad) that emphasize the concept of peace (*salam*).

Major Religion

SUNNI ISLAM

DATE OF ORIGIN Seventh century C.E.

NUMBER OF FOLLOWERS 2.3 million

HISTORY Islam was introduced to the area during the lifetime of the Prophet Muhammad, between approximately 625 and 630 B.C. Sunni Islam as it is practiced in the United Arab Emirates has been influenced by the

A Muslim man kneels on the roadside in preparation for one of his daily prayers. Muslims in the United Arab Emirates perform the same rituals common throughout the Islamic world. © PETER TURNLEY/CORBIS.

Wahhabi movement. This movement was established in Arabia in the mid-eighteenth century by Muhammad Ibn Abd al-Wahhab, who drew upon the teachings of Ibn Taymiyyah (1268–1328), an early interpreter of the Hanbali school of Islamic jurisprudence. The Wahhabis emphasized God's unqualified oneness (*tawhid*), and they were known for rejecting all forms of nonorthodox Islam, including the ideologies and practices of the Shiites. A puritanical group, the Wahabbis repudiated innovation and opposed non-Muslim influences, including the increasing European presence in the Persian Gulf. Muslims of the emirates initially looked to the Wahhabis as a military power to be called upon for support, rather than for guidance in religious matters, and the Wahhabi movement came to be allied with the Qawasim tribes of the emirates.

EARLY AND MODERN LEADERS In the United Arab Emirates religious leaders have traditionally been referred to as *mutawa*'s rather than as sheikhs (*shaykhs*). The *mutawa'* is the person who heads the local *kuttab*, a traditional institute for teaching and memorizing the Koran.

Although religious leaders in the emirates have tended to be local, since the creation of the country in 1971 the president, Shaykh Zayed Bin Sultan al-Nahyan, has played a role as a religious leader. He is a descendant of Zayed the Great, who was influential in the formation of the Trucial States in the late nineteenth and early twentieth centuries. During his presidency Shaykh Zayed has been concerned with preserving the Islamic identity of the state.

MAJOR THEOLOGIANS AND AUTHORS One eminent Muslim scholar from the emirates was Abdul Rahman Bin Muhammad Bin Hafez (1886–1953). His books *Tariqat al-muttaqin* ("The Path of the Devout") and *Khulasat al-fiqh* ("The Essence of Jurisprudence") address issues of the Koran and the *sunnah* (the example of the Prophet Muhammad). Although the prominent twentieth-century scholar Ahmad Bin Abdul Aziz al-Mubarak was born in Saudi Arabia, he spent most of his life in the emirates, where he served as the head of the *shar'iyyah* (religious) courts. He published widely in Islamic law, education, and customs. His books include *Al-asas al-Islami li-manahij al-tarbiyya wa'l-ta'lim* ("The Islamic Foundations of the Educational Curriculum") and *Nizam al-qada' fi'l-Islam* ("The Judicial System in Islam").

HOUSES OF WORSHIP AND HOLY PLACES Before the oil boom of the twentieth century, most of the mosques in the emirates were small, simple buildings without minarets. This was the case, for example, with the unique mosque of Bidiyya, near the city of Buraymi in Abu Dhabi, which was built without the use of wood and which was characterized by four flattened domes. Since then large numbers of mosques of various Islamic architectural designs and with richly ornamented minarets have been constructed. The well-known Jumeirah mosque in Dubai, for instance, was built in the medieval Fatimid tradition. The old Great Mosque, al-Jami' al-Qadim, in Abu Dhabi has been replaced by a modern mosque with blue domes.

WHAT IS SACRED? As with Muslims elsewhere, followers of Islam in the United Arab Emirates hold the Koran to be a sacred text and mosques to be sacred places. Although no animals or plants are held to be sacred, people especially honor the grace (*baraka*) and rootedness (*asalah*) of the palm tree and the camel. Koranic verses and hadiths (traditions of the Prophet Muhammad) that affirm the goodness of palm trees are frequently cited—for example, "We produce therein orchards with date palms and vines, and we cause springs to gush forth therein" (Koran 17:34). Patience is a value associated with the camel, which, because of its exceptional ability to tolerate intense heat and hunger, can live in the desert. In the United Arab Emirates the camel plays a role on social occasions, such as marriages and weddings, and for the payment of hospitality duties and blood money (*diyya*). The slaughtering of camels on these occasions denotes the value placed on honor and hospitality.

HOLIDAYS AND FESTIVALS There are no Muslim holidays and festivals distinctive to the United Arab Emirates. As in other countries, however, Muslims celebrate such festivals as Id al-Fitr, at the end of the feast of Ramadan, and Id al-Adha, at the conclusion of the pilgrimage to Mecca. The birthday of Muhammad (*mawlid*) is also observed.

MODE OF DRESS Dress in the United Arab Emirates is dictated by the stark heat of the sun, traditional Bedouin patterns, and religion. The emphasis for Muslims is modesty. Women wear a traditional full-length garment called a *kandurah.* In addition, they wear an overgarment (*thub*) made of black lace and frequently over this a cloak (*'abayah*). Women also wear a hair veil (*wagayah*) or face veil (*burgo*), characterized by a black mask that covers the lower part of the nose and the mouth and that leaves the eyes shaded by the edge of the hair veil.

The traditional dress of men in the United Arab Emirates is a robe (*kandurah*) whose color varies according to the season. In summer the *kandurah* is white, while in winter it is gray or brown, and it is usually worn with a matching, often Western-style jacket. Men wear a skullcap (*quhfiyya*) and a square scarf (*ghutrah*) on their heads. The attire of dignitaries includes a cloak (*bishit*).

Clerics and religious functionaries often come from neighboring countries, and their dress reflects their national origins. Local religious personnel wear a black toquelike cap, together with a wide scarf, or *rutra.*

DIETARY PRACTICES Muslims in the United Arab Emirates follow Islamic dietary requirements. Alcohol is available, however, and is not banned, as in Saudi Arabia. Following the *sunnah,* people sit on the floor for meals and eat with their right hands and without utensils. Men and women traditionally eat in separate quarters, with the female head of the household directing youths or young children in serving the males. Women eat with the children.

RITUALS Muslims in the United Arab Emirates perform those rituals common throughout the Islamic world. These include the *salat* (prayer) five times a day and, for those who are able, the hajj, or pilgrimage to Mecca. There are, however, no Islamic rituals that are distinctive to the United Arab Emirates.

RITES OF PASSAGE Within the first week after a women gives birth, her family or husband arranges a ritual called *'aqiqa,* in which a small camel or a large sheep is slaughtered and distributed among relatives, neighbors, and friends. Men gather to recite the Koran for the well-being of the mother and the newly born child, and close relatives gather for a meal.

Circumcision for both sexes takes place before the onset of puberty. It is an occasion of great celebration, for with circumcision the child is regarded as having taken the first public step toward a true Islamic identity. Traditional female circumcision is declining and is currently practiced only among local populations. Although once carried out by matriarchs in the community, these minor clitoral operations are now performed primarily in clinics or hospitals.

Marriage is incumbent upon all Muslims. Most marriages continue to be arranged, with a family member, such as an aunt, or occasionally a well-placed woman in the community acting as the negotiator. A marriage contract is drawn up, and a dowry is paid. Wealthy families sometimes sponsor weeks of celebrations. The government, concerned to encourage marriage among the indigenous population, has established a marriage bank (*sanduq al-zawaj*) that gives financial support to men who marry local women, a practice that has resulted in couples marrying at a younger age. Divorce is permitted according to Islamic law.

At death family members wash the body and wrap it in a white funeral cloth. It is then carried to the local mosque, where prayers are said on the deceased's behalf. The Islamic principle of immediate burial in a grave and without a coffin is observed. Families sponsor the recitation of verses from the Koran for the sake of the deceased.

MEMBERSHIP While proselytizing by non-Muslim religions is prohibited in the United Arab Emirates, Islamic religious institutes welcome converts and help them become integrated into the Muslim community. In addition to religious programs publicized through the Internet and mass media, religious literature in various languages is offered to new converts.

SOCIAL JUSTICE Although the legal system of the United Arab Emirates draws on several sources, including those of the West, it gives great weight to Islamic law (Shari'ah), which emphasizes human rights and social justice. Despite the capitalist orientation of the United Arab Emirates, the Islamic spirit of social justice has not suffered and has, in fact, benefited from the country's wealth. Through charitable acts (*sadaqat*) wealthy Muslims help protect the needy. In addition, annual almsgiving (*zakat*) by Muslims provides financial aid on a large scale, often organized by religious institutes, to those who need it.

Even though Western-style education has grown quickly, Islamic education continues to be emphasized. Islamic institutes and departments of Islamic studies constitute major parts of the educational system. Women have been encouraged to participate in both education and the workforce, and by the1990s half of all university students in the United Arab Emirates were female. Women graduates now work in both the government and the private sector.

SOCIAL ASPECTS Compared with other Westernized countries of the Arab world, Islam in the United Arab Emirates has continued to be observed in a conservative way. This is especially true among the native Sunni population who adhere to the Malikite legal tradition.

Although it has become less common, tribal men continue to practice polygamy, limited to four or fewer wives. This is justified as a means of strengthening *'asabiya*, or tribal solidarity, as well as of increasing the population. Because there is a low rate of population growth among the indigenous people, the state uses its affluence to increase the native population. The government encourages marriage among the indigenous population and increases the salary of a native male citizen to whom a child is born.

POLITICAL IMPACT Despite rapid modernization and the participation of the United Arab Emirates in the global economy, both the ruling class and ordinary citizens have maintained an intimate identification with Islam. For the country's leaders identification with Islam and its codes of conduct has served to confirm the legitimacy of their rule. Among university students adherence to Islamic principles has been central in their response to the forces of modernization and secularization from the West. The growth of Islamic fundamentalism in a nearby country such as Iran, however, has sometimes been seen as a potential threat to the political stability of the emirates.

The government of the United Arab Emirates subsidizes all Sunni mosques and employs all Sunni imams. The political content of the sermons delivered in mosques is monitored by the government.

CONTROVERSIAL ISSUES Birth control and abortion are rejected in the United Arab Emirates. Women are not allowed to hold religious positions, although they are involved in traditional religious teaching. Women also participate in the *mutawwi'ah,* the morals police that enforce puritanical Wahhabi law in public. Islamic law (Shari'ah) of the Malikite school is implemented in cases of disputes.

CULTURAL IMPACT Much of the distinctive art of the United Arab Emirates is traditional and not specifically Islamic. Poetry, for example, is much venerated, and there are regular poetry festivals. There are also regional variations in artistic expression. The Shihu and Habus peoples are known for their brightly colored woven saddlebags and distinctive pottery designs, and the Dubai region is known for the wind chimney, which catches air to funnel it downward to cool the home.

Other Religions

Shiite Muslims constitute about 16 percent of the population. The 1979 revolution in Iran, a majority Shiite country, had an impact on Shiites in the United Arab Emirates, as it did in other Persian Gulf states. Although Sunni Islam is the official religion, the Shiite minority is free to congregate and worship in its own mosques, and Shiites conduct meetings and hold distinctive religious activities in *ma'tams*, or *husayniyyas*. The government does not subsidize Shiite mosques or appoint their prayer leaders. As with Sunnis, however, the state monitors activities, including sermons, that take place in Shiite mosques.

Christians, Hindus, and Sikhs constitute about 4 percent of the population. The country's constitution guarantees their human rights and religious freedom. Christians include Roman Catholic, Eastern Orthodox, and Protestant groups, and there are Christian churches located in the major cities. The Hindu and Sikh communities, which are concentrated in Dubai, have their own temples for worship.

el-Sayed el-Aswad

See Also Vol. 1: *Islam, Shiism, Sunnism*

Bibliography

Abul Rahman, Abdul Allah. *Al-imarat fi dhakirat abna'aha.* Sharjah: Itahad kuttab wa Udaba' al-Imarat, 1986.

el-Aswad, el-Sayed. *Al-bait ash-sha'bi: Dirasa anthropolojiyya lil 'imaara ash-sh'abiyya wa ath-thqafa at-taqlidiyya li mugtama' al-imarat.* al-Ain: United Arab Emirates University Press, 1996.

———. "Key Symbols in the Folklore of the Emirates." Translated by Salwa al-Misned and reviewed by the author. *al-Ma'thurat al-Sha'biyyah* (Doha, Qatar) 16, no. 62: 8–27.

Lienhardt, Peter, and Ahmed al-Shahi. *Shaikhdoms of Eastern Arabia.* New York: Palgrave Macmillan, 2001.

Peck, Malcolm C. *Historical Dictionary of the Gulf Arab States.* Lanham, Md.: Scarecrow Press, 1997.

United Kingdom

POPULATION 59,778,002

ANGLICAN (INCLUDING THE CHURCH OF ENGLAND) 39.4 percent

ROMAN CATHOLIC 12.5 percent

PRESBYTERIAN (INCLUDING THE CHURCH OF SCOTLAND) 5.5 percent

OTHER CHRISTIAN 8.2 percent

MUSLIM 2.7 percent

HINDU 1.0 percent

SIKH 0.6 percent

JEWISH 0.5 percent

BUDDHIST 0.3 percent

OTHER 0.3 percent

NO RELIGION 29.0 percent

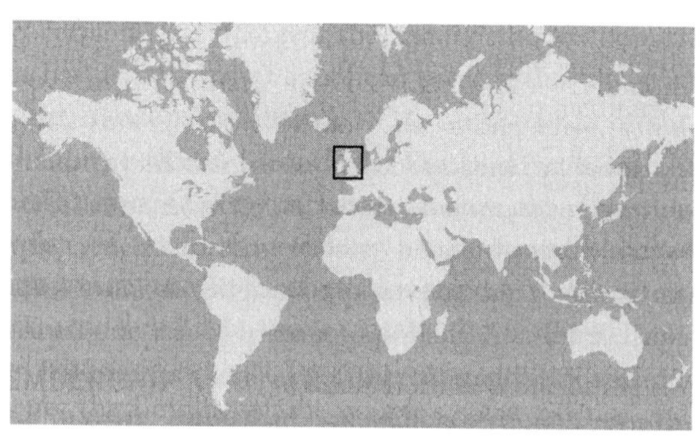

Country Overview

INTRODUCTION The United Kingdom of Great Britain and Northern Ireland occupies most of the British Isles, which lie off the northwestern coast of mainland Europe. The country is composed of four territories—England, Wales, Scotland, and Northern Ireland—with distinct religious histories. Nearly 84 percent of the people live in England, which has one of the most religiously diverse populations in western Europe. Although the English heritage is predominantly Christian, there are substantial numbers of Muslims, Hindus, Sikhs, Jews, and Buddhists. The Church of England is the largest Christian denomination.

The largest religious group in Scotland is the (Presbyterian) Church of Scotland, but there is a substantial Catholic minority. Wales has traditionally been Nonconformist, with chapels generally of a Calvinist hue, though the Anglican Church in Wales has a substantial presence. In Northern Ireland a Protestant, mainly Presbyterian, majority and a Catholic minority have tended to be identified with opposing sides in the political conflict over the future of the province.

English history during the sixteenth and seventeenth centuries was marked by a struggle for supremacy, even survival, between Catholics loyal to Rome, the newly independent Church of England, and dissenting Protestant groups. By the beginning of the eighteenth century the Church of England had become secure. A Catholic minority remained, however, and various Protestant sects took root and grew, including the Quakers and Baptists and later the Methodists.

The contemporary religious position has been greatly influenced by immigration. Large numbers of Irish Catholics came to find work in Britain during the nineteenth and twentieth centuries. After World War II people from former colonies in Africa, the Caribbean, and the Indian subcontinent came to settle in Britain, introducing new churches and non-Christian religions. Many Britons, however, no longer regard themselves as belonging to any religion, and most people do not participate in formal religious practices except at special ceremonies such as weddings and funerals.

RELIGIOUS TOLERANCE The Church of England is the established (official) church in England, though only about half the English population is even loosely affiliated with it. The Church of Scotland serves as the national church in that jurisdiction. Wales has not had an established church since 1920, and there is no official church in Northern Ireland.

In earlier times people not belonging to the Church of England suffered from legal discrimination, but these restrictions were largely dismantled over the course of the nineteenth century. The European Convention on Human Rights, incorporated into domestic law through the Human Rights Act of 1998, provides protection against religious discrimination in the United Kingdom. There is a high degree of religious freedom and tolerance in Britain, though on occasion Muslims and Jews have been the targets of hostility. While religious tensions are still apparent in Northern Ireland, legislation and political agreement have substantially improved the situation there.

Major Religion

CHURCH OF ENGLAND

DATE OF ORIGIN 1534 C.E.

NUMBER OF FOLLOWERS 24 million

HISTORY Christianity arrived in Britain around the second century C.E. and was boosted through the missionary work of Saint Augustine in the sixth century. The new faith had a profound effect on law and culture in the country, and the church as an institution acquired great wealth and influence, as it did elsewhere in Europe. When, in the 1530s, the pope refused to grant King Henry VIII a divorce, the English monarch broke with Rome. The Church of England was separated from the Roman Catholic Church in 1534. Liturgy and practice in the church began to evolve in a Protestant direction, while never entirely forsaking its Catholic roots. Anglicanism (the religious movement that derives from the Church of England and that includes the Episcopal Church in the United States) continues to see itself as pursuing a "middle way" between Catholicism and conventional Protestantism.

Westminster Abbey is among the most significant places of worship in the United Kingdom. It is an ancient church rather than a cathedral because it does not contain a bishop's throne. © ROYALTY-FREE/CORBIS.

The development of a distinctively Anglican liturgy began with the publication of a new prayer book in 1549, and *The Book of Common Prayer,* notably the version published in 1662, has become a cultural landmark. Doctrine was codified under Queen Elizabeth I in the Thirty-nine Articles of 1563. The translation of the Bible commissioned by James I, known as the Authorized or King James Version, was published in 1611 and remained the standard scriptural text through the mid-twentieth century.

Following the death of Henry VIII, the fortunes of Anglicanism rose and fell as successive rulers of England showed sympathy to Catholics or to Puritans. The Glorious Revolution of 1688, and the subsequent Acts of Succession, bound church and state together, with Catholics barred from holding the throne.

Colonization and missionary activity spread the Church of England worldwide, with sister churches belonging to the Anglican Communion coming to exist in all parts of the English-speaking world. Closer to home, the Church of England is linked to the Church in Wales, the Scottish Episcopal Church, and the Church of Ireland.

EARLY AND MODERN LEADERS The reigning monarch is the supreme governor of the Church of England. For all practical purposes, however, the senior figure in the church is the archbishop of Canterbury. Important historical figures to hold this position include Thomas Cranmer (1489–1556), who was condemned to death by the Catholic Queen Mary and burned as a heretic in 1556; William Laud (1573–1645), beheaded during the English Civil War; Gilbert Sheldon (1598–1677), who built the famous Sheldonian Theatre in Oxford; and William Temple (1881–1944), a leading advocate of social reform whose father had also been archbishop. Rowan Williams, who was previously archbishop of Wales and before that professor of theology at the University of Oxford, became archbishop of Canterbury in 2002.

MAJOR THEOLOGIANS AND AUTHORS Important contributors to Anglican thought include Richard Hooker (1554–1600), a great Elizabethan theologian whose work on governance influenced the American founding fathers; John Wesley (1703–91), a founder of the Methodist movement, which became a separate denomination after his death; William Wilberforce (1759–1833), an evangelical antislavery campaigner; and John Henry Newman (1801–90), a leader in the Oxford Movement and later a convert to Catholicism. In the twentieth century the lay theologian C.S. Lewis (1898–1963) restated Christian tenets in response to growing doubt.

A number of great literary figures have had ties to the Church of England and have written on religious themes. These include the poets John Donne (1572–1631), George Herbert (1593–1633), and T.S. Eliot (1888–1965).

HOUSES OF WORSHIP AND HOLY PLACES The territory covered by the Church of England is divided into more than 13,000 parishes. Many churches in rural areas are centuries old, and many of those in cities were built during the Victorian period. Anglican churches are typically more ornate than most Protestant places of worship. It is common, for example, to find stained glass, elaborately carved pulpits and choir stalls, and religious art in the nave or behind the altar in an Anglican church.

Bishops have their seats in cathedrals, buildings that are characteristically large and ancient, although some, like Liverpool cathedral, were built within the past century. Canterbury and Wells cathedrals, York Minster, and Westminster Abbey, an ancient church in which royal weddings have been held and kings crowned but not a cathedral because it does not contain a bishop's throne, number among the most significant places of worship in the United Kingdom.

Other places may be considered holy. Some Anglicans, for example, attach special significance to shrines such as those at Walsingham and Glastonbury Abbey or to newer sites of religious activity and pilgrimage like the Iona Community.

WHAT IS SACRED? Relatively few objects or activities are traditionally regarded as sacred by Anglicans, though there is scope for individual variations in views. The sacraments of the Church of England—baptism and Holy Communion—are sacred rituals, and the objects employed in them, in particular the consecrated wine and wafers, have a special status. Similarly the notion of "consecrated ground"—the churchyard, an adjacent cemetery, the church itself—refers to a holiness attached to these places, within which one is expected to act with decorum. Crosses, images of Christ or the saints, and indeed Bibles and prayer books are to varying degrees held to be sacred, and overt acts of disrespect would previously have been interpreted as blasphemous. As British culture has become more secular, however, it is increasingly difficult to give special protection to what religious people may regard as sanctified.

HOLIDAYS AND FESTIVALS The Advent and Christmas seasons are important periods of the year in Britain, even for people who are not religious. Church attendance on Christmas Eve and Day is higher than at any other time of the year, with special carol services frequently attracting large crowds. The other major, and more purely religious, holiday is Easter. Shrove Tuesday, the last day before the beginning of Lent on Ash Wednesday, is traditionally celebrated as Pancake Day.

Ascension Day (celebrating Christ's ascent into heaven 40 days after Easter) and Pentecost, or Whitsun (the seventh Sunday after Easter, commemorating the descent of the Holy Spirit on the disciples), are other important dates in the Anglican calendar. An English public holiday in late May is often referred to as Whitsun. Although they are not official church holidays, annual harvest festivals are popular services, particularly for children and families, at which people are invited to bring food for distribution to the less well off. Another distinctive practice is Remembrance Sunday (around November 11), when public and religious ceremonies memorialize those who have died in war.

MODE OF DRESS No special dress distinguishes Anglicans from others in England. It is conventional to be reasonably well dressed in a conservative style for attendance at church services, but many people no longer regard this practice as important. There are still traditions regarding dress for special services. Brides usually wear wedding dresses, infants being baptized may have christening robes, and mourners at a funeral often wear black, but even these dress codes are voluntary.

Ordained ministers can often be recognized from their white neck band, sometimes called a "dog collar." In everyday situations, however, clergy often choose to wear ordinary clothing. Priests officiating at services generally wear special vestments, elements of which may have a color corresponding to the church season, with, for example, purple worn during Advent and Lent. It is common for members of the choir or for people assisting the priest at the altar to wear robes as well.

DIETARY PRACTICES The Church of England does not regulate what people may eat. In earlier times it was common to observe practices such as fasting before Communion or abstaining from meat on Fridays, but these traditions are largely obsolete. It is still common, however, for active Anglicans to make modest sacrifices during Lent (for example, by giving up a favorite food or drink).

Unofficial dietary traditions can be found in Britain, but these are not exclusive to Anglicans. They include eating turkey and special cakes and puddings at Christmas or pancakes on Shrove Tuesday. The latter custom arose as people used up eggs and butter in preparation for the Lenten fast.

RITUALS Worship in the Church of England generally takes place on Sundays, though many churches offer midweek services. Anglican services are relatively ritualistic compared with those in most Protestant churches, with a set order that, at least traditionally, requires the congregation to sit (to listen), stand (to sing), or kneel (to pray) at different points in the ceremony. Most services include certain standard prayers, the public reading of passages from the Bible, a sermon, and the singing of traditional hymns or sometimes more contemporary religious songs.

Various types of services may be provided at different times or on different days in order to satisfy the requirements of different groups of churchgoers. Some people prefer the traditional liturgy based on *The Book of Common Prayer;* families may be invited to bring children to special services that offer appropriate words and music; and Communion is performed at some services but not others.

Church weddings remain popular in Britain. Couples applying to marry in church may be asked to demonstrate residence in, or commitment to, the parish. In traditional wedding ceremonies the father escorts the bride down the aisle of the church before "giving away" his daughter to the bridegroom. The man and woman being married make vows and exchange rings.

Funerals were traditionally held in a church, with subsequent burial in the churchyard, but in the late twentieth century more and more people in Britain began to choose cremation, so that many funeral services have come to be conducted at crematoria. For individuals who were reasonably well known, it is common for a small private funeral to be followed days, weeks, or even months later by a memorial service, in which the religious elements tend to take second place to a more secular celebration of the life.

RITES OF PASSAGE Baptism, popularly known as christening, is a sacrament that initiates a person into the Christian community. In the Church of England it has traditionally been administered to infants, though it is also common to see older children and adults being baptized. The church also offers the less formal procedure of "thanksgiving" for celebrating a birth. The official liturgy for baptism involves parents and godparents making religious promises on the child's behalf, while thanksgiving appeals to nominal Anglicans who do not feel comfortable with the undertakings of the traditional christening.

Confirmation is a rite in which adolescents, or sometimes adults, affirm their faith and personally renew the promises made at baptism. It is usual to attend a series of confirmation classes for religious instruction prior to the ceremony. In the past only individuals who had been confirmed were regarded as qualified to receive Communion, though as confirmation becomes less common, this restriction is likely to be eased.

MEMBERSHIP Although 24 million people have been baptized in the Church of England and thus are nominally Anglican, only about 2 million are regular churchgoers. The church is interested in recruiting new adherents and in bringing lapsed Anglicans back into active membership, but it rarely does so aggressively. The evangelical wing of the church tends to be moderate in its approach, while the liberal wing is more concerned to show respect for other faiths than to argue against them. The Alpha Course, a series of talks and discussions generally organized around an evening meal and aimed at introducing nonchurchgoers to Christian beliefs, has become one of the most highly publicized activities.

Discussions have been held with the Methodist Church, the third largest church in England, which originated as an offshoot of the Church of England, over ways of bringing the organizations together. The two churches have come close to agreement on a covenant that may eventually result in union.

SOCIAL JUSTICE The Church of England has spoken out on many issues related to social justice, including racism, poverty, the environment, and foreign policy. The publication in 1985 of a report titled *Faith in the City* is often seen as a watershed in the church's engagement with such issues, demonstrating that it aims to serve the socially disadvantaged and not just the establishment.

The Christian socialist movement drew compassionate attention to social problems in the late nineteenth century. The contemporary church involves itself in practical partnerships such as caring for asylum seekers, supporting urban regeneration schemes and young people's projects, providing counseling, and endorsing groups fighting racism.

SOCIAL ASPECTS The Church of England has attempted to respond to social changes such as premarital cohabitation and childbearing, the rising frequency of divorce, and public acceptance of homosexuality. It proclaims the sanctity of marriage and the importance of the family, while accepting that some people will not meet these ideals. Many Anglican ministers have become willing to perform church weddings for people who are divorced. Most do not automatically condemn nonmarital sexual relations.

POLITICAL IMPACT Although the Church of England has a special constitutional status, its political influence is slight. The public speeches of the archbishop of Canterbury and other leading bishops receive attention, but even Anglican politicians do not feel themselves bound to follow the recommendations of the church. In any event, church leaders generally refrain from making explicit pronouncements on public policy.

Religious influence on political affairs is more commonly felt indirectly, through the activities and decisions of individual Anglicans who hold power. Some prime ministers have been committed Anglicans, from William Gladstone in the nineteenth century to Tony Blair in the twenty-first.

CONTROVERSIAL ISSUES The Church of England includes a broad spectrum of opinion on social issues, and the most awkward divisions are related to internal controversies. The conditions under which people who have been divorced can be married again in church continues to be debated. The ordination of women was resisted by a minority of Anglicans, some of whom left the church to become Catholics, and the question of whether and when women may become bishops remains to be resolved. Although the Church of England tends not to condemn homosexuality, whether in the laity or the clergy, more conservative churches in the Anglican Communion, especially in Africa and Asia, find this view unacceptable. Revised forms of the liturgy have been controversial for many years, with some Anglicans continuing to prefer services from the traditional *Book of Common Prayer.* The position of the institution as the official, or established, church is one that many Anglicans, including some church leaders, have questioned.

CULTURAL IMPACT The cultural impact of the Church of England has been immense. The English language itself has been profoundly influenced by the King James Version of the Bible. The landscape of the country is marked, in reality as well as in art and the popular imagination, by church spires rising above villages and by cathedrals dominating cities. Only the Houses of Parliament can rival Saint Paul's Cathedral or Westminster Abbey as the symbol of London. Sacred music has been extremely important in the cultural life of the nation, with Anglican composers such as Thomas Tallis (1505–85), Orlando Gibbons (1583–1625), Henry Purcell (1659–95), and William Boyce (1711–79) being among the important figures. The English choral tradition is rooted in sacred music such as Handel's *Messiah.* The religious tradition was maintained in the modern period by composers that included Charles Stanford (1852–1924), Herbert Howells (1892–1983), and even Benjamin Britten (1913–76), whose *War Requiem* was commissioned for the dedication of the new Coventry cathedral in 1962.

Other Religions

The Roman Catholic Church is the second largest religious organization in the United Kingdom. Although the number of Catholics in England and Wales—no more than 9 percent of the population—is substantially lower then the number of Anglicans, the Catholic attendance at Mass on a typical Sunday is—at around 1 million—slightly higher than the number of Anglicans in church at the same time. Catholics are even more significant in Scotland, where they make up 16 percent of the population, and they constitute more than 40 percent of the population of Northern Ireland. Although some English Catholics are descended from recusants (those who maintained their allegiance to Rome after the Church of England split from its control), the majority are descended from Irish immigrants.

Catholicism has had an enormous impact on British culture, not only prior to the Anglican split with Rome in the sixteenth century but also subsequently. Many leading figures in public life have been Catholic, and prominent Catholic authors have included Evelyn Waugh (1903–66) and Graham Greene (1904–91).

The cardinal archbishop of Westminster is the leader of the Catholic Church in England and Wales. The church plays an important part in education, with many of the country's state-supported secondary schools being Catholic establishments. In other respects its reputation has suffered; as in some other countries, the church has been accused of doing too little to prevent child abuse by the clergy.

The Church of Scotland, also known as the Kirk, is the largest church in Scotland and the third largest in the United Kingdom. In the 2001 census more than 2 million people in Scotland, 42.4 percent of the population, identified themselves as belonging to the church, though only about 600,000 are officially members.

The Scottish Reformation was led by John Knox in the sixteenth century. The movement, which was opposed by the Catholic monarch Mary, Queen of Scots, was eventually successful, and it resulted in the country becoming Protestant by an act of Parliament. Scotland and England were united under the Stuart dynasty in 1603, and the religious foment of the seventeenth century affected the Kirk. Following the Glorious Revolution of 1688, in which the Catholic King James II was deposed, the Kirk was established as the national church of Scotland in 1690. Periodic rifts, notably the Disruption of 1843, and reunions have produced the Free Church of Scotland and the United Free Church as groups separate from the Kirk.

Unlike the Church of England, which is episcopal (administered by a hierarchy of archbishops, bishops, and priests), the Church of Scotland is presbyterian. Parishes in a district are administered by a group of ministers and elders known as a presbytery. The General Assembly is the national decision-making body of the Kirk.

Other Christian denominations in the United Kingdom include the Methodist, Baptist, United Reformed, Orthodox, and Pentecostal churches. There are also groups such as the Jehovah's Witnesses, Salvation Army, Seventh-day Adventists, Quakers, and Unitarians. In contemporary times there has been substantial growth in independent "house churches," where small groups gather in private homes to worship without clergy or liturgy, and community churches.

Although many, or even most, people in the United Kingdom would describe themselves as being Christian in a broad sense, the majority do not identify themselves with any denomination, and even fewer are members of a church. At least three-quarters of the population do not attend services except on special occasions (for example, for weddings or funerals or for Christmas carols). Church statistics show that baptism, confirmation, church weddings, and other religious practices have declined steadily since World II.

Until the 1970s the principal non-Christian religion in the United Kingdom was Judaism. A Jewish community has existed in Britain for many centuries, and Jews have made large contributions to British society. Although Jews were free to practice their faith for most of the historical period, until the twentieth century they were socially handicapped by official and unofficial discrimination. Nevertheless, some Jews came to prominent positions. One of the greatest figures of the Victorian era, the politician Benjamin Disraeli, was of Jewish descent, though from a family that had converted to Christianity.

Both Orthodox and Reform Judaism are represented in the United Kingdom. Some people who are fairly secular in their practices are nevertheless associated with Orthodox synagogues, and to that extent Orthodoxy in the United Kingdom covers much of the social and religious territory that is occupied by Conservative Judaism in the United States. The head of the Orthodox movement in the United Kingdom is the chief rabbi, who is generally recognized as being the leader of the Jewish community, though strictly he represents only one part of it.

Most British Jews are indistinguishable from the general population in dress and everyday life. Some observant men wear a skullcap, called a *kippa* or a yarmulke, and the highly orthodox, particularly those in the Hasidic community, may wear the distinctive black coats and hats that derive from previous times in eastern Europe. The holy days, rituals, diet, rites of passage, and other practices of Jews in the United Kingdom are the same as those observed by Jews in other parts of the world.

The chief rabbi in the United Kingdom has at different times been criticized by the more and the less orthodox either for being overly accommodating to religious pluralism or, conversely, for being too rigid and sectarian. One particular controversy concerns the inability of some orthodox women to obtain religious divorces from their former husbands. Another surrounds the creation of an *eruv* (a boundary within which activities are less restricted on the Sabbath) in northwest London. The international debate over Israel and the Palestinian territories has been reflected in difficult relations between the British Jewish and Muslim communities.

Following immigration, mainly between the 1950s and 1970s, from the Indian subcontinent, Africa, and the Caribbean, and later from the Balkans, the Middle East, and other areas, Islam has become the largest non-Christian religion in the United Kingdom. The 2001 census found 1.6 million Muslims in the country. There have been Muslims—for example, from Yemen—living in Britain since well before World War II, but it is the presence of large numbers of people whose ethnic origins are in Pakistan and Bangladesh that makes the group so important today.

There are as many as 1,000 mosques in Britain, though more than half of them are simply rooms rather than special buildings. There is no single religious authority or organization representing Muslims in the United Kingdom. One major association is the Muslim Council of Britain, to which several hundred local groups are affiliated. The Imams and Mosques Council is another important organization.

While Muslim religious practices are similar to those found in other parts of the world, in their detail they are often influenced by the national origin of the families concerned. Dress may be wholly Western, particularly among the young, though many individuals—for example, Pakistanis—wear clothes characteristic of their ethnic group. It is not unusual to see women wearing headscarves.

Muslims have become increasingly active politically in the United Kingdom. The controversy surrounding *The Satanic Verses* by Salman Rushdie, himself a British Muslim, served as a catalyst for conflict. The book was viewed as blasphemous by many Muslims, while for secular society freedom of expression trumped religious sensibilities. There has been a move to provide legal protection from religious discrimination, since Muslims, unlike Jews and Sikhs, are not recognized as forming an ethnic category for these purposes.

Immigration has also brought substantial numbers from other faiths to Britain. Among these the largest groups are Hindus, Sikhs, and Buddhists. Asian religious practices have increasingly become integrated into British society, with acceptance of other cultures in schools and workplaces growing. Schools are required to teach elements of Asian religions as part of the curriculum, and it is common for universities and other establishments to provide Muslim prayer rooms alongside Christian chapels.

Many Asian parents bemoan the creeping demise of practices such as arranged marriages, fasting, and family rituals and the fact that religious, clerical, and parental authority is increasingly challenged in ways it would not have been in the more closely knit communities and extended families that have been left behind. Many immigrants have experienced the hostility that can be aroused by outsiders or unfamiliar ways, and there is a constant tension between the desire to integrate and the desire to preserve tradition. In principle, public policy supports diversity as well as assimilation, with many city councils assisting the celebration of non-Christian festivals and some employers providing special leave on religious holidays.

Various New Age and neopagan practices are also found in contemporary Britain.

David Voas

See Also Vol. I: *Anglicanism/Episcopalianism, Christianity, Reformed Christianity, Roman Catholicism*

Bibliography

Bruce, Steve. *Religion in Modern Britain.* Oxford: Oxford University Press, 1995.

Chadwick, Henry, and Allison Ward, eds. *Not Angels, but Anglicans: A History of Christianity in the British Isles.* Norwich, England: Canterbury Press, 2000.

Davie, Grace. *Religion in Britain since 1945: Believing without Belonging.* Oxford: Blackwell, 1994.

Haigh, Christopher. *English Reformations: Religion, Politics, and Society under the Tudors.* Oxford: Clarendon Press, 1993.

Hempton, David. *Religion and Political Culture in Britain and Ireland: From the Glorious Revolution to the Decline of Empire.* Cambridge: Cambridge University Press, 1996.

Hornsby-Smith, Michael. *Catholics in England, 1950–2000: Historical and Sociological Perspectives.* London: Cassell Academic, 2000.

MacCulloch, J.A. *The Religion of the Ancient Celts.* London: Constable and Company, 1991.

Marshall, Peter, and Alec Ryrie, eds. *The Beginnings of English Protestantism.* Cambridge: Cambridge University Press, 2002.

Parsons, Gerald, ed. *Issues.* Vol. 2 of *The Growth of Religious Diversity: Britain from 1945.* London: Routledge, 1994.

———, ed. *Traditions.* Vol. 1 of *The Growth of Religious Diversity: Britain from 1945.* London: Routledge, 1993.

Wolffe, John. *God and Greater Britain: Religion and National Life in Britain and Ireland, 1843–1945.* London: Routledge, 1994.

United States of America

POPULATION 280,562,489

PROTESTANT 52 percent

ROMAN CATHOLIC 24 percent

JEWISH 3 percent

OTHER (OTHER CHRISTIAN, NATIVE AMERICAN RELIGIONS, BUDDHIST, HINDU, MUSLIM, NEW RELIGIOUS MOVEMENTS, SHAKER, MORMON, SEVENTH-DAY ADVENTIST, JEHOVAH'S WITNESS, NONRELIGIOUS) 21 percent

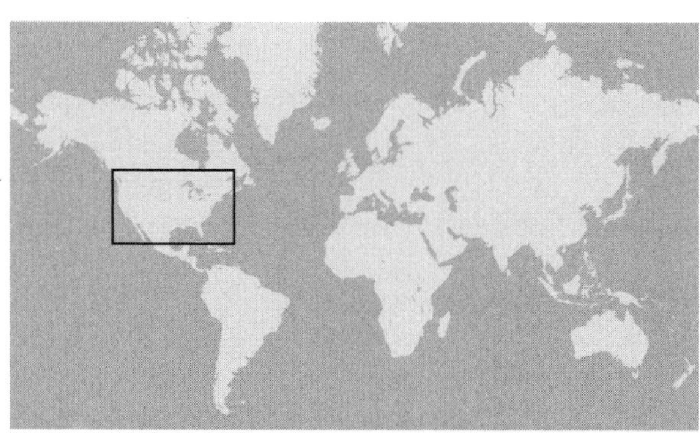

Country Overview

INTRODUCTION The United States of America occupies roughly the middle third of the North American continent and is bordered by Canada to the north, Mexico to the south, and the Atlantic and Pacific Oceans on the east and west, respectively. The states of Alaska (attached to northwestern Canada) and Hawaii (in the middle of the Pacific Ocean) do not abut any of the contiguous 48 states. Its lengthy coastlines, broad expanses of fertile land, and extensive deposits of natural resources, including coal, oil, and timber, have made the United States economically prosperous and thus a magnet for immigrants from around world, who have also been attracted to the country's political and religious freedom. These immigrants have, in turn, arrived with their religious traditions, resulting in a religious pluralism probably never before known in human history, even in the Roman Empire.

The United States has sometimes been described as "the first new nation," referring to its component states voluntarily coming together in 1776 and then under a constitution of their own devising in 1789. The peoples who constituted the new nation at the time of its founding included indigenous Native Americans (misnamed "Indians") with a variety of traditional cultures; enslaved (and, by this time, some free) Africans, mainly from northwestern Africa, whose owners systematically tried, with considerable success, to deprive them of their own cultures; and Europeans, primarily Protestants from Britain and other parts of northwestern Europe but including small numbers of Jews and Roman Catholics as well. Since that time vast numbers of immigrants, at first from Europe and more recently in substantial numbers from Asia, the Middle East, and Latin America, have diversified the U.S. population to a point that it has become virtually a microcosm of the entire world, as is especially apparent in large cities, such as New York, Chicago, Los Angeles, and Miami. In addition, a number of new religious groups have been founded in the United States, including Shakers, Mormons, and

A Baptist pastor preaches during a worship service in Omaha, Nebraska. American Baptists trace their descent from Roger Williams's exile by the Massachusetts Bay Puritans to Rhode Island in the 1630s. AP/WIDE WORLD PHOTOS.

Christian Scientists among Euro-Americans; Peyotism among Native peoples; and the Nation of Islam among African-Americans. As a result, nearly all the world's religious traditions coexist in relative harmony, although the wide variety of Christian denominations still form more than three-fourths of the population. Running counter to this diversity are pressures toward Americanization (involving cultural adaptation in language and many other ways), which has resulted in the gradual transformation of most religious traditions of foreign origin.

RELIGIOUS TOLERANCE A distinctive feature of the American experiment in government has been the religious tolerance mandated by the First Amendment (1791) to the U.S. Constitution, which provides that the federal government shall neither directly support nor interfere with the practice of religion, at least within the broad limits that have emerged through generations of court decisions. The 50 states have all adopted similar measures as well. In practice, patterns and instances of religious intolerance have occurred over the years despite the law and have generally been directed by the Protestant (or more broadly, Christian) majority against minority groups seen as threatening to the status quo and its values. Anti-Catholicism, once common in the nineteenth and early twentieth centuries, is now rare, but expressions of anti-Semitism, though never as toxic as in Europe, still occur. Occasionally Mormons and other minority religious groups have experienced hostility from time to time. In recent years Muslims and Asian and Middle Eastern immigrants have been targeted, especially in the wake of the terrorist attacks in New York City and Washington, D.C., on 11 September 2001.

Major Religions

PROTESTANTISM

ROMAN CATHOLICISM

NATIVE AMERICAN RELIGIONS

A Native American poses in traditional dress. One survey estimates that there were 103,300 practitioners of Native religions in the United States in the early twenty-first century. © PETE SALOUTOS/CORBIS.

PROTESTANTISM

DATE OF ORIGIN 1607 C.E.

NUMBER OF FOLLOWERS 145.9 million

HISTORY The word "Protestantism" denotes those Christian bodies derived, directly or indirectly, from the Protestant Reformation of the sixteenth century and therefore is difficult to discuss as a unified tradition or institution. English Protestants first established permanent settlements in the United States in Virginia in 1607 and New England in 1620. Probably more than 1,000 groups in the United States today could be classified as Protestant. Some of these, such as the Southern Baptist Convention and the United Methodist Church, count their membership in the millions, while many others are independent congregations with only a handful of members. The best way to describe the history of Protestantism in the United States may be to trace the development of several of the most important traditions that have usually been called Protestant. These include the Anabaptist, Anglican, Lutheran, Reformed, Free Church, Wesleyan, and Holiness-Pentecostal. (Other groups that have Protestant backgrounds but are sufficiently distinctive to qualify as "other religions" are dealt with in the section by that name below.)

Anabaptists arose in Switzerland in the 1520s. Two of the major groups who survived early persecution were the Amish and the Mennonites, who had split over issues of church discipline and began to settle in southeastern Pennsylvania in about 1700. The more conservative Amish, who still drive horses and buggies rather than automobiles, can be found today mainly in parts of Pennsylvania and Ohio. The Mennonites, their spiritual cousins who do not reject modern technology, live primarily in Pennsylvania and the Midwest. The Hutterites, who share all property, live primarily on farms in the upper Midwest, as well as the Canadian prairie provinces. All of these groups are pacifist and try to live as simply and traditionally as possible.

Anglicans are followers of the tradition of worship that originated in the Church of England in the sixteenth century. American Anglicans since 1784 have usually been members of the (Protestant) Episcopal Church. Episcopalians worship according to the *Book of Common Prayer,* which today consists of liturgical texts similar to those used by Lutherans and Roman Catholics. The Episcopal Church is often described as a "bridge church," or the "middle way," because its beliefs and practices draw on those of Catholicism, various Protestant traditions, and Eastern Orthodoxy.

Lutherans are followers of the tradition founded by Martin Luther in Germany in 1517. This tradition was the ultimate source for most later Protestant movements, including those in the United States. German and Swedish Lutherans began to arrive in Pennsylvania and vicinity in the mid-1700s; later German and Scandinavian Lutheran immigrants settled primarily in Ohio and the upper Midwest. The largest Lutheran group in the United States today is the Evangelical Lutheran Church in America, made up of many earlier groups that had become Americanized. Two smaller, more conservative groups are the Missouri Synod and Wisconsin Synod Lutherans.

"Reformed" is a term used to describe the movements led by John Calvin and Huldrych Zwingli in Switzerland in the 1520s and '30s and their descendants. Central to the early Reformed churches were a belief in the almighty power of God, the radical influence of original sin on human nature, the predestination of all humans to heaven or hell by God's will, and a simple preaching-centered style of worship. The English Puritans who settled New England beginning in the 1620s were part of this tradition, as were the Presbyterians who migrated from Scotland to the middle colonies in the 1700s and who constitute a major, though much more liberal, denomination today. The Puritans later came to be called Congregationalists after their style of church governance. Many of these churches today, together with their German and Hungarian Reformed counterparts, belong to the liberal United Church of Christ. The descendants of Dutch Reformed immigrants of the nineteenth century today are found in the Reformed Church of America and the Christian Reformed Church.

"Free church" is a generic term for the tradition that includes mainly Baptists, whose roots are both in the Reformed and the Anabaptist traditions. American Baptists trace their descent from Roger Williams's exile by the Massachusetts Bay Puritans to Rhode Island in the 1630s. Their distinctive practice is to baptize only adult believers rather than infants, as most other Christian groups do. Baptists today are divided into many large and small denominations. African-American Baptists usually belong to one of three denominations with the common name National Baptist. The American Baptist churches are a moderate mainline group, while Southern and independent Baptists tend to be much more conservative.

Wesleyan is the name of the tradition stemming from John Wesley, the eighteenth-century Anglican who worked to supplement Church of England worship by organizing small groups to meet outside church for Bible study and spiritual growth. In the United States, Methodists (as Wesley's followers came to be called because of their disciplined spiritual life) first came together as a denomination in 1784 in Baltimore. Through their use of circuit riders (preachers on horseback), they grew rapidly on the southern and western frontiers early in the nineteenth century, but they divided nationally over the slavery issue as the Civil War approached. Today the largest Methodist body is the United Methodist Church, the result of several mergers of smaller groups and now second only to the Southern Baptists among Protestant groups in membership.

The Holiness and Pentecostal traditions both developed from Methodism in the late nineteenth and early twentieth centuries. Holiness denominations, such as today's Church of the Nazarene, focus on Wesley's teaching that, after conversion, believers may have a second religious experience, known as entire sanctification, that would result in a state of holiness, or freedom from voluntary sin. Pentecostals built on this teaching but added the belief that all believers should experience the gifts of the Holy Spirit, especially glossolalia (speaking in tongues).

Today American Protestants may be subdivided into three broad categories. First are the predominantly African-American denominations, mainly Baptist, Methodist, or Pentecostal. Next are the mainline denominations, which range from 1 to 9 million in membership and include members who interpret their traditions in a variety of ways, from the most conservative end of the spectrum to the most liberal. These include the American Baptist Churches, the Disciples of Christ, the Episcopal Church, the Evangelical Lutheran Church in America, the Presbyterian Church (USA), the United Methodist Church, and the United Church of Christ. And finally there are the evangelical denominations, independent congregations, and "parachurch" groups (those whose work is intended to augment rather than rival established denominations). Evangelical Protestants affirm the authority and centrality of the Bible; the need for a personal experience of God's grace (being "born again"); the need to try to convert others by setting an example and evangelizing; and, for many, the second coming of Christ to earth in the near future. Evangelicals can be found to some extent within the inclusive mainline denominations but in greater numbers among Holiness and Pentecostal groups, Southern and independent Baptists, and organizations such as Campus Crusade for Christ and Women Aglow Fellowship. Fundamentalists are ultraconservative evangelicals who stress that the Bible is completely without error.

As H. Richard Niebuhr first pointed out in the 1920s, American Protestant denominations have frequently reflected social, economic, racial, ethnic, and regional divisions among Americans. Episcopalians and Presbyterians have historically attained the highest educational and economic levels, while Baptists and Holiness-Pentecostals were the least prestigious in worldly terms. By the twenty-first century such distinctions had begun to erode. Regionally the South has been dominated by Baptists, Methodists, and Holiness-Pentecostals; Lutherans have been strongest in the upper Midwest, where many Germans and Scandinavians settled; Congregationalists have done best in New England and the areas of the Midwest and Pacific Northwest that were settled in the nineteenth century by New Englanders; and Presbyterianism was originally planted by Scots and Scots-Irish settlers. African-Americans, who have had primarily southern origins, organized their own individual churches and denominations within the Baptist, Methodist, and Holiness-Pentecostal traditions beginning in the late eighteenth century.

EARLY AND MODERN LEADERS There have been many leaders (in addition to the theologians mentioned below under MAJOR THEOLOGIANS AND AUTHORS) in the long and complicated history of Protestantism in the United States. Some denominations have elected national leaders who stay in office for a fixed period, such as the presiding bishop of the Episcopal Church. In recent years few of these leaders have attained a great deal of attention beyond their own denominations. Evangelicals have generally been more likely to generate leaders who attain public recognition than the mainline denominations. In Puritan New England both lay leaders (such as John Winthrop, the first governor of the Massachusetts Bay Colony) and clergy (such as Increase Mather and his son Cotton) were prominent members of a community in which church and state worked in close coordination with one another. By the mid-eighteenth century a new style of evangelical religious leadership, that of revival preacher, emerged; the eminent theologian Jonathan Edwards was also known for the religious revivals that he preached to his congregation. George Whitefield, an Englishman who traveled the colonies preaching wherever he could find an audience, has been described as the first American celebrity because of the attention his work attracted.

During the nineteenth century revivalists (such as Lyman Beecher, Charles G. Finney, and Dwight L. Moody) similarly became public figures. Beecher in the 1820s and '30s also became known for his championship of a number of reform movements, as did Finney, who worked to abolish slavery. Among the twentieth century's mainline Protestant spokesmen were antifundamentalist Harry Emerson Fosdick in the 1920s, the ecumenist Eugene Carson Blake in the 1960s, and, beginning in the 1970s, evangelicals such as Jerry Falwell and Pat Robertson, who were particularly skilled in the use of the mass media. (Other leaders are listed below under SOCIAL JUSTICE.)

MAJOR THEOLOGIANS AND AUTHORS Although many Puritans in colonial New England wrote theology, the most influential in the long run has been Jonathan Edwards, who helped precipitate the widespread religious revivals known as the Great Awakening in the 1740s and who wrote extensively as a latter-day Calvinist, interpreting the revivals and other traditional topics, such as original sin. In the 1830s Charles G. Finney defended revivalism, and in the 1840s Horace Bushnell attacked it. William Ellery Channing in the early nineteenth century defended the liberal creed called Unitarianism, and the Transcendentalist Ralph Waldo Emerson soon afterward challenged even Channing as being too traditional. In the mid-twentieth century the brothers Reinhold and H. Richard Niebuhr adapted the European theology known as neoorthodoxy in an American context. More recently African-American theologians (such as James Cone), feminists (such as Carter Heyward, Phyllis Tribble, and Beverly Harrison), and womanists (or African-American feminists, such as Delores Williams and Katie G. Cannon) have developed distinctive new lines of religious thought, blending traditional Protestant themes with contemporary social issues. Other important twentieth-century theologians include Paul Tillich and Langdon Gilkey.

HOUSES OF WORSHIP AND HOLY PLACES The early Puritan settlers in New England built not churches but meetinghouses, utilitarian structures where the Word of God could be preached effectively and which were not considered sacred in themselves. Anabaptists followed the same logic but worshiped mainly in private homes. This concept of the house of worship as a site for preaching has informed some strains of Protestant building to the present day. By the eighteenth century most Protestant churches in North America began to resemble their European Anglican predecessors, although a central pulpit was retained in many cases. The medieval revivals of the nineteenth century (Romanesque and Gothic) influenced most denominations, especially externally. Since the mid-twentieth century many churches have adopted more modern designs, including circular or semicircular plans intended to diminish the distance between clergy and people.

WHAT IS SACRED The Calvinist (Reformed) strain of piety so influential in colonial times has generally worked against the notion that earthly things or places should be considered holy. Although this attitude has influenced most branches of American Protestantism to some extent, the tendency to regard religiously significant places, such as churches and cemeteries, and persons, such as founders of traditions, as sacred without using such explicit terminology has been widespread. In liturgical traditions, such as the Lutheran and especially the Anglican, such attitudes have tended to emerge with regard to the places and rituals of worship in particular.

HOLIDAYS/FESTIVALS No holidays or holy days other than the Sabbath were considered special in Puritan New England, although today's Thanksgiving Day has early Puritan origins. Since then German and English practices, such as those for Christmas and Easter especially, have been incorporated into American observance. In many cases, however, commercialization has blurred the religious significance of such observances.

MODE OF DRESS Except for Anabaptists and other small sectarian groups, especially those of German origin, who have preserved Reformation-era (sixteenth-century) modes of dress, American Protestants have not usually dressed in any religiously mandated style. Clergy in some traditions, however, wear special robes while conducting services.

DIETARY PRACTICES American Protestants, other than groups not usually classified as Protestant (such as Seventh-day Adventists and Mormons), have seldom advocated specific dietary prohibitions. More general counsel toward temperance in the use of food and drink, however, has been characteristic of evangelicals from John Wesley to contemporary Pentecostal women. Many conservative or fundamentalist groups eschew smoking and drinking alcohol.

RITUALS Worship in Protestant churches varies among traditions. Episcopalians and Lutherans follow a fixed liturgy similar to that of the Roman Catholic Church following the Vatican II council (1962–65). Churches in the Reformed and Wesleyan traditions are usually not as elaborately structured but rather combine the reading of formal prayers, preaching, and hymn-singing by choirs and congregations. The Holiness-Pentecostal tradition favors less formal worship, including the delivery of testimonials to the individual experience of God's grace and, among Pentecostals, speaking in tongues.

Marriage is almost universally recognized as a religious ritual, to be performed by a member of the clergy in a church. Funerals are usually conducted by clergy as well, although ceremonies may take place in a funeral home. Most denominations do not maintain separate cemeteries, as do Catholics and many Jews. Many Protestants now prefer cremation rather than burial of the embalmed body.

RITES OF PASSAGE Most Protestant denominations other than Baptists take their infant children to church for a baptismal or christening ceremony. Some observe confirmation, in which teenagers formally join their congregations as consenting members.

MEMBERSHIP The roots of American religious freedom lie in part in the teachings of some Protestant groups, especially the Baptists. Although some denominations, such as Congregationalists in New England, were initially negative about loss of support from the state, most came rapidly to accept religious pluralism as desirable and also as an opportunity for evangelism. The desirability of spreading the "good news" of the Christian gospel has generally been a priority for American Protestants, especially those known as evangelicals. Since the Second Great Awakening of the early nineteenth century, missionary outreach to both North Americans and foreigners has been a priority for evangelicals, who since the twentieth century have been particularly adept at using mass media, especially television and radio, to propagate their message. In some areas membership in particular groups may be encouraged by social pressure, especially where particular denominations hold majority status or enjoy prestige as an elite group.

SOCIAL JUSTICE During the twentieth century religious leaders could be found across the theological and ideological spectrums. Walter Rauschenbush and Washington Gladden preached a social gospel declaring that Christians were called to the reform of social, political, and economic structures. The revivalist Billy Sunday denounced all things German, such as beer and biblical criticism, during the World War I era. His successor, Billy Graham, began to attract attention for his preaching the imminent second coming of Jesus (premillennialism) in the 1950s and in the early twenty-first century had achieved the status of admired elder statesman in the eyes of Americans of many denominations.

Beginning in the 1950s clergy of different denominations and ethnic backgrounds began to participate in the movement for civil rights for African-Americans, especially in the South, with Baptist minister Martin Luther King, Jr., emerging as one of the most eloquent and effective spokespeople. By the late 1960s many mainline clergy, such as Yale chaplain William Sloan Coffin, began to call for active resistance to U.S. involvement in Southeast Asia. In the 1970s a reaction against Protestant church involvement in liberal causes began to set in, led by such evangelicals as Jerry Falwell of the Moral Majority and Ralph Reed of the Christian Coalition. Such groups have continued into the twenty-first century to focus on sex- and gender-related issues, including abortion, pornography, and gay and women's rights. More liberal groups have generally taken stands against capital punishment and in favor of legalized abortion and full rights for gays and lesbians, without necessarily endorsing such behaviors.

SOCIAL ASPECTS Given the great diversity of belief and practice among U.S. Protestants, it is difficult to generalize about social practice. Until the later twentieth century divorce was forbidden or frowned upon by most groups, even those considered liberal today. In more recent years, however, most mainline churches and many evangelicals recognize the necessity of divorce, even while promoting the traditional family as the norm. Homosexual partnerships are not yet accorded the same status as heterosexual marriage by most, although in some liberal circles the blessing of such unions is practiced.

POLITICAL IMPACT American Protestants have since the nation's colonial beginnings been active in promoting social reform based on their own interpretation of biblical principles. Throughout the nineteenth century they were especially powerful nationally, because no other religious groups had yet attained significant economic and political power outside of a few northeastern cities. Although the Protestant-dominated campaign to bring about the national prohibition of alcoholic beverages resulted in the Eighteenth Amendment to the U.S. Constitution in 1918, its repeal in 1933 signified a diminished Protestant influence on public policy. Franklin D. Roosevelt's New Deal succeeded in the government's taking over many charitable functions previously carried out by churches. The realignment of political parties that followed the desegregation of the South in the 1960s resulted in a major shift of southern—especially southern evangelical—support to the Republican Party, which has since closely aligned itself with evangelical groups and causes.

CONTROVERSIAL ISSUES Since the emergence of Darwinism and biblical criticism in the nineteenth century, American Protestants have been divided over a number of issues. In general, evangelicals are conservative on issues involving morality, although since the 1970s the emphasis has shifted from tobacco and alcohol usage to questions of sexuality and gender. Evangelicals also usually stress a literal interpretation of the Bible and oppose the teaching in public schools of scientific theories of human origin, which seem to contradict such an account. More liberal Protestants, including many found in the mainline denominations, tend to oppose public regulation of morals and are frequently opposed to capital punishment and supportive of the rights of women and minorities, government action to ease economic and social inequality, and free choice on sexual issues, including homosexuality and abortion.

CULTURAL IMPACT During the colonial era, especially in New England, the influence of Protestantism was all-pervasive. During the nineteenth century its impact was less direct. Theological themes dominated much of the fiction of Herman Melville, Nathaniel Hawthorne, and Mark Twain, although their answers were less than orthodox. Some popular writers were at times more direct about their religious views, as in Harriet Beecher Stowe's antislavery polemic in *Uncle Tom's Cabin* (1851). Music and the arts also became more compartmentalized during this period, with secular and sacred themes and styles occupying separate cultural niches. The liturgical arts began to flourish in the later nineteenth century, and stained glass, such as that produced by Tiffany Studios, became prominent in many wealthier churches as the older Protestant suspicion of the arts began to fade. The same separation continued into the twentieth century: While some "secular" writers, such as William Faulkner, explored religious themes in their novels, only a small number of "serious" writers, such as Peter de Vries and John Updike, might be classified as Protestant. In the popular realm, however, Protestant religious themes have been more visible, as in Christian rock music artists of the late twentieth and early twenty-first centuries, such as Amy Grant and Jars of Clay, and in the best-selling *Left Behind* series of millenarian novels.

ROMAN CATHOLICISM

DATE OF ORIGIN 1565 C.E.

NUMBER OF FOLLOWERS 67.3 million

HISTORY The earliest Roman Catholic presence in North America was that of the Spanish, who first settled in what is now the southern rim of the United States, beginning in Florida in 1565. Their empire included most of what is now referred to as the Sunbelt of the United States, stretching from California through Texas to Florida. The French also had an imperial presence in the colonial era, focused on the Mississippi River down to New Orleans. English Catholics first arrived in the 13 original colonies in Maryland in 1634. Catholics remained a small minority in the new nation until massive immigration caused by the great potato famine in Ireland in the decades prior to the American Civil War, together with a growing number of Germans seeking political freedom and economic opportunity, swelled the ranks of the church. Later in the nineteenth century large number of Catholics from Italy and central Europe (Lithuania, Poland, Hungary, and the former Czechoslovakia and Yugoslavia) further swelled Catholic ranks, with considerable conflict developing between predominantly Irish and Irish-American clergy and bishops and lay Catholics from other ethnic backgrounds. During the era between the Civil War (1861–65) and the Great Depression (1929–c. 1939), a vast infrastructure, including churches, schools at all levels, seminaries, convents, hospitals and asylums, and cemeteries, was built up in the growing cities of the East and the Great Lakes region. Religious sisters, again in large numbers from Ireland, helped to staff hospitals and parish schools.

After Congress passed a series of laws in the 1920s severely restricting immigration from Catholic areas of Europe, the Catholic population began to stabilize and Americanize. "Builder bishops," concerned with providing institutions for Catholic needs, set the tone and often ruled autocratically. Catholics, mainly of the working class, had not yet been fully accepted into American life, and their leaders sought to insulate them from secular and Protestant influences. During the early 1960s American Catholic culture was strongly affected by two events. In 1960 John F. Kennedy was the first Catholic to be elected president of the United States; since that time Catholicism largely has ceased to be a political issue. In 1962 Pope John XXIII convened Vatican II, an ecumenical council attended by all the bishops of the Catholic Church, in Rome. This council brought about sweeping changes in Catholic practice, notably celebrating the Mass and other sacraments in vernacular languages, such as English and Spanish, instead of the traditional Latin. A shift in tone from defensiveness to a new openness to other religions also resulted from the council, with considerable impact on Catholics in the United States. Moreover, the GI Bill, passed by Congress in 1944, provided veterans with money for college, leading to a rise in social and economic status for many American Catholics. The resultant move from old ethnic urban neighborhoods to the suburbs further promoted the blending of American Catholics into the population at large. Many of these Catholics became less dependent on Catholic Church teachings and generally ignored Pope Paul VI's 1968 encyclical letter forbidding artificial contraception.

The election of John Paul II as pope in 1978 was another landmark for American Catholics, who now experienced a dramatic reversal of the liberalization that had characterized the 1960s. This Polish pope began to insist on a strict adherence to the norms he advanced, and he removed bishops, priests, and sisters from positions of responsibility when they refused to conform. His appointment of reliable conservatives as bishops over his long pontificate further consolidated his power. Although he did not repeal Vatican II's reforms, such as the vernacular liturgy, he reaffirmed traditional Catholic teaching on matters of sexuality and gender in particular, making it clear that women and married and homosexual men were not welcome in the priesthood. The issue of the priesthood was particularly problematic in the United States, because large numbers of clergy had left the priesthood during the years of turmoil following Vatican II, and seminary enrollments dipped to new lows. Further damaging to the priesthood was a national scandal in the early twenty-first century over the sexual abuse of young people by priests.

Immigration continued, especially in the latter part of the twentieth century, from Mexico, Puerto Rico, Cuba, and other parts of Latin America, as well as from Vietnam and other parts of the old French Indochina. By the twenty-first century Latino Catholics represented a dramatic challenge to a church that had become largely English-speaking and middle class, and a substantial number left to join Pentecostal and other Evangelical Protestant churches. Although a Catholic presence among African-Americans was established early on in Maryland and Louisiana, and many inner-city dwellers prefer Catholic parochial schools to public schools because of the stricter discipline and higher standards of the former, relatively few blacks have abandoned their traditional Protestant allegiances in favor of Catholicism.

EARLY AND MODERN LEADERS Because the Roman Catholic Church is hierarchical in structure, it is not surprising that many of the most influential Catholic leaders have been clergy and especially bishops. John Carroll, first bishop and then archbishop of Baltimore in the early nineteenth century, laid many of the foundations for later Catholic growth. By the end of the nineteenth century, a number of bishops in the Midwest, led by John Ireland of Saint Paul, Minnesota, advocated the embrace of American institutions and culture by Catholics, but their efforts met considerable resistance from other bishops as well as the Vatican.

Twentieth-century leaders include many Catholic bishops who have emerged as spokesmen for the Roman Catholic community, especially those from major cities, such as Chicago's Joseph Bernardin and New York's Francis Spellman. During the 1950s Cardinal Spellman spoke for the Catholic point of view on matters of public policy, such as Communism and sexuality, and his assistant, Bishop Fulton J. Sheen, attracted national attention through his popular television program, *Life Is Worth Living.* At the same time, laity (such as the social activist Dorothy Day) offered alternative paradigms of "grassroots" Catholic leadership, as did increasingly visible members of women's religious orders. By the early twenty-first century American Catholic leadership had grown increasingly conservative, and its authority had been undermined to some degree by the national scandal of sexual abuse of young people by clergy. This scandal resulted in the resignation in 2003 of Cardinal Bernard Law of Boston, who, together with many of his fellow bishops, was harshly criticized for not having dealt with offending priests more firmly.

MAJOR THEOLOGIANS AND AUTHORS The large number of Catholic immigrants and the lack of an educated laity during the nineteenth and early twentieth centuries worked against the development of a distinctively American Catholic intellectual and literary culture, and priests learned their theology from European textbooks. Two converts from Protestantism, Orestes Brownson and Isaac Hecker, produced some original theological work during the mid-nineteenth century, but this had little influence on the broader American Catholic community.

By the 1950s Catholic universities had begun to become centers of scholarship, and intellectuals, such as Father John Tracy Ellis, began to criticize publicly the lack of an American Catholic tradition of learning. During the 1960s the Jesuit John Courtney Murray had considerable influence on Vatican II through his arguments for Catholic recognition of religious liberty for all and his defense of the American system of separation of church and state. At the same time, Thomas Merton, a convert who had become a Trappist monk, produced autobiographical, spiritual, and antiwar writings, which attracted a wide audience. European theologians, such as Karl Rahner, Edward Schillebeeckx, and Hans Küng, attracted considerable attention from U.S. Catholics, as did liberation theologians from Latin America. Charles Curran became noticed in the mid-1980s when he was forbidden by the Vatican to teach theology at the Catholic University of American in Washington, D.C., after refusing to retract what many regarded as rather moderate stands on issues of sexual behavior in particular. Theologians and ethicists prominent at the beginning of the twenty-first century include Lisa Cahill, Bryan Hehir, John Langan, and Richard McBrien.

HOUSES OF WORSHIP AND HOLY PLACES Few Catholic churches predate American independence, except for missions in the former Spanish borderlands. Until Vatican II (1962–65) most Catholic churches were built in revival styles; the Roman and Greek were popular during the early nineteenth century, and styles more directly associated with the European Catholic heritage (Romanesque, Gothic, Renaissance, baroque, and Spanish mission) dominated from the mid-nineteenth to the mid-twentieth century. Liturgical change initiated by Vatican II favored new ground plans, such as the semicircle, in which the priest and altar were no longer isolated from lay worshipers, a model dramatically illustrated by the chapel of the Benedictine monastery in Collegeville, Minnesota. American Catholics also maintain a number of shrines that possess relics of saints and attract especially those seeking cures.

WHAT IS SACRED What is considered sacred is much the same for American Catholics as it is for Catholics in other developed nations. Roman Catholic churches and chapels intended for sacramental worship are consecrated as sacred places. Sacramentals (material aids to worship, such as holy water) are blessed by priests. Saints (men and women who led lives of exemplary holiness and who are believed to have worked miracles) are revered, though not worshiped as gods, and their images are placed in churches, schools, and homes.

HOLIDAYS/FESTIVALS American Catholics do not celebrate any holidays or festivals outside the norm from those observed by Catholics in other developed nations. American Catholics follow the cycle of the liturgical year observed by the Catholic Church as a whole, which begins in Advent (the four weeks prior to Christmas) and continues through Christmas and Epiphany into the Lenten cycle beginning with Ash Wednesday and culminating in Easter. Holy days commemorating events in the life of the Virgin Mary, the mother of Jesus, are distinctive to Catholic (and Eastern Orthodox) worship.

MODE OF DRESS The attire of Roman Catholics in the United States does not differ significantly from that of Catholics in other developed nations. Lay Catholics dress according to the customs and fashions of the general population. Prior to Vatican II (1962–65) clergy generally wore dark clothing with clerical collars, and women in religious orders wore habits that concealed all but hands and face. Now priests and women in orders frequently do not wear distinguishing clothing in public. Priests and deacons wear distinctive vestments during liturgical activity, such as the celebration of the Mass.

DIETARY PRACTICES Prior to Vatican II (1962–65) American Catholics, like Catholics elsewhere, were supposed to refrain from eating meat on Fridays and certain other days. This practice has since then become more relaxed, with meat banned only on a few days in Lent.

RITUALS American Catholics, like Catholics in other developed nations, regard the seven sacraments as the primary rituals, although other significant ceremonies, such as children receiving their first Communion (Eucharist) and women taking religious vows, are also practiced. Five of the sacraments are rites of passage (described below under RITES OF PASSAGE). The other two, in which Catholics are urged to participate frequently, are reconciliation (formerly known as confession or penance), in which individuals confess their transgressions to a priest and then receive absolution, and the Eucharist, in which believers receive bread and wine as the body and blood of Christ in the course of the ritual of the Mass.

RITES OF PASSAGE American Catholic practice does not differ significantly from that of Catholics in other developed nations. Of the Catholic Church's seven sacraments, five are focused on rites of passage. Baptism, usually administered to infants but also to adult converts, marks an individual's initiation into the church. Confirmation, usually performed before age 16, involves a conscious reaffirmation of baptismal vows. Matrimony is the sacramental celebration of marriage. The anointing of the sick, in the past usually restricted to those in danger of death, is now administered to the seriously ill. Ordination to the priesthood is the only sacrament restricted to males.

MEMBERSHIP As its history in the United States indicates, the term "Catholic" (meaning "universal") in "Roman Catholic Church" suggests that universal membership is the ultimately desirable goal. For many centuries until the time of the Protestant Reformation, Catholicism had been the official religion of most of western and central Europe and was carried abroad as Catholic nations (such as Spain) founded extensive overseas empires. Afterward it still remained strong in Ireland, Spain, Portugal, Italy, and much of central Europe. In the United States the Catholic Church had to adapt to the principle of free religious choice, as well as the welcome absence of persecution, and has emulated Protestant evangelization especially through its use of religious orders (such as the Paulists and Maryknoll) as missionaries seeking converts at home and abroad. The loyalty of immigrants from traditionally Catholic countries and their children, as well as a number of conversions, in part through marriage, has allowed the U.S. Catholic Church to attain and maintain the status of the largest single religious group in the nation, approaching (in the twenty-first century) one-quarter of the entire population.

SOCIAL JUSTICE During much of the nineteenth century the American Catholic Church was largely preoccupied with meeting the economic and spiritual needs of immigrants. The encyclical letter *Rerum Novarum* ("Of New Things"), issued by Pope Leo XIII in 1891, articulated the foundation for a distinctive Catholic social philosophy based on the concept of the "just wage"—that is, the amount of money needed for a worker to sustain a wife and family with basic dignity. Although criticized by conservative lay Catholics in the late twentieth century, this affirmation of the rights of labor remains central in contemporary American Catholic teaching. The Catholic Church also opposes capital punishment, although a majority of American Catholics favor it in the same proportion as non-Catholics.

SOCIAL ASPECTS The institutional Catholic Church in the United States has always upheld traditional values, including the centrality of the nuclear family, the indissolubility of marriage other than by church-granted annulment, and the impermissibility of abortion, artificial contraception, and homosexual behavior. Some liberal Catholics are opposed to many of these teachings, and Catholic practice in general does not differ greatly from that of other mainline religious groups.

POLITICAL IMPACT During the late nineteenth and early twentieth centuries, American Catholics were largely working-class immigrants or their children and were involved in the "boss" political systems of Northeastern and Great Lakes cities. Mayor Richard J. Daley of Chicago was one of the last of the prominent big-city bosses whose power was based in considerable part on grassroots ethnic Catholic loyalty. Franklin D. Roosevelt, after his election to the presidency in 1932, appointed many Catholics and Jews to federal judgeships and cabinet- and subcabinet-level posts.

As Catholic World War II veterans gained access to higher education as a result of the GI Bill, they also became more independent politically. The election of John F. Kennedy as the first Catholic U.S. president in 1960 largely removed Catholic identity as an obstacle to political success, even in the once firmly anti-Catholic South. As the Democratic Party became increasingly committed to a pro-choice position on abortion, many previously loyal Catholic Democrats voted for Republicans, most notably Ronald Reagan in 1980 and 1984. Catholics today continue to lean Democratic, but their voting patterns more closely resemble those of other white voters with similar socioeconomic status than a reliably monolithic bloc vote.

CONTROVERSIAL ISSUES Official Catholic teaching cuts across the liberal and conservative lines of American politics. On issues of gender and sexuality, Catholic positions are conservative: Women are not allowed ordination as priests, and homosexual behavior, abortion, artificial contraception, and sexual relations outside of marriage are all prohibited. In the social and economic realm, Catholic teaching stresses economic justice for workers and opposes capital punishment. The opinions and practices of American Catholics, however, tend to be in line with those of other Americans and do not always conform to the teachings of the "official" hierarchical church.

CULTURAL IMPACT Little distinctive cultural production arose from the largely immigrant and working-class American Catholic Church during the nineteenth and early twentieth centuries. The emergence of the popular music and film industries in the 1920s provided opportunities (as did athletics) for Catholics to enter the public eye. Such Catholic entertainers as Bing Crosby, Perry Como, Frank Sinatra, Spencer Tracy, and Gregory Peck all demonstrated the career possibilities for the Catholic minority. It was in the realm of film in particular—in movies about priests and nuns, such as *Going My Way* (1944)—that Catholic themes emerged into the public eye. Later movies, such as *The Exorcist* (1973), dealt with more controversial themes. It was not until the 1950s and '60s that significant American Catholic authors began to emerge as well. Prominent among them have been Flannery O'Connor, who wrote gothic stories about the South, and J.F. Powers, who satirized the lives of priests in the Midwest.

NATIVE AMERICAN RELIGIONS

DATE OF ORIGIN c. 20,000–10,000 B.C.E.
NUMBER OF FOLLOWERS Undetermined

HISTORY Because traditional Native religion has been inextricably linked to the cultures of each of several hundred peoples, and those cultures have been subject to the often traumatic changes brought about by conflict with Euro-Americans and subsequent defeat and displacement, it is possible to trace these developments only in general terms. With the exception of relatively recent developments, such as Peyotism, Native American religions have been practiced since the arrival of Native peoples in North America, most likely across the Bering land bridge from Siberia, in prehistory. Many Native Americans today practice religions of European origin, including Catholicism and several varieties of Protestantism. Most Native peoples possessed belief systems expressed in myths that mainly dealt with the origins of a particular people. These frequently involve stories as to how the earth and its animal and human inhabitants were created by the gods and how those gods imparted to humans the knowledge necessary for survival. They might also address the introduction of evil and death into the world. These narratives were transmitted orally, at least until modern times, and would change subtly or dramatically in their retellings to reflect recent experience.

Prior to the arrival of Europeans in North America, Native life was anything but static and involved frequent wanderings and conflicts that periodically resulted in conquests and relocations. This same pattern continued in the post-Columbian period, but Native technologies of warfare proved no match for those of European origin. Native peoples were also decimated by European-introduced diseases, as well as demoralized by the social disintegration that frequently followed defeat. Beginning during the presidency of Andrew Jackson in the 1830s, Native peoples in the southeastern states were forced to relocate to what is now Oklahoma. Their journey, which came to be known as the Trail of Tears, resulted in considerable suffering and death. Subsequent governmental policies brought about the creation of the reservation system, in which Native peoples were forced to resettle on tracts of land provided by the federal government, almost exclusively west of the Mississippi River. Government policy at times allowed Native Americans to sell their lands, usually at a considerable loss. Many drifted away from the reservations into the cities, where they often found it difficult to adapt successfully. The impact of this massive dislocation on religion manifested itself in the weakening of traditional tribal myth and ritual, conversion of many to Christianity, and an openness to new forms of religious expression after it had become clear that traditional cultural patterns were no longer viable.

The massacre by U.S. soldiers of several hundred Sioux at Wounded Knee (South Dakota) in 1890 was a turning point in the development of Native life and religion. This event had been precipitated in part by the spread of the second Ghost Dance, a movement that had begun in Nevada and California and rapidly spread throughout the Native peoples in the West. According to a vision by the prophet Wodziwob, if the Ghost Dance were performed properly, it would result in the transformation of the earth, the elimination of the Euro-American intruders, and the restoration of the earlier life of the Natives. Its performance alarmed U.S. troops, and the wearing of "ghost shirts" (believed by Native peoples to confer invulnerability) may have emboldened the dancers to take risks. The disastrous result at Wounded Knee put an end to the Ghost Dance and was the last episode of serious resistance to governmental control.

Other movements among Native peoples that represented adaptation to a changed state of affairs rather than overt resistance include the Gaiwiio of the Seneca and the Peyotism that originated in the Southwest. The first movement was founded early in the nineteenth century by a Seneca chief named Handsome Lake. A series of visions prompted him to promulgate a new teaching that combined elements of traditional Seneca lore with others from Christianity and became known as the Gaiwiio. This teaching was originally apocalyptic and predicted the end of the world within three generations. These elements were later discarded, and many Seneca today still follow the Gaiwiio. Peyotism, which began to spread among many tribes following the defeat of Wounded Knee, involves the ritual use of the peyote cactus, which contains a number of consciousness-altering chemicals. The goal of this ceremony is the transformation of individual consciousness rather than social change, and the teachings surrounding it, which differ from place to place, contain various mixtures of Christian and traditional Native elements. Many Peyotists are members of Christian churches as well.

Since the forcible removal of most Native peoples to reservations by the U.S. government beginning in the 1830s, traditional customs have often been displaced by a more Euro-American way of life. Beginning in the 1960s, however, deliberate revivals of traditional customs and rituals have appeared selectively.

In the 2000 census 4.1 million Americans, or 1.5 percent of the population, described themselves as entirely or partially Native American. Of these, a considerable number were Christians but may also have been practitioners to some extent of traditional Native religious rituals or newer movements such as Peyotism. One survey estimates that there were 103,300 practitioners of Native religions in the United States in the early twenty-first century. Because of this selective adherence to custom as well as the decentralized character of Native society, it is impossible to give even rough figures on participation, except to say that peoples such as the Pueblo of the Southwest, who have led relatively stable existences, have generally succeeded in maintaining traditional practices better than others who have been dislocated and assimilated to a greater extent.

EARLY AND MODERN LEADERS Religious leadership among Native peoples has often come from shamans, which are visionaries capable of relating insights from dream journeys to a contemporary situation. Some notable examples in the past have been the "Delaware prophet" associated with Pontiac in the latter's "conspiracy" of 1763; Handsome Lake of the Seneca; Tenskwatawa, the brother of Tecumseh; and Wodziwob and Wovoka, the prophets of the two Ghost Dance movements.

MAJOR THEOLOGIANS AND AUTHORS "Theology" is not a useful term in discussing Native American religions, because it represents a mode of discourse foreign to peoples whose traditions are orally transmitted in narrative form. It was not until the nineteenth century that Native American traditions began to be transcribed into print form. *Black Elk Speaks,* the 1930s transcription of interviews of a Lakota Sioux leader by the Nebraskan poet John Neihardt, is an interesting account of the rituals and historical experience of his people in the late nineteenth century, but Neihardt's rendering is not always reliable. Later twentieth-century writers, such as Vine Deloria, Jr., and Dee Brown, have helped publicize the unfortunate history of Native Americans under U.S. rule. Contemporary Native fiction of high quality includes work by Leslie Marmon Silko, N. Scott Momaday, Linda Hogan, Sherman Alexie, and Louise Erdrich and often deals with religious themes, especially as they reflect and are affected by the breakdown of traditional ways of life.

HOUSES OF WORSHIP AND HOLY PLACES Places for worship vary considerably among the different Native peoples, although most have not used fixed places except under Christian influence. Holy places may consist of already existing natural phenomena (such as the four mountain peaks that define the traditional homeland of the Navajo in the Four Corners region in the Southwest and the cottonwood tree used by the Lakota Sioux for the sun dance) or of human-made artifacts (as illustrated in the Pueblo ceremony involved in the construction of a new house).

WHAT IS SACRED Many Native languages have special words for sacred power, such as *orenda, wakan,* and *manitou.* Such power may be manifested in virtually any part of the natural world; in this aspect "enspiritedness" is a good term to evoke its potentially universal character. Such power can be accessed through ritual, which is usually conducted by a religious specialist—a visionary shaman or a learned medicine man—who is endowed with the power to achieve visions of the supernatural world or who possesses the necessary traditional lore.

HOLIDAYS/FESTIVALS Holidays and festivals are usually calendrical, especially among agricultural peoples, and mark major events in the annual cycle of the life of a people. Events that might be celebrated include the planting and harvesting of crops.

MODE OF DRESS Dress varies greatly from people to people, although the use of some ritual garments, such as masks, is a common part of ritual celebrations. The kachina dancers of the Pueblo are a good example. They don special costumes kept in underground ceremonial chambers, or kivas, when they reenact the emergence of their earliest ancestors from below the surface of the earth.

DIETARY PRACTICES Traditional dietary practices of Native peoples have varied considerably, especially between seminomadic hunting peoples and settled agriculturists. One possible generalization is that the procurement, preparation, and consumption of food have been informed by an awareness of the reciprocal relationship between humans and the plant and animal worlds and that all activities concerning food have been based on ritual practices invoking this reciprocity.

RITUALS Myths were told at, and formed the basis of, Native rituals, including life-cycle ceremonies (see below under RITES OF PASSAGE) and those performed in conjunction with materially essential and socially important activities, such as hunting, harvesting, and warfare. Among the northern Salteaux a hunter would address and propitiate a bear prior to killing it, thus acknowledging the reciprocal role that both played in the broader spiritual economy of the universe. The

Green Corn ceremony of the Creeks (an agricultural people), celebrating the arrival of the first fruits of the annual corn crop in midsummer, included a ritual of individual and collective purification to begin the new year. The Pueblo used a special ritual for dedicating a newly constructed house, ensuring its alignment with the broader cosmic forces. All of these rituals were based on the notion that every aspect of human life, when performed according to correct ritual practice, would integrate those activities into the broader spiritual forces of the cosmos. The Pueblo are among the few Native peoples who have been able to continue to practice many of their traditional customs into the twenty-first century.

RITES OF PASSAGE Rites of passage are a special kind of ritual performed to mediate such life-cycle events as birth, puberty, and death. The Apache had a first moccasin ceremony, marking a baby's first steps, which usually occurred when the baby was between seven months and two years of age. The sun dance of the Plains Indians was a puberty rite in which an adolescent male would undergo painful ordeals designed to induce a vision. Among the Lakota Sioux, young women were sequestered at the time of their first menstrual period and underwent a purification ceremony in a sweat lodge. Funeral practices varied considerably, including permanent interment in burial mounds as well as more temporary arrangements, such as the Huron's practice of placing the remains of the dead on an elevated platform, followed by a ceremony every 15 years in which such remains would be collected and buried prior to the relocation of the entire village. Most of these practices died out after prolonged contact with Euro-Americans in the nineteenth century.

MEMBERSHIP In traditional Native societies the social and religious spheres were coextensive, so that each religious system was unique to a particular people. Pan-Indian movements, such as Peyotism, have not been exclusive; however, because there has never been an effective central organization or authority that transcends individual tribes, their character has varied from place to place as it has been adapted by different peoples at different times.

SOCIAL JUSTICE The new prophetic religious movements among Native peoples in the nineteenth century, such as Handsome Lake's Gaiwiio and the Ghost Dances, can be interpreted as quests for social justice, usually in the form of ignoring or eradicating Euro-American cultural influence and either restoring old ways or selectively adapting to the new. Beginning in the late 1960s pan-Indian movements to arouse Native consciousness have focused on more strictly political issues, such as the recovery of funds mismanaged by the federal government, the improvement of living conditions on reservations, and the ongoing fight against alcoholism, which is common among Native Americans.

SOCIAL ASPECTS Because traditional Native American culture did not differentiate sharply between sacred and secular, rules governing marriage and family life gained their legitimacy as part of a broader tribal culture manifested in myth. Common in traditional Native society was matrilocality—the practice of men living with their wive's people after marriage. Also common was exogamy (marriage outside one's immediate family group). Differentiation of gender roles was also the rule. Men, for example, usually served as warriors and hunters, while women raised children and performed domestic chores. Although unfaithfulness was frowned upon, serial monogamy was common among many peoples, with children raised more as part of an extended kinship group than solely by the nuclear family.

POLITICAL IMPACT Political activity since the 1960s has involved select religious issues. Owing to small numbers, economic weakness, and the division of Native peoples into a large number of tribal groups, political impact has been weak except on a local scale. The ability of Native peoples to claim exemption on treaty grounds from gambling laws has led to the erection of many casinos, some extremely successful. In a few cases, such as that of the Onondaga, opposition to gambling has been based on religious grounds—in this case, the Gaiwiio of Handsome Lake. A more clearly religious issue has been Native opposition to the desecration (by government or private business interests) of traditional burial grounds and religious landscapes; this opposition has had mixed results in the courts.

CONTROVERSIAL ISSUES Various issues concerning the relationship between Native Americans and the broader society have generated controversy since the 1960s. The Lakota Sioux, for example, have denounced the misappropriation of their spiritual traditions by non-Native peoples, such as followers of New Age practices. Commercial efforts to exploit lands sacred to a particular people have met with Native opposition throughout the United States. The ritual use of peyote has provoked a number of court cases; this and other issues resulted in the passage by Congress of the Religious Freedom Act of 1993, which was later declared unconstitutional by the U.S. Supreme Court. The exemption of Native peoples from laws governing gambling and the taking of fish and game have also led to conflict.

CULTURAL IMPACT Throughout the first half or more of the twentieth century, Native peoples were generally depicted in film and fiction as bloodthirsty enemies of Euro-American settlers and were often defeated by the superior power of cowboys and U.S. cavalry. A countertradition of depicting Native peoples as "noble savages" had roots in nineteenth-century European and American romanticism, as in the portraits of them by George Caitlin. This tradition was revived by the 1960s counterculture, as in Carlos Castañeda's best-selling and most likely invented accounts of the shaman Don Juan, who taught enlightenment through consciousness-expanding drugs; it was also perpetuated by the popular film *Dances with Wolves* of 1990. Tony Hillerman's police stories set on the Navajo reservation in the Southwest have been widely praised for their accuracy in depicting Native life, especially religious beliefs and rituals, as well as for their literary interest.

Other Religions

Several traditions with origins in Euro-American Christianity have been founded in the United States and are sufficiently different in fundamental beliefs to place them outside the realm of Protestantism in its usual definitions. Among these traditions are the Shaker, Mormon, Seventh-day Adventist, Christian Scientist, Jehovah's Witness, and Unitarian Universalist.

The Shakers, or United Society of Believers in the Second Appearance of Christ, originated around the time of American independence with the coming of Ann Lee from Britain to the United States. Mother Ann, as she came to be known, was hailed by her disciples as the second, female incarnation of Christ. Her followers organized themselves into about two dozen colonies in the northeastern United States and lived communal lives of celibacy in which the sexes were equal and all goods were held in common. They flourished in the early nineteenth century but today are represented only by a handful of believers at the Shaker community in Sabbathday Lake, Maine.

The Church of Jesus Christ of Latter-day Saints (LDS), or Mormons, originated in the 1820s when Joseph Smith, a young man living in Palmyra, New York, claimed to have had revealed to him a set of golden plates that spoke of a group of Hebrews who had crossed the Atlantic, had founded a new nation in Central America, and were visited by Jesus after his appearance in the Old World. This revelation was translated by Smith and published as the *Book of Mormon.* Together with the Jewish and Christian bibles and other, later revelations to Smith, it forms the basis for the LDS religion. After being forced to flee from several early settlements in the Midwest and enduring the death of their leader, the early Mormons followed Brigham Young to the Great Salt Lake in Utah, where they settled and where their world headquarters, in Salt Lake City, now stands. Although the Mormons were forced to make some compromises with the U.S. government—most notably the abolition of polygamy—their stress on evangelization has led to continual growth. Their major source of strength is still in the American West, but they continue to open new temples (where their distinctive rituals are performed) both in major U.S. cities and through many other parts of the world.

Seventh-day Adventism is a movement based on the religious experiences of Ellen Gould Harmon White. White was a follower of William Miller, who calculated (using biblical texts) that the second coming of Jesus would take place in 1843 or 1844. When Jesus failed to appear, many of Miller's followers rallied behind White, who claimed to have had visions in which she received distinctive teachings on the observation of the Sabbath on Saturday, as well as on proper dietary and sexual practice. The denomination today is noted for its maintenance of well-known health-care facilities in the Midwest.

Christian Science is a movement that was founded by Mary Baker Eddy in late nineteenth-century Boston. Eddy believed that she had been miraculously healed and had thereby found the key to a scientific interpretation of the Jewish and Christian scriptures—that matter is an illusion and that only the mind is real. She also taught that disease and death are therefore illusions as well and that a proper understanding of Christian revelation can overcome them. Her movement flourished in

U.S. cities in the early twentieth century but has since experienced a considerable decline.

Jehovah's Witnesses, a group founded in 1872, have focused on the imminent second coming of Jesus and maintain that the number of full saints is limited to 144,000. Their refusal (on biblical grounds) of blood transfusions and the flag salute has resulted in a number of significant court cases on freedom of religious practice.

Unitarian Universalists (UUs) are the result of a 1961 merger of two liberal, originally Christian groups that began in the late eighteenth century and early nineteenth century in New England. Because their theological positions were essentially alike in their rejection of the doctrines of predestination, original sin, and the Trinity, they eventually overcame differences that were more sociological than theological and merged. Today a majority of UUs do not consider themselves Christian but are open to the insights of a wide variety of religious and philosophical traditions. A smaller, explicitly Christian faction has its center in New England.

"Cult" is a pejorative term usually applied to "new religious movements" (a more neutral term) by those who find them beyond the bounds of acceptability. Most of the religious movements listed above have been labeled "cults" at one time or another. Beginning in the 1970s a new wave of new religious movements began to emerge in the United States, attracting widespread media attention through their unconventional beliefs and practices, which sometimes involved accusations of brainwashing of potential recruits. These movements included the Unification Church (members of which were often called "Moonies," after the name of their founder, Sun Myung Moon, who claimed to have come to create a new perfect human family, a task that Jesus was unable to accomplish); the International Society of Krishna Consciousness, based on a devotional strain in Hinduism; and, most notoriously, the People's Temple of Jim Jones, who led hundreds of his followers in a mass suicide in the South American nation of Guyana in 1978. Many of these movements have been short-lived, but some have survived over a longer term, usually through the alteration of beliefs and practices to be more in line with the American norm.

Although the large majority of Americans since the arrival of Europeans in North America have belonged to Christian churches, including the Eastern Orthodox traditions, a small but significant number of Jews have been present since colonial times. In addition, the Hart-Cellar Act passed by Congress in 1965 opened the door to immigrants from Asia and other parts of the world who had previously been prohibited from entering the United States in significant numbers. These included Hindus from India, Buddhists from East and Southeast Asia, and Muslims from a wide range of countries in Africa, the Middle East, and Asia. Smaller numbers of Sikhs, Jains, and followers of other traditions also arrived in the United States during this period.

Greeks, Russians, and other peoples historically associated with Eastern Orthodoxy began to arrive in the United States in large numbers during the "new immigration" of the late nineteenth and early twentieth centuries and settled primarily in the industrial and mining areas of the Mid-Atlantic and Great Lakes states. The landscapes of these areas are still dotted with Greek Orthodoxy's characteristic round- or onion-domed churches. In 1970 the Orthodox Church in America was declared autocephalous (independent and self-governing). Although it emerged from Russian Orthodoxy, it has lately begun to attract Orthodox Christians of a variety of backgrounds as a panethnic Orthodox community.

Sephardic Jews (from Spain and Portugal) first began to settle in the cities of the eastern seaboard during the colonial era; they prospered but never grew large in number. Much greater numbers of German-speaking Jews began to arrive in the early nineteenth century and settled in such Midwestern cities as Cincinnati as well as in New York City, which would soon become the center of American Jewish life. Still larger numbers of Ashkenazic (northern European) Jews from eastern Europe, who were mainly Yiddish speakers, arrived as part of the new immigration that began in the 1870s and continued until World War I cut off transatlantic travel. The German Jewish community, led by Rabbi Isaac Mayer Wise of Cincinnati, helped institutionalize Reform Judaism (which had originated in Enlightenment Germany) as a new form of Jewish religion adapted to modern life. Reform was opposed not only by the Orthodox community but also by a new, American-born movement known as Conservative Judaism, which rejected both the rigid traditionalism of Orthodoxy as well as the Reform movement's willingness to jettison all aspects of tradition, including the kosher dietary laws. During the twentieth century Jews in the United States continued to assimilate rapidly, attaining levels of education and career achievement in proportions far greater than their small numbers (about 3 percent of the population) would indicate. Although anti-Semitism was less serious in the United States than in Europe, American Jews were nevertheless deeply affected by the Holocaust, and even Reform Jews became more sympathetic to tradition following World War II. Most American Jews, including the roughly 50 percent who today consider themselves Jewish by heritage rather than by religious belief, strongly support the nation of Israel as an international Jewish homeland. By the twenty-first century a major challenge for U.S. Jews was the high rate of intermarriage between Jews and gentiles (non-Jews).

Although an indeterminate number of African slaves may have been Muslims, the first major wave of Islamic immigration to the United States began in the 1920s, when both Muslims and Christians from the Middle East went to work in the auto factories near Detroit. The U.S. Muslim presence remained small until the Hart-Cellar Act of 1965, which encouraged skilled professionals to immigrate. Since then Muslims from a wide variety of countries have settled in the United States, mainly in major cities and their suburbs. Although small mosques, often located in private homes, still exist in many poorer urban areas, well-to-do Muslims have supported the erection of sizable Islamic centers in many suburbs, providing space not only for worship but for a variety of educational and recreational facilities as well. Although the terrorist attacks in New York City and Washington, D.C., on 11 September 2001 generated anti-Muslim sentiment and a handful of violent incidents, Islam remains a rapidly growing faith in the United States. Much of this growth has come not only from immigration but also through the conversion of many African-Americans. The Nation of Islam, associated with W.D. Fard, Elijah Muhammad, and Malcolm X, gained considerable attention during the 1950s and '60s but was not based on historical Islamic tradition. More recently Wallace Deen Muhammad, the son of Elijah Muhammad, has led the American Muslim Mission, a movement recognized by other Muslims.

Hindus, who were scarce in the United States prior to 1965, have, like Muslims, immigrated in considerable numbers in recent years. Also like Muslims, Hindus from all across the Indian subcontinent, accustomed to differing local and regional styles of observance, have had to cooperate with coreligionists of differing cultural backgrounds in the United States. The result has been the building of Hindu temples in the suburbs of most good-sized American cities. These temples differ from any found in India; for example, many in the United States have shrines to a variety of gods and goddesses rather than to a single one, and facilities for education and social interaction are often located on the ground floors of temple buildings.

Buddhism has been taken to the United States by various nations and cultures of East and Southeast Asia since the late nineteenth century, when Japanese and Chinese settled in Hawaii and in the West Coast states. Restrictive laws barred further immigration until 1965, and Buddhism, especially of the Pure Land sect, was practiced mainly in ethnic communities in a few cities, such as Honolulu and San Francisco. Since then many versions of Buddhism have begun to flourish in ethnic communities. The other major locus of U.S. Buddhism has been among Euro-American converts, often highly educated professionals, who are attracted to Zen and occasionally become recognized as Zen masters. Zen centers can now be found throughout the United States, with a mixture of Asian and Euro-American clientele. Tibetan Buddhism has also been popular, especially through the charismatic appeal of the exiled Dalai Lama.

Peter Williams

See Also Vol. 1: *Christianity, Protestantism, Roman Catholicism*

Bibliography

Ahlstrom, Sydney E. *A Religious History of the American People.* New Haven, Conn.: Yale University Press, 1972.

Albanese, Catherine L. *America: Religions and Religion.* 3rd ed. Belmont, Calif.: Wadsworth, 1999.

———, ed. *American Spiritualities: A Reader.* Bloomington: Indiana University Press, 2001.

Balmer, Randall Herbert. *Mine Eyes Have Seen the Glory: A Journey into the Evangelical Subculture in America.* 3rd ed. New York: Oxford University Press, 2000.

Dolan, Jay P. *The American Catholic Experience.* Notre Dame, Ind.: University of Notre Dame Press, 1992.

Gaustad, Edwin Scott, ed. *A Documentary History of Religion in America.* 2nd ed. 2 vols. Grand Rapids, Mich.: Eerdmans, 1993.

Gaustad, Edwin Scott, and Philip L. Barlow. *New Historical Atlas of Religion in America.* New York: Oxford University Press, 2001.

Lippy, Charles H., and Peter W. Williams, eds. *Encyclopedia of the American Religious Experience: Studies of Traditions and Movements.* 3 vols. New York: Scribner, 1988.

Morris, Charles R. *American Catholic.* New York: Random House, 1997.

Raphael, Marc Lee. *Profiles in American Judaism.* San Francisco: Harper and Row, 1984.

Sullivan, Lawrence E., ed., *Native American Religions: North America.* New York: Macmillan, 1989.

Williams, Peter W. *America's Religions.* 2nd ed. Urbana: University of Illinois Press, 2002.

———. *Houses of God: Region, Religion, and Architecture in the United States.* Urbana: University of Illinois Press, 1997.

Uruguay

POPULATION 3,386,575

ROMAN CATHOLIC 64.8 percent

ATHEIST 6.3 percent

PROTESTANT 3.3 percent

JEWISH 1.2 percent

OTHER AND NONAFFILIATED 24.4 percent

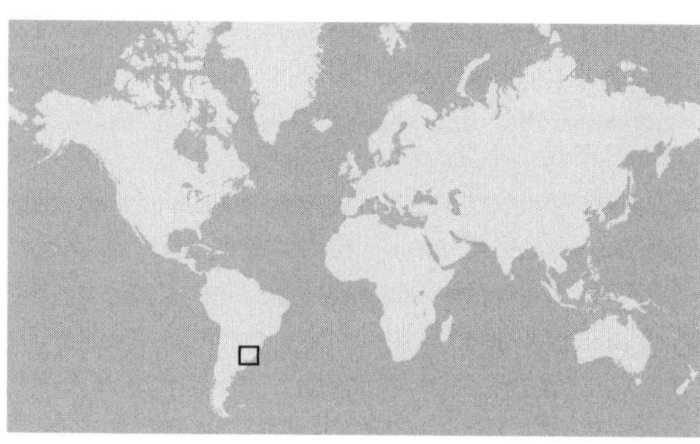

Country Overview

INTRODUCTION The Oriental Republic of Uruguay, on the Atlantic Coast of South America, borders Brazil and Argentina. It is made up mainly of lowlands, and its economy has historically been based on export-led agriculture, primarily beef and leather.

With the highest rates of urbanization (92 percent, with half the population concentrated in the port city of Montevideo) and literacy (98 percent) of all the major Latin American countries, Uruguay's demographics resemble those of many European nations. Roughly 88 percent of the population is Caucasian, of primarily Spanish, French, and Italian descent. The remaining citizens are of African origin (4 percent) or of mixed race (8 percent). At the time of European settlement in the sixteenth and seventeenth centuries, the region was populated sparsely by a seminomadic indigenous tribe known as the Charrua. The colonizers killed off many of the Charrua; others were forcibly absorbed into the European population, leaving no significant indigenous population today.

Both Portugal and Spain laid claim to the territory at different times between 1521 and 1816. Argentina (independent after 1816) and Brazil (independent in 1822) continued to fight for control over Uruguay. In 1828 the British stepped in and brokered a treaty with Argentina guaranteeing Uruguayan sovereignty, but the country spent the next several decades fending off Brazilian and Argentine influence over its political dealings. Since the mid-1800s, Uruguay has slowly evolved a democratic system, despite one period of military rule that lasted from 1973 to 1985. In the early 1900s Uruguay instituted a modern welfare state that guarantees an extensive pension system, unemployment insurance, and a legally mandated forty-hour work week for laborers.

With a significant atheism rate and nearly 27 percent declaring themselves nonreligious (including those who were born into the Catholic faith but do not practice it), the general irreligiosity of the population is the most remarkable feature of Uruguay. In spiritual belief and practice, it resembles northern Europe more than Latin America. Because Uruguay was largely settled between the mid- and late-1800s, when Europe was undergoing secularization and anticlericalism, many immigrants arrived with a distaste toward religion, particularly Catholicism. Neighboring Argentina and Chile, however, experienced a similar immigration pattern and are much more religious. Urbanization and literacy may contribute to the absence of religious fervor. Finally, since religions have traditionally performed social welfare functions, the widespread availability of welfare from the government may lessen the incentive to affiliate with a religious organization.

RELIGIOUS TOLERANCE Uruguay's 1830 constitution declared religious toleration, but separation of church and state was not fully accomplished until 1916. The current constitution guarantees freedom of religion. All registered religious denominations receive equal treatment under the law, including tax-exempt status, and registration is not particularly onerous. Public schools, which the majority of children attend, are not permitted to teach religious doctrine, but private confessional schools, both Catholic and Protestant, are legal. Uruguay has had few instances of religious bigotry or intolerance.

Major Religion

ROMAN CATHOLICISM

DATE OF ORIGIN 1616 C.E.
NUMBER OF FOLLOWERS 2.2 million

HISTORY Portuguese Jesuits introduced Catholicism to the sparse indigenous population in the early seventeenth century. In the 1700s the Spanish colonial province of Rio de la Plata (Argentina) extended its influence over the region, and Uruguay came under the control of the Spanish Catholic Church. The Vatican included colonial Uruguay in the diocese of Buenos Aires.

After it achieved independence in 1828, the Uruguayan government retained the right of the *patronato* (patronage), which allowed it to nominate bishops and approve papal bulls. The Vatican, however, did not agree to a separate Uruguayan diocese and considered the country an apostolic vicariate (a Catholic region assigned diplomatic relations with the Holy See) until 1878. As elsewhere in Latin America, the government expropriated various church landholdings and social

Uruguayan Catholic pilgrims climb a foothill during a celebration. Roughly two-thirds of all Uruguayans identify themselves as Catholic. AP/WIDE WORLD PHOTOS.

functions (such as marriage ceremonies and registering births and deaths) throughout the 1800s, culminating in the formal and complete separation of church and state in 1919. The government has gone as far as giving religious holidays official secular names. Since disestablishment the role of the Catholic Church and Catholicism has been notably unremarkable. Most Catholics are nonpracticing, and the Catholic clergy maintain a relatively low profile in society.

EARLY AND MODERN LEADERS The Uruguayan Catholic Church has not produced many leaders of historical note. Perhaps the most outspoken bishop was Archbishop Mariano Soler (born in 1846), who in the late nineteenth century argued against the separation of church and state and promoted the idea that Catholicism should be declared the state religion. The current head of the Uruguayan Bishop's Conference is Pablo Jaime Galimberti di Vietri.

MAJOR THEOLOGIANS AND AUTHORS With secularism the dominant theme in Uruguayan culture, most intellectuals have avoided religious themes. Theological innovation within the Uruguayan Church itself has been largely absent.

HOUSES OF WORSHIP AND HOLY PLACES Every town in Uruguay has a Catholic parish. The main cathedral or church is typically located in the town's central plaza across from the courthouse or city hall. There are no major pilgrimage sites, though some devoted Uruguayan Catholics journey across the Argentine border to visit the Basilica of Luján.

WHAT IS SACRED? As in many Latin American Catholic societies, the Virgin Mary is a central focus of worship in Uruguay. The Virgin of Treinta y Tres (a small town in rural Uruguay) serves as the country's official patroness. Devout Catholics are known to wear crucifixes, and some will place figurines of various saints in their automobiles, but such displays are uncommon.

HOLIDAYS AND FESTIVALS Uruguayan Catholics celebrate all Roman Catholic holidays, including Christmas and Easter. Because the government does not legally recognize religious holidays, it has provided them with secular names so public employees may take time off. Christmas has been renamed Family Day, and Holy Week has become Tourist Week. Devout Catholics follow rituals similar to those of Southern European Catholics, attending Mass on a regular basis.

MODE OF DRESS Uruguayan Catholics wear everyday dress for services, religious holidays, and celebrations.

DIETARY PRACTICES As elsewhere throughout the Catholic world, Uruguayan Catholics are encouraged to avoid meat (except fish) on Fridays, though observance of this practice has waned.

RITUALS The rituals of the Mass are the same in Uruguay as in other countries. Many weddings involve a religious ceremony, but the only officially recognized marriages are those registered with civil authorities.

RITES OF PASSAGE As in other predominantly Catholic nations, baptism, first Communion, religious marriages, and funeral services are widely observed. Approximately 75 percent of all self-declared Catholics have their children baptized.

MEMBERSHIP Membership in the Catholic Church is open to all Uruguayans. While roughly two-thirds of all Uruguayans identify themselves as Catholic, this identification is largely nominal. Regular participation in religious services is the lowest of any Latin American country; according to the 1995 World Values Survey, only 17 percent of Uruguayan Catholics attend Mass on a weekly basis, while 44 percent report attending less than once a year. In a report commissioned in the late 1970s, the Uruguayan Bishop's Conference estimated weekly Mass attendance at an even lower rate—approximately 4 percent. The church encourages active followers to go through baptism, seek Confirmation, and participate and tithe regularly. It does not aggressively evangelize despite few legal restrictions on proselytizing.

SOCIAL JUSTICE The Uruguayan Catholic Church does not have a strong record in the area of social justice. The episcopacy (bishops and priests) largely remained silent during the military dictatorship of 1973 to 1985. While the military's efforts to quell public opposition to the dictatorship may have played a part in this, the Uruguayan hierarchy and clergy were generally considered to be conservative and accepting of the military government. Near the end of the dictatorship, the episcopacy did release lukewarm statements condemning the human rights situation in the country, but they were never leaders in this criticism. Pockets of parish clergy adopted some of the progressive elements of liberation theology, and a few Christian base communities were created to help impoverished villages improve their standard of living through literacy training and community projects, but these practices were not widespread. Although the Uruguayan government has an extensive welfare system designed to deal with unemployment and poverty, the Catholic Church does maintain charitable services for the poor as in other countries.

SOCIAL ASPECTS The Catholic Church in Uruguay follows Vatican policy in opposing birth control and divorce, but many self-declared Catholics ignore these proscriptions. Birth control is widely available in the country. Civil divorce was legalized in Uruguay in 1912, and Uruguayans have one of the highest divorce rates in Latin America, with estimates that more than half of all marriages end in divorce.

POLITICAL IMPACT Catholicism in Uruguay has produced three political organizations of note: the Circulo Catolico de Obreros de Montevideo (Catholic Workers Circle of Montevideo, a labor union), founded in 1885; the Union Civica (Civic Union, a Catholic political party), founded in 1911; and the Christian Democratic Party, founded in 1962. The early and complete separation of church and state in 1916 has meant that the Catholic episcopacy and clergy have had little influence over political matters. Bishops and priests have occasionally offered statements of concern over poverty but have largely refrained from criticizing political leaders or the political system. Uruguay's current democracy functions comparatively well by Latin American standards and has not come under criticism from Uruguayan religious or lay leaders.

CONTROVERSIAL ISSUES Despite protestations by the Uruguayan Catholic Church, the government legalized first-trimester abortions in 2003. The Uruguayan Catholic hierarchy continues to release statements opposing all forms of abortion. Unauthorized abortions were not uncommon prior to this legislation, though it is difficult to estimate how extensive the practice was. Only Cuba maintains a more liberal abortion law in Latin America.

CULTURAL IMPACT Contemporary Uruguayan culture is highly secular; neither art nor literature reveals any extensive religious influences.

Other Religions

Non-Catholic religions claim a very small portion of the population of Uruguay. Protestant missionaries frequently note the difficulty of winning conversions in Uruguay, largely because of the secular nature of the society. The largest denominations among groups broadly affiliated with Protestants are the Mormons and Jehovah's Witnesses. Mormons claim approximately 65,000 adherents.

Jews make up less than 2 percent of the Uruguayan population. The Jewish population came to Uruguay mostly from Germany and central Europe in the mid-twentieth century. The Jewish population has decreased since the 1990s as some Jews have emigrated because of poor economic conditions in the country. As with Catholicism, Uruguayan Protestants and Jews observe practices similar to their brethren in the United States and Europe; there are no distinctive Uruguayan practices associated with these religions.

Anthony Gill

See Also Vol. I: *Roman Catholicism*

Bibliography

Caetana, Gerardo, and Rober Geymonat. *La secularización uruguaya (1859–1919)*. Montevideo: Ediciones Santillana, 1997.

Gill, Anthony. *Rendering Unto Caesar: The Catholic Church and the State in Latin America.* Chicago: University of Chicago Press, 1998.

Gill, Anthony, and Erik Lundsgaarde. "State Welfare Spending and Religiosity: A Cross-National Analysis." *Rationality and Society.* Forthcoming (2004).

Klaiber, Jeffrey. *The Church, Dictatorships, and Democracy in Latin America.* Maryknoll, N.Y.: Orbis Books, 1998.

Mecham, J. Lloyd. *Church and State in Latin America: A History of Politico-Ecclesiastical Relations.* Chapel Hill: University of North Carolina Press, 1966.

Uzbekistan

POPULATION 25,155,000

MUSLIM 88 percent

EASTERN ORTHODOX 9 percent

OTHER 3 percent

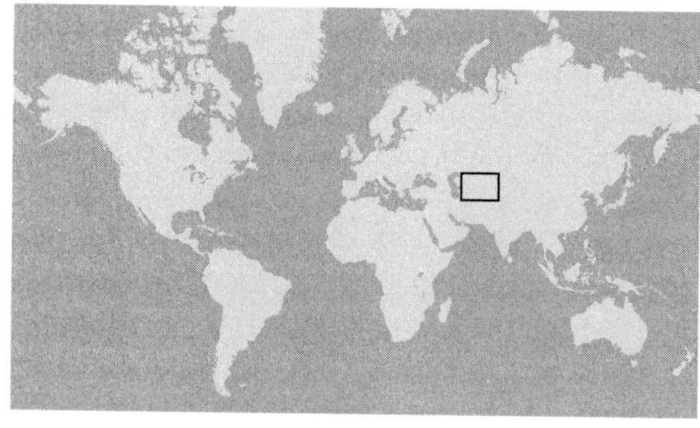

Country Overview

INTRODUCTION Bordered by Kazakhstan to the north, Kyrgyzstan and Tajikistan to the east, Afghanistan to the south, and Turkmenistan to the west, the Republic of Uzbekistan is Central Asia's most populous country. At the juncture of important ancient trade routes, Central Asia was exposed to ideologies and spiritual movements from Indian and Persian cultures. Major cities along the Silk Road included Samarqand, Bukhara, and Khiva, all of which are located in modern Uzbekistan.

Alexander the Great conquered the region in the fourth century B.C.E. Later in the sixth century C.E. Turkic nomads arrived. After a series of battles in Kharasan, Bactria, and Khoresm, Arabs began their rule in the mid-seventh century and introduced Islam to the region. By the end of the eighth century Islam was the dominant religion in Central Asia. The region was conquered by the Mongols in the thirteenth century. A Mongol khan named Öz Beg reigned from 1313 to 1341, and some believe that the Uzbeks claim their descent from this dynasty. The Uzbeks originated as a tribal confederation in the eastern regions of the Golden Horde, a Mongol state founded in the mid-thirteenth century and that encompassed most of Russia. In the fourteenth century Timur Lenk (1336–1405) forged a great empire.

During the sixteenth and seventeenth centuries, the Russian empire had expanded to contiguous lands, and by the middle of the nineteenth century, the Russians began their conquest of Central Asia. In 1924, following the establishment of the Soviet Union, the Soviet Socialist Republic of Uzbekistan was founded. Since 1936 Uzbekistan has included the autonomous Republic of Karakalpakstan within its borders.

During the reform period from 1987 to 1991, Communist leaders of the Central Asian republics feared the demise of their own regimes, and leaders of the Central Asian republics supported the continuation of the Soviet Union until its final moment. When the Soviet Union collapsed in December 1991, it was replaced by the Commonwealth of Independent States, bringing independence to Uzbekistan. Despite religious restrictions, Islam continues to be a cultural and political force.

RELIGIOUS TOLERANCE Traditionally amicable relations have existed among the various religious communities of Uzbekistan. Beginning in the early twenty-first century, however, radical Islamic groups operating outside government structures distributed anti-Semitic literature, prompting some Jews of Uzbekistan to emigrate to Israel. Since the 1980s young Uzbeks have been drawn to what is called "political Islam," including such sects as Wahhabite and Hizb-u-Tahrir, as well as the Islamic Movement of Uzbekistan and Taliban style extremist groups.

Islam Karimov, who had been Uzbekistan's Communist party chief in 1989, was elected president in September 1991. He began a crackdown against political opponents and established controls on Muslims. The Karimov government continues to perceive unauthorized Islamic groups as extremist security threats and forbids them. The level of corruption in the Karimov administration and the extreme poverty experienced since independence from the Soviet Union can perhaps explain the attraction of the young people to such groups.

In May 1998 Parliament passed a law called Freedom of Conscience and Religious Organizations, which begins with the proclamation that "the aim of the present law is to ensure the right of every person to freedom of worship and religion, and the citizens equality irrespective of their religious convictions." The law, however, drastically limits religious activity. It restricts religious rights that conflict with national security, forbids proselytizing, banishes religious subjects in schools, forbids the private instruction of religious principles, forbids the wearing of religious clothing in public by anyone but clerics, and requires religious groups to acquire a license to publish or disseminate materials.

A woman bends over a sacred stone at Shah-i Zinda (Shrine of the Living King), a necropolis built in the eighth century. © FRANCESCO VENTURI/CORBIS.

Major Religion

ISLAM

DATE OF ORIGIN Seventh century C.E.
NUMBER OF FOLLOWERS 22 million

HISTORY At the time of the Arab conquests that began in the seventh century and that introduced Islam to Central Asia, Buddhism, Zoroastrianism, Manichaeanism, Judaism, and Christianity were all represented in Central Asia and the area that would later become Uzbekistan. The region included the cities Bukhara and Samarqand, which became centers of Persian and Islamic culture. By the eleventh century Islam had spread along the trade routes of Central Asia through the efforts of Sufi brotherhoods.

Genghis Khan and the Mongols conquered Uzbekistan in 1220. In the fourteenth century Emir Timur, who claimed descent from Genghis Khan, built the Timurid dynasty that reached from India to Asia Minor with its capital in Samarqand. Sufi brotherhoods reached a peak in the fourteenth century. The most influential Sufi order was the Naqshbandi order, which was founded by Muhammad Baha ad Din Naqshband (1317–89) and patronized by Timur. Until 1501 Central Asia was dominated by the Hanafi school of Sunni Islam. In 1501 Iran was conquered by the Safavids, who ruled until 1727 and made Shiism the dominant religion. The dominance of Shiites in Iran created a religious frontier between Iran and Central Asia.

Beginning with the occupation of Kazan in 1520, the Russians steadily advanced into adjacent lands and Muslim territories. In 1865 Russians occupied Tashkent, and by the nineteenth century Russia had conquered all of Central Asia. In 1924 the Soviet government carved Uzbekistan out of Central Asia. The Soviets attempted to promote Communist mullahs from 1921 to 1927; however, Joseph Stalin tried to abolish Islam from 1927 to 1939. In 1927 the Central Asian Communist organizations, under the supervision of two Communist party members from Moscow, launched the *khujum* (attack) movement, which aimed at counteracting traditions linked to Islam. Following the *khujum,* traditions sanctioned by Islam, such as polygyny, were classified as crimes based on custom. Mosques were closed, and *waqfs*, religious endowments governed by Islamic law, were liquidated. Ultimately the Soviets decided to institute a Muslim board in charge of conservative court mullahs. In 1941 Stalin established four spiritual leaderships for the Soviet Muslims. The Muslim Board of Tashkent was responsible for Central Asia and Kazakhstan, and the head of this board was the only mufti allowed to represent Soviet Islam to the Muslim world beyond the borders of the Soviet Union. During the Soviet era religious texts were preserved in private libraries, and the officially sanctioned Muslim Spiritual Directorate for Central Asia and Kazakhstan (SADUM) was established in 1943. With the onset of World War II, the Soviet government softened its anti-Islamic stance. A strong antireligious campaign, however, resumed after the war and continued to the end of Nikita Khrushchev's regime in 1964. His successor, Leonid Brezhnev, allowed more religious and cultural freedoms among Uzbeks.

Despite 70 years of official atheism during the Soviet period, Islam remains an important social and cultural factor among Uzbeks. In some instances Islam has taken on a political character. Although supportive of Islam as part of the Uzbek heritage, the Karimov administration, which has been in power since independence from the Soviets in 1991, has cracked down on several Islamic movements on the grounds that they destabilize society.

EARLY AND MODERN LEADERS For centuries rulers have fought over the territory of Uzbekistan. Key figures in Uzbekistan's history include Genghis Khan, from whom all the dynasties that followed the Mongols in Central Asia claim descent, and Timur, whose dynasty stretched from Ankara, Turkey, to Delhi, India. During Emir Timur's reign the cities of Samarqand and Bukhara became centers of the arts and sciences.

Of all of the popular uprisings against the Russians in Central Asia, the most significant one was that of 1898, which was led by Muhammad Ali Khalfa, a leader of the Sufi Naqshbandi brotherhood. He called for a holy war against the Russians; however, his revolt was crushed. During the 1920s and 1930s the Basmachi (bandit) movement (which included Muslim clerics who opposed atheism, Muslim nationalists fighting Russian domination, and units of Muslims who had defected from the Red Army) and *jadidis* (young Muslim intellectuals who hoped to achieve independence through social reform) threatened Soviet dominance in Central Asia but were defeated.

In 1988 the Soviet regime suddenly and with no explicable reason curtailed its surveillance on religious activity, which led to a religious revival in Uzbekistan. Under Soviet rule, religious leaders had often been manipulated. Shamsuddin Boboxonov, the director of the Muslim Board of Uzbekistan since 1982, was expelled by popular demand in 1989 and replaced by Muhammad Yusuf. Independence from the Soviet Union led to new Muslim boards that are closely monitored by a Directorate of Spiritual Affairs. In 1993 Muhammed Yusuf, who had been considered too independent by the Karimov administration, was replaced by Hajji Mukhtar Abdullah, a Naqshbandi Sufi.

Islam Karimov, Uzbekistan's Communist Party chief since 1989, was first elected president in December 1991 shortly after Uzbekistan gained its independence. In 1995, in a referendum in which voter's preferences could be observed by election officials, Karimov won with an overwhelming majority. In 2000 he was once again reelected by a substantial majority, and in 2002 his term was extended to December 2007 in a referendum that was much criticized by international organizations.

MAJOR THEOLOGIANS AND AUTHORS Uzbekistan was home to many Muslim mathematicians, astronomers, and scientists as well as Islamic intellectuals. Muhammad Ibn Ismail al-Bukhari, born in Bukhara in the ninth century, traveled throughout the Muslim world collecting the hadith, the traditional sayings of the Prophet Muhammad. His work *Al-Jami al-Sahih* is considered by many Sunni Muslims to be the most authoritative collection of hadith. Muhammad Baha ad Din

Naqshband, a spiritual leader of the fourteenth century, founded the important Sufi order in what is modern Uzbekistan. Babarahim Mashrab, born in Andijan in 1657, became a controversial and popular poet and Sufi dervish. In *The Holy Fool,* his popular folk work that continues to be influential, Mashrab wrote about his life and experiences.

The Sufi Allah Yar (died in 1721 or 1724) was considered a religious authority for his Persian language work *The Path of the Believer,* which was a required text in the religious primary schools, and for *The Weakness of the Pious,* a text aimed at introducing young people to the tenets of Islam. Nineteenth- and early twentieth-century writers include Ahmad Danish (1827–97), Mahmud Khoja Behbudiy (1875–1919), Abdulhamid Cholpan (1897–1938), Abdalrauf Fitrat (1886–1938), Sadriddin Ayni (1878–1954), and Abdullah Qadiri (1894–1938). Many of these modern writers lost their lives during Stalinist purges.

HOUSES OF WORSHIP AND HOLY PLACES Samarqand is home to the Shah-i Zinda compound, Bibi Khanum mosque complex, Gur Emir ensemble, and the Registan Mosque and *madrasahs* (Islamic religious schools). Shah-i Zinda, which means living king, is a necropolis that was built in the eighth century. According to legend, Qusam b. Abbas, Prophet Muhammad's first cousin and a holy man who introduced Islam to the region, entered a well there and is said to still live in an underground palace. Bibi Khanum mosque complex, which was commissioned by Timur for his wife, took five years to construct between 1399 and 1404. The main mosque is flanked by two smaller mosques on the north and south sides to form a rectangle. The magnificent colorful geometric decorations, religious aphorisms, and its main portal with two minarets continue to make it an outstanding example of Islamic architecture. Gur Emir, or grave of Emir, was commissioned by Timur in 1404 for his grandson and heir apparent Muhammad Sultan, and it has become known as the Timurid vault.

Bukhara is known as an important Muslim intellectual center and is also the most complete example of a medieval Central Asian city. Some of its many houses of worship and holy places are Ismail Samani's Tomb, the Magoki-Attori Mosque, the Mausoleum of Chasma Aiub, the Kalyan Minaret, and Sheikh Muhammad Baha ad Din Naqshband's tomb.

The tomb of Sheikh Muhammad Baha ad Din Naqshband, which dates back to 1389, was built adjacent to his school on the site of an ancient pagan temple. Several rulers of Bukhara expanded the school and graves surrounding Naqshband's tomb. This large center of Islamic learning was closed during the Soviet period, and pilgrims were forbidden to visit. In 1988 the Soviets suddenly ceased their strict surveillance of Islam, and the complex was reopened in 1989. At the start of the twenty-first century there were more than 350 mosques and 100 higher schools of religion in Bukhara.

Tashkent, the capital of Uzbekistan, became a Muslim city in the eighth century C.E. and was an important commercial center during the Middle Ages. Wars and earthquakes have destroyed most of its ancient monuments and historical places of worship.

WHAT IS SACRED? Holy places, mosques, shrines, and relics are sacred, and visitors are expected to dress modestly and behave with a certain decorum. While perhaps not sacred in a religious sense, there are certain traditions in Uzbekistan's Muslim community that are treated as if sacred, including loyalty to one's group, respect for elders, and obedience toward parents.

HOLIDAYS AND FESTIVALS Uzbeks share all the major Islamic holidays, such as Ramadan, Id al-Fitr, and Id al-Adha, or the Festival of Sacrifice. Id al-Adha is celebrated throughout the Muslim world as a commemoration of Prophet Abraham's willingness to sacrifice everything for God, including the life of his son Ishmael. Because God spared Ishmael, substituting a sheep in his stead, Muslims honor this occasion by slaughtering an animal and distributing its meat among family, friends, and the needy as a special act of charity. In the *mahalla,* or the traditional urban neighborhood, the entire neighborhood will celebrate holidays together, and in villages everyone may celebrate these important feasts together.

MODE OF DRESS Culture and religion have become intertwined to create a unique Uzbek-Islamic way of dress. Traditional Uzbek attire for men and women adheres to Islamic code while maintaining its regional characteristics. In general, Muslim women cover their hair, and in some cultures they cover their entire body. Muslim men cover their arms up to the elbows and their legs up to the knees. In Uzbekistan traditional women will often wear colorful silk dresses that reach halfway between the knee and ankle with pants or leggings made of the same material under the dress. Both men and women may wear a *doppe,* a boxlike hat. Men may wear a long quilted garment with a sash around the waist called a *chapan.* In the villages a married woman will cover her forehead as well as her head with a scarf.

Since independence from the Soviet Union, scarves and the way they are worn have been the subject of political debate. In a style that has become associated with Uzbeks, women wear a scarf tied in the back of the head that leaves the neck and shoulders uncovered. Wearing a scarf that covers the neck and shoulders as well as the head is considered foreign, and possibly fundamentalist, which is perceived as controversial in Uzbekistan.

DIETARY PRACTICES Practicing Muslims generally do not eat pork or consume alcohol. In Uzbekistan, while a small number of Muslims may eat pork, consumption of alcohol seems to vary according to socioeconomic status and age. Also, it is more acceptable for men than women to drink alcohol.

RITUALS The Five Pillars of Islam—*shahadah* (profession of faith), *salat* (prayer five times a day), *zakat* (alms to the poor), *ruza* (fasting during the month of Ramadan), and hajj (pilgrimage to Mecca)—are followed by practicing Muslims in Uzbekistan.

Weddings, births, circumcisions, and deaths are celebrated by a *toi,* or ceremony and feast. Rural weddings often involve the entire village. In modern times a couple may have both a religious ceremony and a state registration, as well as a celebration that includes Western and local practices. Marriage and parenthood have religious connotations. Navruz, the Persian new year celebration, is also associated with fertility rites. The neighborhood women gather and cook *sumoloq,* which takes 24 hours to prepare and requires constant stirring. During this time the women pray for their daughters to marry and for the childless to bear children. Birth is celebrated with a number of rituals that are not necessarily Islamic in origin. The rituals surrounding death, however, are easily recognizable as Islamic. After death the body is washed and wrapped in a shroud and is often buried the same day or the following day. Culture rather than religion dictates that the family of the deceased host a gathering of family members and neighbors for several days.

RITES OF PASSAGE Birth, circumcision for boys, and marriage all mark rites of passage in Uzbek culture, and they are celebrated with feasts and visitations from extended families and neighbors.

MEMBERSHIP Becoming a Muslim is achieved through birth or conversion. After independence missionary activity was high. Beginning in 1998 with the law on Freedom of Conscience and Religious Organizations, however, missionary efforts were forbidden by the Karimov administration. Although the majority of the population in Uzbekistan claims an Islamic identity, many, in particular the youth, are not well-versed in the tenets of Islamic faith and practices.

SOCIAL JUSTICE On 7 February 2003 the cabinet of Uzbek ministers declared 2003 "the year of the *mahalla.*" The *mahalla* has its roots in the thirteenth century when neighborhoods of densely packed, single dwelling homes were organized around the trades and crafts of the residents. Traditionally the *mahalla* is a place where Sunni and Shiite Muslims interact. The *mahalla* was also a source of social services for community residents. During Soviet rule the government was to supply these services. In the late twentieth century Karimov claimed that reviving the *mahalla* could foster civil society in Uzbekistan. Others viewed it as a way of controlling the Muslims. When the state was unable to provide employment, the *mahalla* stepped in to provide the basic necessities. This practice was also perceived as a duty toward one another as good Muslims.

SOCIAL ASPECTS Uzbekistan is a secular state, but people may choose to follow Islamic laws to guide their lives. Since independence from the Soviets there has been a return to a more traditional view of gender roles, with women caring for the home and children and men acting as the providers. Otins, female Muslim clerics, have been called upon to teach Koranic exegesis to female students in the women's *madrasah*s in Kokand and Bukhara; however, the actual teaching of the Koran remains in men's hands. At feasts men and women will often eat separately, but this has more to do with tradition than Islam. Marriage must be sanctioned by both families.

POLITICAL IMPACT Although the government of Uzbekistan is secular, Karimov swore in as president with a Koran in his hand, and pilgrimages to Mecca are subsidized by the government. The head mufti is present at all major public events. At the same time, there is a deep-seated fear of political Islam. Religious revival in Uzbekistan, which came to the surface in 1998, was tied to rediscovering Islam and Muslim culture and reestablishing links with Muslims beyond the boundaries of the Soviet Union. Breaches between the official and unofficial religious leaders (ulama), who had previously coexisted during the Soviet period, became clear. In 1989 the unofficial ulama publically accused those employed by the Soviet state of corruption and servility.

Since independence the Karimov regime has honored the Islamic heritage of the region with celebrations of ancient mosques and important Islamic figures. The hajj (pilgrimage to Mecca) is officially sponsored by the government, and Karimov has even performed it himself. At the same time, the Karimov regime has been wary of any possible challenges to its authority and has attempted to control Islamic expression. The Muslim Directorate of Uzbekistan, which replaced the Soviet era SADUM, has a monopoly on religious instruction. Mosques that are not controlled by the directorate are illegal. The Karimov government has declared that it will not tolerate the "wrong kind of Islam," which, according to official texts, is fundamentalist and extremist but in practice includes any religious figure or organization that attempts to participate in public life. Beginning in 1999, after an attempt was made on Karimov's life, people have been arbitrarily arrested on suspicion of belonging to an Islamic movement.

CONTROVERSIAL ISSUES The 1998 law called Freedom of Conscience and Religious Organizations, which limits religious activity, has been controversial. The law has been heavily criticized by groups including human rights organizations and religious organizations. It has led to the arrest of thousands of Muslims and some Christians as well.

CULTURAL IMPACT Since the eleventh century Bukhara and Samarqand have been spiritual and intellectual capitals of Islam. For many centuries mystical poetry, music, and ornamental calligraphy from the region has exerted its influence on the rest of the Islamic world. The blue tiles used in the mosques of Samarqand from the Timurid period continue to baffle experts for their enduring vibrancy after six centuries. Repressive measures as well as censorship in Uzbekistan have prompted many contemporary intellectuals and artists to live in exile.

Other Religions

Archaeolgical excavations reveal that many religions existed in Central Asia before the arrival of Islam. Founded 2,500 years ago in the foothills of Nepal, Buddhism spread to northern Pakistan and Afghanistan from roughly the first century B.C.E. to the fourth century C.E. From there it extended along the trade routes, reaching Central Asia, where it left its traces in all five republics. Several Buddhist monuments have been excavated in the Termez region. By the twenty-first century the number of Buddhist followers in contemporary Uzbekistan had dwindled considerably. There is evidence that Zoroastrians, followers of the Persian prophet Zoroaster (c.628–c.551 B.C.E.), lived in the region as well. The Magoki-Attori Mosque in Bukhara was built upon a Zoroastrian temple, which itself was built upon the ruins of a Buddhist temple.

Jewish and Eastern Orthodox groups have existed in Uzbekistan for centuries. Archeaological evidence confirms the presence of Jewish communities in what is today Uzbekistan as far back as the second century C.E. At the start of the twenty-first century, the Jewish community was estimated to be anywhere from 10,000 to 45,000 and included a mix of Orthodox Bukharan Jews, assimilated Jews of Ashkenazi descent, and those returning to religion after a period of Soviet atheism. The number of Russian Orthodox Christians in Uzbekistan also has decreased as they began a wave of emigration to Russia after independence from the Soviet Union. In 1996 the patriarchate of the Russian Orthodox Church in Tashkent celebrated its 125th anniversary.

Mainstream religions—which include state sanctioned Muslim groups, Jewish groups, Russian Orthodoxs, and various other denominations such as Roman Catholics, Lutherans, and Baptists—have official status. A number of minority religious groups, such as the Bahai, Hare Khrishna, and Jehovah's Witnesses, have had a difficult time fulfilling the strict registration requirements set by the law known as Freedom of Conscience and Religious Organizations, which stipulates that a denomination must have branches in at least 8 of Uzbekistan's 13 oblasts (and a minimum of 100 members each) in order to be officially registered.

Roberta Micallef

See Also Vol. I: *Christianity, Eastern Orthodoxy, Islam*

Bibliography

Allworth, Edward. *The Modern Uzbeks.* Stanford, Calif.: Hoover Institution Press, Stanford University, 1990.

———, ed. *Central Asia, 130 Years of Russian Dominance: A Historical Overview.* Durham, N.C.: Duke University Press, 1994.

Capisani, Giampaolo R. *The Handbook of Central Asia.* London: I.B.Tauris, 2000.

Eickelman, Dale. *Russia's Muslim Frontiers.* Bloomington: Indiana University Press, 1993.

Haghayeghi, Mehrdad. *Islam and Politics in Central Asia.* New York: St. Martin's Press, 1995.

Hunter, Shireen. *Central Asia since Independence.* Westport, Conn.: Praeger, 1996.

McChesney, R.D. *Central Asia—Foundations of Change.* Princeton, N.J.: Darwin Press, 1996.

Olcott, Martha Brill. *Central Asia's New States: Independence, Foreign Policy, and Regional Security.* Washington, D.C.: United States Institute of Peace Press, 1996.

Paksoy, H.B., ed. *Central Asia Reader: The Rediscovery of History.* Armonk, N.Y.: M.E. Sharpe, 1994.

Ro'i Yaacov, ed. *Muslim Eurasia: Conflicting Legacies.* London: Frank Cass, 1995.

Roy, Oliver. *The New Central Asia: The Creation of Nations.* New York: New York University Press, 2000.

Smith, Graham, et al. *Nation-Building in the Post-Soviet Borderlands: The Politics of National Identities.* Cambridge: Cambridge University Press, 1998.

Undeland, Charles, and Nicholas Platt. *The Central Asian Republics: Fragments of Empire, Magnets of Wealth.* New York: The Asia Society, 1994.

Westerlund, David, and Ingvar Svanberg, eds. *Islam outside the Arab World.* Richmond, Surrey, England: Curzon Press, 1999.

Vanuatu

POPULATION 196,178

PRESBYTERIAN 32 percent

ANGLICAN 14 percent

ROMAN CATHOLICISM 13 percent

SEVENTH-DAY ADVENTIST 11 percent

CHURCH OF CHRIST 4 percent

ASSEMBLIES OF GOD 4 percent

NEIL THOMAS MINISTRIES 3 percent

OTHER 11.4 percent

INDIGENOUS BELIEFS 7.6 percent

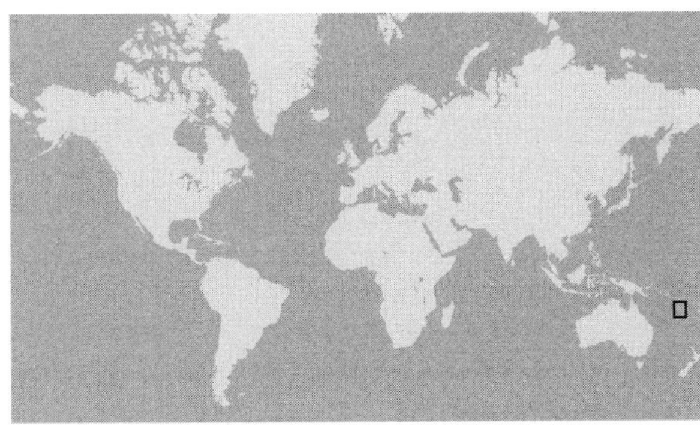

Country Overview

INTRODUCTION The Republic of Vanuatu (known as the New Hebrides before gaining independence in 1980) is an archipelago of 83 islands in the southwestern Pacific Ocean. The interiors of the large islands are mountainous and heavily forested. Five active volcanoes, together with seasonal cyclones, make the islands vulnerable to natural disasters. The country's economy is developing, and the majority of the population are subsistence farmers.

The islands were colonized by Britain and France, who formed a condominium (a jointly ruled government) in 1907, resulting in a system of divided loyalties in Vanuatu that influenced the European languages learned, the quality of education acquired, and the attitude toward the incorporation of the *kastom* (traditional, or customary) religious orientation of the island peoples.

Christianity in Vanuatu combines the philosophical and theological tenets and practices of its various churches with a worldview that has developed out of a long history of pre-Christian orientation to the cosmos. Offerings to creator beings, whose names Christian missionaries frequently used as translation for "God," are still made in some islands. Most illnesses and deaths were, and to a large degree still are, attributed to occult forces; healers frequently combine their traditional expertise with Christian faith healing. In the pre-Christian era, and to an extent still today, the worlds of the living and the dead interpenetrate, and ancestors are extremely important. Encounters with spirits and ghosts, which may be benign and helpful or malign and harmful, are accepted as out of the ordinary but not uncommon. Vanuatu Christianity and contemporary pagan thought are deeply entangled and influence each other.

RELIGIOUS TOLERANCE Religious tolerance is enshrined in the constitution of Vanuatu. Opposition to

Vanuatuan villagers participate in a kava ceremony below Mount Yasur. Although it is discouraged or forbidden by some Christian denominations, ritual kava drinking is an activity that enhances communion with ancestral spirits. © ROGER RESSMEYER/CORBIS.

the proliferation of Christian denominations that have been active in Vanuatu since independence led, in 1995, to the passage in Parliament of the Religious Bodies Act, requiring new churches to be registered. The act has never been enforced, but non-Christian religions, such as Islam, are not permitted to teach their faiths in government schools.

Major Religion

CHRISTIANITY

DATE OF ORIGIN Mid-nineteenth century C.E.
NUMBER OF FOLLOWERS 186,400

HISTORY The first missionaries arrived in Vanuatu in 1839. Initially the islanders did not welcome them. Many missionaries were killed (fewer than 10 of them European); many others died of diseases, such as malaria. Most were Protestant Polynesian teachers whose deaths were rarely well documented. The introduction of European diseases caused massive depopulation. Marist priests began working in the islands in the 1880s after an earlier abortive mission in the 1840s. In the second half of the nineteenth century, thousands of New Hebrideans (now called ni-Vanuatu) were recruited to work on plantations in New Caledonia, Fiji, and northern Australia; many became Christians during their period of indenture.

At the outbreak of World War I, almost every island contained some Christians who were Protestant and anglophone and some who were Catholic and francophone, as well as others who rejected Christianity in favor of traditional life (*kastom*). At the end of World War II, in most of the central and northern islands and the southern island of Tanna, there were still substantial populations of non-Christians, some resolutely opposed to Christianity. By the time independence was declared (1980), few non-Christians remained except in the island of Tanna, where today they outnumber Presbyterians.

Seventh-day Adventists appeared in Vanuatu in the early nineteenth century and have recently enlarged their congregations at the expense of the more established churches. Since the 1970s smaller Christian denominations (including Jehovah's Witnesses, Mormons, Holiness Fellowship, and Assemblies of God) have proliferated in Vanuatu.

EARLY AND MODERN LEADERS Early church leaders were mostly European. On every island many ni-Vanuatu played important roles in the evangelization of their communities. The most influential Christian leaders to emerge also advocated freedom from colonial rule. Father Walter Lini, an Anglican priest who became Vanuatu's first prime minister, led the independence movement and founded the Vanua'aku Party. Another influential leader was francophone Father Gérard Leymang, an ordained Catholic priest. More controversial was Jimmy Steven, the charismatic leader of the 1960s land rights movement Nagriamel. Christened Moses in the Church of Christ and founder of his own Royal Church of Vanuatu, Steven was jailed for his role in the rebellion in Santo that preceded independence in 1980.

MAJOR THEOLOGIANS AND AUTHORS Anglican priest Walter Lini was influential in combining nationalism and liberation theology. Melanesian liberation theology was anticolonial and promoted the inseparability of church and state. Also active in the project of reconciling indigenous beliefs and practices of Vanuatu with Christian theology were Catholic priest Father Gérard Leymang and Chief Willie Bongmatur Malro.

HOUSES OF WORSHIP AND HOLY PLACES The church is the center of Christian worship in Vanuatu, but sites of martyrdom of early missionaries are also considered holy places. Indigenous sacred places exist on all islands and are respected by most Christians.

WHAT IS SACRED? Sacred to most of Vanuatu's Christians are their churches and certain Christian items, ancestral places, and insignia. Some of these have been incorporated into the national emblem of Vanuatu: the leaf of the cycas palm (*namele*), signifying peace, and the spiral curved boar's tusk, a sign of chiefly power, unity, and prosperity.

HOLIDAYS AND FESTIVALS Good Friday, Easter Sunday, and Christmas Day are public holidays. In addition, Vanuatu celebrates Ascension Thursday in May (40 days after Easter), which, though not a public holiday, is a day of special prayer marking the Ascension of Jesus Christ. On 15 August, there is a public holiday to mark Assumption of the Blessed Virgin Mary into heaven. The *kastom* ceremonies that accompany the digging of first yams, Vanuatu's most important crop, are now also celebrated as harvest festivals by the churches from New Year's Day to early April.

MODE OF DRESS Nineteenth-century missionaries disapproved of the traditional clothing of the islanders (penis wrappers or mat skirts for men; girdles and fiber or mat skirts for women), which are still worn in a few villages. Christian men were encouraged to wear trousers and shirts, while women were taught how to make a cotton dress known as a Mother Hubbard, which is still worn today. Western-style dress is favored in the towns, particularly by young people.

DIETARY PRACTICES There are no particular dietary practices observed by Christians in Vanuatu that are not observed elsewhere. Some denominations discourage or forbid the consumption of alcohol and kava (a traditional, popular drink made from the root of the plant *Piper methysticum*). Traditionally, in the north-central region, men ate only boars and women only sows, a practice that continues for some older, more recent converts and traditional people.

RITUALS Whether Christian or not, every local group has some practitioners with acquired or inherited powers who act as mediators between the living and the world of spirits and ancestors, as well as leaders who perform rituals (on behalf of their groups) that frequently involve interaction with the spiritual realm. In many islands ritual kava drinking was a male activity that enhanced communion with ancestral spirits. Ceremonial kava drinking is important in contemporary Vanuatu, particularly in Tanna. Religion and politics were intertwined in the past, as now. Important ritual complexes that culminated in the sacrifice of boars, providing spiritual advancement and status, were widespread until the 1970s in areas where missionaries did not prohibit them, and continue, transformed, in some areas, including Ambae and Tanna.

All the major rituals of the different Christian churches present in Vanuatu are practiced by Vanuatu Christians. Prayer is an important part of events for ni-Vanuatu and accompanies everyday meals and most significant activities of social life, such as opening and closing meetings or work events and feasts.

RITES OF PASSAGE Many important rites of passage—such as birth, marriage, and death—are celebrated by Vanuatu Christians in church ceremonies and in *kastom* (traditional) exchanges of food and wealth between kinsfolk. Similarly, many *kastom* events are accompanied by Christian worship or prayer. Boys in many areas are still circumcised or incised (the foreskin is cut but not removed) in *kastom* ceremonies that are today usually consecrated by church ministers or attended by prayer.

MEMBERSHIP In the 1990s, and especially leading up to the millennium, church membership became more fluid, with individuals moving between denominations. Protestant evangelical campaigns, particularly involving young people, are a popular and common means of securing a renewal of faith in rural areas. Only radio reaches the majority of Vanuatu's population. While leaders recognize a role for the churches in television (introduced in the urban centers in the 1990s), the radio broadcast of Sunday sermons has had a greater significance for the majority of Christians.

SOCIAL JUSTICE The Vanuatu constitution's preamble endorses a commitment to traditional values and Christian principles. The body of the constitution refers to freedom of conscience and worship, and it enjoins children to respect their parents and parents to support and educate their children in both national objectives and Vanuatu culture and customs. All major Vanuatu Christian churches espouse and encourage teaching and activities concerning poverty, education, and human rights.

SOCIAL ASPECTS Ni-Vanuatu consider the family to be the center of social life. Before independence bride-wealth payments (made on behalf of the groom's family to the bride's family) were limited by most churches; the revival of *kastom* life stimulated an inflation of bride-wealth and other goods exchanged between the families of bride and groom. Divorce rates have increased considerably since the 1970s, and it is not uncommon now for children to be born outside of marriage.

POLITICAL IMPACT In the nineteenth century established political leaders saw Christian conversion as a threat to their power and influence and were often militant in opposing missionaries. In some islands hostility between Christians and non-Christians was often intense up to the 1980s, when church leaders emphasized the importance of reconciling custom with Christian commitment, so long as they were not in conflict.

Walter Lini and other Christian leaders emphasized the importance of the political role of the Christian churches and the necessity for political leaders to be ardent Christians. There have been several millenarian movements (in which prophets tell of the imminent return of ancestors or Americans, as in the case of the Jon Frum movement [dating from about 1940] in Tanna) that were anti-European and antimissionary, predicting the arrival of vast wealth, the knowledge of which was selfishly kept by Europeans. Both the Jon Frum movement and the land rights movement Nagriamel (which arose in the 1960s) have survived and, in a transformed fashion, still participate in the national political scene.

CONTROVERSIAL ISSUES The Vanuatu Christian churches do not have a unified view on social issues. For example, a prominent role for women in the church and social life is upheld and promoted by some denominations but not others. While the ordination of women is supported by some Protestants, others oppose it, as do Roman Catholics. Presbyterians support women's issues and rights through their women's groups, but women cannot become ministers. The position is similar for Anglicans, except that women may become deacons but not ministers. The Roman Catholic Church is strong on social justice issues, but there is no role for women in the church—only among the laity. While some traditional cultural practices (such as reciprocal obligations to kinsfolk) are lauded, others (such as sorcery) are condemned.

Sexual activity outside marriage is opposed by all denominations. Attitudes concerning contraception, abortion, and divorce vary. Feminists consider *kastom* attitudes toward women to be oppressive.

CULTURAL IMPACT During the 1970s a serious revival of *kastom* practices began among Christians, and many important techniques and practices were recovered and disseminated through the auspices of the Vanuatu Cultural Centre. Today all cultural and artistic events begin and end with prayer. Ni-Vanuatu poets, such as the late Grace Mera Molisa, have frequently addressed the problematic relationship between *kastom,* Christianity, and modernity in their work.

Other Religions

A small number of non-Christians remain on the islands of Pentecost, Ambrym, Malakula, and Santo; many more remain in Tanna. Their opposition to Christianity is as much a legacy of the colonial period and a political stance as it is a matter of religious adherence. Their contemporary religious views, while pagan, are influenced by a long history of interaction with Christianity.

Since the 1970s revival of *kastom,* practices deemed magical or evil (like sorcery) have been viewed with considerable ambivalence. Evangelical campaigns to rid island communities of sorcery have been limited by its involvement in everyday life as an explanation for success and misfortune.

Mary Patterson

See Also Vol. I: *Anglicanism/Episcopalianism, Christianity, Seventh-day Adventist Church, Roman Catholicism*

Bibliography

Aaron, Daniel Bangtor, et al. *Yumi Stanap: Leaders and Leadership in a New Nation.* Edited by Brian Macdonald-Milne and Pamela Thomas. Suva: Institute of Pacific Studies, University of the South Pacific, 1981.

Allen, Michael, ed. *Vanuatu: Politics, Economics, and Ritual in Island Melanesia.* Sydney and New York: Academic Press, 1981.

Bonnemaison, Joël. *The Tree and the Canoe.* Honolulu: University of Hawai'i Press, 1994.

Bonnemaison, Joël, et al., eds. *Arts of Vanuatu.* Bathurst, Australia: Crawford House Publishing, 1996.

Codrington, R.H. "Religious Beliefs and Practices in Melanesia." *Journal of the Royal Anthropological Institute* 10 (1881): 261–316.

MacClancy, Jeremy. *To Kill a Bird with Two Stones: A Short History of Vanuatu.* Port-Vila: Vanuatu Cultural Centre, 1980.

Miles, William F.S. *Bridging Mental Boundaries in a Postcolonial Microcosm.* Honolulu: University of Hawai'i Press, 1998.

Vatican City

POPULATION 960

ROMAN CATHOLIC 100 percent

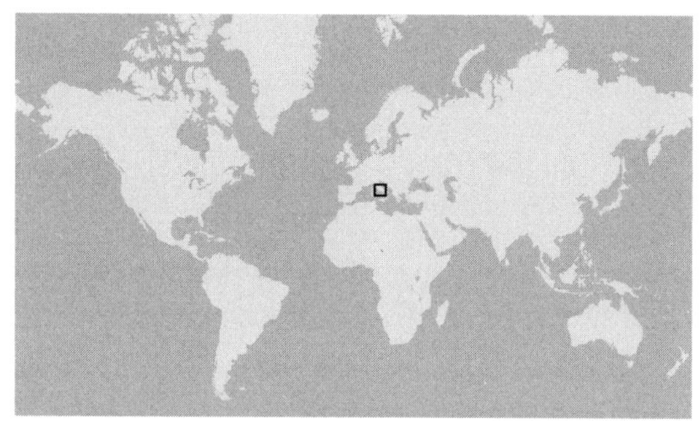

Country Overview

INTRODUCTION The State of the Vatican City, occupying just 0.17 square miles in the center of Rome, is the world's smallest country. It stands on the Vatican Hill, west of the Tiber River and the famed Seven Hills of Rome. The terms Vatican City and the Holy See are often used interchangeably, but they are administratively and functionally distinct from each another. Vatican City is the name of the country, while the Holy See, located within Vatican City, is the central administrative body of the Roman Catholic Church. Vatican City is also the home of the pope, who is both the bishop of Rome and the head of the Roman Catholic Church.

For more than a thousand years the pope ruled various Papal States on the Italian Peninsula, but these lands were annexed during the reunification of Italy in the mid-nineteenth century. In 1870, following the conquest of Rome (including the remaining papal territories) by Italian forces, Rome became the capital of Italy. Pope Pius IX thereupon declared himself a prisoner of the Vatican. The independent Vatican City, with the pope as head of state, was created in 1929 as a result of the three Lateran Treaties signed by Italian dictator Benito Mussolini and Pope Pius XI.

RELIGIOUS TOLERANCE Religious tolerance is not an issue within Vatican City. All permanent residents are Catholic. The million or so yearly visitors, who come from all religious backgrounds, are welcome in Vatican City.

As the head of a religion with about a billion adherents, the pope, however, has increasingly faced questions of religious tolerance. Pope John Paul II (1978–2005) sought to promote Christian unity and peace between members of different religions. At the same time, he consistently stated that the Catholic Church is the true church and that non-Christians are at a disadvantage in seeking salvation when compared with Christians in general and Catholics in particular.

Major Religion

ROMAN CATHOLICISM

DATE OF ORIGIN First century C.E.

NUMBER OF FOLLOWERS 960

HISTORY The early bishops of Rome probably established their see even before the time of Saint Peter, who is recognized as the first pope of the Roman Catholic Church. Peter died on the Vatican Hill in about 64 C.E., and his likely burial place later became the site of Saint Peter's Basilica. Over the years the bishops of Rome, who acquired the title of pope, assumed greater secular power as the Western Roman Empire disintegrated. This secular power led to an accumulation of land and wealth.

In the sixteenth century the Protestant Reformation challenged the supremacy of the pope. Further weakening the church's secular influence and its monopoly in European religious affairs were a series of bloody religious wars, particularly the Thirty Year's War (1618–48); the French Revolution (1789), which resulted in a secularization of many aspects of Christendom; and the rise of the modern secular state.

By the mid-nineteenth century, with the unification of Italy and the seizure of the Papal States, the pope had lost secular control of all his territories, leading Pope Pius IX to declare he was a prisoner in the Vatican. This "imprisonment," maintained by five popes, ended in 1929, when the Italian dictator Benito Mussolini and Pope Pius XI signed the three Lateran Treaties, which established Vatican City, on just 109 acres, as an independent state; compensated the Vatican for territories lost in 1870; established Roman Catholicism as the state church of Italy; and defined other relations between the two countries, forbidding the clergy, for example, from taking part in Italian politics. In 1984 changes were made to the treaties, and Catholicism ceased to be Italy's official religion. The pope, however, retained his secular and religious authority in Vatican City.

EARLY AND MODERN LEADERS The following popes have served as leaders of Vatican City since its creation in 1929: Pius XI (1922–39), Pius XII (1939–58), John XXIII (1958–63), Paul VI (1963–78), John Paul I (1978), John Paul II, (1978–2005), and Benedict XVI (beginning 2005). Other important leaders include those in the Roman Curia, made up of various offices that assist the pope in administering the church. Its members are drawn from the Sacred College of Cardinals. Before being elected Benedict XVI in 2005, Cardinal Joseph Ratzinger, was especially influential in the Curia as prefect of the Congregation of the Doctrine of the Faith.

Pope John Paul II greeting a crowd in St. Peter's Square. John Paul II is one of six popes to serve as leader of Vatican City since its creation in 1929. AP/WIDE WORLD PHOTOS.

MAJOR THEOLOGIANS AND AUTHORS In 1969 Pope Paul VI set up the International Theological Commission to assist the Holy See in examining doctrinal questions. Its members are selected from among outstanding theologians throughout the world.

HOUSES OF WORSHIP AND HOLY PLACES Saint Peter's Basilica and the Sistine Chapel in the Vatican Palace are the best known of the Vatican's houses of worship. The work of famous artists, such as Michelangelo, Raphael, and Brunelleschi, are contained in these sanctuaries. Other important Vatican churches are Saint Paul's, Saint Mary Major, and Saint John Lateran. The last is used by the pope in his capacity as the patriarch of Rome.

WHAT IS SACRED? The Vatican, like the rest of the Roman Catholic world, views the seven sacraments, the Bible, and the great tradition of the church to be sacred. Saints, especially Mary, the mother of Christ, are venerated as exemplars for the living. Within Vatican City the tomb of St. Peter in St. Peter's Basilica is given sacred status. The Vatican Museums also contain many relics, a large number of them brought from the Holy Land by returning pilgrims and Crusaders.

HOLIDAYS AND FESTIVALS The following holidays are celebrated in the Vatican: the Circumcision of Jesus

(1 January); the Epiphany (6 January); Good Friday; Easter Sunday and Easter Monday; the Assumption of Mary into Heaven (15 August); All Saint's Day (1 November); the Immaculate Conception of Mary (8 December); Christmas (25 December); and the Feast of Saint Stephen (26 December). Catholics elsewhere also recognize these holidays, but at the Vatican there is greater pomp when the pope celebrates the Mass. On Christmas the pope blesses the city of Rome and the world. On Easter he conducts special rituals that are open to the public.

In addition, the Vatican celebrates the day on which the current pope was elected. The day on which a new pope is elected is also a holiday.

MODE OF DRESS The pope dresses all in white, a tradition that goes back to the time of Pius V (1566–72), who was a Dominican friar. Cardinals dress in red. Priests who work in the Vatican wear various other kinds of clerical clothing, usually black in color. Nuns wear habits, according to the rules of their institutions; some habits have been adapted to modern styles. Visitors to the Vatican are expected to dress modestly, especially if they plan to visit its shrines and churches.

DIETARY PRACTICES In the Vatican, as in other Roman Catholic communities, various practices of fasting and abstinence are followed during the 40 days of Lent. Generally, for those in good health, the Lenten fast—one full meal per day—is required only on Ash Wednesday and Good Friday. Exceptions are made for the sick. Meat is not eaten on Ash Wednesday and on Fridays during Lent.

RITUALS Of the many rituals associated with Catholicism, the Mass is the primary one. The pope frequently celebrates the Mass in public, often in St. Peter's Square. There are no ordination ceremonies for cardinals, who serve as advisers to the pope and run the administration of the Holy See in Vatican City.

RITES OF PASSAGE As is true in all Roman Catholic communities, the main rites of passage in Vatican City are the seven sacraments, including baptism, first Communion, and confirmation. Promotion in the Vatican hierarchy can also be viewed as a rite of passage. Promotion depends mainly upon the judgment of the pope and upon tradition. In particular, the pope, with the advice of the Roman Curia, appoints bishops and cardinals. In the past someone who was not a member of the clergy could become a cardinal. Today, however, cardinals are selected from the clergy, and the Holy See prefers that the individual be made a bishop before becoming a cardinal, though this is not required.

MEMBERSHIP Because permanent residents must be approved by the pope, either directly or through appointed officials, all residents of the Vatican are Catholic. There is little room for population growth in Vatican City, since its tiny area of 109 acres is filled.

SOCIAL JUSTICE The church's social doctrine is derived mainly from encyclicals (solemn pontifical letters) dealing with problems such as justice, peace, racism, and migration. Although reflections on social justice can be found in many encyclicals, *Centesimus annus, Laborens exercens* and *Sollicitudo rei socialis* are especially important in regard to such issues. Within Vatican City social justice is practiced through welfare provisions, such as health care and pensions, for all residents and workers. Local churches, Catholic associations, wealthy laypeople, and an annual worldwide collection called Peter's Pence contribute to the financing of the Vatican.

SOCIAL ASPECTS The majority of Vatican residents are celibate. Any married residents of Vatican City would be found among the Swiss Guards, the pope's bodyguards, or servants and workers. For married Catholics in Vatican City, the church's teachings on abortion, birth control, and sex prevail. Parents are responsible for the moral and physical well-being of their children.

POLITICAL IMPACT The pope is the absolute ruler of Vatican City. The Curia and its offices aid in his rule. In 2002 governments from 174 nations posted ambassadors or other political representatives to the Vatican state. The pope maintains contact with these representatives and, in turn, has representatives of his own, called nuncios or pontifical delegates, in countries throughout the world.

CONTROVERSIAL ISSUES The Catholic Church's relations with Christian and non-Christian churches are of great importance in Vatican City. The encyclical *Utunum sint* (1995) reopened the question of the authority of the pope and the willingness of the church to collaborate with non-Catholics on matters where they share "a common heritage." It declares that the church wishes to begin a "patient and fraternal dialogue" with its separated brethren about how the pope can exercise his office in a way that fosters Christian unity.

Pope John Paul II (1978–2005), worked for peace, religious tolerance, and ecumenism. He also took strong stands against promiscuity, immodesty, abortion, and birth control. Although the pope was opposed to the ordination of women, debate on this issue has continued in many local Roman Catholic churches. Other controversial issues have included disputes between the Vatican and liberal theologians, priests who have molested children and gone unpunished, and the relationship of Pope Pius XII (1939–58) to Nazi Germany and the Holocaust.

CULTURAL IMPACT The cultural influence of the Roman Catholic Church spread through its many missions, schools, universities, hospitals, publications, and lay movements. The treasures now held in the Vatican Museums, which include paintings, sculptures, and a host of other artifacts from throughout the world, document the church's shaping influence on the roots of Western culture.

Other Religions

There are no members of other religions among the permanent residents of Vatican City.

Frank A. Salamone

See Also Vol. I: *Christianity, Roman Catholicism*

Bibliography

Dawson, Christopher. *Religion and Culture.* London: Sheed and Ward, 1948.

Goffart, Walter. "Christian Pessimism on the Walls of the Vatican Galleria delle Carte Geografiche." *Renaissance Quarterly* 51, no. 3 (1998): 788.

Halperin, S. William. *Italy and the Vatican at War: A Study of Their Relations from the Outbreak of the Franco-Prussian War to the Death of Pius IX.* Chicago: University of Chicago Press, 1939.

Moore, George Foot. *History of Religions.* Vol. I. New York: Charles Scribner's Sons, 1928.

Nachef, Antoine. *Mary's Pope: John Paul II, Mary, and the Church since Vatican II.* Franklin, Wis.: Sheed and Ward, 2000.

Neuvecelle, Jean. *The Vatican: Its Organization, Customs, and Way of Life.* Translated by George Libaire. New York: Criterion Books, 1955.

Tilley, Terrence W. "Christianity and the World Religions: A Recent Vatican Document." *Theological Studies* 60, no. 2 (1999): 318.

Venezuela

POPULATION 24,287,670

ROMAN CATHOLIC 80 percent

PENTECOSTAL 5–7 percent

OTHER PROTESTANT 1 percent

OTHER RELIGIONS 12–14 percent

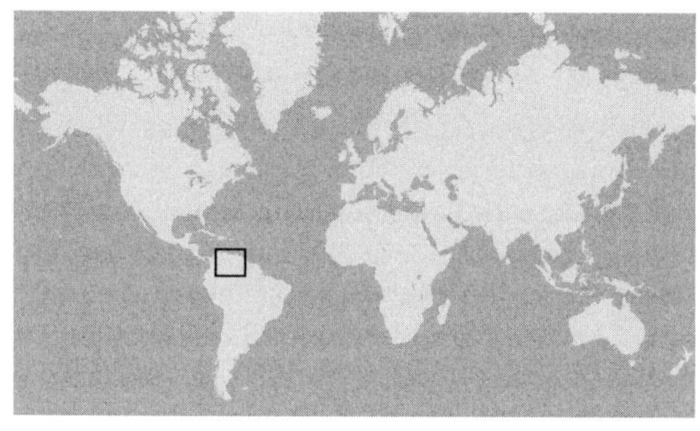

Country Overview

INTRODUCTION The Bolívarian Republic of Venezuela is located on the northern coast of South America. It borders Colombia to the west, Brazil to the south, and Guyana to the east. The Andes Mountains lie to the west and southwest.

The Venezuelan coast, bordered by the Caribbean, was discovered by the Spanish explorer Alonso de Ojeda in 1509. Franciscan and Dominican friars arrived soon thereafter, and many missions were founded among the Indians of the interior. The German Welsers ruled the colony from Coro from 1528 to 1546. After the Spanish regained control, the Jesuits worked among the Indians of the Orinoco Valley, but they were expelled by Charles III in 1767. During the seventeenth and eighteenth centuries, African slaves were imported to work on the coastal sugar and cacao plantations (slavery was abolished in 1854). In 1821 Simon Bolívar led an army that liberated Venezuela from Spanish rule, but during the nineteenth century revolutions devastated the country.

Venezuela became a major oil producer in the twentieth century, attracting American, British, and Dutch companies. Reflecting its missionary background, Venezuela has remained an overwhelmingly Catholic country.

RELIGIOUS TOLERANCE Freedom of worship is guaranteed by the Venezuelan constitution. New religious groups must obtain a license from the Ministry of the Interior before they can establish a religious center, most of which are registered as nonprofit associations.

Most Venezuelans are pragmatic about religious activities, which they view as psychological assistance in the daily struggle for survival. Few children get a formal religious education. Interdenominational marriages are no longer forbidden, and marriages of Catholics with Jews or Moslems are possible. Most Pentecostals feel they are in competition with Catholic institutions, and though their pastors do not like their adherents to marry Catholics, they do acquiesce. There is no prejudice against Jews, whose numbers are relatively small. Many German Jewish immigrants and their children and grandchildren now are nominally Christians and are married to Christians. The Cult of Maria Lionza is popular and tolerated and supplements the worship of saints with beliefs in good and bad spirits.

Major Religion

ROMAN CATHOLICISM

DATE OF ORIGIN c. 1510 C.E.
NUMBER OF FOLLOWERS 19,430,000

HISTORY During colonial times (1523–1821) Spanish friars, including Franciscans, Dominicans, and Capuchines, founded missions in Venezuela's interior and organized parishes in cities and towns. Religious fraternities, some exclusively African-American, were founded to foster interest in religion. Some of the large plantations owned by religious orders used slave labor. At this time most town schools were run by nuns and priests. All important Catholic holidays were celebrated.

During this era only Catholics were permitted to settle in Venezuela, and most settlers were Spanish. A few Jews from Curaçao arrived during the nineteenth century, as did German Protestants and British traders. A temple was erected in Coro around 1840, and Protestant pastors held services for foreigners in Caracas.

After the Wars of Independence in the early nineteenth century, many Spanish friars left Venezuela. This left a shortage of priests because few Venezuelans chose this profession, and illegitimate children were not admitted into seminaries. In the 1870s and 1880s President Guzman Blanco banned Catholic seminaries, closed Catholic schools, and permitted divorce. Cemeteries were secularized. At the same time, however, he founded primary schools to fight illiteracy.

During the first three decades of the twentieth century, dictator Juan Vicente Gomez allowed foreign orders to reopen Catholic missions among the Indians. Some church property was returned, more Catholic schools were founded, and priests were educated in seminaries or emigrated from Spain. It was only after the Second World War that Venezuela and the Vatican signed a modus vivendi by which the government agreed to assist Catholic schools and social institutions. A cardinal was appointed, and diplomatic relations with the Vatican were established. In 1953 the Jesuits founded the Catholic University, and more than 40,000 Venezuelans have graduated from the university since then.

In the early twenty-first century, in spite of conventions and contracts, President Hugo Chavez ceased to assist Catholic schools and the university.

A visitor prays at a statue of the Virgen de Coromoto. The large cathedral was built at the site where the Virgin de Coromoto was said to have appeared in 1652. © PABLO CORRAL VEGA/CORBIS.

EARLY AND MODERN LEADERS Venezuela has not had any particularly significant or influential leaders in the Roman Catholic Church.

MAJOR THEOLOGIANS AND AUTHORS During colonial times a few friars wrote historical accounts of their missionary activities. One was Father Gumilla SJ, who worked among the Indians of the Orinoco Valley. In recent years religious scholars and missionaries, including José Del Rey SJ, Father Cesario Armellada, and Pablo Ojer SJ, have published historical, linguistic, and ethnographic studies of Venezuela.

HOUSES OF WORSHIP AND HOLY PLACES Many colonial churches are well preserved, and the government is responsible for their care. Modern churches are found in urban and rural areas, but often a priest says Mass only once or twice a month. Pilgrims frequently visit the sites where the Virgin Mary is supposed to have appeared. A large cathedral has been built at the site where the Virgin de Coromoto was said to have appeared. The graves of miraculous souls, beatified by the people but not by the church, are visited to obtain a grace.

WHAT IS SACRED? The only great Venezuelan saint is Dr. José Gregório Hernández, a pious medical doctor who died in 1918 in a car accident. He helped the poor and after his death is reported to have performed many miracles. There are a number of his shrines all over the country, with the most important found in his native village, Isnotu, in the Andes. He has not been beatified by the church, mainly because his spirit is also invoked by the followers of the Cult of Maria Lionza. The cult's most sacred place is the mountain range of Sorte in the State of Yaracuy. Pilgrims usually travel there in groups on weekends to perform rituals.

People revere sacred objects, such as medals, pictures, and rosaries, which must be blessed by a priest or washed with holy water. Many people have a small altar at home where they keep a picture of their dead relatives together with statues of saints and other sacred objects intended to ward off evil.

HOLIDAYS AND FESTIVALS Holy Week, with its processions and night services, is the most important event during the religious year. On Holy Wednesday the statue of the Nazareno (Jesus Christ) is carried around, and thousands of candles are lit. Christmas has become very commercialized, with Santa Clauses and plastic Christmas trees adorning stores. Children still occasionally sing the beautiful *aguinaldos* (Christmas carols) during church services or public celebrations. The patron saint's day is still celebrated in many villages with processions as well as dances and drinking.

MODE OF DRESS There is no set mode of dress for Catholics in Venezuela, though people try to dress well when they attend Mass. Widows no longer wear black clothing.

DIETARY PRACTICES During Holy Week and Lent, most people eat fish or the meat of turtles and rodents living in or near fresh water. Hallacas (cornmeal and meat stuffed into banana leaves) and other special dishes are prepared for Christmas.

RITUALS There is a distinction between folk Catholicism and orthodox Catholicism. In folk Catholicism African, Amerindian, and popular Iberian beliefs and practices have intermingled. The saints are invoked to perform miracles, for which they obtain lavish gifts. The cult of the Virgin of Coromoto, the patron of Venezuela, is important. Other Virgins—such as the Virgen de la Chiquinquira in Maracaibo and the Virgen del Valle on Margarita Island—are worshiped. The Virgen de Betania is said to have appeared and spoken to a lady in the 1960s, but this miracle has not been officially recognized. Her shrine in Betania attracts many pilgrims. Folk saints, who are not canonized by the church, are invoked, the most famous of them being Dr. José Gregorio Hernandez.

In African-American villages processions are held during Holy Week. The feast of St. John, which falls near the summer solstice (June 24), is celebrated with drumming and dancing in some villages and with masked dancers who chase away evil spirits in others. In the Andes peasants worship the image of the Christ Child during the Christmas season and celebrate the day of the Holy Innocents with masked dances on December 28. They also celebrate San Isidro Labrador, the patron of peasants, with offerings of the first fruits from their gardens.

In the Cult of Maria Lionza spiritual sessions usually take place on weekends. The faithful gather in front of the altar at a leader's home. The mediums, by means of hyperventilation, drinking rum, or smoking a cigar, fall into a trance. The faithful then approach the mediums to ask questions or be physically examined. At the end of the session, the leader wakes the mediums up by blowing into their ears or washing them with herbal concoctions. In the so-called working sessions the mediums are not in a trance, and they rid clients of evil by blowing tobacco smoke over them or using magic soap, perfumes, or herbal concoctions. The most common ritual has the client lying on the ground while many colorful candles are lit around his or her body.

RITES OF PASSAGE Not all Catholics are baptized as infants, as many villages are visited by priests only a few times a year, but infants are sprinkled with water and blessed by their godparents. In urban areas children are baptized by priests during mass baptisms. Educated Catholics are often parish members and send their children to Catholic schools, where nuns prepare them for First Communion. First Communion and Confirmation are important social events for middle-class Christians but not for peasants. Burial rites are important for the rich and the poor, both of whom usually have burial insurance to cover the costs of a good coffin and a decent burial. Church marriages are rare, as the celebration is expensive. Sometimes a priest visits a village and performs mass marriages for those who have cohabited for many years.

MEMBERSHIP Most Venezuelans consider themselves Catholics, though many are not baptized, and many simultaneously practice Spiritism, Santeria, and the Cult of Maria Lionza. Folk Catholicism in Venezuela has incorporated many concepts and rituals of Amerindian and African derivation.

Since the time of Guzman Blanco, many members of the intellectual elite have considered themselves notreligious or atheists, even though they were educated in Catholic schools. Most Venezuelans do not consider themselves to be members of a particular parish and attend services sporadically and in different churches. Church taxes are unknown.

Charismatic services became popular in the 1970s and attract large crowds of people hoping to solve their problems with the help of the Holy Spirit. Opus Dei has many followers and sponsors student hostels and discussion groups. The Salesians and Capuchines maintain missions among Indians and run schools and dispensaries.

SOCIAL JUSTICE In the past five decades the church has opened many institutions to help the poor and has spoken in favor of social justice and better educational opportunities for everyone. The Jesuits have been leaders in this struggle, founding many schools (Fé y Alegria) in the poorest urban areas. Liberation theology was never popular in Venezuela. The Center Gumilla of the Jesuits, however, propagated similar ideas. Many priests who live in the slums help residents find work and cooperate in self-help projects.

SOCIAL ASPECTS In Venezuela poorer Catholics place little importance on religious weddings, though elaborate church weddings are important among wealthier people, mainly as status symbols. Many Catholics today are divorced and cannot receive Communion but do attend Mass from time to time. Some try to obtain an annulment, and usually the bishops help those who have this problem.

Many middle-class Catholics are active in social-welfare institutions. Some Catholic University students in Caracas work in the poorer sections of the city with delinquents, children, and the sick. A large number of well-to-do Catholics donate generously to Catholic welfare organizations. Banks and industries also offer large sums for church projects, schools, and the Catholic University. Foreign religious orders assist their own orders in Venezuela. The German Adveniat (a charitable Catholic organization) assists parishes, schools, and missions. Upper-class women stage balls, dinners, and other social events to raise money for Catholic dispensaries, hospitals, and schools.

Those who have the money send their children to private schools, most of which are run by nuns and priests. Many schools in the slums are run by religious orders. Cooperation between the church and the government during the second half of the twentieth century has benefited the educational system, as Catholic schools offer a good education to the poor as well as the rich. There are, however, few Catholic youth organizations.

POLITICAL IMPACT The church does not interfere openly in Venezuelan politics. The Copei Party's program is based on Christian social paradigms, and, therefore, during the presidencies of Caldera and Herrera Campins, from the 1970s through the 1990s, the church played a more important role in politics. President Chavez, who at times has claimed to be Catholic, Protestant, or atheist, has attacked the church as being reactionary and bourgeois.

CONTROVERSIAL ISSUES Birth control is no longer an important subject of public discussion in Venezuela, and it seems that many women of all social classes consider it their right to decide how many children to have. Most priests tacitly agree. This fact is borne out by the declining birthrate both in rural and urban areas. Abortion, however, is considered to be a crime by the majority, regardless of religious affiliation, and it is illegal in Venezuela.

Homosexuality is rarely discussed. Celibacy is another issue infrequently mentioned.

CULTURAL IMPACT In Venezuela the Catholic Church publishes a daily journal that has only limited circulation. The Italian order of San Pablo runs a publishing house in Caracas, offering a few monthly publications, and has bookshops in the major cities. Some radio stations transmit religious programs for a few hours every day; and there is one radio station run by the Jesuits. A Caracas television station offers religious programs.

The church sponsors some cultural events, such as church concerts. There are no important Catholic novelists or poets in Venezuela.

Other Religions

Nineteenth-century Protestant missionaries had limited success in converting Venezuelans to Presbyterian or Baptist denominations. The first Pentecostal missionary arrived in Barquisimeto in 1915, but it took more than 20 years for a few churches to be established. In the 1940s the first Pentecostal church was established in Caracas. Most Pentecostal churches were founded in the 1970s and 1980s by native pastors converted by foreign missionaries, who have since left the country. There are a number of different Pentecostal denominations, originating mostly in the Assemblies of God. Sometimes these denominations compete aggressively for adherents.

Pentecostalism is growing rapidly throughout Latin America. Pentecostalism is founded on Methodism and the belief that the Holy Ghost manifests via miracles. Pentecostals experience the power of the spirit expressed in glossolalia (speaking in tongues). They hope to overcome all hardships by faith. They adhere to strict rules of behavior: They do not smoke or drink alcoholic beverages, they dress modestly, and they regularly study the Bible. They are usually serious and hardworking people of the lower classes, though middle-class membership is growing. Their Sunday services are animated with songs, shouts, and testimonies. The pastors are usually excellent and entertaining speakers, although many lack formal education. Pentecostal worship attracts many outsiders, despite its strict moral rules. Rural immigrants find new friends and assistance in these generally small congregations, whose members help each other in emergencies. The churches also afford opportunities for leadership and foster education. Only adults are baptized and thereby accepted into the Pentecostal congregation.

Around 1990 two neo-Pentecostal Brazilian churches, Dios es Amor and Igreja Universal do Reino de Deus (IURD), found adherents in Venezuela; both espouse doctrines of health and wealth. They concentrate on fighting demons and are usually enemies of spiritism, the Cult of Maria Lionza, and Cuban Santeria. Followers of Dios es Amor attend religious services and adhere to a strict moral code, while the IURD has little concern with morals or theology. The IURD, whose temples are run by young Brazilian pastors, offers five services a day, seven days a week. Each day is dedicated to a specific purpose, such as the miraculous healing of illnesses or the exorcism of evil spirits. IURD practices resemble African antiwitchcraft cults more than true Christianity, but the church is very successful. Donations are constantly demanded, and the IURD has opened more than 50 churches throughout Venezuela. It also owns a radio station and transmits a daily television program. Baptism does not confer membership but is considered a cleansing ritual.

The Presbyterian Church has been active in Venezuela for almost a century. The first Lutherans (many were German businessmen) arrived in Venezuela around 1850 and settled in Maracaibo. The Anglican Church prospered when the Shell Oil Company began its activities in Venezuela. Other North American denominations also arrived with the oil companies. These churches never proselytized. The Jehovah's Witnesses are active but not very successful in Venezuela.

The Church of Jesus Christ of Latter-day Saints has been active in Venezuela since the end of the Second World War. Young Mormon missionaries have tried to spread their faith, and though many do not speak Spanish well, they have found a few adherents. There are three Mormon Congregations in Caracas. A large temple was constructed, and a Mormon library contains demographic data on thousands of Venezuelans.

About a half percent of the Venezuelan population is Muslim. Most Muslims are immigrants from the Middle East, particularly Syria and Lebanon, who arrived before and after World War II. The largest mosque in South America, sponsored by the king of Saudi Arabia, was built in Caracas in 1995. Muslim religious services are also held in some cities in Venezuela's interior. Many Muslim women wear headscarves, so the Muslim presence in Venezuela is visible.

The first Jews to arrive in Venezuela during the nineteenth century were Sephardim from Curaçao. Around 1900 Polish and Russian Jews began to immigrate to Venezuela and settled mostly in the larger cities. They were businessmen or artisans, and many of their children studied medicine or law. Before and during World War II well-educated German Jews arrived. There are two large Jewish congregations in Caracas, with synagogues, schools, and other social institutions.

The Cult of Maria Lionza developed in Venezuela beginning in the 1920s and is based on Amerindian shamanism, African-American religions (Cuban Santeria), the teachings of Allan Kardec (a nineteenth-century French spiritist who is popular in South America), and an amalgam of other esoteric concepts. The cult is rooted in Venezuelan traditions and mythology and has nationalist characteristics. It is difficult to estimate how many Venezuelans are worshipers of Maria Lionza, because some attend rituals only when they need spiritual help. The majority of the Maria Lionza faithful belong to the uneducated lower class, while some self-proclaimed leaders are educated members of the middle class. No initiation is necessary for membership, and most leaders claim spirits called them to join the movement. The faithful usually meet in a cult leader's home, where a room is set aside for ritual. An altar is decorated with the images of the spiritual entities that are invoked.

Cult adherents believe in the Christian God, Jesus Christ, and the Holy Spirit but also in the existence of different categories of spirits. Maria Lionza, who gave the cult her name, is a native nature spirit. She is depicted as a white woman with black hair or as sitting on a tapir like an Amazon. She is considered to be the representative of the white race in Venezuela. The cult also believes in the spirit of the Indian chief Guaicaipuro, who represents the Amerindian element in Venezuela. In life he fought the Spaniards after the conquest. Pedro Camejo (Negro Primero), the spirit of a black general in Bolívar's army, represents the black element in Venezuela. African Orishas (the deities of the Yoruba pantheon, who were syncretized with Catholic saints in the Cuban Santeria) are often invoked. Other spirits are the so-called folk saints (*animas milagrosas,* or "miraculous souls"), whose saintliness was proclaimed by the people and not by the church. Simon Bolívar, a Venezuelan general, occupies an important place in the cult and is invoked whenever political issues are discussed.

The Cult of Maria Lionza is considered by some politicians as the true expression of Venezuelan nationalism and a symbol of the racial unity of the people. Venezuelans are proud of their traditions as expressed in the cult.

Angelina Pollak-Eltz

See Also Vol. 1: *Christianity, Pentecostalism, Roman Catholicism*

Bibliography

Barreto, Daisy. *Maria Lionza, Mito e Historia.* Caracas: Universidad Central de Venezuela, 1987.

García Gavidia, Nelly. *El Arte de Curar en El Culto a María Lionza.* Maracaibo: Universidad de Zulia, 1996.

Manara, Bruno. *Maria Lionza.* Caracas: Universidad Central, 1995.

Pollak-Eltz, Angelina. *Estudio Antropológico del Pentecostalismo en Venezuela.* Caracas: Universidad Santa Rosa, 2000.

———. *La Religiosidad Popular en Venezuela.* Caracas: San Pablo, 1994.

———. *Las Religiones Afroamericanas—Hoy.* Caracas: Planeta, 1995.

———. *Maria Lionza, Mito y Culto Venezolano.* Caracas: Universidad Catolica Andres Bello, 1985.

Taussig, Michael. *The Magic of the State.* London and New York: Routledge, 1997.

Vietnam

POPULATION 81,098,416

BUDDHIST 84 percent

CHRISTIAN 10 percent

CAO DAI 3 percent

HOA HAO 2 percent

OTHER 1 percent

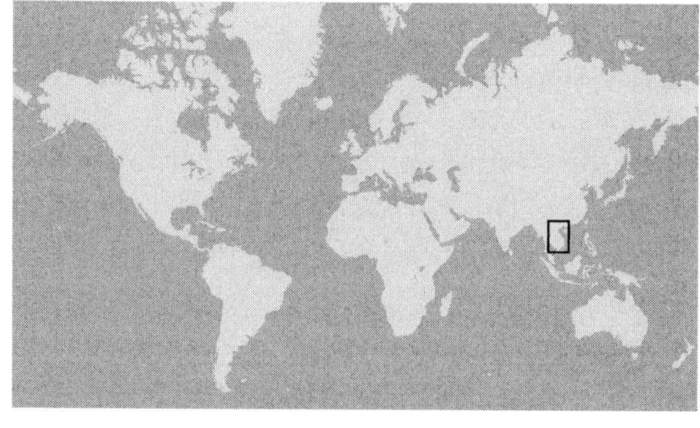

Country Overview

INTRODUCTION Extending south from China in a long, narrow S-curve, Vietnam is a tropical country occupying the east coast of the Indochinese Peninsula. It is often described by Vietnamese as resembling a peasant's carrying pole with a rice basket hanging at each end. The Red River Delta in the north forms one basket, and the Mekong Delta in the south is the other. The narrow stretch of land that is central Vietnam constitutes the carrying pole connecting the two deltas.

Long ago ancient peoples moved into what is today Vietnam from the north and from the islands to the south. Today these people constitute the bulk of the Vietnamese population, with Chinese, Cambodians, and Montagnards being the largest minority groups. China ruled what is today northern Vietnam from 111 B.C.E. until 939 C.E., when the Vietnamese formed an independent state. Over the next 900 years the Vietnamese expanded their territory until they controlled what is now the Socialist Republic of Vietnam. Chinese culture and religion strongly influenced the Vietnamese throughout this period, as they do today.

RELIGIOUS TOLERANCE Religion has long been highly politicized in Vietnam. The 1992 constitution guarantees every citizen of Vietnam "freedom of belief and of religion; he can follow any religion or follow none." It does not, however, guarantee freedom of religion in the fullest sense. It also cautions that no one can "misuse belief and religions to contravene the law and State policies." The observance of Buddhist ritual and practice was drastically reduced after 1975, when the country was unified under a Communist government. The government banned the popular Unified Buddhist Church of Vietnam (UBCV) in 1981, placed its patriarch, Thich Huyen Quang, under house arrest, and tried to replace the UBCV with the state-sponsored and submissive Vietnamese Buddhist Church (VBC). While avoiding overt hostility toward Buddhism or other organized religions, the Communists sought to separate real or potential collaborators from opponents to the regime through a blend of co-optation and control. The heart of the issue was a battle between Buddhist and other religious groups that wanted independence and a regime that viewed religion as an arm of the state. The ongoing concern of the Communist government in this regard was reflected in the establishment in 1985 of a Religious Affairs Committee to coordinate and supervise all religious organizations in Vietnam. Today the attitude of the Communist government toward Buddhism and other faiths remains one of tolerance, but only so long as the clergy and faithful strictly adhere to official guidelines. For example, government approval for holding festivals and reopening cult and worshiping places is still necessary. Government attempts to suppress the UBCV, which now has overseas congregations in Australia, Europe, and the United States, have never been totally successful, in part because many VBC monks are sympathetic with, or tacitly support, the underground UBCV leadership.

Vietnamese villagers walk in a procession to celebrate a Buddhist festival. The attitude of the Communist government toward Buddhism and other faiths remains one of tolerance, but only so long as the clergy and those faithful strictly adhere to official guidelines. © JOHN R. JONES; PAPILIO/CORBIS.

Major Religion

MAHAYANA BUDDHISM

DATE OF ORIGIN 100 C.E.
NUMBER OF FOLLOWERS 68.1 million

HISTORY Buddhism spread first from China into the Red River Delta of northern Vietnam in the second century C.E. It later spread from India into the Mekong Delta region of southern Vietnam, sometime between the third and sixth centuries. The Chinese version of Buddhism, the Mahayana branch, was eventually adopted by most Vietnamese, with the Indian version, the Theravada, or Hinayana, branch, largely confined to the southern delta region.

A second stage in the expansion of Buddhism ran roughly from the seventh to the fourteenth century. With the expulsion of the Chinese in 939 C.E., Buddhism received official support, with pagodas serving as cultural repositories. Between 1010 and 1225 the Ly dynasty made Buddhism the state religion. This period proved to be the high-water mark for official support of Buddhism in Vietnam.

By the end of the eleventh century, Buddhism had planted its roots deeply in Vietnamese culture. At the village and hamlet level it mixed with Confucianism and Taoism to become an indigenous part of the popular beliefs of the Vietnamese people. This adulteration of Buddhism initiated a period of decline, which progressed with the lessening of official support. Beginning with the fifteenth century many Vietnamese rulers favored Confucianism, which played an influential role in public life until the twentieth century. A revival of more orthodox forms of Buddhism began in the early decades of the twentieth century and gained momentum after World War II.

EARLY AND MODERN LEADERS A number of Buddhist monks, or bonzes, through their knowledge, faith, and virtue, achieved prominence during the Nguyen dynasty (1802–1945). In the north, representative bonzes included Tich Truyen at Van Trai Pagoda in Hanoi, Chieu Khoan, also at Van Trai Pagoda, Pho Tich at Van Trai and Thien Quang Pagodas in Hanoi, and Thon Vinh at Ham Long Pagoda in Hanoi. In central Vietnam prominent Buddhist leaders included Nhat Dinh at Linh Huu Pagoda in Hue, Giac Ngo at Bat Nha Pagoda in Phu Yen and at Dieu De Pagoda in Hue, and Mat Hoang at Gia Dinh and Quoc An Pagodas in Hue and at Thap Thap Di Da Pagoda in Binh Dinh. In the south a representative list of prominent Buddhist leaders would include Lieu Thang at Phuong Son Pagoda in Gia Dinh, Vien Quang at Tap Phuong Pagoda in Gia Dinh, and Phuoc An at Hung Long Pagoda in Gia Dinh.

Buddhist clergy were later prominent in the antiwar movement in southern Vietnam in the 1960s and 1970s. In June 1963 Buddhist monk Thich Quang Duc resorted to self-immolation to protest the Diem regime's increasing repression against the Buddhist community. Thich Tri Quang and other Buddhist monks were later arrested as successive Saigon governments resorted to increased persecution and repression.

In the postwar era Thich Quang Do, Thich Don Hau, and Thich Huyen Quang are among the Buddhist monks who provided leadership to the Unified Buddhist Church of Vietnam. Buddhist dissidents are numerous and include Thich Tri Tuu, Thich Hai Tinh, Thich Hai Tang, Thich Long Tri, Thich Khong Tanh, and Thich Tri Luc.

MAJOR THEOLOGIANS AND AUTHORS Buddhist monks Phuc Dien at Lien Tong and Thien Quang Pagodas in Hanoi, An Thien at Dai Giac Pagoda in Ha Bac, and Dieu Nghiem at Tu Quang Pagoda in Phu Yen authored valuable works during the Nguyen dynasty on the history of Buddhism. They also completed detailed notes contributing to a better understanding of ancient Buddhist texts.

HOUSES OF WORSHIP AND HOLY PLACES Buddhist pagodas, shrines, and temples abound in Vietnam. The pagoda (*chua*) is often the largest, most ornate, and best-constructed building in a Vietnamese village. Even in urban areas its design and appearance set it apart. The Vietnamese pagoda is most often constructed in the highly decorative Chinese style. The phoenix, tortoise, dragon, and other legendary figures are intermixed with familiar Buddhist symbols like the Wheel of Life and the swastika (*binh chu van*). Buddha statues are the central figure in most Vietnamese pagodas; wherever found, they are held in high esteem. The pagoda is used for services but even more so for private devotions. The pagoda area often includes rooms for instruction and living quarters for the monks. As part of the contemporary revival of Buddhism throughout Vietnam, a large number of historic pagodas, many renovated or rebuilt, have become major pilgrimage sites. Examples are the Perfume Pagoda complex in the Huong Son Mountains south of Hanoi, Thien Mu Pagoda in Hue, and Vinh Trang Pagoda in My Tho. The village communal house (*dinh*) also functions as a multipurpose institution, serving worldly and spiritual needs.

WHAT IS SACRED? Most Vietnamese adhere to the Mahayana branch of Buddhism, which teaches that Buddha was only one of many "enlightened ones," manifesting the divine power of the universe. Vietnamese adherents to the Theravada branch of Buddhism believe Buddha was the one and only enlightened one, and a great teacher, but not divine. After the Buddha died he was cremated, and his bones were distributed as sacred relics. Many Vietnamese believe his power is still present in these relics and in the many images of the Buddha. Buddhists in Vietnam are expected to honor the Buddha and to pay special homage to objects and images associated with him.

HOLIDAYS AND FESTIVALS Important Buddhist holidays or festivals celebrated in Vietnam include the Buddhist New Year on the 15th day of the first lunar month, Buddha's birthday on the eighth day of the fourth month, Wandering Souls Day on the 15th day of the seventh month, and the Cleaning of the Tombs Day, also called the Festival of Pure Clarity, on the fifth day of the third month. Activities on these festival days often begin at the pagoda and then continue in the village or in private homes. The first and 15th days of each lunar month are also Buddhist holy days in Vietnam.

MODE OF DRESS Buddhist monks and nuns of the Mahayana branch shave their heads and wear brown, gray, saffron, or yellow robes to mark their renunciation of worldly pleasures. Monks of the Theravada branch wear only saffron robes. The dress of Buddhist laity in Vietnam is not constrained by religious practice.

DIETARY PRACTICES The Buddha's Five Commandments include a prohibition against drinking alcohol. That said, it is not uncommon for practicing Buddhists to consume alcohol occasionally in contemporary Vietnam. Buddhist monks are normally vegetarians, but restrictions against eating meat do not extend to the laity.

RITUALS From the beginning the ritual and imagery of the Mahayana branch of Buddhism appealed to the Vietnamese people. Mahayana ceremony easily conformed to indigenous Vietnamese beliefs, which combined folklore with Confucian and Taoist beliefs. Buddhist monks today participate in and lead religious observances and festivals.

RITES OF PASSAGE Birth ceremonies belong mainly to the household proper and are seen as a private matter. Buddhist monks are frequently invited to weddings in Vietnam but do not officiate. At funerals Buddhist monks lead the rites in the home, at cremation or burial, and again at intervals after burial and on the first anniversary of death.

MEMBERSHIP Buddhists believe that humankind is condemned to a cycle of birth, death, and rebirth until discovering the path of enlightenment to nirvana, a world of endless serenity. It is less an organized religion than a religious philosophy consisting of doctrines, branches, and ways of life. In contemporary Vietnam, where Buddhism is the dominant culture, people are Buddhist by birth. In addition, their belief systems and lifestyles often reflect aspects of Confucianism, Taoism, and even animism.

SOCIAL JUSTICE Buddhism brought to the Vietnamese a new look at the universe, the individual, and life. It had an especially strong impact on morals and behavior. In Buddhist thought, human salvation lies in discovering the Four Noble Truths. First, man is born to suffer in successive lives. Second, cravings and desires are the cause of suffering. Third, only the elimination of desire will end suffering. And fourth, the elimination of desire can be achieved only through following the noble Eightfold Path. Both a call for social justice and the foundation of the Buddhist concept of morality and right behavior, the Eightfold Path calls for right views, right aspirations or honesty in judgment, right speech, right behavior, right living or sincerity in making a living, right effort, right thoughts, and right concentration or sincerity in meditation. Vietnamese take these Buddhist precepts seriously and seek to order their lives around them.

SOCIAL ASPECTS For centuries traditional family relationships in Vietnam reflected Confucian teachings and, to a lesser extent, Buddhist practices. Confucian norms strongly influenced the evolution of Vietnamese society as a hierarchical, authoritarian system grounded in five core relationships: subject to ruler, son to father, wife to husband, younger brother to elder brother, and mutual respect between friends. The Buddhist concept of morality and right behavior reinforced these accepted relationships. The extended family, not the nuclear one, was the dominant family structure, often including three or even four generations living under the same roof. Traditionally marriage was regarded as a social contract and arranged by parents through intermediaries. Under the 1986 Law on Marriage and the Family, marriages can still be arranged at the request of the couple but only after the endorsement of the People's Committee. The interest in having children has been reinforced for centuries by Confucian culture, which made it imperative to produce a male heir to continue the family line. Even today young couples visit local Buddhist pagodas in an exercise widely known as praying for a male. Traditional family ties are beginning to break down in urban areas but still dominate in the villages of Vietnam.

POLITICAL IMPACT In contemporary Vietnam the most dramatic demonstration of the power of Buddhism came in the 1960s when Buddhist demonstrations contributed to the overthrow of the Ngo Dinh Diem regime in South Vietnam. Following a pattern throughout Vietnamese history, Buddhists did not replace the Diem government but continued to influence public policy in the south until the Vietnam War ended in 1975. In northern Vietnam a revival of Buddhism in the late 1980s followed almost a half-century of quiescence, a time in which Buddhist priests departed villages and pagodas fell into disrepair. This was also a period in which the Communist government denounced Buddhist folk practices and placed restrictions on monasteries. Following the failure of collectivization and the decline of cooperatives, Vietnamese Buddhists began to return to village pagodas in the 1980s and to solicit government assistance in maintaining them. Pagodas achieved the equivalent of landmark status in 1989, and in the coming decade the government lifted earlier restrictions on monasteries and folk practices and began to contribute to the cost of renovating pagodas.

CONTROVERSIAL ISSUES Despite official support for freedom of worship, questions surrounding religious freedom remain today the most controversial in Vietnam. Issues here have little to do with faith and everything to do with the Communist Party's reluctance to allow anyone to organize outside party control. Religious organizations in Vietnam are well organized, with hierarchical structures and nationwide networks that reach to the grass roots, paralleling the reach of the state. Consequently, questions of autonomy, leadership selection, recruitment, property, and social activism are viewed by the Communists as a direct threat to the regime. Even though the Communist Party has allowed greater individual rights to worship, abuses by local and central governments persist. All faiths, including Buddhism, are under constant threat from corrupt officials and security forces, most especially religions or groups with a history of political opposition to the ruling Communist Party.

CULTURAL IMPACT Buddhism has a strong influence on the mass of the Vietnamese people, and its effects go far beyond religion, touching on behavior, philosophy, the arts, letters, and craft forms. Episodes from the life and teachings of Buddha, together with the effects of good and bad deeds, are the subjects of paintings, engravings, and murals. Sculpture, painting, and architecture have often been inspired by the two key virtues of Buddhism: purity and compassion. Buddhism has also served as a vehicle to take Chinese and Indian art forms to Vietnam and to influence designs in lacquerwork, weaving, embroidery, jewelry, and metalwork. Vietnam's epic poem *Kim Van Kieu* is based on the teachings of Buddha. This poem has been popular for more than a century; Vietnamese children often memorize long passages from its 3,254 verses.

Other Religions

Confucianism, like Buddhism, went to Vietnam from China. The teachings of the philosopher Confucius, born 2,500 years ago, combine politics, ethics, and education, imbuing disciples with a spirit of devotion and reverence. In the mixture of philosophies and religions that have molded the Vietnamese character, Confucianism occupies an important place, as it is an integral part of the cultural environment into which all Vietnamese are born. Living in a time of anarchy and strife, Confucius called, not for the salvation of the soul, but for good government and harmonious relations among men. He taught that individuals should be more conscious of their obligations than of their rights. Vietnamese political culture was forged initially by 1,000 years of Chinese rule (111 B.C.E.–939 C.E.), and once the Vietnamese attained independence, they adopted a Confucian model of government, which lasted several hundred more years. The influence of Confucianism on Vietnamese culture is especially tenacious because it was deeply rooted in the school system until the twentieth century. Education largely consisted of a study of the Confucian classics and ethics. Confucianism remains a source of traditional attitudes and values today, reflected in respect for family, education, and past generations. Most Vietnamese homes have altars dedicated to family ancestors, decorated with candlesticks, incense bowls, and flower trays.

Taoism is both a philosophy and a religion. It had its beginning in China and is thought to have entered Vietnam with conquering Chinese armies around the second or third century B.C.E., although it may have been brought with the Vietnamese when they migrated from China to the Red River Delta. Essentially Taoism is a way of life through which individuals attain harmony with nature as well as the mystical currents of the spiritual world. Taoist worship, rituals, and ceremonies are generally attempts to assist the individual to attune himself to the universe. Taoists are not necessarily spirit worshipers; however, there is an animistic flavor to Taoism. While Taoism has a limited formal organization in Vietnam today, its concepts are reflected in the daily life cycle of most Vietnamese. Moreover, many of the basic beliefs and practices of Taoism have been absorbed into the other religions found in Vietnam.

Christianity has a relatively long history in Vietnam. The first Roman Catholic missionary arrived in Vietnam in the early sixteenth century, and Alexandre de Rhodes, a Spanish Jesuit priest who headed a prominent mission in 1624–45, developed the Vietnamese alphabet. Roman Catholicism persisted in the face of recurrent, often severe persecutions until religious freedom for all Christians was finally guaranteed by treaties with the French regime in the late nineteenth century. Under colonial rule Catholicism established a solid position within Vietnamese society as the French authorities encouraged its propagation as a balance to Buddhism as well as a vehicle to promote Western culture. In the 1950s Catholicism declined in the north, where it was considered a reactionary force after the Communists took power, but it thrived in the south, where it was considered a bulwark against North Vietnam by the regime of Ngo Dinh Diem, himself a Catholic. With the unification of Vietnam in 1975, the Roman Catholic Church experienced the same active state intervention in church affairs as did all other religious organizations. What differentiated the Catholic Church from other religious organizations in Vietnam was an aspect of foreign control, with neocolonial overtones, that alarmed the Communist government. As a result, the Communist Party has yet to normalize relations with the Vatican and has rebuffed attempts by the pope to visit the country, allegedly over the right to appoint bishops. The Vatican contends that it is the right of the Church to select its bishops, but the Vietnamese government counters that only the state has the power to appoint bishops because all religion is state sponsored.

Protestantism was introduced at Da Nang in 1911 by a Canadian missionary under the auspices of the Christian and Missionary Alliance. The establishment of the Evangelical Church of Vietnam was an important outgrowth of this early missionary work. The Montagnard communities in the central highlands of southern Vietnam today constitute the largest single congregation of Protestants in Vietnam. Because of their association with American missionaries, as well as the Montagnard's support for the United States during the Vietnam War, Protestants often suffered more than Catholics after 1975. Although their numbers are still relatively small, Protestantism is the fastest-growing religion in Vietnam. Consequently the government remains concerned about the spread of evangelical Protestantism, and reports of the persecution of members of the Evangelical Church of Vietnam continue into the 21st century.

The Cao Dai religious movement is a self-styled reformed Buddhist sect that flourished after 1926 in the rural areas of the Mekong Delta. The Cao Dai are not accepted by Buddhists in Vietnam as Buddhists. Cao Daism is an amalgam of different beliefs derived from Buddhism, Confucianism, Taoism, and, to a lesser extent, Roman Catholicism, Indian mysticism, and a number of other popular beliefs and practices. It was formed in an effort to create a universally acceptable religion in an area of the world where an intermingling of religious faiths is often found in the same person. The three saints of Cao Daism are the Buddha, Confucius, and Lao-tzu, the founder of Taoism. Three of the Cao Dai movement's spiritual fathers are founder of the Chinese Republic Sun Yat-sen, French poet and novelist Victor Hugo, and Vietnamese prophet Trang Thinh. There are some similarities in the structure and organization of the Cao Dai movement, with its Holy See, and the Roman Catholic Church. Ordinary Cao Dai clergy may marry, and all clergy are required to be vegetarians. Members of the Cao Dai movement can be found throughout Vietnam, but the center of the faith is the Tay Ninh temple in Tay Ninh city. The Cao Dai movement was not recognized by the government as an official religion until 1997, and the Communist regime continues to mistrust its adherents.

Founded in 1939, the Hoa Hao religious movement, named after the native village of founder Huynh Phu So, considers itself a reformed Theravada Buddhist sect; unlike the Cao Dai, it has preserved a distinctive Buddhist coloration. The four major precepts taught by So are to honor parents, love country, respect Buddhism and its teachings, and love fellow men. Devout Hoa Hao members recite four prayers daily: the first to Buddha, the second to the "Reign of the Enlightened King," the third to living and dead parents and relatives, and the fourth to the "mass of small people to whom I wish to have the will to improve themselves, to be charitable, and to liberate themselves from the shackles of ignorance." Centered largely in the southernmost areas of the Mekong Delta, the Hoa Hao movement has never developed more than a rudimentary national organization. The Hoa Hao emphasize simplicity, individual prayer, and social justice as opposed to elaborate ceremonies or the veneration of icons.

Animism, a belief in good and bad spirits, antedates all organized faiths in Vietnam, permeating society in general but most especially society in the rural areas and highlands. Animistic beliefs hold that spirits control all forces in the universe and that the spirits of the dead are instrumental in determining a person's fate. These spirits will provide the living with protection if pacified but will induce misfortune if ignored. Officially condemned as "superstitious practices" by the Communist government, animistic beliefs remain common throughout the country.

Ronald Bruce St John

See Also Vol. I: *Buddhism, Christianity, Confucianism, Mahayana Buddhism, Theravada Buddhism*

Bibliography

Abuza, Zachary. *Renovating Politics in Contemporary Vietnam.* Boulder, Colo.: Lynne Rienner Publishers, 2001.

Beresford, Melanie. *Vietnam: Politics, Economics and Society.* London: Pinter Publishers, 1988.

Dhammaviriyo Kim-Sang. *A Brief History of Theravada Buddhism in Vietnam.* Saigon: Khemarapabha, 1969.

Do Van Minh. *Viet Nam: Where East and West Meet.* Rome: Edizioni Quattro Venti, 1968.

FitzGerald, Frances. *Vietnam: Spirits of the Earth.* New York: Bulfinch Press, 2001.

Gheddo, Piero. *The Cross and the Bo-Tree: Catholics and Buddhists in Vietnam.* New York: Sheed and Ward, 1970.

Gobron, Gabriel. *Histoire et philosophie du caodaïsme.* Paris: Dervy, 1949.

Hickey, Gerald Cannon. *Village in Vietnam.* New Haven: Yale University Press, 1964.

Hue-Tam Ho Tai. *Millenarianism and Peasant Politics in Vietnam.* Cambridge, Mass.: Harvard University Press, 1983.

Jamieson, Neil L. *Understanding Vietnam.* Berkeley: University of California Press, 1993.

Kleinen, John. *Facing the Future, Reviving the Past: A Study of Social Change in a Northern Vietnamese Village.* Singapore: Institute of Southeast Asian Studies, 1999.

McAlister, John T., and Paul Mus. *The Vietnamese and Their Revolution.* New York: Harper Torchbooks, 1970.

Minh Chi, Ha Van Tan, and Nguyen Tai Thu. *Buddhism in Vietnam.* Hanoi: Gioi, 1993.

Oliver, Victor L. *Caodai Spiritism: A Study of Religion in Vietnamese Society.* Leiden: E.J. Brill, 1976.

Porter, Gareth. *Vietnam: The Politics of Bureaucratic Socialism.* Ithaca, N.Y.: Cornell University Press, 1993.

Taylor, Philip. *Fragments of the Present: Searching for Modernity in Vietnam's South.* Honolulu: University of Hawai'i Press, 2001.

Werner, Jayne Susan. *Peasant Politics and Religious Sectarianism: Peasant and Priest in the Cao Dai in Viet Nam.* Monograph Series No. 23. Yale University Southeast Asia Studies, 1981.

Yemen

POPULATION 18,078,000

SUNNI MUSLIM 65 percent

ZAYDI SHIA MUSLIM 34 percent

ISMAILI SHIA MUSLIM LESS THAN 1 percent

JEWISH LESS THAN 1 percent

CHRISTIAN LESS THAN 1 percent

HINDU LESS THAN 1 percent

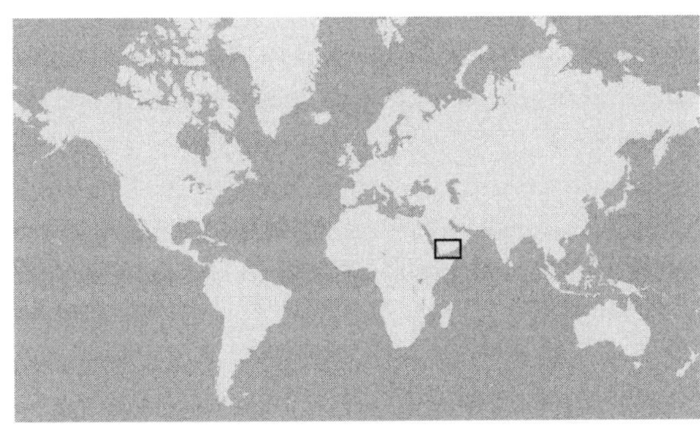

Country Overview

INTRODUCTION The Republic of Yemen is located in the southwestern corner of the Arabian Peninsula. It is bordered by Saudi Arabia to the north, the Red Sea and the Strait of Bab al-Mandab to the west, the Gulf of Aden to the south, and Oman to the east. Islam has been the dominating religion of the area since the seventh century C.E.

The British arrived in the port city of Aden in 1839 and established a protectorate over a large part of the hinterland. By 1873 Yemen had been formally divided into two internationally recognized territories—North Yemen, which had again become part of the Ottoman Empire, and British-controlled South Yemen. After World War I North Yemen gained international recognition as an independent nation-state ruled by the Zaydi imam Yahya Hamid al-Din. Growing demands for reforms (such as a constitutional government) and the fall of the Egyptian and Iraqi monarchies foreshadowed the imamate's decline, however. In 1962 the last imam was ousted in an Egyptian-sponsored coup d'état, and North Yemen was renamed the Yemen Arab Republic (YAR). The new government accused the former ruling elite of sanctioning a hierarchical sociopolitical order and abolished social divisions based on heredity and religious denomination.

Having gained its independence from Britain in 1967, South Yemen became the People's Democratic Republic of Yemen (PDRY), the only Marxist state in the Middle East. Its constitution declared Islam to be the state religion and, as was also done in the YAR, guaranteed non-Muslims freedom of religion. Most members of the religious elite lost their power, and religious endowments (*awqaf*), which had been previously managed by the mosques, came under the control of the state.

The unification of the PDRY and YAR in 1990 introduced an unprecedented level of press freedom and party pluralism, with parliamentary elections taking place for the first time in 1993. A year later, however, the fragile power-sharing agreement between the leaders

Muslim men and boys lean against the wall of the Janad Mosque in al-Janad. During the early Islamic period in Yemen, al-Janad became the center of Muslim traditionalist science. © RICHARD BICKEL/CORBIS.

of the two former states ended in armed struggle and the defeat of the southerners, who had proclaimed a breakaway state in the former South Yemen. President Ali Abdullah Salih, who had ruled the YAR since 1978, asserted supremacy over the whole country and in 1999 won the first direct presidential elections.

RELIGIOUS TOLERANCE The constitution of the Republic of Yemen declares that Islam is the religion of the state and that the Shariah, the divinely revealed law of Islam, is the source of all legislation. Therefore religious tolerance, as it exists in the west as a legal principle, does not exist.

Major Religion

ISLAM

DATE OF ORIGIN 632–34 C.E.
NUMBER OF FOLLOWERS More than 17 million

HISTORY The earliest kingdom in what is now Yemen was that of Saba, whose capital, Marib, was the largest town of ancient South Arabia. Marib, known for its ancient dam and irrigation system, was also an important trading center on the caravan route that carried frankincense from the southern coastal areas of the peninsula to the Mediterranean. The first caravan on this route is mentioned in the Old Testament (1 Kings 10), which refers to the visit of the queen of Saba, or Sheba, to King Solomon of Israel in the tenth century B.C.E.

In the sixth century C.E. Yemen became a province of the Persian Sassanid Empire, and in 628 the last Persian governor converted to Islam. Yemenis accepted Islam during the rule of Muhammad's first successor, the caliph Abu Bakr (573–634). During the early Islamic period the towns of Sanaa and al-Janad became centers of Muslim traditionalist science, exposing the country to ideas from other parts of the Muslim world. The Sanaa school gained fame after the arrival from Basra of the Koran exegete Ma'mar ibn Abd al-Razzaq (died in 770). Following the rise of the local Ziyadid Dynasty in 819, a judge called Abu Qurra Musa ibn Tariq founded a traditionalist school in their capital, Zabid, which became a major center of Sunni learning. Sunni Islam was challenged early by other Islamic groups, however, including the Kharijites, who had opposed the claims of both 'Ali and his rival, Muawiyah, to the caliphate and who captured parts of the Arabian peninsula, including Yemen and Hadramawt, in the late seventh century. Opposition also came from the Mutazilite school, which attempted to establish a rational basis for Islamic belief.

In the tenth century the Sunnis adhered to the doctrines of Abu Hanifa (699–767), Malik ibn Anas (died in 795), and Abu Bakr Muhammad ibn al-Mundir al-Naysaburi (died in 922). A Shafiite, Naysaburi developed legal ideas independently from those held by the founder of the school, Muhammad ibn Idris al-Shafii (767–820). Naysaburi was popular in the region between Ibb and the southern coast that later became the base of the Shafiite school. Another scholar, al-Qasim al-Jumahi al-Qurashi (died in 1045 or 1046), was instrumental in promoting Shafiite doctrine in the south. His disciples spread the doctrine in the areas around Sanaa, al-Janad, Lahj, and Aden. In the twelfth century, when the Shafiite school became more firmly established, the leading scholar Yahya al-Imrani (died in 1163) taught in Dhu Ashraq and Dhu al-Sifal. He popularized the school of Abu Ishaq al-Shirazi (died in 1083), a teacher in Basra and the author of the *Kitab al-Bayan,* a compendium of law that became essential reading for students of the Shafiite school. From the thirteenth century onward Yemeni Shafiites adhered to the Ashari theological school.

The influence of Shiism was minimal in Yemen until the arrival of the Zaydi Shias. Zaydi doctrine focuses on the personal qualities of the imam, who must be a descendant of the Prophet through Ali and Fatima, have excellent knowledge of the Islamic sciences, and be able to use the sword if necessary. In the tenth century Yahya ibn al-Husayn al-Hadi ila l-Haqq, a Zaydi scholar from Medina, became the leader of the first Zaydi imamate (the spiritual and political leadership of an Islamic community) in Yemen. Zaydi doctrine became fully known in Yemen through al-Hadi's writings. He extended his rule from the town of Sada to Najran in the north and, temporarily, to Sanaa in the south. He laid the doctrinal, legal, and military foundations for the imamate, which consolidated itself to a considerable degree by the late twelfth century. Most Zaydi scholars embraced Mutazilite rationalism. Sufism was rejected by the majority of Zaydi imams, not only because of its incompatibility with the Zaydi "rationalist" doctrine and its anti-Shia orientation but also because the imams perceived the Sufi masters and saints as rivals. A Zaydi school of Sufism was founded, however, by a disciple of the Kurdish Sufi Shaykh al-Kurani, 'Ali ibn 'Abdullah ibn Abi 'l-Khayr. From the fourteenth century onward, Sufi orders took hold in Zabid and Taizz.

Another group of Muslims, the Ismaili Shias, were linked to the Fatimid Dynasty of North Africa and Egypt, which brought large areas of Yemen under its control in the ninth century. The Fatimids headed a movement whose followers awaited the appearance of a Mahdi, or messiah, descended from the Prophet through his daughter Fatima and 'Ali in the line of Ismail, son of the imam Jafar al-Sadiq (died in 765). In Yemen the Fatimids found supporters among the Ismaili Sulayhids of Sanaa, whose dynasty controlled much of Yemen from 1038 to 1139. Before they were conquered by the Ayyubids in the twelfth century, Ismaili dynasties had extended their rule to several areas in the south. The Ayyubids and their successors, the Rasulids (1229–1454), strengthened Sunni control of the south.

The Ottomans occupied Yemen from 1539 to 1635, when they were defeated by the forces of the Zaydi imam al-Mansur billah al-Qasim. Thereafter, most of the Sunni areas of the country were governed continuously—except during the second Ottoman occupation (1872–1918)—by Zaydi imams.

In the nineteenth century the Hanbali reform movement of the Wahhabis of Saudi Arabia gained support in western Yemen. Since the late twentieth century this school has attracted followers elsewhere, and it has been represented in a number of religious schools throughout the country.

EARLY AND MODERN LEADERS There have been noteworthy religious leaders in Yemen in addition to the ones mentioned in previous sections. Until his death in 2000, for example, Ahmad ibn Muhammad Zabarah (born in 1908) served as a *mujtahid,* someone who is entitled to form an independent judgment in doctrinal matters and who, as a mufti, issues nonbinding opinions (fatawa). During the imamate Zabarah was the tutor of the crown prince al-Badr, the last imam, and head of the Shariah higher appeal board. He took a liberal view of religious matters and conceded that the imamate should not be confined to the Prophet's descendants as stipulated by orthodox Zaydi law.

One of Zabarah's contemporaries, Abd al-Qadir ibn Abdullah Abd al-Qadir (born in 1908), studied at the famous legal academy, the Madrasa alilmiyya, and later was chairman of the Majlis al-niyabi, a legal council that answers questions from the public on behalf of the imam. After the revolution he became chairman of the first National Council (Majlis al-watani) and president of the High Court. In the 1980s he played a leading role in codifying the Shariah.

Younger Zaydi leaders include Muhammad Izzan and al-Murtada al-Mahatwari. Izzan has sought to revitalize Zaydi Islam and to defend it against the Wahhabi movement. Al-Mahatwari runs a Zaydi center in Sanaa called Markaz al-Badr. One of the most influential and outspoken leaders associated with radical trends within Sunni Islam is 'Abd al-Majid al-Zindani, who cofounded the Reform Party (Islah) and who has promoted new religious schools (*al-mahid al-ilmiyya*) that propagate a form of Sunni Islam that insists on a literal understanding of the Koran and the sunna.

MAJOR THEOLOGIANS AND AUTHORS Qasim ibn Ibrahim al-Rassi (785 [or 786]–860) is credited with having systematized Zaydi teachings. Among his writings are the *Kitab al-radd alal-rawafid min ashab al-ghuluw,* which rejects the hereditary imamate central to Imami-Shia teachings, and the *Kitab al-dalil al-saghir* (The Book of Small Evidence), which stresses that the difference between God and his creation is one of God's fundamental characteristics. Zaydi doctrine became widely known in Yemen through al-Qasim's grandson Yahya ibn al-Husayn (859–911), the ancestor of the vast majority of Yemeni imams. He wrote *Kitab al-Ahkam fi al-halalawa-l-haram* (The Book of Edicts Concerning What Is Forbidden and Allowed) and *al-Muntakhab fil-fiqh* (Selected Writings on Jurisprudence), as well as influential works on the unity of God (*tawhid*) and the fundamental principles of religion (*usul al-din*).

Ibrahim ibn Muhammad al-Wazir (died in 1436), one of the few influential heterodox scholars, considered the canonical hadith collections (compilation of the sayings and deeds of the Prophet) to be much more authoritative than did his more orthodox Zaydi counterparts, dismissed the practice of following one legal school, and rejected the rational sciences associated with the Mutazila. His main book, *Al-Falak al-dawwar,* argues that the Zaydis were never opposed to referring to hadith in elaborating their legal rulings.

Muhammad al-Shawkani (1759–1839) is famous for having attempted to create a jurisprudential conjunction between the Shafiite and Zaydi schools. In contradiction to Zaydi doctrine he argued that it was not mandatory for the supreme leader to be capable of practicing *ijtihad* (a scholar's independent judgment) or to be a descendant of the Prophet. His ideas were favored by those imams of his time who were not *mujtahids* and whose support of dynastic succession violated Zaydi principles, and they also found approval later among republican leaders. Among al-Shawkani's major works are *Al-Badr al-tali bi-mahasin min bad al-qarn al-sabi,* an appraisal of scholarly accomplishments since the seventh century, and *Nayl al-awtar,* which deals with hadith.

Muhammad ibn Muhammad Zabarah (died in 1960), one of the most renowned historians and men of letters of his time, compiled biographical dictionaries of prominent Yemenis (*Nuzhat al-Nadhar fi rijal al-qarn al-rabi ashar* [1979]) and wrote about the Yemeni imams (*Aimmat al-Yaman bi-l-qarn al-rabi ashar li-l-hijrah* [1956]).

Ismail ibn Ali al-Akwa is the founder and director of the General Organization for Antiquities and Libraries in Sanaa, which is directly attached to the prime minister's office. Al-Akwa has published works on Islamic history and science. Among his writings is a comprehensive study of Yemeni teaching institutions (*al-Madaris al-islamiyyah fi-l-yaman* [1980]) and a five-volume study of the Yemeni *hijras* (protected enclaves for religious leaders; *Hijar al-ilm wa maaqiluh fi-l-yaman* [1995]). He has also written about the Yemeni poet Nashwan ibn Said al-Himyari (died in 1117), who was scathing in his treatment of the Zaydi imams and their prerogative to political authority.

HOUSES OF WORSHIP AND HOLY PLACES By the eleventh century Sanaa was home to more than one hundred mosques. At least four of these still exist—the famous Great Mosque, the mosque at Suq al-Halaqah that is associated with Ali ibn Abi Talib, and two mosques (the Jabbanah and Farwah) that were built before the tenth century. Until the late 1950s most people in Sanaa attended Friday prayers at the Great Mosque or the Hanzal mosque. Other well-known mosques in Sanaa are the Tawus; al-Jala, which was originally a synagogue; al-Madrasah; and al-Filayhi. A famous mosque south of Sanaa is the Masjid al-Sayyida Arwa bint Ahmad in Jibla, which was built during the period of Ismaili supremacy in the eleventh century. There are more than 300 mosques in Tarim in Hadramawt, but many of these are now closed. The Sayyid Abdullah al-Aydarus mosque of Aden dates from the fourteenth century.

Yemeni tribes long ago set aside protected enclaves for religious leaders and their families as an expression of respect for the leader's descent and the revealed knowledge they represented. In southern Yemen these enclaves were called *hawtas.* At one time the sultans guaranteed the inviolability of the *hawtas* as well as their exemption from customs duties and other taxes. In northern Yemen such enclaves later served as the prototype for Zaydi *hijras,* which became the central loci of worship, ritual purification, and ascetic practices. Several imams emerged from the *hijras,* and sons of learned families often spent several years in one or two of the reputable enclaves, such as Kawkaban or Shaharah, which produced a number of famous scholars and poets. Since the deposition of the last imam, most of the *hijras* have become moribund.

WHAT IS SACRED? There are no objects regarded as sacred in a strict sense, but sanctity is attributed to certain places—mosques and *hijras,* for example—and to women. Yemenis also speak of the sanctity of religious knowledge, religious scholars (ulama), and death.

HOLIDAYS AND FESTIVALS Like Muslims elsewhere Yemenis celebrate two major religious festivals: the Id al-Fitr, which marks the end of the fasting month of Ramadan, and the Id al-Adha (Feast of the Sacrifices). Both are dedicated to visits to the mosques and family gatherings, during which the meat of the sacrificial animal is consumed. During the Id al-Adha men express their respect for, and reaffirm their enduring responsibility toward, their female relatives, whom they visit and bestow with gifts, usually money, that are referred to as *al-asb.*

MODE OF DRESS Historically a number of dress styles were considered "Islamic" in different parts of Yemen. At times men were required to wear clothes that accorded with their occupational status, which served to distinguish those dedicated to religious knowledge from those in the service sector. These regulations were apparently not formal, however—unlike those pertaining to non-Muslims, who were required to wear clothing that distinguished them from Muslims.

Zaydi jurisprudence prohibits women from wearing male dress, or vice versa. Women are required to cover their whole bodies in the presence of all men except their husbands and male relatives who are within the prohibited degrees. Nowadays only some women in the cities and the *hijras* adhere strictly to this dress code.

DIETARY PRACTICES Common Muslim dietary practices, such as the avoidance of pork, are observed in Yemen. Zaydi law forbids the consumption of shellfish, and rabbit and coconut are held to be undesirable foods, yet few Zaydis abide by these principles.

RITUALS Zaydi law and ritual does not differ more from Sunni Islam than the major schools do among themselves. Unlike the Sunnis, Zaydis pray with arms outstretched rather than folded, but it is not uncommon to find Zaydis and Sunnis praying beside one other. The Zaydi call to prayer includes the Shia pronouncement "Rise to perform the best of works," and "Allah akbar" ("God is most great") must be spoken five times at funerals.

By virtue of the strong Mutazilite component in their religion, the Zaydis have always placed less emphasis on ritual than either the Twelver Shias or the Shafiites. For example, Ashura, the day dedicated to the memory of the life of Imam al-Husayn and one that is linked prominently with the defense of the rights of the House of the Prophet, does not have its own ritual, though some people fast on this day. The ritual on the occasion of Ghadir Khumm, which commemorates the Prophet's designation of Ali as his successor, was introduced in Yemen by Imam al-Mutawakkil Ismail ibn al-Qasim in the seventeenth century and was abolished in 1963. Since the late 1980s it has been revived, particularly in the provinces of Sada and al-Jawf. The Prophet's birthday (*'id milad al-nabi*) is celebrated mainly by women in their homes, while men's ritual activities focus on the birthday of Imam Zayd ibn Ali.

In southern Yemen there are about 20 major shrines that were built for a Sufi known for his miracles as well as for exceptionally pious men of noble descent. Individuals seeking remedy for such misfortunes as infertility visit the tombs of these men, and celebrations of their birthdays last for several days. The festivities center on such towns as Say'un, Qaydun, and Shihr, the site of Salim Umar al-Attas's tomb. Pilgrimages are also made to Ghayl Ba Wazir and to the tomb of Hud (one of the Arab prophets mentioned in the Koran), which is located in the district of Sif, east of Tarim. In the cities women also participate in these rituals.

RITES OF PASSAGE Rites of passage are carried out in Yemen in accordance with Islamic principles but vary considerably from place to place. *Mawlids,* recitals of stories of the Prophet's life, are commonly performed at weddings, postpartum rituals, and funerals. Since women's personal status derives mainly from motherhood, birth is a highly ritualized event. In Sanaa a new mother receives visits from other women for 40 days. When a death occurs, condolences are conveyed to male and female relatives in separate rooms for about 40 days. Celebrations on behalf of children who have finished reading or memorizing the Koran are rarely performed nowadays.

MEMBERSHIP All Muslim doctrinal schools are eager to increase membership through teaching, which now can reach a wider audience via broadcast media, Internet sites, and the distribution of audiocassettes.

SOCIAL JUSTICE The issue of social justice has been debated over the centuries in Yemen by scholars of the different Islamic legal schools. For Zaydi Shias the debate has had a specifically political dimension, focusing as it has on the imam's obligation to implement justice in accordance with the principles of the Shariah. A vast body of legal judgments relates to such matters as the principles of equivalence in marriage, a woman's entitlement to divorce, and a woman's right to maintenance in the event of her husband's prolonged absence.

SOCIAL ASPECTS Heterosexual marriage is considered the basis of society in Yemen. In accordance with the interpretation of Islamic law by the state, the Family Law of 1992 prohibits marriage by minors under the age of 15 and enforces the mandatory registration of marriages. If a man is absent for more than a year and fails to support his wife, she can ask for a divorce, make use of his property, or take a loan in his name. A man wishing to take a second wife is obliged to inform both women of their personal circumstances. Zaydi-Hadawi law prohibits marriage with non-Muslims, but in practice few follow this rule.

POLITICAL IMPACT Since the 1970s Sunni-affiliated Islamists have become ever more internationalized and politicized. The overthrow of the imamate left a religious vacuum that was filled by followers of the Egyptian Muslim Brotherhood, Islamic Jihad, and the Sudanese Brothers, under the leadership of Hasan al-Turabi. The Islah party, founded in 1990, has incorporated many Islamist groups into the political system. The party runs several charities; its activities on behalf of the poor include the sponsorship of weddings in which several couples are married at the same time. The Ittihad al-Quwa al-shabiyya al-yamaniyya (Union of Yemeni Popular Forces) is led by Ibrahim al-Wazir, a liberal thinker who seeks to establish a democratic system in Yemen based on Islamic values. The Hizb al-Haqq (Party of Truth) is affiliated with old, learned Zaydi families and professes to fight oppression and the Wahhabi movement. Also on Yemen's political spectrum are radical, militant religious groups who operate outside the democratic system.

The Sunni reform movement in Yemen is prominently linked with Abd al-Majid al-Zindani, the founder of al-Iman (Faith) University, a religious college dedicated to Salafi-style teaching. (The Salafis advocate a return to the "uncorrupted" Islam of the Prophet and his Companions and insist on a literal adaptation of religious sources. They stress the inseparability of religion and politics and disavow what they describe as "innovations"—visits to the graves of parents or ancestors, for example—and mysticism, as well as democracy, laicism, and gender equality.) In the 1980s the leader of the Salafi movement, Muqbil al-Wadii (died in 2001), established a Salafi teaching center, the Madrasat Dar al-Hadith al-Khayriyya, which attracts students from the Arab world, Southeast Asia, the United States, and the United Kingdom. In 2003 the Hizb al-tahrir al-islami fil wilayat al-yaman (Islamic Liberation Party) was founded. It aims to "liberate the Muslims through the removal of oppressive Arab regimes" and to establish a "just caliphate."

CONTROVERSIAL ISSUES In recent decades changes in family law have caused significant controversy in Yemen. In the late 1970s the Shariah was codified, but it retained many elements of classical jurisprudence (*fiqh*). Thus, in the YAR's law of 1978, marriage and divorce remained the private affairs of men. The Personal Status Act of 1992 was similar to that issued by the YAR in 1978. It was challenged by jurists of the former PDRY, which had one of the most liberal family laws in the Middle East, who argued that the distribution of rights and duties of spouses remained unequal.

Some Islamist groups dispute women's right to vote and to stand for political office. They also denounce shrine visitations, which have been a contentious issue for centuries. These visitations, which involve prayers at the grave and such other rituals as kissing the grave, were denounced as idolatrous and heretical innovations by nineteenth-century Hadrami reformers, and tombs were even destroyed by the Wahhabis. In South Yemen the socialist party considered the visitations to be incompatible with the party's political dogma, not least because they were perceived to promote the interests of the old nobility. After the 1994 war between southern and northern forces, Muslim militias that had fought alongside northern troops attacked holy shrines in various southern towns, as well as the tomb of the Ismaili leader Idris al-Hasan al-Qirshi in Shibam (Haraz).

CULTURAL IMPACT The Great Mosque, erected by order of the Prophet Muhammad, was partly built from fragments of pre-Islamic Sabaean and Himyarite buildings. Wooden decorations with a running vine motif are reminiscent of decorations that appear on the bronze soffit of one of the doorways of the Dome of the Rock in Jerusalem. Some Zaydi imams ruled that minarets must not be raised above the roofs of mosques, in order to distinguish the mosques from churches, and some were opposed to music and dancing. The white domes of the shrines built all over Hadramawt for holy men are characteristic features of this type of religious architecture.

Other Religions

Jews have resided in Yemen since the second century C.E.—five centuries before the advent of Islam. Eventually they were joined by immigrants from Babylon, Persia, Egypt, Spain, and North Africa. Under Islam the Jews lived as "protected people" who could practice their own religion, though with certain restrictions. Most Jewish men in Yemen were craftsmen and petty traders. Many were literate in Hebrew and took responsibility for the education of their sons in the Torah. Men known as *mori,* who were learned in religious traditions, tended to matters pertaining to the synagogues and kosher slaughtering. Yemeni Jewish writers stress that their fellow Jews knew and lived by the *halakha* and credit them with having preserved rabbinical Judaism. Among the most important works written by Yemeni Jews are Nathanael al-Fayumi's *Garden of Knowledge,* which is well known outside Yemen, and David ben Amran's Big Commentary, an exegesis of Jewish dogma. There is still a synagogue in Sanaa, but it is no longer in use. The majority of the Jews left Yemen in 1949 and 1950. Many of those who stayed behind left in the 1990s—apparently for economic rather than political reasons.

The early history of the Christian community of the southern Arabian Peninsula was marked by hostilities between Christians and Jews. The last king of the Himyarites, Dhu Nuwas, adopted Judaism in 523 and killed large numbers of Christians in Najran. The Christian Abyssinians came to their rescue and brought the Himyarite Dynasty to an end in 525. In 897 a peace treaty was arranged between Jews and Christians. According to legend the ancient church al-Qalis was erected where Jesus had once prayed in Sanaa. Remnants of the church can still be seen. Christian communities continued to flourish in Yemen for several centuries after Islam took hold there. During the period of British rule in South Yemen (1839–1967), the descendants of immigrants maintained a Catholic church in Aden that still exists.

Other minority religious groups were able to maintain houses of worship under socialist rule in Yemen. Most notable among these were the Baniyan, members of the Hindu merchant castes of India, who settled in the ports of southern Arabia during the pre-Islamic era. The Hindu quarter in Aden later caused resentment, however, among the city's Shafiite scholars, who argued that Hindus were not members of any of the three religions of the Book and therefore were undesirable residents. The Zaydi imams, however, treated the Hindus much as they treated Jews and Christians, offering them protection and imposing the poll tax (*jizyah*) upon them. After World War I there were still a considerable number of Baniyan in Yemen, but their numbers have since dwindled.

Gabriele vom Bruck

See Also Vol. I: *Islam, Shiism, Sunnism*

Bibliography

Bruck, Gabriele vom. "Being a Zaydi in the Absence of an Imam: Doctrinal Revisions, Religious Instructions, and the (Re-)Invention of Ritual." In *Le Yémen contemporain.* Edited by Rémy Leveau, Franck Mermier, and Udo Steinbach. Paris: Karthala, 1999.

Bujra, Abdalla. "Political Conflict and Stratification in Hadramawt." *Middle Eastern Studies* 3, no. 1 (1966): 355–75.

Haykel, Bernard. "Al-Shawkani and the Jurisprudential Unity of Yemen." *Revue du Monde Musulman et de la Mediterranée* 67, no. 1: 53–65.

———. "The Salafis in Yemen at a Crossroads: An Obituary of Shaykh Muqbil al-Wadi'i of Dammaj (d. 1422/2001)." *Jemen Report* 1 (2002).

Knysh, Alexander. "The Cult of Saints and Islamic Reformism in Early Twentieth-Century Hadramawt." *New Arabian Studies* 4 (1997).

———. "The Cult of Saints in Hadramawt." *New Arabian Studies* 1 (1993).

Lackner, Helen. *P.D.R. Yemen: Outpost of Socialist Development in Arabia.* London: Ithaca Press, 1985.

Madelung, Wilferd. *Der Imam al-Qasim ibn Ibrahim und die Glaubenslehre der Zaiditen.* Berlin: de Gruyter, 1965.

———. "Der Islam im Jemen." In *Jemen: 3000 Years of Art and Civilisation in Arabia Felix.* Edited by Werner Daum. Innsbruck: Pinguin-Verlag; Frankfurt am Main: Umschau-Verlag, 1987.

———. "Zaydiyya." *Encyclopaedia of Islam.* Leiden: E.J. Brill, n.d.

Mermier, Franck. "L'Islam politique au Yémen ou la 'tradition' contre les traditions?" *Monde arab, Maghreb-Machrek* 155 (1997): 6–19.

Serjeant, R.B., and Ronald Lewcock, eds. *Sana: An Arabian Islamic City.* London: World of Islam Festival Trust, 1983.

Stiftl, Ludwig. "Politischer Islam und Pluralismus: Theoretische und empirische Studie am Beispiel des Jemen." Ph.D. thesis, University of Berlin, 1998.

Stothmann, Rudolf. "Al-Zaidiya." *Encyclopaedia of Islam.* Leiden: E.J. Brill, 1974.

Würth, Anna. *Aš-Šaria fi Bab al-Yaman: Recht, Richter und Rechtspraxis an der familienrechtlichen Kammer des Gerichts Süd-Sanaa (Republik Jemen), 1983–1995.* Berlin: Duncker and Humblot, 2000.

Zambia

POPULATION 9,959,037

CHRISTIAN 87.0 percent

MUSLIM 0.4 percent

HINDU 0.1 percent

OTHER 7.2 percent

NONRELIGIOUS 5.3 percent

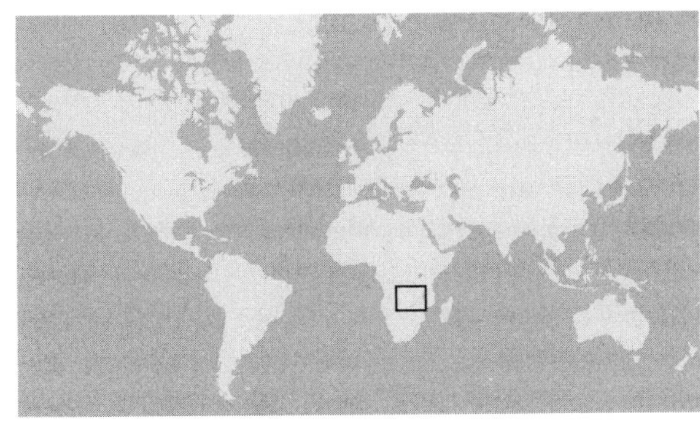

Country Overview

INTRODUCTION The Republic of Zambia, a landlocked country in southern Africa, is situated on a plateau ranging from 1,970 to 5,250 feet (600 to 1,600 meters) above sea level. The country experiences a tropical climate with three seasons: a cool, dry season from April to August; a hot, dry season from August to November; and a warm, wet season from November to April. Drained by four major rivers (the Zambezi, Kafue, Luangwa, and Luapula), Zambia is home to a number of waterfalls, including the famous Victoria Falls. Some of Zambia's geographical features constitute religious symbols among the indigenous people. For example, waterfalls such as the Chishimba and Ntumbachushi falls in the north of the country are said to be inhabited by spirits that can help people in time of need or punish them when they fail to observe certain taboos regarding the falls. In some parts of the country that experience droughts, especially the south with its savannah grassland and scattered trees, the Tonga-speaking inhabitants practice the Lwindi ceremony of asking for rain from the spirits of the dead chiefs. The indigenous people of Zambia are Bantu-speaking people. The most striking features of the country are its underdevelopment and poverty amidst abundant natural and human resources.

A former British protectorate, Zambia (whose name derives from the Zambezi River, which rises in the northwestern part of the country) was known as Northern Rhodesia from 1911 until becoming independent on 24 October 1964. For 74 years the country was under foreign rule, first by the British South Africa Company (1890–1923) and afterward, as a protectorate, by the British Colonial Office. Zambia was the first British protectorate to have been granted republic status immediately after attaining independence.

Religion is important in the lives of the people of Zambia. According to the 2000 census about 65 percent of the population was Protestant, and 22 percent was Catholic. But Christianity and other religions have not replaced the traditional religious beliefs. Alongside the various denominations in Christianity and the major world faiths, specifically Islam, Zambia has witnessed a rapid growth of charismatic Christianity, or neo-Pentecostalism. Charismatic Christianity is becoming a dominant expression of Christianity in the country. Al-

Boys participate in a funeral at a cemetery filled mostly with victims of AIDS. With the advent of HIV and AIDS, the concept of the church family has become even more meaningful. © JOEL STETTENHEIM/CORBIS.

though numerically few, the followers of charismatic churches add to the variety of organized Christian churches, thereby contributing a vibrant dimension to Zambia's Christianity. Charismatic churches are often confused with the various Pentecostal churches because of similarities in their theologies. In fact, most charismatics think that they are Pentecostal.

Until recently Zambia's Christianity was spoken about in terms of three mother bodies, also known as umbrella bodies. The three are the Zambia Episcopal Conference (ZEC), the Christian Council of Zambia (CCZ), and the Evangelical Fellowship of Zambia (EFZ). Officially instituted in 1963, the ZEC is the administrative body of all Roman Catholic dioceses. The CCZ was established in 1945 as the umbrella body of classical Protestant churches. The EFZ was officially formed in 1964 as an umbrella body of Evangelical churches. In 2001 a fourth umbrella body, the Independent Churches Organization of Zambia (ICOZ), was formed to bring together charismatic churches, ministries, fellowships, and centers.

RELIGIOUS TOLERANCE The successive constitutions of Zambia have guaranteed a secular state and freedom of worship and of conscience. The relationship of church and state is generally cordial. Religious education is compulsory in public elementary schools and optional in high schools. The syllabi cover Christianity, Islam, Hinduism, and Bantu religions.

There is a strong ecumenical cooperation among churches in Zambia. The Christian Council of Zambia (CCZ), the Evangelical Fellowship of Zambia (EFZ), and the Zambia Episcopal Conference (ZEC) jointly own Multimedia Zambia. The three church bodies further constitute the Churches Medical Association of Zambia. Together the ZEC and the CCZ run Mindolo Ecumenical Center. The presidential declaration of Zambia as a Christian nation in 1991, however, has negatively affected the long-standing ecumenical spirit. Churches no longer speak with one voice. Most charismatic church leaders will uncritically subscribe to state policies and actions that, to the public and mainline churches, are not for the common good. Most charismatics want to appear obedient to civil authority.

Major Religion

CHRISTIANITY

DATE OF ORIGIN 1882 C.E.

NUMBER OF FOLLOWERS 8.7 million

HISTORY Although David Livingstone (1813–73) was the first missionary to go to Zambia, he did not establish a mission station in the territory. But having traveled through the country writing his *Missionary Travels and Researches,* he became a popular hero. The evangelization of Zambia began in 1882 by Protestant missionaries. The first Christian missionary to stay in Zambia was Frederick Stanley Arnot of the Plymouth Brethren. He lived in the western part of the country from October 1882 to May 1884. In 1885 the Paris Evangelical Missionary Society (including Sotho evangelists) was allowed to establish its first settlement, and in 1887 the London Missionary Society went to the northern part of the country.

In 1892 the Primitive Methodists arrived. The White Fathers joined the London Missionary Society in 1895. The Dutch Reformed missionaries arrived in the east in 1899. Other missionaries who went to Zambia were from the Free Church of Scotland (in 1894) and the Christian Missions in Many Lands (in 1899), the latter a missionary network of the Plymouth Brethren. Among the later groups to send missionaries were the South African Baptists, Seventh-day Adventists, Brethren in Christ, Universities Mission to Central Africa, South African General Mission, Society of Jesus (Jesuits), and Wesleyan Methodists. The largest Protestant denomination is the United Church of Zambia. Created in 1965, it was meant to be the national Protestant church.

The charismatic churches in Zambia owe their origins to the charismatic revival of 1960 in the United States, during which Reverend Dennis Bennett of Saint Mark's Episcopal Church (in Van Nuys, California) claimed to have been baptized in the Holy Spirit. Arriving in Zambia by way of South Africa, the charismatic churches experienced growth that was encouraged by the Scripture Union movement and strengthened by the 1967 visit of Billy Graham.

By 1980 Zambia's Christian population constituted 72 percent of the country's population. As such, Zambia had a higher percentage of Christians than black Africa as a whole, for which the average was 53 percent. The charismatic churches in Zambia are largely concentrated in the towns and are patronized by the working class or middle class. Some of these churches are large, with up to 2,000 people, while others are small.

EARLY AND MODERN LEADERS Kenneth Kaunda, the first president of Zambia (from 1964 to 1991), was a Christian. Son of a Presbyterian minister and missionary, Kaunda spearheaded the independence movement. He later taught a sort of Christian socialism called Zambian Humanism. He argued that it was not atheism but a theistic philosophy. Through Zambian Humanism he united the different ethnic groups in the country.

The healing and exorcism ministry practiced by Archbishop Emmanuel Milingo (born in 1930), a charismatic Catholic clergyman, resulted in the Roman Catholic Church's decision to summon him to Rome in 1983. On behalf of the voiceless and poor, he demanded accountability in governance.

From the charismatic churches, Pastor Nevers Mumba of Victory Bible Church has promoted the charismatic consciousness in Zambia since 1985. In 2003 Mumba was appointed vice president of Zambia. Bishop Joseph Imakando, owner of Bread of Life Church International, is particularly known for his television program, *Hour of Blessing,* which began in January 1997. Pastor Dan Pule developed a partnership between his church, Dunamis, and Trinity Broadcasting Network of the United States in August 1998.

MAJOR THEOLOGIANS AND AUTHORS Zambia's mainline Christianity may have produced theologians, but they are hardly known by the public because they do not publish books. There are, however, a number of Christian authors in the country who are mainly expatriates and mostly Catholic priests belonging to the Franciscans, the Missionaries of Africa, and the Society of Jesus (Jesuits). The work of Brendan Carmody, a Jesuit, has probed the question of African conversion to Christianity and the impact of Jesuit schooling on Zambian boys. Hugo Hinfelaar, a White Father, has traced the religious changes that have occurred among the Bemba-speaking women in Zambia since the last decade of the nineteenth century. Carmody and Hinfelaar have been doing research and publishing their findings since 1980. Charismatics have not yet produced theologians. Nonetheless, Pastor Nevers Mumba of Victory Bible Church has authored a book, *Integrity with Fire,* and a number of charismatics write articles in various newspapers commenting on the social, political, economic, and religious issues in the country.

HOUSES OF WORSHIP AND HOLY PLACES Classical mainline churches have built church halls or chapels in which worship takes place. Anglicans and Catholics have some of the finest chapels in the country. Although some charismatic churches have church halls, too, most of them rent a classroom, school, or cinema hall. Additionally there are those who meet to pray in tents until a hall is rented or built. Bishop Joseph Imakando of Bread of Life Church International has been raising funds to build a cathedral. Pastor Nevers Mumba of Victory Bible Church has not given up the dream of building a coliseum. In terms of holy places, charismatic churches will point to Israel as the holy place. Indeed, Israel is a Holy Land to nearly all Christian churches in Zambia, but some (for example, the Roman Catholic Church) have other holy places, such as sites of Mary's apparitions outside Zambia.

WHAT IS SACRED? In Zambia's Christianity what is sacred is that most important element of Christianity, the transcendent God. Every Sunday as well as every other day of the week God is worshiped in various ways. There is also the feeling that human beings are sacred because they have been created in the image of God. Charismatic Christians emphasize this point in their vernacular choruses and by preaching against smoking, sexual immorality, drinking, and vulgar language. Other Christian churches strongly propagating this type of teaching are the Seventh-day Adventists and the Salvation Army.

HOLIDAYS AND FESTIVALS The most widely celebrated Christian holidays in Zambia are Christmas and Easter. They are national public holidays as well. Not all Christians recognize these holidays, however. For example, the Seventh-day Adventists do not. As elsewhere the two holidays have increasingly become commercialized. Most Zambians will go to church during these festivals and return home to eat, drink, and make merry. Even the poor will try their utmost to have a good meal on Christmas Day. In poor families a dinner of chicken and rice constitutes a Christmas meal, and children are more than delighted to celebrate Christmas in new or decent secondhand clothes they receive as gifts. Charismatic churches may celebrate other festivals, such as marching for Christ or a gospel concert. From 1992 to 2001 charismatic church members marched for Christ on the 29th of every December because that was the day when Zambia was declared a Christian nation.

MODE OF DRESS Zambia is one of the few countries in Africa without a distinctive traditional mode of dress, and among Zambian Christians, Western influence is strong. The men's suit and tie and such women's fashions as Western suits or blouses with skirts or trousers are pervasive. The *citenge* (cloth wrapped around the waist) with a blouse worn on top is the commonest dress among Zambian women, especially the rural and slum women and housewives. Some Christian women have formed groups in which dressing in a sort of uniform is compulsory. Such groups include the Legion of Mary in the Catholic Church or the Women Christian Fellowship in the United Church of Zambia.

Generally, members of a church will dress according to their own tastes. Wearing a miniskirt or tight trousers to worship services is frowned upon in many churches because such clothing is considered to be indecent for the occasion. One particular charismatic church, Deeper Life Church, once encouraged women to cover their heads during praise and worship. Some women were opposed to doing this, so the practice has stopped.

DIETARY PRACTICES Dietary practices are left up to the individual Christian's taste. Seventh-day Adventists, however, will as much as possible adhere to a vegetarian diet and avoid any drink with caffeine or alcohol. Some Adventists also say that it would be wrong for them to eat duck and pig meat and certain types of fish because the Bible does not allow that. They admit, nonetheless, that not all Adventists follow these dietary practices. Other Christians (for example, Catholics) will not eat meat on Fridays throughout Lent or on Good Friday. But generally Catholics are liberal about many other things: beer drinking, smoking, and diet. On the other hand, charismatic Christians are against beer drinking. Their pastors vehemently preach against drinking alcohol and smoking because the human body is the temple of God, and alcohol and tobacco should not contaminate it. There is not much said about dietary practices by many denominations and charismatic churches as part of the church service, although occasionally a pastor will remind his audience to watch their diets to avoid certain illnesses, which nonetheless are believed to be curable through faith in God.

RITUALS Every Christian church in Zambia has rituals surrounding such rites of passage as baptism, marriage, and death. Prayer and worship are other important rituals. Mainline churches of European missionary origins have maintained their rituals in their Western form.

The mode of praying in mainline churches remains essentially European except that rituals and hymns have been vernacularized, and in most churches the modern musical instruments—the organ or piano and the guitar—are complemented by the traditional drums and cymbals. Sermons are in English, in vernacular, or in English with an interpreter.

A charismatic worship service will usually begin with a hymn, which will slowly lead the group into some form of ecstasy: muttering, wailing, sobbing, or speaking in tongues. The pastor will then ask the congregation to look up the reading of the day and proceed by giving a sermon. The pastor will moralize, counsel, and encourage positive thinking in the membership. Toward the end of the worship service, the pastor will pray over those who want to be healed or to be born again. Sometimes the final part of praise and worship will take the form of testimonies when those who feel they have been healed of their ailments during the praise and worship testify to the congregation that Jesus has healed them.

RITES OF PASSAGE The most important and commonly practiced rites of passage in Zambia's Christianity are baptism, marriage, and death. Baptism by immersion is a common rite of passage in charismatic churches. Practitioners profess, "I am born again; I have left my old ways, and I want to follow Jesus." In mainline churches there is either baptism by immersion or sprinkling. In some churches attempts have been made to indigenize rituals such as baptism. In some Catholic parishes catechumens are made to undergo the three stages of separation, marginalization, and integration. Upon completion of their baptism instructions, the catechumens are withdrawn from the public for intensive instruction and testing. Before the actual baptism catechumens enter the liminal stage, a stage linked to being in the womb, invisibility, darkness, death, and the like. (For example, a girl in the initiation rite is represented as possessing nothing during this stage. She is naked or wears only a slip of clothing to show that she has no status or property. The girl's behavior is passive. She must obey her instructors, after which she will be integrated into society as an adult.) Catechumens become full members of the church after baptism.

Among most Zambian Christians marriage is celebrated with pomp and elegance, in many ways similar to traditional Western practices, with a church ceremony followed by a reception. An exciting part of a wedding reception is the entrance dance before the buffet-style meal and cake. The bridesmaids and groomsmen dance to rhumba music, sending the audience into a frenzy. Charismatic weddings also feature this dance. Western influence is conspicuous in funerals held in urban areas. The deceased's body will be brought to the church in a coffin to be prayed over. This is followed by what is known as body viewing, during which time mourners will be reminded not to cry too loudly because in Christianity it is believed that death is a passage to another life. Next is a funeral procession to the cemetery for burial and after that time for speeches, laying of wreaths, the final prayer, and blessings.

MEMBERSHIP Religion continues to have a hold on the majority of the population. Most Zambians claim to be Christian, though for some their belief is only nominal, and there are those who believe without belonging to a church. Every Christian church looks for ways of preserving its members and getting new converts. Most charismatic churches claim to be nondenominational in order to broaden the scope of their congregations. They hold crusades to which people from all denominations go and experience conversion. Other than the Roman Catholic Church (as a single denomination with four community radio stations and one television studio), the churches making the most of the broadcast media and the Internet to evangelize are the charismatics. They also have a program called door-to-door ministering. This is when they invite people for "tea," which usually turns out to be a buffet, followed by singing, preaching, and testimonies.

SOCIAL JUSTICE The Roman Catholic Church sets the tone of the church-state relationship in Zambia. On social justice the Catholic Centre for Justice, Development, and Peace (CCJDP) and the Jesuit Centre for Theological Reflection (JCTR) highlight the plight of the poor resulting from inadequate governance. Backed by the bishops, the CCJDP and the JCTR demand distributive socioeconomic order and engage in civic education. In particular the JCTR has a track record of challenging the state over issues such as budgetary priorities, corruption, and legal and electoral practices. Generally, the ordinary citizens take a fatalistic view of their poverty conditions. Being a civil society, the JCTR demonstrates a compassionate response to the poor and the marginalized.

SOCIAL ASPECTS The concept of church as family propagated by the Catholic African Synod has extended to other churches in Zambia. The concept seeks to strengthen membership from the family to small Christian communities or cells (as charismatic churches call them) to the local Zambian church up to the universal church. With the advent of HIV and AIDS, the concept of family has become even more meaningful because the infected and the affected need the support of their fellow church members.

The need for good parenting in these times is also considered important. Although arranged marriages are no longer practiced, there are charismatic churches that explicitly encourage marriage within churches. Members of these churches usually call themselves brother and sister and make arrangements to marry amongst themselves. In any case, all Christian churches recognize the significance of solid Christian families to ensure there will be good Christians and citizens.

POLITICAL IMPACT Zambia is a secular state. Religion for the most part does not influence politics or public affairs. Many politicians claim to be Christian (or, in the case of Zambians of Indian origins, Hindu or Muslim), but there is a striking absence of the concept of common good in governance. While religion does not have much of an impact on politics (in that it doesn't influence policies or governance), there is Christian rhetoric in politics. During the time of one-party autocratic rule (1972–91), Kenneth Kaunda used Christian rhetoric in politics largely because his political system was aimed at controlling and giving direction to everything in the country. Above all he wanted to show that he was the son of a pastor. When his successor, Frederick Chiluba (Zambia's president from 1991 to 2001), declared Zambia a Christian nation, Chiluba argued that every government policy would be predicated by Christian and biblical principles. He also argued that corruption would end. At the end of his term, however, Chiluba became a victim of corruption and a plunderer of national wealth.

CONTROVERSIAL ISSUES Among the ongoing controversial issues within Christianity in Zambia is the question of inculturation. Some churches, such as the Roman Catholic Church, are inculturating the gospel message of Jesus Christ—that is, making the gospel message meaningful to the people in their cultural and traditional contexts. Other churches demand a total conversion, or a break with traditional Zambian cultural practices and beliefs.

Another issue over which Christians are divided is the involvement of Christian leaders in politics. For example, when born-again Christian Frederick Chiluba became president of Zambia in 1991, many other born-agains blindly supported him. Most mainline churches led by the Roman Catholic Church disagreed with the notion held by born-agains that Chiluba was a God-chosen leader who would make Zambia prosper. Some politicians try to use religion in their political discourses for selfish intentions.

Condoms have been a source of controversy between churches and state. Christian churches led by the Roman Catholic clergy have emphasized abstinence as the surest way of avoiding HIV and AIDS. The state's message is double-edged: Unmarried people are not to engage in sex but should take precautions (using condoms) if they must.

CULTURAL IMPACT The Zambian culture, as expressed in such forms as sculpture, dance, and song, has remained largely unaffected by Christianity. It is possible to come across sculptures and paintings of a black Jesus, Mary, or Joseph, reflecting the process of inculturating the Christian message.

Other Religions

Zambia is traditionally a country of Bantu-speaking people constituting 73 ethnic groups that are culturally related to one another. Each Bantu tribe, clan, village, family, or individual has its own religious practices. Bantu religion can be seen in the people's ceremonies and rituals. The impact of Christianity and colonialism has been enormous, yet many customs, beliefs, and behavioral patterns have survived to this day. There are three types of Bantu religions practiced in Zambia. First, there is the belief in the lineage spirits (spirits of the dead ancestors and recently deceased people), which applies to all the ethnic groups in the country. Second, there is the belief in territorial shrines (places of power in a territory) thought to house influential spirits. And third, there is the belief in the power of the spirits (royal spirits) of the dead chiefs, especially paramount or senior chiefs. Offerings (often referred to as sacrifices) made to the three types of spirits ensure personal and community stability. Crop failure, illnesses such as spirit possession, and personal moral failure are all believed to be caused by these spirits. The Bantu also believe in a powerful but remote spiritual being who is thought to be the creator of all things. The supreme being (known as Lesa in several languages) is readily equated with the Judeo-Christian God, but the concept of a relationship with him through the intercession of Jesus Christ is new.

There are neither images nor temples for God in the Zambian traditional religions. He is prayed to at any convenient time and place—for example, under a tree, on a rock, at the foot of a mountain, near an anthill, at shrines of the deceased chiefs and others who have departed, or in the homes of the living. Shrines have keepers and caretakers who, although they are not called priests, preside over community prayers. The chiefs, especially the senior chiefs, wield political, economic, and social powers. During traditional ceremonies (annually celebrated by major tribes) the chief is both the focus of the celebration and the priest who acts as an intermediary between the people and the spirits.

Islam is a fast-growing religion in Zambia with an explicit ambition to convert as many Zambians as possible. The Muslim community, totaling about 39,800, is made up of indigenous Bantu-speaking people and Zambian citizens of Indian, Pakistan, Tanzanian, Malawian, Iranian, Lebanese, Senegalese, Congolese, Mozambican, and Somalian origins. The giving of alms to the poor has ensured the rapid expansion of this faith. There is an aggressive conversion campaign in the capital city, Lusaka, which has a large number of slums. Spearheading the Islamic revival is the Islamic Council of Zambia, under the chairmanship of Dr. John Mwale, an indigenous Zambian. In 1992 the youth wing of the council attempted unsuccessfully to form a political party with the goal of getting hold of political power.

Since 1991 Zambia has witnessed a proliferation of Islamic literature, available through libraries attached to Islamic centers, information offices, and mosques. The Islamic center in the capital city provides information about Islam to the public by distributing leaflets or pamphlets and by inviting people to the center to read about Islam or to talk to a Muslim. The manifestation of Islamic activity is the building of mosques, which in 1982 numbered 67 but by 2003 rose to just under 100 (of these, two Shiite mosques and the rest Sunni). It is common to see indigenous Zambians wearing the fez and women veiled in the traditional *citenge.* Every Friday afternoon Muslims are seen heading toward their respective mosques to pray, and the poor walk back home with parcels containing some food, which they may have been given at the mosque. Prayer at the mosques is in Arabic. Most indigenous Muslims are quite ignorant about the teachings of the Koran (the holy book of the Muslims), which has not yet been translated into the local languages. Muslims have started building *madrasahs* (schools), which give instruction in Islamic belief and practice, thereby addressing Koranic illiteracy. Mahad-Rashid Islamia, an international theological seminary in Chipata, draws students from Zambia and also from Malawi, Mozambique, Kenya, and other countries. The college trains future *hafiz,* who eventually become sheikhs or imams. Students are taught the Indian language Urdu for conversation in the college, but for lectures and recitation of the Koran they are taught Arabic.

The Bahai faith is also rapidly gaining converts in Zambia. By 2003 there were 20,000 Bahais in Zambia, while their local spiritual assemblies rose from 19 in 1964 to 84 in 2003. The Bahais run a prestigious high school for girls (Banani International School) near the capital city and are involved in community projects aimed at promoting the well-being of the people.

Hinduism is the religion of Zambian Hindus of Indian origins. Hindus have their own halls of worship and celebrate their festivals (such as the Diwali) in their communities. Hindus engage in a great deal of community work to help the underprivileged. It is not believed that any indigenous people practice Hinduism, but there are some who belong to New Age movements with Hindu spirituality.

Yet another religion increasingly popular among indigenous Zambians is Nichiren Buddhism, represented by the lay organization of Soka Gakkai International (SGI). The followers say that it is the highest and most refined Mahayana Buddhism in Zambia, with a membership of slightly more than 3,500. Popularized by Dr. Darlington Kalabula and his Japanese wife, SGI-Zambia has four chapters, 12 districts, and groups in almost half of the Zambian towns. Indigenous Zambians find SGI attractive because it has no commandments. Furthermore, they can immediately see the results of this religion in their lives—they do not have to wait until they reach heaven or paradise.

Austin Cheyeka

See Also Vol. I: *African Indigenous Beliefs, Anglicanism/ Episcopalianism, Christianity, Methodism, Roman Catholicism*

Bibliography

Barrett, David B., George T. Kurian, and Todd M. Johnson, eds. *World Christian Encyclopedia: A Comparative Survey of Churches and Religions in the Modern World.* 2nd ed. New York: Oxford University Press, 2001.

Carmody, Brendan Patrick. *Conversion and Jesuit Schooling in Zambia.* Leiden: E.J. Brill, 1992.

Henkel, Reinhard. *Christian Missions in Africa: A Social Geographical Study of the Impact of Their Activities in Zambia.* Berlin: Dietrich Reimer Verlag, 1989.

Hinfelaar, Hugo. *Bemba-Speaking Women of Zambia in a Century of Religious Change (1892–1992).* Leiden: E.J. Brill, 1994.

Hudson, John. *A Time to Mourn.* Lusaka: Bookworld, 1999.

Ipenburg, At. *"All Good Men": The Development of Lubwa Mission, Chinsali, Zambia, 1905–1967.* Frankfurt am Main: Peter Lang, 1992.

Musonda, D.K. "The Meaning and Value of Life among the Bisa and Christian Morality." D.Th. diss., Pontificale Università Lateranense, Rome, Italy, 1996.

Mwewa, S. Kapita. "Traditional Zambian Eschatology and Ethics Confronting the Advent of Christianity." D.Th. diss., University of Innsbruck, Austria, 1977.

Snelson, Peter. *Educational Development in Northern Rhodesia.* Lusaka: KKF, 1974.

Ter Haar, Gerrie. *The Spirit of Africa: The Healing Ministry of Archbishop Milingo of Zambia.* London: Hurst & Co., 1992.

Weller, John, and Jane Linden. *Mainstream Christianity to 1980 in Malawi, Zambia, and Zimbabwe.* Gweru, Zimbabwe: Mambo Press, 1984.

Zimbabwe

POPULATION 11,376,676

CHRISTIAN 48.5 percent

AFRICAN TRADITIONAL RELIGION 47 percent

BUDDHIST, HINDU, JEWISH, MUSLIM, AND OTHER 4.5 percent

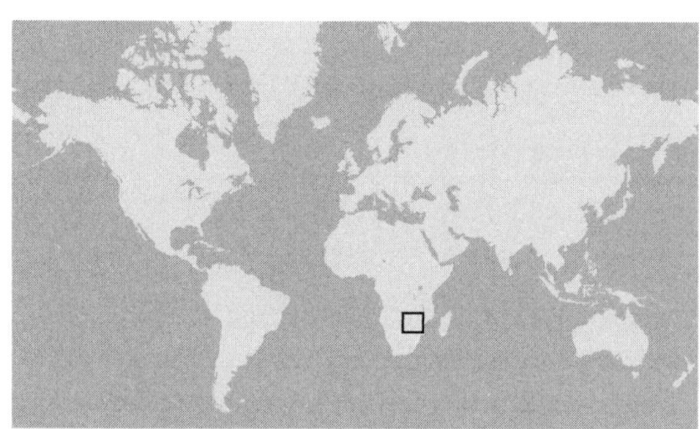

Country Overview

INTRODUCTION The Republic of Zimbabwe, located in southern Africa, is a landlocked country bordered by Zambia to the north, Mozambique to the northeast and east, South Africa to the south, and Botswana to the southwest and west. Natural boundaries include the Zambezi River to the north and the Limpopo River to the south. Eastern Zimbabwe is mountainous, but the rest of the country forms part of the Highveld, a region of high, grassy plains. Agriculture is the main means of sustenance. Their close dependence on the earth has led Zimbabweans to worship a God who supports them when conditions are adverse. During such times, traditionalists and Christians unite to pray. Because Christianity and traditional religion interact so often in the country, there is a degree of syncretism among Zimbabweans.

Christianity was first introduced to the people of "Monomutapa's land," now Zimbabwe, in the sixteenth century. It became a permanent fixture there in the nineteenth century through the efforts of British missionaries in cooperation with British colonialists. When Christianity was introduced, it entered into competition with the traditional religion practiced by both the Ndebele and the Shona peoples. The Ndebele worshiped Inkosi (God), while the Shona believed in Mwari, Nyadenga, or Musikavanhu, each of whose names also means "God." The missionaries preceded the colonialists, encouraging the Ndebele and the Shona to accept the white men, who would offer them a better life—that is, Western culture. The indigenous people were thus colonized. Widespread acceptance of Christianity by Zimbabwe's African population, however, did not occur until late in the twentieth century, when it came about as the result of Zimbabwean initiatives.

Following decades of liberation struggle, Zimbabwe won its independence from Britain in 1980. Formerly called Southern Rhodesia (1911–64) and Rhodesia (1964–79), it had renamed itself Zimbabwe in 1979 after the Dzimbahwe (House Built of Stone), a structure of immense political and cultural significance. The ruins of the Dzimbahwe are located near Maswingo City.

Two religions, Christianity and African traditional religion, are prevalent in contemporary Zimbabwe, with each representing a little less than half of the population. The remaining small minority contains adherents of various religious groups, including Muslims, Hindus, Jews, and Buddhists. Historically the people of Zimbabwe believed that all religious groups worship the same God.

RELIGIOUS TOLERANCE There is religious harmony in Zimbabwe, not only because all of its religions are monotheistic but also because religion is respected by everybody. For this reason even henotheistic religions like Hinduism, which worship one god but do not deny that other gods may exist, are respected. Zimbabweans believe that, since religion is a way of life, no one can legislate how a life of faith is to be lived.

Since the majority of Zimbabwe's population is made up of Africans, who are generally amenable to diversity, it is not surprising to witness ecumenical religious activities, especially at funerals, weddings, family reunions, and other events that bring people together. Several ecumenical organization operate in the country, including the Zimbabwe Council of Churches, Zimbabwe Catholic Bishops' Conference, Evangelical Fellowship of Zimbabwe, and Fambidzano (Conference of Black Churches). It is quite remarkable that there has never been an interreligious battle. Tensions between the country's churches and the government of President Robert Mugabe increased in 2004, however, when some church leaders protested human rights abuses perpetrated by the government.

Christian villagers pray for rain during a drought in Zimbabwe. © GIDEON MENDEL/CORBIS.

Major Religions

CHRISTIANITY

AFRICAN INDIGENOUS BELIEFS

CHRISTIANITY

DATE OF ORIGIN late sixteenth century C.E.
NUMBER OF FOLLOWERS 5.5 million

HISTORY Christianity was initially planted in southern Africa in the sixteenth century by the Jesuit missionary Father Gonçalo da Silveira. He baptized the Thonga rulers and several hundreds of their subjects and converted Monomutapa, the king of what is now Zimbabwe, and his wife but did not make progress after that. A Muslim advised the king that the missionary was in fact a spy representing the viceroy of India. This misinformation resulted in Silveira's murder in 1561. Nevertheless, by 1667 nine places of worship had been established by the Jesuits and the Dominicans. At the end of the century all the missions were destroyed by wars in the region.

The second phase of Christian missionizing in Zimbabwe began in the nineteenth century, with European Protestant missions predominating. The Scottish missionary Robert Moffat played a major role in replanting the church. During this time the missionaries needed the protection of the colonialists, and the colonialists exploited the missionaries' persuasive approach to gain acceptance by the indigenous rulers. The allocation of land by both colonial and indigenous rulers made possible the physical establishment of the missions, and commendations and subsidies from the British government helped legitimate and support them.

According to Gwinyai Muzorewa in *The Origins and Development of African Theology* (1985), "In some instances, Christianity came to Africa with the active assistance of the settlers and traders. Hence confusion resulted as to the intentions of the missionaries and those of the colonizers." This style of church planting colored the character of Christian worship in Zimbabwe, lending Western decorum to the liturgical style and singing of hymns, though services were conducted in the local vernacular. Major missionary societies represented in the country included the London Missionary Society, the Wesleyan Methodist Missionary Society, and the Church Missionary Society, all from Britain.

The plethora of smaller missionary groups present in the early twentieth century is reflected in the numerous Christian denominations in contemporary Zimbabwe. Roman Catholics make up the largest of these. Other denominations tend to dominate in particular regions. For example, the United Methodist Church, which was planted by American missionaries, predominates in the eastern region and is headquartered at Old Mutare, home of the affiliated Africa University. This branch of Methodism had at least 10 mission stations in addition to hundreds of affiliated private schools. Another branch of Methodism, the Methodist Church in Zimbabwe, formerly the Wesleyan Methodist Church, was introduced by the British. The Lutherans had to negotiate for space with the Methodists in Zimbabwe because they serve the same general region. The Seventh-day Adventist Church is based in Matebeleland, in the southwest, where it operates a university. The United Church of Christ is dominant in the southeastern part of the country, where it has a center at Mount Selinda. The Salvation Army represents a significantly smaller population, but it, too, has made an impact among Zimbabweans.

Since the 1940s and '50s the independent church movement has mushroomed all over Zimbabwe. One-fourth to one-third of Zimbabwean Christians belong to independent churches. An extension of the independent church in South Africa, the movement emphasizes a conservative morality. Matthew Chigaga Zwimba founded the first independent church among the Shona in 1915. The healing powers of the founders of the independent churches have attracted many adherents. The most widespread of these groups are the apostolic churches, which originated in southern Africa. They were founded by such African prophets as Johanni Maranke, Samuel Mutendi, and Ndaza.

EARLY AND MODERN LEADERS Among European missionaries in Zimbabwe, the leading figure is Robert Moffat (1795–1883), who sought to develop Zimbabwe politically and economically as well as spiritually. Other missionaries tended to be preoccupied only with their denomination's success. Abel Tendekayi Muzorewa (born in 1925) was the first African to become a bishop in the United Methodist Church. In 1972 Muzorewa led the Pearce Commission, whose objective was to assess black Africans' opinion of the proposals of the white-controlled government regarding such issues as majority rule. He was elected prime minister in 1979, his central message being that Zimbabwe needed a democratic government, which its white rulers had clearly failed to deliver. It was during Muzorewa's time that Zimbabwean youths absconded by the thousands to train as freedom fighters, a development that eventually helped the country gain its independence.

The Reverend Ndabaningi Sithole (1920–2000), a Congregationalist minister and author of *African Nationalism* (1959), was another religious leader who became involved in the nation's politics. Like Muzorewa, Sithole believed that God wants all people to be free. Canaan Sodindo Banana (1936–2003), a Methodist minister and influential liberation theologian, served as the first president of the Republic of Zimbabwe (1980–87) and helped bring ethnic fighting in Matabeleland to an end in 1987. In 2000, however, he was convicted of sexual assault and sodomy.

MAJOR THEOLOGIANS AND AUTHORS Among the first theologians to publish after Zimbabwe gained its independence was Gwinyai Muzorewa (born in the mid-1940s), author of *The Origin and Development of African Theology* (1985). Ambrose Moyo (born in 1943) strongly influenced the development of Zimbabwe's new textbooks for religious education, which introduced African traditional religion as a subject for study. The writings of Alois Maveneka (born in 1947), author of *A Church Self-Reliant and Missionary* (1978), were also useful in educating Zimbabweans to manage their own affairs. But it was Muzorewa's book that marked the official beginning, in book form, of Zimbabwean Christian theology at an international level.

HOUSES OF WORSHIP AND HOLY PLACES In Zimbabwe Catholics, Protestants, and various independent church groups have built churches where they worship on Sunday mornings (and sometimes evenings) or on Saturdays (in the case of the Seventh-day Adventists). Because the church is believed to be a holy place, no other community functions may be performed there except funerals and weddings. The buildings are usually spacious enough to accommodate worshipers and have brick walls and roofs made of tiles or asbestos sheets.

Almost without fail, there is a cross on top of the building, or, at the least, there is one inside at the front of the sanctuary. The altar area is believed to be the "holy of holies."

WHAT IS SACRED? The items most sacred to Zimbabwean Christians are the cross, the Bible, and the sanctuary.

HOLIDAYS AND FESTIVALS The most widely celebrated Christian holiday in Zimbabwe is Christmas. On Christmas Eve, most groups visit selected homes and individuals to sing Christmas carols. Everyone tries to dress up on this day. Easter is also celebrated, though in a rather solemn manner, with fasting, spiritual cleansing, and abstinence from luxurious living. Although during Easter many Christians intensify their praying, Zimbabwean Christians maintain their spiritual commitment year round. Practices vary, but of particular interest are those of the Vapositori, a group of Christians who emulate the lives of the Apostles and John the Baptist. The Vapositori begin their Easter celebration one week before the holiday, and their observance of Christmas begins on Christmas Day and also lasts for one week. For the Vapositori, this is a time to pray, celebrate, enjoy themselves, and get married.

Other holidays include the Day of Pentecost, Boxing Day, and the World Day of Prayer. These are celebrated by all Zimbabweans, including indigenous people who do not know what they commemorate.

MODE OF DRESS The clergy in Zimbabwe generally wear distinctive dress. Elders wear a clerical collar, especially when they are conducting a funeral or visiting the sick or prisoners. Junior members may wear a robe but can not wear the collar until they are ordained. Clerics' robes are usually black, though some wear lighter colors like gray or khaki. Independent church leaders tend to dress lavishly, as their churches emphasize distinctions among members. Independent church members, especially the Vapositori, tend to wear their religious dress—full-length, usually white robes plus a white headdress for women—at all times. Male Vapositori shave their heads. The majority of mainline Protestants wear ordinary work clothes during the week, and during worship they wear whatever they wish. On Sundays when they receive the Lord's Supper and on other special occasions, such as Easter, however, the women wear uniforms designated by their denomination.

DIETARY PRACTICES Christians in Zimbabwe generally follow no specific diet. Seventh-day Adventists, however, observe certain dietary rules. For example, during the observance of the Sabbath, which lasts from Friday evening through sundown on Saturday, they do not cook any meals but eat leftovers instead. They do not eat pork because they believe that, according to the Bible, pigs are unclean animals. Several Apostolic Faith groups also subscribe to this belief. The consumption of intoxicants is considered sinful by most groups, especially the United Methodists and the independent churches.

RITUALS Various Christian groups in Zimbabwe perform special rituals when they assign members to categories of membership, which are usually indicated by their uniforms. Beginners wear simple uniforms, while more senior members are distinguished by the number of badges they wear. Most Protestant groups observe baptism and Holy Communion, while Roman Catholics and some Anglicans celebrate all seven sacraments, including confirmation, holy matrimony, holy orders, penance, and extreme unction.

Other types of rituals include holy matrimony and burial rites. Zimbabwean Christian burial rituals are peculiarly African. For instance, an African mat with both sides cut to symbolize eternal life is placed in the casket beneath the body. After the Christian formula is pronounced, all the women are dismissed, and the elders remain behind "to fix" the grave, making sure that every step is followed properly and that everything is placed to give the grave a dignified appearance. These rituals are performed in the presence and with the consent of the clergy.

RITES OF PASSAGE There are no Christian rites of passage that are distinctive to Zimbabwe.

MEMBERSHIP The number of Christians in Zimbabwe has been growing steadily. Adherents have planned effective methods of evangelization, including the generations-old door-to-door campaign. Whenever there is a revival in a community, the last two days of the meeting are generally devoted to such campaigning. In urban areas, religious broadcasts may reach large numbers of people. Tracts featuring well-known Bible verses are sometimes distributed all over a community. Dispatching two or three witnesses to a school where they will be allowed to address the student body is another powerful method of attracting new members.

SOCIAL JUSTICE The Christian church, along with the national government, has contributed tremendously toward the education of the masses in Zimbabwe. It has successfully taught against certain cultural customs, like the killing of twins at birth. (The Shona regarded having twins as taboo, so they would "bury" twin infants in a calabash, which was then placed by a river.) The church has also built orphanages where they were needed.

SOCIAL ASPECTS Because Christianity came to Zimbabwe from the West, some of its teachings were not just biblical but Western as well. A good example of this was the church's uncompromising insistence on monogamous marriage. In many instances Zimbabwean men who converted to Christianity were instructed to "go and divorce the second, third, or fourth wife" before they were baptized. The church also taught practitioners that, during services, family members were not to sit together but with members of the Men's Organization, Women's Organization, or Youth Organization.

POLITICAL IMPACT In the twentieth century Christianity made the greatest impact on the people of Zimbabwe during the 1970s, when some church leaders took on political roles in order to mobilize the masses to demand majority rule. Up to that time there had been the feeling among believers that Christianity was the religion of the white man and, thus, a means of oppressing the black majority. But Christian churches took the lead in building schools and hospitals and in providing other amenities considered necessary for a comfortable living.

CONTROVERSIAL ISSUES One of the leading controversial issues in Zimbabwe is whether young people should use birth-control pills or other contraceptives. Some churches, intending to cut down on the number of AIDS-related deaths, advocate the use of condoms. With the Roman Catholic Church leading the way, however, some denominations discourage the use of all contraceptives.

Among Zimbabweans a host of questions surrounds the topic of abortion. For example, is abortion acceptable if the mother's life is endangered by her pregnancy? Is abortion an ethical alternative to giving birth to an unwanted child? If impregnated by a rapist, should a woman have to carry the pregnancy to full term? Some believe abortion is ethical provided that it is performed by a physician, but the question remains whether an abortion constitutes the murder of a person. Most mission churches in Zimbabwe are strongly influenced by Western secularism and no longer make a big issue of abortion.

Many Africans were led by Christian missionaries to believe that visiting a traditional healer (*ng'nga;* also *nganga*) is evil. They were told that they should visit doctors trained in the West instead. Many churches in Zimbabwe expel members who visit *ng'ngas*. If the violator is a woman, she is "defrocked" and, in most cases, so embarrassed that she must leave the church. If a person has an illness that the hospitals have failed to treat successfully, he or she usually joins a denomination that allows traditional healing.

The church in Zimbabwe has wrestled with polygamy, though opposition to polygamy originally came from the mother churches overseas. Most African independent church organizations do not oppose it, while others—the leaders of the Apostolic Churches, for instance—actually cherish "decrees" (often presented as the result of revelations received during sleep) that award them young virgins as wives.

In the 1990s the liberation theologian Canaan Banana proposed that the Bible should be revised to include people and events of greater relevance to people in postcolonial societies. The suggestion that such Zimbabwean prophets as Nehanda be included in the Bible has stirred considerable controversy.

CULTURAL IMPACT Christianity has been gradually Westernizing believers in Zimbabwe. It has penetrated all social as well as spiritual aspects of life. Dance, for example, has been modified to reflect Western styles. Western dress has been adopted and is now regarded as the Christian way of dressing. There is little traditional music in Christian homes because it is generally considered unchristian or downright pagan. Architecture in Zimbabwe is generally Western due to the influence of the church.

AFRICAN INDIGENOUS BELIEFS

DATE OF ORIGIN about 3,000 B.C.E

NUMBER OF FOLLOWERS 5.3 million

HISTORY African traditional religion is among the most ancient religions in the world. It is found mainly south of the Sahara. The original practitioners migrated from the north—perhaps from the Sudan—as a group known as the Bantu. Without an individual founder, this religion has survived various cultural invasions and has continued to flourish in its own decentralized structure. Since children born to practitioners are considered adherents from birth, population increase among traditionalists is the same as membership increase.

Practitioners consider African traditional religion to be one of the revealed religions of the world. The God worshiped in this religion is believed to be the same one whose divinity is reverenced by the world's other revealed religions. There are various names for God, all of which designate the oneness and awesomeness of the Creator: Mwari, Inkosi, Unkulunkulu, Mutangakugara, Muwanikwa, Chidzachepo, and Nyadenga. Believing that Nyadenga is Spirit, traditionalists reckon that to communicate with the Supreme Being, they must approach through a spiritual medium, namely their ancestors, who are believed to be most concerned about the welfare of the living. Extending from those who are yet unborn, through the living and the ancestors (immediate, distant, and forgotten), to the Great Ancestor, also known as God the Creator, the hierarchy of beings is believed to be a two-way communication channel between humans and the divine.

African traditional religion permeates all aspects of life; thus, there is no clear distinction between the secular and the sacred. Sacred literature is generally oral. There is no academic elitism in traditional religion; however, there are experts who are consulted when necessary.

Each head of household has the responsibility not only to serve as the family priest but to teach his offspring the central beliefs of traditional religion. A crisis affecting the whole community, such as the war of liberation in the 1960s, may serve more than one purpose. First, such a crisis demonstrates that traditionalists worship the Living God, Mwari, who hears their prayers and answers them. Second, it serves to unite people in a special way. For this reason, traditionalists will never forget the names of their national heroes and heroines—Chaminuka, Mupfemberi (the prophet), Mbuya Nehanda, and Kaguwi—who performed such miracles as sitting on the pointed tip of a spear or making fire without tools or fuel. Mbuya Nehanda in particular is famous for her political astuteness. Her courage empowered numerous youths to arm themselves and fight for their national independence.

EARLY AND MODERN LEADERS In addition to family ancestors, there are district spirit mediums—the spirits of leading figures—who have been installed as national ancestors. They serve as national political advisers as well as religious and spiritual counselors. Most prominent are Mbuya Nehanda, Nyakasikana, Chaminuka, and Kaguwi. Their spirits are believed to have played a major role in Zimbabwe's war of liberation in the 1960s and '70s. Contemporary leaders include the spirits of Chief Tangwena, Chief Mangwende, and a host of other spirit mediums who helped the country's political leadership during the war of liberation.

MAJOR THEOLOGIANS AND AUTHORS Like other religions, African traditional religion has a clear theology based on the belief in one God, the Creator, and the ways in which traditionalists relate to this God. The leading theologian in print is Gwinyai Muzorewa, whose book *The Origin and Development of African Theology* (1985) has remained the benchmark in traditional theology. Other theologians in Zimbabwe continue to maintain the oral tradition.

HOUSES OF WORSHIP AND HOLY PLACES Traditionalists do not build sanctuaries for worship because every home is regarded as God's home and thus is dedicated for worship. Every home also has a *chikuwa* (an earthen platform), however, which is the place in the family's main house where all the sacrifices are offered by the family priest. Another place that is approached with reverence is the grave where the ancestor is buried.

WHAT IS SACRED? For traditionalists all of Creation is holy, as it is all enveloped in spirit. Creatures like the python and the leopard are regarded as sacred, possibly because of the appearance of their skin or coat or due to their habits and natures. The sacred places are those that are believed to be the abodes of the spirits—a pool, a huge tree, or a mountain, for example. The *chikuwa* in each home is the "holy of holies," where only the family priest can place artifacts required for offerings. Wooden or a clay plates are used for such formalities. Any items used in performing these ceremonies must be made of indigenous fabric or material only.

HOLIDAYS AND FESTIVALS In traditional religion one day is set aside as *chisi,* as it is known among the Shona of Zimbabwe. On the *chisi* (unique and, therefore, holy) day, which occurs once every seven days, no one is allowed to work in the fields, and there are no celebrations. Even funerals are interrupted. Violators are severely punished, for this is indeed a holy day (*zuva rinoyera*). Practitioners believe that this is the day when the spirit mediums roam the villages in broad daylight.

MODE OF DRESS Traditionalists dress casually. Special occasions are marked not so much by clothing as by the type of food served. African traditional doctors and those in other cultural professions tend to dress in ways that distinguish them from the rest of the community. Both python and leopard skins are favored because of their dazzling appearance.

DIETARY PRACTICES Traditionalists in Zimbabwe are almost exclusively of African descent. Consequently, most have a totem animal with which they identify and which must not be harmed. If the totem for the chief is Buffalo, for example, the chief and his entire family may never eat the meat of a buffalo.

RITUALS Traditional religion is saturated with rituals. Literally everything is done ritualistically. For example, when one begins a meal, one must spill some food—say, milk, *sadza* (a staple food made from maize or corn meal), or beer—on the floor, thus symbolically sharing with the ancestors. Most elaborate are the burial rituals, in which every step must be accompanied by certain words or actions. The burial includes gathering all the clothes and artifacts of the deceased to "go with him." Some people believe that this is another way traditionalists signify their belief in eternal life. The purpose of all traditional ritual is twofold: to invoke the spirits and to maintain harmony among neighbors and with God.

RITES OF PASSAGE Traditional religion places great emphasis on rites of passage and on the community's role in these rites. For example, it is believed that, in order for a boy to become a man, the community needs to participate in the process. Furthermore, the youth must be conscious of the process. Such rites of passage enable the youth to confirm his identity by consciously "becoming" a man.

Women are also processed through various stages on the way to womanhood. Especially at puberty, girls are trained to clean themselves and to sit properly in the presence of men so that certain parts of their bodies are not exposed. At age 12 or 13, girls are taught to prepare a full meal. Since learning to cook requires practice, girls are expected to cook for the family. Boys also go through a similar training period, taught by either an uncle or grandfather. Later both boys and girls are instructed in how to have sex (without actually engaging), and young men are also taught how to approach young women—all in the context of traditional religion.

MEMBERSHIP Traditional religion does not focus on the number of its members. The community as a whole belongs and does not feel the need to increase in number.

Belonging to the religion presupposes a religious connectedness to the whole universe. For this reason the religion is highly particular about how each practitioner observes the moral guidelines, because a wrong committed by one person will eventually affect the whole community. All wrongs, therefore, must be rectified for the sake of the health of the entire religious body.

SOCIAL JUSTICE Regarding human rights, the predominant teaching of traditional religion is that everyone must respect all human life, no matter how low a person's station in society may be. Life is precious because it is given by the Creator, and no one—not even the community—has the power to take any life. The only power the community has over the individual is authority to forgive the individual, while, at the same time, it requires that the individual forgive the entire community. This is what happens during the final ritual known as the Umbuyiso among the Ndebele and the Chenura among the Shona. Both Umbuyiso and Chenura mean "ritual cleansing." Umbuyiso is intended to perfect the quality of life by using the ancestors in removing all impediments between the living and the spiritual world, the source of blessings.

Traditional religion's influence on everyday living ensures that every citizen is treated with fairness, for it is believed that if a single soul dies "disappointed" because injustice inflicted by any member of the community, the whole community will eventually suffer the consequences. This concern for a just society compels elders to educate their children, albeit informally, in human relations, taboos, and the other social dynamics needed to produce good citizens.

SOCIAL ASPECTS The family is the stronghold in traditional religion. All enculturation and socialization happens within the family. Family values probably constitute the bulk of the education that goes into raising a knowledgeable traditionalist. At a certain age most children are told to sit at the foot of their grandfather or grandmother and learn what it is to be human. For example, grandmothers teach girls that they are different from boys and that they need to guard that difference because there is a purpose for it. All in all, socialization is considered a spiritual as well as a secular exercise because, to be human, one must develop a well-rounded personality.

POLITICAL IMPACT Traditional religion is considered the foundation of Zimbabwean politics. It is believed that, unless a candidate is favored by the four winds (that is, the ancestors), his or her candidacy is in vain. Moreover, the wisdom of national leaders is believed to emanate from the spirits. Finally, a politician can not be a true leader if he or she does not have the special staff given by the traditionalist medium.

CONTROVERSIAL ISSUES Traditional religion is not a culture of argumentation and controversies. To be human is to comply with the community's mores and folkways. In contemporary Zimbabwe, however, there have arisen issues that have caused a stir in the community. Examples include the allocation of land, the role of the chief, and the status of medicine men and medicine women in relation to Western medical practices. Traditionally families were allotted a piece of land by their kraal (village) head or chief, but with the imposition of colonial structures, new rules came into effect. As a result, some people were assigned land far away from their forefathers' graves, making it almost impossible for them to visit the graves when they needed to. Concerning traditional medical practice, in addition to disturbances caused by colonial requirements, the church has also interfered in the name of "being Christian." In short, traditionalist have been pressured to accept non-African values and to believe that these values are superior to those of their traditional faith. The result has been seemingly endless debate among practitioners.

CULTURAL IMPACT Traditional religion is believed to be the cultural reservoir of the people of Zimbabwe. They look to traditional religion to define cultural orthodoxy. This is true in the arts as well, which must be identifiably indigenous in character in order to be received as genuinely African. Even Christians turn to traditionalists to learn how to retain their African dignity. Values—whether cultural, social, or moral—are defined by traditionalists, and matters of spirituality are ultimately defined in terms of traditional life.

Other Religions

Other religions represented in Zimbabwe include Islam, Hinduism, Judaism, and Buddhism. Together their adherents make up about 4.5 percent of the country's population. Buddhists and Muslims tend to be more conspicuous because of their outstanding temples and mosques. Both groups also have unique dietary laws. Most Indians and other Asians in Zimbabwe are Hindus. They do not proselytize; however, their culture has made a significant impact on the rest of the nation, probably because of their social and economic status. Hindus gather to worship in temples in the three major cities of Harare, Bulawayo, and Mutare. Particularly distinctive are their traditional dress, food, and family practices.

Judaism is represented in Zimbabwe by about 600 practitioners. With their congregational headquarters in Harare, Jews are scattered throughout the country. Besides Harare, there are small Jewish communities in Bulawayo and the village of Rusape. Their numbers have declined sharply because of the political instability that has troubled the country since the 1980s. The lively Jewish community in Rusape has taken on local color: Some of its members are indigenous Zimbabweans who claim a genetic as well as spiritual inheritance; some describing themselves as descendants of the Lost Tribes of Israel.

While their communities in Zimbabwe are few, Muslims enjoy the splendor of two major mosques in the country. Like Hindus in the country, Muslims tend to be prominent, middle-class businesspeople. Both men and women wear distinctive clothing. Moreover, since the majority of Muslims in the country are of Asian, Indian, or Arab descent, they differ ethnically from the majority population.

Gwinyai H. Muzorewa

See Also Vol. I: *African Traditional Religions, Christianity*

Bibliography

Dachs, Anthony J., ed. *Christianity South of the Zambezi.* Vol. I. Gwelo, Rhodesia: Mambo Press, 1973.

Daneel, M.L. *Zionism and Faith-Healing in Rhodesia: Aspects of African Independent Churches.* Translated from the Dutch by V.A. February. The Hague: Mouton, 1970.

Gelfand, Michael. *The Genuine Shona: Survival Values of an African Culture.* Gwelo, Rhodesia: Mambo Press, 1973.

———. *The Spiritual Beliefs of the Shona: A Study Based on Field Work among the East-Central Shona.* Gwelo, Rhodesia: Mambo Press, 1977.

Hallencreutz, Carl F., and Ambrose M. Moyo. *Church and State in Zimbabwe.* Gweru, Zimbabwe: Mambo Press, 1988.

Muzorewa, Gwinyai H. *The Origins and Development of African Theology.* Maryknoll, New York: Orbis Books, 1985.

Owomoyela, Oyekan. *Culture and Customs of Zimbabwe.* Westport, Conn.: Greenwood Press, 2002.

Shorter, Aylward. *Prayer in the Religious Traditions of Africa.* Nairobi: Oxford University Press, 1975.

Verstraelen, F.J. *Zimbabwean Realities and Christian Responses: Contemporary Aspects of Christianity in Zimbabwe.* Gweru, Zimbabwe: Mambo Press, 1998.

Index

C

D

E

F

H

I

J

K

L

M

N

O

P

Q

R

S

T

U

V

W

X

Y